SAN BERNARDINO HIGH SCHOOL
1850 "E" STREET
SAN BERNARDINO, CA 92405

501850

CALIFORNIA EDITION

PRENTICE HALL
LITERATURE

Timeless Voices, Timeless Themes

THE BRITISH TRADITION

Prentice
Hall

Upper Saddle River, New Jersey

Glenview, Illinois

Needham, Massachusetts

ISBN 0-13-054808-1

2 3 4 5 6 7 8 9 10   06 05 04 03 02

L PRENTICE HALL
LITERATURE
Timeless Voices, Timeless Themes

COPPER

BRONZE

SILVER

GOLD

PLATINUM

THE AMERICAN EXPERIENCE

THE BRITISH TRADITION

ACKNOWLEDGMENTS

Grateful acknowledgment is made to the following for copyrighted material:

Angel Flores, c/o Barbara Dederick "Eternity" by Arthur Rimbaud from *An Anthology of French Poetry From Nerval to Valery in English Translation with French Originals*, edited by Angel Flores. Reprinted by permission of Barbara Dederick for the Estate of Angel Flores.

Ballantine Books, a division of Random House, Inc. "Homeless" from *Living Out Loud* by Anna Quindlin. Copyright © 1987 by Anna Quindlen. Copyright © 1987 by Anna Quindlen.

Georges Borchardt, Inc. "The First Year of My Life" from *The Stories of Muriel Spark*. Copyright © 1985 by Copyright Administration. Reprinted by permission of Georges Borchardt, Inc., for the author.

Brown University Scholarly Technology Group "The Victorian Web Overview" by George P. Landow from www.stg.brown.edu.

Cambridge University Press, North American Branch Excerpt from "Letter to Thomas Flower Ellis from Thomas Babington Macaulay on the Passing of the Reform Bill" written in 1831, from *The Selected Letters of Thomas Babington Macaulay*, ed. Thomas Pinney, 5 vols. (Cambridge: Cambridge University Press, 1974–80)

Agencia Literaria Carmen Barcells, S.A. and University of Texas Press "Sonnet LXXXIX" and "Sonnet LXIX" from *100 Love Sonnets: Cien Sonetos de Amore*, by Pablo Neruda, translated by Stephen Tapscott. Copyright © 1959 by Pablo Neruda. Copyright © 1986 by the University of Texas Press.

Carol Publishing Group "The Lorelei" by Heinrich Heine from *The Poetry and Prose of Heinrich Heine*, edited by Frederic Ewen. Copyright © 1948, 1976 by The Citadel Press. Used by arrangement with Carol Publishing Group.

(Acknowledgments continue on page R40, which constitutes an extension of this copyright page.)

CONTRIBUTING AUTHORS

The contributing authors guided the direction and philosophy of *Prentice Hall Literature: Timeless Voices, Timeless Themes.* Working with the development team, they helped to build the pedagogical integrity of the program and to ensure its relevance for today's teachers and students.

Kate Kinsella

Kate Kinsella, Ed.D., is a faculty member in the Department of Secondary Education at San Francisco State University. A specialist in second-language acquisition and adolescent reading and writing, she teaches coursework addressing language and literacy development across the secondary curricula. She has taught high-school ESL and directed SFSU's *Intensive English Program* for first-generation bilingual college students. She maintains secondary classroom involvement by teaching an academic literacy class for second-language learners through the University's *Step to College* partnership program. A former Fulbright lecturer and perennial institute leader for TESOL, the California Reading Association, and the California League of Middle Schools, Dr. Kinsella provides professional development nationally on topics ranging from learning-style enhancement to second-language reading. Her scholarship has been published in journals such as the *TESOL Journal,* the *CATESOL Journal,* and the *Social Studies Review.* Dr. Kinsella earned her M.A. in TESOL from San Francisco State University and her Ed.D. in Second Language Acquisition from the University of San Francisco.

Kevin Feldman

Kevin Feldman, Ed.D., is the Director of Reading and Early Intervention with the Sonoma County Office of Education (SCOE). His career in education spans thirty-one years. As the Director of Reading and Early Intervention for SCOE, he develops, organizes, and monitors programs related to K–12 literacy and prevention of reading difficulties. He also serves as a Leadership Team Consultant to the California Reading and Literature Project and assists in the development and implementation of K–12 programs throughout California. Dr. Feldman earned his undergraduate degree in Psychology from Washington State University and has a Master's Degree in Special Education, Learning Disabilities and Instructional Design from U.C. Riverside. He earned his Ed.D. in Curriculum and Instruction from the University of San Francisco.

Colleen Shea Stump

Colleen Shea Stump, Ph.D., is a Special Education supervisor in the area of Resources and Inclusion for Seattle Public Schools. She served as a professor and, since 1993, as chairperson for the Department of Special Education at San Francisco State University. She continues as the lead consultant in the area of collaboration for the California State Improvement Grant and travels the state of California providing professional development training in the areas of collaboration, content literacy instruction, and inclusive instruction. Dr. Stump earned her doctorate at the University of Washington, her M.A. in Special Education from the University of New Mexico, and her B.S. in Elementary Education from the University of Wisconsin–Eau Claire.

Joyce Armstrong Carroll

In her forty-year career, Joyce Armstrong Carroll, Ed. D., has taught on every grade level from primary to graduate school. In the past twenty years, she has trained teachers in the teaching of writing. A nationally known consultant, she has served as president of TCTE and on NCTE's Commission on Composition. More than fifty of her articles have appeared in journals such as *Curriculum Review, English Journal, Media & Methods, Southwest Philosophical Studies, English in Texas,* and the *Florida English Journal.* With Edward E. Wilson, Dr. Carroll co-authored *Acts of Teaching: How to Teach Writing* and co-edited *Poetry After Lunch: Poetry to Read Aloud.* She co-directs the New Jersey Writing Project in Texas.

Edward E. Wilson

A former editor of *English in Texas,* Edward E. Wilson has served as a high-school English teacher and a writing consultant in school districts nationwide. Wilson has served on both the Texas Teacher Professional Practices Commission and NCTE's Commission on Composition. Wilson's poetry appears in Paul Janeczko's anthology *The Music of What Happens.* With Dr. Carroll, he co-wrote *Acts of Teaching: How to Teach Writing* and co-edited *Poetry After Lunch: Poetry to Read Aloud.* Wilson co-directs the New Jersey Writing Project in Texas.

CALIFORNIA PROGRAM ADVISORS

The California program advisors provided ongoing input throughout the development of *Prentice Hall Literature: Timeless Voices, Timeless Themes*. Their valuable insights ensure that the perspectives of the teachers throughout California are represented within this literature series.

Dawn Akuna
Teacher of Reading
Harriet Eddy Middle
School
Elk Grove, CA

Kathy Allen
English Language Arts
Teacher
Palos Verdes
Intermediate School
Palos Verdes, CA

Maxine K. Bigler
Associate Director,
Region II, Migrant
Education, Butte
County Office of
Education
Chico, CA

Cathy Cirimele
Teacher of English
Bullard High School
Fresno, CA

Jesse L. Culbert
English Teacher
Willowbrook Middle
School
Compton, CA

Terry Day
English and Speech
Teacher
Downey High School
Modesto, CA

Yvonne Divans-Hutchinson
Language Arts Teacher
King/Drew Magnet High
School of Medicine
and Science
Los Angeles, CA

Diane Erickson
Teacher of English
Oxford Academy
Cypress, CA

Cynthia Hardy Gayle
Assistant Principal
Rancho del Rey Middle
School
Chula Vista, CA

Joe Glover
Language Arts/ELD
Teacher
Mesa Intermediate
School
Palmdale, CA

Jeannette Hampton
Literacy Coordinator
for Sacramento City
USD, Retired
Fern Bacon Basic
Middle School
Sacramento, CA

Carleen Hemric
Language Arts Teacher
Pershing Middle School
San Diego, CA

Kimberly Wise Johnson, M.Ed.
English Teacher
Arcade Fundamental
Middle School
Sacramento, CA

Keith R. Jones
English/Social Studies
Teacher
Elmhurst Middle School
Oakland, CA

Karen Kessinger
Teacher of English
San Bernardino High
School
San Bernardino, CA

Gail Catherine Kidd
Language Arts Teacher
Center Middle School
Azusa, CA

Alan J. Leonard
English Instructor,
Retired
Anaheim, CA

Catherine C. Linn, Ph.D.
Teacher of Literature
and Writing
Palm Springs High
School
Palm Springs, CA

Karen Lopez
English Teacher
William S. Hart High
School
Newhall, CA

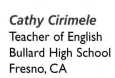

Robert Lopez
ELL Instructor
Gage Middle School
Huntington Park, CA

Celia Monge Mana
Language Arts Teacher
Horace Mann Middle
  School
San Francisco, CA

Kathleen Marshall
English Teacher
Stagg High School
Stockton, CA

Peggy P. Moore
Middle School Educator,
  Retired
Bayshore School
  District
Daly City, CA

Akiko Morimoto
Language Arts Teacher
Washington Middle
  School
Vista, CA

Dewhanne Nyivih
Former English Teacher
Marshall Fundamental
  High School
Pasadena, CA

Judith L. O'Brien
Language Arts
  Instructor
Walter Stiern Middle
  School
Bakersfield, CA

Ann Okamura
Teacher of English
Laguna Creek High
  School
Elk Grove, CA

Judy Plouff
Language Arts/Social
  Studies Teacher
Sherman Oaks Center
  for Enriched Studies
Reseda, CA

Jan Reed
English Curriculum
  Specialist, Retired
Garden Grove USD
Garden Grove, CA

Marian Reimann
Assistant Principal,
  Curriculum and
  Instruction
Sutter Middle School
Winnetka, CA

Lynne Richter
Teacher of English
Fulton Middle School
Van Nuys, CA

Maureen Rippee
English Instructor
Wilson High School
Long Beach, CA

Meredith Ritner
Language Arts Teacher
Alieso Viejo Middle
  School
Alieso Viejo, CA

Sharon Schiesl
Language Arts Teacher
Mendez Fundamental
  Intermediate School
Santa Ana, CA

Carol J. Schowalter
Language Arts Teacher
El Roble Middle School
Claremont, CA

Cheryl Spivak
Language Arts/Reading
  Intervention Teacher
Portola Middle School
Tarzana, CA

Peggy Todd Stover
Teacher of English
Independence High
  School
San Jose, CA

Michael C. Sullivan
Language Arts Teacher
Pacifica High School
Garden Grove, CA

Sandra Sullivan
Language Arts Teacher
Garden Grove High
  School
Garden Grove, CA

Vanna Turner
Language Arts Teacher
Albert Einstein Middle
  School
Sacramento, CA

Linda Valdez
English Teacher
Camarillo High School
Camarillo, CA

Sonia Wilson
English Teacher
Steve Garvey Junior
  High School
Lindsay, CA

Mary Jo Wynne
Language Arts/Social
  Studies Teacher
Assumption of the
  Blessed Virgin Mary
  School
Pasadena, CA

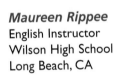

CALIFORNIA GRADE 12 LANGUAGE ARTS STANDARDS

Here is a complete list of the Standards so that you can know what you're expected to learn this year.

READING

1.0 **WORD ANALYSIS, FLUENCY, AND SYSTEMATIC VOCABULARY DEVELOPMENT:** In this strand of standards, you will use your prior knowledge of word origins to learn the meanings of new words and to use these words correctly.

Vocabulary and Concept Development

1.1 Trace the etymology of significant terms used in political science and history.

Over the years, many words in English have changed in meaning and spelling. Words that came to English from other languages may also have evolved from their original forms. Knowing a word's etymology, or history, will help you understand its meaning.

Example:
Vendetta means blood feud. In Italian, the language from which it comes, it means revenge. *Vendetta* came to Italian from the Latin word *vindicta*, meaning vindictive.

1.2 Apply knowledge of Greek, Latin, and Anglo-Saxon roots and affixes to draw inferences concerning the meaning of scientific and mathematical terminology.

Many words in English come from classical languages of long ago and contain distinct references to science or mathematics. Knowing the meanings of word parts (roots, prefixes, and suffixes) will help you figure out the meanings of unfamiliar words.

Example:
botanikos (Greek): of herbs; *-ist* (Greek): a person who does or practices.
Practically every day, botanists discover new uses for plants of the rainforest.

1.3 Discern the meaning of analogies encountered, analyzing specific comparisons as well as relationships and inferences.

An analogy is a statement that two dissimilar things are alike in some way. Examining the relationships expressed in analogies helps us think logically.

Example:
letter : word : : page : book
Relationship: part to whole
microscope : biologist : : telescope : astronomer
Relationship: device or tool

2.0 **READING COMPREHENSION (FOCUS ON INFORMATIONAL MATERIALS):** In this strand of standards you will read material with the purpose of analyzing its organization as well as the arguments and positions it advances.

Structural Features of Informational Materials

2.1 Analyze both the features and the rhetorical devices of different types of public documents (e.g., policy statements, speeches, debates, platforms) and the way in which authors use those features and devices.

Many public documents are expressions of dearly held beliefs, opinions, and convictions and are aimed at swaying the reader to the writer's or speaker's point of view. Understanding the methods used to convey these beliefs, opinions, and convictions will help you evaluate them and rationally decide where you stand on the subject.

Example: **Speech: rhetorical question**
"Are these the remedies for a starving and desperate populace? Will the famished wretch who has braved your bayonets be appalled by your gibbets?"
—from "In Defense of the Lower Classes," George Gordon, Lord Byron

Comprehension and Analysis of Grade-Level-Appropriate Text

2.2 Analyze the way in which clarity of meaning is affected by the patterns of organization, hierarchical structures, repetition of the main ideas, syntax, and word choice in the text.

Studying the methods used by writers of informational material to make their writing understandable and easy to digest will help you express yourselves clearly.

Example: **Syntax: restatement of idea**
"Specifically, when men live, as they do under any industrialized society, as integers who have no weight, no *person* . . . it is unlikely (and in my opinion impossible) that a dramatic picture of them can really overcome the public knowledge of their nature in real life."
—from "On Social Plays," Arthur Miller

2.3 Verify and clarify facts presented in other types of expository texts by using a variety of consumer, workplace, and public documents.

Data presented in informational material is not necessarily true or accurate. Comparing a variety of sources containing similar facts is one way.

2.4 Make warranted and reasonable assertions about the author's arguments by using elements of the text to defend and clarify interpretations.

Many literary discussions revolve around perceptions and statements of an author's arguments and point of view. Reading a text carefully and focusing on pertinent areas will help you understand and explain an author's beliefs about a given topic.

Example: **Clarifying an author's argument**
In 1849, Henry David Thoreau wrote in his essay "Civil Disobedience" that all citizens should speak out about what they think government should be. He states: "Let every man make known what kind of government would command his respect, and that will be one step toward obtaining it."

2.5 Analyze an author's implicit and explicit philosophical assumptions and beliefs about a subject.

Identifying the views and beliefs behind an author's statements and conclusions about a particular topic will help you understand and evaluate the work on many different levels.	*Example:* **Explicit assumptions** In "The Mortgaged Heart," Carson McCullers asserts that the concept of American individualism distinguishes American loneliness from that of the European. Whereas the European is "secure in his ties, and rigid class loyalties," Americans, though outgoing, "tend to seek things out as individuals, alone."

Expository Critique

2.6 Critique the power, validity, and truthfulness of arguments set forth in public documents; their appeal to both friendly and hostile audiences; and the extent to which arguments anticipate and address reader concerns and counterclaims (e.g., appeal to reason, to authority, to pathos and emotion).

Some arguments are powerful and some are less so. Because printed documents do not allow for debate, in order to be effective, they must anticipate and answer the arguments and responses of the reader. Knowing how they do so makes us more knowledgeable consumers of such material.	*Example:* "Someone will need to decide what [the monarchy] can and cannot be allowed to do within the rules. But this is not the real issue. The real issue is how the monarchy as an institution fits into British life, and how its utilitarian functions can become the focus of its existence, now that the magic is mostly torn apart. The answer is elusive. For there's a desire to pretend the magic still exists. The aura of royalty continues to entrance a certain kind of operator, especially if he or she is foreign." —from "Blair and the Queen," Hugo Young, *The Guardian*

3.0   LITERARY RESPONSE AND ANALYSIS: In grade 12, you will read and respond to historically and culturally significant works of literature that will both reflect and enhance your studies of history and social science.

Structural Features of Literature

3.1   Analyze characteristics of subgenres (e.g., satire, parody, allegory, pastoral) that are used in poetry, prose, plays, novels, short stories, essays, and other basic genres.

Literature is usually divided into three major categories: prose, poetry, and drama. Subgenres are categories that help to classify literature with similar elements across periods and genres. At this grade level, you will learn how to identify and understand the elements that make up various subgenres.

Example: **Allegory: a literary work with two or more meanings—a literal and a symbolic.** ". . . Mr. Hooper had ascended the stairs, and showed himself in the pulpit, face to face with the congregation, except for the black veil. That mysterious emblem was never once withdrawn . . . [The sermon] had reference to secret sin, and those said mysteries which we hide from our nearest and dearest, and would fain conceal from our own consciousness . . ."
—from "The Minister's Black Veil," Nathaniel Hawthorne

Narrative Analysis of Grade-Level-Appropriate Text

3.2   Analyze the way in which the theme or meaning of a selection represents a view or comment on life, using textual evidence to support the claim.

A universal theme is a central message or idea about life that is expressed by works of literature from many different times and cultures. In grade 12, you will identify the theme(s) of a selection, explaining how it communicates an idea or thought about life, and use the text to support your assertions.

Example: **Theme: alienation and despair**
Written at the beginning of the twentieth century, T.S. Eliot's poem "The Love Song of J. Alfred Prufrock" is about a speaker who, "like a patient etherized upon the table," questions how and whether to profess his love to a woman. On his way to a tea party, he wanders "through certain half-deserted streets," heavy with "yellow fog" and "yellow smoke."

3.3   Analyze the ways in which irony, tone, mood, the author's style, and the "sound" of language achieve specific rhetorical or aesthetic purposes or both.

At this grade level, you will learn how to identify and understand the way an author uses language, both literal and figurative, and various literary techniques to represent ideas and situations in his or her work.

Example: **Irony**
"Her fancy was running riot along those days ahead of her. . . . She breathed a quick prayer that life might be long. It was only yesterday she had thought with a shudder that life might be too long."
—from "The Story of an Hour," Kate Chopin

3.4 Analyze ways in which poets use imagery, personification, figures of speech, and sounds to evoke readers' emotions.

You will learn how to identify and understand how a poet uses various literary devices to effect a specific emotion in the reader.

Example: **Personification**
"Soon as the sun forsook the eastern main
The pealing thunder shook the heav'nly plain;
Majestic grandeur!"
—from "An Hymn to the Evening,"
Phillis Wheatly

3.5 Analyze recognized works of American literature representing a variety of genres and traditions: a) Trace the development of American literature from the colonial period forward; b) Contrast the major periods, themes, styles, and trends and describe how works by members of different cultures relate to one another in each period; c) Evaluate the philosophical, political, religious, ethical, and social influences of the historical period that shaped the characters, plots, and settings.

American literature has a long and rich history. At this grade level, you will learn how to identify the underlying religious, philosophical, cultural, and political ideas particular to any given period and understand the way in which they shaped the literature of the time. You will also learn how to recognize and explain the similarities and differences between themes, styles, and trends from one period to the next.

Example: **Theme of slavery, struggle for civil rights**
"It was *slavery* . . . that I hated. I had been cheated. I saw through the attempt to keep me in ignorance . . . The feeding and clothing me well, could not atone for taking my liberty from me."
—from "My Bondage and My Freedom," Frederick Douglass

"Ah, Douglass, we have fall'n on evil days,
Such days as thou, not even thou didst know . . ."
—from "Douglass," Paul Laurence Dunbar

3.6 Analyze the way in which authors through the centuries have used archetypes drawn from myth and tradition in literature, film, political speeches, and religious writings (e.g., how the archetypes of banishment from an ideal world may be used to interpret Shakespeare's tragedy *Macbeth*).

An archetype is a style of thought or symbol after which other things are patterned. In grade 12, you will learn how to recognize archetypes and explain how authors utilize them in their work.

Example: **Archetypal animal: serpent**
"So spake the Enemie of Mankind, enclos'd
In Serpent, Inmate bad, and toward EVE
Address'd his way, not with indented wave,
Prone on the ground, as since, but on his reare,
Circular base of rising foulds, that tour'd
Fould above fould a surging Maze, his Head
Crested aloft, and Carbuncle his Eyes . . ."
—from *Paradise Lost*, Book Nine, John Milton

3.7 Analyze recognized works of world literature from a variety of authors: a) Contrast the major literary forms, techniques, and characteristics of the major literary periods (e.g., Homeric Greece, medieval, romantic, neoclassic, modern); b) Relate literary works and authors to the major themes and issues of their eras; c) Evaluate the philosophical, political, religious, ethical, and social influences of the historical period that shaped the characters, plots, and, settings.

Much can be learned from literatures of the world about a people and their culture. At this grade level, you will learn how to identify the underlying religious, philosophical, cultural, and political ideas particular to any given culture and understand the way in which these ideas shaped the literature of the time. You will also learn how to recognize and explain the similarities and differences between themes, styles, and trends from one period to the next.

Literary Criticism

3.8 Analyze the clarity and consistency of political assumptions in a selection of literary works or essays on a topic (e.g., suffrage, women's role in organized labor). (Political approach)

In the political approach to literature, you will look closely at literary and nonfiction works and decide whether the author has presented his or her political views in a clear and effective manner.	*Example:* "The present condition of the Irish, we have no hesitation, has been brought on by ignorant and viscous legislation. The destruction of the potato for one season, though a great calamity, would not have doomed them, fed as they were by the taxes of the state and the charity of the world, to immediate decay . . ." —from "Condition of Ireland: Illustrations of the New Poor Land," *The Illustrated London News*, December 15, 1849

3.9 Analyze the philosophical arguments presented in literary works to determine whether the authors' positions have contributed to the quality of each work and the credibility of the characters. (Philosophical approach)

In the philosophical approach, you will decide whether an author's values and beliefs have contributed to his or her presentation of plot, characters, and themes in a literary work.

WRITING

1.0 WRITING STRATEGIES: In grade 12, you will write clear, coherent, and focused essays. Your writing will exhibit awareness of the audience and purpose, and will contain formal introductions, supporting evidence, and conclusions.

Organization and Focus

1.1 Demonstrate an understanding of the elements of discourse (e.g., purpose, speaker, audience, form) when completing narrative, expository, persuasive, or descriptive writing assignments.

At this grade level, you will write well-organized compositions with a clear purpose, effective voice, and knowledge of audience.

1.2 Use point of view, characterization, style (e.g., use of irony), and related elements for specific rhetorical and aesthetic purposes.

At this grade level, you will learn how to use point of view, characterization, language, both literal and figurative, and various literary techniques to represent ideas and situations in an interesting and effective way in your writing.

Example:
"I was born the first day of the second month of the last year of the First World War. . . . Red sheets of flame shot across the sky. It was 21 March, the fiftieth day of my life, and the German Spring Offensive had started before my morning feed. Infinite slaughter. I scowled at the scene, and made an effort to kick out."
—from "The First Year of My Life," Muriel Spark

The point of view is first person, though the narrator, a baby, claims omniscience. The author's fresh approach is at once amusing and serious as she writes about the year of her birth, 1918 (World War I).

1.3 Structure ideas and arguments in a sustained, persuasive, and sophisticated way and support them with precise and relevant examples.

At this grade level, you will learn how to write effective, persuasive compositions. You will learn how to organize your ideas in complex and purposeful ways and support these ideas with the best possible evidence in order to achieve the desired results.

1.4 Enhance meaning by employing rhetorical devices, including the extended use of parallelism, repetition, and analogy; the incorporation of visual aids (e.g., graphs, tables, pictures); and the issuance of a call for action.

At this grade level, you will learn how to use language in deliberate ways, such as in particular sentence structures and in the repetition of important phrases, to aid in making your ideas and insights powerful. You will also learn how to use visual aids to strengthen your insights.

Example: **Parallelism; call for action**
"And so my fellow Americans: Ask not what your country can do for you—ask what you can do for your country."
—from "Inaugural Address," John F. Kennedy

1.5 Use language in natural, fresh, and vivid ways to establish a specific tone.

You will learn how best to use formal and informal speech, parts of speech, such as adjectives, adverbs, and active verbs, and other sentence parts to create a memorable mood and atmosphere in your writing.

Example: **Tone: personal**
"When I breathe a handful of mint, even pathetic sprigs from my sunbaked Texas earth, I close my eyes. Little chips of ice on the tongue, their cool slide down."
—from "Mint Snowball," Naomi Shihab Nye

Research and Technology

1.6 Develop presentations by using clear research questions and creative and critical research strategies (e.g., field studies, oral histories, interviews, experiments, electronic sources).

In grade 12, you will learn how to construct clear and effective research questions and use a wide variety of research strategies and sources to write well-developed compositions.	*Example:* Question: What was life like on the wagon trail during the settling of the West in the mid-1800s? Source: diary May 11th: "Made" but a few miles yesterday. Forded the Little Osage; the last river, they say, we have to ford. . . . That our wagon is heavily loaded, have only to make minute of what we have stored in it—eight trunks, one valise, three carpet bags, a box of soda crackers . . ." —from "Heading West," Miriam Davis Colt

1.7 Use systematic strategies to organize and record information (e.g., anecdotal scripting, annotated bibliographies).

Keeping a systematic record of your notes will help you understand the complexities of any given topic, while assuring that your composition effectively covers the necessary and important points of your topic.	*Example:* **Annotated bibliography (The Chicago Manual of Style)** Bibliography Adorno, Theodor. *Mahler: A Musical Physiognomy.* Translated by Edmund Jephcott. Chicago, 1996. A classic philosophical/analytical study of Mahler's music.

1.8 Integrate databases, graphics, and spreadsheets into word-processed documents.

At this grade level, you will learn how present your evidence in the most effective way by using computer programs that organize data.

Evaluation and Revision

1.9 Revise text to highlight the individual voice, improve sentence variety and style, and enhance subtlety of meaning and tone in ways that are consistent with the purpose, audience, and genre.

Revising is an important part of the writing process. You will learn how to strengthen your writing style by using a variety of sentence structures, choosing your words precisely and effectively to make your tone more appropriate for your audience, purpose, and context.	*Example:* **Sentence variety, diction and tone** Original: He arrived to the concert late. It was really loud. He was very excited. The band had a lot of energy and was dressed in leather clothing. Revised: Although he was late arriving to Town Hall, he was wild with excitement. The band loudly rocked, with the black leather-clad members infusing each chord with a youthful drive.

2.0 **WRITING APPLICATIONS (GENRES AND THEIR CHARACTERISTICS):** In grade 12, you will use rhetorical strategies of narration, exposition, and persuasion learned in previous grades and write texts of at least 1,500 words, using standard American English. You will learn different research, organizational, and drafting strategies that will aid you in writing effective compositions.

2.1 Write fictional, autobiographical, or biographical narratives: a) **Narrate a sequence of events** and communicate their significance to the audience; b) Locate scenes and incidents in specific places; c) Describe with concrete sensory details the sights, sounds, and smells of a scene and the specific actions, movements, gestures, and feelings of the characters; use interior monologue to depict the characters' feelings; d) Pace the presentation of actions to accommodate temporal, spatial, and dramatic mood changes; e) Make effective use of descriptions of appearance, images, shifting perspectives, and sensory details.

In grade 12, you will master the writing of narratives, including the fictional and the autobiographical, and you will add in such elements as a standard plot line, or a clear sequence of events, character development, concrete details that appeal to the senses, and other details of story-writing.

Example: **Autobiographical narrative**
"That is why, walking across a school campus on this particular December morning, I keep searching the sky. As if I expected to see, rather like hearts, a lost pair of kites hurrying toward heaven."
—from "A Christmas Memory,"
by Truman Capote

2.2 Write responses to literature: a) Demonstrate a comprehensive understanding of the significant ideas in works or passages; b) Analyze the use of imagery, language, universal themes, and unique aspects of the text; c) Support important ideas and viewpoints through accurate and detailed references to the text and to other works; d) Demonstrate an understanding of the author's use of stylistic devices and an appreciation of the effects created; e) Identify and assess the impact of perceived ambiguities, nuances, and complexities within the text.

In grade 12, you will learn how to state clearly your thoughts and opinions on a literary work and to support your ideas and views with the best possible evidence from the text in question and other texts that deal with your thesis. You will show that you understand the effects the author achieves with stylistic devices; you will also identify and evaluate the works' ambiguities, nuances, and complexities.

Example: **Response to literature**
"*Hamlet*, like the sonnets, is full of some stuff that the writer could not drag to light, contemplate, or manipulate into art. And when we search for this feeling, we find it, as in the sonnets, very difficult to localize."
—from "Hamlet," by T.S. Eliot

2.3 Write reflective compositions: a) Explore the significance of personal experiences, events, conditions, or concerns by using rhetorical strategies (e.g., narration, description, exposition, persuasion); b) Draw comparisons between specific incidents and broader themes that illustrate the writer's important beliefs or generalizations about life; c) Maintain a balance in describing individual incidents and relate those incidents to more general and abstract ideas.

A reflective composition is more than just a description of a personal experience; it is a thoughtful piece about your insights and feelings about this experience and how it relates to larger and more universal themes. At this grade level, you will learn how to compose reflective essays, balancing your writing between individual experiences and situations that reflect universal ideas.

Example:
"I went to the woods because I wished to live deliberately, to front only the essential facts of life, and see if I could not learn what it had to teach, and not, when I came to die, discover that I had not lived. . . ."
—from "Walden," Henry David Thoreau

2.4 Write historical investigation reports: a) Use exposition, narration, description, argumentation, exposition, or some combination of rhetorical strategies to support the main proposition; b) Analyze several historical records of a single event, examining critical relationships between elements of the research topic; c) Explain the perceived reason or reasons for the similarities and differences in historical records with information derived from primary and secondary sources to support or enhance the presentation; d) Include information from all relevant perspectives and take into consideration the validity and reliability of sources; e) Include a formal bibliography.

At this grade level, you will learn how to use a wide variety of historical records to examine a topic, and write well-organized historical reports. You will learn research strategies that will aid you in identifying useful historical information, and understanding the ways in which these historical records similarly deal with your topic and the ways in which their treatment of your topic differs. You will include a bibliography.

Example: **Historical essay**
"Harlem was established in 1658 by Dutch settlers, who called it Nieuw Haarlem, after the city in Holland. It was a rural neighborhood until the 19th century . . ."
—from "Harlem: A Paradise of My Own People," Veronica Chambers

2.5 Write job applications and résumés: a) Provide clear and purposeful information and address the intended audience appropriately; b) Use varied levels, patterns, and types of language to achieve intended effects and aid comprehension; c) Modify the tone to fit the purpose and audience; d) Follow the conventional style for that type of document (e.g., résumé, memorandum) and use page formats, fonts, and spacing that contribute to the readability and impact of the document.

Clear and purposeful communication is key to most business transactions. In grade 12, you will learn how to write and correctly format business and career-related documents. Your business transactions, whether compiling a résumé or writing a cover letter, will address their intended audiences appropriately, using suitable vocabulary, tone, and style.

2.6 Deliver multimedia presentations: a) Combine text, images, and sound and draw information from many sources (e.g., television broadcasts, videos, films, newspapers, magazines, CD-ROMs, the Internet, electronic media-generated images); b) Select an appropriate medium for each element of the presentation; c) Use the selected media skillfully, editing appropriately and monitoring for quality; d) Test the audience's response and revise the presentation accordingly.

At this grade level, you will learn how to use a wide variety of media to present your ideas in novel and effective ways. You will learn how to skillfully combine text, images, and sound to draw forth the desired response to your thoughts and insights from a particular audience.

WRITTEN AND ORAL ENGLISH LANGUAGE CONVENTIONS

1.0 WRITTEN AND ORAL ENGLISH LANGUAGE CONVENTIONS: In this strand of standards, you will learn written and oral English language conventions that are essential to mastering listening and speaking skills.

1.1 Demonstrate control of grammar, diction, and paragraph and sentence structure and an understanding of English usage.

In grade 12, you will show that you understand English usage, grammar, diction, and syntax, as well as effective sentence and paragraph structures.

Example:
In his short story "The Tell-Tale Heart," Edgar Allan Poe uses suspense to keep the reader interested in the story's plot. Near the beginning of the narrative, we are told of the horrible deed around which the story revolves: "I was never kinder to the old man than during the whole week before I killed him."

1.2 Produce legible work that shows accurate spelling and correct punctuation and capitalization.

At this grade level, the written work you present in class should be legible, including accurate spelling and correct punctuation and grammar.

1.3 Reflect appropriate manuscript requirements in writing.

Your work should also follow appropriate rules for manuscripts, which may include requirements for a title page, page numbering and margins, line spacing, and the use and citing of material borrowed from sources.

Example: **Integration of source and support material (MLA)**
In "Barn Burning," an illiterate boy reads the labels of cans with "his stomach . . . not from the lettering which meant nothing to his mind but from the scarlet devils and the silver curve of fish" (Faulkner 3).

LISTENING AND SPEAKING

1.0   **LISTENING AND SPEAKING STRATEGIES:** In grade 12, you will learn how to give effective oral presentations: coherent presentations that use verbal and nonverbal strategies to convey ideas clearly and relate to the background and interests of the audience. You will also learn how to evaluate the content of oral communication and formulate judgments.

Comprehension

1.1   Recognize strategies used by the media to inform, persuade, entertain, and transmit culture (e.g., advertisements; perpetuation of stereotypes; use of visual representations, special effects, language).

The media at once reflects and shapes our culture. At this grade level, you will learn the different strategies that the media uses to reflect and transform the culture you live in.

Example: **Advertising: language and perpetuation of stereotype**
Leather seats, a sunroof, and a state-of-the-art stereo . . . still a four-door sedan and still your Dad's car! Act your age and take the highway to 2Cool Motors!

1.2   Analyze the impact of the media on the democratic process (e.g., exerting influence on elections, creating images of leaders, shaping attitudes) at the local, state, and national levels.

In grade 12, you will learn how to identify and understand the ways in which the media shapes your views of political parties and candidates.

Example: **Editorial**
"President Bush described the budget he unveiled Monday as a 'new way of doing business in Washington' that faithfully reflected the 'compassionate conservatism' he espoused during his campaign. . . . Yet a careful reading of the fine print does little to dispel the impression that on the whole the budget's conservatism outweighs its compassion . . ."
—from "Freezing Government," *The New York Times*, April 11, 2001

1.3   Interpret and evaluate the various ways in which events are presented and information is communicated by visual image makers (e.g., graphic artists, documentary filmmakers, illustrators, news photographers).

Visual language, whether expressed in photographs, film, documentaries, cartoons, or graphic illustrations, is a powerful way to communicate ideas. In grade 12, you will learn how to identify and understand how strong and lasting images are created and make judgments on their effectiveness.

Organization and Delivery of Oral Communication

1.4   Use rhetorical questions, parallel structure, concrete images, figurative language, characterization, irony, and dialogue to achieve clarity, force, and aesthetic effect.

Using rhetorical devices, such as rhetorical questions, parallel structures, literal and figurative language, irony, characterization, and dialogue, will help you to construct clear, effective, and memorable speeches.	*Example*: **Speech: rhetorical device: parallel structure** "Neither party expected for the war, the magnitude, or the duration, which it has already attained. Neither anticipated that the *cause* of the conflict might cease with, or even before, the conflict itself should cease." —from "Second Inaugural Address," Abraham Lincoln

1.5   Distinguish between and use various forms of classical and contemporary logical arguments, including: a) Inductive and deductive reasoning, and b) Syllogisms and analogies.

At this grade level, you will learn how to identify the various forms of logical arguments and use these logical methods of organization to construct your own strong and most effective arguments.	*Example*: **Analogy** The basic unit of life is the cell. Your body contains about 10 trillion cells. Complex structures, cells are like factories—they process raw material, produce energy, and expel waste.

1.6   Use logical, ethical, and emotional appeals that enhance a specific tone and purpose.

At this grade level, you will learn when it is appropriate to appeal to an audience to achieve a desired result, and how best to construct your appeals, whether logical, ethical, or emotional.	*Example*: **Speech: logical appeal** "They tell us, sir, that we are weak—unable to cope with so formidable an adversary. But when shall we be stronger? Will it be the next week, or the next year? Will it be when we are totally disarmed, and when a British guard will be stationed in every house? —from "Speech in the Virginia Convention," Patrick Henry

1.7   Use appropriate rehearsal strategies to pay attention to performance details, achieve command of the text, and create skillful artistic staging.

At this grade level, you will learn practice strategies that will help you achieve the best possible results in a dramatic performance.

1.8   Use effective and interesting language, including: a) Informal expressions for effect; b) Standard American English for clarity; c) Technical language for specificity.

At this grade level, you will learn how best to use precise and interesting language, both formal and informal, to achieve the best results in your presentations.	*Example*: **Interesting language** "But, in a larger sense, we cannot dedicate—we cannot consecrate—we cannot hallow—this ground. The brave men, living and dead, who struggled here, have consecrated it, far above our poor power to add or detract." —from "The Gettysburg Address," Abraham Lincoln

1.9 Use research and analysis to justify strategies for gesture, movement, and vocalization, including dialect, pronunciation, and enunciation.

At this grade level, you will learn research strategies for historical material and material from other cultures to help you understand how best to present it to a particular audience.

1.10 Evaluate when to use different kinds of effects (e.g., visual, music, sound, graphics) to create effective productions.

At this grade level, you will learn when it is appropriate to use different kinds of visual and sound effects, and how best to use these effects to achieve a desired purpose.

Analysis and Evaluation of Oral and Media Communications

1.11 Critique a speaker's diction and syntax in relation to the purpose of an oral communication and the impact the words may have on the audience.

At this grade level, you will consider the language and delivery of oral communication and evaluate how they make an impact on the audience.	*Example:* "Look at me! Look at my arm! I have ploughed and planted, and gathered into barns, and no man could head me! And ain't I a woman?" —from "Ain't I a Woman?" Sojourner Truth

1.12 Identify logical fallacies used in oral addresses (e.g., attack ad hominem, false causality, red herring, overgeneralization, bandwagon effect).

Part of being an active listener is recognizing false and unsupported claims, whether in the form of insufficient data or illogical results.	*Example:* **Faulty causality** "Since Governor Jones took office, unemployment in the state among women has decreased by 6 percent. He should be rewarded with your vote for reducing unemployment among women."

1.13 Analyze the four basic types of persuasive speech (i.e., propositions of fact, value, problem, or policy) and understand the similarities and differences in their patterns of organization and the use of persuasive language, reasoning, and proof.

At this grade level, you will be able to distinguish between the various types of persuasive speeches and understand the similarities and differences in persuasive language and patterns of organization.	*Example:* **Reasoning** "It shall be my work this evening to prove to you that in thus voting, I not only committed no crime, but, instead, simply exercised my citizen's right, guaranteed to me and all United States citizens by the national constitution . . ." —from "Woman's Right to Suffrage," Susan B. Anthony

1.14   Analyze the techniques used in media messages for a particular audience and evaluate their effectiveness (e.g., Orson Welles' radio broadcast "War of the Worlds").

At this grade level, you will learn to identify and understand the techniques media uses to create memorable messages and achieve particular aesthetic effects.

2.0   SPEAKING APPLICATIONS (GENRES AND THEIR CHARACTERISTICS): In grade 12, you will learn how to deliver both extemporaneous presentations and well-organized formal presentations employing traditional rhetorical strategies (e.g., narration, exposition, persuasion, description) in standard American English.

2.1   Deliver reflective presentations: a) Explore the significance of personal experiences, events, conditions, or concerns, using appropriate rhetorical strategies (e.g., narration, description, exposition, persuasion); b) Draw comparisons between the specific incident and broader themes that illustrate the speaker's beliefs or generalizations about life; c) Maintain a balance between describing the incident and relating it to more general, abstract ideas.

A reflective presentation is more than just a description of a personal experience; it is a thoughtful piece about your insights and feelings into an experience and how this incident relates to larger and more universal themes. At this grade level, you will learn how to deliver reflective presentations, balancing your efforts between individual experiences and situations that reflect universal ideas.

Example:
"I remember: it happened yesterday or eternities ago. A young Jewish boy discovered the kingdom of the night. I remember his bewilderment, I remember his anguish. It all happened so fast. The ghetto. The deportation. The sealed cattle car . . ."
        —from "Keep Memory Alive," Elie Wiesel

2.2   Deliver oral reports on historical investigations: a) Use exposition, narration, description, persuasion, or some combination of those to support the thesis; b) Analyze several historical records of a single event, examining critical relationships between elements of the research topic; c) Explain the perceived reason or reasons for the similarities and differences by using information derived from primary and secondary sources to support or enhance the presentation; d) Include information on all relevant perspectives and consider the validity and reliability of sources.

At this grade level, you will learn how to use a wide variety of historical records to examine a particular topic, and deliver a well-organized historical report. You will learn research strategies that will aid you in identifying useful historical information, and understanding the ways in which these historical records similarly deal with your topic and the ways in which their treatment of your topic differs. You will use both primary and secondary sources to construct your presentation.

Example:
In their rhetoric leading up to and during the American Revolution, the patriots often espoused the attitude that their fight with the British was just, and they could not lose because God was on the side of the "right." In his "Speech in the Virginia Convention," Patrick Henry refers to the fight as "a holy cause of liberty . . ."

2.3 Deliver oral responses to literature: a) Demonstrate a comprehensive understanding of the significant ideas of literary works (e.g., make assertions about the text that are reasonable and supportable); b) Analyze the imagery, language, universal themes, and unique aspects of the text through the use of rhetorical strategies (e.g., narration, description, persuasion, exposition, a combination of those strategies); c) Support important ideas and viewpoints through accurate and detailed references to the text or to other works; d) Demonstrate an awareness of the author's use of stylistic devices and an appreciation of the effects created; e) Identify and assess the impact of perceived ambiguities, nuances, and complexities within the text.

In grade 12, you will learn how to state clearly your thoughts and opinions on a literary work, and support your ideas and views with the best possible evidence from the text in question and other texts that deal with your thesis. You will show that you understand the effects the author achieves with stylistic devices; you will also identify and evaluate the works' ambiguities, nuances, and complexities.

Example: **Reference to text**
"I am thinking now of what I rate the best [literary work from the late 1950s]: Salinger's *Catcher in the Rye*, perhaps because this one expresses so completely what I have tried to say: a youth, father to what will, must someday be a man . . ."
> —from *Faulkner in the University*, by William Faulkner

2.4 Deliver multimedia presentations: a) Combine text, images, and sound by incorporating information from a wide range of media, including films, newspapers, magazines, CD-ROMs, online information, television, videos, and electronic media-generated images; b) Select an appropriate medium for each element of the presentation; c) Use the selected media skillfully, editing appropriately and monitoring for quality; d) Test the audience's response and revise the presentation accordingly.

At this grade level, you will learn how to use a wide variety of media to present your ideas in novel and effective ways. You will learn how to skillfully combine text, images and sound to draw forth the desired response from a particular audience.

2.5 Recite poems, selections from speeches, or dramatic soliloquies with attention to performance details to achieve clarity, force, and aesthetic effect and to demonstrate an understanding of the meaning (e.g., Hamlet's soliloquy "To Be or Not to Be").

Often what makes a speech, poem, or dramatic monologue compelling is how the speaker uses his or her voice and body language to add meaning to the author's words. In grade 12, you will learn verbal and nonverbal techniques that will aid you in delivering lively and memorable dramatic readings.

From Legend to History: The Old English and Medieval Periods (A.D. 449–1485)

PART 3   A National Spirit

PART 4   Perils and Adventures

SKILLS WORKSHOPS

Celebrating Humanity: The English Renaissance Period (1485–1625)

A Turbulent Time: The Seventeenth and Eighteenth Centuries (1625–1798)

PART 3   The Ties That Bind

PART 4   Focus on Literary Forms: The Essay

SKILLS WORKSHOPS

Rebels and Dreamers: The Romantic Period (1798–1832)

PART 2   Focus on Literary Forms: Lyric Poetry

(*continued*)

Rebels and Dreamers: The Romantic Period (1798–1832) (continued)

SKILLS WORKSHOPS

Progress and Decline: The Victorian Period (1833–1901)

Progress and Decline: The Victorian Period (1833–1901) (continued)

A Time of Rapid Change: The Modern and Postmodern Periods (1901–Present)

(continued)

A Time of Rapid Change: The Modern and Postmodern Periods (1901–Present) (continued)

Part 4   From the National to the Global

SKILLS WORKSHOPS

Resources

COMPARING LITERARY WORKS

READING INFORMATIONAL MATERIALS

CONNECTIONS

WRITING WORKSHOPS

LISTENING AND SPEAKING WORKSHOPS

ASSESSMENT WORKSHOPS

UNIT 1

From Legend to History (A.D. 449–1485)

Sir Gawain and the Green Knight, Bodleian Library, Oxford

66 *Who pulleth out this sword of this stone and anvil, is rightwise king born of all England.* 99

—Sir Thomas Malory,
from *Morte d'Arthur*

Timeline A.D. 449–1485

British Events

- **449** Anglo-Saxon invasion. ▼

- **597** St. Augustine founds Christian monastery at Canterbury, Kent.
- **653** Celtic church begins to spread Christianity among people living in Severn Valley.

- **664** Synod of Whitby establishes Roman Church in England.
- **731 Bede** completes *A History of the English Church and People.*
- **c. 750** Surviving version of *Beowulf* composed.
- **793** Vikings attack Lindisfarne.
- **871** Alfred the Great becomes King of Wessex. ▼

- **c. 975** Saxon monks copy Old English poems into *The Exeter Book.*
- **991** English defeated by Danes at Battle of Maldon.
- **1040** Macbeth kills Duncan I.
- **1042** Edward the Confessor becomes king of Saxons.
- **1066** Normans defeat Saxons at Hastings; William the Conqueror becomes king of England. ▲

World Events

- **476** Western Europe: Fall of Western Roman Empire.
- **496** France: Clovis, king of Franks, converts to Christianity.
- **542** Byzantine Empire: Plague kills half the population of the capital, Constantinople.
- **552** Japan: Buddhism introduced. ▶
- **591** China: Beginning of book printing.

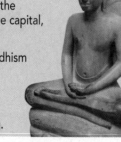

- **637** Middle East: Jerusalem conquered by Arabs.
- **712** Spain: Seville conquered by Moors.
- **732** France: Charles Martel defeats Moors.
- **771** France: Charlemagne becomes king.
- **800** Peru: Incas build city of Machu Picchu.
- **c. 810** Baghdad: Algebra devised.
- **861** North Atlantic: Vikings discover Iceland.

- **c. 900** Western Europe: Feudalism develops.
- **911** France: Normans establish Normandy.
- **982** Greenland: Eric the Red establishes first Viking colony.
- **c. 1020** America: Viking explorer Leif Ericson explores Canadian coast.
- **1045** Spain: Birth of El Cid, national hero who fought Moors.
- **1053** Italy: Normans conquer Sicily.
- **1096** Europe and Middle East: First Crusade begins.

British and World Events

1070   1220   1380   1485

- **1073** Canterbury becomes England's religious center.
- **c. 1130** Oxford becomes a center for learning.
- **1170** Thomas Becket, Archbishop of Canterbury, murdered. ▼
- **1215** King John forced to sign Magna Carta.

- **1233** First coal mined at Newcastle.
- **1258** First commoners allowed in Parliament.
- **1272** Edward I becomes king.
- **1277** England conquers Wales.
- **1295** Edward I assembles Model Parliament.
- **1337** Beginning of the Hundred Years' War with France.
- **1348** Black Death begins sweeping through England.
- **c. 1375** Surviving version of *Sir Gawain and the Green Knight* written.
- **1381** Bible first translated into English.

- **1381** Peasants' Revolt.
- **1386 Chaucer** begins writing *The Canterbury Tales*. ▲
- **1455** Beginning of the Wars of the Roses.
- **c. 1470 Thomas Malory** writes *Morte d'Arthur*.
- **1485** End of the Wars of the Roses.

- **c. 1100** France: *Song of Roland* written.
- **1139** Portugal: Afonso I defeats Moors and assumes title of king.
- **c. 1150** Spain: First paper made.
- **1192** Austria: Duke Leopold imprisons Richard I of England.
- **1194** Iceland: *Elder Edda*, a collection of Norse myths and legends, first appears.
- **1214** China: Mongol leader Genghis Khan captures Peking.

- **1275** China: Marco Polo visits court of Kublai Khan.
- **1291** Europe and Middle East: End of Crusades.
- **1307** Italy: Dante begins writing *The Divine Comedy*.
- **1325** Mexico: Aztecs establish Mexico City and create a dating system with a solar year of 365 days. ▶
- **1341** Italy: Petrarch crowned poet laureate of Rome.

- **1429** France: Joan of Arc leads French in breaking siege of Orléans.
- **1453** France: Hundred Years' War with England ends.
- **1453** Germany: First Gutenberg Bible printed.
- **1461** France: François Villon writes *Grand Testament*.
- **1484** Italy: Botticelli paints *Birth of Venus*.
- **1485** Peru: Incan Empire reaches its zenith.

From Legend to History

(A.D. 449–1485)

Historical Background

The Conquest of Britain Between 800 and 600 B.C., two groups of Celts from southern Europe invaded the British Isles. One group, who called themselves Brythons (now spelled "Britons"), settled on the largest island, Britain. The other, known as Gaels, settled on the second largest island, known to us as Ireland.

The Celts were farmers and hunters. They organized themselves into tightly knit clans, each with a fearsome loyalty to its chieftain. When these clans fell into disagreement with one another, they often looked to a class of priests known as Druids to settle their disputes.

The next conquerors of Britain were the far more sophisticated Romans. In 55 B.C. and again the next year, the Roman general Julius Caesar made hasty invasions. The true conquest of Britain, however, occurred nearly one hundred years later. Disciplined Roman legions spread over the island, establishing camps that soon grew into towns. The Roman rule of Britain lasted for more than 300 years. It ended only when northern European tribes invaded Italy and increased pressure on Rome itself. The last Roman legions departed from Britain to defend Rome in A.D. 407. By that time, the Britons faced a new set of invaders.

Spread of Christianity in Europe, 476-1050

NORWAY SWEDEN
SCOTLAND
IRELAND
DENMARK
ENGLAND
BALTIC SEA
Canterbury
GERMANY
RUSSIA
Paris Worms
Prague
Kiev
ATLANTIC OCEAN
FRANCE
Cluny
SPAIN
CORSICA
ITALY
Rome
Constantinople
BYZANTINE EMPIRE
SARDINIA
MEDITERRANEAN SEA
SICILY
CRETE

Christian areas, 476
Christian areas added by 1050
Muslim areas, 1050

0   250   500 Miles
0   250   500 Kilometers

These invaders were the Anglo-Saxons, from what is now Germany. Some Anglo-Saxons appear to have been deep-sea fishermen; others seem to have been farmers, perhaps seeking soil richer than the sandy or marshy land at home. Gradually, the newcomers took over more and more of what today is England.

The Coming of Christianity By the fourth century, the Romans had accepted Christianity and had introduced it to Britain. A century later, when the Celts fled the Anglo-Saxons, they took their Christian faith with them. Although Rome fell to barbarian tribes in A.D. 476, the Celtic Christian Church continued to thrive.

▲ **Critical Viewing**
This map shows the spread of Christianity throughout Europe. What effects might this religious conversion have had on daily life? **[Analyze Causes and Effects]**

In the late sixth century, a soldier and abbot named Columba, along with some monks, gained converts to Christianity and established monasteries in the north. In 597, the Roman cleric Saint Augustine (not the early Christian Church father) arrived in southeast England and converted King Ethelbert of Kent to Christianity. Augustine set up a monastery at Canterbury in Kent and began preaching his faith to other rulers as well. By providing counsel to quarreling rulers, the Church promoted peace and helped unify the English people.

Danish Invasion In the ninth century, the Norse of Norway and the Danes of Denmark were pressured by their own rising populations and took to the seas. These Vikings carried their piracy to the British Isles. The Norse set their sights on Northumbria, Scotland, Wales, and Ireland, whereas the Danes targeted eastern and southern England.

The Viking invaders sacked and plundered monasteries, destroyed manuscripts, and stole sacred religious objects. They burned entire communities and put villagers to the sword. Although the English fought back valiantly, the Danes made broad inroads. By the middle of the ninth century, most of northern, eastern, and central England had fallen to the invaders.

In 871, a king ascended to the Wessex throne who would become the only ruler in England's history ever to be honored with the epithet "the Great." This king was Alfred, and he earned the title partly by resisting further Danish encroachment. Under a truce concluded in 886, England was formally divided: The Saxons acknowledged Danish rule in the east and north, and the Danes agreed to respect Saxon rule in the south. Alfred the Great became a national hero.

Alfred's achievements went far beyond the field of battle, however. Not only was he instrumental in preserving the remnants of pre-Danish civilization in Britain, but he encouraged a rebirth of learning and education.

Toward the close of the tenth century, however, more Danes from Europe attempted to recapture and widen the Danelaw, the eastern and northern sections of England under Danish control. Once they succeeded, they forced the Saxons to select Danish kings. Then, in 1042, the line of succession returned to a descendant of Alfred the Great. This king, Edward, had acquired the title "the Confessor" because he was a deeply religious Christian. His death in 1066 led to the end of the Anglo-Saxon period of history.

The Norman Conquest The Normans, or "north men," were descendants of Vikings who had invaded the coast of France in the ninth century. William, Duke of Normandy, had family ties to Edward the Confessor, the English king. When Edward died in 1066, the Saxon council of elders chose Harold II to be king. William of Normandy, however, claimed that Edward had promised the throne to him, and he crossed the English Channel to assert his claim by force. At the Battle of Hastings, near a seaside village in southern England, Harold was killed, and William emerged victorious.

▲ **Critical Viewing**
What can you infer about Viking society and technology by studying this sword? **[Make an Inference]**

Over the next five years, William suppressed the Anglo-Saxon nobility and confiscated their lands. He saw to it that Normans controlled the government and that business was conducted in Norman French or in Latin. The Normans gradually remade England along feudal lines. Feudalism had taken root on the European continent at a time when no central government was strong enough to keep order. The feudal system involved an exchange of property for personal service. In theory, all the land belonged to the king, who parceled it out among his powerful supporters. He gave these supporters noble titles—usually "Baron"—and special privileges. As a vassal of his overlord, each baron paid certain fees, or taxes, and supplied a specified number of knights— professional soldiers—should the king require them. In return for their services, knights usually received smaller parcels of land, called manors. The peasants who worked these manors were the lowest class in the feudal system, the serfs.

The Reign of the Plantagenets

Although Norman influence continued for centuries, Norman rule ended in 1154 when Henry Plantagenet, Count of Anjou, came to the throne as Henry II. Henry founded the royal house of Plantagenet and established a record as one of England's ablest kings.

Henry's concern with legal matters led him into direct conflict with the Church. When the archbishop's seat at Canterbury fell vacant, he appointed his friend Thomas Becket to the position, expecting Becket to go along with royal policy. Instead, Becket defied the king and appealed to the Pope. The Pope sided with Becket, provoking Henry to rage.

Some of Henry's knights misunderstood the royal wrath. In 1170, four of them murdered Becket in his cathedral. Henry quickly condemned the crime and tried to atone for it by making a holy journey, or pilgrimage, to Becket's tomb. Thereafter, a pilgrimage to Becket's shrine at Canterbury became a common English means of showing religious devotion.

The Magna Carta

The next king, Richard I, spent most of his reign staging military expeditions overseas. His activities proved costly, and his successor, King John, inherited the debts. John tried to raise money by ordering new taxes on the barons. The barons resisted these measures, bringing England to the brink of civil war. To avert further trouble, King John at last agreed to certain of the barons' conditions by putting his seal on the Magna Carta (Latin for "Great Charter").

In the Magna Carta, the king promised not to tax land without first meeting with the barons. Although the document produced no radical changes in government, many historians believe its restrictions on royal power marked the beginning of constitutional government in England.

▲ **Critical Viewing**
The Bayeux Tapestry is a piece of embroidered linen (231 feet by 19 ½ inches) that tells the story of King Harold's defeat at Hastings in 1066. This small section of the tapestry shows the Normans preparing a meal after their Channel crossing. What conclusions can you draw from this scene about the Normans and their way of life? **[Draw Conclusions]**

Lancasters, Yorks, and Tudors In 1399, the House of Lancaster replaced the Plantagenets on the throne. The Lancastrian kings were Henry IV, Henry V, and Henry VI, all of whom later became central figures in the historical dramas of Shakespeare. Through the fifteenth century, however, the House of York contested Lancastrian rule. The conflicts known as the Wars of the Roses (1455–1485) pitted York against Lancaster. First one house, then the other ruled as they fought over the throne. Eventually, Henry Tudor, a distant cousin and supporter of the Lancastrian kings, led a rebellion against the unpopular Yorkist king Richard III and killed him in battle. Tudor, crowned Henry VII, later married Richard's niece, uniting the houses of York and Lancaster and ending the Wars of the Roses.

Decline of the Feudal System While royal families struggled for supremacy, the social structure of England was changing. After the great plague, called the Black Death, swept across England in 1348 and 1349, a massive labor shortage increased the value of a peasant's work. Landowners began paying their farmers in cash, giving these workers a greater sense of freedom. Along with freedom went frustration, as peasants began to complain about discriminatory laws and heavy taxes. In 1381, peasants in England staged a revolt against serfdom. The revolt was crushed, but many of its causes continued, and so did the peasants' discontent. Gradually, a free peasantry replaced the serfs of the Middle Ages. However, the question of social justice for the lower classes would arise again.

The Structure of Feudal Society

▲ **Critical Viewing** (a) What aspects of feudal society, as diagrammed here, are similar to aspects of modern-day America? (b) What class of modern people is equivalent to the class of knights in feudal society? **[Relate]**

Point/Counterpoint

The Middle Ages: 1000 Years of Darkness?

The Middle Ages are sometimes pictured as a glittering time of chivalrous knights and daring deeds. Were they actually centuries of brutality and chaos? Two historians express opposing points of view.

YES! "It says much about the Middle Ages that in the year 1500, after a thousand years of neglect, the roads built by the Romans were still the best on the continent: . . . The level of everyday violence—deaths in alehouse brawls, during bouts with staves, or even in playing football or wrestling—was shocking. Tournaments were really occasions for . . . mayhem."
—from *A World Lit Only by Fire* by William Manchester

NO! "In the development of single communities and groups of communities there occurs now and again a moment of equilibrium, when institutions are stable and adapted to the needs of those who live under them; when the minds of men are filled with ideas which they find completely satisfying. . . . Such a period were the Middle Ages. . . ."
—from *Medieval Europe* by H.W.C. Davis

Literature of the Period

Anglo-Saxon Literature Anglo-Saxon literature began not with books, but with spoken verse and incantations. The reciting of poems often occurred on ceremonial occasions, such as the celebration of military victories.

Anglo-Saxon Poetry This early verse falls mainly into two categories: heroic poetry, recounting the achievements of warriors, and elegiac poetry, lamenting the deaths of loved ones and the loss of the past. The long poem *Beowulf* is the most famous example of heroic poetry, whereas a famous elegiac poem is "The Wanderer."

Beowulf This epic, or long heroic poem, is the story of a great legendary warrior renowned for his courage, strength, and dignity. Because it is the first such work known to have been composed in the English language, it is considered the national epic of England.

Like most Anglo-Saxon poets, the author of *Beowulf* is unknown. Although versions of the poem were likely recited as early as the sixth century, the text that we have today was composed in the eighth century and not written down until the eleventh. Thus, the poem includes many references to Christian ideas and Latin classics. Clearly evident in *Beowulf*, however, are the values of a warrior society, especially those of dignity, bravery, and prowess in battle.

Anglo-Saxon Prose Before the reign of Alfred the Great, all important prose written in the British Isles was composed in Latin. The monks who transcribed these works regarded the vernacular, the language of the common people, as a "vulgar tongue." The greatest of England's Latin scholars was the Venerable Bede (673–735), whose *History of the English Church and People* gives an account of England from the Roman invasion to his own time.

Another great work of prose from this time is *The Anglo-Saxon Chronicles*, the name given to a group of historical journals written and compiled in monasteries. Unlike Bede's *History*, these records were written in Old English, the earliest form of our own language.

Literature of the English Middle Ages During this period, the first true dramas emerged, the poet Geoffrey Chaucer created a vivid picture of medieval life, romances portrayed the deeds of knights, and anonymous balladeers sang of love and deeds of outlaws.

▲ **Critical Viewing** This gold shoulder clasp comes from the site of a seventh-century grave or commemorative tomb for an Anglo-Saxon king. It is comparable to items buried with Beowulf. Why do you think Anglo-Saxons buried such items with their royal dead? **[Infer]**

Medieval Drama During early Norman times, the Church often sponsored plays as part of religious services. In time, these plays moved from the church building to the churchyard and then to the marketplace. The earliest dramas were miracle plays, or mystery plays, that retold stories from the Bible or dealt with aspects of the lives of saints.

During the turbulent fifteenth century, a new kind of drama arose: the morality play. Morality plays depicted the lives of ordinary people and taught moral lessons.

An Emerging National Identity In 1454, a German silversmith, Johann Gutenberg, perfected a process of printing from movable type. Printing then spread rapidly throughout Europe, and, in 1476, William Caxton set up the first movable-type press in England. English literature no longer needed to be hand-copied by church scribes.

One of Caxton's first projects was the printing of Geoffrey Chaucer's work. Chaucer wrote in Middle English, a language quite close to English as it is spoken today. After centuries of the ebb and flow of conquerors and their languages, the island of England had finally settled on a national identity of its own.

Geoffrey Chaucer Poet Geoffrey Chaucer was born into the merchant class that was adding to the wealth of London and the nation. Chaucer's father was a wine merchant, and young Geoffrey grew up amid the bustle of a successful international business. As a teenager, he entered an aristocratic household as a servant. This apprenticeship led to a career in which he served the nobility as a capable administrator. Chaucer's perch in society, just below the aristocracy, gave him a perfect vantage point for observing all kinds of people.

Nowhere does Chaucer display his keen powers of observation better than in *The Canterbury Tales*. This work, planned as an exchange of tales among pilgrims journeying to the shrine of martyr Thomas Becket at Canterbury, gave Chaucer the opportunity to show a cross section of medieval society. In doing so, he moved literature beyond the themes of courtly love and knightly adventure that dominated the many medieval tales called romances. His compassionate humor and lively realism make him one of the first modern writers.

Although Chaucer completed only 22 of the 120 tales that scholars think he planned to write, these 22 exhibit a great variety. They include the tale of chivalry told by the Knight, the *fabliaux* (French for "short stories") told by

▲ **Critical Viewing**
In the late fifteenth century, the movable-type press began to play an important role in society. This set of letters and its designed border were produced by William Caxton's printing device. Speculate about the effect this device had on English society. **[Speculate]**

the Miller and the Reeve, the animal fable told by the Nun's Priest, and the story based on a fairy tale told by the Merchant. The highly moral Parson, when asked to contribute a tale, declines to tell an "idle story" like those of the other pilgrims. This passage shows how Chaucer introduces a greater dimension of realism by having his fictional storytellers describe their tales and react to previous ones.

Romances, Lyrics, and Ballads Medieval romances were tales describing the adventures of knights. The most popular romances told about King Arthur. For centuries after their defeat by the Anglo-Saxons, the Celts had told stories of this great Celtic hero. Inasmuch as historians cannot say for certain whether Arthur actually lived or not, tales about him are considered legends, a blend of fact and fiction. When the Normans were battling the Anglo-Saxons, they became interested in the old Celtic legends. Because of the Normans' French ties, the tales of Arthur spread not only in England but also in France. In the fifteenth century, Sir Thomas Malory collected these tales in his book *Morte d'Arthur* ("The Death of Arthur").

Europeans of the Middle Ages had a fondness for a harplike instrument called the lyre. In palaces and castles, poets often strummed lyres as they recited their verse. From this custom, English lyric poetry developed. Lyric poems of this period fall into two main categories: secular and religious. The usual topics of secular poetry are love and nature. Religious lyrics might consist of a hymn praising God or a prayer of supplication.

Another popular poetic form was the ballad, a folk song that told a story. Experts find most surviving ballads impossible to date. One series concerns Robin Hood, a legendary hero who may have existed around the turn of the thirteenth century. An outlaw, Robin lives in the woods with his band of "merrye" men, robbing from the rich and helping the poor.

▲ **Critical Viewing**
(a) Which of these two figures is probably Robin Hood? Why? (b) What does the artist's portrayal of Robin Hood suggest about his way of life, his abilities, and his motives? **[Analyze]**

Close-up on History

Two Funerals

To get an overview of British literature, you might begin with two funerals. These ceremonies occur 1,500 years apart, but each honors a person of great importance. Between these two solemn public events—one real and one fictional—the story of British literature unfolds.

One occurred on Saturday, September 6, 1997. It was the funeral of Diana, Princess of Wales. You yourself might have been among the estimated 2.5 billion people worldwide to watch the services for Diana, killed in a tragic auto accident.

The other funeral, from the beginnings of British history and literature, honored Beowulf. He was the king of a Germanic tribe living in southern Sweden, probably during the early sixth century A.D. His death came, after a glorious lifetime of killing enemies and monsters, in a desperate battle with a dragon.

from Beowulf
Translated by Seamus Heaney

The Geat people built a pyre for Beowulf,
stacked and decked it until it stood four-square,
hung with helmets, heavy war-shields
and shining armor, just as he had ordered.
5   Then his warriors laid him in the middle of it,
mourning a lord far-famed and beloved.
On a height they kindled the hugest of all
funeral fires; fumes of woodsmoke
billowed darkly up, the blaze roared
10 and drowned out their weeping, wind died down
and flames wrought havoc in the hot bone-house,
burning it to the core. They were disconsolate
and wailed aloud for their lord's decease.

from "A Farewell to the 'People's Princess'"
by Dan Balz (The Washington Post)

LONDON, Sept. 6—In precedent-shattering ceremonies that were at once sorrowful and uplifting, Diana, Princess of Wales, was remembered today as a woman of "natural nobility" whose life of compassion and style transcended sometimes abusive press coverage and even the royal family itself. Later she was laid to rest on her family's estate, concluding one of the most extraordinary weeks in the modern history of Britain. . . .

A Story Told in Literature A comparison of these funerals shows that in 1,500 years, warring male-centered tribes that valued physical courage and loyalty became a nation of male and female citizens who valued concern for all those in need and the honest expression of feelings as much as physical courage. British literature both recorded and influenced this dramatic change.

THE CHANGING ENGLISH LANGUAGE

The Beginnings of English

BY RICHARD LEDERER

ENGLISH

The rise of English as a planetary language is an unparalleled success story that began long ago, in the middle of the fifth century A.D. Several large tribes of sea rovers—the Angles, Saxons, and Jutes—lived along the continental North Sea coast, from Denmark to Holland. Around A.D. 449, these Teutonic plunderers sailed across the water and invaded the islands then known as Britannia. They found the land pleasant and the people easy to conquer, so they remained there. They brought with them a Low Germanic tongue that, in its new setting, became Anglo-Saxon, or Old English. In A.D. 827, King Egbert first named Britannia *Englaland,* "land of the Angles."

The language came to be called *Englisc.* Old Englisc differs so much from modern English that it is harder for us to learn than German is. Still, we can recognize a number of Anglo-Saxon words: *bedd, candel, eorth, froendscipe, mann, moder,* and *waeter.* Anglo-Saxon words such as these concern the unchanging basics of life. They survived subsequent social upheavals nearly unmodified. English was to gain its more sophisticated words from other languages, as in the case of the multitude of scientific terms that derive from Latin and Greek.

MIDDLE ENGLISH

A dramatic evolution in the language came after yet another

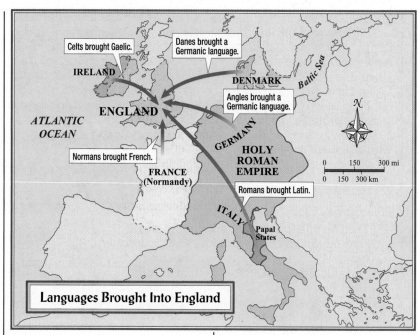

Celts brought Gaelic.

Danes brought a Germanic language.

Angles brought a Germanic language.

Normans brought French.

Romans brought Latin.

IRELAND

DENMARK

Baltic Sea

ENGLAND

ATLANTIC OCEAN

GERMANY

HOLY ROMAN EMPIRE

FRANCE (Normandy)

ITALY

Papal States

N

0   150   300 mi
0   150   300 km

Languages Brought Into England

conquest of England, this one by the Norman French two centuries after the rule of Egbert. The new conquerors came from Normandy, a province of France. These Normans (shortened from *Northmen*) had originally been Viking freebooters from Scandinavia, but they now spoke French and had taken to French customs.

In 1066, under William, Duke of Normandy, the Normans invaded England. In a bloody battle at Hastings they conquered the Saxons and Danes who resisted them, killed the Saxon king, Harold, and forced the nobles to choose Duke William as king of England.

One result was that Old Englisc was flooded by the French spoken by the Normans. Examples of French influence include the words *sir, madam, courtesy, honor, chivalry, dine, table, roast, court,* and *royal.* From this infusion of French words emerged a tongue that today we call Middle English.

ACTIVITY

Read the opening verse of the Prologue to Geoffrey Chaucer's *Canterbury Tales* and look for the words *March, shires,* and *martyr.* Research the origins of these words to gain a fuller understanding of their meanings. Then, write briefly about what their diverse origins suggest about the history of the English language itself.

Earthly Exile, Heavenly Home

Arrival of Williams at Penvesy, (detail from Bayeux Tapestry)

Prepare to Read

The Seafarer ◆ The Wanderer ◆ The Wife's Lament

The Exeter Book

Imagine what life would be like if there were no television sets and if movies played in theaters only on important occasions. On the day a movie was to be shown, the air would crackle with anticipation. People would gather beforehand, chatting excitedly. The next day, everyone would discuss the film, quoting dialogue and reenacting scenes.

Telling the Story This scenario may seem as if it belongs in a movie of its own, but it captures the nature of entertainment during Britain's Anglo-Saxon period, from the fifth to the eleventh century. Few people of the time were able to read, and movies lay centuries in the future. Instead, people turned to traveling storytellers, known as *scops*, who memorized, adapted, and passed along an oral tradition of stories and songs. Through the years, many of these works were lost. Others, however, were eventually written down.

An Early Anthology *The Exeter Book* is a collection of manuscripts that includes pieces of this oral tradition. The book was probably compiled by monks during the reign of Alfred the Great, between A.D. 871 and 899. The later history of *The Exeter Book* is a mystery to scholars, but it has evidently survived some rough treatment. The book has a large burn, several stains from a drinking mug, and marks that suggest it was once used as a cutting board! The book survived this abuse, though, which is fortunate—without *The Exeter Book*, many stories that came out of the oral tradition would have been lost to us forever. "The Seafarer," "The Wanderer," and "The Wife's Lament" were all discovered in this collection.

Guests Who Came to Stay Those who recited and listened to the tales recorded in *The Exeter Book*—the Anglo-Saxons—were not native to Britain. In the 400s, Roman soldiers stationed in Britain had abandoned the island to defend Rome. The native inhabitants of England were soon threatened by Picts from Scotland and Scots from Ireland. One British king invited warlike Germanic tribes from Europe to help him defend Britain. These "guests" proved to be the most dangerous invaders of them all. By the 500s, Angles, Saxons, and other Germanic peoples had settled England themselves, driving out most of the Britons.

A Growing Culture The Angles and Saxons who conquered Britain brought with them a warrior culture, a seafaring tradition, and pagan beliefs, including a grim, fatalistic view of the world. They were followed by missionaries sent by Rome. Eventually, these missionaries converted Britain to Christianity. During this period, various literary forms flourished, including historical and religious prose written by monks as well as the oral poetry of scops. Anglo-Saxon culture at the time of *The Exeter Book* was a blend of traditions, mixing pagan ideas of fate with Christian faith in heaven, the boasts of proud warriors with lessons about humility. Preserved by scops and monks, this culture gave Britain its first literature.

A Quick Look at Anglo-Saxon Culture

- The Anglo-Saxons were expert seafarers who sailed the ocean to raid or settle other lands.

- After the Anglo-Saxons settled England in the 500s, many converted to Christianity. They retained, though, a pagan conviction in the power of fate, and retold Germanic and Scandinavian tales of heroes and monsters.

- Men dominated Anglo-Saxon society, and women had few rights.

Preview

Connecting to the Literature

As you read these poems about people in exile, think about what it would be like to live away from home, unsure of whether you will ever return.

Literary Analysis

Anglo-Saxon Lyrics

A lyric poem expresses the thoughts and feelings of a single speaker. **Anglo-Saxon lyrics** were composed for easy memorization and recitation. They contain these elements:

- Lines with regular rhythms, usually with four strong beats
- **Caesuras,** rhythmic breaks in the middle of lines, where the reciter could pause for breath
- **Kennings,** two-word poetic renamings of people, places, and things, such as the kenning *whales' home* for the sea
- **Assonance,** the repetition of vowel sounds in unrhymed, stressed syllables (for example, "<u>ba</u>tter these <u>ra</u>mparts")
- **Alliteration,** the repetition of initial consonant sounds in accented syllables.

Notice how these elements add a unique flavor to Anglo-Saxon lyrics.

Comparing Literary Works

Each of the lyrics in this grouping is an **elegy,** a lyric poem mourning the loss of someone or something. Though their circumstances vary greatly, each speaker may be said to have lost a home. As you read, notice the similarities and differences among the speakers' experiences.

Reading Strategy

Connecting to Historical Context

Knowing about the period in which a work originated will help you understand it better. Apply the information on the previous page as you read the poems in this grouping. Use a diagram like the one shown.

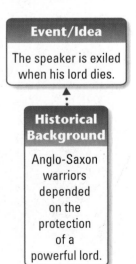

Vocabulary Development

admonish (ad män´ ish) *v.* advise; caution (p. 18)

sentinel (sen´ ti nəl) *n.* person or animal that guards (p. 18)

fervent (fʉr´ vənt) *adj.* having or showing great warmth of feeling (p. 19)

rancor (raŋ´ kər) *n.* ill will (p. 19)

compassionate (kəm pash´ ən it) *adj.* sympathizing; pitying (p. 21)

grievous (grēv´ əs) *adj.* causing sorrow; hard to bear (p. 21)

winsomeness (win´ səm nis) *n.* charm; delightfulness (p. 21)

rapture (rap´ chər) *n.* joy; great pleasure (p. 23)

redress (ri dres´) *n.* compensation, as for a wrong (p. 24)

blithe (blīth) *adj.* cheerful (p. 25)

Ships With Three Men, Fish Bodleian Library, Oxford

▲ **Critical Viewing** Which elements in this picture are true to the seafarer's experience? Which elements are stylized? **[Classify]**

The Seafarer

Translated by Burton Raffel

Background

Each of the poems in this grouping is about exile—a prolonged stay away from home that is forced upon the exiled person. To the Anglo-Saxon people of Britain, *home* meant something different from what it means for people today. An Anglo-Saxon warrior viewed himself as the follower of a particular lord or king, not as a citizen of a nation. In exchange for a warrior's sworn loyalty, a lord dispensed goods—bread, fruit, riches won in raids—and guaranteed security in a dangerous world. Gathering in the mead-hall, a building dedicated to their feasts, a lord and his warriors would share food, drink, entertainment, and fellowship. Smoky, noisy, smelly, and crowded, the mead-hall was home.

This tale is true, and mine. It tells
How the sea took me, swept me back
And forth in sorrow and fear and pain,
Showed me suffering in a hundred ships,
5   In a thousand ports, and in me. It tells
Of smashing surf when I sweated in the cold
Of an anxious watch, perched in the bow
As it dashed under cliffs. My feet were cast
In icy bands, bound with frost,
10 With frozen chains, and hardship groaned
Around my heart. Hunger tore
At my sea-weary soul. No man sheltered
On the quiet fairness of earth can feel
How wretched I was, drifting through winter
15 On an ice-cold sea, whirled in sorrow,
Alone in a world blown clear of love,
Hung with icicles. The hailstorms flew.

Reading Strategy
Connecting to Historical Context What Anglo-Saxon ideas of home and community explain why the speaker feels so strongly about his exile?

✔**Reading Check**
What sufferings has the speaker endured at sea?

The only sound was the roaring sea,
The freezing waves. The song of the swan
20 Might serve for pleasure, the cry of the sea-fowl,
The death-noise of birds instead of laughter,
The mewing of gulls instead of mead.[1]
Storms beat on the rocky cliffs and were echoed
By icy-feathered terns and the eagle's screams;
25 No kinsman could offer comfort there,
To a soul left drowning in desolation.
    And who could believe, knowing but
The passion of cities, swelled proud with wine
And no taste of misfortune, how often, how wearily,
30 I put myself back on the paths of the sea.
Night would blacken; it would snow from the north;
Frost bound the earth and hail would fall,
The coldest seeds. And how my heart
Would begin to beat, knowing once more
35 The salt waves tossing and the towering sea!
The time for journeys would come and my soul
Called me eagerly out, sent me over
The horizon, seeking foreigners' homes.
    But there isn't a man on earth so proud,
40 So born to greatness, so bold with his youth,
Grown so brave, or so graced by God,
That he feels no fear as the sails unfurl,
Wondering what Fate has willed and will do.
No harps ring in his heart, no rewards,
45 No passion for women, no worldly pleasures,
Nothing, only the ocean's heave;
But longing wraps itself around him.
Orchards blossom, the towns bloom,
Fields grow lovely as the world springs fresh,
50 And all these <u>admonish</u> that willing mind
Leaping to journeys, always set
In thoughts traveling on a quickening tide.
So summer's <u>sentinel</u>, the cuckoo, sings
In his murmuring voice, and our hearts mourn
55 As he urges. Who could understand,
In ignorant ease, what we others suffer
As the paths of exile stretch endlessly on?
    And yet my heart wanders away,
My soul roams with the sea, the whales'
60 Home, wandering to the widest corners
Of the world, returning ravenous with desire,
Flying solitary, screaming, exciting me
To the open ocean, breaking oaths

---

1. **mead** liquor made from fermented honey and water.

The British Tradition

Britain, Seafaring Nation

Britain is an island, surrounded by ocean, and its inhabitants have always had a complex relationship with the sea. Throughout British history, the ocean has been both an avenue to new lands and a mighty barrier to strangers, both a gateway to trade and conquest and a scene of terrifying isolation.

From its very beginning, the literature of Britain reflects this complicated connection. "The Seafarer," one of the earliest known British poems, explores the intense hold of the sea on the speaker's heart, an enduring theme. The theme of exile found in this ninth-century poem reappears, for instance, in the twentieth century in Joseph Conrad's sea tales. In the British literary tradition, the sea is a mighty force that tests the human spirit.

admonish (ad män´ ish) *v.*
advise; caution

sentinel (sen´ ti nəl) *n.*
person or animal that guards

Literary Analysis
Anglo-Saxon Lyrics
How does the alliteration of words beginning with *w*, *r*, and *s* affect the sound and meaning of lines 59–62?

On the curve of a wave.
Thus the joys of God

65 Are <u>fervent</u> with life, where life itself
Fades quickly into the earth. The wealth
Of the world neither reaches to Heaven nor remains.
No man has ever faced the dawn
Certain which of Fate's three threats

70 Would fall: illness, or age, or an enemy's
Sword, snatching the life from his soul.
The praise the living pour on the dead
Flowers from reputation: plant
An earthly life of profit reaped

75 Even from hatred and <u>rancor</u>, of bravery
Flung in the devil's face, and death
Can only bring you earthly praise
And a song to celebrate a place
With the angels, life eternally blessed

80 In the hosts of Heaven.
The days are gone
When the kingdoms of earth flourished in glory;
Now there are no rulers, no emperors,
No givers of gold, as once there were,
When wonderful things were worked among them

85 And they lived in lordly magnificence.
Those powers have vanished, those pleasures are dead.
The weakest survives and the world continues,
Kept spinning by toil. All glory is tarnished.
The world's honor ages and shrinks,

90 Bent like the men who mold it. Their faces
Blanch as time advances, their beards
Wither and they mourn the memory of friends.
The sons of princes, sown in the dust.
The soul stripped of its flesh knows nothing

95 Of sweetness or sour, feels no pain,
Bends neither its hand nor its brain. A brother
Opens his palms and pours down gold
On his kinsman's grave, strewing his coffin
With treasures intended for Heaven, but nothing

100 Golden shakes the wrath of God
For a soul overflowing with sin, and nothing
Hidden on earth rises to Heaven.
We all fear God. He turns the earth,
He set it swinging firmly in space,

105 Gave life to the world and light to the sky.
Death leaps at the fools who forget their God.
He who lives humbly has angels from Heaven
To carry him courage and strength and belief.
A man must conquer pride, not kill it,

fervent (fur´ vənt) *adj.* having or showing great warmth of feeling

rancor (raŋ´ kər) *n.* ill will

Literary Analysis
Anglo-Saxon Lyrics and the Elegy What does the speaker mourn in lines 81–90?

**Reading Check**

Why does the seafarer return to the sea time and again?

110 Be firm with his fellows, chaste for himself,
Treat all the world as the world deserves,
With love or with hate but never with harm,
Though an enemy seek to scorch him in hell,
Or set the flames of a funeral pyre
115 Under his lord. Fate is stronger
And God mightier than any man's mind.
Our thoughts should turn to where our home is,
Consider the ways of coming there,
Then strive for sure permission for us
120 To rise to that eternal joy,
That life born in the love of God
And the hope of Heaven. Praise the Holy
Grace of Him who honored us,
Eternal, unchanging creator of earth. Amen.

Review and Assess

Thinking About the Selection

1. **Respond:** Do you agree that "Fate is stronger . . . than any man's mind"? Why or why not?

2. **(a) Recall:** Identify three images related to weather in the first stanza. **(b) Interpret:** What does each convey about the speaker's experiences at sea?

3. **(a) Recall:** What causes the speaker's heart to "begin to beat"? **(b) Generalize:** How can someone dislike something as much as the seafarer dislikes life at sea and yet be drawn to it?

4. **(a) Recall:** What is the seafarer's response to "harps," "rewards," "passion," and the other pleasures of life on the land (lines 44–47)? **(b) Interpret:** Judging from his response to these things, explain whether he is more attached to life on land than he is to life at sea.

5. **(a) Interpret:** What does the speaker mean when he says in lines 58–61 "And yet my heart wanders away, / My soul roams with the sea, . . . / . . . returning ravenous with desire, . . ."?
(b) Draw Conclusions: Is the speaker fully at home on land, on the sea, or in neither place? Explain.

6. **(a) Interpret:** According to the last section of the poem, where is our home? **(b) Synthesize:** Explain the connection between the poem's concluding message and its depiction of the seafarer's wandering existence.

7. **Evaluate:** Can people find a way of life in which they are fully happy, or, like the seafarer, will they always have longings for "another place"? Explain.

The WANDERER

Translated by Charles W. Kennedy

Oft to the wanderer,   weary of exile,
Cometh God's pity,   compassionate love,
Though woefully toiling   on wintry seas
With churning oar   in the icy wave,
5 Homeless and helpless   he fled from fate.
Thus saith the wanderer   mindful of misery,
Grievous disasters,   and death of kin:
     "Oft when the day broke, oft at the dawning,
Lonely and wretched   I wailed my woe.
10 No man is living,   no comrade left.
To whom I dare fully   unlock my heart.
I have learned truly   the mark of a man
Is keeping his counsel   and locking his lips,
Let him think what he will!   For, woe of heart
15 Withstandeth not fate: a failing spirit
Earneth no help.   Men eager for honor
Bury their sorrow   deep in the breast.
     "So have I also,   often in wretchedness
Fettered[1] my feelings,   far from my kin,
20 Homeless and hapless,[2]   since days of old,
When the dark earth covered   my dear lord's face,
And I sailed away   with sorrowful heart,
Over wintry seas,   seeking a gold-lord,
If far or near   lived one to befriend me
25 With gift in the mead-hall   and comfort for grief.
     "Who bears it, knows   what a bitter companion,
Shoulder to shoulder,   sorrow can be,
When friends are no more.   His fortune is exile,
Not gifts of fine gold;   a heart that is frozen,
30 Earth's winsomeness dead.   And he dreams of the hall-men,
The dealing of treasure,   the days of his youth,

---

1. **fettered** (fet´ ərd) chained; restrained.
2. **hapless** (hap´ lis) unlucky.

compassionate (kəm pash´ ən it) *adj.* sympathizing; pitying

grievous (grēv´ əs) *adj.* causing sorrow; hard to bear

Literary Analysis
Anglo-Saxon Lyrics How does the kenning "gold-lord" help you understand the wanderer's goal?

winsomeness (win´ səm nis) *n.* charm; delightfulness.

 **Reading Check**

What is the wanderer's situation?

Wreck of a Transport Ship, J.M.W. Turner, The Bridgeman Art Library, London/New York

▲ **Critical Viewing** Does the scene in this painting match the mood of the poem?
Explain. **[Connect]**

When his lord bade welcome   to wassail³ and feast.
But gone is that gladness,   and never again
Shall come the loved counsel   of comrade and king.
35   "Even in slumber   his sorrow assaileth,
And, dreaming he claspeth   his dear lord again,
Head on knee, hand on knee,   loyally laying,
Pledging his liege⁴   as in days long past.
Then from his slumber   he starts lonely-hearted,
40   Beholding gray stretches   of tossing sea.
Sea-birds bathing,   with wings outspread,
While hailstorms darken,   and driving snow.
Bitterer then   is the bane of his wretchedness,

---

3. **wassail** (wäs´ əl) a toast in drinking a person's health, or a celebration at which such
toasts are made.
4. **liege** (lēj) lord; sovereign.

The longing for loved one: his grief is renewed.
45 The forms of his kinsmen   take shape in the silence:
In rapture he greets them;   in gladness he scans
Old comrades remembered.   But they melt into air
With no word of greeting   to gladden his heart.
Then again surges   his sorrow upon him;
50 And grimly he spurs   his weary soul
Once more to the toil   of the tossing sea.
        "No wonder therefore,   in all the world,
If a shadow darkens   upon my spirit
When I reflect   on the fates of men—
55 How one by one   proud warriors vanish
From the halls that knew them,   and day by day
All this earth ages   and droops unto death.
No man may know wisdom   till many a winter
Has been his portion.   A wise man is patient,
60 Not swift to anger,   nor hasty of speech,
Neither too weak,   nor too reckless, in war,
Neither fearful nor fain,[5]   nor too wishful of wealth,
Nor too eager in vow—   ere he know the event.
A brave man must bide[6]   when he speaketh his boast
65 Until he know surely   the goal of his spirit.
        "A wise man will ponder   how dread is that doom
When all this world's wealth   shall be scattered and waste
As now, over all,   through the regions of earth,
Walls stand rime-covered[7]   and swept by the winds.
70 The battlements crumble,   the wine-halls decay;
Joyless and silent   the heroes are sleeping
Where the proud host fell   by the wall they defended.
Some battle launched   on their long, last journey;
One a bird bore   o'er the billowing sea:
75 One the gray wolf slew;   one a grieving earl
Sadly gave   to the grave's embrace.
The Warden of men   hath wasted this world
Till the sound of music   and revel is stilled,
And these giant-built structures   stand empty of life.
80   "He who shall muse   on these moldering ruins,
And deeply ponder   this darkling life,
Must brood on old legends   of battle and bloodshed,
And heavy the mood   that troubles his heart:
'Where now is the warrior?   Where is the war horse?
85 Bestowal of treasure,   and sharing of feast?
Alas! the bright ale-cup,   the byrny-clad[8] warrior,

---

5. **fain** (fān) archaic word meaning "eager." In this context it means "too eager."
6. **bide** (bīd) wait.
7. **rime** (rīm)-**covered** covered with frost.
8. **byrny** (bər´ nē)-**clad** dressed in a coat of chain-mail armor.

Reading Strategy
Connecting to Historical Context How does your knowledge of Anglo-Saxon life help you appreciate the mood of these lines?

Reading Check
On what aspect of life does the wanderer reflect?

The Wanderer ◆ 23

The prince in his splendor—   those days are long sped
In the night of the past,   as if they never had been!'
And now remains only,   for warriors' memorial,
90 A wall wondrous high   with serpent shapes carved.
Storms of ash-spears   have smitten the earls,
Carnage of weapon,   and conquering fate.
        "Storms now batter   these ramparts of stone;
Blowing snow   and the blast of winter
95 Enfold the earth;   night-shadows fall
Darkly lowering,   from the north driving
Raging hail   in wrath upon men.
Wretchedness fills   the realm of earth,
And fate's decrees   transform the world.
100 Here wealth is fleeting,   friends are fleeting,
Man is fleeting,   maid is fleeting;
All the foundation of earth   shall fail!"
        Thus spake the sage   in solitude pondering.
Good man is he   who guardeth his faith.
105 He must never too quickly   unburden his breast
Of its sorrow, but eagerly   strive for redress;
And happy the man   who seeketh for mercy
From his heavenly Father,   our fortress and strength.

Literary Analysis
Anglo-Saxon Lyrics
How are caesuras
indicated on the page?

redress (ri dres´) *n.*
compensation, as for
a wrong

Review and Assess

Thinking About the Selection

1. **Respond:** In what ways is the wanderer someone with whom you can sympathize?

2. **(a) Recall:** Who are the speakers in the poem? **(b) Analyze:** What is the relationship between the two? **(c) Analyze:** What effect does the use of two speakers have on the reader's picture of the wanderer?

3. **(a) Recall:** Why does the wanderer go into exile? **(b) Analyze:** What images does the poet use to convey his isolation and despair?

4. **(a) Recall:** What are "the fates of men" on which the wanderer reflects? **(b) Connect:** Why might the wanderer's own experiences have led him to such brooding thoughts?

5. **Synthesize:** According to the poem, how might reflection on "the fates of men" lead to wisdom?

6. **Evaluate:** Do you think dwelling on the sorrowful, painful side of life can give a person wisdom and a valuable perspective on life, or do you think it can be harmful? Explain.

The Wife's Lament

Translated by Ann Stanford

I make this song   about me full sadly
my own wayfaring.   I a woman tell
what griefs I had   since I grew up
new or old   never more than now.
5   Ever I know   the dark of my exile.

First my lord went out   away from his people
over the wave-tumult.   I grieved each dawn
wondered where my lord   my first on earth might be.
Then I went forth   a friendless exile
10   to seek service   in my sorrow's need.
My man's kinsmen   began to plot
by darkened thought   to divide us two
so we most widely   in the world's kingdom
lived wretchedly   and I suffered longing.

15   My lord commanded me   to move my dwelling here.
I had few loved ones   in this land
or faithful friends.   For this my heart grieves:
that I should find the man   well matched to me
hard of fortune   mournful of mind
20   hiding his mood   thinking of murder.

Blithe was our bearing   often we vowed
that but death alone   would part us two
naught else.   But this is turned round
now . . .   as if it never were
25   our friendship.   I must far and near

bear the anger   of my beloved.
The man sent me out   to live in the woods
under an oak tree   in this den in the earth.
Ancient this earth hall.   I am all longing.

30   The valleys are dark   the hills high
the yard overgrown   bitter with briars
a joyless dwelling.   Full oft the lack of my lord
seizes me cruelly here.   Friends there are on earth
living beloved   lying in bed
35   while I at dawn   am walking alone
under the oak tree   through these earth halls.
There I may sit   the summerlong day
there I can weep   over my exile
my many hardships.   Hence I may not rest
40   from this care of heart   which belongs to me ever
nor all this longing   that has caught me in this life.

May that young man   be sad-minded always
hard his heart's thought   while he must wear
a blithe bearing   with care in the breast
45   a crowd of sorrows.   May on himself depend
all his world's joy.   Be he outlawed far
in a strange folk-land—   that my beloved sits
under a rocky cliff   rimed with frost
a lord dreary in spirit   drenched with water
50   in a ruined hall.   My lord endures
much care of mind.   He remembers too often
a happier dwelling.   Woe be to them
that for a loved one   must wait in longing.

Literary Analysis
Anglo-Saxon Lyrics and the Elegy What does the wife mourn in this elegy?

Review and Assess

Thinking About the Selection

1. **(a) Recall:** Why was the wife commanded to leave her home?
   (b) Interpret: What do lines 25–26 suggest about her reaction to this event?

2. **Interpret:** How do the setting and her daily life reinforce the idea expressed in the line "I am all longing"?

3. **(a) Generalize:** How might a listener feel about his or her griefs after hearing the wife's lament? **(b) Draw Conclusions:** Explain why the poem presents the wife as an image of pure longing, rather than as a person who will one day move on.

4. **Evaluate:** Is the wife justified in her anger and sorrow? Explain.

Review and Assess

Literary Analysis

Anglo-Saxon Lyrics

1. Find one example in each poem of a feature that could help a storyteller recite that poem, and explain why it would help.
2. (a) Find two examples of **kennings** in the poems, and explain the meaning of each. (b) Explain how these kennings added to the enjoyment of the poems.
3. (a) Find four uses of **alliteration** in lines 80–83 of "The Wanderer." (b) Explain how each reinforces the meaning.
4. (a) Identify two uses each of **assonance** and alliteration in lines 18–20 of "A Wife's Lament." (b) Explain how these effects link words to form strong images.

Comparing Literary Works

5. (a) What makes each of these poems an **elegy**? (b) Which one do you find most moving? Why?
6. Use a graphic organizer like the following to compare the lesson that each poem teaches about suffering.

Poem	Cause of Suffering	Insight Gained

7. Using one example from each poem, compare the ways in which the poems find artistic value, even beauty, in sorrow and longing.

Reading Strategy

Connecting to Historical Context

8. Why is understanding a warrior's relationship to his lord important to appreciating "The Wanderer"?
9. How does understanding the position of Anglo-Saxon women help you understand "A Wife's Lament"?

Extend Understanding

10. **Geography Connection:** The sea is important in British literature. Describe a geographic feature that might be crucial in the literature of another nation. Explain what it might represent.

Integrate Language Skills

Vocabulary Development Lesson

Word Analysis:
Anglo-Saxon Suffix -ness

"The Wanderer" uses the word *winsomeness*, which contains the Anglo-Saxon suffix *-ness*, meaning "the state of being or quality of." Though most English science and math words are formed from Latin or Greek word parts, *-ness* is used in a few. Use your knowlege of the suffix to define these words:

1. obliqueness   **2.** handedness   **3.** randomness

Spelling Strategy

When adding a suffix that begins with a consonant to a word that ends in *e*, retain the final *e*: blithe + -ly = blithely. Add the suffix in parentheses to each word.

1. irate (*-ly*)   **3.** replace (*-ment*)

2. price (*-less*)   **4.** spite (*-ful*)

Concept Development: Synonyms

Synonyms are words that are close to each other in meaning. Replace each italicized word below with a synonym from the vocabulary list on page 15. You may need to change the form of the word.

1. Before being exiled by the king, we were *carefree* and known for our *charm*; we looked forward to the future with *joy*.

2. Being left with nothing, my husband and I sought *compensation*.

3. Our *caring* queen was sympathetic when she learned of our *distressing* situation.

4. The queen *advised* the king to end his *spite* and repeal our banishment.

5. A *spirited* believer in justice, the queen appointed a *guard* to watch over our home.

Grammar and Style Lesson

Compound Predicates

A predicate is the part of a sentence that contains the main verb and states the action or condition of the subject. A **compound predicate** has two or more verbs or verb phrases that relate to the same subject. In this example from "The Seafarer," the subject is *sea*. The three verbs in the compound predicate are underlined.

> **Example:** . . . the sea took me, swept me
> back / And forth in sorrow and
> fear and pain, / Showed me suffer-
> ing in a hundred ships, . . .

As you can see in the example above, compound predicates can be used to create an effect of movement or drama by "piling up" events.

Practice Identify the verbs or verb phrases in the following compound predicates.

1. The world's honor ages and shrinks, . . .

2. The soul . . . knows nothing / Of sweetness or sour, feels no pain, / Bends neither its hands nor its brain. . . .

3. A brother / Opens his palms and pours down gold / On his kinsman's grave. . . .

4. "All this earth ages and droops. . . ."

5. He must never too quickly unburden his breast / Of its sorrow, but eagerly strive for redress. . . .

Writing Application Write a paragraph about a change in the wife's fate in "A Wife's Lament." Use a compound predicate in each sentence.

*W*G *Prentice Hall Writing and Grammar Connection: Chapter 18, Section 1*

Writing Lesson

Analysis of a Literary Theme

Each of the elegies in this grouping speaks movingly on the theme of exile. In an essay, analyze the appearance of the theme of exile in each poem. Compare the ways in which each poem creates beauty out of a painful experience.

Prewriting Reread the selections, taking notes on the theme of exile. Then, write a one- or two-sentence summary of the feelings and imagery associated with exile in each.

Drafting As you draft, use examples showing how each poem creates rich imagery and powerful feelings from the sufferings of exile.

Revising Review your draft, examining the flow of ideas. Consider adding transitions such as *for instance* and *as a result* to clarify the connections between ideas.

Model: Revising to Clarify Connection of Ideas

Even depressing thoughts can have a kind of gloomy

For instance, when

grandeur. ~~When~~ the Wanderer uses images like "Walls

stand rime-covered and swept by the winds. . . ," he

creates a kind of splendor out of destruction.

> Adding the transition words *for instance* clarifies the connection between a general statement and a specific example.

W̶G̶ Prentice Hall Writing and Grammar Connection: Chapter 14, Section 3

Extension Activities

Listening and Speaking In the role of a scop, or traveling storyteller, give an **oral interpretation** of an Anglo-Saxon poem for the class. Use these rehearsal strategies:

1. Mark up a copy of the poem to indicate which words you will emphasize.
2. Add performance notes to the copy as you rehearse.

During your reading, consult your notes. Speak slowly enough so that your audience can follow.

Research and Technology The speakers in these poems had ordinary occupations—wife, sailor, and soldier. With a group, create an Anglo-Saxon **Help Wanted page.** First, investigate Anglo-Saxon occupations. Next, write ads listing the requirements for each job, and assemble them into a Help Wanted page. [**Group Activity**]

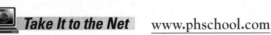 **Take It to the Net**   www.phschool.com

Go online for an additional research activity using the Internet.

CONNECTIONS
Literature Around the World
The Theme of Exile

Exile—the condition of being cut off from one's homeland—may take many different forms. For example, in "The Seafarer," the exile is self-imposed; the seafarer cannot resist the lure of the sea and all its dangers. "The Wanderer," however, experiences exile due to the death in battle of his lord and comrades. In "The Wife's Lament," exile is enforced on the woman by her husband and his conniving relatives.

The following poems also deal with the theme of exile. For Tu Fu, exile is not to be wholly reviled. In some ways, Tu Fu finds himself as a poet only after he is banished from government service.

The same cannot be said of Ovid. For him, exile among the barbarian Scythians near the Black Sea was perhaps more cruel than death. The verses in *Tristia* echo the deep sorrow and longing he felt for his beloved Rome.

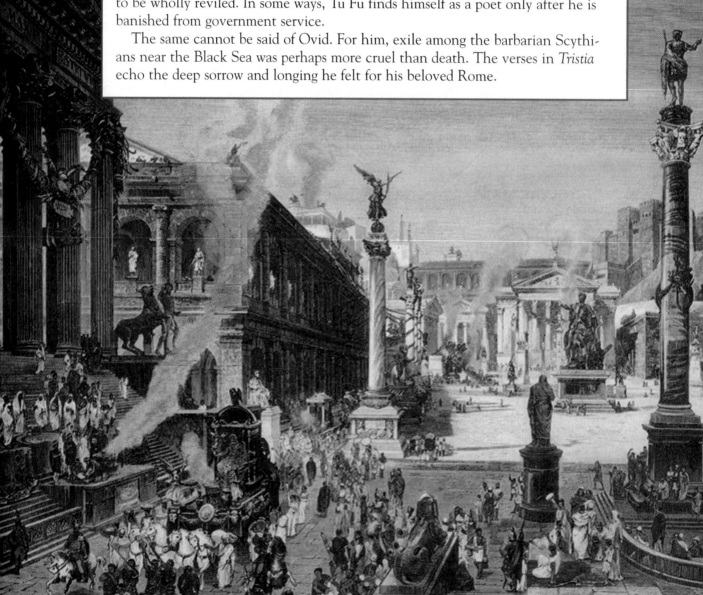

from
TRISTIA

Ovid, Translated by L. R. Lind

Book 10

Since I've been here in the Pontus the Danube has frozen thrice over,
    The waves of the Euxine ocean have hardened as well three times.
And it seems now I've been far from my country just so long a time
    As Dardanian Troy was besieged by the Grecian Army—ten years.
5 So slowly the time goes you'd think it was standing still in its traces
    And the year takes its way as though it were dragging its foot-steps along.
The summer solstice deprives me of nothing at all from the nighttime
    Nor does the winter solstice make shorter each of my days.

Can it be in my case that nature has taken unusual posture
10   And does she make everything long as the wearisome length of my cares?
Or does that time common to all pursue its accustomed progress
    While the time that's peculiar to me is simply more harsh in my life,
I whom the shore of the Euxine, the sea that is falsely denoted,
    Holds now and the left (and ill-omened) land of the Scythian strait?

15 The numberless races around me menace with terrible warfare,
    These people who think it is shameful to live without plundering men;

◀ **Critical Viewing** Judging from this picture of Rome, why might Ovid have missed it so much while in exile? **[Speculate]**

Thematic Connection
Compare Ovid's complaint about the weather with those of the speaker in "The Seafarer."

✔️**Reading Check**
Describe two problems that Ovid finds with his new home.

Nothing beyond me lacks danger; the hill is defended around it
    By the slightest of walls, the strategic position that favors the
        place.
Whenever you least expect it, like a bird the enemy gathered
20   In a dense mass flies past us and, scarce seen, drives its
        booty along.
Often inside of the walls when the gates have been shut quite
    securely,
      We have picked up their poisoned arrows flung into the midst
        of the roads.
It's a rare farmer who dares to till his acres, and he with
      One hand (poor devil) goes plowing, with the other he
        handles his sword.
25 Under his helmet the shepherd blows on straws joined with
    pitch-gum

▲ **Critical Viewing**
What does this Roman statue convey about the might and sophistication of ancient Rome?
[Interpret]

And instead of a wolf the trembling sheep stand in dread
    of war.
We are scarcely defended within the fortress and even within it
    The barbarous crowd mixed with Greeks still inspires our
      hearts with fear.
In fact, the barbarians live with us without discrimination
30   And they possess more than half of the houses which
      shelter us.
Even though you don't fear them you would hate them all when
you see them,
    Their chests covered over with hides and their heads with long
      hanging hair.
And even those men who're believed to descend from Greek
colonizers
    Wear Persian trousers instead of the garments their own
      nation wears.
35 They carry on their relations by means of their common language
    While I am reduced to communication by making signs.
Here I am the barbarian, and I'm understood by no one,
    And the stupid Getae make fun of the Latin words which
      I speak;
And openly often they speak ill of me and with perfect
freedom,
40   Perhaps even holding against me the fact that I'm exiled
      from Rome.
And as it happens, they think I am crazy when to their jabber
    I nod my head to say "yes" and shake it to signify "no."
Add that an unjust justice is enforced with the rigid
sword blade
    And wounds are frequently given in the midst of the
      market place.

45 O harsh Lachesis[1], who gave me, born under a star that's
unlucky,
    The threads of a life that were not shorter than those
      which are mine!
The fact that I lack the sight of my fatherland and of my
comrades
    And that I live here among the Scythian race I lament:
Both of these penalties are grave, but I deserved the loss of
my City;
50   Perhaps I did not deserve to be punished in such a place.
Why do I speak? I'm a madman. I deserved to lose even my
life then
    When I did injury to the power of Caesar the god.

---

1. **Lachesis** (lak´ i sis) in Greek and Roman mythology, one of the three Fates. Lachesis
measures out the length of the thread representing a person's life, while Clotho spins
it and Atropos cuts it short.

Thematic Connection
Unlike the speakers in the
Anglo-Saxon lyrics, Ovid
describes those among
whom he lives. How do
other people make his
exile even lonelier?

OVID

(43 B.C–A.D. 17)
Born in
Sulmona,
Italy, the
writer Publius
Ovidius Naso,
known to us as
Ovid, became
the author of
numerous elegies. Ovid
lived and wrote chiefly in
Rome, a city he loved and
in which he was celebrated
and favored. In A.D. 8,
however, Ovid offended
Emperor Augustus with his
satires and was banished
from Rome to Tomis, near
the Black Sea. Despite
numerous pleas for forgiveness, Ovid was forced to
remain in exile until his
death. *Tristia*, a lament,
was written while Ovid
was in exile.

Far Corners of Earth

Fan mounted as an album leaf: *Evening in Spring Hills*, ink and color on silk. Chinese. The Metropolitan Museum of Art.

Tu Fu

Translated by David Hinton

Chiang-han mountains looming, impassable,
A cloud drifts over this far corner of earth.
Year after year, nothing familiar, nothing
Anywhere but one further end of the road.

5 Here, Wang Ts'an found loss and confusion,
And Ch'ü Yüan cold grief. My heart already
Broken in quiet times—and look at me,
Each day wandering a new waste of highway.

Tu Fu

(712–770)

The poet Tu Fu comes from a background mixing the traditional with the unexpected. The classically educated son of a prominent scholar, he left home at a very early age to travel alone through China. He eventually settled in the nation's capital, where after a few years, he was granted a position in the palace of the crown prince. Within the next few years, rebel forces had sent the emperor into exile, and Tu Fu had fled with his family to the country to live in poverty and write. He eventually returned to political service, but in the political upheavals of the time, exile and return were a recurrent cycle. The bulk of Tu Fu's poetry was written in the last eleven years of his life.

Connecting Literature Around the World

1. Compare Ovid's or Tu Fu's depiction of exile with that found in an Anglo-Saxon poem.
2. Which work finds a universal meaning for exile, a meaning that applies to people in many different situations? Explain.
3. Which most effectively conveys the specific, personal response of the speaker to his or her situation? Explain.

Focus on Literary Forms:
The Epic

Beowulf on the Funeral Pyre, Rockwell Kent

From the fifth through fifteenth centuries, England was a place of upheaval and uncertainty. Invasions, plagues, and political battles raged, and people looked for reassurance in the form of heroes who embodied strength, honor, and virtue. This need for heroes is met in epic tales such as *Beowulf*.

Prepare to Read

from Beowulf

About Beowulf

At the dawn of English literature stands *Beowulf*. Like the epics of other cultures—the *Iliad* and the *Odyssey* of ancient Greece and the *Sundiata* of Mali—*Beowulf* is the self-portrait of a culture. In this adventure-packed poem, the Anglo-Saxons of eighth-century Britain embodied the traditions that shaped their world in one towering figure—Beowulf, sword-wielding slayer of monsters, upholder of the right, warrior-chieftain. The Anglo-Saxons left us few factual records of their life and history. In *Beowulf*, however, they vividly recorded their dreams, aspirations, and fears.

The Stuff of Legend Although the action takes place in sixth-century Scandinavia, *Beowulf* was originally told in Old English, the language spoken by the Anglo-Saxons of England during the years 500 to 1100. Beowulf, a Geat from a region that is today southern Sweden, sets sail to aid the Danish King Hrothgar in his fight against the monster Grendel. A terrifying swampland creature whose eyes burn "with gruesome light," Grendel has been terrorizing Hrothgar's great banquet hall, Herot, for twelve years. The battle between Beowulf, a young warrior of great strength and courage, and Grendel, his bloodthirsty foe, is the first of three mortal battles in this long poem.

Forging an Epic The tales in *Beowulf* originate from a time when stories and poems were passed along by word of mouth. In Anglo-Saxon England, traveling minstrels, called *scops*, captivated audiences with long narrative poems. These poems changed and grew as they were passed from one scop to another. *Beowulf* was told and retold in this fashion throughout England for hundreds of years. In the eleventh century, the epic was finally written down.

Beowulf grew out of other, earlier traditions. The monsters and dragons of the tale, the brave warriors steadfastly loyal to their heroic chief, the descent into the eerie regions below the earth—these were familiar elements of Scandinavian or Celtic folk tales. Even a detail as specific as Beowulf's seizure of Grendel's arm can be traced to earlier tales.

A Guide to Life By forging these various traditions into one unified tale and by adding the later influence of Christianity, the Anglo-Saxon scops created a central reference point for their culture. Listening to *Beowulf*, an Anglo-Saxon could learn of bravery and loyalty, of the monsters that spite and hatred could be, and of the heroism needed to conquer them.

From Oral Tradition to Cyberspace and Beyond The only original manuscript of the complete 3,182-line poem comes to us from Sir Robert Cotton's (1571–1631) collection of medieval manuscripts. In 1731, the manuscript was saved from a fire but did not escape damage—2,000 letters crumbled away from the edges of the manuscript. Thanks to an initiative called the Electronic *Beowulf* Project, the manuscript has now been preserved and made available electronically.

Although much of the attention given to the poem is scholarly, *Beowulf* is far from a museum piece. The adventuresome tale, clanging with blood-curdling battles and the noble ring of bold oaths, continues to thrill readers. In 2000, the celebrated Irish poet Seamus Heaney published his translation of *Beowulf* to public acclaim. Preserved in song, then in writing, then on a hard drive, the memory of Beowulf has stood strong through the ages, finally calling on a modern poet to renew the sounds and spirit of Britain's first epic.

Preview

Connecting to the Literature

It is a familiar but stirring scene: A brave hero battles his archenemy, an evildoer who will stop at nothing to win. The theme of hero and villain goes back more than twelve hundred years, to a time when Anglo-Saxon storytellers sang of the battles of Beowulf, legendary warrior.

Literary Analysis

The Epic

An **epic** is a long narrative poem, sometimes developed orally, that celebrates the deeds of a legendary or heroic figure. Epics are among the earliest forms of literature. Early epics, such as Homer's *Iliad* from ancient Greece, capture the cultural and religious values of the peoples who created and retold them. Common features of epics include the following:

- The hero battles forces that threaten the order of his world.
- The story is told in a serious manner, often in special, elevated language.

Beowulf, the epic of the Anglo-Saxons, uses elements of Anglo-Saxon poetry such as the **kenning** and **caesura**. (For more about these elements, see p. 15.)

Connecting Literary Elements

A **legendary hero** is a larger-than-life character whose accomplishments are celebrated in traditional tales. Beowulf's boastful self-confidence, his feats of strength, and his victories in battle make him a classic legendary hero. Upholding the values of his culture—loyalty, bravery, honor—he can teach modern readers a great deal about the Anglo-Saxon view of the world.

Reading Strategy

Paraphrasing

Although *Beowulf* has been translated into modern English, its long, involved sentences may still be difficult to follow. To aid your understanding, **paraphrase** complex passages—identify the key details in a passage and restate them in your own words. Use a graphic organizer like the one shown.

Vocabulary Development

reparation (rep′ ə rā′ shən) *n.* something making up for a wrong or an injury (p. 41)

solace (säl′ is) *n.* comfort; relief (p. 41)

purge (purj) *v.* purify; cleanse (p. 45)

writhing (rīth′ iŋ) *adj.* making twisting or turning motions (p. 47)

massive (mas′ iv) *adj.* big and solid; bulky (p. 52)

loathsome (lōth′ səm) *adj.* disgusting (p. 52)

> **Original**
>
> High on a wall a Danish watcher / Patrolling along the cliffs saw / The travelers crossing to the shore, their shields / Raised and shining . . . .

Key Details

guard

saw people

come ashore

> **Paraphrase**
>
> A Danish guard saw strangers come ashore, holding up their shields.

Grendel (Frontispiece from *Beowulf*), Patten Wilson, The British Library

▲**Critical Viewing** What details of this painting make Grendel look fearsome? **[Analyze]**

from Beowulf

Translated by Burton Raffel

Background

When *Beowulf* was composed, England was changing from a pagan to a Christian culture. Pagan Anglo-Saxons told grim tales of life ruled by fate, tales in which people struggled against monsters for their place in the world. The missionaries who converted them to Christianity taught them that human beings and their choices of good or evil were at the center of creation. *Beowulf* reflects both pagan and Christian traditions.

The selection opens during an evening of celebration at Herot, the banquet hall of the Danish king Hrothgar (hroth′ gär). Outside in the darkness, however, lurks the murderous monster Grendel.

The Wrath of Grendel

A powerful monster, living down
In the darkness, growled in pain, impatient
As day after day the music rang
Loud in that hall,[1] the harp's rejoicing

5 Call and the poet's clear songs, sung
Of the ancient beginnings of us all, recalling
The Almighty making the earth, shaping
These beautiful plains marked off by oceans,
Then proudly setting the sun and moon

10 To glow across the land and light it;
The corners of the earth were made lovely with trees
And leaves, made quick with life, with each
Of the nations who now move on its face. And then
As now warriors sang of their pleasure:

15 So Hrothgar's men lived happy in his hall
Till the monster stirred, that demon, that fiend,
Grendel, who haunted the moors, the wild
Marshes, and made his home in a hell
Not hell but earth. He was spawned in that slime,

20 Conceived by a pair of those monsters born

---

1. **hall** Herot.

Literary Analysis

The Epic What does the story of Grendel's origins suggest about the beliefs of Anglo-Saxon culture?

✓ Reading Check

What does Grendel resent about Hrothgar and his men?

Of Cain,[2] murderous creatures banished
By God, punished forever for the crime
Of Abel's death. The Almighty drove
Those demons out, and their exile was bitter,
25 Shut away from men; they split
Into a thousand forms of evil—spirits
And fiends, goblins, monsters, giants,
A brood forever opposing the Lord's
Will, and again and again defeated.
30   Then, when darkness had dropped, Grendel
Went up to Herot, wondering what the warriors
Would do in that hall when their drinking was done.
He found them sprawled in sleep, suspecting
Nothing, their dreams undisturbed. The monster's
35 Thoughts were as quick as his greed or his claws:
He slipped through the door and there in the silence
Snatched up thirty men, smashed them
Unknowing in their beds and ran out with their bodies,
The blood dripping behind him, back
40 To his lair, delighted with his night's slaughter.
        At daybreak, with the sun's first light, they saw
How well he had worked, and in that gray morning
Broke their long feast with tears and laments
For the dead. Hrothgar, their lord, sat joyless
45 In Herot, a mighty prince mourning
The fate of his lost friends and companions,
Knowing by its tracks that some demon had torn
His followers apart. He wept, fearing
The beginning might not be the end. And that night
50 Grendel came again, so set
On murder that no crime could ever be enough,
No savage assault quench his lust
For evil. Then each warrior tried
To escape him, searched for rest in different
55 Beds, as far from Herot as they could find,
Seeing how Grendel hunted when they slept.
Distance was safety; the only survivors
Were those who fled him. Hate had triumphed.
        So Grendel ruled, fought with the righteous,
60 One against many, and won; so Herot
Stood empty, and stayed deserted for years,
Twelve winters of grief for Hrothgar, king
Of the Danes, sorrow heaped at his door
By hell-forged hands. His misery leaped
65 The seas, was told and sung in all

Reading Strategy
Paraphrasing What are
the main ideas in the
sentences in lines 34–40?

Literary Analysis
The Epic Terrorized by
Grendel, Hrothgar and his
followers face "Twelve
winters of grief." How
does the length of their
suffering increase the epic
feeling of this tale?

---

2. **Cain** oldest son of Adam and Eve, who murdered his brother Abel.

Men's ears: how Grendel's hatred began,
How the monster relished his savage war
On the Danes, keeping the bloody feud
Alive, seeking no peace, offering
70 No truce, accepting no settlement, no price
In gold or land, and paying the living
For one crime only with another. No one
Waited for <u>reparation</u> from his plundering claws:
That shadow of death hunted in the darkness,
75 Stalked Hrothgar's warriors, old
And young, lying in waiting, hidden
In mist, invisibly following them from the edge
Of the marsh, always there, unseen.
        So mankind's enemy continued his crimes,
80 Killing as often as he could, coming
Alone, bloodthirsty and horrible. Though he lived
In Herot, when the night hid him, he never
Dared to touch King Hrothgar's glorious
Throne, protected by God—God,
85 Whose love Grendel could not know. But Hrothgar's
Heart was bent. The best and most noble
Of his council debated remedies, sat
In secret sessions, talking of terror
And wondering what the bravest of warriors could do.
90 And sometimes they sacrificed to the old stone gods,
Made heathen vows, hoping for Hell's
Support, the Devil's guidance in driving
Their affliction off. That was their way,
And the heathen's only hope, Hell
95 Always in their hearts, knowing neither God
Nor His passing as He walks through our world, the Lord
Of Heaven and earth; their ears could not hear
His praise nor know His glory. Let them
Beware, those who are thrust into danger,
100 Clutched at by trouble, yet can carry no <u>solace</u>
In their hearts, cannot hope to be better! Hail
To those who will rise to God, drop off
Their dead bodies and seek our Father's peace!

The Coming of Beowulf

        So the living sorrow of Healfdane's son[3]
105 Simmered, bitter and fresh, and no wisdom
Or strength could break it: that agony hung
On king and people alike, harsh
And unending, violent and cruel, and evil.

---

3. **Healfdane's** (hā´ alf den´ nəz) **son** Hrothgar.

reparation (rep´ ə rā´ shən) *n.* something making up for wrong or injury

solace (säl´ is) *n.* comfort; relief

✔**Reading Check**

Why do the Danes flee Herot at night?

In his far-off home Beowulf, Higlac's[4]

110 Follower and the strongest of the Geats—greater
And stronger than anyone anywhere in this world—
Heard how Grendel filled nights with horror
And quickly commanded a boat fitted out,
Proclaiming that he'd go to that famous king.

115 Would sail across the sea to Hrothgar,
Now when help was needed. None
Of the wise ones regretted his going, much
As he was loved by the Geats: the omens were good,
And they urged the adventure on. So Beowulf

120 Chose the mightiest men he could find,
The bravest and best of the Geats, fourteen
In all, and led them down to their boat;
He knew the sea, would point the prow
Straight to that distant Danish shore.

125   Then they sailed, set their ship
Out on the waves, under the cliffs.
Ready for what came they wound through the currents,
The seas beating at the sand, and were borne
In the lap of their shining ship, lined

130 With gleaming armor, going safely
In that oak-hard boat to where their hearts took them.
The wind hurried them over the waves,
The ship foamed through the sea like a bird
Until, in the time they had known it would take,

135 Standing in the round-curled prow they could see
Sparkling hills, high and green
Jutting up over the shore, and rejoicing
In those rock-steep cliffs they quietly ended
Their voyage. Jumping to the ground, the Geats

140 Pushed their boat to the sand and tied it
In place, mail[5] shirts and armor rattling
As they swiftly moored their ship. And then
They gave thanks to God for their easy crossing.
     High on a wall a Danish watcher

145 Patrolling along the cliffs saw
The travelers crossing to the shore, their shields
Raised and shining; he came riding down,
Hrothgar's lieutenant, spurring his horse,
Needing to know why they'd landed, these men

Reading Strategy
Paraphrasing Paraphrase
lines 125–131. Remember
that your paraphrase need
not follow the word order
of the original.

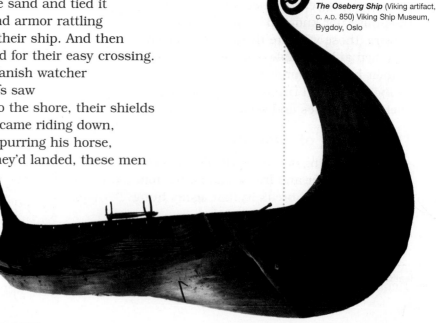

The Oseberg Ship (Viking artifact,
C. A.D. 850) Viking Ship Museum,
Bygdoy, Oslo

---

4. **Higlac's** (hig´ laks) Higlac
was the king of the Geats
(gā´ ats) and Beowulf's
feudal lord and uncle.
5. **mail** flexible body armor
made of metal.

150 In armor. Shaking his heavy spear
In their faces he spoke:
                         "Whose soldiers are you,
You who've been carried in your deep-keeled ship
Across the sea-road to this country of mine?
Listen! I've stood on these cliffs longer
155 Than you know, keeping our coast free
Of pirates, raiders sneaking ashore
From their ships, seeking our lives and our gold.
None have ever come more openly—
And yet you've offered no password, no sign
160 From my prince, no permission from my people for your landing
Here. Nor have I ever seen,
Out of all the men on earth, one greater
Than has come with you; no commoner carries
Such weapons, unless his appearance, and his beauty,
165 Are both lies. You! Tell me your name,
And your father's; no spies go further onto Danish
Soil than you've come already. Strangers,
From wherever it was you sailed, tell it,
And tell it quickly, the quicker the better,
170 I say, for us all. Speak, say
Exactly who you are, and from where, and why."
            Their leader answered him, Beowulf unlocking
Words from deep in his breast:
                         "We are Geats,
Men who follow Higlac. My father
175 Was a famous soldier, known far and wide
As a leader of men. His name was Edgetho.
His life lasted many winters;
Wise men all over the earth surely
Remember him still. And we have come seeking
180 Your prince, Healfdane's son, protector
Of this people, only in friendship: instruct us,
Watchman, help us with your words! Our errand
Is a great one, our business with the glorious king
Of the Danes no secret; there's nothing dark
185 Or hidden in our coming. You know (if we've heard
The truth, and been told honestly) that your country
Is cursed with some strange, vicious creature
That hunts only at night and that no one
Has seen. It's said, watchman, that he has slaughtered
190 Your people, brought terror to the darkness. Perhaps
Hrothgar can hunt, here in my heart,
For some way to drive this devil out—
If anything will ever end the evils
Afflicting your wise and famous lord.
195 Here he can cool his burning sorrow.

Literary Analysis
The Epic How do word choice and other stylistic features of the watchman's speech add a serious, epic tone to his question?

Literary Analysis
The Epic and the Legendary Hero What does Beowulf's way of identifying himself suggest about the values of a warrior culture?

✓ Reading Check
Why does Beowulf sail to Denmark?

from *Beowulf* ◆ 43

Or else he may see his suffering go on
Forever, for as long as Herot towers
High on your hills."

                  The mounted officer
Answered him bluntly, the brave watchman:
200   "A soldier should know the difference between words
And deeds, and keep that knowledge clear
In his brain. I believe your words, I trust in
Your friendship. Go forward, weapons and armor
And all, on into Denmark. I'll guide you
205 Myself—and my men will guard your ship,
Keep it safe here on our shores,
Your fresh-tarred boat, watch it well,
Until that curving prow carries
Across the sea to Geatland a chosen
210 Warrior who bravely does battle with the creature
Haunting our people, who survives that horror
Unhurt, and goes home bearing our love."

          Then they moved on. Their boat lay moored,
Tied tight to its anchor. Glittering at the top
215 Of their golden helmets wild boar heads gleamed,
Shining decorations, swinging as they marched,
Erect like guards, like sentinels, as though ready
To fight. They marched, Beowulf and his men
And their guide, until they could see the gables
220 Of Herot, covered with hammered gold
And glowing in the sun—that most famous of all dwellings,
Towering majestic, its glittering roofs
Visible far across the land.
Their guide reined in his horse, pointing
225 To that hall, built by Hrothgar for the best
And bravest of his men; the path was plain,
They could see their way. . . .

Gilt silver brooch from Gotland (Pre-Viking Scandinavia)
Statens Historiska Museet, Stockholm

◆◆◆◆

Beowulf and his men arrive at Herot and are called to see the King.

◆◆◆◆

               Beowulf arose, with his men
230 Around him, ordering a few to remain
With their weapons, leading the others quickly
Along under Herot's steep roof into Hrothgar's
Presence. Standing on that prince's own hearth,
Helmeted, the silvery metal of his mail shirt
235 Gleaming with a smith's high art, he greeted
The Danes' great lord:

"Hail, Hrothgar!
Higlac is my cousin[6] and my king; the days
Of my youth have been filled with glory. Now Grendel's
Name has echoed in our land: sailors
240 Have brought us stories of Herot, the best
Of all mead-halls,[7] deserted and useless when the moon
Hangs in skies the sun had lit,
Light and life fleeing together.
My people have said, the wisest, most knowing
245 And best of them, that my duty was to go to the Danes'
Great king. They have seen my strength for themselves,
Have watched me rise from the darkness of war,
Dripping with my enemies' blood. I drove
Five great giants into chains, chased
250 All of that race from the earth. I swam
In the blackness of night, hunting monsters
Out of the ocean, and killing them one
By one; death was my errand and the fate
They had earned. Now Grendel and I are called
255 Together, and I've come. Grant me, then,
Lord and protector of this noble place,
A single request! I have come so far,
O shelterer of warriors and your people's loved friend,
That this one favor you should not refuse me—
260 That I, alone and with the help of my men,
May purge all evil from this hall. I have heard,
Too, that the monster's scorn of men
Is so great that he needs no weapons and fears none.
Nor will I. My lord Higlac
265 Might think less of me if I let my sword
Go where my feet were afraid to, if I hid
Behind some broad linden[8] shield: my hands
Alone shall fight for me, struggle for life
Against the monster. God must decide
270 Who will be given to death's cold grip.
Grendel's plan, I think, will be
What it has been before, to invade this hall
And gorge his belly with our bodies. If he can,
If he can. And I think, if my time will have come,
275 There'll be nothing to mourn over, no corpse to prepare
For its grave: Grendel will carry our bloody
Flesh to the moors, crunch on our bones
And smear torn scraps of our skin on the walls

---

6. **cousin** here, used as a general term for relative.
7. **mead-halls** To reward his thanes, the king in heroic literature would build a hall where mead (a drink made from fermented honey) was served.
8. **linden** very sturdy type of wood.

Literary Analysis
The Epic and the Legendary Hero How do Beowulf's boasts of great deeds and his announcement of his plan establish him as a hero?

purge (pʉrj) v. purify; cleanse

Reading Strategy
Paraphrasing Paraphrase Beowulf's plans in lines 264–279.

Reading Check
What does Beowulf ask of Hrothgar?

Of his den. No, I expect no Danes
280 Will fret about sewing our shrouds, if he wins.
And if death does take me, send the hammered
Mail of my armor to Higlac, return
The inheritance I had from Hrethel, and he
From Wayland.[9] Fate will unwind as it must!"

———◆◇◆———

That night Beowulf and his men stay inside Herot. While his men sleep, Beowulf lies awake, eager to meet with Grendel.

———◆◇◆———

The Battle with Grendel

285   Out from the marsh, from the foot of misty
Hills and bogs, bearing God's hatred,
Grendel came, hoping to kill
Anyone he could trap on this trip to high Herot.
He moved quickly through the cloudy night,
290 Up from his swampland, sliding silently
Toward that gold-shining hall. He had visited Hrothgar's
Home before, knew the way—
But never, before nor after that night,
Found Herot defended so firmly, his reception
295 So harsh. He journeyed, forever joyless,
Straight to the door, then snapped it open,
Tore its iron fasteners with a touch
And rushed angrily over the threshold.
He strode quickly across the inlaid
300 Floor, snarling and fierce: his eyes
Gleamed in the darkness, burned with a gruesome
Light. Then he stopped, seeing the hall
Crowded with sleeping warriors, stuffed
With rows of young soldiers resting together.
305 And his heart laughed, he relished the sight,
Intended to tear the life from those bodies
By morning; the monster's mind was hot
With the thought of food and the feasting his belly
Would soon know. But fate, that night, intended
310 Grendel to gnaw the broken bones
Of his last human supper. Human
Eyes were watching his evil steps,
Waiting to see his swift hard claws.
Grendel snatched at the first Geat
315 He came to, ripped him apart, cut

---

9. Wayland from Germanic folklore, an invisible blacksmith.

His body to bits with powerful jaws,
Drank the blood from his veins and bolted
Him down, hands and feet; death
And Grendel's great teeth came together,
320 Snapping life shut. Then he stepped to another
Still body, clutched at Beowulf with his claws,
Grasped at a strong-hearted wakeful sleeper
—And was instantly seized himself, claws
Bent back as Beowulf leaned up on one arm.
325   That shepherd of evil, guardian of crime,
Knew at once that nowhere on earth
Had he met a man whose hands were harder;
His mind was flooded with fear—but nothing
Could take his talons and himself from that tight
330 Hard grip. Grendel's one thought was to run
From Beowulf, flee back to his marsh and hide there:
This was a different Herot than the hall he had emptied.
But Higlac's follower remembered his final
Boast and, standing erect, stopped
335 The monster's flight, fastened those claws
In his fists till they cracked, clutched Grendel
Closer. The infamous killer fought
For his freedom, wanting no flesh but retreat,
Desiring nothing but escape; his claws
340 Had been caught, he was trapped. That trip to Herot
Was a miserable journey for the <u>writhing</u> monster!
        The high hall rang, its roof boards swayed,
And Danes shook with terror. Down
The aisles the battle swept, angry
345 And wild. Herot trembled, wonderfully
Built to withstand the blows, the struggling
Great bodies beating at its beautiful walls;
Shaped and fastened with iron, inside
And out, artfully worked, the building
350 Stood firm. Its benches rattled, fell
To the floor, gold-covered boards grating
As Grendel and Beowulf battled across them.
Hrothgar's wise men had fashioned Herot
To stand forever; only fire,
355 They had planned, could shatter what such skill had put
Together, swallow in hot flames such splendor
Of ivory and iron and wood. Suddenly
The sounds changed, the Danes started
In new terror, cowering in their beds as the terrible
360 Screams of the Almighty's enemy sang
In the darkness, the horrible shrieks of pain
And defeat, the tears torn out of Grendel's
Taut throat, hell's captive caught in the arms

Literary Analysis

The Epic How do the "renamings" of Grendel in line 325 emphasize the weighty significance of the battle that is about to begin?

writhing (rīth´ iŋ) *adj.* making twisting or turning motions

Reading Check

What advantage does Beowulf have in his fight with Grendel?

from *Beowulf* ◆ 47

Of him who of all the men on earth
365 Was the strongest.
                           That mighty protector of men
Meant to hold the monster till its life
Leaped out, knowing the fiend was no use
To anyone in Denmark. All of Beowulf's
Band had jumped from their beds, ancestral
370 Swords raised and ready, determined
To protect their prince if they could. Their courage
Was great but all wasted: they could hack at Grendel
From every side, trying to open
A path for his evil soul, but their points
375 Could not hurt him, the sharpest and hardest iron
Could not scratch at his skin, for that sin-stained demon
Had bewitched all men's weapons, laid spells
That blunted every mortal man's blade.
And yet his time had come, his days
380 Were over, his death near; down
To hell he would go, swept groaning and helpless
To the waiting hands of still worse fiends.
Now he discovered—once the afflictor
Of men, tormentor of their days—what it meant
385 To feud with Almighty God: Grendel
Saw that his strength was deserting him, his claws
Bound fast, Higlac's brave follower tearing at
His hands. The monster's hatred rose higher,
But his power had gone. He twisted in pain,
390 And the bleeding sinews deep in his shoulder
Snapped, muscle and bone split
And broke. The battle was over, Beowulf
Had been granted new glory: Grendel escaped,
But wounded as he was could flee to his den,
395 His miserable hole at the bottom of the marsh,
Only to die, to wait for the end
Of all his days. And after that bloody
Combat the Danes laughed with delight.
He who had come to them from across the sea,
400 Bold and strong-minded, had driven affliction
Off, purged Herot clean. He was happy,
Now, with that night's fierce work; the Danes
Had been served as he'd boasted he'd serve them; Beowulf,
A prince of the Geats, had killed Grendel,
405 Ended the grief, the sorrow, the suffering
Forced on Hrothgar's helpless people
By a bloodthirsty fiend. No Dane doubted
The victory, for the proof, hanging high
From the rafters where Beowulf had hung it, was the monster's
410 Arm, claw and shoulder and all.

Literary Analysis
The Epic Which details
from this description of
the battle between
Beowulf and Grendel add
realism? Which details
add epic grandness?

Reading Strategy
Paraphrasing Paraphrase
the sentence in lines
392–397.

The Danes celebrate Beowulf's victory. That night, though, Grendel's mother kills Hrothgar's closest friend and carries off her child's claw. The next day the horrified king tells Beowulf about the two monsters and their underwater lair.

The Monsters' Lair

"I've heard that my people, peasants working
In the fields, have seen a pair of such fiends
Wandering in the moors and marshes, giant
Monsters living in those desert lands.
415 And they've said to my wise men that, as well as they could see,
One of the devils was a female creature.
The other, they say, walked through the wilderness
Like a man—but mightier than any man.
They were frightened, and they fled, hoping to find help
420 In Herot. They named the huge one Grendel:
If he had a father no one knew him,
Or whether there'd been others before these two,
Hidden evil before hidden evil.
They live in secret places, windy
425 Cliffs, wolf-dens where water pours
From the rocks, then runs underground, where mist
Steams like black clouds, and the groves of trees
Growing out over their lake are all covered
With frozen spray, and wind down snakelike
430 Roots that reach as far as the water
And help keep it dark. At night that lake
Burns like a torch. No one knows its bottom,
No wisdom reaches such depths. A deer,
Hunted through the woods by packs of hounds,
435 A stag with great horns, though driven through the forest
From faraway places, prefers to die
On those shores, refuses to save its life
In that water. It isn't far, nor is it
A pleasant spot! When the wind stirs
440 And storms, waves splash toward the sky,
As dark as the air, as black as the rain
That the heavens weep. Our only help,
Again, lies with you. Grendel's mother
Is hidden in her terrible home, in a place
445 You've not seen. Seek it, if you dare! Save us,
Once more, and again twisted gold,
Heaped-up ancient treasure, will reward you
For the battle you win!"

Golden horn, National Museet, Copenhagen

✓ Reading Check

How does Beowulf's battle with Grendel end?

Beowulf resolves to kill Grendel's monstrous mother. He travels to the lake in which she lives.

The Battle With Grendel's Mother

Then Edgetho's brave son[10] spoke:

"Remember,
450 Hrothgar, O knowing king, now
When my danger is near, the warm words we uttered,
And if your enemy should end my life
Then be, O generous prince, forever
The father and protector of all whom I leave
455 Behind me, here in your hands, my beloved
Comrades left with no leader, their leader
Dead. And the precious gifts you gave me,
My friend, send them to Higlac. May he see
In their golden brightness, the Geats' great lord
460 Gazing at your treasure, that here in Denmark
I found a noble protector, a giver
Of rings whose rewards I won and briefly
Relished. And you, Unferth,[11] let
My famous old sword stay in your hands:
465 I shall shape glory with Hrunting, or death
Will hurry me from this earth!"

As his words ended
He leaped into the lake, would not wait for anyone's
Answer; the heaving water covered him
Over. For hours he sank through the waves;
470 At last he saw the mud of the bottom.
And all at once the greedy she-wolf
Who'd ruled those waters for half a hundred
Years discovered him, saw that a creature
From above had come to explore the bottom
475 Of her wet world. She welcomed him in her claws,
Clutched at him savagely but could not harm him,
Tried to work her fingers through the tight
Ring-woven mail on his breast, but tore
And scratched in vain. Then she carried him, armor
480 And sword and all, to her home; he struggled
To free his weapon, and failed. The fight
Brought other monsters swimming to see

Silver pendant showing the helmet of the Vendel (Early Viking period, 10th century), Statens Historiska Museet, Stockholm

---

10. **Edgetho's brave son** Beowulf. Elsewhere he is identified by such phrases as "the Geats' proud prince" and "the Geats' brave prince."
11. **Unferth** Danish warrior who had questioned Beowulf's bravery before the battle with Grendel.

Her catch, a host of sea beasts who beat at
His mail shirt, stabbing with tusks and teeth
485 As they followed along. Then he realized, suddenly,
That she'd brought him into someone's battle-hall,
And there the water's heat could not hurt him,
Nor anything in the lake attack him through
The building's high-arching roof. A brilliant
490 Light burned all around him, the lake
Itself like a fiery flame.
                              Then he saw
The mighty water witch and swung his sword,
His ring-marked blade, straight at her head;
The iron sang its fierce song,
495 Sang Beowulf's strength. But her guest
Discovered that no sword could slice her evil
Skin, that Hrunting could not hurt her, was useless
Now when he needed it. They wrestled, she ripped
And tore and clawed at him, bit holes in his helmet,
500 And that too failed him; for the first time in years
Of being worn to war it would earn no glory;
It was the last time anyone would wear it. But Beowulf
Longed only for fame, leaped back
Into battle. He tossed his sword aside,
505 Angry; the steel-edged blade lay where
He'd dropped it. If weapons were useless he'd use
His hands, the strength in his fingers. So fame
Comes to the men who mean to win it
And care about nothing else! He raised
510 His arms and seized her by the shoulder; anger
Doubled his strength, he threw her to the floor.
She fell, Grendel's fierce mother, and the Geats'
Proud prince was ready to leap on her. But she rose
At once and repaid him with her clutching claws,
515 Wildly tearing at him. He was weary, that best
And strongest of soldiers; his feet stumbled
And in an instant she had him down, held helpless.
Squatting with her weight on his stomach, she drew
A dagger, brown with dried blood, and prepared
520 To avenge her only son. But he was stretched
On his back, and her stabbing blade was blunted
By the woven mail shirt he wore on his chest.
The hammered links held; the point
Could not touch him. He'd have traveled to the bottom of the earth,
525 Edgetho's son, and died there, if that shining
Woven metal had not helped—and Holy
God, who sent him victory, gave judgment
For truth and right, Ruler of the Heavens,
Once Beowulf was back on his feet and fighting.

Literary Analysis
The Epic How does the setting of this battle add to its epic significance? (Consider what it shows about the realms in which Beowulf has power.)

Reading Strategy
Paraphrasing Paraphrase the sentence describing the combat in lines 498–502

Reading Check
Why does Beowulf toss aside his sword in the fight?

530   Then he saw, hanging on the wall, a heavy
       Sword, hammered by giants, strong
       And blessed with their magic, the best of all weapons
       But so <u>massive</u> that no ordinary man could lift
       Its carved and decorated length. He drew it
535 From its scabbard, broke the chain on its hilt,
       And then, savage, now, angry
       And desperate, lifted it high over his head
       And struck with all the strength he had left,
       Caught her in the neck and cut it through,
540 Broke bones and all. Her body fell
       To the floor, lifeless, the sword was wet
       With her blood, and Beowulf rejoiced at the sight.
           The brilliant light shone, suddenly,
       As though burning in that hall, and as bright as Heaven's
545 Own candle, lit in the sky. He looked
       At her home, then following along the wall
       Went walking, his hands tight on the sword,
       His heart still angry. He was hunting another
       Dead monster, and took his weapon with him
550 For final revenge against Grendel's vicious
       Attacks, his nighttime raids, over
       And over, coming to Herot when Hrothgar's
       Men slept, killing them in their beds,
       Eating some on the spot, fifteen
555 Or more, and running to his <u>loathsome</u> moor
       With another such sickening meal waiting
       In his pouch. But Beowulf repaid him for those visits,
       Found him lying dead in his corner,
       Armless, exactly as that fierce fighter
560 Had sent him out from Herot, then struck off
       His head with a single swift blow. The body
       jerked for the last time, then lay still.
           The wise old warriors who surrounded Hrothgar,
       Like him staring into the monsters' lake,
565 Saw the waves surging and blood
       Spurting through. They spoke about Beowulf,
       All the graybeards, whispered together
       And said that hope was gone, that the hero
       Had lost fame and his life at once, and would never
570 Return to the living, come back as triumphant
       As he had left; almost all agreed that Grendel's
       Mighty mother, the she-wolf, had killed him.
       The sun slid over past noon, went further
       Down. The Danes gave up, left
575 The lake and went home, Hrothgar with them.
       The Geats stayed, sat sadly, watching,
       Imagining they saw their lord but not believing

massive (mas´ iv) *adj.* big and solid

Reading Strategy
Paraphrasing Paraphrase lines 543–562.

loathsome (lōth´ səm) *adj.* disgusting

They would ever see him again.
—Then the sword

Melted, blood-soaked, dripping down
580 Like water, disappearing like ice when the world's
Eternal Lord loosens invisible
Fetters and unwinds icicles and frost
As only He can, He who rules
Time and seasons, He who is truly
585 God. The monsters' hall was full of
Rich treasures, but all that Beowulf took
Was Grendel's head and the hilt of the giants'
Jeweled sword; the rest of that ring-marked
Blade had dissolved in Grendel's steaming
590 Blood, boiling even after his death.
And then the battle's only survivor
Swam up and away from those silent corpses;
The water was calm and clean, the whole
Huge lake peaceful once the demons who'd lived in it
595 Were dead.
Then that noble protector of all seamen
Swam to land, rejoicing in the heavy
Burdens he was bringing with him. He
And all his glorious band of Geats
Thanked God that their leader had come back unharmed;
600 They left the lake together. The Geats
Carried Beowulf's helmet, and his mail shirt.
Behind them the water slowly thickened
As the monsters' blood came seeping up.
They walked quickly, happily, across
605 Roads all of them remembered, left
The lake and the cliffs alongside it, brave men
Staggering under the weight of Grendel's skull,
Too heavy for fewer than four of them to handle—
Two on each side of the spear jammed through it—
610 Yet proud of their ugly load and determined
That the Danes, seated in Herot, should see it.
Soon, fourteen Geats arrived
At the hall, bold and warlike, and with Beowulf,
Their lord and leader, they walked on the mead-hall
615 Green. Then the Geats' brave prince entered
Herot, covered with glory for the daring
Battles he had fought; he sought Hrothgar
To salute him and show Grendel's head.
He carried that terrible trophy by the hair,
620 Brought it straight to where the Danes sat,
Drinking, the queen among them. It was a weird
And wonderful sight, and the warriors stared.

in context   Science Connection

Anglo-Saxon Metalwork
The sword that Beowulf discovers is said to have been magically forged by giants—a story reflecting the scarcity and value of swords in Anglo-Saxon times. To form a sword, highly skilled smiths had to heat ore to the melting point of iron (2,800° F), cool it, and then add carbon. The result was a hard, durable metal. To reach the required temperature, medieval smiths built a fire fueled with charcoal and stoked with huge bellows, or devices for blowing air. Once they had smelted the iron ore, they hammered the molten metal into the proper shape. A smith's work did not stop at a sharp edge but included the ornamentation of the sword hilt. Handsomely adorned, a sword was at once a deadly weapon and a work of art. Both usable iron and the skills needed to work it were scarce, and a sword's noble owner treasured it, treating it as an individual. Some swords—like Beowulf's Hrunting— were given names.

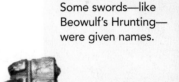

Reading Check

What does Beowulf do after slaying Grendel's mother?

After being honored by Hrothgar, Beowulf and his fellow Geats return home, where he eventually becomes King. Beowulf rules Geatland for fifty years. When a dragon menaces his kingdom, Beowulf, now an old man, determines to slay the beast. Before going into battle, he tells his men about the royal house and his exploits in its service.

The Last Battle

And Beowulf uttered his final boast:
"I've never known fear, as a youth I fought
625 In endless battles. I am old, now,
But I will fight again, seek fame still,
If the dragon hiding in his tower dares
To face me."
          Then he said farewell to his followers,
Each in his turn, for the last time:
630   "I'd use no sword, no weapon, if this beast
Could be killed without it, crushed to death
Like Grendel, gripped in my hands and torn
Limb from limb. But his breath will be burning
Hot, poison will pour from his tongue.
635 I feel no shame, with shield and sword
And armor, against this monster: when he comes to me

▼ **Critical Viewing**
What characteristics do this dragon and Grendel have in common? **[Compare and Contrast]**

The Dragon for "The High Kings," George Sharp

I mean to stand, not run from his shooting
Flames, stand till fate decides
Which of us wins. My heart is firm,
640 My hands calm: I need no hot
Words. Wait for me close by, my friends.
We shall see, soon, who will survive
This bloody battle, stand when the fighting
Is done. No one else could do
645 What I mean to, here, no man but me
Could hope to defeat this monster. No one
Could try. And this dragon's treasure, his gold
And everything hidden in that tower, will be mine
Or war will sweep me to a bitter death!"
650　　　Then Beowulf rose, still brave, still strong,
And with his shield at his side, and a mail shirt on his breast,
Strode calmly, confidently, toward the tower, under
The rocky cliffs: no coward could have walked there!
And then he who'd endured dozens of desperate
655 Battles, who'd stand boldly while swords and shields
Clashed, the best of kings, saw
Huge stone arches and felt the heat
Of the dragon's breath, flooding down
Through the hidden entrance, too hot for anyone
660 To stand, a streaming current of fire
And smoke that blocked all passage. And the Geats'
Lord and leader, angry, lowered
His sword and roared out a battle cry,
A call so loud and clear that it reached through
665 The hoary rock, hung in the dragon's
Ear. The beast rose, angry,
Knowing a man had come—and then nothing
But war could have followed. Its breath came first,
A steaming cloud pouring from the stone,
670 Then the earth itself shook. Beowulf
Swung his shield into place, held it
In front of him, facing the entrance. The dragon
Coiled and uncoiled, its heart urging it
Into battle. Beowulf's ancient sword
675 Was waiting, unsheathed, his sharp and gleaming
Blade. The beast came closer; both of them
Were ready, each set on slaughter. The Geats'
Great prince stood firm, unmoving, prepared
Behind his high shield, waiting in his shining
680 Armor. The monster came quickly toward him,
Pouring out fire and smoke, hurrying
To its fate. Flames beat at the iron
Shield, and for a time it held, protected
Beowulf as he'd planned; then it began to melt,

Literary Analysis
The Epic What does Beowulf's speech in lines 630–649 suggest to you about Anglo-Saxon values?

Detail of a dragon head on the *Mammen* horse collar
(Viking artifact, 10th century), National Museum, Denmark

Reading Check
How does Beowulf plan to fight the dragon?

685 And for the first time in his life that famous prince
Fought with fate against him, with glory
Denied him. He knew it, but he raised his sword
And struck at the dragon's scaly hide.
The ancient blade broke, bit into
690 The monster's skin, drew blood, but cracked
And failed him before it went deep enough, helped him
Less than he needed. The dragon leaped
With pain, thrashed and beat at him, spouting
Murderous flames, spreading them everywhere.
695 And the Geats' ring-giver did not boast of glorious
Victories in other wars: his weapon
Had failed him, deserted him, now when he needed it
Most, that excellent sword. Edgetho's
Famous son stared at death,
700 Unwilling to leave this world, to exchange it
For a dwelling in some distant place—a journey
Into darkness that all men must make, as death
Ends their few brief hours on earth.
            Quickly, the dragon came at him, encouraged
705 As Beowulf fell back; its breath flared,
And he suffered, wrapped around in swirling
Flames—a king, before, but now
A beaten warrior. None of his comrades
Came to him, helped him, his brave and noble
710 Followers; they ran for their lives, fled
Deep in a wood. And only one of them
Remained, stood there, miserable, remembering,
As a good man must, what kinship should mean.

            His name was Wiglaf, he was Wexstan's son
715 And a good soldier; his family had been Swedish,
Once. Watching Beowulf, he could see
How his king was suffering, burning. Remembering
Everything his lord and cousin had given him,
Armor and gold and the great estates
720 Wexstan's family enjoyed, Wiglaf's
Mind was made up; he raised his yellow
Shield and drew his sword—an ancient
Weapon that had once belonged to Onela's
Nephew, and that Wexstan had won, killing
725 The prince when he fled from Sweden, sought safety
With Herdred, and found death.[12] And Wiglaf's father
Had carried the dead man's armor, and his sword,

Gilt bronze winged dragon (Swedish artifact, 8th century),
Statens Historiska Museet, Stockholm

Literary Analysis
The Epic What do these lines reveal about the values of warrior culture?

---

12. Onela's / Nephew . . . found death When Onela seized the throne of Sweden, his two
nephews sought shelter with the king of Geatland, Herdred. Wiglaf's father, Wexstan,
killed the older nephew for Onela.

To Onela, and the king had said nothing, only
Given him armor and sword and all,
730 Everything his rebel nephew had owned
And lost when he left this life. And Wexstan
Had kept those shining gifts, held them
For years, waiting for his son to use them,
Wear them as honorably and well as once
735 His father had done; then Wexstan died
And Wiglaf was his heir, inherited treasures
And weapons and land. He'd never worn
That armor, fought with that sword, until Beowulf
Called him to his side, led him into war.
740 But his soul did not melt, his sword was strong;
The dragon discovered his courage, and his weapon,
When the rush of battle brought them together.
　　　And Wiglaf, his heart heavy, uttered
The kind of words his comrades deserved:
745 　　　"I remember how we sat in the mead-hall, drinking
And boasting of how brave we'd be when Beowulf
Needed us, he who gave us these swords
And armor: all of us swore to repay him,
When the time came, kindness for kindness
750 —With our lives, if he needed them. He allowed us to
　　join him,
Chose us from all his great army, thinking
Our boasting words had some weight, believing
Our promises, trusting our swords. He took us
For soldiers, for men. He meant to kill
755 This monster himself, our mighty king,
Fight this battle alone and unaided,
As in the days when his strength and daring dazzled
Men's eyes. But those days are over and gone
And now our lord must lean on younger
760 Arms. And we must go to him, while angry
Flames burn at his flesh, help
Our glorious king! By almighty God,
I'd rather burn myself than see
Flames swirling around my lord.
765 And who are we to carry home
Our shields before we've slain his enemy
And ours, to run back to our homes with Beowulf
So hard-pressed here? I swear that nothing
He ever did deserved an end
770 Like this, dying miserably and alone,
Butchered by this savage beast: we swore
That these swords and armor were each for us all!"
　　　Then he ran to his king, crying encouragement
As he dove through the dragon's deadly fumes.

Literary Analysis
The Epic and the Legendary Hero
According to Wiglaf, what is Beowulf's relationship with his followers like?

Literary Analysis
The Epic and the Legendary Hero What does Wiglaf's decision suggest about the way in which a legendary hero can inspire heroism in others?

✔**Reading Check**
How do Beowulf's companions react when the dragon breathes flame on him?

Wiglaf and Beowulf kill the dragon, but the old king is mortally wounded. As he dies, Beowulf asks Wiglaf to bring him the treasure that the dragon was guarding.

The Spoils

775   Then Wexstan's son went in, as quickly
  As he could, did as the dying Beowulf
  Asked, entered the inner darkness
  Of the tower, went with his mail shirt and his sword.
  Flushed with victory he groped his way,
780 A brave young warrior, and suddenly saw
  Piles of gleaming gold, precious
  Gems, scattered on the floor, cups
  And bracelets, rusty old helmets, beautifully
  Made but rotting with no hands to rub
785 And polish them. They lay where the dragon left them;
  It had flown in the darkness, once, before fighting
  Its final battle. (So gold can easily
  Triumph, defeat the strongest of men,
  No matter how deep it is hidden!) And he saw,
790 Hanging high above, a golden
  Banner, woven by the best of weavers
  And beautiful. And over everything he saw
  A strange light, shining everywhere,
  On walls and floor and treasure. Nothing
795 Moved, no other monsters appeared;
  He took what he wanted, all the treasures
  That pleased his eye, heavy plates
  And golden cups and the glorious banner,
  Loaded his arms with all they could hold.
800 Beowulf's dagger, his iron blade,
  Had finished the fire-spitting terror
  That once protected tower and treasures
  Alike; the gray-bearded lord of the Geats
  Had ended those flying, burning raids
805 Forever.
     Then Wiglaf went back, anxious
  To return while Beowulf was alive, to bring him
  Treasure they'd won together. He ran,
  Hoping his wounded king, weak
  And dying, had not left the world too soon.
810 Then he brought their treasure to Beowulf, and found
  His famous king bloody, gasping
  For breath. But Wiglaf sprinkled water

Reading Strategy
Paraphrasing What is the main idea in the sentence in lines 779–785?

Head of carved post from the ship burial at Oseberg (Viking, c. A.D. 850). Viking Ship Museum, Bygdoy, Oslo

Over his lord, until the words
Deep in his breast broke through and were heard.
815 Beholding the treasure he spoke, haltingly:
        "For this, this gold, these jewels, I thank
Our Father in Heaven, Ruler of the Earth—
For all of this, that His grace has given me,
Allowed me to bring to my people while breath
820 Still came to my lips. I sold my life
For this treasure, and I sold it well. Take
What I leave, Wiglaf, lead my people,
Help them; my time is gone. Have
The brave Geats build me a tomb,
825 When the funeral flames have burned me, and build it
Here, at the water's edge, high
On this spit of land, so sailors can see
This tower, and remember my name, and call it
Beowulf's tower, and boats in the darkness
830 And mist, crossing the sea, will know it."
        Then that brave king gave the golden
Necklace from around his throat to Wiglaf,
Gave him his gold-covered helmet, and his rings,
And his mail shirt, and ordered him to use them well:
835   "You're the last of all our far-flung family.
Fate has swept our race away,
Taken warriors in their strength and led them
To the death that was waiting. And now I follow them."
        The old man's mouth was silent, spoke
840 No more, had said as much as it could;
He would sleep in the fire, soon. His soul
Left his flesh, flew to glory.

Literary Analysis
The Epic In Beowulf's
death scene, what
is shown about the
importance in warrior
culture of the
commemoration of
individuals after death?

—————————————————— >·◇·< ——————————————————

*Wiglaf denounces the warriors who deserted Beowulf. The Geats
burn their king's body on a funeral pyre and bitterly lament his death.*

—————————————————— >·◇·< ——————————————————

The Farewell

        Then the Geats built the tower, as Beowulf
Had asked, strong and tall, so sailors
845 Could find it from far and wide; working
For ten long days they made his monument,
Sealed his ashes in walls as straight
And high as wise and willing hands
Could raise them. And the riches he and Wiglaf
850 Had won from the dragon, rings, necklaces,
Ancient, hammered armor—all

Reading Check
What is Beowulf's last
request?

The treasures they'd taken were left there, too,
Silver and jewels buried in the sandy
Ground, back in the earth, again
855 And forever hidden and useless to men.
And then twelve of the bravest Geats
Rode their horses around the tower,
Telling their sorrow, telling stories
Of their dead king and his greatness, his glory,
860 Praising him for heroic deeds, for a life
As noble as his name. So should all men
Raise up words for their lords, warm
With love, when their shield and protector leaves
His body behind, sends his soul
865 On high. And so Beowulf's followers
Rode, mourning their beloved leader,
Crying that no better king had ever
Lived, no prince so mild, no man
So open to his people, so deserving of praise.

Review and Assess

Thinking About the Selection

1. **Respond:** Which episode in the epic did you find most thrilling? Why?

2. **(a) Recall:** At the opening of the poem, what annoys Grendel and leads to his attacks? **(b) Interpret:** What universal conflict lies behind his war with the Danes?

3. **(a) Recall:** Why does Beowulf travel to Herot? **(b) Infer:** What do his motives for the trip tell you about his character? **(c) Analyze:** How does the contrast between Grendel and Beowulf turn their conflict into a fight between good and evil?

4. **(a) Infer:** What does Beowulf's speech in lines 246–255 show about how he defines his identity? **(b) Compare and Contrast:** Although Beowulf is brave and Grendel is spiteful, both might be said to act out of pride. Explain.

5. **Synthesize:** Beowulf's defeat of Grendel might be described as the defeat of the "dark side" of the warrior's life. Explain.

6. **(a) Support:** Identify an example from the epic in which the memory of Beowulf's deeds inspires someone. **(b) Synthesize:** Explain how the poem, by keeping Beowulf's memory alive, keeps a culture's values alive.

7. **Evaluate:** Do you think Beowulf's deeds make him a good role model? Explain.

Review and Assess

Literary Analysis

The Epic

1. **Epics** often center on a battle between good and evil. Find evidence in lines 173–198 to indicate that Beowulf is battling for the good.
2. An epic reflects the values of the culture that produced it. Use a chart like the one shown to identify three specific features of *Beowulf* that probably pleased its original audience. For each, draw a conclusion about Anglo-Saxon tastes and values.

Feature	Why Pleasing	Values Reflected
boastful speeches	makes hero seem superhuman	

3. (a) What details show the importance of Christian beliefs in the epic? (b) What details reveal the importance of pagan warrior values, such as a belief in fate, a taste for boasting, a pride in loyalty, and a desire for fame?
4. Frustrated pride may lead to spite, just as a loyalty may lead to vengeance, and eagerness for glory may turn into greed. Explain how each creature Beowulf battles represents an extreme and dangerous form of warrior values and behavior.

Connecting Literary Elements

5. (a) List two heroic characteristics of Beowulf. (b) Find a passage that shows the hero's more human side. Explain your choice.
6. (a) Is Beowulf a believable character, or is he "too heroic"? Explain. (b) How does his believability affect your sympathy for him?

Reading Strategy

Paraphrasing

7. **Paraphrase** lines 843–861 from *Beowulf*.
8. (a) Explain which details you did not understand before paraphrasing. (b) Compare your paraphrase to the original, citing poetic effects that were lost in your paraphrase.

Extend Understanding

9. **Cultural Connection:** Compare the way the epic commemorates Beowulf with the way our culture celebrates its heroes.

Quick Review

An **epic** is an extended narrative poem that celebrates the deeds of a legendary or heroic figure.

A **legendary hero** is a larger-than-life character whose accomplishments reflect a people's values and way of life.

To **paraphrase**, identify key ideas and details in a text and restate them in your own words.

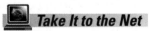 **Take It to the Net**
www.phschool.com
Take the interactive self-test online to check your understanding of the selection.

Integrate Language Skills

Vocabulary Development Lesson

Word Analysis: Latin Root -sol-

The Latin root -sol- means "to comfort." The root appears in the word *solace*, "an easing of grief, loneliness, or discomfort." With the meaning of -sol- in mind, answer the following questions. Provide a definition of each italicized word.

1. Which character in the epic might receive a *consolation* prize?
2. Which character is *inconsolable*?

Spelling Strategy

For words ending in *e*, drop the final *e* when adding the suffix *-ing*: writhe + *-ing* = writhing. Add the suffix *-ing* to these words.

1. raise   2. enrage   3. inquire

Concept Development: Antonyms

Choose the letter of the word that is the antonym, the word opposite in meaning, of the first word.

1. reparation: (a) reimbursement, (b) renewal, (c) theft
2. solace: (a) aggravation, (b) resentment, (c) comfort
3. purge: (a) pollute, (b) purify, (c) complete
4. writhing: (a) valor, (b) churning, (c) still
5. massive: (a) average, (b) tremendous, (c) flimsy
6. loathsome: (a) disgusting, (b) delightful, (c) angry

Grammar and Style Lesson

Appositives and Appositive Phrases

An **appositive** is a noun or pronoun placed next to another noun or pronoun to identify or explain it. An **appositive phrase** is an appositive with modifiers. The underlined appositive phrase below gives additional information about Beowulf:

In his far-off home Beowulf, <u>Higlac's</u>

<u>Follower and the strongest of the Geats</u>—

If an appositive is necessary to identify who or what is being spoken about, it is not set off with commas. If an appositive is not essential to the meaning of the sentence, it should be set off with commas.

Appositive phrases are a key element of epic style, in which naming and renaming things and people is an important poetic act.

Practice In each item, identify the appositive phrase and name what is being described.

1. "We are Geats, / Men who follow Higlac. My father / Was a famous soldier, . . ."
2. "And we have come seeking / Your prince, Healfdane's son, protector / Of this people, only in friendship: instruct us, . . ."
3. . . . Grendel escaped, / But wounded as he was could flee to his den, / His miserable hole at the bottom of the marsh, . . .
4. . . . almost all agreed that Grendel's / Mighty mother, the she-wolf, had killed him.
5. . . . with Beowulf, / Their lord and leader, they walked on the mead-hall / Green.

Writing Application Write a description of Gendel, using two appositive phrases.

WG *Prentice Hall Writing and Grammar Connection: Chapter 19, Section 1*

Writing Lesson

Response to Criticism

Burton Raffel, a translator of *Beowulf*, remarks that "of all the many-sided excellences" of the poem, one of the most satisfying "is the poet's insight into people." In a brief essay, agree or disagree. Your response should clearly set out your position and develop support for it by analyzing scenes from the poem.

Prewriting Begin by taking notes on passages that show either an insight or a lack of insight into people. Concentrate on descriptions of characters' motives or notable actions. Then, take your own position on Raffel's statement.

Drafting In your introduction, state your response to Raffel's comment. Then, discuss scenes from the poem, clearly showing how each supports your point.

Revising Review your draft, placing a star next to each important reference you make to the poem. For each star, make sure you have explained the significance of the passage and its connection to your main point.

Model: Revising to Clarify Connections

☆ When Wiglaf runs back to show Beowulf the treasure, the poet puts the finishing touch on his portrayal of this young warrior. ∧ *It is clear from this action how eager Wiglaf is to win his dying lord's approval and to console him. The episode demonstrates the poet's insight into people and their behavior.*

> With this revision, the writer clarifies the example and shows how it supports the main point.

𝒲𝒢 *Prentice Hall Writing and Grammar Connection: Chapter 14, Section 4*

Extension Activities

Listening and Speaking Give a **dramatic reading** of a passage from *Beowulf*, such as the suspenseful battle with Grendel's mother.

1. Rehearse your reading with a partner, guiding each other about the pace and expressiveness of your reading.
2. Jot down reminders about pacing and expression on a performance copy of the passage.

Present your reading to the class.

Research and Technology Work with a group to prepare a **dictionary** of epic heroes. Include facts about each hero's culture of origin, ancestry, identifying characteristics, accomplishments, and fate. **[Group Activity]**

 **Take It to the Net** www.phschool.com

Go online for an additional research activity using the Internet.

CONNECTIONS
Literature Around the World

The Epic

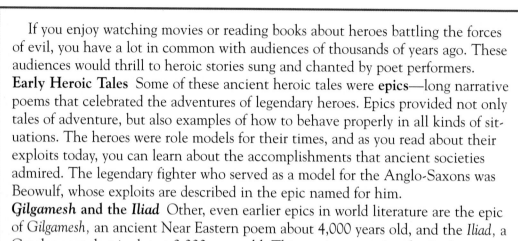

If you enjoy watching movies or reading books about heroes battling the forces of evil, you have a lot in common with audiences of thousands of years ago. These audiences would thrill to heroic stories sung and chanted by poet performers.

Early Heroic Tales Some of these ancient heroic tales were **epics**—long narrative poems that celebrated the adventures of legendary heroes. Epics provided not only tales of adventure, but also examples of how to behave properly in all kinds of situations. The heroes were role models for their times, and as you read about their exploits today, you can learn about the accomplishments that ancient societies admired. The legendary fighter who served as a model for the Anglo-Saxons was Beowulf, whose exploits are described in the epic named for him.

Gilgamesh* and the *Iliad Other, even earlier epics in world literature are the epic of *Gilgamesh*, an ancient Near Eastern poem about 4,000 years old, and the *Iliad*, a Greek poem that is almost 3,000 years old. This section contains the Prologue to *Gilgamesh* and the most famous battle scene from the *Iliad*.

from Gilgamesh
The Prologue

Translated by David Ferry

The Story
of him who knew the most of all men know;
who made the journey; heartbroken; reconciled;

who knew the way things were before the Flood
the secret things, the mystery; who went

5 to the end of the earth, and over; who returned,
and wrote the story on a tablet of stone.

He built Uruk.[1] He built the keeping place
of Anu and Ishtar.[2] The outer wall

shines in the sun like brightest copper; the inner
10 wall is beyond the imagining of kings.

Study the brickwork, study the fortification;
climb the great ancient staircase to the terrace;

study how it is made; from the terrace see
the planted and fallow fields, the ponds and orchards.

15 This is Uruk, the city of Gilgamesh
the Wild Ox, son of Lugalbanda, son

of the Lady Wildcow Ninsun, Gilgamesh
the vanguard and the rear guard of the army,

---

1. **Uruk** (oo´ rook) ancient Sumerian city.
2. **Anu and Ishtar** (ä´ noo; ish´ tär) Anu is the father of the Babylonian
   gods and god of the sky; Ishtar is the Babylonian goddess of love.

Thematic Connection
Compare what Gilgamesh
and Beowulf do for their
respective peoples.

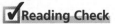

Reading Check
What are two of
Gilgamesh's major
accomplishments?

Shadow of Darkness over the enemy field,
20 the Web, the Flood that rises to wash away

the walls of alien cities, Gilgamesh
the strongest one of all, the perfect, the terror.

It is he who opened passes through the mountains;
and he who dug deep wells on the mountainsides;

25 who measured the world; and sought out Utnapishtim[3]
beyond the world; it is he who restored the shrines;

two-thirds a god, one-third a man, the king.
Go to the temple of Anu and Ishtar:

open the copper chest with the iron locks;
30 the tablet of lapis lazuli[4] tells the story.

---

3. Utnapishtim (o͞ot nə pēsh′ təm) the Mesopotamian Noah, survivor of the great flood.
4. lapis lazuli (lap′ is laz′ yo͞o lĭ) an azure-blue, opaque, semiprecious stone.

Thematic Connection
In *Beowulf*, does the hero appear to be as godlike as Gilgamesh appears to be here? Explain whether this attribute might add to or detract from a character's heroic qualities.

GILGAMESH

Gilgamesh tells about a Sumerian king of that name who lived between 2700 and 2500 B.C. Unlike modern books, but like many epics, the poem does not have a single author. Instead, stories about King Gilgamesh were told and handed down by Sumerians for hundreds of years after his death. When the Babylonians conquered the Sumerians, they inherited the Sumerian cultural tradition. A Babylonian author, borrowing from some of these tales, created a unified epic about the legendary Sumerian king.

◄**Critical Viewing**
What conclusions about the Sumerians led by Gilgamesh can you draw from this Sumerian harp?

from the Iliad

Homer, Translated by Richmond Lattimore

During the Trojan War, fought over Helen of Troy, Achilleus, the greatest Greek warrior, and Hektor, the best Trojan warrior, meet for battle. Hektor has brutally killed Achilleus' friend Patroklos. In this scene, the goddess Athene, disguised as the Trojan warrior Deïphobos, leads Hektor to Achilleus.

"My brother, it is true our father and the lady our mother, taking
my knees in turn, and my companions about me, entreated
that I stay within, such was the terror upon all of them.
But the heart within me was worn away by hard sorrow for you.
5 But now let us go straight on and fight hard, let there be
     no sparing
of our spears, so that we can find out whether Achilleus
will kill us both and carry our bloody war spoils back
to the hollow ships, or will himself go down under your spear."
     So Athene[1] spoke and led him on by beguilement.
10 Now as the two in their advance were come close together,
first of the two to speak was tall helm-glittering Hektor:
"Son of Peleus, I will no longer run from you, as before this
I fled three times around the great city of Priam, and dared not
stand to your onfall. But now my spirit in turn has driven me
15 to stand and face you. I must take you now, or I must be taken.
Come then, shall we swear before the gods? For these are
     the highest
who shall be witnesses and watch over our agreements.
Brutal as you are I will not defile you, if Zeus[2] grants
to me that I can wear you out, and take the life from you.
20 But after I have stripped your glorious armor, Achilleus,
I will give your corpse back to the Achaians.[3] Do you do likewise."

---

1. **Athene** (ə *thē´* nə) daughter of Zeus. She is associated with victory in war and clever thinking and speaking. She protects the Greeks. Here, she is disguised as Deïphobos (dā i fō´ bōs), a Trojan.
2. **Zeus** (zo͞os) the most powerful of the gods, known as "father of men and gods."
3. **Achaians** (ə kē´ ənz) Greeks.

✔ **Reading Check**

What did Hektor do the last time he encountered Achilleus on the battlefield?

Then looking darkly at him swift-footed Achilleus answered:
"Hektor, argue me no agreements. I cannot forgive you.
As there are no trustworthy oaths between men and lions,

25 nor wolves and lambs have spirit that can be brought to
  agreement
but forever these hold feelings of hate for each other,
so there can be no love between you and me, nor shall
  there be
oaths between us, but one or the other must fall
  before then
to glut with his blood Ares the god who fights under the
  shield's guard.

30 Remember every valor of yours, for now the need comes
hardest upon you to be a spearman and a bold warrior.
There shall be no more escape for you, but Pallas Athene
will kill you soon by my spear. You will pay in a lump for
  all those
sorrows of my companions you killed in your spear's fury."

35 So he spoke, and balanced the spear far shadowed, and threw it;
but glorious Hektor kept his eyes on him, and avoided it,
for he dropped, watchful, to his knee, and the bronze spear
  flew over his shoulder
and stuck in the ground, but Pallas Athene snatched it, and gave it
back to Achilleus, unseen by Hektor shepherd of the people.

40 But now Hektor spoke out to the blameless son of Peleus:
"You missed; and it was not, O Achilleus like the immortals,
from Zeus that you knew my destiny; but you thought so; or rather
you are someone clever in speech and spoke to swindle me,
to make me afraid of you and forget my valor and war strength.

45 You will not stick your spear in my back as I run away from you
but drive it into my chest as I storm straight in against you;
if the god gives you that; and now look out for my brazen
spear. I wish it might be taken full length in your body.
And indeed the war would be a lighter thing for the Trojans

50 if you were dead, seeing that you are their greatest affliction."
 So he spoke, and balanced the spear far shadowed, and threw it,
and struck the middle of Peleïdes' shield, nor missed it,
but the spear was driven far back from the shield, and Hektor
  was angered
because his swift weapon had been loosed from his hand in a
  vain cast.

55 He stood discouraged, and had no other ash spear; but lifting
his voice he called aloud on Deïphobos of the pale shield,
and asked him for a long spear, but Deïphobos was not near him.
And Hektor knew the truth inside his heart, and spoke aloud:
"No use. Here at last the gods have summoned me deathward.

60 I thought Deïphobos the hero was here close beside me,
but he is behind the wall and it was Athene cheating me,

▲ **Critical Viewing**
From this vase painting,
what can you deduce
about ancient Greek
attitudes towards
horsemanship and
other battle skills?
[Deduce]

and now evil death is close to me, and no longer far away,
and there is no way out. So it must long since have been pleasing
to Zeus, and Zeus' son who strikes from afar, this way; though
    before this
65 they defended me gladly. But now my death is upon me.
Let me at least not die without a struggle, inglorious,
but do some big thing first, that men to come shall know of it."
    So he spoke, and pulling out the sharp sword that was slung
at the hollow of his side, huge and heavy, and gathering
70 himself together, he made his swoop, like a high-flown eagle
who launches himself out of the murk of the clouds on the flat land
to catch away a tender lamb or a shivering hare; so
Hektor made his swoop, swinging his sharp sword, and Achilleus
charged, the heart within him loaded with savage fury.
75 In front of his chest the beautiful elaborate great shield
covered him, and with the glittering helm with four horns
he nodded; the lovely golden fringes were shaken about it
which Hephaistos[4] had driven close along the horn of the helmet.
And as a star moves among stars in the night's darkening,
80 Hesper,[5] who is the fairest star who stands in the sky, such
was the shining from the pointed spear Achilleus was shaking
in his right hand with evil intention toward brilliant Hektor.
He was eyeing Hektor's splendid body, to see where it might best
give way, but all the rest of the skin was held in the armour,
85 brazen and splendid, he stripped when he cut down the strength
    of Patroklos;[6]
yet showed where the collar-bones hold the neck from
    the shoulders,
the throat, where death of the soul comes most swiftly; in this place
brilliant Achilleus drove the spear as he came on in fury,
and clean through the soft part of the neck the spearpoint
    was driven.
90 Yet the ash spear heavy with bronze did not sever the windpipe,
so that Hektor could still make exchange of words spoken.
But he dropped in the dust, and brilliant Achilleus vaunted
    above him:
"Hektor, surely you thought as you killed Patroklos you would be
safe, and since I was far away you thought nothing of me,
95 O fool, for an avenger was left, far greater than he was,
behind him and away by the hollow ships. And it was I;
and I have broken your strength; on you the dogs and the vultures
shall feed and foully rip you; the Achaians will bury Patroklos."
    In his weakness Hektor of the shining helm spoke to him:
100 "I entreat you, by your life, by your knees, by your parents,

Thematic Connection
Compare the intensity
and suspense of this
battle scene with that
of Beowulf's battle with
Grendel's mother.

---

4. **Hephaistos** (hē fes′ təs) god of fire and the forge. He made Achilleus' armor.
5. **Hesper** (hes′ pər) the evening star.
6. **Patroklos** (pə träk′ lōs) companion and henchman to Achilleus.

☑**Reading Check**
Which hero wins the
combat?

do not let the dogs feed on me by the ships of the Achaians,
but take yourself the bronze and gold that are there in abundance,
those gifts that my father and the lady my mother will give you,
and give my body to be taken home again, so that the Trojans
105 and the wives of the Trojans may give me in death my rite of
      burning."
    But looking darkly at him swift-footed Achilleus answered:
"No more entreating of me, you dog, by knees or parents.
I wish only that my spirit and fury would drive me
to hack your meat away and eat it raw for the things that
110 you have done to me. So there is no one who can hold the dogs off
from your head, not if they bring here and set before me ten times
and twenty times the ransom, and promise more in addition,
not if Priam son of Dardanos should offer to
weigh out your bulk in gold; not even so shall the lady
      your mother
115 who herself bore you lay you on the death-bed and
      mourn you:
no, but the dogs and the birds will have you all for
      their feasting."
    Then, dying, Hektor of the shining helmet spoke to him:
"I know you well as I look upon you, I know that I could not
persuade you, since indeed in your breast is a heart of iron.
120 Be careful now; for I might be made into the gods' curse
upon you, on that day when Paris and Phoibos Apollo[7]
destroy you in the Skaian gates,[8] for all your valor."
    He spoke, and as he spoke the end of death closed in
      upon him,
and the soul fluttering free of the limbs went down into
      Death's house
125 mourning her destiny, leaving youth and manhood behind her.
Now though he was a dead man brilliant Achilleus spoke to him:
"Die: and I will take my own death at whatever time
Zeus and the rest of the immortals choose to accomplish it."

---

7. **Paris and Phoibus Apollo** (par′ is; fē′ bəs ə pôl′ ō) Paris, son of King Priam,
   and Apollo, the archer god of light and of healing who protects the Trojans.
8. **Skaian gates** (skē′ ən) the main gates of Troy.

Connecting Literature Around the World

1. What does the Prologue to *Gilgamesh* suggest about the duties of
   a Sumerian king?
2. (a) What does Hektor ask of Achilleus after he is mortally
   wounded? (b) What conclusions about the values of ancient
   Greece can you draw from this request and Achilleus' response?
3. Compare and contrast a modern leader with Gilgamesh, Achilleus,
   and Beowulf. Consider both their deeds and their values.

Homer

One of the
most powerful
influences on
British and
European
literature
has been the
ancient Greek
epics the *Iliad* and
the *Odyssey*. The
Greeks ascribed these
poems to the blind, half-
legendary poet Homer,
whom they called "The
Poet." Although his birth
and death dates are uncertain, he probably composed
the *Iliad* late in the eighth
century B.C.

  The epic tells about the
legendary Trojan War, set
hundreds of years earlier, in
which Greek forces attacked
the city of Troy in Asia
Minor in quest of the return
of the beautiful Helen, wife
of their chieftain Menelaus.
At the center of the *Iliad*
is the wrath of the mighty
Achilleus, the greatest of
the Greek warriors. Slighted
by Menelaus, Achilleus
withdraws his help from
the Greek cause—until
the Trojan Hektor slays
his best friend, Patroklos,
and provokes him into a
ferocious rage.

A National Spirit

Four Kings of England, British Library, London, Great Britain

Prepare to Read

History of the English Church and People ◆ The Anglo-Saxon Chronicle

Bede (673–735)

It was as if the lights had gone out. In the fifth century, the Roman Empire abandoned Britain. Rome was the center of the most advanced civilization in the West. As part of the Roman Empire, Britain had been connected with a larger world of trade and culture. Roman missionaries taught reading and writing as they preached Christianity. Roman soldiers patrolled Britain's borders. Once Rome withdrew, however, Britain was isolated, threatened by invasion from without and by strife from within.

Keeping Learning Alive Monasteries, particularly in Ireland, kept knowledge alive during these dark times. Monks studied Latin, the language of the Roman Empire. They laboriously copied books. The more scholarly wrote new works.

Much of what we know about England before A.D. 700 is based on the work of one such monk, Bede. A contemporary of the unknown author of *Beowulf*, Bede was the most learned scholar of his day. Although he wrote forty books on various subjects, his reputation would be secure on the basis of one— *A History of the English Church and People*, for which Bede is called the father of English history.

A Daily Reminder Bede was born in Wearmouth (now Sunderland) in northeastern England. At age seven, he entered the nearby monastic school of Jarrow. A diligent student, he stayed on as a priest and scholar. Although Bede lived his whole life at Jarrow, he wrote in Latin, so his work was accessible to scholars throughout the West. His pupils carried his writings to Europe. Famous in his own lifetime for its scholarship, his work has become a part of daily life—Bede helped originate the dating of events from the birth of Christ, a cornerstone of the Western calendar.

A Scholarly Work In the *History*, Bede describes the conquest of Britain by the Anglo-Saxon tribes after the departure of the Romans. His main concern, however, was the expansion of Christianity in England. Bede gathered information from many kinds of documents, interviewed knowledgeable monks, and, in general, proceeded very much like a modern historian.

In the century after his death, Bede's history was translated from Latin into English for King Alfred. In the same century, Bede was honored with the title "the Venerable [respected] Bede."

The Anglo-Saxon Chronicle

In ninth-century Britain, the story of the past existed only in fragments: a poem passed from one person to another; a parchment that listed the names of old kings; a soldier's memories of a battle. Bede's *History* was an exception, but the work was available only in Latin.

During the renaissance of scholarship in King Alfred's reign (A.D. 871–899), a group of monks decided to knit together this fragmentary story. Their efforts resulted in *The Anglo-Saxon Chronicle*, a unique English historic record.

Putting the Pieces Together In writing the *Chronicle*, these monks pulled together parts of Bede's *History*, existing chronologies, royal genealogies (family trees), and other historic documents. They wrote their new manuscript by hand and sent copies to several other monasteries.

A Letter to the Future For the following two centuries, monks added news to the *Chronicle*—ranging from gossip about a local baron to the battles of kings. *The Anglo-Saxon Chronicle* became a kind of chain letter from one generation to the next.

Preview

Connecting to the Literature

When the authors of these selections wrote, there was no videotape or computer disk. The memory of the past took only the most fragile forms—a memorized song, a rare manuscript. These selections are among the few records we have from the time.

Literary Analysis

Historical Writing

Historical writing tells the story of past events using evidence, such as documents from the period, that the writer has evaluated for reliability. Examining the evidence is one way that writers of history take a step back from the shared beliefs of those around them. You can sense this historical "step back" in a sentence from Bede's *History:* "Britain, formerly known as Albion, is an island in the ocean. . . ." The moment Bede wrote that sentence, he left behind his tiny corner of England for a wider world, one that knew little about Britain.

Comparing Literary Works

Both of these selections are accounts from Anglo-Saxon times of early British history. However, the kinds of details they include differ. Bede provides a general background on Britain, while the selection from *The Anglo-Saxon Chronicle* focuses on wars between the Anglo-Saxons and the Danes. In addition, the authors make decisions that may surprise you about what details to include. These selections model the following characteristics:

- Down-to-earth facts
- Fanciful details
- Traces of the author's own loyalties.

As you read, compare the types of details the authors include.

Reading Strategy

Breaking Down Sentences

Bede sometimes writes in long, complicated sentences. To help you interpret them, **break down long sentences** into main and related parts. First, identify the part expressing the main action or actions. Then, identify details that answer *who, what, when, where,* or *why* about these actions. Use a chart like this one to break down long sentences.

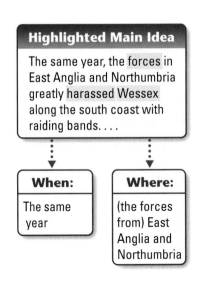

Highlighted Main Idea

The same year, the forces in East Anglia and Northumbria greatly harassed Wessex along the south coast with raiding bands. . . .

When:	**Where:**
The same year	(the forces from) East Anglia and Northumbria

Vocabulary Development

promontories (präm´ ən tôr´ ēz) *n.* peaks of high land sticking out into the water (p. 74)

innumerable (i nōō´ mer ə bəl) *adj.* too many to count (p. 76)

stranded (stran´ did) *v.* forced into shallow water or onto a beach; left helpless (p. 80)

barricaded (bar´ i kād´ id) *v.* blocked (p. 81)

ravaged (rav´ ijd) *v.* destroyed (p. 81)

from
A History of the English Church and People

Bede Translated by *Leo Sherley-Price*

Background

Although the majority of British people in Bede's day were illiterate and written records were scarce, monasteries such as the one to which Bede belonged were dedicated to continuing a tradition of learning. Through the monastery, Bede had access to books and other documents, as well as contact with other learned monks. Using these sources, he was able to generate his history of Britain. His fellow Britons may have been illiterate, but Bede had in mind a larger world of readers for his work—the Church to which he belonged and the Roman civilization in which it participated. Bede wrote his account of Britain for such readers, starting at the beginning with the basics.

The Situation of Britain and Ireland: Their Earliest Inhabitants

Britain, formerly known as Albion, is an island in the ocean, facing between north and west, and lying at a considerable distance from the coasts of Germany, Gaul, and Spain, which together form the greater part of Europe. It extends 800 miles northwards, and is 200 in breadth, except where a number of <u>promontories</u> stretch farther, the coastline round which extends to 3,675 miles. To the south lies Belgic Gaul,[1] from the nearest shore of which travelers can see the

promontories (präm´ ən tôr´ ēz) *n.* peaks of high land sticking out into the water

---

1. **Belgic Gaul** France.

Monks, Bodleian Library, Oxford

▲ **Critical Viewing** The picture includes two events that occurred at different times. In what sense is time like a straight line for Bede? In what sense is it a series of events that all belong to one picture? **[Connect]**

city known as Rutubi Portus, which the English have corrupted to Reptacestir.[2] The distance from there across the sea to Gessoriacum,[3] the nearest coast of the Morini, is 50 miles or, as some write it, 450 furlongs.[4] On the opposite side of Britain, which lies open to the boundless ocean, lie the isles of the Orcades.[5] Britain is rich in grain and timber; it has good pasturage for cattle and draft animals,[6] and vines are cultivated in various localities. There are many land and sea birds of various species, and it is well known for its plentiful springs and rivers abounding in fish. There are salmon and eel fisheries, while seals, dolphins, and sometimes whales are caught. There are also many varieties of shellfish, such as mussels, in which are often found excellent pearls of several colors: red, purple, violet, and green, but mainly white. Cockles[7] are abundant, and a beautiful scarlet dye is extracted from them which remains unfaded by sunshine or rain; indeed, the older the cloth, the more beautiful its color. The country has both salt and hot springs, and the waters flowing from them provide hot baths, in which the people bathe separately according to age and sex. As Saint Basil says: "Water receives its heat when it flows across certain metals, and becomes hot, and even scalding." The land has rich veins of many metals, including copper, iron, lead, and silver. There is also much black jet[8] of fine quality, which sparkles in firelight. When burned, it drives away snakes, and, like amber, when it is warmed by friction, it clings to whatever is applied to it. In old times, the country had twenty-eight noble cities, and <u>innumerable</u> castles, all of which were guarded by walls, towers, and barred gates.

Since Britain lies far north toward the pole, the nights are short in summer, and at midnight it is hard to tell whether the evening twilight still lingers or whether dawn is approaching; for in these northern latitudes the sun does not remain long below the horizon at night. Consequently both summer days and winter nights are long, and when the sun withdraws southwards, the winter nights last eighteen hours. In Armenia,[9] Macedonia,[10] and Italy, and other countries of that latitude, the longest day lasts only fifteen hours and the shortest nine.

At the present time there are in Britain, in harmony with the five books of the divine law, five languages and four nations—English, British, Scots, and Picts. Each of these have their own language, but all are united in their study of God's truth by the fifth, Latin, which

---

2. **Reptacestir** Richborough, part of the city of Sandwich.
3. **Gessoriacum** Boulogne, France.
4. **furlongs** units for measuring distance; a furlong is equal to one eighth of a mile.
5. **Orcades** Orkney Isles.
6. **draft animals** animals used for pulling loads.
7. **Cockles** edible shellfish with two heart-shaped shells.
8. **jet** *n.* type of coal.
9. **Armenia** region between the Black and the Caspian seas, now divided between the nations of Armenia and Turkey.
10. **Macedonia** region in the eastern Mediterranean, divided among Greece, Yugoslavia, and Bulgaria.

Literary Analysis
Historical Writing Find two facts in this paragraph. Then, identify one claim for which you might need more evidence.

Reading Strategy
Breaking Down Sentences Break down the sentence beginning "Cockles" to find the core ideas.

innumerable (i nōō′ mər ə bəl) *adj.* too many to count

has become a common medium through the study of the scriptures. The original inhabitants of the island were the Britons, from whom it takes its name, and who, according to tradition, crossed into Britain from Armorica,[11] and occupied the southern parts. When they had spread northwards and possessed the greater part of the islands, it is said that some Picts from Scythia[12] put to sea in a few long ships and were driven by storms around the coasts of Britain, arriving at length on the north coast of Ireland. Here they found the nation of the Scots, from whom they asked permission to settle, but their request was refused. Ireland is the largest island after Britain, and lies to the west. It is shorter than Britain to the north, but extends far beyond it to the south towards the northern coasts of Spain, although a wide sea separates them. These Pictish seafarers, as I have said, asked for a grant of land to make a settlement. The Scots replied that there was not room for them both, but said: "We can give you good advice. There is another island not far to the east, which we often see in the distance on clear days. Go and settle there if you wish; should you meet resistance, we will come to your help." So the Picts crossed into Britain, and began to settle in the north of the island, since the Britons were in possession of the south. Having no women with them, these Picts asked wives of the Scots, who consented on condition that, when any dispute arose, they should choose a king from the female royal line rather than the male. This custom continues among the Picts to this day. As time went on, Britain received a third nation, that of the Scots, who migrated from Ireland under their chieftain Reuda, and by a combination of force and treaty, obtained from the Picts the settlements that they still hold. From the name of this chieftain, they are still known as Dalreudians, for in their tongue *dal* means a division.

Ireland is broader than Britain, and its mild and healthy climate is superior. Snow rarely lies longer than three days, so that there is no

Cotton Ms Tiberius C II Folio 5 Verso. Page of Bede's *History*, The British Library

▲ **Critical Viewing**
Bede's fellow monks spent years creating books filled with pages such as this one. What can you infer about the values of the society that produced such work? **[Infer]**

☑ **Reading Check**

What are the four nations of England?

---

11. **Armorica** Brittany, France.
12. **Scythia** ancient region in southeastern Europe.

need to store hay in summer for winter use or to build stables for beasts. There are no reptiles, and no snake can exist there, for although often brought over from Britain, as soon as the ship nears land, they breathe its scented air and die. In fact, almost everything in this isle enjoys immunity to poison, and I have heard that folk suffering from snakebite have drunk water in which scrapings from the leaves of books from Ireland had been steeped, and that this remedy checked the spreading poison and reduced the swelling. The island abounds in milk and honey, and there is no lack of vines, fish, and birds, while deer and goats are widely hunted. It is the original home of the Scots, who, as already mentioned, later migrated and joined the Britons and Picts in Britain. There is a very extensive arm of the sea, which originally formed the boundary between the Britons and the Picts. This runs inland from the west for a great distance as far as the strongly fortified British city of Alcuith.[13] It was to the northern shores of this firth[14] that the Scots came and established their new homeland.

---

13. **Alcuith** Dumbarton, Scotland.
14. **firth** narrow arm of the sea.

Literary Analysis
Historical Writing
What purpose guides Bede's choice of details in this selection?

Review and Assess

Thinking About the Selection

1. **Respond:** List three details you found interesting in Bede's history of England.

2. **(a) Recall:** List two pieces of geographical information Bede gives about Britain. **(b) Analyze:** How does this information help explain the nature of life there?

3. **(a) Recall:** What background does Bede give about British scarlet dye? **(b) Infer:** What does this information suggest about the lifestyle or economy of the country?

4. **(a) Interpret:** In what way does Latin unite England? **(b) Interpret:** According to Bede, what factor is most important in uniting people and giving them a common identity?

5. **(a) Compare and Contrast:** Contrast factors in Bede's account that are dividing England with those uniting it. Which seem stronger? **(b) Draw Conclusions:** What overall impression of England does Bede create?

6. **Evaluate:** Does Bede do a good job answering readers' questions about England? Explain, giving three examples of questions a reader would have.

from The ANGLO-SAXON CHRONICLE

Translated by
Anne Savage

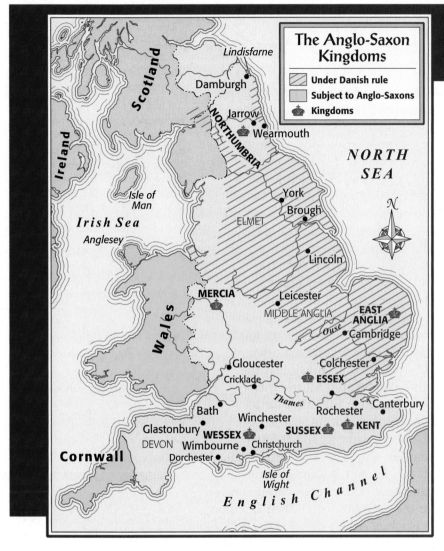

The Anglo-Saxon Kingdoms

- ⬧ Under Danish rule
- Subject to Anglo-Saxons
- 👑 Kingdoms

Scotland · Ireland · Lindisfarne · Damburgh · Jarrow · NORTHUMBRIA · Wearmouth · NORTH SEA · Isle of Man · Irish Sea · Anglesey · York · Brough · ELMET · Lincoln · Wales · MERCIA · Leicester · MIDDLE ANGLIA · EAST ANGLIA · Ouse · Cambridge · Gloucester · Colchester · Cricklade · ESSEX · Thames · Canterbury · Bath · Winchester · Rochester · Glastonbury · WESSEX · SUSSEX · KENT · DEVON · Wimbourne · Christchurch · Dorchester · Cornwall · Isle of Wight · English Channel

896 In the summer of this year, the force[1] split up, one part in East Anglia,[2] one part in Northumbria;[3] and those who were without property got themselves ships and went south over the sea to the Seine.

The force had not, by the grace of God, utterly broken down the English; but they were more greatly broken in those three years by the slaughter of cattle and men, most of all by the fact that many of

---

1. **the force** Danish settlers in England; Vikings.
2. **East Anglia** kingdom of Anglo-Saxon England in the East, including modern Norfolk and Suffolk.
3. **Northumbria** kingdom of Anglo-Saxon England in the North, including the city of York.

▲ **Critical Viewing**
Using the map, explain the relative locations of East Anglia, Wessex, and Kent. **[Interpret]**

☑**Reading Check**
Identify one problem that has weakened the English.

the king's best thanes[4] in the land had died in those three years. One of them was Swithulf, bishop of Rochester; also Ceolmund, ealdorman[5] in Kent, Beorhtulf, ealdorman in Essex, Wulfred, ealdorman in Hampshire, Ealhheard, bishop of Dorchester, Eadulf, king's thane in Sussex, Beornulf, reeve[6] of Winchester, Ecgulf, king's horse-thane, and many others also, though I have named the most distinguished.

The same year, the forces in East Anglia and Northumbria greatly harassed Wessex along the south coast with raiding bands, most of all with the ash-ships[7] they had built many years before. Then King Alfred commanded longships to be built against the ash-ships. They were nearly twice as long as the others; some had sixty oars, some more. They were both swifter and steadier, also higher than the others; nor were they in the Frisian[8] manner or the Danish, but as he himself thought might be most useful.

As it fell out, at a certain time in the same year, six ships came to the Isle of Wight and did much evil there, both in Devon and everywhere along the sea-coast. Then the king commanded men to go there with nine of the new ships, and they went in front of them at the river's mouth in the open sea. The Danes went out with three ships against them, and three stood higher up the river's mouth, beached on dry land; the men from them had gone inland. The English took two of their three ships at the river's mouth, further out, killed the men, and one ship got away—and also on that all the men were killed but five. They got away because the other ships ran aground. They were very awkwardly aground: three were stranded on the same side of the deep water as the Danish ships, and the others all on the other side. But when the tide had ebbed many furlongs[9] from the ships, the Danes went out from their three ships to the other three that were <u>stranded</u> on their side and there fought with them. There were killed Lucumon the king's reeve, Wulfheard the Frisian, Aebbe the Frisian, Aethelhere the Frisian, Athelferth of the king's household, and in all, Frisians and English, sixty-two, and one hundred and twenty of the Danes.

The tide, however, came to the Danish ships before the Christians[10] could shove out, and in this way they rowed out. They were all so damaged that they could not row around Sussex;

Literature in context · Cultural Connection

Anglo-Saxon Pronunciations
General Rules

There are no silent letters in Old English. Most consonants are pronounced as in modern English. For example, *Eadulf* can be pronounced a′ əd oolf′.

H before a vowel is pronounced as it is in modern English. Before a consonant or at the end of a word, it has a "throat-clearing" sound, as in the word *loch* (läkh). For example, *Beorhtulf* was probably pronounced bā′ ōrkh toolf′.

Specific Vowel and Consonant Pronunciations

- *ae = a* in *ash*
- *c* before or after *i* and *e*, or after *a = ch*; otherwise, *c = k*
- *cg = j*
- *ea = a* in *ash* + ə
- *f* between two vowels = *v*
- *g* before or after *i* or *e*, or after *ae = y* as in *year*; otherwise, *g = g* in *get*
- *sc = sh* in *ship*
- *y = ew*

stranded (stran′ did) *v.* forced into shallow water or onto a beach; left helpless

---

4. **thanes** lords in Anglo-Saxon society, ranking below the members of a king's family.
5. **ealdorman** official who managed specific areas of a kingdom.
6. **reeve** official who collected taxes for the king.
7. **ash-ships** ships used by Vikings, propelled by oar and sail.
8. **Frisian** relating to people originally from Frisia, a region now divided between the Netherlands and Germany.
9. **furlongs** units for measuring distance; a furlong is equal to one eighth of a mile.
10. **the Christians** referring here to the English and Frisian forces, in contrast to the unconverted Danes.

but there the sea threw two of them to land, and the men were led to Winchester, to the king. He commanded them to be hanged. The men who were on the one ship badly wounded came to East Anglia. The same summer no less than twenty ships perished with men and all along the south coast. The same year Wulfric the king's horse-thane died; he was also the Welsh-reeve.

900 Alfred, son of Aethelwulf, passed away, six nights before All Saints' Day. He was king over all the English, except for that part which was under Danish rule; and he held that kingdom for one and a half years less than thirty. Then his son Edward received the kingdom. Aethelwald, his father's brother's son, took over the manors at Wimbourne and at Christchurch, without the leave of the king and his counsellors. Then the king rode with the army until he camped at Badbury Rings near Wimbourne, and Aethelwald occupied the manor with those men who were loyal to him, and had <u>barricaded</u> all the gates against them; he said that he would stay there, alive or dead. Then he stole himself away under the cover of night, and sought the force in Northumbria. The king commanded them to ride after, but he could not be overtaken. They captured the woman he had seized without the king's leave and against the bishop's command, because she was hallowed[11] as a nun.

In the same year, Aethelred passed away, who was an ealdorman in Devon, four weeks before King Alfred.

902 Athelwald came here over the sea with all the ships he could get, and in Essex they submitted to him.

903 Aethelwald lured the East Anglian force into breaking the peace, so that they <u>ravaged</u> over the land of Mercia, until they came to Cricklade, went over the Thames there, seized all they could carry off both in and around Braydon and then went homeward again. Then King Edward went after them, as quickly as he could gather his army, and ravaged all their land between Devil's Dyke and Fleam Dyke and the Ouse, and everything up to the northern fens.[12] When he meant to leave there, he had it announced to the army that they would all leave together. The Kentish[13] stayed on there against his command and [the] seven messages he had sent to them. The force came upon them there, and they fought; ealdorman Sigulf was killed there, ealdorman Sigelm, Eadwold the king's thane, abbot[14] Cenulf, Sigebriht son of Sigulf, Eadwald son of Acca, and many besides them although I have named the most distinguished. On the Danish side were killed Eohric their king, atheling[15] Aethelwald, who had lured them into peacebreaking, Byrhtsige son of the atheling Beornoth,

---

11. **hallowed** made holy; given over, in a ceremony, to religious purposes.
12. **Dyke . . . fens** Dykes are barriers made of earth; fens are areas of peaty land covered with water.
13. **The Kentish** inhabitants of Kent, an English kingdom ruled by the kings of Wessex after 825.
14. **abbot** leader of a monastery; chief monk.
15. **atheling** Anglo-Saxon noble, especially one related to the kings of Wessex.

Literary Analysis
Historical Writing Why might the tone of the second sentence in this paragraph suggest the writer is proud of Alfred?

barricaded (bar´ i kād´ id) v. blocked

ravaged (rav´ ijd) v. destroyed

Reading Strategy
Breaking Down Sentences Break down this sentence about Edward into smaller details to clarify its meaning.

**Reading Check**
What new conflict troubles England under Edward?

from *The Anglo-Saxon Chronicle* ◆ 81

hold[16] Ysopa, hold Oscytel, and very many besides them we might not now name. On either hand much slaughter was made, and of the Danes there were more killed, though they had the battlefield. Ealhswith passed away. That same year was the fight at The Holme between the Kentish and the Danes. Ealdorman Aethelwulf died, brother of Ealhswith, King Alfred's mother; and abbot Virgilus of the Scots; and the mass-priest Grimbold. In the same year a new church in Chester was hallowed, and the relics of St. Judoc[17] brought there.

904 The moon darkened.

905 A comet appeared on October 20th.

906 Alfred died, who was town-reeve at Bath; and in the same year the peace was fastened at Tiddingford, just as King Edward advised, both with the East Anglians and the Northumbrians.

---

16. **hold** the equivalent in the Danelaw of a reeve, an official who collected taxes for the king.
17. **relics of St. Judoc** objects associated with Saint Josse, patron of harvests and ships

Review and Assess

Thinking About the Selection

1. **Respond:** Do you think you would have liked living in the era described in the *Chronicle*? Why or why not?

2. **(a) Recall:** What threat did the Anglo-Saxons of Alfred's time face? **(b) Draw Conclusions:** How united does the English opposition to that threat appear to be during his reign? Explain.

3. **(a) Recall:** List two actions Aethelwald takes after Edward becomes king. **(b) Interpret:** What do these actions suggest about the unity of the English under Edward?

4. **(a) Recall:** What does Edward plan to do after pursuing the East Anglian force? **(b) Infer:** What does the Kentish response to this plan and to his commands suggest about Edward's authority? **(c) Draw Conclusions:** What factors made it difficult for one ruler to control all of Britain?

5. **(a) Summarize:** The *Chronicle* lists the deaths of important Anglo-Saxons. Explain how the inclusion of this information creates the sense that the Anglo-Saxons are a nation.
   (b) Draw Conclusions: Explain how the *Chronicle* itself is a sign of national unity.

6. **(a) Evaluate:** Does this excerpt succeed in answering a reader's questions about Anglo-Saxon England? Explain, giving three examples of such questions. **(b) Evaluate:** Does it succeed in creating a picture of important figures such as Alfred? Explain.

Review and Assess

Literary Analysis

Historical Writing

1. What kinds of details indicate that Bede's work is **historical writing,** intended for a wider audience than just inhabitants of Britain?
2. (a) Give an example of evidence Bede offers for a claim he makes. (b) How convincing is this evidence?
3. (a) What knowledge of Anglo-Saxon times does the *Chronicle* assume readers have? (b) Give an example of background information offered by the *Chronicle* that a later reader might not have.
4. Evaluate Bede's *History* and the *Chronicle* as pieces of historical writing. Using a chart like the following, give examples of points where the authors give enough or too little background information or evidence, or where the organization aided or impeded understanding.

Necessary Background	Evidence	Clear Organization

Comparing Literary Works

5. (a) Compare the topics of the two selections. (b) Compare the kinds of details the selections include that a modern historian might consider unsupported or extraneous. (c) Compare the writers' purposes in offering such details.
6. Compare and contrast the impression of England that each selection conveys.

Reading Strategy

Breaking Down Sentences

Read the sentence in Bede that begins "As time went on, Britain received a third nation, . . ." (p. 77). Then, answer these questions:

7. Which words in this sentence state the main action?
8. Answer the questions *who, what, where,* and *how* about the main action.

Extend Understanding

9. **History Connection:** Name three facts in the *Chronicle* and describe the methods a modern historian might use to verify each.

Quick Review

Historical writing tells the story of past events, using evidence from the period.

Breaking down a sentence into the main action and the details that tell more about it helps you better understand the sentence.

 Take It to the Net

www.phschool.com

Take the interactive self-test online to check your understanding of these selections.

Integrate Language Skills

Vocabulary Development Lesson

Word Analysis: Latin Suffix *-ade*

The Latin suffix *-ade* means "the act of," "the result of," or "a gathering of." Knowing the meaning of the suffix can help you see that *barricade* means "the result of barring the way." Use this information to define these words:

1. lemonade
2. motorcade
3. cannonade
4. cavalcade

Spelling Strategy

If a word ends with a consonant and *y*, change the *y* to *ies* to form the plural. *Promontory* becomes *promontories*. Pluralize these words:

1. city
2. boundary
3. treaty

Fluency: Sentence Completion

Choose words from the vocabulary list on page 73 to complete the following sentences.

1. High on the ___?___, the king could see his ships entering the firth.
2. Suddenly, a fleet of Viking ships appeared and savagely ___?___ the king's boats.
3. The fierceness of the attack made it seem there were ___?___ ships.
4. Several of the king's ships ended up ___?___ on the beach.
5. Others tried to sail back out to sea, but the Vikings had ___?___ the harbor.

Grammar and Style Lesson

Compound Sentences

A **compound sentence** is a sentence with two or more independent clauses, clauses that can each stand alone as a sentence.

> IND.CLAUSE
> There are many land and sea birds of various
> IND.CLAUSE
> species, and it is well known for its plentiful
> springs and rivers abounding in fish.

The conjunction or punctuation that joins the parts of a compound sentence expresses the relationship between the parts:

- *and, for, so,* **or a semicolon:** addition; further details or support; sequence; explanation
- *but, yet:* contrast; opposition; exception
- *or, nor:* alternative

Practice Rewrite each pair of sentences below as a compound sentence. Use the conjunction that suggests the indicated relationship between ideas.

1. The Anglo-Saxons referred to them as Danes. We call them Vikings. (contrast)
2. No snakes exist in Ireland. The air there is said to kill them. (further support)
3. Alfred did not set out to rule England. Events dictated otherwise. (contrast)
4. The Dane may have gone to Northumbria. He may have settled in East Anglia. (alternative)
5. Athelwald conquered East Anglia in 902. The next year, he lured the East Anglians into breaking the peace. (addition)

Writing Application Write three compound sentences on Anglo-Saxon life.

W͞G Prentice Hall Writing and Grammar Connection: Chapter 19, Section 4

Writing Lesson

Critical Comparison of Historical Sources

Both Bede and the writers of *The Anglo-Saxon Chronicle* help build a national identity for Britain. By presenting diverse customs, events, and geographical facts as parts of one story, they portray Britain as a unified entity. Write an essay analyzing the vision of national identity in each work.

Prewriting   Take notes on the aspects of Britain covered by each selection. Next, summarize the ingredients, such as geography or political control, that each work includes in its picture of Britain. Then, identify the factors uniting these ingredients in one story.

Drafting   Begin by posing the question your essay answers and stating your conclusions. Develop your points in logical order.

Revising   Highlight each example you use. For each marked passage, ask yourself, In what other way might the writer have treated this information? Consider adding your answers to clarify your insights.

Model: Revising to Elaborate on Critical Insights

Bede is guided by geography when he includes the
The Picts are a separate people, and he could have
treated their story as separate from the story of Anglo-
Saxon England.
settling of the Picts in Scotland in his story. In addition
to geography, though, Bede is thinking of language
and religion.

> The added sentence clarifies the insight by answering the question, *What are the alternative possibilities?*

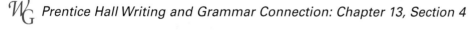 *Prentice Hall Writing and Grammar Connection: Chapter 13, Section 4*

Extension Activities

Listening and Speaking   Develop a short **radio interview** between Bede and a reporter. Adjust the language you use as follows:

- Use informal language for friendly talk.
- Switch to technical language when discussing historical or geographical details.

Tape your interview. **[Group Activity]**

Research and Technology   Produce a **museum exhibit** on medieval seafaring technology. Use research to draw a set of diagrams of a Viking ship. Include images that illuminate Viking life.

 **Take It to the Net**   www.phschool.com

Go online for an additional research activity using the Internet.

READING INFORMATIONAL MATERIALS

Maps

About Maps

The general purpose of a **map** is to present geographical information in a convenient graphic form. To use a map effectively, you should be familiar with the following basic map components:

- A legend or key defines the symbols used on the map.
- A compass rose shows cardinal directions (north, south, east, west).
- A scale shows the ratio between distances on the map and actual distances on the Earth.

Reading Strategy

Using Maps for Verification and Interpretation

To **verify and interpret** information is to check whether it is true and to explore its significance and implications. To verify and interpret textual information using a map, follow the steps below. (The chart shows how these steps might apply to *The Anglo-Saxon Chronicle*.)

1. Identify claims in the text for which geographical information is relevant.
2. Formulate geographical questions based on the text.
3. Obtain a map of the region referenced in the text. Consider whether you need a map that focuses on a specific kind of information.
4. Use the map to answer your questions. Note any discrepancies or additional questions and consult other sources for answers.

Sample Geographical Claims
The Anglo-Saxon Chronicle: Both Anglo-Saxons and Danes, who were enemies, ruled parts of England in the 800s.
Sample Geographical Questions
Which group controlled the most territory?
Type of Map Needed
Historical; should show England in the 800s with political borders.
Answers / Additional Questions
Who controlled the regions of Cornwall and Wales?

Scan the map on the next page. Note regions and facts on the map that are relevant to the selections in this part.

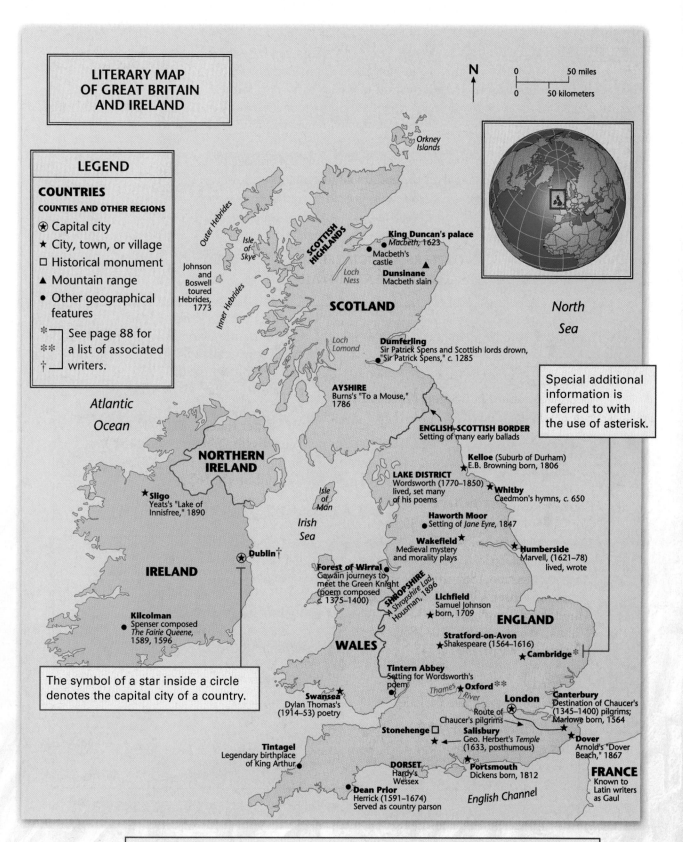

LITERARY MAP OF GREAT BRITAIN AND IRELAND

N

0 ———— 50 miles
0 ———— 50 kilometers

LEGEND

COUNTRIES

COUNTIES AND OTHER REGIONS

✪ Capital city

★ City, town, or village

☐ Historical monument

▲ Mountain range

● Other geographical features

* ⎫
** ⎬ See page 88 for a list of associated writers.
† ⎭

Orkney Islands

Outer Hebrides

Isle of Skye

SCOTTISH HIGHLANDS

Johnson and Boswell toured Hebrides, 1773

Inner Hebrides

Loch Ness

King Duncan's palace
Macbeth, 1623
● Macbeth's castle

▲ **Dunsinane**
Macbeth slain

SCOTLAND

Atlantic Ocean

Loch Lomond

Dumferling
Sir Patrick Spens and Scottish lords drown, "Sir Patrick Spens," c. 1285

AYSHIRE
Burns's "To a Mouse," 1786

ENGLISH–SCOTTISH BORDER
Setting of many early ballads

North Sea

Special additional information is referred to with the use of asterisk.

NORTHERN IRELAND

Isle of Man

Kelloe (Suburb of Durham)
E.B. Browning born, 1806

LAKE DISTRICT
Wordsworth (1770–1850) lived, set many of his poems

★ **Whitby**
Caedmon's hymns, c. 650

★ **Sligo**
Yeats's "Lake of Innisfree," 1890

Irish Sea

● **Haworth Moor**
Setting of *Jane Eyre,* 1847

Wakefield ★
Medieval mystery and morality plays

★ **Humberside**
Marvell, (1621–78) lived, wrote

IRELAND

☆ **Dublin** †

Forest of Wirral
Gawain journeys to meet the Green Knight (poem composed c. 1375–1400)

SHROPSHIRE
A Shropshire Lad, Housman, 1896

Lichfield
Samuel Johnson
★ born, 1709

ENGLAND

Kilcolman
● Spenser composed *The Fairie Queene,* 1589, 1596

Stratford-on-Avon
★ Shakespeare (1564–1616)

★ **Cambridge** *

WALES

The symbol of a star inside a circle denotes the capital city of a country.

Tintern Abbey
Setting for Wordsworth's poem
☐

Thames River

★ **Oxford** **

London
☆

Canterbury
Destination of Chaucer's (1345–1400) pilgrims; Marlowe born, 1564

Swansea ★
Dylan Thomas's (1914–53) poetry

Route of Chaucer's pilgrims

Stonehenge ☐

Salisbury
★ Geo. Herbert's *Temple* (1633, posthumous)

★ **Dover**
Arnold's "Dover Beach," 1867

Tintagel
Legendary birthplace of King Arthur ●

DORSET
Hardy's Wessex

★ **Portsmouth**
Dickens born, 1812

FRANCE
Known to Latin writers as Gaul

● **Dean Prior**
Herrick (1591–1674) Served as country parson

English Channel

Additional information about selected places on the map is found on the next page.

Supplementary Text

Because space on a map is limited, cartographers (mapmakers) may choose to link additional relevant information to a map with some form of cross-reference. In many cases, the cross-reference simply indicates another map on which adjacent regions, not shown on the map, may be found. With specialized maps the link may be to information in another form. For instance, asterisks and daggers are used on the literary map on page 87 to connect locations on the map with the additional information below.

WRITERS ASSOCIATED WITH SELECTED PLACES IN GREAT BRITAIN AND IRELAND

*Cambridge
Authors who studied here include:

Francis **Bacon** 1561–1626
Rupert **Brooke** 1887–1915
George Gordon, Lord **Byron** 1788–1824
Samuel Taylor **Coleridge** 1772–1834
John **Dryden** 1631–1700
E.M. **Forster** 1879–1970
Thomas **Gray** 1716–1771
George **Herbert** 1593–1633
Robert **Herrick** 1591–1674
Christopher **Marlowe** 1564–1593
Andrew **Marvell** 1621–1678
Samuel **Pepys** 1633–1703
Siegfried **Sassoon** 1886–1967
Edmund **Spenser** 1552?–1599
Alfred, Lord **Tennyson** 1809–1892
William **Wordsworth** 1770–1850
Sir Thomas **Wyatt** 1503–1542

T. S. **Eliot** 1888–1965
Gerard Manley **Hopkins** 1844–1889
A.E. **Housman** 1859–1936
Samuel **Johnson** 1709–1784
Richard **Lovelace** 1618–1657
Louis **MacNeice** 1907–1963
Sir Walter **Raleigh** 1552–1618
Percy Bysshe **Shelley** 1792–1822
Sir Philip **Sidney** 1554–1586
Richard **Steele** 1672–1729

†Dublin
Authors associated with the city include:

James **Joyce** 1882–1941
George Bernard **Shaw** 1856–1950
Sir Richard **Steele** 1672–1729
Jonathan **Swift** 1667–1745
Oscar **Wilde** 1854–1900
William Butler **Yeats** 1865–1939

**Oxford
Authors who studied here include:

Joseph **Addison** 1672–1719
Matthew **Arnold** 1822–1888
John **Donne** 1572–1631

Devices such as double asterisks link the information on this page to the map on the previous page.

Check Your Comprehension

1. What is the purpose of the Literary Map of Great Britain and Ireland?
2. Using the map, determine the distance between London and Canterbury.
3. Determine the direction from Oxford to King Duncan's palace.
4. Explain in what part of England the poet John Donne studied.

Applying the Reading Strategy

Using Maps for Verification and Interpretation

Read the excerpt from *A History of the English Church and People* written by Bede, and answer the following questions:

5. Bede claims that Britain "extends 800 miles northwards." According to the literary map, is this an accurate statement?
6. (a) On a copy of the map, mark the general route the Picts took once they reached Britain, according to Bede. (b) Roughly, what distances did they cover? (c) Given Bede's acount of these journeys, were you surprised by your answer? Explain.

Activity

Creating Maps from Textual Descriptions

Read the excerpt from *The Anglo-Saxon Chronicles*, page 79. Then, trace the outlines of the British Isles and of the Anglo-Saxon kingdoms from a map of the period. Next, referring only to the selection, fill in the geographical features and regions decribed in the text. Use a special color to fill in features the locations of which you can only guess. Finally, compare your map to a map of England at the time (you will find one on page 79). Explain what errors you made, and what additional information in the text might have helped you avoid them.

Comparing Informational Materials

The Variety of Maps

1. Compare a tourist map of Great Britain and Ireland to the Literary Map on page 87. Use the chart to help organize your information.
2. Compare the information you can find on the Literary Map with the kind of information you can find in a map of Great Britain and Ireland in an atlas.

Tourist Map	Literary Map

Prepare to Read

from The Canterbury Tales: The Prologue

Geoffrey Chaucer (1343?–1400)

Son of a merchant, page in a royal house, soldier, diplomat, and royal clerk, Geoffrey Chaucer saw quite a bit of the medieval world. His varied experiences helped prepare him to write *The Canterbury Tales*. This masterpiece provides the best contemporary picture we have of fourteenth-century England. Gathering characters from different walks of life, Chaucer takes the reader on a journey through medieval society.

The Poet's Beginning The exact date of Geoffrey Chaucer's birth is unknown, but official records furnish many details of his active life. Born into a middle-class family, Chaucer was sent in his early teens to work as page to the wife of Lionel of Antwerp, a son of the reigning monarch, Edward III. Through this position, middle-class Chaucer was introduced to the aristocratic society of England. In 1359, while serving in the English Army in France, Chaucer was captured and held prisoner. King Edward paid a £16 (sixteen-pound) ransom for his release—a sum that was eight times what a simple laborer might make in a year. In 1366, Chaucer married Philippa Pan, a lady-in-waiting to the queen. Their eldest child, Thomas, continued his father's rise in the world, marrying a noblewoman and acquiring great wealth.

The Poet Matures Chaucer began writing in his twenties, practicing and honing his skills as a poet as he rose through the ranks of medieval society. His early poems were based on the works of European poets. These were followed by various translations of French poetry. His first major work, *The Book of the Duchess*, was probably completed in early 1369, almost one year after the death of Blanche of Lancaster, for whose grieving husband, John of Gaunt, he wrote the poem. As Chaucer grew older, he developed a mature style of his own. In *Troilus and Criseyde*, a later poem drawn from the Greek legend of the Trojan War, Chaucer displays penetrating insight into human character.

The Canterbury Tales

Chaucer wrote *The Canterbury Tales* in his later years. No one knows for certain what prompted him to begin this work. Chaucer's inspiration may have come from his own participation in the pilgrimage to Canterbury. A pilgrimage is a long journey to a shrine or holy site, taken by people who wish to express their devotion. Chaucer certainly had the opportunity to observe many pilgrims starting their journeys— a window of his London home overlooked the pilgrim road that led to Canterbury.

In this masterwork, each character tells a tale on the way to Canterbury. Just as the tellers of *The Canterbury Tales* come from the length and breadth of medieval society, the tales encompass medieval literature—from romance to comedy, from rhyme to prose, from crude humor to religious mysteries. Only 24 of the projected 120 tales were finished, but they stand together as a complete work.

The Father of English Poetry In his own lifetime, Geoffrey Chaucer was considered the greatest English poet. Recognized as a shrewd storyteller, he was also praised by a contemporary as the first to "rain the gold dewdrops of speech and eloquence" into English literature. Throughout history, new generations of poets writing in English have studied his work for inspiration and insight.

Chaucer lies buried in Westminster Abbey. In recognition of his unique position in England's literary tradition, Westminster's honorary burial area for distinguished writers, the Poets' Corner, was established around his tomb.

Preview

Connecting to the Literature

It may have been a class trip you took to a museum or a visit to a famous person's birthplace. Trips taken for inspiration or renewal, even if they are not religious, can loosely be termed pilgrimages. The pilgrims who gather in the Prologue are about to depart on such a journey.

Literary Analysis

Characterization

As you read the Prologue, look for these forms of **characterization**—techniques of revealing character:

- **Direct characterization** presents direct statements about a character, such as Chaucer's statement that the Knight "followed chivalry, / Truth, honor. . . . "

- **Indirect characterization** uses actions, thoughts, and dialogue to reveal a character's personality. By saying "he was not gaily dressed," for instance, Chaucer suggests that the Knight is not vain and perhaps takes the pilgrimage seriously enough to rush to join it straight from battle.

Connecting Literary Elements

Each character in *The Canterbury Tales* represents a different segment of society in Chaucer's time. By noting the virtues and faults of each, Chaucer provides **social commentary,** writing that offers insight into society, its values, and its customs. While reading, draw conclusions from the characters about Chaucer's views on English society.

Reading Strategy

Analyzing Difficult Sentences

Chaucer's Prologue begins with an eighteen-line sentence. To **analyze difficult sentences** such as this one, use the questions *when, who, where, what,* and *how* to identify the essential information each conveys. Use a chart like the one shown to finish analyzing Chaucer's first sentence.

When?	in April
Who?	people; palmers
Where?	
What?	
Why?	
How?	

Vocabulary Development

solicitous (sə lis´ ə təs) *adj.* showing care or concern (p. 98)

garnished (gär´ nisht) *adj.* decorated; trimmed (p. 99)

absolution (ab´ sə lōō´ shən) *n.* act of freeing someone of a sin or criminal charge (p. 100)

commission (kə mish´ ən) *n.* authorization; act of giving authority to an individual (p. 102)

sanguine (saŋ´ gwin) *adj.* confident; cheerful (p. 103)

avouches (ə vouch´ ez) *v.* asserts positively; affirms (p. 104)

prevarication (pri var´ i kā´ shən) *n.* evasion of truth (p. 112)

from *The Canterbury Tales: The Prologue* ◆ 91

A Closer Look

Chaucer's Guided Tour of Medieval Life and Literature

Rich people, poor people, stock brokers, artists, farmers, street vendors . . . With all of the different lifestyles in our culture, you may wonder what single event could gather together people from all parts of society. When modern writers and directors try to imagine such an event, they often picture a disaster or crisis—in times of trouble, the story goes, rich and poor, old and young reach out to each other in a common cause. Geoffrey Chaucer was perhaps luckier than a modern movie director. He found in his own society an orderly, even joyous event that gathered people from diverse backgrounds and occupations— a pilgrimage, or journey to a sacred spot. It is such a pilgrimage that gathers together the diverse characters in his masterpiece, *The Canterbury Tales*.

The Journey Begins Like modern travelers, medieval pilgrims must have been eager to while away their time traveling. Chaucer uses this fact to set his story in motion. *The Canterbury Tales* begins with a Prologue, in which the Narrator, presumably Chaucer himself, meets 29 other pilgrims at the Tabard Inn, located in a suburb of London. As the pilgrims prepare for their journey, the host of the Inn, Harry Bailey, sets a challenge. To make the journey more entertaining, he suggests that each pilgrim tell two stories on the way to Canterbury and two stories on the return trip. The person who tells the best tale will be treated to a feast hosted by the other pilgrims. The pilgrims accept the challenge, and Bailey himself decides to join them and judge the competition.

Each of the following sections of the work consists of one of the pilgrim's tales. Brief transitions, as one storyteller finishes and another begins, link the stories. In this way, the work is actually a story about stories, 24 different tales set within the overarching tale of the pilgrimage.

Snapshots of an Era In the Prologue, Chaucer sketches a brief but vivid portrait of each pilgrim, creating a lively sense of medieval life. In itself, the Prologue is a great literary achievement. As critic Vincent Hopper notes,

> The description of the various pilgrims turn in rapid sequence from an article of clothing to a point of character and back again with no apparent organization or desire for it. Yet so effective is this artful artlessness that each pilgrim stands out sharply as a type of medieval personality and also as a highly individualized character. . . .

Chaucer begins his survey of medieval society with the courtly world, which centered around the nobility. Medieval nobles such as Chaucer's Knight held land granted them by a lord or king, for whom they fought in times of war. In the middle ranks of medieval society were learned professional men, such as

Chaucer's Doctor, and wealthy business-men. The lower orders included craftsmen, storekeepers, peasants, such as Chaucer's Plowman, and minor administrators, such as the Reeve and the Manciple. The various ranks of the Church, a cornerstone of medieval society, are represented by characters from the Prioress to the Summoner.

A Literary Tour In Chaucer's day, there were no science fiction stories or murder mysteries. Instead, popular genres included romances (tales of chivalry), *fabliaux* (short, bawdy, humorous stories), the stories of saint's lives, sermons, and allegories (narratives in which characters represent abstractions such as Pride or Honor). Each pilgrim chooses to tell a type of tale consistent with his or her character—the Knight tells a romance, the Miller a bawdy story—and each of the major forms of medieval literature is represented.

Even while Chaucer revisits old genres, he is perfecting a new poetic form. In the Middle Ages, the meters and sound effects of Old English poetry no longer suited the changing English language. Chaucer adapted French poetic forms to the English of his day. He wrote much of the *Tales* using his own form, the heroic couplet, a pair of rhyming lines with five stressed syllables each. For this important innovation, along with his other achievements, he is known as the father of English poetry.

The Endless Road Traveling with Chaucer's pilgrims, a reader may feel that world is a big place but that, somehow, all of its pieces fit together. *The Canterbury Tales* reminds us that every journey from here to there is filled with stories, waiting to be told.

Character Map of Chaucer's Storytellers

1. The Aristocracy
Status based on birth and tradition

The Knight A man who represents chivalry and honor

The Squire The knight's son, known as a lady's man

The Prioress A high-ranking nun and an elegant, delicate lady

The Nun's Priest A priest who accompanies the nuns on their pilgrimage

The Second Nun A devout nun who believes that idleness leads to sin

Canon's Yeoman The Canon's servant, who joins the pilgrims on their way to Canterbury (not mentioned in the Prologue)

The Monk A lover of hunting

The Friar A talented and wealthy beggar; member of a religious order

3. The Middle Class
Status based on mastery of a trade

The Cook A man skilled as a chef

The Shipman A world-traveler

The Physician A medical doctor

The Wife of Bath A woman who has had five husbands

4. The Virtuous Lower Class
Poor but virtuous

The Parson A poor but virtuous preacher who is the model clergyman, humble and devoted to his flock

2. The Upper Class
Status based on acquired wealth

The Merchant A shrewd trader

The Man of Law A lawyer

The Clerk A lover of learning who spends all of his money on books

The Franklin A wealthy landowner

5. The Degraded Lower Class
Those of low manners or questionable morals

The Manciple A steward for a law school

The Miller A strong, vulgar dealer in grain

The Reeve An old and irritable estate manager

The Summoner An officer of the church who calls people to trial

The Pardoner A seller of religious artifacts who boasts of his cons

from The Canterbury Tales
The Prologue

Geoffrey Chaucer
Translated by Nevill Coghill

Background

In medieval Christianity, pilgrimages—long, annual trips to holy places—were a popular way to express religious devotion. Canterbury, a town 55 miles southeast of London, was a major destination for English pilgrims. The cathedral in Canterbury was the site of Archbishop Thomas à Becket's murder in 1170. Days after the murder and three years before Becket was made a saint, people began flocking to the cathedral to pay their respects.

The first eighteen lines of the Prologue are presented here in Chaucer's original Middle English, followed by the entire Prologue in a modern translation.

> Whan that Aprill with his shourës sootë
> The droghte of March hath percëd to the rootë,
> And bathëd every veyne in swich licour
> Of which vertu engendrëd is the flour;
> 5 Whan Zephirus eek with his sweetë breeth
> Inspirëd hath in every holt and heeth
> The tendrë croppës, and the yongë sonnë
> Hath in the Ram his halvë cours yronnë,
> And smalë fowelës maken melodyë,
> 10 That slepen al the nyght with open ye
> (So priketh hem nature in hir corages);
> Thanne longen folk to goon on pilgrimages,
> And palmeres for to seken straungë strondës,
> To fernë halwës, kowthe in sondry londës;
> 15 And specially from every shirës endë
> Of Engelond to Caunterbury they wendë,
> The hooly blisful martir for to seke,
> That hem hath holpen whan that they were seekë.

When in April the sweet showers fall
And pierce the drought of March to the root, and all
The veins are bathed in liquor of such power
As brings about the engendering of the flower,
5 When also Zephyrus[1] with his sweet breath
Exhales an air in every grove and heath
Upon tender shoots, and the young sun
His half-course in the sign of the Ram[2] has run,
And the small fowl are making melody
10 That sleep away the night with open eye
(So nature pricks them and their heart engages)
Then people long to go on pilgrimages
And palmers[3] long to seek the stranger strands[4]
Of far-off saints, hallowed in sundry lands,
15 And specially, from every shire's end
In England, down to Canterbury they wend
To seek the holy blissful martyr,[5] quick
To give his help to them when they were sick.
It happened in that season that one day
20 In Southwark,[6] at The Tabard,[7] as I lay
Ready to go on pilgrimage and start
For Canterbury, most devout at heart,
At night there came into that hostelry
Some nine and twenty in a company
25 Of sundry folk happening then to fall
In fellowship, and they were pilgrims all
That towards Canterbury meant to ride.
The rooms and stables of the inn were wide;
They made us easy, all was of the best.
30 And shortly, when the sun had gone to rest,
By speaking to them all upon the trip
I soon was one of them in fellowship
And promised to rise early and take the way
To Canterbury, as you heard me say.
35 But nonetheless, while I have time and space,
Before my story takes a further pace,
It seems a reasonable thing to say
What their condition was, the full array
Of each of them, as it appeared to me
40 According to profession and degree,

Literary Analysis
Characterization In these lines, what does the narrator suggest about the pilgrims' motives for going to Canterbury?

Reading Strategy
Analyzing Difficult Sentences *What* does Chaucer say he will do in lines 35–42? *How, or in what manner,* will he do it?

**Reading Check**

Who have gathered at The Tabard?

---

1. **Zephyrus** (zef´ ə rəs) the west wind.
2. **Ram** Aries, the first sign of the zodiac. The pilgrimage began on April 11, 1387.
3. **palmers** pilgrims who wore two crossed palm leaves to show that they had visited the Holy Land.
4. **strands** shores.
5. **martyr** St. Thomas à Becket, the Archbishop of Canterbury, who was murdered in Canterbury Cathedral in 1170.
6. **Southwark** (suth´ ərk) suburb of London at the time.
7. **The Tabard** (ta´ bərd) an inn.

And what apparel they were riding in;
And at a Knight I therefore will begin.
There was a *Knight*, a most distinguished man,
Who from the day on which he first began
45 To ride abroad had followed chivalry,
Truth, honor, generousness and courtesy.
He had done nobly in his sovereign's war
And ridden into battle, no man more,
As well in Christian as heathen places,
50 And ever honored for his noble graces.
      When we took Alexandria,[8] he was there.
He often sat at table in the chair
Of honor, above all nations, when in Prussia.
In Lithuania he had ridden, and Russia,
55 No Christian man so often, of his rank.
When, in Granada, Algeciras sank
Under assault, he had been there, and in
North Africa, raiding Benamarin;
In Anatolia he had been as well
60 And fought when Ayas and Attalia fell,
For all along the Mediterranean coast
He had embarked with many a noble host.
In fifteen mortal battles he had been
And jousted for our faith at Tramissene
65 Thrice in the lists, and always killed his man.
This same distinguished knight had led the van[9]
Once with the Bey of Balat,[10] doing work
For him against another heathen Turk;
He was of sovereign value in all eyes.
70 And though so much distinguished, he was wise
And in his bearing modest as a maid.
He never yet a boorish thing had said
In all his life to any, come what might;
He was a true, a perfect gentle-knight.
75 Speaking of his equipment, he possessed
Fine horses, but he was not gaily dressed.
He wore a fustian[11] tunic stained and dark
With smudges where his armor had left mark;
Just home from service, he had joined our ranks
80 To do his pilgrimage and render thanks.
      He had his son with him, a fine young *Squire*,
A lover and cadet, a lad of fire

Literary Analysis
Characterization What do lines 54–65 indirectly suggest about the Knight's character?

---

8. **Alexandria** site of one of the campaigns fought by Christians against groups who posed a threat to Europe during the fourteenth century. The place names that follow refer to other battle sites in these campaigns, or crusades.
9. **van** the part of the army that goes before the rest (short for *vanguard*).
10. **Bey of Balat** pagan leader.
11. **fustian** (fus´ chən) *n.* coarse cloth of cotton and linen.

With locks as curly as if they had been pressed.
He was some twenty years of age, I guessed.

85 In stature he was of a moderate length,
With wonderful agility and strength.
He'd seen some service with the cavalry
In Flanders and Artois and Picardy[12]
And had done valiantly in little space

90 Of time, in hope to win his lady's grace.
He was embroidered like a meadow bright
And full of freshest flowers, red and white.
Singing he was, or fluting all the day;
He was as fresh as is the month of May.

95 Short was his gown, the sleeves were long and wide;
He knew the way to sit a horse and ride.
He could make songs and poems and recite,
Knew how to joust and dance, to draw and write.
He loved so hotly that till dawn grew pale

100 He slept as little as a nightingale.
Courteous he was, lowly and serviceable,
And carved to serve his father at the table.
    There was a *Yeoman*[13] with him at his side,
No other servant; so he chose to ride.

105 This Yeoman wore a coat and hood of green,
And peacock-feathered arrows, bright and keen
And neatly sheathed, hung at his belt the while
—For he could dress his gear in yeoman style,
His arrows never drooped their feathers low—

110 And in his hand he bore a mighty bow.
His head was like a nut, his face was brown.
He knew the whole of woodcraft up and down.
A saucy brace[14] was on his arm to ward
It from the bow-string, and a shield and sword

115 Hung at one side, and at the other slipped
A jaunty dirk,[15] spear-sharp and well-equipped.
A medal of St. Christopher[16] he wore
Of shining silver on his breast, and bore
A hunting-horn, well slung and burnished clean,

120 That dangled from a baldric[17] of bright green.
He was a proper forester I guess.
    There also was a *Nun*, a Prioress.[18]
Her way of smiling very simple and coy.

The Yeoman, Arthur Szyk for *The Canterbury Tales*

---

12. **Flanders . . . Picardy** regions in Belgium and France.
13. *Yeoman* (yō´ mən) *n.* attendant.
14. **brace** bracelet.
15. **dirk** *n.* dagger.
16. **St. Christopher** patron saint of travelers.
17. **baldric** *n.* belt worn over one shoulder and across the chest to support a sword.
18. **Prioress** *n.* in an abbey, the nun ranking just below the abbess.

✔ **Reading Check**

What is the relationship among the Knight, the Squire and the Yeoman?

Her greatest oath was only "By St. Loy!"[19]
125 And she was known as Madam Eglantyne.
And well she sang a service,[20] with a fine
Intoning through her nose, as was most seemly,
And she spoke daintily in French, extremely,
After the school of Stratford-atte-Bowe;[21]
130 French in the Paris style she did not know.
At meat her manners were well taught withal;
No morsel from her lips did she let fall,
Nor dipped her fingers in the sauce too deep;
But she could carry a morsel up and keep
135 The smallest drop from falling on her breast.
For courtliness she had a special zest,
And she would wipe her upper lip so clean
That not a trace of grease was to be seen
Upon the cup when she had drunk; to eat,
140 She reached a hand sedately for the meat.
She certainly was very entertaining,
Pleasant and friendly in her ways, and straining
To counterfeit a courtly kind of grace,
A stately bearing fitting to her place,
145 And to seem dignified in all her dealings.
As for her sympathies and tender feelings,
She was so charitably <u>solicitous</u>
She used to weep if she but saw a mouse
Caught in a trap, if it were dead or bleeding.
150 And she had little dogs she would be feeding
With roasted flesh, or milk, or fine white bread.
And bitterly she wept if one were dead
Or someone took a stick and made it smart;
She was all sentiment and tender heart.
155 Her veil was gathered in a seemly way,
Her nose was elegant, her eyes glass-gray;
Her mouth was very small, but soft and red,
Her forehead, certainly, was fair of spread,
Almost a span[22] across the brows, I own;
160 She was indeed by no means undergrown.
Her cloak, I noticed, had a graceful charm.
She wore a coral trinket on her arm,
A set of beads, the gaudies[23] tricked in green,
Whence hung a golden brooch of brightest sheen
165 On which there first was graven a crowned *A*,

Reading Strategy
Analyzing Difficult Sentences What two basic qualities does the sentence in lines 141–145 attribute to the Nun?

solicitous (sə lis´ ə təs) *adj.* showing care or concern

Literary Analysis
Characterization What can you infer about the Prioress based on this detailed description of her jewelry?

---

19. St. Loy St. Eligius, patron saint of goldsmiths and courtiers.
20. service daily prayer.
21. Stratford-atte-Bowe nunnery near London.
22. span nine inches.
23. gaudies large green beads that marked certain prayers on a set of prayer beads.

And lower, *Amor vincit omnia.*[24]
　　Another *Nun*, the chaplain at her cell,
Was riding with her, and *three Priests* as well.
　　A *Monk* there was, one of the finest sort
170　Who rode the country; hunting was his sport.
A manly man, to be an Abbot able;
Many a dainty horse he had in stable.
His bridle, when he rode, a man might hear
Jingling in a whistling wind as clear,
175　Aye, and as loud as does the chapel bell
Where my lord Monk was Prior of the cell.
The Rule of good St. Benet or St. Maur[25]
As old and strict he tended to ignore;
He let go by the things of yesterday
180　And took the modern world's more spacious way.
He did not rate that text at a plucked hen
Which says that hunters are not holy men
And that a monk uncloistered is a mere
Fish out of water, flapping on the pier,
185　That is to say a monk out of his cloister.
That was a text he held not worth an oyster;
And I agreed and said his views were sound;
Was he to study till his head went round
Poring over books in cloisters? Must he toil
190　As Austin[26] bade and till the very soil?
Was he to leave the world upon the shelf?
Let Austin have his labor to himself.
　　This Monk was therefore a good man to horse;
Greyhounds he had, as swift as birds, to course.
195　Hunting a hare or riding at a fence
Was all his fun, he spared for no expense.
I saw his sleeves were <u>garnished</u> at the hand
With fine gray fur, the finest in the land,
And on his hood, to fasten it at his chin
200　He had a wrought-gold cunningly fashioned pin;
Into a lover's knot it seemed to pass.
His head was bald and shone like looking-glass;
So did his face, as if it had been greased.
He was a fat and personable priest;
205　His prominent eyeballs never seemed to settle.
They glittered like the flames beneath a kettle;
Supple his boots, his horse in fine condition.
He was a prelate fit for exhibition,
He was not pale like a tormented soul.

The Monk, Arthur Szyk for *The Canterbury Tales*

garnished (gär′ nisht) *adj.* decorated; trimmed

---

24. *Amor vincit omnia* (ä′ môr′ vin′ chit ôm′ nē ä′) "love conquers all" (Latin).
25. **St. Benet or St. Maur** St. Benedict, author of monastic rules, and St. Maurice, one of his followers. Benet and Maur are French versions of Benedict and Maurice.
26. **Austin** English version of St. Augustine, who criticized lazy monks.

✔ Reading Check

What is the Monk's main interest?

210   He liked a fat swan best, and roasted whole.
     His palfrey[27] was as brown as is a berry.
         There was a *Friar*, a wanton[28] one and merry
     A Limiter,[29] a very festive fellow.
     In all Four Orders[30] there was none so mellow
215   So glib with gallant phrase and well-turned speech.
     He'd fixed up many a marriage, giving each
     Of his young women what he could afford her.
     He was a noble pillar to his Order.
     Highly beloved and intimate was he
220   With County folk[31] within his boundary,
     And city dames of honor and possessions;
     For he was qualified to hear confessions,
     Or so he said, with more than priestly scope;
     He had a special license from the Pope.
225   Sweetly he heard his penitents at shrift[32]
     With pleasant <u>absolution</u>, for a gift.
     He was an easy man in penance-giving
     Where he could hope to make a decent living;
     It's a sure sign whenever gifts are given
230   To a poor Order that a man's well shriven,[33]
     And should he give enough he knew in verity
     The penitent repented in sincerity.
     For many a fellow is so hard of heart
     He cannot weep, for all his inward smart.
235   Therefore instead of weeping and of prayer
     One should give silver for a poor Friar's care.
     He kept his tippet[34] stuffed with pins for curls,
     And pocket-knives, to give to pretty girls.
     And certainly his voice was gay and sturdy,
240   For he sang well and played the hurdy-gurdy.[35]
     At sing-songs he was champion of the hour.
     His neck was whiter than a lily-flower
     But strong enough to butt a bruiser down.
     He knew the taverns well in every town
245   And every innkeeper and barmaid too
     Better than lepers, beggars and that crew,
     For in so eminent a man as he
     It was not fitting with the dignity

---

27. **palfrey** *n.* saddle horse.
28. **wanton** *adj.* jolly.
29. **Limiter** friar who is given begging rights for a certain limited area.
30. **Four Orders** There were four orders of friars who supported themselves by begging: Dominicans, Franciscans, Carmelites, and Augustinians.
31. **County folk** The phrase refers to rich landowners.
32. **shrift** *n.* confession.
33. **well shriven** *adj.* absolved of his sins.
34. **tippet** *n.* hood.
35. **hurdy-gurdy** stringed instrument played by cranking a wheel.

Literary Analysis
Characterization and Social Commentary
What do the details about the Monk's habits and tastes indirectly suggest about religious institutions of the time?

absolution (ab´ sə loo´ shən) *n.* act of freeing someone of a sin or of a criminal charge

Literary Analysis
Characterization In lines 244–254, is Chaucer using direct characterization or indirect characterization? Explain.

Of his position, dealing with a scum
250 Of wretched lepers; nothing good can come
Of dealings with the slum-and-gutter dwellers,
But only with the rich and victual-sellers.
But anywhere a profit might accrue
Courteous he was and lowly of service too.
255 Natural gifts like his were hard to match.
He was the finest beggar of his batch,
And, for his begging-district, payed a rent;
His brethren did no poaching where he went.
For though a widow mightn't have a shoe,
260 So pleasant was his holy how-d'ye-do
He got his farthing from her just the same
Before he left, and so his income came
To more than he laid out. And how he romped,
Just like a puppy! He was ever prompt
265 To arbitrate disputes on settling days
(For a small fee) in many helpful ways,
Not then appearing as your cloistered scholar
With threadbare habit hardly worth a dollar,
But much more like a Doctor or a Pope.
270 Of double-worsted was the semi-cope[36]
Upon his shoulders, and the swelling fold
About him, like a bell about its mold
When it is casting, rounded out his dress.
He lisped a little out of wantonness
275 To make his English sweet upon his tongue.
When he had played his harp, or having sung,
His eyes would twinkle in his head as bright
As any star upon a frosty night.
This worthy's name was Hubert, it appeared.
280   There was a *Merchant* with a forking beard
And motley dress, high on his horse he sat,
Upon his head a Flemish[37] beaver hat
And on his feet daintily buckled boots.
He told of his opinions and pursuits
285 In solemn tones, and how he never lost.
The sea should be kept free at any cost
(He thought) upon the Harwich-Holland range,[38]
He was expert at currency exchange.
This estimable Merchant so had set
290 His wits to work, none knew he was in debt,
He was so stately in negotiation,
Loan, bargain and commercial obligation.

---

36. semi-cope cape.
37. Flemish from Flanders.
38. Harwich-Holland range the North Sea between England and Holland.

Reading Strategy
**Analyzing Difficult
Sentences** What is the
main thought in the
sentence in lines 259–263?
What question about this
main idea (*who, what,
where, when, why,* or *how*)
do the other parts of the
sentence help answer?

✔**Reading Check**
How does the Friar earn
his living?

He was an excellent fellow all the same;
To tell the truth I do not know his name.

295   An *Oxford Cleric*, still a student though,
One who had taken logic long ago,
Was there; his horse was thinner than a rake,
And he was not too fat, I undertake,
But had a hollow look, a sober stare;
300 The thread upon his overcoat was bare.
He had found no preferment in the church
And he was too unworldly to make search
For secular employment. By his bed
He preferred having twenty books in red
305 And black, of Aristotle's[39] philosophy,
To having fine clothes, fiddle or psaltery.[40]
Though a philosopher, as I have told,
He had not found the stone for making gold.[41]
Whatever money from his friends he took
310 He spent on learning or another book
And prayed for them most earnestly, returning
Thanks to them thus for paying for his learning.
His only care was study, and indeed
He never spoke a word more than was need,
315 Formal at that, respectful in the extreme,
Short, to the point, and lofty in his theme.
The thought of moral virtue filled his speech
And he would gladly learn, and gladly teach.

        A *Sergeant at the Law* who paid his calls,
320 Wary and wise, for clients at St. Paul's[42]
There also was, of noted excellence.
Discreet he was, a man to reverence,
Or so he seemed, his sayings were so wise.
He often had been Justice of Assize
325 By letters patent, and in full <u>commission</u>.
His fame and learning and his high position
Had won him many a robe and many a fee.
There was no such conveyancer[43] as he;
All was fee-simple[44] to his strong digestion,
330 Not one conveyance could be called in question.
Nowhere there was so busy a man as he;
But was less busy than he seemed to be.

The Student, Arthur Szyk for *The Canterbury Tales*

▲ **Critical Viewing**
What can you infer from this picture about the Oxford Cleric's style of living? List three details supporting your conclusion. **[Infer]**

commission (kə mish´ ən) *n.* authorization; act of giving authority to an individual

---

39. Aristotle's (ar´ is tät´ əlz) referring to the Greek philosopher (384–322 B.C.).
40. psaltery (sôl´ tər ē) ancient stringed instrument.
41. stone . . . gold At the time, alchemists believed that a "philosopher's stone" existed that could turn base metals into gold.
42. St. Paul's London cathedral near the center of legal activities in the city. Lawyers often met near there to discuss cases.
43. conveyancer one who draws up documents for transferring ownership of property.
44. fee-simple unrestricted ownership.

He knew of every judgment, case and crime
Recorded, ever since King William's time.
335 He could dictate defenses or draft deeds;
No one could pinch a comma from his screeds,[45]
And he knew every statute off by rote.
He wore a homely parti-colored coat
Girt with a silken belt of pin-stripe stuff;
340 Of his appearance I have said enough.
 There was a *Franklin*[46] with him, it appeared;
White as a daisy-petal was his beard.
A sanguine man, high-colored and benign,
He loved a morning sop[47] of cake in wine.
345 He lived for pleasure and had always done,
For he was Epicurus'[48] very son,
In whose opinion sensual delight
Was the one true felicity in sight.
As noted as St. Julian[49] was for bounty
350 He made his household free to all the County.
His bread, his ale were the finest of the fine
And no one had a better stock of wine.
His house was never short of bake-meat pies,
Of fish and flesh, and these in such supplies
355 It positively snowed with meat and drink
And all the dainties that a man could think.
According to the seasons of the year
Changes of dish were ordered to appear.
He kept fat partridges in coops, beyond,
360 Many a bream and pike were in his pond.
Woe to the cook whose sauces had no sting
Or who was unprepared in anything!
And in his hall a table stood arrayed
And ready all day long, with places laid.
365 As Justice at the Sessions[50] none stood higher;
He often had been Member for the Shire.[51]
A dagger and a little purse of silk
Hung at his girdle, white as morning milk.
As Sheriff he checked audit, every entry.
370 He was a model among landed gentry.
 A *Haberdasher*, a *Dyer*, a *Carpenter*,
A *Weaver* and a *Carpet-maker* were

---

45. screeds long, boring speeches or pieces of writing.
46. *Franklin* wealthy landowner.
47. sop piece.
48. Epicurus' (ep´ i kyoor´ əs) referring to a Greek philosopher (341–270 B.C.) who believed that happiness is the most important goal in life.
49. St. Julian patron saint of hospitality.
50. Sessions court sessions.
51. Member . . . Shire Parliamentary representative for the county.

sanguine (saŋ´ gwin) *adj.* confident; cheerful

Reading Strategy
Analyzing Difficult Sentences What question do lines 346–348 answer about the main idea in line 345?

Literary Analysis
Characterization What are the Franklin's interests?

**Reading Check**

What are the Cleric's interests?

Among our ranks, all in the livery
Of one impressive guild-fraternity.[52]
375 They were so trim and fresh their gear would pass
For new. Their knives were not tricked out with brass
But wrought with purest silver, which <u>avouches</u>
A like display on girdles and on pouches.
Each seemed a worthy burgess,[53] fit to grace
380 A guild-hall with a seat upon the dais.
Their wisdom would have justified a plan
To make each one of them an alderman;
They had the capital and revenue,
Besides their wives declared it was their due.
385 And if they did not think so, then they ought;
To be called "*Madam*" is a glorious thought,
And so is going to church and being seen
Having your mantle carried like a queen.
        They had a *Cook* with them who stood alone
390 For boiling chicken with a marrow-bone,
Sharp flavoring-powder and a spice for savor.
He could distinguish London ale by flavor,
And he could roast and seethe and broil and fry,
Make good thick soup and bake a tasty pie.
395 But what a pity—so it seemed to me,
That he should have an ulcer on his knee.
As for blancmange,[54] he made it with the best.
        There was a *Skipper* hailing from far west;
He came from Dartmouth, so I understood.
400 He rode a farmer's horse as best he could,
In a woolen gown that reached his knee.
A dagger on a lanyard[55] falling free
Hung from his neck under his arm and down.
The summer heat had tanned his color brown,
405 And certainly he was an excellent fellow.
Many a draught of vintage, red and yellow,
He'd drawn at Bordeaux, while the trader snored.
The nicer rules of conscience he ignored.
If, when he fought, the enemy vessel sank,
410 He sent his prisoners home; they walked the plank.
As for his skill in reckoning his tides,
Currents and many another risk besides,
Moons, harbors, pilots, he had such dispatch
That none from Hull to Carthage was his match.

avouches (ə vouch′ ez) v.
asserts positively; affirms

Literary Analysis
Characterization and Social Commentary
What point is Chaucer making about the relationship between these men and their wives?

Literary Analysis
Characterization
What picture of the Skipper is created by the mixture of details about his heartlessness with details about his competence?

---

52. **guild-fraternity** In the Middle Ages, associations of men practicing the same craft or trade, called guilds, set standards for workmanship and protected their members by controlling competition.
53. **burgess** member of a legislative body.
54. **blancmange** (blə mänzh′) at the time, the name of a creamy chicken dish.
55. **lanyard** loose rope around the neck.

415　Hardy he was, prudent in undertaking;
　　His beard in many a tempest had its shaking,
　　And he knew all the havens as they were
　　From Gottland to the Cape of Finisterre,
　　And every creek in Brittany and Spain;
420　The barge he owned was called *The Maudelayne.*
　　　　　A *Doctor* too emerged as we proceeded;
　　No one alive could talk as well as he did
　　On points of medicine and of surgery,
　　For, being grounded in astronomy,
425　He watched his patient's favorable star
　　And, by his Natural Magic, knew what are
　　The lucky hours and planetary degrees
　　For making charms and magic effigies.
　　The cause of every malady you'd got
430　He knew, and whether dry, cold, moist or hot;[56]
　　He knew their seat, their humor and condition.
　　He was a perfect practicing physician.
　　These causes being known for what they were,
　　He gave the man his medicine then and there.
435　All his apothecaries[57] in a tribe
　　Were ready with the drugs he would prescribe,
　　And each made money from the other's guile;
　　They had been friendly for a goodish while.
　　He was well-versed in Aesculapius[58] too
440　And what Hippocrates and Rufus knew
　　And Dioscorides, now dead and gone,
　　Galen and Rhazes, Hali, Serapion,
　　Averroes, Avicenna, Constantine,
　　Scotch Bernard, John of Gaddesden, Gilbertine.[59]
445　In his own diet he observed some measure;
　　There were no superfluities for pleasure,
　　Only digestives, nutritives and such.
　　He did not read the Bible very much.
　　In blood-red garments, slashed with bluish-gray
450　And lined with taffeta,[60] he rode his way;
　　Yet he was rather close as to expenses
　　And kept the gold he won in pestilences.
　　Gold stimulates the heart, or so we're told.
　　He therefore had a special love of gold.
455　　　　A worthy *woman* from beside Bath[61] city

Reading Strategy
Analyzing Difficult Sentences In the sentence in lines 421–428, what is said about *how* the Doctor practices medicine?

Reading Check

What are two characteristics of the Skipper?

Was with us, somewhat deaf, which was a pity.
In making cloth she showed so great a bent
She bettered those of Ypres and of Ghent.[62]
In all the parish not a dame dared stir
460 Towards the altar steps in front of her,
And if indeed they did, so wrath was she
As to be quite put out of charity.
Her kerchiefs were of finely woven ground;[63]
I dared have sworn they weighed a good ten pound,
465 The ones she wore on Sunday, on her head.
Her hose were of the finest scarlet red
And gartered tight; her shoes were soft and new.
Bold was her face, handsome, and red in hue.
A worthy woman all her life, what's more
470 She'd had five husbands, all at the church door,
Apart from other company in youth;
No need just now to speak of that, forsooth.
And she had thrice been to Jerusalem,
Seen many strange rivers and passed over them;
475 She'd been to Rome and also to Boulogne,
St. James of Compostella and Cologne,[64]
And she was skilled in wandering by the way.
She had gap-teeth, set widely, truth to say.
Easily on an ambling horse she sat
480 Well wimpled[65] up, and on her head a hat
As broad as is a buckler[66] or a shield;
She had a flowing mantle that concealed
Large hips, her heels spurred sharply under that.
In company she liked to laugh and chat
485 And knew the remedies for love's mischances,
An art in which she knew the oldest dances.

　　　A holy-minded man of good renown
There was, and poor, the *Parson* to a town,
Yet he was rich in holy thought and work.
490 He also was a learned man, a clerk,
Who truly knew Christ's gospel and would preach it
Devoutly to parishioners, and teach it.
Benign and wonderfully diligent,
And patient when adversity was sent
495 (For so he proved in great adversity)
He much disliked extorting tithe[67] or fee,

▲ **Critical Viewing**
What does the Wife of
Bath's pose convey about
her character? **[Analyze]**

Reading Strategy
Analyzing Difficult
Sentences What is
the main idea in
lines 493–500?

---

62. **Ypres** (ē′ prə) **and of Ghent** (gent) Flemish cities known for wool making.
63. **ground** composite fabric.
64. **Jerusalem . . . Rome . . . Boulogne . . . St. James of Compostella . . . Cologne** famous pilgrimage sites at the time.
65. **wimpled** wearing a scarf covering the head, neck, and chin.
66. **buckler** small round shield.
67. **tithe** (tīth) one tenth of a person's income, paid as a tax to support the church.

Nay rather he preferred beyond a doubt
Giving to poor parishioners round about
From his own goods and Easter offerings
500 He found sufficiency in little things.
    Wide was his parish, with houses far asunder,
Yet he neglected not in rain or thunder,
In sickness or in grief, to pay a call
      On the remotest, whether great or small,
505 Upon his feet, and in his hand a stave.
This noble example to his sheep he gave,
First following the word before he taught it,
And it was from the gospel he had caught it.
This little proverb he would add thereto
510 That if gold rust, what then will iron do?
For if a priest be foul in whom we trust
No wonder that a common man should rust;
And shame it is to see—let priests take stock—
A soiled shepherd and a snowy flock.
515 The true example that a priest should give
Is one of cleanness, how the sheep should live.
He did not set his benefice to hire[68]
And leave his sheep encumbered in the mire
Or run to London to earn easy bread
520 By singing masses for the wealthy dead,
Or find some Brotherhood and get enrolled.
He stayed at home and watched over his fold
So that no wolf should make the sheep miscarry.
He was a shepherd and no mercenary.
525 Holy and virtuous he was, but then
Never contemptuous of sinful men,
Never disdainful, never too proud or fine,
But was discreet in teaching and benign.
His business was to show a fair behavior
530 And draw men thus to Heaven and their Savior,
Unless indeed a man were obstinate;
And such, whether of high or low estate,
He put to sharp rebuke to say the least.
I think there never was a better priest.
535 He sought no pomp or glory in his dealings,
No scrupulosity had spiced his feelings.
Christ and His Twelve Apostles and their lore
He taught, but followed it himself before.
      There was a *Plowman* with him there, his brother.
540 Many a load of dung one time or other
He must have carted through the morning dew.
He was an honest worker, good and true,

68. set . . . hire pay someone else to perform his parish duties.

Literary Analysis
Characterization and Social Commentary
How does Chaucer use his characterization of the Parson to comment on the way priests ought to behave?

Reading Check

What is the Parson's main characteristic?

Living in peace and perfect charity,
And, as the gospel bade him, so did he,
545 Loving God best with all his heart and mind
And then his neighbor as himself, repined
At no misfortune, slacked for no content,
For steadily about his work he went
To thrash his corn, to dig or to manure
550 Or make a ditch; and he would help the poor
For love of Christ and never take a penny
If he could help it, and, as prompt as any,
He paid his tithes in full when they were due
On what he owned, and on his earnings too.
555 He wore a tabard[69] smock and rode a mare.
There was a *Reeve*,[70] also a *Miller*, there,
A College *Manciple*[71] from the Inns of Court,
A papal *Pardoner*[72] and, in close consort,
A Church-Court *Summoner*,[73] riding at a trot,
560 And finally myself—that was the lot.
        The *Miller* was a chap of sixteen stone,[74]
A great stout fellow big in brawn and bone.
He did well out of them, for he could go
And win the ram at any wrestling show.
565 Broad, knotty and short-shouldered, he would boast
He could heave any door off hinge and post,
Or take a run and break it with his head.
His beard, like any sow or fox, was red
And broad as well, as though it were a spade;
570 And, at its very tip, his nose displayed
A wart on which there stood a tuft of hair.
Red as the bristles in an old sow's ear.
His nostrils were as black as they were wide.
He had a sword and buckler at his side,
575 His mighty mouth was like a furnace door.
A wrangler and buffoon, he had a store
Of tavern stories, filthy in the main.
His was a master-hand at stealing grain.
He felt it with his thumb and thus he knew
580 Its quality and took three times his due—
A thumb of gold, by God, to gauge an oat!
He wore a hood of blue and a white coat.
He liked to play his bagpipes up and down
And that was how he brought us out of town.

Literary Analysis
Characterization and Social Commentary What social commentary does the description of the Plowman provide?

Literary Analysis
Characterization What does the comparison of the Miller's hair color to that of a sow or fox indirectly suggest about his character?

---

69. **tabard** loose jacket.
70. **Reeve** estate manager.
71. **Manciple** buyer of provisions.
72. **Pardoner** one who dispenses papal pardons.
73. **Summoner** one who serves summonses to church courts.
74. **sixteen stone** 224 pounds. A stone equals 14 pounds.

585   The *Manciple* came from the Inner Temple;
      All caterers might follow his example
      In buying victuals; he was never rash
      Whether he bought on credit or paid cash.
      He used to watch the market most precisely
590   And go in first, and so he did quite nicely.
      Now isn't it a marvel of God's grace
      That an illiterate fellow can outpace
      The wisdom of a heap of learned men?
      His masters—he had more than thirty then—
595   All versed in the abstrusest legal knowledge,
      Could have produced a dozen from their College
      Fit to be stewards in land and rents and game
      To any Peer in England you could name,
      And show him how to live on what he had
600   Debt-free (unless of course the Peer were mad)
      Or be as frugal as he might desire,
      And they were fit to help about the Shire
      In any legal case there was to try;
      And yet this Manciple could wipe their eye.

605   The *Reeve* was old and choleric and thin;
      His beard was shaven closely to the skin,
      His shorn hair came abruptly to a stop
      Above his ears, and he was docked on top
      Just like a priest in front; his legs were lean,
610   Like sticks they were, no calf was to be seen.
      He kept his bins and garners[75] very trim;
      No auditor could gain a point on him.
      And he could judge by watching drought and rain
      The yield he might expect from seed and grain.
615   His master's sheep, his animals and hens,
      Pigs, horses, dairies, stores and cattle-pens
      Were wholly trusted to his government.
      And he was under contract to present
      The accounts, right from his master's earliest years.
620   No one had ever caught him in arrears.
      No bailiff, serf or herdsman dared to kick,
      He knew their dodges, knew their every trick;
      Feared like the plague he was, by those beneath.
      He had a lovely dwelling on a heath,
625   Shadowed in green by trees above the sward.[76]
      A better hand at bargains than his lord,
      He had grown rich and had a store of treasure
      Well tucked away, yet out it came to pleasure
      His lord with subtle loans or gifts of goods,

---

75. **garners** *n.* buildings for storing grain.
76. **sward** *n.* turf.

Reading Strategy
Analyzing Difficult Sentences What are the two subjects of the comparison in lines 594–604?

✔**Reading Check**

What is the Miller like?

from *The Canterbury Tales: The Prologue* ◆ 109

630 To earn his thanks and even coats and hoods.
When young he'd learnt a useful trade and still
He was a carpenter of first-rate skill.
The stallion-cob he rode at a slow trot
Was dapple-gray and bore the name of Scot.
635 He wore an overcoat of bluish shade
And rather long; he had a rusty blade
Slung at his side. He came, as I heard tell,
From Norfolk, near a place called Baldeswell.
His coat was tucked under his belt and splayed.
640 He rode the hindmost of our cavalcade.
     There was a *Summoner* with us in the place
Who had a fire-red cherubinnish face,[77]
For he had carbuncles.[78] His eyes were narrow,
He was as hot and lecherous as a sparrow.
645 Black, scabby brows he had, and a thin beard.
Children were afraid when he appeared.
No quicksilver, lead ointments, tartar creams,
Boracic, no, nor brimstone,[79] so it seems,
Could make a salve that had the power to bite,
650 Clean up or cure his whelks[80] of knobby white.
Or purge the pimples sitting on his cheeks.
Garlic he loved, and onions too, and leeks,
And drinking strong wine till all was hazy.
Then he would shout and jabber as if crazy,
655 And wouldn't speak a word except in Latin
When he was drunk, such tags as he was pat in;
He only had a few, say two or three,
That he had mugged up out of some decree;
No wonder, for he heard them every day.
660 And, as you know, a man can teach a jay
To call out "Walter" better than the Pope.
But had you tried to test his wits and grope
For more, you'd have found nothing in the bag.
Then "*Questio quid juris*"[81] was his tag.
665 He was a gentle varlet and a kind one,
No better fellow if you went to find one.
He would allow—just for a quart of wine—
Any good lad to keep a concubine
A twelvemonth and dispense it altogether!
670 Yet he could pluck a finch to leave no feather:

Reading Strategy
Analyzing Difficult Sentences In the sentence in lines 647–650, *what* could not be cured?

Literary Analysis
Characterization In lines 652–659, is the characterization of the Summoner direct or indirect? Explain.

---

77. **fire-red . . . face** In the art of the Middle Ages, the faces of cherubs, or angels, were often painted red.
78. **carbuncles** (kär´ buŋ´ kəlz) *n.* pus-filled boils resulting from a bacterial infection under the skin.
79. **quicksilver . . . brimstone** various chemicals and chemical compounds, used as remedies. *Quicksilver* is a name for mercury. *Brimstone* is a name for sulfur.
80. **whelks** *n.* pustules; pimples.
81. **"*Questio quid juris*"** "The question is, What is the point of law?" (Latin).

And if he found some rascal with a maid
He would instruct him not to be afraid
In such a case of the Archdeacon's curse
(Unless the rascal's soul were in his purse)
675 For in his purse the punishment should be.
"Purse is the good Archdeacon's Hell," said he.
But well I know he lied in what he said;
A curse should put a guilty man in dread,
For curses kill, as shriving brings, salvation.
680 We should beware of excommunication.
Thus, as he pleased, the man could bring duress
On any young fellow in the diocese.
He knew their secrets, they did what he said.
He wore a garland set upon his head
685 Large as the holly-bush upon a stake
Outside an ale-house, and he had a cake,
A round one, which it was his joke to wield
As if it were intended for a shield.
     He and a gentle *Pardoner* rode together,
690 A bird from Charing Cross of the same feather,
Just back from visiting the Court of Rome.
He loudly sang "*Come hither, love, come home!*"
The Summoner sang deep seconds to this song,
No trumpet ever sounded half so strong.
695 This Pardoner had hair as yellow as wax,
Hanging down smoothly like a hank of flax.
In driblets fell his locks behind his head
Down to his shoulder which they overspread;
Thinly they fell, like rat-tails, one by one.
700 He wore no hood upon his head, for fun;
The hood inside his wallet had been stowed,
He aimed at riding in the latest mode;
But for a little cap his head was bare
And he had bulging eyeballs, like a hare.
705 He'd sewed a holy relic on his cap;
His wallet lay before him on his lap,
Brimful of pardons come from Rome all hot.
He had the same small voice a goat has got.
His chin no beard had harbored, nor would harbor,
710 Smoother than ever chin was left by barber.
I judge he was a gelding, or a mare.
As to his trade, from Berwick down to Ware
There was no pardoner of equal grace,
For in his trunk he had a pillowcase
715 Which he asserted was Our Lady's veil.
He said he had a gobbet[82] of the sail

The Pardoner, Arthur Szyk for The Canterbury Tales

▲ **Critical Viewing** How
well does this picture of
the Pardoner match
Chaucer's description of
him in lines 695–710?
[Assess]

☑ **Reading Check**

How does the Summoner
turn religion to personal
profit?

---

82. gobbet piece.

Saint Peter had the time when he made bold
To walk the waves, till Jesu Christ took hold.
He had a cross of metal set with stones
720 And, in a glass, a rubble of pigs' bones.
And with these relics, any time he found
Some poor up-country parson to astound,
On one short day, in money down, he drew
More than the parson in a month or two,
725 And by his flatteries and <u>prevarication</u>
Made monkeys of the priest and congregation.
But still to do him justice first and last
In church he was a noble ecclesiast.
How well he read a lesson or told a story!
730 But best of all he sang an Offertory,[83]
For well he knew that when that song was sung
He'd have to preach and tune his honey-tongue
And (well he could) win silver from the crowd.
That's why he sang so merrily and loud.
735   Now I have told you shortly, in a clause,
The rank, the array, the number and the cause
Of our assembly in this company
In Southwark, at that high-class hostelry
Known as *The Tabard*, close beside *The Bell*.
740 And now the time has come for me to tell
How we behaved that evening; I'll begin
After we had alighted at the inn,
Then I'll report our journey, stage by stage,
All the remainder of our pilgrimage.
745 But first I beg of you, in courtesy,
Not to condemn me as unmannerly
If I speak plainly and with no concealings
And give account of all their words and dealings,
Using their very phrases as they fell.
750 For certainly, as you all know so well,
He who repeats a tale after a man
Is bound to say, as nearly as he can,
Each single word, if he remembers it,
However rudely spoken or unfit,
755 Or else the tale he tells will be untrue,
The things invented and the phrases new.
He may not flinch although it were his brother,
If he says one word he must say the other.
And Christ Himself spoke broad[84] in Holy Writ,
760 And as you know there's nothing there unfit,
And Plato[85] says, for those with power to read,

Literary Analysis
Characterization What facts in lines 719–726 indirectly characterize the Pardoner?

prevarication (pri var´ i kā´ shən) *n.* evasion of truth

Reading Strategy
Analyzing Difficult Sentences Why does Chaucer apologize in the sentence starting with line 745?

---

83. Offertory song that accompanies the collection of the offering at a church service.
84. broad bluntly.
85. Plato Greek philosopher (427?–347? B.C.)

"The word should be as cousin to the deed."
Further I beg you to forgive it me
If I neglect the order and degree
765 And what is due to rank in what I've planned.
I'm short of wit as you will understand.
    Our *Host* gave us great welcome; everyone
Was given a place and supper was begun.
He served the finest victuals you could think,
770 The wine was strong and we were glad to drink.
A very striking man our Host withal,
And fit to be a marshal in a hall.
His eyes were bright, his girth a little wide;
There is no finer burgess in Cheapside.[86]
775 Bold in his speech, yet wise and full of tact,
There was no manly attribute he lacked,
What's more he was a merry-hearted man.
After our meal he jokingly began
To talk of sport, and, among other things
780 After we'd settled up our reckonings,
He said as follows: "Truly, gentlemen,
You're very welcome and I can't think when
—Upon my word I'm telling you no lie—
I've seen a gathering here that looked so spry,
785 No, not this year, as in this tavern now.
I'd think you up some fun if I knew how.
And, as it happens, a thought has just occurred
And it will cost you nothing, on my word.
You're off to Canterbury—well, God speed!
790 Blessed St. Thomas answer to your need!
And I don't doubt, before the journey's done
You mean to while the time in tales and fun.
Indeed, there's little pleasure for your bones
Riding along and all as dumb as stones.
795 So let me then propose for your enjoyment,
Just as I said, a suitable employment.
And if my notion suits and you agree
And promise to submit yourselves to me
Playing your parts exactly as I say
800 Tomorrow as you ride along the way,
Then by my father's soul (and he is dead)
If you don't like it you can have my head!
Hold up your hands, and not another word."
    Well, our consent of course was not deferred,
805 It seemed not worth a serious debate;
We all agreed to it at any rate
And bade him issue what commands he would.

---

86. Cheapside district in London.

***The Literature of
Social Observation***
    The eighteenth-
century poet William
Blake said that the "characters
of Chaucer's pilgrims are the
characters which compose all
ages and nations." Yet Chaucer
did not have the last word on
the subject. Writers after him
continued a tradition of detailed,
ironic observations of social types.
Four centuries later, for instance,
eighteenth-century writers such as
Joseph Addison held up a mirror
to middle-class society, describing
the typical characters of the day
and their follies.

    The tradition of social
commentary bloomed with the
invention of the novel, a form
built around keen observations
of character and society. Yet the
novel emphasized the individual
in a way that earlier literature
often did not. The characters
of nineteenth-century novelist
Charles Dickens, for instance,
take on their social roles with
extravagant, individual style. In
a sense, though, Dickens was only
following Chaucer. In pilgrims such
as the Wife of Bath, the Skipper,
and the Host, you can already
detect a spark of vital individuality,
deeper than any social role.

Reading Check

What concern does the
Host raise?

"My lords," he said, "now listen for your good,
And please don't treat my notion with disdain.
810 This is the point. I'll make it short and plain.
Each one of you shall help to make things slip
By telling two stories on the outward trip
To Canterbury, that's what I intend,
And, on the homeward way to journey's end
815 Another two, tales from the days of old;
And then the man whose story is best told,
That is to say who gives the fullest measure
Of good morality and general pleasure,
He shall be given a supper, paid by all,
820 Here in this tavern, in this very hall,
When we come back again from Canterbury.
And in the hope to keep you bright and merry
I'll go along with you myself and ride
All at my own expense and serve as guide.
825 I'll be the judge, and those who won't obey
Shall pay for what we spend upon the way.
Now if you all agree to what you've heard
Tell me at once without another word,
And I will make arrangements early for it."
830   Of course we all agreed, in fact we swore it
Delightedly, and made entreaty too
That he should act as he proposed to do,
Become our Governor in short, and be
Judge of our tales and general referee,
835 And set the supper at a certain price.
We promised to be ruled by his advice
Come high, come low; unanimously thus
We set him up in judgment over us.
More wine was fetched, the business being done;
840 We drank it off and up went everyone
To bed without a moment of delay.
    Early next morning at the spring of day
Up rose our Host and roused us like a cock,
Gathering us together in a flock,
845 And off we rode at slightly faster pace
Than walking to St. Thomas' watering-place;[87]
And there our Host drew up, began to ease
His horse, and said, "Now, listen if you please,
My lords! Remember what you promised me.
850 If evensong and matins will agree[88]

Literary Analysis
Characterization What
does the Host's decision
to accompany the pilgrims
suggest about him?

---

87. **St. Thomas' watering-place** a brook two miles from the inn.
88. **If evensong . . . agree** "if what you said last night holds true this morning."

Let's see who shall be first to tell a tale.
And as I hope to drink good wine and ale
I'll be your judge. The rebel who disobeys,
However much the journey costs, he pays.
855 Now draw for cut[89] and then we can depart;
The man who draws the shortest cut shall start."

---

89. draw for cut draw lots, as when pulling straws from a bunch; the person who pulls the short straw is "it."

Review and Assess

Thinking About the Selection

1. **Respond:** Which of the pilgrims would you most like to meet? Why?

2. **(a) Recall:** List three characteristics of the Nun. **(b) Deduce:** What details does Chaucer include in his description of the Nun to make gentle fun of her? Explain.

3. **(a) Recall:** Identify two of the main characteristics of the Friar and the Parson. **(b) Compare and Contrast:** What are some of the ways in which the Friar and the Parson differ?

4. **Infer:** Judging from the descriptions of the two, what does Chaucer think can cause a religious person to fail in his or her duty?

5. **Compare and Contrast:** How does Chaucer's attitude towards the Monk differ, if at all, from his attitude towards the Friar? Explain.

6. **(a) Infer:** What does Chaucer seem to dislike about the Skipper? **(b) Infer:** What does he seem to admire about this character? **(c) Draw Conclusions:** Describe Chaucer's overall attitude toward him.

7. **Draw Conclusions:** Judging from his pilgrims, do you think Chaucer believes people are basically good, basically evil, or often a mix of the two? Give examples to support your answer.

8. **(a) Apply:** What modern character types match the characters in the Prologue? **(b) Apply:** What types would Chaucer not have anticipated?

9. **(a) Analyze:** From what segments of medieval society do the pilgrims come? **(b) Draw Conclusions:** What does their participation in a common pilgrimage suggest about the times?

10. **Evaluate:** Do you think Chaucer's view of people is justified? Explain.

Review and Assess

Literary Analysis

Characterization

1. Give three details that Chaucer uses to **characterize** the Doctor. For each, note whether the characterization is **direct** or **indirect.**

2. (a) Find one example of each of the following kinds of details in Chaucer's characterizations: direct statement, physical description, character's action. (b) Explain how your examples of physical description and action indirectly characterize that pilgrim.

3. (a) Identify an example in which Chaucer uses mild sarcasm in describing a character. (b) Explain how his tone changes the meaning of the description.

4. Choose the character sketch you find most effective. Explain the method Chaucer uses to make the sketch so vivid.

Connecting Literary Elements

5. Use a chart like the one below to reflect on the **social commentary** in the Prologue. (a) What social comment does Chaucer make in his sketch of the Pardoner? (b) What does the sketch of the Knight suggest were some of the excellences promoted by medieval society?

Character	Detail		Implication About Society
		···▶	

6. Most of Chaucer's characters are named after a profession. What does this emphasis on social roles suggest about medieval society?

Reading Strategy

Analyzing Difficult Sentences

7. Analyze the sentence in lines 47–50 answering the questions *who, what, how much,* and *how well.*

8. Analyze the sentence in lines 529–533.

9. Find and analyze another long sentence from the Prologue.

Extend Understanding

10. **Cultural Connection:** If Chaucer were writing today, what three kinds of pilgrims might he consider adding to the group?

Quick Review

Characterization is the technique a writer uses to create and develop the personality of a character. Characterization may be **direct**—stated outright—or **indirect**—suggested through details of appearance or action or by the character's statements.

Social commentary is writing that offers insight into a society, its values, and its customs.

Analyze difficult sentences by applying the questions *who, what, where, when, why,* and *how* to them.

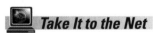 **Take It to the Net**

www.phschool.com

Take the interactive self-test online to check your understanding of this selection.

Integrate Language Skills

Vocabulary Development Lesson

Word Analysis: Latin Suffix -tion

The Latin suffix *-tion* means "the act or process of" or "the result of the act or process of." *To prevaricate* means "to distort the truth." *Prevarication* is the act of distorting the truth. Use your knowledge of *-tion* to define the words below.

1. narration   2. elevation   3. oration

Spelling Strategy

Usually, the ending pronounced *shun* is spelled *tion*, as in *prevarication*. It can also be spelled *sion*, *ssion*, and, in a few cases, *cion*. Fill in the blanks below to spell the *shun* sound correctly.

1. ten__ion   2. expre__ion   3. man__ion

Concept Development: Synonyms

Review the vocabulary list on page 91. Then, match each numbered word with its synonym.

1. solicitous   a. asserts
2. garnished   b. authorization
3. sanguine   c. an act freeing from sin
4. avouches   d. confident
5. commission   e. caring
6. absolution   f. decorated
7. prevarication   g. lying

Grammar and Style

Past and Past Perfect Tenses

The **past tense** is a verb form showing an action or a condition that began and ended in the past. The **past perfect tense** indicates an action or a condition that ended before another past action began.

> PAST PERFECT TENSE
> This estimable Merchant so <u>had set</u> / His wits
> PAST TENSE
> to work, none <u>knew</u> he was in debt. . . .

Practice Recount each pair of events. Show sequence by using the past and the past perfect.

1. Narrator meets pilgrims / stays at inn
2. Nun plans trip / wears nice clothing
3. Cleric is poor / finds no preferment
4. Wife goes to Rome / joins the group
5. Pardoner sells relic / lies about its origin

Writing Application Using verbs in both the past and past perfect tenses, describe a modern pilgrim.

W/*G* *Prentice Hall Writing and Grammar Connection: Chapter 21, Section 2*

Extension Activities

Writing Write a **critical response** to the poet William Blake's assertion that the "characters of Chaucer's pilgrims are the characters which compose all ages and nations." Use examples from the Prologue to explain why you agree or disagree with Blake's idea that Chaucer's characterizations can apply to people today.

Listening and Speaking With two partners, perform a **dialogue** for three of the pilgrims, discussing the trip you are about to take. Prepare by rereading the sections of the Prologue describing your characters. Use language and expressions appropriate to each character. **[Group Activity]**

Prepare to Read

The Nun's Priest's Tale

Literary Analysis

Parody

A **parody** is a humorous imitation of another work or type of work. For example, an epic is a long narrative poem that uses grand language to tell of noble characters and dramatic events. To create a parody of epic style called **mock-heroic style,** a writer

- applies epic language to ordinary characters and trivial events
- uses the combination of lowly subject matter and impressive descriptions to develop amusing, even ridiculous, contrasts

Note Chaucer's use of mock-heroic style in "The Nun's Priest's Tale."

Connecting Literary Elements

In addition to parodying epic style, "The Nun's Priest's Tale" also parodies a fable. A **fable** is a brief tale that

- points out a moral truth
- usually features animal characters

By using nonhuman characters, a fable may protect the vanity of people even as it prods them into seeing a truth about their own follies. Chaucer's parody of a fable uses animal characters to suggest a moral truth, but it may leave you unsure of what that truth is.

Reading Strategy

Using Context Clues

When you encounter an unfamiliar word, you can often figure out its meaning by using **context clues**—words and phrases in the surrounding passage that shed light on the word. Common context clues are synonyms, antonyms, and examples that clarify a word's meaning. Use a chart like the following to find context clues as you read.

Vocabulary Development

capital (kap´ət əl) *n.* wealth in the form of money or property (p. 120)

timorous (tim´ ər es) *adj.* timid (p. 122)

derision (di rizh´ ən) *n.* contempt or ridicule (p. 126)

maxim (maks´ im) *n.* general truth or rule of conduct, expressed in brief form (p. 130)

stringent (strin´ jənt) *adj.* strict (p. 132)

cant (kant) *n.* insincere or meaning-less talk (p. 134)

Passage

"She was so full of torment and dismay / That in the very flames she chose her part and burnt . . ."

↓

Unfamiliar Word

dismay

↓

Context Clue

torment

↓

Relation to Unfamiliar Word

similar in meaning

↓

Conclusion

If *dismay* is anything like *torment*, it must name an unpleasant feeling of some kind.

The Nun's Priest's Tale

Geoffrey Chaucer
Translated by Nevill Coghill

Review and Anticipate

Each pilgrim in the Prologue agrees to tell two tales on the way to Canterbury. The teller of this tale, the Nun's Priest, is briefly mentioned in the Prologue. The character reappears when the Knight objects to a tragic tale told by the Monk. Just when it looks as if the storytelling game might end in bitterness, the Host spots the Nun's Priest and asks him to tell a tale. The new storyteller is described as riding a "jade," an old, filthy cart horse. Yet, he vows to be "merry," and Chaucer describes him as both "sweet" and "goodly." Predict what kind of story such a character might tell in such a predicament. When you have finished reading the tale, review your prediction and determine how accurate it was.

Once, long ago, there dwelt a poor old widow
In a small cottage, by a little meadow
Beside a grove and standing in a dale.
This widow-woman of whom I tell my tale
5 Since the sad day when last she was a wife
Had led a very patient, simple life.
Little she had in <u>capital</u> or rent,
But still, by making do with what God sent,
She kept herself and her two daughters going.
10 Three hefty sows—no more—were all her showing,
Three cows as well; there was a sheep called Molly.
     Sooty her hall, her kitchen melancholy,
And there she ate full many a slender meal;
There was no *sauce piquante*[1] to spice her veal,
15 No dainty morsel ever passed her throat,
According to her cloth she cut her coat.
Repletion[2] never left her in disquiet
And all her physic was a temperate diet,
Hard work for exercise and heart's content.
20 And rich man's gout did nothing to prevent
Her dancing, apoplexy[3] struck her not;
She drank no wine, nor white nor red had got.
Her board was mostly served with white and black,
Milk and brown bread, in which she found no lack;
25 Broiled bacon or an egg or two were common,
She was in fact a sort of dairy-woman.
     She had a yard that was enclosed about
By a stockade and a dry ditch without,
In which she kept a cock called Chanticleer.
30 In all the land for crowing he'd no peer;
His voice was jollier than the organ blowing
In church on Sundays, he was great at crowing.
Far, far more regular than any clock
Or abbey bell the crowing of this cock.
35 The equinoctial wheel and its position[4]
At each ascent he knew by intuition;
At every hour—fifteen degrees of movement—
He crowed so well there could be no improvement.
His comb was redder than fine coral, tall
40 And battlemented like a castle wall,
His bill was black and shone as bright as jet,

capital (kap′ ət əl) *n.*
wealth in the form
of money or property

Reading Strategy
Using Context Clues
What related words and
facts in this sentence help
you get a sense of the
meaning of *board* in
line 23?

---

1. *sauce piquante* (pē′ kənt) French for a pleasantly sharp sauce, used for fancy and
   expensive meals.
2. **Repletion** (ri plē′ shən) *n.* the state of having eaten too much.
3. **apoplexy** old-fashioned term for a stroke.
4. **equinoctial . . . position** Chaucer and his contemporaries accounted for changes in
   the positions of stars and planets by imagining that the heavens circled the Earth
   once a day, moving fifteen degrees each hour.

English Travelers Setting Forth, from *The Canterbury Tales,* The British Library

▲ **Critical Viewing** Why might people traveling in the manner of these pilgrims enjoy "The Nun's Priest's Tale"? **[Speculate]**

Like azure were his legs and they were set
On azure toes with nails of lily white,
Like burnished gold his feathers, flaming bright.
45   This gentlecock was master in some measure
Of seven hens, all there to do his pleasure.
They were his sisters and his paramours,
Colored like him in all particulars;

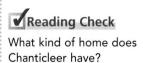

Reading Check

What kind of home does Chanticleer have?

She with the loveliest dyes upon her throat
50 Was known as gracious Lady Pertelote.
Courteous she was, discreet and debonair,
Companionable too, and took such care
In her deportment, since she was seven days old
She held the heart of Chanticleer controlled,
55 Locked up securely in her every limb;
O such happiness his love to him!
And such a joy it was to hear them sing,
As when the glorious sun began to spring,
In sweet accord *My love is far from land*[5]
60 —For in those far off days I understand
All birds and animals could speak and sing.
        Now it befell, as dawn began to spring,
When Chanticleer and Pertelote and all
His wives were perched in this poor widow's hall
65 (Fair Pertelote was next him on the perch),
This Chanticleer began to groan and lurch
Like someone sorely troubled by a dream,
And Pertelote who heard him roar and scream
Was quite aghast and said, "O dearest heart,
70 What's ailing you? Why do you groan and start?
Fie, what a sleeper! What a noise to make!"
"Madam," he said, "I beg you not to take
Offense, but by the Lord I had a dream
So terrible just now I had to scream;
75 I still can feel my heart racing from fear.
God turn my dream to good and guard all here.
And keep my body out of durance vile![6]
I dreamt that roaming up and down a while
Within our yard I saw a kind of beast,
80 A sort of hound that tried or seemed at least
To try and seize me. . . would have killed me dead!
His color was a blend of yellow and red,
His ears and tail were tipped with sable fur
Unlike the rest; he was a russet cur.
85 Small was his snout, his eyes were glowing bright.
It was enough to make one die of fright.
That was no doubt what made me groan and swoon."
        "For shame," she said, "you timorous poltroon![7]
Alas, what cowardice! By God above,
90 You've forfeited my heart and lost my love.
I cannot love a coward, come what may.
For certainly, whatever we may say,

Reading Strategy
Using Context Clues
Which context clues
might help you figure
out the meaning of
aghast in line 69?

timorous (tim´ ər es) *adj.*
timid

---

5. *My love is far from land* refrain of a popular song.
6. durance vile long imprisonment.
7. poltroon (päl trōōn´) *n.* coward.

All women long—and O that it might be!—
For husbands tough, dependable and free,
95 Secret, discreet, no niggard,[8] not a fool
That boasts and then will find his courage cool
At every trifling thing. By God above,
How dare you say for shame, and to your love,
That anything at all was to be feared?
100 Have you no manly heart to match your beard?
And can a dream reduce you to such terror?
Dreams are a vanity, God knows, pure error.
Dreams are engendered in the too-replete
From vapors in the belly, which compete
105 With others, too abundant, swollen tight.
    "No doubt the redness in your dream tonight
Comes from the superfluity and force
Of the red choler in your blood. Of course.
That is what puts a dreamer in the dread
110 Of crimsoned arrows, fires flaming red,
Of great red monsters making as to fight him,
And big red whelps and little ones to bite him;
Just so the black and melancholy vapors
Will set a sleeper shrieking, cutting capers
115 And swearing that black bears, black bulls as well,
Or blackest fiends are haling him to Hell.
And there are other vapors that I know
That on a sleeping man will work their woe,
But I'll pass on as lightly as I can.
120   "Take Cato[9] now, that was so wise a man,
Did he not say, 'Take no account of dreams'?
Now, sir," she said, "on flying from these beams,
For love of God do take some laxative;
Upon my soul that's the advice to give
125 For melancholy choler; let me urge
You free yourself from vapors with a purge.
And that you may have no excuse to tarry
By saying this town has no apothecary,
I shall myself instruct you and prescribe
130 Herbs that will cure all vapors of that tribe,
Herbs from our very farmyard! You will find
Their natural property is to unbind
And purge you well beneath and well above.
Now don't forget it, dear, for God's own love!
135 Your face is choleric and shows distension;
Be careful lest the sun in his ascension

---

8. **niggard** stingy person.
9. **Cato** Dionysius Cato, supposed author of a book of maxims used in elementary education.

Literary Analysis
Parody How does the serious, dramatic quality of Pertelote's complaint (lines 88–101) lend comedy to this passage?

Literary Analysis
Parody Why is the thought of a barnyard hen quoting classical authors humorous?

Reading Check

How does Pertelote respond to Chanticleer's complaint that he was frightened by a dream?

Should catch you full of humors,[10] hot and many.
And if he does, my dear, I'll lay a penny
It means a bout of fever or a breath
140 Of tertian ague.[11] You may catch your death.
　　　"Worms for a day or two I'll have to give
As a digestive, then your laxative.
Centaury, fumitory, caper-spurge
And hellebore will make a splendid purge;
145 And then there's laurel or the blackthorn berry,
Ground-ivy too that makes our yard so merry;
Peck them right up, my dear, and swallow whole.
Be happy, husband, by your father's soul!
Don't be afraid of dreams. I'll say no more."
150 　　"Madam," he said, "I thank you for your lore,
But with regard to Cato all the same,
His wisdom has, no doubt, a certain fame,
But though he said that we should take no heed
Of dreams, by God in ancient books I read
155 Of many a man of more authority
Than ever Cato was, believe you me,
Who say the very opposite is true
And prove their theories by experience too.
Dreams have quite often been significations
160 As well of triumphs as of tribulations
That people undergo in this our life.
This needs no argument at all, dear wife,
The proof is all too manifest indeed.
　　　"One of the greatest authors one can read
165 Says thus: there were two comrades once who went
On pilgrimage, sincere in their intent.
And as it happened they had reached a town
Where such a throng was milling up and down
And yet so scanty the accommodation,
170 They could not find themselves a habitation,
No, not a cottage that could lodge them both.
And so they separated, very loath,
Under constraint of this necessity
And each went off to find some hostelry,
175 And lodge whatever way his luck might fall.
　　　"The first of them found refuge in a stall
Down in a yard with oxen and a plow.

Reading Strategy
Using Context Clues
What is the meaning of
tribulations in line 160?
What context clue helped
you figure it out?

▼ **Critical Viewing**
How do the position and
facial expression of the
subject of this illustration
for the tale suggest he is
telling a story? **[Support]**

The Nun's Priest, detail from the Ellesmere Manuscript,
The Huntington Library, San Marino, California

---

10. **humors** People in Chaucer's time believed that bodily
fluids, called humors, were responsible for one's health
and disposition. An excess of the fluid called yellow
bile resulted in a choleric, or quick-tempered, personality. In lines 108 and 125, Chaucer seems to use the
word *choler* as a synonym for the term *humor.*
11. **tertian ague** (tʉr′ shən ā′ gyōō′) malarial fever.

His friend found lodging for himself somehow
Elsewhere, by accident or destiny,
180 Which governs all of us and equally.
   "Now it so happened, long ere it was day,
This fellow had a dream, and as he lay
In bed it seemed he heard his comrade call,
'Help! I am lying in an ox's stall
185 And shall tonight be murdered as I lie.
Help me, dear brother, help or I shall die!
Come in all haste!' Such were the words he spoke;
The dreamer, lost in terror, then awoke.
But once awake he paid it no attention,
190 Turned over and dismissed it as invention,
It was a dream, he thought, a fantasy.
And twice he dreamt this dream successively.
   "Yet a third time his comrade came again,
Or seemed to come, and said, 'I have been slain.
195 Look, look! my wounds are bleeding wide and deep,
Rise early in the morning, break your sleep
And go to the west gate. You there shall see
A cart all loaded up with dung,' said he,
'And in that dung my body has been hidden.
200 Boldly arrest that cart as you are bidden.
It was my money that they killed me for.'
   "He told him every detail, sighing sore,
And pitiful in feature, pale of hue.
This dream, believe me, Madam, turned out true;
205 For in the dawn, as soon as it was light,
He went to where his friend had spent the night
And when he came upon the cattle-stall
He looked about him and began to call.
   "The innkeeper, appearing thereupon,
210 Quickly gave answer, 'Sir, your friend has gone.
He left the town a little after dawn.'
The man began to feel suspicious, drawn
By memories of his dream—the western gate,
The dung-cart—off he went, he would not wait,
215 Towards the western entry. There he found,
Seemingly on its way to dung some ground,
A dung-cart loaded on the very plan
Described so closely by the murdered man.
So he began to shout courageously
220 For right and vengeance on the felony,
'My friend's been killed! There's been a foul attack,
He's in that cart and gaping on his back!
Fetch the authorities, get the sheriff down
—Whosever job it is to run the town—
225 Help! My companion's murdered, sent to glory!'

Literary Analysis
Parody and Fable Why is it unexpected for a character in an animal fable to tell a story, such as this one, that teaches a lesson?

✓**Reading Check**
Why does Chanticleer tell the story of the two comrades?

"What need I add to finish off the story?
People ran out and cast the cart to ground,
And in the middle of the dung they found
The murdered man. The corpse was fresh and new.
230   "O blessed God, that art so just and true,
Thus thou revealest murder! As we say,
'Murder will out.' We see it day by day.
Murder's a foul, abominable treason,
So loathsome to God's justice, to God's reason,
235 He will not suffer its concealment. True,
Things may lie hidden for a year or two,
But still 'Murder will out,' that's my conclusion.
    "All the town officers in great confusion
Seized on the carter and they gave him hell,
240 And then they racked the innkeeper as well,
And both confessed. And then they took the wrecks
And there and then they hanged them by their necks.
    "By this we see that dreams are to be dreaded.
And in the self-same book I find embedded,
245 Right in the very chapter after this
(I'm not inventing, as I hope for bliss)
The story of two men who started out
To cross the sea—for merchandise no doubt—
But as the winds were contrary they waited.
250 It was a pleasant town, I should have stated,
Merrily grouped about the haven-side.
A few days later with the evening tide
The wind veered round so as to suit them best;
They were delighted and they went to rest
255 Meaning to sail next morning early. Well,
To one of them a miracle befell.
    "This man as he lay sleeping, it would seem,
Just before dawn had an astounding dream.
He thought a man was standing by his bed
260 Commanding him to wait, and thus he said:
'If you set sail tomorrow as you intend
You will be drowned. My tale is at an end.'
    "He woke and told his friend what had occurred
And begged him that the journey be deferred
265 At least a day, implored him not to start.
But his companion, lying there apart,
Began to laugh and treat him to derision.
'I'm not afraid,' he said, 'of any vision,
To let it interfere with my affairs;
270 A straw for all your dreamings and your scares.
Dreams are just empty nonsense, merest japes;[12]

Reading Strategy
Using Context Clues
Which context clues help
clarify the meaning of
loathsome in line 234?

Literary Analysis
Parody and Fable Why
does this tale lack
"punch"?

derision (di rizh´ ən) *n.*
contempt or ridicule

---

12. japes jokes.

Why, people dream all day of owls and apes,
All sorts of trash that can't be understood,
Things that have never happened and never could.
275 But as I see you mean to stay behind
And miss the tide for wilful sloth of mind,
God knows I'm sorry for it, but good day!'
And so he took his leave and went his way.
    "And yet, before they'd covered half the trip
280 —I don't know what went wrong—there was a rip
And by some accident the ship went down,
Her bottom rent,[13] all hands aboard to drown
In sight of all the vessels at her side,
That had put out upon the self-same tide.
285   "So, my dear Pertelote, if you discern
The force of these examples, you may learn
One never should be careless about dreams,
For, undeniably, I say it seems
That many are a sign of trouble breeding.
290   "Now, take St. Kenelm's life which I've been reading;
He was Kenulphus' son, the noble King
Of Mercia. Now, St. Kenelm dreamt a thing
Shortly before they murdered him one day.
He saw his murder in a dream, I say.
295 His nurse expounded it and gave her reasons
On every point and warned him against treasons
But as the saint was only seven years old
All that she said about it left him cold.
He was so holy how could visions hurt?
300   "By God, I willingly would give my shirt
To have you read his legend as I've read it;
And, Madam Pertelote, upon my credit,
Macrobius wrote of dreams and can explain us
The vision of young Scipio Africanus,[14]
305 And he affirms that dreams can give a due
Warnings of things that later on come true.
    "And then there's the Old Testament—a manual
Well worth your study; see the *Book of Daniel*.
Did Daniel think a dream was vanity?
310 Read about Joseph too and you will see
That many dreams—I do not say that all—
Give cognizance of what is to befall.
    "Look at Lord Pharaoh, king of Egypt! Look
At what befell his butler and his cook.
315 Did not their visions have a certain force?
But those who study history of course

Literary Analysis
Parody How does the explanation in lines 297–298 help turn this section into a parody of a scholarly debate about dreams?

---

13. **rent** torn.
14. **Scipio Africanus** (sip′ ē ō af′ ri kā′ nəs) famous Roman general (237–183 B.C.).

☑**Reading Check**

What happens in each of Chanticleer's examples?

Woman Feeding Chickens, from an Italian manuscript (c. 1385), Österreichische National Bibliothek, Vienna

▲ **Critical Viewing** Contrast the tone of this barnyard scene with the tone of Chanticleer's scholarly discussion of dreams. **[Compare and Contrast]**

Meet many dreams that set them wondering.
　　　"What about Croesus too, the Lydian king,
Who dreamt that he was sitting in a tree,
320　Meaning he would be hanged? It had to be.
　　　"Or take Andromache, great Hector's wife;[15]
The day on which he was to lose his life
She dreamt about, the very night before,
And realized that if Hector went to war
325　He would be lost that very day in battle.
She warned him; he dismissed it all as prattle
And sallied forth to fight, being self-willed,
And there he met Achilles and was killed.
The tale is long and somewhat overdrawn,
330　And anyhow it's very nearly dawn,
So let me say in very brief conclusion
My dream undoubtedly foretells confusion,
It bodes me ill, I say. And, furthermore,
Upon your laxatives I set no store,
335　For they are venomous. I've suffered by them
Often enough before and I defy them.
　　　"And now, let's talk of fun and stop all this.
Dear Madam, as I hope for Heaven's bliss.
Of one thing God has sent me plenteous grace,
340　For when I see the beauty of your face,
That scarlet loveliness about your eyes,
All thought of terror and confusion dies.
For it's as certain as the Creed, I know,
Mulier est hominis confusio[16]
345　(A Latin tag, dear Madam, meaning this:
'Woman is man's delight and all his bliss').
For when at night I feel your feathery side,
Although perforce I cannot take a ride
Because, alas, our perch was made too narrow,
350　Delight and solace fill me to the marrow
And I defy all visions and all dreams!"
　　　And with that word he flew down from the beams,
For it was day, and down his hens flew all,
And with a chuck he gave the troupe a call
355　For he had found a seed upon the floor.
Royal he was, he was afraid no more.
He feathered Pertelote in wanton play
And trod her twenty times ere prime of day.
Grim as a lion's was his manly frown
360　As on his toes he sauntered up and down;

---

15. **Andromache** (an dräm´ ə kē) . . . **wife** the wife of Hector, the greatest warrior of
Troy at the time of the Trojan War.
16. *Mulier est hominis confusio* Latin for "woman is man's ruin."

Literary Analysis
Parody References to ancient literature and to the Bible appear in scholarly works of Chaucer's time, adding to their serious tone. What effect do the references in lines 303–330 have?

Literary Analysis
Parody In what way does Chanticleer's mistranslation of the Latin tag in line 344 make fun of the literary practice of backing up opinions with references?

✔**Reading Check**
What does Chanticleer do after concluding the debate on dreams?

He scarcely deigned to set his foot to ground
And every time a seed of corn was found
He gave a chuck, and up his wives ran all.
Thus royal as a prince who strides his hall
365 Leave we this Chanticleer engaged on feeding
And pass to the adventure that was breeding.
     Now when the month in which the world began,
March, the first month, when God created man,
Was over, and the thirty-second day
370 Thereafter ended, on the third of May
It happened that Chanticleer in all his pride,
His seven wives attendant at his side,
Cast his eyes upward to the blazing sun,
Which in the sign of *Taurus* then had run
375 His twenty-one degrees and somewhat more,
And knew by nature and no other lore
That it was nine o'clock. With blissful voice
He crew triumphantly and said, "Rejoice,
Behold the sun! The sun is up, my seven.
380 Look, it has climbed forty degrees in heaven,
Forty degrees and one in fact, by this.
Dear Madam Pertelote, my earthly bliss,
Hark to those blissful birds and how they sing!
Look at those pretty flowers, how they spring!
385 Solace and revel fill my heart!" He laughed.
     But in that moment Fate let fly her shaft;
Ever the latter end of joy is woe,
God knows that worldly joy is swift to go.
A rhetorician[17] with a flair for style
390 Could chronicle this <u>maxim</u> in his file
Of Notable Remarks with safe conviction.
Then let the wise give ear; this is no fiction
My story is as true, I undertake,
As that of good Sir Lancelot du Lake[18]
395 Who held all women in such high esteem.
Let me return full circle to my theme.
     A coal-tipped fox of sly iniquity[19]
That had been lurking round the grove for three
Long years, that very night burst through and passed
400 Stockade and hedge, as Providence forecast,
Into the yard where Chanticleer the Fair
Was wont, with all his ladies, to repair.
Still, in a bed of cabbages, he lay
Until about the middle of the day

---

17. rhetorician (ret´ ə rish´ ən) *n.* person skilled in public speaking or writing.
18. Sir Lancelot du Lake the most celebrated of King Arthur's Knights of the Round Table.
19. iniquity (i nik´ wi tē) *n.* wickedness.

Reading Strategy
Using Context Clues Use context clues to define *deigned* in line 361.

Literary Analysis
Parody and Fable What moral is Chaucer offering in lines 387–391?

maxim (maks´ im) *n.* general truth or rule of conduct, expressed in brief form

**Reading Check**
Who has entered Chanticleer's yard?

Chaucer Reciting Troilus and Cressida Before a Court Gathering (Frontispiece) Corpus Christi College

▲ **Critical Viewing** Judging from this scene, what was a storytelling event in Chaucer's time like? **[Interpret]**

405 Watching the cock and waiting for his cue,
As all these homicides so gladly do
That lie about in wait to murder men.
O false assassin, lurking in thy den!
O new Iscariot, new Ganelon!
410 And O Greek Sinon,[20] thou whose treachery won
Troy town and brought it utterly to sorrow!
O Chanticleer, accursed be that morrow
That brought thee to the yard from thy high beams!
Thou hadst been warned, and truly, by thy dreams
415 That this would be a perilous day for thee.
     But that which God's foreknowledge can foresee
Must needs occur, as certain men of learning
Have said. Ask any scholar of discerning;
He'll say the Schools are filled with altercation
420 On this vexed matter of predestination[21]
Long bandied by a hundred thousand men.
How can I sift it to the bottom then?
The Holy Doctor St. Augustine shines
In this, and there is Bishop Bradwardine's
425 Authority, Boethius'[22] too, decreeing
Whether the fact of God's divine foreseeing
Constrains me to perform a certain act
—And by "constraint" I mean the simple fact
Of mere compulsion by necessity—
430 Or whether a free choice is granted me
To do a given act or not to do it
Though, ere it was accomplished, God foreknew it.
Or whether Providence is not so stringent
And merely makes necessity contingent.
435   But I decline discussion of the matter;
My tale is of a cock and of the clatter
That came of following his wife's advice
To walk about his yard on the precise
Morning after the dream of which I told.
440   O woman's counsel is so often cold!
A woman's counsel brought us first to woe.
Made Adam out of Paradise to go
Where he had been so merry, so well at ease.

---

20. **Iscariot . . . Ganelon . . . Sinon** Each of these men was famous for betrayal. Judas Iscariot betrayed Jesus Christ; Ganelon betrayed Charlemagne's greatest knight, Roland; and Sinon convinced King Priam to bring the Trojan horse, filled with Greek troops, into Troy.

21. **predestination** (prē des′ tə nā′ shən) *n.* the idea that God arranges beforehand everything that happens.

22. **Bishop Bradwardine's . . . Boethius'** (bō ē′ thē əs) Bishop Bradwardine was a well-known theologian of Chaucer's time. Boethius (A.D. 480–524) was a famous Roman philosopher.

Literary Analysis
Parody Is an attack by a fox on a henyard really comparable to the betrayals of Iscariot, Ganelon, and Sinon? Explain.

stringent (strin′ jənt) *adj.* strict

Reading Strategy
Using Context Clues
Which context clues could help you interpret the word *counsel* in line 441?

But, for I know not whom it may displease
445 If I suggest that women are to blame,
Pass over that; I only speak in game.
Read the authorities to know about
What has been said of women; you'll find out
These are the cock's words, and not mine, I'm giving;
450 I think no harm of any woman living.
Merrily in her dust-bath in the sand
Lay Pertelote. Her sisters were at hand
Basking in sunlight. Chanticleer sang free,
More merrily than a mermaid in the sea
455 (For *Physiologus*[23] reports the thing
And says how well and merrily they sing).
And so it happened as he cast his eye
Towards the cabbage at a butterfly
It fell upon the fox there, lying low.
460 Gone was all inclination then to crow.
"Cok cok," he cried, giving a sudden start,
As one who feels a terror at his heart,
For natural instinct teaches beasts to flee
The moment they perceive an enemy,
465 Though they had never met with it before.
This Chanticleer was shaken to the core
And would have fled. The fox was quick to say
However, "Sir! Whither so fast away?
Are you afraid of me, that am your friend?
470 A fiend, or worse, I should be, to intend
You harm, or practice villainy upon you;
Dear sir, I was not even spying on you!
Truly I came to do no other thing
Than just to lie and listen to you sing.
475 You have as merry a voice as God has given
To any angel in the courts of Heaven;
To that you add a musical sense as strong
As had Boethius who was skilled in song.
My Lord your Father (God receive his soul!),
480 Your mother too—how courtly, what control!—
Have honored my poor house, to my great ease;
And you, sir, too, I should be glad to please.
For, when it comes to singing, I'll say this
(Else may these eyes of mine be barred from bliss),
485 There never was a singer I would rather
Have heard at dawn than your respected father.
All that he sang came welling from his soul
And how he put his voice under control!
The pains he took to keep his eyes tight shut

23. *Physiologus* book on nature written in Latin meter.

Literary Analysis
Parody In what way does Chaucer's description of Chanticleer's reaction both show Chanticleer's lack of heroism and make fun of scholarly explanations?

✓**Reading Check**
What compliments does the fox pay Chanticleer?

490 In concentration—then the tip-toe strut,
The slender neck stretched out, the delicate beak!
No singer could approach him in technique
Or rival him in song, still less surpass.
I've read the story in *Burnel the Ass*,[24]
495 Among some other verses, of a cock
Whose leg in youth was broken by a knock
A clergyman's son had given him, and for this
He made the father lose his benefice.
But certainly there's no comparison
500 Between the subtlety of such a one
And the discretion of your father's art
And wisdom. Oh, for charity of heart,
Can you not emulate your sire and sing?"
    This Chanticleer began to beat a wing
505 As one incapable of smelling treason,
So wholly had this flattery ravished reason.
Alas, my lords! there's many a sycophant[25]
And flatterer that fill your courts with <u>cant</u>
And give more pleasure with their zeal forsooth
510 Than he who speaks in soberness and truth.
Read what *Ecclesiasticus*[26] records
Of flatterers. 'Ware treachery, my lords!
    This Chanticleer stood high upon his toes,
He stretched his neck, his eyes began to close,
515 His beak to open; with his eyes shut tight
He then began to sing with all his might.
    Sir Russel Fox then leapt to the attack,
Grabbing his gorge he flung him o'er his back
And off he bore him to the woods, the brute,
520 And for the moment there was no pursuit.
O Destiny that may not be evaded!
Alas that Chanticleer had so paraded!
Alas that he had flown down from the beams!
O that his wife took no account of dreams!
525 And on a Friday too to risk their necks!
O Venus, goddess of the joys of sex,
Since Chanticleer thy mysteries professed
And in thy service always did his best,
And more for pleasure than to multiply
530 His kind, on thine own day is he to die?
    O Geoffrey, thou my dear and sovereign master[27]

Literary Analysis
Parody and Fable What happens to the reader's faith in fables if every character in the tale, including a fox bent on trickery, tells them for his or her own ends?

Reading Strategy
Using Context Clues Judging from the information in the previous lines, what is the meaning of *emulate* in line 503?

cant (kant) *n.* insincere or meaningless talk

---

24. ***Burnel the Ass*** twelfth-century poem in which a rooster gains revenge after being mistreated by a priest's son.
25. **sycophant** (sik´ ə fənt) *n.* person who seeks favor by flattering influential people.
26. ***Ecclesiasticus*** not Ecclesiastes, but a book of proverbs included with the Apocrypha in the Authorized Version of the Bible.
27. **O Geoffrey . . . master** Geoffrey de Vinsauf, twelfth-century author of a book on rhetoric.

Who, when they brought King Richard to disaster
And shot him dead, lamented so his death,
Would that I had thy skill, thy gracious breath,
535 To chide a Friday half so well as you!
(For he was killed upon a Friday too.)
Then I could fashion you a rhapsody
For Chanticleer in dread and agony.
    Sure never such a cry or lamentation
540 Was made by ladies of high Trojan station,
When Ilium fell and Pyrrhus with his sword
Grabbed Priam by the beard, their king and lord,
And slew him there as the *Aeneid* tells,[28]
As what was uttered by those hens. Their yells
545 Surpassed them all in palpitating fear
When they beheld the rape of Chanticleer.
Dame Pertelote emitted sovereign shrieks
That echoed up in anguish to the peaks
Louder than those extorted from the wife
550 Of Hasdrubal,[29] when he had lost his life
And Carthage all in flame and ashes lay.
She was so full of torment and dismay
That in the very flames she chose her part
And burnt to ashes with a steadfast heart.
555 O woeful hens, louder your shrieks and higher
Than those of Roman matrons when the fire
Consumed their husbands, senators of Rome,
When Nero burnt their city and their home,
Beyond a doubt that Nero was their bale![30]
560   Now let me turn again to tell my tale;
This blessed widow and her daughters two
Heard all these hens in clamor and halloo
And, rushing to the door at all this shrieking,
They saw the fox towards the covert streaking
565 And, on his shoulder, Chanticleer stretched flat.
"Look, look!" they cried, "O mercy, look at that!
Ha! Ha! the fox!" and after him they ran,
And stick in hand ran many a serving man,
Ran Coll our dog, ran Talbot, Bran and Shaggy,
570 And with a distaff in her hand ran Maggie,
Ran cow and calf and ran the very hogs
In terror at the barking of the dogs;
The men and women shouted, ran and cursed,
They ran so hard they thought their hearts would burst,
575 They yelled like fiends in Hell, ducks left the water

Literary Analysis
Parody To what epic story does Chaucer allude in lamenting Chanticleer's abduction?

Literary Analysis
Parody What do the comparisons in lines 539–559 add to the mock-heroic style of the tale?

---

28. **Sure never . . . Aeneid tells** reference to the destruction of Troy as described in the *Aeneid,* an epic by the Roman poet Virgil.
29. **Hasdrubal** (haz′ droo bel) Carthaginian general.
30. **bale** *n.* evil; harm.

✔**Reading Check**

By what means does the fox capture Chanticleer?

Quacking and flapping as on point of slaughter,
Up flew the geese in terror over the trees,
Out of the hive came forth the swarm of bees;
So hideous was the noise—God bless us all,
580 Jack Straw and all his followers in their brawl[31]
Were never half so shrill, for all their noise,
When they were murdering those Flemish boys,
As that day's hue and cry upon the fox.
They grabbed up trumpets made of brass and box,
585 Of horn and bone, on which they blew and pooped,
And therewithal they shouted and they whooped
So that it seemed the very heavens would fall.
     And now, good people, pay attention all.
See how Dame Fortune quickly changes side
590 And robs her enemy of hope and pride!
This cock that lay upon the fox's back
In all his dread contrived to give a quack
And said, "Sir Fox, if I were you, as God's
My witness, I would round upon these clods
595 And shout, 'Turn back, you saucy bumpkins all!
A very pestilence upon you fall!
Now that I have in safety reached the wood
Do what you like, the cock is mine for good;
I'll eat him there in spite of every one.'"
600   The fox replying, "Faith, it shall be done!"
Opened his mouth and spoke. The nimble bird,
Breaking away upon the uttered word,
Flew high into the tree-tops on the spot.
And when the fox perceived where he had got,
605 "Alas," he cried, "alas, my Chanticleer,
I've done you grievous wrong, indeed I fear
I must have frightened you; I grabbed too hard
When I caught hold and took you from the yard.
But, sir, I meant no harm, don't be offended,
610 Come down and I'll explain what I intended;
So help me God I'll tell the truth—on oath!"
"No," said the cock, "and curses on us both,
And first on me if I were such a dunce
As let you fool me oftener than once.
615 Never again, for all your flattering lies,
You'll coax a song to make me blink my eyes;
And as for those who blink when they should look,
God blot them from his everlasting Book!"
"Nay, rather," said the fox, "his plagues be flung
620 On all who chatter that should hold their tongue."

31. **Jack Straw . . . brawl** Jack Straw was one of the leaders of the Peasants' Revolt (1381),
in which angry peasants and workers destroyed property and killed wealthy people.

Reading Strategy
Using Context Clues
What does context
suggest about the
meaning of *contrived*?

Literary Analysis
Parody and Fable
What morals can you find
expressed in the closing
passages of the tale?
Does an ordinary fable
have this many morals?

Lo, such it is not to be on your guard
Against the flatterers of the world, or yard,
And if you think my story is absurd,
A foolish trifle of a beast and bird,
625 A fable of a fox, a cock, a hen,
Take hold upon the moral, gentlemen.
      St. Paul himself, a saint of great discerning,
Says that all things are written for our learning;
So take the grain and let the chaff be still.
630 And, gracious Father, if it be thy will
As saith my Savior, make us all good men,
And bring us to his heavenly bliss.
      Amen.

Review and Assess

Thinking About the Selection

1. **Respond:** In which part of the tale did you find the mismatch between Chaucer's style and the events of the story most amusing? Why?

2. **(a) Recall:** Why do Chanticleer and Pertelote argue at the beginning of the tale? **(b) Analyze:** What seems to be Pertelote's main reason for her position? **(c) Connect:** In what sense do both Pertelote's and Chanticleer's positions turn out to be correct?

3. **(a) Recall:** What "evidence" does Chanticleer use to support his position? **(b) Draw Conclusions:** What does his use of this type of evidence suggest about the persuasive power of stories?

4. **(a) Recall:** How is the fox able to catch Chanticleer? **(b) Infer:** What does his success show about Chanticleer's character? **(c) Draw Conclusions:** What does this event show about the power of words over Chanticleer?

5. **(a) Recall:** How does Chanticleer escape from the fox? **(b) Infer:** What characteristic of the fox enables Chanticleer to escape? **(c) Draw Conclusions:** What does this event show about the powerful attraction of words for the fox?

6. **(a) Synthesize:** What general lesson about the power of words do the fates of Chanticleer and the fox suggest? **(b) Support:** The tale uses formal language to describe an everyday, brutal barnyard occurrence. What additional lesson does this contrast between style and reality suggest about the power of words?

7. **Apply:** In your own experience, do people attach too much importance to how a person or thing is described, neglecting the reality? Explain, making a connection to Chaucer's tale.

Review and Assess

Literary Analysis

Parody

1. Epic heroes are often boastful, as is the hero in this **parody**. (a) Give two examples of Chanticleer's boastfulness. (b) Why is his boastfulness humorous?
2. Find three passages describing trivial things in a grand style. Explain how each is an example of **mock-heroic style**.
3. Is Chaucer's parody affectionate, or does he dislike epics? Explain.
4. (a) What kind of writing might Chaucer be parodying in the debate on dreams? (b) What makes the debate a parody, rather than a serious discussion?

Connecting Literary Elements

5. Chanticleer, the fox, and the narrator present different morals for this **fable**. Compare three of them, using a chart like the one shown.

Character/Speaker:_____

Moral	Why Moral Suits Character	What Moral Implies About Power of Words

6. Each moral of the story addresses what goes wrong when words are taken too seriously or not seriously enough. Explain.
7. (a) By including multiple morals, each reflecting the concerns of a different character, the tale encourages you to take its words less seriously. Explain. (b) How does having characters suggest and even argue about the moral make the tale a parody?

Reading Strategy

Using Context Clues

8. Define each of the following words as it is used in the tale, explaining which **context clues** helped you determine its meaning: (a) *forfeited* in line 90, (b) *surpass* in line 493, (c) *nimble* in line 601.

Extend Understanding

9. **Science Connection:** Chanticleer argues that dreams foretell the future. What value does modern science find in dreams?

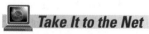

Integrate Language Skills

Vocabulary Development Lesson

Word Analysis: Latin Root -cap-

The Latin root -cap- means "head" or "main part." *Capital* can mean "the chief part of a person's fortune." Use the meaning of -cap- to explain each phrase.

1. a capital city
2. a capital crime
3. per capita income
4. a captain of industry

Spelling Strategy

The sound *zhun* at the end of words is nearly always spelled *sion*, as in *derision*. Only rarely is it spelled *tion*. Complete the following words.

1. illu __?__
2. equa __?__
3. vi __?__

Fluency: Definitions

For each word from the vocabulary list on page 118, write the letter of its definition in the right column.

1. capital
2. timorous
3. derision
4. maxim
5. stringent
6. cant

a. meaningless talk
b. principle
c. fearful
d. strict; severe
e. scorn; ridicule
f. money or property

Grammar and Style Lesson

Pronoun Case

Pronouns in the **nominative case**—*I, he, she, we, they, who*—are used for subjects and subject complements. Pronouns in the **objective case**—*me, him, her, us, them, whom*—are used for direct and indirect objects and for objects of prepositions.

SUBJECT
Nominative Case: She had a yard that was enclosed about. . . .

DIRECT OBJECT
Objective Case: apoplexy struck her not . . .

Practice In the items below, identify each pronoun and its case.

1. Repletion never left her in disquiet. . . .
2. Alas that he had flown down . . . !
3. . . . I could fashion you a rhapsody. . . .
4. They saw the fox towards the covert streaking. . . .
5. "No," said the cock, "and curses on us both, . . ."

Writing Application Write a brief news report on Chanticleer's fight with the fox. Use pronouns in both nominative and objective cases.

W͜G *Prentice Hall Writing and Grammar Connection: Chapter 22, Section 1*

Extension Activities

Listening and Speaking With a partner, present a **dramatic reading** of the debate on dreams for the class. Adjust your tone of voice and reading speed to convey indignation, humor, and excitement, as appropriate. [Group Activity]

Writing Using what you know about the style, write a **mock-heroic narrative** that makes everyday occurrences seem like events in a tragedy or a heroic tale.

Prepare to Read

The Pardoner's Tale

Literary Analysis

Exemplum (Anecdote)

A medieval clergyman giving a sermon would illustrate his main point with an anecdote, or brief story, called an **exemplum,** Latin for "example." "The Pardoner's Tale" is an exemplum against the sin of greed. The Pardoner uses the tale to illustrate the point of one of his sermons, "Love of money is the root of all evil." As you read the tale, consider how it illustrates this point—and aids the Pardoner in his swindles.

Connecting Literary Elements

To teach its lesson effectively, an exemplum must be easily understood and remembered by the listeners. For this reason, an exemplum may use certain basic storytelling patterns, or **archetypal narrative elements,** found in folk literature around the world. These elements include the following:

- Characters, events, and other things that come in threes
- A test of characters' moral fiber leading to their destiny
- A mysterious guide who helps point the way
- A just ending that rewards good or punishes evil

Because it includes such elements, the basic story in "The Pardoner's Tale" was able to survive retelling after retelling as it traveled from ancient India to Persia (present-day Iran) across the Middle East to Europe, finally coming to England. Note the elements in the tale that make the story and its moral memorable and clear.

Reading Strategy

Rereading for Clarification

Rereading passages in a work can clarify characters' identities, the sequence or causes of events, and even puzzling language. As you read "The Pardoner's Tale," reread earlier passages to clarify any lines that puzzle you. Use a diagram like the one shown to clarify difficult passages.

Vocabulary Development

pallor (pal´ ər) n. unnatural lack of color; paleness (p. 146)

hoary (hôr´ ē) adj. white or gray with age (p. 146)

prating (prāt´ iŋ) n. chatter (p. 146)

tarry (tar´ ē) v. to delay or linger (p. 148)

apothecary (ə päth´ ə ker´ ē) n. pharmacist; druggist (p. 148)

Passage

"He gathered lots and hid them in his hand. . . ."

Reread Earlier Passage

"'We draw for lots and see the way it goes; / The one who draws the longest, lucky man, . . .'"

Clarification

"Drawing lots" must be like drawing straws: The one who draws the longest is "it."

from # The Pardoner's Tale

Geoffrey Chaucer
Translated by Nevill Coghill

Review and Anticipate

In the Prologue, Chaucer describes the Pardoner as a cleric full of "flatteries and prevarication." By selling pardons—documents officially forgiving the purchaser's sins—and supposedly holy relics, the swindling Pardoner earns more in one short day than a poor country parson earns in a month or two. Even while exposing the Pardoner's dishonesty, Chaucer praises the Pardoner's persuasive skills: "How well he read a lesson or told a story!" Now, when it is the Pardoner's turn to tell a story, he himself explains his methods: All his sermons illustrate the biblical text *Radix malorum est cupiditas* ("Love of money is the root of all evil"). He finds that preaching against the sin of avarice, or greed, is the best way to get people to pay him large sums of money for his pardons and relics! After providing this boastful explanation, he then proceeds to tell one of the stories from his sermons. As you read, think of answers to the question, What effect would the Pardoner's story have on an audience of poorly educated country folk?

The Pardoner's Prologue

"My lords," he said, "in churches where I preach
I cultivate a haughty kind of speech
And ring it out as roundly as a bell;
I've got it all by heart, the tale I tell.
5 I have a text, it always is the same
And always has been, since I learnt the game,
Old as the hills and fresher than the grass,
Radix malorum est cupiditas."[1]

The Pardoner explains how he introduces himself to a congregation, showing official documents and offering relics as cures for various problems. Next, he explains how he preaches.

"Then, priestlike in my pulpit, with a frown,
10 I stand, and when the yokels[2] have sat down,
I preach, as you have heard me say before,
And tell a hundred lying mockeries[3] more.
I take great pains, and stretching out my neck
To east and west I crane about and peck
15 Just like a pigeon sitting on a barn.
My hands and tongue together spin the yarn
And all my antics[4] are a joy to see.
The curse of avarice and cupidity[5]
Is all my sermon, for it frees the pelf.[6]
20 Out come the pence, and specially for myself,
For my exclusive purpose is to win
And not at all to castigate[7] their sin.
Once dead what matter how their souls may fare?
They can go blackberrying, for all I care!
25   "Believe me, many a sermon or devotive
Exordium[8] issues from an evil motive.
Some to give pleasure by their flattery
And gain promotion through hypocrisy,
Some out of vanity, some out of hate;

Reading Strategy
Reading for Clarification
Reread lines 14–15 for an example of the "antics" to which the Pardoner refers in line 17.

---

1. *Radix malorum est cupiditas* Latin for "Greed is the root of all evil."
2. **yokels** (yō´ kəlz) *n.* unsophisticated people living in a rural area.
3. **mockeries** (mäk´ ər ēz) *n.* stories that are untrue.
4. **antics** (an´ tikz) *n.* playful, silly, or ludicrous acts.
5. **avarice** (av´ ə ris) **and cupidity** (kyo͞o pid´ ə tē) *n.* desire to gain wealth; greed (synonyms).
6. **pelf** (pelf) *n.* ill-gotten gains of money or wealth.
7. **castigate** (kas´ ti gāt´) *v.* to punish severely.
8. **Exordium** (eg zôr´ dē əm) *n.* the opening part of an oration.

30 Or when I dare not otherwise debate
I'll put my discourse into such a shape,
My tongue will be a dagger; no escape
For him from slandering falsehood shall there be,
If he has hurt my brethren[9] or me.
35 For though I never mention him by name
The congregation guesses all the same
From certain hints that everybody knows,
And so I take revenge upon our foes
And spit my venom forth, while I profess
40 Holy and true—or seeming holiness.
  "But let me briefly make my purpose plain;
I preach for nothing but for greed of gain
And use the same old text, as bold as brass,
Radix malorum est cupiditas.
45 And thus I preach against the very vice
I make my living out of—avarice.
And yet however guilty of that sin
Myself with others I have power to win
Them from it, I can bring them to repent;
50 But that is not my principal intent.
Covetousness[10] is both the root and stuff
Of all I preach. That ought to be enough.
  "Well, then I give examples thick and fast
From bygone times, old stories from the past.
55 A yokel mind loves stories from of old,
Being the kind it can repeat and hold.
What! Do you think, as long as I can preach
And get their silver for the things I teach,
That I will live in poverty, from choice?
60 That's not the counsel of my inner voice!
No! Let me preach and beg from kirk[11] to kirk
And never do an honest job of work,
No, nor make baskets, like St. Paul, to gain
A livelihood. I do not preach in vain.
65 There's no apostle I would counterfeit;
I mean to have money, wool and cheese and wheat
Though it were given me by the poorest lad
Or poorest village widow, though she had
A string of starving children, all agape.
70 No, let me drink the liquor of the grape
And keep a jolly wench in every town!
  "But listen, gentlemen; to bring things down
To a conclusion, would you like a tale?

▲ Critical Viewing Do the Pardoner's garments in the illustration support his claims about his success? Explain. **[Connect]**

☑ Reading Check

What vice does the Pardoner admit to having, even though he preaches against it?

---

9. **brethren** (breth´ rən) *n.* brothers.
10. **covetousness** (kuv´ ət əs nis) *n.* greed, especially for what belongs to others.
11. **kirk** *n.* church.

Now as I've drunk a draught of corn-ripe ale,
75 By God it stands to reason I can strike
On some good story that you all will like.
For though I am a wholly vicious man
Don't think I can't tell moral tales. I can!
Here's one I often preach when out for winning;
80 Now please be quiet. Here is the beginning."

The Pardoner's Tale

It's of three rioters I have to tell
Who, long before the morning service bell,[12]
Were sitting in a tavern for a drink.
And as they sat, they heard the hand-bell clink
85 Before a coffin going to the grave;
One of them called the little tavern-knave[13]
And said "Go and find out at once—look spry!—
Whose corpse is in that coffin passing by;
And see you get the name correctly too."
90 "Sir," said the boy, "no need, I promise you;
Two hours before you came here I was told.
He was a friend of yours in days of old,
And suddenly, last night, the man was slain,
Upon his bench, face up, dead drunk again.
95 There came a privy[14] thief, they call him Death,
Who kills us all round here, and in a breath
He speared him through the heart, he never stirred.
And then Death went his way without a word.
He's killed a thousand in the present plague,[15]
100 And, sir, it doesn't do to be too vague
If you should meet him; you had best be wary.
Be on your guard with such an adversary,
Be primed to meet him everywhere you go,
That's what my mother said. It's all I know."
105   The publican[16] joined in with, "By St. Mary,

Literary Analysis
Exemplum Which details in the opening sentence enable the audience to form a quick opinion of the main characters?

Reading Strategy
Rereading for Clarification What earlier line explains the reference to the "adversary" in line 102?

---

12. **long before . . . bell** long before 9:00 A.M.
13. **tavern-knave** serving boy.
14. **privy** secretive.
15. **plague** the Black Death, which killed over a third of the population of Europe from 1347–1351. The plague reached England in 1348.
16. **publican** innkeeper.

What the child says is right; you'd best be wary,
This very year he killed, in a large village
A mile away, man, woman, serf at tillage,[17]
Page in the household, children—all there were.
110 Yes, I imagine that he lives round there.
It's well to be prepared in these alarms,
He might do you dishonor." "Huh, God's arms!"
The rioter said, "Is he so fierce to meet?
I'll search for him, by Jesus, street by street.
115 God's blessed bones! I'll register a vow!
Here, chaps! The three of us together now,
Hold up your hands, like me, and we'll be brothers
In this affair, and each defend the others,
And we will kill this traitor Death, I say!
120 Away with him as he had made away
With all our friends. God's dignity! Tonight!"
         They made their bargain, swore with appetite,
These three, to live and die for one another
As brother-born might swear to his born brother.
125 And up they started in their drunken rage
And made towards this village which the page
And publican had spoken of before.
Many and grisly were the oaths they swore,
Tearing Christ's blessed body to a shred;[18]
130 "If we can only catch him, Death is dead!"
         When they had gone not fully half a mile,
Just as they were about to cross a stile,
They came upon a very poor old man
Who humbly greeted them and thus began,
135 "God look to you, my lords, and give you quiet!"
To which the proudest of these men of riot
Gave back the answer, "What, old fool? Give place!
Why are you all wrapped up except your face?
Why live so long? Isn't it time to die?"
140   The old, old fellow looked him in the eye
And said, "Because I never yet have found,
Though I have walked to India, searching round
Village and city on my pilgrimage,
One who would change his youth to have my age.
145 And so my age is mine and must be still
Upon me, for such time as God may will.
         "Not even Death, alas, will take my life;
So, like a wretched prisoner at strife
Within himself, I walk alone and wait

---

17. **tillage** plowing.
18. **Tearing . . . shred** their oaths included such expressions as "God's arms"
    and "God's blessed bones."

Literary Analysis
Exemplum and Archetypal Elements What details of the publican's comments build the danger of the situation?

Reading Strategy
Rereading for Clarification What lines explain the "bargain" the rioters are said to have made in line 122?

Reading Check
What do the three rioters swear to do?

150 About the earth, which is my mother's gate,
Knock-knocking with my staff from night to noon
And crying, 'Mother, open to me soon!
Look at me, mother, won't you let me in?
See how I wither, flesh and blood and skin!
155 Alas! When will these bones be laid to rest?
Mother, I would exchange—for that were best—
The wardrobe in my chamber, standing there
So long, for yours! Aye, for a shirt of hair[19]
To wrap me in!' She has refused her grace,
160 Whence comes the pallor of my withered face.
        "But it dishonored you when you began
To speak so roughly, sir, to an old man,
Unless he had injured you in word or deed.
It says in holy writ, as you may read,
165 'Thou shalt rise up before the hoary head
And honor it,' And therefore be it said
'Do no more harm to an old man than you,
Being now young, would have another do
When you are old'—if you should live till then.
170 And so may God be with you, gentlemen,
For I must go whither I have to go.'
        "By God," the gambler said, "you shan't do so,
You don't get off so easy, by St. John!
I heard you mention, just a moment gone,
175 A certain traitor Death who singles out
And kills the fine young fellows hereabout.
And you're his spy, by God! You wait a bit.
Say where he is or you shall pay for it,
By God and by the Holy Sacrament!
180 I say you've joined together by consent
To kill us younger folk, you thieving swine!"
        "Well, sirs," he said, "if it be your design
To find out Death, turn up this crooked way
Towards that grove, I left him there today
185 Under a tree, and there you'll find him waiting.
He isn't one to hide for all your prating.
You see that oak? He won't be far to find.
And God protect you that redeemed mankind,
Aye, and amend you!" Thus that ancient man.
190   At once the three young rioters began
To run, and reached the tree, and there they found
A pile of golden florins[20] on the ground,
New-coined, eight bushels of them as they thought.
No longer was it Death those fellows sought,

Reading Strategy
Rereading for Clarification
Who is "she" in line 159? What earlier lines give you the answer?

pallor (pal′ ər) *n.* unnatural lack of color; paleness

hoary (hôr′ ē) *adj.* white or gray with age

Literary Analysis
Exemplum and Archetypal Elements What archetypal role does the old man play?

prating (prāt′ iŋ) *n.* chatter

---

19. **shirt of hair** here, a shroud.
20. **florins** coins.

195 For they were all so thrilled to see the sight,
The florins were so beautiful and bright,
That down they sat beside the precious pile.
The wickedest spoke first after a while.
"Brothers," he said, "you listen to what I say.

200 I'm pretty sharp although I joke away.
It's clear that Fortune has bestowed this treasure
To let us live in jollity and pleasure.
Light come, light go! We'll spend it as we ought.
God's precious dignity! Who would have thought

205 This morning was to be our lucky day?
    "If one could only get the gold away,
Back to my house, or else to yours, perhaps
For as you know, the gold is ours, chaps—
We'd all be at the top of fortune, hey?

210 But certainly it can't be done by day.
People would call us robbers—a strong gang,
So our own property would make us hang.
No, we must bring this treasure back by night
Some prudent way, and keep it out of sight.

215 And so as a solution I propose
We draw for lots and see the way it goes;
The one who draws the longest, lucky man,
Shall run to town as quickly as he can
To fetch us bread and wine—but keep things dark—

220 While two remain in hiding here to mark
Our heap of treasure. If there's no delay,
When night comes down we'll carry it away,
All three of us, wherever we have planned."
    He gathered lots and hid them in his hand

225 Bidding them draw for where the luck should fall.
It fell upon the youngest of them all,
And off he ran at once towards the town.
    As soon as he had gone, the first sat down
And thus began a parley[21] with the other:

230 "You know that you can trust me as a brother;
Now let me tell you where your profit lies;
You know our friend has gone to get supplies
And here's a lot of gold that is to be
Divided equally amongst us three.

235 Nevertheless, if I could shape things thus
So that we shared it out—the two of us—
Wouldn't you take it as a friendly act?"
    "But how?" the other said. "He knows the fact
that all the gold was left with me and you;

240 What can we tell him? What are we to do?"

---

21. **parley** discussion.

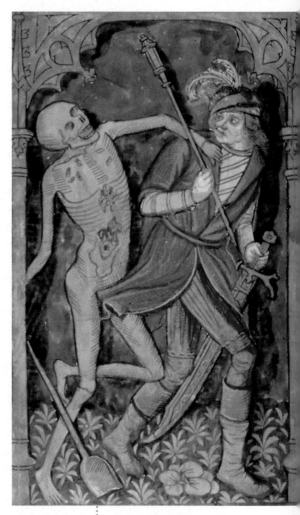

▲ **Critical Viewing**
What moral might medieval illustrations like this one have served to teach? **[Hypothesize]**

Literary Analysis
Exemplum Into what new sin does greed lead the rioters?

☑ **Reading Check**

What does the old man say the rioters will find under the tree? What do they find there?

"Is it a bargain," said the first, "or no?
For I can tell you in a word or so
What's to be done to bring the thing about."
"Trust me," the other said, "you needn't doubt
245 My word. I won't betray you, I'll be true."
"Well," said his friend, "you see that we are two,
And two are twice as powerful as one.
Now look; when he comes back, get up in fun
To have a wrestle; then, as you attack,
250 I'll up and put my dagger through his back
While you and he are struggling, as in game;
Then draw your dagger too and do the same.
Then all this money will be ours to spend,
Divided equally of course, dear friend.
255 Then we can gratify our lusts and fill
The day with dicing at our own sweet will."
Thus these two miscreants[22] agreed to slay
The third and youngest, as you heard me say.
The youngest, as he ran towards the town,
260 Kept turning over, rolling up and down
Within his heart the beauty of those bright
New florins, saying, "Lord, to think I might
Have all that treasure to myself alone!
Could there be anyone beneath the throne
265 Of God so happy as I then should be?"
And so the Fiend,[23] our common enemy,
Was given power to put it in his thought
That there was always poison to be bought,
And that with poison he could kill his friends.
270 To men in such a state the Devil sends
Thoughts of this kind, and has a full permission
To lure them on to sorrow and perdition;[24]
For this young man was utterly content
To kill them both and never to repent.
275 And on he ran, he had no thought to <u>tarry</u>,
Came to the town, found an <u>apothecary</u>
And said, "Sell me some poison if you will,
I have a lot of rats I want to kill
And there's a polecat too about my yard
280 That takes my chickens and it hits me hard;
But I'll get even, as is only right,
With vermin that destroy a man by night."
The chemist answered, "I've a preparation
Which you shall have, and by my soul's salvation

Reading Strategy
Rereading for Clarification
What does the first rioter mean by "as in game"? Which earlier lines explain this meaning?

Literary Analysis
Exemplum What new sin does greed lead the youngest rioter to contemplate?

tarry (tar´ ē) v. to delay or linger

apothecary (ə päth´ ə ker´ ē) n. pharmacist; druggist

---

22. **miscreants** villains.
23. **Fiend** Satan.
24. **perdition** damnation.

285 If any living creature eat or drink
A mouthful, ere he has the time to think,
Though he took less than makes a grain of wheat,
You'll see him fall down dying at your feet;
Yes, die he must and in so short a while
290 You'd hardly have the time to walk a mile,
The poison is so strong, you understand."
        This cursed fellow grabbed into his hand
The box of poison and away he ran
Into a neighboring street, and found a man
295 Who lent him three large bottles, He withdrew
And deftly poured the poison into two.
He kept the third one clean, as well he might,
For his own drink, meaning to work all night
Stacking the gold and carrying it away.
300 And when this rioter, this devil's clay,
Had filled his bottles up with wine, all three,
Back to rejoin his comrades sauntered he.
        Why make a sermon of it? Why waste breath?
Exactly in the way they'd planned his death
305 They fell on him and slew him, two to one.
Then said the first of them when this was done,
"Now for a drink. Sit down and let's be merry,
For later on there'll be the corpse to bury."
And, as it happened, reaching for a sup,
310 He took a bottle full of poison up
And drank and his companion, nothing loth,
Drank from it also, and they perished both.
        There is, in Avicenna's long relation[25]
Concerning poison and its operation,
315 Trust me, no ghastlier section to transcend
What these two wretches suffered at their end.
Thus these two murderers received their due,
So did the treacherous young poisoner too.

        O cursed sin! O blackguardly excess!
320 O treacherous homicide! O wickedness!
O gluttony that lusted on and diced!
O blasphemy that took the name of Christ
With habit-hardened oaths that pride began!
Alas, how comes it that a mortal man,
325 That thou, to thy Creator, Him that wrought thee,
That paid His precious blood for thee and bought thee,
Art so unnatural and false within?
        Dearly beloved, God forgive your sin

▲ **Critical Viewing**
Compare this illustration to the one on page 147. What point might the artist make by depicting contrasting individuals being taken by death? **[Compare and Contrast]**

Literary Analysis
Exemplum In addition to avarice, or greed, against what sins does the exemplum preach in the final lines?

☑**Reading Check**

How does each rioter meet his end?

---

25. Avicenna's long relation book on medicines written by Avicenna (980–1037), an
Arab physician, which contains a chapter on poisons.

And keep you from the vice of avarice!
330 My holy pardon frees you all of this,
Provided that you make the right approaches,
That is with sterling rings, or silver brooches.
Bow down your heads under this holy bull![26]
Come on, you women, offer up your wool!
335 I'll write your name into my ledger; so!
Into the bliss of Heaven you shall go.
For I'll absolve you by my holy power,
You that make offering, clean as at the hour
When you were born. . . . That, sirs, is how I preach.
340 And Jesu Christ, soul's healer, aye, the leech
Of every soul, grant pardon and relieve you
Of sin, for that is best I won't deceive you.

---

26. holy bull an official proclamation by the Catholic Church.

Review and Assess

Thinking About the Selection

1. **Respond:** Were you surprised by the fate of the rioters? Why or why not?

2. **(a) Recall:** When the story opens, what are the rioters doing, and what captures their attention? **(b) Generalize:** What sort of people are they? Explain how you know.

3. **(a) Recall:** What pledge do the rioters make to one another? **(b) Evaluate:** Do the rioters try to keep that pledge? Explain.

4. **(a) Recall:** What do the rioters find under the tree? **(b) Interpret:** The old man has said that death is under the tree. In what sense is his statement accurate?

5. **(a) Recall:** What reason does the young rioter give the apothecary for needing the poison? **(b) Interpret:** In what sense is he lying? In what sense is he telling the truth?

6. **Draw Conclusions:** The Pardoner is quite open about the manipulative use to which he puts the tale. Do the Pardoner's reasons for telling the story detract from its moral truth? Explain.

7. **(a) Extend:** The tale refers to the time of the plague. What does the tale suggest about the effects of such a disaster on society? Support your answer. **(b) Apply:** Can stories such as this one encourage people to behave well even in times of crisis? Explain.

8. **Make a Judgment:** Do you think the desire for gain is ultimately destructive, as the Pardoner's tale suggests, or can it lead to positive consequences? Explain.

Review and Assess

Literary Analysis

Exemplum (Anecdote)

1. Explain how the **exemplum** of "The Pardoner's Tale" proves that greed is the root of all evil.

2. Identify two ways in which the tale differs from modern short stories.

3. (a) Why is it ironic that the Pardoner tells this story? (b) What point might Chaucer be making about moral tales by assigning this one to a rogue?

4. Compare this exemplum with Chaucer's parody of an animal fable, "The Nun's Priest's Tale" (p. 119). (a) In each, how does the character of the one delivering the moral affect the reader's response? (b) Do these narratives suggest that stories cannot be trusted, or that stories can be true regardless of the teller's motives? Explain, using examples from the selections.

Connecting Literary Elements

5. On a chart like the one shown, explain how the tale illustrates the archetypal elements listed.

Patterns of Three	Test of Characters	Mysterious Guide	Just Ending

6. What other familiar elements does the story include?

7. Why do you think many tales feature things that come in threes?

8. (a) What role does the old man perform in the story? (b) What makes him mysterious? (c) What might he symbolize?

Reading Strategy

Rereading for Clarification

9. In line 112, the publican tells the rioters, "He might do you dishonor." Reread the previous lines to explain his meaning.

10. In line 319, the Pardoner speaks of "blackguardly excess" as well as homicide. Reread earlier portions to clarify what he means.

Extend Understanding

11. **Career Connection:** What person or profession in current-day America most reminds you of the Pardoner? Why?

Quick Review

An **exemplum** is a story used to illustrate the moral message of a sermon.

Archetypal narrative elements are basic story patterns found in tales the world over.

When you come across something puzzling in a selection, go back to earlier passages and **reread for clarification**.

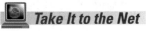 **Take It to the Net**
www.phschool.com
Take the interactive self-test online to check your understanding of these selections.

Integrate Language Skills

Vocabulary Development Lesson

Word Analysis: Greek Prefix *apo-*

The word *apothecary*, meaning "druggist," combines the Greek prefix *apo-*, meaning "away; off; separate," with a form of a Greek word for "put." An apothecary is one who "puts away" (stores) prescriptions. The prefix is also used in a number of scientific and mathematical terms. Using a dictionary, explain how the meaning of *apo-* contributes to these words:

1. apostrophe
2. apogee
3. apophysis
4. apology
5. apostle

Concept Development: Analogies

Using the words from the vocabulary list on page 140, complete the following analogies:

1. whisper : murmur :: ___?___ : dawdle
2. baker : bread :: ___?___ : medicine
3. riot : parade :: ___?___ : sermon
4. rosy : pink :: ___?___ : white
5. blindness : sight :: ___?___ : color

Spelling Strategy

The ending *-er* is more common among nouns than *-or*. Many words ending in *-or* name a quality or role, like *pallor* and *juror*. Choose between these two spellings to complete these words:

1. dishon__   2. chamb__   3. trait__

Grammar and Style Lesson

Clauses With *who* and *whom*

The nominative pronoun **who** is used as the subject of a clause. The objective pronoun **whom** is used for objects in a clause. Review these examples:

Subject: There are three men **who** are sitting in a tavern.

Predicate Nominative: The rioters did not know **who** the old man was.

Direct Object: Little troubled the men, **whom** the publican served.

Object of a Preposition: Death awaited those for **whom** greed ruled.

Practice Complete each sentence by choosing the correct pronoun form.

1. Death is a thief (who, whom) kills us all.
2. He is the one (who, whom) Death chose.
3. Those (who, whom) love gold too well may find Death instead.
4. The Pardoner knows (who, whom) his audience is.
5. He knows from (who, whom) to get money.

Writing Application Write a paragraph about three modern rioters, using four clauses with *who* or *whom*. Include a clear moral for your story, as the Pardoner does for his.

*W*G *Prentice Hall Writing and Grammar Connection: Chapter 22, Section 2*

Writing Lesson

Storyboard for an Animated Fable

Both "The Nun's Priest's Tale" and "The Pardoner's Tale" use simple characters and situations to convey a moral. Develop a storyboard—a script with pictures—for an animated version of such a fable. Include dialogue and descriptions of the action.

Prewriting   Choose a traditional story that conveys a moral, or create one of your own. To keep the characters simple, assign to each only one or two exaggerated traits.

Drafting   As you draft, develop the right pace. Establish a basic situation quickly, and then build suspense about the resolution. At the climax, move quickly between one character's action and another's.

Model: Using Storyboard Format

[Wolf moves in towards flock.] **Wolf:** Hi, folks!

[Mid-shot: Wolf chatting with sheep.] **Wolf:** That was before I made my first million.

[Wolf turns away; hood falls off; sheep is hit with sudden realization.]

Revising   Review your storyboard. Make sure that your tale clearly conveys the moral. If any part of the story moves at the wrong pace, adjust it.

 Prentice Hall Writing and Grammar Connection: Chapter 5, Section 3

Extension Activities

Listening and Speaking Give a **critical talk** for the class on the following idea: Chaucer had the survivor's ability to view life in purely practical terms—to be both engaged in and detached from a situation. In your talk, do the following:

- Explain the idea.
- Show whether or not it fits Chaucer's presentation of the Pardoner.

Invite comments from the class.

Research and Technology In a group, develop a **multimedia report** on the Black Death. Assign each member an aspect of the plague: its history, its social effects, and its influence on the arts. Include maps and timelines. [**Group Activity**]

 Take It to the Net   www.phschool.com

Go online for an additional research activity using the Internet.

CONNECTIONS
Literature Past and Present
A National Spirit

A thousand years ago, the bloody wars of kings and queens defined Britain's national identity in a decisive way. *The Anglo-Saxon Chronicle* tells how Alfred, ninth-century warrior-king of a small kingdom in southern England, fought off the invading Danes and united all of Britain's Anglo-Saxon kingdoms under his rule. The business of kings and queens—their births and deaths, marriages and friendships, rivalries and assassinations—continued to govern the nation's destiny for centuries after Alfred's time.

The New Royalty Beginning in the 1640s, though, when the people revolted and executed their king, the real power to govern has shifted to the country's Parliament and prime minister. Modern kings and queens have little to do with running the country. Their official duties are ceremonial—handing out awards or receiving foreign dignitaries. Yet government officials in Britain still act in the name of "Her Majesty." And even while the gossip columns dissect the private lives of the royal family, the appearance of Queen Elizabeth II in public, waving from a car or balcony, still has a thrilling effect on her subjects.

National Symbols A national identity binds together diverse people who may have few things in common. To anchor the idea of a nation in their hearts as well as in their minds, people look to emotionally charged symbols of national identity. Britain's monarch remains the foremost symbol of the British nation. Following is an especially important article about the royal family that appeared in *The London Times* on February 7, 1952. It gives a brief biography of Elizabeth II, Britain's new queen. (The report of George VI's death appeared in the same paper.)

Elizabeth II:
A New Queen

The London Times 2/7/52

DEATH OF THE KING
THE NEW QUEEN EXPECTED
IN LONDON TO-DAY
PUBLIC PROCLAMATION TO BE
MADE TO-MORROW

It is with profound regret that we announce the death of the King at Sandringham early yesterday.

The following statement was issued from Buckingham Palace:

"It was announced from Sandringham at 10:45 A.M. today, February 6, 1952, that the King, who retired to rest last night in his usual health, passed peacefully away in his sleep early this morning."

The London Times 2/7/52

THE NEW QUEEN
AN OUTSTANDING REPRESENTATIVE
OF HER GENERATION

Princess Elizabeth Alexandra Mary was born a little before three o'clock on the morning of April 21, 1926, at No. 17, Bruton Street, the London home of her grandparents, the late Lord and Lady Strathmore. At the age of five weeks she was baptized at Buckingham Palace by the late Lord Lang of Lambeth, then Dr. Cosmo Gordon Lang, Archbishop of York.

At that time the Prince of Wales, though unmarried, was not quite 32; and there was no expectation that the newly born Princess, especially as she might some day have a brother, would ever come very close to the succession. Even if there had been, it would probably not have been allowed to influence her early upbringing, which the Duke and Duchess of York deliberately kept as simple as possible. In infancy her time was divided between her parents' home in Piccadilly and the various country houses of her maternal grandparents in England and Scotland; and Lady Strathmore took charge of her when the Duke and Duchess went to Australia in 1927 to inaugurate the new capital.

King George V was devoted to his grandchild, and at his desire she was sent, at the age of two and a half, to keep him company at

Thematic Connection
Contrast the spirit of these comments on royal succession—the inheriting of a throne—with the problems after Alfred's death reported in *The Anglo-Saxon Chronicle*.

✔**Reading Check**
What effect did Elizabeth's status have on her upbringing?

Bognor during his convalescence after his dangerous illness in 1928. The birth of her sister in August, 1930, brought her a playmate who was destined to be by far her closest friend until she was fully grown up. Her nursery days, spent mostly in the country and in constant association with horses, dogs, and other pets, may be said to have ended with the death of King George V in 1936 and the abdication of her uncle at the end of the same year. At this date the family moved from Piccadilly to Buckingham Palace, and the position of the Princess as Heiress-Presumptive took on new importance.

It was not, however, allowed to overshadow her education. She did not go to school but was taught, under the close personal direction of the Queen, by a governess, Miss Marion Crawford, who joined the household in 1933.

The outbreak of war found the Royal Family at Balmoral; but the Princesses were soon moved to Windsor, where the quiet routine of lessons continued through the darkest and most stirring days. Gradually, subjects specially appropriate to a future queen, notably constitutional history, were introduced into the curriculum; and the Provost of Eton took a large part in the Princess's instruction. She became a good musician and singer; and in regular participation in amateur theatricals she not only showed a marked talent for acting but overcame the tendency to shyness which at one time looked like becoming a handicap to her in the great position that lay ahead.

On her sixteenth birthday in 1942 the Princess registered for national service, and soon after her eighteenth birthday—when special legislation was passed to qualify her to act as a Counsellor of State in the King's absence from the realm—she was gazetted to a commission in the A.T.S. [Auxiliary Territorial Service]. This was at her own insistence, the King withdrawing his original ruling that her duties as heir precluded her entry to any of the services. She in fact became an efficient driver in the mechanical transport branch of the A.T.S.

PUBLIC CAREER

Her public career may be said to have begun with her broadcast to the children of the Empire during the Battle of Britain; but it was only when war ended that she began to emerge into full publicity as a leading figure in ceremonial and social life. Naturally most of her appearances were made under the wing of one or both of her parents. But she was accompanied only by members of her own staff—her first lady in waiting had been appointed in July—when she went to Greenock in November 1944, and launched the great battleship H.M.S. Vanguard. The commissioning of this ship was the principal event of her notable visit to Northern Ireland—again without her parents—in the summer of 1946; and it was in the Vanguard that she embarked with the rest of the Royal Family on February 1, 1947, for their tour of South Africa and Rhodesia.

▼ **Critical Viewing**
What feelings might this photograph of Elizabeth's wartime service have inspired in her future subjects? **[Apply]**

This was the Princess's first journey outside the British Isles, and the beginning of her introduction to those dominions beyond the seas over which, equally with the United Kingdom, she will now reign.

Although she was content to remain somewhat in the background, especially in the early part of the tour, South Africans rapidly became conscious of her as a personality, and her character made a great and favorable impression. A speech at the opening of the graving dock, named after herself, at East London seemed to mark the emergence of a new representative of the younger generation; and at her coming of age, which she celebrated in Cape Town, she broadcast to the Empire, and especially to the young, in vigorous and vibrant terms which carried the impression farther.

She was already outstandingly qualified to be the representative figure among the girls who came to womanhood with her. She had absorbed an admirably balanced education and entered into the gaieties appropriate to her age, from the racecourse to the ballroom. But she already combined with a capacity for enjoyment a high seriousness which even at that time made her insist upon doing thoroughly everything that her hand found to do, and spare herself nothing that belonged to her preparation for the greater responsibilities that she knew lay ahead.

Soon after the return of the Royal Family from South Africa, the nation learnt with joy on July 9, 1947, that the King had gladly given his consent to the betrothal of the Heiress-Presumptive to Lieutenant Philip Mountbatten, R.N., son of the late Prince Andrew of Greece and Princess Andrew (Princess Alice of Battenberg). Messages of congratulation to the betrothed couple from the people of the Commonwealth and from all parts of the world showed clearly the affection in which Princess Elizabeth was held, and the four months of their engagement during which preparations for the royal wedding went forward were a period of intense and eager expectation for the nation. The feelings of the nation were expressed by the then Prime Minister, Mr. Attlee, when, on October 22, he moved a congratulatory Address to their Majesties on the occasion of the royal marriage, and said: "Her royal Highness has shown, in the public duties which she has undertaken, the same unerring graciousness and understanding, and the same human simplicity, which has endeared the Royal House to the people of this country," and by Mr. Churchill, who prophesied that millions would welcome the joyous event as a flash of color on the hard road we had to travel.

On the eve of the wedding came the announcement that Lieutenant Mountbatten had been made Duke of Edinburgh.

MARRIAGE

The marriage was solemnized in Westminster Abbey on November 20, when the royal processions were watched by countless thousands. The ceremony was performed by the Archbishop of Canterbury in the presence of three generations of the Royal Family, and was followed by scenes of rich pageantry and of homely greetings from people gathered

Thematic Connection
Contrast the virtues attributed to Elizabeth with those King Alfred displays in *The Anglo-Saxon Chronicle.*

☑ Reading Check
What role did Elizabeth play in World War II?

from all parts of the British Isles as the bride and bridegroom left for Winchester, on their journey to Broadlands, near Romsey, where they spent their honeymoon.

Early in the New Year they set out on their public life together, and in May paid an official visit to Paris, where they were greeted with a welcome of great warmth and spontaneity. Then early in June it was announced that the Princess would soon cancel all her engagements. On November 14 her son, Prince Charles, was born. In 1949 Princess Elizabeth resumed her busy public life and during that year the Duke of Edinburgh returned to sea. He was stationed at Malta and in November was joined there by his wife.

At the end of March, 1950, the Princess paid a second visit to Malta and while there it was announced that her Royal Highness was expecting a baby. Princess Anne was born in August. In November Princess Elizabeth joined the Duke of Edinburgh and together they visited Athens. In the spring of 1951 they went to Rome, where they were received by the Pope, and it was in Rome that her Royal Highness celebrated her twenty-fifth birthday.

Returning to England in time for the opening of the Festival of Britain, she embarked upon a program of public duties more formidable even than those of the years immediately before. It fell to her more than once on great state occasions to stand in the place of her father and to speak for him.

When, last September, the King underwent an operation, Princess Elizabeth and the Duke of Edinburgh deferred their departure for Canada, but the King's progress enabled them to leave by air on October 7. Their six weeks' tour, probably the most strenuous ever undertaken by royal personages, took them across Canada in a memorable series of visits and ceremonies. Not least successful was their visit to Washington, where they were welcomed by President Truman. Upon their return, a "brilliant mission" accomplished, they were ceremonially received in Liverpool on November 17, and given an official welcome at Guildhall two days later.

After spending Christmas with the Royal Family at Sandringham, the Princess and the Duke left London Airport last Thursday on the first stage of the journey which was to have taken them to Ceylon, Australia, and New Zealand, but which has been so untimely cut short only four days after they reached their hunting lodge at Nyeri, in Kenya.

Connecting Literature Past and Present

1. Contrast the impression of the new queen with the impression of Alfred created by *The Anglo-Saxon Chronicle*.

2. The *Times* article implies that common sentiment—pride and mourning—binds Britain together. Contrast this idea with ideas of nationality found in Bede, *The Anglo-Saxon Chronicle*, and *The Canterbury Tales*.

Newspapers and Royalty

Open any newspaper in Britain and you're bound to find an article about a member of the royal family. Whether opening Parliament, visiting a hospital, or yachting in the Caribbean, the royal family makes the news.

The Times (formerly *The London Times*) is one of the most significant and respected British newspapers. Founded in 1785, its offices occupied the original premises in Fleet Street, London, until 1974.

Prepare to Read

from Sir Gawain and the Green Knight ◆ *from* Morte d'Arthur

Knights of Legend

Medieval Europe depended on a few powerful words—the promise of loyalty a knight gave to his lord. By A.D. 1000, a simple promise had blossomed into a social order called feudalism.

A Society of Promises
Feudalism was a system both of government and of landownership. In exchange for a nobleman's oath of loyalty, a king would give him lands. The nobleman ruled these lands, judging legal cases, imposing taxes, and maintaining an army—powers granted him in exchange for his promise of loyalty to his king.

The Code of Chivalry As an expression of feudal ideals of honor, nobles developed a code of conduct called chivalry. This code demanded that knights be brave warriors and virtuous Christians who would selflessly fight for justice.

King Arthur and His Knights
The ideals of chivalry gave rise to legends and songs, such as the tales of King Arthur and his Knights of the Round Table. In the eleventh century, as feudalism established itself throughout Europe, stories about Arthur's court became widespread.

Sir Gawain and the Green Knight In *Sir Gawain and the Green Knight*, a medieval poem, the chivalry of Gawain, Arthur's loyal nephew, is tested by three challenges. In meeting them, Gawain proves admirable but not invulnerable. As one critic writes, the hero "gains in human credibility what he loses in ideal perfection."

We know little about the poet of *Sir Gawain*, who is credited with three other poems in alliterative verse. In his work, though, with its combination of humor and fervent ideals, he has helped shape an enduring vision of personal integrity.

Sir Thomas Malory (1405?–1471)

When people today hear the name Sir Thomas Malory, they may think of knights in shining armor, daring quests, and heroic rescues. They may not think of a convicted felon who spent much of his life in jail! The Malory they recall is the author of the most complete surviving collection of Arthurian legends, *Morte d'Arthur*. Yet, some historians have claimed that he is the same Thomas Malory who was jailed for such crimes as cattle-stealing, extortion, and assault—and who once escaped custody by swimming a moat!

Malory the Prisoner Few facts about Malory's life are known with certainty. It is said that he loved hunting and tournaments as well as Arthurian lore. Scholars generally hold that the author of *Morte d'Arthur* spent much of his life in prison. Some maintain, though, that he was jailed as a prisoner of war, not as a rustler.

A Book From Behind Bars Whatever the reason for his imprisonment, Malory probably wrote *Morte d'Arthur* from behind bars. Even as a prisoner, a knight such as Malory would have been granted access to books, such as the Arthurian texts that Malory translated and adapted.

A Legend Reborn *Morte d'Arthur* is not merely a retelling of existing legends. Fired by his own belief in the ideals of knighthood—and perhaps embittered by the decline of these ideals in a time of civil war—Malory forged the Arthurian legends into a visionary cycle of bold adventure, spiritual quests, and heart-rending betrayal. This great work was given its name by William Caxton, the man who established the first printing press in England. Caxton published *Morte d'Arthur* after its author's death, ensuring its enduring fame.

Preview

Connecting to the Literature

Most days, you probably aren't out slaying dragons. If you aid the distressed through volunteer work, though, or if you loyally stand by friends, you are following the knightly code of chivalry, a code modeled in the selections that follow.

Literary Analysis

Medieval Romance

Romances are narratives based in fantasy that tell of strange, sometimes supernatural events in exotic settings. **Medieval romances** are adventure stories that feature kings, knights, and damsels in distress and tell of quests, battles, and doomed love. The best-remembered romances concern King Arthur and his knights. As you read these romances, look for themes of love and honor in a blend of realism and fantasy.

Comparing Literary Works

Though their form and style differ, the romances in this grouping are based on the same group of **legends,** anonymous traditional stories about the past. Legends may be based in fact. They typically feature these elements:

- Heroic figures and memorable deeds
- Quests, contests, or tests
- Patterned events (for instance, events repeated three times).

Medieval writers often fashioned their romances by embellishing legends with detailed descriptions, plot twists, and sophisticated characterization (descriptions of the reactions and motives of characters). As you read these selections, compare the ways in which they adapt legends as literature.

Reading Strategy

Summarizing

To **summarize** a passage or a work, identify and restate its main ideas. As you read, use a chart like the one shown to track key ideas and details.

Vocabulary Development

assay (as´ ā) *v.* prove or test (p. 164)

adjure (ə joor´) *v.* request solemnly; appeal to earnestly (p. 166)

feigned (fānd) *v.* made a false show of; pretended (p. 171)

adroitly (ə droit´ lē) *adv.* with physical or mental skill (p. 172)

largesse (lär jes´) *n.* nobility of spirit (p. 174)

righteous (rī´chəs) *adj.* acting in a just, upright manner; doing what is right (p. 177)

entreated (en trēt´ id) *v.* made an earnest appeal; pleaded (p. 178)

peril (per´ əl) *n.* exposure to harm or injury (p. 179)

interred (in turd´) *v.* buried (p. 183)

Passage

"Ah, traitor unto me and untrue," said King Arthur, "now hast thou betrayed me twice. Who would have weened that thou that has been to me so loved and dear . . . , and would betray me for the riches of this sword."

Summary

King Arthur charges his knight with betraying him twice out of greed.

---

from Sir Gawain and the Green Knight

Translated by Marie Borroff

Background

The legend of King Arthur is probably based on the life of a Celtic warrior who fought the Anglo-Saxon invaders of England in the late fifth and early sixth centuries. His role as a defender of England made him a hero to the Britons, the island's Celtic inhabitants. They told stories celebrating his just rule and championship of the oppressed and abused.

By the time the Arthurian legends were transformed into written literature, the Britons had long since been defeated by the Anglo-Saxons. The fact that the tales came from a vanished world only fueled their power as literature. The Arthurian stories set an ideal for knights, and ideals are never fully realized in the present. Their true home may be the legendary past, or a future yet to come.

The selection begins at the start of a New Year's Eve feast at King Arthur's Court in Camelot. Before anyone has started eating, the festivities are interrupted by an immense green knight who suddenly appears at the hall door. The knight rides a green horse and is armed with a gigantic ax.

This horseman hurtles in, and the hall enters;
Riding to the high dais,[1] recked he no danger;
Not a greeting he gave as the guests he o'erlooked,
Nor wasted his words, but "Where is," he said,
5 "The captain of this crowd? Keenly I wish
To see that sire with sight, and to himself say my say."
    He swaggered all about
    To scan the host so gay;
    He halted, as if in doubt
10   Who in that hall held sway.

---

1. **dais** (dā′ is) *n.* platform.

There were stares on all sides as the stranger spoke,
For much did they marvel what it might mean
That a horseman and a horse should have such a hue,
Grow green as the grass, and greener, it seemed.
15 Then green fused on gold more glorious by far.
All the onlookers eyed him, and edged nearer,
And awaited in wonder what he would do,
For many sights had they seen, but such a one never,
So that phantom and fairy the folk there deemed it,
20 Therefore chary² of answer was many a champion bold,
And stunned at his strong words stone-still they sat
In a swooning silence in the stately hall.
As all were slipped into sleep, so slackened their speech apace.
    Not all, I think, for dread,
25   But some of courteous grace
    Let him who was their head
    Be spokesman in that place.

Then Arthur before the high dais that entrance beholds,
And hailed him, as behooved, for he had no fear.
30 And said "Fellow, in faith you have found fair welcome;
The head of this hostelry Arthur am I;
Leap lightly down, and linger, I pray,
And the tale of your intent you shall tell us after."
"Nay, so help me," said the other, "He that on high sits,
35 To tarry here any time, 'twas not mine errand;
But as the praise of you, prince, is puffed up so high,
And your court and your company are counted the best,
Stoutest under steel-gear on steeds to ride,
Worthiest of their works the wide world over,
40 And peerless to prove in passages of arms,
And courtesy here is carried to its height,
And so at this season I have sought you out.
You may be certain by the branch that I bear in hand
That I pass here in peace, and would part friends,
45 For had I come to this court on combat bent,
I have a hauberk³ at home, and a helm beside,
A shield and a sharp spear, shining bright,
And other weapons to wield, I ween well, to boot,
But as I willed no war, I wore no metal.
50 But if you be so bold as all men believe,
You will graciously grant the game that I ask by right."
    Arthur answer gave
    And said, "Sir courteous knight,
    If contest here you crave,
55   You shall not fail to fight."

---

2. **chary** (cher´ ē) *adj.* not giving freely.
3. **hauberk** (hô´ bərk) *n.* coat of armor.

Reading Strategy
Summarizing What are three main points of the Green Knight's speech in lines 34–51?

**Reading Check**

What is uncanny about the Knight who enters Arthur's court?

"Nay, to fight, in good faith, is far from my thought;
There are about on these benches but beardless children,
Were I here in full arms on a haughty[4] steed,
For measured against mine, their might is puny.

60 And so I call in this court for a Christmas game,
For 'tis Yule, and New Year, and many young bloods about;
If any in this house such hardihood claims,
Be so bold in his blood, his brain so wild,
As stoutly to strike one stroke for another,

65 I shall give him as my gift this gisarme[5] noble,
This ax, that is heavy enough, to handle as he likes,
And I shall bide the first blow, as bare as I sit.
If there be one so wilful my words to <u>assay</u>,
Let him leap hither lightly, lay hold of this weapon;

70 I quitclaim it forever, keep it as his own,
And I shall stand him a stroke, steady on this floor,
So you grant me the guerdon to give him another, sans blame.[6]
　　In a twelvemonth[7] and a day
　　He shall have of me the same;

75 　　Now be it seen straightway
　　Who dares take up the game."

If he astonished them at first, stiller were then
All that household in hall, the high and the low;
The stranger on his green steed stirred in the saddle,

80 And roisterously his red eyes he rolled all about,
Bent his bristling brows, that were bright green,
Wagged his beard as he watched who would arise.
When the court kept its counsel he coughed aloud,
And cleared his throat coolly, the clearer to speak:

85 "What, is this Arthur's house," said that horseman then,
"Whose fame is so fair in far realms and wide?
Where is now your arrogance and your awesome deeds,
Your valor and your victories and your vaunting words?
Now are the revel and renown of the Round Table

90 Overwhelmed with a word of one man's speech,
For all cower and quake, and no cut felt!"
With this he laughs so loud that the lord grieved;
The blood for sheer shame shot to his face, and pride.
　　With rage his face flushed red,

95 　　And so did all beside.
　　Then the king as bold man bred
　　Toward the stranger took a stride.

assay (as´ ā) *v.* prove or test

Literary Analysis
Medieval Romance
What aspect of medieval romances does the Green Knight's appearance illustrate?

---

4. **haughty** (hôt´ ē) *adj.* lofty.
5. **gisarme** (gi zärm´) *n.* battle-ax.
6. **I shall . . . blame** "I will stand firm while he strikes me with the ax provided that you reward me with the opportunity to do the same to him without being blamed for it."
7. **twelvemonth** a year.

Three Knights Returning From a Tournament

And said, "Sir, now we see you will say but folly,
Which whoso has sought, it suits that he find.
100 No guest here is aghast of your great words.
Give to me your gisarme, in God's own name,
And the boon you have begged shall straight be granted."
He leaps to him lightly, lays hold of his weapon;
The green fellow on foot fiercely alights.
105 Now has Arthur his ax, and the haft[8] grips,
And sternly stirs it about, on striking bent.
The stranger before him stood there erect,
Higher than any in the house by a head and more;
With stern look as he stood, he stroked his beard,
110 And with undaunted countenance drew down his coat,
No more moved nor dismayed for his mighty dints
Than any bold man on bench had brought him a drink of wine.
        Gawain by Guenevere
        Toward the king doth now incline:
115   "I beseech, before all here,
        That this melee may be mine."

"Would you grant me the grace," said Gawain to the king,
"To be gone from this bench and stand by you there,
If I without discourtesy might quit this board,

✔ Reading Check

What challenge does the Green Knight make to Arthur's court?

---

8. haft *n.* handle of a weapon or tool.

120 And if my liege lady[9] misliked it not,
　　 I would come to your counsel before your court noble.
　　 For I find it not fit, as in faith it is known,
　　 When such a boon is begged before all these knights,
　　 Though you be tempted thereto, to take it on yourself
125 While so bold men about upon benches sit,
　　 That no host under heaven is hardier of will,
　　 Nor better brothers-in-arms where battle is joined;
　　 I am the weakest, well I know, and of wit feeblest;
　　 And the loss of my life would be least of any;
130 That I have you for uncle is my only praise;
　　 My body, but for your blood, is barren of worth;
　　 And for that this folly befits not a king,
　　 And 'tis I that have asked it, it ought to be mine,
　　 And if my claim be not comely let all this court judge in sight."
135 　　　The court assays the claim,
　　　　 And in counsel all unite
　　　　 To give Gawain the game
　　　　 And release the king outright.

　　 Then the king called the knight to come to his side,
140 And he rose up readily, and reached him with speed,
　　 Bows low to his lord, lays hold of the weapon,
　　 And he releases it lightly, and lifts up his hand,
　　 And gives him God's blessing, and graciously prays
　　 That his heart and his hand may be hardy both.
145 "Keep, cousin," said the king, "what you cut with this day,
　　 And if you rule it aright, then readily, I know,
　　 You shall stand the stroke it will strike after."
　　 Gawain goes to the guest with gisarme in hand,
　　 And boldly he bides there, abashed not a whit.
150 Then hails he Sir Gawain, the horseman in green:
　　 "Recount we our contract, ere you come further.
　　 First I ask and <u>adjure</u> you, how you are called
　　 That you tell me true, so that trust it I may."
　　 "In good faith," said the good knight, "Gawain am I
155 Whose buffet befalls you,[10] whate'er betide after,
　　 And at this time twelvemonth take from you another
　　 With what weapon you will, and with no man else alive."
　　　　 The other nods assent:
　　　　 "Sir Gawain, as I may thrive,
160 　　　 I am wondrous well content
　　　　 That you this dint[11] shall drive."

---

9. liege (lēj) **lady** Guenevere, the wife of the lord, Arthur, to whom Gawain is bound to give service and allegiance.
10. Whose . . . you "whose blow you will receive."
11. dint n. blow.

"Sir Gawain," said the Green Knight, "By God, I rejoice
That your fist shall fetch this favor I seek,
And you have readily rehearsed, and in right terms,
165 Each clause of my covenant with the king your lord,
Save that you shall assure me, sir, upon oath,
That you shall seek me yourself, wheresoever you deem
My lodgings may lie, and look for such wages[12]
As you have offered me here before all this host."
170 "What is the way there?" said Gawain, "Where do you dwell?
I heard never of your house, by Him that made me,
Nor I know you not, knight, your name nor your court.
But tell me truly thereof, and teach me your name,
And I shall fare forth to find you, so far as I may,
175 And this I say in good certain, and swear upon oath."
"That is enough in New Year, you need say no more,"
Said the knight in the green to Gawain the noble,
"If I tell you true, when I have taken your knock,
And if you handily have hit, you shall hear straightway
180 Of my house and my home and my own name;
Then follow in my footsteps by faithful accord.
And if I spend no speech, you shall speed the better:
You can feast with your friends, nor further trace my tracks.[13]
        Now hold your grim tool steady
185   And show us how it hacks."
        "Gladly, sir; all ready,"
        Says Gawain; he strokes the ax.

The Green Knight upon ground girds him with care:
Bows a bit with his head, and bares his flesh:
190 His long lovely locks he laid over his crown,
Let the naked nape for the need be shown
Gawain grips to his ax and gathers it aloft—
The left foot on the floor before him he set—
Brought it down deftly upon the bare neck,
195 That the shock of the sharp blow shivered the bones
And cut the flesh cleanly and clove it in twain,[14]
That the blade of bright steel bit into the ground.
The head was hewn off and fell to the floor;
Many found it at their feet, as forth it rolled;
200 The blood gushed from the body, bright on the green,
Yet fell not the fellow, nor faltered a whit,
But stoutly he starts forth upon stiff shanks,
And as all stood staring he stretched forth his hand,

Reading Strategy
Summarizing How would
you summarize the event
in lines 188–213?

---

12. **wages** *n.* payment; that is, a strike with the ax.
13. **If I tell you . . . tracks** The Green Knight tells Gawain that he will let him know
where he lives after he has taken the blow. If he is unable to speak following the
blow, there will be no need for Gawain to know.
14. **clove it in twain** split it in two.

✔**Reading Check**

What does Gawain do
to the Green Knight?

Laid hold of his head and heaved it aloft,
205 Then goes to the green steed, grasps the bridle,
Steps into the stirrup, bestrides his mount,
And his head by the hair in his hand holds,
And as steady he sits in the stately saddle
As he had met with no mishap, nor missing were his head.
210   His bulk about he haled,
          That fearsome body that bled;
          There were many in the court that quailed
          Before all his say was said.

For the head in his hand he holds right up;
215 Toward the first on the dais directs he the face,
And it lifted up its lids, and looked with wide eyes,
And said as much with its mouth as now you may hear:
"Sir Gawain, forget not to go as agreed,
And cease not to seek till me, sir, you find,
220 As you promised in the presence of these proud knights.
To the Green Chapel come, I charge you, to take
Such a dint as you have dealt—you have well deserved
That your neck should have a knock on New Year's morn.
The Knight of the Green Chapel I am well-known to many,
225 Wherefore you cannot fail to find me at last;
Therefore come, or be counted a recreant[15] knight."
With a roisterous rush he flings round the reins,
Hurtles out at the hall door, his head in his hand,
That the flint fire flew from the flashing hooves.
230 Which way he went, not one of them knew
Nor whence he was come in the wide world so fair.
          The king and Gawain gay
          Make a game of the Green Knight there,
          Yet all who saw it say
235   'Twas a wonder past compare.

Though high-born Arthur at heart had wonder,
He let no sign be seen, but said aloud
To the comely queen, with courteous speech,
"Dear dame, on this day dismay you no whit;
240 Such crafts are becoming at Christmastide,
Laughing at interludes, light songs and mirth,
Amid dancing of damsels with doughty knights.
Nevertheless of my meat now let me partake,
For I have met with a marvel, I may not deny."
245 He glanced at Sir Gawain, and gaily he said,
"Now, sir, hang up your ax, that has hewn enough,"
And over the high dais it was hung on the wall

Literary Analysis
Medieval Romance
What two characteristics of a medieval romance are reflected in lines 214–231?

Reading Strategy
Summarizing Sum up Arthur's reaction to the Green Knight's visit.

---

15. recreant *adj.* cowardly.

That men in amazement might on it look,
And tell in true terms the tale of the wonder.
250 Then they turned toward the table, those two together,
The good king and Gawain, and made great feast,
With all dainties double, dishes rare,
With all manner of meat and minstrelsy both,
Such happiness wholly had they that day in hold.
255   Now take care, Sir Gawain,
     That your courage wax not cold
     When you must turn again
     To your enterprise foretold.

The following November, Sir Gawain sets out to fulfill his promise to the Green Knight. For weeks, he travels alone through the cold, threatening woods of North Wales. Then, after he prays for shelter, he comes upon a wondrous castle on Christmas Eve, where he is greeted warmly by the lord of the castle and his lady. The lord assures Sir Gawain that the Green Chapel is nearby and promises to provide him with a guide to lead him there on New Year's Day. Before the lord and Sir Gawain retire for the night, they agree to exchange whatever they receive during the next three days. Sir Gawain keeps his pledge for the first two days, but he fails to give the lord the magic green girdle that the lady gives him on the third day, because she gives it with the promise that it will protect him from harm. The next day, Gawain sets out for the Green Chapel. His guide urges him not to proceed, but Gawain feels that it would be dishonorable not to fulfill his pledge. He is determined to accept his fate; however, he wears the magic green girdle that the lady has given him.

Gawain Receiving the Green Girdle. Woodcut by Fritz Kredel from John Gardner, *The Complete Works of the Gawain Poet.* The University of Chicago Press, 1965.

▲ **Critical Viewing**
Does the simple, stylized look of this woodcut suit the style of the selection? Explain. **[Assess]**

✔ **Reading Check**
What happens after Gawain chops off the Green Knight's head?

He puts his heels to his horse, and picks up the path;
260 Goes in beside a grove where the ground is steep,
Rides down the rough slope right to the valley;
And then he looked a little about him—the landscape was wild,
And not a soul to be seen, nor sign of a dwelling,
But high banks on either hand hemmed it about,
265 With many a ragged rock and rough-hewn crag;
The skies seemed scored by the scowling peaks.
Then he halted his horse, and hoved there a space,
And sought on every side for a sight of the Chapel,

But no such place appeared, which puzzled him sore,
270 Yet he saw some way off what seemed like a mound,
A hillock high and broad, hard by the water,
Where the stream fell in foam down the face of the steep
And bubbled as if it boiled on its bed below.
The knight urges his horse, and heads for the knoll;
275 Leaps lightly to earth; loops well the rein
Of his steed to a stout branch, and stations him there.
He strides straight to the mound, and strolls all about,
Much wondering what it was, but no whit the wiser;
It had a hole at one end, and on either side,
280 And was covered with coarse grass in clumps all without,
And hollow all within, like some old cave,
Or a crevice of an old crag—he could not discern aright.
 "Can this be the Chapel Green?
 Alack!" said the man, "Here might
285 The devil himself be seen
 Saying matins[16] at black midnight!"

"Now by heaven," said he, "it is bleak hereabouts;
This prayer house is hideous, half covered with grass!
Well may the grim man mantled in green
290 Hold here his orisons,[17] in hell's own style!
Now I feel it is the Fiend, in my five wits,
That has tempted me to this tryst,[18] to take my life;
This is a Chapel of mischance, may the mischief take it!
As accursed a country church as I came upon ever!"
295 With his helm on his head, his lance in his hand,
He stalks toward the steep wall of that strange house.
Then he heard, on the hill, behind a hard rock,
Beyond the brook, from the bank, a most barbarous din:
Lord! it clattered in the cliff fit to cleave it in two,
300 As one upon a grindstone ground a great scythe!
Lord! it whirred like a mill-wheel whirling about!
Lord! it echoed loud and long, lamentable to hear!
Then "By heaven," said the bold knight, "That business up there
Is arranged for my arrival, or else I am much misled.
305 Let God work! Ah me!
 All hope of help has fled!
 Forfeit my life may be
 But noise I do not dread."

Then he listened no longer, but loudly he called,
310 "Who has power in this place, high parley to hold?

---

16. matins n. morning prayers.
17. orisons n. prayers.
18. tryst (trist) n. meeting.

For none greets Sir Gawain, or gives him good day;
If any would a word with him, let him walk forth
And speak now or never, to speed his affairs."
"Abide," said one on the bank above over his head,
315 "And what I promised you once shall straightway be given."
Yet he stayed not his grindstone, nor stinted its noise,
But worked awhile at his whetting before he would rest,
And then he comes around a crag, from a cave in the rocks,
Hurtling out of hiding with a hateful weapon,
320 A Danish ax[19] devised for that day's deed,
With a broad blade and bright, bent in a curve,
Filed to a fine edge—four feet it measured
By the length of the lace that was looped round the haft.
And in form as at first, the fellow all green,
325 His lordly face and his legs, his locks and his beard,
Save that firm upon two feet forward he strides,
Sets a hand on the ax-head, the haft to the earth;
When he came to the cold stream, and cared not to wade,
He vaults over on his ax, and advances amain
330 On a broad bank of snow, overbearing and brisk of mood.
    Little did the knight incline
    When face to face they stood;
    Said the other man, "Friend mine,
    It seems your word holds good!"

335 "God love you, Sir Gawain!" said the Green Knight then,
"And well met this morning, man, at my place!
And you have followed me faithfully and found me betimes,
And on the business between us we both are agreed:
Twelve months ago today you took what was yours,
340 And you at this New Year must yield me the same.
And we have met in these mountains, remote from all eyes:
There is none here to halt us or hinder our sport;
Unhasp your high helm, and have here your wages;
Make no more demur[20] than I did myself
345 When you hacked off my head with one hard blow."
"No, by God," said Sir Gawain, "that granted me life,
I shall grudge not the guerdon[21] grim though it prove;
And you may lay on as you like till the last of my part be paid."
    He proffered, with good grace,
350   His bare neck to the blade,
    And <u>feigned</u> a cheerful face:
    He scorned to seem afraid.

Literary Analysis
Medieval Romance and Legend Which details in lines 309–334 strike you as belonging to the legend retold by the poem? Which details sound more literary?

feigned (fānd) v. made a false show of; pretended

✔**Reading Check**

What is the Green Knight doing when Gawain arrives at the Green Chapel?

---

19. Danish ax long-bladed ax.
20. demur (dē mʉr) protest; delay.
21. guerdon n. reward.

Then the grim man in green gathers his strength,
Heaves high the heavy ax to hit him the blow.
355 With all the force in his frame he fetches it aloft,
With a grimace as grim as he would grind him to bits;
Had the blow he bestowed been as big as he threatened,
A good knight and gallant had gone to his grave.
But Gawain at the great ax glanced up aside
360 As down it descended with death-dealing force,
And his shoulders shrank a little from the sharp iron.
Abruptly the brawny man breaks off the stroke,
And then reproved with proud words that prince among knights.
"You are not Gawain the glorious," the green man said,
365 "That never fell back on field in the face of the foe,
And now you flee for fear, and have felt no harm:
Such news of that knight I never heard yet!
I moved not a muscle when you made to strike,
Nor caviled[22] at the cut in King Arthur's house;
370 My head fell to my feet, yet steadfast I stood,
And you, all unharmed, are wholly dismayed—
Wherefore the better man I, by all odds, must be."
        Said Gawain, "Strike once more;
        I shall neither flinch nor flee;
375   But if my head falls to the floor
        There is no mending me!"

"But go on, man, in God's name, and get to the point!
Deliver me my destiny, and do it out of hand,
For I shall stand to the stroke and stir not an inch
380 Till your ax has hit home—on my honor I swear it!"
"Have at thee then!" said the other, and heaves it aloft,
And glares down as grimly as he had gone mad.
He made a mighty feint, but marred not his hide;
Withdrew the ax <u>adroitly</u> before it did damage.
385 Gawain gave no ground, nor glanced up aside,
But stood still as a stone, or else a stout stump
That is held in hard earth by a hundred roots.
Then merrily does he mock him, the man all in green:
"So now you have your nerve again, I needs must strike;
390 Uphold the high knighthood that Arthur bestowed,
And keep your neck-bone clear, if this cut allows!"
Then was Gawain gripped with rage, and grimly he said,
"Why, thrash away, tyrant, I tire of your threats;
You make such a scene, you must frighten yourself."
395 Said the green fellow, "In faith, so fiercely you speak
That I shall finish this affair, nor further grace allow."
        He stands prepared to strike

22. caviled raised trivial objections.

Literary Analysis
Medieval Romance
In what way do Gawain's actions in lines 359–387 fit the ideals of knighthood? In what way might they depart from those ideals?

adroitly (ə drɔit′ lē) *adv.* with physical or mental skill

And scowls with both lip and brow;
No marvel if the man mislike
400   Who can hope no rescue now.

He gathered up the grim ax and guided it well:
Let the barb at the blade's end brush the bare throat;
He hammered down hard, yet harmed him no whit
Save a scratch on one side, that severed the skin;
405 The end of the hooked edge entered the flesh,
And a little blood lightly leapt to the earth.
And when the man beheld his own blood bright on the snow,
He sprang a spear's length with feet spread wide,
Seized his high helm, and set it on his head,
410 Shoved before his shoulders the shield at his back,
Bares his trusty blade, and boldly he speaks—
Not since he was a babe born of his mother
Was he once in this world one half so blithe—
"Have done with your hacking—harry me no more!
415 I have borne, as behooved, one blow in this place;
If you make another move I shall meet it midway
And promptly, I promise you, pay back each blow with brand.
   One stroke acquits me here;
   So did our covenant stand
420   In Arthur's court last year—
   Wherefore, sir, hold your hand!"

He lowers the long ax and leans on it there,
Sets his arms on the head, the haft on the earth,
And beholds the bold knight that bides there afoot,

▲ **Critical Viewing**
Compare the scenes in the picture with the text. What episodes are included or omitted? **[Compare and Contrast]**

Reading Strategy
Summarizing What is the key point of Gawain's speech in lines 414–421?

☑**Reading Check**

What happens on the Green Knight's third stroke with the the ax?

from *Sir Gawain and the Green Knight* ◆ *173*

425 How he faces him fearless, fierce in full arms,
And plies him with proud words—it pleases him well.
Then once again gaily to Gawain he calls,
And in a loud voice and lusty, delivers these words:
"Bold fellow, on this field your anger forbear!
430 No man has made demands here in manner uncouth,
Nor done, save as duly determined at court.
I owed you a hit and you have it; be happy therewith!
The rest of my rights here I freely resign.
Had I been a bit busier, a buffet, perhaps,
435 I could have dealt more directly; and done you some harm.
First I flourished with a feint, in frolicsome mood,
And left your hide unhurt—and here I did well
By the fair terms we fixed on the first night;
And fully and faithfully you followed accord:
440 Gave over all your gains as a good man should.
A second feint, sir, I assigned for the morning
You kissed my comely wife—each kiss you restored.
For both of these there behooved but two feigned blows by right.
    True men pay what they owe;
445   No danger then in sight.
    You failed at the third throw,
    So take my tap, sir knight.

"For that is my belt about you, that same braided girdle,
My wife it was that wore it; I know well the tale,
450 And the count of your kisses and your conduct too,
And the wooing of my wife—it was all my scheme!
She made trial of a man most faultless by far
Of all that ever walked over the wide earth;
As pearls to white peas, more precious and prized,
455 So is Gawain, in good faith, to other gay knights.
Yet you lacked, sir, a little in loyalty there,
But the cause was not cunning, nor courtship either,
But that you loved your own life; the less, then, to blame."
The other stout knight in a study stood a long while,
460 So gripped with grim rage that his great heart shook.
All the blood of his body burned in his face
As he shrank back in shame from the man's sharp speech.
The first words that fell from the fair knight's lips:
"Accursed be a cowardly and covetous heart!
465 In you is villainy and vice, and virtue laid low!"
Then he grasps the green girdle and lets go the knot,
Hands it over in haste, and hotly he says:
"Behold there my falsehood, ill hap betide it!
Your cut taught me cowardice, care for my life,
470 And coveting came after, contrary both
To <u>largesse</u> and loyalty belonging to knights.

Literary Analysis
Medieval Romance
What theme of medieval romance is suggested in lines 441–443?

Reading Strategy
Summarizing How would you summarize Sir Gawain's response to the Green Knight in lines 459–477?

largesse (lär jes´) *n.* nobility of spirit

Now am I faulty and false, that fearful was ever
Of disloyalty and lies, bad luck to them both! and greed.
    I confess, knight, in this place,
475   Most dire is my misdeed;
    Let me gain back your good grace,
    And thereafter I shall take heed."

Then the other laughed aloud, and lightly he said,
"Such harm as I have had, I hold it quite healed.
480 You are so fully confessed, your failings made known,
And bear the plain penance of the point of my blade,
I hold you polished as a pearl, as pure and as bright
As you had lived free of fault since first you were born.
And I give you sir, this girdle that is gold-hemmed
485 And green as my garments, that, Gawain, you may
Be mindful of this meeting when you mingle in throng
With nobles of renown—and known by this token
How it chanced at the Green Chapel, to chivalrous knights.
And you shall in this New Year come yet again
490 And we shall finish out our feast in my fair hall with cheer."

Review and Assess

Thinking About the Selection

1. **Respond:** If you were King Arthur, would you have allowed Sir Gawain to accept the Green Knight's challenge? Why?

2. **(a) Recall:** How do Arthur's knights first respond to the Green Knight's challenge? **(b) Analyze:** Why does the Green Knight laugh at their response? **(c) Draw Conclusions:** Judging from Arthur's reaction, how important is honor in Arthur's court?

3. **(a) Recall:** What does Gawain offer to do? **(b) Analyze:** How does he manage to make his offer seem humble, not boastful? **(c) Infer:** Why are the offer and his manner of making it appropriate for a knight?

4. **(a) Interpret:** In lines 464–477, how does Sir Gawain react when he considers his own actions? **(b) Draw Conclusions:** What do you think Sir Gawain has learned from his second encounter with the Green Knight?

5. **Make a Judgment:** In your opinion, has Sir Gawain failed to live up to his knightly ideals? Explain.

6. **Take a Position:** Using the example of Sir Gawain, explain whether you think it is more important to achieve one's goals or to learn from one's mistakes.

from **Morte d'Arthur**

Sir Thomas Malory

This selection begins after King Arthur has traveled to France at the insistence of his nephew, Gawain, to besiege his former friend and knight, Lancelot, for his involvement with Queen Guenevere. However, the king's attempts to punish Lancelot are halfhearted, and he is soon forced to abandon them altogether when he learns that his illegitimate son, Mordred, has seized control of England. Arthur leads his forces back to England, and Mordred attacks them upon their landing. Gawain is killed in the fighting, but before he dies, he manages to send word to Lancelot that Arthur is in need of his assistance.

So upon Trinity Sunday at night King Arthur dreamed a wonderful dream, and in his dream him seemed[1] that he saw upon a chafflet[2] a chair, and the chair was fast to a wheel, and thereupon sat King Arthur in the richest cloth of gold that might be made. And the King thought there was under him, far from him, an hideous deep black water, and therein was all manner of serpents, and worms, and wild beasts, foul and horrible. And suddenly the King thought that the wheel turned upside down, and he fell among the serpents, and every beast took him by a limb. And then the King cried as he lay in his bed, "Help, help!"

And then knights, squires, and yeomen awaked the King, and then he was so amazed that he wist[3] not where he was. And then so he awaked until it was nigh day, and then he fell on slumbering again, not sleeping nor thoroughly waking. So the King seemed[4] verily that

---

1. **him seemed** It seemed to him.
2. **chafflet** platform.
3. **wist** knew.
4. **the King seemed** It seemed to the King.

▲ **Critical Viewing** Using your knowledge of chivalry, draw conclusions about King Arthur's decision to set his knights at a round table. **[Draw Conclusions]**

King Arthur's Round Table and the Holy Grail, Art Resource, NY

there came Sir Gawain unto him with a number of fair ladies with him. So when King Arthur saw him, he said, "Welcome, my sister's son. I weened ye had been dead. And now I see thee on-live, much am I beholden unto Almighty Jesu. Ah, fair nephew and my sister's son, what been these ladies that hither be come with you?"

"Sir," said Sir Gawain, "all these be ladies for whom I have foughten for when I was man living. And all these are those that I did battle for in <u>righteous</u> quarrels, and God hath given them that grace, at their great prayer, because I did battle for them for their right, that they should bring me hither unto you. Thus much hath given me leave God, for to warn you of your death. For and ye fight as tomorn[5] with

righteous (rī´chəs) *adj.* acting in a just, upright manner; doing what is right

✔**Reading Check**

What kind of dreams is Arthur having?

---

5. **and . . . tomorn** "if you fight tomorrow."

Sir Mordred, as ye both have assigned, doubt ye not ye must be slain, and the most party of your people on both parties. And for the great grace and goodness that Almighty Jesu hath unto you, and for pity of you and many more other good men there shall be slain, God hath sent me to you of his special grace to give you warning that in no wise ye do battle as tomorn, but that ye take a treaty for a month from today. And proffer you largely[6] you so that tomorn ye put in a delay. For within a month shall come Sir Lancelot with all his noble knights and rescue you worshipfully and slay Sir Mordred and all that ever will hold with him."

Then Sir Gawain and all the ladies vanished. And anon the King called upon his knights, squires, and yeomen, and charged them wightly[7] to fetch his noble lords and wise bishops unto him. And when they were come the King told them of his avision,[8] that Sir Gawain had told him and warned him that, and he fought on the morn, he should be slain. Then the King commanded Sir Lucan the Butler and his brother Sir Bedivere the Bold, with two bishops with them, and charged them in any wise to take a treaty for a month from today with Sir Mordred. "And spare not: proffer him lands and goods as much as ye think reasonable."

So then they departed and came to Sir Mordred where he had a grim host of an hundred thousand, and there they <u>entreated</u> Sir Mordred long time. And at the last Sir Mordred was agreed for to have Cornwall and Kent by King Arthur's days, and after that, all England, after the days of King Arthur.

Then were they condescended[9] that King Arthur and Sir Mordred should meet betwixt both their hosts, and each of them should bring fourteen persons. And so they came with this word unto Arthur. Then said he, "I am glad that this is done," and so he went into the field.

And when King Arthur should depart, he warned all his host that, and they see any sword drawn, "Look ye come on fiercely and slay that traitor Sir Mordred, for I in no wise trust him." In like wise Sir Mordred warned his host that "And ye see any manner of sword drawn, look that ye come on fiercely, and so slay all that ever before you standeth, for in no wise I will not trust for this treaty." And in the same wise said Sir Mordred unto his host, "For I know well my father will be avenged upon me."

And so they met as their pointment[10] was and were agreed and accorded thoroughly. And wine was fetched and they drank together. Right so came an adder out of a little heathbush, and it stung a knight in the foot. And so when the knight felt him so stung, he looked down and saw the adder. And anon he drew his sword to slay

---

6. **proffer you largely** make generous offers.
7. **wightly** quickly.
8. **avision** dream.
9. **condescended** agreed.
10. **pointment** arrangement.

Reading Strategy
Summarizing What are three key points of Sir Gawain's speech in the dream?

Literary Analysis
Medieval Romance What characteristic of medieval romance is illustrated by the dream and Arthur's response to it?

entreated (en trēt′ id) v. made an earnest appeal; pleaded

the adder, and thought none other harm. And when the host on both parties saw that sword drawn, then they blew beams,[11] trumpets, horns, and shouted grimly. And so both hosts dressed them together. And King Arthur took his horse and said, "Alas, this unhappy day!" and so rode to his party, and Sir Mordred in like wise.

And never since was there never seen a more dolefuller battle in no Christian land, for there was but rushing and riding, lunging and striking; and many a grim word was there spoken of either to other, and many a deadly stroke. But ever King Arthur rode throughout the battle[12] of Sir Mordred many times and did full nobly, as a noble king should do, and at all times he fainted never. And Sir Mordred did his devoir[13] that day and put himself in great <u>peril</u>.

And thus they fought all the long day, and never stinted[14] till the noble knights were laid to the cold earth. And ever they fought still till it was near night, and by then was there an hundred thousand laid dead upon the down. Then was King Arthur wood-wroth[15] out of measure when he saw his people so slain from him. And so he looked about him and could see no more of all his host, and good knights left no more on-live, but two knights: the t'one was Sir Lucan the Butler and the other his brother Sir Bedivere. And yet they were full sore wounded.

"Jesu, mercy," said the King, "where are all my noble knights become? Alas that ever I should see this doleful day! For now," said King Arthur, "I am come to mine end. But would to God," said he, "that I wist now where were that traitor Sir Mordred that has caused all this mischief."

Then King Arthur looked about and was ware where stood Sir Mordred leaning upon his sword among a great heap of dead men.

"Now give me my spear," said King Arthur unto Sir Lucan, "for yonder I have espied the traitor that all this woe hath wrought."

"Sir, let him be," said Sir Lucan, "for he is unhappy. And if ye pass this unhappy day ye shall be right well revenged upon him. And, good lord, remember ye of your night's dream, and what the spirit of Sir Gawain told you tonight, and yet God of his great goodness hath preserved you hitherto. And for God's sake, my lord, leave off by this, for, blessed be God, ye have won the field: for yet we been here three on-live, and with Sir Mordred is not one on-live. And therefore if ye leave off now, this wicked day of destiny is past."

"Now, tide[16] me death, tide me life," said the King, "now I see him yonder alone, he shall never escape mine hands. For at a better avail shall I never have him."

"God speed you well!" said Sir Bedivere.

peril (per´ əl) *n.* exposure to harm or injury

Literary Analysis
Medieval Romance and Legend What features of this account seem more typical of legend than of written forms of story telling?

---

11. **beams** type of trumpet.
12. **battle** battalion.
13. **devoir** (də vwär´) *n.* duty (from the French; obsolete).
14. **stinted** stopped.
15. **wood-wroth** wild with rage.
16. **tide** befall.

Reading Check

What happens to the truce between Arthur and Mordred?

The Nine Heroes Tapestries: Christian Heroes: Arthur, probably Nicolas Bataille, Paris; The Metropolitan Museum of Art

▲ **Critical Viewing** What can you deduce about King Arthur's character from his depiction in this tapestry? **[Deduce]**

Then the King got his spear in both his hands and ran toward Sir Mordred, crying and saying, "Traitor, now is thy deathday come!"

And when Sir Mordred saw King Arthur he ran until him with his sword drawn in his hand, and there King Arthur smote Sir Mordred under the shield, with a thrust of his spear, throughout the body more than a fathom. And when Sir Mordred felt that he had his death's wound, he thrust himself with the might that he had up to the burr[17] of King Arthur's spear, and right so he smote his father King Arthur with his sword holden in both his hands, upon the side of the head, that the sword pierced the helmet and the casing of the brain. And therewith Sir Mordred dashed down stark dead to the earth.

Reading Strategy
Summarizing Summarize the events leading to the death of Mordred and the mortal wounding of King Arthur.

---

17. burr hand guard.

And noble King Arthur fell in a swough[18] to the earth, and there he swooned oftentimes, and Sir Lucan and Sir Bedivere ofttimes heaved him up. And so, weakly betwixt them, they led him to a little chapel not far from the seaside, and when the King was there, him thought him reasonably eased. Then heard they people cry in the field. "Now go thou, Sir Lucan," said the King, "and do me to wit[19] what betokens that noise in the field."

So Sir Lucan departed, for he was grievously wounded in many places. And so as he walked he saw and harkened by the moonlight how that pillagers and robbers were come into the field to pill and to rob many a full noble knight of brooches and bracelets and of many a good ring and many a rich jewel. And who that were not dead all out there they slew them for their harness and their riches. When Sir Lucan understood this work, he came to the King as soon as he might and told him all what he had heard and seen. "Therefore by my read,"[20] said Sir Lucan, "it is best that we bring you to some town."

"I would it were so," said the King, "but I may not stand, my head works so. Ah, Sir Lancelot," said King Arthur, "this day have I sore missed thee. And alas that ever I was against thee, for now have I my death, whereof Sir Gawain me warned in my dream."

Then Sir Lucan took up the King the t'one party[21] and Sir Bedivere the other party; and in the lifting up the King swooned and in the lifting Sir Lucan fell in a swoon that part of his guts fell out of his body, and therewith the noble knight's heart burst. And when the King awoke he beheld Sir Lucan how he lay foaming at the mouth and part of his guts lay at his feet.

"Alas," said the King, "this is to me a full heavy sight to see this noble duke so die for my sake, for he would have helped me that had more need of help than I. Alas that he would not complain him for his heart was so set to help me. Now Jesu have mercy upon his soul."

Then Sir Bedivere wept for the death of his brother.

"Now leave this mourning and weeping gentle knight," said the King, "for all this will not avail me. For wit thou well, and might I live myself, the death of Sir Lucan would grieve me evermore. But my time passeth on fast," said the King. "Therefore," said King Arthur unto Sir Bedivere, "take thou here Excalibur my good sword and go with it to yonder water's side; and when thou comest there I charge thee throw my sword in that water and come again and tell me what thou sawest there."

"My lord," said Sir Bedivere, "your commandment shall be done, and I shall lightly[22] bring you word again."

So Sir Bedivere departed. And by the way he beheld that noble sword, that the pommel and the haft[23] was all precious stones. And

---

18. **swough** forcible movement
19. **me to wit** "let me know."
20. **read** advice.
21. **party** side.
22. **lightly** quickly.
23. **pommel . . . haft** hilt and hand guard.

Literary Analysis
Medieval Romance What note of realism does this paragraph strike?

Literary Analysis
Medieval Romance What note of fantasy does this paragraph strike?

**Reading Check**

What happens in the combat between Arthur and Mordred?

then he said to himself, "If I throw this rich sword in the water, thereof shall never come good, but harm and loss." And then Sir Bedivere hid Excalibur under a tree. And so, as soon as he might, he came again unto the King and said he had been at the water and had thrown the sword into the water.

"What saw thou there?" said the King.

"Sir," he said, "I saw nothing but waves and winds."

"That is untruly said of thee," said the King. "And therefore go thou lightly again and do my commandment; as thou art to me loved and dear, spare not, but throw it in."

Then Sir Bedivere returned again and took the sword in his hand. And yet him thought sin and shame to throw away that noble sword. And so eft[24] he hid the sword and returned again and told the King that he had been at the water and done his commandment.

"What sawest thou there?" said the King.

"Sir," he said, "I saw nothing but waters wap and waves wan."[25]

"Ah, traitor unto me and untrue," said King Arthur, "now hast thou betrayed me twice. Who would have weened that thou that has been to me so loved and dear, and thou art named a noble knight, and would betray me for the riches of this sword. But now go again lightly, for thy long tarrying putteth me in great jeopardy of my life, for I have taken cold. And but if thou do now as I bid thee, if ever I may see thee I shall slay thee mine own hands, for thou wouldest for my rich sword see me dead."

Then Sir Bedivere departed and went to the sword and lightly took it up, and so he went to the water's side; and there he bound the girdle about the hilts, and threw the sword as far into the water as he might. And there came an arm and an hand above the water and took it and clutched it, and shook it thrice and brandished; and then vanished away the hand with the sword into the water. So Sir Bedivere came again to the King and told him what he saw.

"Alas," said the King, "help me hence, for I dread me I have tarried overlong."

Then Sir Bedivere took the King upon his back and so went with him to that water's side. And when they were at the water's side, even fast[26] by the bank floated a little barge with many fair ladies in it;

▲ **Critical Viewing**
Compare the mood of this depiction of Arthur's departure with that of Malory's account. **[Compare and Contrast]**

Literary Analysis
Medieval Romance
What element does the appearance of the hand add to the tale?

---

24. **eft** again.
25. **waters . . . wan** waters lap and waves grow dark.
26. **fast** close.

and among them all was a queen; and all they had black hoods, and all they wept and shrieked when they saw King Arthur.

"Now put me into that barge," said the King; and so he did softly. And there received him three ladies with great mourning, and so they set them down. And in one of their laps King Arthur laid his head, and then the queen said, "Ah, my dear brother, why have ye tarried so long from me? Alas, this wound on your head hath caught over-much cold." And anon they rowed fromward the land, and Sir Bedivere beheld all those ladies go froward him.

Then Sir Bedivere cried and said, "Ah, my lord Arthur, what shall become of me, now ye go from me and leave me here alone among mine enemies?"

"Comfort thyself," said the King, "and do as well as thou mayest, for in me is no trust for to trust in. For I must into the vale of Avilion[27] to heal me of my grievous wound. And if thou hear nevermore of me, pray for my soul."

But ever the queen and ladies wept and shrieked, that it was pity to hear. And as soon as Sir Bedivere had lost sight of the barge he wept and wailed, and so took the forest and went all that night.

And in the morning he was ware, betwixt two bare woods, of a chapel and an hermitage. Then was Sir Bedivere glad, and thither he went, and when he came into the chapel he saw where lay an hermit groveling on all fours, close thereby a tomb was new dug. When the hermit saw Sir Bedivere he knew him well, for he was but little tofore Bishop of Canterbury, that Sir Mordred put to flight.

"Sirs," said Sir Bedivere, "what man is there here <u>interred</u> that you pray so fast for?"

"Fair son," said the hermit. "I wot not verily but by guessing. But this same night, at midnight, here came a number of ladies and brought here a dead corpse and prayed me to inter him. And here they offered an hundred tapers, and gave me a thousand gold coins."

"Alas," said Sir Bedivere, "that was my lord King Arthur, which lieth here buried in this chapel."

Then Sir Bedivere swooned, and when he awoke he prayed the hermit that he might abide with him still, there to live with fasting and prayers:

"For from hence will I never go," said Sir Bedivere, "by my will, but all the days of my life here to pray for my lord Arthur."

"Sir, ye are welcome to me," said the hermit, "for I know you better than ye think that I do: for ye are Sir Bedivere the Bold, and the full noble duke Sir Lucan the Butler was your brother."

Then Sir Bedivere told the hermit all as you have heard tofore, and so he stayed with the hermit that was beforehand Bishop of Canterbury. And there Sir Bedivere put upon him poor clothes, and served the hermit full lowly in fasting and in prayers.

Thus of Arthur I find no more written in books that been authorized, neither more of the very certainty of his death heard I nor read, but

Literary Analysis
Medieval Romance and Legend Does the description of Sir Bedivere's reaction sound more like a description you might find in a folk tale or in a modern short story? Explain.

interred (in turd´) v. buried

✓**Reading Check**
What happens after Sir Bedivere casts the sword in the water?

---

27. **Avilion** legendary island where Arthur is said to dwell until his return.

thus was he led away in a ship wherein were three queens; that one was King Arthur's sister, Queen Morgan le Fay, the other was the Queen of North Galis, and the third was the Queen of the Waste Lands.

Now more of the death of King Arthur could I never find, but that these ladies brought him to his grave, and such one was interred there which the hermit bare witness that was once Bishop of Canterbury. But yet the hermit knew not in certain that he was verily the body of King Arthur; for this tale Sir Bedivere, a knight of the Table Round, made it to be written.

Yet some men say in many parts of England that King Arthur is not dead, but carried by the will of our Lord Jesu into another place; and men say that he shall come again, and he shall win the Holy Cross. Yet I will not say that it shall be so, but rather I would say: here in this world he changed his life. And many men say that there is written upon the tomb this:

HIC IACET ARTHURUS, REX QUONDAM, REXQUE FUTURUS[28]

---

28. **HIC . . . FUTURUS** Here lies Arthur, who was once king and king will be again.

Review and Assess

Thinking About the Selection

1. **Respond:** If Arthur had asked you to throw his sword into the water, would you have hesitated? Why or why not?

2. **(a) Recall:** What warning does King Arthur receive in his dream? **(b) Recall:** How do circumstances frustrate his attempt to heed this warning? **(c) Interpret:** How does this series of events make the ending of the tale seem fated?

3. **(a) Recall:** What is the relationship between Mordred and Arthur? **(b) Interpret:** How does the conflict between them emphasize the theme of betrayal in the tale?

4. **(a) Compare and Contrast:** How does the description of Sir Lucan's death contrast with the speech in which Arthur bemoans his passing? **(b) Draw Conclusions:** What conclusions can you draw about the range of medieval taste in literature?

5. **(a) Recall:** How does Sir Bedivere respond when Arthur asks him to throw Excalibur in the water? **(b) Interpret:** What lesson about loyalty does the tale of Sir Bedivere and the sword suggest?

6. **Generalize:** At the tale's end, rightful authority has been betrayed and may yet return, but it is not here now. What idea of leadership and loyalty in the present does this ending suggest?

7. **Apply:** Do you think leaders are "Arthurs"—those who should receive perfect obedience—or should people sometimes question their leader's decisions? Explain.

Review and Assess

Literary Analysis
Medieval Romance

1. Identify three characteristics of Sir Gawain that make him an ideal hero for a **medieval romance.** Explain each answer.

2. (a) Identify one way in which Sir Gawain falls short of the ideals of chivalry. (b) What do his shortcomings suggest about the theme of human weakness in medieval romances?

3. In the excerpt from *Morte d'Arthur*, how do the supernatural events surrounding King Arthur's death link the story to the future?

Comparing Literary Works

4. Which of these elements of romance is least emphasized in *Sir Gawain*: chivalry, a far-off setting, the supernatural, adventure, or love? Explain. (b) Which is least emphasized in *Morte d'Arthur*?

5. What characteristics of a **legend** do the two selections share?

6. Identify a feature or section of each work that the writer may have added to the original legend. Explain your choices.

7. (a) Compare the characterization of Gawain in lines 459–477 of *Sir Gawain* with Malory's description of Bedivere as he reacts to Arthur's imminent death. Use a graphic organizer like the one below. (b) Explain which author has done more to add literary elements, such as plot twists, descriptions, and characterization.

	Gawain's Reactions	Bedivere's Reactions
What He Says		
What He Does		
What He Feels		

Reading Strategy
Summarizing

8. If you were retelling *Sir Gawain and the Green Knight* for an audience of fifth graders, which key events would you emphasize?

9. As Sir Bedivere, **summarize** for a curious traveler who is visiting your hermitage the events leading up to King Arthur's death.

Extend Understanding

10. **Contemporary Connection:** Explain why you think the legend of King Arthur has remained popular to this day.

Quick Review

Medieval romances are narratives featuring adventure, love, the supernatural, and the ideals of chivalry.

A **legend** is a traditional story telling of heroic figures or deeds, which may be based in fact.

To **summarize** a work or passage, identify and restate its main ideas.

 Take It to the Net
www.phschool.com

Take the interactive self-test online to check your understanding of these selections.

Integrate Language Skills

Vocabulary Development Lesson

Word Analysis: Root *-droit-*

The word *adroitly*, meaning "with skill," is based on the root *-droit-*, meaning "right." This root meaning reveals a historical bias toward right-handedness.

1. Given that the prefix *mal-* means "bad," what might *maladroit* mean?
2. *Gauche* means "socially maladroit." Which of these two might it also mean: "left" or "right"?

Spelling Strategy

The *-esse* in *largesse* comes from the English adaptation of medieval French spelling patterns. Using a dictionary, explain the influence the origin of the following words has had on their spelling.

1. finesse   2. knight   3. neighbor

Fluency: Definitions

For each word from the vocabulary list on page 161, write the letter of its definition.

1. assay: (a) test, (b) deny, (c) ignore
2. adjure: (a) reject, (b) request, (c) withhold
3. feigned: (a) asked, (b) refused, (c) pretended
4. adroitly: (a) rightly, (b) boldly, (c) skillfully
5. largesse: (a) nobility, (b) insignificance, (c) wisdom
6. righteous: (a) awkward, (b) virtuous, (c) dishonorable
7. entreated: (a) pleaded, (b) requested, (c) refused
8. peril: (a) safety, (b) security, (c) danger
9. interred: (a) kept, (b) delayed, (c) buried

Grammar and Style Lesson

Comparative and Superlative Forms

The **comparative form** of a modifier compares one thing with another. It is formed by adding *-er* to short modifiers and by using *more* with most modifiers of two or more syllables.

The **superlative form** compares more than two things. It is formed by adding *-est* to one-syllable modifiers and by using *most* with modifiers of two or more syllables.

Comparative Form: Grow green as the grass, and <u>greener</u>, it seemed. / Then green fused on gold <u>more glorious</u> by far.

Superlative Form: . . . thereupon sat King Arthur in the <u>richest</u> cloth of gold that might be made.

Practice Identify the comparative and superlative forms of modifiers in the following passages.

1. She made trial of a man most faultless by far. . . .
2. ". . . I am the weakest, well I know, and of wit feeblest; . . ."
3. "And the loss of my life would be least of any; . . ."
4. ". . . he would have helped me that had more need of help than I."
5. Thus of Arthur I find no more written in books that [have] been authorized, . . .

Writing Application Use comparatives and superlatives to compare characters from the selections.

Writing Lesson

Interior Monologue

As Sir Gawain approaches the Green Chapel, he reacts in a monologue. In an **interior monologue,** a character speaks only to himself to reveal thoughts and feelings. Write a monologue in which Gawain reacts to another event in the story. In your monologue, create a distinctive voice as you develop Gawain's situation. Consider having Gawain react to unfolding events, giving your monologue narrative interest.

Prewriting   List characteristics of Gawain, and jot down notes on the dramatic situation he is confronting.

Drafting   Writing in the first person, have Gawain "discuss" the situation with himself. Make sure that key details explaining the situation emerge early in your draft. Refer to your prewriting notes to ensure that you clearly convey Gawain's character. Have Gawain's reactions help tell the story to readers.

Model: Using Reactions to Develop a Situation

By St. Peter's sail, will no one answer this strange knight's challenge? I would, forsooth, were it not presumptuous-seeming and—what! Arthur himself is answering!

> When Gawain interrupts himself to remark on a new disturbance, the reader sees the situation through the character's reactions.

Revising   Star sections of your draft in which Gawain's feelings are especially strong. Review these passages, replacing dull phrases with vivid expressions of his personality or reactions.

WG *Prentice Hall Writing and Grammar Connection: Chapter 5, Section 2*

Extension Activities

Listening and Speaking Write a **proposal for a multimedia presentation** on Arthurian legends. Discuss using materials such as these:

- Clips from movies
- Reproductions of fine art
- Computer games
- Audio excerpts of songs and music
- Graphics, such as maps and charts

Explain which type of media would be most effective in conveying each major idea or theme.

Research and Technology With a group, research and give a brief **oral report** on medieval illuminated manuscripts. Use a variety of strategies for research, such as Internet searches and interviews with experts at a museum. Based on your research, draw conclusions about medieval trade, lifestyles, and values. **[Group Activity]**

 **Take It to the Net**   www.phschool.com

Go online for an additional research activity using the Internet.

Prepare to Read

Letters of Margaret Paston ◆ Four Ballads

Margaret Paston (1423–1484)

Brokering deals, managing staff, fighting lawsuits—tasks like these challenge today's top executives. Yet, in fifteenth-century England, they fell to Margaret Paston simply because her family owned land.

Margaret Paston, born Margaret Mautby, came to these responsibilities through her marriage to John Paston, a lawyer and son of a well-to-do landowner. The Paston family, having recently emerged from the upper segment of the peasantry, was eager to increase its landholdings and rise in society. Just holding onto their estates, though, proved to be a challenge. The Pastons lived in a time of social turmoil and violence. They were sued, threatened, and bullied over the years by those who wanted their holdings.

Throughout the Pastons' married life, John Paston was frequently called away to London on business for his law practice. As a result, Margaret was left to run the estates, settle rent disputes, and defend their manors against takeovers—which she did admirably.

The Legacy of the Pastons While John was away, he and Margaret exchanged letters frequently. In the letters, the Pastons often discuss the everyday business of running an estate as well as local political matters, providing historians with a detailed insight into the life of the times. Sometimes, the letters read like a medieval soap opera, as when they tell of the secret marriage of one daughter to the family's bailiff and the marriage of another daughter to her father's rival's son.

The letters between the Pastons are part of a collection of more than 1,000 papers. Although they were originally preserved as evidence for impending lawsuits, today they offer us an invaluable, vivid glimpse into fifteenth-century life.

Folk Ballads

Long before most people in Britain could read or write, they listened to ballads. A ballad is a song or poem that tells a story in short verses and simple words. Much like modern country-western songs, medieval ballads tell of the fate of lovers (usually tragic), of sensational crimes, of the dangers of the working life, and of historical disasters.

The Ballad's Origins The first folk ballads in England may have appeared during the twelfth century. Ballads were passed along orally for many centuries. As a result, they were subject to constant variation in both text and tune, as singers' memories altered or as they added ideas.

Most ballads consist of a sixteen-bar melody with two beats to the measure. Consistency among ballads emerged in the fifteenth century as people wrote them down.

Border Ballads The ballads in this grouping originated in the rugged border region between England and Scotland. Their language is a Scots dialect of English. Folk ballads typically thrived in areas such as the Border, where a formal, written literature had yet to develop.

Ballads and Literature Ballads did eventually join the literary tradition. In 1765, ballad enthusiast Bishop Thomas Percy published *Reliques of Ancient English Poetry*, an extensive collection of ballads. People then began to appreciate the ballads for their literary value as well as for the fascinating glimpses they offered into life in the past. Percy's collection even had its own dramatic story. Just as a housemaid was about to light a fire with an old manuscript, Percy intervened, saving a collection of treasures from the past. Later poets, and even contemporary songwriters such as American Bob Dylan, have drawn on this rich tradition.

Preview

Connecting to the Literature

Trouble always moves people to words: asking for advice, calling for assistance, or just seeking the comfort of talk. In her letters, Margaret Paston talks about her troubles—and what she has done about them.

Literary Analysis

Letter and Folk Ballad

A **letter** addresses a specific person or group and is meant to be read within a specific time. The best letters preserve a moment of life. As you read Paston's letters, note what they reveal about medieval times.

A **folk ballad,** is a narrative poem, intended to be sung and without a known author. While some ballads are humorous, many starkly insist on the doom that haunts our loves and lives. Most ballads use these features:

- Four-line stanzas in which the second and fourth lines rhyme
- Repeated key phrases or a regularly repeated section, called a refrain
- Dialogue

As you read the ballads, note the views of life they express.

Comparing Literary Works

In different ways—by recording a local event or by expressing a common attitude—letters and ballads can serve as **primary sources**—documents from the past that report or indicate events or values of the time. Primary sources include letters, inscriptions, legal documents, and songs. Compare the information these selections offer about medieval life.

Reading Strategy

Understanding Dialect

A **dialect** is a form of a language, spoken by people in a particular region or group. To understand the Scottish-English dialect of these ballads, read unfamiliar words aloud. Their sound and context may lead you to the corresponding current English word. Also, consult footnotes for guidance. To help you decode dialect, use a chart like the one here.

Phrase in Dialect	The wind sae cauld blew…
Meaning Suggested	**sound:** cauld = cold **context:** How does the wind blow?
Meaning Given in Footnote	

Vocabulary Development

aldermen (ôl′ dər mən) *n.* chief officers in a shire, or district (p. 191)

enquiry (en kwīr′ ē) *n.* question; investigation (p. 191)

succor (suk′ ər) *v.* help; aid; relieve (p. 191)

certify (sʉrt′ ə fī′) *v.* declare a thing true or accurate; verify; attest (p. 191)

remnant (rem′ nənt) *n.* what is left over; remainder; residue (p. 191)

ransacked (ran′ sakt′) *v.* searched through for plunder; pillaged; robbed (p. 192)

asunder (ə sun′ dər) *adv.* into parts or pieces (p. 192)

assault (ə sôlt′) *v.* violently attack (p. 192)

Letters of *Margaret Paston*

Margaret Paston

Background

His father, King Henry V, had brought much of France under English rule, but Henry VI's weakness as a ruler plunged England into chaos. Some English nobles took advantage of his weak government, terrorizing the countryside with small armies. Overseas, the French fought to regain their lands, while back in England a power struggle broke out for the throne. The House of York, a noble family, disputed the right of Henry's family, the House of Lancaster, to rule. Eventually, their quarrel plunged the country into the Wars of the Roses. In the midst of this upheaval and uncertainty, many families such as the Pastons were able to rise from poverty by taking properties to which they had a questionable (or at least easily challenged) legal claim.

Hellesdon, one of the Paston manors, was coveted by the Duke of Suffolk. The duke bribed the mayor of Norwich, a town northeast of London, to assist him in launching a campaign of terror to force the Pastons to surrender their property. Although Margaret Paston, along with a garrison of sixty, successfully repelled the first attacks, Hellesdon eventually was seized and plundered by the duke. In the first two letters, Margaret writes to her husband in London with the news.

Margaret Paston to John Paston
17 October 1465
Norwich

. . . The Duke came to Norwich on Tuesday at 10 o'clock with some 500 men. And he sent for the mayor and <u>aldermen</u> with the Sheriffs, desiring them in the King's name that they should make <u>enquiry</u> of the constables of every ward in the City as to what men had gone to help or <u>succor</u> your men at any time during these gatherings and, if they could find any, that they should take and arrest and correct them, and <u>certify</u> to him the names by 8 o'clock on Wednesday. Which the Mayor did and will do anything that he may for him and his men. . . .

I am told that the old Lady [the Dowager Duchess] and the Duke are fiercely set against us on the information of Harleston, the bailiff of Costessey . . . and such other false shrews which would have this matter carried through for their own pleasure. . . . And as for Sir John Heveningham, Sir John Wingfield and other worshipful men, they are but made their doggebolds [lackeys], which I suppose will cause their disworship hereafter. I spoke with Sir John Heveningham and informed him of the truth of the matter and of all our demeaning at Drayton, and he said he would that all things were well, and that he would inform my Lord what I told him, but that Harleston had all the influence with the Duke here, and at this time he was advised by him and Dr. Aleyn.

The lodge and the <u>remnant</u> of your place was beaten down on Tuesday and Wednesday and the Duke rode on Wednesday to Drayton and so forth to Costessey while the lodge at Hellesdon was being beaten down. And this night at midnight Thomas Slyforth . . . and others had a cart and fetched away featherbeds and all our stuff that was left at the parson's and Thomas Waters' house to be kept. . . . I pray you send me word how I shall act—whether you wish that I abide at Caister or come to you at London. . . .

Margaret Paston to John Paston
27 October 1465
Norwich

. . . Please you to know that I was at Hellesdon on Thursday last and saw the place there, and, in good faith, nobody would believe how foul and horrible it appears unless they saw it. There come many people daily to wonder at it, both from Norwich and many other

◀ Critical Viewing
The Pastons' manors were often attacked by their enemies. Judging from this photograph of a manor house, how easy would it have been to defend such a manor? Explain. **[Speculate]**

---

aldermen (ôl′ dər mən) *n.* chief officers in a shire, or district

enquiry (en kwir′ ē) *n.* question; investigation

succor (suk′ ər) *v.* help; aid; relieve

certify (surt′ ə fī′) *v.* declare a thing true or accurate; verify; attest

remnant (rem′ nənt) *n.* what is left over; remainder; residue

✓Reading Check

What has the Duke done against the Pastons?

places, and they speak of it with shame. The Duke would have been a £1000 better off if it had not happened, and you have the more good will of the people because it was so foully done. They made your tenants of Hellesdon and Drayton, with others, break down the walls of both the place and the lodge—God knows full much against their wills, but they dare not refuse for fear. I have spoken with your tenants of Hellesdon and Drayton and comforted them as well as I can. The Duke's men <u>ransacked</u> the church and bore away all the goods that were left there, both of ours and of the tenants, and even stood upon the high altar and ransacked the images and took away those that they could find, and put the parson out of the church till they had done, and ransacked every man's house in the town five or six times. . . . As for lead, brass, pewter, iron, doors, gates and other stuff of the house, men from Costessey and Cawston have it, and what they might not carry away they have hewn <u>asunder</u> in the most spiteful manner. . . .

At the reverence of God, if any worshipful and profitable settlement may be made in your matters, do not forsake it, to avoid our trouble and great costs and charges that we may have and that may grow hereafter. . . .

———◆◇◆———

The following letter was sent to Sir John Paston, Margaret's knighted son. Caister, a castle with many manors and estates, had been willed to the Paston family by Sir John Fastolf, for whom John Paston worked as financial advisor. There followed years of legal wrangles during which the Pastons faced numerous challenges to the will. Because her husband had died the year before, Margaret turned to her son Sir John for help defending Caister. Sir John sent his younger brother, also named John, to protect the castle. John failed, however, surrendering the castle after his protector, King Edward IV, was captured during the Wars of the Roses.

———◆◇◆———

Margaret Paston to Sir John Paston
11 July 1467
Norwich

. . . Also this day was brought me word from Caister that Rising of Fritton had heard in divers places in Suffolk that Fastolf of Cowhawe gathers all the strength he may and intends to <u>assault</u> Caister and to enter there if he may, insomuch that it is said that he has five score men ready and daily sends spies to know what men guard the place. By whose power or favor or support he will do this I know not, but you know well that I have

ransacked (ran′ sakt′) *v.* searched through for plunder; pillaged; robbed

asunder (ə sun′ dər) *adv.* into parts or pieces

assault (ə sôlt′) *v.* violently attack

Literature in context *History Connection*

Land Rights

When the Pastons struggled to retain their land, they were fighting history. In the Middle Ages, land ownership was bound up with social privilege, and laws kept large tracts of land in the hands of aristocrats. Even if a nobleman wanted to sell a small part of his land to a lower-class family, he could not: Inheritance laws forbade aristocrats from dividing up their estates. The Pastons were fortunate to live during a time of social turmoil, when the grip of tradition and law had been loosened. At the same time, the chaos of the day threatened their own hold on the lands they had acquired. For women such as Margaret Paston, the situation was especially difficult, since women had only limited rights to property.

been afraid there before this time, when I had other comfort than I had now: I cannot guide nor rule soldiers well and they set not by [do not respect] a woman as they should by a man. Therefore I would that you should send home your brothers or else Daubeney to take control and to bring in such men as are necessary for the safeguard of the place. . . . And I have been about my livelode to set a rule therein, as I have written to you, which is not yet all performed after my desire, and I would not go to Caister till I had done. I do not want to spend more days near thereabouts, if I can avoid it; so make sure that you send someone home to keep the place and when I have finished what I have begun I shall arrange to go there if it will do any good—otherwise I had rather not be there. . . .

. . . I marvel greatly that you send me no word how you do, for your enemies begin to grow right bold and that puts your friends in fear and doubt. Therefore arrange that they may have some comfort, so that they be not discouraged, for if we lose our friends, it will be hard in this troublous world to get them again . . .

Literary Analysis
Letter and Primary Sources What does this letter show about the position of medieval women?

Review and Assess

Thinking About the Selection

1. **Respond:** Would you have liked Margaret Paston? Why?

2. **(a) Recall:** What has the Duke done at Hellesdon?
   (b) Draw Conclusions: Explain what Margaret Paston's references to those who aid the Duke and her conversation with Sir Heveningham show about the Pastons' relationship with the Duke.

3. **(a) Infer:** When the Duke forces the tenants to assist him, what effect does Margaret Paston hope his act will have?
   (b) Draw Conclusions: What do Margaret Paston's actions among the tenants show about the relationship she wants to have with the lower classes?

4. **(a) Analyze:** To what extent does Margaret Paston use emotional appeals in her requests for help to her husband and son? To what extent does she use reason? **(b) Draw Conclusions:** What were relations like among the Paston family?

5. **(a) Generalize:** What do the letters suggest to you about life in the Middle Ages? **(b) Evaluate:** What do you think is the most important difference, positive or negative, between life then and life today? Why?

6. **Apply:** What professions today involve tasks comparable to those performed by the Pastons? Explain your answer.

Twa Corbies

Background

During the Middle Ages, death before the age of thirty-five was the norm. The stark facts of mortality intruded on any medieval picture of life, and it promoted the unsentimentalized outlook of medieval folk ballads. Ballads tell of adventure, love, and disaster with an unflinching attention to the limits of life and the dangerous depths of passion.

As I was walking all alane,
I heard twa corbies[1] making a mane.[2]
The tane unto the tither did say,
"Whar sall we gang and dine the day?"

5 "In behint yon auld fail dyke,[3]
I wot[4] there lies a new-slain knight;
And naebody kens[5] that he lies there
But his hawk, his hound, and his lady fair.

"His hound is to the hunting gane,
10 His hawk to fetch the wild-fowl hame,
His lady's ta'en anither mate,
So we may mak our dinner sweet.

"Ye'll sit on his white hause-bane,[6]
And I'll pike out his bonny blue e'en;[7]
15 Wi' ae lock o' his gowden hair
We'll theek[8] our nest when it grows bare.

"Mony a one for him maks mane,
But nane sall ken whar he is gane.
O'er his white banes, when they are bare,
20 The wind sall blaw for evermair."

▲ **Critical Viewing**
Compare the feelings evoked by the ravens shown with those evoked by the "twa corbies."
[Compare and Contrast]

1. **twa corbies** two ravens.
2. **mane** moan.
3. **fail dyke** bank of earth.
4. **wot** know.
5. **kens** knows.
6. **hause-bane** neck-bone.
7. **e'en** eyes.
8. **theek** thatch.

Lord Randall

"O where hae ye been, Lord Randall, my son?
O where hae ye been, my handsome young man?"
"I hae been to the wild wood; mother, make my bed soon,
For I'm weary wi' hunting, and fain¹ wald² lie down."

5   "Where gat ye your dinner, Lord Randall, my son?
Where gat ye your dinner, my handsome young man?"
"I dined wi' my true-love; mother, make my bed soon,
For I'm weary wi' hunting, and fain wald lie down."

"What gat ye to your dinner, Lord Randall, my son?
10 What gat ye to your dinner, my handsome young man?"
"I gat eels boil'd in broo;³ mother, make my bed soon,
For I'm weary wi' hunting, and fain wald lie down."

"What became of your bloodhounds, Lord Randall, my son?
What became of your bloodhounds, my handsome young man?"
15 "O they swell'd and they died; mother, make my bed soon,
For I'm weary wi' hunting, and fain wald lie down."

"O I fear ye are poison'd, Lord Randall, my son!
O I fear ye are poison'd, my handsome young man!"
"O yes! I am poison'd; mother, make my bed soon,
20 For I'm sick at the heart, and I fain wald lie down."

---

1. **fain** gladly.   2. **wald** would.   3. **broo** broth.

Reading Strategy
Understanding Dialect
Use sound, context, and a footnote to give the modern equivalents of "gat ye to your dinner" and "boil'd in broo."

Review and Assess
Thinking About the Selections

1. **Infer:** In "Twa Corbies," what does the ravens' discussion of the knight's animals and lady suggest about his fate?

2. **Interpret:** What do the images of the knight's hair and the wind across his bones suggest about the effect of death on identity?

3. **(a) Infer:** In "Lord Randall," who has caused Lord Randall to feel sick? **(b) Interpret:** What two meanings might line 20 have?

4. **(a) Analyze:** How might love itself be like a poison? **(b) Draw Conclusions:** What idea of love does "Lord Randall" express?

5. **Evaluate:** These poems are about extraordinary situations. Are their messages relevant to ordinary life? Explain.

Get Up and Bar the Door

It fell about the Martinmas time,[1]
    And a gay time it was then,
When our goodwife got puddings to make,
    She's boild them in the pan.

5   The wind sae cauld blew south and north.
    And blew into the floor;
Quoth our goodman to our goodwife,
    "Gae out and bar the door."

"My hand is in my hussyfskap,[2]
10   Goodman, as ye may see;
An it should nae be barrd this hundred year,
    It's no be barrd for me."[3]

They made a paction[4] tween them twa.
    They made it firm and sure.
15 That the first word whaeer shoud speak,
    Shoud rise and bar the door.

Then by there came two gentlemen,
    At twelve o'clock at night,
And they could neither see house nor hall,
20   Nor coal nor candlelight.

"Now whether is this a rich man's house,
    Or whether it is a poor?"
But neer a word wad ane o' them[5] speak,
    For barring of the door.

---

1. **Martinmas time** November 11.
2. **hussyfskap** household duties.
3. **An it should . . . me** "If it has to be barred by me, then it will not be barred in a hundred years."
4. **paction** agreement.
5. **them** the man and his wife.

▲ Critical Viewing

What does this painting tell you about domestic life in medieval times? **[Infer]**

Literary Analysis

Folk Ballad How does the rhyme scheme of lines 17–20 illustrate the typical ballad stanza?

25 And first they[6] ate the white puddings,
   And then they ate the black:
Tho muckle[7] thought the goodwife to hersel,
   Yet neer a word she spake.

   Then said the one unto the other,
30   "Here, man, take ye my knife;
   Do ye tak aff the auld man's beard,
      And I'll kiss the goodwife."

   "But there's nae water in the house,
      And what shall we do than?"
35 "What ails ye at the pudding broo,[8]
      That boils into[9] the pan?"

   O up then started our goodman,
      An angry man was he:
   "Will ye kiss my wife before my een,
40   And scad[10] me wi pudding bree?"[11]

   Then up and started our goodwife,
      Gied three skips on the floor:
   "Goodman, you've spoken the foremost word;
      Get up and bar the door."

---

6. **they** the strangers.
7. **muckle** much.
8. **What . . . broo** "What's the matter with pudding water?"
9. **into** in.
10. **scad** scald.
11. **bree** broth.

Reading Strategy
Understanding Dialect
Restate lines 30–31 in
modern English.

Literary Analysis
Folk Ballad Why might
listeners find this ballad
both amusing and
insightful?

Review and Assess

Thinking About the Selection

1. **Respond:** Whom do you like better—the goodman or the goodwife? Explain.

2. **(a) Recall:** What agreement do the goodman and his wife make? **(b) Analyze:** What are their main motives in making this agreement?

3. **(a) Summarize:** What new dilemma do the goodman and his wife face when the strangers arrive? **(b) Interpret:** In what sense does the wife "win"?

4. **Interpret:** What serious point about stubborness does the ballad make?

5. **Evaluate:** Which of the two characters is more foolish? Why?

Veronica Veronese, Dante Gabriel Rossetti, Delaware Art Museum

▲ **Critical Viewing** How does the artist's choice of color and the posture of
the subject suit the description of the fictional Barbara Allan? **[Interpret]**

Barbara Allan

It was in and about the Martinmas time,[1]
    When the green leaves were a-fallin';
That Sir John Graeme in the West Country
    Fell in love with Barbara Allan.

5 He sent his man down through the town
    To the place where she was dwellin':
"O haste and come to my master dear,
    Gin[2] ye be Barbara Allan."

O slowly, slowly rase[3] she up,
10   To the place where he was lyin',
And when she drew the curtain by:
    "Young man, I think you're dyin'."

"O it's I'm sick, and very, very sick,
    And 'tis a' for Barbara Allan."
15 "O the better for me ye sal[4] never be,
    Though your heart's blood were a-spillin'.

"O dinna ye mind,[5] young man," said she,
    "When ye the cups were fillin',
That ye made the healths gae round and round,
20   And slighted Barbara Allan?"

---

1. **Martinmas time** November 11.
2. **Gin** if.
3. **rase** rose.
4. **sal** shall.
5. **dinna ye mind** don't you remember.

Literary Analysis
Folk Ballad and Primary Sources What does the phrase "his man" tell you about the society of the time?

✔Reading Check
How does Barbara Allan react to Sir John's confession of love?

He turned his face unto the wall,
    And death with him was dealin':
"Adieu, adieu, my dear friends all,
    And be kind of Barbara Allan."

25 And slowly, slowly rase she up,
    And slowly, slowly left him;
And sighing said she could not stay,
    Since death of life had reft[6] him.

She had not gane a mile but twa,[7]
30   When she heard the dead-bell knellin',
And every jow[8] that the dead-bell ga'ed[9]
    It cried, "Woe to Barbara Allan!"

"O mother, mother, make my bed,
    O make it soft and narrow:
35 Since my love died for me today,
    I'll die for him tomorrow."

6. **reft** deprived.
7. **not . . . twa** gone but two miles.
8. **jow** stroke.
9. **ga'ed** made.

Literary Analysis
Folk Ballad What phrase repeated from earlier in the poem appears in lines 25–28?

Review and Assess

Thinking About the Selection

1. **Respond:** Which character—Sir John or Barbara Allan—do you find more sympathetic? Why?

2. **(a) Recall:** According to Sir John, why is he "sick, and very, very sick"? **(b) Recall:** What reason does Barbara Allan give for acting unconcerned about his plight? **(c) Interpret:** What is another reason she might put on a show of indifference?

3. **Interpret:** Do you think Barbara Allan was in love with Sir John before her visit, or do you think the knowledge that he is dying for her inspires her with love? Explain.

4. **(a) Analyze:** At what point does the ballad make you critical of Barbara Allan? **(b) Analyze:** At what point does it make you sympathize with her?

5. **(a) Support:** Explain how, in the poem, Barbara Allan's pride is an obstacle to her happiness in love. **(b) Support:** Explain how, in the poem, death is the ultimate expression of love.

6. **Evaluate:** Do you agree with the view of love in the poem, or do you think the view is too extreme? Explain.

Review and Assess

Literary Analysis

Letter and Folk Ballad

1. What does the content and style of Margaret Paston's **letters** reveal about the kind of life she led? Support your answer with examples.
2. What does the style of the letters reveal about family life in her time? Explain.
3. Choose two of the **ballads,** and explain how repetition and dialogue add to the drama of each.
4. Compare and contrast the theme of love in each of the folk ballads. Explain which show a lighter side of love and which, a darker side.

Comparing Literary Works

5. (a) What do both Paston's letters and the ballads suggest about violence in fifteenth-century society? (b) Explain which of these **primary sources** indicates the causes of violence at the time.
6. Use a Venn diagram like the one shown to compare the kinds of historical information you can find in Paston's letters and the ballads.

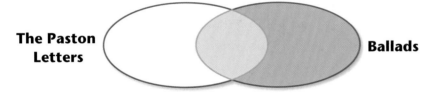

The Paston Letters   **Ballads**

7. If you were researching the roles of women in medieval times, which of these selections would be most effective as primary sources? Explain

Reading Strategy

Understanding Dialect

8. Identify the standard modern English words whose pronunciation is similar to the italicized **dialect** words: (a) And *naebody kens* that he lies there. . . . (b) But *neer* a word *wad ane* o' them speak, . . .
9. Find three other dialect words in the ballads, and explain the strategy you used to decode the meaning of each.

Extend Understanding

10. **History Connection:** What primary sources could a future historian use to reconstruct present-day life?

Quick Review

Letters are written for a specific audience on a specific occasion and usually contain a date, greeting, body, and closing.

A **folk ballad** is a traditional narrative poem meant to be sung.

Primary sources are documents, inscriptions, songs, and other records from the past that shed light on the time period when they were created.

Dialect is a distinctive form of a language, spoken by people in a particular region or group.

 Take It to the Net
www.phschool.com
Take the interactive self-test online to check your understanding of these selections.

Integrate Language Skills

Vocabulary Development Lesson

Word Analysis: Latin Root -cert-

Margaret Paston uses the phases "certify to him the names of. . . ." The root of *certify*, *-cert-*, comes from the Latin *certus*, which means "sure." *Certify* means "to make sure," or "to verify offically." Use your knowledge of the root *-cert-* to choose the best definition for the words that follow.

1. ascertain: (a) question, (b) sort through, (c) determine definitely
2. certificate: (a) written proof of qualifications, (b) bill for receipt of goods, (c) application form for a diploma
3. certitude: (a) vagueness, (b) sureness, (c) righteousness
4. certified: (a) guaranteed, (b) imprisoned, (c) doubtful

Fluency: Definitions

Match each vocabulary word with its definition.

1.	aldermen	a.	looted
2.	enquiry	b.	attack
3.	succor	c.	officials
4.	certify	d.	guarantee
5.	remnant	e.	remainder
6.	ransacked	f.	into pieces
7.	asunder	g.	assist
8.	assault	h.	investigation

Spelling Strategy

The ô sound in words may be spelled *au*, as in *assault*, *vault*, *cautious*, and *auction*. It is less commonly spelled *aw*, as in *awl* and *shawl*. Choose between these spellings to complete the following words.

1. f__lt
2. m__l
3. h__l
4. b__l

Grammar and Style Lesson

Direct Address

These folk ballads employ **direct address**—the use of a person's name or title or a descriptive phrase referring to the person when the speaker directly addresses someone.

> **Direct Address:** "O where hae ye been, <u>Lord Randall, my son?</u>"

In writing, terms of direct address are set off by commas. Direct address helps readers identify characters and adds drama by mimicking spoken language in which speakers may indicate strong feelings by calling someone by name.

Practice In your notebook, identify each phrase that serves as a term of direct address.

1. ". . . mother, make my bed soon, . . ."
2. "My hand is in my hussyfskap, / Goodman, as ye may see; . . ."
3. "Here, man, take ye my knife; . . . "
4. "O dinna ye mind, young man," said she, . . .
5. "Adieu, adieu, my dear friends all, / And be kind of Barbara Allan. . . . "

Writing Application Write a brief dialogue between Margaret Paston and her husband. Use at least three instances of direct address.

*W*G *Prentice Hall Writing and Grammar Connection: Chapter 27, Section 2*

Writing Lesson

Investigative Report

Margaret Paston's letters shed some light on life in fifteenth-century England. Draw three conclusions from her letters about events and life in her time. Then, check your conclusions in secondary sources. Write an investigative report in which you evaluate the accuracy and value of Paston's letters as a primary source.

Prewriting   Review the letters, and formulate three historical conclusions based on them. Then, do research to locate resources on the Paston letters and on fifteenth-century England.

Drafting   Begin your draft with background on the Paston letters. Introduce the three conclusions you have reached, and then explain what other sources indicated about your hypotheses. Conclude with an evaluation of the letters based on your investigation.

Revising   Review your draft, highlighting repetitious or out-of-sequence ideas. Cut or reorder these passages.

Model: Revising for Logical Organization

The Paston's claims to their land were easily disputed because of the family's lower class origins.

The question of whether the Pastons "really" owned their land is probably a false one. At the time, a claim to land depended on the goodwill of one's neighbors, who could easily argue that a person was a serf and so not entitled to own land. ←

> The circled detail belongs in the paragraph introduced by the topic sentence shown.

WG *Prentice Hall Writing and Grammar Connection: Chapter 13, Section 4*

Extension Activities

Research and Technology With a group, research the origins of several medieval holidays, such as Martinmas. Make a **holidays chart** that:

- Lists each holiday
- Describes the way in which it was celebrated
- Explains its origins

Incorporate graphics in your chart.
[Group Activity]

Listening and Speaking With a classmate, write and present a **phone conversation** between Margaret and John. Research English accents, and apply what you learn as you speak your parts.

 **Take It to the Net**   www.phschool.com

Go online for an additional research activity using the Internet.

Medieval literature has all the punch of a good television adventure series. Deception and betrayal, power and triumph make for exciting stories, whether written hundreds of years ago or today. From the legendary adventures of Malory's King Arthur to the real-life battles of Margaret Paston, perils and adventures abound in medieval literature.

Warrior Heroes Several memorable warrior heroes spring from the literature of the period, including Spain's El Cid and France's Roland, from *The Song of Roland*. In the *Niebelungenlied*, the Germanic hero Siegfried risks life and limb to claim his love, the princess Kriemhild. In order to marry Kriemhild, he must first win the hand of the maiden warrior Brunhild for Kriemhild's brother, Gunther. Disguised as Gunther, Siegfried wins Brunhild. The two couples marry, but when Brunhild discovers the trick, she seeks revenge. Kriemhild foolishly reveals Siegfried's vulnerable spot to Gunther's servant Hagen, and Siegfried's doom is sealed, as told in this excerpt. In the second half of the poem, though, Kriemhild avenges Siegfried.

The Nibelungenlied:
How Siegfried Was Slain *translated by A. T. Hatto*

*T*he fearless warriors Gunther and Hagen treacherously proclaimed a hunt in the forest where they wished to chase the boar, the bear, and the bison—and what could be more daring? Siegfried rode with their party in magnificent style. They took all manner of food with them; and it was while drinking from a cool stream that the hero was to lose his life at the instigation of Brunhild, King Gunther's queen.

Bold Siegfried went to Kriemhild while his and his companions' hunting-gear was being loaded onto the sumpters in readiness to cross the Rhine,[1] and she could not have been more afflicted. "God grant that I may see you well again, my lady," he said, kissing his dear wife, "and that your eyes may see me too. Pass the time pleasantly with your relations who are so kind to you, since I cannot stay with you at home."

Kriemhild thought of what she had told Hagen, but she dared not mention it and began to lament that she had ever been born. "I dreamt last night—and an ill-omened dream it was—" said lord Siegfried's noble queen, weeping with unrestrained passion, "that two boars chased you over the heath and the flowers were dyed with blood! How can I help weeping so? I stand in great dread of some attempt against your life.—What if we have offended any men who have the power to vent their malice on us? Stay away, my lord, I urge you."

"I shall return in a few days time, my darling. I know of no people here who bear me any hatred. Your kinsmen without exception wish me well, nor have I deserved otherwise of them."

"It is not so, lord Siegfried. I fear you will come to grief. Last night I had a sinister dream of how two mountains fell upon you and hid you from my sight! I shall suffer cruelly if you go away and leave me." But he clasped the noble woman in his arms and after kissing and caressing her fair person very tenderly, took his leave and went forthwith. Alas, she was never to see him alive again.

They rode away deep into the forest in pursuit of their sport. Gunther and his men were accompanied by numbers of brave knights, but Gernot and Giselher stayed at home. Ahead of the hunt many horses had crossed the Rhine laden with their bread, wine, meat, fish, and various other provisions such as a king of Gunther's wealth is bound to have with him.

The proud and intrepid hunters were told to set up their lodges on a spacious isle in the river on which they were to hunt, at the skirt of the greenwood over toward the spot where the game would have to break cover. Siegfried, too, had arrived there, and this was reported to the King. Thereupon the sportsmen everywhere manned their relays.[2]

"Who is going to guide us through the forest to our quarry, brave warriors?" asked mighty Siegfried.

---

1. **sumpters . . . Rhine** Sumpters are pack horses, and the Rhine River flows from eastern Switzerland north through Germany, then west through the Netherlands into the North Sea.
2. **relays** fresh horses to relieve tired ones.

Thematic Connection
Compare the role of dreams here and in *Morte d'Arthur.*

**Reading Check**

Who has planned the hunt on which Siegfried is going?

"Shall we split up before we start hunting here?" asked Hagen. "Then my lords and I could tell who are the best hunters on this foray into the woods. Let us share the huntsmen and hounds between us and each take the direction he likes—and then all honor to him that hunts best!" At this, the hunters quickly dispersed.

"I do not need any hounds," said lord Siegfried, "except for one tracker so well fleshed that he recognizes the tracks which the game leave through the wood: then we shall not fail to find our quarry."

An old huntsman took a good sleuth-hound and quickly led the lord to where there was game in abundance. The party chased everything that was roused from its lair, as good hunting-men still do today. Bold Siegfried of the Netherlands killed every beast that his hound started, for his hunter was so swift that nothing could elude him. Thus, versatile as he was, Siegfried outshone all the others in that hunt.

The very first kill was when he brought down a strong young tusker,[3] after which he soon chanced on an enormous lion. When his hound had roused it he laid a keen arrow to his bow and shot it so that it dropped in its tracks at the third bound. Siegfried's fellow-huntsmen acclaimed him for this shot. Next, in swift succession, he killed a wisent, an elk, four mighty aurochs,[4] and a fierce and monstrous buck—so well mounted was he that nothing, be it hart or hind, could evade him. His hound then came upon a great boar, and, as this turned to flee, the champion hunter at once blocked his path, bringing him to bay; and when in a trice the beast sprang at the hero in a fury, Siegfried slew him with his sword, a feat no other hunter could have performed with such ease. After the felling of this boar, the tracker was returned to his leash and Siegfried's splendid bag was made known to the Burgundians.

"If it is not asking too much, lord Siegfried," said his companions of the chase, "do leave some of the game alive for us. You are emptying the hills and woods for us today." At this the brave knight had to smile.

There now arose a great shouting of men and clamor of hounds on all sides, and the tumult grew so great that the hills and the forest reechoed with it—the huntsmen had unleashed no fewer than four and twenty packs! Thus, many beasts had to lose their lives there, since each of these hunters was hoping to bring it about that *he* should be given the high honors of the chase. But when mighty Siegfried appeared beside the campfire there was no chance of that.

The hunt was over, yet not entirely so. Those who wished to go to the fire brought the hides of innumerable beasts, and game in plenty—what loads of it they carried back to the kitchen to the royal retainers! And now the noble King had it announced to those fine hunters that he wished to take his repast, and there was one great blast of the horn to tell them that he was back in camp.

Thematic Connection
Compare Siegfried's prowess at the hunting with the virtues Gawain shows in *Gawain and the Green Knight*.

---

3. **tusker** (tusk´ ər) wild boar.
4. **wisent** (vē´ zant). . . **aurochs** (ô´ räks´) European bison and wild oxen.

◀ **Critical Viewing**
Like Siegfried, Gunther, and his men, the hunters in this picture seem to enjoy the sport as a group activity. What practical reason may they have had for hunting in a group? **[Infer]**

At this, one of Siegfried's huntsmen said: "Sir, I have heard a horn-blast telling us to return to our lodges.—I shall answer it." There was much blowing to summon the companions.

"Let us quit the forest, too," said lord Siegfried. His mount carried him at an even pace, and the others hastened away with him but with the noise of their going they started a savage bear, a very fierce beast.

"I shall give our party some good entertainment," he said over his shoulder. "Loose the hound, for I can see a bear which will have to come back to our lodges with us. It will not be able to save itself unless it runs very fast." The hound was unleashed, and the bear made off at speed. Siegfried meant to ride it down but soon found that his way was blocked and his intention thwarted, while the mighty

☑ **Reading Check**

What delays Siegfried on his return to the lodges?

Connections: from The Nibelungenlied ◆ 207

beast fancied it would escape from its pursuer. But the proud knight leapt from his horse and started to chase it on foot, and the animal, quite off its guard, failed to elude him. And so he quickly caught and bound it, without having wounded it at all—nor could the beast use either claws or teeth on the man. Siegfried tied it to his saddle, mounted his horse, and in his high-spirited fashion led it to the campfire in order to amuse the good knights.

And in what magnificent style Siegfried rode! He bore a great spear, stout of shaft and broad of head; his handsome sword reached down to his spurs; and the fine horn which this lord carried was of the reddest gold. Nor have I ever heard tell of a better hunting outfit: he wore a surcoat of costly black silk and a splendid hat of sable,[5] and you should have seen the gorgeous silken tassels on his quiver, which was covered in panther-skin for the sake of its fragrant odor![6] He also bore a bow so strong that apart from Siegfried any who wished to span it would have had to use a rack. His hunting suit was all of otter-skin, varied throughout its length with furs of other kinds from whose shining hair clasps of gold gleamed out on either side of this daring lord of the hunt. The handsome sword that he wore was Balmung, a weapon so keen and with such excellent edges that it never failed to bite when swung against a helmet. No wonder this splendid hunter was proud and gay. And (since I am bound to tell you all) know that his quiver was full of good arrows with gold mountings and heads a span[7] in width, so that any beast they pierced must inevitably soon die.

Thus the noble knight rode along, the very image of a hunting man. Gunther's attendants saw him coming and ran to meet him to take his horse—tied to whose saddle he led a mighty bear! On dismounting, he loosed the bonds from its muzzle and paws, whereupon all the hounds that saw it instantly gave tongue. The beast made for the forest and the people were seized with panic. Affrighted by the tumult, the bear strayed into the kitchen—and how the cooks scuttled from their fire at its approach! Many caldrons were sent flying and many fires were scattered, while heaps of good food lay among the ashes. Lords and retainers leapt from their seats, the bear became infuriated, and the King ordered all the hounds on their leashes to be loosed—and if all had ended well they would have had a jolly day! Bows and spears were no longer left idle, for the brave ones ran toward the bear, yet there were so many hounds in the way that none dared shoot. With the whole mountain thundering with people's cries the bear took to flight before the hounds and none could keep up with it but Siegfried, who ran it down and then dispatched it with his sword. The bear was later carried to the campfire, and all who had witnessed this feat declared that Siegfried was a very powerful man.

Thematic Connection
Compare Siegfried's social standing, as shown by his clothing, with that of a character in the ballads.

---

5. **surcoat . . . sable** (saˊ bəl) A surcoat is a loose, short cloak worn over armor, and sable is the costly fur of the marten.
6. **panther-skin . . . odor** The odor of panther skin was supposed to lure other animals and therefore help with the hunt.
7. **span** nine inches.

The proud companions were then summoned to table. There were a great many seated in that meadow. Piles of sumptuous dishes were set before the noble huntsmen, but the butlers who were to pour their wine were very slow to appear. Yet knights could not be better cared for than they and if only no treachery had been lurking in their minds those warriors would have been above reproach.

"Seeing that we are being treated to such a variety of dishes from the kitchen," said lord Siegfried, "I fail to understand why the butlers bring us no wine. Unless we hunters are better looked after, I'll not be a companion of the hunt. I thought I had deserved better attention."

"We shall be very glad to make amends to you for our present lack," answered the perfidious[8] King from his table. "This is Hagen's fault—he wants us to die of thirst."

"My very dear lord," replied Hagen of Troneck, "I thought the day's hunting would be away in the Spessart and so I sent the wine there. If we go without drink today I shall take good care that it does not happen again."

"Those fellows!" said lord Siegfried. "It was arranged that they were to bring along seven panniers of spiced wine and mead[9] for me. Since that proved impossible, we should have been placed nearer the Rhine."

"You brave and noble knights," said Hagen of Troneck, "I know a cool spring nearby—do not be offended!—let us go there."—A proposal which (as it turned out) was to bring many knights into jeopardy.

Siegfried was tormented by thirst and ordered the board to be removed all the sooner in his eagerness to go to that spring at the foot of the hills. And now the knights put their treacherous plot into execution.

Word was given for the game which Siegfried had killed to be conveyed back to Worms on wagons, and all who saw it gave him great credit for it.

Hagen of Troneck broke his faith with Siegfried most grievously, for as they were leaving to go to the spreading lime-tree he said: "I have often been told that no one can keep up with Lady Kriemhild's lord when he cares to show his speed. I wish he would show it us now."

"You can easily put it to the test by racing me to the brook," replied gallant Siegfried of the Netherlands. "Then those who see it shall declare the winner."

"I accept your challenge," said Hagen.

"Then I will lie down in the grass at your feet, as a handicap," replied brave Siegfried, much to Gunther's satisfaction. "And I will tell you what more I shall do. I will carry all my equipment with me, my spear and my shield and all my hunting clothes." And he quickly strapped on his quiver and sword. The two men took off their outer clothing and stood there in their white vests. Then they ran through the clover like a pair of wild panthers. Siegfried appeared first at the brook.

---

8. **perfidious** (pər fid´ ē əs) *adj.* treacherous.
9. **panniers** (pan´ yərz) . . . **mead** (mēd) Panniers are baskets, and mead is an alcoholic liquor made of fermented honey and water.

Thematic Connection
Compare Gunther and Hagen's plotting with Arthur's plans before battle in *Morte d'Arthur*. Draw a conclusion about politics and trust in medieval society.

Thematic Connection
What other contests appear in the medieval romances in this section?

**Reading Check**

What challenge from Hagen does Siegfried accept?

Gunther's magnificent guest who excelled so many men in all things quickly unstrapped his sword, took off his quiver, and after leaning his great spear against a branch of the lime, stood beside the rushing brook. Then he laid down his shield near the flowing water, and although he was very thirsty he most courteously refrained from drinking until the King had drunk. Gunther thanked him very ill for this.

The stream was cool, sweet, and clear. Gunther stooped to its running waters and after drinking stood up and stepped aside. Siegfried in turn would have liked to do the same, but he paid for his good manners. For now Hagen carried Siegfried's sword and bow beyond his reach, ran back for the spear, and searched for the sign on the brave man's tunic. Then, as Siegfried bent over the brook and drank, Hagen hurled the spear at the cross, so that the hero's heart's blood leapt from the wound and splashed against Hagen's clothes. No warrior will ever do a darker deed. Leaving the spear fixed in Siegfried's heart, he fled in wild desperation, as he had never fled before from any man.

When lord Siegfried felt the great wound, maddened with rage he bounded back from the stream with the long shaft jutting from his heart. He was hoping to find either his bow or his sword, and, had he succeeded in doing so, Hagen would have had his pay. But finding no sword, the gravely wounded man had nothing but his shield. Snatching this from the bank he ran at Hagen, and King Gunther's vassal was unable to elude him. Siegfried was wounded to death, yet he struck so powerfully that he sent many precious stones whirling from the shield as it smashed to pieces. Gunther's noble guest would dearly have loved to avenge himself. Hagen fell reeling under the weight of the blow and the riverside echoed loudly. Had Siegfried had his sword in his hand it would have been the end of Hagen, so enraged was the wounded man, as indeed he had good cause to be.

The hero's face had lost its color and he was no longer able to stand. His strength had ebbed away, for in the field of his bright countenance he now displayed Death's token. Soon many fair ladies would be weeping for him.

The lady Kriemhild's lord fell among the flowers, where you could see the blood surging from his wound. Then—and he had cause—he rebuked those who had plotted his foul murder. "You vile cowards," he said as he lay dying. "What good has my service done me now that you have slain me? I was always loyal to you, but now I have paid for it. Alas, you have wronged your kinsmen so that all who are born in days to come will be dishonored by your deed. You have cooled your anger on me beyond all measure. You will be held in contempt and stand apart from all good warriors."

▲ **Critical Viewing**
What aspects of the scene does the artist emphasize? What does he omit? What conclusion can you draw based on his choices?
[Draw Conclusions]

The knights all ran to where he lay wounded to death. It was a sad day for many of them. Those who were at all loyal-hearted mourned for him, and this, as a gay and valiant knight, he had well deserved.

The King of Burgundy too lamented Siegfried's death.

"There is no need for the doer of the deed to weep when the damage is done," said the dying man. "He should be held up to scorn. It would have been better left undone."

"I do not know what you are grieving for," said Hagen fiercely. "All our cares and sorrows are over and done with. We shall not find many who will dare oppose us now. I am glad I have put an end to his supremacy."

"You may well exult," said Siegfried. "But had I known your murderous bent I should easily have guarded my life from you. I am sorry for none so much as my wife, the lady Kriemhild. May God have mercy on me for ever having got a son who in years to come will suffer the reproach that his kinsmen were murderers. If I had the strength I would have good reason to complain. But if you feel at all inclined to do a loyal deed for anyone, noble King," continued the mortally wounded man, "let me commend my dear sweetheart to your mercy. Let her profit from being your sister. By the virtue of all princes, stand by her loyally! No lady was ever more greatly wronged through her dear friend. As to my father and his vassals, they will have long to wait for me."

The flowers everywhere were drenched with blood. Siegfried was at grips with Death, yet not for long, since Death's sword ever was too sharp. And now the warrior who had been so brave and gay could speak no more.

When those lords saw that the hero was dead they laid him on a shield that shone red with gold, and they plotted ways and means of concealing the fact that Hagen had done the deed. "A disaster has befallen us," many of them said. "You must all hush it up and declare with one voice that Siegfried rode off hunting alone and was killed by robbers as he was passing through the forest."

"I shall take him home," said Hagen of Troneck. "It is all one to me if the woman who made Brunhild so unhappy should come to know of it. It will trouble me very little, however much she weeps."

Connecting Literature Around the World

1. (a) What do you learn about Siegfried's character from the chase and killing the bear? (b) What does his death scene show about the values of his culture?

2. In "How Siegfried Was Slain," love comes hand in hand with danger: for example, Brunhild's passion for Siegfried provokes her to instigate his murder. Choose an English ballad to compare with "How Siegfried Was Slain," exploring the idea of love and danger in both works.

The Nibelungenlied

The epic poem the *Nibelungenlied* is one of the great works of Germanic literature. The title means "Song of the Nibelungs, or Burgundians," the people among whom it is set.

Composed in the thirteenth century by an unknown Austrian, the poem's themes of betrayal, forgiveness, and salvation still resonate for modern readers. The basic story derives from Old Norse traditions; forms of the story appear in the collections of Germanic and Norse literature called the Eddas. Its anonymous author integrated these various stories and traditions into a unified epic work. It has influenced German literature for centuries.

Writing About Literature

Analyzing Literary Periods

In the Middle Ages, what one's father did for a living, or whom one married, determined one's place in a complex social hierarchy. From peasants to kings, from monks to warriors, characters in romances, ballads, and epics reflect the rigid social structure of their time. Their actions and thoughts are often determined by what is expected of them: A hero responds courageously, and a wife loves devotedly. Write an essay that explains whether or not characters of the Middle Ages ever break the boundaries of their roles and exhibit individuality. Refer to the box at right for the specific details of the assignment.

Prewriting

Find a focus. To respond to the question, think about the medieval characters you have encountered in the unit. Answer the following questions to help you evaluate each of them.

- What is the character's social position?
- What were the expectations for that position during this period?
- How do the character's thoughts, words, and actions reflect his or her social role?
- Do any of the character's thoughts, words, or actions reflect a unique personality? Does the character have an individual difficulty with or question about his or her role?

Review at least four or five characters, writing your notes in a chart like the one shown. Then, choose the three characters that best support your ideas about individuality in the Middle Ages.

Model: Listing to Find a Focus

Character	Social Position	Elements Reflecting Social Position	Elements Reflecting Individuality
Beowulf in *Beowulf*	Warrior/ Hero	He acts heroically. He protects his followers.	As a young man, he boasts. As an older man, he is more humble.

Gather details. After you choose the characters you will discuss, return to the text and gather details about their words, thoughts, and actions. Look for specific passages you may want to quote. Pay special attention to sections in which characters reflect on themselves or in which they act in a defining way.

Write a working thesis. Your thesis summarizes your response to the question. Writing your thesis as you collect details will focus your search. As you think more about a topic, you can modify your thesis.

Assignment: Individuality in Medieval Characters

Are characters in medieval literature solely defined by their role in society, or do they also exhibit signs of individuality? Write an analytical essay in which you explain your response using at least three examples from this unit.

Criteria:

- Include a thesis statement that summarizes your response to the essay question.
- Analyze three characters from different works in this unit.
- Approximate length: 1,500 words.

Read to Write

As you reread the texts, look for characters that behave in unexpected ways. Are they stepping outside their social roles?

Drafting

Organize. A logical organization connects your ideas. It can also strengthen your argument. For example, you could discuss the characters in chronological order, but a thematic order would sharpen your response. Prepare an outline to help you adjust your organization and ensure that you include all of your best ideas in your first draft.

Model: Using a Logical Organization

I. **Little individuality:** Beowulf is defined by his role as a hero.

II. **Some individuality:** Gawain doesn't always live up to the role of knight.

III. **Lots of individuality:** The responses of the wife in "The Wife's Lament" are vivid and individual.

Provide support. As you draft, include quotations from works to support each major point you make. For each quotation, write a clause or sentence showing its relevance to the idea you are illustrating.

Revising and Editing

Review content: Check your analysis for thoroughness. Review your exploration of each character. Make sure that you have included enough insights to offer a complete analysis.

Review style: Use transitions to link ideas. If your sentences sound choppy and disconnected, consider combining some of them.

Choppy	Revised
The wife acts according to her role. She waits patiently. It tortures her. She appears to be the model medieval wife. Her attitude is individual.	The wife acts according to her role, waiting patiently although it tortures her. Though she might appear to be the model medieval wife, her attitude is in fact individual.

Publishing and Presenting

Give a lecture. Develop a brief talk to share the ideas you have developed in your essay. You might prepare a character chart for display to help your audience follow your analysis. Be sure to provide time for your listeners to ask questions.

Prentice Hall Writing and Grammar Connection: Chapter 14

Write to Learn

An outline is a guide, not a prison. Your writing may take an unexpected turn as you start drafting. Follow your new ideas. You can review your fresh thoughts for accuracy and relevance when you revise.

Write to Explain

Make sure that you explain why each of your examples supports your thesis.

Writing WORKSHOP

Narration: Autobiographical Narrative

An **autobiographical narrative** is a work in which the writer tells a story from his or her life. In this workshop, you will write a narrative relating a significant incident that happened to you or to someone important to you.

Assignment Criteria Your narrative should have the following elements:

- Characters, with a focus on one main character
- A setting with specifically located scenes and incidents
- A sequence of events that forms a plot
- Conflict or tension between characters or between a character and another force
- Insights that the main character gained from the experience

To preview the criteria on which your narrative may be assessed, see the Rubric on page 217.

Prewriting

Choose a topic. Select an event or incident that marks a significant change or insight—for example, an event that gave you or someone you know a new way of looking at life. The strongest narratives involve a conflict and its resolution.

- If you want to write about an incident that happened to you, you might list events from your life and select a memorable one.
- If you are writing about a person in your life, choose an incident that reveals something meaningful about him or her.

Pace the action. As you collect details, categorize them according to the part of the story to which they belong. Make sure you gather enough details to cover all important parts of the story. Approximate how much space and emphasis you will give to elements such as background information, setting, the event itself, and any lessons learned. The plan at right works for many narratives.

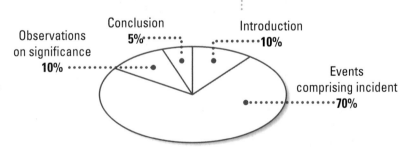

Conclusion 5%

Observations on significance 10%

Introduction 10%

Events comprising incident 70%

Flesh out the setting and characters. To enliven your narrative, list concrete details you will include. Sensory images will convey the sights, sounds, and smells of scenes. Details recording characters' acts, movements, thoughts, words, and gestures will add depth and realism.

Student Model

Before you begin drafting your narrative, read this student model and review the characteristics of a powerful narrative.

Mircea Vlaicu
Palm Springs, CA

A Toast to the Future

I came to this country on a plane. Just a kid, not even eight years old yet, I sat on the center aisle of a huge 747 in Chicago waiting to fly to Los Angeles. These names—Chicago, Los Angeles—were abstract to me. All I knew was that I was in America, the place where everybody drives a nice car and lives in a great house or apartment and the bad guys always lose. At least, that was what the television back in Romania had shown me.

> Mircea clearly establishes the setting of his story.

I was very thirsty, sitting in that center aisle. I kept asking my mom when they were going to bring us drinks. I don't know how much time went by before the cart came around, but it finally arrived.

> The narrative centers on the conflict of cultures.

That moment was my first real encounter with America. There were so many cans to choose from, so many colors. I had no idea which one to take. I chose the blue one since blue was my favorite color. I opened it up and poured it in my clear plastic cup. The soda was also clear, and I was very disappointed. Out of all those different cans I had to choose club soda, a drink I already knew the taste of. But I was wrong. I took a sip, and to my joyous surprise, it was sweet and refreshing and the bubbles tickled the inside of my mouth. It tasted nothing like club soda. It was a good experience, to be surprised by the taste of a drink.

> Mircea devotes several sentences to the choice of sodas, using pacing to focus his reader's attention and build interest.

That day was more than nine years ago. I have lived in America now for nearly ten years. I have since passed through feelings of isolation and fears of being different. I have learned to make friends and to lead life as I want to.

> Vivid sensory details draw a reader into Mircea's experience.

Today, I struggle to hold on to everything about myself that makes me un-American. I try not to forget the Romanian language, I try to remember that I was not born in America. I think about Romania every day. I will not forget it, ever. A Romanian flag hangs in my bedroom alongside pictures of American rock stars. The thought of my homeland always makes me feel a certain way. A kind of bittersweet feeling, calm, a glimpse of home, a feeling of happiness. I picture a warm sunny day on which I am walking alone on the little winding street that surrounded our building complex.

When I think of the future, though, I have a simple hope. I hope the future will be like the moment one tastes the first sip of sweet, crisp, bubbly soda, when a second before it looked like just plain old club soda.

> Mircea clearly states the insight he has gained and poetically links it to the incident he narrates.

Drafting

Start out strong. A strong opening should catch the readers' interest and make them want to continue reading. Consider one of these options:

- **Start with a character:** A description or anecdote about the main character is effective if your narrative centers around a relationship.

- **Start with dialogue:** Besides intriguing the reader, dialogue can provide quick insight into a situation.

- **Start with the setting:** This approach works well if time and place are critical elements of your narrative.

Follow your pacing plan. Use the pacing plan you developed earlier to make sure you do not bog down in details. Establish background information quickly, and then set your main incident in motion.

End well. Devise an interesting closing. You might put the finishing touch on your story or leave readers hoping for more. Consider ending with an epilogue about what happened after the incident, a summary of the main character's insights, or an unanswered question related to the conflict.

Choose a Starting Point

Character
Bob doesn't say much, no matter what may be going on, but when you see that gleam in his eye, you know mischief is afoot.

Setting
The wind whistled through the cracks in the attic window.

Dialogue
"I said, did anybody leave this package on the counter?"

Revising

Revise to clarify the place and time. Make sure that shifts in place and time in your narrative are clearly indicated.

1. Star any places where there is a time or location change.

2. Underline in red the words you have used to indicate the change. Have a partner check to make sure that each shift comes through clearly.

3. Clarify time or place shifts by adding descriptive words or transitional phrases. To highlight the impact of shifts, insert paragraph breaks.

Model: Revising to Clarify Time and Place

¶*That day was more than nine years ago. I have lived in America now for nearly ten years.*

   It was a good experience, to be surprised by the taste of a drink. Today, I struggle to hold on to everything about myself that makes me un-American.

> Mircea added information to show a gap in time.

Revise to eliminate unnecessary tense changes. Even though you may be moving back and forth in time in your narrative, be careful that you have not changed tenses unnecessarily—for example, that you have not moved from present to past without a good reason.

Example: It *was* midnight when the vote tally *is* complete.

Corrected: It *was* midnight when the vote tally *was* completed.

Compare the model and nonmodel. Note the changes in tense, and consider why they were made.

Nonmodel	Model
All I know is that I was in America, the place where everybody drives a nice car...	All I knew was that I was in America, the place where everybody drives a nice car...

Publishing and Presenting

Choose one of the following ways to share your narrative.

Organize a storytelling festival. With a group, plan a storytelling festival at school. Advertise for participants and for attendees. Participants might share booths at the festival and take scheduled turns reading their works.

Publish a literary magazine. Collect narratives and other writings of your classmates for publication in a student magazine.

- Group selections by genre (fiction or autobiography) or theme.
- Have writers provide illustrations and introductions for their works.
- Produce copies of your magazine, and distribute them.

W͞G Prentice Hall Writing and Grammar Connection: Chapter 4

Speaking Connection
For tips on presenting a narrative orally, see the **Listening and Speaking Workshop**, p. 218.

Rubric for Self-Assessment

Evaluate your narrative using the following criteria and rating scale:

Criteria	Rating Scale Not very				Very
How well-portrayed is the main character?	1	2	3	4	5
How clearly and vividly is the setting established?	1	2	3	4	5
How smoothly does the narrative move from set-up to incident to resolution?	1	2	3	4	5
How effectively do the details convey the main character's conflict?	1	2	3	4	5
How clearly conveyed are the insights gained by the main character?	1	2	3	4	5

Listening and Speaking WORKSHOP

Delivering Autobiographical Presentations

In an **autobiographical presentation,** a speaker tells the story of an event, period, or person in his or her life. (To review the characteristics of effective autobiographical narration, see the Writing Workshop, pp. 214–217.) Follow the steps below when preparing an autobiographical presentation. Use the checklist on this page to ensure that you have met all the requirements for an effective autobiographical presentation.

Generate Your Presentation

Like a written autobiographical incident, an effective oral autobiographical presentation begins with clear organization.

Outline your subject. Before drafting, develop a logical organization. Begin your draft with a clear introduction and end with a conclusion clearly stating the significance of the story.

Grab the audience's attention. As you draft, prepare to capture your audience's attention with the following elements:

- Figurative language—images, comparisons, and sound devices that enrich descriptions
- Characterization—the vivid portrayal of a character through narration, description, and dialogue
- Dialogue—direct conversation between characters

Choose sound and visual effects. Consider adding visuals and sound effects to enhance your presentation. Choose effects carefully, taking care not to clutter your story with too many of them.

> ### Generating Your Presentation
>
> - Do your ideas follow logical order?
> - Did you connect your story to a concluding observation or insight?
> - Do you use strategies to grab audience attention?
> - Have you carefully reviewed your choices of sound or visual effects?

Practice Your Presentation

Once you have drafted your presentation, practice delivering it until you are confident. Follow these tips:

Practice with a classmate. Practice in front of a "live" audience to become comfortable. As you practice, use your draft as a reminder, not as a text to be read word for word. Look up from your draft frequently.

Rehearse with audiovisual effects. Your effects will be a nuisance, not an enhancement, if you do not practice with them. Make sure they are well integrated in your presentation.

Find points of emphasis. Look for places in your presentation to create emphasis with your voice. For instance, slowing your delivery and lowering the pitch of your voice will convey seriousness.

Activity: **Presentation and Feedback** Rehearse your autobiographical speech until you feel comfortable. Then, present your speech to your classmates. Ask them for feedback on your presentation.

Assessment WORKSHOP

Sequential Order

In the reading sections of some tests, you are required to read a passage and answer questions on the sequential order of events. Use the following strategies to help you answer such questions:

- Do not mistake the order of statements in the passage for the order of events.
- To help clarify sequential order, determine the logical relations between causes and effects or actions and consequences.
- To determine the sequence of events, watch for key sequence words such as *first, next, then,* and *finally.*

Test-Taking Strategy

As you read, assign sequential numbers to events, indicating which happened first, which happened next, and which happened last.

Sample Test Item

Directions: Read the passage, and then answer the question that follows.

To wash a car the correct way, start by hosing the car down to loosen and wash away the surface grime. Spray the hubcaps. Next, prepare a bucket of warm, soapy water, and grab two sponges. Starting with the hood, use a soapy sponge to rub the car's surface gently. Work from front to back, along each side, and end with the trunk lid. Wash and rinse small sections of the surface as you go. When you have finished washing and rinsing the entire surface, buff the car with a chamois cloth.

1. When should you rinse off the soap?

   A Before you wash the car

   B After you spray the tires

   C After you wash each section

   D Before you wash the car's hood

Answer and Explanation

The correct answer is **C,** because you should wash and rinse small sections of the car at a time. Answer *A* is clearly incorrect. *B* is incorrect because this step occurs before you soap the car. *D* is not correct because you must wash the hood before rinsing it.

▶ Practice

Directions: Read the passage, and then answer the question that follows.

While we were in search of some good water, we came upon a village of the natives about half a league from the place where the ships lay; the inhabitants on discovering us abandoned their houses, and took to flight, carrying off their goods to the mountains. I ordered that nothing which they had left should be taken. Presently, we saw several of the natives advancing towards our party, and one of them came up to us, to whom we gave some hawk's bells and glass beads. We asked him, in return, for water.

1. When did the natives abandon their houses?

   A After the travelers received water

   B Before the travelers landed

   C After the natives discovered the travelers

   D After the natives received hawk's bells and glass beads

2. When did the travelers ask for water?

   A When they arrived

   B When they saw the natives

   C Before the natives left

   D After they gave the natives gifts

The Peasants' Wedding, Pieter Brueghel

> **❝ What a piece of work is a man! how noble in reason! how infinite in faculties! in form and moving how express and admirable! in action how like an angel! ❞**
>
> —William Shakespeare,
> from *Hamlet*

Timeline 1485–1625

British Events

- **1485** Henry VII becomes the first Tudor king.
- **c. 1500** *Everyman* first performed.
- **1512** First masque performed.
- **1516 Thomas More** publishes *Utopia*.

- **1534** Henry VIII issues Act of Supremacy. ▲
- **1534** Church of England established.
- **1535 Thomas More** executed. ◄
- **1541** John Knox leads Calvinist reformation in Scotland.
- **1547** Henry VIII dies.
- **1549** The *Book of Common Prayer* issued.

- **1558** Elizabeth I becomes queen. ►
- **1560** Thomas Tallis publishes English cathedral music.
- **1563** More than 20,000 Londoners die in plague.
- **1564 William Shakespeare** born. ▼

World Events

- **1492** Columbus lands in Western Hemisphere.
- **1497** Africa: Vasco da Gama rounds Cape of Good Hope.
- **1503** Italy: Leonardo da Vinci paints *Mona Lisa*.
- **1509** Italy: Michelangelo paints ceiling of Sistine Chapel.
- **1513** North America: Ponce de León explores Florida.
- **1518** Africa: Algiers and Tunisia founded.

- **1521** Italy: Pope Leo X excommunicates Martin Luther.
- **1532** Peru: Pizarro conquers Incas.
- **1532** France: Rabelais publishes *Gargantua and Pantagruel*, Book 1.
- **1534** Spain: St. Ignatius Loyola founds Jesuit brotherhood.
- **1535** Spain: King Charles I captures Tunis.
- **1540** Poland: Copernicus completes treatise on astronomy.

- **1554** Italy: Cellini completes bronze statue of Perseus.
- **1556** India: Akbar the Great comes to power.
- **1566** Belgium: Bruegel paints *The Wedding Dance*.
- **1567** South America: 2 million Indians die of typhoid.
- **1567** Brazil: Rio de Janeiro founded by Portuguese.

British and World Events

- **1611** King James Bible published. ▼
- **1620** Francis Bacon publishes *Novum Organum.*
- **1623** First patent laws passed.
- **1625** James I dies.

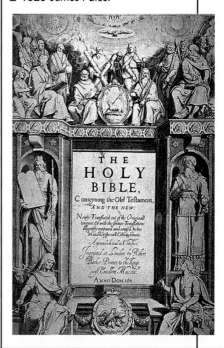

- **1580** Francis Drake returns from circumnavigating the globe.
- **c. 1582 Sir Philip Sidney** writes *Astrophel and Stella.*
- **1588** English navy defeats Spanish Armada. ▲
- **1590 Edmund Spenser** publishes *The Faerie Queene,* Part I.
- **1594 Shakespeare** writes *Romeo and Juliet.*
- **1599** Globe theater opens.

- **1600** East India Company founded.
- **1603 Elizabeth I** dies; James I becomes king.
- **1606** Guy Fawkes executed for Gunpowder Plot.
- **1606** Royal debt amounts to more than £600,000.
- **1609** *The Faerie Queene* by **Edmund Spenser** is published in its entirety.

- **1580** France: Montaigne's *Essays* published.
- **1582** Italy: Pope Gregory XIII introduces new calendar. ▼
- **1595** South America: Sir Walter Raleigh explores Orinoco River.

- **1605** Spain: Cervantes publishes Part I of *Don Quixote.*
- **1607** North America: British colony established at Jamestown.
- **1608** North America: French colony of Quebec established.
- **1609** Italy: Galileo builds first telescope. ▶

- **1618** Germany: Kepler proposes laws of planetary motion.
- **1618** Europe: Beginning of the Thirty Years' War, a series of European conflicts fought for various reasons.
- **1620** North America: Pilgrims land at Plymouth Rock.
- **1620** China: Death of the T'ai-Ch'ang emperor after a one-month reign sparks new conflicts.

Celebrating Humanity
THE ENGLISH RENAISSANCE
(1485–1625)

Historical Background

The Renaissance, one of the most exciting periods in history, was both a worldly and a religious age. It blossomed first in the Italian city-states (1350–1550), where commerce and a wealthy middle class supported learning and the arts. Slowly, Renaissance ideas spread northward, giving rise to the English Renaissance (1485–1625). During the Renaissance, scholars reacted against what they saw as the "dark ages" of medieval Europe, and they revived the learning of ancient Greece and Rome. They wanted to bring about a rebirth of civilization.

The Age of Exploration The Renaissance thirst for knowledge prompted a great burst of exploration by sea. Navigators ventured far and wide, aided by the development of the compass and by advances in astronomy, which freed them from the need to cling to the shores of the Atlantic. Their explorations reached a high point with Columbus's arrival in the Western Hemisphere in 1492.

England's participation in the Age of Exploration began in 1497, when the Italian-born explorer John Cabot, sailing in the service of an English company, reached Newfoundland (an island off the east coast of what is now Canada) and perhaps also the mainland. Cabot thus laid the basis for future English claims in North America.

Religion Along with the Renaissance spirit, a growing sense of nationalism led many Europeans to question the authority of the Roman Catholic Church. Many people had grievances against the Church. Some felt that Church officials were corrupt; others questioned Church teachings and hierarchy.

The edition of the New Testament by the great Dutch scholar Desiderius Erasmus (1466–1536) raised serious questions about standard interpretations of the Bible. Because of his friendship with such English writers as Thomas More (1478–1535), Erasmus focused attention on issues of morality and religion that continued to be central concerns of the English Renaissance.

Although Erasmus himself remained a Roman Catholic, he helped pave the way for a split in the Church that began in 1517, when a German monk named Martin Luther (1483–1546) nailed a list of dissenting beliefs to the door of a German church. Although this was not his intent, Luther's protest

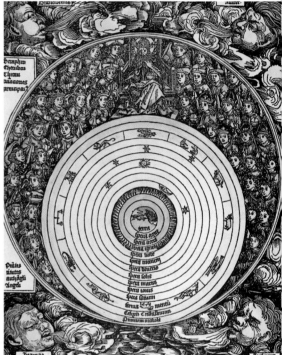

▲ **Critical Viewing**
Ptolemy was a second century A.D. astronomer and mathematician. Renaissance thinkers believed in his Earth-centered model of the universe, shown above. Compare and contrast this view of the universe with our view of the universe today. **[Compare and Contrast]**

resulted in the division of the Church and a new Christian denomination that became known as Lutheranism. The process that Luther started has come to be called the Protestant Reformation.

The Tudors The ending of the Wars of the Roses and the founding of the Tudor dynasty in 1485 opened a new era in English life. Monarchs assured stability by increasing their own power and undercutting the strength of the nobles. At the same time, they dramatically changed England's religious practices and helped transform the country from a small island nation into one of the world's great powers.

▲ **Critical Viewing**
The English navy gained supremacy on the sea after defeating the Spanish Armada in 1588. Examine this painting of the battle between the two navies, and infer the types of war tactics used by the English that may have contributed to their success. **[Infer]**

The first Tudor monarch, Henry VII, inherited an England that had been depleted and exhausted by years of civil war. By the time he died in 1509, he had rebuilt the nation's treasury and established law and order. In doing so, he restored the prestige of the monarchy and set the stage for his successors.

Henry VII was succeeded by his handsome and athletic son, Henry VIII. Like his father, Henry VIII was a practicing Catholic. He even wrote a book against Martin Luther, for which a grateful Pope granted him the title "Defender of the Faith."

Henry VIII's good relationship with the Pope did not last, however. Because his marriage to Catherine of Aragon had not produced a son, Henry tried to obtain an annulment from the Pope so that he could marry Anne Boleyn. When the Pope refused, Henry remarried anyway. This defiance of papal authority led to an open break with the Roman Catholic Church. Henry seized the Catholic Church's English property and dissolved the powerful monasteries. He even had his former friend and leading advisor, Thomas More, executed because More had refused to renounce his Catholic faith.

Henry married six times. His first two marriages produced two daughters, Mary and Elizabeth. His third wife, Jane Seymour, bore a son, Edward, who was still a child when Henry died in 1547.

Religious Turmoil Henry VIII's son became King Edward VI at the age of nine and died at the age of fifteen. During his brief reign, a series of parliamentary acts dramatically changed the nation's religious practices. English replaced Latin in church ritual, and the Anglican prayer book, the Book of Common Prayer, became required in public worship. By the time of Edward's death in 1553, England was well on its way to becoming a Protestant nation.

Roman Catholicism made a turbulent comeback, however, when Edward's half sister Mary took the throne. Mary I was a Catholic, and she restored Roman practices to the Church of England. She also restored the authority of the Pope over the English Church. Ordering the execution of about 300

Protestants, Queen Mary earned the nickname "Bloody Mary" and strengthened anti-Catholic sentiment in England.

Elizabeth I When Mary I died after a five-year reign, her half sister, Elizabeth, came to the throne. Strong and clever, Elizabeth I was probably England's ablest monarch since William the Conqueror. She had received a Renaissance education and had read widely in the Greek and Latin classics. Becoming a great patron of the arts, she gathered around her the best writers of her day.

Elizabeth also put an end to the religious turmoil that had existed during Mary I's reign. She reestablished the monarch's supremacy over the Church of England and restored the Book of Common Prayer. Overall, she instituted a policy of religious compromise, enforcing reforms that she felt both moderate Catholics and Protestants could accept.

Elizabeth's one outstanding problem was her Catholic cousin Mary Stuart, queen of Scotland by birth and next in line for the throne of England. Because Catholics did not recognize Henry VIII's marriage to Elizabeth's mother, Anne Boleyn, they considered Mary Stuart the queen of England. Imprisoned by Elizabeth for eighteen years, Mary instigated numerous Catholic plots against her. Following the recommendations of her advisors, Elizabeth stepped up punishment of the Catholics but let her royal cousin live. Finally, Parliament insisted on Mary's execution. She was beheaded in 1587, a Catholic martyr.

Close-up on Society

High Fashion in the Elizabethan Age

Noblewomen looked like dolls on display, tightly laced into dresses that resembled giant bells. Noblemen were arrayed like showy peacocks in close-fitting jackets and wide collars that seemed to serve up their heads on plates of lace. High fashion was indeed a statement during Elizabeth's reign. As shown in the accompanying pictures—one of Queen Elizabeth and one of Sir Walter Raleigh—clothing was elaborate and theatrical in an age that loved the drama and dramatized itself.

Two devices that helped create these effects were the ruff and the farthingale, both of which came from the Spanish court. Even after the English navy defeated the Spanish Armada in 1588, Spanish fashions held sway among the English nobility. The ruff was a pleated, starched collar worn by both sexes. It varied in size, but as you can see from the picture of Raleigh, above, it could expand to the size of a very large platter. The farthingale was a linen underskirt stretched over a thick iron wire that supported a skirt or dress and gave it a bell shape.

Toward the end of Elizabeth's reign, fashions became a little less showy. Men began to wear a falling collar more like that of today, and a simpler doublet, or close-fitting jacket. Women changed their bell-shaped gowns for drum-shaped ones, and in the early seventeenth century, the farthingale itself was replaced by padding.

▲ **Critical Viewing** These portraits show Queen Elizabeth and Sir Walter Raleigh dressed in elaborate fashions. Speculate about the types of lives led by the people who could afford these clothes. **[Speculate]**

Stuarts and Puritans The English Renaissance continued after Elizabeth died in 1603, although a new dynasty—the Stuarts—came to the throne of England. Determined to avoid a dispute over the throne and a return of civil strife, Elizabeth had named King James VI of Scotland as her successor, making him James I of England. James's claim to the throne of England rested on his descent from King Henry VII of England through his mother, Mary Stuart, Elizabeth's old antagonist. Unlike Mary, however, James was a Protestant.

The years of James I's reign are sometimes described as the Jacobean Era, from *Jacobus*, the Latin word for James. Like his predecessor, James I was a strong supporter of the arts. He also took measures to expand England's position as a world power, sponsoring the establishment of its first successful American colony—Jamestown, Virginia.

During his reign, however, James and Parliament struggled for power, a conflict that would later erupt into war. Guided by the idea of the "divine right of kings," James I often treated Parliament with contempt, and they quarreled over taxes and foreign wars. James I also persecuted the Puritans, who were strongly represented in the House of Commons. Prompted by the king's religious intolerance, a group of Puritans migrated to America and established the Plymouth Colony in 1620.

Art in the Historical Context

Hans Holbein the Younger, Portraitist of the English Court

During the English Renaissance, the visual arts did not flourish as they had in Italy and other European countries. Perhaps that is why the greatest English painter of this period was a German, Hans Holbein the Younger (1497–1543). Born in south Germany, Holbein traveled to Switzerland and eventually settled in England.

Working at the English court, Holbein painted many of its most prominent figures, including Sir Thomas More. In this portrait, Holbein focuses on the most powerful man in early sixteenth-century England, King Henry VIII.

Holbein's portrait of King Henry VIII is not much larger than 2 1/2 feet by two feet, but some scholars have argued that it makes Henry seem very large indeed.

▶ **Critical Viewing** Considering details such as body language, costume, facial expression, position, and pose, support or refute this analysis of the painting by the art critic H. W. Janson: ". . . the [frontal view] and physical bulk of Henry VIII create an overpowering sensation of the king's ruthless commanding presence." **[Draw Conclusions]**

The Hireling Shepherd, William Holman Hunt © Manchester City Art Galleries

▲ Critical Viewing
This picture dates from the nineteenth century, but it portrays the type of pastoral scene that appealed to many Elizabethan poets. Why do you think the lives of shepherds and shepherdesses like these interested court poets? [Infer]

Literature of the Period

The Elizabethan Age produced an explosion of cultural energy. English architects designed and constructed beautiful mansions. Composers turned out new hymns to fit the Anglican service and popularized the English madrigal, a love song performed without musical accompaniment, often by several harmonizing voices. Painters and sculptors were busy, too. Although the Renaissance masters generally were not English, some—like the German artist Hans Holbein the Younger (1497–1543), court painter to Henry VIII—did move to England.

Like painting and sculpture, literature expressed the spirit of the Renaissance. Narratives, poetry, dramas, and comedies reflected the ideas of the times. They also provided a forum for subtle and satirical criticisms of social institutions such as the monarchy and the Church.

Elizabethan Poetry During the reign of Elizabeth I, English literature came of age. The most significant literary developments took place in the area of poetry. Favoring lyric poetry, rather than the narrative poems enjoyed by their medieval predecessors, the Elizabethan poets perfected the sonnet and began experimenting with other poetic forms.

The Sonnet: Sidney, Spenser, and Shakespeare One of the most popular literary forms during the Elizabethan Age was the sonnet cycle, a series of sonnets that fit loosely together to form a story. A sonnet is a fourteen-line poem which in English is usually in iambic pentameter and whose rhyme scheme varies. The first of the great Elizabethan sonnet cycles was *Astrophel and Stella* by Sir Philip Sidney. Sidney also helped adapt classical verse forms to the English language.

Another major Elizabethan poet was Edmund Spenser, who wrote intricate verse filled with rich imagery. His sonnet cycle *Amoretti* is unique in that it was addressed to his wife.

The brilliant lyric poet William Shakespeare, also the era's greatest dramatist, brought the Elizabethan sonnet to new heights. Shakespeare changed the pattern and rhyme scheme of the Petrarchan, or Italian, sonnet, employing a form now known as the English, or Shakespearean, sonnet. The Petrarchan sonnet is divided into an octave, with a rhyme scheme *abbaabba*, and a sestet, with a rhyme scheme *cdecde, cdcdcd,* or a similar pattern, avoiding a closing couplet. The Shakespearean sonnet is divided into four quatrains and a closing couplet, with a rhyme scheme *abab cdcd efef gg.*

Pastoral Poetry: Marlowe and Raleigh Christopher Marlowe (1564–1593) was also a noted playwright and a gifted lyric poet. Marlowe helped popularize pastoral verse, which idealizes the rustic simplicity of rural life, in such poems as "The Passionate Shepherd to His Love."

Marlowe's poem inspired Sir Walter Raleigh (1552?–1618) to write a famous response, "The Nymph's Reply to the Shepherd." Poet, historian, courtier, soldier, and explorer, Raleigh was a typical Renaissance man whose adventurous life mirrored the restless spirit of his day.

Elizabethan Drama During the Elizabethan Age, playwrights turned away from religious subjects and began writing more complex and sophisticated plays. Drawing upon the classical models of ancient Greece and Rome, they reintroduced tragedies and dramas.

Christopher Marlowe as Playwright Besides being a leading poet, Christopher Marlowe became the first major Elizabethan dramatist in the 1580s, writing such plays as *Tamburlaine the Great* and *The Tragical History of Doctor Faustus.* Had Marlowe lived past the age of thirty, he might well have rivaled Shakespeare as England's greatest playwright.

William Shakespeare as Playwright Shakespeare began his involvement with the theater as an actor. By 1592, he was a popular playwright, whose works were performed even at Elizabeth I's court.

After the Globe theater was built in 1599, many of Shakespeare's plays were performed

▼ **Critical Viewing** What could readers learn about Shakespeare's *Romeo and Juliet* from this illustration? **[Infer]**

Romeo and Juliet

there. Shakespeare wrote thirty-seven plays, among them many of the greatest dramas of all time. He wrote nine tragedies, including *Romeo and Juliet*, *Hamlet*, and *Macbeth*; several comedies, including *The Merchant of Venice* and *A Midsummer Night's Dream*; ten histories (plays based on historical characters), including *Richard II*, *Richard III*, and *Henry V*; and a number of plays often classified as "tragic comedies" or "romances," such as *The Tempest*.

Filled with powerful and beautiful language, his works display his deep understanding of human nature. Because of their eloquent language and depth, Shakespeare's plays have retained their popularity through the centuries. Fellow poet and playwright Ben Jonson said of Shakespeare, "He was not of an age, but for all time."

Elizabethan and Jacobean Prose Prose took a back seat to poetry and drama during the English Renaissance. Scholars still preferred to write in Latin, and their English prose had a Latin flavor. Because they used long words and ornate sentences, their work is often difficult to read today.

A Writer's Voice

William Shakespeare's Farewell in *The Tempest*

The Tempest, which may have been Shakespeare's last play, is often regarded as his farewell to the theater. One speech, given by a character named Prospero, seems to embody this farewell. Prospero has just staged an elaborate, magical play-within-a-play in which "spirits" are the actors, but he quickly ends it when he recalls what he still must do to thwart his enemies.

In his speech, the references to the vanishing scenery of the play could also refer to a vanishing world: "The cloud-capped towers, the gorgeous palaces, / The solemn temples, the great globe itself. . . ." This double reference to reality and play is supported by his pun on the word *globe*, which could refer to the Earth or to the Globe theater, where so many of Shakespeare's dramas were staged. In good Elizabethan fashion, Shakespeare equates life with theater, at the same time suggesting the illusory quality of life.

from *The Tempest,* Act IV, Scene i

Our revels° now are ended. These our actors,   °Entertainments
As I foretold you, were all spirits and
Are melted into air, into thin air;
And, like the baseless fabric° of this vision,   °Structure without
5 The cloud-capped towers, the gorgeous places,   foundation
The solemn temples, the great globe itself,
Yea, all which it inherit,° shall dissolve,   °All who inhabit it
And, like this insubstantial pageant faded,
Leave not a rack° behind. We are such stuff   °A drifting cloud
10 As dreams are made on, and our little life
Is rounded with a sleep. . . .

The Prose of Sidney, Nashe, and Raleigh Several Elizabethan poets also contributed major works of prose. Sir Philip Sidney's *Defence of Poesie* (about 1582) is one of the earliest works of English literary criticism. Thomas Nashe's *The Unfortunate Traveler* (1594), a fictional tale, was a forerunner of the novel. *History of the World*, another important work of prose, was written by Sir Walter Raleigh during his imprisonment in the Tower of London.

Sir Francis Bacon Perhaps the leading prose writer of the English Renaissance was Sir Francis Bacon, a high government official under James I. "I have taken all knowledge to be my province," Bacon wrote, and his literary output reflects his scholarship in many fields. *Novum Organum* (1620), his greatest work, made major contributions to natural science and philosophy. Bacon is also known for his formal essays, short prose works focusing on single topics.

The King James Bible The most monumental prose achievement of the entire English Renaissance is undoubtedly the English translation of the Bible commissioned by King James on the advice of Protestant clergymen. Fifty-four scholars labored for seven years to bring this magnificent work to fruition. The King James Bible, or Authorized Version, is among the most widely quoted and influential works in the English language.

The Achievements of the Renaissance The English Renaissance moved England out of its medieval past and into the modern world. No writers since have surpassed the literary achievements of Shakespeare or the majestic language of the King James Bible. They provide the standard against which all English literature has been judged right down to the present time.

▲ **Critical Viewing** Doctors could do little to stop epidemics of smallpox, measles, influenza, and yellow fever. Study this picture to speculate about the measures taken in epidemics: (a) Why has the door been padlocked? (b) Why is a fire burning before the house? **[Speculate]**

THE CHANGING ENGLISH LANGUAGE

"A Man of Fire-New Words"

BY RICHARD LEDERER

THE AGELESS BARD

Shakespeare's plays, which he wrote in London between approximately 1590 and 1613, have been in almost constant production since their creation. Because the playwright dealt with universal truths and conflicts in human nature, his tragedies, comedies, and history plays continue to draw audiences from all walks of life, just as they did in their own day. Time has proved the truth of what Shakespeare's contemporary, Ben Jonson, said of him: "He was not of an age but for all time."

WORD-MAKER SUPREME

William Shakespeare's words, as well as his works, were not just of an age, but for all time. He was, quite simply, the greatest word maker who ever lived—an often neglected aspect of his genius.

Of the 20,138 different words that Shakespeare employs in his plays, sonnets, and other poems, his is the first known use of more than 1,700 of them. The most verbally innovative of our authors, Shakespeare made up more than 8.5 percent of his written vocabulary. Reading his works is like witnessing the birth of language itself.

"I pitied thee, / Took pains to make thee speak," says Prospero to Caliban in *The Tempest*. "I endow'd thy purposes / With words that made them known." Shakespeare is our Prospero; he dressed our thoughts with words and set our tongue teeming with phrases.

Consider the following list of thirty representative words that, as far as we can tell, Shakespeare was the first to use in writing. So great is his influence on his native tongue that we find it hard to imagine a time when these words did not exist.

aerial	amazement	assassination	auspicious
baseless	bedroom	bump	castigate
countless	courtship	critic	dishearten
dislocate	dwindle	exposure	frugal
generous	gloomy	hurry	impartial
invulnerable	lapse	laughable	lonely
majestic	monumental	perusal	pious
sneak	useless		

The striking compound that Shakespeare fashioned to describe Don Adriano de Armando in *Love's Labour's Lost* is an important label for the playwright himself: "a man of fire-new words." No day goes by that we do not speak and hear, and read and write using his legacy.

ACTIVITY

Oscar Wilde once quipped, "Now we sit through Shakespeare in order to recognize the quotations." Unrivaled in his invention of words, William Shakespeare is unequaled as a phrase-maker.

Complete the following expressions, each of which first saw the light in one of his plays:

1. Neither a _____ or a _____ be
2. All the world's a _____
3. With bated _____
4. Break the _____
5. Come full _____
6. Eaten me out of house and _____
7. A foregone _____
8. Laugh yourselves into _____
9. Not _____ an inch
10. Too much of a good _____

PART 1 · Lovers and Their Lines

Prepare to Read

from Spenser's Sonnets ◆ *from* Sidney's Sonnets

Edmund Spenser (1552–1599)

Born into a working-class family, Edmund Spenser attended the Merchant Taylors' School on a scholarship and managed to work his way through Cambridge University. During his university years, Spenser published his first poems.

Pay for Poetry Unlike many other poets of the day, Spenser depended on the payments he received for his work. When the queen's treasurer balked at paying him, he sent this verse to the queen: "I was promised on a time / To have reason for my rhime. / From that time unto this season / I have received nor rhime, nor reason." Spenser was paid immediately.

The Faerie Queene In 1580, Spenser took a position as secretary to the Lord Deputy of Ireland. On a visit to Ireland in 1589, Sir Walter Raleigh (see p. 244) read and was impressed with one of Spenser's unfinished poems. He persuaded Spenser to take the first three books of this long poem to London for publication. That poem became Spenser's greatest work, *The Faerie Queene*.

Written in an intentionally archaic style, *The Faerie Queene* recounts the adventures of several knights, each representing a virtue. This allegory of good and evil, dedicated to Queen Elizabeth I (who appears as the Faerie Queene in the poem), brought Spenser a small pension.

A Poet's Poet Spenser was an innovative poet. In *The Farie Queene*, he created a new type of nine-line stanza, which was later named for him. He also created a sonnet form, known as the Spenserian sonnet, containing a unique structure and rhyme scheme. His sonnet sequence *Amoretti* is unique among such works—it is addressed to the poet's own wife, not some inaccessible, idealized beauty.

Sir Philip Sidney (1554–1586)

Sir Philip Sidney was a courtier, scholar, poet, and soldier—a true "Renaissance man." He attended both Oxford and Cambridge, and furthered his knowledge by traveling extensively through Europe. He became a favorite in the court of Queen Elizabeth I.

Groomed for Success Nephew of the earl of Leicester and son of the statesman Sir Henry Sidney, Philip Sidney was certainly well connected. Throughout his life, though, he carried himself with remarkable modesty. His schoolmate and, later, biographer Fulke Greville remarked on his "staidness of mind, [and] lovely and familiar gravity."

A Brave Soldier Around 1580, Sidney fell out of favor with the queen when he wrote a letter urging her not to marry the duke of Anjou. Eventually, he regained status with her and was knighted in 1583. In 1586, during a military engagement against the Spanish Catholics in Holland, Sidney was severely wounded. As he lay on the battlefield, he bravely insisted that the water offered to him be given to another wounded soldier. Twenty-six days later he died, to the great grief of his country.

Pioneering Sonneteer Sidney wrote the first great sonnet sequence in English, *Astrophel and Stella*. Before Sidney, Sir Thomas Wyatt and others had written excellent sonnets, but Sidney's were the first linked by subject matter and theme. Each sonnet addresses an aspect of Astrophel's love for Stella. This sonnet sequence was inspired by Penelope Devereux (Stella), to whom Sir Philip (Astrophel) had been engaged. The engagement was later broken, and Penelope married Lord Rich. Yet, for most readers, Stella's name will forever be linked with Astrophel's.

Preview

Connecting to the Literature

Expressing your heart is never easy, yet Elizabethan sonneteers like Spenser and Sidney were able to pour their hearts out in just fourteen lines.

Literary Analysis

The Sonnet

A **sonnet** is a fourteen-line lyric poem with a single theme. Each line in a sonnet is usually in iambic pentameter—five groups of two syllables, each with the accent on the second syllable. Sonnets take definite forms.

- The **Petrarchan sonnet** is divided into an eight-line octave, rhyming *abba abba,* followed by a six-line sestet, rhyming *cdecde.* Often, the octave poses a problem that is answered in the sestet.

- The **Spenserian sonnet** rhymes *abab bcbc cdcdee.* Note the *abab* rhyme scheme in these lines of Spenser's:

> One day I wrote her name upon the <u>strand,</u>
> But came the waves and washèd it <u>away:</u>
> Again I wrote it with a second <u>hand,</u>
> But came the tide, and made my pains his <u>prey.</u>

In a **sonnet sequence,** the one hundred or so sonnets are linked by theme or person addressed. As you read these sonnets, identify their form and how they are linked.

Comparing Literary Works

Notable writers of the Elizabethan Age such as Spenser and Sidney made their mark by writing sonnet sequences. To connect one hundred or more poems without growing dull, they used a basic fictional situation:

- The speaker in the sequence is in love—some sonnets may explain the depth of his love, while others may praise his beloved.

- His love is unfulfilled—poems may dramatize his hopes and disappointments or analyze the nature of love.

As you read, compare Spenser's and Sidney's uses of this basic situation.

Reading Strategy

Paraphrasing

To **paraphrase** a poem, read until you find a complete thought. Then, restate that thought in your own words. Use a chart like this one to help.

Vocabulary Development

deign (dān) *v.* condescend; lower oneself (p. 236)

assay (a sā´) *v.* try (p. 238)

devise (di vīz´) *v.* work out or create; plan (p. 238)

wan (wän) *adj.* sickly; pale (p. 239)

languished (laŋ´ gwisht) *adj.* weakened; dulled (p. 239)

balm (bäm) *n.* ointment or other thing that heals or soothes (p. 240)

Poet's Lines

"One day I wrote her name upon the strand, / But came the waves and washèd it away:"

↓

Paraphrase

One day the speaker wrote his beloved's name in the sand at the beach, but the waves came and erased his writing.

Sonnet 1
Edmund Spenser

Background

Elizabethans believed that they lived in an orderly world based on a grand universal design. For example, they imagined that the heavens were so perfectly balanced that the planets and stars created a glorious music, which they called the "music of the spheres." It is hardly surprising that the sonnet, a perfectly designed little poem, became wildly popular. In many sonnets, lovers are idealized and compared to other "perfect" things, such as the sun and stars.

Happy ye leaves when as those lily hands,
Which hold my life in their dead doing[1] might,
Shall handle you and hold in love's soft bands,
Like captives trembling at the victor's sight,
5 And happy lines, on which with starry light,
Those lamping[2] eyes will <u>deign</u> sometimes to look
And read the sorrows of my dying spright,[3]
Written with tears in heart's close[4] bleeding book.
And happy rhymes bathed in the sacred brook
10 Of Helicon[5] whence she derived is,
When ye behold that angel's blessed look,
My soul's long lacked food, my heaven's bliss.
Leaves, lines, and rhymes, seek her to please alone,
Whom if ye please, I care for other none.

deign (dān) *v.* condescend; lower oneself

1. **doing** killing.
2. **lamping** flashing.
3. **spright** spirit.
4. **close** secret.
5. **sacred . . . Helicon** In Greek mythology, the Helicon mountains were the home of the Muses, goddesses of the arts, and the site of the Hippocrene, the fountain from which the waters of poetic inspiration flowed.

Sonnet 35

Edmund Spenser

My hungry eyes through greedy covetize,[1]
Still[2] to behold the object of their pain,
With no contentment can themselves suffice:
But having pine[3] and having not complain.

5   For lacking it they cannot life sustain,
And having it they gaze on it the more:
In their amazement like Narcissus[4] vain
Whose eyes him starved: so plenty makes me poor.
Yet are mine eyes so fillèd with the store

10 Of that fair sight, that nothing else they brook,
But loathe the things which they did like before,
And can no more endure on them to look.
All this world's glory seemeth vain to me,
And all their shows but shadows, saving she.

---

1. **covetize** *v.* excessive desire.
2. **Still** *adv.* always.
3. **pine** *v.* yearn.
4. **Narcissus** in Greek mythology, a youth who fell in love with his own reflection in a pool, wasted away with yearning, and was changed after his death into the narcissus flower.

▼ **Critical Viewing**
How does the sight of the distant horizon, as in this photograph, suggest the "desire" eyes may have to see, referred to in Sonnet 35? **[Speculate]**

✔**Reading Check**
What does the speaker long for, even though it causes him pain?

Sonnet 75

Edmund Spenser

One day I wrote her name upon the strand,[1]
But came the waves and washèd it away:
Again I wrote it with a second hand,
But came the tide, and made my pains his prey.
5 "Vain man," said she, "that dost in vain <u>assay</u>,
A mortal thing so to immortalize,
For I myself shall like to this decay,
And eek[2] my name be wipèd out likewise."
"Not so," quod[3] I, "let baser things <u>devise</u>
10 To die in dust, but you shall live by fame:
My verse your virtues rare shall eternize,
And in the heavens write your glorious name.
Where whenas death shall all the world subdue,
Our love shall live, and later life renew."

assay (a sā´) v. try

devise (di vīz´) v. work out or create; plan

---

1. **strand** beach.
2. **eek** also.
3. **quod** said.

Review and Assess

Thinking About the Selections

1. **Respond:** Which of Spenser's sonnets do you like the best? Why?

2. **(a) Recall:** In Sonnet 1, what are the three things the speaker addresses? **(b) Interpret:** What does the speaker hope their combined effect will be on the lady?

3. **(a) Recall:** In Sonnet 35, what do the speaker's eyes desire? **(b) Interpret:** Describe the state that desire produces in him.

4. **(a) Interpret:** In Sonnet 75, why does the lady say the speaker's efforts are futile? **(b) Summarize:** Summarize the speaker's response. **(c) Draw Conclusions:** What connection does the poem make between immortality and poetry?

5. **Compare and Contrast:** Compare and contrast the relationship between the speaker and his love in each of the sonnets.

6. **Take a Position:** Are these speakers overreacting to their situations? Explain.

Sonnet 31

Sir Philip Sidney

With how sad steps, O Moon, thou climb'st the skies!
How silently, and with how <u>wan</u> a face!
What, may it be that even in heavenly place
That busy archer[1] his sharp arrows tries?
5 Sure, if that long-with-love-acquainted eyes
Can judge of love, thou feel'st a lover's case.
I read it in thy looks, thy <u>languished</u> grace,
To me, that feel the like, thy state descries.[2]
Then even of fellowship, O Moon, tell me
10 Is constant love deemed there but want of wit?[3]
Are beauties there as proud as here they be?
Do they above love to be loved, and yet
Those lovers scorn whom that love doth possess?
Do they call virtue there ungratefulness?

---

1. **busy archer** Cupid, the Roman god of love.
2. **descries** reveals.
3. **wit** intelligence.

wan (wän) *adj.* sickly; pale

languished (laŋ´ gwisht) *adj.* weakened; dulled

✔**Reading Check**

What does the speaker claim he and the moon have in common?

▲ **Critical Viewing** Which details of this photograph of the moon convey the mood of Sonnet 31? **[Evaluate]**

Sonnet 39

Sir Philip Sidney

Come sleep! O sleep, the certain knot of peace,
The baiting place[1] of wit, the <u>balm</u> of woe,
The poor man's wealth, the prisoner's release,
The indifferent[2] judge between the high and low;
5 With shield of proof[3] shield me from out the prease[4]
Of those fierce darts Despair at me doth throw:
O make in me those civil wars to cease;
I will good tribute pay, if thou do so.
Take thou of me smooth pillows, sweetest bed,
10 A chamber deaf to noise, and blind to light,
A rose garland, and a weary head:
And if these things, as being thine by right,
Move not thy heavy grace, thou shalt in me,
Livelier than elsewhere, Stella's image see.

---

1. **baiting place** place for refreshment.
2. **indifferent** impartial.
3. **proof** proven strength.
4. **prease** crowd.

balm (bäm) *n.* ointment or other thing that heals and soothes

Literary Analysis
The Sonnet How does the rhyme scheme of lines 1–8 make this sonnet different from a typical Spenserian or Petrarchan sonnet?

Review and Assess

Thinking About the Selections

1. **Respond:** Do you sympathize with the speakers? Explain.

2. **(a) Recall:** In Sonnet 31, how does the moon appear to the speaker? **(b) Infer:** To what does the speaker attribute the moon's mood? **(c) Analyze:** How does the speaker reveal his own situation by addressing the moon?

3. **(a) Recall:** What benefits does the speaker attribute to sleep in lines 1–4 of Sonnet 39? **(b) Recall:** What "reward" does he promise sleep in lines 13–14? **(c) Interpret:** Judging from this "reward," why does he crave sleep?

4. **Draw Conclusions:** What conclusion can you draw about each speaker's relationship with his lady?

5. **Generalize:** Do you think both sonnets express moods that people in love always experience? Explain.

Review and Assess

Literary Analysis

The Sonnet

1. Reread Sidney's Sonnets 31 and 39, and analyze their rhyme schemes. Do these **sonnets** more closely follow the **Spenserian** or the **Petrarchan** form? Explain.

2. Review Spenser's three sonnets. Then, explain what poets can achieve in a **sonnet sequence** that they cannot in individual poems. Consider such factors as shifting moods and developing characters.

3. Using a chart like the one here, compare and contrast one of Sidney's sonnets with one of Spenser's.

Petrarchan/ Spenserian?	Speaker's Situation	Addressed to . . .	Types of Images	Speaker's Conclusion

Comparing Literary Works

4. (a) Compare the person or thing addressed in each of the sonnets. (b) Explain how the basic sonnet sequence situation justifies or motivates each choice of addressee.

5. (a) Compare the dominant purpose of each sonnet—to express hope, to persuade, to complain, and so on. (b) Explain how the sonnet sequence situation justifies or motivates each purpose.

6. Explain how, in each sonnet, the writer goes beyond the basic sonnet situation to give a general insight into the nature of love or life.

Reading Strategy

Paraphrasing

7. Reread the octave of Sidney's Sonnet 39. (a) Write a **paraphrase** of lines 1–4. (b) Paraphrase lines 5–8.

8. Reread and then paraphrase the sestet of Sonnet 39. You may break the sestet into smaller sections for paraphrasing.

Extend Understanding

9. **Cultural Connection:** Renaissance poets compared their beloveds to "perfect" things in nature or to timeless figures from mythology. Do any songwriters idealize love today? If so, to what "perfect" things do they compare their loves?

Quick Review

The **sonnet** is a fourteen-line lyric poem with a single theme.

A **sonnet sequence** is a group of sonnets linked by theme, subject, or the person addressed.

The **Spenserian sonnet** has the following rhyme scheme: *abab bcbc cdcdee.*

The **Petrarchan sonnet** has the following rhyme scheme: *abba abba cdecde.*

The **basic sonnet sequence situation** involves the speaker's unfulfilled love for his beloved.

To **paraphrase**, restate an author's ideas in your own words.

 Take It to the Net
www.phschool.com
Take the interactive self-test online to check your understanding of these selections.

Integrate Language Skills

Vocabulary Development Lesson

Related Words: Forms of *languished*

Languished is the past participle of the verb *languish*, which means "to become weak." Other forms of this word are *languid*, an adjective that means "drooping" or "weak," and the noun *languor*, meaning "weakness." Choose from these related words to complete each sentence below.

1. His ___?___ was caused by overexertion.
2. The worker's movements were ___?___ at the end of the day.
3. Everyone ___?___ in the heat.

Fluency: Words in Context

Write a paragraph describing the plight of a longing lover using forms of all the words on the vocabulary list on page 235.

Spelling Strategy

The long *a* sound can be spelled in several different ways. Two examples are *ei* as in *deign* and *ay* as in *assay*. In your notebook, complete the spelling of the long *a* sound in each word.

1. m__be
2. r__ndeer
3. n__ghbor
4. p__ment

Grammar and Style Lesson

Capitalization of Proper Nouns

A **proper noun** is the name of a specific person, place, or thing. It begins with a capital letter. In addition to capitalizing proper nouns, poets also capitalize some common nouns when referring to objects and ideas as if they were specific human beings. Note the following examples from Spenser's Sonnet 1 and Sidney's Sonnet 31.

> **Proper Noun:** And happy rhymes bathed in the sacred brook Of <u>Helicon</u> whence she derived is, . . .
>
> **Direct Address:** With how sad steps, O <u>Moon</u>, thou climb'st the skies!

In the second example, Sidney capitalizes *moon*, ordinarily an uncapitalized common noun, because he is addressing the moon as if it were a person.

Practice Identify the proper noun in each item.

1. Both poets had met Elizabeth.
2. . . . In their amazement like Narcissus vain . . .
3. Then even of fellowship, O Moon, tell me. . . .
4. . . . Of those fierce darts Despair at me doth throw: . . .
5. . . . thou shalt in me, / Livelier than elsewhere, Stella's image see.

Writing Application Rewrite the following sentences, capitalizing the proper nouns.

After staring at the moon for a while, romeo the cat howled as though his heart were broken. The moon dimmed as though she too felt romeo's pain. Softly, luna's whispering tones floated down through the night air to cupid's wounded victim. "Let morpheus soothe you, and when you awaken, all will be well."

W̶G *Prentice Hall Writing and Grammar Connection: Chapter 26*

Writing Lesson

Introduction to a Sonnet Sequence

Write an introduction to Spenser's or Sidney's sonnet sequence. In addition to an insight to interest readers, include a summary of two of the poems from the sequence.

Prewriting   Choose one of the authors, and do background research on his sequence. Then, choose two poems from the sequence. Divide each into parts, following the meaning. Jot down a paraphrase of each section.

Model: Taking Notes for a Summary

SECTION	LINES	SUMMARY
Beginning	1–4	The man twice writes his love's name in the sand, but the waves wash it away.
Middle	5–8	
	9–12	
End	13–14	

> This chart organizes Spenser's Sonnet 75 into three sections: beginning, middle, and end, with space to summarize each part.

Drafting   Introduce the sonnet sequence, explaining when it was written and the variety of poems it contains. Then, summarize the two sonnets, clearly noting the beginning, middle, and end of each. Indicate connections with transitions such as *as a result* and *however*.

Revising   Review your introduction. Draw a square at points in your draft where ideas shift. Check the square when you have used a transition to indicate the connection between ideas. Otherwise, consider adding transitions to help readers follow the sequence of ideas.

𝒲𝒢 *Prentice Hall Writing and Grammar Connection: Chapter 14, Section 2*

Extension Activities

Listening and Speaking With a small group, prepare Sonnet 75 as a **scene with dialogue.**

1. Rewrite the poem as a dialogue.
2. Appoint a director, who should suggest effective ways to deliver lines.
3. Rehearse until you have command of lines and the director is satisfied.

Present your scene to the class. **[Group Activity]**

Research and Technology Do further research on the lives and works of Spenser and Sidney, and write a **biographical report** comparing the two and their contributions to literature. Include timelines of their lives and important events of their era.

 **Take It to the Net**   www.phschool.com

Go online for an additional research activity using the Internet.

Pastoral Poetry

Pastoral poems are lyrics that celebrate the pleasures of a simple life in the country. In their pastoral poetry, Renaissance poets use a number of traditional conventions borrowed from ancient Greek and Roman poetry, such as making the speaker a shepherd who addresses or describes a shepherdess with whom he is in love and presenting an idealized world of nature.

Christopher Marlowe's "The Passionate Shepherd to His Love" is a well-known example of pastoral poetry. It has inspired a number of responses to the invitation issued in the poem by Marlowe's shepherd. The most famous and—some have argued—the best response was written by Sir Walter Raleigh in 1600.

Christopher Marlowe
1564–1593

Killed before the age of thirty, Christopher Marlowe nonetheless managed to achieve renown as a brilliant playwright and poet. He spent his college days writing plays and serving as a government agent. *Tamburlaine*, his first drama, dazzled the public with its dynamic characterization of the tyrant-hero, and his tragedy *Doctor Faustus* is often performed even today.

A Life of Intrigue Marlowe has been described as a scoundrel, a ladies' man, and a hothead; however, it is clear that he was full of personal magnetism, for his numerous friends—and even his enemies—were drawn to him like moths to a flame. When the council of Queen Elizabeth I wrote a letter implying that Marlowe had performed important government services, rumors flew about that he was a spy. Marlowe was knifed to death in a tavern brawl in 1593. To this day, scholars question whether his death was really caused by his drunken refusal to pay his bill or whether he was murdered because of his undercover activities.

Sir Walter Raleigh
1554?–1618

Sir Walter Raleigh is famed for being a courtier, a navigator, a poet, and a historian.

A Charmed Life A favorite of Queen Elizabeth I, Raleigh was given estates and prestigious appointments. In 1584, he set up a colony on Roanoke Island, Virginia. Returning home, Raleigh introduced tobacco and potatoes into England and Ireland.

Disaster While away, Raleigh was replaced in the queen's affection by the Earl of Essex, and when it was discovered that Raleigh had been secretly married to one of the queen's maids, he and his wife were imprisoned in the Tower of London for a time. Following the death of the queen in 1603, Raleigh was accused of conspiring against James I and was again sent to the Tower of London, where he lived for thirteen years. He was eventually released to seek out gold along the Orinoco river in Venezuela, but the expedition was plagued by ill luck and he lost his fleet and his son. Upon his return, Raleigh was beheaded at Whitehall under the old sentence of treason.

The Passionate Shepherd to His Love

CHRISTOPHER MARLOWE

Come live with me, and be my love,
And we will all the pleasures prove[1]
That valleys, groves, hills, and fields,
Woods, or steepy mountain yields.

5 And we will sit upon the rocks,
Seeing the shepherds feed their flocks,
By shallow rivers to whose falls
Melodious birds sing madrigals.

And I will make thee beds of roses,
10 And a thousand fragrant posies,
A cap of flowers, and a kirtle[2]
Embroidered all with leaves of myrtle;

A gown made of the finest wool,
Which from our pretty lambs we pull;
15 Fair lined slippers for the cold,
With buckles of the purest gold;

A belt of straw and ivy buds,
With coral clasps and amber studs;
And if these pleasures may thee move,
20 Come live with me, and be my love.

The shepherds' swains shall dance and sing
For thy delight each May morning;
If these delights thy mind may move,
Then live with me and be my love.

---

1. **prove** experience.
2. **kirtle** skirt.

The Nymph's Reply to the Shepherd

SIR WALTER RALEIGH

If all the world and love were young
And truth in every shepherd's tongue
These pretty pleasures might me move
To live with thee, and be thy love.

5 Time drives the flocks from field to fold,
When rivers rage and rocks grow cold,
And Philomel[1] becometh dumb,
The rest complains of cares to come.

The flowers do fade, and wanton fields
10 To wayward winter reckoning yields:
A honey tongue, a heart of gall,
Is fancy's spring, but sorrow's fall.

Thy gowns, thy shoes, thy beds of roses,
Thy cap, thy kirtle,[2] and thy posies
15 Soon break, soon wither, soon forgotten,
In folly ripe, in reason rotten.

Thy belt of straw and ivy buds,
Thy coral clasps and amber studs,
All these in me no means can move
20 To come to thee and be thy love.

But could youth last and love still breed,
Has joy no date[3] nor age no need,
Then these delights my mind might move,
To live with thee and be thy love.

---

1. **Philomel** the nightingale.
2. **kirtle** skirt.
3. **date** ending.

Position Statements

About Position Statements

A **position statement** is an essay presenting the views of an individual or group on a particular issue. It features these elements:

- An introductory statement identifying the issue, the position argued for, and, where appropriate, the person or group taking the position
- Arguments in support of the position
- The use of support such as expert opinion and statistics

In an **apology,** a kind of position statement, a writer defends a belief or activity against criticism. In *The Defense of Poesy*, Sir Philip Sidney (1554–1586) takes on a big case—the defense of art against those who see it as idleness or, worse, a source of immorality. Sidney may have been writing in reply to Stephen Gosson's pamphlet "The Schoole of Abuse" (1579). (For more on Sidney, see page 234.)

The issues Sidney addresses were inherited from the ancient Greek philosophers Plato (428/27–348/47 B.C.) and Aristotle (384–322 B.C.): the moral worth of art and the relationship of art with Nature. The "speaking picture" of heroes painted by literature, he argues, leads people to virtue more effectively than either philosophy or nature can.

Reading Strategy

Analyzing Expert Opinions and Allusions

Expert opinions are judgments about an issue made by people who have studied the issue extensively and whose work is respected by other experts. Such opinions may be used to support a position. In *The Defense*, for example, Sidney refers to the opinions of a respected authority on art, the Greek philosopher Aristotle.

Allusions, brief references to literary works and historical figures, are another form of support. Because Sidney's subject is literature, he uses allusions as examples supporting his points. He also gains authority for his points by alluding to respected authors, such as the ancient poet Homer.

Read the excerpt from *The Defense*. Use a chart like this one to record each expert opinion and allusion (consult reference sources if necessary).

Expert Opinions/Allusions	Source/Reference
Cyclops	Greek mythology; Homer's *Odyssey*
Aristotle	

from The Defense of Poesy

Sir Philip Sidney

There is no art delivered unto mankind that has not the works of Nature for his principal object, without which they could not consist, and on which they so depend, as they become actors and players, as it were, of what Nature will have set forth. So does the astronomer look upon the stars, and, by that he sees set down what order Nature has taken therein. So do the geometrician and arithmetician in their diverse sorts of quantities. . . .

Only the poet, disdaining to be tied to any such subjection, lifted up with the vigor of his own invention, grows in effect into another Nature, in making things either better than Nature brings forth, or, quite anew, forms such as never were in Nature, as the Heroes, Demigods, Cyclops, Chimeras, Furies, and such like: so as he goes hand in hand with Nature, not enclosed within the narrow warrant of her gifts, but freely ranging within the zodiac of his own wit.

Nature never set forth the earth in so rich tapestry as divers poets have done, neither with so pleasant rivers, fruitful trees, sweet-smelling flowers, nor whatsoever else may make the too much loved earth more lovely. Her world is brazen,[1] the poets only deliver a golden. But let those things alone, and go to man (for whom as the other things are, so it seems in him her uttermost cunning is employed), and know whether she have brought forth so true a lover as Theagenes, so constant a friend as Pylades, so valiant a man as Orlando, so right a prince as Xenophon's Cyrus, and so excellent a man every way as Virgil's Aeneas[2]. Neither let this be jestingly conceived because the works of the one be essential, the other in imitation or fiction, for every understanding knows the skill of each artificer stands in that Idea or foreconceit of the work, and not in the work itself. And that the poet has that Idea is manifest, by delivering them forth in such excellency as he had imagined them. Which delivering forth also is not wholly imaginative, as we are wont to say by them that build castles in the air, but so far substantially it works, not only to make a Cyrus, which had been but a particular excellence, as Nature might have done, but to bestow a Cyrus upon the world to make many Cyruses, if they will learn aright why and how that maker made him.

. . .

[Definition] Poesy, therefore, is an art of imitation, for so Aristotle terms it in the word *mimesis*; that is to say, a representing, counterfeiting, or figuring forth—to speak metaphorically, a speaking picture—with this end, to teach and delight.

. . .

[W]hen by the balance of experience it was found that the

The writer introduces a generalization to form the foundation for his position.

The ancient Roman poet Virgil was revered by Sidney's readers. This allusion commanded his audience's respect.

Sidney advances his argument by defending the products of poetry.

Sidney cites expert opinions to support his case.

---

1. **brazen** (brā´ zən) *adj.* made of brass, a metal alloy of inferior value to gold.

2. **Theagenes . . . Aeneas** Heroes of ancient Greek, ancient Roman, and medieval literature and histories.

astronomer looking to the stars might fall in a ditch, that the inquiring philosopher might be blind in himself, and the mathematician might draw forth a straight line with a crooked heart, then, lo, did proof, the overruler of opinions, make manifest that all these are but serving sciences, which, as they have a private end in themselves, so yet are they all directed to the highest end of the mistress knowledge, by the Greeks [called] *architektonike*,[3] which stands (as I think) in the knowledge of a man's self, in the ethic and politic consideration, with the end of well doing and not of well knowing only; even as the saddler's next end is to make a good saddle, but his further end to serve a nobler faculty, which is horsemanship; so the horseman's to soldiery, and the soldier not only to have the skill, but to perform the practice of a soldier. So that, the ending end of all earthly learning being virtuous action, those skills that most serve to bring forth that, have a most just title to be princes over all the rest. Wherein we can show the poet is worthy to have it before any other competitors.

. . .

The philosopher . . . and the historian are they which would win the goal, the one by precept,[4] the other by example. But both, not having both, do both halt. For the philosopher, setting down with thorny arguments the bare rule, is so hard

of utterance, and so misty to be conceived, that one that has no other guide but him shall wade in him till he be old before he shall find sufficient cause to be honest: for his knowledge stands so upon the abstract and general, that happy is that man who may understand him, and more happy that can apply what he does understand. On the other side, the historian, wanting the precept, is so tied, not to what should be but to what is, to the particular truth of things and not to the general reason of things, that his example draws no necessary consequence, and therefore a less fruitful doctrine.

Now does the peerless poet perform both: for whatsoever the philosopher says should be done, he gives a perfect picture of it by some one by whom he presupposes it was done; so as he couples the general notion with the particular example. A perfect picture, I say, for he yields to the powers of the mind an image of that whereof the philosopher bestows but a wordish description, which does neither strike, pierce, nor possess the sight of the soul so much as that other does. . . . [No] doubt the philosopher with his learned definitions, be it of virtues or vices, matters of public policy or private government, replenishes the memory with many infallible grounds of wisdom, which, notwithstanding, lie dark before the imaginative and judging power, if they be not illuminated, or figured forth, by the speaking picture of poesy.[5]

Here, Sidney introduces his next argument.

Sidney strengthens his position by testing his ideas against possible counterclaims.

The excerpt concludes with a persuasive image—"the speaking picture" of poetry.

---

3. *architektonike* (är kə tek tän´ ik ā) *n.* Greek for "construction." The ancient Greek philosophers Plato (428/27 B.C.–348/47 B.C.) and Aristotle (384–322 B.C.) used the term to refer to purposeful, knowledgeable activity.
4. **precept** (prē´ sept´) *n.* rule of conduct.

5. **speaking picture of poesy** The idea that poetry and painting are alike was made famous by the Roman poet Horace (65 B.C.–8 B.C.) who wrote, *ut pictura poesis* (Latin: "as is painting so is poetry").

Check Your Comprehension

1. Why does Sidney claim that art is less "subjected" to nature than other activities?
2. According to Sidney, what is the ultimate goal of poetry?
3. (a) To what other types of occupations does Sidney compare poetry? (b) Why does he say that the poet's occupation is the highest of these?

Applying the Reading Strategy

Analyzing Expert Opinions and Allusions

4. What point does Sidney illustrate using allusions to Greek mythology?
5. (a) What does Sidney assume his readers know about Cyrus? (b) What does he assume they think of Cyrus?
6. What effect might Sidney's references to the expert opinions of Greek philosophers, using the Greek words, have on readers? Explain.

Activity

Analyzing Philosophical Allusions

Position statements offer opinions and theories about facts. These opinions and theories are based on **philosophical assumptions,** the basic concepts and judgments that shape a writer's viewpoint. A writer may explicitly discuss and argue for his or her assumptions, or a writer may simply use these assumptions to guide his or her thoughts. Using a chart like the one shown, identify an assumption that Sidney makes about each of the following: the purpose of skilled activity in general, the function of art, and the work done by historians. For each, summarize a related argument that starts from this assumption, and then note your own reaction to the assumption.

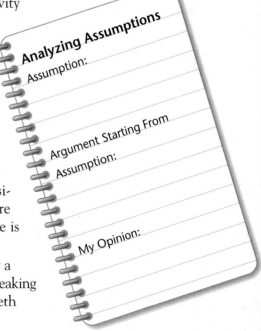

Analyzing Assumptions

Assumption:

Argument Starting From Assumption:

My Opinion:

Comparing Informational Materials

Comparing Position Statements

1. Read Sir Thomas More's *Utopia* (p. 266), a position statement on the duties of a king. Compare More's *Utopia* to Sidney's *Defense*. Which piece is more persuasive? Explain.
2. Read Queen Elizabeth I's speech (p. 268). Draw a conclusion about how Sidney would view the "speaking picture" of a good monarch (herself) that Elizabeth paints in the speech.

Prepare to Read

Sonnet 29 ◆ Sonnet 106 ◆ Sonnet 116 ◆ Sonnet 130

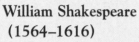

William Shakespeare (1564–1616)

Shakespeare may be the most admired author of all time. If he were living today, he would be a celebrity, and the facts of his life would be widely available in magazine articles, books, Web pages, and chat rooms. Instead, we know few facts about him, and these few had to be painstakingly traced from legal and church records or deduced from references in his work.

Bare-Bones Biography Shakespeare was born in the country town of Stratford-on-Avon and probably attended the town's free grammar school. When he was eighteen, he married twenty-six-year-old Anne Hathaway. They had a daughter, Susanna, and twins, Hamnet and Judith.

Shakespeare acquired a public reputation as an actor and a playwright. In addition, he was part owner of a London theater called the Globe, where many of his plays were performed. (For more about Shakespeare and his work as a dramatist, see pages 290–298.)

The Sonnet In the years 1592–1594, London's theaters were closed because of an outbreak of the plague. This general misfortune may have had at least one benefit: It may have provided the time that Shakespeare needed to write some of his 154 sonnets.

In writing a long sequence of sonnets, Shakespeare was being fashionable. Elizabethan poets enjoyed the sonnet form, writing fourteen-line lyric poems to both real and imaginary lovers. The great Italian poet Petrarch (1304–1374) began the writing of sonnet sequences, and Henry Howard, Earl of Surrey, developed the English form of the sonnet that Shakespeare used.

Petrarch set the thematic course of the sonnet for generations to come. His sequence charts each pang and longing of the speaker's unfulfilled love for an idealized lady. This poetic device led to endless inventiveness—the beloved's beauty invites extravagant comparisons, and she provides a focus for the poet's ingenuity.

Shakespeare's Sequence Like the sonnet sequences of other poets, Shakespeare's 154 sonnets are numbered. Most of them are addressed to a handsome, talented, young man, urging him to marry and have children who can carry on his talents. The speaker also warns the young man about the destructive powers of time, age, and moral weakness. Midway through the sequence, the sonnets focus on a rival poet who has also addressed poems to the young man. Twenty-five of the later sonnets are addressed to a "dark lady" who is romantically involved with both the speaker and the young man. These later sonnets focus on the grief she causes by her betrayal of the speaker.

A Mystery Scholars fiercely debate the identity of the young man (Mr. W. H.), the "dark lady," and the rival poet. Leading candidates for the role of Mr. W. H. are Henry Wriothesley, third earl of Southampton, to whom Shakespeare dedicated his narrative poems, and William Herbert, third earl of Pembroke. Those favoring Southampton claim Mrs. John Davenant was the "dark lady," but the Pembroke side believes she was Mary Fitton, a woman of doubtful reputation. The many nominees for the rival poet include Edmund Spenser, Christopher Marlowe, Ben Jonson, and John Donne—even the name of Chaucer, a poet who had been dead for two hundred years, has been proposed!

Scholarly debates aside, readers treasure Shakespeare's masterful use of the sonnet to bring the fundamental experiences of life—time, death, love, and friendship—into tight focus.

Preview

Connecting to the Literature

Feelings may sink you into gloom or send you floating with joy. If you are a Shakespeare, your strong feelings will erupt in a sonnet!

Literary Analysis

The Shakespearean Sonnet

Shakespeare uses a variation of the sonnet form, a variation that has since been named after him. Like other sonnets, a **Shakespearean sonnet** has fourteen lines, with five iambic feet to the line (an iambic foot is an unstressed syllable followed by a stressed one).

Unlike Petrarchan and Spenserian sonnets, a Shakespearean sonnet follows the rhyme scheme *abab cdcd efef gg*, giving it this structure:

- three **quatrains,** or four-line stanzas
- a rhyming **couplet**—often a dramatic statement that resolves, restates, or redefines the central problem of the sonnet

Notice the artful way in which Shakespeare uses the first twelve lines of each sonnet to present a problem that he resolves or restates in the couplet.

Comparing Literary Works

Though all Shakespearean sonnets have fourteen rhyming lines, there are no rules about the number or type of sentences they contain. Shakespeare uses this freedom of **syntax,** or sentence structure, to create dazzling dramatic effects. By saving his main idea until the end of one long sentence, he makes Sonnet 106 build and build like a lawyer's statement to a jury. Using alternating short clauses, setting up and then delivering punchlines, he turns Sonnet 130 into a miniature comedy routine. As you read, compare the effects Shakespeare achieves with syntax.

Reading Strategy

Relating Structure to Theme

As you read, **relate structure to theme.** Notice how Shakespeare builds on or varies his theme—his main concern—from quatrain to quatrain, using the couplet to deliver a dramatic concluding statement. Use a chart like the one shown to record the main idea of each section of a sonnet.

Quatrain 1
Speaker has bad luck, which causes him to feel isolated. He pities himself and bemoans his condition.
Theme: *bad fortune; self-pity*

Quatrain 2
Theme:

Relation of 1 and 2
Change in Theme:

Vocabulary Development

scope (skōp) *n.* range of perception or understanding (p. 253)

sullen (sul´ ən) *adj.* gloomy; dismal (p. 253)

chronicle (krän´ i kəl) *n.* historical record of events in chronological order (p. 254)

prefiguring (prē fig´ yər iŋ) *v.* resembling and so suggesting beforehand (p. 254)

impediments (im ped´ ə mənts) *n.* obstacles (p. 255)

alters (ôl´ tərz) *v.* changes (p. 255)

Autumn, 1865, Frederick Walker, Victoria and Albert Museum

▲ **Critical Viewing** What details suggest that the person in this painting shares the mood of the speaker of Sonnet 29? **[Analyze]**

SONNET 29
WILLIAM SHAKESPEARE

When in disgrace with fortune and men's eyes,
I all alone beweep my outcast state,
And trouble deaf heaven with my bootless[1] cries,
And look upon myself and curse my fate,

5   Wishing me like to one more rich in hope,
Featured like him, like him with friends possessed,
Desiring this man's art, and that man's <u>scope</u>,
With what I most enjoy contented least.
Yet in these thoughts myself almost despising,

10   Haply[2] I think on thee, and then my state,
Like to the lark at break of day arising
From <u>sullen</u> earth, sings hymns at heaven's gate;
     For thy sweet love remembered such wealth brings
     That then I scorn to change my state with kings.

---

1. bootless futile.
2. haply *adv.* by chance

scope (skōp) *n.* range of perception or understanding

sullen (sul´ ən) *adj.* gloomy; dismal

✔ Reading Check

What is the speaker's state of mind at the end of the poem?

Sonnet 106
William Shakespeare

When in the <u>chronicle</u> of wasted time
I see descriptions of the fairest wights,[1]
And beauty making beautiful old rhyme,
In praise of ladies dead and lovely knights,
5 Then in the blazon[2] of sweet beauty's best
Of hand, of foot, of lip, of eye, of brow,
I see their antique pen would have express'd
Even such a beauty as you master now.
10 So all their praises are but prophecies
Of this our time, all you <u>prefiguring</u>;
And, for they look'd but with divining eyes,
They had not skill enough your worth to sing:
    For we, which now behold these present days,
    Have eyes to wonder, but lack tongues to praise.

chronicle (krän´ i kəl) *n.* historical record of events in chronological order

prefiguring (prē fig´ yer iŋ) *v.* resembling and so suggesting beforehand

---

1. **wights** (wītz) *n.* human beings; people.
2. **blazon** *n.* coat of arms; emblem.

Review and Assess

Thinking About the Selections

1. In Sonnet 29, did you find the shift in the speaker's mood believable? Explain.

2. **(a) Recall:** With whom is the speaker in Sonnet 29 in "disgrace"? **(b) Analyze:** What overall effect does this disgrace have on the speaker's state of mind?

3. **(a) Recall:** According to line 12 of Sonnet 29, what causes the shift in the speaker's mood? **(b) Analyze:** How would you describe the shifting moods in the sonnet? **(c) Interpret:** How do the last two lines summarize the theme?

4. **(a) Recall:** In Sonnet 106, what is ancient poetry "prefiguring"? **(b) Compare and Contrast:** Compare the ways in which writers past and present fail. **(c) Synthesize:** How are their failures a testament to the lady's beauty?

5. **Evaluate:** Based on what he reveals of himself, assess the character of the speaker in each sonnet.

6. **Make a Judgment:** Which sonnet, if either, presents a more convincing picture of love? Explain your answer.

Justa. Bartolome Esteban Murillo

◀ **Critical Viewing**
Which elements of this portrait seem idealized? Which seem realistic? **[Classify]**

SONNET 116
WILLIAM SHAKESPEARE

Let me not to the marriage of true minds
Admit <u>impediments</u>. Love is not love
Which <u>alters</u> when it alteration finds,
Or bends with the remover to remove.
5 O, no! It is an ever-fixèd mark
That looks on tempests and is never shaken;
It is the star to every wandering bark,[1]
Whose worth's unknown, although his height be taken.[2]
Love's not Time's fool, though rosy lips and cheeks
10 Within his bending sickle's compass[3] come;
Love alters not with his brief hours and weeks,
But bears it out even to the edge of doom.[4]
      If this be error, and upon me proved,
      I never writ, nor no man ever loved.

impediments (im ped′ ə mənts) *n.* obstacles

alters (ôl′ tərs) *v.* changes

---

1. **star . . . bark** the star that guides every wandering ship: the North Star.
2. **Whose . . . be taken** whose value is unmeasurable, although navigators measure its height in the sky.
3. **compass** range; scope.
4. **doom** Judgment Day.

✔**Reading Check**

According to the speaker, how long does true love last?

SONNET 130
WILLIAM SHAKESPEARE

My mistress' eyes are nothing like the sun,
Coral is far more red than her lips' red;
If snow be white, why then her breasts are dun;
If hairs be wires, black wires grow on her head.
5 I have seen roses damasked,[1] red and white,
But no such roses see I in her cheeks;
And in some perfumes is there more delight
Than in the breath that from my mistress reeks.[2]
I love to hear her speak. Yet well I know
10 That music hath a far more pleasing sound.
I grant I never saw a goddess go;[3]
My mistress, when she walks, treads on the ground.
    And yet, by heaven, I think my love as rare
    As any she belied[4] with false compare.

---

1. **damasked** variegated.
2. **reeks** emanates.
3. **go** walk.
4. **belied** (bē līd´) misrepresented.

Literary Analysis
The Shakespearean Sonnet Identify the rhyme scheme of the sonnet's first quatrain. Which line does not begin with an iambic foot?

Review and Assess

Thinking About the Selections

1. **Respond:** Which speaker's idea of love do you prefer? Why?

2. **(a) Recall:** To what is love compared in the second quatrain of Sonnet 116? **(b) Analyze:** Why is love similar to this object?

3. **(a) Recall:** Identify two images in Sonnet 116 that show the effects of time. **(b) Compare and Contrast:** Compare the effects of time on love with the ideal of love in the poem.

4. **(a) Recall:** How are the mistress's eyes, lips, cheeks, breath, and voice inferior, according to Sonnet 130? **(b) Interpret:** Why does the speaker say she "treads on the ground"?

5. **(a) Recall:** In Sonnet 130, what does the final couplet say about the speaker's feelings? **(b) Interpret:** What general truth does the couplet suggest? **(c) Draw Conclusions:** In his sonnets, Petrarch worshiped his mistress. Why has Sonnet 130 been called anti-Petrarchan?

6. **Apply:** In which of these sonnets does the speaker's attitude toward love seem more typical of our times? Explain.

Review and Assess

Literary Analysis

The Shakespearean Sonnet

1. (a) Identify the three quatrains and the couplet of the **Shakespearean sonnet,** Sonnet 29. (b) Which rhyming words represent the *b*'s, *e*'s, and *g*'s of the rhyme scheme?

2. Using a chart organized like the one below, show how Shakespeare conveys his message in the sonnet form in Sonnet 106.

Theme: _____	
Message of Quatrain 1	**Message of Quatrain 2**
⋮ **Connection to Theme:** ▼	⋮ **Connection to Theme:** ▼

3. Explain whether the couplet in Sonnet 116 affirms the rest of the sonnet or represents a sudden shift in attitude.

Comparing Literary Works

4. Explain how Shakespeare uses references to other poetry in Sonnets 106 and 130 to make these sonnets seem more in touch with life.

5. Which two of the sonnets use complex **syntax,** featuring sentences full of phrases and clauses?

6. (a) Compare the complex syntax of these two sonnets with the syntax of the other two sonnets. (b) Why does Shakespeare use each type of syntax?

Reading Strategy

Relating Structure to Theme

7. (a) List the main idea of each section of Sonnets 106 and 116. (b) Does each idea correspond to a quatrain or couplet? Explain.

8. If Shakespeare had adapted one of these sonnets to the Petrarchan form (an eight-line octet followed by a six-line sestet), how might the new form have affected the way he presented his message?

Extend Understanding

9. **Cultural Connection:** Which sonnet do you think best expresses modern attitudes? Support your choice with examples.

Quick Review

A **Shakespearean sonnet** consists of three four-line quatrains and a final two-line couplet. Each line is normally written in iambic pentameter—it contains five pairs of syllables, with the first syllable in each pair unstressed and the second stressed. The rhyme scheme is usually *abab cdcd efef gg.*

Syntax is the sentence structure a writer uses.

When you **relate structure to theme,** you note how variations of the theme—the work's central concern—are tied to different parts of the work.

 Take It to the Net
www.phschool.com
Take the interactive self-test online to check your understanding of these selections.

Integrate Language Skills

Vocabulary Development Lesson

Word Analysis: Greek Root -chron-

The word *chronicle* contains the Greek root *-chron-*, meaning "time." A chronicle is a record of events arranged in the order in which they occurred. Match the following related words with their definitions.

1. chronic
2. chronology
3. chronicler
4. chronological
5. chronometer
6. synchronized

  a. person who records events by date
  b. arranged in order of occurrence
  c. lasting over a long time
  d. a list of important events by date
  e. keeping the same time
  f. device for measuring time

Concept Development: Synonyms

Identify the synonym for each word below.

1. scope: (a) shovel, (b) range, (c) exploration
2. sullen: (a) strained, (b) dull, (c) sulky
3. impediments: (a) obstacles, (b) utensils, (c) commands
4. alters: (a) argues, (b) sacrifices, (c) changes
5. chronicle: (a) record, (b) paper, (c) dates
6. prefiguring: (a) guessing, (b) foreshadowing, (c) introducing

Spelling Strategy

Many words end in *-le* or *-el*. Usually, when a *k* sound precedes the ending, *-le* is used, as in *chronicle*, *sparkle*, and *tickle*. In your notebook, use *el* or *le* to complete each of the following words.

1. tentac__   2. barnac__   3. crack__

Grammar and Style Lesson

Participles as Adjectives

A **participle** is a verb form ending with *-ing* or *-ed*. A participle can act as an **adjective,** a word that modifies a noun or pronoun. For clarity, a participle must always appear near the noun or pronoun that it modifies.

In these examples, the participles are underlined.

For thy sweet love <u>remembered</u> such wealth brings . . . (modifies *love*)

And, for they look'd but with <u>divining</u> eyes, . . . (modifies *eyes*)

Though they function as adjectives, participles remind readers of the associated verbs, and so give a more active tone to a writer's descriptions.

Practice Copy each of the following sentences. Then, underline each participle, and draw an arrow to the noun that it modifies.

1. When in the chronicle of wasted time / I see descriptions of the fairest wights, . . .
2. It is the star to every wandering bark, . . .
3. . . . rosy lips and cheeks / Within his bending sickle's compass come; . . .
4. It is an ever-fixèd mark. . . .
5. Yet well I know / That music hath a far more pleasing sound.

Writing Application Write a brief review of your favorite sonnet. Include three participles.

W͞G *Prentice Hall Writing and Grammar Connection: Chapter 19, Section 2*

Writing Lesson

Analysis of a Sonnet's Imagery

In his sonnets, Shakespeare uses contrasts in imagery—word pictures—to suggest the complexities of love. Analyze the imagery in one of his sonnets, quoting from the poem to support your ideas.

Prewriting   Describe the images in a sonnet of your choice. Next to each image, note the idea that it expresses and its relationship to other images in the poem. Use a chart like the one shown here.

Model: Gathering Details

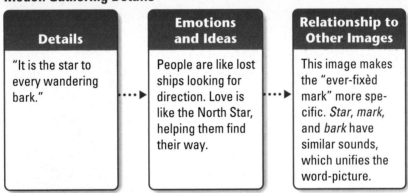

Details	Emotions and Ideas	Relationship to Other Images
"It is the star to every wandering bark."	People are like lost ships looking for direction. Love is like the North Star, helping them find their way.	This image makes the "ever-fixèd mark" more specific. *Star, mark,* and *bark* have similar sounds, which unifies the word-picture.

Drafting   Begin by summarizing the main ideas and feelings conveyed by the sonnet's imagery. Then, use the details you have gathered to support your ideas. Note especially relationships of similarity, contrast, and development among images.

Revising   Review your analysis. If necessary, refine your main idea to fit the details or add details to support the main idea.

W̸G Prentice Hall Writing and Grammar Connection: Chapter 14, Section 3

Extension Activities

Listening and Speaking Hold a **sonnet recital,** taking turns reciting sonnets with classmates.

- On a copy of the poem you choose, mark words to emphasize and shifts in tone.
- Rehearse using facial expressions and tone of voice to convey emotions.

After the recital, discuss the works.
[Group Activity]

Research and Technology Use the Internet, CD-ROM encyclopedias, or recordings from your public library to research Elizabethan music. Analyze the distinguishing characteristics of the music. Present your findings in a **multimedia report.**

 **Take It to the Net**   www.phschool.com

Go online for an additional research activity using the Internet.

A Rebirth of Love and Poetry

The years 1350 to 1550 marked a rebirth of interest in the literature of ancient Greece and Rome. It also marked a rebirth of interest in the nature of human experience, including love. The Italian poet Francesco Petrarcha, known by the English as Petrarch (pe´ trärk´), perfected a new type of poem to write about love in a new way.

The Invention of the Modern Sonnet A **sonnet** is a fourteen-line lyric with an elaborate rhyme scheme. In his sequence of 366 sonnets, Petrarch invented many of the attitudes and conventions that would be imitated by all proper poet-lovers, including the poets of the English Renaissance. Armed with this new tool of self-exploration, poets could disclose every aspect of love as they experienced it.

The Immortal Sonnet The sonnet continues to be a thriving form. While Petrarch devoted hundreds of sonnets to an unattainable, idealized woman, the modern Chilean poet Pablo Neruda seems to address an intimate companion in his sonnets.

Portrait of Laura, Biblioteca Laurenziana, Firenze

Sonnet 18

Francesco Petrarch
Translated by Noti

Ashamed sometimes thy beauties should remain
As yet unsung, sweet lady, in my rhyme;
When first I saw thee I recall the time.
Pleasing as none shall ever please again.
5 But no fit polish can my verse attain,
Not mine is strength to try the task sublime:
My genius, measuring its power to climb,
From such attempt doth prudently refrain.
Full oft I oped my lips to chant thy name;
10 Then in mid-utterance the lay was lost:
But say what muse can dare so bold a flight?
Full oft I strove in measure to indite;
But ah, the pen, the hand, the vein I boast,
At once were vanquish'd by the mighty theme!

▲ **Critical Viewing**
Petrarch invented the idea of the "unattainable woman." What details in this portrait reflect such an ideal? **[Analyze]**

Sonnet 28

Francesco Petrarch
Anonymous Translator

Alone, and lost in thought, the desert glade
Measuring I roam with ling'ring steps and slow;
And still a watchful glance around me throw,
Anxious to shun the print of human tread:
5 No other means I find, no surer aid
From the world's prying eye to hide my woe:
So well my wild disorder'd gestures show,
And lovelorn looks, the fire within me bred,
That well I deem each mountain, wood and plain,
10 And river knows, what I from man conceal,
What dreary hues my life's fond prospects dim.
Yet whate'er wild or savage paths I've ta'en,
Where'er I wander, love attends me still,
Soft whisp'ring to my soul, and I to him.

Thematic Connection
What attitudes toward love do Sidney and Spenser share with Petrarch?

Sonnet 69

Pablo Neruda
Translated by Stephan Tapscott

Maybe nothingness is to be without your presence,
without you moving, slicing the noon
like a blue flower, without you walking
later through the fog and the cobbles,

5 without the light you carry in your hand,
golden, which maybe others will not see,
which maybe no one knew was growing
like the red beginnings of a rose.

Francesco Petrarch

(1304–1374)

Along with Dante, Petrarch was among the great Italian poets of the fourteenth century. Born in Arezzo, Italy, he moved to Avignon, France, when he was eight. In 1320, Petrarch returned to Italy to study law but began to write poetry.

He returned to Avignon in 1326, where he first saw the famous Laura, whom he celebrates in his love poetry. Laura died in the Great Plague of 1348.

In short, without your presence: without your coming
10   suddenly, incitingly,[1] to know my life,
gust of a rosebush, wheat of wind:

since then I am because you are,
since then you are, I am, we are,
and through love I will be, you will be, we'll be.

Sonnet 89

Pablo Neruda
Translated by Stephan Tapscott

When I die, I want your hands on my eyes:
I want the light and wheat of your beloved hands
to pass their freshness over me once more:
I want to feel the softness that changed my destiny.

5   I want you to live while I wait for you, asleep.
I want your ears still to hear the wind, I want you
to sniff the sea's aroma that we loved together,
to continue to walk on the sand we walk on.

I want what I love to continue to live,
10   and you whom I love and sang above everything else
to continue to flourish, full-flowered:

so that you can reach everything my love directs you to,
so that my shadow can travel along in your hair,
so that everything can learn the reason for my song.

---

1. **incitingly** *adv.* in a way that sets in motion or stimulates to action.

Connecting Literature Around the World

1. Of all the sonnets you read in Part One: Lovers and Their Lines, including Petrarch's and Neruda's, which were your favorites? Why?
2. Compare and contrast the expressions of love in Neruda's Sonnet 89 with those in Spenser's Sonnet 1.

Pablo Neruda

(1904–1973)

Pablo Neruda was born in Parral, Chile, the son of a railway worker. He was only twenty when his book *Twenty Love Poems and a Desperate Song* earned him recognition as one of Chile's best young poets.

Much of Neruda's work expresses political sentiments. However, he never lost his sense of poetry's irrational magic. In 1971, he received the Nobel Prize for Literature.

PART 2

The Influence of the Monarchy

King Henry VIII of England,
after Hans Holbein

Queen Elizabeth I of England,
Unknown Artist

King James I of England,
John De Critz the Elder,
Galleria Platina, Palazzo Pitti,
Florence, Italy

Prepare to Read

from Utopia ◆
Elizabeth I: Speech Before Her Troops

Sir Thomas More (1477–1535)

Even the king who had him put to death respected him. Sir Thomas More—devoted husband and father, passionate defender of the common citizen, sophisticated legal advisor, and deeply religious man—ultimately came to grief through the very quality that made him admirable: his integrity.

Early Career Trained in Latin, logic, and the law, More pursued a successful legal and political career. He championed the cultural movement know as Humanism, writing poems on behalf of the renewal of scholarship and religion advocated by the Dutch Humanist Desidirius Erasmus (1469–1536).

Opposing the King More entered King Henry VIII's service full-time in 1518 and soon became an important advisor. At times, his opinions made him a friend, and at other times, a bitter enemy of the king.

The final break with the king came when Henry asked Pope Clement VII for a divorce from Catherine of Aragon. She had not born him a male child, and Henry was eager for an heir. The pope denied the request, and in 1534, Henry broke with the Roman Catholic Church, establishing the Church of England, with himself as the head.

A devout Catholic, More opposed the king's divorce, arousing his anger. In 1535, the king had More beheaded for his refusal to swear an oath that violated his beliefs.

An Ideal Kingdom More, however, had a kind of revenge. His book *Utopia*, an account of an ideal kingdom (the title means "not a place"), exposes the injustices of his time. It still stands today as a challenge to leaders to pursue social justice.

Elizabeth I (1533–1603)

The Elizabethan Age was a period rich in cultural activity and political success. It owes its name to an equally energetic ruler, Queen Elizabeth I. Elizabeth's path to the throne, though, was fraught with peril and sadness, and serious political challenges awaited her once she arrived.

A Tumultuous Childhood Elizabeth grew up surrounded by danger and intrigue. When she was not yet three years old, her mother, Anne Boleyn, was executed by her father, Henry VIII. After her father's death, Elizabeth's brother, Edward VI, inherited the throne. At his death six years later, Elizabeth's half sister, Mary, took the throne. Ever suspicious of Elizabeth, Mary even had her jailed at one point. Finally, in 1558, after Mary's death, Elizabeth was crowned queen of England and Ireland.

A Triumphant Ruler Once on the throne, Elizabeth met problems with decisive action and subtle diplomacy. Reigning as a single woman, she wielded her unmarried status as a political tool, taking suitors from all factions as a way of keeping the peace. During her reign, England won significant victories against its archenemy, Spain. With the destruction of the Spanish Armada (navy), England entered its long term as the world's supreme naval power.

The Elizabethan Age Today, Elizabeth I is regarded as one of the finest English monarchs. Highly intelligent, beloved by her subjects, she governed during a time of artistic achievement, military success, and economic advance. The young girl who grew up in danger left her name on a glorious era: the Elizabethan Age.

Preview

Connecting to the Literature

Picture a crowd wandering around a mall. Now, picture a basketball team racing downcourt, flipping passes back and forth. To turn a crowd into a team, you need unity. With rousing words, Elizabeth I and More try to unify the English people.

Literary Analysis

Theme: The Monarch as Hero

The literature of the English Renaissance (1485–1625) contains many depictions of the **monarch as hero,** the ruler as a perfect or larger-than-life person. Writers created heroic portraits to inspire confidence and loyalty in citizens. Praising, or even flattering, rulers in power could also help a writer establish strong connections with the court.

Look for this **theme** in these selections.

Comparing Literary Works

In *Utopia*, More paints a picture of the heroic monarch with brisk logic, connecting the qualities of a monarch with the effects of his or her actions. By contrast, Elizabeth I needs no arguments—as she gives her speech, she acts out the part of the heroic monarch, from the armor she wears to her offer to join the troops on the front lines. Compare the different **persuasive devices** these writers use to bring their audience to accept their presentation of the heroic monarch. These include the following techniques:

- **Reasoned argument**—the use of one idea to logically support another.
- **Charged language**—words with strong positive or negative connotations used to create a memorable perspective on an issue.

Reading Strategy

Summarizing

To understand a difficult work, **summarize** it by restating the main ideas. As you read these selections, track main ideas with a chart like the one shown.

Vocabulary Development

confiscation (kän´ fis kā´ shən) *n.* act of seizing private property (p. 267)

sloth (slôth) *n.* laziness; idleness (p. 267)

subsequently (sub´ si kwənt lē) *adv.* at a later time (p. 267)

abrogated (ab´rō gāt´ id) *v.* repealed; annulled (p. 267)

forfeited (fôr´ fit id) *v.* gave up, as a penalty (p. 267)

fraudulent (frô´ jə lənt) *adj.* characterized by deceit or trickery (p. 267)

treachery (trech´ ər ē) *n.* betrayal of trust, faith, or allegiance (p. 269)

stead (sted) *n.* position of a person as filled by a replacement (p. 270)

> **More's Sentence**
>
> Let him curb crime, and by his wise conduct prevent it rather than allow it to increase, only to punish it subsequently.

> **Main Idea**
>
> A good king should try to prevent crime.

from Utopia
Sir Thomas More

Gardens at Llancerch, Denbigshire, Yale Center for British Art, New Haven, Connecticut

▲ **Critical Viewing**
How does this painting illustrate the orderliness of the well-run kingdom More advocates? **[Apply]**

Background

Running a kingdom is expensive. Waging wars and living in royal style requires money, and raising enough money was often a problem for the kings and queens of England. Henry VIII's father, Henry VII (ruled 1485–1509), approached the problem in several ways. He avoided costly wars, and he encouraged trade, which he then taxed. He also taxed the poor harshly and took advantage of outdated laws that gave monarchs the right to impose fines in certain matters. (More refers to such laws when he speaks of "laws already abrogated by disuse.") As a result, he acquired a large fortune for the Crown. In *Utopia*, More casts a critical eye on some of the ways in which monarchs like Henry VIII collected wealth.

Reading Strategy
Summarize Summarize the main ideas in the first two sentences.

Suppose I should maintain that men choose a king not for his sake, but for theirs, that by his care and efforts they may live comfortably and safely. And that therefore a prince ought to take more care of his people's happiness than of his own, as a shepherd ought to take more care of his flock than of himself. Certainly it is wrong to think that the poverty of the people is a safeguard of public peace. Who quarrel more than beggars do? Who long for a change more earnestly than the dissatisfied? Or who rushes in to create disorders [with] such desperate boldness as the man who has nothing to lose and everything to gain? If a king is so hated and scorned by his subjects that he can rule them only by insults, ill-usage, <u>confiscation</u>, and impoverishment, it would certainly be better for him to quit his kingdom than to keep the name of authority when he has lost the majesty of kingship through his misrule. It is less befitting the dignity of a king to reign over beggars than over rich and happy subjects. Thus Fabricius, a man of noble and exalted spirit, said he would rather govern rich men than be rich himself. When a ruler enjoys wealth and pleasure while all about him are grieving and groaning, he acts as a jailor rather than as a king. He is a poor physician who cannot cure a disease except by throwing his patient into another. A king who can only rule his people by taking from them the pleasures of life shows that he does not know how to govern free men. He ought to shake off either his <u>sloth</u> or his pride, for the people's hatred and scorn arise from these faults in him. Let him live on his own income without wronging others, and limit his expenses to his revenue. Let him curb crime, and by his wise conduct prevent it rather than allow it to increase, only to punish it <u>subsequently</u>. Let him not rashly revive laws already <u>abrogated</u> by disuse, especially if they have been long forgotten and never wanted. And let him never seize any property on the ground that it is <u>forfeited</u> as a fine, when a judge would regard a subject as wicked and <u>fraudulent</u> for claiming it.

confiscation (kän´ fis kā´ shən) *n.* act of seizing private property

sloth (slôth) *n.* laziness; idleness

subsequently (sub´ si kwənt lē) *adv.* at a later time

abrogated (ab´ rō gāt´ id) *v.* repealed; annulled

forfeited (fôr´ fit id) *v.* gave up, as a penalty

fraudulent (frô´ jə lənt) *adj.* characterized by deceit or trickery

Review and Assess

Thinking About the Selection

1. **Respond:** Do you think More's ideas would lead to greater fairness?

2. **(a) Recall:** What reason does More give for viewing poverty as a threat to a nation? **(b) Analyze:** How does he connect this idea to the notion that a king should rule for the sake of his people?

3. **(a) Recall:** According to More, what does a king lose when he rules by "insults, ill-usage, confiscation, and impoverishment"? **(b) Infer:** What assumption about monarchs or the monarchy does this point reveal?

4. **Generalize:** Explain how More appeals to the self-interest and even the vanity of kings to strengthen his argument.

5. **(a) Summarize:** What general rule for good leadership does More advocate in this selection? **(b) Apply:** How do More's views of good government resemble modern democratic ideals?

Portrait of Queen Elizabeth I, Anonymous Artist, Private Collection

▲ **Critical Viewing** What does this rendering of Elizabeth indicate about the importance of pageantry—ceremony and theatrical presence—in her court? Explain your reasoning. **[Interpret]**

Speech Before Her Troops

QUEEN ELIZABETH I

Background

In 1587, Protestant Queen Elizabeth agreed to have her Catholic cousin, Mary, Queen of Scots, executed. This act gave Philip II, the Catholic king of Spain and England's archenemy, an excuse to attack England with the Spanish Armada (navy). As nerves grew frayed and soldiers began to grumble about delays in pay, Elizabeth, wearing a white gown and a silver breast-plate, appeared before her land troops to rally them. She delivered the following speech. (At the time, the Armada had already been defeated, but the news had not yet reached Elizabeth and her troops. Invasion seemed imminent.)

As the speech shows, the physical presence of a monarch had a special significance in Elizabeth's day. The touch of a monarch, it was said, could cure certain diseases, and people acknowledged the presence of royalty with gestures such as the removal of hats. In her speech, Queen Elizabeth makes effective use of people's reverence for the monarch's person.

My loving people, we have been persuaded by some, that are careful of our safety, to take heed how we commit ourselves to armed multitudes,[1] for fear of <u>treachery</u>; but I assure you, I do not desire to live to distrust my faithful and loving people. Let tyrants fear; I have always so behaved myself that, under God, I have placed my chiefest strength and safeguard in the loyal hearts and good will of my subjects. And therefore I am come amongst you at this time, not as for my recreation or sport, but being resolved, in the midst and heat of the battle, to live or die amongst you all; to lay down, for my God, and for my kingdom, and for my people, my honor and my blood, even the dust. I know I have but the body of a weak and feeble woman; but I

treachery (trech′ ər ē) *n.* betrayal of trust, faith, or allegiance

**Reading Check**

What have Elizabeth's advisers cautioned her about?

1. **armed multitudes** troops such as she is addressing

have the heart of a king, and of a king of England, too; and think foul scorn that Parma[2] or Spain, or any prince of Europe, should dare to invade the borders of my realms: to which, rather than any dishonor should grow by me, I myself will take up arms; I myself will be your general, judge, and rewarder of every one of your virtues in the field. I know already, by your forwardness, that you have deserved rewards and crowns; and we do assure you, on the word of a prince, they shall be duly paid you. In the mean my lieutenant general shall be in my <u>stead</u>, than whom never prince commanded a more noble and worthy subject; not doubting by your obedience to my general, by your concord in the camp, and by your valor in the field, we shall shortly have a famous victory over the enemies of my God, of my kingdom, and of my people.

stead (sted) *n.* position of a person as filled by a replacement

---

2. **Parma** Alessandro Farnese (1545–1592), duke of the state of Parma and Piacenza in Italy and King Philip of Spain's representative in the Netherlands. Philip had him prepare troops for the invasion of England.

Review and Assess
Thinking About the Selection

1. **Respond:** If you were a British soldier at the time, how would you have responded to Elizabeth's speech?

2. **(a) Recall:** What have Elizabeth's advisors warned her not to do? **(b) Recall:** According to her speech, why does she do it anyway? **(c) Interpret:** What effect is this introduction designed to have on her audience?

3. **(a) Recall:** Name two concerns of Elizabeth's audience that she addresses. **(b) Analyze:** How does she put these concerns to rest?

4. **(a) Recall:** What does Elizabeth promise to do rather than permit her country to be dishonored? **(b) Analyze:** Which criticism of her capacity to rule is she answering?

5. **(a) Analyze:** Explain two ways in which Elizabeth's physical "person"—for instance, her presence on the scene or her femininity—plays a role in this speech. **(b) Apply:** Does the physical presence of leaders today count as much as it did in Elizabeth's time? Explain.

Review and Assess

Literary Analysis

Theme: The Monarch as Hero

1. (a) How idealistic is More's presentation of the **theme of the monarch as hero?** (b) How realistic?

2. (a) Explain how More paints a picture of a rather unheroic monarch even as he describes an ideal monarch. (b) What effect might More have hoped this picture would have?

3. Elizabeth says, "I know I have but the body of a weak and feeble woman; but I have the heart of a king, and of a king of England, too. . . ." Relate this assertion to the idea of a heroic monarch.

Comparing Literary Works

4. (a) Identify a **persuasive device** in each work. (b) Do these devices appeal to logic, ethics, or feelings? Explain.

5. (a) Analyze how Elizabeth's speech turns her appearance among the troops into a persuasive device. Use a chart like the one below, noting under the appropriate heading each reference she makes to the reasons for her appearance. (b) Do you think this device is more effective than one of More's arguments? Explain.

6. (a) Contrast the role of persuasive arguments in More's work with their role in Elizabeth's speech. (b) Which work has stronger arguments? Explain. (c) Which is more persuasive? Explain.

Reading Strategy

Summarizing

7. **Summarize** More's *Utopia*, listing each main idea.

8. Summarize Elizabeth's speech.

Extend Understanding

9. **Career Connection:** Motivational speakers inspire audiences to achieve goals. What tips might a speaker learn from these authors?

Quick Review

A **theme** is the central idea, concern, or purpose of a literary work.

In the literature presenting the **theme of the monarch as hero,** a ruler is portrayed as a larger-than-life person with noble qualities.

A **persuasive device** is the use of words to lead an audience to accept a particular position or attitude. Persuasive devices include **arguments,** ideas supported by their logical connections to other ideas, and **charged language,** words with strong positive or negative connotations.

To **summarize,** restate the main ideas of a work.

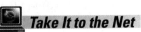 **Take It to the Net**
www.phschool.com
Take the interactive self-test online to check your understanding of these selections.

Integrate Language Skills

Vocabulary Development Lesson

Word Analysis: Latin Root -sequent-

The word *subsequently*, meaning "at a later time," is derived from the Latin root *-sequent-*, meaning "following in time or order." Use the meaning of *-sequent-* to match each word below with its definition.

1. consequence
2. sequential
3. non sequitur
4. subsequent

a. something that does not follow
b. result of an action
c. at a later time
d. coming in order

Spelling Strategy

Either *i*, *ei*, or *ie* can spell the short *i* sound, as in the words *different*, *forfeited*, and *kerchief*. Correct the misspellings in the following passage.

A surfiet of unfair laws will yield disloyalty. The people must be considered, no matter how mischeivous they seem.

Concept Development: Analogies

An analogy compares two relationships to show their basic similarity. For each analogy below, analyze the relationship between the first and second words. Then, in your notebook, write the vocabulary word from page 265 that forms the same relationship with the third word.

1. lending : borrowing :: grant : ____?____
2. front : back :: beforehand : ____?____
3. built : constructed :: repealed : ____?____
4. goal : ambition :: place : ____?____
5. honorable : untrustworthy :: authentic : ____?____
6. nervousness : calm :: ____?____ : energy
7. goodness : virtue :: betrayal : ____?____
8. praised : honored :: surrendered ____?____

Grammar and Style Lesson

Complex Sentences

Complex sentences contain a main clause and one or more subordinate clauses. The main clause can stand by itself as a sentence. The subordinate clauses modify the main clause.

> SUB. CLAUSE
> **Example:** When a ruler enjoys wealth . . .
> SUB. CLAUSE
> when all about him are grieving, . . .
> MAIN CLAUSE
> he acts as a jailor. . . .

Writers use complex sentences to show the connections between ideas or events.

Practice Copy the sentences below, underlining main clauses once and subordinate clauses twice.

1. He is a poor king who rules unfairly.
2. A king should not seize property when a subject would be wrong to do the same.
3. Elizabeth's advisors warned her that appearing before the troops was risky.
4. She knew that the troops were upaid.
5. Her general, than whom there was no better commander, led the troops.

Writing Application Using three complex sentences, write your own description of an ideal leader.

WG *Prentice Hall Writing and Grammar Connection: Chapter 19, Section 4*

Writing Lesson

Letter to an Editor

Thomas More and Queen Elizabeth I have definite ideas about the characteristics of a good leader. In a letter to the editor, apply their criteria of good leadership—or the example they set in their lives—to a contemporary leader.

Prewriting Review the selections and the biographical information on page 264, taking notes on the writers' ideas about and their practice of leadership. Then, research a modern leader, taking notes on his or her leadership skills as shown in news stories.

Drafting Begin by stating the ideas of leadership you will apply, and then apply these ideas in an analysis of the leader you have chosen.

Revising Reread your draft, highlighting passages in which you express parallel ideas—ideas that are similar to one another. Consider rewriting marked passages using parallel phrases.

Model: Using Parallelism to Create Persuasive Tone

When a senator suddenly changes his or her mind about

an important issue, he or she begins to look irresponsible.
When a senator makes and then apologizes for hasty,
~~A congressperson who makes and then apologizes for hasty and~~
inaccurate statements, he or she starts to look careless.
~~inaccurate statements seems careless.~~

> By rewriting the second sentence to begin with a subordinate clause, the writer uses parallelism to create a persuasive rhythm and to convey confidence.

 Prentice Hall Writing and Grammar Connection: Chapter 7, Section 4

Extension Activities

Listening and Speaking Form two groups, and prepare for a **debate** on this question: Do More's ideas apply to today's leaders? Use the following persuasive devices:

- strong arguments
- effective emotional appeals
- charged language
- vivid images

Hold your debate before the class. **[Group Activity]**

Research and Technology Create a large **illustrated timeline** of the Elizabethan Age, indicating major achievements and events. Use library and Internet references to identify entries. Collect information on notecards, and organize the cards chronologically as you plan the timeline.

 Take It to the Net www.phschool.com

Go online for an additional research activity using the Internet.

Prepare to Read

from The King James Bible

The King James Bible (completed 1611)

For centuries, the Bible was the cornerstone of European culture—the ultimate reference for rulers and priests, the ultimate authorization for laws and religious practices, a treasury of images and subjects for art. Yet, the book that shaped the lives of Europeans was inaccessible to the majority of them. During the Reformation of the 1500s, a time of religious dispute and division, the need for a closer study of the Bible was widely acknowledged, which led to translations of the work into the vernacular, or common languages. For the first time, this grounding work became widely accessible.

The King James Bible, the authoritative English translation, was created at the command of King James I, who ascended the English throne upon the death of Queen Elizabeth I. In 1604, James commissioned fifty-four scholars and clergymen to compare all known texts of the Bible and prepare the definitive English edition.

Early Bibles To understand the magnitude of King James's project, consider the nature of the work to be translated. The Bible, a collection of books developed over more than 1,200 years, consists of two main parts—the Old Testament, written in Hebrew, and the New Testament, written in Greek. In about A.D. 405, St. Jerome finished translating the Bible into Latin. This translation, the Vulgate, remained the standard Bible of the West for centuries. King James's translators, though, were to review the original sources, as well as translations of the work.

A Systematic Plan The project was carefully organized from the start. The books of the Bible were divided among six groups of scholars in Westminster, Oxford, and Cambridge. A set of fifteen guidelines for the project was drafted, governing everything from the translation of names to the procedure for review.

The groups took four years to produce their initial drafts. Then, two scholars from each region spent nine months in London reviewing and revising the draft. The preface to the first edition acknowledged the importance of rewriting during the project—"Neither did we disdain to revise that which we had done, and to bring back to the anvil that which we had hammered."

After laboring for seven years, the group produced one of the great works of English literature. The King James Bible has been called "the only classic ever created by a committee."

Early English Bibles The King James Bible was not the first English translation of the book. The reformer John Wycliffe had translated the Bible into English in the late 1300s. It was William Tyndale's sixteenth-century version, though, that most influenced James's translators.

Tyndale's Legacy Tyndale was a Protestant chaplain and tutor in England. As Protestants across Europe challenged the authority of the Catholic Church, Tyndale decided to translate the Bible. Facing clerical opposition at home, he fled to what is now Germany, where he published his translation of the New Testament. Before he had completed work on the Old Testament, however, he was arrested for heresy and executed near Brussels, Belgium, in 1536.

As England became more Protestant, Tyndale came to be viewed, not as a heretic, but as a hero. King James's committee closely followed the magnificent diction and rhythms of Tyndale's groundbreaking translation.

A Lasting Vision Generations of English-speakers have grown up reading the King James Bible. It has contributed hundreds of phrases to the language— "fat of the land," "out of the mouths of babes," "suffer fools gladly"—and left a lasting mark on English prose style.

Preview

Connecting to the Literature

Not too long ago, the development of the Web opened up a world of information. Yet, that event was small compared to an earlier "information revolution"—the translation of the Bible into modern languages.

Literary Analysis

Psalm, Sermon, and Parable

The Bible conveys themes of faith in a few genres, including these:

- **Psalms**—sacred songs or lyric poems in praise of God. The Old Testament's Book of Psalms contains 150 such pieces.
- **Sermons**—speeches offering religious or moral instruction. Given by Jesus on a mountainside in Galilee, the Sermon on the Mount contains the basic teachings of Christianity.
- **Parables**—simple stories from which a moral or religious lesson can be drawn. The most famous are in the New Testament.

Notice the different impact and features of each genre.

Comparing Literary Works

Psalms, sermons, and parables all convey deep messages about life. Each type of writing communicates messages in a manner suited to its form.

- Psalms are songs. To engage an audience, psalms may feature vivid, memorable **metaphors**—comparisons of unlike things.
- To help listeners understand, sermons may feature **analogies**—explanations comparing abstract relationships to familiar ones.
- Parables are **narratives**—they tell a story illustrating a message.

As you read, compare the methods by which each selection conveys its message and the appeal and effectiveness of each.

Reading Strategy

Inferring Meaning

Some portions of the Bible require you to **make inferences**—to uncover meaning that is implied but not directly stated. To make inferences, identify key details in the text and then examine the relation of one detail to another. Use a chart like the one shown.

Vocabulary Development

righteousness (rī′ chəs nis) *n.* the characteristic of acting in a just, virtuous manner (p. 277)

stature (stach′ ər) *n.* height; level of achievement (p. 278)

prodigal (präd′ i gəl) *adj.* recklessly wasteful (p. 279)

entreated (en trēt′ id) *v.* begged; pleaded with (p. 280)

transgressed (trans grest′) *v.* overstepped or broke (a law or commandment) (p. 280)

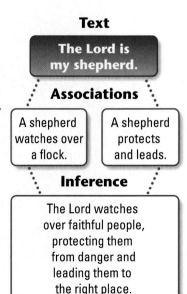

Text

The Lord is my shepherd.

Associations

A shepherd watches over a flock.

A shepherd protects and leads.

Inference

The Lord watches over faithful people, protecting them from danger and leading them to the right place.

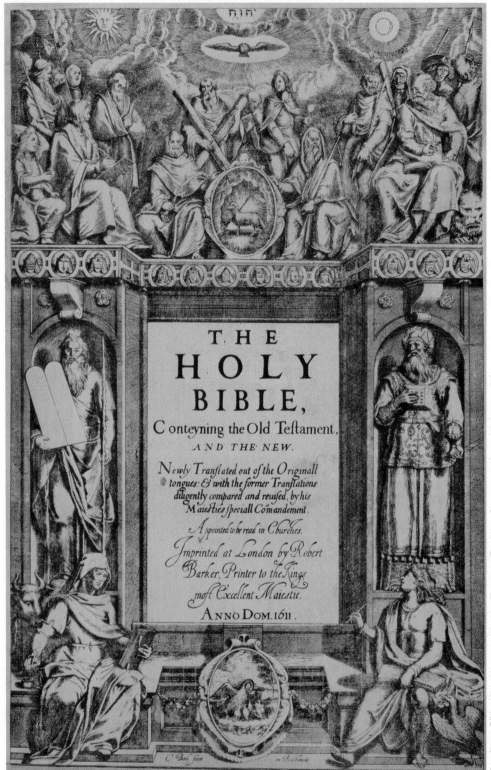

King James Bible, 1611, title page of the New Testament, The Folger Shakespeare Library, Washington, D.C.

▲ **Critical Viewing** What can you infer about the King James Bible from the style of the art on this title page? **[Infer]**

Psalm 23

from The King James Bible

Background

Up to the middle 1400s, Bibles were painstakingly copied by hand. The resulting manuscripts, though often quite beautiful, were rare and costly. When the German inventor Johann Gutenberg devised a method of printing with movable type, widespread distribution of the Bible began.

1 The Lord is my shepherd; I shall not want.

2 He maketh me to lie down in green pastures: he leadeth me beside the still waters.

3 He restoreth my soul: he leadeth me in the paths of <u>righteousness</u> for his name's sake.

4 Yea, though I walk through the valley of the shadow of death, I will fear no evil: for thou art with me; thy rod and thy staff they comfort me.

5 Thou preparest a table before me in the presence of mine enemies; thou anointest my head with oil; my cup runneth over.

6 Surely goodness and mercy shall follow me all the days of my life: and I will dwell in the house of the Lord forever.

righteousness (rī´ chəs nis) *n.* the characteristic of acting in a just, virtuous manner

Review and Assess

Thinking About the Selection

1. **Respond:** Which phrases in Psalm 23 are familiar to you?

2. **(a) Recall:** What image is developed in the opening verses?
   (b) Infer: Why might this image provide comfort to listeners?
   (c) Draw Conclusions: How does the inclusion of the images of the valley of death and of enemies strengthen the psalm?

3. **Draw Conclusions:** What is the message of the psalm?

4. **Evaluate:** Does the psalm offer comfort, express hope of comfort, or both?

5. **Apply:** What images of comfort and guidance might a modern psalm writer use?

from The Sermon on the Mount

from The King James Bible Matthew 6: 24-30

24 No man can serve two masters: for either he will hate the one, and love the other; or else he will hold to the one, and despise the other. Ye cannot serve God and mammon.[1]

25 Therefore I say unto you, Take no thought for your life, what ye shall eat, or what ye shall drink; nor yet for your body, what ye shall put on. Is not the life more than meat, and the body than raiment?[2]

26 Behold the fowls of the air: for they sow not, neither do they reap, nor gather into barns; yet your heavenly Father feedeth them. Are ye not much better than they?

27 Which of you by taking thought can add one cubit unto his <u>stature</u>?

28 And why take ye thought for raiment? Consider the lilies of the field, how they grow; they toil not, neither do they spin:

29 And yet I say unto you, That even Solomon[3] in all his glory was not arrayed like one of these.

30 Wherefore, if God so clothe the grass of the field, which to day is, and to morrow is cast into the oven, *shall he* not much more *clothe* you, O ye of little faith?

---

1. **mammon** (mam´ ən) *n.* money, personified as a false god.
2. **raiment** (rā´ mənt) *n.* clothing; wearing apparel.
3. **Solomon** (säl´ ə mən) *n.* tenth-century B.C. king of Israel.

Literary Analysis
Psalm, Sermon, and Parable Why is the strategy of asking the audience questions particularly suited to a sermon?

stature (stach´ ər) *n.* height; level of achievement

Review and Assess

Thinking About the Selection

1. **Respond:** How do you view worries about the future?

2. **(a) Recall:** What human activities do the fowls and lilies of the parable avoid? **(b) Analyze:** How does this "omission" affect their lives? **(c) Interpret:** Describe the attitude towards life that Jesus advocates.

3. **Draw Conclusions:** Does Jesus, the speaker of this sermon, mean that his followers should literally "take no thought for life"? Explain.

4. **Speculate:** Explain what a life lived like the lilies might be like.

The Parable of the Prodigal Son

from The King James Bible Luke 15: 11–32

11 And he said, A certain man had two sons:

12 And the younger of them said to *his* father, Father, give me the portion of goods that falleth *to me*. And he divided unto them *his* living.

13 And not many days after the younger son gathered all together, and took his journey into a far country, and there wasted his substance with riotous living.

14 And when he had spent all, there arose a mighty famine in that land; and he began to be in want.

15 And he went and joined himself to a citizen of that country; and he sent him into his fields to feed swine.

16 And he would fain[1] have filled his belly with the husks that the swine did eat: and no man gave unto him.

17 And when he came to himself, he said, How many hired servants of my father's have bread enough and to spare, and I perish with hunger!

18 I will arise and go to my father, and will say unto him, Father, I have sinned against heaven, and before thee,

19 And am no more worthy to be called thy son: make me as one of thy hired servants.

20 And he arose, and came to his father. But when he was yet a great way off, his father saw him, and had compassion, and ran, and fell on his neck, and kissed him.

21 And the son said unto him, Father, I have sinned against heaven, and in thy sight, and am no more worthy to be called thy son.

22 But the father said to his servants, Bring forth the best robe, and put *it* on him; and put a ring on his hand, and shoes on *his* feet:

23 And bring hither the fatted calf, and kill *it*; and let us eat, and be merry:

24 For this my son was dead, and is alive again; he was lost, and is found. And they began to be merry.

---

1. **fain** *adv.* gladly.

---

prodigal (präd´ i gəl) *adj.* recklessly wasteful

The British Tradition

Church and State in Literature

These excerpts from the Bible teach trust and calm, but religion has led to some unrelenting conflicts in the history of Great Britain. English literature often reflects this turmoil. When Henry VIII broke with Rome and created the Church of England, statesman Sir Thomas More was beheaded for maintaining his Catholic views. Later writers were not deterred from expressing their opinions on religious matters, as Jonathan Swift did in *Gulliver's Travels*, a parody of religious disputes of the day.

The translation of the Bible from which this parable is taken was one response to religious conflict. By creating the King James Bible, a standard authorized by a king, James I hoped to avert conflict over religious matters.

✔ Reading Check

How does the father respond to his prodigal son's return?

25 Now his elder son was in the field: and as he came and drew nigh to the house, he heard music and dancing.

26 And he called one of the servants, and asked what these things meant.

27 And he said unto him, Thy brother is come; and thy father hath killed the fatted calf, because he hath received him safe and sound.

28 And he was angry, and would not go in: therefore came his father out, and <u>entreated</u> him.

29 And he answering said to *his* father, Lo, these many years do I serve thee, neither <u>transgressed</u> I at any time thy commandment: and yet thou never gavest me a kid, that I might make merry with my friends:

30 But as soon as this thy son was come, which hath devoured thy living with harlots, thou hast killed for him the fatted calf.

31 And he said unto him, Son, thou art ever with me, and all that I have is thine.

32 It was meet² that we should make merry, and be glad: for this thy brother was dead, and is alive again; and was lost, and is found.

---

2. meet *adj.* fitting.

entreated (en trēt′ id) *v.* begged; pleaded with

transgressed (trans grest′) *v.* overstepped or broke (a law or commandment)

Review and Assess

Thinking About the Selection

1. **Respond:** If you were the elder son, how would you have reacted to the father's response at the end? Why?

2. **(a) Recall:** What causes the younger son to return home?
   (b) Compare and Contrast: Contrast the father's and the older son's responses to the younger son's return. Why do they respond differently?

3. **(a) Recall:** How does the younger son express his repentance?
   (b) Deduce: How truly repentant do you think the younger son is? **(c) Draw Conclusions:** What does the parable suggest about the importance of the motives for repentance?

4. **(a) Recall:** What specific complaint does the older son make?
   (b) Assess: How effectively does the father address his concerns?

5. **(a) Interpret:** Why does the father say that the younger son is "alive again"? **(b) Apply:** In what circumstances might the lesson of the parable apply today?

6. **Take a Position:** Do you think mercy and forgiveness are more important than, less important than, or equal in importance to justice? Explain, using examples from the parable.

Review and Assess

Literary Analysis

Psalm, Sermon, and Parable

1. (a) What is the message of the selection from the Sermon on the Mount? (b) Why is the form of a **sermon** suited to this lesson?
2. (a) What is the chief moral lesson of the Parable of the Prodigal Son? (b) Why is the form of a **parable** suited to this lesson?

Comparing Literary Works

3. (a) Contrast the styles of the **psalm,** the sermon, and the parable. (b) How is the style of each selection appropriate to its purpose?
4. The **metaphor** of the shepherd in Psalm 23, the **analogy** of the birds in the Sermon on the Mount, and the **narrative** in the Parable of the Prodigal Son are all designed to appeal to their original audience of simple, rural folk. Explain, using a chart like the one below.

Images: Familiar / Unfamiliar?	Simple / Difficult?	Memorable? Why?

5. Of the following, which did you find easiest to understand: the metaphor of the shepherd, the analogy of the lilies, or the lesson of the prodigal son? For each, explain what was clear and what was complex.

Reading Strategy

Inferring Meaning

6. **Make inferences** about the meaning of this quotation from Psalm 23: "I will dwell in the house of the Lord forever."
7. What inference can you make from the fact that this excerpt from the Sermon on the Mount closes with "O ye of little faith?"
8. After reading the Parable of the Prodigal Son, what inference can you make about the value the Bible places on forgiveness?

Extend Understanding

9. **Career Connection:** If you wanted to commission a new translation of the Bible, would you choose a committee of translators or a single translator? Why?

Quick Review

A **sermon** is a speech offering religious or moral instruction.

A **parable** is a short, simple story from which a moral or religious lesson can be drawn.

A **psalm** is a sacred song or lyric poem in praise of God.

A **metaphor** is an implied comparison, in which a thing is described as if it were another kind of thing.

An **analogy** is an extended comparison in which the relationship between two things is explained by comparing it with another relationship.

A **narrative** is a story telling a sequence of events.

To **make inferences,** draw conclusions about the implied meaning of a text based on information it presents.

 Take It to the Net
www.phschool.com
Take the interactive self-test online to check your understanding of the selection.

Integrate Language Skills

Vocabulary Development Lesson

Word Analysis: Latin Root -stat-

The word *stature*, meaning "height when standing," comes from the Latin root -*stat*-, sometimes spelled -*stit*-, which means "to stand" or "to set up." Use this meaning to match the following words with their definitions.

1. statue   a. to set up a procedure
2. stationary   b. standing still; not moving
3. institute   c. a figure that stands

Spelling Strategy

Remember that the word-ending -*ious*, found in *precious*, is more common, but that some words, such as *righteous*, end with -*eous*. In your notebook, correct any misspellings among the following words.

1. religeous   2. deliceous   3. bountious

Concept Development: Synonyms

For each item, choose the letter of the word that is the synonym of (the word closest in meaning to) the word from the vocabulary list on page 275.

1. righteousness: (a) justness, (b) neatness, (c) error
2. stature: (a) depth, (b) standing, (c) interference
3. prodigal: (a) brilliant, (b) wasteful, (c) repugnant
4. entreated: (a) agreed, (b) financed, (c) begged
5. transgressed: (a) sinned, (b) traveled, (c) crossed

Grammar and Style Lesson

Infinitive Phrases

An **infinitive phrase** consists of an infinitive (the base form of the verb preceded by *to*) and its modifiers and complements. It can function as a noun, an adjective, or an adverb.

> **Noun:** The younger son chose <u>to take his inheritance.</u> (*What* did he choose?)
>
> **Adjective:** Soon, he had no more money <u>to spend.</u> (*What* kind of money?)
>
> **Adverb:** <u>To avoid starvation,</u> he returned to his home. (*Why* did he return?)

Infinitive phrases are often used to give reasons and explain motives, so they are often found in writing about ethics and conduct.

Practice In your notebook, identify each infinitive phrase in the following sentences and identify its function (noun, adjective, or adverb).

1. He kneeled to seek his father's forgiveness.
2. The father decided to hold a celebration.
3. He made plans to feast his son lavishly.
4. The elder brother did not want to attend the feast.
5. To persuade the elder brother, the father explained his joy.

Writing Application Write a paragraph evaluating the father's decision to welcome the prodigal's return in the Parable of the Prodigal Son. Use at least three infinitive phrases to add variety to your writing.

W/G *Prentice Hall Writing and Grammar Connection: Chapter 19, Section 2*

Writing Lesson

Parable in King James Style

Write a parable that supports a moral in which you believe. Study the style of the Parable of the Prodigal Son, and adapt it to your purposes.

Prewriting   Choose a moral to teach, and sketch the plot of a story to illustrate it. Then reread the Parable of the Prodigal Son, taking notes on the style in which it is told, noting sentence length, typical sentence beginnings, and word choice.

Drafting   Follow your notes as you draft, setting out the events of your story in clear sequence. Emphasize those elements—character traits or events—that will lead the reader to understand your lesson.

Revising   Highlight parts of your work that do not fit the general style you have adopted. Rewrite marked passages for consistency.

Model: Revising for Consistent Style

And, lo, the bully descended like a wolf on the

playground. "Out of my way, meathead," he said.
laid about him mightily.
And he ~~started wailing on the nearest person.~~

> The revision maintains the style: formal, simple, biblical-sounding narration contrasting with the characters' slang dialogue.

W *Prentice Hall Writing and Grammar Connection: Chapter 5, Section 3*

Extension Activities

Listening and Speaking Prepare a **retelling** of the Parable of the Prodigal Son for an audience of young children. As you rehearse, choose language appropriate to your audience:

- Speak in language that listeners will readily understand.
- Include vivid words and phrases to hold their interest.
- Use informal expressions to help listeners connect the story to their experiences.

Deliver your version to a suitable audience.

Research and Technology Working in a small group, write an **evaluative report** comparing one of the selections here with two other translations of the same passage. As you review the translations, consider how word choice, tone, and style affect the meaning and impact of the text. Write up the group's impressions in an essay, citing sources accurately. **[Group Activity]**

 **Take It to the Net**   www.phschool.com

Go online for an additional research activity using the Internet.

from A Man *for* All Seasons

Robert Bolt

Being a king in the 1500s was no easy job. On the one hand, you were the ultimate authority in the land. On the other hand, you had to keep the Church, the Parliament, and the nobles on your side. Being a friend of a king was even tougher. Sir Thomas More tried to balance friendship and loyalty in his relationship with King Henry VIII. In the end, he was executed by his friend, the king.

A Test of Strength More's troubles started with a power struggle between Church and King. Henry VIII sought an annulment of his marriage to Catherine of Aragon. When his request was denied, he remarried and formed his own church, the Church of England. He then demanded that officials swear an oath of supremacy, recognizing his power over the power of the Pope. More's conscience would not permit him to swear such an oath, and he was put to death as a result.

Diminishing Power In later history, parliamentary authority has grown while royal power has diminished, virtually disappearing in Europe by the end of World War I. The present government of England is a constitutional monarchy, in which the reigning monarch serves mainly as a symbol.

Abiding Interest The monarchy remains, however, a popular theme in literature and movies. In the following excerpt from the screenplay of the movie *A Man for All Seasons*, Henry VIII tries to force More to side with him against the Church.

HENRY. I am a fool.

MORE. How so, Your Grace?

HENRY. [*A pause, during which the music fades to silence*] What else but a fool to live in a Court, in a licentious[1] mob—when I have friends, with gardens.

MORE. Your Grace—

HENRY. No courtship, no ceremony, Thomas. Be seated. You are my friend, are you not? [MORE *sits.*]

MORE. Your Majesty.

HENRY. [*Eyes lighting on the chain on the table by* MORE] And thank God I have a friend for my Chancellor.[2] [*Laughingly, but implacably, he takes up the chain and lowers it over* MORE'S *head.*] Readier to be friends, I trust, than he was to be Chancellor.

MORE. My own knowledge of my poor abilities—

HENRY. I will judge of your abilities, Thomas . . . Did you know that Wolsey named you for Chancellor?

MORE. Wolsey!

HENRY. Aye, before he died. Wolsey named you and Wolsey was no fool.

MORE. He was a statesman of incomparable ability, Your Grace.

HENRY. Was he? Was he so? [*He rises.*] Then why did he fail me? Be seated—it was villainy then! Yes, villainy. I was right to break him; he was all pride, Thomas; a proud man; pride right through. And he failed me! [MORE *opens his mouth.*] He failed me in the one thing that mattered! The one thing that matters, Thomas, then or now. And why? He wanted to be Pope! Yes, he wanted to be the Bishop of Rome. I'll tell you something, Thomas, and you can check this for yourself—it was never merry in England while we had Cardinals amongst us. [*He nods significantly at* MORE, *who lowers his eyes.*] But look now— [*Walking away*] —I shall forget the feel of that . . . great tiller[3] under my hands . . . I took her down to Dogget's Bank, went about and brought her up in Tilbury Roads. A man could sail clean round the world in that ship.

MORE. [*With affectionate admiration*] Some men could, Your Grace.

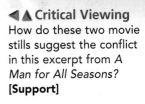

◀▲ **Critical Viewing**
How do these two movie stills suggest the conflict in this excerpt from *A Man for All Seasons*? **[Support]**

1. **licentious** (lī sen´ shəs) *adj.* disregarding accepted rules and standards.
2. **Chancellor** (chan´ sə lər) *n.* More's position as an important advisor to the king.
3. **tiller** (til´ ər) *n.* bar or handle for turning a boat's rudder.

✔**Reading Check**

What does Henry say was a flaw of Wolsey?

HENRY. [*Offhand*] Touching this matter of my divorce, Thomas; have you thought of it since we last talked?

MORE. Of little else.

HENRY. Then you see your way clear to me?

MORE. That you should put away Queen Catherine, Sire? Oh, alas [*He thumps the chair in distress.*] as I think of it I see so clearly that I cannot come with Your Grace that my endeavor is not to think of it at all.

HENRY. Then you have not thought enough! . . . [*With real appeal*] Great God, Thomas, why do you hold out against me in the desire of my heart—the very wick of my heart?

MORE. [*Draws up his sleeve, baring his arm*] There is my right arm. [*A practical proposition*] Take your dagger and saw it from my shoulder, and I will laugh and be thankful, if by that means I can come with Your Grace with a clear conscience.

HENRY. [*Uncomfortably pulls at the sleeve*] I know it, Thomas, I know . . .

MORE. [*Rises, formally*] I crave pardon if I offend.

HENRY. [*Suspiciously*] Speak then.

MORE. When I took the Great Seal your Majesty promised not to pursue me on this matter.

HENRY. Ha! So I break my word, Master More! No no, I'm joking . . . I joke roughly . . . [*He wanders away.*] I often think I'm a rough fellow . . . Yes, a rough young fellow. [*He shakes his head indulgently.*] Be seated . . . That's a rosebay.[4] We have one like it at Hampton—not so red as that though. Ha—I'm in an excellent frame of mind. [*Glances at the rosebay*] Beautiful. [*Reasonable, pleasant*] You must consider, Thomas, that I stand in peril of my soul. It was no marriage; she was my brother's widow. Leviticus: "Thou shalt not uncover the nakedness of thy brother's wife." Leviticus, Chapter eighteen, Verse sixteen.[5]

MORE. Yes, Your Grace. But Deuteronomy—[6]

HENRY. [*Triumphant*] Deuteronomy's ambiguous!

MORE. [*Bursting out*] Your Grace, I'm not fit to meddle in these matters—to me it seems a matter for the Holy See—

Thematic Connection
What does More's offer suggest about his loyalty to King Henry?

---

4. **rosebay** (rōz´ bā) *n.* any of the genus (rhododendron) of trees or shrubs with showy flowers of pink, white, or purple.
5. **Leviticus** (lə´ vit´ i kəs), **Chapter eighteen, Verse sixteen** reference to the third book of the Pentateuch in the Bible, containing the laws relating to priests and their assistants, the Levites.
6. **Deuteronomy** (dōōt´ ər än´ ə mē) fifth book of the Pentateuch in the Bible, in which the laws of Moses are set down.

HENRY. [*Reprovingly*] Thomas, Thomas, does a man need a Pope to tell him when he's sinned? It was a sin, Thomas; I admit it; I repent. And God has punished me; I have no son . . . Son after son she's borne me, Thomas, all dead at birth, or dead within the month; I never saw the hand of God so clear in anything . . . I have a daughter, she's a good child, a well-set child—But I have no son. [*He flares up.*] It is my bounden duty to put away the Queen, and all the Popes back to St. Peter shall not come between me and my duty! How is it that you cannot see? Everyone else does.

MORE. [*Eagerly*] Then why does Your Grace need my poor support?

HENRY. Because you are honest. What's more to the purpose, you're known to be honest . . . There are those like Norfolk who follow me because I wear the crown, and there are those like Master Cromwell who follow me because they are jackals with sharp teeth and I am their lion, and there is a mass that follows me because it follows anything that moves—and there is you.

MORE. I am sick to think how much I must displease Your Grace.

HENRY. No, Thomas, I respect your sincerity. Respect? Oh, man, it's water in the desert . . . How did you like our music? That air they played, it had a certain—well, tell me what you thought of it.

MORE. [*Relieved at this turn; smiling*] Could it have been Your Grace's own?

HENRY. [*Smiles back*] Discovered! Now I'll never know your true opinion. And that's irksome, Thomas, for we artists, though we love praise, yet we love truth better.

MORE. [*Mildly*] Then I will tell Your Grace truly what I thought of it.

HENRY. [*A little disconcerted*] Speak then.

MORE. To me it seemed—delightful.

HENRY. Thomas—I chose the right man for Chancellor.

MORE. I must in fairness add that my taste in music is reputedly deplorable.[7]

HENRY. Your taste in music is excellent. It exactly coincides with my own. Ah music! Music! Send them back without me, Thomas; I will live here in Chelsea and make music.

MORE. My house is at Your Grace's disposal.

HENRY. Thomas, you understand me; we will stay here together and make music.

Thematic Connection
What does Bolt's characterization of Henry add to the picture of English monarchs painted in More's *Utopia* and Elizabeth's "Speech"?

Reading Check
What issue does More want to avoid discussing with King Henry?

---

7. **deplorable** (dē plôr´ ə bəl) *adj.* regrettable or wretched.

MORE. Will Your Grace honor my roof after dinner?

HENRY. [*Walking away, blowing moodily on his whistle*] Mm? Yes, I expect I'll bellow for you . . .

MORE. My wife will be more—

HENRY. Yes, yes. [*He turns, his face set.*] Touching this other business, mark you, Thomas, I'll have no opposition.

MORE. [*Sadly*] Your Grace?

HENRY. No opposition, I say! No opposition! Your conscience is your own affair; but you are my Chancellor! There, you have my word—I'll leave you out of it. But I don't take it kindly, Thomas, and I'll have no opposition! I see how it will be; the bishops will oppose me. The full-fed, hypocritical, "Princes of the Church"! Ha! As for the Pope! Am I to burn in Hell because the Bishop of Rome, with the King of Spain's knife to his throat, mouths me Deuteronomy? Hypocrites! They're all hypocrites! Mind they do not take you in, Thomas! Lie low if you will, but I'll brook no opposition—no noise! No words, no signs, no letters, no pamphlets—Mind that, Thomas—no writings against me!

MORE. Your grace is unjust. I am Your Grace's loyal minister. If I cannot serve Your Grace in this great matter of the Queen—

HENRY. I have no Queen! Catherine is not my wife and no priest can make her so, and they that say she is my wife are not only liars . . . but traitors! Mind it, Thomas!

MORE. Am I a babbler, Your Grace? [*But his voice is unsteady.*]

HENRY. You are stubborn . . . [*Wooingly*] If you could come with me, you are the man I would soonest raise—yes, with my own hand.

MORE. [*Covers his face*] Oh, Your Grace overwhelms me!

Connecting Literature and Media

1. (a) Identify three characteristics of Henry indicated in the screenplay. (b) Do these characteristics make him seem more like an ordinary person than a king? Explain.
2. What does Henry's speech, beginning "No opposition, I say!" suggest about the effect of his authority on his personality?
3. Explain how—in the screenplay, in More's *Utopia,* and in Elizabeth's speech—people's perceptions of a monarch become as important as the actual power he or she wields.

Robert Bolt

(1924–1995)

Robert Bolt was a successful British playwright and writer of screenplays. He was born in Manchester and educated at Manchester University. He served three years in the army and air force before trying his hand as a playwright. He was teaching when his first play, *Flowing Cherry,* was produced in London. Its great success led Bolt to leave the classroom for the stage.

Bolt wrote the screenplay for several successful movies besides *A Man for All Seasons,* including *Dr. Zhivago, Lawrence of Arabia,* and *Ryan's Daughter.*

PART 3 Focus on Literary Forms: Drama

The Globe Theatre, London

"All the world's a stage," exclaims one of Shakespeare's characters, and the audience agreed. Elizabethan England had a dramatic sense of itself as a new power, acting its part on the world's stage. Playwrights like Marlowe and Shakespeare created bold new dramas, letting the English language strut and swagger.

The Elizabethan Theater

English drama came of age during the reign of Elizabeth I, developing into a sophisticated and very popular art form. Although playwrights like Shakespeare were mainly responsible for the great theatrical achievements of the time, the importance of actors, audiences, and theater buildings should not be underestimated.

Before the reign of Elizabeth I, theater companies traveled about the country putting on plays wherever they could find an audience, often performing in the open courtyards of inns. Spectators watched either from the ground or from balconies or galleries above.

England's First Playhouse

When Shakespeare was twelve years old, an actor named James Burbage built London's first theater, called simply The Theater, just beyond the city walls in Shoreditch. Actors—even prominent and well-to-do actors like James Burbage—occupied a strange place in London society: They were frowned upon by the city fathers but were wildly popular with the common people, who clamored to see them perform in plays. Though actors were considered rogues and vagabonds by some, they were held in sufficient repute to be called on frequently to perform at court. A man like Burbage enjoyed a reputation somewhat like a rock star's today.

The Globe In 1597, the city fathers closed down The Theater. In late 1598, Richard Burbage (James Burbage's son) and his men dismantled it and hauled it in pieces across the Thames to Southwark. It took them six months to rebuild it, and when they did, they renamed it the Globe.

Scholars disagree about what the Globe actually looked like because there are no surviving drawings from the time or detailed written descriptions. Shakespeare refers to the building in *Henry V* as "this wooden O," so we have a sense that it was round or octagonal. It is presumed that an important influence on the design of the theater was the bear-baiting and bull-baiting rings built in Southwark. These "sports" arenas were circular, open to the sky, and had galleries all around.

The building had to have been small enough to ensure that the actors would be heard, but we know that performances could draw audiences as large as 2,500 to 3,000 people. These truly packed houses must have been quite uncomfortable at times—especially when you consider that people of the era didn't bathe or change their clothes very often! Those who paid an admission price of a penny (not an inconsiderable sum of money then) stood throughout the performance. Some of the audience even sat in a gallery behind the performers. Their seats were the second-most expensive in the house, and though they saw

only the actors' backs and probably could not hear very well, they were content to be seen by the other members of the audience.

Actors of the period had none of the elaborate technology that helps modern actors. There were no sets or lighting at the Globe. Plays were performed in the bright afternoon sunlight, and a playwright's words alone had to create moods like the one in the eerie first scene of *Macbeth*. Holding an audience spellbound was made even more difficult by the fact that most people in the audience were eating and drinking throughout the performance.

The first Globe met its demise in 1613, when a cannon fired as part of a performance of *Henry VIII* ignited the theater's thatched roof. Everyone escaped unharmed, but the Globe burned to the ground. Although the theater was rebuilt, the Puritans had it permanently closed in 1642.

The New Globe

Almost four centuries after the original Globe opened, an actor stood onstage in the replica of the Globe and recited these lines from Shakespeare's *Henry V*: "Can this cockpit hold / The vasty fields of France? Or may we cram / Within this wooden O the very casques / That did affright the air at Agincourt?"

Building a replica of Shakespeare's Globe was the American actor Sam Wanamaker's dream. After long years of fund-raising and construction, the theater opened to its first full season on June 8, 1997, with a production of *Henry V*. Like the earlier Globe, this one is made of wood, with a thatched roof and lime plaster covering the walls. The stage and the galleries are covered, but the "bear pit," where the modern-day groundlings stand, is open to the skies, exposing the spectators to the weather.

Perhaps the most striking aspect of seeing Shakespeare's plays performed at the Globe is the immediacy of the action. The performers, as Benedict Nightingale noted in the *London Times*, "are talking to you, asking you questions, involving you in their fears." At the Globe, the audience is part of the debate. Is that not what theater is all about?

▲ **Critical Viewing**
Judging from these photographs of the reconstructed Globe, what part of the theater might the upper-class audience members have occupied? Explain.
[Speculate]

Shakespeare on Stage

A play on the page is only half a play. The script is a recipe for a performance—incomplete until it is staged in a theater, in a reader's mind, or on screen. When a play is staged, actors and directors bring the words to life through their interpretations. Decisions about scenery, costumes, props, timing, and casting, as well as ideas about a character's gestures, walk, expressions, and motivations, can call forth contrasting meanings from even the most familiar play.

Shakespeare's plays have been produced for more than four hundred years and call forth brilliant performances and daring reinterpretations. The best interpretations of his plays shed new light by asking imaginative questions that the texts themselves answer. The following is a tiny sampling of the questions posed by Shakespearean productions in the last century.

Character and Motivation

Shakespeare's Lady Macbeth conspires with her husband to murder their king, leading generations of actresses to ask about the source of Lady Macbeth's evil.

Inhuman Monster? Sarah Siddons, who played the role of Lady Macbeth about two hundred years ago, portrayed Lady Macbeth as a driven woman, in whom "the passion of ambition has almost obliterated all the characteristics of human nature. . . ."

▼ **Critical Viewing** What decisions about staging might the director of a play in this theater need to make? **[Hypothesize]**

Evil Beauty? Vivien Leigh found in Lady Macbeth an evil beauty who gives a goodnight kiss to the man she is plotting to murder that same evening.

Weak Woman? At the other end of the spectrum, nineteenth-century actress Ellen Terry played Lady Macbeth as "essentially feminine," noting that she faints after the murder of the king.

Setting and Action

Realism? Some directors attempt to keep faith with a playwright's vision by staging the action in as realistic a manner as possible. To bring new realism to the woodland setting of *A Midsummer Night's Dream*, the director of a 1905 production brought live rabbits onstage! The famous actor Laurence Olivier brought unintentional realism to the part of Macbeth. Following his director's instructions, he played the part so enthusiastically that one night, he injured the actor playing Macduff in their staged sword fight. On another occasion, with a substitute Macduff, Olivier fought the sword battle so vigorously that his sword broke and flew into the audience.

Relevance? Orson Welles also struck a note of realism in his 1936 version of *Macbeth*, but he did so by radically departing from Shakespeare's text: He set the play in Haiti instead of Scotland! By using an all-black cast and modeling Macbeth after a famous Haitian dictator, Welles found a new application for Shakespeare's message about power. The 1986 Stratford-on-Avon version of *Romeo and Juliet* also attempted to emphasize Shakespeare's contemporary significance: A live rock band set the musical mood for the production.

◀ ▲ **Critical Viewing**
What does the fact that Shakespere's *Macbeth* can be staged in such different ways as these suggest about its power?
[Draw Conclusions]

A Closer Look

Shakespeare on Film

William Shakespeare wrote for the same audience that moviemakers write for today. Rich and poor, smart and not-so-smart, sentimentalists and action-lovers, fans of heartbreak and fans of comedy—all crowded into the Globe theater to watch Shakespeare's plays. Hundreds of years later, a similarly diverse audience pours into multiplexes and video stores for movies. Not surprisingly, film versions of many Shakespearean plays are readily available.

Filmmakers have taken varied approaches to Shakespeare's plays, approaches that reflect changing popular tastes and interests. The variety of styles in which the plays have been filmed also reflects their richness. The timeless themes, powerful characters, and resonant language of the plays form a treasure house of the imagination, from which a creative film-maker can borrow materials for his or her own work.

Romeo and Juliet Shakespeare's *Romeo and Juliet* has been filmed more often than any other play in history.

- In 1908, the first movie version, a ten-minute silent short, was created. Lines from the play were displayed on title cards while the actors mimed the action.
- In 1936, Hollywood director George Cukor produced a full-length feature film of the play. Cukor needed three months to construct the set, a four-acre re-creation of Verona. The shooting itself lasted six months, running the budget up to $2 million—at the time, the most MGM had ever paid for a film.
- In 1996, Australian filmmaker Baz Luhrmann created an "updated" version of *Romeo and Juliet* starring Leonardo DiCaprio. Characters cruise around in sharp-looking cars, wear designer clothes, and carry automatic weapons—not swords—while a television newscast provides narration.
- The 1998 film *Shakespeare in Love*, cowritten by playwright Tom Stoppard, hypothesizes about the events that led Shakespeare to write *Romeo and Juliet*. In the movie, lines from the play weave together Shakespeare's life with the play he is writing.

Hamlet Like *Romeo and Juliet*, Shakespeare's tragedy *Hamlet* also had its film debut during the silent film era.

- The most famous cinematic translation of *Hamlet* to film is the 1948 version starring Laurence Olivier as Hamlet. Olivier's performance as the melancholic prince, who broods over his father's murder but is unable to act, is considered a high point of dramatic art.
- In 1990, director Franco Zeffirelli filmed *Hamlet* with Mel Gibson in the title role. Zeffirelli followed modern tastes in film, shooting the play on location and encouraging actors to deliver lines as prose rather than as poetry.
- Six years later, Kenneth Branagh directed another version of the brooding tragedy. He presented the play nearly whole, editing out few lines, a project never before attempted. The result runs 242 minutes long.

Macbeth

- One of the best-known film versions of *Macbeth* was created by David Bradley for a mere $5 thousand. Costumes were bought at rummage sales, props were purchased at junk stores, helmets were fashioned from papier-mâché, swords were cut from wood, and Bradley's mother made sandwiches for the cast and crew.
- In 1971, director Roman Polanski chose to film his version of the play during the winter: The weather, he felt, set a bleak tone suited to the grim atmosphere of *Macbeth*. To keep his cast from falling ill, Polanski insisted that they take daily dosages of vitamin C.
- Perhaps the most successful adaptation of *Macbeth* is, paradoxically, one that retains none of the original language: Japanese director Akira Kurosawa's *Throne of Blood*. The dialogue and setting of the film is Japanese, but Kurosawa carefully builds his drama directly from Shakespeare's story. Critics have hailed the film as a masterpiece for its dramatic visual effects and editing.

◄ ▼ **Critical Viewing** What effect does the work of popular actors—such as Claire Danes, Gwyneth Paltrow, and Mel Gibson—have on Shakespeare's accessibility? Explain. **[Hypothesize]**

Prepare to Read

Macbeth

William Shakespeare (1564–1616)

Because of his deep understanding of human nature, his compassion for all types of people, and the power and beauty of his language, William Shakespeare is regarded as the greatest writer in English. Nearly four hundred years after his death, Shakespeare's plays continue to be read widely and produced throughout the world. They have the same powerful impact on today's audiences as they had when they were first staged.

Timeline of Praise No other writer in English has won such universal and enthusiastic praise from critics and fellow writers. Here are just a few samples of that praise, shown on a timeline from Shakespeare's day to our own:

The Playwright in His Own Time It is a myth that we know absolutely nothing about Shakespeare's life. As critic Irving Ribner attests, "we know more about him than we do about virtually any other of his contemporary dramatists, with the exception of Ben Jonson." Shakespeare was born on April 23, 1564, in Stratford-on-Avon, which is northwest of London. (The date is based on a record of his baptism on April 26.) Stratford, with a population of about two thousand in Shakespeare's day, was the market town for a fertile agricultural region.

Shakespeare's father, John, was a successful glove maker and businessman who held a number of positions in the town's government. His mother, whose maiden name was Mary Arden, was the daughter of John's landlord. Their marriage, therefore, boosted the Shakespeare family's holdings. Nevertheless, there is evidence that in the late 1570s, John Shakespeare began to suffer financial reverses.

Shakespeare's Education No written evidence of Shakespeare's boyhood exists—not even a name on a school attendance list. However, given his

---

Timeline of Praise

Ben Jonson (1572–1637)
"He was not of an age, but for all time!"

Samuel Johnson (1709–1784)
"Shakespeare is, above all writers, at least above all modern writers, the poet of nature: the poet that holds up to his readers a faithful mirror of manners and life."

A.C. Bradley (1851–1935)
"Where his power of art is fully exerted, it really does resemble that of nature."

| 1600 | 1700 | 1800 | 1900 |

John Dryden (1631–1700)
"He was the man who of all modern, and perhaps ancient, poets had the largest and most comprehensive soul."

Samuel Taylor Coleridge (1772–1834)
"The Englishman, who, without reverence, a proud and affectionate reverence, can utter the name of William Shakespeare, stands disqualified for the office of critic."

T. S. Eliot (1888–1965)
"About any one so great as Shakespeare, it is probable that we can never be right . . ."

Speaking Shakespeare

You may not realize the extent to which you already "speak" Shakespeare. For example, have you ever used or heard any of these common phrases?

He's full of *the milk of human kindness.* (I, v, 17)
Don't worry about it, *what's done is done!* (III, ii, 12)
That will last until *the crack of doom.* (IV, i, 117)
She finished the jobs in *one fell swoop.* (IV, iii, 219)

Shakespeare invented each of these now common phrases, which were unknown in English before their appearance in *Macbeth*. Look for them as you read and discover if their meanings have changed since Shakespeare's time.

father's status, it is highly probable that he attended the Stratford Grammar School, where he acquired a knowledge of Latin.

Although Shakespeare did not go on to study at a university, his attendance at the grammar school from ages seven to sixteen would have provided him with a good education. Discipline at such a school was strict, and the school day lasted from 6:00 A.M. in the summer (7:00 in the winter) until 5:00 P.M. From 11:00 to 1:00, students were dismissed to eat lunch with their families. At 3:00, they were allowed to play for a quarter of an hour!

Shakespeare's Marriage and Family Shakespeare's name enters the official records again in November 1582, when he received a license to marry Anne Hathaway. The couple had a daughter, Susanna, in 1583, and twins, Judith and Hamnet, in 1585. Beyond names and years in which his children were born, we know little about his family life. Some writers have made much of the fact that Shakespeare left his wife and children behind when he went to London not long after his twins were born. However, he visited his family in Stratford regularly during his years as a playwright, and they may have lived with him for a time in London.

His Career as Actor and Playwright It is uncertain how Shakespeare became connected with the theater in the late 1580s and early 1590s. By 1594, however, he had become a part owner and the principal playwright of the Lord Chamberlain's Men, one of the most successful theater companies in London.

In 1599, the company built the famous Globe theater on the south bank of the Thames River, in Southwark. This is where most of Shakespeare's plays were performed. When James I became king in 1603, after the death of Elizabeth I, James took control of the Lord Chamberlain's Men and renamed the company the King's Men.

Retirement In about 1610, Shakespeare retired to Stratford, where he continued to write plays. He was a prosperous middle-class man, who profited from his share in a successful theater company. Six years later, on April 23, 1616, he died and was buried in Holy Trinity Church in Stratford. Because it was a common practice to move bodies after burial to make room for others, Shakespeare wrote the following as his epitaph:

Blest be the man that spares these stones,
And curst be he that moves my bones.

His Literary Record Shakespeare did not think of himself as a man of letters. He wrote his plays to be performed and did not bring out editions of them for the reading public. The first published edition of his work, called the First Folio, was issued in 1623 by two members of his theater company, John Heminges and Henry Condell. It contained thirty-six of the thirty-seven plays now attributed to him.

Shakespeare's varied output includes romantic comedies, like *A Midsummer Night's Dream* and *As You Like It;* history plays, like *Henry IV,* Parts 1 and 2; tragedies, like *Romeo and Juliet, Hamlet, Othello, King Lear,* and *Macbeth;* and later romances, like *The Tempest.* In addition to his plays, he wrote 154 sonnets and three longer poems.

Prepare to Read

Macbeth

Shakespeare's Sources

Fact and Legend By Shakespeare's time, the story of the eleventh-century Scottish king Macbeth was a mixture of fact and legend. Shakespeare and his contemporaries, however, probably regarded the account of Macbeth in Raphael Holinshed's *Chronicles of England, Scotland, and Ireland* as completely factual. The playwright drew on the *Chronicles* as a source for the play, yet, as you will see, he freely adapted the material for his own purposes.

Holinshed's *Chronicles* Holinshed's account contains a description of a meeting between Macbeth and the witches. His account also tells how Macbeth and his friends, angry at the naming of King Duncan's son Malcolm as Prince of Cumberland, ambush and slay Duncan. However, the historical Macbeth's claim to the throne has some basis. (See page 382 for an explanation of the ancient Scottish custom of choosing kings.) Finally, Holinshed indicates that Banquo is Macbeth's accomplice in the assassination. Lady Macbeth, prominent in Shakespeare's play, does not play a significant role in Holinshed.

Shakespeare's *Macbeth* Shakespeare took what he needed from the *Chronicles* and shaped it into a tragic plot. Seeing the theatrical possibilities of the meeting with the witches, Shakespeare staged such an encounter in Act I, Scene iii. However, he changed Holinshed's account in order to make King Duncan an innocent victim: Shakespeare's Macbeth does not have a legitimate claim to the throne. Further, Shakespeare used another story in the *Chronicles*—one in which a wife urges her husband to kill a friend and guest—as the basis for the character Lady Macbeth. She becomes Macbeth's co-conspirator, replacing Banquo. Read on to discover Shakespeare's political motives for holding Banquo innocent.

A Tribute to the King

A Dangerous Plot *Macbeth* is set in eleventh-century Scotland. However, Shakespeare wrote the play with an eye on seventeenth-century events in England. In November 1605, a group of Catholics seeking revenge for the increasing oppression of Catholics plotted to blow up the king and Parliament. With the help of Guy Fawkes, a soldier of fortune, they rented a cellar directly below the House of Lords, in which to stockpile barrels of gunpowder. Incredibly, the conspirators succeeded in storing thirty-six barrels of gunpowder there. To appreciate the magnitude of the threat, imagine modern terrorists smuggling tons of explosives into the Capitol building in Washington, D.C.

The Plot Revealed The plot was revealed when a lord, who happened to be a brother-in-law of one of the conspirators, was anonymously warned by letter not to attend the opening of Parliament. This warning helped the authorities break the case, and they arrested Guy Fawkes as he entered the cellar. Fawkes and some of the other chief conspirators were executed. Although their numbers were few, their plan was so frightening that it led, for a time, to increased persecution of all English Catholics. In England, Guy Fawkes Day is still commemorated on November 5 each year with fireworks, bonfires, and the burning of effigies representing Guy Fawkes.

Sympathy for the King In *Macbeth*, Shakespeare capitalized on the sympathy generated for the king by this incident. He chose the Scottish setting for his play, knowing that James's family, the Stuarts, first came to the Scottish throne in the eleventh century. One of the most virtuous characters in the play, Banquo, was thought to be the father of the first of the Stuart kings. Knowing that James I had written a book on witches, Shakespeare included the three hags in the play.

Preview

Connecting to the Literature

If you have ever been elbowed aside by a team member eager for glory, you have experienced the effects of fierce ambition. In *Macbeth,* ambition causes a brave soldier to become an evil plotter.

Literary Analysis

Elizabethan Drama

During the late sixteenth century, **Elizabethan drama** came into full bloom. Playwrights turned away from religious subjects and began writing more sophisticated plays. Drawing on models from ancient Greece and Rome, writers reintroduced **tragedies**—plays in which disaster befalls a hero or heroine. Dramatists also began writing their plays in carefully crafted unrhymed verse, using rich language and vivid imagery.

Because the Globe, like other Elizabethan theaters, had no lighting, plays were performed in broad daylight. There were also no sets, so the words of the play had to create the illusion of time and place for the audience.

Connecting Literary Elements

In a play, a **soliloquy** is a long speech, usually made by a character who is alone (*soliloquy* comes from the Latin *solus,* meaning "alone") and thus reveals private thoughts and feelings to the audience, but not to other characters. In Shakespeare's tragedies, the greatest works of Elizabethan drama, tragic characters reveal secret desires or troubling fears through their soliloquies. For example, as you read the following soliloquies in this act, use a chart like the one shown here to note the inner struggles each reveals.

- Lady Macbeth's soliloquy, Act I, Scene v
- Macbeth's soliloquy, Act I, Scene vii

Reading Strategy

Using Text Aids

Like many dramas, Shakespeare's plays were meant to be performed, not read. Playwrights and editors, however, provide **text aids,** explanatory features that help you interpret the plays. These aids include stage directions in brackets and notes on the side of the text. Use these aids when you read.

Vocabulary Development

valor (val´ ər) *n.* marked courage or bravery (p. 302)

treasons (trē´ zənz) *n.* betrayals of one's country or oath of loyalty (p. 308)

imperial (im pir´ ē əl) *adj.* of an empire; having supreme authority (p. 308)

liege (lēj) *n.* lord or king (p. 309)

sovereign (säv´ rən) *adj.* supreme in power, rank, or authority (p. 314)

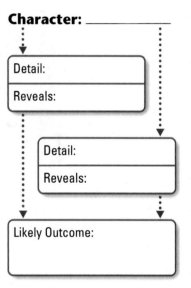

Character: _____

Detail:

Reveals:

Detail:

Reveals:

Likely Outcome:

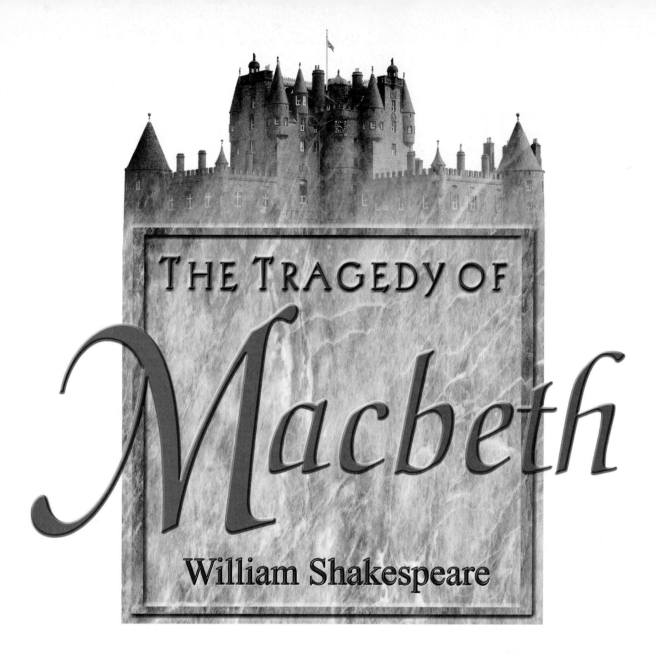

THE TRAGEDY OF Macbeth

William Shakespeare

Background

The Elizabethans viewed the universe, in its ideal state, as both orderly and interconnected. They believed that a great chain linked all beings, from God on high to the lowest beasts and plants. They also believed that universal order was based on parallels between different realms. Just as the sun ruled in the heavens, for example, the king ruled in the state and the father in the family. Because everything was linked, a disturbance in one area would cause a disturbance in others. In keeping with this concept of order, a Shakespearean tragedy shows how a tragic hero's bad choices can disturb the whole universe. As *Macbeth* gets underway, notice the parallel disorders in the mind of the hero, the weather, and the kingdom.

CHARACTERS

DUNCAN, King of Scotland
MALCOLM }
DONALBAIN } his sons
MACBETH ⎫
BANQUO ⎥
MACDUFF ⎥
LENNOX ⎬ noblemen
ROSS ⎥ of Scotland
MENTEITH ⎥
ANGUS ⎥
CAITHNESS ⎭
FLEANCE, son to Banquo
SIWARD, Earl of Northumberland,
    general of the English forces
YOUNG SIWARD, his son

SEYTON, an officer attending on Macbeth
SON TO MACDUFF
AN ENGLISH DOCTOR
A SCOTTISH DOCTOR
A PORTER
AN OLD MAN
THREE MURDERERS
LADY MACBETH
LADY MACDUFF
A GENTLEWOMAN attending
    on Lady Macbeth
HECATE
WITCHES
APPARITIONS
LORDS, OFFICERS, SOLDIERS, ATTENDANTS,
    AND MESSENGERS

Setting: Scotland; England

Act I

Scene i. An open place.

[*Thunder and lightning. Enter* THREE WITCHES.]

    FIRST WITCH. When shall we three meet again?
      In thunder, lightning, or in rain?

    SECOND WITCH. When the hurlyburly's done,
      When the battle's lost and won.

5 **THIRD WITCH.** That will be ere the set of sun.

    FIRST WITCH. Where the place?

    SECOND WITCH.   Upon the heath.

    THIRD WITCH. There to meet with Macbeth.

    FIRST WITCH. I come, Graymalkin.[1]

    SECOND WITCH. Paddock[2] calls.

    THIRD WITCH.   Anon![3]

10 **ALL.** Fair is foul, and foul is fair.
      Hover through the fog and filthy air.   [*Exit.*]

Scene ii. A camp near Forres, a town in northeast Scotland.

[*Alarum within.*[1] *Enter* KING DUNCAN, MALCOLM, DONALBAIN, LENNOX,
with ATTENDANTS, *meeting a bleeding* CAPTAIN.]

▲**Critical Viewing** Examine Fuseli's rendering of the witches. Does the mood he creates correspond to the mood in Act I, Scene i? Why or why not? **[Connect]**

KING. What bloody man is that? He can report,
    As seemeth by his plight, of the revolt
    The newest state.

MALCOLM.   This is the sergeant[2]
    Who like a good and hardy soldier fought
5   'Gainst my captivity. Hail, brave friend!
    Say to the king the knowledge of the broil[3]
    As thou didst leave it.

CAPTAIN.   Doubtful it stood,
    As two spent swimmers, that do cling together
    And choke their art.[4] The merciless Macdonwald—
10   Worthy to be a rebel for to that
    The multiplying villainies of nature
    Do swarm upon him—from the Western Isles[5]
    Of kerns and gallowglasses[6] is supplied;
    And fortune, on his damnéd quarrel[7] smiling,
15   Showed like a rebel's whore:[8] but all's too weak:
    For brave Macbeth—well he deserves that name—
    Disdaining fortune, with his brandished steel,
    Which smoked with bloody execution,
    Like <u>valor's</u> minion[9] carved out his passage

2. sergeant officer.

3. broil battle.

4. choke their art prevent each other from swimming.

5. Western Isles the Hebrides, off Scotland.

6. Of kerns and gallow-glasses with lightly armed Irish foot soldiers and heavily armed soldiers.

7. damned quarrel accursed cause.

8. Showed . . . whore falsely appeared to favor Macdonwald.

9. minion favorite.

valor (val´ ər) *n.* marked courage or bravery

20

Till he faced the slave;
Which nev'r shook hands, nor bade farewell to him,
Till he unseamed him from the nave to th' chops,[10]
And fixed his head upon our battlements.

KING. O valiant cousin! Worthy gentleman!

25 **CAPTAIN.** As whence the sun 'gins his reflection[11]
Shipwracking storms and direful thunders break,
So from that spring whence comfort seemed to come
Discomfort swells. Mark, King of Scotland, mark:
No sooner justice had, with valor armed,
30 Compelled these skipping kerns to trust their heels
But the Norweyan lord,[12] surveying vantage,[13]
With furbished arms and new supplies of men,
Began a fresh assault.

KING.   Dismayed not this
Our captains, Macbeth and Banquo?

CAPTAIN.   Yes;
35 As sparrows eagles, or the hare the lion.
If I say sooth,[14] I must report they were
As cannons overcharged with double cracks;[15]
So they doubly redoubled strokes upon the foe.
Except[16] they meant to bathe in reeking wounds,
40 Or memorize another Golgotha,[17]
I cannot tell—
But I am faint; my gashes cry for help.

KING. So well thy words become thee as thy wounds;
They smack of honor both. Go get him surgeons.

[*Exit* CAPTAIN, *attended.*]

[*Enter* ROSS *and* ANGUS.]

Who comes here?

45 **MALCOLM.**   The worthy Thane[18] of Ross.

LENNOX. What a haste looks through his eyes! So should he look
That seems to[19] speak things strange.

ROSS.   God save the king!

KING. Whence cam'st thou, worthy Thane?

ROSS.   From Fife, great King;
Where the Norweyan banners flout the sky
50 And fan our people cold.
Norway[20] himself, with terrible numbers,
Assisted by that most disloyal traitor
The Thane of Cawdor, began a dismal[21] conflict;
Till that Bellona's bridegroom, lapped in proof,[22]

Literary Analysis
Elizabethan Drama What offstage scene does the captain describe in this speech (lines 7–23)?

10. **unseamed . . . chops** split him open from the navel to the jaws.

11. **'gins his reflection** rises.

12. **Norweyan lord** king of Norway.

13. **surveying vantage** seeing an opportunity.

14. **sooth** truth.

15. **cracks** explosives.

16. **except** unless.

17. **memorize . . . Golgotha** (gôlʹ gə thə) make the place as memorable for slaughter as Golgotha, the place where Christ was crucified.

18. **Thane** Scottish title of nobility.

19. **seems to** seems about to.

20. **Norway** king of Norway.

21. **dismal** threatening.

22. **Bellona's . . . proof** Macbeth is called the mate of Bellona, the goddess of war, clad in tested armor.

Literary Analysis
Elizabethan Drama How do Lennox's words here (lines 46–47) supply a clue for the actor playing Ross?

✓**Reading Check**

What role has Macbeth played in the battle?

55 Confronted him with self-comparisons,[23]
Point against point, rebellious arm 'gainst arm,
Curbing his lavish[24] spirit: and, to conclude,
The victory fell on us.

KING. Great happiness!

ROSS. That now
Sweno, the Norways' king, craves composition;[25]
60 Nor would we deign him burial of his men
Till he disbursed, at Saint Colme's Inch,[26]
Ten thousand dollars to our general use.

KING. No more that Thane of Cawdor shall deceive
Our bosom interest:[27] go pronounce his present[28] death,
65 And with his former title greet Macbeth.

ROSS. I'll see it done.

KING. What he hath lost, noble Macbeth hath won.

[*Exit.*]

Scene iii. A heath near Forres.

[*Thunder. Enter the* THREE WITCHES.]

FIRST WITCH. Where hast thou been, sister?

SECOND WITCH. Killing swine.[1]

THIRD WITCH. Sister, where thou?

FIRST WITCH. A sailor's wife had chestnuts in her lap,
And mounched, and mounched, and mounched.
5 "Give me," quoth I.
"Aroint thee,[2] witch!" the rump-fed ronyon[3] cries.
Her husband's to Aleppo[4] gone, master o' th' Tiger:
But in a sieve[5] I'll thither sail,
And, like a rat without a tail,[6]
10 I'll do, I'll do, and I'll do.

SECOND WITCH. I'll give thee a wind.

FIRST WITCH. Th' art kind.

THIRD WITCH. And I another.

FIRST WITCH. I myself have all the other;
15 And the very ports they blow,[7]
All the quarters that they know
I' th' shipman's card.[8]
I'll drain him dry as hay:
Sleep shall neither night nor day
20 Hang upon his penthouse lid;[9]
He shall live a man forbid:[10]

23. self-comparisons counter movements.

24. lavish insolent.

25. composition terms of peace.

26. St. Colme's Inch island near Edinburgh, Scotland.

27. our bosom interest my heart's trust.

28. present immediate.

Reading Strategy
Using Text Aids What information about the setting for Scene iii do you learn from the italicized stage directions?

1. Killing swine It was commonly believed that witches killed domestic animals.

2. Aroint thee Be off.

3. rump-fed ronyon fat-rumped, scabby creature.

4. Aleppo trading center in Syria.

5. sieve It was commonly believed that witches often sailed in sieves.

6. rat . . . tail According to popular belief, witches could assume the form of any animal, but the tail would always be missing.

7. they blow to which the winds blow.

8. card compass.

9. penthouse lid eyelid.

10. forbid cursed.

Weary sev'nights[11] nine times nine
Shall he dwindle, peak,[12] and pine:
Though his bark cannot be lost,
25 Yet it shall be tempest-tossed.
Look what I have.

SECOND WITCH. Show me, show me.

FIRST WITCH. Here I have a pilot's thumb,
Wracked as homeward he did come.

[Drum within.]

30 **THIRD WITCH.** A drum, a drum!
Macbeth doth come.

ALL. The weird[13] sisters, hand in hand,
Posters[14] of the sea and land,
Thus do go about, about:
35 Thrice to thine, and thrice to mine,
And thrice again, to make up nine.
Peace! The charm's wound up.

[Enter MACBETH and BANQUO.]

MACBETH. So foul and fair a day I have not seen.

BANQUO. How far is 't called to Forres? What are these
40 So withered, and so wild in their attire,
That look not like th' inhabitants o' th' earth,
And yet are on 't? Live you, or are you aught
That man may question? You seem to understand me,
By each at once her choppy[15] finger laying
45 Upon her skinny lips. You should be women,
And yet your beards forbid me to interpret
That you are so.

MACBETH.   Speak, if you can: what are you?

FIRST WITCH. All hail, Macbeth! Hail to thee, Thane of Glamis!

SECOND WITCH. All hail, Macbeth! Hail to thee, Thane of Cawdor!

50 **THIRD WITCH.** All hail, Macbeth, that shalt be King hereafter!

BANQUO. Good sir, why do you start, and seem to fear
Things that do sound so fair? I' th' name of truth,
Are you fantastical,[16] or that indeed
Which outwardly ye show? My noble partner
55 You greet with present grace[17] and great prediction
Of noble having[18] and of royal hope,
That he seems rapt withal:[19] to me you speak not.
If you can look into the seeds of time,
And say which grain will grow and which will not,

11. **sev'nights** weeks.

12. **peak** waste away.

13. **weird** destiny-serving.

14. **Posters** swift travelers.

Literary Analysis
Elizabethan Drama
What descriptive details does Banquo use in his speech about the witches (lines 39–47)?

15. **choppy** chapped.

16. **fantastical** imaginary.

17. **grace** honor.

18. **having** possession.

19. **rapt withal** entranced by it.

 **Reading Check**

What has Macbeth earned through his exploits?

Macbeth and the Witches, Clarkson Stanfield, Leicestershire Museums, Art Galleries and Records Service

▲ **Critical Viewing** Which of the two soldiers on the right do you think is Macbeth? Explain your reasoning. **[Deduce]**

60   Speak then to me, who neither beg nor fear
        Your favors nor your hate.

FIRST WITCH. Hail!

SECOND WITCH. Hail!

THIRD WITCH. Hail!

65   **FIRST WITCH.** Lesser than Macbeth, and greater.

SECOND WITCH. Not so happy,[20] yet much happier.

THIRD WITCH. Thou shalt get kings, though thou be none.
        So all hail, Macbeth and Banquo!

FIRST WITCH. Banquo and Macbeth, all hail!

70   **MACBETH.** Stay, you imperfect[21] speakers, tell me more:
        By Sinel's[22] death I know I am Thane of Glamis;
        But how of Cawdor? The Thane of Cawdor lives,
        A prosperous gentleman; and to be King
        Stands not within the prospect of belief,
75   No more than to be Cawdor. Say from whence
        You owe[23] this strange intelligence?[24] Or why

Literary Analysis
Elizabethan Drama How could Elizabethan actors have made this scene with the witches mysterious without help from special lighting effects?

20. **happy** fortunate.

21. **imperfect** incomplete.

22. **Sinel's** (sī´ nəlz) Macbeth's father's.

23. **owe** own.

24. **intelligence** information.

Upon this blasted heath you stop our way
With such prophetic greeting? Speak, I charge you.

[WITCHES *vanish*.]

BANQUO. The earth hath bubbles as the water has,
80   And these are of them. Whither are they vanished?

MACBETH. Into the air, and what seemed corporal[25] melted
    As breath into the wind. Would they had stayed!

BANQUO. Were such things here as we do speak about?
    Or have we eaten on the insane root[26]
85   That takes the reason prisoner?

MACBETH. Your children shall be kings.

BANQUO.   You shall be King.

MACBETH. And Thane of Cawdor too. Went it not so?

BANQUO. To th' selfsame tune and words. Who's here?

[*Enter* ROSS *and* ANGUS.]

ROSS. The King hath happily received, Macbeth,
90   The news of thy success; and when he reads[27]
    Thy personal venture in the rebels' fight,
    His wonders and his praises do contend
    Which should be thine or his.[28] Silenced with that,
    In viewing o'er the rest o' th' selfsame day,
95   He finds thee in the stout Norweyan ranks,
    Nothing afeard of what thyself didst make,
    Strange images of death.[29] As thick as tale
    Came post with post,[30] and every one did bear
    Thy praises in his kingdom's great defense,
    And poured them down before him.

100 **ANGUS.**   We are sent
    To give thee, from our royal master, thanks;
    Only to herald thee into his sight,
    Not pay thee.

ROSS. And for an earnest[31] of a greater honor,
105   He bade me, from him, call thee Thane of Cawdor;
    In which addition,[32] hail, most worthy Thane!
    For it is thine.

BANQUO. [*Aside*] What, can the devil speak true?

MACBETH. The Thane of Cawdor lives: why do you dress me
    In borrowed robes?

ANGUS.   Who was the thane lives yet,
110   But under heavy judgment bears that life
    Which he deserves to lose. Whether he was combined[33]

25. **corporal** real.

26. **insane root** henbane or hemlock, believed to cause insanity.

Reading Strategy
Using Text Aids What does Banquo mean by the "insane root" (line 84)?

27. **reads** considers.

28. **His wonders . . . his** His admiration contends with his desire to praise you.

29. **Nothing . . . death** killing, but not being afraid of being killed.

30. **As thick . . . post** as fast as could be counted came messenger after messenger.

31. **earnest** pledge.

32. **In which addition** with this new title.

33. **combined** allied.

✔**Reading Check**

What do the witches promise Macbeth and Banquo?

With those of Norway, or did line[34] the rebel
With hidden help and vantage,[35] or that with both
He labored in his country's wrack,[36] I know not;

115　But <u>treasons</u> capital, confessed and proved,
Have overthrown him.

MACBETH.　　　　　　　[*Aside*] Glamis, and Thane of Cawdor:
The greatest is behind.[37] [*To* ROSS *and* ANGUS]
Thanks for your pains.
[*Aside to* BANQUO] Do you not hope your children shall be
kings,
When those that gave the Thane of Cawdor to me
Promised no less to them?

120　**BANQUO.** [*Aside to* MACBETH] That, trusted home,[38]
Might yet enkindle you unto[39] the crown,
Besides the Thane of Cawdor. But 'tis strange:
And oftentimes, to win us to our harm,
The instruments of darkness tell us truths,

125　Win us with honest trifles, to betray 's
In deepest consequence.
Cousins,[40] a word, I pray you.

MACBETH.　　　　　　　[*Aside*] Two truths are told,
As happy prologues to the swelling act
Of the <u>imperial</u> theme.[41]—I thank you, gentlemen.—

130　[*Aside*] This supernatural soliciting
Cannot be ill, cannot be good. If ill,
Why hath it given me earnest of success,
Commencing in a truth? I am Thane of Cawdor:
If good, why do I yield to that suggestion[42]

135　Whose horrid image doth unfix my hair
And make my seated[43] heart knock at my ribs,
Against the use of nature?[44] Present fears

34. line support.

35. vantage assistance.

treasons (trē´ zenz) *n.*
betrayals of one's country
or oath of loyalty

36. wrack ruin.

37. behind still to come.

Reading Strategy
Using Text Aids Using the
side notes, how would you
rephrase lines 120–121 in
modern English?

38. home fully.

39. enkindle you unto
encourage you to hope for.

40. Cousins often used as
a term of courtesy between
fellow noblemen.

41. swelling . . . theme
stately idea that I will be
King.

imperial (im pir´ ē əl) *adj.*
of an empire; having
supreme authority

42. suggestion thought of
murdering Duncan.

43. seated fixed.

44. Against . . . nature in an
unnatural way.

Literature in context Vocabulary Connection

The Etymology of Power
　　Even the language of *Macbeth* reinforces the theme of
power. For example, if you look up the word *imperial*, you will
find that it comes from the Latin noun *imperium*, meaning
"power." The word *treason* is from the Latin verb *tradere*,
which means "to hand over." The word *liege* comes from Latin
through medieval German; it has been influenced by two
words: one means "free" and the other is a verb meaning
"to bind." Many of the words related to political power in this
drama came from Latin—one of history's greatest languages.

Are less than horrible imaginings.
My thought, whose murder yet is but fantastical

140 Shakes so my single[45] state of man that function
Is smothered in surmise, and nothing is
But what is not.

BANQUO.   Look, how our partner's rapt.

MACBETH. [*Aside*] If chance will have me King, why, chance may crown me,
Without my stir.

BANQUO.   New honors come upon him,
145 Like our strange[46] garments, cleave not to their mold
But with the aid of use.

MACBETH.   [*Aside*] Come what come may,
Time and the hour runs through the roughest day.

BANQUO. Worthy Macbeth, we stay upon your leisure.[47]

MACBETH. Give me your favor.[48] My dull brain was wrought
150 With things forgotten. Kind gentlemen, your pains
Are registered where every day I turn
The leaf to read them. Let us toward the King.
[*Aside to* BANQUO] Think upon what hath chanced,
   and at more time,
The interim having weighed it,[49] let us speak
Our free hearts[50] each to other.

155 **BANQUO.**   Very gladly.

MACBETH. Till then, enough. Come, friends.   [*Exit.*]

Scene iv. Forres. The palace.

[*Flourish.*[1] *Enter* KING DUNCAN, LENNOX, MALCOLM, DONALBAIN, *and* ATTENDANTS.]

KING. Is execution done on Cawdor? Are not
Those in commission[2] yet returned?

MALCOLM.   My liege,
They are not yet come back. But I have spoke
With one that saw him die, who did report
5 That very frankly he confessed his treasons,
Implored your Highness' pardon and set forth
A deep repentance: nothing in his life
Became him like the leaving it. He died
As one that had been studied[3] in his death,
10 To throw away the dearest thing he owed[4]
As 'twere a careless[5] trifle.

Reading Strategy
Using Text Aids What does the stage direction for line 153 indicate to the actor playing Macbeth?

45. **single** unaided, weak.

46. **strange** new.

47. **stay upon your leisure** await your convenience.

48. **favor** pardon.

49. **The interim . . . it** when we have had time to think about it.

50. **Our free hearts** our minds freely.

1. **Flourish** trumpet fanfare.

2. **in commission** commissioned to oversee the execution.

liege (lēj) *n.* lord or king

3. **studied** rehearsed.

4. **owed** owned.

5. **careless** worthless.

✓**Reading Check**

As Macbeth thinks about what the witches have promised, what "horrid image" frightens him?

KING.   There's no art
To find the mind's construction[6] in the face:
He was a gentleman on whom I built
An absolute trust.

[*Enter* MACBETH, BANQUO, ROSS, *and* ANGUS.]

                     O worthiest cousin!
15   The sin of my ingratitude even now
      Was heavy on me: thou art so far before,
      That swiftest wing of recompense is slow
      To overtake thee. Would thou hadst less deserved,
      That the proportion both of thanks and payment
20   Might have been mine![7] Only I have left to say,
      More is thy due than more than all can pay.

MACBETH. The service and the loyalty I owe,
      In doing it, pays itself.[8] Your Highness' part
      Is to receive our duties: and our duties
25   Are to your throne and state children and servants;
      Which do but what they should, by doing every thing
      Safe toward[9] your love and honor.

KING.   Welcome hither.
      I have begun to plant thee, and will labor
      To make thee full of growing. Noble Banquo,
30   That hast no less deserved, nor must be known

6. mind's construction
person's character.

7. Would . . . mine If you
had been less worthy, my
thanks and payment could
have exceeded the rewards
you deserve.

8. pays itself is its own
reward.

9. Safe toward with sure
regard for.

▼ **Critical Viewing** How does this Scottish
castle reflect the mood of the play? **[Connect]**

No less to have done so, let me enfold thee
And hold thee to my heart.

BANQUO.   There if I grow,
The harvest is your own.

KING.   My plenteous joys,
Wanton[10] in fullness, seek to hide themselves
35 In drops of sorrow. Sons, kinsmen, thanes,
And you whose places are the nearest, know,
We will establish our estate upon
Our eldest, Malcolm,[11] whom we name hereafter
The Prince of Cumberland: which honor must
40 Not unaccompanied invest him only,
But signs of nobleness, like stars, shall shine
On all deservers. From hence to Inverness,[12]
And bind us further to you.

MACBETH. The rest is labor, which is not used for you.[13]
45 I'll be myself the harbinger,[14] and make joyful
The hearing of my wife with your approach;
So, humbly take my leave.

KING.   My worthy Cawdor!

MACBETH. [*Aside*] The Prince of Cumberland! That is a step
On which I must fall down, or else o'erleap,
50 For in my way it lies. Stars, hide your fires;
Let not light see my black and deep desires:
The eye wink at the hand;[15] yet let that be
Which the eye fears, when it is done, to see.   [*Exit.*]

KING. True, worthy Banquo; he is full so valiant,
55 And in his commendations I am fed;
It is a banquet to me. Let's after him,
Whose care is gone before to bid us welcome.
It is a peerless kinsman.   [*Flourish. Exit.*]

Scene v. Inverness. Macbeth's castle.

[*Enter* MACBETH'S WIFE, *alone, with a letter.*]

LADY MACBETH. [*Reads*] "They met me in the day of
success; and I have learned by the perfect'st report
they have more in them than mortal knowledge.
When I burned in desire to question them further,
5 they made themselves air, into which they vanished.
Whiles I stood rapt in the wonder of it, came
missives[1] from the King, who all-hailed me 'Thane
of Cawdor'; by which title, before, these weird sisters
saluted me, and referred me to the coming on
10 of time, with 'Hail, King that shalt be!' This have I

Literary Analysis
Elizabethan Drama
From what area of human activity do King Duncan and Banquo draw the imagery in this passage (lines 28–33)?

10. Wanton unrestrained.

11. establish . . . Malcolm make Malcolm the heir to my throne.

12. Inverness Macbeth's castle.

13. The rest . . . you anything not done for you is laborious.

14. harbinger advance representative of the army or royal party who makes arrangements for a visit.

15. wink at the hand be blind to the hand's deed.

Reading Strategy
Using Text Aids What do the stage directions with line 48 tell you about how Macbeth is to deliver this speech?

1. missives messengers.

 **Reading Check**

What action of Duncan's upsets Macbeth?

thought good to deliver thee,[2] my dearest partner of
greatness, that thou mightst not lose the dues of
rejoicing, by being ignorant of what greatness is
promised thee. Lay it to thy heart, and farewell."

15 Glamis thou art, and Cawdor, and shalt be
What thou art promised. Yet do I fear thy nature;
It is too full o' th' milk of human kindness
To catch the nearest[3] way. Thou wouldst be great,
Art not without ambition, but without
20 The illness[4] should attend it. What thou wouldst highly,
That wouldst thou holily; wouldst not play false,
And yet wouldst wrongly win. Thou'dst have, great Glamis,
That which cries "Thus thou must do" if thou have it;
And that which rather thou dost fear to do
25 Than wishest should be undone.[5] Hie thee hither,
That I may pour my spirits in thine ear,
And chastise with the valor of my tongue
All that impedes thee from the golden round[6]
Which fate and metaphysical aid doth seem
To have thee crowned withal.

[*Enter* MESSENGER.]

30   What is your tidings?

MESSENGER. The King comes here tonight.

LADY MACBETH.   Thou'rt mad to say it!
Is not thy master with him, who, were't so,
Would have informed for preparation?

MESSENGER. So please you, it is true. Our thane is coming.
35 One of my fellows had the speed of him,[7]
Who, almost dead for breath, had scarcely more
Than would make up his message.

LADY MACBETH.   Give him tending;
He brings great news.   [*Exit* MESSENGER.]
                    The raven himself is hoarse
That croaks the fatal entrance of Duncan
40 Under my battlements. Come, you spirits
That tend on mortal[8] thoughts, unsex me here,
And fill me, from the crown to the toe, top-full
Of direst cruelty! Make thick my blood,
Stop up th' access and passage to remorse[9]
45 That no compunctious visitings of nature[10]
Shake my fell[11] purpose, nor keep peace between
Th' effect[12] and it! Come to my woman's breasts,
And take my milk for gall,[13] you murd'ring ministers,[14]
Wherever in your sightless[15] substances
50 You wait on[16] nature's mischief! Come, thick night,

---

2. deliver thee report to
you.

Literary Analysis
Elizabethan Drama and
Soliloquy What does
Lady Macbeth's soliloquy
in lines 15–30 reveal about
her ambitions and plans?

3. nearest quickest.

4. illness wickedness.

5. that which . . . undone
What you are afraid of doing
you would not wish undone
once you have done it.

6. round crown.

7. had . . . him
overtook him.

8. mortal deadly.

9. remorse compassion.

10. compunctious . . .
nature natural feelings of pity.

11. fell savage.

12. effect fulfillment.

13. milk for gall kindness in
exchange for bitterness.

14. ministers agents.

15. sightless invisible.

16. wait on assist.

◄ Critical Viewing This is an artist's rendering of nineteenth-century actress Ellen Terry playing Lady Macbeth. Judging by the picture, how do you think Terry would have spoken lines 38–53 in Act I, Scene v? **[Deduce]**

And pall[17] thee in the dunnest[18] smoke of hell,
That my keen knife see not the wound it makes,
Nor heaven peep through the blanket of the dark,
To cry "Hold, hold!"

[*Enter* MACBETH.]

                                   Great Glamis! Worthy Cawdor!
55   Greater than both, by the all-hail hereafter!
      Thy letters have transported me beyond
      This ignorant[19] present, and I feel now
      The future in the instant.[20]

      MACBETH.   My dearest love,
      Duncan comes here tonight.

      LADY MACBETH.   And when goes hence?

      MACBETH. Tomorrow, as he purposes.

17. **pall** enshroud.

18. **dunnest** darkest.

19. **ignorant** unknowing.

20. **instant** present.

✔Reading Check

What does Lady Macbeth feel is Macbeth's weakness?

Macbeth, Act I, Scene v ◆ 313

60 **LADY MACBETH.** O, never
Shall sun that morrow see!
Your face, my Thane, is as a book where men
May read strange matters. To beguile the time,[21]
Look like the time; bear welcome in your eye,
65 Your hand, your tongue: look like th' innocent flower,
But be the serpent under 't. He that's coming
Must be provided for: and you shall put
This night's great business into my dispatch;[22]
Which shall to all our nights and days to come
70 Give solely <u>sovereign</u> sway and masterdom.

    MACBETH. We will speak further.

    LADY MACBETH. Only look up clear.[23]
To alter favor ever is to fear.[24]
Leave all the rest to me.   [*Exit.*]

Scene vi. Before Macbeth's castle.

[*Hautboys.[1] Torches. Enter* KING DUNCAN, MALCOLM, DONALBAIN, BANQUO, LENNOX, MACDUFF, ROSS, ANGUS, *and* ATTENDANTS.]

    KING. This castle hath a pleasant seat;[2] the air
Nimbly and sweetly recommends itself
Unto our gentle[3] senses.

    BANQUO. This guest of summer,
The temple-haunting martlet,[4] does approve[5]
5 By his loved mansionry[6] that the heaven's breath
Smells wooingly here. No jutty,[7] frieze,
Buttress, nor coign of vantage,[8] but this bird
Hath made his pendent bed and procreant cradle.[9]
Where they most breed and haunt,[10] I have observed
The air is delicate.

[*Enter* LADY MACBETH.]

10 **KING.** See, see, our honored hostess!
The love that follows us sometime is our trouble,
Which still we thank as love. Herein I teach you
How you shall bid God 'ield us for your pains
And thank us for your trouble.[11]

    LADY MACBETH. All our service
15 In every point twice done, and then done double,
Were poor and single business[12] to contend
Against those honors deep and broad wherewith
Your Majesty loads our house: for those of old,
And the late dignities heaped up to them,
We rest your hermits.[13]

---

21. beguile the time deceive the people tonight.

22. dispatch management.

23. look up clear appear innocent.

sovereign (säv´ rən) *adj.* supreme in power, rank, or authority

24. To alter . . . fear to show a disturbed face will arouse suspicion.

1. *Hautboys* oboes announcing the arrival of royalty.

2. seat location.

3. gentle soothed.

4. temple-haunting martlet martin, a bird that usually nests in churches. In Shakespeare's time, *martin* was a slang term for a person who is easily deceived.

5. approve show.

6. mansionry nests.

7. jutty projection.

8. coign of vantage advantageous corner.

9. procreant (prō´ krē ənt) **cradle** nest where the young are hatched.

10. haunt visit.

11. The love . . . trouble Though my visit inconveniences you, you should ask God to reward me for coming, because it was my love for you that prompted my visit.

12. single business feeble service.

13. rest your hermits remain your dependents bound to pray for you. Hermits were often paid to pray for another person's soul.

20 KING.   Where's the Thane of Cawdor?
We coursed[14] him at the heels, and had a purpose
To be his purveyor:[15] but he rides well,
And his great love, sharp as his spur, hath holp[16] him
To his home before us. Fair and noble hostess,
We are your guest tonight.

25 LADY MACBETH.   Your servants ever
Have theirs, themselves, and what is theirs, in compt,[17]
To make their audit at your Highness' pleasure,
Still[18] to return your own.

KING.   Give me your hand.
Conduct me to mine host: we love him highly,
30 And shall continue our graces towards him.
By your leave, hostess.   [*Exit.*]

Scene vii. *Macbeth's castle.*

[*Hautboys. Torches. Enter a* SEWER,[1] *and diverse* SERVANTS *with dishes and service over the stage. Then enter* MACBETH.]

MACBETH. If it were done[2] when 'tis done, then 'twere well
It were done quickly. If th' assassination
Could trammel up the consequence, and catch,
With his surcease, success;[3] that but this blow
5 Might be the be-all and the end-all—here,
But here, upon this bank and shoal of time,
We'd jump the life to come.[4] But in these cases
We still have judgment here; that we but teach
Bloody instructions, which, being taught, return
10 To plague th' inventor: this even-handed[5] justice
Commends[6] th' ingredients of our poisoned chalice[7]
To our own lips. He's here in double trust:
First, as I am his kinsman and his subject,
Strong both against the deed; then, as his host,
15 Who should against his murderer shut the door,
Not bear the knife myself. Besides, this Duncan
Hath borne his faculties[8] so meek, hath been
So clear[9] in his great office, that his virtues
Will plead like angels trumpet-tongued against
20 The deep damnation of his taking-off;
And pity, like a naked newborn babe,
Striding the blast, or heaven's cherubin[10] horsed
Upon the sightless couriers[11] of the air,
Shall blow the horrid deed in every eye,
25 That tears shall drown the wind. I have no spur
To prick the sides of my intent, but only
Vaulting ambition, which o'erleaps itself
And falls on th' other—

---

14. coursed chased.

15. purveyor advance supply officer.

16. holp helped.

17. compt trust.

18. Still always.

Literary Analysis
Elizabethan Drama What details does Banquo use in Scene vi, lines 3–10 to paint a word picture of Macbeth's castle?

1. sewer chief butler.

2. done over and done with.

3. If . . . success if the assassination could be done successfully and without consequence.

4. We'd . . . come I would risk life in the world to come.

5. even-handed impartial.

6. commends offers.

7. chalice cup.

8. faculties powers.

9. clear blameless.

10. cherubin angels.

11. sightless couriers unseen messengers (the wind).

Literary Analysis
Elizabethan Drama and Soliloquy What doubts does Macbeth reveal in his soliloquy (lines 1–28)?

**Reading Check**

What deed does Lady Macbeth urge her husband to perform?

[*Enter* LADY MACBETH.]

How now! What news?

LADY MACBETH. He has almost supped. Why have you
left the chamber?

MACBETH. Hath he asked for me?

30 **LADY MACBETH.**   Know you not he has?

MACBETH. We will proceed no further in this business:
He hath honored me of late, and I have bought[12]
Golden opinions from all sorts of people,
Which would be worn now in their newest gloss,
Not cast aside so soon.

35 **LADY MACBETH.**   Was the hope drunk
Wherein you dressed yourself? Hath it slept since?
And wakes it now, to look so green and pale
At what it did so freely? From this time
Such I account thy love. Art thou afeard
40 To be the same in thine own act and valor
As thou art in desire? Wouldst thou have that
Which thou esteem'st the ornament of life,[13]
And live a coward in thine own esteem,
Letting "I dare not" wait upon[14] "I would,"
Like the poor cat i' th' adage?[15]

45 **MACBETH.**   Prithee, peace!
I dare do all that may become a man;
Who dares do more is none.

LADY MACBETH.   What beast was 't then
That made you break[16] this enterprise to me?
When you durst do it, then you were a man;
50 And to be more than what you were, you would
Be so much more the man. Nor time nor place
Did then adhere,[17] and yet you would make both.
They have made themselves, and that their[18] fitness now
Does unmake you. I have given suck, and know
55 How tender 'tis to love the babe that milks me:
I would, while it was smiling in my face,
Have plucked my nipple from his boneless gums,
And dashed the brains out, had I so sworn as you
Have done to this.

MACBETH.   If we should fail?

LADY MACBETH.   We fail?
60 But[19] screw your courage to the sticking-place[20]
And we'll not fail. When Duncan is asleep—
Whereto the rather shall his day's hard journey
Soundly invite him—his two chamberlains

---

12. bought acquired.

Reading Strategy
Using Text Aids In
line 42, what does Lady
Macbeth mean by the
"ornament of life"?

13. ornament of life
the crown.

14. wait upon follow.

15. poor . . . adage from an
old proverb about a cat who
wants to eat fish but is afraid
of getting its paws wet.

16. break reveal.

17. Did then adhere
was then suitable (for the
assassination).

18. that their their very.

19. But only.

20. sticking-place the notch
that holds the bowstring of a
taut crossbow.

65 Will I with wine and wassail²¹ so convince,²²
That memory, the warder of the brain,
Shall be a fume, and the receipt of reason
A limbeck only:²³ when in swinish sleep
Their drenchéd natures lies as in a death,
70 What cannot you and I perform upon
Th' unguarded Duncan, what not put upon
His spongy²⁴ officers, who shall bear the guilt
Of our great quell?²⁵

MACBETH.   Bring forth men-children only;
For thy undaunted mettle²⁶ should compose
Nothing but males. Will it not be received,
75 When we have marked with blood those sleepy two
Of his own chamber, and used their very daggers,
That they have done 't?

LADY MACBETH.   Who dares receive it other,²⁷
As we shall make our griefs and clamor roar
Upon his death?

MACBETH.   I am settled, and bend up
80 Each corporal agent to this terrible feat.
Away, and mock the time²⁸ with fairest show:
False face must hide what the false heart doth know.   [Exit.]

21. **wassail** carousing.

22. **convince** overpower.

23. **That . . . only** that memory, the guardian of the brain, will be confused by the fumes of the drink, and the reason become like a still, distilling confused thoughts.

24. **spongy** sodden.

25. **quell** murder.

26. **mettle** spirit.

27. **other** otherwise.

28. **mock the time** mislead the world.

Review and Assess

Thinking About Act I

1. **Respond:** What mood did Act I evoke in you? Explain.

2. **(a) Recall:** What statements do the witches and Macbeth make about "foul and fair"? **(b) Interpret:** What meaning (or meanings) does each remark have?

3. **(a) Recall:** Describe Banquo's and Macbeth's reactions to the witches. **(b) Compare and Contrast:** Compare and contrast their reactions to the witches.

4. **(a) Recall:** In his soliloquy at the beginning of Scene vii, what arguments against killing Duncan does Macbeth express? **(b) Analyze Cause and Effect:** Which of these arguments seems to influence him the most? Explain.

5. **(a) Recall:** What is Lady Macbeth's opinion of her husband's character? **(b) Analyze:** How does she use her knowledge of his character to convince him to kill Duncan?

6. **Speculate:** Does the meeting with the witches suggest that evil is something people choose or a force that seeks out people? Explain.

Review and Assess

Literary Analysis

Elizabethan Drama

1. (a) What vivid image, typical of **Elizabethan drama,** does Shakespeare create when Macbeth says to Ross, "why do you dress me / In borrowed robes?" (Act I, Scene iii, lines 108–109)? (b) What uneasiness in Macbeth does this word picture reveal?

2. How does Macbeth's encounter with the witches show that the play will probably be a **tragedy**?

3. Using a chart like this one, analyze the details of setting in the lines shown. Then, indicate how modern sets and lighting might produce such a setting.

Shakespeare's Words		Modern Sets and Lighting
I, i, 10–11	....▶	
I, vi, 3–10		

Connecting Literary Elements

4. What do each of the following **soliloquies** reveal about their speaker's thoughts and plans: (a) Lady Macbeth, Act I, Scene v, lines 1–30 and (b) Macbeth, Act I, Scene vii, lines 1–28?

5. In Act I, which type of speech directed to the audience is more effective in revealing Macbeth's thoughts: asides or a soliloquy? Explain.

6. Do Lady Macbeth's and Macbeth's soliloquies add to the sense that the characters are moving toward disaster? Why or why not?

Reading Strategy

Using Text Aids

7. Use **text aids** such as stage directions and side notes to describe the action in these scenes: (a) Act I, Scene i, (b) beginning of Act I, Scene v.

8. Use the side notes to describe the following terms: (a) anon, (b) Thane, (c) cousins.

Extend Understanding

9. **Social Studies Connection:** Identify a person in history who is similar to a character in *Macbeth*. Then, explain your choice.

Quick Review

Elizabethan drama is written in unrhymed verse, contains rich language and vivid imagery, and depends on words to set a scene. Many Elizabethan dramas are **tragedies,** in which disaster befalls a hero or heroine.

A **soliloquy** is a long speech in which a character who is alone reveals his or her thoughts to the audience.

By **using text aids** such as stage directions and notes, readers can supplement their reading of a drama.

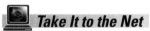 **Take It to the Net**
www.phschool.com

Take the interactive self-test online to check your understanding of the selection.

Integrate Language Skills

Vocabulary Development Lesson

Concept Development: Power Words

Liege refers to the role of the king as chief lord in a feudal system. *Sovereign* contains a form of the Latin root *super,* meaning "above" and can be used as a noun or an adjective.

1. Why might "my *liege*" be an appropriate phrase to use when addressing a king?
2. Name a modern-day *sovereign*.

Spelling Strategy

When *i* and *e* spell the long *e* sound, they usually appear as *ie,* as in *liege.* In your notebook, complete the spelling of these words with *ie* or *ei.*

1. rel__f   2. caff__ne   3. ach__ve

Grammar and Style Lesson

Action Verbs and Linking Verbs

Action verbs depict physical or mental actions. **Linking verbs**—like *seem* and forms of the verb *to be*—connect the subject of a sentence with a word that renames or describes it.

> **Action Verb:** The Thane of Cawdor <u>lives.</u>
>
> **Linking Verb:** You <u>shall be</u> King.

Practice Identify each verb in these sentences from *Macbeth* as an action or a linking verb.

1. Fair is foul, and foul is fair. (I, i, 10)

W̶G *Prentice Hall Writing and Grammar Connection: Chapter 17, Section 2*

Concept Development: Antonyms

In your notebook, write the letter of the word that is the antonym (opposite in meaning) of the first word.

1. valor: (a) courage, (b) bravery, (c) cowardice
2. treason: (a) loyalty, (b) betrayal, (c) treachery
3. imperial: (a) royal, (b) submissive, (c) powerful
4. liege: (a) authority, (b) king, (c) peasant
5. sovereign: (a) insignificant, (b) supreme, (c) solid

2. But I am faint; my gashes cry for help. (I, ii, 42)
3. Speak then to me, . . . (I, iii, 60)
4. Stars, hide your fires; . . . (I, iv, 50)
5. It is too full o' th' milk of human kindness. . . . (I, v, 17)

Writing Application Write a brief paragraph predicting what will happen in Act II. Base your predictions on the events of Act I, and use at least two linking verbs and two action verbs.

Extension Activities

Writing Write the **speech of welcome** that Macbeth might have addressed to Duncan as Duncan entered Macbeth's castle. Use prose or blank verse, and include vivid images designed to make Duncan feel at home.

Research and Technology With a group, view different film versions of *Macbeth.* Use what you learn to present an **oral report** on the ways that famous actresses have portrayed Lady Macbeth in Act I. **[Group Activity]**

Prepare to Read

Macbeth, Act II

Literary Analysis

Blank Verse

Blank verse—unrhymed iambic pentameter—was invented during the English Renaissance to reflect natural speech. An **iamb** consists of an unstressed syllable followed by a stressed syllable (˘ ´). In iambic pentameter, there are five such feet (units) to the line. *Macbeth* is written mainly in blank verse:

> Methŏúght Ĭ héard ă vóice crўy, "Sléep nŏ móre!" (II, ii, 34)

For interest, Shakespeare varies his meter, as when he begins this line with a **trochaic foot** (´ ˘): "List'ning their fear, I could not say 'Amen'" (II, ii, 28). Another variation is the **anapestic foot** (˘ ˘ ´). As you read, listen for the rhythm as well as the meaning of the dialogue.

Connecting Literary Elements

Shakespeare interrupts his blank verse with **prose,** which is writing that is not divided into poetic lines and lacks a definite rhythm. In his tragedies, lower-ranking characters often speak in prose to provide **comic relief,** a humorous break from a tense mood. Notice this effect as you read the porter's speech at the start of Act II, Scene iii.

Reading Strategy

Reading Verse for Meaning

To **read blank verse for meaning,** follow sentences past line endings. For instance, you must follow this sentence past the end of the line to learn what the owl does:

> "It was the owl that shrieked, the fatal bellman,
> Which gives the stern'st good-night. . . ." (II, ii, 3–4).

Use a chart like this one to distinguish between lines and sentences.

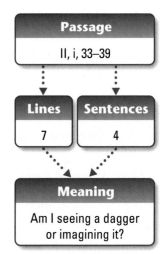

Passage
II, i, 33–39

Lines	Sentences
7	4

Meaning
Am I seeing a dagger or imagining it?

Vocabulary Development

augment (ôg ment´) *v.* make greater; enlarge (p. 322)

palpable (pal´ pə bəl) *adj.* capable of being touched or felt (p. 322)

stealthy (stel´ thē) *adj.* sly (p. 322)

multitudinous (mul´ tə tōōd´ 'n əs) *adj.* existing in great numbers (p. 326)

equivocate (ē kwiv´ ə kāt´) *v.* to use terms that have two or more meanings to mislead purposely or deceive (p. 326)

predominance (prē däm´ ə nəns) *n.* superiority (p. 332)

Review and Anticipate

In Act I, we learn that Macbeth has distinguished himself in battle.
Returning from the battlefield, he and Banquo meet three witches who
predict that Macbeth will not only be rewarded by King Duncan, but that
he will become king himself. However, the witches also greet Banquo as a
father of kings. Motivated by the witches' prophecies, Macbeth considers
killing Duncan. The assassination becomes more likely when the king
decides to visit Macbeth's castle. Lady Macbeth, on hearing about the
witches' predictions and the king's visit, resolves that she and her husband
will kill Duncan. When Macbeth hesitates, she urges him on. As
Act II begins, they are about to perform this evil deed.

▼ **Critical Viewing**
What sort of person
would be worthy of
wearing a crown such as
this one? **[Generalize]**

Scene i. Inverness. Court of Macbeth's castle.

[*Enter* BANQUO, *and* FLEANCE, *with a torch before him.*]

BANQUO. How goes the night, boy?

FLEANCE. The moon is down; I have not heard the clock.

BANQUO. And she goes down at twelve.

FLEANCE.   I take't, 'tis later, sir.

BANQUO. Hold, take my sword. There's husbandry¹ in heaven.
5   Their candles are all out. Take thee that² too.
       A heavy summons³ lies like lead upon me,
       And yet I would not sleep. Merciful powers,
       Restrain in me the cursèd thoughts that nature
       Gives way to in repose!

[*Enter* MACBETH, *and a* SERVANT *with a torch.*]

                                    Give me my sword!
10   Who's there?

MACBETH. A friend.

BANQUO. What, sir, not yet at rest? The King's a-bed:
       He hath been in unusual pleasure, and
       Sent forth great largess to your offices:⁴
15   This diamond he greets your wife withal,
       By the name of most kind hostess; and shut up⁵
       In measureless content.

MACBETH.   Being unprepared,
       Our will became the servant to defect,
       Which else should free have wrought.⁶

Reading Strategy
**Reading Verse for
Meaning** Which line
endings in lines 12–17
do *not* require a pause?

1. **husbandry** thrift.

2. **that** probably his
sword belt.

3. **summons** weariness.

4. **largess . . . offices** gifts
to your servants' quarters.

5. **shut up** retired.

6. **Being . . . wrought**
Because we did not have
enough time to prepare, we
were unable to entertain as
lavishly as we wanted to.

✓**Reading Check**

Where and when do
Macbeth and Banquo
meet?

BANQUO.   All's well.

20   I dreamt last night of the three weird sisters:
To you they have showed some truth.

MACBETH.   I think not of them.
Yet, when we can entreat an hour to serve,
We would spend it in some words upon that business,
If you would grant the time.

BANQUO.   At your kind'st leisure.

25 **MACBETH.** If you shall cleave to my consent, when 'tis,[7]
It shall make honor for you.

BANQUO.   So[8] I lose none
In seeking to <u>augment</u> it, but still keep
My bosom franchised[9] and allegiance clear,
I shall be counseled.

MACBETH.   Good repose the while!

30 **BANQUO.** Thanks, sir. The like to you!

[Exit BANQUO with FLEANCE.]

MACBETH. Go bid thy mistress, when my drink is ready,
She strike upon the bell. Get thee to bed.

[Exit SERVANT.]

Is this a dagger which I see before me,
The handle toward my hand? Come, let me clutch thee.
35   I have thee not, and yet I see thee still.
Art thou not, fatal vision, sensible[10]
To feeling as to sight, or art thou but
A dagger of the mind, a false creation,
Proceeding from the heat-oppressèd brain?
40   I see thee yet, in form as <u>palpable</u>
As this which now I draw.
Thou marshal'st[11] me the way that I was going;
And such an instrument I was to use.
Mine eyes are made the fools o' th' other senses,
45   Or else worth all the rest. I see thee still;
And on thy blade and dudgeon[12] gouts[13] of blood,
Which was not so before. There's no such thing.
It is the bloody business which informs[14]
Thus to mine eyes. Now o'er the one half-world
50   Nature seems dead, and wicked dreams abuse[15]
The curtained sleep; witchcraft celebrates
Pale Hecate's offerings;[16] and withered murder,
Alarumed by his sentinel, the wolf,
Whose howl's his watch, thus with his <u>stealthy</u> pace,
55   With Tarquin's[17] ravishing strides, towards his design
Moves like a ghost. Thou sure and firm-set earth,

7. **cleave . . . 'tis** Join
my cause when the time
comes.

8. **So** provided that.

augment (ôg ment´) v. to
make greater; enlarge

9. **bosom franchised** heart
free (from guilt)

10. **sensible** able to be felt.

palpable (pal´ pə bəl) *adj.*
capable of being touched
or felt

11. **marshal'st** leads.

12. **dudgeon** wooden hilt.

13. **gouts** large drops.

14. **informs** takes shape.

15. **abuse** deceive.

16. **Hecate's** (hek´ə tēz)
offerings offerings to Hecate,
the Greek goddess of witchcraft.

stealthy (stel´ thē) *adj.* sly

17. **Tarquin's** of Tarquin, a
Roman tyrant.

Hear not my steps, which way they walk, for fear
Thy very stones prate of my whereabout,
And take the present horror from the time,
60 Which now suits with it.[18] Whiles I threat, he lives:
Words to the heat of deeds too cold breath gives.

[*A bell rings.*]

I go, and it is done: the bell invites me.
Hear it not, Duncan, for it is a knell
That summons thee to heaven, or to hell.   [*Exit.*]

18. **take . . . it** remove the horrible silence which suits this moment.

Scene ii. *Macbeth's castle.*

[*Enter* LADY MACBETH.]

LADY MACBETH. That which hath made them drunk hath made
          me bold;
     What hath quenched them hath given me fire. Hark! Peace!
     It was the owl that shrieked, the fatal bellman,
     Which gives the stern'st good-night.[1] He is about it.
5   The doors are open, and the surfeited grooms[2]
     Do mock their charge with snores. I have drugged their possets,[3]
     That death and nature do contend about them,
     Whether they live or die.

MACBETH.   [*Within*] Who's there? What, ho?

LADY MACBETH. Alack, I am afraid they have awaked
10   And 'tis not done! Th' attempt and not the deed
     Confounds[4] us. Hark! I laid their daggers ready;
     He could not miss 'em. Had he not resembled
     My father as he slept, I had done 't.

[*Enter* MACBETH.]

                              My husband!

MACBETH. I have done the deed. Didst thou not hear a noise?

15 LADY MACBETH. I heard the owl scream and the crickets cry.
     Did not you speak?

MACBETH.   When?

LADY MACBETH.   Now.

MACBETH.   As I descended?

LADY MACBETH. Ay.

MACBETH. Hark!
     Who lies i' th' second chamber?

LADY MACBETH.   Donalbain.

20 MACBETH. This is a sorry[5] sight.

1. **bellman . . . good-night** It was customary for a bell to be rung at midnight outside a condemned person's cell on the night before an execution.

2. **surfeited grooms** overfed servants.

3. **possets** warm bedtime drinks.

4. **Confounds** ruins.

Literary Analysis
Blank Verse Notice that the iambic pentameter of line 16 is shared in dialogue between Macbeth and Lady Macbeth. Why might the playwright have chosen this artistry?

5. **sorry** miserable.

**Reading Check**

What deed have Macbeth and Lady Macbeth performed?

LADY MACBETH. A foolish thought, to say a sorry sight.

MACBETH. There's one did laugh in 's sleep, and one cried
      "Murder!"
That they did wake each other. I stood and heard them.
But they did say their prayers, and addressed them
Again to sleep.

25 **LADY MACBETH.** There are two[6] lodged together.

MACBETH. One cried "God bless us!" and "Amen" the other,
    As they had seen me with these hangman's hands:
    List'ning their fear, I could not say "Amen,"
    When they did say "God bless us!"

LADY MACBETH.   Consider it not so deeply.

30 **MACBETH.** But wherefore could not I pronounce "Amen"?
    I had most need of blessing, and "Amen"
    Stuck in my throat.

LADY MACBETH.   These deeds must not be thought
    After these ways; so, it will make us mad.

MACBETH. Methought I heard a voice cry "Sleep no more!
35   Macbeth does murder sleep"—the innocent sleep,
    Sleep that knits up the raveled sleave[7] of care,
    The death of each day's life, sore labor's bath,
    Balm of hurt minds, great nature's second course,[8]
    Chief nourisher in life's feast—

LADY MACBETH.   What do you mean?

40 **MACBETH.** Still it cried "Sleep no more!" to all the house:
    "Glamis hath murdered sleep, and therefore Cawdor
    Shall sleep no more: Macbeth shall sleep no more."

LADY MACBETH. Who was it that thus cried? Why, worthy Thane,
    You do unbend[9] your noble strength, to think
45   So brainsickly of things. Go get some water,
    And wash this filthy witness[10] from your hand.
    Why did you bring these daggers from the place?
    They must lie there: go carry them, and smear
    The sleepy grooms with blood.

MACBETH.   I'll go no more.
50   I am afraid to think what I have done;
    Look on 't again I dare not.

LADY MACBETH.   Infirm of purpose!
    Give me the daggers. The sleeping and the dead
    Are but as pictures. 'Tis the eye of childhood
    That fears a painted devil. If he do bleed,
55   I'll gild[11] the faces of the grooms withal,
    For it must seem their guilt.   *[Exit. Knock within.]*

6. **two** Malcolm and Donalbain, Duncan's sons.

7. **knits . . . sleave** straightens out the tangled threads.

8. **second course** main course; sleep.

9. **unbend** relax.

10. **witness** evidence.

11. **gild** paint.

▲ **Critical Viewing** How do these images from a poster advertising a production of *Macbeth* capture the suspense created in Act II? **[Connect]**

MACBETH.   Whence is that knocking?
How is 't with me, when every noise appalls me?
What hands are here? Ha! They pluck out mine eyes!
Will all great Neptune's ocean wash this blood
60   Clean from my hand? No; this my hand will rather
The <u>multitudinous</u> seas incarnadine,[12]
Making the green one red.

[*Enter* LADY MACBETH.]

LADY MACBETH. My hands are of your color, but I shame
To wear a heart so white. [*Knock.*] I hear a knocking
65   At the south entry. Retire we to our chamber.
A little water clears us of this deed:
How easy is it then! Your constancy
Hath left you unattended.[13] [*Knock.*] Hark! more knocking.
Get on your nightgown, lest occasion call us
70   And show us to be watchers.[14] Be not lost
So poorly in your thoughts.

MACBETH. To know my deed, 'twere best not know myself. [*Knock.*]
Wake Duncan with thy knocking! I would thou couldst!

[*Exit.*]

Scene iii. *Macbeth's castle.*

[*Enter a* PORTER.[1] *Knocking within.*]

PORTER. Here's a knocking indeed! If a man were porter
of hell gate, he should have old[2] turning the key.
[*Knock.*] Knock, knock, knock! Who's there, i' th'
name of Beelzebub?[3] Here's a farmer, that
5   hanged himself on th' expectation of plenty.[4] Come
in time! Have napkins enow[5] about you; here you'll
sweat for 't. [*Knock.*] Knock, knock! Who's there, in
th' other devil's name? Faith, here's an equivocator,
that could swear in both the scales against
10   either scale;[6] who committed treason enough for
God's sake, yet could not <u>equivocate</u> to heaven. O,
come in, equivocator. [*Knock.*] Knock, knock, knock!
Who's there? Faith, here's an English tailor come
hither for stealing out of a French hose:[7]
15   come in, tailor. Here you may roast your goose.[8]
[*Knock.*] Knock, knock; never at quiet! What are you?
But this place is too cold for hell. I'll devil-porter it no
further. I had thought to have let in some of all
professions that go the primrose way to th'
20   everlasting bonfire. [*Knock.*] Anon, anon!
[*Opens an entrance.*] I pray you, remember the porter.

multitudinous (mul′ tə tood′ 'n əs) *adj.* existing in great numbers

12. incarnadine (in kär′ nə dīn) redden.

13. Your constancy . . . unattended Your firmness of purpose has left you.

14. watchers up late.

Literary Analysis
Blank Verse, Prose, and Comic Relief How do the shift from verse to prose in Scene iii and the porter's remarks affect the mood?

1. porter doorkeeper.

2. should have old would have plenty of.

3. Beelzebub (bē el′ zə bub′) the chief devil.

4. A farmer . . . plenty a farmer who hoarded grain, hoping that the prices would come up as a result of a bad harvest.

5. enow enough.

equivocate (ē kwiv′ə kāt′) *v.* to use terms that have two or more meanings to mislead purposely or deceive

6. an equivocator . . . scale a liar who could make two contradictory statements and swear that both were true.

7. stealing . . . hose stealing some cloth from the hose while making them.

8. goose pressing iron.

[*Enter* MACDUFF *and* LENNOX.]

MACDUFF. Was it so late, friend, ere you went to bed,
  That you do lie so late?

PORTER. Faith, sir, we were carousing till the second
25 cock:[9] and drink, sir, is a great provoker of three
  things.

MACDUFF. What three things does drink especially
  provoke?

PORTER. Marry, sir, nose-painting, sleep, and urine.
30 Lechery, sir, it provokes and unprovokes; it provokes
  the desire, but it takes away the performance: therefore much drink may be said to be an equivocator
  with lechery: it makes him and it mars him; it
  sets him on and it takes him off; it persuades him
35 and disheartens him; makes him stand to and not
  stand to; in conclusion equivocates him in a sleep,
  and giving him the lie, leaves him.

MACDUFF. I believe drink gave thee the lie[10] last night.

PORTER. That it did, sir, i' the very throat on me: but I
40 requited him for his lie, and, I think, being too strong
  for him, though he took up my legs sometime, yet I
  make a shift to cast[11] him.

MACDUFF. Is thy master stirring?

[*Enter* MACBETH.]

  Our knocking has awaked him; here he comes.

LENNOX. Good morrow, noble sir.

45 **MACBETH.**   Good morrow, both.

MACDUFF. Is the king stirring, worthy Thane?

MACBETH.   Not yet.

MACDUFF. He did command me to call timely[12] on him:
  I have almost slipped the hour.

MACBETH.   I'll bring you to him.

MACDUFF. I know this is a joyful trouble to you;
50 But yet 'tis one.

MACBETH. The labor we delight in physics pain.[13]
  This is the door.

MACDUFF.   I'll make so bold to call,
  For 'tis my limited service.[14]   [*Exit* MACDUFF.]

LENNOX. Goes the king hence today?

9. **second cock** 3:00 A.M.

10. **gave thee the lie** laid you out.

11. **cast** vomit.

Literary Analysis
Blank Verse Why is it appropriate for the dialogue in lines 43–44 to change back from prose to blank verse?

12. **timely** early.

13. **labor . . . pain** Labor that we enjoy cures discomfort.

14. **limited service** assigned duty.

✔**Reading Check**

To what gate does the porter compare the gate of Macbeth's castle?

MACBETH.   He does: he did appoint so.

55 **LENNOX.** The night has been unruly. Where we lay,
     Our chimneys were blown down, and, as they say,
     Lamentings heard i' th' air, strange screams of death,
     And prophesying with accents terrible
     Of dire combustion[15] and confused events
60   New hatched to th' woeful time: the obscure bird[16]
     Clamored the livelong night. Some say, the earth
     Was feverous and did shake.

     MACBETH.   'Twas a rough night.

     LENNOX. My young remembrance cannot parallel
     A fellow to it.

[*Enter* MACDUFF.]

65 **MACDUFF.** O horror, horror, horror! Tongue nor heart
     Cannot conceive nor name thee.

     MACBETH AND LENNOX.   What's the matter?

     MACDUFF. Confusion[17] now hath made his masterpiece.
     Most sacrilegious murder hath broke ope
     The Lord's anointed temple,[18] and stole thence
     The life o' th' building. ◆

70 **MACBETH.**   What is 't you say? The life?

     LENNOX. Mean you his Majesty?

     MACDUFF. Approach the chamber, and destroy your sight
     With a new Gorgon:[19] do not bid me speak;
     See, and then speak yourselves. Awake, awake!

                              [*Exit* MACBETH *and* LENNOX.]
75   Ring the alarum bell. Murder and Treason!
     Banquo and Donalbain! Malcolm! Awake!
     Shake off this downy sleep, death's counterfeit,

Reading Strategy
Reading Verse for Meaning Read lines 55–62 aloud. How many sentences are there in these lines?

15. combustion confusion.

16. obscure bird bird of darkness, the owl.

17. Confusion destruction.

18. The Lord's anointed temple the King's body.

Reading Strategy
Reading Verse for Meaning In the latter part of Macduff's speech, lines 75–81, where should you *not* pause at the ends of lines?

19. Gorgon Medusa, a mythological monster whose appearance was so ghastly that those who looked at it turned to stone.

*L*iterature
in context Cultural Connection

◆ Elizabethan Concepts of Monarchy
    For the Elizabethans, the monarch was God's representative on Earth. For this reason, the expression "the Lord's anointed" is used to describe the head of state. Killing the ruler, therefore, was not just an act of political assassination; it was also a horrifying desecration of religious values. When Macduff, for example, reports the murder of Duncan, he calls it a "Most sacrilegious murder" and refers to the destruction of "The Lord's anointed temple" (II, iii, 68–69), comparing the king's body to a sacred temple.

And look on death itself! Up, up, and see
The great doom's image![20] Malcolm! Banquo!
As from your graves rise up, and walk like sprites,[21]
To countenance[22] this horror. Ring the bell.

[*Bell rings. Enter* LADY MACBETH.]

LADY MACBETH. What's the business,
That such a hideous trumpet calls to parley[23]
The sleepers of the house? Speak, speak!

MACDUFF.   O gentle lady,
'Tis not for you to hear what I can speak:
The repetition, in a woman's ear,
Would murder as it fell.

[*Enter* BANQUO.]

                                    O Banquo, Banquo!
Our royal master's murdered.

LADY MACBETH.   Woe, alas!
What, in our house?

BANQUO.   Too cruel anywhere.
Dear Duff, I prithee, contradict thyself,
And say it is not so.

[*Enter* MACBETH, LENNOX, *and* ROSS.]

MACBETH. Had I but died an hour before this chance,
I had lived a blessèd time; for from this instant
There's nothing serious in mortality:[24]
All is but toys.[25] Renown and grace is dead,
The wine of life is drawn, and the mere lees[26]
Is left this vault[27] to brag of.

[*Enter* MALCOLM *and* DONALBAIN.]

DONALBAIN. What is amiss?

MACBETH.   You are, and do not know 't.
The spring, the head, the fountain of your blood
Is stopped; the very source of it is stopped.

MACDUFF. Your royal father's murdered.

MALCOLM.   O, by whom?

LENNOX. Those of his chamber, as it seemed, had done 't:
Their hands and faces were all badged[28] with blood;
So were their daggers, which unwiped we found
Upon their pillows. They stared, and were distracted.
No man's life was to be trusted with them.

MACBETH. O, yet I do repent me of my fury,
That I did kill them.

80

85

90

95

100

105

20. great doom's image
likeness of Judgment Day.

21. sprites spirits.

22. countenance be in
keeping with.

23. parley war conference.

24. serious in mortality
worthwhile in mortal life.

25. toys trifles.

26. lees dregs.

27. vault world.

Literary Analysis
Blank Verse Where is
there a pause in line 100?
How does it reinforce the
meaning?

28. badged marked.

✔**Reading Check**

According to Macbeth,
why did he kill the
grooms?

Lady Macbeth Seizing the Daggers, Henry Fuseli, The Tate Gallery, London

▲ **Critical Viewing** This painting depicts the moment when Macbeth comes from murdering Duncan (II, ii, 14). However, it also captures the nature of the relationship between Macbeth and Lady Macbeth in the first part of the play. What do their facial expressions and body language suggest about that relationship? **[Interpret]**

MACDUFF. Wherefore did you so?

MACBETH. Who can be wise, amazed, temp'rate and furious,
110 Loyal and neutral, in a moment? No man.
The expedition²⁹ of my violent love
Outrun the pauser, reason. Here lay Duncan,
His silver skin laced with his golden blood,
And his gashed stabs looked like a breach in nature
115 For ruin's wasteful entrance: there, the murderers,
Steeped in the colors of their trade, their daggers
Unmannerly breeched with gore.³⁰ Who could refrain,

29. expedition haste.

30. breeched with gore covered with blood.

That had a heart to love, and in that heart
Courage to make 's love known?

LADY MACBETH.   Help me hence, ho!

MACDUFF. Look to the lady.

120   **MALCOLM.** [*Aside to* DONALBAIN] Why do we hold our tongues,
That most may claim this argument for ours?[31]

DONALBAIN. [*Aside to* MALCOLM] What should be spoken here,
Where our fate, hid in an auger-hole,[32]
May rush, and seize us? Let's away:
Our tears are not yet brewed.

125   **MALCOLM.** [*Aside to* DONALBAIN] Nor our strong sorrow
Upon the foot of motion.[33]

BANQUO.   Look to the lady.

[LADY MACBETH *is carried out.*]
And when we have our naked frailties hid,[34]
That suffer in exposure, let us meet
And question[35] this most bloody piece of work,
130   To know it further. Fears and scruples[36] shake us.
In the great hand of God I stand, and thence
Against the undivulged pretense[37] I fight
Of treasonous malice.

MACDUFF.   And so do I.

ALL.   So all.

MACBETH. Let's briefly[38] put on manly readiness,
And meet i' th' hall together.

135   **ALL.**   Well contented.

[*Exit all but* MALCOLM *and* DONALBAIN.]

MALCOLM. What will you do? Let's not consort with them.
To show an unfelt sorrow is an office[39]
Which the false man does easy. I'll to England.

DONALBAIN. To Ireland, I; our separated fortune
140   Shall keep us both the safer. Where we are
There's daggers in men's smiles; the near in blood,
The nearer bloody.[40]

MALCOLM.   This murderous shaft that's shot
Hath not yet lighted,[41] and our safest way
Is to avoid the aim. Therefore to horse;
145   And let us not be dainty of leave-taking,
But shift away. There's warrant[42] in that theft
Which steals itself[43] when there's no mercy left.

[*Exit.*]

31. That most . . . ours who are the most concerned with this topic.

32. auger-hole tiny hole, an unsuspected place because of its size.

33. Our tears . . . motion We have not yet had time for tears nor to turn our sorrow into action.

34. when . . . hid when we have put on our clothes.

35. question investigate.

36. scruples doubts.

37. undivulged pretense hidden purpose.

38. briefly quickly.

Reading Strategy
Reading Verse for Meaning How do the brief sentences in lines 136–138 reinforce the meaning?

39. office function.

40. the near . . . bloody The closer we are in blood relationship to Duncan, the greater our chance of being murdered.

41. lighted reached its target.

42. warrant justification.

43. that theft . . . itself stealing away.

**Reading Check**

What do Malcolm and Donalbain decide to do?

Scene iv. *Outside Macbeth's castle.*

[*Enter* ROSS *with an* OLD MAN.]

    OLD MAN. Threescore and ten I can remember well:
Within the volume of which time I have seen
Hours dreadful and things strange, but this sore[1] night
Hath trifled former knowings.

    ROSS.   Ha, good father,
5 Thou seest the heavens, as troubled with man's act,
Threatens his bloody stage. By th' clock 'tis day,
And yet dark night strangles the traveling lamp:[2]
Is 't night's <u>predominance</u>, or the day's shame,
That darkness does the face of earth entomb,
When living light should kiss it?

10 **OLD MAN.**   'Tis unnatural,
Even like the deed that's done. On Tuesday last
A falcon, tow'ring in her pride of place,[3]
Was by a mousing owl hawked at and killed.

    ROSS. And Duncan's horses—a thing most strange
        and certain—
15 Beauteous and swift, the minions of their race,
Turned wild in nature, broke their stalls, flung out,
Contending 'gainst obedience, as they would make
War with mankind.

    OLD MAN.   'Tis said they eat[4] each other.

    ROSS. They did so, to th' amazement of mine eyes,
That looked upon 't.

[*Enter* MACDUFF.]

20   Here comes the good Macduff.
How goes the world, sir, now?

    MACDUFF.   Why, see you not?

    ROSS. Is 't known who did this more than bloody deed?

    MACDUFF. Those that Macbeth hath slain.

    ROSS.   Alas, the day!
What good could they pretend?[5]

    MACDUFF.   They were suborned:[6]
25 Malcolm and Donalbain, the king's two sons,
Are stol'n away and fled, which puts upon them
Suspicion of the deed.

    ROSS.   'Gainst nature still.
Thriftless ambition, that will ravin up[7]
Thine own life's means! Then 'tis most like

---

1. **sore** grievous.

2. **traveling lamp** the sun.

predominance (prē däm′ ə nəns) *n.* superiority

3. **tow'ring . . . place** soaring at its summit.

4. **eat** ate.

Literary Analysis
Blank Verse What rhythmic variation in the blank verse do you find at the beginning of line 23?

5. **pretend** hope for.

6. **suborned** bribed.

7. **ravin up** devour greedily.

30   The sovereignty will fall upon Macbeth.

MACDUFF. He is already named, and gone to Scone[8]
To be invested.

ROSS.   Where is Duncan's body?

MACDUFF. Carried to Colmekill,
The sacred storehouse of his predecessors
And guardian of their bones.

35   ROSS.   Will you to Scone?

MACDUFF. No, cousin, I'll to Fife.[9]

ROSS.   Well, I will thither.

MACDUFF. Well, may you see things well done there.
    Adieu,
Lest our old robes sit easier than our new!

ROSS. Farewell, father.

40   OLD MAN. God's benison[10] go with you, and with those
That would make good of bad, and friends of foes!

[*Exit.*]

8. **Scone** (skōōn) where Scottish kings were crowned.

9. **Fife** where Macduff's castle is located.

10. **benison** blessing.

Review and Assess

Thinking About Act II

1. **Respond:** Whom do you blame more for the murder of King Duncan—Macbeth or Lady Macbeth? Explain.

2. **(a) Recall:** Describe Macbeth's and Lady Macbeth's reactions to the murder just after it is committed. **(b) Compare and Contrast:** Compare and contrast their reactions to the deed.

3. **(a) Recall:** What kind of gate does the porter imagine he is tending? **(b) Interpret:** In what way is the porter's playful fantasy a comment on Macbeth's situation?

4. **(a) Recall:** What two strange occurrences are reported in this act? **(b) Interpret:** Why would Shakespeare include reports of such occurrences at this point in the play? **(c) Connect:** In what way do these strange occurrences relate to the Elizabethan notion of an orderly and interconnected universe?

5. **(a) Analyze:** What question does Ross ask that indicates he doubts that the grooms committed the murder? Explain. **(b) Infer:** Is Ross satisfied by the answer? Explain.

6. **Speculate:** Do you think a political assassination like the one Macbeth commits is ever justifiable? Why or why not?

Review and Assess

Literary Analysis

Blank Verse

1. To analyze Shakespeare's use of **blank verse,** complete a chart like this one by identifying the rhythm of each of the lines indicated.

Line	Iambic Feet	Trochaic or Anapestic Feet
"It is the bloody business which informs...."		
"'Macbeth does murder sleep' —the innocent sleep, ..."		

2. Mark stressed and unstressed syllables in Act II, Scene ii, lines 59–62.
3. Identify three metrical variations in Act II, Scene ii, lines 59–62.

Connecting Literary Elements

4. (a) Contrast the porter's speech (Act II, Scene iii, lines 1–21) with the two speeches at the end of II, ii, to show that the porter's speech is written in **prose** form. (b) Why might prose be suitable for a "low" character? (c) How does the speech offer **comic relief**?

5. The nineteenth-century English writer Thomas De Quincey argued that the scene with the porter reinforces the shock of the king's murder by a striking contrast: ". . . the re-establishment of the goings-on of the world in which we live, first makes us profoundly sensible of the awful [episode] that had suspended them." Do you agree or disagree? Explain.

Reading Strategy

Reading Verse for Meaning

6. (a) How many sentences are there in Act II, Scene i, lines 62–64? (b) In **reading these lines for meaning,** would you pause at any of the line ends? Explain.

7. In your own words, express the meaning of the sentences in Act II, Scene i, lines 62–64.

Extend Understanding

8. **Psychology Connection:** Macbeth has a strong imagination. In what way does this trait both prompt him to commit a crime and make it hard for him to commit it?

Quick Review

Blank verse is unrhymed iambic pentameter—an iamb is an unstressed syllable followed by a stressed syllable. In **iambic pentameter,** there are five such feet to the line.

The following variations in blank verse break the regular iambic rhythm: **trochaic feet** (stressed, unstressed) and **anapestic feet** (unstressed, unstressed, stressed).

Prose is writing presented in sentences and paragraphs without a predictable rhythm.

Comic relief provides a humorous break in an otherwise tense mood.

To **read verse for meaning,** focus on sentences, not lines.

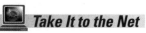 **Take It to the Net**
www.phschool.com
Take the interactive self-test online to check your understanding of the selection.

Integrate Language Skills

Vocabulary Development Lesson

Word Analysis: Latin Root -voc-

The Latin root -voc- means "voice" or "calling." *Equivocate* means "to speak in two equal voices," or "to mislead." Knowing this root, define each of the words below.

1. vocalist   **2.** vocal   **3.** invocation

Spelling Strategy

Many words end in an unstressed syllable spelled with a consonant + le. To add -ly, drop the le: *palpable* becomes *palpably*. To add other endings, drop the final e, except when it helps to spell a separate syllable, as in *trickled*. In your notebook, add the suffixes indicated.

1. capable + ly   **2.** nestle + ing   **3.** dazzle + ment

Concept Development: Synonyms

In your notebook, write the letter of the word that is the synonym of the first word.

1. augment: (a) add, (b) reduce, (c) move
2. palpable: (a) imperceptible, (b) touchable, (c) obvious
3. stealthy: (a) reputable, (b) sneaky, (c) open
4. multitudinous: (a) scarce, (b) agitated, (c) many
5. equivocate: (a) mislead, (b) declare, (c) ruin
6. predominance: (a) equality, (b) superiority, (c) inferiority

Grammar and Style Lesson

Commonly Confused Words:
Lie and *Lay*

Do not confuse *lie* with *lay*. **Lie** (past: *lay*; past participle: *lain*) means "to lie down or on," and **lay** (past and past participle: *laid*) means "to place."

> **Examples:** He <u>lies</u> silently in wait.
>
> She <u>lays</u> the knives on the table.

Practice Choose the correct form of *lie* or *lay* for each item.

1. Macbeth kills Duncan as the king ____?____ in bed.

2. Lady Macbeth thought the daggers should ____?____ beside King Duncan.
3. Lady Macbeth went to ____?____ the daggers beside King Duncan.
4. Macbeth intended to ____?____ down.
5. After the murder, Duncan's dead body was ____?____ to rest.

Writing Application Write a speech in prose in which the porter tells a friend about the murder of Duncan. Use *lie* and *lay* correctly.

W̶G *Prentice Hall Writing and Grammar Connection: Chapter 25, Section 2*

Extension Activities

Listening and Speaking In a group, present a **debate** on this proposition: Ross is a self-seeking flatterer, not a loyal Scot. [**Group Activity**]

Writing As a detective, create an **investigational journal** of Duncan's murder. Record clues at the scene and each person's testimony.

Prepare to Read

Macbeth, Act III

Literary Analysis

Conflict

Conflict—the struggle between two forces—is what creates drama.
- An **external conflict** is a struggle between two characters or groups.
- An **internal conflict** is a struggle within a character.

The **climax** of a play is the point at which the internal and external conflicts are greatest. The action rises to the climax—the moment of highest tension—and then falls as the conflicts are resolved.

In Act III of *Macbeth*, notice how the rising action leads the new king to a state dinner and the sight of a guest—a guest who should not be there!

Connecting Literary Elements

Macbeth makes this critical remark to Banquo at Act III, Scene i, line 27: "Fail not our feast."

This invitation is an example of dramatic irony, a device that playwrights use to heighten conflict. **Dramatic irony** occurs when the words or actions of a character take on a meaning for the audience or readers different from the one the character intends. Observe how Macbeth's remark takes on dramatic irony as events unfold, and becomes a different kind of invitation, answered by a different kind of guest.

Reading Strategy

Reading Between the Lines

By connecting a character's remark to later events, you are **reading between the lines**—linking different parts of the play and finding their deeper meanings. Reading line by line tells you *what* happens, but reading between the lines tells you *why*. Fill in a chart like this one to help you read between the lines of Act III.

Vocabulary Development

indissoluble (in´ di säl´ yōō bəl) *adj.* not able to be dissolved or undone (p. 337)

dauntless (dônt´ lis) *adj.* fearless; cannot be intimidated (p. 338)

jocund (jäk´ ənd) *adj.* cheerful; jovial (p. 342)

infirmity (in fʉr´ mə tē) *n.* physical or mental defect; illness (p. 347)

malevolence (mə lev´ ə ləns) *n.* ill will; spitefulness (p. 351)

> **Link to I, iii, 65–69**
>
> Witches prophesy that Banquo would father kings. Macbeth may view Fleance, Banquo's son, as a threat.

> **Macbeth's Lines, III, i, 35**
>
> Banquo is going for a ride. Macbeth asks, "Goes Fleance with you?"

> **Link to Future Actions**
>
> Is Macbeth planning the murder of Banquo and Fleance?

Review and Anticipate

In Act II, Lady Macbeth drugs Duncan's guards, enabling Macbeth to kill the king. Macbeth then kills the guards, too, so that he can more easily blame them for the king's murder. Duncan's sons, Malcolm and Donalbain, flee, afraid that they will be assassinated by a kinsman eager to claim the throne. Because they run away, some suspect them of killing their father. As the act closes, it seems that Macbeth will be named king.

Act III begins with Macbeth on the throne—as the witches had predicted. All seems to be going well for him, but he feels threatened by Banquo.

Act III

Scene i. Forres. The palace.

[*Enter* BANQUO.]

    BANQUO. Thou hast it now: King, Cawdor, Glamis, all,
        As the weird women promised, and I fear
        Thou play'dst most foully for 't. Yet it was said
        It should not stand[1] in thy posterity,
5   But that myself should be the root and father
        Of many kings. If there come truth from them—
        As upon thee, Macbeth, their speeches shine—
        Why, by the verities on thee made good,
        May they not be my oracles as well
10   And set me up in hope? But hush, no more!

[*Sennet[2] sounded. Enter* MACBETH *as King,* LADY MACBETH, LENNOX, ROSS, LORDS, *and* ATTENDANTS.]

    MACBETH. Here's our chief guest.

    LADY MACBETH.   If he had been forgotten,
        It had been as a gap in our great feast,
        And all-thing[3] unbecoming.

    MACBETH. Tonight we hold a solemn[4] supper, sir,
        And I'll request your presence.

15 **BANQUO.**   Let your Highness
        Command upon me, to the which my duties
        Are with a most <u>indissoluble</u> tie
        For ever knit.

    MACBETH. Ride you this afternoon?

    BANQUO.   Ay, my good lord.

20 **MACBETH.** We should have else desired your good advice
        (Which still hath been both grave and prosperous[5])

◀ **Critical Viewing**
After wielding a dagger like this against Duncan, can Macbeth expect to rule in peace? Explain. **[Predict]**

1. stand continue.

2. *Sennet* trumpet call.

3. all-thing altogether.

4. solemn ceremonious.

5. grave and prosperous weighty and profitable.

indissoluble (in′ di säl′ yo͞o bəl) *adj.* not able to be dissolved or undone

✔ **Reading Check**

What does Banquo suspect about Macbeth?

In this day's council; but we'll take tomorrow.
Is't far you ride?

BANQUO. As far, my lord, as will fill up the time
25   'Twixt this and supper. Go not my horse the better,[6]
I must become a borrower of the night
For a dark hour or twain.

MACBETH. Fail not our feast.

BANQUO. My lord, I will not.

MACBETH. We hear our bloody cousins are bestowed
30   In England and in Ireland, not confessing
Their cruel parricide, filling their hearers
With strange invention.[7] But of that tomorrow,
When therewithal we shall have cause of state
Craving us jointly.[8] Hie you to horse. Adieu,
35   Till you return at night. Goes Fleance with you?

BANQUO. Ay, my good lord: our time does call upon 's.

MACBETH. I wish your horses swift and sure of foot,
And so I do commend you to their backs.
Farewell.   [*Exit* BANQUO.]
40   Let every man be master of his time
Till seven at night. To make society
The sweeter welcome, we will keep ourself
Till suppertime alone. While[9] then, God be with you!

        [*Exit* LORDS *and all but* MACBETH *and a* SERVANT.]

Sirrah,[10] a word with you: attend those men
45   Our pleasure?

ATTENDANT. They are, my lord, without the palace gate.

MACBETH. Bring them before us.   [*Exit* SERVANT.]
To be thus[11] is nothing, but[12] to be safely thus—
Our fears in Banquo stick deep,
50   And in his royalty of nature reigns that
Which would be feared. 'Tis much he dares;
And, to[13] that <u>dauntless</u> temper of his mind,
He hath a wisdom that doth guide his valor
To act in safety. There is none but he
55   Whose being I do fear: and under him
My genius is rebuked,[14] as it is said
Mark Antony's was by Caesar. He chid[15] the sisters,
When first they put the name of King upon me,
And bade them speak to him; then prophetlike
60   They hailed him father to a line of kings.
Upon my head they placed a fruitless crown
And put a barren scepter in my gripe,[16]

6. Go not . . . better unless my horse goes faster than I expect.

7. invention lies.

8. cause . . . jointly matters of state demanding our joint attention.

9. While until.

10. Sirrah common address to an inferior.

11. thus king.

12. but unless.

dauntless (dônt´ lis) *adj.* fearless; cannot be intimidated

13. to added to.

14. genius is rebuked guardian spirit is cowed.

15. chid scolded.

16. gripe grip.

Thence to be wrenched with an unlineal hand,
No son of mine succeeding. If 't be so,
For Banquo's issue have I filed[17] my mind;
For them the gracious Duncan have I murdered;
Put rancors in the vessel of my peace
Only for them, and mine eternal jewel[18]
Given to the common enemy of man,[19]
To make them kings, the seeds of Banquo kings!
Rather than so, come, fate, into the list,
And champion me to th' utterance![20] Who's there?

[*Enter* SERVANT *and* TWO MURDERERS.]

Now go to the door, and stay there till we call.

[*Exit* SERVANT.]

Was it not yesterday we spoke together?

MURDERERS. It was, so please your Highness.

MACBETH.   Well then, now
Have you considered of my speeches? Know
That it was he in the times past, which held you
So under fortune,[21] which you thought had been
Our innocent self: this I made good to you
In our last conference; passed in probation[22] with you,
How you were born in hand,[23] how crossed, the instruments,
Who wrought with them, and all things else that might
To half a soul[24] and to a notion[25] crazed
Say "Thus did Banquo."

FIRST MURDERER.   You made it known to us.

MACBETH. I did so; and went further, which is now
Our point of second meeting. Do you find
Your patience so predominant in your nature,
That you can let this go? Are you so gospeled,[26]
To pray for this good man and for his issue,
Whose heavy hand hath bowed you to the grave
And beggared yours for ever?

FIRST MURDERER.   We are men, my liege.

MACBETH. Ay, in the catalogue ye go for[27] men;
As hounds and greyhounds, mongrels, spaniels, curs,
Shoughs, water-rugs[28] and demi-wolves, are clept[29]
All by the name of dogs: the valued file[30]
Distinguishes the swift, the slow, the subtle,
The housekeeper, the hunter, every one
According to the gift which bounteous nature
Hath in him closed,[31] whereby he does receive
Particular addition,[32] from the bill

Line numbers:
65, 70, 75, 80, 85, 90, 95, 100

17. **filed** defiled.

18. **eternal jewel** soul.

19. **common . . . man** the Devil.

20. **champion me to th' utterance** Fight against me to the death.

21. **held . . . fortune** kept you from good fortune.

22. **passed in probation** reviewed the proofs.

23. **born in hand** deceived.

24. **half a soul** halfwit.

25. **notion** mind.

26. **gospeled** ready to forgive.

27. **go for** pass as.

28. **Shoughs** (shuks), **water-rugs** shaggy dogs, long-haired dogs.

29. **clept** called.

30. **valued file** classification by valuable traits.

31. **closed** enclosed.

32. **addition** distinction (to set it apart from other dogs).

Reading Strategy
Reading Between the Lines What does the first murderer mean in line 91 when he answers Macbeth, "We are men"?

Reading Check

Why does Macbeth fear Banquo?

That writes them all alike: and so of men.
Now if you have a station in the file,[33]
Not i' th' worst rank of manhood, say 't,
And I will put that business in your bosoms
105 Whose execution takes your enemy off,
Grapples you to the heart and love of us,
Who wear our health but sickly in his life,[34]
Which in his death were perfect.

SECOND MURDERER.   I am one, my liege,
Whom the vile blows and buffets of the world
110 Hath so incensed that I am reckless what
I do to spite the world.

FIRST MURDERER.   And I another
So weary with disasters, tugged with fortune,
That I would set[35] my life on any chance,
To mend it or be rid on 't.

MACBETH.   Both of you
Know Banquo was your enemy.

115 **BOTH MURDERERS.**   True, my lord.

MACBETH. So is he mine, and in such bloody distance[36]
That every minute of his being thrusts
Against my near'st of life:[37] and though I could
With barefaced power sweep him from my sight
120 And bid my will avouch[38] it, yet I must not,
For certain friends that are both his and mine,
Whose loves I may not drop, but wail his fall[39]
Who I myself struck down: and thence it is
That I to your assistance do make love,
125 Masking the business from the common eye
For sundry weighty reasons.

SECOND MURDERER.   We shall, my lord,
Perform what you command us.

FIRST MURDERER.   Though our lives—

MACBETH. Your spirits shine through you. Within this hour at most
I will advise you where to plant yourselves,
130 Acquaint you with the perfect spy o' th' time,
The moment on 't;[40] for 't must be done tonight,
And something[41] from the palace; always thought[42]
That I require a clearness:[43] and with him—
To leave no rubs[44] nor botches in the work—
135 Fleance his son, that keeps him company,
Whose absence is no less material to me
Than is his father's, must embrace the fate

33. file ranks.

34. wear . . . life are sick as long as he lives.

35. set risk.

36. distance disagreement.

37. near'st of life most vital parts.

38. avouch justify.

39. wail his fall (I must) bewail his death.

Literary Analysis
Conflict What conflict does Macbeth express in lines 116–126?

40. the perfect . . . on't exact information of the exact time.

41. something some distance.

42. thought remembered.

43. clearness freedom from suspicion.

44. rubs flaws.

Of that dark hour. Resolve yourselves apart:[45]
I'll come to you anon.

45. Resolve yourselves apart Make your own decision.

MURDERERS.   We are resolved, my lord.

140 **MACBETH.** I'll call upon you straight.[46] Abide within.
It is concluded: Banquo, thy soul's flight,
If it find heaven, must find it out tonight.   [*Exit.*]

46. straight immediately.

Scene ii. *The palace.*

[*Enter* MACBETH'S LADY *and a* SERVANT.]

LADY MACBETH. Is Banquo gone from court?

SERVANT. Ay, madam, but returns again tonight.

LADY MACBETH. Say to the King, I would attend his leisure
For a few words.

SERVANT.   Madam, I will.   [*Exit.*]

LADY MACBETH.   Nought's had, all's spent,
5   Where our desire is got without content:
'Tis safer to be that which we destroy
Than by destruction dwell in doubtful joy.

[*Enter* MACBETH.]
How now, my lord! Why do you keep alone,
Of sorriest fancies your companions making,
10   Using those thoughts which should indeed have died
With them they think on? Things without all remedy
Should be without regard: what's done is done.

MACBETH. We have scotched[1] the snake, not killed it:
She'll close[2] and be herself, whilst our poor malice
15   Remains in danger of her former tooth.[3]
But let the frame of things disjoint,[4] both the worlds[5] suffer,
Ere we will eat our meal in fear, and sleep
In the affliction of these terrible dreams
That shake us nightly: better be with the dead,
20   Whom we, to gain our peace, have sent to peace,
Than on the torture of the mind to lie
In restless ecstasy.[6] Duncan is in his grave;
After life's fitful fever he sleeps well.
Treason has done his worst: nor steel, nor poison,
25   Malice domestic, foreign levy,[7] nothing,
Can touch him further.

LADY MACBETH.   Come on.
Gentle my lord, sleek o'er your rugged looks;
Be bright and jovial among your guests tonight.

MACBETH. So shall I, love; and so, I pray, be you:

Reading Strategy
Reading Between the Lines In Scene ii, lines 4–7, what has Lady Macbeth realized about her actions?

1. scotched wounded.

2. close heal.

3. in . . . tooth in as much danger as before.

4. frame of things disjoint universe collapse.

5. both the worlds heaven and earth.

6. ecstasy frenzy.

7. Malice . . . levy civil and foreign war.

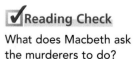

Reading Check

What does Macbeth ask the murderers to do?

Mrs. Siddons as Lady Macbeth, G. H. Harlow, Garrick Club, London

◀ **Critical Viewing**
This artist depicted actress Sarah Siddons (1755–1831) playing Lady Macbeth. How does Mrs. Siddons's body language suggest the same inner conflict as do lines 4–7 in Act III, ii? **[Connect]**

Literary Analysis
Conflict and Irony What is ironic about Macbeth's idea about disguising the couple's real conflict with Banquo (Scene ii, lines 30–35)?

30   Let your remembrance apply to Banquo;
Present him eminence,[8] both with eye and tongue:
Unsafe the while, that we must lave[9]
Our honors in these flattering streams
And make our faces vizards[10] to our hearts,
Disguising what they are.

35   **LADY MACBETH.**   You must leave this.

MACBETH. O, full of scorpions is my mind, dear wife!
Thou know'st that Banquo, and his Fleance, lives.

LADY MACBETH. But in them nature's copy's not eterne.[11]

MACBETH. There's comfort yet; they are assailable.
40   Then be thou jocund. Ere the bat hath flown
His cloistered flight, ere to black Hecate's summons
The shard-borne[12] beetle with his drowsy hums

8. Present him eminence
Honor him.

9. Unsafe . . . lave We are unsafe as long as we have to wash.

10. vizards (viz´ ərdz) masks.

11. nature's . . . eterne
Nature's lease is not eternal.

jocund (jäk´ ənd) *adj.*
cheerful; jovial

12. shard-borne borne on scaly wings.

Hath rung night's yawning peal, there shall be done
A deed of dreadful note.

LADY MACBETH.   What 's to be done?

45 **MACBETH.** Be innocent of the knowledge, dearest chuck,[13]
Till thou applaud the deed. Come, seeling[14] night,
Scarf up[15] the tender eye of pitiful day,
And with thy bloody and invisible hand
Cancel and tear to pieces that great bond[16]
50 Which keeps me pale! Light thickens, and the crow
Makes wing to th' rooky[17] wood.
Good things of day begin to droop and drowse,
Whiles night's black agents to their preys do rouse.
Thou marvel'st at my words: but hold thee still;
55 Things bad begun make strong themselves by ill:
So, prithee, go with me.   [*Exit.*]

Scene iii. Near the palace.

[*Enter* THREE MURDERERS.]

FIRST MURDERER. But who did bid thee join with us?

THIRD MURDERER.   Macbeth.

SECOND MURDERER. He needs not our mistrust; since he delivers
Our offices[1] and what we have to do
To the direction just.[2]

FIRST MURDERER.   Then stand with us.
5 The west yet glimmers with some streaks of day.
Now spurs the lated traveler apace
To gain the timely inn, and near approaches
The subject of our watch.

THIRD MURDERER.   Hark! I hear horses.

BANQUO. [*Within*] Give us a light there, ho!

SECOND MURDERER.   Then 'tis he. The rest
10 That are within the note of expectation[3]
Already are i' th' court.

FIRST MURDERER.   His horses go about.[4]

THIRD MURDERER. Almost a mile: but he does usually—
So all men do—from hence to th' palace gate
Make it their walk.

[*Enter* BANQUO *and* FLEANCE, *with a torch.*]

SECOND MURDERER. A light, a light!

THIRD MURDERER.   'Tis he.

---

13. chuck term of endearment.

14. seeling eye-closing. Falconers sometimes sewed a hawk's eyes closed in order to train it.

15. Scarf up blindfold.

16. great bond between Banquo and fate.

17. rooky full of rooks, or crows.

Reading Strategy
Reading Between the Lines To what specific action do you think Macbeth is indirectly referring in lines 45–56?

1. offices duties.

2. direction just exact detail.

3. within . . . expectations on the list of expected guests.

4. His . . . about His horses have been taken to the stable.

**Reading Check**

What does Macbeth tell Lady Macbeth and what does he hold back from her?

15 **FIRST MURDERER.**   Stand to 't

BANQUO. It will be rain tonight.

FIRST MURDERER.   Let it come down.

[*They set upon* BANQUO.]

BANQUO. O, treachery! Fly, good Fleance, fly, fly, fly!

[*Exit* FLEANCE.]

Thou mayst revenge. O slave! [*Dies.*]

THIRD MURDERER. Who did strike out the light?

FIRST MURDERER.   Was't not the way?[5]

20 **THIRD MURDERER.** There's but one down; the son is fled.

SECOND MURDERER. We have lost best half of our affair.

FIRST MURDERER. Well, let 's away and say how much is done.

[*Exit.*]

Scene iv. The palace.

[*Banquet prepared. Enter* MACBETH, LADY MACBETH, ROSS, LENNOX, LORDS, *and* ATTENDANTS.]

MACBETH. You know your own degrees;[1] sit down:
At first and last, the hearty welcome.

LORDS. Thanks to your Majesty.

MACBETH. Ourself will mingle with society[2]
5   And play the humble host.
Our hostess keeps her state,[3] but in best time
We will require[4] her welcome.

LADY MACBETH. Pronounce it for me, sir, to all our friends,
For my heart speaks they are welcome.

[*Enter* FIRST MURDERER.]

10 **MACBETH.** See, they encounter thee with their hearts' thanks.
Both sides are even: here I'll sit i' th' midst:
Be large in mirth; anon we'll drink a measure[5]
The table round. [*Goes to* MURDERER] There's blood upon thy face.

MURDERER. 'Tis Banquo's then.

15 **MACBETH.** 'Tis better thee without than he within.[6]
Is he dispatched?

MURDERER. My lord, his throat is cut; that I did for him.

MACBETH. Thou art the best o' th' cutthroats.
Yet he's good that did the like for Fleance;
20   If thou didst it, thou art the nonpareil.[7]

---

5. way thing to do.

1. degrees ranks. At state banquets guests were seated according to rank.

2. society company.

3. keeps her state remains seated on her throne.

4. require request.

5. measure toast.

6. thee . . . within you outside than he inside.

7. nonpareil without equal.

MURDERER. Most royal sir, Fleance is 'scaped.

MACBETH. [*Aside*] Then comes my fit again: I had else been perfect,
Whole as the marble, founded as the rock,
As broad and general as the casing[8] air:
25 But now I am cabined, cribbed, confined, bound in
To saucy[9] doubts and fears.—But Banquo's safe?

MURDERER. Ay, my good lord: safe in a ditch he bides,
With twenty trenchèd[10] gashes on his head,
The least a death to nature.[11]

MACBETH.   Thanks for that.
30 [*Aside*] There the grown serpent lies; the worm that's fled
Hath nature that in time will venom breed,
No teeth for th' present. Get thee gone. Tomorrow
We'll hear ourselves[12] again.   [*Exit* MURDERER.]

LADY MACBETH.   My royal lord,
You do not give the cheer.[13] The feast is sold
35 That is not often vouched, while 'tis a-making,
'Tis given with welcome.[14] To feed were best at home;
From thence, the sauce to meat is ceremony;[15]
Meeting were bare without it.

[*Enter the* GHOST *of* BANQUO *and sits in* MACBETH'S *place.*]

MACBETH.   Sweet remembrancer!
Now good digestion wait on appetite,
And health on both!

40 **LENNOX.**   May't please your Highness sit.

MACBETH. Here had we now our country's honor roofed,[16]
Were the graced person of our Banquo present—

8. **as . . . casing** as unrestrained as the surrounding.

9. **saucy** insolent.

10. **trenchèd** trenchlike.

11. **nature** natural life.

12. **hear ourselves** talk it over.

13. **give the cheer** make the guests feel welcome.

14. **The feast . . . welcome** The feast at which the host fails to make the guests feel welcome while the food is being prepared is no more than a bought dinner.

15. **From . . . ceremony** Ceremony adds a pleasant flavor to the food.

16. **our . . . roofed** the most honorable men in the country under one roof.

✔**Reading Check**

What do the murderers fail to do?

Literature in context Cultural Connection

Stagecraft at the Globe

It took some sophisticated Elizabethan theatrics to manage entrances and exits such as those of Banquo's ghost. (Macbeth reacts to the ghost in this picture.) The outer stage at the Globe theater thrust forward into the ground-floor audience. Actors standing at the edge of the stage could therefore play to a surrounding crowd. Behind the outer stage was a smaller area called the rear stage, which was open to the audience but enclosed by a wall at the back and cloth hangings on the sides. A trapdoor in the floor of the rear stage was the means by which Banquo's ghost made an entrance. The trapdoor operated silently, and it also had the advantage of not being completely visible to the audience.

Who may I rather challenge for unkindness
Than pity for mischance![17]

ROSS.   His absence, sir,
45   Lays blame upon his promise. Please 't your Highness
To grace us with your royal company?

MACBETH. The table's full.

LENNOX. Here is a place reserved, sir.

MACBETH. Where?

LENNOX. Here, my good lord. What is 't that moves your Highness?

MACBETH. Which of you have done this?

50 **LORDS.**   What, my good lord?

MACBETH. Thou canst not say I did it. Never shake
Thy gory locks at me.

ROSS. Gentlemen, rise, his Highness is not well.

LADY MACBETH. Sit, worthy friends. My lord is often thus,
55   And hath been from his youth. Pray you, keep seat.
The fit is momentary; upon a thought[18]
He will again be well. If much you note him,
You shall offend him and extend his passion.[19]
Feed, and regard him not.—Are you a man?

60 **MACBETH.** Ay, and a bold one, that dare look on that
Which might appall the devil.

LADY MACBETH.   O proper stuff!
This is the very painting of your fear.
This is the air-drawn dagger which, you said,
Led you to Duncan. O, these flaws[20] and starts,
65   Impostors to true fear, would well become
A woman's story at a winter's fire,
Authorized[21] by her grandam. Shame itself!
Why do you make such faces? When all's done,
You look but on a stool.

MACBETH.   Prithee, see there!
70   Behold! Look! Lo! How say you?
Why, what care I? If thou canst nod, speak too.
If charnel houses[22] and our graves must send
Those that we bury back, our monuments
Shall be the maws of kites.[23]   [*Exit* GHOST.]

75 **LADY MACBETH.**   What, quite unmanned in folly?

MACBETH. If I stand here, I saw him.

LADY MACBETH.   Fie, for shame!

17. Who . . . mischance
whom I hope I may reproach
for being absent due to
discourtesy rather than pity
because he has had an
accident.

Reading Strategy
**Reading Between the
Lines** How might you
connect Macbeth's
agitation with his
knowledge that
Fleance has escaped?

Literary Analysis
Conflict How does the
incident with Banquo's
ghost convey Macbeth's
inner conflict?

18. upon a thought in a
moment.

19. passion suffering.

20. flaws gusts of wind;
outbursts of emotion.

21. Authorized vouched for.

22. charnel houses vaults
containing human bones dug
up in making new graves.

23. our . . . kites Our tombs
shall be the bellies of birds
of prey.

Scene from Macbeth, Cattermole, The Folger Shakespeare Library, Washington, D.C.

◀ **Critical Viewing**
In what ways does the artist's use of light and shadow suggest the conflict in Act III, Scene iv? **[Interpret]**

MACBETH. Blood hath been shed ere now, i' th' olden time,
Ere humane statute purged the gentle weal;[24]
Ay, and since too, murders have been performed
Too terrible for the ear. The times has been
80 That, when the brains were out, the man would die,
And there an end; but now they rise again,
With twenty mortal murders on their crowns,[25]
And push us from our stools. This is more strange
Than such a murder is.

LADY MACBETH. My worthy lord,
Your noble friends do lack you.

85 **MACBETH.** I do forget.
Do not muse at me, my most worthy friends;
I have a strange <u>infirmity</u>, which is nothing
To those that know me. Come, love and health to all!
Then I'll sit down. Give me some wine, fill full.

[*Enter* GHOST.]

90 I drink to th' general joy o' th' whole table,
And to our dear friend Banquo, whom we miss;
Would he were here! To all and him we thirst,[26]
And all to all.

LORDS. Our duties, and the pledge.

MACBETH. Avaunt![27] and quit my sight! Let the earth hide thee!
95 Thy bones are marrowless, thy blood is cold;

24. Ere . . . weal before humane laws civilized the state and made it gentle.

25. mortal . . . crowns deadly wounds on their heads.

infirmity (in fur´ mə tē) *n.* physical or mental defect; illness

26. thirst drink.

27. Avaunt Be gone!

✔ **Reading Check**

Why is Macbeth startled at the feast?

Macbeth, Act III, Scene iv ◆ 347

Thou hast no speculation[28] in those eyes
Which thou dost glare with.

LADY MACBETH.   Think of this, good peers,
But as a thing of custom, 'tis no other.
Only it spoils the pleasure of the time.

100 **MACBETH.** What man dare, I dare.
Approach thou like the rugged Russian bear,
The armed rhinoceros, or th' Hyrcan[29] tiger;
Take any shape but that,[30] and my firm nerves
Shall never tremble. Or be alive again,
105 And dare me to the desert[31] with thy sword.
If trembling I inhabit[32] then, protest me
The baby of a girl. Hence, horrible shadow!
Unreal mock'ry, hence!   [*Exit* GHOST.]
                    Why, so: being gone,
I am a man again. Pray you, sit still.

LADY MACBETH. You have displaced the mirth, broke the
110 good meeting,
With most admired[33] disorder.

MACBETH.   Can such things be,
And overcome us[34] like a summer's cloud,
Without our special wonder? You make me strange
Even to the disposition that I owe,[35]
115 When now I think you can behold such sights,
And keep the natural ruby of your cheeks,
When mine is blanched with fear.

ROSS.   What sights, my lord?

LADY MACBETH. I pray you, speak not: He grows worse and worse;
Question enrages him: at once, good night.
120 Stand not upon the order of your going,[36]
But go at once.

LENNOX.   Good night; and better health
Attend his Majesty!

LADY MACBETH.   A kind good night to all!
                    [*Exit* LORDS.]

MACBETH. It will have blood, they say: blood will have blood.
Stones have been known to move and trees to speak;
125 Augures and understood relations[37] have
By maggot-pies and choughs[38] and rooks brought forth
The secret'st man of blood.[39] What is the night?

LADY MACBETH. Almost at odds[40] with morning, which is which.

MACBETH. How say'st thou, that Macduff denies his person
At our great bidding?

---

28. **speculation** sight.

29. **Hyrcan** (hər´ kən) from Hyrcania, a province of the ancient Persian and Macedonian empires south of the Caspian Sea.

30. **that** Banquo's shape.

31. **desert** place where neither of us could escape.

32. **inhabit** remain indoors.

33. **admired** amazing.

34. **overcome us** come over us.

35. **disposition. . . owe** my own nature.

Reading Strategy
Reading Between the Lines Do Lady Macbeth's remarks in this scene suggest that she, too, sees the ghost? Why or why not?

36. **Stand . . . going** Do not wait to depart in order of rank.

37. **Augures and understood relations** omens and the relationship between the omens and what they represent.

38. **maggot-pies and choughs** (chufs) magpies and crows.

39. **man of blood** murderer.

40. **at odds** disputing.

130 **LADY MACBETH.**   Did you send to him, sir?

MACBETH. I hear it by the way, but I will send:
There's not a one of them but in his house
I keep a servant fee'd.[41] I will tomorrow,
And betimes[42] I will, to the weird sisters:
135 More shall they speak, for now I am bent[43] to know
By the worst means the worst. For mine own good
All causes shall give way. I am in blood
Stepped in so far that, should I wade no more,
Returning were as tedious as go o'er.
140 Strange things I have in head that will to hand,
Which must be acted ere they may be scanned.[44]

LADY MACBETH. You lack the season of all natures,[45] sleep.

MACBETH. Come, we'll to sleep. My strange and self-abuse[46]
Is the initiate fear that wants hard use.[47]
145 We are yet but young in deed.   [*Exit.*]

Scene v. A witches' haunt.

[*Thunder. Enter the* THREE WITCHES, *meeting* HECATE.]

FIRST WITCH. Why, how now, Hecate! you look angerly.

HECATE. Have I not reason, beldams[1] as you are,
Saucy and overbold? How did you dare
To trade and traffic with Macbeth
5 In riddles and affairs of death;
And I, the mistress of your charms,
The close contriver[2] of all harms,
Was never called to bear my part,
Or show the glory of our art?
10 And, which is worse, all you have done
Hath been but for a wayward son,
Spiteful and wrathful; who, as others do,
Loves for his own ends, not for you.
But make amends now: get you gone,
15 And at the pit of Acheron[3]
Meet me i' th' morning: thither he
Will come to know his destiny.
Your vessels and your spells provide,
Your charms and everything beside.
20 I am for th' air; this night I'll spend
Unto a dismal and a fatal end:
Great business must be wrought ere noon.
Upon the corner of the moon
There hangs a vap'rous drop profound;
25 I'll catch it ere it come to ground:
And that distilled by magic sleights[4]

41. **fee'd** paid to spy.

42. **betimes** quickly.

43. **bent** determined.

Literary Analysis
Conflict How do lines 136–139 in Scene iv mark a turning point in Macbeth's inner conflict?

44. **scanned** examined.

45. **season . . . natures** preservative of all living creatures.

46. **My . . . self-abuse** my strange delusion.

47. **initiate . . . use** beginner's fear that will harden with experience.

1. **beldams** hags.

2. **close contriver** secret inventor.

3. **Acheron** (ak´ ər än´) hell; in Greek mythology the river of Hades.

4. **sleights** devices.

**Reading Check**

Why will Macbeth visit "the weird sisters" again?

Shall raise such artificial sprites[5]
As by the strength of their illusion
Shall draw him on to his confusion.[6]
30 He shall spurn fate, scorn death, and bear
His hopes 'bove wisdom, grace, and fear:
And you all know security[7]
Is mortals' chiefest enemy.

[*Music and a song.*]

Hark! I am called; my little spirit, see,
35 Sits in a foggy cloud and stays for me.   [*Exit.*]

[*Sing within,* "Come away, come away," *etc.*]

FIRST WITCH. Come, let's make haste; she'll soon be
back again.   [*Exit.*]

Scene vi. The palace.

[*Enter* LENNOX *and another* LORD.]

LENNOX. My former speeches have but hit[1] your thoughts,
Which can interpret farther.[2] Only I say
Things have been strangely borne.[3] The gracious Duncan
Was pitied of Macbeth: marry, he was dead.
5 And the right-valiant Banquo walked too late;
Whom, you may say, if 't please you, Fleance killed,
For Fleance fled. Men must not walk too late.
Who cannot want the thought,[4] how monstrous
It was for Malcolm and for Donalbain
10 To kill their gracious father? Damnèd fact![5]
How it did grieve Macbeth! Did he not straight,
In pious rage, the two delinquents tear,
That were the slaves of drink and thralls[6] of sleep?
Was not that nobly done? Ay, and wisely too;
15 For 'twould have angered any heart alive
To hear the men deny 't. So that I say
He has borne all things well: and I do think
That, had he Duncan's sons under his key—
As, an 't[7] please heaven, he shall not—they should find
20 What 'twere to kill a father. So should Fleance.
But, peace! for from broad[8] words, and 'cause he failed
His presence at the tyrant's feast, I hear,
Macduff lives in disgrace. Sir, can you tell
Where he bestows himself?

LORD.   The son of Duncan,
25 From whom this tyrant holds the due of birth,[9]
Lives in the English court, and is received
Of the most pious Edward[10] with such grace

---

5. artificial sprites spirits created by magic.

6. confusion ruin.

7. security overconfidence.

1. hit coincided with.

2. Which . . . farther from which you can draw your own conclusions.

3. borne managed.

4. cannot . . . thought can fail to think.

5. fact deed.

6. thralls slaves.

7. an 't if it.

8. broad unguarded.

9. due of birth birthright; claim to the throne.

10. Edward Edward the Confessor, king of England 1042–1066.

That the <u>malevolence</u> of fortune nothing
Takes from his high respect.[11] Thither Macduff
30   Is gone to pray the holy King, upon his aid[12]
To wake Northumberland and warlike Siward;[13]
That by the help of these, with Him above
To ratify the work, we may again
Give to our tables meat, sleep to our nights,
35   Free from our feasts and banquets bloody knives,
Do faithful homage and receive free honors:[14]
All which we pine for now. And this report
Hath so exasperate the King that he
Prepares for some attempt of war.

LENNOX.   Sent he to Macduff?

40 **LORD.** He did: and with an absolute "Sir, not I,"
The cloudy[15] messenger turns me his back,
And hums, as who should say "You'll rue the time
That clogs[16] me with this answer."

LENNOX.   And that well might
Advise him to a caution, t' hold what distance
45   His wisdom can provide. Some holy angel
Fly to the court of England and unfold
His message ere he come, that a swift blessing
May soon return to this our suffering country
Under a hand accursed!

LORD.   I'll send my prayers with him.   [*Exit.*]

---

malevolence (mə lev′ə ləns) *n.* ill will; spitefulness

11. with . . . respect does not diminish the high respect he is given.

12. upon his aid to aid Malcolm.

13. To . . . Siward to call to arms the commander of the English forces, the Earl of Northumberland, and his son Siward.

14. free honors honors given to freemen.

15. cloudy disturbed.

16. clogs burdens.

Review and Assess

Thinking About Act III

1. **(a) Recall:** In the banquet scene, what complaint does Macbeth make about murdered men? **(b) Analyze:** Is there anything humorous or even ridiculous in this complaint? Why or why not? **(c) Connect:** Does Shakespeare use humor for comic relief in this scene, as he does in the earlier scene with the porter? Explain.

2. **(a) Recall:** What does Macbeth think as he anticipates the murder of Banquo? **(b) Compare and Contrast:** Compare and contrast Macbeth's thoughts about Banquo's murder with his thoughts before the murder of Duncan.

3. **Synthesize:** Has the relationship between Macbeth and Lady Macbeth changed? Explain.

4. **Generalize:** What does this act suggest about the effects of evil on evildoers? Explain.

Review and Assess

Literary Analysis

Conflict

1. (a) Why is Macbeth involved in an **external conflict** with Banquo? (b) In what way does Macbeth fail to resolve this conflict?

2. Complete a chart like the one below to show the intensification of **conflict** and the movement toward a climax in Act III.

3. (a) How is Macbeth's behavior at the banquet a sign of an **internal conflict?** (b) How does he temporarily resolve this conflict?

4. Macbeth is personifying evil. Who do you think will lead the forces of good in a campaign against him? How do you know?

Connecting Literary Elements

5. (a) Identify three examples of **dramatic irony** in Macbeth's speeches to Banquo in Act III, Scene i, lines 20–38. (b) In what way do these examples heighten the tension?

6. How does the dramatic irony in Act III, Scene iv, lines 41–44 create an expectation of a tense encounter?

Reading Strategy

Reading Between the Lines

7. "What man dares, I dare," proclaims Macbeth (III, iv, 100). **Read between the lines** by identifying another remark on manhood earlier in the play.

8. Using Macbeth's and Lady Macbeth's remarks, define their idea of manhood.

9. Some critics suggest that the third murderer is Macbeth himself. By reading between the lines, support or refute this interpretation.

Extend Understanding

10. **Media Connection:** What camera shots would you use to film the banquet scene for a movie version of *Macbeth*? Explain.

Integrate Language Skills

Vocabulary Development Lesson

Word Analysis: Latin Prefix *mal-*

The Latin prefix *mal-* means "bad or badly, poorly, or wrong." For example, *malevolence* means "ill will." Define the words below. Then, use a dictionary to verify your definitions.

1. maladjusted
2. malformed
3. malcontent
4. malady

Fluency: Words in Context

Use all the words from the vocabulary list on page 336 to write a brief profile of Macbeth.

Spelling Strategy

Nouns ending in *-ence* usually end in *-ent* and *-ently* in their adjectival and adverbial forms: the noun *malevolence* becomes *malevolent* (adjective) and *malevolently* (adverb). In your notebook, write the adjectival and adverbial forms for these nouns:

1. permanence   2. diligence   3. intelligence

Grammar and Style Lesson

Subject and Verb Agreement

Verbs **agree with their subjects in number**—singular subjects must have singular verbs and plural subjects must have plural verbs.

> **Singular:** "After life's fitful fever $\underset{\text{S}}{\text{he}}$ $\underset{\text{V}}{\text{sleeps}}$ well."
>
> **Plural:** "Our $\underset{\text{S}}{\text{fears}}$ in Banquo $\underset{\text{V}}{\text{stick}}$ deep, . . ."

Practice Choose the correct form of the verb. Do not be misled by words that come between the subject and the verb.

1. Macbeth, of all the Scottish kings, (is, are) most evil.
2. Scotland, country of stark contrasts, (is, are) the setting of *Macbeth*.
3. Malcolm, despite his worries, (does, do) what must be done.
4. Lady Macbeth, expressing some concerns, (begin, begins) to doubt what she has done.
5. Not everyone in this country of ghosts (support, supports) Macbeth.

Writing Application As a Scottish lord, write a note to Malcolm at the English court reporting on conditions in Scotland. Be sure that subjects and verbs agree—even when they are separated by phrases.

W͛G Prentice Hall Writing and Grammar Connection: Chapter 23, Section 1

Extension Activities

Writing As a lord returning from Macbeth's banquet, write a **diary entry** about the strange events you have just witnessed. Use fresh and vivid language to convey a tone of shock, outrage, bewilderment, or some combination of these.

Research and Technology Scan critical works for comments on the banquet scene in *Macbeth*. To record your findings, compile an **annotated bibliography,** a list of your sources together with a summary of what each says about the scene.

Prepare to Read

Macbeth, Act IV

Literary Analysis

Imagery

Imagery is the language that writers use to re-create sensory experiences and stir emotions. It is what helps you see, hear, feel, smell, and taste, rather than just read or listen to words. Shakespeare uses imagery to pack sensory experiences and strong emotions into almost every line. Further, he creates these patterns of images that run through the whole play:

- Blood
- Ill-fitting clothes
- Babies and children, sometimes killed by Macbeth and sometimes threatening him

These images reinforce important themes in the play. The last group of images suggests that Macbeth is in some way warring against the future, which babies and children represent. As you read, link patterns of images to the play's central ideas.

Connecting Literary Elements

Some images are powerful because they are **archetypal**—they relate to ideas and emotions expressed by people in many cultures. In Act IV, for example, **images of a fallen world**—shrieking, groaning, and bleeding—indicate that Macbeth's Scotland resembles an underworld region where the dead are punished. Look for such archetypal images as you read.

Reading Strategy

Using Your Senses

You will enjoy a literary work more if you **use your senses** to experience the imagery it contains. Fill out an imagery chart like this one to ensure that you read with your senses. The chart analyzes the passage in Act IV, Scene i, lines 52–55.

Line	Images Senses
IV, i, 52	"untie the winds" hearing; touch
IV, i, 53	"yesty waves" sight

Vocabulary Development

pernicious (pər nish´ əs) *adj.* fatal; deadly (p. 360)

judicious (jōō dish´ əs) *adj.* showing good judgment (p. 361)

sundry (sun´ drē) *adj.* various; miscellaneous (p. 365)

intemperance (in tem´ pər əns) *n.* lack of restraint (p. 366)

avarice (av´ ə ris) *n.* greed (p. 366)

credulous (krej´ ōō ləs) *adj.* tending to believe too readily (p. 367)

Review and Anticipate

Macbeth hires murderers to kill Banquo and Banquo's son, Fleance. The murderers botch the job, killing Banquo but allowing Fleance to escape. Then, at a state banquet, Macbeth is shocked to see the ghost of Banquo sitting in the king's chair. Macbeth decides to visit the witches again, determined to know "the worst." At the end of Act III, we learn that Malcolm is in England preparing to invade Scotland and that Macduff has gone to join him.

Act IV will be a turning point in the play. Macbeth seeks help from the witches to secure his power. The forces of good, however, are beginning to gather against him.

Act IV

Scene i. *A witches' haunt.*

[*Thunder. Enter the* THREE WITCHES.]

FIRST WITCH. Thrice the brinded[1] cat hath mewed.

SECOND WITCH. Thrice and once the hedge-pig[2] whined.

THIRD WITCH. Harpier[3] cries. 'Tis time, 'tis time.

FIRST WITCH. Round about the caldron go:
5   In the poisoned entrails throw.
Toad, that under cold stone
Days and nights has thirty-one
Swelt'red venom sleeping got,[4]
Boil thou first i' th' charmèd pot.

10 **ALL.** Double, double, toil and trouble;
Fire burn and caldron bubble.

SECOND WITCH. Fillet of a fenny snake,
In the caldron boil and bake;
Eye of newt and toe of frog,
15   Wool of bat and tongue of dog,
Adder's fork[5] and blindworm's[6] sting,
Lizard's leg and howlet's[7] wing,
For a charm of pow'rful trouble,
Like a hell-broth boil and bubble.

20 **ALL.** Double, double, toil and trouble;
Fire burn and caldron bubble.

THIRD WITCH. Scale of dragon, tooth of wolf,
Witch's mummy, maw and gulf[8]
Of the ravined[9] salt-sea shark,

▲ **Critical Viewing**
What is the significance of a burning cauldron—like this one—to the play? **[Connect]**

1. **brinded** striped.

2. **hedge-pig** hedgehog.

3. **Harpier** one of the spirits attending the witches.

4. **Swelt'red . . . got** venom sweated out while sleeping.

5. **fork** forked tongue.

6. **blindworm's** small, limbless lizard's.

7. **howlet's** small owl's.

8. **maw and gulf** stomach and gullet.

9. **ravined** ravenous.

✓**Reading Check**

What are the witches doing as the act begins?

Poster for Macbeth, His Majesty's Theater, 1911, Edmund Dulac

▲ **Critical Viewing** Has this artist captured the spirit of the witches as it is portrayed in IV, i? Explain. **[Evaluate]**

25 Root of hemlock digged i' th' dark,
 Liver of blaspheming Jew,
 Gall of goat, and slips of yew
 Slivered in the moon's eclipse,
 Nose of Turk and Tartar's lips,[10]
30 Finger of birth-strangled babe
 Ditch-delivered by a drab,
 Make the gruel thick and slab:[11]
 Add thereto a tiger's chaudron,[12]
 For th' ingredience of our caldron.

35 **ALL.** Double, double, toil and trouble;
 Fire burn and caldron bubble.

 SECOND WITCH. Cool it with a baboon's blood,
 Then the charm is firm and good.

[*Enter* HECATE *and the other* THREE WITCHES.]

 HECATE. O, well done! I commend your pains;
40 And every one shall share i' th' gains:
 And now about the caldron sing,
 Like elves and fairies in a ring,
 Enchanting all that you put in.

[*Music and a song:* "Black Spirits," *etc. Exit* HECATE *and the other* THREE WITCHES.]

 SECOND WITCH. By the pricking of my thumbs,
45 Something wicked this way comes:
 Open, locks,
 Whoever knocks!

[*Enter* MACBETH.]

 MACBETH. How now, you secret, black, and midnight hags!
 What is 't you do?

  ALL.   A deed without a name.

50 **MACBETH.** I conjure you, by that which you profess,
 Howe'er you come to know it, answer me:
 Though you untie the winds and let them fight
 Against the churches; though the yesty[13] waves
 Confound[14] and swallow navigation up;
55 Though bladed corn be lodged[15] and trees blown down;
 Though castles topple on their warders' heads;
 Though palaces and pyramids do slope[16]
 Their heads to their foundations; though the treasure
 Of nature's germens[17] tumble all together,
60 Even till destruction sicken, answer me
 To what I ask you.

 FIRST WITCH.   Speak.

10. blaspheming Jew . . . Tartar's lips For many in Shakespeare's audience, the words "Jew," "Turk," and "Tartar" evoked stereotypical enemies of Christianity.

11. slab sticky.

12. chaudron (shō´ drən) entrails.

Reading Strategy
Using Your Senses
How do you picture the strange world described in Scene i ?

13. yesty foamy.

14. Confound destroy.

15. lodged beaten down.

16. slope bend.

17. nature's germens seeds of all life.

**Reading Check**

What does Macbeth demand of the witches?

SECOND WITCH.   Demand.

THIRD WITCH.   We'll answer.

FIRST WITCH. Say, if th' hadst rather hear it from our mouths,
Or from our masters?

    MACBETH.   Call 'em, let me see 'em.

FIRST WITCH. Pour in sow's blood, that hath eaten

65   Her nine farrow;¹⁸ grease that's sweaten
From the murderer's gibbet¹⁹ throw
Into the flame.

    ALL.   Come, high or low,
Thyself and office²⁰ deftly show!

[*Thunder.* FIRST APPARITION: *an Armed Head.*²¹]

    MACBETH. Tell me, thou unknown power—

FIRST WITCH.   He knows thy thought:

70   Hear his speech, but say thou nought.

FIRST APPARITION. Macbeth! Macbeth! Macbeth! Beware Macduff!
Beware the Thane of Fife. Dismiss me: enough.

                       [*He descends.*]

MACBETH. Whate'er thou art, for thy good caution thanks:
Thou hast harped²² my fear aright. But one word more—

75 **FIRST WITCH.** He will not be commanded. Here's another,
More potent than the first.

[*Thunder.* SECOND APPARITION: *a Bloody Child.*²³]

    SECOND APPARITION. Macbeth! Macbeth! Macbeth!

    MACBETH. Had I three ears, I'd hear thee.

    SECOND APPARITION. Be bloody, bold, and resolute! Laugh to scorn

80   The pow'r of man, for none of woman born
Shall harm Macbeth.   [*Descends.*]

    MACBETH. Then live, Macduff: what need I fear of thee?
But yet I'll make assurance double sure,
And take a bond of fate.²⁴ Thou shalt not live;

85   That I may tell pale-hearted fear it lies,
And sleep in spite of thunder.

[*Thunder.* THIRD APPARITION: *a Child Crowned, with a tree in his hand.*²⁵]

                 What is this,
That rises like the issue of a king,
And wears upon his baby-brow the round
And top of sovereignty?²⁶

    ALL.   Listen, but speak not to 't.

Literary Analysis
Imagery How do the apparitions that Macbeth sees in Scene i, lines 68, 75, and 86 connect with the patterns of imagery in the play?

18. farrow young pigs.

19. gibbet (jib´ it) gallows.

20. office function.

21. *an Armed Head* symbol of Macduff.

22. harped hit upon.

23. *a Bloody Child* symbol of Macduff at birth.

24. take . . . fate get a guarantee from fate (by killing Macduff).

25. *a Child . . . hand* symbol of Malcolm.

26. top of sovereignty crown.

90　**THIRD APPARITION.** Be lion-mettled, proud, and take no care
　　　Who chafes, who frets, or where conspirers are:
　　　Macbeth shall never vanquished be until
　　　Great Birnam Wood to high Dunsinane Hill
　　　Shall come against him.　　　　　　　　　　[*Descends.*]

　　　MACBETH.　　　　　　　　That will never be.
95　　Who can impress²⁷ the forest, bid the tree
　　　Unfix his earth-bound root? Sweet bodements,²⁸ good!
　　　Rebellious dead, rise never, till the Wood
　　　Of Birnam rise, and our high-placed Macbeth
　　　Shall live the lease of nature,²⁹ pay his breath
100　To time and mortal custom.³⁰ Yet my heart
　　　Throbs to know one thing. Tell me, if your art
　　　Can tell so much: shall Banquo's issue ever
　　　Reign in this kingdom?

　　　ALL.　　　　　　　　Seek to know no more.

　　　MACBETH. I will be satisfied. Deny me this,
105　And an eternal curse fall on you! Let me know.
　　　Why sinks that caldron? And what noise is this?

[*Hautboys.*]

　　　FIRST WITCH. Show!

　　　SECOND WITCH. Show!

　　　THIRD WITCH. Show!

110　**ALL.** Show his eyes, and grieve his heart;
　　　Come like shadows, so depart!

[*A show of eight* KINGS *and* BANQUO, *last* KING *with a glass³¹ in his hand.*]

　　　MACBETH. Thou art too like the spirit of Banquo. Down!
　　　Thy crown does sear mine eyelids. And thy hair,
　　　Thou other gold-bound brow, is like the first.
115　A third is like the former. Filthy hags!
　　　Why do you show me this? A fourth! Start, eyes!
　　　What, will the line stretch out to th' crack of doom?
　　　Another yet! A seventh! I'll see no more.
　　　And yet the eighth appears, who bears a glass
120　Which shows me many more: and some I see
　　　That twofold balls and treble scepters³² carry:
　　　Horrible sight! Now I see 'tis true;
　　　For the blood-boltered³³ Banquo smiles upon me,
　　　And points at them for his.³⁴ What, is this so?

125　**FIRST WITCH.** Ay, sir, all this is so. But why
　　　Stands Macbeth thus amazedly?
　　　Come, sisters, cheer we up his sprites,
　　　And show the best of our delights:

27. impress force into service.

28. bodements prophecies.

29. lease of nature natural lifespan.

30. mortal custom natural death.

31. glass mirror.

Literary Analysis
Imagery What does Macbeth learn from the images of the eight kings?

32. twofold . . . scepters coronation emblems and insignia of the kingdoms of England, Scotland, and Ireland, united in 1603 when James VI of Scotland became James I of England.

33. blood-boltered with his hair matted with blood.

34. his his descendants.

✔**Reading Check**

What do the three apparitions tell Macbeth, and what further vision does he see?

I'll charm the air to give a sound,
130 While you perform your antic round,[35]
That this great king may kindly say
Our duties did his welcome pay.

[*Music.* THE WITCHES *dance, and vanish.*]

MACBETH. Where are they? Gone? Let this <u>pernicious</u> hour
Stand aye accursèd in the calendar!
Come in, without there!

[*Enter* LENNOX.]

135 **LENNOX.**   What's your Grace's will?

MACBETH. Saw you the weird sisters?

LENNOX.   No, my lord.

MACBETH. Came they not by you?

LENNOX.   No indeed, my lord.

MACBETH. Infected be the air whereon they ride,
And damned all those that trust them! I did hear
140 The galloping of horse. Who was 't came by?

LENNOX. 'Tis two or three, my lord, that bring you word
Macduff is fled to England.

MACBETH.   Fled to England?

LENNOX. Ay, my good lord.

MACBETH. [*Aside*] Time, thou anticipat'st[36] my dread exploits.
145 The flighty purpose never is o'ertook
Unless the deed go with it.[37] From this moment
The very firstlings of my heart[38] shall be
The firstlings of my hand. And even now,
To crown my thoughts with acts be it thought and done:
150 The castle of Macduff I will surprise;
Seize upon Fife; give to th' edge o' th' sword
His wife, his babes, and all unfortunate souls
That trace[39] him in his line. No boasting like a fool;
This deed I'll do before this purpose cool:
155 But no more sights!—Where are these gentlemen?
Come, bring me where they are.

[*Exit.*]

Scene ii. *Macduff's castle.*

[*Enter* MACDUFF'S WIFE, *her* SON, *and* ROSS.]

LADY MACDUFF. What had he done, to make him fly the land?

ROSS. You must have patience, madam.

---

35. antic round grotesque circular dance.

pernicious (pər nish' əs) *adj.* fatal; deadly

36. anticipat'st foretold.

37. The flighty . . . it The fleeting plan is never fulfilled unless it is carried out at once.

38. firstlings . . . heart first thoughts, impulses.

39. trace succeed.

LADY MACDUFF.   He had none:
His flight was madness. When our actions do not,
Our fears do make us traitors.

ROSS.   You know not
5   Whether it was his wisdom or his fear.

LADY MACDUFF. Wisdom! To leave his wife, to leave his babes,
His mansion and his titles,[1] in a place
From whence himself does fly? He loves us not;
He wants the natural touch:[2] for the poor wren,
10   The most diminutive of birds, will fight,
Her young ones in her nest, against the owl.
All is the fear and nothing is the love;
As little is the wisdom, where the flight
So runs against all reason.

ROSS.   My dearest coz,[3]
15   I pray you, school[4] yourself. But, for your husband,
He is noble, wise, <u>judicious</u>, and best knows
The fits o' th' seasons,[5] I dare not speak much further:
But cruel are the times, when we are traitors
And do not know ourselves;[6] when we hold rumor
20   From what we fear,[7] yet know not what we fear,
But float upon a wild and violent sea
Each way and move. I take my leave of you.
Shall not be long but I'll be here again.
Things at the worst will cease, or else climb upward
25   To what they were before. My pretty cousin,
Blessing upon you!

LADY MACDUFF. Fathered he is, and yet he's fatherless.

ROSS. I am so much a fool, should I stay longer,
It would be my disgrace and your discomfort.[8]
I take my leave at once.   [*Exit* ROSS.]

30   **LADY MACDUFF.**   Sirrah, your father's dead;
And what will you do now? How will you live?

SON. As birds do, mother.

LADY MACDUFF.   What, with worms and flies?

SON. With what I get, I mean; and so do they.

LADY MACDUFF. Poor bird! thou'dst never fear the net nor lime,[9]
35   The pitfall nor the gin.[10]

SON. Why should I, mother? Poor birds they are not set for.
My father is not dead, for all your saying.

LADY MACDUFF. Yes, he is dead: how wilt thou do for a father?

SON. Nay, how will you do for a husband?

Literary Analysis

Imagery What image is suggested by Lady Macduff's use of the words "fly" and "flight" in lines 8 and 13?

1. **titles** possessions.

2. **wants . . . touch** lacks natural affection.

3. **coz** cousin.

4. **school** control.

judicious (jōō dish′ əs) *adj.* showing good judgment

5. **fits o' th' season** disorders of the time.

6. **when . . . ourselves** when we are treated as traitors but do not know of any treason.

7. **when . . . fear** believe rumors based on our fears.

8. **It . . . discomfort:** I would disgrace myself and embarrass you by weeping.

Literary Analysis

Imagery What does the imagery in Scene ii, 34–35 suggest about what might happen?

9. **lime** birdlime, a sticky substance smeared on branches to catch birds.

10. **gin** trap.

✓**Reading Check**

Where has Macduff gone, and how will Macbeth revenge himself against Macduff?

40 **LADY MACDUFF.** Why, I can buy me twenty at any market.

SON. Then you'll buy 'em to sell[11] again.

LADY MACDUFF. Thou speak'st with all thy wit, and yet i' faith,
With wit enough for thee.[12]

SON. Was my father a traitor, mother?

45 **LADY MACDUFF.** Ay, that he was.

SON. What is a traitor?

LADY MACDUFF. Why, one that swears and lies.[13]

SON. And be all traitors that do so?

LADY MACDUFF. Every one that does so is a traitor, and must
be hanged.

50 **SON.** And must they all be hanged that swear and lie?

LADY MACDUFF. Every one.

SON. Who must hang them?

LADY MACDUFF. Why, the honest men.

SON. Then the liars and swearers are fools; for there are liars and
55 swearers enow[14] to beat the honest men and hang up them.

LADY MACDUFF. Now, God help thee, poor monkey! But how wilt
thou do for a father?

SON. If he were dead, you'd weep for him. If you would not, it were
60 a good sign that I should quickly have a new father.

LADY MACDUFF. Poor prattler, how thou talk'st!

[*Enter a* MESSENGER.]

MESSENGER. Bless you, fair dame! I am not to you known,
Though in your state of honor I am perfect.[15]
65 I doubt[16] some danger does approach you nearly:
If you will take a homely[17] man's advice,
Be not found here; hence, with your little ones.
To fright you thus, methinks I am too savage;
To do worse to you were fell[18] cruelty,
70 Which is too nigh your person. Heaven preserve you!
I dare abide no longer.   [*Exit* MESSENGER.]

LADY MACDUFF.   Whither should I fly?
I have done no harm. But I remember now
I am in this earthly world, where to do harm
Is often laudable, to do good sometime
75 Accounted dangerous folly. Why then, alas,
Do I put up that womanly defense,
To say I have done no harm?—What are these faces?

11. **sell** betray.

12. **for thee** for a child.

13. **swears and lies** takes
an oath and breaks it.

14. **enow** enough.

15. **in . . . perfect** I am fully
informed of your honorable
rank.

16. **doubt** fear.

17. **homely** simple.

18. **fell** fierce.

Reading Strategy
Using Your Senses What
do the content of the
messenger's speech and
the context suggest about
his dress, appearance,
and manner?

[*Enter* MURDERERS.]

    MURDERER. Where is your husband?

    LADY MACDUFF. I hope, in no place so unsanctified
      Where such as thou mayst find him.

80   **MURDERER.**   He's a traitor.

    SON. Thou li'st, thou shag-eared[19] villain!

    MURDERER.   What, you egg!

                  [*Stabbing him.*]
    Young fry[20] of treachery!

    SON.   He has killed me, mother:
    Run away, I pray you!   [*Dies.*]

        [*Exit* LADY MACDUFF *crying "Murder!" followed by* MURDERERS.]

19. **shag-eared** hairy-eared.

20. **fry** offspring.

**Reading Check**

Whom do Macbeth's men kill?

▼ **Critical Viewing**
This engraving shows the murderers menacing Macduff's family. In what way does the artist capture the defiance reflected in Act IV, Scene ii, line 81? **[Interpret]**

Scene iii. England. Before the King's palace.

[*Enter* MALCOLM *and* MACDUFF.]

MALCOLM. Let us seek out some desolate shade, and there
Weep our sad bosoms empty.

MACDUFF.   Let us rather
Hold fast the mortal◆ sword, and like good men
Bestride our down-fall'n birthdom.¹ Each new morn
5   New widows howl, new orphans cry, new sorrows
Strike heaven on the face, that it resounds
As if it felt with Scotland and yelled out
Like syllable of dolor.²

MALCOLM.   What I believe, I'll wail;
What know, believe; and what I can redress,
10   As I shall find the time to friend,◆ I will.
What you have spoke, it may be so perchance.
This tyrant, whose sole◆ name blisters our tongues,
Was once thought honest:◆ you have loved him well;
He hath not touched you yet. I am young; but something
15   You may deserve of him through me;³ and wisdom⁴
To offer up a weak, poor, innocent lamb
T' appease an angry god.

MACDUFF. I am not treacherous.

Literary Analysis
Imagery How do the images in Scene iii, lines 1–4 help establish a contrast between Malcolm and Macduff?

1. Bestride . . . birthdom
Protectively stand over our native land.

2. Like . . . dolor similar cry of anguish.

3. deserve . . . me earn by betraying me to Macbeth.

4. wisdom It is wise.

*L*iterature
in context Vocabulary Connection

◆ *Shifting Meanings*
   Because language is always changing, some words used by Shakespeare have shifted in meaning.

Mortal (IV, iii, 3) means "deadly," which is somewhat unlike its current meaning, "subject to death or decay."

Friend (IV, iii, 10), which today is a noun, is used as a verb meaning "to be friendly."

Sole (IV, iii, 12), which now means "single" or "one and only," is used as an intensifier meaning "very."

Honest (IV, iii, 13) has the broad sense of "good."

Recoil (IV, iii, 19) means "to give way" rather than "to shrink back."

Transpose (IV, iii, 21) means "to transform," not "to transfer" or "shift."

Jealousies (IV, iii, 29) means "suspicions" rather than "envious feelings."

   As you read, be alert to shifts in meaning like these, and use the context of a word or phrase as well as the side notes to help you determine Shakespeare's meaning.

MALCOLM.   But Macbeth is.
    A good and virtuous nature may recoil♦

20 In an imperial charge. But I shall crave your pardon;
    That which you are, my thoughts cannot transpose:♦
    Angels are bright still, though the brightest⁵ fell:
    Though all things foul would wear⁶ the brows of grace,
    Yet grace must still look so.⁷

MACDUFF.   I have lost my hopes.

25 **MALCOLM.** Perchance even there where I did find my doubts.
    Why in that rawness⁸ left you wife and child,
    Those precious motives, those strong knots of love,
    Without leave-taking? I pray you,
    Let not my jealousies♦ be your dishonors.

30 But mine own safeties.⁹ You may be rightly just
    Whatever I shall think.

MACDUFF.   Bleed, bleed, poor country:
    Great tyranny, lay thou thy basis sure,
    For goodness dare not check thee: wear thou thy wrongs:
    The title is affeered.¹⁰ Fare thee well, lord:

35 I would not be the villain that thou think'st
    For the whole space that's in the tyrant's grasp
    And the rich East to boot.

MALCOLM.   Be not offended:
    I speak not as in absolute fear of you.
    I think our country sinks beneath the yoke;

40 It weeps, it bleeds, and each new day a gash
    Is added to her wounds. I think withal
    There would be hands uplifted in my right;¹¹
    And here from gracious England¹² have I offer
    Of goodly thousands: but, for all this,

45 When I shall tread upon the tyrant's head,
    Or wear it on my sword, yet my poor country
    Shall have more vices than it had before,
    More suffer, and more <u>sundry</u> ways than ever,
    By him that shall succeed.

MACDUFF.   What should he be?

50 **MALCOLM.** It is myself I mean, in whom I know
    All the particulars of vice so grafted¹³
    That, when they shall be opened,¹⁴ black Macbeth
    Will seem as pure as snow, and the poor state
    Esteem him as a lamb, being compared
    With my confineless harms.¹⁵

55 **MACDUFF.**   Not in the legions
    Of horrid hell can come a devil more damned
    In evils to top Macbeth.

5. the brightest Lucifer.

6. would wear desire to wear.

7. so like itself.

8. rawness unprotected state or condition.

9. safeties protections.

10. affeered legally confirmed.

Literary Analysis
Imagery Why are the images Malcolm uses to describe Scotland in lines 39–41 more effective than a simple statement that the country is in trouble and getting worse?

11. in my right on behalf of my claim.

12. England king of England.

sundry (sun´ drē) *adj.* various; miscellaneous

13. grafted implanted.

14. opened in bloom.

15. confineless harms unbounded evils.

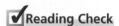
Reading Check

How does Malcolm describe himself to Macduff?

MALCOLM. I grant him bloody,
Luxurious,[16] avaricious, false, deceitful,
Sudden,[17] malicious, smacking of every sin
60 That has a name: but there's no bottom, none,
In my voluptuousness: your wives, your daughters,
Your matrons and your maids, could not fill up
The cistern of my lust, and my desire
All continent impediments[18] would o'erbear,
65 That did oppose my will. Better Macbeth
Than such an one to reign.

MACDUFF. Boundless <u>intemperance</u>
In nature[19] is a tyranny; it hath been
Th' untimely emptying of the happy throne,
And fall of many kings. But fear not yet
70 To take upon you what is yours: you may
Convey[20] your pleasures in a spacious plenty,
And yet seem cold, the time you may so hoodwink.
We have willing dames enough. There cannot be
That vulture in you, to devour so many
75 As will to greatness dedicate themselves,
Finding it so inclined.

MALCOLM. With this there grows
In my most ill-composed affection[21] such
A stanchless[22] <u>avarice</u> that, were I King,
I should cut off the nobles for their lands,
80 Desire his jewels and this other's house:
And my more-having would be as a sauce
To make me hunger more, that I should forge
Quarrels unjust against the good and loyal,
Destroying them for wealth.

MACDUFF. This avarice
85 Sticks deeper, grows with more pernicious root
Than summer-seeming[23] lust, and it hath been
The sword of[24] our slain kings. Yet do not fear.
Scotland hath foisons[25] to fill up your will
Of your mere own.[26] All these are portable,[27]
90 With other graces weighed.

MALCOLM. But I have none: the king-becoming graces,
As justice, verity, temp'rance, stableness,
Bounty, perseverance, mercy, lowliness,
Devotion, patience, courage, fortitude,
95 I have no relish of them, but abound
In the division of each several crime,[28]
Acting it many ways. Nay, had I pow'r, I should
Pour the sweet milk of concord into hell,
Uproar the universal peace, confound[29]

16. **luxurious** lecherous.

17. **Sudden** violent.

18. **continent impediments** restraints.

intemperance (in tem´ pər əns) *n.* lack of restraint

19. **nature** man's nature.

20. **Convey** secretly manage.

21. **affection** character.

avarice (av´ ə ris) *n.* greed

22. **stanchless** never-ending.

23. **summer-seeming** summerlike.

24. **of** that killed.

25. **foisons** (foi´ zənz) plenty.

26. **mere own** own property.

27. **portable** bearable.

28. **division . . . crime** variations of each kind of crime.

29. **confound** destroy.

All unity on earth.

100　**MACDUFF.**　　　　　O Scotland, Scotland!

MALCOLM. If such a one be fit to govern, speak:
I am as I have spoken.

MACDUFF.　　　　　Fit to govern!
No, not to live. O nation miserable!
With an untitled[30] tyrant bloody-sceptered,
105　When shalt thou see thy wholesome days again,
Since that the truest issue of thy throne[31]
By his own interdiction[32] stands accursed,
And does blaspheme his breed?[33] Thy royal father
Was a most sainted king: the queen that bore thee,
110　Oft'ner upon her knees than on her feet,
Died[34] every day she lived. Fare thee well!
These evils thou repeat'st upon thyself
Hath banished me from Scotland. O my breast,
Thy hope ends here!

MALCOLM.　　　　　Macduff, this noble passion,
115　Child of integrity, hath from my soul
Wiped the black scruples, reconciled my thoughts
To thy good truth and honor. Devilish Macbeth
By many of these trains[35] hath sought to win me
Into his power; and modest wisdom[36] plucks me
120　From over-<u>credulous</u> haste: but God above
Deal between thee and me! For even now
I put myself to thy direction, and
Unspeak mine own detraction,[37] here abjure
The taints and blames I laid upon myself,
125　For[38] strangers to my nature. I am yet
Unknown to woman, never was forsworn,
Scarcely have coveted what was mine own,
At no time broke my faith, would not betray
The devil to his fellow, and delight
130　No less in truth than life. My first false speaking
Was this upon myself. What I am truly,
Is thine and my poor country's to command:
Whither indeed, before thy here-approach,
Old Siward, with ten thousand warlike men,
135　Already at a point,[39] was setting forth.
Now we'll together, and the chance of goodness
Be like our warranted quarrel![40] Why are you silent?

MACDUFF. Such welcome and unwelcome things at once
'Tis hard to reconcile.

[*Enter a* DOCTOR.]

140　**MALCOLM.** Well, more anon. Comes the King forth, I pray you?

Literary Analysis
Imagery How does the image in Act IV, Scene iii, line 98 echo those in Act I, Scene v, line 17 and Act I, Scene v, lines 47–48?

30. untitled having no right to the throne.

31. truest… throne child of the true king.

32. interdiction exclusion.

33. blaspheme his breed slander his ancestry.

34. Died prepared for heaven.

35. trains enticements.

36. modest wisdom prudence.

credulous (krej′ ͝oo ləs) *adj.* tending to believe too readily

37. detraction slander.

38. For as.

39. at a point prepared.

40. the chance . . . quarrel May our chance of success equal the justice of our cause.

☑**Reading Check**
What response by Macduff convinces Malcolm that Macduff is being honest?

DOCTOR. Ay, sir. There are a crew of wretched souls
    That stay[41] his cure: their malady convinces
    The great assay of art;[42] but at his touch,
    Such sanctity hath heaven given his hand,
    They presently amend.[43]

145 **MALCOLM.**   I thank you, doctor.

                               [*Exit* DOCTOR.]

MACDUFF. What's the disease he means?

MALCOLM.   'Tis called the evil:[44]
    A most miraculous work in this good King,
    Which often since my here-remain in England
    I have seen him do. How he solicits heaven,
150   Himself best knows: but strangely-visited people,
    All swoll'n and ulcerous, pitiful to the eye,
    The mere[45] despair of surgery, he cures,
    Hanging a golden stamp[46] about their necks,
    Put on with holy prayers: and 'tis spoken,
155   To the succeeding royalty he leaves
    The healing benediction. With this strange virtue
    He hath a heavenly gift of prophecy,
    And sundry blessings hang about his throne
    That speak him full of grace.

[*Enter* ROSS.]

MACDUFF.   See, who comes here?

160 **MALCOLM.** My countryman; but yet I know him not.

MACDUFF. My ever gentle[47] cousin, welcome hither.

MALCOLM. I know him now: good God, betimes[48] remove
    The means that makes us strangers!

ROSS.   Sir, amen.

MACDUFF. Stands Scotland where it did?

ROSS.   Alas, poor country!
165   Almost afraid to know itself! It cannot
    Be called our mother but our grave, where nothing[49]
    But who knows nothing is once seen to smile;
    Where sighs and groans, and shrieks that rent the air,
    Are made, not marked, where violent sorrow seems
170   A modern ecstasy.[50] The dead man's knell
    Is there scarce asked for who,[51] and good men's lives
    Expire before the flowers in their caps,
    Dying or ere they sicken.

MACDUFF.   O, relation
    Too nice,[52] and yet too true!

---

41. stay wait for.

42. convinces . . . art defies the efforts of medical science.

43. presently amend immediately recover.

44. evil scrofula (skräf′ yə lə), skin disease called "the king's evil" because it was believed that it could be cured by the king's touch.

45. mere utter.

46. stamp coin.

47. gentle noble.

48. betimes quickly.

Reading Strategy

Using Your Senses How does the description in lines 164–173 help you envision the condition of Scotland?

49. nothing no one.

50. modern ecstasy ordinary emotion.

51. The dead . . . who People can no longer keep track of Macbeth's victims.

52. nice exact.

MALCOLM.   What's the newest grief?

175 **ROSS.** That of an hour's age doth hiss the speaker;[53]
Each minute teems[54] a new one.

MACDUFF.   How does my wife?

ROSS. Why, well.

MACDUFF.   And all my children?

ROSS.   Well too.

MACDUFF. The tyrant has not battered at their peace?

ROSS. No; they were well at peace when I did leave 'em.

180 **MACDUFF.** Be not a niggard of your speech: how goes 't?

ROSS. When I came hither to transport the tidings,
Which I have heavily borne, there ran a rumor
Of many worthy fellows that were out;[55]
Which was to my belief witnessed[56] the rather,
185 For that I saw the tyrant's power[57] afoot.
Now is the time of help. Your eye in Scotland
Would create soldiers, make our women fight,
To doff[58] their dire distresses.

MALCOLM.   Be 't their comfort
We are coming thither. Gracious England hath
190 Lent us good Siward and ten thousand men;
An older and a better soldier none
That Christendom gives out.

ROSS.   Would I could answer
This comfort with the like! But I have words

53. That . . . speaker Report of the grief of an hour ago is hissed as stale news.

54. teems gives birth to.

Literary Analysis
Imagery Why do you think Ross uses such an exaggerated image in lines 186–188?

55. out in rebellion.

56. witnessed confirmed.

57. power army.

58. doff put off.

Reading Check

What report from Scotland does Ross bring?

▼ **Critical Viewing**
How does this castle compare with your image of Inverness? **[Connect]**

That would be howled out in the desert air,
Where hearing should not latch[59] them.

195 **MACDUFF.**   What concern they?
The general cause or is it a fee-grief[60]
Due to some single breast?

ROSS.   No mind that's honest
But in it shares some woe, though the main part
Pertains to you alone.

MACDUFF.   If it be mine,
200   Keep it not from me, quickly let me have it.

ROSS. Let not your ears despise my tongue for ever,
Which shall possess them with the heaviest sound
That ever yet they heard.

MACDUFF.   Humh! I guess at it.

ROSS. Your castle is surprised; your wife and babes
205   Savagely slaughtered. To relate the manner,
Were, on the quarry[61] of these murdered deer,
To add the death of you.

MALCOLM.   Merciful heaven!
What, man! Ne'er pull your hat upon your brows;
Give sorrow words. The grief that does not speak
210   Whispers the o'er-fraught heart[62] and bids it break.

MACDUFF. My children too?

ROSS.   Wife, children, servants, all
That could be found.

MACDUFF.   And I must be from thence!
My wife killed too?

ROSS.   I have said.

MALCOLM.   Be comforted.
Let's make us med'cines of our great revenge,
215   To cure this deadly grief.

MACDUFF. He has no children. All my pretty ones?
Did you say all? O hell-kite![63] All?
What, all my pretty chickens and their dam
At one fell swoop?

MALCOLM. Dispute it[64] like a man.

220 **MACDUFF.**   I shall do so;
But I must also feel it as a man.
I cannot but remember such things were,
That were most precious to me. Did heaven look on,
And would not take their part? Sinful Macduff,

---

59. latch catch.

60. fee-grief personal grief.

Literary Analysis
Imagery How does the image in line 206 emphasize the ghastly fate of Macduff's family?

61. quarry heap of game slain in a hunt.

62. o'er-fraught over-burdened.

63. hell-kite hellish bird of prey.

64. Dispute it Counter your grief.

225 They were all struck for thee! Naught[65] that I am,
　　Not for their own demerits but for mine
　　Fell slaughter on their souls. Heaven rest them now!

　　MALCOLM. Be this the whetstone of your sword. Let grief
　　Convert to anger; blunt not the heart, enrage it.

230 MACDUFF. O, I could play the woman with mine eyes,
　　And braggart with my tongue! But, gentle heavens,
　　Cut short all intermission; front to front[66]
　　Bring thou this fiend of Scotland and myself;
　　Within my sword's length set him. If he 'scape,
235 Heaven forgive him too!

　　MALCOLM.　　　　　　　This time goes manly.
　　Come, go we to the King. Our power is ready;
　　Our lack is nothing but our leave.[67] Macbeth
　　Is ripe for shaking, and the pow'rs above
　　Put on their instruments.[68] Receive what cheer you may.
240 The night is long that never finds the day.　　　　[Exit.]

65. **Naught** wicked.

66. **front to front** face to face.

67. **Our . . . leave** We need only to take our leave.

68. **Put . . . instruments** urge us onward as their agents.

Review and Assess

Thinking About Act IV

1. **Respond:** Do you blame Macduff for abandoning his family? Why or why not?

2. **(a) Recall:** What are the predictions made by the second and third apparitions? **(b) Analyze:** Why does Macbeth readily accept these predictions?

3. **(a) Recall:** What happens to Macduff's family? **(b) Infer:** What does the fate of Macduff's family suggest about Macbeth's state of mind?

4. **(a) Recall:** How does Malcolm test Macduff? **(b) Analyze:** What does this test reveal about both Malcolm and Macduff? Explain.

5. **(a) Recall:** How does Macduff respond when asked to take the news about his family "like a man"? **(b) Interpret:** How would you characterize Macduff, based on his reaction to the murder of his wife and son? **(c) Compare and Contrast:** Compare and contrast Macduff's understanding of manhood with definitions of it earlier in the play.

6. **(a) Hypothesize:** If Shakespeare were alive today, would he argue that evildoers are primarily influenced by genetics, upbringing, or their own free choice? Base your answer on evidence from Act IV. **(b) Evaluate:** Would you agree with his position? Explain.

Review and Assess

Literary Analysis

Imagery

1. Identify a passage in Act IV that has vivid **imagery.** Using a chart like the one shown, indicate the emotions that the images express.

2. (a) In Act IV, Scene i and Act IV, Scene ii, find images that show children and babies are in danger from Macbeth and also threaten him. (b) Why is Macbeth at war with the future, which babies and children represent?

3. (a) Find two passages in Act IV, Scene iii with images of sickness. (b) Explain how these images relate to the conflict between Macbeth and Malcolm.

Connecting Literary Elements

4. In Act IV, Scene iii, identify two **archetypal images of a fallen world** that describe Scotland in terms of weeping, bleeding, or both.

5. What do the images of a fallen world and the references to the Christian underworld indicate about Macbeth's rule over Scotland? Explain.

Reading Strategy

Using Your Senses

6. Indicate how Malcolm's description of Scotland in Act IV, Scene iii, lines 39–41 appeals to the **senses** of touch, sight, and sound.

7. Why does reading this description of Scotland with your senses give a greater urgency to the dialogue between Macduff and Malcolm in Act IV, Scene iii?

Extend Understanding

8. **Social Studies Connection:** To flatter James I, Shakespeare transformed Banquo from a co-conspirator to an innocent victim. Did Shakespeare's politically motivated decision make *Macbeth* less effective as a drama? Why or why not?

Quick Review

Imagery is the language that writers use to re-create sensory experiences and stir emotions.

An **archetypal image** is one that has a powerful appeal in many different cultures. One such image is that of a **fallen world** where, according to the beliefs of many, the dead are confined.

By **using your senses,** you can experience the imagery in a literary text.

 Take It to the Net

www.phschool.com

Take the interactive self-test online to check your understanding of the selection.

Integrate Language Skills

Vocabulary Development Lesson

Word Analysis: Latin Root -cred-

The root -cred- means "belief." To be *credulous* is "to believe something too readily." Use the word parts shown below to build five -cred- words. Then, write the meanings of these words, and verify your definitions by referring to a dictionary.

in-   *-ulous*   *-ible*   *-ulity*

Spelling Strategy

The letter *c* combines with the *i* of the suffix *-ious* to spell the *sh* sound, as in *pernicious* and *judicious*. In your notebook, correctly spell the following words with *ci* or *sh*.

1. suspi__ous   2. avari__ous   3. __oemaker

Fluency: Words in Context

In your notebook, answer each question.

1. Whose influence in this play is the most *pernicious*? Why?
2. Which character do you think is the most *judicious*? Why?
3. If you were staging IV, i, what *sundry* items might you use as props?
4. Does *intemperance*, rather than *ambition*, cause Macbeth's downfall? Explain.
5. Is ambition a kind of *avarice*? Why or why not?
6. How would you refute someone's claim that Malcolm is too *credulous* to rule Scotland?

Grammar and Style Lesson

Possessive Forms

To form the **possessive forms** of most singular nouns and plural nouns not ending in *s*, add an apostrophe and *s*. For plural nouns ending in *s*, just add an apostrophe, but do not use an apostrophe to make a word plural. Shakespeare uses both singular and plural possessives in this act:

> **Singular:** adder's traitor's baboon's
>
> **Plural:** witches' warders' men's

Practice In your notebook, write the possessive for the following nouns.

1. the Macbeths   3. Ross   5. the women
2. the nobles   4. Fleance   6. Lennox

Writing Application Using the possessive forms of these characters' names or designations, briefly explain what role they play in the drama: Banquo, Lady Macbeth, and the witches.

W͞G *Prentice Hall Writing and Grammar Connection: Chapter 27, Section 6*

Extension Activities

Writing Write a **motivational flier** that will inspire young, working-class Englishmen to join the army that will be invading Scotland. Use repetition and parallelism, the expression of similar ideas in similar grammatical structures.

Listening and Speaking With a small group, role-play an **interview** between Malcolm's staff and a young Englishman who wants to join their cause. Have the staff test the young man's motivation and abilities. [**Group Activity**]

Prepare to Read

Macbeth, Act V

Literary Analysis

Shakespearean Tragedy

Shakespearean tragedy usually contains these elements:

- A central character of high rank and personal quality, yet with a **tragic flaw** or weakness
- Causally related events that lead this character to disaster, at least partly through his or her flaw
- Lively action that creates a vivid spectacle
- The use of comic scenes to temper and offset the mood of sadness

In viewing the destruction of the central character, members of the audience experience a mixture of pity, fear, and awe that lifts them out of their everyday lives.

As you read, look for the elements of Shakespearean tragedy in this act and recall their appearance in previous acts.

Connecting Literary Elements

Viewing a Shakespearean tragedy is often an uplifting experience despite the disasters that befall the hero. The source of this positive experience is the **tragic impulse,** which shows the tragic hero confronting his or her limits in a noble way. Notice, for instance, how Shakespeare gives Macbeth a streak of reckless bravery in Act V.

Reading Strategy

Inferring Beliefs of the Period

As products of a certain era, great plays reflect the **beliefs** of their period. Infer those beliefs by looking carefully at the ideas the characters express and comparing them to modern ideas on the same subject.

In Act V, Scene i, for example, you have the opportunity to watch a doctor in action. Listen carefully to what he says about a case of mental disturbance. Then, use a chart like the one shown to compare his ideas with those that a modern psychiatrist might express.

Vocabulary Development

perturbation (pʉr´ tər bā´ shən) *n.* disturbance (p. 375)

pristine (pris´ tēn´) *adj.* original; unspoiled (p. 381)

clamorous (klam´ ər əs) *adj.* noisy (p. 384)

harbingers (här´ bin jərz) *n.* forerunners (p. 384)

Comparison of Beliefs

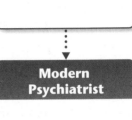

Doctor in *Macbeth*

Modern Psychiatrist

Review and Anticipate

In Act IV, Macbeth learns from the witches that he must "Beware Macduff!" but that he need not fear any man "of woman born." He also learns that he will never be vanquished until the forest itself marches against him. However, he sees a vision indicating that Banquo will indeed father a long line of kings.

Armed with his new knowledge, Macbeth orders the murder of Macduff's wife and son. Macduff himself is in England to join forces with Malcolm and is overcome when he hears the news. Nevertheless, he and Malcolm will lead an army against Macbeth.

Act V will determine the outcome as Macbeth, grown reckless in evil, battles against Malcolm and his men.

Act V

Scene i. Dunsinane. In the castle.

[*Enter a* DOCTOR OF PHYSIC *and a* WAITING-GENTLEWOMAN.]

DOCTOR. I have two nights watched with you, but can perceive no truth in your report. When was it she last walked?

GENTLEWOMAN. Since his Majesty went into the field.[1] I have seen
5   her rise from her bed, throw her nightgown upon her, unlock her closet,[2] take forth paper, fold it, write upon 't, read it, afterwards seal it, and again return to bed; yet all this while in a most fast sleep.

DOCTOR. A great <u>perturbation</u> in nature, to receive at
10   once the benefit of sleep and do the effects of watching![3] In this slumb'ry agitation, besides her walking, and other actual performances, what, at any time, have you heard her say?

15 **GENTLEWOMAN.** That, sir, which I will not report after her.

DOCTOR. You may to me, and 'tis most meet[4] you should.

GENTLEWOMAN. Neither to you nor anyone, having no witness to confirm my speech.

[*Enter* LADY MACBETH, *with a* taper.]

Lo you, here she comes! This is her very guise,[5] and, upon my
20   life, fast asleep! Observe her; stand close.[6]

DOCTOR. How came she by that light?

GENTLEWOMAN. Why, it stood by her. She has light by her continually. 'Tis her command.

25 **DOCTOR.** You see, her eyes are open.

▲ **Critical Viewing**
Who will slay Macbeth with a sword like this one? **[Predict]**

1. **field** battlefield.

2. **closet** chest.

perturbation (pur´ tər bā´ shən) *n.* disturbance

3. **effects of watching** deeds of one awake.

4. **meet** suitable.

5. **guise** custom.

6. **close** hidden.

✔ **Reading Check**
Why has the gentlewoman summoned the doctor?

Lady Macbeth Sleepwalking, Henry Fuseli, Louvre, Paris

▲ **Critical Viewing** Identify four details from the sleepwalking scene (V, i) that the artist illustrates in this picture. **[Connect]**

GENTLEWOMAN. Ay, but their sense[7] are shut.

DOCTOR. What is it she does now? Look, how she rubs her hands.

GENTLEWOMAN. It is an accustomed action with her, to seem thus washing her hands: I have known her continue in this a quarter of an hour.

LADY MACBETH. Yet here's a spot.

DOCTOR. Hark! She speaks. I will set down what comes from her, to satisfy[8] my remembrance the more strongly.

LADY MACBETH. Out, damned spot! Out, I say! One: two: why, then 'tis time to do 't. Hell is murky. Fie, my lord, fie! A soldier, and afeard? What need we fear who knows it, when none can call our pow'r to accompt?[9] Yet who would have thought the old man to have had so much blood in him?

DOCTOR. Do you mark that?

LADY MACBETH. The Thane of Fife had a wife. Where is she now? What, will these hands ne'er be clean? No more o' that, my lord, no more o' that! You mar all with this starting.

DOCTOR. Go to, go to! You have known what you should not.

GENTLEWOMAN. She has spoke what she should not, I am sure of that. Heaven knows what she has known.

LADY MACBETH. Here's the smell of the blood still. All the perfumes of Arabia will not sweeten this little hand. Oh, oh, oh!

DOCTOR. What a sigh is there! The heart is sorely charged.[10]

GENTLEWOMAN. I would not have such a heart in my bosom for the dignity[11] of the whole body.

DOCTOR. Well, well, well—

GENTLEWOMAN. Pray God it be, sir.

DOCTOR. This disease is beyond my practice. Yet I have known those which have walked in their sleep who have died holily in their beds.

LADY MACBETH. Wash your hands; put on your nightgown; look not so pale! I tell you yet again, Banquo's buried. He cannot come out on 's[12] grave.

DOCTOR. Even so?

LADY MACBETH. To bed, to bed! There's knocking at the gate. Come, come, come, come, give me your hand!

---

7. **sense** powers of sight.

8. **satisfy** support.

9. **to accompt** into account.

Literary Analysis
Shakespearean Tragedy
Does the sleepwalking scene suggest that Lady Macbeth is a tragic heroine? Explain.

10. **charged** burdened.

11. **dignity** worth.

12. **on 's** of his

**Reading Check**
What does Lady Macbeth do and say as she sleepwalks?

70   What's done cannot be undone. To bed, to bed, to bed!

                                      [*Exit* LADY MACBETH.]

DOCTOR. Will she go now to bed?

GENTLEWOMAN. Directly.

DOCTOR. Foul whisp'rings are abroad. Unnatural deeds
    Do breed unnatural troubles. Infected minds
    To their deaf pillows will discharge their secrets.
75   More needs she the divine than the physician.
    God, God forgive us all! Look after her;
    Remove from her the means of all annoyance,[13]
    And still keep eyes upon her. So good night.
    My mind she has mated[14] and amazed my sight:
80   I think, but dare not speak.

GENTLEWOMAN.   Good night, good doctor.

                                             [*Exit.*]

Scene ii. *The country near Dunsinane.*

[*Drum and colors. Enter* MENTEITH, CAITHNESS, ANGUS, LENNOX, SOLDIERS.]

MENTEITH. The English pow'r[1] is near, led on by Malcolm,
    His uncle Siward and the good Macduff.
    Revenges burn in them; for their dear causes
    Would to the bleeding and the grim alarm
    Excite the mortified man.[2]

5 **ANGUS.**   Near Birnam Wood
    Shall we well meet them; that way are they coming.

CAITHNESS. Who knows if Donalbain be with his brother?

LENNOX. For certain, sir, he is not. I have a file[3]
    Of all the gentry: there is Siward's son,
10   And many unrough[4] youths that even now
    Protest[5] their first of manhood.

MENTEITH.   What does the tyrant?

CAITHNESS. Great Dunsinane he strongly fortifies.
    Some say he's mad; others, that lesser hate him,
    Do call it valiant fury: but, for certain,
15   He cannot buckle his distempered cause
    Within the belt of rule.[6]

ANGUS.   Now does he feel
    His secret murders sticking on his hands;
    Now minutely revolts upbraid his faith-breach.[7]
    Those he commands move only in command,
20   Nothing in love. Now does he feel his title

Reading Strategy
Inferring Beliefs of the Period What can you infer about medicine during this time from the doctor's words in lines 72–80?

13. **annoyance** injury.

14. **mated** baffled.

1. **pow'r** army.

2. **Would . . . man** would incite a dead man to join the bloody, grim call to arms.

3. **file** list.

4. **unrough** beardless.

5. **Protest** assert.

Literary Analysis
Shakespearean Tragedy Do you agree with those whom Caithness quotes in Scene ii, line 13? Is Macbeth "mad"? Why or why not?

6. **rule** self-control.

7. **minutely . . . faith-breach** Every minute revolts rebuke his disloyalty.

Hang loose about him, like a giant's robe
Upon a dwarfish thief.

MENTEITH.   Who then shall blame
His pestered[8] senses to recoil and start,
When all that is within him does condemn
Itself for being there?

25 CAITHNESS.   Well, march we on,
To give obedience where 'tis truly owed.
Meet we the med'cine of the sickly weal,[9]
And with him pour we, in our country's purge,
Each drop of us.[10]

LENNOX.   Or so much as it needs
30 To dew the sovereign flower and drown the weeds.[11]
Make we our march towards Birnam.

[*Exit, marching.*]

8. **pestered** tormented.

9. **med'cine . . . weal** Malcolm and his supporters are "the medicine" that will heal "the sickly" commonwealth.

10. **Each . . . us** every last drop of our blood.

11. **dew . . . weeds** water the royal flower (Malcolm) and drown the weeds (Macbeth).

Scene iii. Dunsinane. In the castle.

[*Enter* MACBETH, DOCTOR, *and* ATTENDANTS.]

MACBETH. Bring me no more reports; let them fly all![1]
Till Birnam Wood remove to Dunsinane
I cannot taint[2] with fear. What's the boy Malcolm?
Was he not born of woman? The spirits that know
5 All mortal consequences[3] have pronounced me thus:
"Fear not, Macbeth; no man that's born of woman
Shall e'er have power upon thee." Then fly, false thanes,
And mingle with the English epicures.[4]
The mind I sway[5] by and the heart I bear
10 Shall never sag with doubt nor shake with fear.

[*Enter* SERVANT.]

The devil damn thee black, thou cream-faced loon.[6]
Where got'st thou that goose look?

SERVANT. There is ten thousand—

MACBETH.   Geese, villain?

SERVANT.   Soldiers, sir.

MACBETH. Go prick thy face and over-red thy fear.
15 Thou lily-livered boy. What soldiers, patch?[7]
Death of thy soul! Those linen[8] cheeks of thine
Are counselors to fear. What soldiers, whey-face?

SERVANT. The English force, so please you.

MACBETH. Take thy face hence.   [*Exit* SERVANT.]
Seyton!—I am sick at heart.

1. **let . . . all** let them all desert me!

2. **taint** become infected.

3. **mortal consequences** future human events.

4. **epicures** gluttons.

5. **sway** move.

6. **loon** fool.

7. **patch** fool.

8. **linen** pale as linen.

✔Reading Check

Why is Macbeth unafraid even though Malcolm's army is marching against him?

20　When I behold—Seyton, I say!—This push[9]
　　Will cheer me ever, or disseat[10] me now.
　　I have lived long enough. My way of life
　　Is fall'n into the sear,[11] the yellow leaf,
　　And that which should accompany old age,
25　As honor, love, obedience, troops of friends,
　　I must not look to have; but, in their stead,
　　Curses not loud but deep, mouth-honor, breath,
　　Which the poor heart would fain deny, and dare not.
　　Seyton!

[*Enter* SEYTON.]

　　SEYTON. What's your gracious pleasure?

30　**MACBETH.**　　　　　　　　　　　　What news more?

　　SEYTON. All is confirmed, my lord, which was reported.

　　MACBETH. I'll fight, till from my bones my flesh be hacked.
　　Give me my armor.

　　SEYTON.　　　　　　　　'Tis not needed yet.

　　MACBETH. I'll put it on.
35　Send out moe[12] horses, skirr[13] the country round.
　　Hang those that talk of fear. Give me mine armor.
　　How does your patient, doctor?

　　DOCTOR.　　　　　　　　　　Not so sick, my lord,
　　As she is troubled with thick-coming fancies
　　That keep her from her rest.

　　MACBETH.　　　　　　　　　Cure her of that.
40　Canst thou not minister to a mind diseased,
　　Pluck from the memory a rooted sorrow,
　　Raze out[14] the written troubles of the brain,
　　And with some sweet oblivious antidote
　　Cleanse the stuffed bosom of that perilous stuff
　　Which weighs upon the heart?

9. push effort.

10. disseat unthrone.

11. the sear withered state.

Literary Analysis
Shakespearean Tragedy Do lines 20–28 evoke sympathy for Macbeth? Explain.

12. moe more.

13. skirr scour.

Reading Strategy
Inferring Beliefs of the Period Would a modern psychiatrist answer as the doctor does in lines 45–46? Why or why not?

14. Raze out erase.

45 **DOCTOR.**   Therein the patient
         Must minister to himself.

   MACBETH. Throw physic[15] to the dogs, I'll none of it.
         Come, put mine armor on. Give me my staff.
         Seyton, send out.—Doctor, the thanes fly from me.—
50   Come, sir, dispatch. If thou couldst, doctor, cast
         The water[16] of my land, find her disease
         And purge it to a sound and <u>pristine</u> health,
         I would applaud thee to the very echo,
         That should applaud again.—Pull 't off,[17] I say.—
55   What rhubarb, senna, or what purgative drug,
         Would scour these English hence? Hear'st thou of them?

   DOCTOR. Ay, my good lord; your royal preparation
         Makes us hear something.

   MACBETH.   Bring it[18] after me.
         I will not be afraid of death and bane[19]
60   Till Birnam Forest come to Dunsinane.

   DOCTOR. [*Aside*] Were I from Dunsinane away and clear,
         Profit again should hardly draw me here.   [*Exit.*]

Scene iv. *Country near Birnam Wood.*

[*Drum and colors.* Enter MALCOLM, SIWARD, MACDUFF, SIWARD'S SON,

MENTEITH, CAITHNESS, ANGUS, *and* SOLDIERS, *marching.*]

   MALCOLM. Cousins, I hope the days are near at hand
         That chambers will be safe.[1]

   MENTEITH.   We doubt it nothing.

   SIWARD. What wood is this before us?

   MENTEITH.   The Wood of Birnam.

   MALCOLM. Let every soldier hew him down a bough
5   And bear 't before him. Thereby shall we shadow[2]
         The numbers of our host, and make discovery[3]
         Err in report of us.

   SOLDIERS.   It shall be done.

   SIWARD. We learn no other but the confident tyrant
         Keeps still in Dunsinane, and will endure
         Our setting down before 't.[4]

10 **MALCOLM.**   'Tis his main hope,
         For where there is advantage to be given
         Both more and less[5] have given him the revolt,
         And none serve with him but constrained things
         Whose hearts are absent too.

15. physic medicine.

16. cast the water diagnose the illness.

pristine (pris tēn´) *adj.* original; unspoiled

17. Pull 't off Pull off a piece of armor, which has been put on incorrectly in Macbeth's haste.

18. it his armor.

19. bane destruction.

Literary Analysis
Shakespearean Tragedy
How does Malcolm's order in Scene iv, lines 4–7 increase the sense of tension surrounding the play's outcome and Macbeth's fate?

1. That . . . safe that people will be safe in their own homes.

2. shadow conceal.

3. discovery those who see us.

4. setting down before 't laying seige to it.

5. more and less people of high and low rank.

**Reading Check**

How will Malcolm's men disguise themselves?

MACDUFF.   Let our just censures

15   Attend the true event,[6] and put we on
     Industrious soldiership.

     SIWARD.   The time approaches,
     That will with due decision make us know
     What we shall say we have and what we owe.[7]
     Thoughts speculative their unsure hopes relate,
20   But certain issue strokes must arbitrate:[8]
     Towards which advance the war.[9]   *[Exit, marching.]*

Scene v. Dunsinane. Within the castle.

[Enter MACBETH, SEYTON, *and* SOLDIERS, *with drum and colors.]*

     MACBETH. Hang out our banners on the outward walls.
     The cry is still "They come!" Our castle's strength
     Will laugh a siege to scorn. Here let them lie
     Till famine and the ague[1] eat them up.
5   Were they not forced[2] with those that should be ours,
     We might have met them dareful,[3] beard to beard,
     And beat them backward home.

           [A cry within of women.]
                     What is that noise?

     SEYTON. It is the cry of women, my good lord.   *[Exit.]*

     MACBETH. I have almost forgot the taste of fears:
10   The time has been, my senses would have cooled
     To hear a night-shriek, and my fell[4] of hair

---

6. **our . . . event** True judgment awaits the actual outcome.

7. **owe** own.

8. **strokes . . . arbitrate** Fighting must decide.

9. **war** army.

1. **ague** fever.

2. **forced** reinforced.

3. **dareful** boldly.

4. **fell** scalp.

𝓛iterature
in context   History Connection

The Real Macbeth

     As Malcolm's forces close in on Macbeth, it is worth considering the differences between Shakespeare's king and the historical Macbeth. The real Macbeth, who ruled Scotland from 1040 to 1057, did become king by killing King Duncan. However, Macbeth's claim to the throne was legitimate due to the ancient Scottish custom of tanistry.

     According to this system, kingships were not passed from father to son. Instead, the ablest, oldest male in an extended royal family was chosen by a family council or chose himself by declaring war on his competitors. The real Macbeth took the second course, declared war on King Duncan, and killed him fairly in battle. Eventually, Duncan's son Malcolm led a Northumbrian invasion force into Scotland. In 1057, he killed Macbeth.

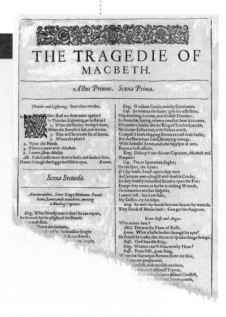

Would at a dismal treatise[5] rouse and stir
As life were in 't. I have supped full with horrors.
Direness, familiar to my slaughterous thoughts,
Cannot once start[6] me.

[*Enter* SEYTON.]

15   Wherefore was that cry?

SEYTON. The queen, my lord, is dead.

MACBETH. She should[7] have died hereafter;
There would have been a time for such a word.[8]
Tomorrow, and tomorrow, and tomorrow
20   Creeps in this petty pace from day to day,
To the last syllable of recorded time;
And all our yesterdays have lighted fools
The way to dusty death. Out, out, brief candle!
Life's but a walking shadow, a poor player
25   That struts and frets his hour upon the stage
And then is heard no more. It is a tale
Told by an idiot, full of sound and fury
Signifying nothing.

[*Enter a* MESSENGER.]

Thou com'st to use thy tongue; thy story quickly!

30 **MESSENGER.** Gracious my lord,
I should report that which I say I saw,
But know not how to do 't.

MACBETH.   Well, say, sir.

MESSENGER. As I did stand my watch upon the hill,
I looked toward Birnam, and anon, methought,
The wood began to move.

35 **MACBETH.**   Liar and slave!

MESSENGER. Let me endure your wrath, if 't be not so.
Within this three mile may you see it coming;
I say a moving grove.

MACBETH.   If thou speak'st false,
Upon the next tree shalt thou hang alive,
40   Till famine cling[9] thee. If thy speech be sooth,[10]
I care not if thou dost for me as much.
I pull in resolution, and begin
To doubt th' equivocation of the fiend
That lies like truth: "Fear not, till Birnam Wood
45   Do come to Dunsinane!" And now a wood
Comes toward Dunsinane. Arm, arm, and out!
If this which he avouches[11] does appear,

5. treatise story.

6. start startle.

7. should inevitably would.

8. word message.

Literary Analysis
Shakespearean Tragedy and the Tragic Impulse
This speech in lines 17–28 is a powerful expression of life's futility. Is Macbeth's story really "a tale/Told by an idiot, full of sound and fury / Signifying nothing"? Why or why not?

Literary Analysis
Shakespearean Tragedy
In lines 42–50, how does Macbeth's allusion to the witches' prophecies disclose a growing awareness of his own doom?

9. cling wither.

10. sooth truth.

11. avouches asserts.

✔Reading Check

To what two things does Macbeth compare life when he hears that Lady Macbeth is dead?

◄ Critical Viewing
Do you think this picture portrays the fight between Macbeth and Young Siward (V, vii, 10–11) or that between Macbeth and Macduff (V, viii, 34–35)? Explain. **[Make a Judgment]**

There is nor flying hence nor tarrying here.
I 'gin to be aweary of the sun,
50 And wish th' estate o' th' world were now undone.
Ring the alarum bell! Blow wind, come wrack!
At least we'll die with harness[12] on our back.   [*Exit.*]

12. **harness** armor.

Scene vi. Dunsinane. Before the castle.

[*Drum and colors. Enter* MALCOLM, SIWARD, MACDUFF, *and their army,*

with boughs.]

    MALCOLM. Now near enough. Your leavy[1] screens throw down,
    And show like those you are. You, worthy uncle,
    Shall, with my cousin, your right noble son,
    Lead our first battle.[2] Worthy Macduff and we
5   Shall take upon 's what else remains to do,
    According to our order.[3]

    SIWARD.   Fare you well.
    Do we find the tyrant's power[4] tonight,
    Let us be beaten, if we cannot fight.

    MACDUFF. Make all our trumpets speak; give them all breath.
10 Those <u>clamorous</u> <u>harbingers</u> of blood and death.

                    [*Exit. Alarums continued.*]

1. **leavy** leafy.

2. **battle** battalion.

3. **order** plan.

4. **power** forces.

clamorous (klam′ ər əs) *adj.* noisy

harbingers (här′ bin jərs) *n.* forerunners

Scene vii. *Another part of the field.*

[*Enter* MACBETH.]

> MACBETH. They have tied me to a stake; I cannot fly,
> But bearlike I must fight the course.[1] What's he
> That was not born of woman? Such a one
> Am I to fear, or none.

[*Enter* YOUNG SIWARD.]

> YOUNG SIWARD. What is thy name?

5 > MACBETH.   Thou'lt be afraid to hear it.

> YOUNG SIWARD. No; though thou call'st thyself a hotter name
> Than any is in hell.

> MACBETH.   My name's Macbeth.

> YOUNG SIWARD. The devil himself could not pronounce a title
> More hateful to mine ear.

> MACBETH.   No, nor more fearful.

10 > YOUNG SIWARD. Thou liest, abhorrèd tyrant; with my sword
> I'll prove the lie thou speak'st.

> [*Fight, and* YOUNG SIWARD *slain.*]

> MACBETH.   Thou wast born of woman.
> But swords I smile at, weapons laugh to scorn,
> Brandished by man that's of a woman born.   [*Exit.*]

[*Alarums. Enter* MACDUFF.]

> MACDUFF. That way the noise is. Tyrant, show thy face!
15 > If thou be'st slain and with no stroke of mine,
> My wife and children's ghosts will haunt me still.
> I cannot strike at wretched kerns, whose arms
> Are hired to bear their staves.[2] Either thou, Macbeth,
> Or else my sword, with an unbattered edge,
20 > I sheathe again undeeded.[3] There thou shouldst be;
> By this great clatter, one of greatest note
> Seems bruited.[4] Let me find him, Fortune!
> And more I beg not.   [*Exit. Alarums.*]

[*Enter* MALCOLM *and* SIWARD.]

> SIWARD. This way, my lord. The castle's gently rend'red:[5]
25 > The tyrant's people on both sides do fight;
> The noble thanes do bravely in the war;
> The day almost itself professes yours,
> And little is to do.

> MALCOLM.   We have met with foes
> That strike beside us.[6]

---

1. **bearlike . . . .course** Like a bear chained to a stake being attacked by dogs, I must fight until the end.

Literary Analysis
Shakespearean Tragedy
In Scene vii, does Macbeth show signs of bravery or is he just overconfident because of what the witches said? Explain.

2. **staves** spears.

3. **undeeded** unused.

4. **bruited** reported.

5. **gently rend'red** easily surrendered.

6. **strike . . . us** deliberately miss us.

 **Reading Check**

What is the outcome of the hand-to-hand combat between Macbeth and Young Siward?

SIWARD.   Enter, sir, the castle.

[*Exit. Alarum.*]

Scene viii. Another part of the field.

[*Enter* MACBETH.]

MACBETH. Why should I play the Roman fool, and die
On mine own sword?[1] Whiles I see lives,[2] the gashes
Do better upon them.

[*Enter* MACDUFF.]

MACDUFF.   Turn, hell-hound, turn!

MACBETH. Of all men else I have avoided thee.
5   But get thee back! My soul is too much charged
With blood of thine already.

MACDUFF.   I have no words:
My voice is in my sword, thou bloodier villain
Than terms[3] can give thee out!

[*Fight. Alarum.*]

MACBETH.   Thou losest labor:
As easy mayst thou the intrenchant[4] air
10 With thy keen sword impress[5] as make me bleed:
Let fall thy blade on vulnerable crests;
I bear a charmèd life, which must not yield
To one of woman born.

MACDUFF.   Despair thy charm,
And let the angel[6] whom thou still hast served
15 Tell thee, Macduff was from his mother's womb
Untimely ripped.[7]

MACBETH. Accursèd be that tongue that tells me so,
For it hath cowed my better part of man![8]
And be these juggling fiends no more believed,
20 That palter[9] with us in a double sense;
That keep the word of promise to our ear,
And break it to our hope. I'll not fight with thee.

MACDUFF. Then yield thee, coward,
And live to be the show and gaze o' th' time:[10]
25 We'll have thee, as our rarer monsters[11] are,
Painted upon a pole,[12] and underwrit,
"Here may you see the tyrant."

MACBETH.   I will not yield,
To kiss the ground before young Malcolm's feet,
And to be baited with the rabble's curse.
30 Though Birnam Wood be come to Dunsinane,

---

1. play . . . sword die like Brutus or Cassius, who killed themselves with their own swords in the moment of defeat.

2. While . . . lives so long as I see living men.

3. terms . . . out words can describe you.

4. intrenchant incapable of being cut.

5. impress make a dent in.

6. angel fallen angel; fiend.

7. his . . . ripped Macduff's mother died before giving birth to him.

8. better. . . man courage.

9. palter juggle.

10. gaze o' th' time spectacle of the age.

11. monsters freaks.

12. Painted . . . pole pictured on a banner stuck on a pole by a showman's booth.

And thou opposed, being of no woman born,
Yet I will try the last. Before my body
I throw my warlike shield. Lay on, Macduff;
And damned be him that first cries "Hold, enough!"

[*Exit, fighting. Alarums.*]

[*Re-enter fighting, and* MACBETH *slain. Exit* MACDUFF, *with* MACBETH.
Retreat and flourish.[13] *Enter, with drum and colors,*
MALCOLM, SIWARD, ROSS, THANES, *and* SOLDIERS.]

35 **MALCOLM.** I would the friends we miss were safe arrived.

SIWARD. Some must go off;[14] and yet, by these I see,
So great a day as this is cheaply bought.

MALCOLM. Macduff is missing, and your noble son.

ROSS. Your son, my lord, has paid a soldier's debt:
40   He only lived but till he was a man;
The which no sooner had his prowess confirmed
In the unshrinking station[15] where he fought,
But like a man he died.

SIWARD.   Then he is dead?

ROSS. Ay, and brought off the field. Your cause of sorrow
45   Must not be measured by his worth, for then
It hath no end.

SIWARD.   Had he his hurts before?

ROSS. Ay, on the front.

SIWARD.   Why then, God's soldier be he!
Had I as many sons as I have hairs,
I would not wish them to a fairer death:
And so his knell is knolled.

50 **MALCOLM.**   He's worth more sorrow,
And that I'll spend for him.

SIWARD.   He's worth no more:
They say he parted well and paid his score:
And so God be with him! Here comes newer comfort.

[*Enter* MACDUFF, *with* MACBETH'S *head.*]

MACDUFF. Hail, King! for so thou art: behold, where stands
55   Th' usurper's cursèd head. The time is free.[16]
I see thee compassed with thy kingdom's pearl,[17]
That speak my salutation in their minds,
Whose voices I desire aloud with mine:
Hail, King of Scotland!

ALL.   Hail, King of Scotland!
[*Flourish.*]

60 **MALCOLM.** We shall not spend a large expense of time
     Before we reckon with your several loves,[18]
     And make us even with you.[19] My thanes and kinsmen,
     Henceforth be earls, the first that ever Scotland
     In such an honor named. What's more to do,
65   Which would be planted newly with the time[20]—
     As calling home our exiled friends abroad
     That fled the snares of watchful tyranny,
     Producing forth the cruel ministers
     Of this dead butcher and his fiendlike queen,
70   Who, as 'tis thought, by self and violent hands
     Took off her life—this, and what needful else
     That calls upon us, by the grace of Grace
     We will perform in measure, time, and place:[21]
     So thanks to all at once and to each one,
75   Whom we invite to see us crowned at Scone.

[Flourish. Exit all.]

18. **reckon . . . loves** reward each of you for your devotion.

19. **make . . . you** pay what we owe you.

20. **What's . . . time** what remains to be done at the beginning of this new age.

21. **in measure . . . place** fittingly at the appropriate time and place.

Review and Assess

Thinking About Act V

1. **Respond:** Does the ending of the play inspire in you feelings of pity and an almost wondrous sense of fear? Why or why not?

2. **(a) Recall:** What does the doctor see in the sleepwalking scene, and what does he speculate about the causes for what he sees? **(b) Analyze:** How have Macbeth and Lady Macbeth reversed roles by the end of the play?

3. **(a) Recall:** What does Macbeth say when he hears of Lady Macbeth's death? **(b) Draw Conclusions:** What does his reaction to her death reveal about their relationship and his state of mind?

4. **(a) Recall:** What does Macbeth say about the witches when he learns that Birnam Wood is apparently moving and that Macduff "was from his mother's womb / Untimely ripped"? **(b) Infer:** What growing realization do these statements about the witches seem to reflect? **(c) Draw Conclusions:** What is Macbeth's state of mind in his final battle with Macduff? Explain.

5. **(a) Recall:** What occurs in Act V, Scene viii, lines 35–75? **(b) Evaluate:** Would the play be complete if it ended with Macbeth's death but omitted these lines? Why or why not?

6. **Speculate:** Do you think that a tragedy could be written about an ordinary person living today? Why or why not?

Review and Assess

Literary Analysis

Shakespearean Tragedy

1. Identify all the elements of **Shakespearean tragedy** in *Macbeth*, citing examples from the play.

2. Use a chart like this one to show how Banquo's response to the witches emphasizes Macbeth's **tragic flaw.**

3. What role does Lady Macbeth play in Macbeth's choice of evil?

4. (a) How does Macbeth's tragic flaw lead him to disaster? (b) Once Macbeth kills Duncan, can he turn back? Why or why not?

5. Find three passages that show how the intensity of Macbeth's imagination adds to the tragedy. Support your choices.

Connecting Literary Elements

6. (a) What positive qualities does Macbeth display in Act V? Explain. (b) How do Macbeth's positive qualities contribute to the **tragic impulse** revealed in the play?

7. How does the tragic impulse involve a conflict between limitations and the ability to go beyond limitations? Support your answer with references to the play.

Reading Strategy

Inferring Beliefs of the Period

8. What do the doctor's remarks lead you to **infer** about Elizabethan concepts of and treatments for mental illness?

9. Compare and contrast Elizabethan concepts of mental illness with those of today.

Extend Understanding

10. **Philosophy Connection:** Is tragedy an inescapable part of life at any time, or is it a perspective on life that makes sense only in certain eras? Explain.

Quick Review

In **Shakespearean tragedy,** a central character possessing both nobility and a **tragic flaw** or weakness is caught up in events that lead to his or her downfall.

The **tragic impulse** celebrates the way in which the tragic hero confronts his or her limitations in a noble way.

To **infer the beliefs** of the period, compare the ideas expressed by the characters with modern ideas on the same subject.

 Take It to the Net

www.phschool.com

Take the interactive self-test online to check your understanding of these selections.

Integrate Language Skills

Vocabulary Development Lesson

Word Analysis: Latin Root -turb-

The root -turb- means "to disturb." To experience *perturbation* is to experience "a great disturbance." Knowing the meaning of the root -turb-, define the italicized words below. Then, verify your definitions with a dictionary.

1. Macbeth encounters *turbulence* in battle.
2. The eleventh century was a *turbulent* time in Scotland.
3. Elizabethans believed that a *perturbation* in the heavens meant disorder in society.
4. Macbeth was very *perturbed* by Fleance's escape.
5. After being stirred, the witches' potion was *turbid*.

Fluency: Sentence Completion

Fill in each blank with a word from the vocabulary list on page 374.

1. The movement of Birnam Wood began with a ___?___ rustling of trees.
2. The first trees that approached Dunsinane were ___?___ of the army.
3. Farmers were shocked to see the untouched, ___?___ wood suddenly move.
4. These farmers confessed to feeling a ___?___ in their hearts.

Spelling Strategy

Add -ous to some nouns to make adjectives: *famous* from *fame* (dropping the final e). In your notebook, turn each noun into an adjective.

1. treason   2. glamor   3. nerve

Grammar and Style Lesson

Pronouns and Antecedents

Pronouns, which take the place of nouns, agree with their **antecedents,** the nouns that they replace, in these ways:

- in gender (male, female, or neuter)
- number (singular or plural)
- person (first person, second person, or third person)

In this example of pronoun-antecedent agreement from Act V, the pronoun is set in boldface and the antecedent is underlined.

> **Example:** The English pow'r is near, led on by <u>Malcolm</u>, **his** uncle Siward and the good Macduff. (*Malcolm*, singular and masculine takes *his*, a singular masculine pronoun.)

Practice Identify the antecedents and the gender, number, and person of the italicized pronouns.

1. "Who knows if Donalbain be with *his* brother?"
2. "What does the tyrant? / Great Dunsinane *he* strongly fortifies."
3. "Make all our trumpets speak; give *them* all breath."
4. "I cannot strike at wretched kerns, whose arms / Are hired to bear *their* staves."
5. "Had I as many sons as I have hairs, / I would not wish *them* to a fairer death: . . ."

Writing Application Write a lead paragraph for a news story about Malcolm's victory. Be sure that pronouns agree with their antecedents.

W͞G Prentice Hall Writing and Grammar Connection: Chapter 23, Section 2

Writing Lesson

Response to Criticism

A. C. Bradley wrote about *Macbeth:* "darkness, we may even say blackness, broods over this tragedy. . . . all the scenes which at once recur to memory take place either at night or in some dark spot." In an essay, evaluate this statement, supporting your response with specific references to the play.

Prewriting List the play's memorable scenes, circling those that fit Bradley's description. Based on this list, decide whether you agree with the criticism. Then, determine the effect of the connection between darkness and the play's theme.

Drafting Introduce the drama and the quotation. Then, choose two or three key scenes to analyze. As you draft, refer to specific characters, settings, or events to make your argument.

Model: Including References and Citations

The play begins in the darkness of a thunderstorm—the stage is lit only by the flash of lightning. Three witches appear, chanting. "When shall we three meet again?/In thunder, lightning, or in rain?" (I, i, 1-2) As the witches plan, they choose only dark weather, a perfect beginning for a play that examines the darkness of the human heart.

> A direct reference to dialogue strengthens the analysis. Parenthetical citations indicate act, scene, and line numbers.

Revising Review your draft to ensure you have developed an analysis of each scene. If necessary, revise your conclusion to clearly address the effectiveness of darkness in the play.

WG Prentice Hall Writing and Grammar Connection: Chapter 14, Section 2

Extension Activities

Listening and Speaking With a group, cover the battle described in Act V for radio in a **battle-field report.**

- Use vivid images and figurative language.
- Include battlefield interviews.

After agreeing on a sequence of battlefield descriptions and interviews, perform your coverage for the class. **[Group Activity]**

Research and Technology Research some of the many books on Shakespearean tragedy, and produce an **annotated bibliography.** Next to each entry, briefly describe the source and evaluate its reliability.

 Take It to the Net   www.phschool.com

Go online for an additional research activity using the Internet.

CONNECTIONS
Literature Past and Present
What Makes a Tragedy?

Shakespeare did not invent tragedy, though *Macbeth* is one of the best-known tragedies. The honor of creating this literary form goes to the ancient Greeks. Tragedy may have evolved from the festivals they held honoring the god Dionysus, who ruled the grape harvest and the production of wine.

A Recipe for Tragedy The destruction of a noble character as a result of his or her choices is an essential ingredient of tragedy, whether Greek or Elizabethan. In the ancient Greek tragedy *Oedipus the King,* Oedipus, like Macbeth, is an aristocrat who comes to grief through his own actions. Unlike Macbeth, who chooses to transgress the social order, Oedipus acts with the best intentions. He is blind to his own crimes. Oedipus' blindness suggests that for the Greeks, tragedy is fundamental to human existence and is not merely the product of a character flaw.

The Tragic Message Tragedy shows us a powerful personality confronting the limits of life—facing the fact that we do not control circumstances or the outcome of our actions. In the destruction of the tragic hero, tragedy celebrates this conflict between action and fate. It affirms and finds a kind of joy in the contradictions of life.

Oedipus the King Oedipus is perhaps the most famous tragic hero. Abandoned as an infant because of a prophecy, he has unwittingly killed his father, King Laius. After saving the city of Thebes from a monster, the Sphinx, Oedipus is rewarded with the Theban crown and marriage to Queen Jocasta, who is actually his mother. These unintended crimes—the murder and marriage—have brought a plague on Thebes. In this scene from the play, Oedipus does not yet know what he has done.

from Oedipus The King

Sophocles *Translated by David Grene*

PART I

[**SCENE:** *In front of the palace of Oedipus at Thebes. To the right of the stage near the altar stands the priest with a crowd of children. Oedipus emerges from the central door.*]

    OEDIPUS. Children, young sons and daughters of old Cadmus,[1]
      why do you sit here with your suppliant crowns?[2]
      The town is heavy with a mingled burden
      of sounds and smells, of groans and hymns and incense;
5   I did not think it fit that I should hear
      of this from messengers but came myself,—
      I Oedipus whom all men call the Great.

                             [*He turns to the* PRIEST.]

      You're old and they are young; come, speak for them.
      What do you fear or want, that you sit here
10 suppliant? Indeed I'm willing to give all
      that you may need; I would be very hard
      should I not pity suppliants like these.

    PRIEST. O ruler of my country, Oedipus,
      you see our company around the altar;
15 you see our ages; some of us, like these,
      who cannot yet fly far, and some of us
      heavy with age; these children are the chosen
      among the young, and I the priest of Zeus.
      Within the market place sit others crowned
20 with suppliant garlands,[3] at the double shrine
      of Pallas[4] and the temple where Ismenus
      gives oracles by fire.[5] King, you yourself
      have seen our city reeling like a wreck
      already; it can scarcely lift its prow
25 out of the depths, out of the bloody surf.
      A blight is on the fruitful plants of the earth,
      a blight is on the cattle in the fields,

Thematic Connection

How does *Macbeth* also use images of natural disaster to express the significance of the hero's crime?

✔**Reading Check**

Why has the priest come to talk to Oedipus?

---

1. **Cadmus** (kad´ məs) mythical founder of Thebes, a city in central Greece.
2. **suppliant** (sup´ lē ənt) **crowns** wreaths worn by people who ask favors of the gods.
3. **suppliant garlands** branches wound in wool that were placed on the altar and left there until the suppliant's request was granted.
4. **double shrine of Pallas** two temples of Athena.
5. **temple where Ismenus / gives oracles by fire** temple of Apollo, located by the Ismenus River, where the priests foretold the future from the ashes of sacrifices.

a blight is on our women that no children
are born to them; a God that carries fire,
30   a deadly pestilence,[6] is on our town,
strikes us and spares not, and the house of Cadmus
is emptied of its people while black Death
grows rich in groaning and in lamentation.[7]
We have not come as suppliants to this altar
35   because we thought of you as of a God,
but rather judging you the first of men
in all the chances of this life and when
we mortals have to do with more than man.
You came and by your coming saved our city,
40   freed us from tribute which we paid of old
to the Sphinx,[8] cruel singer. This you did
in virtue of no knowledge we could give you,
in virtue of no teaching; it was God
that aided you, men say, and you are held
45   with God's assistance to have saved our lives.
Now Oedipus, Greatest in all men's eyes,
here falling at your feet we all entreat you,
find us some strength for rescue.
Perhaps you'll hear a wise word from some God
50   perhaps you will learn something from a man
(for I have seen that for the skilled of practice
the outcome of their counsels live the most).
Noblest of men, go, and raise up our city,
go,—and give heed. For now this land of ours
55   calls you its savior since you saved it once.
So, let us never speak about your reign
as of a time when first our feet were set
secure on high, but later fell to ruin.
Raise up our city, save it and raise it up.
60   Once you have brought us luck with happy omen;
be no less now in fortune.
If you will rule this land, as now you rule it,
better to rule it full of men than empty.
For neither tower nor ship is anything
65   when empty, and none live in it together.

    OEDIPUS. I pity you, children. You have come full of longing,
but I have known the story before you told it

---

6. **pestilence** (pes´ tə ləns) *n.* fatal, contagious disease of epidemic proportions.
7. **lamentation** (lam´ ən tā´ shən) *n.* act of expressing deep sorrow and grief.
8. **Sphinx** (sfiŋks) *n.* winged female monster with the head of a woman and the body of
a lion. She ate Theban men who could not answer her riddle: "What is it that walks
on four legs at dawn, two legs at midday, and three legs in the evening, and has
only one voice; when it walks on most feet, it is weakest?" By answering the riddle
correctly—"Man, who crawls in infancy, walks upright in his prime, and leans on a
cane in old age"—Oedipus saved Thebes and became its king.

Thematic Connection
Explain how both
Sophocles here and
Shakespeare in *Macbeth*
establish their heroes'
credentials.

only too well. I know you are all sick,
yet there is not one of you, sick though you are,
70 that is as sick as I myself.
Your several sorrows each have single scope
and touch but one of you. My spirit groans
for city and myself and you at once.
You have not roused me like a man from sleep;
75 know that I have given many tears to this,
gone many ways wandering in thought,
but as I thought I found only one remedy
and that I took. I sent Menoeceus' son
Creon, Jocasta's brother, to Apollo,
80 to his Pythian temple,[9]
that he might learn there by what act or word
I could save this city. As I count the days,
it vexes me what ails him; he is gone
far longer than he needed for the journey.
85 But when he comes, then, may I prove a villain,
if I shall not do all the God commands.

PRIEST. Thanks for your gracious words. Your servants here
signal that Creon is this moment coming.

OEDIPUS. His face is bright. O holy Lord Apollo,
90 grant that his news too may be bright for us and bring us safety.

PRIEST. It is happy news,
I think, for else his head would not be crowned
with sprigs of fruitful laurel.[10]

OEDIPUS.   We will know soon,
he's within hail. Lord Creon, my good brother,
95 what is the word you bring us from the God?

[CREON enters.]

CREON. A good word,—for things hard to bear themselves
if in the final issue all is well I count complete good fortune.

OEDIPUS. What do you mean?
What you have said so far
100 leaves me uncertain whether to trust or fear.

CREON. If you will hear my news before these others
I am ready to speak, or else to go within.

OEDIPUS. Speak it to all;
the grief I bear, I bear it more for these
105 than for my own heart.

---

9. **Pythian** (pith′ ē ən) **temple** shrine of Apollo at Delphi, below Mount Parnassus in
central Greece.
10. **sprigs of fruitful laurel** laurel symbolized triumph; a crown of laurel signified
good news.

Thematic Connection
Contrast Oedipus'
attitude towards political
power with Macbeth's.

Reading Check

What is Oedipus'
response to the priest's
request?

CREON. I will tell you, then, what I heard from the God.
King Phoebus[11] in plain words commanded us
to drive out a pollution from our land,
pollution grown ingrained within the land;
110   drive it out, said the God, not cherish it, till it's past cure.

OEDIPUS. What is the rite
of purification? How shall it be done?

CREON. By banishing a man, or expiation[12]
of blood by blood, since it is murder guilt
115   which holds our city in this destroying storm.

OEDIPUS. Who is this man whose fate the God pronounces?

CREON. My Lord, before you piloted the state
we had a king called Laius.

OEDIPUS. I know of him by hearsay. I have not seen him.

120 **CREON.** The God commanded clearly: let some one
punish with force this dead man's murderers.

OEDIPUS. Where are they in the world? Where would a trace
of this old crime be found? It would be hard to guess where.

CREON. The clue is in this land;
125   that which is sought is found;
the unheeded thing escapes:
so said the God.

OEDIPUS.   Was it at home,
or in the country that death came upon him,
or in another country traveling?

130 **CREON.** He went, he said himself, upon an embassy,
but never returned when he set out from home.

OEDIPUS. Was there no messenger, no fellow traveller
who knew what happened? Such a one might tell
something of use.

135 **CREON.** They were all killed save one. He fled in terror
and he could tell us nothing in clear terms
of what he knew, nothing, but one thing only.

OEDIPUS. What was it?
If we could even find a slim beginning
140   in which to hope, we might discover much.

CREON. This man said that the robbers they encountered
were many and the hands that did the murder
were many; it was no man's single power.

Thematic Connection
Oedipus' words in lines 122–123 have more meaning than he knows—he himself is the murderer he asks about. Compare this double meaning with the double meaning of the witches' prophecies in *Macbeth*.

---

11. **King Phoebus** (fē´ bəs) Apollo, god of sun.
12. **expiation** (eks´ pē ā´ shən) *n.* Act of making amends for wrongdoing.

OEDIPUS. How could a robber dare a deed like this
145 were he not helped with money from the city,
money and treachery?[13]

CREON.   That indeed was thought.
But Laius was dead and in our trouble
there was none to help.

OEDIPUS. What trouble was so great to hinder you
150 inquiring out the murder of your king?

CREON. The riddling Sphinx induced[14] us to neglect
mysterious crimes and rather seek solution
of troubles at our feet.

OEDIPUS. I will bring this to light again. King Phoebus
155 fittingly took this care about the dead,
and you too fittingly.
And justly you will see in me an ally,
a champion of my country and the God.
For when I drive pollution from the land
160 I will not serve a distant friend's advantage,
but act in my own interest. Whoever
he was that killed the king may readily
wish to dispatch me with his murderous hand;
so helping the dead king I help myself.
165 Come, children, take your suppliant boughs and go;
up from the altars now. Call the assembly
and let it meet upon the understanding
that I'll do everything. God will decide
whether we prosper or remain in sorrow.

170 **PRIEST.** Rise, children—it was this we came to seek,
which of himself the king now offers us.
May Phoebus who gave us the oracle
come to our rescue and stay the plague.

[*Exeunt all but the* CHORUS.]

---

13. **treachery** (trech′ ər ē) *n.* disloyalty or treason.
14. **induced** (in do͞ost′) *v.* persuaded; caused.

Connecting Literature Past and Present

1. In this scene from *Oedipus the King*, is there any evidence of the tension between fate and intention? Explain.
2. Compare the role of the witches in Act I of *Macbeth* with that of Apollo's spokespersons, the priest and Creon, in this scene from *Oedipus the King*.

Sophocles

Sophocles
(*c.* 496–406 B.C.)

Sophocles' life paralleled the splendid rise and tragic fall of fifth-century B.C. Athens. As a young man, he performed in a public celebration of Athens' great naval victory over the Persians at Salamis. He died only two years before Athens surrendered to Sparta in the Peloponnesian War.

Sophocles' life also corresponded with the rise and fall of the Golden Age of Greek tragedy. His career as a dramatist began in 468 B.C., when he entered an annual theatrical competition and defeated the brilliant established playwright Aeschylus. Over the next sixty-two years, Sophocles wrote more than 120 plays. Unfortunately, only seven of his plays have survived, *Oedipus the King* among them.

Writing About Literature

Compare and Contrast Literary Trends

In literature of the Renaissance, writing often celebrated formal techniques. Readers found beauty and satisfaction in a well-crafted poem with wittily presented sentiments. Although the simplest way to share an idea or feeling is to state it directly, the popular writing styles of the Renaissance featured indirect, ornate statements. They relied on conventions: standard forms, subjects, comparisons, and references. How well did Renaissance writers express experience within these constraints? Write an essay on this topic, completing the assignment described in the yellow box, reviewing and analyzing the selections in this unit.

Prewriting

Find a focus. First, you need to select the two works you will compare and contrast. You can use charts like the pair shown here to take notes on works or passages you have read. Use these questions to help you categorize the writing:

● What formal conventions or styles is the writer following?

● What ideas or thoughts does the writer want to express?

● What is the main goal of the writing: formal beauty and wit or direct communication? How can you tell?

Model: Categorizing to Select Works to Compare

Writing That Emphasizes Form and Style	Writing That Emphasizes Direct Communication
Sidney, Sonnet 31 Creates clever lyrical images within the sonnet form	**Shakespeare, Sonnet 130** Uses direct language and challenges conventional compliments
Spenser, Sonnet 1 Uses complex language and rigid form	**The Parable of the Prodigal Son** Uses direct language to tell a moral story

Gather details. After you select two works, read them together to find the most important similarities and differences. You might use a Venn diagram to collect your ideas. Use the criteria in the assignment—the contrast between crafted writing and direct statements—to guide you.

Test your ideas. Once you have selected and reviewed two works, test your ideas about them. Look for details in each that would permit you to categorize them differently.

Write a working thesis. Your thesis should connect the works you have chosen with the contrast in the assignment. Writing your thesis statement early will help you focus on key distinctions between works.

Read to Write

Think about the writer's motivation as you reread the texts. Did the writer want to dazzle an audience with gorgeous language or express a personal or moral idea?

Drafting

Prepare an outline. Preparing a detailed outline can help you organize your comments and guide your first draft. Each subsection of your outline can become a single, focused paragraph.

> ### Model: Making a Detailed Outline
>
> **C.** Shakespeare's "Sonnet 130" uses conventional form, but turns conventional compliments upside down to create a direct statement.
>   **1.** follows rigid sonnet form
>   **2.** but uses simple, direct language
>   **a.** "the breath that from my mistress reeks"
>   **b.** "black wires grow on her head"

Cite specific examples. Your essay will be more effective if you use quotations from the works you are comparing. Choose examples that make the contrast between the two works clear. Read your quotations aloud to make sure they support your analysis.

Revising and Editing

Review content: Test logical connections. Make sure that your ideas flow logically within each sentence and each paragraph, and within the essay as a whole. Check the connections in your comparison to be sure that every link in your analysis is sensible.

> **Illogical connection:** In this sonnet, Shakespeare pokes fun at poetic conventions, but he concludes with a direct expression of love.
>
> **Logical connection:** In this sonnet, Shakespeare pokes fun at poetic conventions, but he then shows the true power of poetry by concluding with a poetic yet believable, direct expression of love.

Review style: Vary sentence length. Using a variety of sentence lengths builds interest and flow. You might look for paragraphs that include only long sentences. In such cases, add a short, emphatic sentence to grab your readers' attention.

Publishing and Presenting

Prepare a dramatic presentation. Rehearse readings of the two works you chose to compare. Direct performers to emphasize the qualities you discuss in your essay. After the presentation, share your analysis.

W͟G Prentice Hall Writing and Grammar Connection: Chapter 14

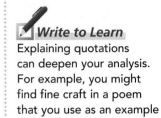
Write to Learn
Explaining quotations can deepen your analysis. For example, you might find fine craft in a poem that you use as an example of direct communication.

Write to Explain
Remember to explain your reason for including each quotation—do not just quote a line and expect your readers to understand why you included it.

Writing WORKSHOP

Persuasion: Persuasive Essay

A **persuasive essay** is a work in which the writer presents a case for or against some position. In this workshop, you will write a composition persuading your audience to accept your viewpoint on a subject and take some action.

Assignment Criteria Your persuasive essay should include the following elements:

- An issue of concern or importance to you
- A clear statement of your position and the action you want taken
- Support for the position, including clearly organized facts, examples, and statistics
- An understanding of the knowledge level, experiences, needs, and concerns of your intended audience
- Language and arguments that are fair but convincing

To preview the criteria on which your persuasive essay may be assessed, see the Rubric on page 403.

Prewriting

Choose a topic. Select a topic on which you not only have a strong opinion but that you can support with several convincing reasons, facts, and examples. If necessary, conduct a **news scan.** Read newspapers or listen to newsbroadcasts to learn about current issues. Political controversies as well as decisions affecting school life are potential topic sources. Avoid issues on which your only opinion is "I like (or dislike)—" in favor of those on which you can take a clearly articulated stand.

> **Weak:** I really dislike the proposed changes to update the mall.
>
> **Better:** Rather than piecemeal projects, our community needs a coherent revitalization plan.

Determine the purpose and audience. Successful persuasion involves focusing on the change you want to effect and using arguments that will convince your particular audience. Spend time defining your purpose so that your goal is reasonable. Then, match your arguments to your audience.

Do the research. Gather facts to support your arguments. Use libraries, the Internet, personal interviews, or other resources. Make note also of any facts that contradict your position, so you can prepare counterarguments.

Focusing on Purpose and Audience		
Specific Purpose	**Audience**	**Arguments to Convince This Audience**
To persuade seniors to apply early to college	Seniors at my school	• Choosing early admissions may improve your chances of acceptance. • Applications will just hang over your head if you delay.

Student Model

Before you begin drafting your persuasive essay, read this student model and review the characteristics of a persuasive composition.

Jason Heflin
Lakeland, FL

Not Now, but Right Now!

It sneaks up on you at all hours of the day or night, a floating cloud of angst. Suddenly, a feeling bubbles up from the pit of your stomach, an achy, acidic feeling of panic. "Which college is the right college? Can I get in? And how will I afford tuition, books, food, and housing?" These fears are definitely part of your senior year experience, but two simple words hold the secret to reduced stress: Apply early. It is as simple as that. Apply early, both for college admission and scholarships, and you will sleep easier at night.

Think for a moment of how the college admissions process works. Like a thousand cattle trying to pass through the same gate at once, vast numbers of people across the nation apply each year for a limited number of places at colleges. Academic records of applicants aside, admissions boards work on a first come, first served basis. The longer you wait to apply, the less likely you are to make the cut, no matter how qualified you may be.

Now think for a moment of how the scholarship application process works. Even if you are lucky enough to land a spot in a college, you still have to pay for it, and college costs are steadily rising. Funds are available from corporations, foundations, and colleges, but you must compete for them, and you must act quickly. All scholarships have important deadlines to meet. Due to the high volume of candidates, scholarship foundations can easily afford to disqualify someone who has failed to fulfill all criteria, however minor. A late scholarship application has almost no chance whatsoever. And without financial aid, college is out of reach for all but the richest students.

The modern world places so much importance on attending college that uncertainty about acceptance and funding can lead to overwhelming stress. An enormous weight is lifted from your shoulders once you can say, "I know where I am going to college, and I know how I am going to pay for it."

Your senior year is a time of closing chapters, a time to enjoy the last days at home with friends and family, a time to remember the joys of childhood and adolescence before jumping into the great unknown, adulthood. Waiting until January to apply for college is like leaping blindly, without a net. Take some pressure off yourself by getting applications in on time or, better yet, early. With just two simple words in mind, you can enjoy the bittersweet pleasures of the last year of high school in peace: Apply early.

Jason has selected a topic of concern to himself and his audience.

In his introduction, Jason clearly states his position and the action he recommends.

The vivid language of this image helps readers grasp and appreciate Jason's point.

Jason uses clearly organized facts to support his position.

Jason concludes strongly, showing his grasp of the experiences and concerns of his readers.

Drafting

Give your position maximum impact. Present your view on the issue in your first paragraph. You might want to build up to your view, stating it in the final sentence of the paragraph.

Elaborate with strong arguments and appeals. Use arguments of these types:

- **Inductive reasoning:** Specific facts used to lead to a general truth.
- **Deductive reasoning:** A general truth applied to a particular case.

You can use these forms of reasoning to make the following kinds of appeals:

- **Logical appeals:** If one thing happens, something else will follow.
- **Ethical appeals:** If a thing has a certain characteristic, and all things with that characteristic are good, then that thing is good.
- **Emotional appeals:** If a thing has a certain characteristic, and all things with that characteristic are horrible, then you should reject that thing.

Call for action. Conclude your essay with a clear call for action, a statement of what you want done.

Revising

Revise to strengthen the language. Strengthen your arguments by improving the way you state ideas.

1. Highlight passages that are vague or lack force.

2. On a self-sticking note, jot down a sentence summarizing your point in each passage. Stick the note next to the passage.

3. Review your flags, and brainstorm for charged words, vivid images and dramatic analogies to help you make your points.

4. Include effective new ideas in your draft.

Developing Opening Paragraphs

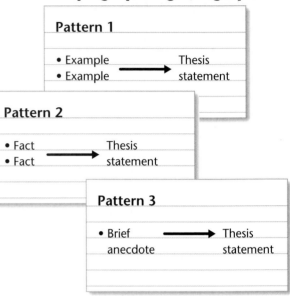

Pattern 1

- Example
- Example → Thesis statement

Pattern 2

- Fact
- Fact → Thesis statement

Pattern 3

- Brief anecdote → Thesis statement

Many people apply at the same time, so competition is fierce.
Images, analogies: *Race, stampede, cattle run.*

Model: Strengthening Language

Like a thousand cattle trying to pass through the same gate at once, vast numbers of people across the nation apply each year for a limited number of places at colleges.

Think for a moment of how the college admissions process works. ~~Getting in can be tough.~~ Academic records of applicants aside, admissions boards work on a first come, first served basis.

Jason replaced a vague phrase with a vivid analogy.

Revise for parallel structure. Review your draft for concepts that are related or contrasting. Consider expressing these concepts using parallelism, the expression of related ideas in similar grammatic structures.

Not parallel: . . . a place for meeting and shopping. People could also have lunch there. . . .

Parallel: . . . a place to meet, to shop, and to have lunch.

Compare the model and nonmodel. Why is the model more effective?

Nonmodel	Model
As you wait to apply, your chances of making the cut are going down, no matter how qualified you may be.	The longer you wait to apply, the less likely you are to make the cut, no matter how qualified you may be.

Publishing and Presenting

Present your persuasive essay orally. Use your essay as the basis of an oral presentation. Follow these suggestions:

- Rehearse reading your essay in front of a friend or family member so you can learn to present it in a natural way.
- As you read, think of the role you are playing—that of a dynamic, persuasive speaker. Do not *read* your speech word by word, but "speak" it in a natural manner.
- Speak clearly, changing the rate, pitch, and tone of your voice as needed. For instance, slowing down dramatically as you state your main point is an effective way of drawing an audience in.
- If gestures feel natural to you, use them occasionally for emphasis.

W̶G Prentice Hall Writing and Grammar Connection: Chapter 7

Rubric for Self-Assessment

Evaluate your narrative using the following criteria and rating scale:

Criteria	Rating Scale				
	Not very				Very
How clearly is your position stated?	1	2	3	4	5
How effective and well-organized is your support for your position?	1	2	3	4	5
How well are your arguments reasoned?	1	2	3	4	5
How appropriately do your arguments and examples fit your audience and purpose?	1	2	3	4	5
How strong and fair are the language and arguments you have used?	1	2	3	4	5

Listening and Speaking WORKSHOP

Analyzing Advertising

A television commercial may last only thirty seconds, but it is packed with enticements and factual claims. A commercial is a kind of **advertisement,** a persuasive message in print or in broadcast form, sponsored by an individual or a group to achieve a goal, such as selling a product or persuading people to adopt an opinion. To **analyze an advertisement,** identify the key persuasive elements it contains, following the steps outlined here.

Taking an Advertisement Apart

To analyze an advertisement, identify the following key elements:

● **Concept**—central theme of the ad; for instance, that a specific toothpaste will improve the user's popularity

● **Hook**—a memorable or catchy jingle or slogan

● **Charged language**—words that imply a certain view of the product; for instance, *efficient, cool, fabulous*

● **Characterization**—the creation of memorable, sympathetic, odd, or repulsive characters

● **Special effects**—visual and sound effects used to grab viewer attention

Interpreting Its Meaning

To understand how these elements are intended to work in the advertisement, ask yourself the following questions. For each answer you give, identify the elements—concept, hook, language, characters, or effects—that support your answer.

● Who is the targeted audience of this advertisement?

● What is the message of this ad?

● What is the overall mood of the commercial? Is it exciting, scary, or funny?

● Is the viewer expected to identify or sympathize with the characters or to reject or condemn them?

● What cultural values (generosity, sharing, winning) are illustrated in the ad?

Sum up your analysis by answering this question: How does the ad use persuasive elements to send its message?

 **Activity:** View and Analyze — Compare and contrast two commercials using the questions listed above. Use a chart like the one shown to guide your analysis.

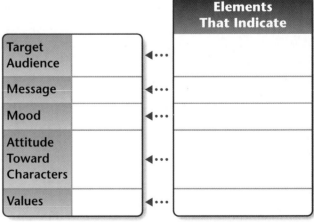

		Elements That Indicate
Target Audience		
Message		
Mood		
Attitude Toward Characters		
Values		

On certain tests, you are required to recognize forms of propaganda and to distinguish between fact and opinion. Use the following strategies to help you answer questions testing these skills:

- As you read, remember that a propaganda statement is one that distorts or conceals facts and manipulates emotions to advance a particular cause.
- Realize that charged language, exaggeration, and name-calling are tactics often used in propaganda to manipulate opinion.

Test-Taking Strategies

- Question the significance and validity of claims made in the passage.
- Look for symbols—highly positive or negative images—used to influence your opinions.

Sample Test Item

Directions: Read the passage, and answer the question that follows.

(1) More than 5,000 people voted last week in favor of building a new shopping center, but the opposition won out.
(2) The margin of victory is irrelevant.
(3) Those radical voters who opposed the center are obviously self-serving elitists who do not care about anyone but themselves. (4) This month's unemployment figures for Braden are 12 percent, which represents an increase of some 3 percent over the figures for last year. (5) These figures mean that unemployment in Braden is worsening. (6) But the people who voted against the mall probably do not care about creating new jobs.

1. Which of the statements can be labeled as propaganda?

   A Statements 1, 2, 6

   B Statements 2, 5

   C Statements 2, 3, 6

   D Statements 2, 4

Answer and Explanation

The correct answer is *C.* Statements 1 and 4 state facts. Statement 5 is supported by the facts in the selection. Statements 2, 3, and 6 are propaganda because they use exaggeration and name-calling unjustified by the facts cited.

Practice

Directions: Read the passage, and answer the questions that follow.

(1) The first new Tiger automobiles rolled off the assembly line at the Dearborn assembly plant on Monday.
(2) The cars, which feature such luxury appointments as programmable destination mapping, retail at $48,000 each.
(3) Nothing compares with the Tiger's luxury. (4) Tigers are available in 17 colors, ranging from Dark Midnight to Dazzle Red. (5) And they offer 37 percent better gas mileage over last year's model.
(6) When you are behind the wheel of a Tiger, you are the envy of every driver on the road.

1. Which statements might be considered propaganda?

   A Statement 1

   B Statements 4, 5

   C Statements 2, 4

   D Statements 3, 6

2. The purpose of Statement 5 is to

   A state a fact.

   B conceal a fact.

   C inspire desire.

   D state an opinion.

King Charles I After the Battle of Naseby, (June 14, 1645)

" *Methinks I see in
my mind a noble . . .
nation rousing herself
like a strong man
after sleep, and shaking
her invincible locks.* "

—John Milton,
from *Areopagitica*

Timeline 1625–1798

British Events

- **1627** Sir Francis Bacon publishes *The New Atlantis*. ▼

- **1628** William Harvey explains blood circulation.
- **1633** John Donne's *Songs and Sonnets* published.
- **1635** Public mail service established.
- **1638** John Milton publishes *Lycidas*.

- **1640** Charles I summons Long Parliament.
- **1642** English Civil War begins.
- **1642** Puritans close theaters.
- **1646** John Suckling publishes *Fragmenta Aurea*.
- **1647** George Fox founds Society of Friends (Quakers).
- **1648** Robert Herrick publishes *Hesperides*.
- **1649** Charles I beheaded.
- **1649** Richard Lovelace publishes *Lucasta*.
- **c. 1650** Early newspaper ads appear.
- **c. 1650** Full-bottomed wigs come into fashion.
- **1653** Oliver Cromwell becomes Lord Protector.

- **1658** Oliver Cromwell dies.
- **1658** Puritan government collapses.
- **1660** Monarchy restored.
- **1660** Theaters reopened.
- **1660** Samuel Pepys begins *Diary*.
- **1662** Royal Society chartered.
- **1663** Drury Lane Theater opens.
- **1666** Great Fire of London.
- **1667** John Milton's *Paradise Lost* published. ▲
- **1668** John Dryden publishes *An Essay of Dramatic Poesy*.

World Events

- **c. 1600** Japan: Kabuki theater developed. ▼

- **1614** North America: Dutch found New Amsterdam.

- **1640** India: English settlement established at Madras.
- **1640** North America: *Bay Psalm Book* published in Massachusetts.
- **1642** Holland: Rembrandt paints *The Nightwatch*.
- **1643** France: Louis XIV becomes king.
- **1644** China: Ming Dynasty ends.
- **1650** North America: Anne Bradstreet's collection of poems *The Tenth Muse Lately Sprung Up in America* published.
- **1651** North America: William Bradford finishes *Of Plymouth Plantation*.

- **1662** France: Louis XIV begins building palace at Versailles. ▼
- **1664** North America: Britain seizes New Netherlands.
- **1664** France: Molière's *Tartuffe* first produced.
- **1666** Italy: Stradivari labels first violin.

British and World Events

- **1685** James II becomes king.
- **1687** Sir Isaac Newton publishes his *Principia*.
- **1688** Glorious Revolution.
- **1689** Bill of Rights becomes law.
- **1690** John Locke publishes his *Two Treatises of Government*. ▼

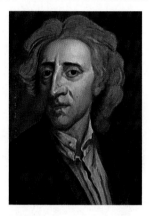

- **1702** First daily newspaper begins publication.
- **1707** Great Britain created by Act of Union.

- **1712 Alexander Pope** publishes *The Rape of the Lock*.
- **1714** George I becomes king.
- **1719** First organized cricket match takes place. ▲
- **1719 Daniel Defo**e publishes *Robinson Crusoe*.
- **1726 Jonathan Swift** publishes *Gulliver's Travels*.
- **1735** William Hogarth paints *The Rake's Progress*.
- **1745** Last Jacobite rebellion in Scotland.
- **1749** Henry Fielding publishes *Tom Jones*.
- **1751 Thomas Gray** publishes "Elegy in a Country Churchyard."

- **1755 Samuel Johnson** publishes *Dictionary of the English Language.*
- **1756** Britain enters Seven Years' War.
- **1775** Actress Sarah Siddons debuts at Drury Lane Theater. ▼

- **1791 James Boswell** publishes *The Life of Samuel Johnson.*
- **1793** England goes to war with France.

- **1680** Dodo becomes extinct.
- **1682** North America: La Salle claims Louisiana for France.
- **1684** China: All ports open to foreign trade.
- **1685** France: Louis XIV revokes Edict of Nantes, provoking persecution of Protestants.
- **1690** India: Calcutta founded by British.
- **1703** Russia: Peter the Great begins building St. Petersburg.

- **1715** France: Louis XV succeeds to throne.
- **1721** Germany: Bach composes *Brandenburg Concertos*. ▶
- **1727** Brazil: First coffee planted.
- **1740** Prussia: Frederick the Great succeeds to the throne.
- **1748** France: Montesquieu publishes *The Spirit of the Laws*.
- **1752** North America: Benjamin Franklin invents lightning rod.

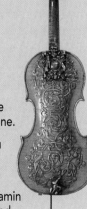

- **1759** Canada: British troops capture Quebec.
- **1773** North America: Boston Tea Party.
- **1775** North America: American Revolution begins.
- **1784** France: First school for the blind established.
- **1789** France: Revolution begins with storming of the Bastille.

A Turbulent Time:

THE SEVENTEENTH AND EIGHTEENTH CENTURIES (1625–1798)

Historical Background

In 1649, the English shocked the world by beheading their king and abolishing the monarchy. In the decades before civil wars tore England apart, revolutions in science and religion had already unsettled people's worldview. The new astronomy had exiled the Earth from the center of the universe to the vastness of infinite space. New religious creeds had altered or abolished the traditions of centuries. John Donne wrote, with his newfound insecurity, "Tis all in pieces, all coherence gone." By the 1700s, though, a monarch was back on the throne, and a new, competitive society had sprung up, with a looser social structure and greater freedom in religion and politics.

▲ Critical Viewing
(a) Describe the style in which Charles's execution is rendered in this picture. (b) How would the mood of the picture and your sense of the event be different if the picture were more realistic? [Interpret]

Charles I and Parliament Charles I, crowned in 1625, frequently clashed with Parliament over money. King Charles needed money for his wars, and Parliament refused to fund them. The king then extorted loans from his wealthy subjects and pressed the poor into service as soldiers and sailors. Parliament tried to prevent such abuses of power, so Charles eventually dissolved Parliament and would not call it into session for eleven years.

Charles I also turned up the flame under a simmering religious controversy. He insisted that clergymen "conform," or observe all the ceremonies of the Anglican Church. Puritans—Calvinists who wished to purify the Church of its Catholic traditions—were enraged by some of these requirements. Radical Puritans believed that each group of worshipers, moved by the members' divinely granted consciences, had the right to choose its own minister—an idea dangerously close to democracy. For these and other ideas, "dissenters" were persecuted and tortured as criminals.

The Civil War Charles's problems grew worse after he was forced to fight Scottish rebels outraged by his insistence on religious conformity. Desperate for money, he summoned a hostile Parliament, which passed wave upon wave of reforms. Angered when Charles tried to outmaneuver the reformers, Parliament condemned him as a tyrant in 1642. Civil war broke out. In 1645, Parliament's forces, led by Oliver Cromwell, defeated the royalist army and, in 1647, took Charles as a prisoner. Radical Puritans, who by then dominated Parliament, tried the king and convicted him of treason. Charles I was beheaded on January 30, 1649.

Cromwell led the new government, called the English Commonwealth. Facing discontent at home and wars abroad, he dissolved Parliament in 1653 and named himself Lord Protector. Until his death in 1658, he ruled as a virtual dictator.

Civil war had not led to the free society that many who had fought against the king expected. Their hopes, coupled with economic hardships, brought unrest. The Commonwealth also fueled discontent by outlawing gambling, horse racing, newspapers, fancy clothes, public dancing, and the theater.

The Restoration By the time of Cromwell's death, England had had enough of taxation, violence, and disorder. Two chaotic years later, Parliament offered the crown to the exiled son of Charles I, who became Charles II in 1660. The monarchy was restored.

In sharp contrast to the drab Puritan leaders, Charles II and his court copied the plush fashions of Paris. An avid patron of the arts and sciences, Charles invited Italian composers and Dutch painters to live and work in London.

Point/Counterpoint

Royal Victim or Devious King?

Was Charles I at least partly a victim of circumstances, or was he a schemer whose plotting backfired and led to his own downfall? Two scholars disagree about this question.

Royal Victim "We may perhaps set aside the personal appeal which the royal martyr and sainted cavalier has always made, but we should not forget that all along he had had a large share of legality, if not of equity, honesty, and intelligence, on his side. And the king lacked not only revenue but a national civil service, a solid framework of royal authority . . . we cannot . . . idealize the Long Parliament as an assembly of political Galahads, and the behavior of the victorious army . . . was scarcely in accord with the doctrine of the supremacy of law for which they had fought."
—**Douglas Bush**, *English Literature in the Earlier Seventeenth Century*

Devious King "Cromwell and his associates negotiated seriously with the king to preserve the monarchy and the changes that had been accomplished. Charles invariably eluded them, reaching a peak of deviousness when he agreed to accept a presbyterian church and so launched the Scots against the English in the second Civil War in 1648. Cromwell . . . finally came to believe that it was necessary to get rid of Charles Stuart . . . and Charles was seized and brought to trial . . . He was convicted on the charge of high treason against the state and executed on January 30, 1649."
—**R. K. Webb**, "Elizabethans and Puritans," *The Columbia History of the World*

European Political Thinkers

Thinker	Major Ideas	Quotation
Thomas Hobbes *Leviathan* (1651) 	People are driven by selfishness and greed. To avoid chaos, they give up their freedom to a government that will ensure order. Such a government must be strong and able to suppress rebellion.	"The condition of man [in the state of nature] . . . is a condition of war of everyone against everyone."
John Locke *Two Treatises of Government* (1690)	People have a natural right to life, liberty, and property. Rulers have a responsibility to protect those rights. People have the right to change a government that fails to do so.	"Men being . . . by nature all free, equal, and independent, no one can be put out of this estate and subjected to the political power of another without his own consent."
Baron de Montesquieu *The Spirit of the Laws* (1748)	The powers of government should be separated into executive, legislative, and judicial branches, to prevent any one group from gaining too much power.	"In order to have . . . liberty, it is necessary that government be set up so that one man need not be afraid of another."

◀ **Critical Viewing**
Compare Locke's and Hobbes's notions of the purpose of government.
[Read a Chart]

A Glorious Revolution Religious differences resurfaced with Charles II's successor, James II, a devout Catholic. Parliament eventually invited Mary, the Protestant daughter of James II, to rule England jointly with her husband, William of Orange. Rather than fight, James escaped to France. The people of England hailed the event as the "Glorious Revolution of 1688" because not a drop of blood had been shed.

In 1689, William and Mary agreed to respect a Bill of Rights passed by Parliament. This bill guaranteed Parliament the right to approve all taxes and forbade the monarch to suspend the law. England thus attained a limited, or constitutional, monarchy. In ensuing decades, two political factions crystallized in Parliament: the conservative, aristocratic Tories and the Whigs, drawn largely from Britain's growing merchant class. A cabinet of ministers drawn from Parliament, and eventually unified under the leadership of a prime minister, began to rule the country.

An Agricultural Revolution By the late 1600s, new farm tools made it possible for farms to produce much more food. With more food available, the population surged upward. Because fewer farmhands were needed, many people left the countryside. In the growing towns, they became the factory hands who ran the machines of the early Industrial Revolution.

The Industrial Age British inventions after 1750 made the spinning and weaving of cloth much more efficient. The steam engine was perfected and adapted to run a power loom. Factories were built to produce vast quantities of cotton cloth. Merchants sold the goods all over the world, adding more gold to the nation's coffers. As late as the 1790s, the majority of British people still earned their living as farmers. Yet, the economic revolution of the 1700s increased Britain's wealth enormously.

The Enlightenment The scientific revolution that made industry possible stemmed from a larger development in thought known as the Enlightenment. Enlightenment thinkers in all fields believed that, through reason and observation of nature, human beings could discover the order underlying all things. In 1687, Sir Isaac Newton published one of the touchstone works of the Enlightenment, a monumental study of gravity.

By 1750, Britain was rapidly industrializing and the social theories of the Enlightenment were eclipsed. Mills and factories belched smoke into the country air. Men, women, and children toiled at machines for twelve to fourteen hours a day. Poor people crowded into the towns and cities, unable to find regular work and barely able to survive. By the late 1700s, "progress" seemed to mean misery for millions. Writers and intellectuals began to lose faith in the ability of human reason to solve every problem.

Literature of the Period

The Schools of Jonson and Donne In his writing, Ben Jonson (1572–1637) strove for the perfection and harmony he found in his beloved classical authors, turning away from the ornate style of Elizabethan times to create his own modern, strong voice. He wrote poems, plays, and masques (court entertainments). His critical opinion exercised a powerful influence on other poets of the time. Among the best-known "Sons of Ben" were Robert Herrick (1591–1674), Sir John Suckling (1609–1642), and Richard Lovelace (1618–1657).

John Donne (1572–1631) pioneered a new, witty, cerebral style later known as metaphysical poetry. Metaphysical poetry is characterized by an unusual degree of intellectualism. Even Donne's love poems are frequently structured like ingenuous, subtle arguments that raid the worlds of science, law, and philosophy for surprising but strangely accurate comparisons. In "A Valediction: Forbidding Mourning," for example, he compares parted lovers to the two legs of a drawing compass. In "A Valediction: Of Weeping," he compares his tears, which reflect his lover's face, to coins that are stamped with her image.

The most notable followers of John Donne were George Herbert (1593–1633) and Andrew Marvell (1621–1678). Herbert's mother was a friend of Donne's, and in many ways the life of Herbert parallels Donne's. He keenly felt the tension between wordly ambition and religious devotion. Tempted for a time by the sparkling life at the court of James I, he later became an Anglican deacon. Herbert's best poems are the religious lyrics collected in *The Temple*. Marvell's best lyrics blend the brilliance of Donne and the classical finish of Jonson. They offer observations on nature, love, and God that, at first, seem urbane and perhaps conventional, but on closer

A Living Tradition

The Poet Laureate of Brooklyn Invokes George Herbert

Recently, D. Nurkse, the poet laureate of Brooklyn, New York, and author of *Voices Over Water* and *Leaving Xaia,* wrote a response to George Herbert's dialogue with God in *The Temple,* quoting from Herbert's poem "Love (III)"

> "At the end of the twentieth century, George Herbert's voice carries intimately from the seventeenth, pitched just above a breath, often strangely uncertain. He describes his poetry to a friend as "a picture of the many spiritual conflicts" between the soul and God. . . . Always the voice persists, hushed in fear of its own unpredictability ("Love bade me welcome: yet my soul drew back"), its strangely powerful freedom. [To] this conversation with the unknown . . . the reader is invited as a guest. . . ."

Love (III) by George Herbert

Love bade me welcome: yet my soul drew back,
　　Guilty of dust and sin.
But quick-eyed Love, observing me grow slack
　　From my first entrance in,
5　Drew nearer to me, sweetly questioning,
　　If I lacked any thing.

"A guest," I answered, "worthy to be here":
　　Love said, "You shall be he."
"I the'unkind, ungrateful? Ah my dear
10　I cannot look on thee."
Love took my hand, and smiling did reply,
　　"Who made the eyes but I?"

"Truth Lord, but I have marred° them: let my shame　　°spoiled
　　Go where it doth deserve."
15　"And know you not," says Love, "who bore the blame?"
　　"My dear, then I will serve."
"You must sit down," says Love, "and taste my meat":
　　So I did sit and eat.

Marriage à la Mode: The Marriage Contract,
1743, William Hogarth. Reproduced by
courtesy of the Trustees, National Gallery
of Art, London.

inspection, prove profound. His best-known poem, "To His Coy Mistress," is
one of the best lyrics in English literature.

The Puritan Writers Perhaps the greatest poet of the seventeenth century
was a Puritan, not a Cavalier: John Milton. The Puritan movement also produced the best-selling prose writer of the century, John Bunyan. Only the Bible
sold more copies than Bunyan's religious narrative, *The Pilgrim's Progress.*

John Milton Like Ben Jonson, John Milton (1608–1674) was a learned
disciple of the classical Greek and Latin authors. However, unlike the
Elizabethan humanists and Cavalier poets, he was also a profound Calvinist
and studied the Old Testament in Hebrew.

Milton was born in London to a prosperous middle-class family. He
received a good basic education, studied at Cambridge, and spent the next
six years reading and studying on his own. In the 1640s, as the battle between
Charles I and Parliament grew hotter, Milton began writing political pamphlets for the Puritan cause. One of his greatest contributions to the
"pamphlet wars" was *Areopagitica*, a ringing call for freedom of the press.

Milton supported the Commonwealth and Protectorate and even defended
the execution of Charles I. As Cromwell's rule turned to a dictatorship,
however, Milton lost hope in the possibility of forming a just society on
Earth. Having gone completely blind by 1652 as a result of his labors for the
Commonwealth, he set about composing an epic that would explain why
God allows suffering in this world. That epic, *Paradise Lost*, reflects Milton's
humanistic love of poetry and his Puritan devotion to God.

▲ **Critical Viewing**
In William Hogarth's
satirical *Signing the
Marriage Contract,*
the fathers of the
bride and groom
(both seated) dis-
cuss the property
the bride will give
her new husband.
What conclusions
can you draw about
the characters' atti-
tudes and Hogarth's
opinion of them?
[Draw Conclusions]

John Bunyan A tinker by trade, John Bunyan (1628–1688) had little education beyond reading the Bible. Like many others of his time, he wandered from town to town in rural England, preaching wherever people would listen. After the restoration of Charles II, Bunyan was imprisoned, and it was there that he wrote *The Pilgrim's Progress*. This allegory, in which events have a hidden meaning, relates how a man flees sin to lead a holy life.

Literature of the Age of Reason Enlightenment writers discovered the qualities they admired most—harmony, restraint, and clarity—among the writers of ancient Greece and Rome, such as Homer, Virgil, and Horace. Neoclassical writers—English writers who imitated the styles of classical writers—often referred to the myths, gods, and heroes of ancient times. They favored generalities rather than the viewpoint of the individual, displayed a fondness for satires that poked fun at society's follies, and often expressed their thoughts in aphorisms—short, quotable sentences—such as, "The proper study of mankind is man."

John Dryden From 1660 to 1700, a period known as the Restoration, John Dryden (1631–1700) dominated literature. Named poet laureate, England's official poet for life, by Charles II, he wrote plays, satirical poems, and celebratory poems that hailed the achievements of humanity. His essays about drama and his other prose compositions represent the first modern prose.

Restoration Theater The Restoration was also noted for its plays, especially its comedies. When Charles II became king, he reopened the London theaters. The Restoration theaters, fancier and more costly than those of Shakespeare's time, did a thriving business.

Alexander Pope The poetry of Alexander Pope (1688–1744), written in the early 1700s, is a shining example of neoclassical style, exhibiting wit, elegance, and moderation. All these qualities show forth in his most famous work, *The Rape of the Lock*, a satire on the war between the sexes. Pope also had enormous influence as a critic.

Jonathan Swift A close friend of Pope's, Jonathan Swift (1667–1745) was a scornful critic of England's rising merchant class, whom he viewed as shameless money-grubbers. In his great satires, *Gulliver's Travels* and *A Modest Proposal*, he presents human nature as

▼ **Critical Viewing**
Unlike Elizabethan theaters, Restoration theaters had a proscenium arch separating the stage from the audience, real changes of scenery, lighting, and female actors. How do you think these changes affected the way that theater goers experienced plays? **[Speculate]**

deeply flawed, suggesting that moral progress must begin with a recognition of our intellectual and moral limitations.

Daniel Defoe The first English novel, *Robinson Crusoe* by Daniel Defoe (1660–1731), appeared in this period. This new form of fiction would, in the 1800s, become the favorite reading matter of the growing middle classes.

Addison and Steele England's first literary periodicals, *The Tatler* and *The Spectator*, also appeared in the early 1700s. Written by Joseph Addison (1672–1719) and Richard Steele (1672–1729), these one-page papers included crisply written, reflective essays and news addressed to the middle classes.

The Age of Johnson Samuel Johnson (1709–1784) dominated his age not only with his writings but also with his conversation and acquaintanceships. A brilliant and inexhaustible talker, he befriended most of the writers, painters, and actors of his time. His wise advice helped nurture the careers of many younger talents. *The Dictionary of the English Language*, published in 1755, is his most important work. It is the first dictionary to be considered a standard and authoritative reference work on English.

The Eclipse of the Enlightenment By the late 1700s, the "progress" that had once been celebrated by Enlightenment thinkers seemed to be causing millions to suffer. As they lost faith in the power of human reason, writers turned away from the standards of neoclassicism. Writing in the language of everyday life, writers such as Thomas Gray charged their poems with fresh new emotion. The Age of Reason was coming to an end. Emerging voices would make the 1800s a new literary age.

▲ **Critical Viewing**
The landscape paintings of Richard Wilson (1714–1782) influenced the work of nineteenth-century Romantic painters such as John Constable and J.W.M. Turner. What feelings do Wilson's use of light and his choice of a vantage point inspire in you? **[Respond]**

NO HARMLESS DRUDGE, HE

BY RICHARD LEDERER

On April 15, 1755, Dr. Samuel Johnson—blind in one eye, impoverished, and incompletely educated—produced the first modern *Dictionary of the English Language*. "Languages are the pedigrees of nations," he proclaimed, and, in compiling his wordbook, Johnson conferred a pedigree on the English-speaking nations. In garnering the rich, exuberant vocabulary of eighteenth-century England, the *Dictionary of the English Language* marks a turning point in the history of our tongue.

JOHNSON'S FIRSTS

Johnson set himself the task of making a different kind of dictionary, one of the first that would include all the words in the English language, not just the difficult ones. In addition, he would show how to divide words into syllables and where words came from. He would establish a consistent system of defining words and draw from his own gigantic learning to provide, for the first time in any dictionary, illustrative quotations from famous writers. Johnson's lexicon, like its modern descendants, is a report on the way writers actually used the English language.

Underfunded and working almost alone in a Fleet Street garret room, Johnson defined some 43,000 words and illuminated their meanings with more than 114,000 supporting quotations drawn from every area of literature. Laboring for almost nine years, he captured the majesty of the English language and gave it a dignity that was long overdue.

Johnson defined a lexicographer as "a writer of dictionaries, a harmless drudge that busies himself in tracing the original and detailing the signification of words."

However, he was obviously far more than a harmless drudge, and his two-volume dictionary was by far the most comprehensive and readable that had appeared. The reputation of the *Dictionary of the English Language* was so great that it dominated the field until the turn of this century.

From Johnson's *Dictionary*

dedication. A servile address to a patron

excise. A hateful tax levied upon commodities, and adjudged not by the common judges of property, but wretches hired by those to whom excise is paid.

gambler. (A cant word, I suppose, for game, or gamster.) A knave whose practice it is to invite the unwary to game and cheat them.

opera. An exotic and irrational entertainment.

parasite. One that frequents rich tables, and earns his welcome by flattery.

patron. One who supports with insolence, and is paid with flattery.

pensioner. A slave of state hired by a stipend to obey his master. In England it is generally understood to mean pay given to a state hireling for treason to his country.

Tory. One who adheres to the ancient constitution of the state, and the apostolical hierarchy of the church of England, opposed to a whig.

whig. The name of a faction.

ACTIVITIES

1. How do the definitions in the box at left differ from those you would find in current dictionaries? For example, what can you tell about Johnson's political loyalties from his definition of Tory and Whig? What can you tell about Johnson's political opinions from his definition of *excise*?

2. Reviewing Johnson's definitions, write three definitions in his style.

3. Secure a copy from your school or local library of *Johnson's Dictionary: A Modern Selection*, edited by E. L. McAdam, Jr., and George Milne (Pantheon Books). Browse through it and report any interesting and unusual definitions to the class.

4. Research the techniques of modern dictionary makers. Then, compare and contrast their techniques with Johnson's.

The War Against Time

A Musical Garden Party, (detail), The Metropolitan Museum of Art

Prepare to Read

Works of John Donne

John Donne (1572?–1631)

Donne's life and poetry seem to fall neatly into two contradictory parts. Wild, young Jack Donne wrote clever love poems read by sophisticated aristocrats. In later life, sober Dr. John Donne, Dean of St. Paul's and the most popular preacher in England, published widely read meditations and sermons. Contradiction and conflict were the stuff of Donne's life; they are also at the heart of his poetic style. As Jack or as John, Donne the writer excelled at dramatizing—and wittily resolving—the contradictions of life.

Religious Conflict A distant relative of Sir Thomas More, Donne was raised a Catholic. In the England of Queen Elizabeth I, Catholics faced prejudice and restrictive laws. Although Donne studied at Oxford and Cambridge, he never obtained his degree, probably because of his refusal to compromise his Catholicism by swearing an oath acknowledging the supremacy of the king over the church. Later, he abandoned Catholicism and joined the official Church of England. To this day, scholars debate whether Donne experienced a genuine conversion or made a shrewd move to gain advancement in court society.

A Secret Marriage After taking part in two naval expeditions against the Spanish, Donne served as private secretary to one of the queen's highest ranking officials, Sir Thomas Egerton. Bright, clever, and charming, Donne secretly wed Anne More, his employer's niece, in 1601. Again, scholars throw doubt on Donne's motives. Some hold that he married for love; others maintain that he hoped his marriage to the daughter of an influential family would promote his career. If Donne counted on this possibility, though, he was sadly mistaken. Anne's father disapproved of the union, and so Donne's marriage temporarily ruined his chances for social advancement.

For many years, the devoted couple lived plagued by poverty and illness, in the midst of which Donne still managed to write influential poetry. He eked out a living writing religious tracts and serving as temporary secretary to several aristocrats. Donne finally attained a secure position in 1615 when, at the insistence of King James, he entered the clergy.

Success After serving as a royal chaplain, Donne became dean of St. Paul's Cathedral in London in 1621, a post he held until his death. He became one of the most popular preachers of his day. No longer the writer of sly or witty passionate verses, he published widely read sermons and religious meditations. Jack Donne's days were over, and John Donne's fame was spreading.

A Modern Individual Even after his death, John Donne's reputation has been subject to dramatic changes. His writings, popular during his lifetime, soon went out of favor. At the beginning of the twentieth century, however, interest in Donne's poetry rekindled. Earlier critics had faulted Donne for overworking his ideas. The noted modern poet T. S. Eliot, though, found in Donne's work a valuable unification of intellect and feeling.

Renewed interest in Donne might stem from a kind of self-recognition by modern readers. The conflicts Donne faced have a distinctively contemporary flavor. His family's faith and his secret marriage pitted the private man against the demands of the world. Society in his time, as in ours, was no longer ready with clear answers to the question, Where do I fit in? Donne, in his contradictory life and complex poetry, had to invent his own answers.

Preview

Connecting to the Literature

In a dark and lonely place, a person may whistle a tune to keep his or her spirits up. Donne is perhaps our greatest whistler in the dark. In his poems, he confronts the uncertainties of parting and death, filling the silence with extravagant improvisations.

Literary Analysis

Metaphysical Poetry

Donne and his followers wrote **metaphysical poetry**—poetry characterized by intellectual displays and concern with metaphysical, or philosophical, issues. It uses the following poetic devices:

- **Conceits** are extended comparisons that link objects or ideas not commonly associated, often mixing abstract ideas and emotional matters. In one of his poems, for example, Donne compares two lovers to the two legs of a drawing compass.
- **Paradoxes** are images or descriptions that appear self-contradictory but that reveal a deeper truth. Donne uses a paradox in Holy Sonnet 10 when he writes, "Death, thou shalt die."

Interpret the conceits and paradoxes you find in Donne's work.

Comparing Literary Works

Donne's work falls into two distinctive periods—the youthful phase in which he wrote love poems such as "Song" and a later phase in which he wrote religious works such as Holy Sonnet 10. His appointment as a clergyman in 1621 is a key cause of this shift. The works in this section are arranged in rough chronological order. As you read, compare the influence of Donne's changing life on his subject-matter and attitude towards life. Also, note the features of his style that do not change.

Reading Strategy

Recognizing the Speaker's Situation and Motivation

To understand these poems, imagine the **speaker's situation** and figure out his **motivation** for addressing another person, often his beloved. Use a chart like the one here to help you as you read.

Vocabulary Development

profanation (präf´ ə nā´ shən) *n.* action showing disrespect for something sacred (p. 424)

laity (lā´ i tē) *n.* those not initiated into a priesthood (p. 424)

trepidation (trep´ ə dā´ shən) *n.* trembling (p. 424)

breach (brēch) *n.* a break (p. 425)

contention (kən ten´ shən) *n.* dispute; argument (p. 429)

piety (pī´ ə tē) *n.* devotion to sacred duties (p. 429)

intermit (in´ tər mit´) *v.* stop for a time (p. 429)

covetousness (kuv´ ət əs nis) *n.* greediness (p. 430)

Speaker's Words
"Sweetest love, I do not go, For weariness of thee, . . ."

Situation
He has to leave his beloved.

Motivation
He is reassuring her that he is not leaving because he is tired of her.

Fair Is My Love, Edwin A. Abbey. The Harris Museum and Art Gallery, Preston

Song

John Donne

Sweetest love, I do not go,
    For weariness of thee,
Nor in hope the world can show
    A fitter love for me;
5   But since that I
Must die at last, 'tis best
To use[1] myself in jest,
    Thus by feigned[2] deaths to die.

Yesternight the sun went hence,
10   And yet is here today;
He hath no desire nor sense,
    Nor half so short a way;
        Then fear not me,
But believe that I shall make
15 Speedier journeys, since I take
    More wings and spurs than he.

▲ **Critical Viewing**
How does the relationship
of the man and woman in
this painting compare
with the relationship
described in the poem?
[Compare and Contrast]

---

1. **use** condition.
2. **feigned** (fānd) *adj.* imagined.

O how feeble is man's power,
    That if good fortune fall,
Cannot add another hour,
20   Nor a lost hour recall!
            But come bad chance,
And we join to it our strength,
And we teach it art and length,
    Itself o'er us to advance.

25 When thou sigh'st, thou sigh'st not wind,
    But sigh'st my soul away;
When thou weep'st, unkindly kind,
    My life's blood doth decay.
        It cannot be
30 That thou lovest me as thou say'st,
If in thine my life thou waste,
    That art the best of me.

Let not thy divining heart
    Forethink me any ill,
35 Destiny may take thy part,
    And may thy fears fulfill;
        But think that we
Are but turned aside to sleep.
They who one another keep
40   Alive, ne'r parted be.

Review and Assess

Thinking About the Selection

1. **Respond:** Do you agree with the speaker when, in lines 17–24, he says that we add to our own misfortunes? Why?

2. **(a) Recall:** What does the speaker say his reason is for leaving? **(b) Infer:** To what remark of his beloved might he be responding in this poem?

3. **(a) Analyze:** How would you outline the speaker's argument? **(b) Speculate:** What might the argument's effect on the beloved be?

4. **Draw Conclusions:** Imagine that the speaker's beloved is in tears as he is leaving. Why might the speaker have chosen to present his feelings in the form of witty arguments?

5. **Generalize:** The speaker uses exaggeration to persuade his beloved. Do you think exaggeration is a useful or a valid persuasive tool?

The **British** **Tradition**

Mind and Feeling

The twentieth-century poet T. S. Eliot celebrated Donne as one of the best —and last—poets to integrate mind and heart: "A thought to Donne was an experience; it modified his sensibility [feeling and perception]." Eliot praised Donne's "direct sensuous apprehension of thought" and his "re-creation of thought into feeling."

Eliot claimed that later poets did not "feel their thought as immediately as the odor of a rose" and that "[in] the seventeenth century a dissociation of sensibility set in, from which we have never recovered." Critics might counter that Eliot himself helped restore this integration to poetry.

A Valediction:[1]
Forbidding Mourning

John Donne

As virtuous men pass mildly away,
    And whisper to their souls to go,
Whilst some of their sad friends do say
    The breath goes now, and some say, No;

5 So let us melt, and make no noise,
    No tear-floods, nor sigh-tempests move,
'Twere profanation of our joys
    To tell the laity our love.

Moving of th'earth brings harms and fears,
10   Men reckon what it did and meant;
But trepidation of the spheres,[2]
    Though greater far, is innocent.

Dull sublunary[3] lovers' love
    (Whose soul is sense) cannot admit
15 Absence, because it doth remove
    Those things which elemented it.[4]

But we by a love, so much refined,
    That our selves know not what it is,
Inter-assurèd of the mind,[5]
20   Care less, eyes, lips, and hands to miss.

Our two souls therefore, which are one,
    Though I must go, endure not yet

profanation (präf´ ə nā´ shən) *n.* action showing disrespect for something sacred

laity (lā´ i tē) *n.* those not initiated into a priesthood

trepidation (trep´ ə dā´ shən) *n.* trembling

Reading Strategy
Recognizing the Speaker's Situation and Motivation Why does the speaker turn parting into a proof of the strength of his love?

---

1. **valediction** farewell speech.
2. **trepidation of the spheres** movements of the stars and planets that are inconsistent with a perfect circular orbit.
3. **sublunary** (sub´ lo͞o nər´ ē) referring to the region below the moon, considered in early astronomy to be the domain of changeable and perishable things.
4. **Those things . . . elemented it** the basic materials or parts of their love.
5. **Inter-assurèd of the mind** mutually confident of each other's thoughts.

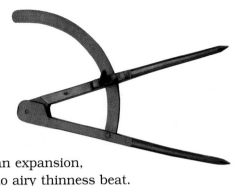

◀ **Critical Viewing** Why is a comparison of lovers to a compass such as this one unexpected? **[Connect]**

A <u>breach</u>, but an expansion,
  Like gold to airy thinness beat.

breach (brēch) *n.* a break

25 If they be two, they are two so
    As stiff twin compasses[6] are two;
  Thy soul the fixed foot, makes no show
    To move, but doth, if th'other do.

  And though it in the center sit,
30   Yet when the other far doth roam,
  It leans, and hearkens after it,
    And grows erect, as that comes home.

  Such wilt thou be to me, who must
    Like th'other foot, obliquely[7] run;
35 Thy firmness makes my circle just,[8]
    And makes me end where I begun.

---

6. **twin compasses** the two legs of a drawing compass.
7. **obliquely** at an angle; not straight.
8. **just** true; perfect.

Review and Assess

Thinking About the Selection

1. **Respond:** If you were the woman addressed by the speaker, how persuasive would you find his reassurances? Explain.

2. **(a) Recall:** According to the speaker, how should he and his beloved part? **(b) Infer:** What does he think that this manner of parting shows about their love? **(c) Interpret:** Describe two other claims the speaker makes to show how special their love is.

3. **Draw Conclusions:** The poem compares the lovers to the legs of a compass—she is fixed in place while he moves. What does the comparison indicate about their relationship?

4. **Support:** The speaker links love with the order and stability of the world. Support this insight with details from the poem.

5. **Apply:** Do you, like the speaker, see love as a union of two souls, or do you think that lovers should be independent? Explain.

HOLY SONNET 10

JOHN DONNE

Sir Thomas Aston at the Deathbed of His Wife, John Souch, Manchester City Art Galleries

▲ **Critical Viewing** The painting shows Lady Aston both when she is alive and when she is dead. Compare the relationship between death and life implied by the painting with that developed in "Holy Sonnet 10." **[Compare and Contrast]**

Background

Writers in Donne's day often depended on the support of patrons, wealthy supporters of the arts. The young Donne did not publish his poems (most were printed only after his death). Instead, they were circulated among a select literary audience that included patrons such as the Countess of Bedford. After Donne was dismissed from his position with Sir Thomas Egerton, he and his family depended in part on patrons for financial support. When he became a clergyman, Donne no longer needed to capture the interest of patrons with his wit. He continued, though, to write impassioned, witty verse such as the Holy Sonnets.

Death be not proud, though some have called thee
Mighty and dreadful, for thou art not so;
For those whom thou think'st thou dost overthrow,
Die not, poor death, nor yet canst thou kill me.
5 From rest and sleep, which but thy pictures[1] be,
Much pleasure; then from thee much more must flow,
And soonest our best men with thee do go,
Rest of their bones, and soul's delivery.[2]
Thou art slave to fate, chance, kings, and desperate men,
10 And dost with poison, war, and sickness dwell,
And poppy,[3] or charms can make us sleep as well
And better than thy stroke; why swell'st[4] thou then?
One short sleep past, we wake eternally,
And death shall be no more; Death, thou shalt die.

1. **pictures** images.
2. **And . . . delivery** Our best men go with you to rest their bones and find freedom for their souls.
3. **poppy** opium.
4. **swell'st** swell with pride.

Literary Analysis
Metaphysical Poetry
What paradox does the speaker use to end his argument with Death?

Review and Assess

Thinking About the Selection

1. **Respond:** Do you picture death as arrogant? Explain.

2. **(a) Recall:** What "pictures" of death does the speaker mention? **(b) Infer:** What positive lesson about death does the speaker draw from this resemblance?

3. **(a) Interpret:** In what sense is death a slave (line 9)? **(b) Connect:** How does this point justify the opening line?

4. **(a) Interpret:** What does the statement "Death, thou shalt die" mean? **(b) Draw Conclusions:** Why might the speaker react to death by challenging its "strength" and "pride"?

5. **Evaluate:** Does the speaker sound like a man talking himself out of fear or like one who has triumphed over fear? Explain.

MEDITATION 17
JOHN DONNE

▲ **Critical Viewing** The bells in this tower might ring on the occasion of someone's death, as Donne notes. On what other occasions might they ring? **[Deduce]**

Nunc lento sonitu dicunt, Morieris.
(Now, this bell tolling softly for another,
says to me, Thou must die.)

Perchance he for whom this bell tolls may be so ill as that he knows not it tolls for him; and perchance I may think myself so much better than I am as that they who are about me and see my state may have caused it to toll for me, and I know not that. The church is catholic,[1] universal, so are all her actions; all that she does belongs to all. When she baptizes a child, that action concerns me; for that child is thereby connected to that head which is my head too, and ingrafted into that body[2] whereof I am a member. And when she buries a man, that action concerns me: all mankind is of one author and is one volume; when one man dies, one chapter is not torn out of the book, but translated into a better language; and every chapter must be so translated. God employs several translators; some pieces are translated by age, some by sickness, some by war, some by justice; but God's hand is in every translation, and his hand shall bind up all our scattered leaves again for that library where every book shall lie open to one another. As therefore the bell that rings to a sermon calls not upon the preacher only, but upon the congregation to come, so this bell calls us all; but how much more me, who am brought so near the door by this sickness. There was a <u>contention</u> as far as a suit[3] (in which both <u>piety</u> and dignity, religion and estimation,[4] were mingled) which of the religious orders should ring to prayers first in the morning; and it was determined that they should ring first that rose earliest. If we understand aright the dignity of this bell that tolls for our evening prayer, we would be glad to make it ours by rising early, in that application, that it might be ours as well as his whose indeed it is. The bell doth toll for him that thinks it doth; and though it <u>intermit</u> again, yet from that minute that that occasion wrought upon him, he is united to God. Who casts not up his eye to the sun when it rises? but who takes off his eye from a comet when that breaks out? Who bends not his ear to any bell which upon any occasion rings? but who can remove it from that bell which is passing a piece of himself out of this world? No man is an island, entire of itself; every man is a piece of the continent, a part of the main.[5] If a clod be washed away by the sea, Europe is the less, as well as if a promontory were, as well as if a manor of thy friend's or of thine own were. Any man's death diminishes me because I am involved in mankind, and therefore never send to know for whom the bell tolls; it tolls for thee. Neither can we call this a begging of misery or a borrowing of misery,

---

1. **catholic** applying to humanity generally.
2. **head . . . body** In the Bible, St. Paul calls Jesus the head (spiritual leader) of all men (1 Corinthians 11:3) and a body in which the faithful are unified (1 Corinthians 12:12).
3. **suit** lawsuit.
4. **estimation** self-esteem.
5. **main** mainland.

Literary Analysis
Metaphysical Poetry
In this passage, to what does Donne compare mankind?

contention (kən ten´ shən) *n.* dispute; argument

piety (pī´ ə tē) *n.* devotion to sacred duties

intermit (in´ tər mit´) *v.* stop for a time

Literary Analysis
Metaphysical Poetry
What extended metaphor does Donne use here to show a single individual's relationship to all of mankind?

✔**Reading Check**

According to Donne, for whom does the bell toll?

as though we were not miserable enough of ourselves but must fetch in more from the next house, in taking upon us the misery of our neighbors. Truly it were an excusable <u>covetousness</u> if we did; for affliction is a treasure, and scarce any man hath enough of it. No man hath affliction enough that is not matured and ripened by it, and made fit for God by that affliction. If a man carry treasure in bullion, or in a wedge of gold, and have none coined into current money,[6] his treasure will not defray him as he travels. Tribulation is treasure in the nature of it, but it is not current money in the use of it, except we get nearer and nearer our home, heaven, by it. Another man may be sick too, and sick to death, and this affliction may lie in his bowels as gold in a mine and be of no use to him; but this bell that tells me of his affliction digs out and applies that gold to me, if by this consideration of another's danger, I take mine own into contemplation and so secure myself by making my recourse to my God, who is our only security.

covetousness (kuv´ ət əs nis) *n.* greediness

---

6. current money currency; wealth in spendable form

Review and Assess

Thinking About the Selection

1. **Respond:** Do you think suffering is ever a good thing? Explain.

2. **(a) Recall:** What event does the tolling bell announce?
   (b) Analyze: Why does Donne say the tolling bell applies to him as well as to others?

3. **(a) Recall:** What reason does Donne give for saying, "Any man's death diminishes me"? **(b) Interpret:** What does Donne mean by "No man is an island, entire of itself; every man is a piece of the continent"? **(c) Analyze:** How does the comparison of humanity to a continent support the idea that one death affects all people?

4. **(a) Analyze:** In Donne's metaphor, when does the "treasure" of affliction turn into "current [spendable] money"?
   (b) Interpret: Why does Donne find affliction valuable?
   (c) Connect: In what sense does the tolling bell "apply" one person's affliction to another?

5. **Draw Conclusions:** Donne says that, once one takes the bell as tolling for oneself, one is "united to God." In urging people to think about their own deaths, what might he be implying about people's attachment to worldly things such as money, success, and popularity?

6. **Apply:** Do you think the statement "No man is an island" applies more, less, or about the same in today's world, compared to how it applied in Donne's time? Explain.

Review and Assess

Literary Analysis

Metaphysical Poetry

1. Identify and interpret a **conceit** that the speaker in "Song" uses to reassure his beloved. Explain what things are being compared.

2. (a) What **paradox** does the speaker use in the fourth stanza of "Song"? (b) Explain the truth underlying this contradiction.

3. (a) Identify a conceit in Holy Sonnet 10. (b) Explain the speaker's point in making the comparison.

4. In Meditation 17, Donne uses a conceit comparing suffering and treasure. (a) Use a chart like the one shown to analyze the forms of treasure he discusses. (b) Explain how each relates to suffering.

Main Idea: There are two forms of suffering, just as there are two forms of treasure.		
First Form of Treasure: _____	Second Form of Treasure: _____	Relationship Between Forms of Treasure: _____

Comparing Literary Works

5. (a) What important differences distinguish "Song" and "Valediction" from Holy Sonnet 10? (b) Identify an element of metaphysical poetry that all three share, giving examples from each.

6. In the poems, the speaker uses conceits and paradoxes to move from uncertainty (his own or his listener's) to certainty. In Meditation 17, he uses these devices to inspire uncertainty in his listener. Explain, using examples from each work.

Reading Strategy

Recognizing the Speaker's Situation and Motivation

7. (a) In each of Donne's works, who is the speaker and what is the **speaker's situation**? (b) What is each speaker's **motivation**?

8. Choose a line from each work, and describe how knowledge of the speaker's situation and motivation helps you understand the text.

Extend Understanding

9. **World Events Connection:** During World War II, the British used the phrase "No man is an island" to justify joining the fight against Nazi Germany. Would Donne approve? Explain.

Quick Review

Metaphysical poetry is characterized by the use of conceits and paradoxes.

A **conceit** is an extended comparison linking objects or ideas that are not commonly associated.

A **paradox** is an image or a description that appears to contradict itself but really reveals a deeper truth.

An **analogy** compares the relationship between one pair of things with the relationship between another pair.

To **recognize a speaker's situation and motivation,** picture the speaker's circumstances and determine his or her reasons for speaking or acting.

 Take It to the Net
www.phschool.com

Take the interactive self-test online to check your understanding of these selections.

Works of John Donne ◆ 431

Integrate Language Skills

Vocabulary Development Lesson

Word Analysis: Latin Prefix *inter-*

The Latin prefix *inter-* means "between" or "among." It appears in the word *intermit,* meaning "to put a space between" or "to pause." The prefix also appears in many words that describe relationships in society. Use the meaning of the prefix to help you define the following words:

1. interstate
2. international
3. interdependent
4. intermediary

Spelling Strategy

In English, the suffix *-ity,* used in the word *laity,* is more common than the suffix *-ety.* Often, *-ety* is used to avoid two *i*'s in a row when a word stem ends in an *i,* as in the word *anxiety.*

Complete the following words with *-ity* or *-ety.*

1. facil__
2. soci__
3. agil__

Concept Development: Synonyms

Choose the letter of the word or phrase closest in meaning to each vocabulary word.

1. contention: (a) gathering, (b) campsite, (c) dispute
2. piety: (a) roundness, (b) partiality, (c) devotion
3. intermit: (a) interfere, (b) pause, (c) deny
4. covetousness: (a) greed, (b) agreement, (c) sloth
5. profanation: (a) violation, (b) arson, (c) prediction
6. laity: (a) the uninitiated, (b) those who stand, (c) professionals
7. trepidation: (a) hunger, (b) trembling, (c) calm
8. breach: (a) birth, (b) pants, (c) break

Grammar and Style Lesson

Active and Passive Voice

In the **active voice,** a verb expresses an action performed by its subject. In the **passive voice,** the subject receives the action of the verb. The passive voice uses a form of *to be* with the past participle (the form usually ending in *-ed*) of the main verb.

Active Voice:	Donne <u>compares</u> death to sleep. (Subject, *Donne,* performs action.)
Passive Voice:	Sleep <u>is compared</u> to death by Donne. (Subject, *Sleep,* receives action.)

In many cases, writers prefer the active voice because it creates a more forceful impression.

Practice In your notebook, rewrite the following sentences in the active voice.

1. Their love is expanded by separation.
2. His soul is sighed away by her sighs.
3. His life's blood is weakened by her weeping.
4. It has been said that death is mighty.
5. Life is not conquered by death.

Writing Application The passive voice helps hide who did what to whom, so it is often used in press releases. Using the passive voice, write a brief press release explaining Donne's loss of his job with Anne More's uncle. (See the biography on p. 420 for details.) For instance, you might begin "It was decided that . . .".

W̶G̶ Prentice Hall Writing and Grammar Connection: Chapter 21, Section 4

Writing Lesson

Persuasive Speech Based on Donne's Work

Many of Donne's works are written as speeches. Adapt one of them to a contemporary situation, writing the speech Donne's speaker might make today.

Prewriting   Review the selection of your choice to identify the speaker's situation, audience, and persuasive purpose. Outline Donne's arguments, and then list images and comparisons from contemporary experience that could be used in their place.

Drafting   Begin with an emphatic statement or vivid image. Develop the images and arguments supporting your point in language suited to a contemporary audience.

Revising   Review your draft to evaluate its unity. If you find parts that do not clearly connect to your theme and to one another, consider eliminating or rewriting them. You might make a post-draft outline of the ideas in your draft to aid you.

Model: Making a Post-Draft Outline to Revise for Unity

Paragraph A: Topic _____

    1. Connection to purpose: _____

    2. Connection to next paragraph: _____

Paragraph B: Topic _____

> Using a format like this one, a writer can analyze the unity of a draft.

 Prentice Hall Writing and Grammar Connection: Chapter 7, Section 4

Extension Activities

Listening and Speaking

With a partner, prepare a **dramatic reading** of two of Donne's poems. Use these tips:

1. Determine the appropriate tone of voice, whether comforting, cajoling, or challenging.
2. Analyze the text to find appropriate points at which to add dramatic gestures.
3. Help each other find places to add emphasis.

Perform your readings for the class.

Research and Technology What Donne called "trepidations of the spheres" are known as "perturbations" in modern astronomy. Compile a **science report** about these movements. Include maps and tables, incorporating them into your word-processor file.

 **Take It to the Net**   www.phschool.com

Go online for an additional research activity using the Internet.

Prepare to Read

On My First Son ◆ Still to Be Neat ◆ Song: To Celia

Ben Jonson (1572–1637)

Ben Jonson lived a nearly mythic life. Even in his physical stature, he seemed a little larger than life—he was a big man with boundless energy and enormous courage. Brilliant in his poetry and dangerous in a duel, a classical scholar and a veteran soldier, an astute critic and a brassy talker, Jonson had a colorful, sometimes violent career that culminated in his reputation as an esteemed judge of literature. The friend as well as the chief rival of Shakespeare and Donne, he set literary tastes for a generation of poets. From bricklayer to poet laureate, his life story is a true "rags to riches" tale.

A Poet at War Adopted in infancy, Jonson worked for his stepfather, a bricklayer, while attending the equivalent of high school under a private tutor. Too poor to study at a university, Jonson joined the army and fought in the wars for Dutch independence from Spain. The brawny Jonson at one point met an enemy champion in single combat before the massed armies of Holland and Spain. Jonson won.

Scandal and Success After returning to England, Jonson became an actor. Despite his turbulent life—jailed for his part in a "slanderous" play, almost hanged for killing a fellow actor in a duel, and even suspected of plotting against the king— Jonson became a major dramatist. Some say William Shakespeare acted in his first play, and the chief acting companies of the day, including Shakespeare's company, performed his later dramas.

Jonson was so successful that he was granted a handsome pension by King James I and treated as if he were poet laureate of England. Over the years, he wrote masques—elaborate entertainments—for the royal court, where he was a favorite writer.

Dictator of Taste Jonson became extremely influential in literary affairs of the day, functioning as a virtual dictator of taste. Historic accounts help us picture him at the Mermaid Tavern, surrounded by admirers and engaged in duels of wit with Shakespeare. His followers, including Robert Herrick and Sir John Suckling, took to calling themselves the "Sons of Ben" or "Tribe of Ben."

The Importance of a Poet Jonson's own opinion of his work and status may be judged by the fact that when he published his collected works in 1616, he entitled the volume *The Works of Benjamin Jonson*—a style of title used largely with celebrated ancient authors. With this gesture, Jonson may have become the first English-language poet to claim true professional dignity for himself. The esteem in which the occupation of poet is held in later times owes something to Jonson's self-confidence.

Varied Styles Jonson's experiences ranged from tavern brawls to elegant entertainments, and his poetic styles are equally varied. He favored satire in his dramas, poking fun at contemporary character types in plays such as *Volpone* and *The Alchemist*. In contrast, his masques provided the king's court with lavish pageants, often based on Greek and Roman myths and topped off with flattering references to the king and queen—far from the satirical bite of his stage plays.

Jonson wrote many of his poems in an impersonal style, one suited to inscriptions on monuments. Others are filled with nasty wit. As diverse as his styles are, though, one of his consistent strengths is the clear, direct expression of ideas.

A Lasting Influence In his varied experiences and diverse literary output, Jonson might seem to sum up the age in which he lived. Yet his importance does not end with the seventeenth century. Jonson's influence on writers is still felt today, and his plays continue to be produced. What Jonson said of Shakespeare can also be said of him: "He was not of an age, but for all time."

Preview

Connecting to the Literature

Mottos emblazoned on T-shirts or inscribed on mugs reflect the same urge that brought Ben Jonson to write—the desire to pass on memorable sayings.

Literary Analysis

Epigrams

An **epigram** (from the Greek for "inscription") is a short poem in which the writer strives for brevity, clarity, and permanence. Ben Jonson's famous lines have the qualities of an epigram: "Drink to me only with thine eyes, / And I will pledge with mine." Epigrams include these features:

- Short lines with bouncy rhythms
- Paradoxical twists, as in the lines quoted above
- Parallel phrases or clauses, as in the line "Still to be neat, still to be dressed, . . ."

As you read, analyze the elements that make Jonson's lines memorable.

Comparing Literary Works

Jonson writes epigrammatic poems on a variety of subjects. You may be impressed by his range of feeling in them. "On My First Son" is a sharp testament to a personal grief. By contrast, you may find "Song: To Celia" quite generalized—as if it might have been written by anyone to anyone. Compare the sentiment—personal or generalized—of each poem.

Reading Strategy

Hypothesizing

To read actively, **hypothesize** by making informed guesses about the people, events, or ideas in the work. Reading further, check your hypothesis against new information, using a chart like the one shown.

Vocabulary Development

In his poems, Johnson uses **archaic words,** words that are no longer in general use. Familiarize yourself with the following words before you read.

thou you (second-person singular; used instead of *you* with family and friends)

thy your (second-person singular; used with family and friends)

thine yours or, before a word beginning with a vowel, your (second-person singular; used with family and friends)

wast were (used with *thou*)

wert were (used with *thou*)

hast have (used with *thou*)

hath has (used with *he, she, it*)

dost do (used with *thou*, usually as a helping verb)

doth does (used with *he, she, it,* usually as a helping verb)

Hypothesis	
Line 1: Speaker is a father whose son has gone away or died.	
Proved	**Disproved**
Lines 3–7: Boy lived 7 years and "scaped world's, and flesh's rage."	_____ _____ _____ _____ _____

On My
First Son

Ben Jonson

Background

Ben Jonson was indebted to ancient Greek and Roman poets, whose work shaped his taste for clear, brief expression. Like ancient poets, Jonson composed poetry with a definite social function. Jonson's poems praising other writers appeared at the beginning of their books. Poems such as "On My First Son" marked the occasion of a death. Songs such as "Still to Be Neat" were written by Jonson for his masques (royal entertainments).

Farewell, thou child of my right hand,[1] and joy;
    My sin was too much hope of thee, loved boy,
Seven years thou wert lent to me, and I thee pay,
    Exacted by thy fate, on the just[2] day.
5 O, could I lose all father,[3] now. For why
    Will man lament the state he should envy?
To have so soon scaped world's, and flesh's rage,
    And, if no other misery, yet age?
Rest in soft peace, and, asked, say here doth lie
10   Ben Jonson his best piece of poetry.
For whose sake, henceforth, all his vows be such,
    As what he loves may never like[4] too much.

---

1. **child . . . hand** literal translation of the Hebrew name Benjamin, the name of Jonson's son. Jonson's son was born in 1596 and died in 1603.
2. **just** exact.
3. **lose . . . father** shed an identity as a father.
4. **like** possibly meant in the old sense of "please."

Review and Assess

Thinking About the Selection

1. **Respond:** Do you think the speaker in "On My First Son" is wise in not wanting to love anything so strongly again? Explain.

2. **(a) Recall:** What is the sin the speaker refers to in line 2?
   (b) Interpret: Why does the speaker call this feeling a sin?

3. **(a) Interpret:** Why does the speaker wish to "lose all father, now"? **(b) Interpret:** What does he vow in lines 11–12?
   (c) Draw Conclusions: Why would grief lead to these reactions?

4. **(a) Interpret:** Does the speaker ever present his feelings of grief directly? Explain. **(b) Evaluate:** Why might this manner of presenting grief strengthen the impression made on the reader?

5. **(a) Apply:** Contrast the ideas in lines 5–8 with contemporary attitudes. **(b) Evaluate:** Which makes more sense to you?

Portrait of Mrs. Richard Brinsley Sheridan, Thomas Gainsborough, National Gallery of Art, Washington, D.C.

▲ **Critical Viewing** Given his sentiments in the poem, of what details of this women's appearance would Jonson approve? Explain. **[Connect]**

Still to Be Neat

Ben Jonson

Still[1] to be neat, still to be dressed,
As you were going to a feast;
Still to be powdered, still perfumed;
Lady, it is to be presumed,
5 Though art's hid causes[2] are not found,
All is not sweet, all is not sound.

Give me a look, give me a face,
That makes simplicity a grace;
Robes loosely flowing, hair as free;
10 Such sweet neglect more taketh me
                Than all th'adulteries[3] of art.
They strike mine eyes, but not my heart.

---

1. **still** always.
2. **causes** reasons.
3. **adulteries** adulterations; corruptions.

Review and Assess

Thinking About the Selection

1. **Respond:** Do you agree with the speaker about the attractiveness of a spontaneous look? Why or why not?

2. **(a) Recall:** To what style of dress and grooming is the speaker reacting in the first stanza? **(b) Interpret:** What are the "hid causes" that he suspects lie behind this style? **(c) Infer:** Why does he prefer the style of "sweet neglect"?

3. **(a) Analyze:** How does Jonson use repetition to support his meaning? **(b) Evaluate:** How might Jonson's ideas about fashion apply to his own poem?

4. **Relate:** Which trends in modern advertising can you connect with the ideas in the poem?

Song: To Celia

Ben Jonson

Drink to me only with thine eyes,
And I will pledge with mine:
Or leave a kiss but in the cup,
And I'll not look for wine.
5 The thirst that from the soul doth rise,
Doth ask a drink divine:
But might I of Jove's[1] nectar sup,
I would not change for thine.

I sent thee late[2] a rosy wreath,
10 Not so much honoring thee,
As giving it a hope, that there
It could not withered be.
But thou thereon did'st only breathe,
And sent'st it back to me;
15 Since when it grows and smells, I swear,
Not of itself, but thee.

---

1. **Jove's** Jupiter's. In Roman mythology, Jupiter is the ruler of the gods.
2. **late** recently.

Review and Assess

Thinking About the Selection

1. **(a) Recall:** For what does the soul thirst in lines 5–6 of "Song: To Celia"? **(b) Interpret:** Explain how this idea of the soul's thirst extends the image in lines 1–2.

2. **(a) Analyze:** Which images suggest sensory experiences? **(b) Analyze:** Which words or images suggest emotional states? **(c) Generalize:** What do these two categories of image suggest about the process of falling in love?

3. **(a) Assess:** How much do you know about the speaker of "Song: To Celia" or his beloved? **(b) Make a Judgment:** How would more information affect your appreciation of the poem?

4. **Evaluate:** Does Jonson's poem seem artificial or false by today's standards, or does it capture true sentiment? Explain.

Review and Assess

Literary Analysis

Epigrams

1. Would any lines from "On My First Son" be suitable for engraving on the subject's tombstone? Explain.

2. Identify three pairs of parallel phrases or clauses in "Still to Be Neat."

3. Explain how the phrase "sweet neglect" in "Still to Be Neat" appears self-contradictory but makes memorable sense.

4. Use a chart like the one shown to identify and characterize lines that give "Song: To Celia" the style of an **epigram.**

"Bouncy" Rhythms	Parallelism	Witty Wordings	Paradoxes
Lines:	Lines:	Lines:	Lines:

Comparing Literary Works

5. (a) Identify two details in "On My First Son" that make it a sincere, personal statement of grief. Explain your choices. (b) Identify two details in "Song" that give it a formal, impersonal quality. Explain your choices. (c) Are both types of poem valuable? Explain.

6. (a) Which details in "Still to Be Neat" give it a generalized quality? (b) Which details make it seem heartfelt? (c) Compare the sentiment in this poem with the sentiment of the other two.

Reading Strategy

Hypothesizing

7. (a) Using only lines 1–4 of "On My First Son," make a **hypothesis** about the speaker's feelings for his son. (b) Do lines 5–8 of the poem support your hypothesis? Explain.

8. Basing your answer on lines 11–12 of "On My First Son," what final hypothesis can you make about the speaker's reaction to his son's death?

Extend Understanding

9. **Career Connection:** In what modern occupations might Jonson's witty, epigrammatic style be effective? Why?

Quick Review

An **epigram** is a short poem in which the poet strives for brevity, clarity, and memorability.

To **hypothesize,** stop and make informed guesses and predictions based on the information you have read to that point.

 Take It to the Net
www.phschool.com
Take the interactive self-test online to check your understanding of these selections.

Integrate Language Skills

Vocabulary Development Lesson

Concept Development: Archaic Words

Ben Jonson's poetry and many other works of English literature contain **archaic words**—words that are no longer in general use. Choose the correct archaic word to complete each sentence.

1. (Thy / Thine) looks are like the nectar of the gods.
2. Thou (wert / doth) too dear to me.
3. She (hast / hath) dressed neatly once again.

Spelling Strategy

When a word ends in a consonant and *y*, change the *y* to *i* before adding most suffixes, as when Jonson adds *-es* to *adultery* to form *adulteries*. When adding the suffixes *-ing* and *-ish*, however, keep the final *y*. Write the words formed by each of the following combinations.

1. *envy* + *-able* 2. *misery* + *-es* 3. *reply* + *-ing*

Fluency: Archaic Words

"Translate" the following passage from Jonson's "To the Memory of My Beloved Master, William Shakespeare" into modern English.

> For, if I thought my judgment were
>   of years,
> I should commit thee surely with
>   thy peers,
> And tell, how far thou didst our Lyly
>   outshine,
> Or sporting Kyd, or Marlowe's mighty
>   line.
> And though thou hadst small Latin, and
>   less Greek,
> From thence to honor thee, I would not
>   seek
> For names; but call forth thund'ring
>   Aeschylus. . . .

Grammar and Style Lesson

Modifiers: Placement of *only*

Modifiers should always be placed as close as possible to the words they modify. Changing the placement of a modifier such as *only* can change the meaning of a sentence.

> **Example:** Drink to me <u>only</u> with thine eyes. (Drink only with your eyes, not with anything else.)
>
> <u>Only</u> drink to me with thine eyes. (Only gaze at the speaker; don't do anything else.)

Poets such as Jonson face a complex task. They must place modifiers close to the words they modify while at the same time creating the right rhythm.

Practice Add the word *only* to the following sentences to convey the meanings in parentheses.

1. Drink to me with thine eyes. (just to me, no one else)
2. Drink to me with thine eyes. (use your eyes, no one else's)
3. Give me a look. (just a look, nothing else)
4. They strike mine eyes. (they, and no others)
5. They strike mine eyes. (only my eyes, not my heart)

Writing Application Write a paragraph about Ben Jonson, using information from page 434. Use the modifier *only* at least twice.

*W*G *Prentice Hall Writing and Grammar Connection: Chapter 20, Section 5*

Writing Lesson

Critical Response

Critic Douglas Bush defends what some have called the dullness of Jonson's style: ". . . Jonson demanded . . . the ageless classical virtues of clarity, unity, symmetry, and proportion. . . . His poems are wholes, not erratic displays of verbal fireworks." Drawing on details from the selections, write a response to this idea.

Prewriting   Using parts of the quotation above as heads (for example, "Clarity"), categorize examples from Jonson's poems that illustrate or contradict Bush's defense. Then, write a brief summary of your own reaction to Jonson's style.

Drafting   Begin with a summary of Bush's point and of your position. As you draft, support generalizations with quotations from Jonson.

Revising   Highlight generalizations in your draft and check off supporting details for each. At points where there are few or no checkmarks, consider adding support.

Model: Adding Support by Connecting General to Specific

For instance, the lines "But might I of Jove's nectar sup / I would not change for thine" unify the images of drinking. The reference to Jove, though, is artificial.

Jonson may achieve unity, but in some cases it is at the

expense of spontaneous feeling. What is the virtue of formal

unity if the poem seems lifeless?

> Added details from the poem strengthen support for the generalization.

Prentice Hall Writing and Grammar Connection: Chapter 14, Section 4

Extension Activities

Listening and Speaking Hold a **debate** between supporters of "natural" styles (grunge, long hair) and supporters of "artificial" styles (black-colored clothes, dyed hair). Each side should prepare

- A generalization that sums up its position
- A deductive argument—an argument applying a general truth to a specific case
- Visual images that illustrate and support its arguments

Hold your debate for the class. **[Group Activity]**

Research and Technology Research and write a **biographical report** on Ben Jonson's life. Begin by writing a list of questions about him. Then, check various sources, including writings from the time and modern commentaries, to answer your questions. Include a list of sources, annotated with your comments, at the end of your report.

 **Take It to the Net**   www.phschool.com

Go online for an additional research activity using the Internet.

Prepare to Read

To His Coy Mistress ◆ To the Virgins, to Make Much of Time ◆ Song

Andrew Marvell (1621–1678)

Marvell showed an extraordinary adaptability in a turbulent time. Although he was the son of a Puritan minister and frowned on the abuses of the monarchy, he enjoyed close friendships with supporters of Charles I in the king's dispute with Parliament. He also opposed the government of Oliver Cromwell, leader of the Puritan rebellion and then ruler of England.

Beginning in 1651, however, Marvell worked for Lord Fairfax, the commanding general of the Parliamentary army. Still later, he tutored Cromwell's ward. Marvell gained the sponsorship of the Puritan and great English poet John Milton, whose assistant he became.

Marvell wrote masterful poetry in various veins—some works share the metaphysical qualities of Donne's verse, while others have the classical qualities recommended by Jonson. Thought of chiefly as a satirist until the nineteenth century, much of his work has become classic.

Robert Herrick (1591–1674)

Born into a family of London goldsmiths, Herrick went to Cambridge when he was twenty-two and graduated at the age of twenty-nine. After graduation, he served as a military chaplain. As a reward for his services, he was assigned to a parish in rural England. Here, he performed his churchly duties and wrote religious verse and musical love poems.

Although not politically active, Herrick was evicted from his parish by the Puritans and allowed back only with the Restoration of Charles II. While barred from his church, Herrick returned to his native and beloved London, where he published his poetry in *Noble Numbers* and *Hesperides* (the title comes from an ancient Greek name for a mythical garden at the edge of the world).

Published during a turbulent time and largely ignored by his contemporaries, these verses are highly regarded today.

Sir John Suckling (1609–1642)

In some ways, Sir John Suckling lived a life more romantic than Marvell's or Herrick's. A privileged young courtier, Suckling inherited his vast estates when he was only eighteen. He later served as a gentleman in the privy chamber of Charles I. Praised as the cleverest of conversationalists, Suckling was said to be able to compose a poem at a moment's notice. He incorporated some of his best lyrics, including the poem "Song," into plays that he lavishly produced at his own expense.

Suckling's military exploits proved less successful than his poems, however. The cavalry troop he raised and lavishly uniformed for the king was defeated in Scotland, and Suckling was mocked for caring more about his men's uniforms than about their military abilities. After joining a failed Royalist plot to rescue a royal minister from prison, he fled to France, where he died in despair at the age of thirty-three. His poems, though, preserve the dash and spirit of his younger days.

Preview

Connecting to the Literature

It is easy for students to feel that life is one big, totally booked schedule. It is just as easy to figure out how the authors of these selections would respond: Make room for some enjoyment, before it is too late!

Literary Analysis

Carpe Diem Theme

Each poem in this grouping expresses a version of the **carpe diem theme** (kär´ pē dē´ em). *Carpe diem* is Latin for "Seize the day." The theme might be summed up, "Time is fleeting, so act decisively to enjoy life." Marvell expresses this theme in an extended fashion. First, he playfully describes to his beloved the centuries he would spend wooing her, if they had all of time. Then, he dryly reminds her that life does in fact come to an end, so she must act. Look for the various treatments of this theme in these selections.

Comparing Literary Works

Marvell approaches the *carpe diem* theme with a mix of whimsical fancy and passionate urgency. Herrick delivers a more traditional version of the theme, using familiar imagery to remind his readers of the seasons of life. Suckling gives the theme a new twist—his speaker advises a friend to abandon, not act on, love. As you read, compare the ways in which the poets address the same basic theme.

Reading Strategy

Inferring the Speaker's Attitude

To recognize the tone of a poem, you must **infer the speaker's attitude** toward the subject or audience.

- First, focus on the connotations (positive and negative associations) of the words and images the speaker uses.
- Then, determine what attitude would lead a speaker to choose these words and images.

You may find that the speaker's attitude shifts from one stanza to another, affecting the overall tone of the work. As you read, use a chart like the one shown here to note details that convey the speaker's attitude.

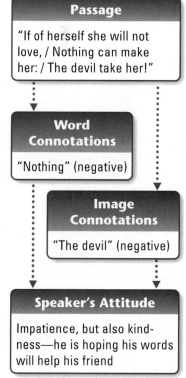

Passage

"If of herself she will not love, / Nothing can make her: / The devil take her!"

↓

Word Connotations

"Nothing" (negative)

↓

Image Connotations

"The devil" (negative)

↓

Speaker's Attitude

Impatience, but also kindness—he is hoping his words will help his friend

Vocabulary Development

coyness (koi´ nis) *n.* shyness; aloofness, often as part of a flirtation (p. 447)

amorous (am´ ə rəs) *adj.* full of love or desire (p. 448)

languish (laŋ´ gwish) *v.* to become weak; droop (p. 448)

prime (prīm) *n.* best stage of a thing or process (p. 449)

wan (wän) *adj.* sickly pale; faint or weak (p. 450)

The Interrupted Sleep, François Boucher. The Metropolitan Museum of Art

▲ **Critical Viewing** In what way do both the painting and the poem illustrate the traditional roles of men and women in courtship? **[Compare and Contrast]**

To His Coy Mistress

Andrew Marvell

Background

By the seventeenth century, the English language had become a fluid combination of Anglo-Saxon, Gaelic, Latin, and French. It was more than a tool for basic communication. Through it, one could express philosophical ideas, convey abstract theories, and indulge in humorous wordplay. These poems show the range of this language, from witty puns to fanciful imagery.

Had we but world enough, and time,
This coyness lady were no crime.
We would sit down, and think which way
To walk, and pass our long love's day.
5 Thou by the Indian Ganges' side
Should'st rubies find; I by the tide
Of Humber[1] would complain. I would
Love you ten years before the Flood,
And you should if you please refuse
10 Till the conversion of the Jews.[2]
My vegetable love should grow
Vaster than empires, and more slow;
An hundred years should go to praise
Thine eyes, and on thy forehead gaze;
15 Two hundred to adore each breast,
But thirty thousand to the rest;
An age at least to every part,
And the last age should show your heart.
For, lady, you deserve this state,[3]
20 Nor would I love at lower rate.
But at my back I always hear
Time's wingèd chariot hurrying near:
And yonder all before us lie
Deserts of vast eternity.
25 Thy beauty shall no more be found,
Nor, in thy marble vault, shall sound

coyness (koi′ nis) *n.* shyness; aloofness, often as part of flirtation

---

1. **Humber** river flowing through Hull, Marvell's home town.
2. **conversion of the Jews** according to Christian tradition, the Jews were to be converted immediately before the Last Judgment.
3. **state** dignity.

✔ **Reading Check**

What is the lady's crime?

My echoing songs; then worms shall try
That long-preserved virginity,
And your quaint honor turn to dust,
30 And into ashes all my lust:
The grave's a fine and private place,
But none I think do there embrace.
        Now therefore, while the youthful hue
Sits on thy skin like morning dew,
35 And while thy willing soul transpires[4]
At every pore with instant fires,
Now let us sport us while we may,
And now, like <u>amorous</u> birds of prey,
Rather at once our time devour
40 Than <u>languish</u> in his slow-chapped[5] power.
Let us roll all our strength, and all
Our sweetness, up into one ball,
And tear our pleasures with rough strife
Thorough[6] the iron gates of life:
45 Thus, though we cannot make our sun
Stand still, yet we will make him run.

---

4. **transpires** breathes out.
5. **slow-chapped** slow-jawed.
6. **thorough** through.

amorous (am´ ə res) *adj.*
full of love or desire

languish (laŋ´ gwish) *v.* to
become weak; droop

Literary Analysis
Carpe Diem **Theme**
What new twist does the
speaker apply in order
to "solve" the problem
of fleeting time?

Review and Assess

Thinking About the Selection

1. **Respond:** If you were the lady, how would you respond
   to the speaker? Why?

2. **(a) Recall:** Name three things the speaker and his mistress
   would do and the time each would take if time were not an
   issue. **(b) Connect:** How do these images relate to the charge
   the speaker makes against his lady in lines 1–2?

3. **(a) Infer:** Why would the speaker be willing to spend so
   much time waiting for his mistress? **(b) Interpret:** How does
   this willingness take the sting out of his complaint?

4. **(a) Analyze:** What future does the speaker foresee for himself
   and his love in lines 25–30? **(b) Connect:** How do the images
   in lines 21–30 answer the images in the first part of the poem?

5. **Draw Conclusions:** Why does the speaker save the urgent
   requests in lines 33–46 for the end?

6. **(a) Compare and Contrast:** Compare the attitudes toward
   time at the beginning, middle, and end. **(b) Evaluate:** Is
   Marvell's idea of love realistic or idealistic? Explain.

To the Virgins, to Make Much of Time

Robert Herrick

Gather ye rosebuds while ye may,
    Old time is still a-flying;
And this same flower that smiles today
    Tomorrow will be dying.

5 The glorious lamp of heaven, the sun,
    The higher he's a-getting,
The sooner will his race be run,
    And nearer he's to setting.

That age is best which is the first,
10   When youth and blood are warmer;
But being spent, the worse, and worst
    Times still succeed the former.

Then be not coy, but use your time,
    And, while ye may, go marry;
15 For, having lost but once your prime,
    You may forever tarry.[1]

---

1. tarry (tar´ ē) *v.* delay.

Literary Analysis
***Carpe Diem* Theme and Tone** Which images in lines 5–8 capture the *carpe diem* theme?

prime (prīm) *n.* best stage of a thing or process

Review and Assess

Thinking About the Selection

1. **Respond:** How did you respond to Herrick's images?
2. **(a) Recall:** What advice does the speaker give women in lines 1–4? **(b) Interpret:** What does the advice mean? **(c) Analyze:** How do the images he uses convey the idea of passing time?
3. **(a) Interpret:** What does the poem suggest about passing time? **(b) Connect:** How does the last stanza answer these concerns?
4. **Hypothesize:** What response could an opponent offer Herrick?

Song

Sir John Suckling

Why so pale and <u>wan</u>, fond lover?
    Prithee, why so pale?
Will, when looking well can't move her,
    Looking ill prevail?
5   Prithee, why so pale?

Why so dull and mute, young sinner?
    Prithee, why so mute?
Will, when speaking well can't win her,
    Saying nothing do't?
10   Prithee, why so mute?

Quit, quit, for shame; this will not move,
    This cannot take her.
If of herself she will not love,
    Nothing can make her:
15   The devil take her!

wan (wän) *adj.* sickly pale; faint or weak

Reading Strategy
Inferring Speaker's Attitude What is the difference between the speaker's attitude toward his listener in lines 6–10 and his attitude in lines 11–15?

Review and Assess

Thinking About the Selection

1. **Respond:** Do you think "Song" would make a good popular song? Why?

2. **(a) Recall:** How does the young lover look and act according to the first ten lines of "Song"? **(b) Analyze:** Explain why the speaker treats the friend's behavior as if it were an attempt to achieve a goal.

3. **(a) Interpret:** In the final stanza, what helpful shift in perspective does the speaker encourage? **(b) Draw Conclusions:** What attitude toward love does the last stanza reflect?

4. **(a) Analyze:** What features of the poem make it suitable as song lyrics? **(b) Hypothesize:** Which would be a good audience for such a song: uneducated farmers, young aristocrats, or both? Explain, using details from the poem.

5. **Apply:** How effective would Suckling's advice be for a modern lover? Explain.

Review and Assess

Literary Analysis

Carpe Diem Theme

1. (a) Identify the part of "To His Coy Mistress" that most clearly states the *carpe diem* **theme**. (b) Contrast the images in these lines with the conventional images of time and death in lines 21–32. (c) How does Marvell's *carpe diem* imagery add power to his plea?

2. (a) Explain how Herrick's images imply that the course of human life—including marriage—is part of the natural order. (b) Does this implication add authority to his advice? Explain.

3. In what sense does the speaker in Suckling's "Song" advise his listener to "seize the day"?

Comparing Literary Works

4. Of "To His Coy Mistress" and "To the Virgins," which do you find expresses the *carpe diem* message most persuasively? Why?

5. Contrast the treatment of the theme in the three poems, using a chart like the following.

Carpe Diem Images	Qualities: Fanciful? Simple?	Statement of Plea	Humorous? Passionate? Reasonable?

Reading Strategy

Inferring the Speaker's Attitude

6. (a) Judging from the exaggerated images he uses, infer the speaker's attitude toward his beloved in lines 1–20 of "To His Coy Mistress." (b) How does the speaker's attitude shift in lines 21–32?

7. (a) Explain where and in what way the speaker's attitude in Suckling's "Song" undergoes a change. (b) Compare his attitude toward love with the speaker's attitude in "To the Virgins."

Extend Understanding

8. **World Events Connection:** Review the biographies of these authors (p. 444), and explain how the message of these poems is suited to the turbulent times in which they were written.

Integrate Language Skills

Vocabulary Development Lesson

Word Analysis: Related Forms of *prime*

When Herrick refers to a person's "prime," he means both the first part of adulthood and the best years of a person's life. *Prime* comes from a Latin word meaning "first in importance" or "first in time." Using this information, define the italicized forms of the word *prime* below.

1. The party will hold a *primary*.
2. What is his *primary* reason for going to college?
3. Who is the *prime minister* of Great Britain?
4. Every television actor wants a *prime-time* show.
5. This *primer* will help you start learning computer programming.
6. Babbage's difference engine was a *primitive* form of computer.
7. These trees are survivors of the *primeval* forest once covering the land.

Fluency: Apply Word Meaning

Identify each statement as true or false.

1. Flushed with rage, his cheeks were <u>wan</u>.
2. *The <u>Prime</u> of Miss Jean Brodie* is probably about a woman on her deathbed.
3. A plant without water may <u>languish</u>.
4. An <u>amorous</u> couple is affectionate.
5. <u>Coyness</u> indicates commitment.

Spelling Strategy

The letters *ui* can represent several different sounds: long *i* (*guide*), short *i* (*biscuit*), *oo* (*fruit*), or *wi* (*languish*). For each of the following, give a word spelled with *ui* that matches the definition.

1. a path that returns to its beginning (circ___)
2. a set of formal clothes (s___)
3. to tell apart (disting___)
4. to conceal the identity of (disg___)

Grammar and Style Lesson

Irregular Forms of Adjectives

Herrick's poem contains comparative and superlative forms of the adjectives *good* and *bad*. These forms are **irregular.** Instead of adding *-er* to *good* for the comparative form and *-est* for the superlative, the comparative and superlative forms of *good* and *bad* are as follows:

Regular: good, bad

Comparative: better, worse

Superlative: best, worst

Practice Identify the forms used to compare *good* and *bad* in the following lines. Label each form as comparative or superlative.

> That age is best which is the first,
> When youth and blood are warmer;
> But being spent, the worse, and worst
> Times still succeed the former.

Writing Application Write a paragraph comparing three different periods in your life. Use correct comparative and superlative forms of *good* and *bad* in your writing.

WG *Prentice Hall Writing and Grammar Connection: Chapter 24, Section 1*

Writing Lesson

Witty Poem

The speakers in these poems spin clever arguments and witty phrases to persuade their listeners to "seize the day." Write a poem in which you use humor and wordplay to win an argument.

Prewriting   Identify the speaker of your poem, the speaker's purpose, and the audience. Decide on the type of humor and argument that will work with this audience.

Drafting   To give your poem a persuasive tone, be confident in your argument. Use fresh, natural, vivid words and images, and build a sense of urgency by issuing playful commands to your audience. Include puns or other forms of wordplay.

Revising   Review your draft, bracketing "dead spots"—phrases or ideas that lack urgency or vividness or that are too familiar to sound fresh. Revise these sections to give them the punchy, persuasive tone you need.

Model: Revising to Achieve a Persuasive Tone

I can't believe you're

[~~You spend your time just~~] sitting there, E-mailing your life

                       he-male's

away. / Come on and take your ~~boyfriend's~~ dare. [~~Let's~~

Get up! Let's go! It's May!

~~have some fun~~] this May.

> The new wording of the first and last lines has a much more urgent tone than the wording in the first draft. The wordplay "he-male" should win a smile from the listener.

W̶G̶ *Prentice Hall Writing and Grammar Connection: Chapter 6, Connected Assignment*

Extension Activities

Listening and Speaking With a partner, present a **phone skit** based on "Song."

1. Choose roles: lovelorn friend or exasperated giver of advice.
2. "Translate" the poem into advice you might give a lovelorn friend today. Then, work out the friend's reply to each stanza.
3. Rehearse your role play by sitting back to back and speaking into phones.

Perform your skit for your class. [**Group Activity**]

Research and Technology The lives of each of these poets was affected by the English Civil War. Do research on their lives and on the war. Write a **comparative biographical essay** comparing the impact of the war on each of their lives. Incorporate timelines and other graphics to illustrate your comparisons.

 **Take It to the Net**   www.phschool.com

Go online for an additional research activity using the Internet.

CONNECTIONS
Literature and Music
The War Against Time

The poets in this section wrote during one of the most turbulent periods of English history, the years leading up to and including the Civil War. Religious persecution and political strife prompted a new awareness of the uncertainty of life. Against this backdrop of conflict, poets like Marvell and Herrick remind us that time is fleeting and advise us to seize each moment, rather than postponing decisions.

Songs That Reflect on Time The elusiveness of time, central to the works of these seventeenth-century poets, is still a popular theme in today's literature, movies, and songs. Songwriter Suzanne Vega's "Freeze Tag" presents a moment frozen in time as two people hesitate over whether to become a couple. The central message of the song echoes the *carpe diem* ("seize the day") theme of Marvell and Herrick. Tracy Chapman's "New Beginning" describes a world in turmoil. Her socially conscious lyrics encourage people to stop time, erase the past, and re-create the world.

"Seize the Day" The fast pace of today's world often robs us of the opportunity to make the most of our time. The advice given by the seventeenth-century poets to "seize the day" and make the most of life is still valid today.

Freeze Tag

Suzanne Vega

We go to the playground
in the wintertime
the sun is fading fast
upon the slides into the past
upon the swings of indecision
in the wintertime

in the dimming diamonds
scattering in the park
in the tickling
and the trembling
of freeze tag
in the dark

✔ **Reading Check**

What is the setting of
the song?

We play that we're actors
on a movie screen
I will be Dietrich
and you can be Dean

you stand
with your hand
in your pocket
and lean against the wall
You will be Bogart
and I will be
Bacall
And we can only say yes now
to the sky, to the street, to the night

Slow fade now to black
Play me one more game
of chivalry
you and me
do you see
where I've been hiding
in this hide-and-seek?

We go to the playground
in the wintertime
the sun is fading fast
upon the slides into the past
upon the swings of indecision
in the wintertime
wintertime
wintertime

We can only say yes now,
to the sky, to the street, to the night
We can only say yes now
to the sky, to the street, to the night

Thematic Connection
Compare Vega's way of presenting the moment of decision with Marvell's image of the ball in "To His Coy Mistress."

Suzanne Vega

(b. 1959)

Songwriter Suzanne Vega grew up in New York's Spanish Harlem. By age fourteen, she had begun writing music. By the time she was sixteen, she was performing in coffeehouses. Her sweet folk style, along with her fresh, direct observations of life and poetic lyrics, appeals to a diverse audience. Vega won nominations for the Grammy Awards for record of the year, song of the year, and best female pop performance in 1987.

Connecting Literature and Music

1. Compare the images of fleeting time used in the opening stanza with those used by Herrick in "To the Virgins."
2. (a) Compare the games in "Freeze Tag" with the "game" Marvell's speaker plays in the opening of "To His Coy Mistress." (b) How might such games help romance along?
3. (a) Contrast the attitudes toward the passing moment in Vega's song and in Marvell's poem. (b) Which attitude do you think is more justified? Explain.

New Beginning

Tracy Chapman

The whole world's broke and it ain't worth fixing
It's time to start all over, make a new beginning
There's too much pain, too much suffering
Let's resolve to start all over make a new beginning
Now don't get me wrong—I love life and living
But when you wake up and look around at everything
            that's going down—
All wrong
You see we need to change it now, this world with too
            few happy endings
We can resolve to start all over make a new beginning

Refrain:
Start all over
Start all over
Start all over
Start all over

The world is broken into fragments and pieces
That once were joined together in a unified whole
But now too many stand alone—There's too much
        separation
We can resolve to come together in the new beginning

(Refrain)

We can break the cycle—We can break the chain
We can start all over—In the new beginning
We can learn, we can teach
We can share the myths the dream the prayer
The notion that we can do better
Change our lives and paths
Create a new world and

(Refrain)

The whole world's broke and it ain't worth fixing
It's time to start all over, make a new beginning
There's too much fighting, too little understanding
It's time to stop and start all over
Make a new beginning

(Refrain)

We need to make new symbols
Make new signs
Make a new language
With these we'll define the world

(Refrain)

Connecting Literature and Music

1. Contrast the idea that we should "start all over" with the decision that Herrick proposes in "To the Virgins."

2. Compare Donne's idea in Meditation 17 that we are all near death with Chapman's idea that "the whole world's broke."

3. Whose ideas come closest to your own? Explain.

Tracy Chapman

(b. 1964)

Tracy Chapman grew up in a working-class neighborhood in Cleveland, Ohio. At an early age, she taught herself to play the guitar and began to write music. Chapman's love of music and knowledge motivated her to seek the best education possible. After winning a scholarship to a prestigious prep school, she observed that her wealthy classmates were often ignorant of the harsh realities of poverty. Chapman uses her music to combat such ignorance and to raise awareness of social issues and spiritual concerns.

Whitehall, January 30th, 1649, (Execution of Charles I),
Ernest Crofts, Forbes Magazine

Prepare to Read

Poetry of John Milton

John Milton (1608–1674)

John Milton is regarded as one of the greatest poets of the English language, yet he owes this regard to comparatively few poems. Much of his work is in Latin, not English, and during the fifteen years he spent writing political pamphlets and other prose works, he wrote little poetry. Although other poets have surpassed him in quantity, Milton's masterpiece, the epic *Paradise Lost*, is enough to establish him as the equal of Chaucer and Shakespeare. Milton himself never lacked self-confidence, setting his sights on poetic greatness at the start of his career.

A Privileged Childhood Milton was born in London to a middle-class family and grew up in a highly cultured environment. His father, a professional scribe who drew up contracts and lent money, was also a composer and musician of considerable ability. Deeply religious, Milton's father was devoted to the Protestant cause. At the age of thirteen, Milton started his formal education, the equivalent of high school. He was also tutored at home. He mastered Greek, Latin, and Hebrew, as well as several modern European languages. After this thorough education, Milton went on to college.

God's Poet When Milton entered Christ's College at Cambridge University, he had already decided to prepare himself for a career as a great poet ("God's poet" was how he described himself). It appears that for a time he also considered entering the ministry. The religious and political situation at the time, though, was quite uncertain, so Milton devoted himself to a life of study. After earning his degrees from Cambridge, he withdrew to his father's house, first at Hammersmith, then at Horton in Buckinghamshire, for nearly six years, where, it is said, he read everything that was written in the ancient and modern languages at his command. It was during this long period of study that he wrote one of his best-known poems, "Lycidas." That work, together with the poems "L'Allegro" and "Il Penseroso," written during his student days, marked the young Milton as a gifted poet destined for fame.

A Man of Ideals Following his studies, Milton went to continental Europe for a planned two-year Grand Tour, during which he called on the astronomer Galileo (1564–1642). While he was away, Parliament rebelled against King Charles I, eventually replacing the monarchy with a government led by Oliver Cromwell. Learning of the revolt, Milton cut short his trip and returned to England. He began writing pamphlets for the Puritan cause, criticizing the control of the bishops over the English church.

Public Service, Private Loss In 1649, when the Puritans decided to execute Charles I, Milton wrote a treatise defending this act. Impressed by Milton's brilliantly presented opinions, Cromwell made him Secretary of State for Foreign Tongues. This position required Milton to translate official documents into Latin and to write in defense of the new government against Royalist attacks. It was while serving in this position that he lost his eyesight.

In 1660, Milton's fortunes took a turn for the worse. The monarchy was restored, and Milton was imprisoned for a time. (His friend, the poet Andrew Marvell, may have been instrumental in gaining his release.) Blind and stripped of most of his property, Milton withdrew once again into words—he wrote *Paradise Lost* (1667), the greatest epic of the English language.

Preview

Connecting to the Literature

At the pauses in life, you may ask, How far have I come? How far yet to go? In these poems, the speaker pauses to reflect on his journey.

Literary Analysis

The Italian Sonnet; Epic Poetry

An **Italian**, or **Petrarchan**, **sonnet** is a fourteen-line lyric poem. The first eight lines, called the octave, rhyme *abbaabba* and present a problem. A six-line sestet with a variable rhyme scheme responds to the octave. Note how, in Milton's Italian sonnets, one part flows into the next.

An **epic** is a long narrative poem about a hero. For seventeenth-century English writers, ancient epic poets such as Homer—the blind, half-mythical author of the *Iliad* and the *Odyssey*—set the standard for literary greatness. Notice how Milton uses the following features of Homeric epics in *Paradise Lost*:

- A story that begins in the middle of the action (*in medias res*)
- An opening invocation in which the poet calls for divine aid in telling his story
- Extended similes, comparisions using *like* or *as*

Comparing Literary Works

Writing an epic is an ambitious task—the writer of a successful epic is the spokesperson for an entire culture. In his poems, Milton reflects on his own ambitions for poetic greatness, addressing his insecurities about them and the setbacks he faces. Compare the ways in which Milton addresses the theme of poetic ambition, both in reflections on his own life and in his character Satan's angry desires.

Reading Strategy

Breaking Down Sentences

Break down sentences into smaller elements to clarify the meaning. Identify main clauses, which can stand by themselves, and supporting clauses, which cannot. Use a chart like the one shown as you read.

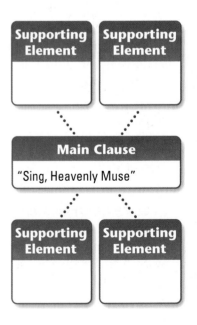

Vocabulary Development

semblance (sem′ bləns) *n.* appearance; image (p. 465)

illumine (i lo͞o′ mən) *v.* light up (p. 470)

transgress (trans gres′) *v.* violate a law or command (p. 470)

guile (gīl) *n.* artful trickery (p. 470)

obdurate (äb′ door it) *adj.* stubborn (p. 470)

tempestuous (tem pes′ cho͞o əs) *adj.* turbulent; stormy (p. 471)

transcendent (tran sen′ dənt) *adj.* exceeding beyond all limits (p. 471)

suppliant (sup′ lē ənt) *adj.* imploring (p. 472)

ignominy (ig′ nə min′ ē) *n.* humiliation; dishonor (p. 472)

A Closer Look

Making "Darkness Visible": Milton's Epic Ambition

People tell stories for different reasons. Some tell stories to keep their hopes up. Some tell stories to mark what they have left behind. In the 1650s, the aged John Milton decided to retell the central story of his culture—the Biblical story of the creation, fall, and redemption of humanity—in two epics, the poems *Paradise Lost* and *Paradise Regained*. With these works, Milton gave his nation a gift, reaffirming Britain's core values after a decade of war.

Storytelling and Adversity When you consider Milton's circumstances, you will see that his reasons for telling this story were strong. By 1652, Milton was completely blind. Unable to write himself, he dictated the poem to his daughters, who copied down each word. As he worked, the world crumbled around him. The monarchy he had opposed was restored to England, and he went to jail for a time. Blind, disgraced, and disillusioned, Milton nevertheless persevered. Over perhaps ten years, he dictated nearly 11,000 lines of poetry. The result, critics agree, is the greatest epic in the English language, *Paradise Lost*.

An Overview *Paradise Lost* is divided into twelve books, and like many epics, it begins in the middle. Milton introduces Satan who, with his angel allies, has done the unthinkable—rebelled against God. At the opening of the epic, Satan's army has just lost the war. Expelled from heaven, they have plummeted into Hell. Milton is equal to the challenge of describing Hell, a place devoid of light, life, and even form: "one great furnace flamed, yet from those flames / No light, but rather darkness visible / Served only to discern sights of woe."

Satan's war with Heaven is Milton's invention. The remainder of the story is the familiar one of Christian tradition. God has forbidden Adam and Eve to eat of the fruit of the Tree of the Knowledge of Good and Evil. Bent on revenge, Satan tempts Eve into eating of the apple. She then persuades Adam to partake. This event, the Fall of Adam and Eve, leads to their (and so humanity's) expulsion from the Garden of Eden. Adam is caught between gladness and sorrow over his sin, for the angel has told him that the world will receive a Savior as a result of the Fall. Adam and Eve leave Paradise with a sense of hopeful resolution: "The World was all before them, where to choose / Their place of rest, and Providence their guide. . . ."

A Cosmic Commentary Apart from telling this grand story, large portions of *Paradise Lost* are dedicated to another grand project—"justifying the ways of God to man." In the story, God sends the angel Raphael to Paradise to warn Adam of the necessity of obedience. In their conversation, Milton is able to speak on a few issues that were controversial in his day.

▼ **Critical Viewing**
What feelings does this portrayal of Adam and Eve convey?
[Interpret]

- **Reason and Free Will** Humanity can see the difference between right and wrong. With that ability comes the freedom to choose between the two.

- **Free Will and Predestination** God knows everything that is, was, and will be. Yet God's foreknowledge of a person's actions does not mean that the person's choices were determined in advance, by God. People have free will.

By affirming free will, Milton broke with some of the sternest Puritans of his day, who held that men and women were predestined to salvation or damnation. Milton's epic story finds individuals responsible for their own actions and fate and so grants them dignity.

Words in the Void In a sense, *Paradise Lost* is Milton's answer to the great historical crisis through which Britain had just passed. Puritans, including Milton, had challenged the official Church of England. They demanded a return to what they saw as the original principles of the Christian religion. At the same time, religious controversy had contributed to the Civil War (1642–1649) waged against King Charles I. Casting aside centuries of tradition and sentiment, Parliament eventually put its own king to death.

These upheavals shattered the symbolic centers of English life and culture, Church and King. Into the resulting void, Milton pronounced the rolling, often majestic phrases of *Paradise Lost*. He helped the nation find its bearings again by retelling the central story of its culture. In the dark, defiant figure of the rebel angel Satan, he commemorated the destructive forces that had recently torn through the nation. At the same time, the fall of Satan symbolically puts rebellious urges into their proper place—the netherworld of Hell. It was these tasks, perhaps, that drove the blind Milton to rise above adversity and deliver this epic to his country.

Milton's Legacy Over the centuries Milton's story of the Fall has become as well known as the biblical version. It has influenced writers as diverse as the poets William Blake, the visionary, and John Keats, the introspective dreamer, as well as the novelist George Eliot, a formidable social critic. By the nineteenth century, study of Milton's epic was considered an essential part of a respectable education, and even relatively uneducated people could be expected to have two books in their homes—the King James Bible and *Paradise Lost*. In telling a story to heal his own time, Milton fed the imaginations of generations to come.

Satan Smitten by Michael, Gustave Doré, for *Paradise Lost*

▲ **Critical Viewing**
Milton describes the light in Hell as "darkness visible." Explain whether the engraving captures this quality. **[Interpret]**

Sonnet VII

("How soon hath Time")

John Milton

Background

While sonnet writers of the Elizabethan Age, such as Spenser, Sidney, and Shakespeare, had mustered all the force of wit and words to chart the experiences of romantic love, Milton found other topics for his sonnets. The form proved strong enough to accommodate a variety of subjects, as Milton shows in these reflections on the limitations placed on human life.

How soon hath Time, the subtle thief of youth,
    Stolen on his wing my three and twentieth year!
    My hasting days fly on with full career,[1]
    But my late spring no bud or blossom showeth.
5 Perhaps my <u>semblance</u> might deceive[2] the truth,
    That I to manhood am arrived so near,
    And inward ripeness doth much less appear,
    That some more timely-happy spirits[3] endueth.[4]
    Yet be it less or more, or soon or slow,
10   It shall be still[5] in strictest measure even
    To that same lot,[6] however mean or high,
Toward which Time leads me, and the will of Heaven;
    All is, if I have grace to use it so,
    As ever in my great Taskmaster's eye.

semblance (sem´ bləns) *n.*
appearance; image

---

1. **career** speed.
2. **deceive** prove false.
3. **timely-happy spirits** others who seem to be more accomplished poets at the age of twenty-four.
4. **endueth** endows.
5. **still** always.
6. **lot** fate.

Review and Assess

Thinking About the Selection

1. **Respond:** Do you usually judge people by how much they have accomplished by a certain age? Why or why not?

2. **(a) Recall:** What occasion leads Milton to the thoughts in the poem? **(b) Infer:** Judging from the image in lines 1–2, how does Milton view this occasion?

3. **(a) Recall:** To what season does Milton compare his time of life? **(b) Infer:** Why does he say that this season "no bud or blossom showeth"? **(c) Interpret:** What is his feeling about this situation?

4. **(a) Interpret:** What is the connection between the "bud or blossom" of line 4 and the "semblance" of line 5? **(b) Interpret:** How does the contrast between outward appearance and inward state in lines 5–8 apply to Milton's career as a poet?

5. **(a) Infer:** To what does Milton trust himself and his life in lines 9–14? **(b) Interpret:** In what way does this act of trust answer his worries in the first part of the poem? **(c) Evaluate:** Do you think this "answer" is a valid and effective response to concern about one's progress in life? Explain.

John Milton, 1878, Mihaly von Munkacsy

▲ **Critical Viewing** How does Milton's pose in this portrait reflect the theme of the poem? **[Speculate]**

Sonnet XIX
("When I consider how my light is spent")
John Milton

When I consider how my light is spent
    Ere half my days, in this dark world and wide,
    And that one talent[1] which is death to hide,
    Lodged with me useless, though my soul more bent
5 To serve therewith my Maker, and present
    My true account, lest he returning chide;
    "Doth God exact day labor, light denied?"
    I fondly[2] ask; but Patience to prevent
That murmur, soon replies, "God doth not need
10   Either man's work or his own gifts; who best
    Bear his mild yoke, they serve him best. His state
Is kingly. Thousands[3] at his bidding speed
    And post[4] o'er land and ocean without rest:
    They also serve who only stand and wait."

Literary Analysis
The Italian Sonnet and Poetic Ambition
What setback to his poetic ambition does Milton describe in this sonnet?

---

1. **talent** allusion to the parable of the talents (Matthew 25: 14–30). The servant who earns interest for his master on five talents (a large unit of money) is commended. The servant who hides and then returns a talent is condemned to "outer darkness."
2. **fondly** foolishly.
3. **thousands** thousands of angels.
4. **post** travel.

Review and Assess
Thinking About the Selection

1. **(a) Recall:** According to the poem, at what point in his life did the speaker's eyesight fail? **(b) Infer:** In line 2, how does his way of identifying this point in his life emphasize the despair he feels?

2. **(a) Recall:** What has happened to the speaker's "one talent"? **(b) Infer:** Why does blindness have this effect on his talent?

3. **(a) Connect:** In lines 3–6, what connection does the speaker make between the use of one's talent and service to God? **(b) Interpret:** What dilemma does this connection create for him? **(c) Interpret:** What does his complaint in line 7 mean?

4. **(a) Infer:** What answers the speaker? **(b) Interpret:** How does this new speaker interpret the idea of service to God?

5. **Apply:** Do you think that this poem could inspire a contemporary person who is facing a physical challenge? Explain.

from PARADISE LOST

John Milton

Paradise Lost, 1688, From the British Library

▲ **Critical Viewing** Is this illustration an accurate visual representation of Milton's Hell? Explain. **[Evaluate]**

Background

Paradise Lost was written as the dust was settling after years of war and turmoil. From 1642 to 1660, the government of England went from a monarchy to a commonwealth (rule by Parliament) to a protectorate (rule by one man, Oliver Cromwell) to a monarchy. During this two-decade period, no matter which side a person was on, he or she experienced both defeat and triumph.

Perhaps Milton wrote *Paradise Lost* because he sensed that the nation needed an anchor, a literary work that would once again help define and unite a culture. His explanation of God's reason for allowing suffering in the world, and the dark, proud figure of the rebel Satan pitted against God in civil war, must have led readers to reflect on England's own civil war.

Of man's first disobedience, and the fruit
Of that forbidden tree, whose mortal[1] taste
Brought death into the world, and all our woe,
With loss of Eden, till one greater Man[2]
5 Restore us, and regain the blissful seat,
Sing Heavenly Muse,[3] that on the secret top
Of Oreb, or of Sinai,[4] didst inspire
That shepherd, who first taught the chosen seed,
In the beginning how the Heavens and Earth
10 Rose out of Chaos: or if Sion hill[5]
Delight thee more, and Siloa's brook[6] that flowed
Fast[7] by the oracle of God, I thence
Invoke thy aid to my adventurous song,
That with no middle flight intends to soar
15 Above the Aonian mount,[8] while it pursues
Things unattempted yet in prose or rhyme.
And chiefly thou O Spirit,[9] that dost prefer
Before all temples the upright heart and pure,
Instruct me, for thou know'st; thou from the first

Literary Analysis
Epic Poetry What epic convention does Milton follow in his opening sentence?

---

1. **mortal** deadly.
2. **one . . . Man** Christ.
3. **Heavenly Muse** Urania, the muse of astronomy and sacred poetry in Greek mythology. Here, Milton associates Urania with the holy spirit that inspired Moses ("That shepherd") to receive and interpret the word of God for the Jews ("the chosen seed"). To convey the message of God to his people, Moses wrote the first five books of the Bible, including Genesis, the book on which *Paradise Lost* is based.
4. **Oreb** (ôr´ eb) **. . . Sinai** (sī´ nī´) alternate names for the mountain where God communicated the laws to Moses.
5. **Sion** (sī´ ən) **hill** hill near Jerusalem on which the temple ("the oracle of God") stood.
6. **Siloa's** (sī lō´ əz) **brook** stream near Sion hill.
7. **fast** close.
8. **Aonian** (ā ō´ nē ən) **Mount** Mount Helicon in Greek mythology, home of the Muses. Milton is drawing a comparison between the epic he is now presenting and the epics written by the classical poets, Homer and Virgil.
9. **Spirit** the Holy Spirit, the voice that provided inspiration for the Hebrew prophets.

✔**Reading Check**

Whom does Milton call to help him tell his story?

20 Wast present, and with mighty wings outspread
    Dovelike sat'st brooding on the vast abyss
    And mad'st it pregnant: what in me is dark
    <u>Illumine</u>, what is low raise and support;
    That to the height of this great argument[10]
25 I may assert Eternal Providence,
    And justify the ways of God to men.
            Say first, for Heaven hides nothing from thy view
    Nor the deep tract of Hell, say first what cause
    Moved our grand[11] parents in that happy state,
30 Favored of Heaven so highly, to fall off
    From their Creator, and <u>transgress</u> his will
    For[12] one restraint,[13] lords of the world besides?[14]
    Who first seduced them to that foul revolt?
    The infernal Serpent; he it was, whose <u>guile</u>
35 Stirred up with envy and revenge, deceived
    The mother of mankind, what time his pride
    Had cast him out from Heaven, with all his host
    Of rebel angels, by whose aid aspiring
    To set himself in glory above his peers,
40 He trusted to have equaled the Most High,
    If he opposed; and with ambitious aim
    Against the throne and monarchy of God
    Raised impious war in Heaven and battle proud,
    With vain attempt. Him the Almighty Power
45 Hurled headlong flaming from the ethereal sky
    With hideous ruin and combustion down
    To bottomless perdition, there to dwell
    In adamantine[15] chains and penal fire,
    Who durst defy the Omnipotent to arms.
50 Nine times the space that measures day and night
    To mortal men, he with his horrid crew
    Lay vanquished, rolling in the fiery gulf,
    Confounded though immortal. But his doom
    Reserved him to more wrath; for now the thought
55 Both of lost happiness and lasting pain
    Torments him; round he throws his baleful eyes
    That witnessed[16] huge affliction and dismay,
    Mixed with <u>obdurate</u> pride and steadfast hate.
    At once as far as angels' ken,[17] he views

illumine (i lōō′ mən) *v.* light up

transgress (trans gres′) *v.* violate a law or command

guile (gīl) *n.* artful trickery

Literary Analysis
Epic Poetry and Poetic Ambition What does the story Milton has chosen to retell reveal about his poetic ambition?

obdurate (äb′ door it) *adj.* stubborn

---

10. **argument** theme.
11. **grand** first in importance and in time.
12. **For** because of.
13. **one restraint** commandment that Adam and Eve should not eat of the fruit of the tree of knowledge.
14. **besides** in every other respect.
15. **adamantine** (ad′ ə man′ tēn′) *adj.* unbreakable.
16. **witnessed** gave evidence of.
17. **ken** view; scope of knowledge

60 The dismal situation waste and wild:
   A dungeon horrible, on all sides round,
   As one great furnace flamed, yet from those flames
   No light, but rather darkness visible
   Served only to discover sights of woe,
65 Regions of sorrow, doleful shades, where peace
   And rest can never dwell, hope never comes
   That comes to all; but torture without end
   Still urges,[18] and a fiery deluge, fed
   With ever-burning sulfur unconsumed:
70 Such place eternal justice had prepared
   For these rebellious, here their prison ordained
   In utter darkness, and their portion set
   As far removed from God and light of Heaven
   As from the center thrice to the utmost pole.[19]
75 O how unlike the place from whence they fell!
   There the companions of his fall, o'erwhelmed
   With floods and whirlwinds of <u>tempestuous</u> fire,
   He soon discerns, and weltering by his side
   One next himself in power, and next in crime,
80 Long after known in Palestine, and named
   Beelzebub.[20] To whom the archenemy,
   And thence in Heaven called Satan, with bold words
   Breaking the horrid silence thus began:
        "If thou beest he; but O how fallen! how changed
85 From him, who in the happy realms of light
   Clothed with <u>transcendent</u> brightness didst outshine
   Myriads though bright: if he whom mutual league,
   United thoughts and counsels, equal hope
   And hazard in the glorious enterprise,
90 Joined with me once, now misery hath joined
   In equal ruin: into what pit thou seest
   From what height fallen, so much the stronger proved
   He with his thunder:[21] and till then who knew
   The force of those dire arms? Yet not for those,
95 Nor what the potent Victor in his rage
   Can else inflict, do I repent or change,
   Though changed in outward luster, that fixed mind
   And high disdain, from sense of injured merit,
   That with the Mightiest raised me to contend,
100 And to the fierce contention brought along
   Innumerable force of spirits armed

---

18. urges afflicts.
19. Center . . . . pole three times the distance from the center of the universe (Earth) to the outermost sphere of the universe.
20. Beelzebub (bē el′ zə bub′) traditionally, the chief devil, or Satan. In this poem, Satan's chief lieutenant among the fallen angels.
21. He . . . thunder God.

◀ **Critical Viewing**
What traditional associations between sin and death explain this artist's rendering of one of Milton's fallen angels? **[Hypothesize]**

tempestuous (tem pes′ chōō əs) *adj.* turbulent; stormy

transcendent (tran sen′ dənt) *adj.* exceeding beyond all limits

Literary Analysis
Epic Poetry What details in these lines suggest that Satan is a suitable hero for an epic?

✔ **Reading Check**
Whom does Satan discover lying next to him?

That durst dislike his reign, and me preferring,
His utmost power with adverse power opposed
In dubious battle on the plains of Heaven,
105 And shook his throne. What though the field be lost?
All is not lost; the unconquerable will,
And study[22] of revenge, immortal hate,
And courage never to submit or yield:
And what is else not to be overcome?
110 That glory never shall his wrath or might
Extort from me. To bow and sue for grace
With suppliant knee, and deify his power
Who from the terror of this arm so late
Doubted[23] his empire, that were low indeed,
115 That were an ignominy and shame beneath
This downfall; since by fate the strength of gods
And this empyreal substance[24] cannot fail,
Since through experience of this great event,
In arms not worse, in foresight much advanced,
120 We may with more successful hope resolve
To wage by force or guile eternal war
Irreconcilable, to our grand Foe,
Who now triumphs, and in the excess of joy
Sole reigning holds the tyranny of Heaven."
125   So spake the apostate angel, though in pain,
Vaunting aloud, but racked with deep despair;
And him thus answered soon his bold compeer.[25]
    "O prince, O chief of many thronèd Powers,
That led the embattled Seraphim[26] to war
130 Under thy conduct, and in dreadful deeds
Fearless, endangered Heaven's perpetual King,
And put to proof his high supremacy,
Whether upheld by strength, or chance, or fate!
Too well I see and rue the dire event[27]
135 That with sad overthrow and foul defeat
Hath lost us Heaven, and all this mighty host
In horrible destruction laid thus low,
As far as gods and heavenly essences
Can perish: for the mind and spirit remains
140 Invincible, and vigor soon returns,
Though all our glory extinct, and happy state
Here swallowed up in endless misery.

22. **study** pursuit.
23. **Doubted** feared for.
24. **empyreal** (em pir´ ē əl) **substance** the indestructible substance of which Heaven, or the empyrean, is composed.
25. **compeer** comrade; equal.
26. **Seraphim** (ser´ ə fim´) the highest order of angels.
27. **event** outcome.

Literary Analysis

Epic Poetry In what way does Milton's vision of the opposition between Satan and God fit the expectation that epics tell of famous battles?

suppliant (sup´ lē ənt) *adj.* imploring

ignominy (ig´ nə min´ ē) *n.* humiliation; dishonor

Reading Strategy

Breaking Down Sentences Rewrite lines 134–142 in your own words, putting the ideas in the main clause first.

But what if he our conqueror (whom I now
Of force[28] believe almighty, since no less
145 Than such could have o'erpowered such force as ours)
Have left us this our spirit and strength entire
Strongly to suffer and support our pains,
That we may so suffice[29] his vengeful ire,
Or do him mightier service as his thralls
150 By right of war, whate'er his business be
Here in the heart of Hell to work in fire,
Or do his errands in the gloomy deep?
What can it then avail though yet we feel
Strength undiminished, or eternal being
155 To undergo eternal punishment?"
Whereto with speedy words the Archfiend replied:
    "Fallen cherub, to be weak is miserable,
Doing or suffering:[30] but of this be sure,
To do aught[31] good never will be our task,
160 But ever to do ill our sole delight,
As being the contrary to his high will
Whom we resist. If then his providence
Out of our evil seek to bring forth good,
Our labor must be to pervert that end,
165 And out of good still[32] to find means of evil;
Which oft times may succeed, so as perhaps
Shall grieve him, if I fail not,[33] and disturb
His inmost counsels from their destined aim.
But see the angry Victor[34] hath recalled
170 His ministers of vengeance and pursuit
Back to the gates of Heaven: the sulfurous hail
Shot after us in storm, o'erblown hath laid
The fiery surge, that from the precipice
Of Heaven received us falling, and the thunder,
175 Winged with red lightning and impetuous rage,
Perhaps hath spent his shafts, and ceases now
To bellow through the vast and boundless deep.
Let us not slip[35] the occasion, whether scorn,
Or satiate[36] fury yield it from our Foe.
180 Seest thou yon dreary plain, forlorn and wild,
The seat of desolation, void of light,
Save what the glimmering of these livid flames

Paradise Lost, 1688, (detail)
John Milton British Library

▲ **Critical Viewing**
Milton's angels go to war. What is war-like about this depiction of an angel? **[Interpret]**

Literary Analysis
Epic What assumptions about the epic struggle between good and evil does Milton make in lines 159–168?

---

28. **Of force** necessarily.
29. **suffice** satisfy.
30. **doing or suffering** whether one is active or passive.
31. **aught** anything.
32. **still** always.
33. **if . . . not** unless I am mistaken.
34. **angry Victor** God.
35. **slip** fail to take advantage of.
36. **satiate** (sā′ shē āt′) satisfied.

✔**Reading Check**

What dose Satan tell Beelzebub their sole purpose will be?

Casts pale and dreadful? Thither let us tend
From off the tossing of these fiery waves,
185 There rest, if any rest can harbor there,
And reassembling our afflicted powers,[37]
Consult how we may henceforth most offend
Our Enemy, our own loss how repair,
How overcome this dire calamity,
190 What reinforcement we may gain from hope,
If not what resolution from despair."

      Thus Satan talking to his nearest mate,
With head uplift above the wave, and eyes
That sparkling blazed; his other parts besides
195 Prone on the flood, extended long and large,
Lay floating many a rood,[38] in bulk as huge
As whom the fables name of monstrous size,
Titanian, or Earthborn, that warred on Jove,
Briareos or Typhon,[39] whom the den
200 By ancient Tarsus[40] held, or that sea beast
Leviathan,[41] which God of all his works
Created hugest that swim the ocean stream:
Him haply slumbering on the Norway foam
The pilot of some small night-foundered skiff,
205 Deeming some island, oft, as seamen tell,
With fixed anchor in his scaly rind
Moors by his side under the lee, while night
Invests[42] the sea, and wished morn delays:
So stretched out huge in length the Archfiend lay
210 Chained on the burning lake, nor ever thence
Had risen or heaved his head, but that the will
And high permission of all-ruling Heaven
Left him at large to his own dark designs,
That with reiterated crimes he might
215 Heap on himself damnation, while he sought
Evil to others, and enraged might see
How all his malice served but to bring forth
Infinite goodness, grace and mercy shown
On man by him seduced, but on himself
220 Treble confusion, wrath and vengeance poured.

The British Tradition

Renewing the Literary Tradition

We value a poet like Milton for his originality, but like many poets, he creates what is original by returning to a tradition—a developing body of work widely read and respected by a culture. By going back to past works, Milton is able to define his own poetic tasks and tools in unique ways. To create *Paradise Lost,* he borrowed the form of the epic from ancient Greek and Roman writers and drew on the Bible for the story of Adam and Eve. The result, though, is a new, disenchanted vision of the human condition with all its stark limitations.

Like Milton, modern poets, including Derek Walcott and Seamus Heaney, also consciously return to a tradition. When Walcott reflects on the place of black writers in a tradition dominated by whites, when he calls on African storytelling traditions, or when Heaney retranslates the Anglo-Saxon epic *Beowulf,* they explore their own poetic vision by reworking their literary heritage.

---

37. **afflicted powers** overthrown armies.
38. **rood** old unit of measure equal to seven or eight yards.
39. **Titanian** (tī tā´ nē ən) . . . **Earthborn** . . . **Briareos** (brī ar´ ē əs) . . . **Typhon** (tī´ fən) In classical mythology, both the Titans, led by Briareos, who had a hundred hands, and the Giants (Earthborn), led by Typhon, a hundred-headed serpent monster, fought with Jove. As punishment for their rebellion, both Briareos and Typhon were thrown into the underworld.
40. **Tarsus** (tär´ səs) capital of Cilicia (sə lish´ə). Typhon is said to have lived in Cilicia near Tarsus.
41. **Leviathan** (lə vī´ ə thən) in the Bible, a great sea monster.
42. **Invests** covers.

Forthwith upright he rears from off the pool
His mighty stature; on each hand the flames
Driven backward, slope their pointing spires, and rolled
In billows leave in the midst a horrid vale.
225 Then with expanded wings he steers his flight
Aloft, incumbent[43] on the dusky air
That felt unusual weight, till on dry land
He lights, if it were land that ever burned
With solid, as the lake with liquid fire;
230 And such appeared in hue, as when the force
Of subterranean wind transports a hill
Torn from Pelorus, or the shattered side
Of thundering Etna,[44] whose combustible
And fueled entrails thence conceiving fire,
235 Sublimed[45] with mineral fury, aid the winds,
And leave a singèd bottom all involved[46]
With stench and smoke: such resting found the sole
Of unblessed feet. Him followed his next mate,
Both glorying to have scaped the Stygian[47] flood
240 As gods, and by their own recovered strength,
Not by the sufferance[48] of supernal[49] power.
"Is this the region, this the soil, the clime,"
Said then the lost Archangel, "this the seat
That we must change[50] for Heaven, this mournful gloom
245 For that celestial light? Be it so, since he
Who now is sovereign can dispose and bid
What shall be right: farthest from him is best,
Whom reason hath equaled, force hath made supreme
Above his equals. Farewell happy fields,
250 Where joy forever dwells. Hail horrors! Hail
Infernal world! and thou, profoundest Hell
Receive thy new possessor, one who brings
A mind not to be changed by place or time.
The mind is its own place, and in itself
255 Can make a Heaven of Hell, a Hell of Heaven.
What matter where, if I be still the same,
And what I should be, all but less than he
Whom thunder hath made greater? Here at least
We shall be free; the Almighty hath not built
260 Here for his envy, will not drive us hence:

---

43. **incumbent** lying.
44. **Pelorus** (pə lôr´ əs) . . . **Etna** volcanic mountains in Sicily.
45. **Sublimed** vaporized.
46. **involved** enveloped.
47. **Stygian** (stij´ ē ən) of the river Styx, which, in Greek mythology, encircled Hades (hā´ dēz´), the home of the dead.
48. **sufferance** permission.
49. **supernal** (sə p♯rn´ əl) heavenly.
50. **change** exchange.

Reading Strategy
Breaking Down Sentences Put the ideas in lines 221–222 in a more natural order. Then, explain how Milton's wording makes the description more dramatic.

Literary Analysis
Epic Poetry and Poetic Ambition In what way is the attitude expressed in lines 250–258 fitting both for a hero and a poet?

**Reading Check**

In what manner do Satan and Beelzebub travel to land?

Here we may reign secure, and in my choice
To reign is worth ambition though in Hell:
Better to reign in Hell than serve in Heaven.
But wherefore[51] let we then our faithful friends,
265 The associates and copartners of our loss
Lie thus astonished[52] on the oblivious[53] pool,
And call them not to share with us their part
In this unhappy mansion, or once more
With rallied arms to try what may be yet
Regained in Heaven, or what more lost in Hell?"

---

51. **wherefore** why.
52. **astonished** stunned.
53. **oblivious** causing forgetfulness.

Review and Assess

Thinking About the Selection

1. **Respond:** What part of Milton's description of Hell do you find the most vivid? Explain.

2. **(a) Recall:** Summarize the story of Adam and Eve as Milton tells it in lines 28–36. **(b) Connect:** How is the fall of Adam and Eve connected to the fall of Satan and his cohorts?

3. **(a) Recall:** Lines 59–74 describe Hell. What does Milton describe as its main features? **(b) Interpret:** Explain Satan's reaction in lines 94–99 to his fall into Hell.

4. **(a) Infer:** In lines 116–124, what kind of war does Satan propose to wage against Heaven? **(b) Interpret:** Judging from lines 105–116, what is his motive for such a war? **(c) Hypothesize:** How will this war lead to the fall of Adam and Eve?

5. **(a) Interpret:** Explain how Satan's attitude toward Hell in lines 250–252 proves that he is "one who brings / A mind not to be changed by place or time" (lines 252–253).
   (b) Draw Conclusions: Explain how the mind "Can make a Heaven of Hell, a Hell of Heaven" (lines 254–255).

6. **(a) Analyze:** In lines 256–263, what three things does Satan imply are infinitely more important than the place in which he happens to be? **(b) Summarize:** Characterize Satan, supporting your description with quotations. **(c) Evaluate:** To what extent does Satan seem admirable? To what extent despairing? Explain.

7. **(a) Interpret:** What does Milton mean when he says he wants to "justify the ways of God to men" (line 26)? **(b) Assess:** How good a start has Milton made toward this goal?

Review and Assess

Literary Analysis

The Italian Sonnet; Epic Poetry

1. (a) Which **Italian sonnet** has the more regular pattern of rhymes in the sestet? (b) Does this regularity strengthen the "solution" the sestet gives to the problem set out in the octave? Explain.
2. (a) In Sonnet XIX, how does sentence structure break with the pattern of octave and sestet? (b) What effect is achieved?
3. (a) What major event has occurred before the beginning of Milton's **epic**? (b) How does picking up the story after this event follow the conventions of epic form?
4. A traditional epic hero is noble. How does Milton make Satan a suitable epic hero?

Comparing Literary Works

5. In Sonnets VII and XIX, Milton reflects on setbacks to his poetic ambition. Use a chart like the one shown to compare the two poems.

Speaker's Situation	Effect on Ambition	Solution	How Solution Helps

6. (a) Explain how, by writing *Paradise Lost*, Milton aspires to the literary greatness of Homer and the Bible. Provide lines from the poem in support. (b) Compare Milton's ambition with the moral of Sonnet XIX: "They also serve who only stand and wait."
7. (a) What ideas about the power of a poet might lines 254–255 of *Paradise Lost* suggest? (b) What parallel can you draw between the situation of Satan and the ambition of a poet?

Reading Strategy

Breaking Down Sentences

8. (a) Identify the main clause in lines 1–8 of Sonnet XIX.
   (b) Explain what each supporting clause adds to its meaning.

Extend Understanding

9. **Art Connection:** With what artistic depictions of Hell are you familiar? Share your recollections with the class.

Quick Review

An **Italian sonnet** is a fourteen-line poem with an eight-line octave and a six-line sestet. The rhyme scheme of the octave is *abbaabba*, and the rhyme scheme of the sestet varies.

An **epic** is a long narrative poem featuring a larger-than-life hero, and reflecting the values of the society in which it was created.

When you **break down sentences,** you identify the main clause and then determine what the other, supporting, phrases and clauses add to the meaning of the sentence.

 Take It to the Net
www.phschool.com
Take the interactive self-test online to check your understanding of the selection.

Integrate Language Skills

Vocabulary Development Lesson

Word Analysis: Latin Root -lum-

The Latin root -lum-, found in *illumine*, means "light" or "lamp." It is the base of many scientific words about light. Use this fact to match each word with its definition.

1. illumine
2. luminous
3. lumen
4. luminescence
5. illuminant

a. a unit of light
b. emission of light with little heat
c. light up
d. something that gives off light
e. giving off light

Spelling Strategy

The sound *in* at the end of words may be spelled *ine*, as in *illumine*, or *en*, as in *darken*. For each item below, fill in the blanks to spell the *in* sound correctly.

1. determ__   2. fam__   3. sull__

Concept Development: Synonyms

Synonyms are words that have the same or nearly the same meaning as each other. Review the vocabulary list on page 461. Then, for each numbered vocabulary word from the selections, identify its synonym and write its letter in your notebook.

1. transcendent
2. ignominy
3. tempestuous
4. suppliant
5. transgress
6. obdurate
7. semblance
8. guile
9. illumine

a. appearance
b. stubborn
c. violate
d. trickery
e. stormy
f. surpassing
g. pleading
h. light
i. disgrace

Grammar and Style Lesson

Usage: *who* and *whom*

Who is used as the subject of a verb. **Whom** is used as the object of a verb or of a preposition.

Subject: Poets <u>who</u> become great do not always publish early. [*Who* is the subject of the verb *become*.]

Object of a Verb: Fame comes to those <u>whom</u> fate chooses. [*Whom* is the direct object of *chooses*.]

Object of a Preposition: Fame may not come to the poet to <u>whom</u> it matters most. [*Whom* is the object of the preposition *to*.]

Practice Choose *who* or *whom* to complete each sentence correctly.

1. With ___?___ did the serpent quarrel?
2. ___?___ lay chained on the burning lake?
3. To ___?___ did Eve offer the apple?
4. ___?___ condemned the pair to eternal punishment?
5. ___?___ did Adam and Eve blame for their fate?

Writing Application Describe a setback you have experienced. In your writing, use *who* and *whom* at least once each.

WG *Prentice Hall Writing and Grammar Connection: Chapter 22, Section 2*

Writing Lesson

Critical Analysis of a Literary Theme

Eighteenth-century poet William Blake said that Milton "wrote in fetters when he wrote of Angels & God, and at liberty when of Devils & Hell." In an essay, explain why villains such as Milton's Satan engage the imagination so readily.

Prewriting   Review the excerpt from Milton's epic. Take notes on the character of Satan, and write two sentences explaining his appeal. Then, jot down notes on other villains with whom you are familiar.

Drafting   Begin with an analysis of Satan's appeal, and relate your observations about other villains to this analysis. Draw a conclusion about why villains can be fascinating.

Revising   Circle key words in your draft—terms that you use to identify central themes or character features. For each key word, write a "thought shot"—a list of associated terms. Review each list for ideas that will help you elaborate on your insights.

Model: Using Thought Shots to Elaborate

defiance
disobedience
tantrums rebellion
hopeless rebellion

He is not a spoiled child throwing a tantrum, though; he

knows exactly how hopeless his situation is. By setting him so

completely against his circumstances, his

Satan is defiant. His (defiance) makes him seem noble.

> The added images and ideas clarify and deepen the writer's insight.

Prentice Hall Writing and Grammar Connection: Chapter 14, Section 4

Extension Activities

Listening and Speaking Douglas Bush writes of *Paradise Lost*, "Its characterization of Satan is one of the supreme achievements of world literature." Prepare a **speech** defending or opposing Bush's opinion. Include the following:

1. Arguments evaluating the characterization of Satan against a standard you define
2. Emotional appeals based on your own response to the character of Satan
3. Supporting details from the poem

Deliver your speech to the class.

Research and Technology Milton's blindness did not prevent him from writing *Paradise Lost*. With a group, produce a **documentary** on the achievements of community members with disabilities. Divide the following tasks: conducting interviews, videotaping, researching, and writing a script. Present your documentary to the class. **[Group Activity]**

 Take It to the Net   www.phschool.com

Go online for an additional research activity using the Internet.

Prepare to Read

from Eve's Apology in Defense of Women ◆ To Lucasta, on Going to the Wars ◆ To Althea, From Prison

Amelia Lanier (1569–1645)

Amelia Lanier (also spelled "Lanyer") saw the need for women's rights three hundred years before the women's movement for equality. Daring to question her society's vision of women and the limited roles it allowed them, she anticipated future ideas of justice for women.

From Court Life to Working Woman Lanier had ties to the royal court, where her father, Baptista Bassano, was a musician to Queen Elizabeth I. Lanier's husband, Alphonso, and her son, Henry, were also court musicians. Despite her court connections, however, Lanier and her husband were not wealthy. When her husband died in 1613, Lanier sought to make a living by opening a school outside London.

A Radical Work In 1611, Lanier published a volume of poetry called *Salve Deus Rex Judaeorum* (*Hail, God, King of the Jews*). In this groundbreaking work, of which "Eve's Apology in Defense of Women" is a section, Lanier questioned the privileges of the upper class and called for women's social and religious equality with men.

Although a woman sat on the throne of England during much of Lanier's lifetime, few women in her day published poetry. The poems in *Salve Deus Rex Judaeoroum* reflect her sense that women were underrepresented in the culture of the time. Sections of the work praise her female patrons, while others re-evaluate the role of women in stories from the Bible.

"Dark Lady" or Visionary? In later times, Lanier was perhaps more famous as a possibility for Shakespeare's "dark lady" (the mysterious woman to whom he addresses some of his sonnets) than for her poetry. As scholars have explored the political undercurrents of past literature, though, interest in Lanier has revived. Today, Lanier is considered a visionary feminist who spoke out against injustice.

Richard Lovelace (1618–1657)

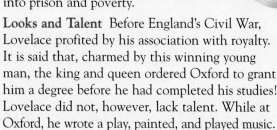

Richard Lovelace, son of a wealthy family and firm supporter of his king, had the misfortune to live at a time when the English monarchy was under violent assault. The Civil War that culminated in the execution of the king plunged the privileged Lovelace into prison and poverty.

Looks and Talent Before England's Civil War, Lovelace profited by his association with royalty. It is said that, charmed by this winning young man, the king and queen ordered Oxford to grant him a degree before he had completed his studies! Lovelace did not, however, lack talent. While at Oxford, he wrote a play, painted, and played music.

The Price of Loyalty Lovelace was about twenty-six when Parliament challenged the king's authority and civil war broke out. Perhaps because of his personal charm, Lovelace was chosen to demand that Parliament restore the king's authority. Parliament was not impressed, though, and Lovelace was immediately arrested.

A Daring Life While imprisoned, Lovelace wrote "To Althea, From Prison," a moving affirmation of the value of personal integrity, even if it meant imprisonment. When released, he rejoined Charles's forces and spent his fortune equipping the king's army. Upon Charles's defeat in 1645, Lovelace joined the wars against Spain.

An Untimely End Returning to England years later, Lovelace was again imprisoned by the Puritans. During this time, he prepared for publication the volume that included "To Lucasta, on Going to the Wars." No one knows for certain how Lovelace's life ended, but it is believed that the charming young man who had won the heart of his king and queen died in discouragement and poverty at the age of thirty-nine.

Preview

Connecting to the Literature

If you don't like the way things are, you can always speak up, but sometimes speaking up means paying a price. Unpopularity and punishment can be the costs of speaking out on controversial issues. Both Lanier and Lovelace had the courage to take such risks, speaking their minds in the face of opposition.

Literary Analysis

Tradition and Reform

Although they may seem to be opposites, tradition and reform go hand in hand.

- **Tradition** consists of a society's approved values, beliefs, roles, and practices.
- **Reform** attempts to change traditional practices and ideas.

Lanier is a clear reformer, fighting against stereotypes of women, while Lovelace fights for tradition, going to war and to prison for his king and his honor. As you read, note the appearance of themes of tradition and reform in their works.

Comparing Literary Works

Even when reformers' proposals are radical, they are often based on traditional beliefs. Lanier, for example, turns to the Bible, a traditional text, to support her new ideas about the equality between men and women. Lovelace, a supporter of the traditional power of his king, finds a new kind of freedom in love and integrity.

Both use a key strategy for interpreters of a tradition: They explore the multiple meanings of value terms such as *strength, honor,* and *freedom.* By redefining such terms, they find new ways to apply traditional ideas. As you read, compare the ways in which literary and political traditions and the spirit of reform weave their way through these works.

Reading Strategy

Using Historical Context

As you read a work, place it in its **historical context** by identifying ideas and assumptions that are typical of its era. Consider also which ideas may be responses to events of the period. To place Lanier's and Lovelace's poems in their context, complete a chart like the one shown for each work.

Poem
"Eve's Apology"

Historical Context
Seventeenth-century women's rights were restricted; story of Eve was used to justify these restrictions

Connection

Vocabulary Development

breach (brēch) *n.* breaking or being broken; failure to observe the terms of an agreement (p. 483)

discretion (di skresh´ ən) *n.* care in what one does and says (p. 483)

inconstancy (in kän´ stən sē) *n.* fickleness; changeableness (p. 484)

from *Eve's Apology in Defense of Women*

AMELIA LANIER

Background

During the late sixteenth and early seventeenth centuries, a war of words raged, known as the *querelle des femmes*—"the debate about women." Each side fired off pamphlets and poems against the other. The issue: Were women by nature idle, vain, and immoral, or were they by nature good? Most of the debaters, pro or con, turned to the biblical story of Eve to support their points. Eve, their assumption went, was the first woman and the image of all women after her, so all women share her nature. Lanier's poem, making the same assumption, joins the controversy with powerful pro-woman arguments.

But surely Adam cannot be excused;
Her fault though great, yet he was most to blame.
What weakness offered, strength might have refused;
Being lord of all, the greater was his shame;
5 Although the serpent's craft had her abused,
God's holy word ought all his actions frame;
     For he was lord and king of all the earth,
     Before poor Eve had either life or breath,

Who being framed by God's eternal hand
10 The perfectest man that ever breathed on earth,

Literary Analysis
Tradition and Reform On what tradition does Lanier draw in these lines?

And from God's mouth received that strait command,
The <u>breach</u> whereof he knew was present death;
Yea, having power to rule both sea and land,
Yet with one apple won to lose that breath
15   Which God had breathèd in his beauteous face,
      Bringing us all in danger and disgrace;

And then to lay the fault on patience's back,
That we (poor women) must endure it all;
We know right well he did <u>discretion</u> lack,
20 Being not persuaded thereunto at all.
If Eve did err, it was for knowledge sake;
The fruit being fair persuaded him to fall.
      No subtle serpent's falsehood did betray him;
      If he would eat it, who had power to stay him?

25 Not Eve, whose fault was only too much love,
Which made her give this present to her dear,
That what she tasted he likewise might prove,
Whereby his knowledge might become more clear;
He never sought her weakness to reprove
30 With those sharp words which he of God did hear;
      Yet men will boast of knowledge, which he took
      From Eve's fair hand, as from a learned book.

breach (brēch) *n.* breaking or being broken; failure to observe the terms of an agreement

discretion (di skresh′ ən) *n.* care in what one does and says

Review and Assess

Thinking About the Selection

1. **(a) Recall:** Who does Lanier blame more for the Fall—Adam or Eve? **(b) Connect:** How does the second stanza connect Adam's "superiority" to Eve with his blameworthiness?

2. **(a) Recall:** According to Lanier, what motive did Eve have for tasting of the Tree of Knowledge? **(b) Recall:** According to Lanier, why did Eve offer Adam a taste of the apple? **(c) Summarize:** Describe Eve's character according to Lanier.

3. **(a) Recall:** According to the last stanza, what should Adam have done? **(b) Infer:** What view of Adam is suggested by Lanier's description of him?

4. **Interpret:** According to the poem, in what way do men apply a double standard to the story of the Fall?

5. **Generalize:** Explain why the interpretation of this story was so important in seventeenth-century arguments about the nature of women.

6. **Take a Position:** Do you think Lanier's argument is convincing? Why or why not?

To Lucasta, on Going to the Wars

Richard Lovelace

Background

Tensions between the Church of England and the Puritans who wished to reform it had risen to a dangerous level. Foreign wars had led to a money shortage. Charles I made the situation worse by mishandling Parliament, by pressuring nobles for money, and by forcing commoners to serve in his armies. In 1642, England's Parliament went to war against England's king. Lovelace, a loyal supporter of Charles, was twice imprisoned by the king's opponents.

Tell me not, Sweet, I am unkind,
    That from the nunnery
Of thy chaste breast, and quiet mind,
    To war and arms I fly.

5 True, a new mistress now I chase,
    The first foe in the field;
And with a stronger faith embrace
    A sword, a horse, a shield.

Yet this inconstancy is such,
10   As you too shall adore;
I could not love thee, Dear, so much,
    Loved I not honor more.

▲ **Critical Viewing**
Like the speaker in "To Lucasta," the knight in the background of this image is going to war. Do the knight and the poem's speaker seem to be leaving in the same spirit? Explain. **[Compare and Contrast]**

inconstancy (in kän′ stən sē) *n.* fickleness; changeableness

Going to the Battle, Edward Burn-Jones, Fitzwilliam Museum, Cambridge

To Althea, from Prison

Richard Lovelace

When love with unconfined wings
    Hovers within my gates,
And my divine Althea brings
    To whisper at the grates;
5   When I lie tangled in her hair
    And fettered to her eye,
The gods[1] that wanton[2] in the air
    Know no such liberty.

When flowing cups run swiftly round,
10   With no allaying Thames,[3]
Our careless heads with roses bound,
    Our hearts with loyal flames;
When thirsty grief in wine we steep,

---

1. **gods** The word *gods* is replaced by *birds* in some versions of this poem.
2. **wanton** play.
3. **cups . . . Thames** (temz) wine that has not been diluted by water (from the river Thames).

✔ Reading Check

What makes the speaker feel free, even while he is in prison?

When healths[4] and drafts[5] go free,
15 Fishes that tipple in the deep,
Know no such liberty.
When, like committed linnets,[6] I
With shriller throat shall sing
The sweetness, mercy, majesty,
20 And glories of my King;
When I shall voice aloud how good
He is, how great should be,
Enlarged[7] winds that curl the flood,
Know no such liberty.

25 Stone walls do not a prison make,
Nor iron bars a cage;
Minds innocent and quiet take
That for an hermitage;[8]
If I have freedom in my love,
30 And in my soul am free,
Angels alone that soar above,
Enjoy such liberty.

---

4. **healths** toasts.
5. **drafts** drinks.
6. **committed linnets** caged finches.
7. **enlarged** released.
8. **hermitage** (hʉr´ mi tij) *n.* a place of religious seclusion

Review and Assess

Thinking About the Selections

1. **Respond:** If you were Lucasta or Althea, would you be persuaded by Lovelace's arguments? Why or why not?

2. **(a) Recall:** In lines 1–4 of "To Lucasta," where is the speaker going? **(b) Infer:** How does he expect Lucasta to respond?

3. **(a) Recall:** What does the speaker "now . . . chase" in line 5? **(b) Interpret:** In what sense does the speaker admit to having two loves? **(c) Draw Conclusions:** In the final two lines, why does the strength of the speaker's love for Lucasta depend on the strength of his other love?

4. **(a) Recall:** In "To Althea," what are three things the poet does in prison? **(b) Interpret:** Explain the kind of "liberty" expressed in each of these activities.

5. **(a) Recall:** In the fourth stanza of "To Althea," which two freedoms does the poet say are most important? **(b) Interpret:** What is the meaning of lines 25–26? **(c) Evaluate:** Do you agree with Lovelace's views on freedom? Explain.

Literary Analysis
Tradition and Reform
In lines 25–28, how does Lovelace use the multiple associations of *walls* to shift from the idea of a prison to the idea of a place of religious seclusion?

Review and Assess

Literary Analysis

Tradition and Reform

1. (a) In "Eve's Apology," what traditional assumptions is Lanier trying to **reform**? (b) What **tradition** does she use to aid her? (c) How does she reinterpret this tradition to make her point?

2. How does Lanier's use of a Bible story make it easier for her to communicate with readers, even if they disagree with her arguments?

3. (a) In "To Althea, From Prison," what tradition does Lovelace defend? (b) Compare the spirit of lines 29–32 with the principles of a reformer such as Gandhi or Martin Luther King, Jr.

Comparing Literary Works

4. (a) Which poem in this grouping best represents tradition? Explain. (b) Which poem best represents reform? Explain.

5. (a) In "Eve's Apology," lines 1–8, what conclusion about the Fall does Lanier draw from Adam's strength? (b) Explain how she shifts between meanings of the word *weakness*—meaning both "moral weakness" and "powerlessness to influence"—to make her point. (c) Using a chart like the one below, compare this shift to a similar shift in the meaning of *freedom* in "To Althea."

Meaning 1	Meaning 2	Reasoning Behind Shift	Valid?

6. Explain why redefining key traditional terms like *weakness* might be important to a poet trying to reform a tradition.

Reading Strategy

Using Historical Context

7. Explain the historical facts about education that help you understand lines 31–32 of "Eve's Apology."

8. Explain how **historical context** helps you interpret the third stanza of "To Althea."

Extend Understanding

9. **World Events Connection:** Name an example of a reform movement of today, and compare its message with Lanier's or Lovelace's.

Quick Review

Tradition consists of a society's approved values, beliefs, roles, and practices. **Reform** refers to attempts to change traditional practices.

To **use historical context** to help you understand a work, consider the common assumptions and important events of the era in which the work was written and decide to what extent the piece reflects them.

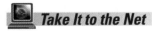 **Take It to the Net**
www.phschool.com
Take the interactive self-test online to check your understanding of these selections.

Integrate Language Skills

Vocabulary Development Lesson

Fluency: Terms With *breach*

Use your knowledge of the word *breach*, meaning "a breaking or state of being broken," to write a definition of the italicized terms below.

1. The woman sued her fiancé for *breach of promise*.
2. The policewoman arrested the girls for a *breach of the peace*.
3. After his *breach of etiquette*, he was never invited back.
4. Selling the land to someone else would be a *breach of contract*.
5. From the shore, he watched the *breach of the whale*.
6. Unwilling to commit a *breach of honor*, he accepted the challenge.

Concept Development: Synonyms

For each word, choose the letter of its synonym.

1. discretion: (a) prudence, (b) falseness, (c) speed
2. inconstancy: (a) faithlessness, (b) doubt, (c) anger
3. breach: (a) promise, (b) help, (c) violation

Spelling Strategy

The endings *-ant* and *-ent* are both used to form adjectives. To spell the related noun, match the vowel in the ending of the adjective. For example, *constant* becomes *constancy*, while *insistent* becomes *insistence*.

Correctly spell each word below. If a word is spelled correctly, write *correct*.

1. eloquence 2. competance 3. dominence

Grammar and Style Lesson

Correlative Conjunctions

Correlative conjunctions are paired conjunctions that connect two words or groups of words of equal significance. Correlative conjunctions include *either . . . or*; *both . . . and*; *neither . . . nor*; *whether . . . or*; and *not only . . . but also*.

> **Example:** For he was lord and king of all the earth,
>
> Before poor Eve had <u>either</u> life <u>or</u> breath, ...

Practice Rewrite each item, using correlative conjunctions to combine the sentences.

1. Lanier did not put man before God. She did not put woman before God, either.
2. When in prison, Lovelace was able to feel free. When spending time with friends, he was also able to feel free.
3. Lanier believed that men had to take responsibility for sin. She believed that women also had to take responsibility.
4. Richard Lovelace fought for the king. He also fought for honor.
5. Lanier was traditional in her poem. Lanier was radical in her poem.

Writing Application Write a brief paragraph defining your idea of freedom and explaining how it compares to Lovelace's views in "To Althea, From Prison." Use at least two pairs of correlative conjunctions in your paragraph.

W͡G Prentice Hall Writing and Grammar Connection: Chapter 17, Section 4

Writing Lesson

Essay Connecting Literature With Experience

Lovelace strengthens his poetry by linking broad themes—freedom and honor—to his own experiences. Write an essay in which you draw general conclusions from personal experience about one of these themes. Compare your experiences and conclusions with Lovelace's.

Prewriting   Jot down notes on experiences that have shaped your views of freedom or honor. Then, write a summary of Lovelace's view of the topic and the experiences that led him to that view.

Drafting   Begin your draft with a summary comparing your experiences to Lovelace's. Support your comparison by linking specific incidents and quotations from Lovelace with your broader point.

Model: Relating Broad Themes to Personal Experience

• **Broad Theme:** Lovelace says freedom is a state of mind.

• **Personal Experience:** I hated taking piano lessons
   because I was made to. When my friend asked me to
   teach her "Chopsticks," I saw music in a new light
   and began practicing devotedly.

• **Link experience to theme:** Being "made to" practice
   piano was only a constraint when I did not embrace it.

> This organization allows the writer to explore the experience fully before analyzing its larger meaning.

Revising   Review your draft, strengthening connections between incidents, quotations, and general points.

Prentice Hall Writing and Grammar Connection: Chapter 4, Section 2

Extension Activities

Listening and Speaking Write and perform a rhymed **ballad** about a reform you support.

1. Use a question-and-answer dialogue format. Question why the cause is worthy of support, and provide answers.
2. Use strong images to dramatize the cause.
3. Repeat a catchy phrase as your refrain.

After rehearsing, perform your ballad in class.

Research and Technology Research and write a **report with spreadsheets** on the English Civil War. Include in your report a spreadsheet documenting an aspect of the subject, such as the regional distribution of Royalists and Puritans.

 **Take It to the Net**   www.phschool.com

Go online for an additional research activity using the Internet.

The turmoil of seventeenth-century England makes it a ripe subject for dramatic treatment. In this scene from his movie *Cromwell* (1970), director Ken Hughes presents the trial of King Charles I by Parliament, with Oliver Cromwell, the Parliamentary general who would become leader of England, among the spectators. Standing beside Cromwell are Sir Thomas Fairfax, commander in chief of the Parliamentary army; Henry Ireton, a leader in the Parliamentary cause; and Haselrig Holles Strode, a leading opponent of the king.

from Cromwell: The Movie
Ken Hughes

INT. THE GREAT HALL WESTMINISTER DAY (Jan 29th, 1648)

LONG SHOT. *The chamber is packed to suffocation.* NOBLES *and their* LADIES *jam the raised tiered seats at the back of the court.* PARLIAMENTARIANS *fill the benches either side, whilst the public benches are filled to overflowing with all manner of persons, old soldiers, cripples, men and women of all classes.* TROOPERS *of the* CROMWELL *army guard all entrances, whilst the public benches are ringed by* PIKEMEN. *The noise and clamor is tremendous.*

A long table set up for the JUDGES *is empty and faces the open court. The* COURT CRIER *bangs a staff for silence.*

CRIER.   HO YEZ HO YEZ HO YEZ !!!

The JUDGES *enter, 40* COMMISSIONERS *including 3* HIGH COURT JUDGES, LAWYERS, ARMY OFFICERS, HASELRIG HOLLES STRODE, *and of course* HENRY IRETON. SIR THOMAS FAIRFAX, OLIVER CROMWELL, *and the* SOLICITOR GENERAL SIR EDWARD COOKE. *Ahead of them, a sword and mace are carried by an* OFFICER, *which are placed on a table before the judges' bench. The* PRESIDENT OF THE COURT *is* JOHN BRADSHAW, *a tough judge of the High Court, now in his late thirties. Each man carries documents and papers.*

CRIER.   ALL MANNER OF PERSONS THAT HAVE ANYTHING TO DO WITH THIS COURT COME FORWARD AND GIVE YOUR ATTENDANCE. EVERY MAN TO KEEP SILENCE UPON PAIN OF IMPRISONMENT GOD SAVE THE KING !!!

The noise subsides. In the public seats, MANCHESTER *and* ESSEX, SIR EDWARD HYDE. PRESIDENT BRADSHAW *bangs his gavel.*

PRESIDENT BRADSHAW. LET THE PRISONER BE BROUGHT IN.

Doors open and GUARDS *call for the prisoner. A murmur runs through the court. Many people stand on chairs to get a better view.*

A hush falls over the entire chamber as the tiny figure of CHARLES *appears in the doorway. He wears a plain dark cloak, carries a silver topped cane, and wears the* STAR *and* BLUE RIBBON *and* GEORGE *of the* GARTER.[1] *He stands for a moment looking about the court, then seeing the chair in the center of the floor, he walks toward it alone and unaided.*

As he sits, he drops his stick. It clatters to the floor in the silence. He sits there looking down at it. Behind him a SOLDIER *leans on his musket and regards the King without moving.*

CHARLES *realizes that no one is coming to pick it up, so he carefully picks it up himself, then sits back and faces the bench.*

PRESIDENT BRADSHAW. THE CLERK OF ARRAIGNS WILL READ THE CHARGES.

The CLERK OF ARRAIGNS *stands and reads from a document.*

CLERK OF ARRAIGNS. CHARLES STUART, KING OF ENGLAND, YOU STAND BEFORE THIS COURT CHARGED WITH HIGH TREASON IN THAT BEING ADMITTED KING OF ENGLAND AND THEREIN TRUSTED WITH POWER TO GOVERN ACCORDING TO THE LAWS OF THE LAND, YOU DID, OUT OF WICKEDNESS AND DESIGN, ERECT AND UPHOLD IN YOURSELF, AN UNLIMITED AND TYRANNICAL POWER, TO RULE ACCORDING TO YOUR WILL, AND TO OVERTHROW THE RIGHTS AND LIBERTIES OF THE PEOPLE. . . .

A murmur of protest from ROYALISTS *and others.* CLOSE SHOT MANCHESTER *and* ESSEX *in the gallery. The* PRESIDENT *bangs his gavel.*

CRIER. SILENCE! SILENCE !

CLERK OF ARRAIGNS. AND THAT FOR THE ACCOMPLISHMENT OF SUCH DESIGN AND THE PROTECTING OF YOURSELF IN THESE WICKED PRACTICES, YOU DID TRAITOROUSLY AND MALICIOUSLY LEVY A CRUEL WAR AGAINST PARLIAMENT AND THE PEOPLE AND ARE THEREFORE GUILTY OF ALL THE TREASONS, . . . BURNINGS, SPOILS, DESOLATIONS, DAMAGES, AND MISCHIEFS TO THE NATION COMMITTED IN THE SAID WAR! THUS ON BEHALF OF THE PEOPLE OF ENGLAND, THIS COURT IMPEACHES YOU AS A TYRANT, TRAITOR, MURDERER, AND PUBLIC ENEMY TO THE COMMONWEALTH OF ENGLAND.

CHARLES *looks up with a smile and chuckles aloud. At this his* SUPPORTERS *in the public benches roar with forced laughter. There are shouts of* "GOD SAVE THE KING"! *and counter shouts from the army of* "TRAITOR."

---

1. **Star and Blue Ribbon and George of the Garter** star, blue silk ribbon, and badge depicting St. George and the dragon, all representing the Order of the Garter. Membership in the Order is highest British military and civil honor.

Thematic Connection
What information does this scene reveal to you about the legal institutions of England during this era?

Thematic Connection
Compare the idea of monarchy implied in this passage with Lovelace's depiction of monarchy in "To Althea."

**Reading Check**
Who has been brought before the court?

CRIER. SILENCE! SILENCE!

SOLDIERS *yell at the public to be quiet.*

SOLDIERS. QUIET! SIT DOWN!

PRESIDENT BRADSHAW. SIR, YOU HAVE HEARD THE CHARGES AGAINST YOU. THE COURT EXPECTS AN ANSWER.

CHARLES *shifts in his chair, glances at his fingers, speaks with a half smile.*

CHARLES. First I must know by what authority I was brought here, and by what authority you sit in judgment upon me. Remember I am still your lawful king. I know no authority in this land above mine except that of Almighty God. Therefore, let me know by what authority I am brought here and I shall answer.

PRESIDENT BRADSHAW. IT IS NOT FOR THE PRISONER TO QUESTION THE COURT.

CHARLES. I am no ordinary prisoner, sir!

PRESIDENT BRADSHAW. AN ANSWER SIR! THE COURT DEMANDS AN ANSWER!

CHARLES. THEN I REFUSE AN ANSWER!

PRESIDENT BRADSHAW. SIR! YOU ARE BEFORE A COURT OF JUSTICE.

CHARLES. Well, sir, I see that I am before a power!

UPROAR.

CROWD. GOD SAVE THE KING! TO THE BLOCK WITH HIM etc.

CLERK. SILENCE!

PRESIDENT BRADSHAW. THE COURT WILL KEEP SILENT! Mr. Solicitor General, are your witnesses prepared?

SOLICITOR GENERAL. They are my Lord.

PRESIDENT BRADSHAW. Then let them be brought forth.

LONG SHOT. *A murmur runs through the crowd as they await the witnesses. The* KING *sits silent and alone in his chair.*

SOLICITOR GENERAL. Call witness Humfrey Browne.

USHER. CALL WITNESS HUMFREY BROWNE!

DISSOLVE

Connecting Literature and Media

1. What do you think Lovelace's reaction would have been if he had witnessed the trial scene depicted in *Cromwell*?
2. Compare the king's attitude with that of Milton's Satan.

Ken Hughes

(1922–2001)
Ken Hughes began his career in film at the age of fourteen, when he won an amateur filmmaking contest. At sixteen, he joined the British Broadcasting Company (BBC) where he worked his way up to sound engineer.

During his military service, Hughes studied his craft by created training films for the military. Hughes directed the popular film *The Trials of Oscar Wilde* in 1960. Subsequently, he directed several high-budget films, including *Cromwell* in 1970.

PART 3

The Ties That Bind

Illustration From *Gulliver's Travels*

Prepare to Read

from The Diary ◆
from A Journal of the Plague Year

Samuel Pepys (1633–1703)

Samuel Pepys (pēps) is an unusual literary celebrity. Not only does his fame rest on a single work, but that work was never intended for publication! The work in question is Pepys's *Diary*, which he wrote in shorthand and in his own private code. Undeciphered until the nineteenth century, the *Diary* provides a fascinating glimpse of London from 1660 to 1669, when Pepys's failing eyesight forced him to abandon the project.

An Ideal Observer Pepys was in a good position to report on the era. The son of a London tailor, he attended Cambridge University. After graduation he became the secretary of his influential cousin, the future Earl of Sandwich. Later, he married Elizabeth Marchant de Saint-Michel, a girl of fifteen. *The Diary* contains many details of their troubled marriage.

In 1660, the year the monarchy was restored, he received his first government post as a clerk for the navy. From there, his rise to fame and fortune was rapid, though not always smooth.

Why Did He Write? Pepys would probably have been shocked to learn that his coded diary would be "translated" and read centuries after his death. He wrote for his own pleasure. Writing about his accomplishments —and rereading his own accounts—made him feel proud.

The Value of his Writing Pepys has sometimes been dismissed as a shallow gossiper, interested only in advancing his career. However, he was respected by his contemporaries, and his *Diary* reveals his intelligence, diplomacy, honesty, and powers of observation. Readers who wish to learn about life in seventeenth-century London are greatly in his debt.

Daniel Defoe (1660–1731)

"A false, shuffling, prevaricating rascal"— that was how fellow author Joseph Addison described Daniel Defoe. In many ways, Addison was not far from wrong. Constantly in debt, Defoe often engaged in shady business deals and declared bankruptcy in 1692, owing a small fortune to his creditors. He was also a sometime government spy and propagandist who even upgraded his own name, originally *Foe*, by adding an aristocratic *De*.

An Innovative Novelist Despite all his flaws, we remember Defoe for an important literary achievement. He practically invented the modern realistic novel. He did so with two books that were written as the memoirs of fictional characters. *Robinson Crusoe* (1719) presents an almost documentary narrative of a man marooned on a desert island. *Moll Flanders* (1722) tells a satirical tale of a poor woman seeking respectability. During his lifetime, Defoe's books were considered so realistic that they were sold as nonfiction. In fact, the first-person narrators were so convincing that Defoe was even accused of "forging a story, and imposing it on the world for truth."

Factual Fiction Defoe brought an even greater factual background to *A Journal of the Plague Year* (1722), his fictional account of the great plague that devastated England from 1664 to 1665. To construct this vivid narrative, Defoe studied official documents, interviewed survivors of the plague, and may have drawn on his own memories as a young child.

The vivid historical re-creation of the plague is a triumph of Defoe's energetic, detailed style in a genre that set English fiction on a new path.

Preview

Connecting to the Literature

Humans are not yet germproof or fireproof. That is why you can sympathize with those caught up in the twin disasters described in these accounts.

Literary Analysis

Diaries and Journals

A **diary** or **journal** is a daily account of a writer's experiences and reactions. Most often, diaries or journals record life's little adventures and misadventures. However, diaries or journals that become literature can provide insights into historical events or periods:

- Pepys's *Diary* describes not only his personal life, but also historical events that he witnessed, like the plague and the Great Fire.
- Defoe's *A Journal of the Plague Year* also describes the plague that struck London, though it is actually a well-researched fictional novel posing as a journal.

In reading, note how these personal accounts reveal details of public events.

Comparing Literary Works

In journals and diaries, **first-person narrators** describe their own experience and refer to themselves as "I." Their individual perspectives help bring readers into a private world and create a strong sense of intimacy and immediacy.

However, as you read, remember that Pepys did not write his *Diary* for others, while Defoe wrote with other readers in mind. Contrast the qualities of the real Pepys with those of the fictional narrator in the *Journal*.

Reading Strategy

Drawing Conclusions

As you read, set up a chart like this one to keep track of details that each writer includes and the **conclusions,** or generalizations, that you draw from them.

Details from *The Diary*

He hires a boat.	He has servants.

Conclusion

He may be well-to-do.

Vocabulary Development

apprehensions (ap´ rē hen´ shənz) *n.* fears; concerns (p. 497)

abated (ə bāt´ id) *v.* lessened (p. 497)

lamentable (lam´ ən tə bəl) *adj.* distressing (p. 499)

combustible (kəm bus´ tə bəl) *adj.* capable of igniting and burning; flammable (p. 499)

malicious (mə lish´ əs) *adj.* deliberately harmful; destructive (p. 501)

discoursing (dis´ kôrs´ iŋ) *v.* talking about; discussing (p. 502)

distemper (dis tem´ pər) *n.* infectious disease, such as the plague (p. 505)

importuning (im´ pôr tō͞on´ iŋ) *v.* pleading with (p. 507)

prodigious (prō dij´ əs) *adj.* enormous; huge (p. 508)

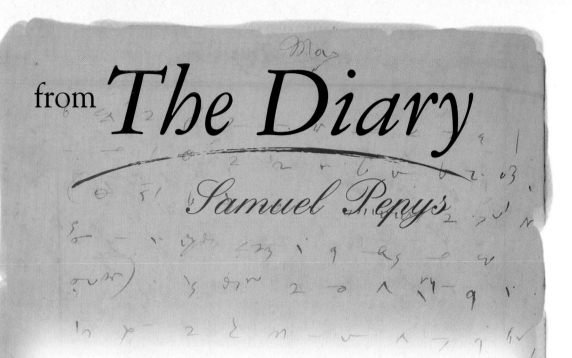

from *The Diary*

Samuel Pepys

Background

In the 1660s, following years of upheaval and a short period of peace, London was struck by twin disasters. The first of these was a plague that began in 1664. A frequently fatal infectious disease, the bubonic plague that ravaged London is usually spread by fleas from an infected host, such as the black rat. However, the disease was poorly understood at the time, and within a year or so, it had killed nearly 70,000 of London's 460,000 inhabitants.

Then, in 1666, just as the city was beginning to recover, the Great Fire of London broke out, destroying more than 13,000 buildings. Like the plague, the Great Fire of London also had a devastating effect on the city.

▲ **Critical Viewing** What evidence on this page of *The Diary* suggests that Pepys never meant to share his writing with the world? **[Infer]**

The Plague

Sept. 3, 1665. (Lord's Day.) Church being done, my Lord Bruncker, Sir J. Minnes, and I up to the vestry[1] at the desire of the Justices of the Peace, Sir Theo. Biddulph and Sir W. Boreman and Alderman Hooker, in order to the doing something for the keeping of the plague from growing; but Lord! to consider the madness of the people of the town, who will (because they are forbid) come in crowds along with the dead corps[2] to see them buried; but we agreed on some orders for the prevention thereof.[3] Among other stories, one was very passionate, methought of a complaint brought against a man in the town for taking a child from London from an infected house. Alderman Hooker told us it was the child of a very able citizen in Gracious Street, a saddler,[4] who had buried all the rest of his children of the plague, and himself and wife now being shut up and in despair of escaping, did desire only to save the life of this little child; and so prevailed to have it received stark-naked into the arms of a friend, who brought it (having put it into new fresh clothes) to Greenwich; where upon hearing the story, we did agree it should be permitted to be received and kept in the town. Thence with my Lord Bruncker to Captain Cocke's, where we mighty merry and supped, and very late I by water to Woolwich, in great <u>apprehensions</u> of an ague. . . .

Sept. 14, 1665. When I come home I spent some thoughts upon the occurrences of this day, giving matter for as much content on one hand and melancholy on another, as any day in all my life. For the first; the finding of my money and plate,[5] and all safe at London, and speeding in my business of money this day. The hearing of this good news to such excess, after so great a despair of my Lord's doing anything this year; adding to that, the decrease of 500 and more, which is the first decrease we have yet had in the sickness since it begun: and great hopes that the next week it will be greater. Then, on the other side, my finding that though the bill[6] in general is <u>abated</u>, yet the city within the walls is increased, and likely to continue so, and is close to our house there. My meeting dead corpses of the plague, carried to be buried close to me at noonday through the city in Fanchurch Street. To see a person sick of the sores, carried close by me by Grace church in a hackney coach.[7] My finding the Angell Tavern at the lower end of Tower Hill, shut up, and more than that, the alehouse at the Tower Stairs, and more than that, the person was then dying of the plague when I was last there, a little while ago, at night, to write a short letter there, and I overheard the mistress of the

---

1. **vestry** (ves′ trē) *n.* church meeting-room.
2. **corps** corpses.
3. **but we . . . thereof** Funeral processions were forbidden in London during the plague. However, the law was often ignored.
4. **saddler** *n.* person who makes, sells, and repairs saddles.
5. **plate** valuable serving dishes and flatware.
6. **bill** weekly list of burials.
7. **hackney coach** carriage for hire.

Reading Strategy
Drawing Conclusions
What conclusions can you draw about Pepys from the entry for "Sept. 3, 1665"? Explain.

apprehensions (ap′ rē hen′ shənz) *n.* fears; concerns

abated (ə bāt′ id) *v.* lessened

✔**Reading Check**

What gives Pepys "much content" and what makes him "melancholy"?

The Great Fire of London, 1666

house sadly saying to her husband somebody was very ill, but did not think it was of the plague. To hear that poor Payne, my waiter, hath buried a child, and is dying himself. To hear that a laborer I sent but the other day to Dagenhams, to know how they did there, is dead of the plague; and that one of my own watermen, that carried me daily, fell sick as soon as he had landed me on Friday morning last, when I had been all night upon the water (and I believe he did get his infection that day at Brainford), and is now dead of the plague. To hear that Captain Lambert and Cuttle are killed in the taking these ships; and that Mr. Sidney Montague is sick of a desperate fever at my Lady Carteret's, at Scott's Hall. To hear that Mr. Lewes hath another daughter sick. And, lastly, that both my servants, W. Hewer and Tom Edwards, have lost their fathers, both in St. Sepulcher's parish, of the plague this week, do put me into great apprehensions of melancholy, and with good reason. But I put off the thoughts of sadness as much as I can, and the rather to keep my wife in good heart and family also. After supper (having eat nothing all this day) upon a fine tench[8] of Mr. Shelden's taking, we to bed.

The Fire of London

Sept. 2, 1666. (Lord's day.) Some of our maids sitting up late last night to get things ready against our feast today, Jane called us up about three in the morning, to tell us of a great fire they saw in the

---

8. **tench** *n.* type of fish.

▲ **Critical Viewing**
What line from Pepys's account of the fire would be an appropriate caption for this painting? Why? **[Connect]**

Literary Analysis
Diaries and Journals
What does the abbreviated language in the entry for "Sept. 14" suggest about the audience for whom Pepys was writing? Explain.

city. So I rose and slipped on my night-gown, and went to her window, and thought it to be on the back side of Mark Lane at the farthest; but, being unused to such fires as followed, I thought it far enough off; and so went to bed again and to sleep. About seven rose again to dress myself, and there looked out at the window, and saw the fire not so much as it was and farther off. So to my closet to set things to rights after yesterday's cleaning. By and by Jane comes and tells me that she hears that above 300 houses have been burned down tonight by the fire we saw, and that it is now burning down all Fish Street, by London Bridge. So I made myself ready presently, and walked to the Tower,[9] and there got up upon one of the high places, Sir J. Robinson's little son going up with me; and there I did see the houses at that end of the bridge all on fire, and an infinite great fire on this and the other side the end of the bridge; which, among other people, did trouble me for poor little Michell and our Sarah on the bridge. So down, with my heart full of trouble, to the Lieutenant of the Tower, who tells me that it begun this morning in the King's baker's house in Pudding Lane, and that it hath burned St. Magnus's Church and most part of Fish Street already. So I down to the waterside, and there got a boat and through bridge, and there saw a <u>lamentable</u> fire. Poor Michell's house, as far as the Old Swan, already burned that way, and the fire running farther, that in a very little time it got as far as the steel yard, while I was there. Everybody endeavoring to remove their goods, and flinging into the river or bringing them into lighters that lay off; poor people staying in their houses as long as till the very fire touched them, and then running into boats, or clambering from one pair of stairs by the waterside to another. And among other things, the poor pigeons, I perceive, were loth to leave their houses, but hovered about the windows and balconies till they were, some of them burned, their wings, and fell down. Having stayed, and in an hour's time seen the fire rage every way, and nobody, to my sight, endeavoring to quench it, but to remove their goods, and leave all to the fire, and having seen it get as far as the steel yard, and the wind mighty high and driving it into the city; and everything, after so long a drought, proving <u>combustible</u>, even the very stones of churches, and among other things the poor steeple by which pretty Mrs.— lives, and whereof my old schoolfellow Elborough is parson, taken fire in the very top, and there burned till it fell down. I to Whitehall (with a gentleman with me who desired to go off from the Tower, to see the fire, in my boat), and there up to the King's closet in the chapel, where people come about me, and I did give them an account dismayed them all, and word was carried in to the King. So I was called for, and did tell the King and Duke of York what I saw, and that unless his Majesty did command houses to be pulled down nothing could stop the fire. They seemed much troubled, and the King commanded me to go to my Lord Mayor from him, and

---

9. **Tower** Tower of London.

lamentable (lam´ ən tə bəl) *adj.* distressing

combustible (kəm bus´ tə bəl) *adj.* capable of igniting and burning; flammable

**Reading Check**

What does Pepys learn about the fire from his visit to the Tower?

command him to spare no houses, but to pull down before the fire every way. The Duke of York bid me tell him that if he would have any more soldiers he shall; and so did my Lord Arlington afterwards, as a great secret. Here meeting with Captain Cocke, I in his coach, which he lent me, and Creed with me to Paul's,[10] and there walked along Watling Street, as well as I could, every creature coming away loaden with goods to save, and here and there sick people carried away in beds. Extraordinary good goods carried in carts and on backs. At last met my Lord Mayor in Canning Street, like a man spent, with a handkerchief about his neck. To the King's message he cried, like a fainting woman, "Lord! what can I do? I am spent: people will not obey me. I have been pulling down houses; but the fire overtakes us faster than we can do it." That he needed no more soldiers; and that, for himself, he must go and refresh himself, having been up all night. So he left me, and I him, and walked home, seeing people all almost distracted, and no manner of means used to quench the fire. The houses, too, so very thick thereabouts, and full of matter for burning, as pitch and tar, in Thames Street; and warehouses of oil, and wines, and brandy, and other things. Here I saw Mr. Isaake Houblon, the handsome man, prettily dressed and dirty, at his door at Dowgate, receiving some of his brothers' things, whose houses were on fire; and, as he says, have been removed twice already; and he doubts (as it soon proved) that they must be in a little time removed from his house also, which was a sad consideration. And to see the churches all filling with goods by people who themselves should have been quietly there at this time. By this time it was about twelve o'clock; and so home. Soon as dined, and walked through the city, the streets full of nothing but people and horses and carts loaden with goods, ready to run over one another, and removing goods from one burned house to another. They now removing out of Canning Street (which received goods in the morning) into Lumbard Street, and farther; and among others I now saw my little goldsmith, Stokes, receiving some friend's goods, whose house itself was burned the day after. I to Paul's Wharf, where I had appointed a boat to attend me, and took in Mr. Carcasse and his brother, whom I met in the street, and carried them below and above bridge to and again to see the fire, which was now got farther, both below and above, and no likelihood of stopping it. Met with the King and Duke of York in their barge, and with them to Queenhithe, and there called Sir Richard Browne to them. Their order was only to pull down houses apace, and so below bridge at the waterside; but little was or could be done, the fire coming upon them so fast. Good hopes there was of stopping it at the Three Cranes above, and at Buttolph's Wharf below bridge, if care be used; but the wind carries it into the city, so as we know not by the waterside what it do there. River full of lighters and boats taking in goods, and good goods swimming in the water, and only I

---

10. **Paul's** St. Paul's Cathedral.

Reading Strategy
Drawing Conclusions
What conclusion about the fire can you draw from the fact that goods were removed "from one burned house to another"?

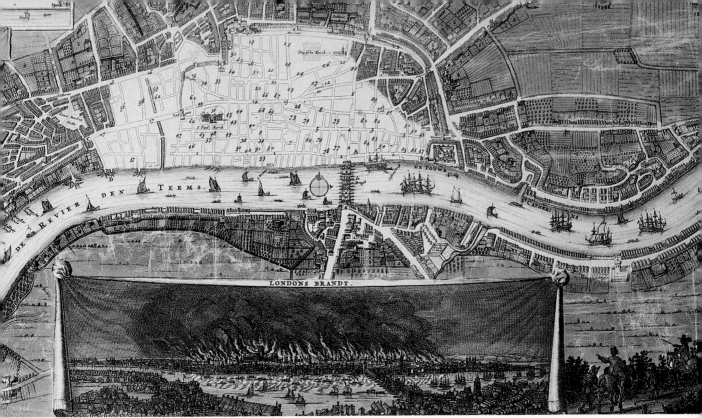

The Great Fire, 1666, Marcus Willemsz Doornik, Guildhall Library, Corporation of London

observed that hardly one lighter or boat in three that had the goods
of a house in, but there was a pair of virginals[11] in it. Having seen as
much as I could now, I away to Whitehall by appointment, and there
walked to St. James's Park, and there met my wife and Creed and
Wood and his wife, and walked to my boat; and there upon the water
again, and to the fire up and down, it still increasing, and the wind
great. So near the fire as we could for smoke; and all over the
Thames, with one's face in the wind, you were almost burned with a
shower of firedrops. This is very true; so as houses were burned by
these drops and flakes of fire, three or four, nay, five or six houses,
one from another. When we could endure no more upon the water, we
to a little alehouse on the Bankside, over against the Three Cranes,
and there stayed till it was dark almost, and saw the fire grow; and,
as it grew darker, appeared more and more, and in corners and upon
steeples, and between churches and houses, as far as we could see
up the hill of the city, in a most horrid <u>malicious</u> bloody flame, not
like the fine flame of an ordinary fire. Barbary and her husband away
before us. We stayed till, it being darkish, we saw the fire as only one
entire arch of fire from this to the other side the bridge, and in a bow
up the hill for an arch of above a mile long: it made me weep to see it.
The churches, houses, and all on fire and flaming at once; and a horrid noise the flames made, and the cracking of houses at their ruin.

11. **virginals** *n.* small, legless harpsichords.

So home with a sad heart, and there find everybody <u>discoursing</u> and lamenting the fire; and poor Tom Hater come with some of his few goods saved out of his house, which is burned upon Fish Street Hill. I invited him to lie at my house, and did receive his goods, but was deceived in his lying there, the news coming every moment of the growth of the fire; so as we were forced to begin to pack up our own goods, and prepare for their removal; and did by moonshine (it being brave dry, and moonshine, and warm weather) carry much of my goods into the garden, and Mr. Hater and I did remove my money and iron chests into my cellar, as thinking that the safest place. And got my bags of gold into my office, ready to carry away, and my chief papers of accounts also there, and my tallies into a box by themselves. So great was our fear, as Sir W. Batten hath carts come out of the country to fetch away his goods this night. We did put Mr. Haters, poor man, to bed a little; but he got but very little rest, so much noise being in my house, taking down of goods.

3rd. About four o'clock in the morning, my Lady Batten sent me a cart to carry away all my money, and plate, and best things, to Sir W. Rider's at Bednall Green. Which I did, riding myself in my nightgown in the cart; and, Lord! to see how the streets and the highways are crowded with people running and riding, and getting of carts at any rate to fetch away things. I find Sir W. Rider tired with being called up all night, and receiving things from several friends. His house full of goods, and much of Sir W. Batten's and Sir W. Pen's. I am eased at my heart to have my treasure so well secured. Then home, with much ado to find a way, nor any sleep all this night to me nor my poor wife.

discoursing (dis′ kôrs′ iŋ) *v.* talking about; discussing

Review and Assess

Thinking About the Selection

1. **Recall:** Does Pepys's *Diary* make the plague and fire seem real to you? Why or why not?

2. **(a) Recall:** According to the entry for September 3, 1665, what happened to the saddler's family? **(b) Infer:** What does Pepys's reaction to these events tell you about his personality?

3. **(a) Recall:** What does Pepys recommend to the King and the Duke of York during the fire? **(b) Evaluate:** Was the recommendation a good one? Why or why not?

4. **(a) Classify:** Briefly describe the main types of things Pepys does during the plague and the fire. **(b) Draw Conclusions:** Explain why each of the following adjectives does or does not apply to him: *curious, observant, helpful,* and *competent.*

5. **(a) Compare and Contrast:** Which do you think was a greater disaster—the plague or the Great Fire? Why? **(b) Relate:** What modern disasters compare with these events? Explain.

from A Journal of the Plague Year

Daniel Defoe

The face of London was now indeed strangely altered, I mean the whole mass of buildings, city, liberties, suburbs, Westminster, Southwark, and altogether; for as to the particular part called the city, or within the walls, that was not yet much infected. But in the whole the face of things, I say, was much altered; sorrow and sadness sat upon every face; and though some parts were not yet overwhelmed, yet all looked deeply concerned; and as we saw it apparently coming on, so everyone looked on himself and his family as in the utmost danger. Were it possible to represent those times exactly to those that did not see them, and give the reader due ideas of the horror that everywhere presented itself, it must make just impressions upon their minds and fill them with surprise. London might well be said to be all in tears; the mourners did not go about the streets indeed, for nobody put on black or made a formal dress of mourning for their nearest friends; but the voice of mourning was truly heard in the streets. The shrieks of women and children at the windows and doors of their houses, where their dearest relations were perhaps dying, or just dead, were so frequent to be heard as we passed the streets, that it was enough to pierce the stoutest heart in the world to hear them. Tears and lamentations were seen almost in every house, especially in the first part of the visitation; for toward the latter end men's hearts were hardened, and death was so always before their eyes, that they did not so much concern themselves for the loss of their friends, expecting that themselves should be summoned the next hour. . . .

I went all the first part of the time freely about the streets, though not so freely as to run myself into apparent danger, except when they dug the great pit in the churchyard of our parish of Aldgate. A terrible pit it was, and I could not resist my curiosity to go and see it. As near as I may judge, it was about forty feet in length, and about fifteen or sixteen feet broad, and, at the time I first looked at it, about nine feet deep; but it was said they dug it near twenty feet deep afterwards in one part of it, till they could go no deeper for the water; for they had, it seems, dug several large pits before this. For though the plague was long a-coming to our parish, yet, when it did come, there was no parish in or about London where it raged with such violence as in the two parishes of Aldgate and Whitechapel.

Literary Analysis
Diaries and Journals
Where in the first paragraph does the narrator indicate that he is providing a personal account intended to be read by others? Explain.

☑ **Reading Check**

In what ways was the "face of London . . . strangely altered"?

The Dead Cart, The British Library

▲ **Critical Viewing** The cart in this picture carries the bodies of people killed by the plague. What can you infer about the plague's impact on daily life from the number of people on the street and from the gestures of the men in conversation? **[Infer]**

I saw they had dug several pits in another ground, when the distemper began to spread in our parish, and especially when the dead carts began to go about, which was not, in our parish, till the beginning of August. Into these pits they had put perhaps fifty or sixty bodies each; then they made larger holes, wherein they buried all that the cart brought in a week, which, by the middle to the end of August, came to from 200 to 400 a week; and they could not well dig them larger, because of the order of the magistrates confining them to leave no bodies within six feet of the surface; and the water coming on at about seventeen or eighteen feet, they could not well, I say, put more in one pit. But now, at the beginning of September, the plague raging in a dreadful manner, and the number of burials in our parish increasing to more than was ever buried in any parish about London of no larger extent, they ordered this dreadful gulf to be dug, for such it was rather than a pit.

distemper (dis tem´ pər) *n.* infectious disease such as the plague

They had supposed this pit would have supplied them for a month or more when they dug it, and some blamed the churchwardens for suffering[1] such a frightful thing, telling them they were making preparations to bury the whole parish, and the like; but time made it appear the churchwardens knew the condition of the parish better than they did, for the pit being finished the 4th of September, I think, they began to bury in it the 6th, and by the 20th, which was just two weeks, they had thrown into it 1114 bodies, when they were obliged to fill it up, the bodies being then come to lie within six feet of the surface. I doubt not but there may be some ancient persons alive in the parish who can justify the fact of this, and are able to show even in what place of the churchyard the pit lay better than I can. The mark of it also was many years to be seen in the churchyard on the surface, lying in length parallel with the passage which goes by the west wall of the churchyard out of Houndsditch, and turns east again into Whitechapel, coming out near the Three Nuns' Inn.

It was about the 10th of September that my curiosity led, or rather drove, me to go and see this pit again, when there had been near 400 people buried in it; and I was not content to see it in the daytime, as I had done before, for then there would have been nothing to have been seen but the loose earth; for all the bodies that were thrown in were immediately covered with earth by those they called the buriers, which at other times were called bearers; but I resolved to go in the night and see some of them thrown in.

Reading Strategy
Drawing Conclusions
From the information in the paragraph beginning, "It was . . . ," what do you conclude about the narrator's motives? Explain.

There was a strict order to prevent people coming to those pits, and that was only to prevent infection. But after some time that order was more necessary, for people that were infected and near their end, and delirious also, would run to those pits, wrapped in blankets or rugs, and throw themselves in, and, as they said, bury themselves. I cannot say that the officers suffered any willingly to lie there; but I have heard that in a great pit in Finsbury, in the parish of

**Reading Check**

What provisions does the parish make for disposing of the bodies of plague victims?

---

1. **suffering** allowing.

Cripplegate, it lying open then to the fields, for it was not then walled about, [some] came and threw themselves in, and expired there, before they threw any earth upon them; and that when they came to bury others, and found them there, they were quite dead, though not cold.

This may serve a little to describe the dreadful condition of that day, though it is impossible to say anything that is able to give a true idea of it to those who did not see it, other than this, that it was indeed very, very, very dreadful, and such as no tongue can express.

I got admittance into the churchyard by being acquainted with the sexton who attended, who, though he did not refuse me at all, yet earnestly persuaded me not to go, telling me very seriously, for he was a good, religious, and sensible man, that it was indeed their business and duty to venture, and to run all hazards, and that in it they might hope to be preserved; but that I had no apparent call to it but my own curiosity, which, he said, he believed I would not pretend was sufficient to justify my running that hazard. I told him I had been pressed in my mind to go, and that perhaps it might be an instructing sight, that might not be without its uses. "Nay," says the good man, "if you will venture upon that score, name of God go in; for, depend upon it, 't will be a sermon to you, it may be, the best that ever you heard in your life. 'T is a speaking sight," says he, "and has a voice with it, and a loud one, to call us all to repentance"; and with that he opened the door and said, "Go, if you will."

His discourse had shocked my resolution a little, and I stood wavering for a good while, but just at that interval I saw two links[2] come over from the end of the Minories, and heard the bellman, and then appeared a dead cart, as they called it, coming over the streets; so I could no longer resist my desire of seeing it, and went in. There was nobody, as I could perceive at first, in the churchyard, or going into it, but the buriers and the fellow that drove the cart, or rather led the horse and cart; but when they came up to the pit they saw a man go to and again,[3] muffled up in a brown cloak, and making motions with his hands under his cloak, as if he was in a great agony, and the buriers immediately gathered about him, supposing he was one of those poor delirious or desperate creatures that used to pretend, as I have said, to bury themselves. He said nothing as he walked about, but two or three times groaned very deeply and loud, and sighed as he would break his heart.

When the buriers came up to him they soon found he was neither a person infected and desperate, as I have observed above, or a person distempered in mind, but one oppressed with a dreadful weight of grief indeed, having his wife and several of his children all in the cart that was just come in with him, and he followed in an agony and excess of sorrow. He mourned heartily, as it was easy to see, but with a kind of masculine grief that could not give itself vent by tears; and

Literary Analysis
Diaries, Journals, and First-Person Narrators In the paragraph beginning, "His discourse . . . ," which details make Defoe's fictional narrator seem like a real person? Why?

---

2. **links** torches.
3. **to and again** to and fro.

calmly defying the buriers to let him alone, said he would only see the bodies thrown in and go away, so they left <u>importuning</u> him. But no sooner was the cart turned round and the bodies shot into the pit promiscuously,[4] which was a surprise to him, for he at least expected they would have been decently laid in, though indeed he was afterwards convinced that was impracticable; I say, no sooner did he see the sight but he cried out aloud, unable to contain himself. I could not hear what he said, but he went backward two or three steps and fell down in a swoon. The buriers ran to him and took him up, and

---

4. **promiscuously** mixed together without care or thought.

importuning (im′ pôr tōōn′ iŋ) *v.* pleading with

✔Reading Check

What touching scene does the narrator observe in the churchyard?

▼ **Critical Viewing** Explain how the *Journal* helps you make sense of details in this picture. **[Connect]**

in a little while he came to himself, and they led him away to the Pie Tavern over against the end of Houndsditch, where, it seems, the man was known, and where they took care of him. He looked into the pit again as he went away, but the buriers had covered the bodies so immediately with throwing in earth, that though there was light enough, for there were lanterns, and candles in them, placed all night round the sides of the pit, upon heaps of earth, seven or eight, or perhaps more, yet nothing could be seen.

This was a mournful scene indeed, and affected me almost as much as the rest; but the other was awful and full of terror. The cart had in it sixteen or seventeen bodies: some were wrapped up in linen sheets, some in rags, some little other than naked, or so loose that what covering they had fell from them in the shooting out of the cart, and they fell quite naked among the rest; but the matter was not much to them, or the indecency much to anyone else, seeing they were all dead, and were to be huddled together into the common grave of mankind, as we may call it, for here was no difference made, but poor and rich went together; there was no other way of burials, neither was it possible there should, for coffins were not to be had for the <u>prodigious</u> numbers that fell in such a calamity as this.

prodigious (prō′ dij′ əs) *adj.* enormous; huge

Review and Assess

Thinking About the Selection

1. **Recall:** Which passages in *A Journal of the Plague Year* seem especially vivid to you? Why?

2. **(a) Recall:** What was the purpose of the great pit dug in Aldgate? **(b) Infer:** Why do you think the narrator describes the pit in such detail?

3. **(a) Recall:** What prompts the narrator to visit the pit? **(b) Interpret:** What does the Sexton mean when he says that visiting the pit will "be a sermon" to the narrator?

4. **(a) Summarize:** Retell the incident concerning the man in the brown cloak. **(b) Draw Conclusions:** In what way does this incident add a new dimension of meaning to the previous general descriptions of the plague? Explain.

5. **(a) Compare and Contrast:** Compare and contrast Pepys's true account of the plague with Defoe's fictional account of it. **(b) Assess:** Which description do you find more effective? Why?

6. **Generalize:** Do you think that literary works should avoid mixing fiction and nonfiction? Why or why not?

7. **Apply:** Compare Defoe's approach to that of a television reporter reporting from a news scene.

Review and Assess

Literary Analysis

Diaries and Journals

1. Using specific references, show how the texts by Pepys and Defoe are good examples of **diaries** or **journals.**

2. Find a passage in each work that reflects the immediacy of real life and one that teaches you about history. Explain your choices.

3. (a) Use a chart like this one to determine which of the questions in the left column can be answered by reading Pepys's *Diary*.
(b) What do your results suggest about diaries as sources of historical information? Explain.

Questions About the Great Fire	Answer in *Diary?* Yes/No	Pepys's Answer
What parts of the city were most damaged?		
How many houses were destroyed?		
What was the total monetary damage?		

Comparing Literary Works

4. What clues in Pepys's *Diary* and Defoe's *Journal* indicate that both these works are told by **first-person narrators**? Explain.

5. Which of these works would be more changed if it were written by a third-person narrator who did not participate in the action? Explain.

6. For which of these works would it be easier to capture the first-person narrative in a film version? Why?

Reading Strategy

Drawing Conclusions

7. Referring to the entry dated "Sept. 14, 1665," in Pepys's *Diary*, **draw a conclusion** about Pepys's position in society.

8. (a) Which narrator—Pepys or Defoe's fictional narrator—seems more observant to you? (b) On what details do you base your conclusion?

Extend Understanding

9. **Science Connection:** What do the selections reveal about medical knowledge in the late seventeenth century?

Integrate Language Skills

Vocabulary Development Lesson

Word Analysis: Latin Prefix *dis-*

The prefix *dis-* can mean "apart," "not," "cause to be the opposite of," or "the opposite of." In *distemper, dis-* makes "the opposite of" *temper* or "balance"—in other words, that state of imbalance called "disease."

Use your knowledge of *dis-* to define each of the following words.

1. disable
2. dismiss
3. disobey
4. dissatisfied

Spelling Strategy

In the words *combustible* and *lamentable*, the related suffixes *-ible* and *-able* mean "capable of" or "worthy of." New words, such as *skiable*, always use the suffix *-able*.

On your paper, add *-ible or -able* to each word.

1. machine-wash
2. forget
3. suggest
4. flex

Fluency: Words in Context

Identify the word from the vocabulary list on page 495 that best completes each sentence.

1. The flames of the fire seemed ___?___, as if they wanted to devour the city.
2. The wooden buildings were ___?___.
3. People fleeing the flames began ___?___ boatmen to take them aboard.
4. The fire did a ___?___ amount of damage.
5. When the fire at last ___?___, 13,000 buildings had been destroyed.
6. Worried people were ___?___ about raising money to rebuild their homes.
7. They also worried about quelling the spread of ___?___.
8. Many Londoners had ___?___ about another fire.
9. Others just wished to forget the ___?___ episode.

Grammar and Style Lesson

Gerunds

Both Pepys and Defoe use **gerunds**, verb forms that end in *-ing* and function as nouns. Do not mistake gerunds for participles, which also end in *-ing* but serve as verbs and adjectives.

Gerund: In the dark, the <u>wailing</u> continued.

Present Participle as Verb: Those whose loved ones had died were <u>wailing</u>.

Present Participle as Adjective: The <u>wailing</u> mourner bowed his head in sorrow.

Practice In your notebook, identify the gerund in the sentence or write *none* if there is no gerund.

1. The plague was a time for deep mourning.
2. Suffering was everywhere in evidence.
3. Lamenting people were fleeing London.
4. The ranks of the dead and dying were swelling daily.
5. Still shuddering, London had just finished burying its dead when the fire broke out.

Writing Application Write a paragraph describing a dramatic event. Use at least four gerunds in your description.

W̶G̶ Prentice Hall Writing and Grammar Connection: Chapter 19, Section 2

Writing Lesson

Response to Criticism

Critic Brian Fitzgerald says Defoe "used literature to express his views on social and other questions and only secondarily as a craftsman and artist." In an essay, support or refute Fitzgerald's comment.

Prewriting Note details from Defoe's *Journal* that show him expressing views on social conditions. Then, gather examples that show him to be a craftsman, such as vivid images, figures of speech, and passages creating a mood.

Drafting Write a thesis statement supporting or refuting Fitzgerald's remark. Referring to your prewriting notes, back up your thesis statement with details from Defoe's writing.

Revising Check your essay for accuracy by highlighting statements that can be proved true or false. Then, verify these statements using Defoe's *Journal* or a reference source.

> **Model: Checking for Accuracy**
>
> In this excerpt from the *Journal*, Defoe uses statistics or measurements ten times to describe accurately the conditions of plague-ridden London. However, his literary artistry is just as evident as his precision.

> The author has highlighted a fact that must be checked by reviewing the excerpt from Defoe's *Journal*.

 Prentice Hall Writing and Grammar Connection: Chapter 14, Section 3

Extension Activities

Listening and Speaking Many seventeenth-century Londoners heard their news from a town crier. Plan a **performance as a town crier,** calling out news at the time of the plague or fire.

- Research how town criers performed their jobs.
- Apply what you learn to devise effective gestures and vocal styles for the job.

After your performance, share your insights into this early news format.

Research and Technology With a group, write a **fact-check report** on Pepys's account of the fire or Defoe's account of the plague. Identify facts presented in the selection, and divide them among group members, who should check them in reference sources. Assemble your findings in a report. **[Group Activity]**

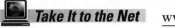 **Take It to the Net** www.phschool.com

Go online for an additional research activity using the Internet.

Prepare to Read

from Gulliver's Travels

Jonathan Swift (1667–1745)

While Swift was writing *Gulliver's Travels*, he had already started to suffer from the inner ear disease that eventually disabled him. "I always expect tomorrow to be worse," he wrote in a letter, "but I enjoy today as well as I can." The result of the author's determination to keep up his spirits was that rarest of books, a literary masterpiece that is loved by children and adults alike.

Finding His Way Swift was born in Dublin, Ireland, to English parents, although his father died before he was born. With the assistance of relatives, he received a good education and then obtained an appointment in the household of Sir William Temple, a wealthy diplomat who lived on an estate in Surrey, England. Swift hoped for a career in politics, but receiving no support from Sir William, he decided on a career in the church. After Temple's death in 1699, he was given a small parish near London.

The satirical writing Swift had done while in the Temple household was out of character for a clergyman, but its brilliance was widely acknowledged in 1704 when he published his satires as two separate books: *A Tale of a Tub*, which satirizes excesses in religion and learning, and *The Battle of the Books*, which describes a comic encounter between ancient and modern literature.

Ambition and Achievement In Swift's day, religion was interwoven with politics. When the authorship of Swift's religious satires became known, Swift lost favor in the eyes of many church officials and also lost opportunities for advancement. Although he failed to achieve his goal of becoming a bishop in the Church of England, Swift remained a staunch defender of the Anglican faith. His political allegiance, however, shifted completely in 1710 when he left the Whig party to join the Tory party favored by Queen Anne. He benefited immediately from this move. As the leading party writer for the government, he wrote many pamphlets and wielded considerable political influence. He also continued to write anonymous satires, ridiculing the English policy in Ireland in works such as *Drapier's Letters* (1724).

The Story Behind *Gulliver's Travels* Swift's most famous book, the novel *Gulliver's Travels*, began as a humorous assignment from the Scriblerus Club, a group of Swift's sharp-witted literary friends. These writers, who delighted in making fun of literary pretensions, gave Swift the project of writing a series of amusing, imaginary journeys because they knew he enjoyed reading travel books. The result was *Gulliver's Travels* (1726), which was an instant triumph. Ten thousand copies were sold in the first three weeks following its publication.

Later Years Although embittered by his failure to be named a bishop, Swift served for more than thirty years as dean of St. Patrick's Cathedral in Dublin. His caustic wit did not flag, as shown in the savage satire *A Modest Proposal* (1729), on starvation in Ireland.

In his later years, Swift suffered from a disease of the inner ear that affected both his memory and his sense of balance. His death in 1745 deprived the world of a generous and learned man who despised the fanaticism, selfishness, and pride to which humanity is often prey, but who admired certain individuals.

Swift's Epitaph Swift wrote his own epitaph, which still hangs in St. Patrick's Cathedral as a reminder of his memorable career: "The body of Jonathan Swift, Doctor of Sacred Theology, dean of this cathedral church, is buried here, where fierce indignation can no more lacerate his heart. Go, traveler, and imitate, if you can, one who strove with all his strength to champion liberty."

Preview

Connecting to the Literature

Jonathan Swift's strange distortions of humanity seem to be the products of pure fantasy—until you realize that you are seeing your own failings and foibles in his funhouse mirror.

Literary Analysis

Satire

Satire is writing that uses humor to expose and ridicule human vice and folly. This type of writing can be good-humored or bitter in its attack on what is evil, harmful, or just plain foolish. Satire can appear in many genres—from stories and novels to poems and songs.

Although satirists like to unmask evils, they also mask their targets in order to avoid the dangers involved in naming real people, places, or beliefs. Swift uses masks such as these:

- Imaginary lands, like Lilliput and Brobdingnag
- Made-up characters, like the King of Brobdingnag
- Fictional conflicts of belief, like that between Big-Endians and Little-Endians

Swift expects you to pull off these fictional masks as you read so that you can identify the real targets of his satire.

Connecting Literary Elements

Swift uses masks in another way, too. He disguises his true meanings by attacking vice and folly indirectly through **irony,** a contradiction between reality and appearance or between the actual and intended meaning of words. Use a chart like this one to decode his irony.

Reading Strategy

Interpreting

Satirists cannot expose folly if you, the reader, fail to interpret the fictional and ironic masks they use to disguise their true targets. To **interpret,** or figure out, a satire, follow these tips:

- Use background and footnotes to identify historical references.
- Recognize and figure out ironic meanings.

Vocabulary Development

conjecture (kən jek´ chər) *v.* guess (p. 515)

expostulate (eks päs´ chə lāt´) *v.* reason earnestly with (p. 517)

schism (siz´ əm) *n.* division of a group into factions (p. 517)

expedient (ek spē´ dē ənt) *n.* device used in an emergency (p. 518)

habituate (hə bich´ o͞o āt´) *v.* make used to (p. 521)

odious (ō´ dē əs) *adj.* hateful; disgusting (p. 522)

Statement or Situation

"Many . . . volumes have been published" about the best way to break an egg.

↓

Ironic Contradiction

Appearance vs. Reality
(Serious Debate)   (Silly Topic)

↓

Interpretation

Swift shows how crazy people get about silly issues. See footnotes for the historical link.

from Gulliver's TRAVELS

Jonathan Swift

Background

Swift's era was marked by religious and political strife. Reacting against the intolerance displayed in these conflicts, he ridiculed those whose pride overcame their reason. His novel *Gulliver's Travels* satirizes such intolerance by means of four imaginary voyages of Lemuel Gulliver, the narrator, a well-educated but unimaginative ship's surgeon. In "A Voyage to Lilliput," for example, Swift focuses on disputes between the established Church of England and Roman Catholicism, calling the followers of each Little-Endians and Big-Endians, respectively. He also satirizes the religious wars between Protestant England and Catholic France, disguising them as a conflict between Lilliput and Blefuscu. In "A Voyage to Brobdingnag," he suggests that the politicians leading England are guilty of "ignorance, idleness, and vice."

from A Voyage to Lilliput

After being shipwrecked, Gulliver swims to shore and drifts off to sleep. When he awakens, he finds that he has been tied down by the Lilliputians (lil′ ə pyōō′ shənz), a race of people who are only six inches tall. Though he is held captive and his sword and pistols are taken from him, Gulliver gradually begins to win the Lilliputians' favor because of his mild disposition, and he is eventually granted his freedom. Through Gulliver's exposure to Lilliputian politics and court life, the reader becomes increasingly aware of the remarkable similarities between the English and Lilliputian affairs of state. The following excerpt begins during a discussion between the Lilliputian Principal Secretary of Private Affairs and Gulliver concerning the affairs of the Lilliputian empire.

We are threatened with an invasion from the island of Blefuscu,[1] which is the other great empire of the universe, almost as large and powerful as this of his Majesty. For as to what we have heard you affirm, that there are other kingdoms and states in the world, inhabited by human creatures as large as yourself, our philosophers are in much doubt, and would rather <u>conjecture</u> that you dropped from the moon, or one of the stars; because it is certain, that an hundred mortals of your bulk would, in a short time, destroy all the fruits and cattle of his Majesty's dominions. Besides, our histories of six thousand moons make no mention of any other regions, than the two great empires of Lilliput and Blefuscu. Which two mighty powers have, as I was going to tell you, been engaged in a most obstinate war for six and thirty moons past. It began upon the following occasion. It is allowed on all hands, that the primitive way of breaking eggs before we eat them, was upon the larger end; but his present Majesty's grandfather, while he was a boy, going to eat an egg, and breaking it according to the ancient practice, happened to cut one of his fingers. Whereupon the Emperor, his father, published an edict, commanding all his subjects, upon great penalties, to break the smaller end of their eggs. The people so highly resented this law that our histories tell us there have been six rebellions raised on that account; wherein one emperor lost his life, and another his crown.[2] These civil commotions were constantly fomented by the monarchs of Blefuscu; and when they were quelled, the exiles always fled for refuge to that empire. It is computed that eleven thousand persons have, at several times, suffered death rather than submit to break their eggs at the smaller end. Many hundred large volumes have been published upon this controversy; but the books of the Big-Endians have been long

conjecture (kən jek′ chər) *v.* guess

Literary Analysis
Satire Why do you think Swift chooses the correct way to break eggs as the cause of conflict between Lilliput and Blefuscu?

---

1. **Blefuscu** represents France.
2. **It is allowed . . . crown** Here, Swift satirizes the dispute in England between the Catholics (Big-Endians) and Protestants (Little-Endians). King Henry VIII who "broke" with the Catholic church, King Charles I, who "lost his life," and King James, who lost his "crown," are each referred to in the passage.

✔**Reading Check**
What sparked the war between Lilliput and Blefuscu?

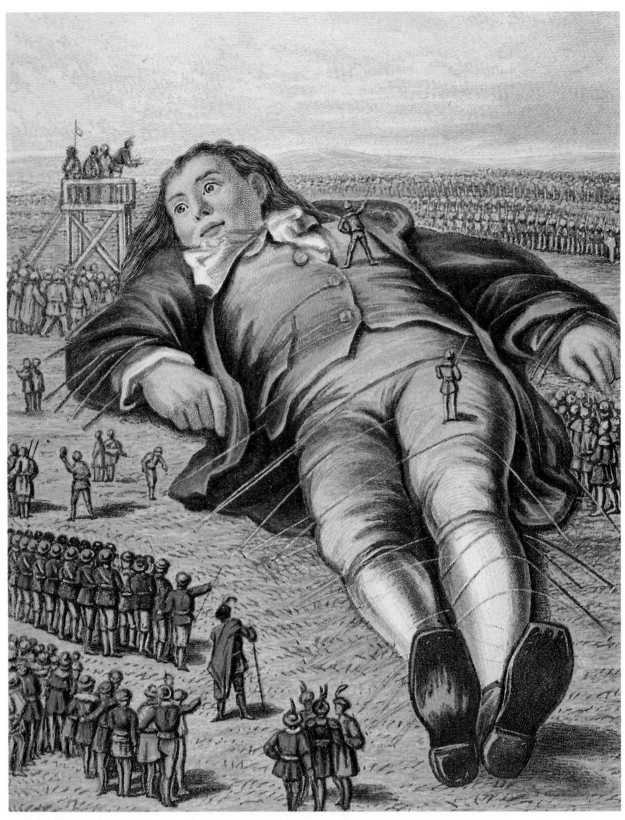

▲ **Critical Viewing** What passages in the text reveal that Lilliputians now trust Gulliver more than they did in the episode depicted here? **[Infer]**

forbidden, and the whole party rendered incapable by law of holding employments.[3] During the course of these troubles, the emperors of Blefuscu did frequently <u>expostulate</u> by their ambassadors, accusing us of making a <u>schism</u> in religion, by offending against a fundamental doctrine of our great prophet Lustrog, in the fifty-fourth chapter of the *Brundecral* (which is their Alcoran).[4] This, however, is thought to be a mere strain upon the text, for the words are these: That all true believers shall break their eggs at the convenient end; and which is the convenient end, seems, in my humble opinion, to be left to every man's conscience, or at least in the power of the chief magistrate[5] to determine. Now the Big-Endian exiles have found so much credit in the Emperor of Blefuscu's court, and so much private assistance and encouragement from their party here at home, that a bloody war hath been carried on between the two empires for six and thirty moons with various success; during which time we have lost forty capital ships, and a much greater number of smaller vessels, together with thirty thousand of our best seamen and soldiers; and the damage received by the enemy is reckoned to be somewhat greater than ours. However, they have now equipped a numerous fleet, and are just preparing to make a descent upon us; and his Imperial Majesty, placing great confidence in your valor and strength, hath commanded me to lay this account of his affairs before you.

I desired the Secretary to present my humble duty to the Emperor, and to let him know, that I thought it would not become me, who was a foreigner, to interfere with parties; but I was ready, with the hazard of my life, to defend his person and state against all invaders.

The empire of Blefuscu is an island situated to the north-northeast side of Lilliput, from whence it is parted only by a channel of eight hundred yards wide. I had not yet seen it, and upon this notice of an intended invasion, I avoided appearing on that side of the coast, for fear of being discovered by some of the enemy's ships, who had received no intelligence of me, all intercourse between the two empires having been strictly forbidden during the war, upon pain of death, and an embargo laid by our Emperor upon all vessels whatsoever. I communicated to his Majesty a project I had formed of seizing the enemy's whole fleet; which, as our scouts assured us, lay at anchor in the harbor ready to sail with the first fair wind. I consulted the most experienced seamen upon the depth of the channel, which they had often plumbed, who told me, that in the middle at high water it was

---

3. **the whole party . . . employments** The Test Act (1673) prevented Catholics from holding office.
4. **Alcoran** Koran, the sacred book of Muslims.
5. **chief magistrate** ruler.

expostulate (eks päs′ chə lāt′) *v.* reason earnestly with

schism (siz′ əm) *n.* division of a group into factions

£iterature
in context Vocabulary Connection

The Vocabulary of Religious Conflict
   The word *schism*, which Swift uses in describing the conflict between Big-Endians and Little-Endians, is an important term in the history of religious conflict. This term comes from the Greek word *schizein*, meaning "divide," and it can mean simply "to cleave or cut." Traditionally, it has been applied to a split in an organized group (especially a church), the act of trying to cause such a split, or a sect formed by the split. By using this word in describing the controversy between Big-Endians and Little-Endians, Swift signals readers that his fiction refers to a significant religious conflict.

✓**Reading Check**
How does Gulliver plan to defend the Lilliputians against invasion?

seventy *glumgluffs* deep (which is about six feet of European measure), and the rest of it fifty *glumgluffs* at most. I walked to the northeast coast over against Blefuscu, where, lying down behind a hillock, I took out my small pocket perspective-glass, and viewed the enemy's fleet at anchor, consisting of about fifty men of war, and a great number of transports. I then came back to my house and gave order (for which I had a warrant) for a great quantity of the strongest cable and bars of iron. The cable was about as thick as packthread, and the bars of the length and size of a knitting-needle. I trebled the cable to make it stronger, and for the same reason I twisted three of the iron bars together, bending the extremities into a hook. Having thus fixed fifty hooks to as many cables, I went back to the northeast coast and, putting off my coat, shoes, and stockings, walked into the sea in my leathern jerkin, about half an hour before high water. I waded with what haste I could, and swam in the middle about thirty yards until I felt ground; I arrived at the fleet in less than half an hour. The enemy was so frightened when they saw me, that they leaped out of their ships, and swam to shore, where there could not be fewer than thirty thousand souls. I then took my tackling, and, fastening a hook to the hole at the prow of each, I tied all the cords together at the end. While I was thus employed, the enemy discharged several thousand arrows, many of which struck in my hands and face and, besides the excessive smart, gave me much disturbance in my work. My greatest apprehension was for my eyes, which I should have infallibly lost, if I had not suddenly thought of an <u>expedient</u>. I kept among other little necessaries a pair of spectacles in a private pocket, which, as I observed before, had escaped the Emperor's searchers. These I took out and fastened as strongly as I could upon my nose and thus armed went on boldly with my work in spite of the enemy's arrows, many of which struck against the glasses of my spectacles, but without any other effect further than a little to discompose them. I had now fastened all the hooks and, taking the knot in my hand, began to pull, but not a ship would stir, for they were all too fast held by their anchors, so that the boldest part of my enterprise remained. I therefore let go the cord, and, leaving the hooks fixed to the ships, I resolutely cut with my knife the cables that fastened the anchors, receiving above two hundred shots in my face and hands; then I took up the knotted end of the cables to which my hooks were tied and, with great ease, drew fifty of the enemy's largest men-of-war after me.

The Blefuscudians, who had not the least imagination of what I intended, were at first confounded with astonishment. They had seen me cut the cables and thought my design was only to let the ships run adrift or fall foul on each other; but when they perceived the whole fleet, moving in order, and saw me pulling at the end, they set up such a scream of grief and despair that it is almost impossible to describe or conceive. When I had got out of danger, I stopped a while to pick out the arrows that stuck in my hands and face, and rubbed on some of the same ointment that was given me at my first arrival, as I have

expedient (ek spē′ dē ənt) *n.* device used in an emergency

Literary Analysis
Satire and Irony What is ironic about Gulliver using spectacles as a shield in a military operation?

◄ **Critical Viewing**
What specific details from the text does this picture illustrate? **[Connect]**

formerly mentioned. I then took off my spectacles, and, waiting about an hour until the tide was a little fallen, I waded through the middle with my cargo and arrived safe at the royal port of Lilliput.

The Emperor and his whole court stood on the shore expecting the issue of this great adventure. They saw the ships move forward in a large half-moon but could not discern me, who was up to my breast in water. When I advanced to the middle of the channel, they were yet

✔ **Reading Check**

Summarize the action Gulliver takes against the fleet of Blefuscu.

more in pain, because I was under water to my neck. The Emperor concluded me to be drowned, and that the enemy's fleet was approaching in a hostile manner; but he was soon eased of his fears; for, the channel growing shallower every step I made, I came in a short time within hearing, and holding up the end of the cable by which the fleet was fastened, I cried in a loud voice, Long live the most puissant[6] Emperor of Lilliput! This great prince received me at my landing with all possible encomiums and created me a *Nardac* upon the spot, which is the highest title of honor among them.

His Majesty desired I would take some other opportunity of bringing all the rest of his enemy's ships into his ports. And so unmeasurable is the ambition of princes, that he seemed to think of nothing less than reducing the whole empire of Blefuscu into a province and governing it by a viceroy; of destroying the Big-Endian exiles and compelling that people to break the smaller end of their eggs, by which he would remain sole monarch of the whole world. But I endeavored to divert him from this design by many arguments drawn from the topics of policy as well as justice, and I plainly protested that I would never be an instrument of bringing a free and brave people into slavery. And when the matter was debated in council, the wisest part of the ministry were of my opinion.

This open bold declaration of mine was so opposite to the schemes and politics of his Imperial Majesty that he could never forgive me; he mentioned it in a very artful manner at council, where I was told that some of the wisest appeared, at least, by their silence, to be of my opinion; but others, who were my secret enemies, could not forbear some expressions, which by a sidewind reflected on me. And from this time began an intrigue between his Majesty and a junta of ministers maliciously bent against me, which broke out in less than two months and had like to have ended in my utter destruction. Of so little weight are the greatest services to princes when put into the balance with a refusal to gratify their passions.

from A Voyage to Brobdingnag

Gulliver's second voyage leads him to Brobdingnag (bräb´ diŋ nag´), an island located near Alaska that is inhabited by giants twelve times as tall as Gulliver. After being sold to the Queen of Brobdingnag, Gulliver describes the English social and political institutions to the King, who reacts to his description with contempt and disgust.

It is the custom that every Wednesday (which, as I have before observed, was their Sabbath) the King and Queen, with the royal issue of both sexes, dine together in the apartment of his Majesty, to whom I was now become a favorite; and at these times my little chair

Literary Analysis
Satire Which satirical details in the first paragraph of "A Voyage to Brobdingnag" relate to England and which relate to humanity in general? Explain.

---

6. puissant (pyoo´ i sənt) powerful.

and table were placed at his left hand before one of the saltcellars. This prince took a pleasure in conversing with me, inquiring into the manners, religion, laws, government, and learning of Europe, wherein I gave him the best account I was able. His apprehension was so clear, and his judgment so exact, that he made very wise reflections and observations upon all I said. But I confess, that after I had been a little too copious in talking of my own beloved country, of our trade, and wars by sea and land, of our schisms in religion, and parties in the state, the prejudices of his education prevailed so far, that he could not forbear taking me up in his right hand, and stroking me gently with the other, after an hearty fit of laughing, asked me whether I were a Whig or a Tory.[7] Then turning to his first minister, who waited behind him with a white staff, near as tall as the mainmast of the *Royal Sovereign*,[8] he observed how contemptible a thing was human grandeur, which could be mimicked by such diminutive insects as I. And yet, said he, I dare engage, those creatures have their titles and distinctions of honor, they contrive little nests and burrows, that they call houses and cities; they make a figure in dress and equipage;[9] they love, they fight, they dispute, they cheat, they betray. And thus he continued on, while my color came and went several times, with indignation to hear our noble country, the mistress of arts and arms, the scourge of France, the arbitress of Europe, the seat of virtue, piety, honor and truth, the pride and envy of the world, so contemptuously treated. . . .

He laughed at my odd kind of arithmetic (as he was pleased to call it) in reckoning the numbers of our people by a computation drawn from the several sects among us in religion and politics. He said he knew no reason why those who entertain opinions prejudicial to the public should be obliged to change or should not be obliged to conceal them. And, as it was tyranny in any government to require the first, so it was weakness not to enforce the second; for, a man may be allowed to keep poisons in his closets, but not to vend them about as cordials.

He observed, that among the diversions of our nobility and gentry[10] I had mentioned gaming.[11] He desired to know at what age this entertainment was usually taken up, and when it was laid down. How much of their time it employed; whether it ever went so high as to affect their fortunes. Whether mean vicious people by their dexterity in that art might not arrive at great riches, and sometimes keep our very nobles in dependence, as well as <u>habituate</u> them to vile companions, wholly take them from the improvement of their minds, and force them, by the losses they received, to learn and practice that infamous dexterity upon others.

---

7. **Whig . . . Tory** British political parties.
8. *Royal Sovereign* one of the largest ships in the British Navy.
9. **equipage** (ek´ wi pij´) horses and carriages.
10. **gentry** the class of landowning people ranking just below the nobility.
11. **gaming** gambling.

Reading Strategy
Interpreting What does the King's laughing question about whether Gulliver is "a Whig or a Tory" suggest about Swift's attitude towards disputes between these parties?

habituate (hə bich´ ōō āt´) v. make used to

✔**Reading Check**

What does the King of Brobdingnag say in response to Gulliver's account of European customs and history?

from *Gulliver's Travels* ◆ 521

He was perfectly astonished with the historical account I gave him of our affairs during the last century, protesting it was only an heap of conspiracies, rebellions, murders, massacres, revolutions, banishments, the very worst effects that avarice, faction, hypocrisy, perfidiousness, cruelty, rage, madness, hatred, envy, lust, malice, and ambition could produce.

His Majesty in another audience was at the pains to recapitulate the sum of all I had spoken; compared the questions he made with the answers I had given; then taking me into his hands, and stroking me gently, delivered himself in these words, which I shall never forget, nor the manner he spoke them in. "My little friend Grildrig, you have made a most admirable panegyric upon your country. You have clearly proved that ignorance, idleness, and vice are the proper ingredients for qualifying a legislator. That laws are best explained, interpreted, and applied by those whose interest and abilities lie in perverting, confounding, and eluding them. I observe among you some lines of an institution, which in its original might have been tolerable, but these half erased, and the rest wholly blurred and blotted by corruptions. It doth not appear from all you have said how any one perfection is required toward the procurement of any one station among you, much less that men are ennobled on account of their virtue, that priests are advanced for their piety or learning, soldiers for their conduct or valor, judges for their integrity, senators for the love of their country, or counselors for their wisdom. As for yourself," continued the King, "who have spent the greatest part of your life in traveling, I am well disposed to hope you may hitherto have escaped many vices of your country. But, by what I have gathered from your own relation, and the answers I have with much pains wringed and extorted from you, I cannot but conclude the bulk of your natives to be the most pernicious race of little <u>odious</u> vermin that nature ever suffered to crawl upon the surface of the earth."

Nothing but an extreme love of truth could have hindered me from concealing this part of my story. It was in vain to discover my resentments, which were always turned into ridicule; and I was forced to rest with patience while my noble and most beloved country was so injuriously treated. I am heartily sorry as any of my readers can possibly be that such an occasion was given, but this prince happened to be so curious and inquisitive upon every particular that it could not consist either with gratitude or good manners to refuse giving him what satisfaction I was able. Yet thus much I may be allowed to say in my own vindication that I artfully eluded many of his questions and gave to every point a more favorable turn by many degrees than the strictness of truth would allow. For I have always borne that laudable partiality to my own country, which Dionysius Halicarnassensis[12] with so much justice recommends to an historian.

odious (ō′ dē əs) *adj.* hateful; disgusting

Literary Analysis
Satire and Irony In Gulliver's remark that he "artfully eluded" the King's questions, what is the difference between the intended meaning and the actual meaning?

---

12. Dionysius (dī′ ə nīsh′ əs) **Halicarnassensis** (hal′ ə kär na sen′ sis) Greek writer who lived in Rome and attempted to persuade the Greeks to submit to their Roman conquerors.

I would hide the frailties and deformities of my political mother and place her virtues and beauties in the most advantageous light. This was my sincere endeavor in those many discourses I had with that mighty monarch, although it unfortunately failed of success.

But great allowances should be given to a king who lives wholly secluded from the rest of the world, and must therefore be altogether unacquainted with the manners and customs that most prevail in other nations: the want of which knowledge will ever produce many prejudices, and a certain narrowness of thinking, from which we and the politer countries of Europe are wholly exempted. And it would be hard indeed, if so remote a prince's notions of virtue and vice were to be offered as a standard for all mankind.

To confirm what I have now said, and further to show the miserable effects of a confined education, I shall here insert a passage which will hardly obtain belief. In hopes to ingratiate myself farther into his Majesty's favor, I told him of an invention discovered between three and four hundred years ago, to make a certain powder, into an heap of which the smallest spark of fire falling, would kindle the whole in a moment, although it were as big as a mountain, and make it all fly up in the air together, with a noise and agitation greater than thunder. That a proper quantity of this powder rammed into an hollow tube of brass or iron, according to its bigness, would drive a ball of iron or lead with such violence and speed as nothing was able to sustain its force. That the largest balls, thus discharged, would not only destroy whole ranks of an army at once, but batter the strongest walls to the ground, sink down ships, with a thousand men in each, to the bottom of the sea; and when linked together by a chain, would cut through masts and rigging, divide hundreds of bodies in the middle, and lay all waste before them. That we often put this powder into large hollow balls of iron, and discharged them by an engine into some city we were besieging, which would rip up the pavement, tear the houses to pieces, burst and throw splinters on every side, dashing out the brains of all who came near. That I knew the ingredients very well, which were cheap, and common; I understood the manner of compounding them, and could direct his workmen how to make those tubes of a size proportionable to all other things in his Majesty's kingdom, and the largest need not be above two hundred foot long; twenty or thirty of which tubes, charged with the proper quantity

A Voyage to Brobdingnag, Illustration from a nineteenth-century edition of *Gulliver's Travels*

▲ **Critical Viewing**
Compare the relationship between Gulliver and the King of Brobdingnag as portrayed by the artist with that portrayed in the text. **[Compare and Contrast]**

☑ **Reading Check**

What is the King's opinion of most of Gulliver's countrymen?

of powder and balls, would batter down the walls of the strongest town in his dominions in a few hours, or destroy the whole metropolis, if ever it should pretend to dispute his absolute commands. This I humbly offered to his Majesty as a small tribute of acknowledgment in return of so many marks that I had received of his royal favor and protection.

The King was struck with horror at the description I had given of those terrible engines and the proposal I had made. He was amazed how so impotent and groveling an insect as I (these were his expressions) could entertain such inhuman ideas, and in so familiar a manner as to appear wholly unmoved at all the scenes of blood and desolation which I had painted as the common effects of those destructive machines; whereof he said some evil genius, enemy to mankind, must have been the first contriver. As for himself, he protested that although few things delighted him so much as new discoveries in art or in nature, yet he would rather lose half his kingdom than be privy to such a secret, which he commanded me, as I valued my life, never to mention any more.

Review and Assess

Thinking About the Selection

1. **Respond:** Would you like to travel with Gulliver? Explain.

2. **(a) Recall:** Describe the conflict between Big-Endians and Little-Endians over the breaking of eggs. **(b) Infer:** Do these two groups take their dispute seriously? Why or why not? **(c) Analyze:** What evidence is there that Swift does not want you to take the dispute seriously? Explain.

3. **(a) Recall:** Citing the text, give one example of how the King of Brobdingnag shows affection toward Gulliver and one example of how he shows distaste for Gulliver's ideas. **(b) Interpret:** Show how the final disagreement between Gulliver and the King reflects a difference between ingenuity and wisdom.

4. **(a) Recall:** What is the most important physical difference between Lilliputians and Brobdingnagians? **(b) Interpret:** How does this physical difference suggest other important ways in which they differ? Explain. **(c) Synthesize:** How do Lilliputians and Brobdingnagians each represent a different way of viewing humanity?

5. **(a) Support:** In the final paragraph of "A Voyage to Brobdingnag," how does Swift use the King's reactions to express his own hopes for humankind? **(b) Assess:** Do you think these hopes are valid? Why or why not?

6. **Take a Position:** Do you think that satires like Swift's can ever change people's behavior? Why or why not?

Review and Assess

Literary Analysis

Satire

1. Use a chart like the one shown to indicate three targets of Swift's **satire**.

Items in Text		Targets of Swift's Satire
	....▶	
	....▶	
	....▶	

2. (a) Compare and contrast Gulliver's impression of the Lilliputians with the King of Brobdingnag's impression of Europeans. (b) How does the comparison add to the satire?

3. Summarize the universal and timeless points Swift wants to make with his satire.

Connecting Literary Elements

4. (a) Find an example of **irony** that depends on a difference between appearance and reality. (b) Explain your choice.

5. (a) Find an example of irony in which the real meaning of a passage is the opposite of the expressed meaning. (b) Explain your choice.

6. Why might a satirist offer ironic, rather than direct, criticisms of institutions like church and state?

Reading Strategy

Interpreting

7. To **interpret** Gulliver's remark that many have "suffered death rather than submit to break their eggs at the smaller end," what historical facts should you know? Why?

8. In interpreting Gulliver's reference to the King of Brobdingnag's "narrowness of thinking," can you assume that Swift supports his central character's remark? Explain.

9. Why is it necessary to interpret a satirical work like *Gulliver's Travels*?

Extend Understanding

10. **Social Studies Connection:** If Swift were alive today, what recent events might he satirize? Why?

Quick Review

Satire is writing that uses humor to expose and ridicule human vice and folly.

Irony is a difference or contradiction between reality and appearance or between what is meant and what is said.

Interpreting is using clues to determine the meaning of a passage.

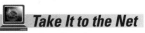 **Take It to the Net**

www.phschool.com

Take the interactive self-test online to check your understanding of the selection.

Integrate Language Skills

Vocabulary Development Lesson

Word Analysis: Latin Root -jec-

The Latin root -jec- means "throw." This root is found in many scientific words, such as *conjecture*, which means "to guess by 'throwing' facts or inferences together."

Choose the letter of the best definition for each word below.

1. inject
2. eject
3. project
4. trajectory
5. projectile
6. reject
7. abject
8. deject

  a. to "throw" forward
  b. to "throw" into
  c. to "throw" out of
  d. object designed to be "thrown" or shot
  e. path along which an object is "thrown"
  f. "thrown" away; hopeless
  g. state of being "thrown" down; depression
  h. "throw" back at

Concept Development: Antonyms

For each numbered vocabulary word, identify the letter of the term that is the best antonym (opposite in meaning).

1. conjecture
2. expostulate
3. schism
4. expedient
5. habituate
6. odious

  a. fusion
  b. unworkable device
  c. certainty
  d. pleasant
  e. alienate
  f. keep silent

Spelling Strategy

When adding *ex-* to words, you usually do not include a hyphen, as in *expedient*. You do add a hyphen when *ex-* means "former," as in *ex-president*. On your paper, add *ex-* to these words.

1. change
2. ambassador
3. tension

Grammar and Style Lesson

Usage: *between* and *among*

Use the preposition **between** when referring to only two things or people or groups. Use the preposition **among** when referring to more than two.

> The channel was <u>between</u> Lilliput and Blefuscu.
>
> Gulliver stood <u>among</u> the boats of the fleet.

Practice In your notebook, fill in each blank with the correct preposition: *between* or *among*.

1. A channel eight hundred yards wide lies ___?___ the two countries.

2. ___?___ the Lilliputians, a Big-Endian faction refused to accept the Emperor's edict.
3. Wednesday is the Sabbath ___?___ the Brobdingnagians.
4. The difference in size ___?___ Gulliver and the Lilliputians was remarkable.
5. The King notices that gambling is ___?___ the pastimes Gulliver mentions.

Writing Application Write four sentences comparing Gulliver with the people he meets on his journeys. Use *between* and *among* twice each.

W͜G Prentice Hall Writing and Grammar Connection: Chapter 25, Section 2

Writing Lesson

Satirical Essay

In his novel, Swift uses irony and fantasy to ridicule human vices and follies. Write your own satirical essay that targets and ironically mocks a foolish behavior or trend in today's world.

Prewriting   Target your satire by choosing a particular behavior, trend, or attitude to attack. Then, list some of the arguments its supporters use so you can exaggerate them in your essay.

Drafting   Refer to your prewriting notes, and select the most outrageous arguments for the behavior, trend, or attitude you are satirizing. Include them in a punchy, ironic lead that pretends to support what you are attacking. Continue by offering further support in a way that seems positive but is actually ridiculous.

Revising   Read your satire aloud to a classmate. If there are passages that fall flat, look for ways to enhance your satire with irony.

Model: Revising to Add Irony

I think the president should   *a*
~~When adults, who should know better,~~ ride ~~these~~ little

on his way up to give the State of the Union address.

~~scooters, they look like overgrown kids.~~

> The author adds irony to the satire by pretending to advocate something that is actually ridiculous.

 Prentice Hall Writing and Grammar Connection: Chapter 11, Section 2

Extension Activities

Listening and Speaking With a small group, devise a **special-effects plan** for a filmed version of the voyages to Lilliput and Brobdingnag.

- Review the story. Then, brainstorm for visual, musical, sound, and graphic effects to enhance the narrative.
- Decide where in the story they would be most effective.

Compose an oral summary of your plan that one or more group members can present to the class. **[Group Activity]**

Research and Technology Write a **research report** on the seventeenth-century religious disputes between Catholics and Protestants that Swift satirizes as a conflict between Big-Endians and Little-Endians. Explain in detail the references Swift makes in his novel, and enhance your report with graphics, timelines, statistical charts, and diagrams.

 **Take It to the Net**   www.phschool.com

Go online for an additional research activity using the Internet.

Prepare to Read

from An Essay on Man ◆ *from* The Rape of the Lock

Alexander Pope
(1688–1744)

Despite a crippling childhood disease and persistent ill health, Alexander Pope determined at a young age to become a great poet. He triumphantly achieved his boyhood ambition by the time he was in his twenties, capturing the attention of the leading literary figures of England with *An Essay on Criticism* (1711) and *The Rape of the Lock* (1712–1714). A brilliant satirist in verse, Pope gave his name to the literary era in which he wrote, which is now called the Age of Pope and Swift.

A Struggle Against Prejudice Born into the Roman Catholic family of a London linen merchant, Pope was a member of a persecuted religious minority. After the expulsion of King James II in 1688, English Catholics could not legally vote, hold office, attend a university, or live within ten miles of London. Probably to comply with the rule of residency, his family moved first to the village of Hammersmith and then to Binfield, near Windsor Forest. In this rural setting, Pope spent his formative years writing poetry, studying the classics, and educating himself.

"[T]his long Disease, my Life" In addition to facing religious prejudice, Pope had severe physical problems. Deformed by tuberculosis of the bone, or Pott's disease, Pope stood only about four and a half feet tall—"that little Alexander the women laugh at," he said about himself. Pope also suffered from nervousness and excruciating headaches throughout his life. In a line from his poem *Epistle to Dr. Arbuthnot* (1735), he refers jokingly but also with sadness to "this long Disease, my Life."

Around 1719, two years after his father's death, Pope moved to Twickenham (traditionally pronounced twit´ nəm), a village on the Thames, where he lived for the remainder of his life.

Literary Friendships Although Pope is more often remembered for his wasplike sting in quarrels than for his cordiality—he was called "the Wasp of Twickenham"—he befriended many literary figures of his day. For example, in the coffeehouses of London, he associated with Richard Steele and Joseph Addison, essayists and founders of two prominent periodicals of the time.

Satiric Scribblers Pope also associated with a group that included writers Jonathan Swift and John Gay. Pope joined with these men and others in forming the Scriblerus Club, whose purpose was to ridicule what its members regarded as "false tastes in learning."

Meeting regularly, the members wined, dined, and joked with one another. For example, when Pope read aloud to the group his revised version of *The Rape of the Lock*, one member, Thomas Parnell, humorously objected that Pope had stolen a passage from an old manuscript. Parnell even pretended to produce this manuscript, which was really his own translation of Pope's English into bad Latin.

Although the club did not continue for long, its emphasis on fun and satire probably inspired Swift's masterwork *Gulliver's Travels*; Gay's *Beggar's Opera*, the most successful play of the century; and Pope's *The Dunciad*, which is an assault on his literary enemies.

A Turn to Philosophy In the 1730s, Pope's writing moved out of the satirical mode to become increasingly philosophical. Leaving humor behind, he embarked on a massive work concerning morality and government but completed only *An Essay on Man* and *Moral Essays*. Nevertheless, the entire body of his work is so noteworthy that critics and fellow writers alike frequently accord him exceptionally high praise. The twentieth-century poet Edith Sitwell, for example, called Pope "perhaps the most flawless artist our race has yet produced."

Preview

Connecting to the Literature

Violating social rules may cause some people to disapprove of you. In the upper-class society of Pope's time, the unwritten rules were so elaborate that Pope made fun of them in *The Rape of the Lock*.

Literary Analysis

Mock Epic

A **mock epic** is a long, humorous narrative poem that treats a trivial subject in the grand style of a true epic like Homer's *Iliad* or Milton's *Paradise Lost*. For example, in *The Rape of the Lock*, Pope applies to the theft of a lady's lock of hair such epic elements as these:

- Boasting speeches of heroes and heroines
- Elaborate descriptions of warriors and their weapons
- Involvement of gods and goddesses in the action
- **Epic similes,** or elaborate comparisons in the style of Homer that sometimes use the words *like, as,* or *so*

As you read, look for the epic elements that convey Pope's affectionate mockery.

Comparing Literary Works

One of these works is a mock epic that pokes fun; the other is a serious look at human nature. In both works, Pope uses a figure of speech from **rhetoric,** or public speaking, called **antithesis**—placing side by side, and in similar grammatical structures, strongly contrasting words, clauses, sentences, or ideas. Using a chart like this one to identify examples of antithesis in both poems, note how the contrast in each example is between what is lofty and what is low or trivial. Also, observe how Pope uses this device to satirize behavior in *The Rape of the Lock* and to define the human condition in *An Essay on Man*.

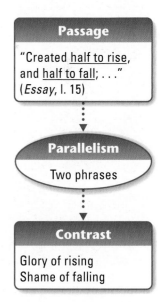

Passage

"Created <u>half to rise</u>, and <u>half to fall</u>; . . ." (*Essay*, l. 15)

Parallelism

Two phrases

Contrast

Glory of rising
Shame of falling

Reading Strategy

Recognizing Author's Purpose

As you read *The Rape of the Lock*, find evidence of Pope's **purpose,** or reason for writing—to ridicule and to entertain.

Vocabulary Development

stoic (stō′ ik) *n.* person indifferent to joy, grief, pleasure, or pain (p. 531)

disabused (dis′ ə byo͞ozd′) *adj.* freed from false ideas (p. 531)

obliquely (ə blēk′ lē) *adv.* at a slant; indirectly (p. 534)

plebeian (plē bē′ ən) *adj.* common; not aristocratic (p. 535)

destitute (des′ tə to͞ot′) *adj.* lacking (p. 536)

assignations (as′ ig nā′ shənz) *n.* appointments to meet (p. 538)

from
An Essay on Man

Alexander Pope

▲ **Critical Viewing** Compare and contrast the perspective on humanity indicated by this Rodin sculpture with Pope's perspective in *An Essay on Man*. **[Compare and Contrast]**

An Essay on Man is an examination of human nature, society, and morals. In the following passage, Pope cautions against intellectual pride by vividly describing the uncertain "middle state" in which humans have been placed.

Know then thyself, presume not God to scan;
The proper study of mankind is man.
Placed on this isthmus of a middle state,
A being darkly wise, and rudely great:
5 With too much knowledge for the skeptic side,
With too much weakness for the <u>stoic's</u> pride,
He hangs between; in doubt to act, or rest;
In doubt to deem himself a god, or beast;
In doubt his mind or body to prefer;
10 Born but to die, and reasoning but to err;
Alike in ignorance, his reason such,
Whether he thinks too little, or too much:
Chaos of thought and passion, all confused;
Still by himself abused, or <u>disabused</u>;
15 Created half to rise, and half to fall;
Great lord of all things, yet a prey to all;
Sole judge of truth, in endless error hurled:
The glory, jest, and riddle of the world!

stoic (stō´ ik) *n.* person indifferent to joy, grief, pleasure, or pain

disabused (dis´ ə byo͞ozd´) *adj.* freed from false ideas

Review and Assess

Thinking About the Selection

1. **Respond:** Do you react negatively or positively to Pope's picture of human nature? Explain.

2. **(a) Recall:** What does Pope say should be the object of man's study? **(b) Speculate:** Why do you think Pope says, "presume not God to scan"?

3. **(a) Recall:** According to Pope, what prevents man from being a skeptic or a stoic? **(b) Analyze Cause and Effect:** What is the result of man's being neither skeptic nor stoic? Explain.

4. **(a) Recall:** What does each "half" of man do?
   (b) Interpret: In your own words, express how man can be both a "lord of all things" and "a prey to all."

5. **Connect:** What twentieth-century events suggest that humans are any or all of the following: "The glory, jest, and riddle of the world!" Explain.

from The Rape of the Lock

Alexander Pope

Background

The Rape of the Lock is based on an actual incident. Two families, the Petres and the Fermors, became involved in a dispute when Robert Petre flirtatiously cut a lock of hair from the head of lovely Arabella Fermor.

The first of the poem's five cantos opens with a formal statement of theme and an invocation to the Muse for poetic inspiration. Then, Belinda, the poem's heroine, receives a warning from the sylph Ariel that a dreadful event will take place in her immediate future. In Canto II, during a boat ride on the Thames, an adventurous baron admires Belinda's hair and is determined to cut two bright locks from her head and keep them as a prize. Aware of the baron's desires, Ariel urges the spirits to protect Belinda.

Canto III

    Close by those meads, forever crowned with flowers,
    Where Thames with pride surveys his rising towers,
    There stands a structure of majestic frame,[1]
    Which from the neighboring Hampton takes its name.
5 Here Britain's statesmen oft the fall foredoom
    Of foreign tyrants, and of nymphs at home;
    Here thou, great Anna![2] whom three realms obey,
    Dost sometimes counsel take—and sometimes tea.
       Hither the heroes and the nymphs resort,
10 To taste awhile the pleasures of a court;

---

1. **structure . . . frame** Hampton Court, a royal palace near London.
2. **Anna** Queen Anne, who ruled England, Ireland, and Scotland from 1702 through 1714.

The Barge, 1895–96 Aubrey Beardsley

▲ **Critical Viewing** Does the artist's portrayal of Belinda, who is shown here, correspond to Pope's portrayal of her in Canto III? Explain. **[Connect]**

◀ **Critical Viewing**
Where in the poem does Pope make a trivial occasion seem important, as the artist does here? Explain. **[Connect]**

The Rape of the Lock, 1895–96, Aubrey Beardsley

In various talk th' instructive hours they passed,
Who gave the ball, or paid the visit last;
One speaks the glory of the British Queen,
And one describes a charming Indian screen;
15 A third interprets motions, looks, and eyes;
At every word a reputation dies.
Snuff, or the fan,³ supply each pause of chat,
With singing, laughing, ogling, and all that.
  Meanwhile, declining from the noon of day,
20 The sun <u>obliquely</u> shoots his burning ray;
The hungry judges soon the sentence sign,

obliquely (ə blēk′ lē) *adv.*
at a slant; indirectly

---

3. snuff . . . fan At the time, gentlemen commonly took snuff and
ladies usually carried a fan.

And wretches hang that jurymen may dine;
The merchant from th' Exchange[4] returns in peace,
And the long labors of the toilet[5] cease.
25 Belinda now, whom thirst of fame invites,
Burns to encounter two adventurous knights,
At omber[6] singly to decide their doom;
And swells her breast with conquests yet to come.
Straight the three bands prepare in arms to join,
30 Each band the number of the sacred nine.[7]
Soon as she spreads her hand, th' aerial guard
Descend, and sit on each important card:
First Ariel perched upon a Matadore,[8]
Then each, according to the rank they bore;
35 For sylphs, yet mindful of their ancient race,
Are, as when women, wondrous fond of place.
　　　Behold, four kings in majesty revered,
With hoary whiskers and a forky beard;
And four fair queens whose hands sustain a flower,
40 Th' expressive emblem of their softer power;
Four knaves in garbs succinct,[9] a trusty band,
Caps on their heads, and halberts[10] in their hand;
And particolored troops, a shining train,
Draw forth to combat on the velvet plain.
45 　　　The skillful nymph reviews her force with care:
Let spades be trumps! she said, and trumps they were.
　　　Now move to war her sable Matadores,
In show like leaders of the swarthy Moors.
Spadillio[11] first, unconquerable Lord!
50 Led off two captive trumps, and swept the board.
As many more Manillio[12] forced to yield,
And marched a victor from the verdant field.[13]
Him Basto[14] followed, but his fate more hard
Gained but one trump and one <u>plebeian</u> card.
55 With his broad saber next, a chief in years,
The hoary majesty of spades appears,
Puts forth one manly leg, to sight revealed,
The rest, his many-colored robe concealed.

Reading Strategy
Recognizing Author's Purpose How do the remarks in lines 33–36 serve both to satirize and to entertain?

plebeian (plē bē′ ən) *adj.*
common; not aristocratic

---

4. **Exchange** London financial center where merchants, bankers, and brokers conducted business.
5. **toilet** dressing tables.
6. **omber** popular card game.
7. **sacred nine** reference to the nine Muses of Greek mythology.
8. **Matadore** powerful card that could take a trick.
9. **succinct** (sək siŋkt′) belted.
10. **halberts** long-handled weapons.
11. **Spadillio** ace of spades.
12. **Manillio** two of spades.
13. **Verdant field** the card table, covered with a green cloth.
14. **Basto** ace of clubs.

✔**Reading Check**

In what way do Belinda and her friends pass the time?

The rebel knave, who dares his prince engage,
60 Proves the just victim of his royal rage.
Even mighty Pam,[15] that kings and queens o'erthrew
And mowed down armies in the fights of loo,
Sad chance of war! now <u>destitute</u> of aid,
Falls undistinguished by the victor spade!
65   Thus far both armies to Belinda yield;
Now to the baron fate inclines the field.
His warlike Amazon her host invades,
Th' imperial consort of the crown of spades.
The club's black tyrant first her victim died,
70 Spite of his haughty mien, and barbarous pride.
What boots[16] the regal circle on his head,
His giant limbs, in state unwieldy spread;
That long behind he trails his pompous robe,
And, of all monarchs, only grasps the globe?
75   The baron now his diamonds pours apace;
Th' embroidered king who shows but half his face,
And his refulgent queen, with powers combined
Of broken troops an easy conquest find.
Clubs, diamonds, hearts, in wild disorder seen,
80 With throngs promiscuous strew the level green.
Thus when dispersed a routed army runs,
Of Asia's troops, and Afric's sable sons,
        With like confusion different nations fly,
Of various habit, and of various dye,
85 The pierced battalions disunited fall,
In heaps on heaps; one fate o'erwhelms them all.
        The knave of diamonds tries his wily arts,
And wins (oh shameful chance!) the queen of hearts.
At this, the blood the virgin's cheek forsook,
90 A livid paleness spreads o'er all her look;
She sees, and trembles at th' approaching ill,
Just in the jaws of ruin, and codille.[17]
And now (as oft in some distempered state)
On one nice trick depends the general fate.
95 An ace of hearts steps forth; the king unseen
Lurked in her hand, and mourned his captive queen.
He springs to vengeance with an eager pace,
And falls like thunder on the prostrate ace.
The nymph exulting fills with shouts the sky;
100 The walls, the woods, and long canals reply.
        Oh thoughtless mortals! ever blind to fate,
Too soon dejected, and too soon elate.

destitute (des´ tə tōōt) *adj.*
lacking

Literary Analysis
Mock Epic and Antithesis
Why are lines 97–98 an
example of antithesis?

---

15. **Pam** knave of clubs, the highest card in the game called "loo."
16. **What boots** of what benefit is.
17. **codille** term meaning the defeat of a hand of cards.

Sudden, these honors shall be snatched away,
And cursed forever this victorious day.

105   For lo! the board with cups and spoons is crowned,
The berries crackle, and the mill turns round;[18]
On shining altars of Japan[19] they raise
The silver lamp; the fiery spirits blaze;
From silver spouts the grateful liquors glide,
110 While China's earth[20] receives the smoking tide.
At once they gratify their scent and taste,
And frequent cups prolong the rich repast.
Straight hover round the fair her airy band;
some, as she sipped, the fuming liquor fanned,
115 Some o'er her lap their careful plumes displayed,
Trembling, and conscious of the rich brocade.
Coffee (which makes the politician wise,
And see through all things with his half-shut eyes)
Sent up in vapors to the baron's brain
120 New stratagems, the radiant lock to gain.
Ah cease, rash youth! desist ere 'tis too late,
Fear the just gods, and think of Scylla's fate![21]
Changed to a bird, and sent to flit in air,
She dearly pays for Nisus' injured hair!
125   But when to mischief mortals bend their will,
How soon they find fit instruments of ill!
Just then, Clarissa drew with tempting grace
A two-edged weapon from her shining case:
So ladies in romance assist their knight,
130 Present the spear, and arm him for the fight.
He takes the gift with reverence, and extends
The little engine[22] on his fingers' ends;
This just behind Belinda's neck he spread,
As o'er the fragrant steams she bends her head.
135 Swift to the lock a thousand sprites repair,
A thousand wings, by turns, blow back the hair;
And thrice they twitched the diamond in her ear;
Thrice she looked back, and thrice the foe drew near.
Just in that instant, anxious Ariel sought
140 The close recesses of the virgin's thought;
As on the nosegay in her breast reclined,
He watched th' ideas rising in her mind,
Sudden he viewed, in spite of all her art,

---

18. **The berries . . . round** Coffee beans are ground in a hand mill at the table.
19. **altars of Japan** small imported lacquer tables.
20. **China's earth** earthenware cups imported from China.
21. **Scylla's** (sil´ əz) **fate** Scylla, the daughter of King Nisus, was turned into a sea bird because she cut off the lock of her father's hair on which his safety depended and sent it to his enemy.
22. **engine** instrument.

The **British Tradition**

Neoclassical Style and The Heroic Couplet

  Lines 105–106 or any of the rhyming lines in the poem demonstrate Pope's use of the closed heroic couplet, a rhyming pair of iambic pentameter lines that are "closed" because they express a complete thought. This type of couplet is typical of the Neoclassical style of the eighteenth century, which had these characteristics: a reliance on Greek and Roman models, a stress on human limitations, and a concept of the poet as a kind of public speaker addressing society as a whole.

  In keeping with the Neoclassical outlook, the closed heroic couplet allows Pope to indicate human follies and frailties with devices from public speaking like antithesis.

  By way of contrast with Pope's couplets, note how Browning in "My Last Duchess," page 836, uses open couplets that flow on rather than encapsulating a thought. These open couplets allow Browning to imitate speech rhythms and the "flow" of human character expressing itself.

✔**Reading Check**

What is the baron plotting to do?

An earthly lover lurking at her heart.[23]

145 Amazed, confused, he found his power expired,
Resigned to fate, and with a sigh retired.
     The peer now spreads the glittering forfex[24] wide,
T' enclose the lock; now joins it, to divide.
Even then, before the fatal engine closed,
150 A wretched sylph too fondly interposed;
Fate urged the shears, and cut the sylph in twain,
(But airy substance soon unites again).
The meeting points the sacred hair dissever
From the fair head, forever, and forever!
155   Then flashed the living lightning from her eyes,
And screams of horror rend th' affrighted skies.
Not louder shrieks to pitying heaven are cast,
When husbands, or when lap dogs breathe their last;
Or when rich China vessels fallen from high,
160 In glittering dust, and painted fragments lie!
     "Let wreaths of triumph now my temples twine,"
The victor cried, "the glorious prize is mine!"
While fish in streams, or birds delight in air,
Or in a coach and six the British Fair,
165 As long as *Atalantis*[25] shall be read,
Or the small pillow grace a lady's bed,
While visits shall be paid on solemn days,
When numerous wax lights in bright order blaze,
While nymphs take treats, or <u>assignations</u> give,
170 So long my honor, name, and praise shall live!
What time would spare, from steel receives its date,[26]
And monuments, like men, submit to fate!
Steel could the labor of the gods destroy,
And strike to dust th' imperial towers of Troy;
175 Steel could the works of mortal pride confound,
And hew triumphal arches to the ground.
What wonder then, fair nymph! thy hairs should feel,
The conquering force of unresisted steel?

from Canto V

In Canto IV, after Umbriel, "a dusky, melancholy sprite," empties a bag filled with "the force of female lungs, sighs, sobs, and passions, and the war of tongues" onto Belinda's head, the lady erupts over the loss of her lock. Then she "bids her beau," Sir Plume, to "demand the precious hairs," but Plume is unable to persuade the baron to return the hair.

---

23. **earthly lover . . . heart** If in her heart Belinda wants the baron to succeed, they cannot protect her.
24. **forfex** scissors.
25. **Atalantis** popular book of scandalous gossip.
26. **receives its date** is destroyed.

Reading Strategy
Recognizing Author's Purpose Why does the author describe the scene in lines 145–160 in such an elevated manner?

assignations (as´ ig nā´ shənz) *n.* appointments to meet

The Battle of the Beaux and Belles Aubrey Beardsley

▲ **Critical Viewing** In what ways is the elaborate decorative style of the drawing similar to the language of the poem? **[Evaluate]**

In the beginning of Canto V, Clarissa, a level-headed nymph, tries to bring an end to the commotion, but rather than being greeted with applause, her speech is followed by a battle cry.

"To arms, to arms!" the fierce virago[27] cries,
And swift as lightning to the combat flies.
All side in parties, and begin th' attack;
Fans clap, silks rustle, and tough whalebones crack;
5 Heroes' and heroines' shouts confusedly rise,
And bass and treble voices strike the skies.
No common weapons in their hands are found,
Like gods they fight, nor dread a mortal wound.
    So when bold Homer makes the gods engage,
10 And heavenly breasts with human passions rage;
'Gainst Pallas, Mars, Latona, Hermes[28] arms;
And all Olympus[29] rings with loud alarms:
Jove's[30] thunder roars, heaven trembles all around,
Blue Neptune[31] storms, the bellowing deeps resound;
15 Earth shakes her nodding towers, the ground gives way,
And the pale ghosts start at the flash of day!
    Triumphant Umbriel on a sconce's height[32]
Clapped his glad wings, and sat to view the fight;
Propped on their bodkin spears,[33] the sprites survey
20 The growing combat, or assist the fray.
    While through the press enraged Thalestris[34] flies,
And scatters death around from both her eyes,
A beau and witling[35] perished in the throng,
One died in metaphor, and one in song.
25 "O cruel nymph! a living death I bear,"
Cried Dapperwit, and sunk beside his chair.
A mournful glance Sir Fopling[36] upwards cast,
"Those eyes are made so killing"—was his last.
Thus on Maeander's[37] flowery margin lies
30 Th' expiring swan, and as he sings he dies.
    When bold Sir Plume had drawn Clarissa down,

---

27. **virago** (vi rā′ gō) scolding woman.
28. **Pallas . . . Hermes** gods who directed the Trojan War. Pallas and Hermes supported the Greeks, while Mars and Latona sided with the Trojans.
29. **Olympus** mountain which was supposed to be the home of the Greek gods.
30. **Jove's** referring to Jupiter, the ruler of the Gods in Roman mythology: identified with Zeus in Greek mythology.
31. **Neptune** Roman god of the sea; identified with Poseidon in Greek mythology.
32. **sconce's height** candleholder attached to the wall.
33. **bodkin spears** large needles.
34. **Thalestris** (thə lēs′ tris) an Amazon (a race of female warriors supposed to have lived in Scythia) who played a role in the medieval tales of Alexander the Great.
35. **witling** person who fancies himself or herself a wit.
36. **Dapperwit . . . Sir Fopling** names of amusing characters in comedies of the time.
37. **Maeander's** referring to a river in Asia.

Fashions of the Times

Pope's focus on Belinda's hair indicates the importance that women's hairstyles played in the upper-class obsession with fashion at this time. During the eighteenth century, the world's first fashion magazine was launched by the French, suggesting that nation's leadership in setting styles. Leonard, hairdresser to the French queen Marie Antoinette (1755–1793), whose picture appears below, established a fashion in which women's hairdos rose as high as four feet. These "hair statues" were augmented with horsehair pads and decorated with gauze and feathers. English hairdressers quickly took up the challenge, decorating women's heads with horse-drawn carriages, zoos of miniature lions and tigers, and, if accounts can be believed, a lit stove complete with pots and pans!

Chloe[38] stepped in, and killed him with a frown;
She smiled to see the doughty hero slain,
But, at her smile, the beau revived again.
35   Now Jove suspends his golden scales in air,
Weighs the men's wits against the lady's hair;
The doubtful beam long nods from side to side;
At length the wits mount up, the hairs subside.
        See, fierce Belinda on the baron flies,
40 With more than usual lightning in her eyes;
Nor feared the chief th' unequal fight to try,
Who sought no more than on his foe to die.
But this bold lord with manly strength endued,
She with one finger and a thumb subdued:
45 Just where the breath of life his nostrils drew,
A charge of snuff the wily virgin threw;
The gnomes direct, to every atom just,
The pungent grains of titillating dust.
Sudden with starting tears each eye o'erflows,
50 And the high dome re-echoes to his nose.
        "Now meet thy fate," incensed Belinda cried,
And drew a deadly bodkin[39] from her side . . .
        "Boast not my fall," he cried, "insulting foe!
Thou by some other shalt be laid as low.
55 Nor think, to die dejects my lofty mind;
All that I dread is leaving you behind!
Rather than so, ah let me still survive,
And burn in Cupid's flames—but burn alive."
        "Restore the lock!" she cries; and all around
60 "Restore the lock!" the vaulted roofs rebound.
Not fierce Othello in so loud a strain
Roared for the handkerchief that caused his pain.[40]
But see how oft ambitious aims are crossed,
And chiefs contend till all the prize is lost!
65 The lock, obtained with guilt, and kept with pain,
In every place is sought, but sought in vain.
With such a prize no mortal must be blessed,
So Heaven decrees! with Heaven who can contest?
        Some thought it mounted to the lunar sphere,
70 Since all things lost on earth are treasured there.
There heroes' wits are kept in ponderous vases,
And beaux' in snuffboxes and tweezer cases.
There broken vows and deathbed alms are found,

---

38. Chloe (klō´ ē) heroine of the ancient Greek pastoral romance, *Daphnis and Chloe*.
39. bodkin ornamental pin shaped like a dagger.
40. Not . . . pain In Shakespeare's *Othello*, the hero is convinced that his wife is being unfaithful to him when she cannot find the handkerchief that he had given her. Actually, the handkerchief had been taken by the villain, Iago, who uses it as part of his evil plot.

Reading Check

For what prize are Belinda and her friends fighting?

And lovers' hearts with ends of riband bound . . .
75   But trust the Muse—she saw it upward rise,
Though marked by none but quick, poetic eyes . . .
A sudden star, it shot through liquid[41] air
And drew behind a radiant trail of hair . . . .[42]
    Then cease, bright Nymph! to mourn thy ravished hair,
80 Which adds new glory to the shining sphere!
Not all the tresses that fair head can boast,
Shall draw such envy as the lock you lost.
For, after all the murders of your eye,[43]
When, after millions slain, yourself shall die;
85 When those fair suns shall set, as set they must,
And all those tresses shall be laid in dust,
This lock, the Muse shall consecrate to fame,
And midst the stars inscribe Belinda's name.

---

41. liquid clear.
42. trail of hair The word comet comes from a Greek word meaning long-haired.
43. murders . . . eye lovers struck down by her glances.

Review and Assess

Thinking About the Selection

1. **Respond:** Are the characters in this poem ridiculous, strange, attractive, heroic, or some combination of these? Explain.

2. **(a) Recall:** What happens during the game of cards?
   (b) Infer: What does the way in which Belinda and the baron play reveal about them?

3. **(a) Recall:** What does Clarissa help the baron do to Belinda, and what struggle results from it? **(b) Compare and Contrast:** Compare and contrast the card game with the final conflict in the poem. **(c) Synthesize:** What is really at stake in all of the poem's conflicts?

4. **(a) Recall:** What happens to the lock of hair in lines 79–88 of Canto V? **(b) Analyze:** In what way is the claim that Pope makes in these lines ridiculous? In what way is it true? Explain.

5. **(a) Interpret:** What do you think is Pope's basic criticism of the rituals he describes in the poem? Explain.
   (b) Support: Which passage or passages indicate that Pope has some positive feelings about the rituals he criticizes? Explain.

6. **Apply:** Pope based this poem on an actual incident. What contemporary incident might inspire a mock epic? Explain.

7. **Take a Position:** Are elaborate social rituals, like the ones Pope mocks, always ridiculous? Why or why not?

Review and Assess

Literary Analysis

Mock Epic

1. Use a chart like the one shown to identify epic elements and the trivial activities to which they apply in *The Rape of the Lock*, Pope's **mock epic.**

Epic Element	Lines in Poem	Activity
Hero's boasts		
Gods and goddesses		
Description of warriors		

2. (a) Why are lines 8–16 in Canto V an **epic simile**? (b) How does this simile add to the absurdity of the action Pope is describing?

3. Which of the epic elements Pope uses adds most to his criticism of upper-class courtship rituals? Explain.

4. Referring to a specific passage, show that Pope's criticism of upper-class rituals is affectionate rather than stern.

Comparing Literary Works

5. Explain how line 12 of *An Essay on Man* and Canto III, lines 13–14 of *The Rape of the Lock* are examples of **antithesis.**

6. In what way does antithesis help Pope describe the human condition in *An Essay* and mock upper-class pretensions in *The Rape of the Lock*?

7. Is antithesis a device that is equally essential in both poems? Why or why not?

Reading Strategy

Recognizing Author's Purpose

8. Show how in Canto III, 105–120, Pope's **purpose** is both to poke fun at a social ritual and to entertain readers.

9. How does Pope's use of little spirits like Ariel in Canto III, 135–154 help him fulfill his purpose of poking affectionate fun at upper-class society?

Extend Understanding

10. **Social Studies Connection:** What do you think causes social rituals to become as elaborate as those Pope satirizes?

Integrate Language Skills

Vocabulary Development Lesson

Word Analysis: Words From Political Science

Many English words concerning social or political divisions have Latin origins. *Plebeian*, meaning "ordinary or common," comes from the Latin word *plebs*, meaning "the common people." The opposite of *plebeian* is *patrician*, meaning "noble."

Patrician comes from the Latin *pater* ("father"). Roman senators were known as *patres*, or "fathers," of Rome. Other words derived from *pater* include *paternal* and *patron*.

For each pair below, explain who would act the plebeian and who the patrician.

1. Belinda and her maid
2. a coachman and the baron
3. in omber, Basto and a four of hearts

Concept Development: Synonyms

Choose the letter of the synonym of each numbered word.

1. plebeian
2. obliquely
3. assignations
4. stoic
5. destitute
6. disabused

a. lacking
b. person indifferent to pleasure and pain
c. undeceived
d. indirectly
e. meetings
f. common

Spelling Strategy

To add suffixes to words ending with a consonant and *y*, you usually change the *y* to *i* before adding the suffix: *haughty* becomes *haughtier*. Correctly spell the combinations below.

1. merry +-*ly*   2. wily +-*er*   3. easy +-*ly*

Grammar and Style Lesson

Inverted Word Order

A sentence with **inverted word order** is one that does not follow the normal word order of subject-verb-complement (s-v-c), as in this example from *The Rape of the Lock*:

>   s   c   v
> The hungry judges soon the sentence sign,
> (Canto III, 21)

More typical of poetry than prose, inverted order can emphasize words or ideas by placing them at the beginning or end of a sentence. It can also create a more regular rhythm or intensify sound effects, which can be critical in poetry. You should use this device in prose, however, only in rare cases.

Practice For each item, identify the subject, verb, and complement. Rewrite each in standard order.

1. Here Britain's statesmen oft the fall foredoom . . . (III, 5)
2. His warlike Amazon her host invades, . . . (III, 67)
3. The baron now his diamonds pours apace; . . . (III, 75)
4. From silver spouts the grateful liquors glide, . . . (III, 109)
5. Then flashed the living lightning from her eyes, . . . (III, 155)

Looking at Style For each item above, explain the emphasis or the rhythm that the order creates.

WG *Prentice Hall Writing and Grammar Connection: Chapter 18, Section 2*

Writing Lesson

Imitating an Author's Style

Pope's amusing rhymes and serious treatment of trivial matters make for a distinctive style. Imitate that style as you write a mock-heroic scene or episode.

Prewriting   Choose a trivial conflict that you can treat in a mock-heroic way—for example, a dispute over fashions or sports. Then, jot down ideas for applying epic elements—like warriors' boasts and the interventions of gods and goddesses—to this petty struggle.

Drafting   As you write your poem, apply stylistic devices like repetition of key words, antithesis, and parallel grammatical structures.

Model: Using Parallelism and Antithesis

Here the heroes and their girlfriends resort
To taste the pleasures of the basketball court;
In various talk the after-school hours they passed,
Who <u>dribbled best</u> or <u>slam-dunked the baddest.</u>
One worries about low grades from all his teachers,
While another praises high-flying basketball sneakers.

> By adapting a passage from Pope (Canto III, 9–14), the writer includes one example of parallelism (underlined) and one of antithesis (highlighted).

Revising   Read your poem aloud to a few classmates. If some parts sound uninteresting, add examples of antithesis or parallelism, and be sure you have used epic elements to describe petty events.

W̶G Prentice Hall Writing and Grammar Connection: Chapter 20, Section 6

Extension Activities

Listening and Speaking Let An *Essay on Man* inspire you to write a **graduation speech.** Summarize Pope's concept of human nature, and link it to the choices graduates must make. Use appeals like these:

- *ethical*—explain what values to apply
- *logical*—show how actions lead to results
- *emotional*—use words that create good feelings

Practice the speech, adding gestures that will stress your ideas. Then, present it to the class.

Research and Technology Help readers of Pope's mock epic by creating a **glossary** of literary terms in the poem. First, note terms you will explain and where in the poem each appears. Then, use reference books to write brief explanations. Alphabetize the annotated terms, including the line reference with each.

 **Take It to the Net**   www.phschool.com

Go online for an additional research activity using the Internet.

Prepare to Read

from A Dictionary of the English Language ◆ *from the* Life of Samuel Johnson

Samuel Johnson (1709–1784)

With his fine mind and dazzling conversation, Samuel Johnson was at the center of a circle that included most of Britain's leading artists and intellectuals. So great was his influence on English literature that the second half of the eighteenth century is often called the Age of Johnson.

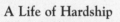

A Life of Hardship
Samuel Johnson overcame severe physical and economic hardships. The son of a bookseller in Lichfield, England, he suffered a series of childhood illnesses that left him weak and disfigured. Bright enough to read Shakespeare as a young boy, he was too poor to attend the schools of the aristocracy and pursued his education largely by reading books in his father's shop. Although he was able to enter Oxford in 1728, lack of funds forced him to leave early.

A Great Work In 1737, Johnson moved to London to try to earn his living as a writer; in 1746, he began work on his *Dictionary of the English Language*. This landmark effort took nine years to complete—difficult years during which his wife died and he continued to be dogged by poverty. When at last the *Dictionary* was published, however, it ensured Johnson's place in literary history. Still, it was not until 1762, when he received a pension from the king, that he did not have to rely on writing for a living. In 1775, he received an honorary degree from Oxford, the school he had been forced to leave.

James Boswell (1740–1795)

James Boswell is perhaps the greatest biographer in English letters. In his *Life of Samuel Johnson*, he writes with vigor about his fascinating subject, training his eye on the picturesque and the grotesque.

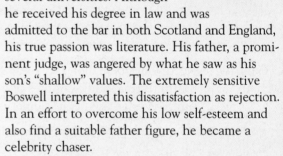

Celebrity Chaser
Born into an aristocratic family in Edinburgh, Scotland, Boswell was educated at several universities. Although he received his degree in law and was admitted to the bar in both Scotland and England, his true passion was literature. His father, a prominent judge, was angered by what he saw as his son's "shallow" values. The extremely sensitive Boswell interpreted this dissatisfaction as rejection. In an effort to overcome his low self-esteem and also find a suitable father figure, he became a celebrity chaser.

In Samuel Johnson, he found not only a friendly celebrity but also the father figure he apparently sought. Deciding to become Johnson's biographer, he devoted many years to compiling detailed records of Johnson's life.

Twentieth-Century Author Boswell's *Life of Samuel Johnson* (1791) was an acclaimed book from its first appearance. Then, in the 1920s, scholars discovered Boswell's private papers, long thought to have been destroyed. In 1950, they began publishing the journals they found among these papers—the first volume was *Boswell's London Journal* (1762–1763)—and the great biographer was reborn as a twentieth-century author!

Preview

Connecting to Literature

Think of the new words constantly entering the language. Johnson's *Dictionary* was one man's heroic attempt to master a changing language.

Literary Analysis

Dictionary; Biography

A **dictionary** defines words and may provide information about their pronunciation, history, and usage. Samuel Johnson compiled the first standard dictionary of the English language. As you read, look for features he initiated that are still in use today.

A **biography** is the account of someone's life written by another person. Just as Johnson's *Dictionary* was a landmark, so was Boswell's *Life of Samuel Johnson*. In reading it, note how Boswell uses many details from his own personal knowledge to reveal Johnson's character.

Comparing Literary Works

Both these selections were natural products of the Enlightenment, the eighteenth-century intellectual movement that stressed the setting down of knowledge. As you read these key works, note one of the qualities of this time period—an elevated language that revealed respect for knowledge. Compare the **diction,** or word choice, of these two works, and notice the attitude that the language reveals.

Reading Strategy

Establishing a Purpose

To ensure the efficiency of your reading, **establish a purpose,** or goal, before you begin. For example, you might want to learn about Johnson's writing style, to understand the process of compiling a dictionary, or to analyze Johnson's attitudes. As you read, complete a chart like the one shown with details related to your purpose.

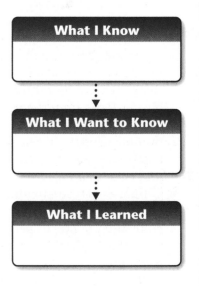

What I Know

⋮

What I Want to Know

⋮

What I Learned

Vocabulary Development

recompense (rek´ əm pens´) *n.* reward; payment (p. 548)

caprices (kə prēs´ iz) *n.* whims (p. 548)

adulterations (ə dul´ tər ā´ shənz) *n.* impurities; added ingredients that are improper or inferior (p. 549)

propagators (präp´ ə gāt´ ərz) *n.* those who cause something to happen or to spread (p. 550)

risible (riz´ ə bəl) *adj.* prompting laughter (p. 550)

abasement (ə bās´ mənt) *n.* condition of being put down or humbled (p. 555)

credulity (krə dōō´ lə tē) *n.* tendency to believe too readily (p. 558)

malignity (mə lig´ nə tē) *n.* strong desire to harm others (p. 558)

pernicious (pər nish´ əs) *adj.* causing serious injury; deadly (p. 560)

inculcated (in kul´ kāt´ id) *v.* impressed upon the mind by repetition (p. 560)

from **A Dictionary** *of the* **English Language**

SAMUEL JOHNSON

Background

Eighteenth-century thinkers sensed that their era had made great advances in knowledge, and they set down in writing the scientific, philosophical, and historic facts and ideas that were part of this new understanding. Among the intellectual pioneers of this period were Samuel Johnson and James Boswell, whose dictionary and biography, respectively, set the standard for nonfiction works of their type. The eighteenth century also saw the birth of the first *Encyclopedia Britannica* (1768–1771) as well as Adam Smith's *Wealth of Nations* (1776), which revolutionized the study of economics. As you read the following selections, notice how just as Johnson captures in his dictionary the changing English language, Boswell captures in his biography the changeable personality of Johnson.

from **The Preface**

It is the fate of those who toil at the lower employments of life, to be rather driven by the fear of evil, than attracted by the prospect of good; to be exposed to censure, without hope of praise; to be disgraced by miscarriage, or punished for neglect, where success would have been without applause, and diligence without reward.

Among these unhappy mortals is the writer of dictionaries; whom mankind have considered, not as the pupil, but the slave of science, the pioneer of literature, doomed only to remove rubbish and clear obstructions from the paths through which learning and genius press forward to conquest and glory, without bestowing a smile on the humble drudge that facilitates their progress. Every other author may aspire to praise; the lexicographer can only hope to escape reproach, and even this negative <u>recompense</u> has been yet granted to very few.

I have, notwithstanding this discouragement, attempted a dictionary of the English language, which, while it was employed in the cultivation of every species of literature, has itself been hitherto neglected; suffered to spread under the direction of chance, into wild exuberance; resigned to the tyranny of time and fashion: and exposed to the corruptions of ignorance and <u>caprices</u> of innovation.

When I took the first survey of my undertaking, I found our speech copious without order and energetic without rule: wherever I turned

recompense (rek´ əm pens´) *n.* reward; payment

caprices (kə prēs´ iz) *n.* whims

A

DICTIONARY

OF THE

ENGLISH LANGUAGE:

IN WHICH

The WORDS are deduced from their ORIGINALS,

AND

ILLUSTRATED in their DIFFERENT SIGNIFICATIONS

BY

EXAMPLES from the beſt WRITERS.

TO WHICH ARE PREFIXED,

A HISTORY of the LANGUAGE,

AND

AN ENGLISH GRAMMAR.

By SAMUEL JOHNSON, A.M.

IN TWO VOLUMES

VOL. I.

Cum tabulis animum cenſoris ſumet honeſti;
Audebit quæcunque parum ſplendoris habebunt,
Et ſine pondere erunt, et honore indigna ferentur,
Verba movere loco; quamvis invita recedant,
Et verſentur adhuc intra penetralia Veſtæ:
Obſcurata diu populo bonus eruet, atque
Proferet in lucem ſpecioſa vocabula rerum,
Quæ priſcis memorata Catonibus atque Cethegis,
Nunc ſitus informis premit et deſerta vetuſtas.   HOR.

LONDON,
Printed by W. STRAHAN,
For J. and P. KNAPTON; T. and T. LONGMAN; C. HITCH and L. HAWES;
A. MILLAR; and R. and J. DODSLEY.
MDCCLV.

◀ **Critical Viewing**
What does this title page of Johnson's *Dictionary* tell you about the contents? **[Infer]**

my view, there was perplexity to be disentangled and confusion to be regulated; choice was to be made out of boundless variety, without any established principle of selection; <u>adulterations</u> were to be detected, without a settled test of purity; and modes of expression to be rejected or received, without the suffrages of any writers of classical reputation or acknowledged authority.

Having therefore no assistance but from general grammar, I applied myself to the perusal of our writers; and noting whatever might be of use to ascertain or illustrate any word or phrase, accumulated in time the materials of a dictionary, which, by degrees, I reduced to method,

adulterations (ə dul´ tər ā´ shənz) *n.* impurities; added ingredients that are improper or inferior

✔**Reading Check**

In what condition did Johnson find the English language when he began work?

establishing to myself, in the progress of the work, such rules as experience and analogy suggested to me; experience, which practice and observation were continually increasing; and analogy, which, though in some other words obscure, was evident in others. . . .

In hope of giving longevity to that which its own nature forbids to be immortal, I have devoted this book, the labor of years, to the honor of my country, that we may no longer yield the palm of philology, without a contest to the nations of the continent. The chief glory of every people arises from its authors. Whether I shall add anything by my own writings to the reputation of English literature, must be left to time. Much of my life has been lost under the pressures of disease; much has been trifled away; and much has always been spent in provision for the day that was passing over me; but I shall not think my employment useless or ignoble, if by my assistance foreign nations and distant ages gain access to the propagators of knowledge, and understand the teachers of truth; if my labors afford light to the repositories of science, and add celebrity to Bacon, to Hooker, to Milton, and to Boyle.[1]

When I am animated by this wish, I look with pleasure on my book, however defective, and deliver it to the world with the spirit of a man that has endeavored well. That it will immediately become popular, I have not promised to myself. A few wild blunders, and risible absurdities, from which no work of such multiplicity was ever free, may for a time furnish folly with laughter, and harden ignorance into contempt; but useful diligence will at last prevail, and there never can be wanting some who distinguish desert; who will consider that no dictionary of a living tongue ever can be perfect, since, while it is hastening to publication, some words are budding, and some falling away; that a whole life cannot be spent upon syntax and etymology, and that even a whole life would not be sufficient; that he, whose design includes whatever language can express, must often speak of what he does not understand; that a writer will sometimes be hurried by eagerness to the end, and sometimes faint with weariness under a task which Scaliger[2] compares to the labors of the anvil and the mine; that what is obvious is not always known, and what is known is not always present; that sudden fits of inadvertency will surprise vigilance, slight avocations[3] will seduce attention, and casual eclipses of the mind will darken learning; and that the writer shall often in vain trace his memory at the moment of need, for that which yesterday he knew with intuitive readiness, and which will come uncalled into his thoughts tomorrow.

In this work, when it shall be found that much is omitted, let it not be forgotten that much likewise is performed; and though no book was ever spared out of tenderness to the author, and the world is

Literary Analysis
Dictionary What do the first five paragraphs reveal about how Johnson's task differed from that of dictionary makers today?

propagators (präp´ ə gāt´ ərz) *n.* those who cause something to happen or to spread

risible (riz´ ə bəl) *adj.* prompting laughter

---

1. **Bacon . . . Boyle** writers quoted by Johnson in the *Dictionary*.
2. **Scaliger** Joseph Justus Scaliger (1540–1609), a scholar who suggested that criminals should be condemned to writing dictionaries.
3. **avocations** things that call one away or distract one from something.

little solicitous to know whence proceed the faults of that which it condemns; yet it may gratify curiosity to inform it, that the *English Dictionary* was written with little assistance of the learned, and without any patronage of the great; not in the soft obscurities of retirement, or under the shelter of academic bowers, but amidst inconvenience and distraction, in sickness and in sorrow. It may repress the triumph of malignant criticism to observe that if our language is not here fully displayed, I have only failed in an attempt which no human powers have hitherto completed. If the lexicons of ancient tongues, now immutably fixed and comprised in a few volumes, be yet, after the toil of successive ages, inadequate and delusive; if the aggregated knowledge and cooperating diligence of the Italian academicians did not secure them from the censure of Beni;[4] if the embodied critics of France, when fifty years had been spent upon their work, were obliged to change its economy[5] and give their second edition another form, I may surely be contented without the praise of perfection, which, if I could obtain, in this gloom of solitude, what would it avail me? I have protracted my work till most of those whom I wished to please have sunk into the grave,[6] and success and miscarriage are empty sounds: I therefore dismiss it with frigid tranquility, having little to fear or hope from censure or from praise.

Selected Entries from **A Dictionary**

athle´ tick. Strong of body; vigorous; lusty; robust.
> Science distinguishes a man of honor from one of those *athletick* brutes, whom undeservedly we call heroes. Dryden.

bang. A blow; a thump; a stroke: a low word.
> I am a bachelor. That's to say, they are fools that marry; you'll bear me a *bang* for that. Shakespeare, *Julius Caesar*.

to ba´rbecue. A term used in the West Indies for dressing a hog whole; which, being split to the backbone, is laid flat upon a large gridiron, raised about two foot above a charcoal fire, with which it is surrounded.
> Oldfield, with more than harpy throat endu'd,
> Cries, send me, gods, a whole hog *barbecu'd*. Pope.

bu´ffleheaded. A man with a large head, like a buffalo; dull; stupid; foolish.

cream. The unctuous or oily part of milk, which, when it is cold, floats on the top, and is changed by the agitation of the churn into butter; the flower of milk.

---

4. **Beni** Paolo Beni severely criticized the first Italian dictionary.
5. **economy** organization.
6. **sunk . . . grave** Johnson's wife had died three years earlier.

Reading Strategy
Establishing a Purpose If your purpose were to find out more about Samuel Johnson's feelings about writing his dictionary, what information in the last two paragraphs would be helpful?

**Reading Check**

Why according to Johnson, can "no dictionary of a living tongue ever . . . be perfect"?

electri'city. A property in some bodies, whereby, when rubbed so as to grow warm, they draw little bits of paper, or such like substances, to them. Quincy.

    Such was the account given a few years ago of electricity; but the industry of the present age, first excited by the experiments of Gray, has discovered in electricity a multitude of philosophical wonders. Bodies electrified by a sphere of glass, turned nimbly round, not only emit flame, but may be fitted with such a quantity of the electrical vapor as, if discharged at once upon a human body, would endanger life. The force of this vapor has hitherto appeared instantaneous, persons at both ends of a long chain seeming to be struck at once. The philosophers are now endeavoring to intercept the strokes of lightning.

to fu'rnace. To throw out as sparks from a furnace. A bad word.
        He *furnaces*
    The thick sighs from him. Shakespeare's
    Cymbeline.

gang. A number herding together; a troop; a company; a tribe; a herd. It is seldom used but in contempt or abhorrence.

ha'tchet-face. An ugly face; such, I suppose, as might be hewn out of a block by a hatchet.
    An ape his own dear image will embrace;
    An ugly beau adores a *hatchet-face.* Dryden.

lifegua'rd. The guard of a king's person.

mo'dern. In Shakespeare, vulgar; mean; common.
    We have our philosophical persons to make *modern*
    and familiar things supernatural and causeless.
    Shakespeare.

pa'tron. One who countenances, supports or protects. Commonly a wretch who supports with insolence, and is paid with flattery.

pi'ckle. Condition; state. A word of contempt and ridicule.
    How cam'st though in this *pickle?* Shakespeare.

plu'mper. Something worn in the mouth to swell out the cheeks.
    She dex'trously her *plumpers* draws, That serve to fill
    her hollow jaws. Swift's *Miscellanies.*

shill-I-shall-I. A corrupt reduplication of *shall I?* The question of a man hesitating. To stand *shill-I-shall-I*, is to continue hesitating and procrastinating.
    I am somewhat dainty in making a resolution, because

Literary Analysis
Dictionary and Diction What effect does Johnson's word choice have on his definition of *patron?*

when I make it, I keep it; I don't stand shill-I-shall-I then; if I say't, I'll do't. Congreve's *Way of the World.*

to sneeze. To emit wind audibly by the nose.

wi´llow. A tree worn by forlorn lovers.

to wipe. To cheat; to defraud.
> The next bordering lords commonly encroach one upon another, as one is stronger, or lie still in wait to wipe them out of their lands. Spenser, *On Ireland.*

you´ngster, you´nker. A young person.
> In contempt.

youth. The part of life succeeding to childhood and adolescence; the time from fourteen to twenty-eight.

Review and Assess

Thinking About the Selections

1. **Respond:** Are Johnson's definitions fair? funny? prejudiced? Explain.

2. **(a) Recall:** Among what class of workers does Johnson place writers of dictionaries? **(b) Infer:** What does this ranking suggest about his experience in compiling his *Dictionary*?

3. **(a) Recall:** What did the English language lack when Johnson undertook his work? **(b) Infer:** What do you think Johnson hoped his *Dictionary* would make available to English speakers and writers?

4. **(a) Recall:** What is Johnson's definition of *modern*? **(b) Compare and Contrast:** Compare and contrast Johnson's definition of this word with our definition of it today. Explain what different values each represents. **(c) Draw Conclusions:** What does your comparison indicate about the nature of language?

5. **(a) Analyze:** Which definitions are most revealing of Johnson's character and situation? **(b) Draw Conclusions:** What do these definitions reveal about Johnson?

6. **(a) Speculate:** Why do you think *electricity* receives such a long definition? **(b) Connect:** In what ways is Johnson similar to the scientists whose work he eagerly discusses in this entry?

7. **Apply:** What does Johnson's use of quotations suggest about the role of authors in shaping meanings?

8. **Take a Position:** Do you find Johnson's definitions more or less useful than those in modern dictionaries? Explain.

from the Life of Samuel Johnson

James Boswell

Boswell Meets Johnson
1763

This is to me a memorable year; for in it I had the happiness to obtain the acquaintance of that extraordinary man whose memoirs I am now writing; an acquaintance which I shall ever esteem as one of the most fortunate circumstances in my life. Though then but two-and-twenty, I had for several years read his works with delight and instruction, and had the highest reverence for their author, which had grown up in my fancy into a kind of mysterious veneration, by figuring to myself a state of solemn elevated abstraction, in which I supposed him to live in the immense metropolis of London. . . .

Mr. Thomas Davies[1] the actor, who then kept a bookseller's shop in Russel Street, Covent Garden, told me that Johnson was very much his friend, and came frequently to his house, where he more than once invited me to meet him; but by some unlucky accident or other he was prevented from coming to us.

At last, on Monday the 16th day of May, when I was sitting in Mr. Davies's back parlor, after having drunk tea with him and Mrs. Davies, Johnson unexpectedly came into the shop; and Mr. Davies having perceived him through the glass door in the room in which

---

1. **Thomas Davies** English bookseller and unsuccessful actor (1712–1785).

we were sitting, advancing towards us—he announced his aweful[2] approach to me, somewhat in the manner of an actor in the part of Horatio, when he addresses Hamlet on the appearance of his father's ghost, "Look, my Lord, it comes,"[3] I found that I had a very perfect idea of Johnson's figure, from the portrait of him painted by Sir Joshua Reynolds[4] soon after he had published his *Dictionary*, in the attitude of sitting in his easy chair in deep meditation, which was the first picture his friend did for him, which Sir Joshua very kindly presented to me, and from which an engraving has been made for this work. Mr. Davies mentioned my name, and respectfully introduced me to him. I was much agitated; and recollecting his prejudice against the Scotch, of which I had heard much, I said to Davies, "Don't tell where I come from." "From Scotland," cried Davies roguishly. "Mr. Johnson," said I, "I do indeed come from Scotland, but I cannot help it." I am willing to flatter myself that I meant this as light pleasantry to soothe and conciliate him, and not as an humiliating <u>abasement</u> at the expense of my country. But however that might be, this speech was somewhat unlucky; for with that quickness of wit for which he was so remarkable, he seized the expression "come from Scotland," which I used in the sense of being of that country; and, as if I had said that I had come away from it, or left, retorted, "That, Sir, I find, is what a very great many of your countrymen cannot help." This stroke stunned me a good deal; and when we had sat down, I felt myself not a little embarrassed, and apprehensive of what might come next. He then addressed himself to Davies: "What do you think of Garrick?[5] He has refused me an order for the play for Miss Williams, because he knows the house will be full, and that an order would be worth three shillings." Eager to take any opening to get into conversation with him, I ventured to say, "O, Sir, I cannot think Mr. Garrick would grudge such a trifle to you." "Sir," said he, with a stern look, "I have known David Garrick longer than you have done: and I know no right you have to talk to me on the subject." Perhaps I deserved this check; for it was rather presumptuous in me, an entire stranger, to express any doubt of the justice of his animadversion upon his old acquaintance and pupil. I now felt myself much mortified, and began to think that the hope which I had long indulged of obtaining his acquaintance was blasted. And, in truth, had not my ardor been uncommonly strong, and my resolution uncommonly persevering, so rough a reception might have deterred me forever from making any further attempts. Fortunately, however, I remained upon the field not wholly discomfited; and was soon rewarded by hearing some of his conversation, of which I preserved the following short

---

2. **aweful** awe-inspiring.
3. **Horatio ". . . it comes"** from Shakespeare's *Hamlet* (Act I, Scene iv).
4. **Sir Joshua Reynolds** celebrated portrait painter at the time (1723–1792).
5. **Garrick** David Garrick (1717–1779), a famous actor who had been educated by Johnson. Garrick was also one of the managing partners of the Drury Lane Theatre in London.

Reading Strategy
Establishing a Purpose
If your purpose were to find out more about eighteenth-century English theater, on what details of the third paragraph would you focus?

abasement (ə bās´ mənt) *n.* condition of being put down or humbled

Reading Check

Why is 1763 "a memorable year" for Boswell?

minute,[6] without marking the questions and observations by which it was produced.

"People," he remarked, "may be taken in once, who imagine that an author is greater in private life than other men. Uncommon parts require uncommon opportunities for their exertion."

"In barbarous society, superiority of parts is of real consequence. Great strength or great wisdom is of much value to an individual. But in more polished times there are people to do everything for money; and then there are a number of other superiorities, such as those of birth and fortune, and rank, that dissipate men's attention, and leave no extraordinary share of respect for personal and intellectual superiority. This is wisely ordered by Providence, to preserve some equality among mankind."

"Sir, this book (*The Elements of Criticism*,[7] which he had taken up) is a pretty essay, and deserves to be held in some estimation, though much of it is chimerical."

Speaking of one[8] who with more than ordinary boldness attacked public measures and the royal family, he said, "I think he is safe from the law, but he is an abusive scoundrel; and instead of applying to my Lord Chief Justice to punish him, I would send half a dozen footmen and have him well ducked."[9]

"The notion of liberty amuses the people of England, and helps to keep off the *taedium vitae.*[10] When a butcher tells you that his heart bleeds for his country, he has, in fact, no uneasy feeling."

"Sheridan[11] will not succeed at Bath with his oratory. Ridicule has gone down before him, and, I doubt,[12] Derrick[13] is his enemy."

"Derrick may do very well, as long as he can outrun his character; but the moment his character gets up with him, it is all over."

It is, however, but just to record, that some years afterwards, when I reminded him of this sarcasm, he said, "Well, but Derrick has now got a character that he need not run away from."

I was highly pleased with the extraordinary vigor of his conversation, and regretted that I was drawn away from it by an engagement at another place. I had, for a part of the evening, been left alone with him, and had ventured to make an observation now and then, which he received very civilly; so that I was satisfied that though there was a roughness in his manner, there was no ill nature in his disposition. Davies followed me to the door, and when I complained to him a little of the hard blows which the great man had given me he kindly took

Literary Analysis
Biography Has Boswell sufficiently supported his statement about the "extraordinary vigor" of Johnson's conversation? Why or why not?

---

6. **minute** note.
7. **The Elements of Criticism** one of the works of Scottish philosophical writer Henry Home (1696–1782).
8. **one** John Wilkes (1727–1797), an English political agitator.
9. **ducked** tied to a chair at the end of a plank and plunged into water.
10. *taedium vitae* (tē´ dē əm vī´ tē) boredom.
11. **Sheridan** Thomas Sheridan (1719–1788), an Irish actor and author. At the time, Sheridan was reading lectures at the Oratory at Bath.
12. **doubt** fear.
13. **Derrick** the Master of Ceremonies of the Oratory at Bath.

◀ **Critical Viewing**
This engraving shows the ghost of Samuel Johnson haunting Boswell. In what ways does the relationship between the men that it portrays reflect the relationship suggested by Boswell's *Life*? **[Interpret]**

upon him to console me by saying, "Don't be uneasy. I can see he likes you very well."

Johnson's Character

The character of Samuel Johnson has, I trust, been so developed in the course of this work, that they who have honored it with a perusal, may be considered as well acquainted with him. As, however, it may be expected that I should collect into one view the capital and distinguishing features of this extraordinary man, I shall endeavor to acquit myself of that part of my biographical undertaking, however difficult it may be to do that which many of my readers will do better for themselves.

His figure was large and well formed, and his countenance of the cast of an ancient statue; yet his appearance was rendered strange and somewhat uncouth by convulsive cramps, by the scars of that distemper[14] which it was once imagined the royal touch could cure,[15]

---

14. **distemper** scrofula, a type of tuberculosis that causes swelling and scarring of the neck.
15. **royal touch . . . cure** it was at one time believed that the touch of an English monarch had the power to heal. As a child Johnson was taken to Queen Anne to receive her touch in the hope that it would cure him.

**Reading Check**

What quality of Johnson's conversation pleased Boswell?

and by a slovenly mode of dress. He had the use only of one eye; yet so much does mind govern and even supply the deficiency of organs, that his visual perceptions, as far as they extended, were uncommonly quick and accurate. So morbid was his temperament, that he never knew the natural joy of a free and vigorous use of his limbs: when he walked, it was like the struggling gait of one in fetters; when he rode, he had no command or direction of his horse, but was carried as if in a balloon. That with his constitution and habits of life he should have lived seventy-five years, is a proof that an inherent *vivida vis*[16] is a powerful preservative of the human frame.

Man is, in general, made up of contradictory qualities; and these will ever show themselves in strange succession, where a consistency in appearance at least, if not in reality, has not been attained by long habits of philosophical discipline. In proportion to the native vigor of the mind, the contradictory qualities will be the more prominent, and more difficult to be adjusted; and, therefore, we are not to wonder that Johnson exhibited an eminent example of this remark which I have made upon human nature. At different times, he seemed a different man, in some respects; not, however, in any great or essential article, upon which he had fully employed his mind, and settled certain principles of duty, but only in his manners and in the display of argument and fancy in his talk. He was prone to superstition, but not to credulity. Though his imagination might incline him to a belief of the marvelous and the mysterious, his vigorous reason examined the evidence with jealousy.[17] He was a sincere and zealous Christian, of high Church of England and monarchical principles, which he would not tamely suffer to be questioned; and had, perhaps, at an early period, narrowed his mind somewhat too much, both as to religion and politics. His being impressed with the danger of extreme latitude in either, though he was of a very independent spirit, occasioned his appearing somewhat unfavorable to the prevalence of that noble freedom of sentiment which is the best possession of man. Nor can it be denied, that he had many prejudices; which, however, frequently suggested many of his pointed sayings that rather show a playfulness of fancy than any settled malignity. He was steady and inflexible in maintaining the obligations of religion and morality; both from a regard for the order of society, and from a veneration for the Great Source of all order; correct, nay, stern in his taste; hard to please, and easily offended; impetuous and irritable in his temper, but of a most humane and benevolent heart, which showed itself not only in a most liberal charity, as far as his circumstances would allow, but in a thousand instances of active benevolence. He was afflicted with a bodily disease, which made him often restless and fretful; and with a constitutional melancholy, the clouds of which darkened the brightness of his fancy, and gave a gloomy cast to his whole course of thinking: we, therefore,

credulity (krə dōō′ lə tē) *n.* tendency to believe too readily

malignity (mə lig′ nə tē) *n.* strong desire to harm others

---

16. *vivida vis* lively force.
17. **jealousy** suspicion.

ought not to wonder at his sallies of impatience and passion at any time; especially when provoked by obtrusive ignorance, or presuming petulance; and allowance must be made for his uttering hasty and satirical sallies even against his best friends. And, surely, when it is considered, that, "amidst sickness and sorrow," he exerted his faculties in so many works for the benefit of mankind, and particularly that he achieved the great and admirable Dictionary of our language, we must be astonished at his resolution. The solemn text, "of him to whom much is given, much will be required," seems to have been ever present to his mind, in a rigorous sense, and to have made him dissatisfied with his labors and acts of goodness, however comparatively great; so that the unavoidable consciousness of his superiority was, in that respect, a cause of disquiet. He suffered so much from this, and from the gloom which perpetually haunted him and made solitude frightful, that it may be said of him, "If in this life only he had hope, he was of all men most miserable."[18] He loved praise, when it was brought to him; but was too proud to seek for it. He was somewhat susceptible of flattery. As he was general and unconfined in his studies, he cannot be considered as master of any one particular science; but he had accumulated a vast and various collection of learning and knowledge, which was so arranged in his mind, as to be ever in readiness to be brought forth. But his superiority over other learned men consisted chiefly in what may be called the art of thinking, the art of using his mind; a certain continual power of seizing the useful substance of all that he knew and exhibiting it in a clear and forcible manner; so that knowledge, which we often see to be no better than lumber[19] in men of dull understanding, was, in him, true, evident, and actual wisdom. His moral precepts are practical; for they are drawn from an intimate acquaintance with human nature. His maxims carry conviction; for they are founded on the basis of common sense, and a very attentive and minute survey of real life. His mind was so full of imagery, that he might have been perpetually a poet; yet it is remarkable, that, however rich his prose is in this respect, his poetical pieces, in general, have not much of that splendor, but are rather distinguished by strong sentiment and acute observation, conveyed in harmonious and energetic verse, particularly in heroic couplets. Though usually grave, and even aweful, in his deportment, he possessed uncommon and peculiar powers of wit and humor; he frequently indulged himself in colloquial pleasantry; and the heartiest merriment was often enjoyed in his company; with this great advantage, that as it was entirely free from any poisonous tincture of vice or impiety, it was salutary to those who shared in it. He had accustomed himself to such accuracy in his common conversation, that he at all times expressed his thoughts with great force, and an elegant choice of language, the effect of which was aided by his having a loud voice, and a slow deliberate

Literary Analysis
Biography In what part of his biography— the beginning, middle, or end—would it be appropriate for Boswell to present this analysis of Johnson's character? Why?

Reading Check

What are some of Johnson's "contradictory qualities"?

---

18. **"If . . . miserable"** from I Corinthians 15:19.
19. **lumber** rubbish.

utterance. In him were united a most logical head with a most fertile imagination, which gave him an extraordinary advantage in arguing: for he could reason close or wide, as he saw best for the moment. Exulting in his intellectual strength and dexterity, he could, when he pleased, be the greatest sophist[20] that ever contended in the lists of declamation; and, from a spirit of contradiction and a delight in showing his powers, he would often maintain the wrong side with equal warmth and ingenuity; so that, when there was an audience, his real opinions could seldom be gathered from his talk; though when he was in company with a single friend, he would discuss a subject with genuine fairness: but he was too conscientious to make error permanent and <u>pernicious</u>, by deliberately writing it; and, in all his numerous works, he earnestly <u>inculcated</u> what appeared to him to be the truth; his piety being constant, and the ruling principle of all his conduct.

Such was Samuel Johnson, a man whose talents, acquirements, and virtues, were so extraordinary, that the more his character is considered the more he will be regarded by the present age, and by posterity, with admiration and reverence.

pernicious (pər nish´ əs) *adj.* causing serious injury; deadly

inculcated (in kul´ kāt´ id) *v.* impressed upon the mind by repetition

---

20. **sophist** (säf´ ist) *n.* one who makes clever, apparently plausible arguments.

Review and Assess

Thinking About the Selection

1. **Respond:** Basing your answer on this excerpt from *Life*, would you have liked Samuel Johnson? Explain.

2. **(a) Recall:** How did Boswell meet Johnson? **(b) Infer:** What does their conversation at that meeting tell you about each of them?

3. **(a) Recall:** What are some of the topics Johnson discusses that Boswell records "without marking the questions and observations" that produced them? **(b) Infer:** What do Johnson's opinions on these topics suggest about his interests and knowledge?

4. **(a) Recall:** Briefly summarize Boswell's remarks on Johnson's character. **(b) Evaluate:** Would Johnson have been less interesting if he had been less "contradictory"? Explain.

5. **Compare and Contrast:** In what ways is Boswell's *Life* similar to and different from modern biographies you have read? Explain.

6. **Hypothesize:** What makes biography, the genre Boswell helped establish, so popular today?

Review and Assess

Literary Analysis

Dictionary; Biography

1. Use a chart like this to compare the definition of a word in Johnson's *Dictionary* with the definition of the same word in a modern historical **dictionary.**

Johnson's *Dictionary*	Modern Dictionary	Similarities/ Differences

2. Judging his *Dictionary* by the aims he expresses in the Preface, decide whether Johnson achieved his goals.

3. (a) Find three examples of facts and three of opinions in the **biography** written by Boswell. (b) Which is more revealing of Johnson's character, the facts or the opinions? Why?

Comparing Literary Works

4. Using examples from the Preface to the *Dictionary* and the *Life*, show how **diction** in the eighteenth century was very formal.

5. Citing specific passages, contrast Johnson's mixed tone of discouragement and pride with Boswell's unmixed tone of admiration.

6. Whose diction and tone, Johnson's or Boswell's, are more welcoming to readers? Why?

Reading Strategy

Establishing a Purpose

7. List details you would record if your purpose in reading the Preface to the *Dictionary* were to learn about the history of dictionary-making.

8. If your purpose in reading Boswell's *Life* were to learn about Johnson's sense of humor, list details that you would note.

Extend Understanding

9. **History Connection:** How do both the *Dictionary* and the *Life* demonstrate an eighteenth-century goal of bringing order to messy reality?

Integrate Language Skills

Vocabulary Development Lesson

Word Analysis: Latin Root -dict-

The Latin root -dict- conveys the idea of something said—in *dictionary*, the words "said" in a language, and in *diction*, the words "said" by an author. It is often the root of words used in political science or history, such as *dictator*, "a ruler whose pronouncements are the final word." Knowing the meaning of -dict-, infer the meaning of each italicized word below. Then, use a dictionary to verify your definitions.

1. In a war, nations seek to *interdict* the flow of goods to their enemies.
2. The legal system in the United States requires that a person be *indicted* before being tried.
3. Legislatures debate laws, but dictators issue *edicts*.

Fluency: Word Use

As a young college graduate newly arrived in eighteenth-century London, write a letter introducing yourself to Samuel Johnson and requesting a job assisting him with the *Dictionary*. To impress Johnson, correctly use each of these vocabulary words in the course of your letter: *recompense*, *caprices*, *adulterations*, *propagators*, *risible*, *abasement*, *credulity*, *malignity*, *pernicious*, and *inculcated*.

Spelling Strategy

In English, -*ity* is a common noun ending, as in *credulity*. However, use -*ety* when -*ity* would result in two *i*'s in a row, as in *anxiety*. In your notebook, spell each word by adding -*ity* or -*ety*.

1. capac__   2. vari__   3. conform__

Grammar and Style Lesson

Parenthetical Expressions

A **parenthetical expression** is a phrase or clause that interrupts the main part of a sentence to comment on it or to give additional information. To avoid confusion, it is usually set off with a comma or commas, as in these examples from *The Life of Samuel Johnson*.

> The character of Samuel Johnson has, <u>I trust</u>, been so developed in the course of this work, . . .
>
> Man is, <u>in general</u>, made up of contradictory qualities; . . .

Parenthetical expressions allow writers to refine their meaning or quickly connect ideas.

Practice In your notebook, rewrite each sentence, adding commas to set off parenthetical expressions.

1. Boswell I have heard was a young man when he first met Johnson.
2. Johnson on the other hand was much older.
3. Many in Johnson's circle were contemptuous of Boswell by the way.
4. Sad to say the poet Thomas Gray made very critical comments about Boswell.
5. Johnson in contrast was kind to Boswell.

Writing Application Write a paragraph expressing your opinion of Johnson's *Dictionary*. Correctly use two parenthetical expressions.

W͟G Prentice Hall Writing and Grammar Connection: Chapter 27, Section 2

Writing Lesson

Comparative Analysis of Dictionaries

Johnson was a pioneer dictionary-maker. Assess how far the field has come by writing a comparative analysis of his *Dictionary* and a modern historical dictionary.

Prewriting Locate a modern historical dictionary, such as *The Oxford English Dictionary*. Use a chart like this one to compare Johnson's definitions with modern definitions of the same words.

Model: Using a Chart to Compare

	Pronunciation & Part of Speech	Derivation	Definition	Historical Quotations
Johnson's				
Modern				

Drafting Referring to your chart, draft a thesis statement summarizing the similarities and differences. Support each point of your thesis with a separate paragraph of comparison and contrast, citing specific passages from each dictionary.

Revising Have classmates read your analysis and determine whether it clearly explains similarities and differences between the dictionaries. If not, check that your structure is consistent, with a paragraph devoted to each point you discuss.

W̧G Prentice Hall Writing and Grammar Connection: Chapter 9, Sections 3 and 4

Extension Activities

Listening and Speaking Working with a group, perform a **reenactment** of Boswell's meeting with Johnson as Boswell describes it. Keep this checklist in mind as you rehearse:

- Have you memorized your lines?
- Are you speaking loudly enough?
- Are your movements appropriate?

Rehearse until everyone is comfortable. Then, stage the reenactment for the class. [**Group Activity**]

Research and Technology Using Boswell's *London Journal (1762–1763)* and any Web site about him, write a **biographical sketch** of Boswell during the period in which he first met Johnson. In your sketch, compare and contrast the Boswell revealed in his own journals with the Boswell who emerges in *The Life of Samuel Johnson*.

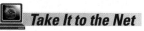 **Take It to the Net** www.phschool.com

Go online for an additional research activity using the Internet.

READING INFORMATIONAL MATERIALS

Scientific Reports

About Scientific Reports

Science is the branch of knowledge that deals with observed facts and the relationships among those facts, experimentally confirmed. A **scientific report** is a written work that explains the results of an experiment or analyzes the causes and effects of a natural event. An informative scientific report will present the following information:

1. The phenomenon, or pattern of events, under investigation
2. A hypothesis—an educated guess—explaining the phenomenon
3. Predictions based on the hypothesis
4. A detailed description of the steps taken to test the predictions
5. An explanation showing how the experiment serves as a test of the hypothesis. Often, an experiment is designed to keep a given set of conditions the same while changing another condition. This procedure is called "isolating a variable."
6. A simply stated conclusion explaining what the results of the experiment demonstrate

Reading Strategy

Evaluating Scientific Reasoning

Unlike the speaker in a novel or an advertisement, the speaker in a scientific report does not address the feelings of the reader or offer personal intuitions or value judgments. Instead, the speaker takes a self-effacing role, presenting what he or she has seen, done, and thought in such a way that any reader can reproduce, or attempt to reproduce, the same experience. The report offers the speaker's experience as what "anyone" might see and think given a specified set of circumstances. At the same time, the clarity and decisiveness of a thinker's work can convey the experimenter's excitement and intellectual passion.

As you read, use a graphic organizer like the following to evaluate whether Newton has provided the appropriate types of arguments and information.

Section of Report	Clear and Specific	Unclear or General	Missing
List of materials			
Sequence of steps			
Report of results			
Logical explanation linking results to conclusions			

Letter on Light and Color
Sir Isaac Newton

Letter sent to the Royal Society

February 6, 1672

Sir,

To perform my late promise to you, I shall without further ceremony acquaint you that in the beginning of the year 1666 (at which time I applied myself to the grinding of optic glasses of other figures than spherical) I procured me a triangular glass prism to try therewith the celebrated phenomena of colors. And in order thereto having darkened my chamber and made a small hole in my window-shuts to let in a convenient quantity of the sun's light, I placed my prism at his entrance that it might be thereby refracted[1] to the opposite wall. It was at first a very pleasing divertissement to view the vivid and intense colors produced thereby; but after a while, applying myself to consider more circumspectly, I became surprised to see them in an *oblong*[2] form, which according to the received laws of refraction I expected should have been *circular.*

> Newton explains the phenomenon he is investigating, as well as his initial prediction.

They were terminated at the sides with straight lines, but at the ends the decay of light was so gradual that it was difficult to determine justly what was their figure; yet they seemed *semicircular.*

Comparing the length of this colored spectrum with its breadth, I found it about five times greater, a disproportion so extravagant that it excited me to a more than ordinary curiosity of examining from whence it might proceed. I could scarce think that the various thickness of the glass or the termination with shadow or darkness could have any influence on light to produce such an effect; yet I thought it not amiss first to examine those circumstances, and so tried what would happen by transmitting light through parts of the glass of divers thicknesses, or by setting the prism without so that the light might pass through it and be refracted before it was terminated by the hole. But I found none of those circumstances material. The fashion of the colors was in all these cases the same.

Then I suspected whether by any unevenness in the glass or other contingent irregularity these colors might be thus dilated. And to try this, I took another prism like the former and so placed it that the light, passing through them both, might be refracted contrary ways, and so by the latter returned into that course from which the former had diverted it. For by this means I thought the regular effects of the first prism would be destroyed by the second prism but the irregular ones more augmented by the multiplicity of refractions. The event was that the light which by the first prism was diffused into an oblong form was by the second reduced into an orbicular[3] one with as much regularity as when it did not at all pass through them. So that, whatever was the cause of that length, 'twas not any contingent irregularity.

> Newton isolates a variable—color— by eliminating other variables such as impurities or irregularities in his prisms.

. . .

---

1. **refracted** (ri frakt´ id) *v.* bent when passing from one medium to another (as from air to glass).
2. **oblong** (äb´ lôŋ´) *adj.* rectangular.
3. **orbicular** (ôr bik´ yoo lər) *adj.* circular.

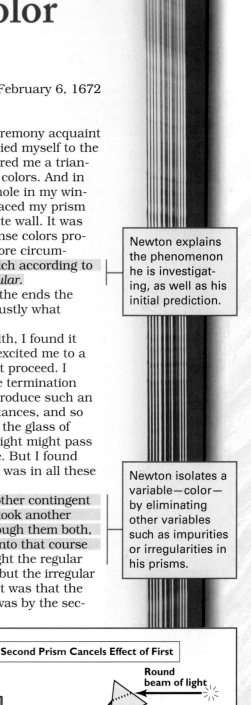

Second Prism Cancels Effect of First

Round beam of light

Prism 2

Prism I

Round (not oblong) beam

The gradual removal of these suspicions at length led me to the *experimentum crucis*, which was this: I took two boards, and placed one of them close behind the prism at the window, so that the light might pass through a small hole made in it for the purpose and fall on the other board, which I placed at about 12 feet distance, having first made a small hole in it also, for some of that incident light to pass through. Then I placed another prism behind this second board so that the light, through both the boards, might pass through that also, and be again refracted before it arrived at the wall. This done, I took the first prism in my hand, and turned it to and fro slowly about its axis, so much as to make the several parts of the image cast on the second board successively pass through the hole in it, that I might observe to what places on the wall the second prism would refract them. And I saw by the variation of those places that the light tending to that end of the image towards which the refraction of the first prism was made did in the second prism suffer a refraction considerably greater than the light tending to the other end. And so the true cause of the length of that image was detected to be no other than that light consists of *rays differently refrangible*,[6] which, without any respect to a difference in their incidence, were, according to their degrees of refrangibility, transmitted towards divers parts of the wall.

. . .

Newton sums up his conclusions.

1. As the rays of light differ in degrees of refrangibility, so they also differ in their disposition to exhibit this or that particular color. Colors are not qualifications of light, derived

from refractions or reflections of natural bodies (as 'tis generally believed), but original and connate properties which in divers rays are divers. Some rays are disposed to exhibit a red color and no other; some a yellow and no other, some a green and no other, and so of the rest. Nor are there only rays proper and particular to the more eminent colors, but even to all their intermediate gradations.

2. To the same degree of refrangibility ever belongs the same color, and to the same color ever belongs the same degree of refrangibility. The least refrangible rays are all disposed to exhibit a red color, and contrarily those rays which are disposed to exhibit a red color are all the least refrangible. So the most refrangible rays are all disposed to exhibit a deep violet color, and contrarily those which are apt to exhibit such a violet color are all the most refrangible. And so to all the intermediate colors in a continued series belong intermediate degrees of refrangibility. And this analogy 'twixt colors and refrangibility is very precise and strict; the rays always exactly agreeing in both or proportionally disagreeing in both.

---

6. **refrangible** (ri fran´ jə bəl) *adj.* able to be refracted.

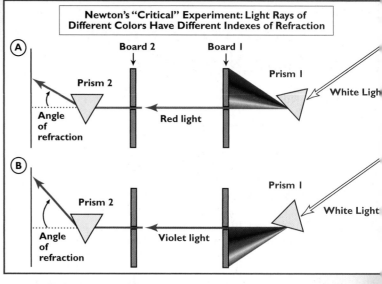

Newton's "Critical" Experiment: Light Rays of Different Colors Have Different Indexes of Refraction

> Newton clearly outlines his steps in this "crucial" experiment.

> Newton clearly states the conclusions to which the experiment has led him.

Check Your Comprehension

1. (a) Why does Newton decide to shine light through two prisms?
   (b) What results does he get? (c) What conclusions does he draw?
2. What are Newton's two major conclusions about the nature of light?

Apply the Reading Strategy

Evaluating Scientific Reasoning

3. (a) Explain how Newton's "crucial experiment" allows him to isolate just one variable—the color of the light that is being refracted.
   (b) What related property of light does he measure in the experiment?
   (c) Why is the repetition of the experiment necessary to confirm his conclusions?
4. (a) Explain how Newton uses the narrative of his path of reasoning to create a sense of drama. (b) Do these feelings and drama detract from the objectivity of his report? Explain.

Activity

Working With Color

Using the information presented in the "Letter on Light and Color," conduct Newton's experiments. Then, answer the following questions, using a chart like the one shown:

1. Does Newton present enough information for you to conduct an accurate experiment? If not, what information is missing?
2. Did you arrive at the same conclusion as Sir Isaac Newton? If not, how do you account for the different results?

	Newton's Experiment	My Experiment
Steps / materials		
Results		
Explanation of any discrepancies		

Comparing Informational Materials

Comparing Research Projects

Read or review Samuel Johnson's "Preface" to *A Dictionary of the English Language* (p. 548). Then, write a brief essay comparing Johnson's project of bringing order to a language "energetic without rule" with Newton's project of finding a rule behind what he sees.

Prepare to Read

Elegy Written in a Country Churchyard ◆
A Nocturnal Reverie

Thomas Gray (1716–1771)

The uncertainty of life was something that Thomas Gray understood all too well. The only one of twelve Gray children to survive infancy, he suffered from convulsions as a child. On at least one occasion, his mother was forced to open a vein to relieve the pressure on his brain.

Lavishing affection on her sickly son, Gray's mother saved money from the shop she kept in London and sent Gray to Eton and Cambridge.

A Quiet Life After making the Grand Tour of Europe with his friend the author Horace Walpole, Gray lived with his mother and aunts in the sleepy village of Stoke Poges. There, in the summer of 1742, he wrote his first important poems. The church and graveyard at Stoke Poges probably inspired his best-known poem, "Elegy Written in a Country Churchyard."

A Near Mishap This beloved poem nearly went astray. Gray sent a copy to Walpole, and it fell into the hands of a dishonest editor. It was retrieved only after a struggle. In the end, the poem came to belong to its readers: It contains some of the best-remembered lines in English poetry.

A Lonely Romantic After age thirty, Gray returned to Cambridge, where he studied classical literature and Celtic and Norse mythology. He died after an attack of gout. His literary output was small—he wrote slowly, striving for perfection—but his poems are counted among the finest in the English language. In them, he expresses new, Romantic yearnings in the formal style of his times. The poet Matthew Arnold suggested that if Gray had lived in another era, his accomplishments might have been even greater.

Anne Finch, Countess of Winchilsea (1661–1720)

Anne Kingsmill Finch, Countess of Winchilsea, lived in an era that rejected women intellectuals. Even her friend Alexander Pope poked fun at her, satirizing her as the character Phoebe Clinket in the play *Three Hours After Marriage*. Despite this mockery, Finch pursued her interest in poetry, publishing a volume of verse in 1713, during an era when publication by women was rare.

An Uncertain Childhood Anne Kingsmill's father died when she was only five months old, and three years later her mother died as well. For eight years, she and her sister, Bridget, lived with their grandmother, while their brother, William, lived with an uncle. The children were reunited under their uncle's care in 1672. By the standards of the day, the girls' education was quite progressive. Anne studied classic Greek and Roman literature, the Bible, French, Italian, history, poetry, and drama.

A Poet and Countess In 1682, Anne Kingsmill left home to become a maid of honor to the wife of the duke of York, later James II. In the duke's household, she met her husband, Heneage Finch.

When James II was driven from power in 1688, the Finches endured a period of poverty until Heneage Finch inherited the title Earl of Winchilsea and an estate at Eastwell in Kent. Many of Anne Finch's poems celebrate the rural pleasures of Eastwell.

Though she was not the most famous of poets, her work had an impact on later writers. In 1801, Romantic poet William Wordsworth praised her in the Preface to the *Lyrical Ballads*.

Preview
Connecting to the Literature

When the bustle of the day has died down, your thoughts may turn inward. Gray and Finch share feelings gathered at the end of the day from contemplative walks.

Literary Analysis
Pre-Romantic Poetry

Eighteenth-century **Pre-Romantic poetry** shares characteristics of two different styles. Like earlier, Neoclassical poetry, Pre-Romantic poetry is characterized by these features:

- The polished expression of ideas
- The use of balanced phrases and sophisticated vocabulary

At the same time, Pre-Romantic poetry anticipates the Romantics. It introduces these new elements:

- A new focus on nature and the life of common folk
- The expression of heightened, sometimes nameless feelings

Look for these characteristics as you read the following poems.

Connecting Literary Elements

Like the Romantics who come after them, Gray and Finch express heightened feelings in their poetry. In these poems, each discovers a feeling about life as a whole. Gray's stroll through a country churchyard lets him feel the tragedy of life and discover its true value. Finch's stroll allows her to feel the mind's deep connection with nature. As you read, compare the feelings and lessons the poets discover.

Reading Strategy
Paraphrasing

To aid your understanding, **paraphrase** passages in the poems that follow by identifying key ideas and expressing them in your own words. Use a chart like the one shown.

Original
"Now fades the glimmering landscape on the sight, . . ."

Paraphrase
Nightfall is making it difficult to see the landscape.

Vocabulary Development

penury (pen′ yoo rē) *n.* poverty (p. 573)

circumscribed (sur′ kəm skrībd′) *v.* limited; confined (p. 573)

ingenuous (in jen′ yoo əs) *adj.* naive; simple (p. 573)

ignoble (ig nō′ bəl) *adj.* not noble; common (p. 573)

nocturnal (näk tur′ nəl) *adj.* occurring at night (p. 577)

temperate (tem′ pər it) *adj.* mild (p. 577)

venerable (ven′ ər ə bəl) *adj.* commanding respect because of age, character, or social rank (p. 577)

forage (fôr′ ij) *n.* food grazed for by animals (p. 577)

▲ **Critical Viewing** The churchyard in this photograph looks untended and forgotten. How does the photograph reflect the meaning of Gray's poem? **[Deduce]**

Elegy Written in a Country Churchyard

Thomas Gray

Background

In the eighteenth century, many writers championed reason, clarity, and logic. These values led to the articulate, eloquent couplets of Alexander Pope. They also led to the major scientific discoveries of Sir Isaac Newton, of whom Pope wrote: "God said, Let Newton be! And there was light!" These values might be thought of as belonging to daylight. In contrast, the poems in this grouping are set at twilight or at night. They stress emotion—the not-always-reasonable reaction to circumstances—and mystery—those longings and intuitions of human experience that are not clearly communicable or analyzable. By stressing these "nighttime" qualities, these poets anticipate the artistic movement called Romanticism.

The curfew tolls the knell of parting day,
    The lowing herd winds slowly o'er the lea,[1]
The plowman homeward plods his weary way,
    And leaves the world to darkness and to me.

5 Now fades the glimmering landscape on the sight,
    And all the air a solemn stillness holds,
Save where the beetle wheels his droning flight,
    And drowsy tinklings lull the distant folds;

Save that from yonder ivy-mantled tower,
10   The moping owl does to the moon complain
Of such as, wandering near her secret bower,
    Molest her ancient solitary reign.

Beneath those rugged elms, that yew tree's shade,
    Where heaves the turf in many a moldering heap,
15 Each in his narrow cell forever laid,
    The rude[2] forefathers of the hamlet sleep.

---

1. **lea** meadow.
2. **rude** uneducated.

Reading Check

At what time of day is the poem set?

The breezy call of incense-breathing morn,
        The swallow twittering from the straw-built shed,
The cock's shrill clarion, or the echoing horn,[3]
20   No more shall rouse them from their lowly bed.

For them no more the blazing hearth shall burn,
        Or busy housewife ply her evening care;
No children run to lisp their sire's return,
        Or climb his knees the envied kiss to share.

25 Oft did the harvest to their sickle yield,
        Their furrow oft the stubborn glebe[4] has broke;
How jocund[5] did they drive their team afield!
        How bowed the woods beneath their sturdy stroke!

Let not Ambition mock their useful toil,
30   Their homely joys, and destiny obscure;
Nor Grandeur hear with a disdainful smile
        The short and simple annals of the poor.

The boast of heraldry,[6] the pomp of power,
        And all that beauty, all that wealth e'er gave,
35 Awaits alike the inevitable hour.
        The paths of glory lead but to the grave.

Nor you, ye proud, impute to these the fault,
        If memory o'er their tomb no trophies[7] raise,
Where through the long-drawn aisle and fretted vault[8]
40   The pealing anthem swells the note of praise.

Can storied urn,[9] or animated[10] bust,
        Back to its mansion call the fleeting breath?
Can honor's voice provoke[11] the silent dust,
        Or Flattery soothe the dull cold ear of Death?

45 Perhaps in this neglected spot is laid
        Some heart once pregnant with celestial fire;
Hands, that the rod of empire might have swayed,
        Or waked to ecstasy the living lyre.

Reading Strategy
Paraphrasing Restate the main ideas in lines 17–20 in your own words.

Literary Analysis
Pre-Romantic Poetry What images and phrasings in lines 33–36 show formal polish?

---

3. **clarion . . . horn** A clarion is a trumpet. The horn is a hunter's horn.
4. **glebe** soil.
5. **jocund** cheerful.
6. **heraldry** noble descent.
7. **trophies** symbolic figures or pictures depicting the achievements of the dead man.
8. **fretted vault** church ceiling decorated with intersecting lines.
9. **storied urn** funeral urn with an epitaph inscribed on it.
10. **animated** lifelike.
11. **provoke** call forth.

But Knowledge to their eyes her ample page
50   Rich with the spoils of time did ne'er unroll;
Chill <u>Penury</u> repressed their noble rage,
        And froze the genial current of the soul.

Full many a gem of purest ray serene
        The dark unfathomed caves of ocean bear:
55 Full many a flower is born to blush unseen,
        And waste its sweetness on the desert air.

Some village Hampden,[12] that, with dauntless breast,
        The little tyrant of his fields withstood,
Some mute inglorious Milton[13] here may rest,
60   Some Cromwell[14] guiltless of his country's blood.

The applause of listening senates to command,
        The threats of pain and ruin to despise,
To scatter plenty o'er a smiling land,
        And read their history in a nation's eyes,

65 Their lot forbade: nor <u>circumscribed</u> alone
        Their growing virtues, but their crimes confined
Forbade to wade through slaughter to a throne,
        And shut the gates of mercy on mankind,

The struggling pangs of conscious truth to hide,
70   To quench the blushes of <u>ingenuous</u> shame,
Or heap the shrine of Luxury and Pride
        With incense kindled at the Muse's flame.

Far from the madding[15] crowd's <u>ignoble</u> strife,
        Their sober wishes never learned to stray;
75 Along the cool sequestered vale of life
        They kept the noiseless tenor[16] of their way.

Yet even these bones from insult to protect
        Some frail memorial still erected nigh,
With uncouth rhymes and shapeless sculpture decked,[17]
80   Implores the passing tribute of a sigh.

---

12. **Hampden** John Hampden (1594–1643), an English statesman who defied King Charles I, resisting the king's efforts to circumvent Parliament.
13. **Milton** English poet, John Milton (1608–1674).
14. **Cromwell** Oliver Cromwell (1599–1658), English revolutionary leader who defeated King Charles I and ruled England as Lord Protector of the Commonwealth from 1653 to 1658.
15. **madding** frenzied.
16. **tenor** general tendency or course.
17. **Some . . . decked** contrasts with "the storied urn[s] or animated bust[s]" (line 41) inside the church.

penury (pen′ yōō rē) *n.* poverty

Literary Analysis
Pre-Romantic Poetry
How do the images in lines 53–56 give the reader a powerful sense of what is unknown or lost?

circumscribed (sur′ kəm skrībd) *v.* limited; confined

ingenuous (in jen′ yōō əs) *adj.* naive; simple

ignoble (ig nō′ bəl) *adj.* not noble; common

Reading Check
About whom is the speaker speculating?

Their name, their years, spelt by the unlettered Muse,[18]
    The place of fame and elegy supply:
And many a holy text around she strews,
    That teach the rustic moralist to die.

85 For who, to dumb Forgetfulness a prey,
    This pleasing anxious being e'er resigned,
Left the warm precincts of the cheerful day,
    Nor cast one longing lingering look behind?

On some fond breast the parting soul relies,
90   Some pious drops[19] the closing eye requires;
Even from the tomb the voice of Nature cries,
    Even in our ashes live their wonted fires.

For thee,[20] who, mindful of the unhonored dead,
    Dost in these lines their artless tale relate;
95 If chance, by lonely contemplation led,
    Some kindred spirit shall enquire thy fate,

Haply[21] some hoary-headed swain[22] may say,
    "Oft have we seen him at the peep of dawn
Brushing with hasty steps the dews away,
100   To meet the sun upon the upland lawn.

"There at the foot of yonder nodding beech,
    That wreathes its old fantastic roots so high,
His listless length at noontide would he stretch,
    And pore upon the brook that babbles by.

105 "Hard by yon wood, now smiling as in scorn,
    Muttering his wayward fancies he would rove;
Now drooping, woeful wan, like one forlorn,
    Or crazed with care, or crossed in hopeless love.

"One morn I missed him on the customed hill,
110   Along the heath, and near his favorite tree;
Another came; nor yet beside the rill,[23]
    Nor up the lawn, nor at the wood was he;

"The next, with dirges due in sad array
    Slow through the churchway path we saw him borne.

---

18. **the unlettered Muse** In Greek mythology, the Muses were goddesses who inspired artists and writers. *Unlettered* means "uneducated."
19. **drops** tears.
20. **thee** Gray himself.
21. **haply** perhaps.
22. **hoary-headed swain** white-haired country laborer.
23. **rill** brook.

115 Approach and read (for thou canst read) the lay
    Graved on the stone beneath yon aged thorn."[24]

The Epitaph

Here rests his head upon the lap of Earth
    A youth, to Fortune and to Fame unknown.
Fair Science[25] frowned not on his humble birth,
120   *And melancholy marked him for her own.*

Large was his bounty, and his soul sincere,
    Heaven did a recompense as largely send:
He gave to misery (all he had) a tear,
    He gained from Heaven ('twas all he wished) a friend.

125 *No farther seek his merits to disclose,*
    Or draw his frailties from their dread abode
(There they alike in trembling hope repose),
    The bosom of his Father and his God.

---

24. **thorn** hawthorn tree.
25. **Science** learning.

Review and Assess

Thinking About the Selection

1. **Respond:** Which lines do you find memorable? Why?
2. **(a) Recall:** Who are the forefathers to whom the speaker refers in line 16? **(b) Interpret:** In line 35, what is the "inevitable hour" that the rich and ambitious share with their forefathers?
3. **(a) Recall:** According to lines 45–48, what types of people might lie among the forefathers? **(b) Infer:** Why did the forefathers not fulfill their potential? **(c) Interpret:** In what way do the images of the gem and the flower in lines 53–56 express the idea of unfulfilled potential?
4. **(a) Summarize:** What mark have the forefathers left on history? **(b) Connect:** According to lines 77–84, how is their memory preserved? **(c) Interpret:** What do lines 85–92 suggest about the need to be remembered after death?
5. **(a) Summarize:** By what standards is the life of the speaker measured in "The Epitaph"? **(b) Draw Conclusions:** What insight into life does the speaker reach?
6. **(a) Evaluate:** Do you find the feelings in the poem artificial or moving? Explain.

A Nocturnal Reverie

Anne Finch, Countess of Winchilsea

▲ **Critical Viewing** What visual elements in this picture help create a mood like that of the poem? **[Analyze]**

In such a night, when every louder wind
Is to its distant cavern safe confined;
And only gentle Zephyr[1] fans his wings,
And lonely Philomel,[2] still waking, sings;
5 Or from some tree, famed for the owl's delight,
She, hollowing clear, directs the wanderer right:
In such a night, when passing clouds give place,
Or thinly veil the heavens' mysterious face;
When in some river, overhung with green,
10 The waving moon and trembling leaves are seen;
When freshened grass now bears itself upright,
And makes cool banks to pleasing rest invite,
Whence springs the woodbind, and the bramble-rose,
And where the sleepy cowslip sheltered grows;
15 Whilst now a paler hue the foxglove takes,
Yet checkers still with red the dusky brakes:[3]
When scattered glow-worms, but in twilight fine,
Show trivial beauties watch their hour to shine;
Whilst Salisbury[4] stands the test of every light,
20 In perfect charms, and perfect virtue bright:
When odors, which declined repelling day,
Through <u>temperate</u> air uninterrupted stray;
When darkened groves their softest shadows wear,
And falling waters we distinctly hear;
25 When through the gloom more <u>venerable</u> shows
Some ancient fabric,[5] awful in repose,
While sunburnt hills their swarthy looks conceal,
And swelling haycocks thicken up the vale:
When the loosed horse now, as his pasture leads,
30 Comes slowly grazing through the adjoining meads,[6]
Whose stealing pace, and lengthened shade we fear,
Till torn-up <u>forage</u> in his teeth we hear:

---

1. **Zephyr** (zef´ ər) in Greek myth, the west wind; a breeze.
2. **Philomel** (fil´ ō mel´) in Greek myth, nightingale.
3. **brakes** overgrown areas; thickets.
4. **Salisbury** This may refer to a Lady Salisbury, daughter of a friend, not to the town of Salisbury.
5. **ancient fabric** edifice or large, imposing building.
6. **meads** archaic term for meadows.

nocturnal (näk tʉr´ nəl) *adj.* occurring at night

temperate (tem´ pər it) *adj.* mild

venerable (ven´ ər ə bəl) *adj.* commanding respect because of age, character, or social rank

forage (fôr´ ij) *n.* food grazed for by animals

✔**Reading Check**

Name three sights to which the speaker refers.

Cottage and Pond, Moonlight, Thomas Gainsborough, Victoria and Albert Museum, London

When nibbling sheep at large pursue their food,
And unmolested kine[7] rechew the cud;
35 When curlews cry beneath the village walls,
And to her straggling brood the partridge calls;
Their shortlived jubilee the creatures keep,
Which but endures, whilst tyrant man does sleep;
When a sedate content the spirit feels,
40 And no fierce light disturbs, whilst it reveals;
But silent musings urge the mind to seek
Something, too high for syllables to speak;
Till the free soul to a composedness charmed,
Finding the elements of rage disarmed,
45 O'er all below a solemn quiet grown,
Joys in the inferior world, and thinks it like her own:
In such a night let me abroad remain,
Till morning breaks, and all's confused again;
Our cares, our toils, our clamors are renewed,
50 Or pleasures, seldom reached, again pursued.

---

7. kine archaic plural of *cow*; cattle.

Review and Assess

Thinking About the Selection

1. **Respond:** Could you share the speaker's mood? Explain.

2. **(a) Recall:** Describe the setting of the poem, listing specific images from lines 1–24. **(b) Analyze:** What mood do these images create?

3. **(a) Analyze:** Outline the steps that lead from the speaker's "sedate content" to her joy (lines 39–46). **(b) Interpret:** How does the natural world charm the speaker to "composedness"?

4. **(a) Infer:** What is the relation between people and their "pleasures" in line 50? **(b) Compare and Contrast:** What is the main difference between the pursuit of pleasures and the "composedness" caused by nature?

5. **Hypothesize:** If the speaker were taking a nocturnal walk in modern times, do you think her reactions to nature would be the same? Explain.

6. **Evaluate:** Do you think the speaker's attitude toward the morning is justified? Explain.

The *British*
Tradition

The Literature of Nature
Anne Finch's poem contributed to the revolutionary literary trend called Romanticism. Before Anne Finch, Renaissance poets had idealized nature, but their focus was the pleasures of a simple country life, conceived in a conventional, idealized manner. Later, eighteenth-century writers saw nature as a source of moral lessons or as a power to be mastered. Pre-Romantics like Finch, though, respond to nature with their hearts. They found in natural scenes a mirror for their moods and deepest longings.

Later, the Romantic Lord Byron went so far as to celebrate the ocean's fathomless power as a mirror of divine in his "Apostrophe to the Ocean" (p. 720). Byron's ocean is different from Finch's farmland—darker, more awesome—but it was poets like Finch who prepared the way for his vision.

Review and Assess

Literary Analysis

Pre-Romantic Poetry

1. (a) What kinds of people does Gray celebrate in his "Elegy"?
   (b) What emotions does he convey about their lives and deaths?
2. (a) What is similar about Gray's concern for the unknown dead of a village graveyard and Finch's loving attention to humble "creatures"? (b) What is **Pre-Romantic** about this type of subject?
3. Explain how lines 39–50 of "A Nocturnal Reverie" affirm mystery and emotion over achievement and striving.
4. Both poets choose a nighttime setting. How is this choice a reflection of Pre-Romantic ideals?

Comparing Literary Works

5. (a) Reread lines 89–92 of Gray's "Elegy." What feelings do they convey? (b) Compare these feelings to the feelings in lines 39–46 of "A Nocturnal Reverie," using a chart like the one shown.

Lines	Stated Ideas	Feelings Expressed	Message About Life

6. On her walk, Finch discovers that nature can charm the mind to "composedness." In her poem, what does this feeling imply about humanity's place in the world?
7. Contrast this idea of humanity's place with that expressed in line 36 of Gray's "Elegy."

Reading Strategy

Paraphrasing

8. Paraphrase the key ideas in lines 29–32 of Gray's "Elegy."
9. Paraphrase the wish in lines 47–50 of "A Nocturnal Reverie."
10. Compare your paraphrases to the originals. What is lost?

Extend Understanding

11. **World Events Connection:** How do Gray's thoughts on the common man anticipate the democratic ideals of the American Revolution, some thirty years later?

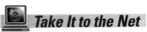

Integrate Language Skills

Vocabulary Development Lesson

Word Analysis: Latin Prefix *circum-*

The Latin prefix *circum-* means "around." The word *circumscribed* literally means "having a line around" and thus means "limited." Use the meaning of *circum-* to define each word below.

1. circumnavigating
2. circumvented
3. circumlocutions
4. circumspect
5. circumference

Spelling Strategy

When adding *-ly* to form an adverb from an adjective ending in *-le*, drop the *-le*: for example, venerable + *-ly* = venerably. Write the adverb form of each word below.

1. reasonable
2. ample
3. terrible

Concept Development: Synonyms and Antonyms

In your notebook, indicate whether each pair of words below is composed of synonyms—words sharing nearly the same meaning—or antonyms—words that have opposite meanings.

1. penury, wealth
2. circumscribed, infinite
3. ingenuous, sophisticated
4. ignoble, lowly
5. nocturnal, daytime
6. temperate, moderate
7. venerable, respected
8. forage, fodder

Grammar and Style Lesson

Pronoun-Antecedent Agreement

Pronouns **agree** with their **antecedents**—the words to which they refer—in number and gender.

| Singular: | The <u>plowman</u> homeward plods **his** weary way, . . . (singular, masculine) |
| Plural: | No <u>children</u> run to lisp **their** sire's return, . . . (plural) |

There are a few special cases of agreement. For two singular antecedents joined by *and*, the pronoun is plural. For two singular antecedents joined by *or* or *nor*, the pronoun is singular. When a plural and a singular antecedent are joined by *or*, use a plural pronoun. When the antecedent is a singular indefinite pronoun such as *each*, *every*, or *none*, use a singular pronoun.

Practice Correct errors in pronoun-antecedent agreement in each item, indicating those that are correct already.

1. Finch wrote her poems at a rural estate.
2. Both Finch and Gray set his poems at nighttime.
3. Did Gray or Finch base his or her work on personal experience?
4. In Finch's poem, either the nightingale or the owl sang their song.
5. The woodbine and the bramble-rose wafted its scent into the nighttime air.

Writing Application Write a paragraph on Gray's churchyard, using four pronouns. Be sure that your pronouns agree with their antecedents.

W͞G *Prentice Hall Writing and Grammar Connection: Chapter 23, Section 2*

Writing Lesson

Reflective Essay

Both Gray and Finch draw on specific experiences to reflect on a theme of significance to many people. Think of a time and place that inspired you, and write a reflective essay about the general meaning of your experience.

Prewriting   Jot down the sensory details of the setting that inspired you. Then, take notes on whatever occurs to you about the place.

Drafting   As you draft, refer to the details you have gathered. Clearly link the details of your experience to your general reflections and feelings.

Revising   Analyze your essay, drawing arrows to show connections between specific details and general feelings and thoughts. Review your marked-up draft, noting details or general ideas not connected by arrows. Add details or transitions to clarify the connections of these passages to the rest of your draft.

Model: Revising to Connect the Personal and the General

The wind, whipping through my hair, scattered the heaps of leaves spilling out under the autumn sun.

No one would listen to me, so I jumped on my bike. Before my ride was over, I had forgotten about my anger and learned that sometimes, getting away is the best answer.

The added sentence gives details supporting the circled general point (which has no arrow attached).

W/G Prentice Hall Writing and Grammar Connection: Chapter 6, Section 2

Extension Activities

Listening and Speaking Perform a **group reading** of Gray's poem.

- Divide the poem into sections, following the theme, and assign sections to readers.
- Determine where to shift the speed, pitch, or volume. The opening rural descriptions might benefit from a slow reading at a low volume and pitch. A higher, faster reading might suit later stanzas.

Rehearse your reading, and perform it for your class. [**Group Activity**]

Research and Technology In her poem, Finch re-creates a reverie, or daydream, she experienced. Write a **daydream report,** using magazines and the Internet to research the latest findings on the brain activity involved in dreams and daydreams. If possible, integrate spreadsheet charts and graphics into your word-processing draft.

 **Take It to the Net**   www.phschool.com

Go online for an additional research activity using the Internet.

CONNECTIONS
Literature Around the World
The Ties That Bind

Constant Experiences The experiences that bind people together in a community are various. As Pepys and Defoe show, a disaster—a fire or plague—can bring people together, showing them that they share a common destiny. Yet, the deepest ties that bind people together are constant experiences, not isolated incidents. Johnson affirms one important source of national identity when he compiles his *Dictionary*. With the publication of the *Dictionary*, the English language, which connects all who speak it, became touchable and portable.

Touchstone Works Like Johnson's *Dictionary*, the collected sayings of the Chinese philosopher Confucius, *The Analects*, and Thomas Jefferson's Declaration of Independence affirm the links among a people. *The Analects* states the beliefs of Confucianism, which for centuries was the dominant political and ethical philosophy of China. Jefferson's Declaration delineates the bond that united Americans in their struggle to become a nation. Both works define fundamental sources of unity among people. At the same time, the reverence shown to each helps define a national identity.

from The Analects

Confucius

Translated by Arthur Waley

The Master said, He who rules by moral force is like the pole-star, which remains in its place while all the lesser stars do homage[1] to it.

The Master said, Govern the people by regulations, keep order among them by chastisements,[2] and they will flee from you, and lose all self-respect. Govern them by moral force, keep order among them by ritual, and they will keep their self-respect and come to you of their own accord.

The Master said, High office filled by men of narrow views, ritual performed without reverence,[3] the forms of mourning observed without grief—these are things I cannot bear to see!

Chi K'ang-tzu asked Master K'ung about government, saying, Suppose I were to slay those who have not the Way in order to help on those who have the Way, what would you think of it? Master K'ung replied saying, You are there to rule, not to slay. If you desire what is good, the people will at once be good. The essence of the gentleman is that of wind; the essence of small people is that of grass. And when a wind passes over the grass, it cannot choose but bend.

Tzu-kung asked about government. The Master said, sufficient food, sufficient weapons, and the confidence of the common people. Tzu-kung said, Suppose you had no choice but to dispense with one of these three, which would you forgo? The Master said, Weapons. Tzu-kung said, Suppose you were forced to dispense with one of the two that were left, which would you forgo? The Master said, Food. For from of old death has been the lot of all men; but a people that no longer trusts its rulers is lost indeed.

Master Yu said, Those who in private life behave well towards their parents and elder brothers, in public life seldom show a disposition to resist the authority of their superiors. And as for such men starting a revolution, no instance of it has ever occurred. It is upon the trunk that a gentleman works. When that is firmly set up, the Way grows. And surely proper behavior towards parents and elder brothers is the trunk of Goodness?

---

1. **homage** (häm´ ij) *n.* anything given or done to show honor or respect.
2. **chastisements** (chas tīz´ mənts) *n.* acts of scolding or condemning.
3. **reverence** (rev´ ər əns) *n.* feeling or attitude of deep respect, love, and awe.

Confucius

(551–479 B.C.)

Confucius was a Chinese philosopher and reformer who taught respect for tradition during a time of conflict and corruption. In this dark period of Chinese history, he wandered the land and instructed any young men who appeared to have a talent for learning. In the end, the man who sought to revive tradition founded a new tradition of his own. As set out in *The Analects* and developed in centuries of commentary, Confucian beliefs formed the official state doctrine of China until the overthrow of the imperial system in 1911. Confucian thinking still exerts a strong underground influence in China.

from The Declaration of Independence
Thomas Jefferson

When in the course of human events, it becomes necessary for one people to dissolve the political bands which have connected them with another, and to assume among the powers of the earth, the separate and equal station to which the laws of nature and of nature's God entitle them, a decent respect to the opinions of mankind requires that they should declare the causes which impel them to the separation. We hold these truths to be self-evident: that all men are created equal; that they are endowed by their Creator with certain unalienable[1] rights; that among these are life, liberty and the pursuit of happiness; that to secure these rights, governments are instituted among men, deriving their just powers from the consent of the governed; that whenever any form of government becomes destructive of these ends, it is the right of the people to alter or to abolish it, and to institute new government, laying its foundation on such principles and organizing its powers in such form, as to them shall seem most likely to effect their safety and happiness. Prudence, indeed, will dictate that governments long established should not be changed for light and transient causes; and accordingly all experience hath shown, that mankind are more disposed to suffer while evils are sufferable than to right themselves by abolishing the forms to which they are accustomed. But when a long train of abuses and usurpations,[2] pursuing invariably the same object, evinces a design to reduce them under absolute despotism, it is their right, it is their duty, to throw off such government, and to provide new guards for their future security. Such has been the patient sufferance of these colonies; and such is now the necessity which constrains them to alter their former systems of government. The history of the present king of Great Britain is a history of repeated injuries and usurpations, all having in direct object the establishment of an absolute tyranny over these states.

---

1. **unalienable** (ən āl′ yən ə bəl) *adj.* of that which may not be taken or given away.
2. **usurpations** (yo͞o′ zər pā′ shənz) *n.* unlawful seizures of power.

Connecting Literature Around the World

1. Contrast Confucius' idea of the ways in which tradition and ritual work to bind people together with the ways consent and obligation work in the Declaration.
2. How might Pope, Johnson, or Gray respond to Confucius and Jefferson?

Thomas Jefferson

(1743–1826)

Thomas Jefferson was an American Revolutionary leader, a political philosopher, author of The Declaration of Independence, and third President of the United States. In 1774, Jefferson wrote *A Summary View of the Rights of British America*, in which he argued that the connection between the colonies and the crown was voluntary and that England therefore had no ultimate right to rule American communities. The eloquence and power of this document made Jefferson the obvious choice to be the writer of the Declaration.

Girl Writing by Lamplight, William Henry Hunt, The Mass Gallery, London

Focus on Literary Forms:
The Essay

The titles of the new eighteenth-century periodicals—*The Rambler, The Spectator, The Tatler*—expressed the fun of getting out into the world, looking, listening, and telling. In the pages of these periodicals, the informal essay came to life. Like a friendly guide, it was whispering into the public's ear, advising it what to think and telling it that it *was* a public!

Prepare to Read

On Spring ◆ The Aims of *The Spectator*

Samuel Johnson (1709–1784)

Samuel Johnson was determined to make his living as a writer. After a few unsuccessful projects, he finally moved to London in 1737. There, he got the break he needed.

Success in the City When Johnson arrived in London, he turned to *The Gentleman's Magazine*, the most successful magazine of the day, and bombarded its editors with ideas. He became an influential contributor. Then, from 1750 to 1752, Johnson published his own magazine, *The Rambler*, a popular biweekly collection of essays and moral tales.

A Man of Leisure In 1762, Johnson was awarded an annual pension of 300 pounds, which made him something of a man of leisure. The next year, he and twenty-two-year-old James Boswell met for the first time. From that fateful meeting sprang a lasting relationship that eventually resulted in Boswell's biography, *The Life of Samuel Johnson*.

Late Works In 1765, Johnson published an acclaimed edition of Shakespeare. His last important work, *The Lives of the Poets*, appeared in ten volumes between 1779 and 1781. This work, a group of fifty-two critical biographies, covers about two hundred years of English literary history.

Classics and Commerce Johnson's style is meticulously balanced, yet he wrote much of his work to meet the needs of the moment. Even the classic essays in *Lives of the Poets* were written for the market—a publisher commissioned them to dress up a new edition of English poetry. Late in life, Johnson won a more permanent kind of recognition, receiving honorary degrees from Oxford and from Trinity College, Dublin. He is buried in Westminster Abbey. (For more on Johnson's life and his *Dictionary*, see p. 546.)

Joseph Addison (1672–1719)

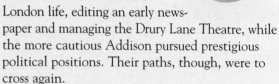

Born in a village in Wiltshire, England, Joseph Addison was educated at the Charterhouse School in London, where he became a friend of classmate Richard Steele. Both young men went on to Oxford, but, after their school days, their paths diverged. The impetuous Steele immersed himself in London life, editing an early newspaper and managing the Drury Lane Theatre, while the more cautious Addison pursued prestigious political positions. Their paths, though, were to cross again.

Scholar, Poet, and Bureaucrat A Fellow of Magdalen College, Oxford, Addison was invited by John Dryden to do translations of Virgil. After four years of European study and travel, he produced an epic, *The Campaign*, celebrating a notable English victory. In 1706, Addison was named undersecretary of state and later went on to other important posts.

A Reunion In 1709, the story is told, Addison happened to read an article in *The Tatler*, a new literary magazine that had become all the rage in London coffeehouses. The article was signed "Isaac Bickerstaff," but Addison immediately recognized the style of his old school friend Richard Steele. Addison soon became a contributor to *The Tatler*. When publication of *The Tatler* ended, the two founded another journal, *The Spectator*.

A Lifetime Partnership As a team, Addison and Steele became the most celebrated journalists in England. Their essays in *The Tatler* and *The Spectator* earned them a permanent place in English literature. Almost every magazine you can buy today uses an informal, popular style derived from the one they originated.

Preview

Connecting to the Literature

As a small child, you probably bubbled over with questions about the world. As you grew older, though, you probably began to ask questions about yourself. Writing essays is a way to explore such questions.

Literary Analysis

Essay

An **essay** is a short prose piece that explores a topic as if the author were letting you overhear his or her thoughts. Meaning an "attempt" or a "test," the word *essay* was first applied to writing by the French essayist Michel Montaigne (1533–1592).

Johnson's and Addison's essays can be seen as "tests," or experiments, to discover connections between experiences and so learn about the self. As you read, notice how the writers link their observations and anecdotes to form ideas and arguments.

Comparing Literary Works

The essay flourished during a time of social change, and Johnson and Addison wrote essays that help their readers ask and answer questions about themselves—what should I do? Who am I?

In the eighteenth century, England's middle class—lawyers, shopkeepers, merchants—was growing. Neither aristocrats nor laborers, this new class needed a self-definition, and essayists provided one. From Johnson's moral instruction to Addison's humorous observations, the essay set new ideals for—or exposed new follies in—the rising middle classes. As you read, compare the way each essay helps readers ask and answer the question, Who am I?

Reading Strategy

Drawing Inferences

To appreciate a writer's attitudes, you need to **draw inferences**—reach logical conclusions about what the writer leaves unstated. Use a chart like the one shown to make inferences as you read the essays.

Vocabulary Development

procured (prō kyoord´) *v.* got; obtained through some effort (p. 589)

divert (də vurt´) *v.* amuse; entertain; distract (p. 590)

speculation (spek´ yoo lā´ shən) *n.* train of thought on a subject using hypotheses (p. 591)

transient (tran´ shənt) *adj.* temporary; passing (p. 592)

affluence (af´ loo əns) *n.* abundant wealth (p. 593)

contentious (kən ten´ shəs) *adj.* quarrelsome (p. 593)

trifles (trī´ fəlz) *n.* things of little value or importance (p. 594)

embellishments (em bel´ ish məntz) *n.* decorative touches; ornamentation (p. 594)

"On Spring"

Topic

People's hopes for future happiness

↓

Details

Everyone is "in quest of future happiness," but the expected "blessing" of the future does not come. Still, we "press forward again with equal eagerness"— we never learn!

↓

Inference: Author's Attitude

Disapproving but also understanding; mildly amused

On Spring

Samuel Johnson

Background

The first daily newspapers began appearing in England in 1702. As the nation's middle classes grew, the market for words and information grew more sophisticated. Through the magazines they founded and edited, Johnson, Addison, and Steele helped develop a new, popular taste for sophisticated writing about books, ideas, and fashions.

TUESDAY, APRIL 3, 1750

> *Et nunc omnis ager, nunc omnis parturit arbos,*
> *Nunc frondent silvae, nunc formosissimus annus.*

> Now ev'ry field, now ev'ry tree is green;
> Now genial nature's fairest face is seen.

VIRGIL, *Eclogues III*, v. 56; TRANSLATOR, ELPHINSTON

Every man is sufficiently discontented with some circumstances of his present state, to suffer his imagination to range more or less in quest of future happiness, and to fix upon some point of time, in which, by the removal of the inconvenience which now perplexes him, or acquisition of the advantage which he at present wants, he shall find the condition of his life very much improved.

When this time, which is too often expected with great impatience, at last arrives, it generally comes without the blessing for which it was desired; but we solace ourselves with some new prospect,[1] and press forward again with equal eagerness.

It is lucky for a man, in whom this temper prevails, when he turns his hopes upon things wholly out of his own power; since he forbears then to precipitate his affairs,[2] for the sake of the great event that is to complete his felicity, and waits for the blissful hour, with less neglect of the measures necessary to be taken in the meantime.

---

1. **solace ourselves with some new prospect** comfort ourselves with something new to look forward to.
2. **forbears then to precipitate his affairs** refrains from rushing his affairs.

▲ **Critical Viewing**
Relate the qualities of the flowers in the photograph to Johnson's description of spring. **[Connect]**

I have long known a person of this temper, who indulged his dream of happiness with less hurt to himself than such chimerical[3] wishes commonly produce, and adjusted his scheme with such address, that his hopes were in full bloom three parts of the year, and in the other part never wholly blasted. Many, perhaps, would be desirous of learning by what means he <u>procured</u> to himself such a cheap and lasting satisfaction. It was gained by a constant practice of referring the removal of all his uneasiness to the coming of the next spring; if his health was impaired, the spring would restore it; if what he wanted was at a high price, it would fall in value in the spring.

The spring, indeed, did often come without any of these effects, but he was always certain that the next would be more propitious; nor was ever convinced that the present spring would fail him before the middle of summer; for he always talked of the spring as coming till it was past, and when it was once past, everyone agreed with him that it was coming.

By long converse with this man, I am, perhaps, brought to feel immoderate pleasure in the contemplation of this delightful season; but I have the satisfaction of finding many, whom it can be no shame to resemble, infected with the same enthusiasm; for there is, I believe, scarce any poet of eminence, who has not left some testimony of his fondness for the flowers, the zephyrs, and the warblers of the spring. Nor has the most luxuriant imagination been able to describe the serenity and happiness of the golden age,[4] otherwise than by giving a perpetual spring, as the highest reward of uncorrupted innocence.

There is, indeed, something inexpressibly pleasing, in the annual renovation of the world, and the new display of the treasures of nature. The cold and darkness of winter, with the naked deformity of every object on which we turn our eyes, make us rejoice at the succeeding season, as well for what we have escaped, as for what we may enjoy; and every budding flower, which a warm situation brings early to our view, is considered by us as a messenger to notify the approach of more joyous days.

The spring affords to a mind, so free from the disturbance of cares or passions as to be vacant to calm amusements, almost every thing that our present state makes us capable of enjoying. The variegated verdure[5] of the fields and woods, the succession of grateful odors, the voice of pleasure pouring out its notes on every side, with the gladness apparently conceived by every animal, from the growth of his food, and the clemency of the weather, throw over the whole earth an air of gaiety, significantly expressed by the smile of nature.

Yet there are men to whom these scenes are able to give no delight, and who hurry away from all the varieties of rural beauty, to lose

procured (prō kyoord′) *v.* got; obtained through some effort

Literary Analysis
Essay Johnson tests the value of his feelings of pleasure in spring. What test does he use?

---

3. **chimerical** unrealistic; fantastic.
4. **golden age** in mythology, the time in the past when the world was free from suffering and evil.
5. **variegated verdure** varied greenery, striped or spotted with different colors.

Reading Check
What does Johnson's friend perpetually look forward to enjoying?

their hours, and <u>divert</u> their thoughts by cards, or assemblies, a tavern dinner, or the prattle of the day.

It may be laid down as a position which will seldom deceive, that when a man cannot bear his own company there is something wrong. He must fly from himself, either because he feels a tediousness in life from the equipoise[6] of an empty mind, which, having no tendency to one motion more than another but as it is impelled by some external power, must always have recourse to foreign objects; or he must be afraid of the intrusion of some unpleasing ideas, and, perhaps, is struggling to escape from the remembrance of a loss, the fear of a calamity, or some other thought of greater horror.

Those whom sorrow incapacitates to enjoy the pleasures of contemplation, may properly apply to such diversions, provided they are innocent, as lay strong hold on the attention; and those, whom fear of any future affliction chains down to misery, must endeavor to obviate the danger.

My considerations shall, on this occasion, be turned on such as are burthensome to themselves merely because they want subjects for reflection, and to whom the volume of nature is thrown open, without affording them pleasure or instruction, because they never learned to read the characters.[7]

A French author has advanced this seeming paradox, that *very few men know how to take a walk*; and, indeed, it is true, that few know how to take a walk with a prospect of any other pleasure, than the same company would have afforded them at home.

There are animals that borrow their color from the neighboring body, and, consequently, vary their hue as they happen to change their place. In like manner it ought to be the endeavor of every man to derive his reflections from the objects about him; for it is to no purpose that he alters his position, if his attention continues fixed to the same point. The mind should be kept open to the access of every new idea, and so far disengaged[8] from the predominance of particular thoughts, as easily to accommodate itself to occasional entertainment.

A man that has formed this habit of turning every new object to his entertainment, finds in the productions of nature an inexhaustible stock of materials upon which he can employ himself, without any temptations to envy or malevolence; faults, perhaps, seldom totally avoided by those, whose judgment is much exercised upon the works of art. He has always a certain prospect of discovering new reasons for adoring the sovereign author of the universe, and probable hopes of making some discovery of benefit to others, or of profit to himself. There is no doubt but many vegetables and animals have qualities that might be of great use, to the knowledge of which there is not required much force of penetration, or fatigue of study,

---

divert (də vʉrt´) *v.* amuse; entertain; distract

Literary Analysis
Essay What duties does Johnson propose for his readers in this paragraph?

Literary Analysis
Essay What new idea of a person's present state of mind does Johnson try out here?

---

6. **equipoise** balanced state.
7. **the characters** nature's signs.
8. **disengaged** free.

but only frequent experiments, and close attention. What is said by the chemists of their darling mercury, is, perhaps, true of everybody through the whole creation, that if a thousand lives should be spent upon it, all its properties would not be found out.

Mankind must necessarily be diversified by various tastes, since life affords and requires such multiplicity of employments, and a nation of naturalists is neither to be hoped, or desired; but it is surely not improper to point out a fresh amusement to those who languish in health, and repine in plenty, for want of some source of diversion that may be less easily exhausted, and to inform the multitudes of both sexes, who are burthened with every new day, that there are many shows which they have not seen.

He that enlarges his curiosity after the works of nature, demonstrably multiplies the inlets to happiness; and, therefore, the younger part of my readers, to whom I dedicate this vernal[9] speculation, must excuse me for calling upon them, to make use at once of the spring of the year, and the spring of life; to acquire, while their minds may be yet impressed with new images, a love of innocent pleasures, and an ardor for useful knowledge; and to remember, that a blighted spring makes a barren year, and that the vernal flowers, however beautiful and gay, are only intended by nature as preparatives to autumnal fruits.

speculation (spek´ yōo lā´ shən) *n.* train of thought on a subject using hypotheses

---

9. **vernal** concerning spring

Review and Assess

Thinking About the Selection

1. **(a) Recall:** According to Johnson, to what feelings and thoughts does a person's "present state" usually lead?
   (b) Analyze: What problem does he find with this habit of thought and feeling?

2. **(a) Recall:** What is unique about the way in which Johnson's friend looks forward to spring? **(b) Connect:** How is his friend's habit a humorous solution to the problem Johnson has identified?

3. **(a) Analyze:** According to Johnson's descriptions, how does spring give us joy in relation to the past, the present and the future? **(b) Draw Conclusions:** What relationship does Johnson find between happiness and the way we experience time?

4. **Compare and Contrast:** In what way are those who "cannot bear their own company" like those who expect future happiness?

5. **(a) Interpret:** How would you sum up Johnson's idea of happiness? **(b) Evaluate:** Do you think Johnson's ideas offer a practical prescription for happiness? Explain.

The Aims of
The Spectator

Joseph Addison

The Spectator, No. 10,
Monday, March 12, 1711

It is with much satisfaction that I hear this great city inquiring day by day after these my papers, and receiving my morning lectures with a becoming seriousness and attention. My publisher tells me that there are already three thousand of them distributed every day. So that if I allow twenty readers to every paper, which I look upon as a modest computation, I may reckon about three-score thousand[1] disciples in London and Westminster, who I hope will take care to distinguish themselves from the thoughtless herd of their ignorant and unattentive brethren. Since I have raised to myself so great an audience, I shall spare no pains to make their instruction agreeable, and their diversion useful. For which reasons I shall endeavor to enliven morality with wit, and to temper wit with morality, that my readers may, if possible, both ways find their account in the speculation of the day. And to the end that their virtue and discretion may not be short, <u>transient</u>, intermitting[2] starts of thought, I have resolved to refresh their memories from day to day, till I have recovered them out of that desperate state of vice and folly into which the age is fallen. The mind that lies fallow[3] but a single day sprouts up in follies that are only to be killed by a constant and assiduous culture. It was said of Socrates[4] that he brought philosophy down from heaven, to inhabit among men; and I shall be ambitious to have it said of me that I have brought philosophy out of closets and libraries, schools and colleges, to dwell in clubs and assemblies, at tea tables and in coffeehouses.

I would therefore in a very particular manner recommend these my speculations to all well-regulated families that set apart an hour in every morning for tea and bread and butter; and would earnestly advise them for their good to order this paper to be punctually served up, and to be looked upon as part of the tea equipage. . . .

In the next place, I would recommend this paper to the daily perusal of those gentlemen whom I cannot but consider as my good brothers

> **Literary Analysis**
> **Essay** How does Addison make a personal connection with his readers in his opening paragraph?

> **transient** (tran´ shənt) *adj.* temporary; passing

---

1. **three-score thousand** sixty thousand.
2. **intermitting** pausing at times; not constant.
3. **fallow** unused; unproductive.
4. **Socrates** ancient Greek philosopher (470?–399 B.C.), immortalized as a character in Plato's dialogues, who cross-examined ancient Athenians about their lives and values.

and allies, I mean the fraternity of spectators, who live in the world without having anything to do in it; and either by the <u>affluence</u> of their fortunes or laziness of their dispositions have no other business with the rest of mankind but to look upon them. Under this class of men are comprehended all contemplative tradesmen, titular physicians, fellows of the Royal Society, Templars[5] that are not given to be <u>contentious</u>, and statesmen that are out of business; in short, everyone that considers the world as a theater, and desires to form a right judgment of those who are the actors on it.

There is another set of men that I must likewise lay a claim to, whom I have lately called the blanks of society, as being altogether unfurnished with ideas, till the business and conversation of the day has supplied them. I have often considered these poor souls with an eye of great commiseration, when I have heard them asking the first man they have met with, whether there was any news stirring? and by that means gathering together materials for thinking. These needy persons do not know what to talk of till about twelve o'clock in the morning; for by that time they are pretty good judges of the weather, know which way the wind sits, and whether the Dutch mail[6] be come in. As they lie at the mercy of the first man they meet, and are grave or impertinent all the day long, according to the notions which they have imbibed in the morning, I would earnestly entreat them not to stir out of their chambers till they have read this paper, and do promise them that I will daily instil into them such sound and wholesome sentiments as shall have a good effect on their conversation for the ensuing twelve hours.

But there are none to whom this paper will be more useful than to the female world. I have often thought there has not been sufficient pains taken in finding out proper employments and diversions for the fair ones. Their amusements seem contrived for them, rather as they are women, than as they are reasonable creatures; and are more adapted to the sex than to the species. The toilet[7] is their great sense of business, and the right adjusting of their hair the principal employment of their lives. The sorting of a suit of ribbons is reckoned a very good morning's work; and if they make

Literature in context World Events

Rise of the Middle Class

In this essay, Addison addresses members of a new and rising social group, the British middle classes. By the mid-1700s, England enjoyed growing prosperity and a high rate of literacy. The careers available in law, medicine, teaching, banking, and government service expanded. As a result, more and more English citizens had the leisure, education, and money needed to enjoy such cultural pursuits as music, art, and reading.

Addison knows his audience, quickly tapping their interests in this essay. He refers, for instance, to the coffeehouses that provided their middle-class patrons with newspapers, gossip, and political debate as well as refreshments. He has great fun with the new custom of the shopping trip, a product of the eighteenth-century boom in the number of shops. Tongue half in cheek, Addison informs his audience of his intentions: to improve and amuse them.

affluence (af´ lōō əns) *n.* abundant wealth

contentious (kən ten´ shəs) *adj.* quarrelsome

Reading Check

To what four groups does Addison recommend his paper?

---

5. **titular physicians, fellows of the Royal Society, Templars** physicians in title only; members of a group dedicated to scientific research; lawyers or law students with offices in the Inner or Middle Temple.
6. **Dutch mail** mail from Europe bearing news of the war.
7. **toilet** act of dressing and grooming oneself.

an excursion to a mercer's or a toyshop,[8] so great a fatigue makes them unfit for anything else all the day after. Their more serious occupations are sewing and embroidery, and their greatest drudgery the preparation of jellies and sweetmeats. This, I say, is the state of ordinary women; though I know there are multitudes of those of a more elevated life and conversation, that move in an exalted sphere of knowledge and virtue, that join all the beauties of the mind to the ornaments of dress, and inspire a kind of awe and respect, as well as love, into their male beholders. I hope to increase the number of these by publishing this daily paper, which I shall always endeavor to make an innocent if not an improving entertainment, and by that means at least divert the minds of my female readers from greater <u>trifles</u>. At the same time, as I would fain give some finishing touches to those which are already the most beautiful pieces in human nature, I shall endeavor to point all those imperfections that are the blemishes, as well as those virtues which are the <u>embellishments</u>, of the sex.

trifles (trī´ fəlz) *n.* things of little value or importance

embellishments (em bel´ ish məntz) *n.* decorative touches; ornamentation

---

8. **suit of ribbons . . . mercer's or a toyshop** A suit of ribbons was a set of matching ribbons; a mercer's store sold fabrics, ribbons, and so on; a toyshop sold small items of little value.

Review and Assess

Thinking About the Selection

1. **Respond:** If you had read Addison's essay in 1711, would you have wanted to become a regular reader of *The Spectator*? Why?

2. **(a) Recall:** What reason does Addison give for making the instruction of his readers "agreeable"? **(b) Support:** Addison felt that *The Spectator* would set high standards for readers. Identify two expressions of this attitude.

3. **(a) Recall:** How does Addison define the "spectators" of society? **(b) Infer:** What is Addison's attitude toward the "blanks of society" and toward women? Is he sympathetic, mocking, or both? Explain. **(c) Draw Conclusions:** Describe Addison's attitude toward his audience, giving three examples.

4. **(a) Draw Conclusions:** What kinds of things would Addison like to change about society? **(b) Draw Conclusions:** What is Addison's attitude toward his own aims? Explain.

5. **(a) Speculate:** Do you think readers would identify with Addison's audience as he describes its members, or would they identify with Addison as the spectator? **(b) Apply:** Do modern media encourage "spectatorship" as Addison defines it? Explain.

6. **Take a Position:** Compare the attitudes towards human foolishness—whether tolerant, amused, or impatient—that Johnson and Addison display. Of which do you approve?

Review and Assess

Literary Analysis

Essay

1. (a) Explain how Johnson, in the **essay** "On Spring," introduces the idea of a state of mind that does not involve discontent. (b) How does the essay "test" the idea of enjoyment of the present?
2. In his essay for *The Spectator*, Addison describes audiences for his paper. How does he "test" the usefulness of his paper?
3. (a) What attitude does Addison encourage in readers toward themselves? (b) Connect this attitude with the ideal of self-knowledge.

Comparing Literary Works

4. Using a chart like the one shown, compare Johnson's analysis of those who "cannot bear their own company" with Addison's portrait of his four readers.

Passage	Analytic / Descriptive?	General / Of a Specific Era?	Logical / Humorous?

5. (a) Which writer works with a general idea of human nature? Explain. (b) Which writer shows a sharper sense of specific social types? Explain.
6. Judging from his essay, Addison believes that having a sense of humor about oneself is an important aspect of self-knowledge. How might Johnson respond to this assumption?

Reading Strategy

Drawing Inferences

7. **Draw inferences** about the author's attitude in the following passages: (a) Johnson's story of his friend, (b) Johnson's view of men who do not enjoy spring, (c) Addison's description of the "blanks."
8. Draw an inference about Johnson's attitude toward science based on his remark about "a nation of naturalists."

Extend Understanding

9. **Career Connection:** Based on the essay "On Spring," what modern careers do you think Johnson would support? Explain.

Integrate Language Skills

Vocabulary Development Lesson

Word Analysis: Latin Root -spec-

The root -spec-, meaning "to look," helps form the word *speculation*, meaning "reflection"—the result of looking at a subject. It also forms scientific words involving the idea of light or looking. Using a dictionary, explain how this root contributes to each word's meaning:

1. spectrum
3. spectroscope
2. spectrograph
4. specimen

Spelling Strategy

The *sh* sound in words that end with the sound *shun* or *shus* is usually spelled *ti*, as in *speculation* and *contentious*. Write the letters that spell the *sh* sound in each of these words:

1. conversa__on
3. establi__ment
2. propi__ous
4. suspi__ous

Concept Development: Synonyms

Review the words in the vocabulary list on page 587. Then, for each word below, write the letter of its synonym.

1. embellishments: (a) food, (b) decorations, (c) remarks
2. divert: (a) distract, (b) horrify, (c) inform
3. trifles: (a) trivia, (b) wonders, (c) dangers
4. contentious: (a) mild, (b) argumentative, (c) proud
5. procured: (a) lent, (b) killed, (c) got
6. affluence: (a) speed, (b) poverty, (c) wealth
7. transient: (a) powerful, (b) passing, (c) near
8. speculation: (a) reflection, (b) fear, (c) belief

Grammar and Style Lesson

Adjective Clauses

An **adjective clause** has a subject and a verb, and it modifies a noun or pronoun in a sentence. The clause usually begins with a relative pronoun, such as *that, which, who, whom,* or *whose.*

Example: The mind <u>that lies fallow but a single day</u> sprouts up in follies. . . .

Practice Copy these items, identifying each adjective clause and the word that it modifies.

1. I have long known a person of this temper, who indulged his dream of happiness. . . .
2. . . . every budding flower, which a warm situation brings early to our view, is considered by us as a messenger. . . .

3. I . . . recommend these my speculations to all well-regulated families that set apart an hour in every morning for tea and bread and butter; . . .
4. . . . I mean the fraternity of spectators, who live in the world without having anything to do in it; . . .
5. There is another set of men that I must likewise lay a claim to, whom I have lately called the blanks of society, . . .

Writing Application Write a paragraph comparing your response to spring with that of Johnson's friend. In your writing, use at least two sentences with adjective clauses. Underline these clauses, and circle the words they modify.

$\mathcal{W}_G$ *Prentice Hall Writing and Grammar Connection: Chapter 19, Section 3*

Writing Lesson

Essay on Human Behavior

These essays offer sharp insights into human habits and character. Write an essay about a type of human behavior that interests you. In your essay, address readers in a friendly, confiding way as you explore your subject and test your ideas. Take care to balance examples from experience with general points.

Prewriting   Do some people-watching in a public setting, such as a mall, the school lunchroom, or a bus. Jot down details of people's behavior, noting contrasts or unexpected twists.

Drafting   Focus your essay on a few examples. For each, offer conclusions about the habit, character, or outlook it represents.

Revising   Highlight specific stories in your draft in one color and general statements in another. Then, evaluate whether your draft needs more generalizations or more specific details.

Model: Revising to Balance the Specific and the General

> *Clearly, our brains find ways to economize the attention we pay to the world.*

The parent sits there, absorbed in a magazine, until the child sets a collision course for the magazine rack. One nanosecond before impact, the parent's radar clicks in—"Now sit down!" he or she commands, barely looking up.

> The added sentence balances the specific incident described with a general point.

W̶G̶ *Prentice Hall Writing and Grammar Connection: Chapter 6, Section 4*

Extension Activities

Listening and Speaking   Write and perform a brief **monologue** in which you poke fun at a contemporary "blank of society"—the surfer, perhaps, or the slacker. To prepare, follow these suggestions:

- Write down details of how the "blank" might behave in a specific situation.
- Use understatement, exaggeration, and irony to humorously convey your points.
- Use informal slang for humorous effect and Standard American English for clarity.

Present your monologue to the class.

Research and Technology   With a group, produce an **analysis of the audience** for Johnson's and Addison's magazines. Assign these tasks: explaining the changes in society that led to the popularity of these magazines; explaining the social status of the readers; and relating the nature of the writers' audience to their style. Include spreadsheets in your analysis. [**Group Activity**]

 **Take It to the Net**   www.phschool.com

Go online for an additional research activity using the Internet.

CONNECTIONS
Literature Past and Present
The Essay

Testing It Out The sixteenth-century French writer Montaigne (män tän´) first applied the word *essay*, meaning "an attempt or a trial," to a form of writing. In his essays, Montaigne explored ideas, "testing" them out. In the eighteenth century, the essay found a home in periodicals created by men like Addison and Steele. There, essays such as Johnson's "On Spring" and Addison's "Aims of *The Spectator*" entertained and informed a wide readership.

Seeing It Afresh Anna Quindlen's essay "Homeless" is a direct descendant of these periodical essays. It also appeared in a periodical, *The New York Times*. Quindlen's column is briefer and more politically oriented than those earlier essays, but, like them, it speaks directly to readers about their world. She works to help readers to see a problem that is everywhere around them and to see it differently—not as "the homeless," but as people without homes.

Homeless

Anna Quindlen

Her name was Ann, and we met in the Port Authority Bus Terminal[1] several Januarys ago. I was doing a story on homeless people. She said I was wasting my time talking to her; she was just passing through, although she'd been passing through for more than two weeks. To prove to me that this was true, she rummaged through a tote bag and a manila envelope and finally unfolded a sheet of typing paper and brought out her photographs.

They were not pictures of family, or friends, or even a dog or cat, its eyes brown-red in the flashbulb's light. They were pictures of a house. It was like a thousand houses in a hundred towns, not suburb, not city, but somewhere in between, with aluminum siding and a chain-link fence, a narrow driveway running up to a one-car garage and a patch of backyard. The house was yellow. I looked on the back for a date or a name, but neither was there. There was no need for discussion. I knew what she was trying to tell me, for it was something I had often felt. She was not adrift, alone, anonymous, although her bags and her raincoat with the grime shadowing its creases had made me believe she was. She had a house, or at least once upon a time had had one. Inside were curtains, a couch, a stove, potholders. You are where you live. She was somebody.

I've never been very good at looking at the big picture, taking the global view, and I've always been a person with an overactive sense of place, the legacy of an Irish grandfather. So it is natural that the thing that seems most wrong with the world to me right now is that

---

1. **Port Authority Bus Terminal** major bus terminal located in New York City.

Thematic Connection
Compare and contrast the opening of Quindlen's essay with the opening of Johnson's or Addison's.

✔**Reading Check**
What does Ann show the author?

▲ **Critical Viewing** Contrast details in this photograph with the details Quindlen uses to define *home*. **[Connect]**

there are so many people with no homes. I'm not simply talking about shelter from the elements, or three square meals a day or a mailing address to which the welfare people can send the check—although I know that all these are important for survival. I'm talking about a home, about precisely those kinds of feelings that have wound up in cross-stitch and French knots on samplers over the years.

Home is where the heart is. There's no place like it. I love my home with a ferocity totally out of proportion to its appearance or location. I love dumb things about it: the hot-water heater, the plastic rack you drain dishes in, the roof over my head, which occasionally leaks. And yet it is precisely those dumb things that make it what it is—a place of certainty, stability, predictability, privacy, for me and for my family. It is where I live. What more can you say about a place than that? That is everything.

Yet it is something that we have been edging away from gradually during my lifetime and the lifetimes of my parents and grandparents. There was a time when where you lived often was where you worked

Thematic Connection
Analyze the way Quindlen tests her own concept of home.

and where you grew the food you ate and even where you were buried. When that era passed, where you lived at least was where your parents had lived and where you would live with your children when you became enfeebled. Then, suddenly, where you lived was where you lived for three years, until you could move on to something else and something else again.

And so we have come to something else again, to children who do not understand what it means to go to their rooms because they have never had a room, to men and women whose fantasy is a wall they can paint a color of their own choosing, to old people reduced to sitting on molded plastic chairs, their skin blue-white in the lights of a bus station, who pull pictures of houses out of their bags. Homes have stopped being homes. Now they are real estate.

People find it curious that those without homes would rather sleep sitting up on benches or huddled in doorways than go to shelters. Certainly some prefer to do so because they are emotionally ill, because they have been locked in before and they are [darned] if they will be locked in again. Others are afraid of the violence and trouble they may find there. But some seem to want something that is not available in shelters, and they will not compromise, not for a cot, or oatmeal, or a shower with special soap that kills the bugs. "One room," a woman with a baby who was sleeping on her sister's floor, once told me, "painted blue." That was the crux of it; not size or location, but pride of ownership. Painted blue.

This is a difficult problem, and some wise and compassionate people are working hard at it. But in the main I think we work around it, just as we walk around it when it is lying on the sidewalk or sitting in the bus terminal—the problem, that is. It has been customary to take people's pain and lessen our own participation in it by turning it into an issue, not a collection of human beings. We turn an adjective into a noun: the poor, not poor people; the homeless, not Ann or the man who lives in the box or the woman who sleeps on the subway grate.

Sometimes I think we would be better off if we forgot about the broad strokes and concentrated on the details. Here is a woman without a bureau. There is a man with no mirror, no wall to hang it on. They are not the homeless. They are people who have no homes. No drawer that holds the spoons. No window to look out upon the world. My [word]. That is everything.

Thematic Connection

In what way is Quindlen's commentary in this passage like Addison's commentary in "The Aims of The Spectator"?

Anna Quindlen

(b. 1953)

Anna Quindlen is currently a best-selling novelist. However, she first won recognition as a columnist for *The New York Times*. She provided a fresh voice in the editorial pages of that paper, addressing controversial issues like homelessness in a sensitive and caring way. Her commentary won her the highest award in journalism, the Pulitzer Prize.

Connecting Literature Past and Present

1. In what ways does Quindlen test our perceptions of the homeless?
2. In what way do both Johnson and Quindlen use their essays to explore core human experiences?

Writing About Literature

Compare and Contrast Literary Themes

Words are the tools that a writer uses to communicate, but not every writer looks at words in the same way. Some writers use words to describe the world as accurately as possible. Samuel Johnson produced a dictionary that precisely defined words so that they could be used as tools for this purpose. Other writers, however, use words to redefine the world. They stretch the meanings of words to show the reader a new perspective, as when John Donne describes the parting of two lovers as an "expansion" of their love ("A Valediction," p. 424). In an essay, compare and contrast the ways that two writers from the seventeenth and eighteenth centuries viewed words.

See the box to the right for the details of the assignment.

Prewriting

Find a focus. Review the literature in the unit. Use a chart like the one below to help you analyze how writers look at words. As you take notes, consider these questions to narrow your focus:

- Is the writer using words in a direct, descriptive way?
- Does the writer use words playfully or satirically?
- Does the writer use a given set of words to describe a situation with which such words are not typically associated?
- Does the writer take a situation and transform it by redescribing it as another type of situation?
- Does the writer report facts with precision?

Model: Taking Notes to Focus on a Theme

Work	Key Words	Writer's Attitude Toward Words
"A Valediction: Forbidding Mourning" by Donne	"breach," "expansion," "twin compasses"	Donne uses the language of science to redefine parting.
A Journal of the Plague Year by Defoe	"pit. . . . forty feet in length," "1114 bodies"	Defoe uses words with journalistic precision to make his fiction seem real.

Gather details. Select two works to compare, and analyze each text carefully. Note the words and phrases that best capture the way each writer looks at words.

Write a working thesis. Write a thesis sentence identifying the key similarities or differences between the works you will compare. Use this sentence to guide you as you gather additional details.

Assignment: Words at Work

Write an essay comparing the ways two seventeenth- or eighteenth-century writers treat words, whether as tools to describe the world accurately or as the means to see the world from an unusual perspective.

Criteria:

- Include a thesis statement that summarizes the main point of your comparison.
- Thoroughly analyze two writers' views of words by carefully discussing representative works.
- Approximate length: 1,500 words

Read to Write

Review at least four writers and their work before choosing two to compare. Choose two works that show a strong contrast in the writer's view of words.

Drafting

Organize. A logical and clear organization matches the needs of your essay. In the outline below, the writer chose to discuss Defoe first because his use of words is straightforward, whereas Donne uses words to create a new perspective. Even though Defoe's work is chronologically later, it makes sense to discuss it first in this essay.

Elaborate with specific examples. As you plan and structure your ideas, make sure that you have adequate support for each statement. Use an informal outline to keep track of the examples you plan to use.

Write to Learn
The gaps in your outline may help you identify weaknesses in your analysis. If you are having trouble finding examples to include, consider looking in a different passage or choosing a different selection to discuss.

Model: Including Examples in an Informal Outline

II. In *A Journal of the Plague Year*, Defoe uses words to describe the world accurately:

    A. He includes detailed descriptions: a pit is "about forty feet in length, and about fifteen or sixteen feet broad, . . ."

    B. Words are journalistic, even when reporting emotions: "This was a mournful scene indeed. . . ."

III. In "Valediction," Donne uses words to show a new perspective:

    A. Crying is renamed as "tear-floods" and "sigh-tempests."

    B. Separating is not a "breach, but an expansion."

Revising and Editing

Review content: Eliminate contradictions. Comparing works can create a confusing draft. Make sure that you have not included any contradictions or unnecessary details that detract from your argument.

Write to Explain
Establish clear contrasts with words like *however*, *instead*, and *whereas* or phrases like *on the other hand* and *on the contrary*.

Contradictory Statement: Fiction always invents a new world, so Defoe uses the plain-spoken language of journalism to present a realistic description of the plague.

Logical Statement: Even though he is writing fiction, Defoe uses the plain-spoken language of journalism to present realistic descriptions.

Review style: Analyze your own word choice. Review your word choices to make sure that they are effective and say what you mean. Replace flat or repetitive language with active and striking words.

Publishing and Presenting

Submit your work to a literary magazine. Prepare your essay for a school literary magazine, adding background information for readers.

Prentice Hall Writing and Grammar Connection: Chapter 14

Writing WORKSHOP

Narration: Reflective Essay

A **reflective essay** is a work in which the writer explores how he or she came to hold certain views. In this workshop, you will write a reflective composition tracing how personal experiences, events, or concerns helped shape your beliefs about life.

Assignment Criteria A good reflective essay balances accounts of specific incidents with statements of general insights. Your reflective composition should include the following elements:

- A statement of a general view that you have gained from experience
- Descriptions of the incidents that helped shape that general view
- A balance between individual incidents and more general ideas
- Clear connections between beliefs and events
- A consistent tone

To preview the criteria on which your reflective essay may be assessed, see the Rubric on page 607.

Prewriting

Choose a topic. To write a strong reflective essay, you need to tie two elements together. One element is a belief that you hold about life, and the other is an event or events that led you to that belief or that show its effect on you. To find these elements, **freewrite** on either of these subjects:

- Important events or experiences in your life
- Beliefs that you hold strongly

Review your freewriting for connections between general beliefs and specific incidents.

Compile your ideas. Chart your freewriting ideas as shown here. If you find that connections among the ideas are still vague, freewrite again until you have a clearer grasp of their relationship.

Write three focus statements. Review your notes, and then sum up your *insight* in a single, clear sentence. Then, write another sentence summarizing the *experiences* leading to this insight. Finally, write a sentence explaining the *connection* between the insight and the experiences. Refer to these focus statements as you draft.

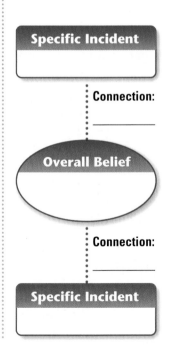

Specific Incident

Connection:
_____

Overall Belief

Connection:
_____

Specific Incident

Student Model

Before you begin drafting your reflective essay, read this student
model and review the characteristics of a powerful reflective composition.

Ashley Philips
Ruston, LA

Coming Home

North Carolina novelist T. R. Pearson told me recently that when he
was a teenager, he had set his stories in New York City, though he had
never been there. "I thought New York was where it was," he laughed,
adding that the fiction he had produced during this period was uniformly
bad. Almost accidentally, he had begun to write about the life he really
knew—life in little towns like Reidsville, North Carolina. It was only then
that he succeeded at what he was attempting. Pearson's remarks set me
thinking about my own life. Like Tom Pearson, I had spent a part of my life
attempting something foreign and feeling unhappy with the result.

When I was in grade school, I read through every book in our classroom and did special reports. Research thrilled me. Books were the most
important part of my life. I knew who I was. And I was happy.

In freshman year, though, I decided that my own life paled compared
with that of my older friend Julie. Julie was popular and dated the most
popular boys in our school. She was a cheerleader and a Student Council
member. She was also the most confident person I knew, and she welcomed
an understudy. I borrowed Julie's clothes and copied her hairstyles, right
down to the huge hair bows that were her signature. By the end of the year
I had decided to run for cheerleader.

I giggled and flirted my way through the next two years. Through it
all, I felt as if I was putting on an act. In the middle of my junior year, I
received my first ACT results. I was not happy with my scores. I began to
reevaluate my life. I decided not to run for cheerleader. I paid less attention
to who was popular and concentrated on friendships that were comfortable
and fun. I threw myself into my science project and was exhilarated when
I took top honors at the state science fair. By the end of the year, a teacher
had invited me to serve as editor of a literary magazine. I felt that I was
home again.

This December, as I sat listening to T. R. Pearson discuss the path that
had led him to his true subject, I felt I knew exactly what he was talking
about. It was a warm December day. A late fall sun filtered through the
pine trees onto my English teacher's deck. Four other students and I sat in
deck chairs and listened to Pearson speak about writing. It all felt so natural.
This, I thought, is the kind of world I want to live in. I realized then that you
can never get anywhere if you leave your true self behind. At that moment,
I could not, for all the world, remember why cheerleading or Julie's boys or
big hair bows had ever mattered.

Ashley sets up a
clear connection
between the narra-
tive that follows
and her general
point: Success
depends on being
true to oneself.

By carefully
selecting details,
Ashley includes
just enough inci-
dents to support
and balance her
general insight.

Ashley's short, deci-
sive self-descriptions
establish a consis-
tent tone.

Ashley reports
incidents that
clearly lead to her
realization.

In her conclusion,
Ashley clearly
states her general
insight.

Drafting

Decide where to start. A well-organized reflective essay will alternate between generalizations and specific incidents. Your opening paragraph will probably include both—a statement of the overall belief on which the essay is based and a brief indication of how you arrived at that position.

Experiment with ways to present these two elements effectively. For instance, you might open with a statement of belief but include only one or two tantalizing details about the incidents that led you to it.

Establish a tone. Your essay will be stronger if you establish a recognizable tone from the beginning and stay with it throughout. A serious, straightforward tone is certainly acceptable, but also consider using one of these:

- **Ironic tone:** A good tone to use if your examples show that things do not always work out as expected or intended
- **Humorous tone:** A logical choice if your examples are amusing

Model: Experimenting with Specific Tones

Ironic Tone

I welcomed my coach's criticism as warmly as any self-centered ten-year-old might. I was quite comfortable postponing any action until the following year, by which time I expected the matter would be forgotten.

Humorous Tone

Having a little brother is not as big a pain as people say. It's worse. Yet after years of his tattling and tagging along, one incident brought home to me how important family is—even little brothers. I no longer want to sell him to the circus. Not unless they've raised their prices.

Know when to end. If you have made your points well, an elaborate conclusion is not necessary. Just write a brief summarizing paragraph.

Revising

Revise to balance narration with ideas. Make sure that you balance the specifics of the incidents you narrate with your general ideas.

1. Bracket any segments of the essay that describe specific incidents.

2. Have a partner read these sections and mark in red any points at which you have included detail that does little to set a scene or to advance ideas.

3. Consider your partner's suggestions, and rewrite as needed, cutting unnecessary details or replacing them with more compelling ones.

[I giggled and flirted my way through the next two years.]
✓[During that time, my Dad got a new job and we moved to a different neighborhood.] Through it all, I felt as if I was putting on an act. [In the middle of my junior year, I received my first ACT results.] I was not happy with my scores.

> Ashley deleted this incident because it did not contribute toward her insight or provide necessary background.

Revise to strengthen connections. To work well, your reflective essay must clearly show the connections between events and the generalizations to which they have led you. Sometimes these connections can be clarified simply by the use of appropriate transitional words.

Examples: "And that is how . . ." "After this happened, . . ."
"Suddenly I understood "As a result, . . ."
that . . ."

Compare the model and nonmodel. Notice how connections have been clarified in the model.

Nonmodel	Model
Pearson's remarks set me thinking about my own life. I had spent a part of my life attempting something foreign and feeling unhappy with the result.	Pearson's remarks set me thinking about my own life. Like Tom Pearson, I had spent a part of my life attempting something foreign and feeling unhappy with the result.

Publishing and Presenting

Present your essay orally. Use your reflective essay as the basis of an oral presentation. Follow these suggestions:

- Rehearse your presentation so that you can deliver it without awkward pauses.
- Avoid distracting movements, like foot tapping or paper shuffling.
- Match the tone of your voice to the tone of your essay.
- Try to "tell" incidents or events rather than reading them verbatim.

Prentice Hall Writing and Grammar Connection: Chapter 4

Read to Write
To review a model of a reflective essay, read Anna Quindlen's essay "Homeless," p. 598. Note how she skillfully builds from a specific encounter with a homeless person to a general reflection on the meaning of "home."

Rubric for Self-Assessment

Evaluate your reflective essay using the following criteria and rating scale:

Criteria	Rating Scale Not very				Very
How well does the essay convey the general belief on which it is based?	1	2	3	4	5
How effectively and succinctly are the incidents presented?	1	2	3	4	5
How well does the essay balance incidents with generalizations?	1	2	3	4	5
How clearly are connections between incidents and generalizations established?	1	2	3	4	5
How well is tone established through word choice?	1	2	3	4	5

Listening and Speaking WORKSHOP

Analyzing Persuasive Techniques

In a **persuasive speech,** the speaker's goal is to change the audience's attitudes, beliefs, or actions. The techniques that a speaker uses to achieve this general goal depend on the speaker's specific focus. Review the four major focuses for a persuasive speech and the various types of persuasive devices. Then, analyze a persuasive speech or presentation, such as a radio editorial, campaign speech, or student presentation, identifying the type of speech and the techniques utilized.

Four Types of Persuasive Speeches

Persuasive speeches can be categorized by the type of proposition, or central point, for which they argue. The four basic types are shown in the chart at right.

Type	Purpose	Support
Proposition of Fact	To prove a claim about facts	Expert opinions; research findings; inductive arguments
Proposition of Value	To apply values to facts	Appeals to widely shared values; deductive arguments; factual claims
Proposition to Create Concern	To establish that a situation is an important problem	Appeals to widely shared values; expert opinions; research findings; powerful images and comparisons
Proposition of Policy	To support a course of action	Appeals to widely shared values; expert opinions; research findings; inductive arguments; powerful images and comparisons

Persuasive Techniques

Persuasive speakers use a wide variety of techniques and elements, depending on the type of proposition they are advocating and their audience. Some techniques address the listener's mind, some address the heart, while others address the ear. Techniques include the following:

- **Deductive arguments** apply a general principle to a specific case to reach a conclusion.
- **Inductive arguments** make a generalization based on a selection of representative cases.
- **Emotional appeals** are statements intended to move a listener to feel a certain way about a situation.
- **Effective diction,** or word choice, ensures clarity and vivid, memorable formulations of main points.
- **Rhetorical devices**—such as repetition, rhetorical questions (questions to which the expected answer is obvious), and vivid comparisons—add force and make points memorable.

Not all persuasive techniques are suitable for each type of proposition. For instance, emotional appeals can be an effective element for a proposition of value but would not be effective if used for a proposition of fact.

(Activity: Listen and Analyze) Analyze a persuasive presentation such as a radio editorial or a classmate's speech, identifying the type of speech and the persuasive techniques used.

In the reading sections of certain tests, you may be required to read a passage and interpret the writer's point of view in it. Use the following strategies to help you answer questions testing this skill:

- As you read, look for clues to the writer's attitude toward the subject.
- Remember that a writer can reveal his or her attitude in direct statements, or indirectly through choice of words or through choice of details.
- While reading the passage, consider the writer's tone. Is it positive, negative, humorous, or serious?
- Look for changes in the writer's point of view over the course of a passage.

Test-Taking Strategies

- As you read, ask yourself what other viewpoint the writer might have taken.
- Look for charged words that indicate feelings or opinions, whether negative or positive.

Sample Test Item

Directions: Read the passage, and then answer the question that follows.

The nine African Americans who were the first to integrate Little Rock Central High School are among the heroes of the civil rights movement. On their first day at school, they were turned away by a violent mob. Only after President Eisenhower sent troops to protect the courageous "Little Rock Nine" were they able to attend classes.

1. What is the writer's attitude toward the nine students?

   A envy

   B admiration

   C distaste

   D fear

Answer and Explanation

The correct answer is *B;* the author uses words such as "heroes" and "courageous" to describe the students. The tone of the passage is positive, so answers *A* and *C* are incorrect. At no time does the writer express fear of the students, so *D* is not correct.

Practice

Directions: Read the passage, and then answer the questions that follow.

A blaze caused by an unattended campfire destroyed 3,500 acres of Balsam Forest. This is one more reason to support banning fires at Balsam. Since 1984, more than 300 fires have burned there, causing one death and the destruction of acres of prime forest. Campfires are simply impossible to control, especially in dry months. Tell your legislator today to vote for a ban on campfires at Balsam Forest.

1. Which statement best expresses the writer's point of view?

   A Fires are dangerous to people.

   B Preserving forest land is desirable.

   C Only adults should light fires.

   D The lumber industry needs help.

2. Which of the following programs might the author also support?

   A courses in building fires safely

   B a study of damage caused by fires

   C fire extinguishers in the park

   D a ban on camping at Balsam in the summer

UNIT 4

Rebels and Dreamers
(1798–1832)

Two Men Observing the Moon, Caspar David Friedrich, Staatl. Kunstsammlungen, Neue Meister, Dresden, Germany

❝ *Come forth into the light of things, Let Nature be your teacher.* ❞

— William Wordsworth,
from "The Tables Turned"

British Events

- **1798 William Wordsworth** and **Samuel Taylor Coleridge** publish *Lyrical Ballads*.

- **1801** Act of Union creates United Kingdom of Great Britain and Ireland.

- **1801** Union Jack becomes official flag. ▼

- **1803** J.M.W. Turner's *Calais Pier* exhibited in London.

- **1805** Battle of Trafalgar.

- **1807** Thomas Moore writes *Irish Melodies*.

- **1812 Byron** publishes *Childe Harold's Pilgrimage*.

- **1813 Jane Austen** publishes *Pride and Prejudice*. ◄

- **1814** George Stephenson constructs first successful steam locomotive. ▼

- **1815** John MacAdam constructs roads of crushed stone.

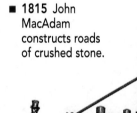

World Events

- **1799** France: Napoleon becomes head of revolutionary government.

- **1799** Egypt: Rosetta Stone, key to deciphering hieroglyphics, discovered.

- **1802** Haiti: Toussaint L'Ouverture leads rebellion against French rule.

- **1803** United States: Louisiana Territory purchased from France.

- **1804** Germany: Beethoven composes *Symphony No. 3.*

- **1804** France: Napoleon crowns himself emperor.

- **1807** United States: Fulton's steamboat navigates Hudson River. ▲

- **1810** South America: Simón Bolivar leads rebellions against Spanish rule.

- **1812** United States: War with Britain declared.

- **1813** Mexico: Independence declared.

- **1815** Belgium: Napoleon defeated at Waterloo.

British and World Events

- **1818** **Mary Wollstonecraft Shelley** publishes *Frankenstein or the Modern Prometheus.* ▲

- **1819** Peterloo Massacre in Manchester.

- **1819** **Percy Bysshe Shelley** writes "Ode to the West Wind."

- **1820** **John Keats** publishes "Ode on a Grecian Urn."

- **1825** Horse-drawn buses begin operating in London.

- **1825** John Nash begins rebuilding of Buckingham Palace.

- **1827** System for purifying London water installed.

- **1829** Robert Peel establishes Metropolitan Police in London.

- **1830** Liverpool-Manchester railway opens. ▲

- **1831** Michael Faraday demonstrates electromagnetic induction. ◄

- **1832** First Reform Act extends voting rights.

- **1816** France: René Läennec invents stethoscope.

- **1819** United States: Washington Irving writes "Rip Van Winkle."

- **1819** First steamship crosses Atlantic.

- **1821** Greece: War with Turkey begins.

- **1821** Germany: Heinrich Heine publishes *Poems.*

- **1823** Russia: Aleksandr Pushkin begins writing *Eugene Onegin.*

- **1825** Russia: Bolshoi Ballet founded.

- **1826** Germany: Mendelssohn composes *Overture to A Midsummer Night's Dream.*

- **1826** United States: James Fenimore Cooper publishes *The Last of the Mohicans.*

- **1830** France: Stendhal publishes *The Red and the Black.*

- **1831** United States: Edgar Allan Poe publishes *Poems.*

- **1831** France: Victor Hugo publishes *The Hunchback of Notre Dame.*

Rebels and Dreamers

THE ROMANTIC PERIOD
(1798–1832)

Historical Background

After nearly a century of progress in science and industry, the faith of poets in reason was eroded. Whereas eighteenth-century poets had celebrated the power of human understanding—their most bitter satire could say no more than "humanity is unreasonable"—Wordsworth marked the end of the century with the warning, "Our meddling intellect / Misshapes the beauteous forms of things— / We murder to dissect."

In the ensuing period, which was named the Romantic Period by historians during the late 1800s, nearly all the attitudes and tendencies of eighteenth-century classicism and rationalism were redefined or changed dramatically. To understand how these changes occurred, it is necessary to examine not only the impact of events in Britain, but also the effects of the social and political upheaval that began taking place in other parts of the world.

The Battle of Trafalgar, October 21, 1805, J.M.W. Turner, The Granger Collection, Ltd.

Revolution and Reaction Some of the defining events for British thought and politics at the end of the eighteenth century took place not in England but in France. The French Revolution began on July 14, 1789, when a mob stormed the Bastille, a Paris prison for political prisoners. The successful revolutionaries placed limits on the powers of King Louis XVI, established a new government, and approved a document called the Declaration of the Rights of Man and of the Citizen, which affirmed the principles of "liberty, equality, and fraternity." France became a constitutional monarchy.

In England, the ruling class felt threatened by the events in France, which seemed to strike at the roots of social order. Most intellectuals, including such important writers of the Romantic Age as William Wordsworth, at first enthusiastically supported the revolution and the democratic ideals on which it was based.

▲ **Critical Viewing**
The Romantic painter J.M.W. Turner depicted the defeat of the French fleet by the British at Trafalgar. Using the details in this painting, describe the experience of participating in a sea battle.
[Speculate]

The Reign of Terror As royalists, moderates, and radicals jockeyed for power, the French Revolution became more and more chaotic. In 1792, France declared war against Austria and Prussia, touching off an invasion by troops from those countries. Fuming with patriotic indignation, a radical group called the Jacobins gained control of the French legislative assembly, abolished the monarchy, and declared the nation a republic. Mobs attacked and killed many prisoners—including former aristocrats and priests—in the bloody "September massacres."

Within weeks, the revolutionaries had tried and convicted Louis XVI on a charge of treason and sent him to the guillotine early in 1793. The Jacobins, under the leadership of Maximilien de Robespierre, then began what is called the Reign of Terror. Over the course of about a year, they sent some 17,000 royalists, moderates, and even radicals to the guillotine—including, finally, Robespierre himself.

At the same time, France's new "citizen army" was making war across Europe in the name of liberty. In 1793, France declared war on Britain. Thus began a series of wars that would drag on for twenty-two years.

British Reaction The September massacres and the Reign of Terror were so shocking that even those Britons who had sympathized with the French

Close-up on History

The Napoleonic Wars

Britain's battles with France took a new turn after 1799, when a military leader named Napoleon Bonaparte seized control of France. Napoleon had grandiose plans for French expansion, and he was a brilliant military leader. After a brief break in Franco-British hostilities from 1802 to 1803, war resumed in earnest.

Napoleon, who had declared himself emperor of France, planned an invasion of Britain, but he had to abandon the plan after a British fleet under Lord Nelson defeated the French and Spanish fleets at the Battle of Trafalgar, off Spain, in 1805. Napoleon's armies had fought well against Britain's European allies, however, and by 1807 they controlled almost all of Europe as far east as the borders of Russia.

In 1812, Napoleon finally overextended himself by invading Russia. There, his armies were defeated by a combination of factors: the hardships of the Russian winter, the vastness of the landscape, and the strategic retreats of the Russian army, which involved the destruction of goods and property that the French might use. At the same time, Napoleon was experiencing reverses in the west. His forces were defeated in the Peninsular War (1808–1814) in Portugal and Spain, and, in 1814, British and allied armies closed in on him and forced him to abandon his throne.

Napoleon was not finished, however. Exiled to the Mediterranean island of Elba, he plotted to return, and, in 1815, he escaped to France. Resuming his rule for a period known as the Hundred Days, he met final defeat on the battlefield at Waterloo, Belgium, in 1815. His victorious opponent was the Duke of Wellington, the British hero of the Peninsular War.

Revolution now turned against it. Conservative Britons demanded a crackdown on reformers, whom they denounced as dangerous Jacobins. Adding to British alarm was the success of France's new "citizen army," which had expelled the Austrian and Russian invaders and then set out to "liberate" other European nations from despotic rule. British leaders did not want France or any other

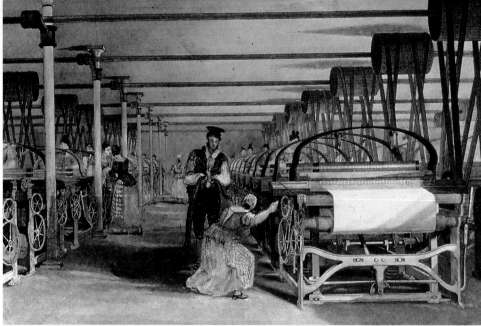

Power Loom, Anonymous, 18th Century

nation to win dominance on the European continent. The Tory government, led by William Pitt (the Younger), outlawed all talk of parliamentary reform outside the halls of Parliament, banned public meetings, and suspended certain basic rights. Liberal-minded Britons had no political outlet for their hopes and dreams. Many turned to literature and art instead.

Society's Problems Throughout the long wars with France, Britain's government ignored the problems caused by the Industrial Revolution—overcrowded factory towns, unpleasant and unsafe working conditions in the factories, and long working hours for low pay. The working class grew steadily larger and more restless. In the factory towns of northern England, workers protested in the violent Luddite Riots (1811–1813) the loss of jobs to new machinery. Some attempted to organize into unions.

Britain's government claimed to be following a hands-off policy, but in fact it sided openly with factory owners against workers, even helping to crush the workers' attempts to form unions. In Manchester, mounted soldiers charged a peaceful mass meeting of cotton workers and killed several of them in what came to be known as the Peterloo Massacre (1819). To many, it seemed that British society was splitting into two angry camps—the working classes, who demanded reform, and the ruling classes, who fiercely resisted reform.

A new generation of Tories emerged in the 1820s, and a trickle of reforms began. A law was passed in 1824 permitting Britain's first labor unions to organize, and in 1829 the Catholic Emancipation Act restored economic and religious freedoms to Roman Catholics.

The trickle grew into a stream following a Whig victory in the election of 1830. The Reform Bill of 1832 brought sweeping changes to British political life. By extending voting rights to the small but important middle class (males only), this law threatened the traditional dominance of landowning aristocrats in Parliament. Moreover, in 1833 Parliament passed the first law governing factory safety. In that same year, it also abolished slavery.

▲ **Critical Viewing**
Early cotton mills employed mostly women and children. (a) What does the clothing of the workers in this picture suggest about factory conditions of the time? (b) Describe the tasks that you see being performed. **[Draw Conclusions]**

Literature of the Period

The Beginnings of Romanticism British Romantic writers responded to the climate of their times. Their new interest in the trials and dreams of the common people and their desire for radical change developed out of the democratic idealism that characterized the early part of the French Revolution. Their deep attachment to nature and to a pure, simple past was a response to the misery and ugliness born of industrialization. For the Romantics, the faith in science and reason, so characteristic of eighteenth-century thought and literature, no longer applied in a world of tyranny and factories.

Rousseau and Goethe Many of the ideas that influenced the British Romantics, though, first arose on continental Europe well before the turn of the century. Swiss-born writer Jean-Jacques Rousseau (1712–1778), a leading philosopher of eighteenth-century France, saw society as a force that, throughout history, deformed and imprisoned an originally free human nature. "Man is born free," he wrote, "and everywhere he is in chains." His ideas influenced both American and French revolutionaries.

Tea Time, David Emil

A group of later eighteenth-century writers and artists living in German-speaking Europe began incorporating Rousseau's ideas into poetry, fiction, and drama. The most famous of this group, Johann Wolfgang von Goethe (1749–1832), found in the German literature of the Middle Ages a primitive simplicity much in keeping with Rousseau's ideas and values. These works, not unlike the Anglo-Saxon *Beowulf*, were filled with myth, adventure, and passion. The Romantic Movement takes its name from this interest in medieval romances. Goethe's own works show a new attention to feelings and express an ideal of self-fulfillment and growth through experience.

▲ **Critical Viewing**
By the early 1800s, tea was truly a national drink, popular with all classes. Which details illustrate how relaxing the custom of drinking tea can be? **[Interpret]**

The Romantic Age in British Poetry Romanticism was a movement that affected not only literature but also all the other arts. In music, it produced such brilliant European composers as Germany's Ludwig van Beethoven (1770–1827) and Austria's Franz Schubert (1797–1828), but there was no one of comparable stature in Britain. In painting, Romanticism influenced the intensely personal and warmly spontaneous rural landscapes of Britain's John Constable (1776–1837) and the dramatic seascapes of J.M.W. Turner (1775–1851). However, it is for literature, especially poetry, that Britain's Romantic Age is most famous.

Wordsworth and Coleridge William Wordsworth (1770–1850) provided an early statement of the goals of Romantic poetry in the preface to *Lyrical Ballads* (1798), a collaboration with his friend Samuel Taylor Coleridge

(1772–1834). The preface defined poetry as "the spontaneous overflow of powerful feelings" and explained that poetry "takes its origin from emotion recollected in tranquility." An emphasis on the emotions, then, was central to the new Romantic poetry.

Equally important was subject matter. The new poetry, said Wordsworth, dealt with "incidents and situations from common life" over which the poet throws "a certain coloring of imagination, whereby ordinary things should be presented . . . in an unusual way."

Finally, Wordsworth's preface spoke about incorporating human passions with "the beautiful and permanent forms of nature." An emphasis on nature would become another important characteristic of British Romantic verse.

The Romantic view of nature was quite different from that of most eighteenth-century literature. Nature was not a force to be tamed and analyzed scientifically; rather, it was a wild, free force that could inspire poets to instinctive spiritual understanding.

Lyrical Ballads was cooly received at first, but with time, it came to be regarded as the cornerstone of Britain's Romantic Age. Also with time, Wordsworth and Coleridge became respected members of Britain's literary establishment. Their political thinking, deeply marked by events in France, grew more conservative, and their literary ideas began to seem less radical than they once had.

▲ **Critical Viewing**
Why do you think that ruins like these appealed to Romantic writers? **[Speculate]**

Point /Counterpoint

Wordsworth, Visionary Poet or Comfortable Country Gentleman?

Was Wordsworth a poet with a revolutionary new vision of the natural world or a country gentleman who merely appreciated a tamed landscape? Two critics express these opposite perspectives on Britain's most famous Romantic poet.

Visionary Poet
"Wordsworth's 'philosophic' . . . poems . . . give us a clear and comprehensive expression of what we today so strikingly lack—an organic, unitary vision of man and nature, of the human mind, the earth, and the heavens, all activated by one spirit, all in harmonious relationship. . . ."
—**George W. Meyer,**
Major British Writers

Country Gentleman
"Wordsworth's 'Nature' is of course a Nature freed of wild beasts and danger by eons of human work, a Nature in which the poet, enjoying a comfortable income, lives on the products of industrialism even while he enjoys the natural scene 'unspoilt' by industrialism."
—**Christopher Caudwell,**
Illusion and Reality

The Second Generation of Romantic Poets Wordsworth and Coleridge blazed the way for a new generation of British Romantic poets—the so-called "second generation" of poets, which included George Gordon, Lord Byron; Percy Bysshe Shelley; and John Keats. Coming of age during the Napoleonic Era, these younger poets rebelled even more strongly than did Wordsworth and Coleridge against the British conservatism of the time. All three died abroad after tragically short lives, and their viewpoints were those of disillusioned outsiders.

George Gordon, Lord Byron Byron (1788–1824) was a member of the House of Lords. Although critics responded unfavorably to his early poetry, Byron persisted and finally achieved success when he published the first two cantos of *Childe Harold's Pilgrimage* (1812). Handsome, egotistical, and aloof, Byron became the darling of elegant society, but not for long. Shocked by his radical politics and scandalous love affairs, London hostesses began to shun him, and Byron left Britain in 1816, never to return.

A Writer's Voice

George Gordon, Lord Byron, and the Byronic Hero

The critic Northrop Frye declared that Byron "probably had more influence outside England than any other English poet except Shakespeare." One source of this influence was the mysterious "Byronic hero," a role model for young readers and an influence on novelists like Balzac.

In this description of the Byronic hero by Frye, you may recognize features that still characterize today's heroes of literature and film: "an inscrutable figure with hollow cheeks and blazing eyes, wrapped in a cloud of gloom, full of mysterious and undefined remorse, an outcast from society . . . he will not brook questioning, though he himself questions all established social standards, . . ."

This hero appears in various forms throughout Byron's tales in verse and his verse dramas. At the beginning of *A Dramatic Poem, Manfred*, for example, the protagonist, despite his accomplishments, feels no satisfaction and does not love anyone or anything.

> Philosophy and science, and the springs
> Of wonder, and the wisdom of the world,
> I have essay'd,° and in my mind there is   °Tried
> A power to make these subject to itself—
> 5 But they avail° not: I have done men good   °Help
> And I have met with good even among men—
> But this avail'd not: I have had my foes,
> And none have baffled°, many fallen before me—   °Hindered
> But this avail'd not:—Good, or evil, life,
> 10 Powers, passions, all I see in other beings,
> Have been to me as rain unto the sands,
> Since that all-nameless hour. I have no dread,
> And feel the curse to have no natural fear,
> Nor fluttering throb, that beats with hopes or wishes,
> 15 Or lurking love of something on the earth. . . .

Percy Bysshe Shelley Byron's friend Shelley (1792–1822) was also an aristocrat and political radical, more consistently radical, in fact, than Byron. In poems such as "Song to the Men of England" (1819), Shelley urged England's lower classes to rebel. Like Byron, Shelley was shunned for his radical ideas; he left Britain for good in 1818. In his lifetime, he did not attain the fame that Byron did. Yet, he is now remembered for the fervor he brought to lyric poetry in such intensely personal and emotional verses as "To a Skylark" (1820).

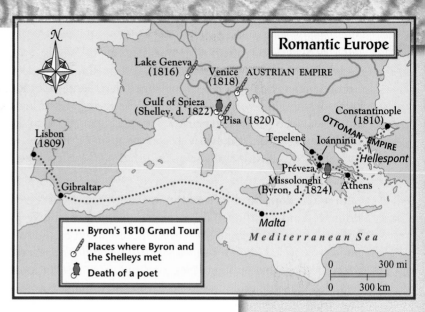

John Keats Keats (1795–1821), the third great figure in the second generation of Romantic poets, was also a master of lyrical poetry. Unlike Byron and Shelley, Keats was born outside upper-class society, the son of a London stable keeper. Keats trained to be a doctor but abandoned his medical career to pursue his passion for poetry.

He produced many of his greatest poems in a burst of creativity during the first nine months of 1819—works like *The Fall of Hyperion* and "Ode on a Grecian Urn." In many of these poems, Keats tried to reconcile the eternal, and therefore almost inhuman, beauty of art with the realities of human suffering. The famous line at the end of "Ode on a Grecian Urn"— "Beauty is truth, truth beauty"—represents one response to this dilemma, but it is not a final answer for Keats. Unfortunately, Keats contracted tuberculosis. Hoping to recuperate in a warmer climate, he traveled to Italy, where he died at the age of twenty-five.

The Romantic Age in British Prose Poetry was the dominant literary form during the Romantic Age, but many significant prose works also appeared, mainly in the form of essays and novels. This was a dry period for drama—only two theaters were licensed to produce plays, and they tended to feature popular spectacles rather than serious plays. However, Byron and Shelley did write closet dramas, or verse works intended to be read rather than produced on stage.

Lamb, Hazlitt, and De Quincey British readers of the Romantic Age could find brilliant literary criticism and topical essays in a variety of new periodicals. *The London Magazine*, although it appeared from only 1820 to 1829, attracted major contributions from the three greatest essayists of the era: Charles Lamb (1775–1834), William Hazlitt (1778–1830), and Thomas De Quincey (1785–1859). Lamb, in particular, transformed the informal essay of the eighteenth century into a more personal, more introspective Romantic composition.

▲ **Critical Viewing**
The second generation of Romantics traveled and lived in Europe. (a) How many years passed between Byron's Grand Tour of Europe and his move to Pisa? (b) When and where in Europe did Shelley and Byron die? **[Read a Map]**

Mary Shelley Unlike the Romantic poets, the novelists of the Romantic Age did not make a sharp break with the past. The Gothic novel first appeared in the middle of the eighteenth century. It featured a number of standard ingredients, including brave heroes and heroines, threatening scoundrels, vast eerie castles, and ghosts. The fascination of the Romantics with mystery and the supernatural made such novels quite popular during the Romantic Age. One of the most successful was *Frankenstein, or the Modern Prometheus* (1818), written by Shelley's wife Mary Wollstonecraft Shelley (1797–1851).

Jane Austen The Romantic novel of manners continued in the tradition of earlier writers by turning a satirical eye on British customs. The most highly regarded writer of novels of manners was Jane Austen (1775–1817), whose works include *Sense and Sensibility* (1811) and *Pride and Prejudice* (1813). Her incisive portrayals of character and her social satire are more reflective of the classical sensibility of the eighteenth century than of the notions of the new Romantic age.

Sketch for Hadleigh Castle, John Constable

▲ **Critical Viewing**
John Constable (1776–1837) is a painter linked with the Romantics. What mood does Constable create with the clouds in this scene? Why? (b) How is this mood related to the beliefs of Romanticism? Explain. **[Interpret]**

Sir Walter Scott Passionately devoted to his native Scotland, Sir Walter Scott (1771–1832) used his knowledge of Scottish history to create what amounted to a new literary form, the historical novel. It was characterized by a focus on historical events and settings, with attention to local flavor and regional speech. It also featured a Romantic treatment of realistic themes.

The close of Britain's Romantic Age is usually considered to be the year 1832, the year that the First Reform Bill was passed. However, the ideas of Romanticism remained a strong influence on following generations of writers. In fact, even today we can detect elements of Romanticism in many major works of contemporary fiction and poetry, as well as in television dramas, movies, and popular songs.

THE CHANGING ENGLISH LANGUAGE

The Romantic Age

BY RICHARD LEDERER

THE SUN NEVER SET ON THE BRITISH EMPIRE

During the Romantic Age, Britannia ruled the waves and English ruled much of the land. Great Britain's smashing conquests in the Napoleonic Wars at the beginning of the nineteenth century—culminating in Nelson's famous victory at Trafalgar in 1805—established an undisputed naval supremacy. This, in turn, gave Great Britain control over most of the world's commerce. As British ships traveled throughout the world, they left the language of the mother country in their wake but also came home from foreign ports laden with cargoes of words from other languages freighted with new meanings for English speakers.

WORDS, WORDS, WORDS

The biggest and fattest unabridged English dictionaries hold more than 600,000 words, compared to German in second place with 185,000 words, and then Russian and French at 130,000 and 100,000. One reason we have accumulated the world's largest and most varied vocabulary is that English continues to be the most hospitable and democratic language that has ever existed, unique in the number and variety of its borrowed words. Although Anglo-Saxon is the foundation of the English language, more than seventy percent of our words have been imported from other lands, ancient and modern, far and near. No wonder Ralph Waldo Emerson waxed ecstatic about "English speech, the sea which receives tributaries from every region under heaven" and Dorothy Thompson, employing a more prosaic metaphor, referred to "that glorious and imperial mongrel, the English language."

The following are words that became part of the English language as a result of England's great economic expansion.	
Country	**Borrowed Words**
India	*bandanna, bungalow, calico, cashmere, china, cot, curry, juggernaut, jungle, loot, nirvana, polo, punch* (beverage), *thug,* and *verandah*
Asia	*gingham, indigo, mango,* and *typhoon*
New Zealand	*kiwi*
Australia	*boomerang* and *kangaroo*
Africa	*banana, boorish, chimpanzee, gorilla, gumbo,* and *zebra*

ACTIVITIES

1. Open your dictionary at random and examine the etymology of the words listed at the top of fifteen pages. Record the earliest source for each word. Words noted as *AS* or *OE* are native; the rest are borrowed. What is the ratio of native versus borrowed words? Among the borrowed words, what percentage are derived from Latin? from Greek? from French? from other languages? Compare your results with those of your classmates and discuss the implications.

2. Now choose a passage from a newspaper or magazine. Analyze the first thirty words of that passage in the manner described above. Do you notice a different ratio of native to borrowed words? Discuss your conclusions regarding random dictionary entries versus the words in actual sentences.

PART 1 Fantasy and Reality

Prepare to Read

To a Mouse ◆ To a Louse ◆ Woo'd and Married and A'

Robert Burns (1759–1796)

Known as "The Voice of Scotland," Robert Burns wrote his first verse when he was fifteen. It was a love poem to a girl named Nellie, who was helping the Burns family with the harvest on their farm in Scotland. "Thus with me," Burns later wrote, "began Love and Poesy."

Poor But Learned Beginnings Burns was born at Alloway, in Ayrshire. Although poverty kept him from a full formal education, with his father's encouragement he read widely, studying the Bible, Shakespeare, and Alexander Pope. His mother, though herself illiterate, instilled in him a love of Scottish folk songs, legends, and proverbs.

Literary Triumph In 1786, Burns published his first collection of poems, *Poems, Chiefly in the Scottish Dialect*, through a small local press. The collection, which included "To a Mouse," was a huge success, applauded by critics and country folk alike. The new literary hero was invited to the Scottish capital, where he was swept into the social scene and hailed as the "heaven-taught plowman." When he died, thousands of people from all social levels followed his coffin to the grave.

A Lasting Contribution Although Burns died while just in his thirties, having suffered for years from a weak heart, his brief career resulted in a lasting contribution to literature. Burns's poems, written for the most part in dialect, are marked by their natural, direct, and spontaneous quality. Burns certainly drew on the ballad tradition of Scotland, but while some of the poet's work had its origins in folk tunes, "it is not," as critic James Douglas writes, "easy to tell where the vernacular ends and the personal magic begins."

Joanna Baillie (1762–1851)

When Joanna Baillie's (bā′ lēz) *Plays on the Passions* was published anonymously in 1798, it created a great literary sensation in London. Debates raged over which famous man of letters had written the plays. It was not until 1800 that the true author was revealed—an unassuming thirty-eight-year-old Scottish woman named Joanna Baillie. Even her literary friends were astounded, and she became an instant celebrity.

A Gregarious Tomboy Born in Lanarkshire, Scotland, the daughter of a minister, young Joanna Baillie was a tomboy who loved horseback riding and who resisted the stern moral education given by her father. She blossomed when she and her sister, Agnes, were sent away to boarding school in 1772. Joanna Baillie became an outgoing leader who led the other girls on boisterous outdoor adventures and staged plays that she herself wrote.

A Spinster's Life in London When Baillie's father died in 1778, the family depended on the kindness of a wealthy uncle for support. He provided the two sisters with a lifetime income. When their brother married in 1791, the sisters and their mother started a household of their own. They began a busy social life amid London's bustling literary scene, welcoming many important writers of the day into their home.

Success and Critical Acclaim With Baillie's literary success, the two sisters were able to travel, and they often returned to Scotland to visit Sir Walter Scott, who helped in the production of Baillie's plays. Best known in her day for her dramatic works, Baillie also wrote poetry. Like her fellow Scot Robert Burns, she wrote poems in the dialect of her homeland, many of them on nature and rustic manners.

Preview
Connecting to the Literature

If a poem is written in your language, then, in a sense, it belongs to you. These poets write in Scottish dialect to give poetry back to Scotland.

Literary Analysis
Dialect

Dialect is the language, and particularly the speech habits, of a specific social class, region, or group. A dialect may vary from the standard form of a language in grammar, in pronunciation, and in the use of certain expressions. In literature, dialect helps achieve these goals:

- Establishing character, mood, and setting
- Adding "texture" or charm for readers who do not speak the dialect

By writing in dialect, Burns and Baillie broke with tradition and gave their poetry to the common folk who spoke that dialect. Note, however, the poetic effect of the dialect even for those who do not speak it.

Comparing Literary Works

Using dialect was just one way in which late-eighteenth-century poets returned poetry to the common people. Poets like Burns and Baillie also introduced subjects drawn from everyday life, such as the mouse in Burns's "To a Mouse." This shift was part of the artistic rebellion known as Romanticism.

Before Romanticism, poets devoted their "serious" poetry to "lofty" topics, such as the fate of kings. The Romantics greatly expanded the range of subjects considered suitable for poetry, and many wrote poems based on the everyday experiences of common folk. Compare the results Burns and Baillie achieve. Ask yourself, does an "everyday" subject limit the poet's message, or does the poet reach a general truth?

Reading Strategy
Translating Dialect

You may not know Scottish dialect, but you may be able to interpret words in dialect using context, by referencing a footnote, or even by noticing a resemblance to a Standard English word. Use a chart like the one shown to help you translate the Scottish dialect in the poems.

Footnotes	*sleekit*[3]
	3. sleek
Context	*saunt an' sinner*
	saunt = saint
Word Similarities	*dinna*
	do not
Missing Letters	*woo'd, a'*
	wooed, all

Vocabulary Development

dominion (də min′ yən) *n.* rule; authority (p. 627)

impudence (im′ pyo͞o dəns) *n.* lack of shame; rudeness (p. 629)

winsome (win′ səm) *adj.* having a charming appearance or way (p. 632)

discretion (di skresh′ ən) *n.* good judgment; prudence (p. 633)

inconstantly (in kän′ stənt lē) *adv.* changeably; in a fickle way (p. 633)

To a Mouse

On Turning Her up in Her Nest with the Plow, November, 1785

Robert Burns

Background

Before Robert Burns published his poetry, works of literature were almost always modeled on the classics, in which structure, grammar, and vocabulary were polished and complex. Robert Burns ignored these conventions and boldly put poetry in the hands of the people, writing in their language, Scottish dialect, and using common folk as subject matter.

▼ **Critical Viewing**
What facial qualities of a mouse might have inspired Burns's poem? [Hypothesize]

Wee, sleekit,[1] cow'rin', tim'rous beastie,
O, what a panic's in thy breastie!
Thou need na start awa sae hasty,
    Wi' bickering brattle![2]
5 I wad be laith[3] to rin an' chase thee
    Wi' murd'ring pattle![4]

I'm truly sorry man's <u>dominion</u>
Has broken Nature's social union,
An' justifies that ill opinion,
10   Which makes thee startle,
At me, thy poor, earth-born companion,
    An' fellow-mortal!

I doubt na, whyles,[5] but thou may thieve;
What then? poor beastie, thou maun[6] live!
15 A daimen icker in a thrave[7]
    'S a sma' request:
I'll get a blessin' wi' the lave,[8]
    And never miss't!

Thy wee bit housie, too, in ruin!
20 Its silly wa's[9] the win's are strewin'!
An' naething, now, to big[10] a new ane,
    O' foggage[11] green!
An' bleak December's winds ensuin',
    Baith snell[12] an' keen!

25 Thou saw the fields laid bare and waste,
An' weary winter comin' fast,
An' cozie here, beneath the blast,
    Thou thought to dwell,
Till crash! the cruel coulter[13] past
30   Out through thy cell.

That wee bit heap o' leaves an' stibble,
Has cost thee mony a weary nibble!

---

1. **sleekit** sleek.
2. **Wi' . . . brattle** with a quick pattering sound.
3. **wad be laith** would be loath.
4. **pattle** paddle for cleaning a plow.
5. **whyles** at times.
6. **maun** must.
7. **A . . . thrave** an occasional ear of grain in a bundle.
8. **lave** rest.
9. **silly wa's** feeble walls.
10. **big** build.
11. **foggage** rough grass.
12. **snell** sharp.
13. **coulter** plow blade.

dominion (də min´ yən) *n.*
rule; authority

Reading Strategy
Translating Dialect Use
context clues to determine
the meaning of "win's" in
line 20.

**Reading Check**

How does the speaker
uncover the mouse?

Now thou's turned out, for a' thy trouble,
　　But[14] house or hald,[15]
35　To thole[16] the winter's sleety dribble,
　　An' cranreuch[17] cauld!

But, Mousie, thou art no thy lane,[18]
In proving foresight may be vain:
The best laid schemes o' mice an' men
　　Gang aft a-gley,[19]
An' lea'e us nought but grief an' pain,
　　For promised joy.

Still thou art blest, compared wi' me!
The present only toucheth thee:
45　But, och! I backward cast my e'e
　　On prospects drear!
An' forward, though I canna see,
　　I guess an' fear!

---

14. **But** without.
15. **hald** property.
16. **thole** withstand.
17. **cranreuch** (krən´ rəkh) frost.
18. **no thy lane** not alone.
19. **Gang aft a-gley** go often awry.

Review and Assess

Thinking About the Selection

1. **Respond:** How would you have reacted to the plight of the mouse? Explain.

2. **(a) Recall:** For what reason does the speaker apologize to the mouse? **(b) Infer:** How does the speaker feel about the grain the mouse steals? **(c) Interpret:** What does the speaker's reaction show about his ideas of justice?

3. **(a) Infer:** What has happened to the mouse's attempt to prepare for winter? **(b) Interpret:** Which two famous lines in the poem express the poem's theme? **(c) Paraphrase:** Restate the theme in your own words.

4. **(a) Interpret:** What comparison does the speaker draw between himself and the mouse in the last stanza? **(b) Evaluate:** Do you agree with the speaker about the mouse's advantage? Explain.

5. **Apply:** What value do you place on foresight? Explain.

6. **Evaluate:** Does dialect add to the quality of folk-wisdom in the poem, or does it distract from the meaning? Explain.

To a Louse

On Seeing One on a Lady's Bonnet at Church

Robert Burns

The Bow, Talbot Hughes, Warrington Museum and Art Gallery, Great Britain

◀ **Critical Viewing**
Does this lady's pose and costume link her to the lady in the poem? Explain. **[Connect]**

Ha! whare ye gaun, ye crowlin' ferlie!¹
Your <u>impudence</u> protects you sairly:²
I canna say but ye strunt³ rarely,
    Owre gauze and lace;
5 Though faith! I fear ye dine but sparely
    On sic a place.

impudence (im′ pyo͞o dəns)
n. lack of shame; rudeness

✔**Reading Check**

Where is the louse crawling?

---

1. **crowlin′ ferlie** crawling wonder.
2. **sairly** wondrously.
3. **strunt** strut.

Ye ugly, creepin', blastit wonner,[4]
Detested, shunned by saunt an' sinner,
How dare ye set your fit[5] upon her,
10   Sae fine a lady?
Gae somewhere else, and seek your dinner
        On some poor body.

Swith![6] in some beggar's haffet[7] squattle;[8]
There ye may creep, and sprawl, and sprattle[9]
15 Wi' ither kindred, jumping cattle,
        In shoals and nations:
Whare horn nor bane[10] ne'er dare unsettle
        Your thick plantations.

Now haud[11] ye there, ye're out o' sight,
20 Below the fatt'rels,[12] snug an' tight;
Na, faith ye yet![13] ye'll no be right
        Till ye've got on it,
The vera tapmost, tow'ring height
        O' Miss's bonnet.

25 My sooth! right bauld ye set your nose out,
As plump and gray as onie grozet;[14]
O for some rank, mercurial rozet,[15]
        Or fell,[16] red smeddum,[17]
I'd gie you sic a hearty dose o't,
30   Wad dress your droddum![18]

I wad na been surprised to spy
You on an auld wife's flannen toy;[19]
Or aiblins some bit duddie boy,[20]
        On's wyliecoat;[21]

4. **blastit wonner** blasted wonder.
5. **fit** foot.
6. **swith** swift.
7. **haffet** locks.
8. **squattle** sprawl.
9. **sprattle** struggle.
10. **horn nor bane** comb made of horn or bone.
11. **haud** hold.
12. **fatt'rels** ribbon ends.
13. **Na, faith ye yet!** "Confound you!"
14. **onie grozet** (gräz´ it) any gooseberry.
15. **rozet** (räz´ it) rosin.
16. **fell** sharp.
17. **smeddum** powder.
18. **Wad . . . droddum** "would put an end to you."
19. **flannen toy** flannel cap.
20. **Or . . . boy** or perhaps on some little ragged boy.
21. **wyliecoat** (wī´ lē kōt´) undershirt.

35 But Miss's fine Lunardi![22] fie,
        How daur ye do't?

    O, Jenny, dinna toss your head,
    An' set your beauties a' abread![23]
    Ye little ken what cursèd speed
40   The blastie's[24] makin'!
    Thae[25] winks and finger-ends, I dread,
        Are notice takin'!

    O wad some Pow'r the giftie gie us
    To see oursels as ithers see us!
45 It wad frae monie a blunder free us
        And foolish notion:
    What airs in dress an' gait wad lea'e us,
        And ev'n devotion!

---

22. **Lunardi** balloon-shaped bonnet, named for Vincenzo Lunardi,
    a balloonist of the late 1700's.
23. **abread** abroad.
24. **blastie's** creature's.
25. **Thae** those.

Review and Assess

Thinking About the Selection

1. **Respond:** Did this poem make you laugh? Why or why not?
2. **(a) Recall:** What is the louse doing? **(b) Recall:** What does the speaker command it to do instead? **(c) Interpret:** What social assumptions about cleanliness does the speaker's command reflect?
3. **(a) Draw Conclusions:** What impression of Jenny does the speaker create? **(b) Analyze:** How do the references to her clothing and the contrast between her and "some poor body" contribute to this impression?
4. **(a) Infer:** In the lines 37–42, why does the speaker warn Jenny against tossing her head? **(b) Infer:** What is the reaction of others in the church to Jenny's gesture? **(c) Draw Conclusions:** Why is the contrast between this gesture and the progress of the louse particularly embarrassing?
5. **(a) Interpret:** Paraphrase the generalization that the speaker makes in the last stanza. **(b) Evaluate:** Do you agree that we would profit if we could "see oursels as ithers see us"? Explain.
6. **Make a Judgement:** Do you think caring about the impression we make on others is foolish vanity? Explain.

Woo'd and Married and A'

Joanna Baillie

The bride she is <u>winsome</u> and bonny,
    Her hair it is snooded[1] sae sleek,
And faithfu' and kind is her Johnny,
    Yet fast fa' the tears on her cheek.
5 New pearlins[2] are cause of her sorrow,
    New pearlins and plenishing[3] too;
The bride that has a' to borrow
    Has e'en right mickle[4] ado.
      Woo'd and married and a'!
10   Woo'd and married and a'!
    Is na' she very weel aff
      To be woo'd and married at a'?

Her mither then hastily spak,
    "The Lassie is glaikit[5] wi' pride;
15 In my pouch I had never a plack[6]
    On the day when I was a bride.
E'en tak to your wheel and be clever,
    And draw out your thread in the sun;
The gear[7] that is gifted it never
20   Will last like the gear that is won.
      Woo'd and married and a'!
      Wi' havins and toucher[8] sae sma'!
    I think ye are very weel aff
      To be woo'd and married at a'."

---

1. **snooded** bound up with a ribbon.
2. **pearlins** lace trimmings.
3. **plenishing** furnishings.
4. **mickle** much.
5. **glaikit** foolish.
6. **plack** farthing; a small coin equal to one fourth of a penny.
7. **gear** wealth or goods.
8. **havins and toucher** possessions and dowry.

winsome (win´ səm) *adj.* having a charming appearance or way

Literary Analysis
Dialect What feelings or qualities does the use of dialect add to the mother's advice to her daughter?

The Village Wedding, (detail) Sir Luke Fildes, Christopher Wood Gallery, London

25 "Toot, toot," quo' her gray-headed faither,
       "She's less o' a bride than a bairn,[9]
    She's ta'en like a cout[10] frae the heather,
       Wi' sense and <u>discretion</u> to learn.
    Half husband, I trow, and half daddy,
30   As humor <u>inconstantly</u> leans,
    The chiel maun be patient and steady[11]
       That yokes wi' a mate in her teens.
          A kerchief sae douce[12] and sae neat
          O'er her locks that the wind used to blaw!
35 I'm baith like to laugh and to greet[13]
          When I think of her married at a'!"

    Then out spak the wily bridegroom,
       Weel waled[14] were his wordies, I ween,
    "I'm rich, though my coffer be toom,[15]

---

9. **bairn** child.
10. **cout** colt.
11. **The chiel maun . . . steady** The man must be patient and steady.
12. **douce** respectable.
13. **greet** weep.
14. **waled** chosen.
15. **toom** empty.

▲ Critical Viewing
Compare and contrast the setting and costumes in this painting with the scene described in the poem. **[Compare and Contrast]**

discretion (di skresh′ ən) *n.* good judgment; prudence

inconstantly (in kän′ stənt lē) *adv.* changeably; in a fickle way

Reading Check

What is the father's opinion of his daughter?

40   Wi' the blinks o' your bonny blue e'en.[16]
     I'm prouder o' thee by my side,
          Though thy ruffles or ribbons be few,
     Than if Kate o' the Croft were my bride
          Wi' purfles[17] and pearlins enow.
45   Dear and dearest of ony!
                Ye're woo'd and buikit[18] and a'!
          And do ye think scorn o' your Johnny,
          And grieve to be married at a'?"

     She turn'd, and she blush'd, and she smiled,
50   And she looked sae bashfully down;
     The pride o' her heart was beguiled,
          And she played wi' the sleeves o' her gown.
     She twirled the tag o' her lace,
          And she nipped her boddice sae blue,
55   Syne blinkit sae sweet in his face,
          And aff like a maukin[19] she flew.
                Woo'd and married and a'!
          Wi' Johnny to roose[20] her and a'!
          She thinks hersel very weel aff
60   To be woo'd and married at a'!

---

16. **e'en** eyes.
17. **purfles** embroidered trimmings.
18. **buikit** "booked"; entered as married in the official registry.
19. **maukin** hare.
20. **roose** praise.

Review and Assess

Thinking About the Selection

1. **(a) Recall:** Why is the bride unhappy at the beginning of the poem? **(b) Infer:** Does either parent seem sympathetic to the daughter's unhappiness? Explain.

2. **(a) Recall:** How does the bridegroom respond to his bride's unhappiness? **(b) Analyze Cause and Effect:** Describe the effect the bridegroom's words have on his young bride. **(c) Draw Conclusions:** How would you describe the personality of the bridegroom?

3. **(a) Recall:** Which speaker succeeds in changing the bride's outlook? **(b) Draw Conclusions:** Judging from the final stanza, do you think the marriage will be a happy one? Explain.

4. **Make a Judgement:** Do you think the poet is unkind to the young bride, or does she show insight into people? Explain.

Review and Assess

Literary Analysis

Dialect

1. What does the use of **dialect** in the poems by Burns suggest about the speaker's social status?
2. What does dialect contribute to the setting of Joanna Baillie's "Woo'd and Married and A'"?
3. Find at least two examples in "To a Mouse" of the following pronunciation patterns for Scottish English: (a) Final consonants are dropped, and (b) the letter *o* is replaced by either *ae* or *a*.
4. How would the overall effect of these poems have been different if they had been written in Standard English?

Comparing Literary Works

5. Using a chart like the one shown, analyze the subject matter of the poems in this grouping.

Poem	Subject	Message

6. (a) Which poem conveys the message that applies most generally? Explain. (b) Which poem conveys a message that applies only to some people? Explain.
7. Do you think the use of everyday subjects in these poems limits the messages they convey? Explain.
8. What subject matter would you be surprised to find in poetry today? Explain.

Reading Strategy

Translating Dialect

9. List and define ten words in dialect that appear in these poems. For each, explain the techniques you used to arrive at a definition.
10. Choose one stanza from a Burns or Baillie poem, and translate it into Standard English.

Extend Understanding

11. **History Connection:** What difficulties might dialect present to historians? Explain.

Quick Review

Dialect is the form of a language spoken by a particular social class, region, or group. It differs from the standard language in pronunciation, vocabulary, or grammar.

To **translate dialect** into Standard English, read footnotes, notice context clues, look for similarities to words you know, and fill in missing letters in words.

 Take It to the Net
www.phschool.com
Take the interactive self-test online to check your understanding of these selections.

Integrate Language Skills

Vocabulary Development Lesson

Word Analysis: Anglo-Saxon Suffix *-some*

Baillie calls the bride in her poem *winsome*, meaning "charming." The Anglo-Saxon suffix *-some* means "tending to" or "tending toward being." Literally, *winsome* means "tending to win over or to delight." Using this meaning of the suffix and a dictionary, define each word below.

1. handsome
2. lithesome
3. worrisome
4. awesome
5. tiresome

Spelling Strategy

The suffix that sounds like *shun* at the end of a word may be spelled *tion, ssion,* or *cion.* The spelling *ssion* is used when a related verb ends in *-mit* or *-ess: permit/permission* and *confess/confession.* In your notebook, correctly complete the spelling of each word including the *shun* sound.

1. discre__   2. posse__   3. omi__

Concept Development: Synonyms

Synonyms are words that share the same, or nearly the same, meaning. In your notebook, write the letter of the word that is the best synonym of the word from the vocabulary list on page 625. Then, use a dictionary to explain any differences in meaning between the synonyms in each pair.

1. dominion: (a) incapability, (b) rule, (c) pride
2. impudence: (a) rudeness, (b) shyness, (c) test
3. winsome: (a) competitive, (b) bold, (c) attractive
4. discretion: (a) disappointment, (b) good judgment, (c) gratitude
5. inconstantly: (a) changeably, (b) emptily, (c) sadly

Grammar and Style Lesson

Interjections

Interjections are words or phrases expressing emotion that function independently of a sentence. A comma separates a mild interjection from the rest of the sentence. An exclamation mark follows a stronger interjection. A question mark is used when the interjection takes the form of a question.

> **Examples:** <u>O</u>, what a panic's in thy breastie!
>
> But, <u>och!</u> I backward cast my e'e. . . .

Practice Identify the interjection in each line, and correctly punctuate the sentence.

1. What then poor beastie, thou maun live!
2. Ha whare ye gaun, ye crowlin' ferlie!
3. Though faith I fear ye dine but sparely. . . .
4. My sooth right bauld ye set your nose out, . . .
5. O Jenny, dinna toss your head, . . .

Writing Application Write a short paragraph about a funny incident. Use at least two interjections, punctuated correctly.

W̶G̶ Prentice Hall Writing and Grammar Connection: Chapter 17, Section 4

Writing Lesson

Comparison of Characters

Burns and Baillie paint brilliant miniature portraits of Scottish common folk. In an essay, compare the vain churchgoer in Burns's "To a Louse" with the moping young bride in Baillie's "Woo'd and Married and A'."

Prewriting Jot down notes on the two characters, identifying similarities and differences between them.

Drafting Choose a method of organization and follow it consistently as you draft. For instance, you might compare each character point by point, focusing first on social position and then on basic attitudes.

Revising Mark up your draft, highlighting details about one character in one color and details about the other in another color. If the pattern of highlights shows that you have departed from your chosen form of organization, reorganize passages. If you have more highlights of one color than of another, consider adding details for better balance.

> **Model: Revising to Better Balance Comparisons**
>
> The young bride is clearly emotional. Upset as she is about her poverty, she is easily reassured by the groom's flattery—which has nothing to do with money.

She seems to be driven by vanity, just like the vain churchgoer in Burns's poem.

The added sentence balances the discussion of the two characters in this paragraph.

Prentice Hall Writing and Grammar Connection: Chapter 14, Section 4

Extension Activities

Listening and Speaking With a group, prepare an **authentic dialect reading** of the poems in this group.

1. Listen to recordings of Burns's poetry.
2. Mark a photocopy of the poems with the correct pronunciations of words in dialect.
3. Rehearse, offering one another suggestions about pronunciation, expression, and gestures.

When you have prepared throughly, present your readings to the class. **[Group Activity]**

Research and Technology Assemble a **multimedia presentation** about Scotland that includes photographs, recordings, and maps. Make photocopies, and code each piece of art to indicate in which part of your presentation you might use it (for example, use **L** for land and **H** for history). To organize your visuals, start a folder for each category. Share your work with classmates.

 **Take It to the Net** www.phschool.com

Go online for an additional research activity using the Internet.

Prepare to Read

The Lamb ◆ The Tyger ◆ The Chimney Sweeper ◆ Infant Sorrow

William Blake (1757–1827)

"I must create a system or be enslaved by another man's." So spoke William Blake, an artist and poet who strove in his work to break free from the patterns of thought that defined common experience. As if to underscore the difference between his views and the ordinary, he claimed that mystical visions were the source of his inspiration.

Finding His Way Blake's visions began when, at the age of four, he thought he saw God at his window. Four years later, Blake said, he saw a tree filled with angels. While Blake's "spells" might have seemed a cause for concern, Blake's parents were followers of the mystical teachings of Emanuel Swedenborg, a Swedish spiritualist. They believed that their son had a "gift of vision" and did all they could to nurture this gift.

Blake's father was a poor Londoner who owned a small hosiery shop. He sent Blake to drawing school, and Blake pursued his own education at home through wide reading. Already well educated by the age of twelve, Blake wrote some of the simple, eloquent poems that became part of a collection entitled *Poetical Sketches* (1783). He became an engraver's apprentice and then went on to study at the Royal Academy.

Striking Out on His Own Formal study did not last long, however. The president of the Academy, noted painter Sir Joshua Reynolds, discouraged Blake's original style and pushed him toward more conventional work. The rebellious Blake left the school and eventually set up his own print shop. He was to live most of his days eking out a living as an engraver, barely making enough to support himself and his wife, Catherine.

Innocence and Experience When Blake was thirty-two, he published *Songs of Innocence*, a series of poems that he had composed when he was younger. The poems explored his favorite themes—the destiny of the human spirit and the possibility of renewing our perceptions. In these poems, Blake suggested that by recapturing the wonderment of childhood, we can achieve the goal of true self-knowledge and integration with the world. To print the collection, he developed a unique process whereby the words and illustrations were etched onto metal plates and then printed on paper. Blake often painted in colors and details on each page by hand. The result was a true integration of text and picture. Because the process was time consuming, few books could be produced. To support himself, Blake worked for other authors as an illustrator and sold what he could of his own works for one pound per copy. He also continued to write, and in 1794 he brought out a companion to *Songs of Innocence*, entitled *Songs of Experience*.

A Mature Vision Exploring the darker side of life, *Songs of Experience* reflected Blake's growing disillusionment and more mature vision. He came to believe that a return to innocence was not, at least by itself, sufficient for people to attain true self-awareness: They must also recognize and accept the parts of themselves that religion and morality teach them to reject. Thus, Blake's credo was that there must be a union of opposites, or a fusion of innocence and experience.

An Unrecognized Genius Blake's talent was barely recognized by his peers or by the public during his lifetime. It was only late in his life that a small group of admiring painters sought him out. Despite the lack of recognition, Blake filled his seventy years with constant creative activity. Years after his death, he came to be regarded as one of the most important poets of his time.

Preview

Connecting to the Literature

For a child, the tooth-fairy story can be a cherished belief. When such beliefs are disproved, a child may experience sadness, even mistrust, before finding a new, mature confidence. Like such a child, Blake passes from the innocence of "The Lamb" to the darker awareness of "The Tyger."

Literary Analysis

Symbols

In literary works, a **symbol** is a word, image, or idea that represents something else. Often, a symbol is something tangible, or solid, that stands for and helps readers understand something intangible, like an emotion. A symbol appears in the following line from Blake:

> And wash in a river and shine in the Sun.

Washing "in a river" symbolizes the Christian rite of baptism, in which a believer is cleansed of sin. To help you interpret Blake's symbols, use a graphic organizer like the one shown.

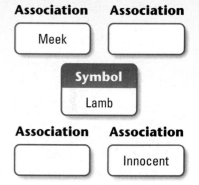

Comparing Literary Works

Using symbols, Blake defines a unique **poetic vision** or philosophy—a comprehensive view of life, the world, and our ordinary perceptions. In the poems that follow, you will be struck by the extreme contrasts this vision includes. As you read, compare the aspects of life that Blake explores through symbols:

- The world seen from the perspective of "innocence" versus the world seen from the perspective of "experience"
- Suffering seen from "above"—suffering one rises beyond—versus suffering one is trapped inside

Reading Strategy

Using Visuals as a Key to Meaning

When you read literature, such as these poems, that is accompanied by illustrations, **use the visuals as a key to meaning.** Look closely at the details of Blake's illustrations, and consider how they support or add to the author's words.

Vocabulary Development

vales (vālz) *n.* valleys; hollows; depressed stretches of ground (p. 640)

symmetry (sim´ ə trē) *n.* balanced form; the beauty resulting from such balance (p. 641)

aspire (ə spīr´) *v.* have high ambitions; yearn or seek after (p. 641)

The Lamb

William Blake

Background

Blake illustrated his poems with striking, integrated designs. These illustrations seem to swirl through the words and become part of their meaning. Blake claimed that many of the images he drew as illustrations were likenesses of his inner visions. They have a childlike feeling and are very different from the strict, formal styles of his time.

> Little Lamb who made thee
> Dost thou know who made thee
> Gave thee life & bid thee feed.
> By the stream & o'er the mead;
> 5   Gave thee clothing of delight,
> Softest clothing wooly bright;
> Gave thee such a tender voice,
> Making all the <u>vales</u> rejoice!
> Little Lamb who made thee
> 10   Dost thou know who made thee
>
> Little Lamb I'll tell thee,
> Little Lamb I'll tell thee!
> He is called by thy name,
> For he calls himself a Lamb:
> 15   He is meek & he is mild,
> He became a little child:
> I a child & thou a lamb,
> We are called by his name.
> Little Lamb God bless thee.
> 20   Little Lamb God bless thee.

▲ Critical Viewing
What view of nature is expressed by the style of Blake's drawing? **[Infer]**

vales (vāls) *n.* valleys; hollows; depressed stretches of ground

The Tyger

William Blake

Tyger Tyger, burning bright,
In the forests of the night;
What immortal hand or eye,
Could frame thy fearful <u>symmetry</u>?

5   In what distant deeps or skies
Burnt the fire of thine eyes!
On what wings dare he <u>aspire</u>?
What the hand, dare seize the fire?

From a manuscript of "The Tyger" by William Blake, The Metropolitan Museum of Art

01141_lt712u04blak_125%

symmetry (sim´ ə trē) *n.*
balanced form; the
beauty resulting
from such balance

aspire (ə spīr´) *v.* have
high ambitions; yearn or
seek after

◀ **Critical Viewing**
Compare and contrast
the tiger's expression
with the poem's image of
the animal. **[Compare and
Contrast]**

✔ **Reading Check**

Who does the speaker ask
the tiger about?

And what shoulder, & what art,
10　Could twist the sinews of thy heart?
And when thy heart began to beat,
What dread hand? & what dread feet?

What the hammer? what the chain,
In what furnace was thy brain?
15　What the anvil? what dread grasp,
Dare its deadly terrors clasp?

When the stars threw down their spears
And water'd heaven with their tears:
Did he smile his work to see?
20　Did he who made the Lamb make thee?

Tyger, Tyger burning bright,
In the forests of the night:
What immortal hand or eye,
Dare frame thy fearful symmetry?

Review and Assess

Thinking About the Selections

1. **(a) Recall:** What two questions does the speaker ask at the beginning of "The Lamb"? **(b) Analyze:** How does the speaker extend these questions into a description of the lamb? **(c) Interpret:** Sum up the characteristics of the lamb.

2. **(a) Recall:** How does the speaker of "The Lamb" identify himself? **(b) Infer:** What does the speaker have in common with the lamb and the lamb's creator? **(c) Deduce:** Considering the opening of the second stanza, what is an important difference between the speaker and the lamb?

3. **(a) Recall:** What question is asked in the first stanza of "The Tyger"? **(b) Interpret:** What does this question suggest about the tiger's nature? **(c) Draw Conclusions:** What does this question suggest about the tiger's creator?

4. **(a) Recall:** What two questions are asked in stanza 5 of "The Tyger"? **(b) Draw Conclusions:** What deeper question about the creator is Blake asking in this stanza?

5. **(a) Analyze:** Are the questions in the poem ever answered? **(b) Synthesize:** What does this fact suggest about Blake's purpose in writing "The Tyger"?

6. **Apply:** Do you think the world is best viewed as a lamb, as a tiger, as both, or as neither? Explain.

The Chimney Sweeper

William Blake

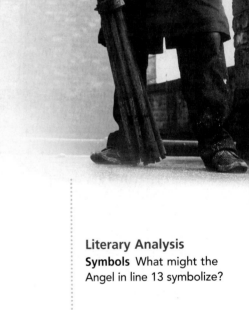

When my mother died I was very young,
And my father sold me while yet my tongue,
Could scarcely cry weep weep weep weep.
So your chimneys I sweep & in soot I sleep.

5   There's little Tom Dacre, who cried when his head
That curl'd like a lambs back, was shav'd, so I said.
Hush Tom never mind it, for when your head's bare,
You know that the soot cannot spoil your white hair.

And so he was quiet, & that very night,
10   As Tom was a sleeping he had such a sight,
That thousands of sweepers Dick, Joe, Ned & Jack
Were all of them lock'd up in coffins of black

And by came an Angel who had a bright key,
And he open'd the coffins & set them all free.
15   Then down a green plain leaping laughing they run
And wash in a river and shine in the Sun.

Then naked & white, all their bags left behind,
They rise upon clouds, and sport in the wind.
And the Angel told Tom if he'd be a good boy,
20   He'd have God for his father & never want joy.

And so Tom awoke and we rose in the dark
And got with our bags & our brushes to work.
Tho' the morning was cold, Tom was happy & warm,
So if all do their duty, they need not fear harm.

Literary Analysis
Symbols What might the Angel in line 13 symbolize?

✓ **Reading Check**

Why does Tom Dacre cry?

Infant Sorrow

William Blake

My mother groand![1] my father wept.
Into the dangerous world I leapt,
Helpless, naked, piping loud;
Like a fiend hid in a cloud.

5   Struggling in my father's hands,
Striving against my swaddling bands;
Bound and weary, I thought best
To sulk upon my mother's breast.

---

1. **groand** groaned; an example of Blake's often eccentric spelling.

Review and Assess

Thinking About the Selections

1. **(a) Recall:** How does the child in the first stanza of "The Chimney Sweeper" become a chimney sweep? **(b) Interpret:** What do these events suggest about the life of chimney sweeps?

2. **(a) Recall:** Describe Tom's dream. **(b) Interpret:** Connect the dream with the final line. **(c) Evaluate:** Does Blake stand firmly behind the lesson in the final line? Explain.

3. **(a) Recall:** In "Infant Sorrow," what are the reactions of the parents and the child to the child's birth? **(b) Interpret:** What do these reactions indicate about the moment?

4. **(a) Intepret:** Aside from the tight "swaddling bands," in what larger sense is the speaker bound? **(b) Generalize:** What general truth about human life does the infant's predicament suggest?

5. **Evaluate:** Is the infant's final reaction characteristic of the way people deal with frustration? Explain.

6. **Compare and Contrast:** How does each poem inspire readers to rethink assumptions about life and death?

Review and Assess

Literary Analysis

Symbols

1. (a) In "The Lamb," what associations does the lamb have for Blake? (b) Identify two ideas that the **symbol** of the lamb represents.
2. (a) What might the images of fire in "The Tyger" symbolize? (b) The speaker in "The Tyger" asks who made the tiger. What does the existence of the tiger imply for Blake?
3. (a) How does the symbolism of "The Lamb" add to your understanding of the second stanza of "The Chimney Sweeper"? (b) What might the "bright key" in "The Chimney Sweeper" symbolize?

Comparing Literary Works

4. Compare the ways the idea of creation, an important part of Blake's **poetic vision,** is used in "The Lamb" and "The Tyger." Consider how this idea helps to express contrary views of the world.
5. (a) Using a chart like the one shown for each poem, compare the contrasting ideas of suffering in "The Chimney Sweeper" and "Infant Sorrow." (b) Does the ending of each poem confirm or challenge these ideas? Explain.

Who Is Suffering?	Why?	Is the Suffering Unjust?	Suggested Solution	Is the Solution Adequate?

Reading Strategy

Using Visuals as a Key to Meaning

6. (a) **Using visuals as a key,** explain in what way the mood of the illustration for "The Lamb" relates to the poem. (b) Compare Blake's picture of a tiger to the tiger in the poem.
7. In general, do illustrations enhance your understanding and enjoyment of a literary work? Why or why not?

Extend Understanding

8. **World Events Connection:** "The Chimney Sweeper" addresses the issue of child labor. In what form does the problem exist today?

Quick Review

Symbols are words, images, or ideas that represent something else, such as an emotion or an abstract concept.

A poet's **poetic vision** is a view of the world, shaped by specific and sometimes opposed traditions, problems, experiences, and values.

When a literary work is accompanied by illustrations, **use the visuals as a key to meaning** by comparing details in the illustrations with details in the text.

 Take It to the Net
www.phschool.com
Take the interactive self-test online to check your understanding of these selections.

Integrate Language Skills

Vocabulary Development Lesson

Word Analysis: Latin Root *-spir-*

In "The Tyger," Blake uses the word *aspire*, meaning "to yearn or seek after." *Aspire* contains the Latin root *-spir-*, meaning "breath" or "life." When you aspire to something, you "live for it." Many scientific words that have to do with breathing contain the root *-spir-*. Look up the meaning of each word below. Give a definition incorporating the meaning of *-spir-*.

1. respiration
2. respirator
3. transpiration
4. aspirate
5. spiracle
6. spirometer

Fluency: Words in Context

Use words from the vocabulary list on page 639 to replace each italicized item.

1. They traveled through *valleys* and over hills.
2. The *formal balance* of the animal's body made it look graceful and powerful.
3. The students *desire* to attend a top college.

Spelling Strategy

Both the letter *i* and the letter *y* can represent either the short *i* sound or the long *i* sound in words. Complete each word using an *i* or a *y*.

1. asp__re
2. s__mmetry
3. th__
4. s__news

Grammar and Style Lesson

Commonly Confused Words: *rise* and *raise*

Blake describes children's spirits that "rise upon clouds." **Rise** means "to go up" or "to get up." It is sometimes confused with the verb **raise,** which means "to lift or elevate." *Raise* is always followed by a direct object, a noun or pronoun that tells who or what is raised. *Rise* never takes a direct object.

I <u>rise</u> early in the morning.

He <u>raises</u> a question about the tiger.

The forms of *rise* are as follows:

rise, rose, risen

The forms of *raise* are as follows:

raise, raised, raised

Practice In your notebook, write the correct form of *rise* or *raise* to complete each sentence. Remember that *rise* never takes an object, while *raise* always does.

1. You can ___?___ your grades by studying.
2. His grade-point average ___?___ last semester.
3. We ___?___ money for our school at the silent auction.
4. I have ___?___ early every day this week.
5. Have you ever ___?___ the flag on the flagpole?

Writing Application Write a paragraph about the plight of chimney sweepers. Use forms of both *rise* and *raise* at least two times in your paragraph, choosing the correct word each time.

*W*G *Prentice Hall Writing and Grammar Connection: Chapter 25, Section 2*

Writing Lesson

Comparative Literary Analysis

"The Lamb" and "The Tyger" explore the same subject from different points of view. Write a comparative analysis exploring the connection between the view presented in each poem and the period of Blake's life in which it was written.

Prewriting Review the biographical information on page 638. Develop a thesis statement on the relationship you find between each poem and the period of Blake's life in which it was written.

Drafting Begin with an introduction that includes your thesis statement. Then, support your thesis by elaborating on your comparison of the poems and their connection to Blake's life.

Revising Review your essay, circling particularly striking details or ideas. Consider moving these details to the beginning or end of a paragraph to add emphasis.

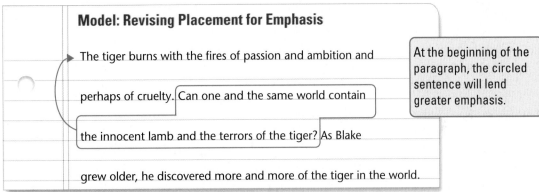

Model: Revising Placement for Emphasis

The tiger burns with the fires of passion and ambition and perhaps of cruelty. Can one and the same world contain the innocent lamb and the terrors of the tiger? As Blake grew older, he discovered more and more of the tiger in the world.

> At the beginning of the paragraph, the circled sentence will lend greater emphasis.

WG *Prentice Hall Writing and Grammar Connection: Chapter 14, Section 4*

Extension Activities

Listening and Speaking A number of composers have set Blake's poems to music. Follow their example, and prepare a **musical reading** of Blake's poetry.

1. Choose one or two poems to set to music. Read each poem aloud, analyzing the mood.
2. Find music that creates a mood similar to that expressed in each poem.

Present your reading, introducing the piece by explaining your choice of music.

Research and Technology Choose a product, and generate an **advertisement** for it. Center your advertisement on a single visual symbol, like Blake's Tyger, that represents one or more of the attributes you wish your audience to associate with the product. Use a word-processing program to lay out your final ad.

 **Take It to the Net** www.phschool.com

Go online for an additional research activity using the Internet.

Prepare to Read

Introduction to *Frankenstein*

Mary Wollstonecraft Shelley (1797–1851)

Perhaps you have sat around on a rainy day with your friends exchanging thrilling "tales of terror." The classic Gothic novel *Frankenstein* was born from just such an entertainment. One day in 1816, Mary Shelley, her husband (the poet Percy Bysshe Shelley), the poet Lord Byron, and another friend challenged one another to write ghost stories. Mary Shelley's contribution, a horrific tale of the creation of a monster, eventually became the full-length novel *Frankenstein*.

When *Frankenstein* was first published in 1818, it was praised by the novelist Sir Walter Scott as an "extraordinary tale" in which the author revealed "uncommon powers of poetic imagination." Since then, *Frankenstein* has thrilled countless readers and has been interpreted and reinterpreted by generations of filmmakers.

Literary and Political Legacy Writing was in Mary Shelley's blood: Her mother, Mary Wollstonecraft Godwin (who died at Mary's birth), wrote one of the first feminist books ever published, *A Vindication of the Rights of Woman* (1792). Her father, William Godwin, was a leading reformer, author, and political philosopher who attracted a following of gifted thinkers and disciples. As a child, Mary Shelley knew some of the most famous writers of the day, including the poet Samuel Taylor Coleridge and the essayist Charles Lamb.

Exile From Her Father's House Four years after his wife's death, Godwin married a widow, Mary Jane Clairmont, whom his daughter grew to resent bitterly. Although Mary Shelley adored her father, it was agreed that to ease the situation in the tense household, the girl, now fourteen would go to live in Dundee, Scotland, in the home of William Baxter, her father's friend. After two years in Scotland, she returned to her father's home in London.

Love and Loss Upon her return, Mary Shelley (then still named Godwin) met her future husband, Percy Bysshe Shelley. Shelley was a radical young poet who had become William Godwin's admirer after reading his book *Political Justice*. Mary Godwin, only sixteen, fell in love with her father's follower. The two ran away together to the continent and later married.

Eventually, the couple settled in Italy, where they lived blissfully for an all-too-short time. (Their great friend, Lord Byron, also lived in Italy at the time.) Within a few years, the Shelleys suffered the death of two of their children. Then, tragedy struck again. In 1822, only eight years after Mary Shelley had first met him, Percy Shelley drowned, leaving the twenty-four-year-old Mary and their two-year-old son penniless.

A Career of Her Own After Percy's death, Mary returned to England, where she continued writing to support herself and her son. She produced other novels, including: *Valperga* (1823) and *The Fortunes of Perkin Warbeck* (1830), which are historical works; *The Last Man* (1826), a tale of a great plague that destroys the human race; the autobiographical *Lodore* (1835); and *Falkner* (1837), a mystery tale. *The Last Man* is believed by many to be her best work, although she is usually remembered for *Frankenstein*.

A Lasting Legacy At the age of forty-eight, Mary Shelley became an invalid. She died six years later of a brain tumor. It is ironic that Shelley, author of a work warning of the dangers of technology, died in the opening year of The Great Exhibition, a fair celebrating technological progress. In *Frankenstein*, Shelley dramatically questioned the cost of technology to the human soul—a theme writers continue to explore today.

Preview

Connecting to the Literature

When Mary Shelley heard speculations about where the science of her time was going, she could not sleep—her mind was filled with visions. With these imaginings, Mary Shelley tapped into deep fears of technology and ensured the success of her novel *Frankenstein.*

Literary Analysis

The Gothic Tradition

The novel *Frankenstein* is a classic example of **Gothic literature,** a form of literature in which events take the reader from the reasoned order of the everyday world into the dark and dreadful world of the supernatural. Gothic literature, popular in the late eighteenth and early nineteenth centuries, is set in dark, mysterious castles, dark towers, eerie monasteries with underground passages, or other places with a disquieting, mysterious atmosphere. As you read, note Gothic characteristics of Shelley's writing.

Connecting Literary Elements

In a Gothic novel, the "spell" of reason is broken as the characters plunge deeper into the supernatural. The popularity of this form in the late 1700s was part of the new **Romantic Movement** in literature. The Romantics rejected the idea that reason could explain everything and pledged their faith in the powers of nature and the imagination. For the Romantics, the imagination, unlike reason, had these traits:

- It was a creative force comparable to that of nature.
- It was the fundamental source of morality and truth, enabling people to sympathize with others and to picture the world.

As you read, notice how Shelley's account of the creative process reflects the high value the Romantics placed on the imagination.

Reading Strategy

Predicting

Involved readers naturally try to **predict,** or make reasoned guesses about, what will happen next in a literary work. As you read, use a chart like the one shown to make, check, and, if necessary, revise predictions.

Vocabulary Development

appendage (ə pen´ dij) *n.* something added on (p. 651)

ungenial (un jē´ nyəl) *adj.* disagreeable; characterized by bad weather (p. 651)

acceded (ak sēd´ id) *v.* yielded (to); agreed (p. 652)

platitude (plat´ ə tood´) *n.* statement lacking originality (p. 652)

phantasm (fan´ taz´ əm) *n.* supernatural form or shape; ghost; figment of the imagination (p. 653)

incitement (in sīt´ mənt) *n.* act of urging; encouragement (p. 654)

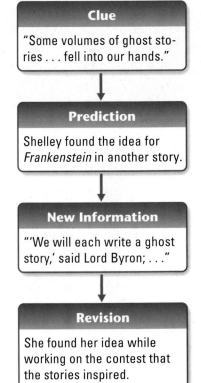

Clue

"Some volumes of ghost stories . . . fell into our hands."

↓

Prediction

Shelley found the idea for *Frankenstein* in another story.

↓

New Information

"'We will each write a ghost story,' said Lord Byron; . . ."

↓

Revision

She found her idea while working on the contest that the stories inspired.

Introduction to
Frankenstein

Mary Wollstonecraft Shelley

Background

In Greek mythology, Prometheus was one of the Titans—a race of giants who were said to have existed before humans and who engaged the gods in battle. Later myths say Prometheus created the first human beings. During the Romantic Era, Prometheus drew renewed attention. Percy Bysshe Shelley wrote a verse play about Prometheus entitled *Prometheus Unbound.* The complete title of Mary Shelley's novel about a doctor who attempts to create a man is *Frankenstein, or the Modern Prometheus.*

A View of Chamonix and Mt. Blanc, Julius Schnorr von Carolsfeld, Austrian Gallery, Vienna

The Publishers of the Standard Novels, in selecting *Frankenstein* for one of their series, expressed a wish that I should furnish them with some account of the origin of the story. I am the more willing to comply, because I shall thus give a general answer to the question, so very frequently asked me: "How I, then a young girl, came to think of, and to dilate upon, so very hideous an idea?" It is true that I am very averse to bringing myself forward in print; but as my account will only appear as an appendage to a former production, and as it will be confined to such topics as have connection with my authorship alone, I can scarcely accuse myself of a personal intrusion. . . .

In the summer of 1816, we[1] visited Switzerland, and became the neighbors of Lord Byron. At first we spent our pleasant hours on the lake or wandering on its shores; and Lord Byron, who was writing the third canto of *Childe Harold*, was the only one among us who put his thoughts upon paper. These, as he brought them successively to us, clothed in all the light and harmony of poetry, seemed to stamp as divine the glories of heaven and earth, whose influences we partook with him.

But it proved a wet, ungenial summer, and incessant rain often confined us for days to the house. Some volumes of ghost stories, translated from the German into French,[2] fell into our hands. There was "The History of the Inconstant Lover,"[3] who, when he thought to clasp the bride to whom he had pledged his vows, found himself in

1. **we** Mary Shelley, her husband Percy Bysshe Shelley, and their two children.
2. **volumes . . . French** *Fantasmagoriana,* or *Collected Stories of Apparitions of Specters, Ghosts, Phantoms, Etc.,* published anonymously in 1812.
3. **"The History . . . Lover"** The true name of the story is "The Dead Fiancée."

◀ **Critical Viewing**
Based on the second paragraph of her essay, do you think Shelly might have liked this painting? Why?

appendage (ə pen´ dij) *n.* something added on

ungenial (un jēn´ yəl) *adj.* disagreeable; characterized by bad weather

**Reading Check**
What has the author set out to explain?

the arms of the pale ghost of her whom he had deserted. There was the tale of the sinful founder of his race,[4] whose miserable doom it was to bestow the kiss of death on all the younger sons of his fated house, just when they reached the age of promise. His gigantic, shadowy form, clothed like the ghost in Hamlet, in complete armor but with the beaver[5] up, was seen at midnight, by the moon's fitful beams, to advance slowly along the gloomy avenue. The shape was lost beneath the shadow of the castle walls; but soon a gate swung back, a step was heard, the door of the chamber opened, and he advanced to the couch of the blooming youths, cradled in healthy sleep. Eternal sorrow sat upon his face as he bent down and kissed the foreheads of the boys, who from that hour withered like flowers snapped upon the stalk. I have not seen these stories since then, but their incidents are as fresh in my mind as if I had read them yesterday.

"We will each write a ghost story," said Lord Byron; and his proposition was <u>acceded</u> to. There were four of us.[6] The noble author began a tale, a fragment of which he printed at the end of his poem of Mazeppa. Shelley, more apt to embody ideas and sentiments in the radiance of brilliant imagery, and in the music of the most melodious verse that adorns our language, than to invent the machinery of a story, commenced one founded on the experiences of his early life. Poor Polidori had some terrible idea about a skull-headed lady, who was so punished for peeping through a keyhole—what to see I forget—something very shocking and wrong of course; but when she was reduced to a worse condition than the renowned Tom of Coventry,[7] he did not know what to do with her, and was obliged to despatch her to the tomb of the Capulets,[8] the only place for which she was fitted. The illustrious poets also, annoyed by the <u>platitude</u> of prose, speedily relinquished their uncongenial task.

I busied myself to *think of a story*—a story to rival those which had excited us to this task. One which would speak to the mysterious fears of our nature and awaken thrilling horror—one to make the reader dread to look round, to curdle the blood, and quicken the beatings of the heart. If I did not accomplish these things, my ghost story would be unworthy of its name. I thought and pondered—vainly. I felt that blank incapability of invention which is the greatest misery of authorship, when dull Nothing replies to our anxious invocations. *Have you thought of a story?* I was asked each morning, and each morning I was forced to reply with a mortifying negative. . . .

Many and long were the conversations between Lord Byron and Shelley, to which I was a devout but nearly silent listener. During one of these, various philosophical doctrines were discussed, and among

---

Literary Analysis
The Gothic Tradition
What elements of the Gothic tradition are incorporated in the image of a shape "lost beneath the shadow of the castle walls"?

acceded (ak sēd´ id) *v.* yielded (to); agreed

platitude (plat´ ə tōōd´) *n.* statement lacking originality

Reading Strategy
Predicting By what means do you think Shelley will find a story idea?

---

4. **the tale . . . race** "Family Portraits."
5. **beaver** hinged piece of armor that covers the face.
6. **four of us** Byron, the two Shelleys, and John William Polidori, Byron's physician.
7. **Tom of Coventry** "Peeping Tom" who, according to legend, was struck blind for looking at Lady Godiva as she rode naked through Coventry.
8. **tomb of the Capulets** the place where Romeo and Juliet died.

others the nature of the principle of life and whether there was any probability of its ever being discovered and communicated. They talked of the experiments of Dr. Darwin* (I speak not of what the Doctor really did or said that he did, but, as more to my purpose, of what was then spoken of as having been done by him), who preserved a piece of vermicelli in a glass case till by some extraordinary means it began to move with voluntary motion. Not thus, after all, would life be given. Perhaps a corpse would be reanimated: galvanism[9] had given token of such things. Perhaps the component parts of a creature might be manufactured, brought together, and endued with vital warmth.

Night waned upon this talk, and even the witching hour had gone by, before we retired to rest. When I placed my head on my pillow, I did not sleep, nor could I be said to think. My imagination, unbidden, possessed and guided me, gifting the successive images that arose in my mind with a vividness far beyond the usual bounds of reverie. I saw—with shut eyes but acute mental vision—I saw the pale student of unhallowed arts kneeling beside the thing he had put together. I saw the hideous <u>phantasm</u> of a man stretched out, and then, on the working of some powerful engine, show signs of life and stir with an uneasy, half vital motion. Frightful must it be, for supremely frightful would be the effect of any human endeavor to mock the stupendous mechanism of the Creator of the world. His success would terrify the artist; he would rush away from his odious handiwork, horror-stricken. He would hope that, left to itself, the slight spark of life which he had communicated would fade; that this thing, which had received such imperfect animation, would subside into dead matter; and he might sleep in the belief that the silence of the grave would quench forever the transient existence of the hideous corpse which he had looked upon as the cradle of life. He sleeps; but he is awakened; he opens his eyes; behold the horrid thing stands at his bedside, opening his curtains, and looking on him with yellow, watery, but speculative eyes.

I opened mine in terror. The idea so possessed my mind, that a thrill of fear ran through me, and I wished to exchange the ghastly image of my fancy for the realities around. I see them still: the very room, the dark parquet,[10] the closed shutters, with the moonlight struggling through, and the sense I had that the glassy lake and white high Alps were beyond. I could not so easily get rid of my hideous phantom: still it haunted me. I must try to think of something else. I recurred to my ghost story—my tiresome unlucky

---

9. **galvanism** use of electric current to induce twitching in dead muscles.
10. **parquet** (pär kā´) flooring made of wooden pieces arranged in a pattern.

Literature in context Science Connection

♦ *The Romantics and Science*

As Shelley's Introduction suggests, the Romantics had a two-sided relationship with science. They rejected the eighteenth-century view that the universe could be explained as if it were a giant machine. Fascinated by nature, however, they eagerly read about the new sciences of life. The "Dr. Darwin" referred to by Shelley is the physician, botanist, and poet Erasmus Darwin (1731–1802), grandfather of the Charles Darwin who pioneered the theory of evolution. Erasmus Darwin wrote, "Organic forms with chemic changes strive, / Live but to die, and die but to revive." This sentiment fit well with the Romantic vision of nature as a productive power that is eternally changing, like the larva that have turned into butterflies in the photograph.

phantasm (fan´ taz´ əm) *n.* supernatural form or shape; ghost; figment of the imagination

✔ **Reading Check**

That night, what does Mary Shelley imagine?

ghost story! O! if I could only contrive one which would frighten my reader as I myself had been frightened that night!

Swift as light and as cheering was the idea that broke in upon me. "I have found it! What terrified me will terrify others, and I need only describe the specter which had haunted my midnight pillow." On the morrow I announced that I had *thought of a story.* I began that day with the words, *It was on a dreary night of November,* making only a transcript of the grim terrors of my waking dream.

At first I thought but of a few pages—of a short tale—but Shelley urged me to develop the idea at greater length. I certainly did not owe the suggestion of one incident, nor scarcely of one train of feeling, to my husband, and yet but for his <u>incitement</u>, it would never have taken the form in which it was presented to the world. From this declaration I must except the preface. As far as I can recollect, it was entirely written by him.

And now, once again, I bid my hideous progeny go forth and prosper. I have an affection for it, for it was the offspring of happy days, when death and grief were but words, which found no true echo in my heart. Its several pages speak of many a walk, many a drive, and many a conversation, when I was not alone; and my companion was one who, in this world, I shall never see more. But this is for myself: my readers have nothing to do with these associations.

incitement (in sīt´ mənt) *n.* act of urging; encouragement

Review and Assess

Thinking About the Selection

1. **Respond:** Do you share Shelley's interest in ghost stories? Why or why not?

2. **(a) Recall:** What special set of circumstances inspired the four friends to attempt to write ghost stories?
   (b) Compare and Contrast: Compare the difficulty Shelley has with the reason her companions give up their efforts.

3. **(a) Recall:** What gives Shelley her idea for a story?
   (b) Connect: What does the intensity of her vision suggest about her reaction to Dr. Darwin's experiments?

4. **(a) Compare and Contrast:** Why is the relationship between student and monster in her vision both similar to and different from the relationship between the Creator and humanity?
   (b) Draw Conclusions: Why might the similarities of these relationships be "supremely frightful"?

5. **Synthesize:** What does the selection reveal about the relationship between Shelley and her husband?

6. **Make a Judgment:** In your opinion, has later history borne out Shelley's dread of science? Explain.

Review and Assess

Literary Analysis

The Gothic Tradition

1. Which characteristics of the **Gothic tradition**—horror, supernatural elements, medieval elements—do the ghost stories described by Shelley in her third paragraph share? List examples in a chart like the one shown.

Gothic Characteristic	Example in Shelley

2. In which passage does Shelley describe a connection between the world of reason and a terrifying supernatural world?

3. Explain why Shelley's idea for *Frankenstein* fits the Gothic tradition.

4. Compare the ingredients of Gothic tales with those used in current horror movies and books.

Connecting Literary Elements

5. (a) How does Shelley respond to the discussion of Darwin's experiments? (b) How does her experience echo the idea of the **Romantic imagination**—a power similar to nature's creative force?

6. (a) Contrast Shelley's first efforts to find an idea with her final inspiration. (b) How does this contrast reflect the Romantic contrast between reason and imagination?

7. What "truth" does Shelley's imagined vision suggest about the dangerous possibilities of science?

Reading Strategy

Predicting

8. Explain whether you were able to **predict** how Shelley would be affected by the discussion of Darwin's experiments.

9. Based on clues in the Introduction, predict the theme of *Frankenstein*. Explain your reasoning.

Extend Understanding

10. **Science Connection:** What scientific experiments today are comparable to Darwin's? Explain, indicating whether you find such experiments as horrifying as Shelley found Darwin's to be.

Integrate Language Skills

Vocabulary Development Lesson

Related Words: *phantasm* and *fantasy*

Shelley uses the word *phantasm*, meaning "supernatural form or shape" or "figment of the imagination," to describe her monster. *Phantasm* and the more familiar word *fantasy* are related. Based on this connection, define the following terms, explaining how each relates to the word *fantasy*.

1. phantom   2. phantasmagoric

Spelling Strategy

In most words ending with the sound *seed*, the sound is spelled *cede*, as in *accede*. Three English words end in *ceed: exceed, proceed,* and *succeed*. In your notebook, fill in the letters that spell the *seed* sound in the following words.

1. con____   2. pro____   3. pre____

Concept Development: Synonyms

For each numbered word, write the letter of the word that is closest to it in meaning.

1. appendage: (a) offspring, (b) fragment, (c) addition
2. ungenial: (a) friendly, (b) cruel, (c) disagreeable
3. acceded: (a) defied, (b) broken, (c) agreed
4. platitude: (a) innovation, (b) cliché, (c) statement
5. phantasm: (a) reality, (b) illusion, (c) creation
6. incitement: (a) deterrent, (b) apparition, (c) motivation

Grammar and Style Lesson

Past Participial Phrases

Shelley frequently uses past participial phrases. A **past participial phrase** includes a past participle —a verbal form usually ending in *-ed*—plus its modifiers and complements. The phrase functions as an adjective and modifies a noun or pronoun.

In this example, the underlined past participial phrase modifies *stories*:

Some volumes of ghost stories, <u>translated from the German into French</u>, fell into our hands.

By using past participial phrases, writers can convey much information in a single sentence. Instead of writing a series of short sentences, they can combine ideas in a single sentence to vary sentence length.

Practice Identify the participial phrase in each passage. Then, indicate the word it modifies.

1. These, as he brought them successively to us, clothed in all the light . . . of poetry, . . .
2. . . . he advanced to the couch of the blooming youths, cradled in healthy sleep.
3. His gigantic, shadowy form, clothed like the ghost in *Hamlet*, in complete armor. . . .
4. The illustrious poets also, annoyed by the platitude of prose, . . .
5. He would hope that, left to itself, the slight spark of life which he had communicated would fade; . . .

Writing Application Using at least two past participial phrases, describe Shelley's vision.

W͟G Prentice Hall Writing and Grammar Connection: Chapter 19, Section 2

Writing Lesson

Essay Comparing and Contrasting Impressions of a Work

You've probably seen the story of Dr. Frankenstein and his monster depicted in movies. Write an essay in which you compare the impressions you had of *Frankenstein* before you read Shelley's Introduction with your impressions afterwards.

Prewriting To gather and organize details, use a chart like the one shown. First, list points you want to compare. Then, note your impressions of each before and after reading Shelley's Introduction.

Model: Organizing Details

Impressions: The Monster	
Before Reading	**After Reading**
Scary and strong, but gentle inside	

Drafting Decide how to present the details in your chart. One possibility is to describe all of your impressions before reading and then to describe all of your impressions after reading. Another approach is to use one paragraph to compare and contrast your impressions of the monster and another to compare and contrast your impressions of Dr. Frankenstein.

Revising Reread the body of your essay to make sure its organization is logical. Then, be sure your closing paragraph summarizes how your impressions did or did not change.

 Prentice Hall Writing and Grammar Connection: Chapter 9, Section 3

Extension Activities

Listening and Speaking Stories such as *Frankenstein* were once broadcast on radio. In a group, re-create a horror story as a **radio play.**

1. Collaborate on a script.
2. Select effective background music and sound effects.
3. Choose actors and rehearse the play.

Tape-record your performance, and play it for the class. **[Group Activity]**

Research and Technology Mary Shelley was horrified at the idea of a scientist reconstituting life. Today, animals are cloned in laboratories. Prepare a **science report** on the process of cloning. Add graphics to your word-processed report to help explain the process.

 **Take It to the Net**   www.phschool.com

Go online for an additional research activity using the Internet.

CONNECTIONS
Literature Around the World
Fantasy and Reality

A Gothic Explosion Although the Romantic Movement led writers to focus on the experience of the common people, it also inspired them to explore more fantastic realms. The popularity of Gothic stories like Mary Shelley's *Frankenstein* reached beyond England into other cultures and countries. One of the masters of the Gothic tradition is the American writer Edgar Allan Poe.

The Oval Portrait

EDGAR ALLAN POE

The chateau into which my valet had ventured to make forcible entrance, rather than permit me, in my desperately wounded condition, to pass a night in the open air, was one of those piles of commingled gloom and grandeur which have so long frowned among the Apennines,[1] not less in fact than in the fancy of Mrs. Radcliffe.[2] To all appearance it had been temporarily and very lately abandoned. We established ourselves in one of the smallest and least sumptuously furnished apartments. It lay in a remote turret of the building. Its decorations were rich, yet tattered and antique. Its walls were hung with tapestry and bedecked with manifold and multiform armorial trophies, together with an unusually great number of very spirited modern paintings in frames of rich golden arabesque.[3] In these paintings, which depended from the walls not only in their main surfaces, but in very many nooks which the bizarre architecture of the chateau rendered necessary—in these paintings my incipient delirium, perhaps, had caused me to take deep interest; so that I bade Pedro to close the heavy shutters of the room—since it was already night—to light the tongues of a tall candelabrum which stood by the head of my bed—and to throw open far and wide the fringed curtains of black velvet which enveloped the bed itself. I wished all this done that I might resign myself, if not to sleep, at least alternately to the contemplation of these pictures, and the perusal of a small volume which had been found upon the pillow, and which purported to criticize and describe them.

Long—long I read—and devoutly, devotedly I gazed. Rapidly and gloriously the hours flew by, and the deep midnight came. The position of the candelabrum displeased me, and outreaching my hand with

Thematic Connection
What details make the setting seem fantastic?

---

1. **Appennines** (ap´ ə nīnz) mountain range located in Italy.
2. **Mrs. Radcliffe** Ann Radcliffe (1764–1823), English novelist.
3. **arabesque** (ar´ ə besk´) complex and elaborate design.

difficulty, rather than disturb my slumbering valet, I placed it so as to throw its rays more fully upon the book.

But the action produced an effect altogether unanticipated. The rays of the numerous candles (for there were many) now fell within a niche of the room which had hitherto been thrown into deep shade by one of the bed-posts. I thus saw in vivid light a picture all unnoticed before. It was the portrait of a young girl just ripening into womanhood. I glanced at the painting hurriedly, and then closed my eyes. Why I did this was not at first apparent even to my own perception. But while my lids remained thus shut, I ran over in mind my reason for so shutting them. It was an impulsive movement to gain time for thought—to make sure that my vision had not deceived me—to calm and subdue my fancy for a more sober and more certain gaze. In a very few moments I again looked fixedly at the painting.

That I now saw aright I could not and would not doubt; for the first flashing of the candles upon that canvas had seemed to dissipate the dreamy stupor which was stealing over my senses, and to startle me at once into waking life.

The portrait, I have already said, was that of a young girl. It was a mere head and shoulders, done in what is technically termed a vignette[4] manner; much in the style of the favorite heads of Sully.[5] The arms, the bosom and even the ends of the radiant hair, melted imperceptibly into the vague yet deep shadow which formed the back-ground of the whole. The frame was oval, richly gilded and filigreed in *Moresque*.[6] As a thing of art nothing could be more admirable than the painting itself. But it could have been neither the execution of the work, nor the immortal beauty of the countenance, which had so suddenly and so vehemently moved me. Least of all, could it have been that my fancy, shaken from its half slumber, had mistaken the head for that of a living person. I saw at once that the peculiarities of the design, of the *vignetting*, and of the frame, must have instantly dispelled such idea—must have prevented even its momentary entertainment. Thinking earnestly upon these points, I remained, for an hour perhaps, half sitting, half reclining, with my vision riveted upon the portrait. At length, satisfied with the true secret of its effect, I fell back within the bed. I had found the spell of the picture in an absolute *life-likeliness* of expression, which at first startled, finally confounded, subdued and appalled me. With deep and reverent awe I replaced the candelabrum in its former position. The cause of my deep agitation being thus shut from view, I sought eagerly the volume which discussed the paintings and their histories. Turning to the number which designated the oval portrait, I there read the vague and quaint words which follow:

Elizabeth Beale Bordley, Gilbert Stuart, Courtesy of the Museum of American Art of the Pennsylvania Academy of the Fine Arts, Philadelphia, Bequest of Elizabeth Mifflin

▲ **Critical Viewing**
Does this portrait, like the one in the story, capture "Life" itself? Explain.
[Connect]

**Reading Check**

What does the narrator find so disturbing about the portrait?

---

4. **vignette** (vin yet´) *n.* picture or photograph with no definite border.
5. **Sully** Thomas Sully (1783–1872), American painter born in England.
6. **Moresque** (mô resk´) decoration characterized by intricate tracery and bright colors.

"She was a maiden of rarest beauty, and not more lovely than full of glee. And evil was the hour when she saw, and loved, and wedded the painter. He, passionate, studious, austere, and having already a bride in his Art; she a maiden of rarest beauty, and not more lovely than full of glee: all light and smiles, and frolicksome as the young fawn: loving and cherishing all things: hating only the Art which was her rival: dreading only the pallet and brushes and other untoward instruments which deprived her of the countenance of her lover. It was thus a terrible thing for this lady to hear the painter speak of his desire to portray even his young bride. But she was humble and obedient, and sat meekly for many weeks in the dark high turret-chamber where the light dripped upon the pale canvas only from overhead. But he, the painter, took glory in his work, which went on from hour to hour and from day to day. And he was a passionate, and wild and moody man, who became lost in reveries; so that he would not see that the light which fell so ghastlily in that lone turret withered the health and the spirits of his bride, who pined visibly to all but him. Yet she smiled on and still on, uncomplainingly, because she saw that the painter, (who had high renown), took a fervid and burning pleasure in his task, and wrought day and night to depict her who so loved him, yet who grew daily more dispirited and weak. And in sooth some who beheld the portrait spoke of its resemblance in low words, as of a mighty marvel, and a proof not less of the power of the painter than of his deep love for her whom he depicted so surpassingly well. But at length, as the labor drew nearer to its conclusion, there were admitted none into the turret; for the painter had grown wild with the ardor of his work, and turned his eyes from the canvas rarely, even to regard the countenance of his wife. And he *would* not see that the tints which he spread upon the canvas were drawn from the cheeks of her who sat beside him. And when many weeks had passed, and but little remained to do, save one brush upon the mouth and one tint upon the eye, the spirit of the lady again flickered up as the flame within the socket of the lamp. And then the brush was given, and then the tint was placed; and, for one moment, the painter stood entranced before the work which he had wrought; but in the next, while he yet gazed, he grew tremulous and very pallid, and aghast, and crying with a loud voice, 'This is indeed *Life* itself!' turned suddenly to regard his beloved:—*She was dead!*"

Connecting Literature Around the World

1. In what way do both this tale and Shelley's *Frankenstein* address the theme of excessive ambition?
2. (a) Do any of the poems in this section try to "capture" life as the artist in Poe's story does? Explain. (b) Might any of the poems be as disturbing to a reader as the "life-like" portrait is to Poe's narrator? Explain.

Edgar Allan Poe

(1809–1849)

Poe's real-life troubles must have inspired his dark imaginings. An orphan before he was three years old, he was taken in by the Allans, a prosperous family in Richmond, Virginia. Poe quarreled with his foster father, John Allan, and was eventually disowned.

Poe's writing career was a mixture of literary success and financial failure. He won recognition as a poet, critic, and short-story writer while earning a meager living as a magazine editor in Richmond, Philadelphia, and New York City.

PART 2

Focus on Literary Forms:
Lyric Poetry

The Wanderer over the Sea of Clouds,
Caspar David Friedrich, Kunsthalle, Hamburg

Lyric poems express a writer's thoughts and feelings. The ancient Greeks, who set this type of poem to lyre music, gave the lyric its name. Romantic poets of the nineteenth century devoted themselves to lyric poetry, "singing" about nature and society's injustices.

Prepare to Read

Poetry of William Wordsworth

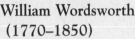

William Wordsworth (1770–1850)

Writing poetry may seem like a quiet, meditative activity, a matter of words, not deeds—hardly the scene of upheavals and crises. Yet in 1798, a revolution shook the world of poetry. In that year, William Wordsworth took generations of assumptions about the proper style, words, and subject matter for a poem and calmly put them aside.

A Revolution in Poetry In the 1802 Preface to *Lyrical Ballads*, a collection of Wordworth's and Samuel Taylor Coleridge's works, Wordsworth announced, "There will . . . be found in these volumes little of what is usually called poetic diction; as much pains has been taken to avoid it as is ordinarily taken to produce it; . . ."

Gone were the flowery language, the wittily crafted figures of speech, the effusive praise, and the tragic complaints that had defined poetry in the past. In their place, Wordsworth offered an intensified presentation of ordinary life and nature using common language. Wordsworth's revolution took literature in a dramatic new direction, building the movement known as Romanticism.

The Lake District Wordsworth's revolution was rooted in his early love for nature. Born in the beautiful Lake District of England, Wordsworth spent his youth roaming the countryside. In later years, too, he found peace and reassurance in the gentle hills and serene lakes of this landscape. This region of northwestern England became the cradle of the Romantic Movement, inspiring many personal commentaries and poetic tributes.

Revolution and Love By the time Wordsworth was thirteen, both his parents had died. Nonetheless, he was able to pursue his education and entered Cambridge University in 1787. After graduating, he traveled through Europe, spending considerable time in France. There, he embraced the ideals of the newly born French Revolution—ideals that stressed social justice and individual rights. Growing emotionally as well as intellectually, Wordsworth fell in love with Annette Vallon.

Disillusionment and Crisis Wordsworth's involvement with the Revolution and with Vallon ended abruptly when lack of funds and family pressure forced him to return home. Two months later, in 1793, England declared war on France, and the Revolution became increasingly violent. His dreams of liberty betrayed, Wordsworth lapsed into a depression. His beloved sister, Dorothy, and fellow poet Samuel Taylor Coleridge helped him through this crisis.

From Politics to Art In 1798, Wordsworth published *Lyrical Ballads* with Coleridge. With the publication of this work, Wordsworth translated his revolutionary hopes from politics to literature. His democratic ideals appeared in his use of the language of ordinary people rather than specialized "poetic" words. The "ballads" showed how the lives and experiences of ordinary people, when properly viewed, were really *extra*ordinary.

Poetry and Autobiography Critics agree that Wordsworth's greatest work is his autobiography in poetry, *The Prelude*. Wordsworth completed a version of this poem in 1799, which he expanded considerably by 1805. As he wrote to a friend, *The Prelude* told the story of "the growth of my own mind." The poem is not always factually accurate, but, as noted by critic Stephen Gill, in its combination of "satire and narrative, description and meditation, the visionary and the deliberately banal," it was unique.

Eventually, Wordsworth's radical new approach to poetry gained acceptance, while he himself grew more conservative in his politics. A new generation of Romantics, more radical than Wordsworth and Coleridge, arose. Wordsworth's position was secure, however: We remember him as the father of English Romanticism.

Preview

Connecting to the Literature

Rock music and recycling belong to modern America, not eighteenth-century England. Yet Wordsworth's poems show a resemblance to rock's celebration of individual feeling and to environmentalists' respect for nature.

Literary Analysis

Romanticism and the Lyric

Romanticism was a late-eighteenth-century European literary movement. While the earlier Neoclassical writers, such as Pope and Johnson, favored reason, wit, and outward elegance, the works of many Romantic poets include these elements:

- Simplicity or directness of language
- The expression of spontaneous, intensified feelings
- Profound responses to nature, in which nature appears to reflect the soul and contemplation of nature leads to a deeper awareness of self

English Romanticism began with William Wordsworth. The **lyric,** a poem in which a single speaker expresses personal emotions and observations, was particularly suited to his vision.

Comparing Literary Works

The Romantics adopted a new, freer **diction,** or choice of words. As you read, you will notice that Wordsworth's poetry favors simple words but that his work also relies heavily on abstract terms. Compare the different types of words Wordsworth chooses—whether specific and concrete like *sycamore* or abstract like *a sense sublime.* Evaluate whether he succeeds in forging a new style that appeals to the ear, heart, and mind.

Reading Strategy

Using Literary Context

Literary context is the climate of literary practices and assumptions that influence a writer. Wordsworth is one of those rare writers who brings about a change in literary context. Use a chart like the one shown to identify details and qualities in his work that were revolutionary at the time.

Literary Context: Romanticism
Celebration of Common Folk
Love of Nature
Admiration for French Revolution
Loss of Faith in Reason

Vocabulary Development

recompense (rek´ əm pens´) *n.* payment in return for something (p. 669)

roused (rouzd) *v.* stirred up (p. 672)

presumption (prē zump´ shən) *n.* audacity (p. 673)

anatomize (ə nat´ ə mīz´) *v.* to dissect in order to examine structure (p. 674)

confounded (kən found´ id) *adj.* confused; mixed together indiscriminately; bewildered (p. 674)

sordid (sôr´ did) *adj.* dirty (p. 675)

stagnant (stag´ nənt) *adj.* motionless; foul (p. 676)

A Closer Look

Poetry and Friendship in the Romantic Age

> . . . I have been on a visit to Wordsworth's at Racedown. . . .
> Wordsworth is a very great man, the only man *at all times* and *in all
> modes of excellence* I feel myself inferior. . . . (Samuel Coleridge, in a
> letter to Robert Southey, 1797)

Great art is not created in a vacuum. In ancient
Greece, great works of art and intellect were born
within communities of artists and thinkers, the result of
apprenticeship and debate. Hundreds of years later, in
the Renaissance city of Florence, Italy, artists gathered
in schools and workshops produced breathtaking
achievements in the visual arts and architecture.
In Elizabethan England, Shakespeare, spurred
on by his competition with rival playwright
Ben Jonson, reached new heights of dramatic
art. Like these earlier flowerings of creative
activity, the Romantic movement was sparked
and nurtured by social relationships. Where
apprenticeship and rivalry had urged past
artists to higher achievements, friendship was
a dominant force pushing Romantic poets to
make their breakthroughs.

England: The Lake District

London

A Paradox There is a paradox here. Of all poetry, that of the British Romantics
might seem likeliest to be the product of solitary writers. With their emphasis on
subjective responses to nature, on their own emotions, and on radical social views,
Romantic writers might seem to have had little use for society and community.

An Inspiring Friendship In fact, a strong network of friendships helped create the poetic vision of the age. The friendship between William Wordsworth
and Samuel Taylor Coleridge lies at the center of the new movement in poetry.
Their friendship was one of great intensity. Both men, of course, loved poetry,
which they discussed with enthusiasm. They were also both fierce partisans of
the French Revolution in its early days. Lovers of nature, they shared the joy of
walking in the hills of England's Lake District, where Wordsworth lived with his
sister Dorothy. Coleridge visited them frequently and at times lived nearby.

Complementary Talents When the two poets lived near enough to
each other, they met and talked every day. Wordsworth's understanding of
himself as a poet became increasingly clear to him, perhaps owing to what
he described as "the power [Coleridge] possessed of throwing out in profusion
grand, central truths from which might be evolved the most comprehensive
systems." Coleridge, a voracious reader who delved deeply into philosophy,

helped expand his friend's intellectual life. As a writer he worked very quickly, inspiring more spontaneity from the deliberately paced Wordsworth.

While Coleridge made his mark on Wordsworth, he also fell under Wordsworth's spell. Wordsworth was a great observer of nature and everyday life. He was also an astute reader. It was he who suggested that Coleridge center "The Rime of the Ancient Mariner" around a crime at sea. Friendship with Wordsworth heightened Coleridge's own poetic powers. It is no accident that his greatest poetry was written during their years of deepest friendship.

The Lake Poets Coleridge and Wordsworth were at the center of a circle of poets and writers, often referred to as the Lake Poets because of their attachment to England's Lake District and its natural beauty. The circle included Charles Lamb, Thomas de Quincey, William Hazlitt, and Robert Southey (see the chart for more information). Dorothy Wordsworth, too, was a key member of the circle. Her descriptive journals of her life and travels with her brother and Coleridge fed the imaginations of both poets, and provide a sense of the life they shared, as this quotation suggests:

> *Saturday, 4th October 1800.*—A very rainy, or rather showery and gusty, morning; for often the sun shines. . . . Coleridge came in while we were at dinner, very wet. We talked till twelve o'clock. He had sat up all the night before, writing essays for the newspapers. . . . Exceedingly delighted with the second part of [Coleridge's poem] *Christabel.*

Later Years The friendship between Wordsworth and Coleridge broke down around 1810, owing in part to Coleridge's reliance on painkillers. They were never fully reconciled. Even so, nearly twenty-five years after their break, Wordsworth would say, on the occasion of Coleridge's death, that Coleridge was "the most *wonderful* man he had ever known." This tradition of friendship was carried on by the next generation of Romantics as well, most notably in the friendship between Percy Bysshe Shelley and Lord Byron.

▲▼ **Critical Viewing** What connection can you make between the beauty of the scene in the photograph on the previous page and the information in the chart? **[Connect]**

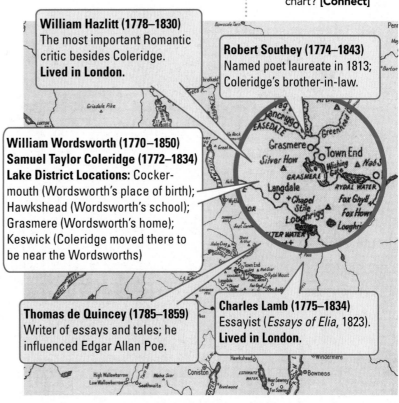

William Hazlitt (1778–1830) The most important Romantic critic besides Coleridge. **Lived in London.**

Robert Southey (1774–1843) Named poet laureate in 1813; Coleridge's brother-in-law.

William Wordsworth (1770–1850) Samuel Taylor Coleridge (1772–1834) Lake District Locations: Cockermouth (Wordsworth's place of birth); Hawkshead (Wordsworth's school); Grasmere (Wordsworth's home); Keswick (Coleridge moved there to be near the Wordsworths)

Thomas de Quincey (1785–1859) Writer of essays and tales; he influenced Edgar Allan Poe.

Charles Lamb (1775–1834) Essayist (*Essays of Elia*, 1823). **Lived in London.**

Lake District Writers and Their Visitors

Lines Composed a Few Miles Above Tintern Abbey

William Wordsworth

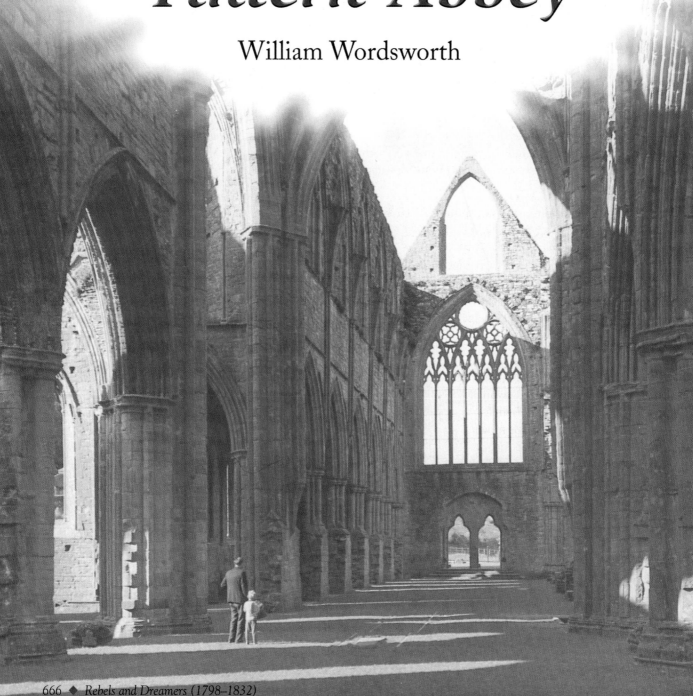

Background

This poem was written in 1798 during Wordsworth's second visit to the valley of the River Wye and the ruins of Tintern Abbey, once a great medieval church, in Wales. Wordsworth had passed through the region alone five years earlier. This time he brought his sister along to share the experience. Of this visit and the poem it inspired, Wordsworth wrote, "No poem of mine was composed under circumstances more pleasant for one to remember than this."

Five years have past; five summers, with the length
Of five long winters! and again I hear
These waters, rolling from their mountain springs
With a soft inland murmur. Once again

5 Do I behold these steep and lofty cliffs,
That on a wild secluded scene impress
Thoughts of more deep seclusion; and connect
The landscape with the quiet of the sky.
The day is come when I again repose

10 Here, under this dark sycamore, and view
These plots of cottage ground, these orchard tufts,
Which at this season, with their unripe fruits,
Are clad in one green hue, and lose themselves
'Mid groves and copses. Once again I see

15 These hedgerows, hardly hedgerows, little lines
Of sportive wood run wild: these pastoral farms,
Green to the very door; and wreaths of smoke
Sent up, in silence, from among the trees!
With some uncertain notice, as might seem

20 Of vagrant dwellers in the houseless woods,
Or of some hermit's cave, where by his fire
The hermit sits alone.
                  These beauteous forms,
Through a long absence, have not been to me
As is a landscape to a blind man's eye:

25 But oft, in lonely rooms, and 'mid the din
Of towns and cities, I have owed to them
In hours of weariness, sensations sweet,
Felt in the blood, and felt along the heart;
And passing even into my purer mind,

30 With tranquil restoration—feelings too
Of unremembered pleasure: such, perhaps,
As have no slight or trivial influence
On that best portion of a good man's life.
His little, nameless, unremembered, acts

Literary Analysis

Romanticism and the Lyric How do the sensory observations Wordsworth includes reflect what you know about Romanticism?

◀ **Critical Viewing**
What elements in this photograph help it capture awe and excitement comparable to Wordsworth's on his return to the Wye? **[Connect]**

✔ **Reading Check**

Name two sights that strike Wordsworth on his return to the Wye.

35 Of kindness and of love. Nor less, I trust,
   To them I may have owed another gift,
   Of aspect more sublime; that blessed mood,
   In which the burthen[1] of the mystery,
   In which the heavy and the weary weight
40 Of all this unintelligible world
   Is lightened—that serene and blessed mood,
   In which the affections gently lead us on—
   Until, the breath of this corporeal frame[2]
   And even the motion of our human blood
45 Almost suspended, we are laid asleep
   In body, and become a living soul;
   While with an eye made quiet by the power
   Of harmony, and the deep power of joy,
   We see into the life of things.

                          If this
50 Be but a vain belief, yet, oh! how oft—
   In darkness and amid the many shapes
   Of joyless daylight; when the fretful stir
   Unprofitable, and the fever of the world,
   Have hung upon the beatings of my heart—
55 How oft, in spirit, have I turned to thee,
   O sylvan[3] Wye! thou wanderer through the woods,
   How often has my spirit turned to thee!

            And now, with gleams of half-extinguished thought,
   With many recognitions dim and faint,
60 And somewhat of a sad perplexity,
   The picture of the mind revives again;
   While here I stand, not only with the sense
   Of present pleasure, but with pleasing thoughts
   That in this moment there is life and food
65 For future years. And so I dare to hope,
   Though changed, no doubt, from what I was when first
   I came among these hills; when like a roe[4]
   I bounded o'er the mountains, by the sides
   Of the deep rivers, and the lonely streams,
70 Wherever nature led: more like a man
   Flying from something that he dreads, than one
   Who sought the thing he loved. For nature then
   (The coarser pleasures of my boyish days,
   And their glad animal movements all gone by)
75 To me was all in all—I cannot paint

Literary Analysis
Romanticism and the Lyric How do the images in lines 40–49 reflect Romantic ideas of the relation between nature and the soul?

Reading Strategy
Using Literary Context What changing attitude about the importance of reason is reflected in Wordsworth's contrast of childhood with adulthood?

---

1. **burthen** burden.
2. **corporeal** (kôr pôr´ ē əl) **frame** body.
3. **sylvan** (sil´ vən) wooded.
4. **roe** type of deer.

What then I was. The sounding cataract
Haunted me like a passion; the tall rock,
The mountain, and the deep and gloomy wood,
Their colors and their forms, were then to me
80 An appetite; a feeling and a love,
That had no need of a remoter charm,
By thought supplied, nor any interest
Unborrowed from the eye. That time is past,
And all its aching joys are now no more,
85 And all its dizzy raptures. Not for this
Faint[5] I, nor mourn nor murmur; other gifts
Have followed; for such loss, I would believe,
Abundant <u>recompense</u>. For I have learned
To look on nature, not as in the hour
90 Of thoughtless youth; but hearing oftentimes
The still, sad music of humanity,
Nor harsh nor grating, though of ample power
To chasten and subdue. And I have felt
A presence that disturbs me with the joy
95 Of elevated thoughts; a sense sublime
Of something far more deeply interfused,
Whose dwelling is the light of setting suns,
And the round ocean and the living air,
And the blue sky, and in the mind of man;
100 A motion and a spirit, that impels
All thinking things, all objects of all thought,
And rolls through all things. Therefore am I still
A lover of the meadows and the woods
And mountains; and of all that we behold
105 From this green earth; of all the mighty world
Of eye, and ear—both what they half create,
And what perceive; well pleased to recognize
In nature and the language of the sense,
The anchor of my purest thoughts, the nurse,
110 The guide, the guardian of my heart, and soul
Of all my moral being.

                              Nor perchance,
If I were not thus taught, should I the more
Suffer[6] my genial spirits[7] to decay;
For thou art with me here upon the banks
115 Of this fair river; thou my dearest Friend,[8]
My dear, dear Friend, and in thy voice I catch
The language of my former heart, and read

---

5. **Faint** lose heart.
6. **Suffer** allow.
7. **genial spirits** creative powers.
8. **Friend** his sister Dorothy.

The British Tradition

The Evolution of the Self

On returning to the Wye, Wordsworth discovers his own deeper self in experiences of nature bound together by memory. His discovery contributed to a new, Romantic idea of the self. For the Romantics, the self was a journey of self-discovery, not a collection of personal quirks or facts. The Romantic poet set out to recover his or her deeper self through nature, memory, and lyric poetry. For the Romantics, writing a poem became an act of self-definition and discovery.

This Romantic idea of the self—always divided yet always recovering itself—inspired later works such as Tennyson's *In Memoriam, A. H. H.* Centuries later, Wordsworth's vision of the self and its journey still resonates in modern culture.

recompense (rek′ əm pens′) *n.* payment in return for something

 **Reading Check**

What natural sights inspire in Wordsworth a sense of the unity of things—of "something far more deeply interfused, . . ."?

Tintern Abbey, J. M. W. Turner, British Museum

◄ **Critical Viewing**
Compare the appreciation
of light and sky shown by
Romantic painter J.M.W.
Turner with Wordsworth's
descriptions in the poem.
[Connect]

My former pleasures in the shooting lights
Of thy wild eyes. Oh! yet a little while
120 May I behold in thee what I was once,
My dear, dear Sister! and this prayer I make
Knowing that Nature never did betray
The heart that loved her; 'tis her privilege,
Through all the years of this our life, to lead
125 From joy to joy; for she can so inform
The mind that is within us, so impress
With quietness and beauty, and so feed
With lofty thoughts, that neither evil tongues,
Rash judgments, nor the sneers of selfish men,
130 Nor greetings where no kindness is, nor all
The dreary intercourse of daily life,
Shall e'er prevail against us, or disturb
Our cheerful faith, that all which we behold
Is full of blessings. Therefore let the moon
135 Shine on thee in thy solitary walk;
And let the misty mountain winds be free
To blow against thee: and, in after years,
When these wild ecstasies shall be matured

Reading Strategy
Using Literary Context
Many Neoclassical poets
personified nature in a
conventional way as a
goddess. What makes
Wordsworth's personifi-
cation in lines 122–134
more personal?

Into a sober pleasure; when thy mind
140 Shall be a mansion for all lovely forms,
Thy memory be as a dwelling place
For all sweet sound and harmonies; oh! then,
If solitude, or fear, or pain, or grief,
Should be thy portion, with what healing thoughts
145 Of tender joy wilt thou remember me,
And these my exhortations! Nor, perchance—
If I should be where I no more can hear
Thy voice, nor catch from thy wild eyes these gleams
Of past existence—wilt thou then forget
150 That on the banks of this delightful stream
We stood together; and that I, so long
A worshipper of Nature, hither came
Unwearied in that service: rather say
With warmer love—oh! with far deeper zeal
155 Of holier love. Nor wilt thou then forget,
That after many wanderings, many years
Of absence, these steep woods and lofty cliffs,
And this green pastoral landscape, were to me
More dear, both for themselves and for thy sake!

Literary Analysis
Romanticism, the Lyric, and Diction Does Wordsworth use simple or difficult words to describe old age? Are they specific or general?

Review and Assess

Thinking About the Selection

1. **(a) Recall:** How long has it been since the poet visited Tintern Abbey? **(b) Infer:** At what time of year does the poet make his second visit to the area? How do you know?

2. **(a) Recall:** How have the poet's memories of his first visit helped him? **(b) Interpret:** In line 36 of the poem, the poet mentions "another gift" that his contact with this rural scene bestowed upon him. Briefly describe this gift.

3. **Compare and Contrast:** Explain the difference in the poet's attitude on his first and on his second visit to Tintern Abbey.

4. **(a) Summarize:** What wish for his sister does the poet express toward the end of the poem? **(b) Connect:** What connection can you see between this wish, Wordsworth's thoughts in lines 22–31, and his hopes in lines 62–65? **(c) Draw Conclusions:** Is memory as important a force in the poem as nature? Explain.

5. **Evaluate:** Does Wordsworth express a deep truth about our relationships with nature, or are his reactions exaggerated? Support your answer.

6. **Take a Position:** Do you agree with Wordsworth's ideas about our relationship with nature? Why or why not?

from The Prelude

William Wordsworth

Background

In 1790, Wordsworth witnessed the early, optimistic days of the French Revolution. The country seemed on the verge of achieving true freedom from outdated, oppressive feudal institutions. Caught up in the revolutionary fervor, Wordsworth felt he was seeing "France standing on the top of golden hours." The war between England and France (declared in 1793) and the violent turn taken by the French Revolution, known as the Reign of Terror (1793–1794), dashed Wordsworth's hopes.

> O pleasant exercise of hope and joy!
> For mighty were the auxiliars which then stood
> Upon our side, us who were strong in love!
> Bliss was it in that dawn to be alive,
> 5 But to be young was very Heaven! O times,
> In which the meager, stale, forbidding ways
> Of custom, law, and statute, took at once
> The attraction of a country in romance!
> When Reason seemed the most to assert her rights
> 10 When most intent on making of herself
> A prime enchantress—to assist the work,
> Which then was going forward in her name!
> Not favored spots alone, but the whole Earth,
> The beauty wore of promise—that which sets
> 15 (As at some moments might not be unfelt
> Among the bowers of Paradise itself)
> The budding rose above the rose full blown.
> What temper at the prospect did not wake
> To happiness unthought of? The inert
> 20 Were <u>roused</u>, and lively natures rapt away!
> They who had fed their childhood upon dreams,
> The play-fellows of fancy, who had made
> All powers of swiftness, subtlety, and strength
> Their ministers,—who in lordly wise had stirred
> 25 Among the grandest objects of the sense,
> And dealt with whatsoever they found there
> As if they had within some lurking right
> To wield it;—they, too, who of gentle mood
> Had watched all gentle motions, and to these

Literary Analysis
Romanticism and the Lyric What connection can you find between the spirit described in these lines and the spirit of Wordsworth's "rebellion" against old styles of poetry?

roused (rouzd) *v.* stirred up

Storming of the Bastille, 14 July 1789,
Anonymous, Chateau, Versailles, France

◀ **Critical Viewing**
Compare and contrast the impression of the French Revolution conveyed by this poem to the one conveyed by this picture.
[Compare and Contrast]

30   Had fitted their own thoughts, schemers more mild,
     And in the region of their peaceful selves;—
     Now was it that *both* found, the meek and lofty
     Did both find helpers to their hearts' desire,
     And stuff at hand, plastic as they could wish,—
35   Were called upon to exercise their skill,
     Not in Utopia,—subterranean fields,—
     Or some secreted island, Heaven knows where!
     But in the very world, which is the world
     Of all of us,—the place where, in the end,
40   We find our happiness, or not at all!

             .   .   .

         But now, become oppressors in their turn,
     Frenchmen had changed a war of self-defense
     For one of conquest, losing sight of all
     Which they had struggled for: now mounted up,
45   Openly in the eye of earth and heaven,
     The scale of liberty. I read her doom,
     With anger vexed, with disappointment sore,
     But not dismayed, nor taking to the shame
     Of a false prophet. While resentment rose
50   Striving to hide, what nought could heal, the wounds
     Of mortified <u>presumption</u>, I adhered
     More firmly to old tenets, and, to prove
     Their temper, strained them more; and thus, in heat
     Of contest, did opinions every day
55   Grow into consequence, till round my mind
     They clung, as if they were its life, nay more,
     The very being of the immortal soul.

             .   .   .   .

presumption (prē zump´ shən) *n.* audacity

✔**Reading Check**

To which two kinds of people did the Revolution appeal?

I summoned my best skill, and toiled, intent
To <u>anatomize</u> the frame of social life,
60   Yea, the whole body of society
Searched to its heart. Share with me, Friend! the wish
That some dramatic tale, endued with shapes
Livelier, and flinging out less guarded words
Than suit the work we fashion, might set forth
65   What then I learned, or think I learned, of truth,
And the errors into which I fell, betrayed
By present objects, and by reasonings false
From their beginnings, inasmuch as drawn
Out of a heart that had been turned aside
70   From Nature's way by outward accidents,
And which are thus <u>confounded</u>, more and more
Misguided, and misguiding. So I fared,
Dragging all precepts, judgments, maxims, creeds,
Like culprits to the bar; calling the mind,
75   Suspiciously, to establish in plain day
Her titles and her honors; now believing,
Now disbelieving; endlessly perplexed
With impulse, motive, right and wrong, the ground
Of obligation, what the rule and whence
80   The sanction; till, demanding formal *proof*,
And seeking it in every thing, I lost
All feeling of conviction, and, in fine,
Sick, wearied out with contrarieties,
Yielded up moral questions in despair.

anatomize (ə nat´ ə mīz´)
v. to dissect in order to
examine structure

confounded (kən found´ id)
adj. confused; mixed
together indiscriminately;
bewildered

Review and Assess

Thinking About the Selection

1. **(a) Recall:** With what phrase does the speaker describe the
    early days of the French Revolution? **(b) Generalize:** What
    basic values does his reaction reflect? **(c) Interpret:** What role
    did reason seem to play in the Revolution?

2. **(a) Recall:** What change in the course of the French Revolution
    caused a conflict in Wordsworth? **(b) Interpret:** What two
    reactions to this turn of events does Wordsworth describe?

3. **(a) Interpret:** What does Wordsworth say happened to him
    when his heart "had been turned aside / From Nature's way"?
    (b) Interpret: At the end of the excerpt, how has Wordsworth
    resolved his conflict? **(c) Draw Conclusions:** What change in
    his attitude toward reason does this experience bring about?

4. **Make a Judgment:** Do you think Wordsworth has given up
    political hopes too easily? Explain.

The World Is Too Much with Us

William Wordsworth

The world is too much with us; late and soon,
Getting and spending, we lay waste our powers:
Little we see in Nature that is ours;
We have given our hearts away, a <u>sordid</u> boon![1]
5 This Sea that bares her bosom to the moon;
The winds that will be howling at all hours,
And are upgathered now like sleeping flowers;
For this, for everything, we are out of tune;
It moves us not.—Great God! I'd rather be
10 A Pagan suckled in a creed outworn;
So might I, standing on this pleasant lea,[2]
Have glimpses that would make me less forlorn;
Have sight of Proteus[3] rising from the sea;
Or hear old Triton[4] blow his wreathèd horn.

---

1. **boon** favor.
2. **lea** meadow.
3. **Proteus** (prō´ tē əs) in Greek mythology, a sea god who could change his appearance at will.
4. **Triton** in Greek mythology, a sea god with the head and upper body of a man and the tail of a fish.

▲ **Critical Viewing**
Do you agree with Wordsworth that an image such as this one "moves us not"? Explain.
[Make a Judgment]

sordid (sôr´ did) *adj.* dirty

✔**Reading Check**

According to the speaker, in what way do we "lay waste our powers"?

London, 1802

William Wordsworth

Milton![1] thou should'st be living at this hour:
England hath need of thee: she is a fen[2]
Of <u>stagnant</u> waters: altar, sword, and pen,
Fireside, the heroic wealth of hall and bower,

5   Have forfeited their ancient English dower
Of inward happiness. We are selfish men;
Oh! raise us up, return to us again;
And give us manners, virtue, freedom, power.
Thy soul was like a Star, and dwelt apart:

10 Thou hadst a voice whose sound was like the sea:
Pure as the naked heavens, majestic, free,
So didst thou travel on life's common way,
In cheerful godliness; and yet thy heart
The lowliest duties on herself did lay.

stagnant (stagʹ nənt) *adj.* motionless; foul

---

1. **Milton** seventeenth-century English poet John Milton.
2. **fen** (fen) *n.* area of low, flat, marshy land.

Review and Assess

Thinking About the Selections

1. **Respond:** When have you felt that "The world is too much with us"?

2. **(a) Recall:** In "The World Is Too Much with Us," what activities cause people to exhaust their "powers"?
   (b) Interpret: What does the speaker mean by the "world"?

3. **(a) Recall:** According to the speaker, with what are we "out of tune"? **(b) Interpret:** Why is being out of tune with these experiences such a loss? **(c) Interpret:** What relationship with nature does the poet envision at the end of the sonnet?

4. **(a) Recall:** According to "London, 1802," what is England like?
   (b) Analyze: What lacks or missing qualities have caused this condition? **(c) Interpret:** How would Milton's return help?

5. **Compare and Contrast:** How are the problems criticized in the two poems similar? How are they different?

6. **Apply:** Do Wordsworth's criticisms of England also apply to modern America? Explain.

Review and Assess

Literary Analysis

Romanticism and the Lyric

1. Identify a passage from the poems that illustrates Wordsworth's idealized view of nature.

2. Find a passage that reflects the **Romantic** belief in the dignity and importance of ordinary people and their language.

3. Romantic **lyrics** focused on the speaker's personal development. What lessons from Wordsworth's growth might readers adopt?

Comparing Literary Works

4. Using a chart like the one shown, find examples in the poems of **diction** that is specific and simple, abstract but simple, or abstract and difficult. Then, summarize your results.

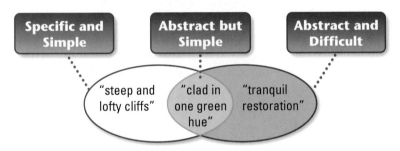

5. Wordsworth's subjects in these poems range widely, from natural scenes to politics to modern life. Does his diction vary to match his subject? Support your answer with details from the poems.

Reading Strategy

Using Literary Context

6. Imagine that you are a Neoclassical writer—a sociable city-dweller who writes polished, witty, rational verse. Explain how you might react to lines 76–80 of "Tintern Abbey."

7. (a) What do the hopes described in *The Prelude* tell you about the Romantic **literary context**? (b) What do lines 66–84 suggest about Romantic dissatisfaction with the Neoclassical context?

Extend Understanding

8. **Cultural Connection:** Would Wordsworth have appreciated modern technology such as computers and the Internet? Explain.

Integrate Language Skills

Vocabulary Development Lesson

Word Analysis: Forms of *anatomize*

The verb *anatomize*, meaning "cut into constituent parts" or "dissect," comes from the Greek word *atomos*, meaning "that which cannot be cut further; the smallest part." When Wordsworth tries to "anatomize" society, he tries to "dissect," or analyze, it into the parts that make it up. Several scientific words come from this Greek word. In your notebook, match each word with its meaning.

1. anatomy
2. atom
3. anatomist
4. atomism

a. one who studies the structure of the body
b. the study of parts
c. the smallest part into which something can be divided
d. the theory that the world is made of tiny, indivisible particles

Concept Development: Synonyms

For each numbered word, write the letter of the word that is closest to it in meaning.

1. roused
2. sordid
3. stagnant
4. confounded
5. anatomize
6. presumption
7. recompense

a. audacity
b. dissect
c. dirty
d. perplexed
e. stirred
f. reward
g. foul

Spelling Strategy

In Standard American English, the suffix *-ize* is common, as in the word *anatomize*. The suffix *-ise* is used in only about thirty common words, including *exercise*. Correct each misspelled word below.

1. criticised   2. advertize   3. recognising

Grammar and Style Lesson

Present Participial Phrases

A **present participial phrase** consists of a verb form ending in *-ing* and its complements and modifiers. The entire phrase functions as an adjective. In this example, the phrase modifies the pronoun *I*.

So might I, <u>standing on this pleasant lea,</u> . . .

By using present participial phrases, writers place their readers in the middle of an action that is already underway, drawing them in.

Practice Identify the present participial phrase in each sentence, and tell the word it modifies.

1. Today's world is full of Romantics calling for social change and praising nature.
2. Hoping to change the world, they write and take action.
3. You can search the Internet if you are trying to locate modern-day Romantics.
4. Essayists publish works on the Web advocating a return to nature and the land.
5. The irony of "Romanticism on the Web," reflecting the clash of technology and nature, is acknowledged by many.

Writing Application Write a paragraph about an experience you have had with nature. Use two or more present participial phrases. Circle the phrases and underline the noun or pronoun each modifies.

$W\!G$ *Prentice Hall Writing and Grammar Connection: Chapter 19, Section 2*

Writing Lesson

Response to Criticism

Author Thomas Wolfe defined the true Romantic feeling as "not the desire to escape life, but to prevent life from escaping you." In an essay, explain whether or not Wordsworth's poetry is captured by this definition.

Prewriting Discuss Wolfe's claim with a partner. Then, look in Wordsworth's poems for lines that reflect the desire "to prevent life from escaping you." If you cannot find any, you might challenge Wolfe's claim.

Drafting Begin your essay by relating Wolfe's quotation to Wordsworth's poetry. As you draft, organize your examples in logical order, and use quotations to support your evaluation.

Revising Review the lines of poetry you have analyzed, and circle key words they include. Add sentences to your draft if necessary to explain finer shades of meaning in these key words.

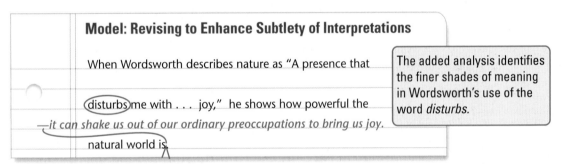

Model: Revising to Enhance Subtlety of Interpretations

When Wordsworth describes nature as "A presence that

(disturbs) me with . . . joy," he shows how powerful the
—it can shake us out of our ordinary preoccupations to bring us joy.
natural world is.

> The added analysis identifies the finer shades of meaning in Wordsworth's use of the word *disturbs*.

 Prentice Hall Writing and Grammar Connection: Chapter 14, Section 3

Extension Activities

Listening and Speaking The Romantic Movement affected arts other than literature. With two classmates, research Romanticism in the arts and assemble a **photo essay presentation.**

1. Use informal expressions for liveliness and technical language for precision.
2. Provide captions explaining each example.

Share your photo essay in an oral presentation, such as a slide show. **[Group Activity]**

Research and Technology Write a **cultural analysis** connecting Romanticism with the ecology movement. Develop a research strategy to find out about an active environmental group. In your analysis, identify Romantic influences in the group's statements.

 Take It to the Net www.phschool.com

Go online for an additional research activity using the Internet.

READING INFORMATIONAL MATERIALS

Book Reviews

About Book Reviews

A **response to literature** is a piece of writing that discusses a reader's reaction to a work. A response might show why a story is moving, point out the beauties of a poem, or analyze the short-comings of a play. One type of response to literature is a book review. **Book reviews** include these elements:

- A report of the reviewer's reactions to and insights into a work
- General observations about works of this type
- Insight into the relationship of the work reviewed to the writer's life or other works, past, present, or to come
- A recommendation about the work to readers

Reading Strategy

Analyzing a Writer's Basic Assumptions

A good book reviewer uses a rich set of assumptions about what is important or valuable in literary writing. Applying these assumptions to a book, the critic can measure its value. To understand these measurements and, ultimately, to make up your own mind about the work, identify a reviewer's scale of values, **analyzing his or her assumptions**. Begin with these questions:

1. To what general ideas, such as originality or good taste, does the reviewer repeatedly refer?
2. What are the more powerful evaluative terms the reviewer uses? Look for words like *compelling* or *sentimental*.
3. Which of these ideas and terms does the reviewer take in a positive sense? Which in a negative sense?
4. Do any of these ideas or terms come in pairs of opposites that could define a scale of values, from best to worst?

As you read, use a chart like the one shown to analyze Jeffrey's scale of poetic values.

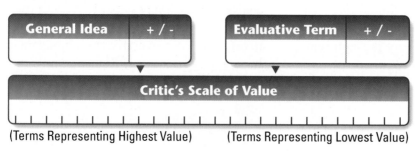

General Idea	+ / -

Evaluative Term	+ / -

Critic's Scale of Value

(Terms Representing Highest Value)   (Terms Representing Lowest Value)

Early Reviews of Wordsworth

Francis Jeffrey

Book reviews,

The Edinburgh Review, 1807 and 1814

Jeffrey describes a distinctive general characteristic he has found in the poetry of Wordsworth and others. He offers an insight into the sources of this characteristic.

With Mr. Wordsworth and his friends, it is plain that their peculiarities of diction[1] are things of choice, and not of accident. They write as they do, upon principle and system; and it evidently costs them much pains to keep *down* to the standard which they have proposed to themselves. They are, to the full, as much mannerists,[2] too, as the poetasters[3] who ring changes on the commonplaces of magazine versification; and all the difference between them is, that they borrow their phrases from a different and scantier *gradus ad Parnassum.*[4] If they were, indeed, to discard all imitation and set phraseology, and to bring in no words merely for show or for

Through the use of terms such as *freedom, originality, authority, vulgar,* and *plebeian,* Jeffrey defines two scales of value: high-class versus vulgar, individuality versus polish.

meter—as much, perhaps, might be gained in freedom and originality, as would infallibly be lost in allusion and authority; but, in point of fact, the new poets are just as great borrowers as the old; only that, instead of borrowing from the more popular passages of their illustrious predecessors, they have preferred furnishing themselves from vulgar ballads and plebeian nurseries.

. . .

Long habits of seclusion, and an excessive ambition of originality, can alone account for the disproportion which seems to exist between this author's taste and his genius; or for the devotion with which he has sacrificed so many precious gifts at the shrine of those paltry idols which he has set up for himself among his lakes and his mountains. Solitary musings, amidst such scenes, might no doubt be expected to nurse up the mind to the majesty of poetical conception (though it is remarkable, that all the greater poets lived, or had lived, in the full current

---

1. **diction** (dik´ shən) *n.* choice of words; style of expression.
2. **mannerists** artists using an exaggerated or artificial style.
3. **poetasters** (pō´ ət as´ tərz) *n.* inferior poets.
4. ***gradus ad Parnassum*** (grä´ dəs ad pär nas´ ǒom) *n.* dictionary for writing poetry (Latin for "step to Parnassus," mountain of Apollo and the Muses, deities of the arts).

of society), but the collision of equal minds—the admonition of prevailing impressions—seems necessary to reduce its redundancies, and repress that tendency to extravagance or puerility, into which the self-indulgence and self-admiration of genius is so apt to be betrayed, when it is allowed to wanton, without awe or restraint, in the triumph and delight of its own intoxication. That its flights should be graceful and glorious in the eyes of men, it seems almost to be necessary that they should be made in the consciousness that men's eyes are to behold them,—and that the inward transport and vigor by which they are inspired, should be tempered by an occasional reference to what will be thought of them by those ultimate dispensers of glory. An habitual and general knowledge of the few settled and permanent maxims, which form the canon[5] of general taste in all large and polished societies—a certain tact, which informs us at once that many things, which we still love and are moved by in secret, must necessarily be despised as childish, or derided as absurd, in all such societies—though it will not stand in the place of genius, seems necessary to the success of its exertions; and though it will never enable anyone to produce the higher beauties of art, can alone secure the talent which does produce them, from errors that must render it useless.

Those who have most of the talent, however, commonly acquire this knowledge with the greatest facility; and if Mr. Wordsworth, instead of confining himself almost entirely to the society of the dalesmen[6] and cottagers and little children, who form the subjects of his book, had condescended to mingle a little more with the people that were to read and judge of it, we cannot help thinking that its texture might have been considerably improved: at least it appears to us to be absolutely impossible, that anyone who had lived or mixed familiarly with men of literature and ordinary judgment in poetry, (of course we exclude the coadjutors[7] and disciples of his own school) could ever have fallen into such gross faults, or so long mistaken them for beauties. His first essays we looked upon in a good degree as poetical paradoxes—maintained experimentally, in order to display talent, and court notoriety;—and so maintained, with no more serious belief in their truth, than is usually generated by an ingenious and animated defense of other paradoxes. But when we find that he has been for twenty years exclusively employed upon articles of this very fabric, and that he has still enough of raw material on hand to keep him so employed for twenty years to come, we cannot refuse him the justice of believing that he is a sincere convert to his own system. . . .

Here Jeffrey makes a general observation on the ingredients for successful poetry: genius guided by tact.

Jeffrey relates the work that he is reviewing to the author's earlier work, giving the reader a more general sense of Wordsworth as a writer.

---

5. **canon** (kan´ ən) n. group of established, basic rules.

6. **dalesmen** simple farmers.
7. **coadjutors** (ko aj´ ə tərz) n. assistants.

Check Your Comprehension

1. Judging from this review, what details of Wordsworth's poetry made his work revolutionary at the time?
2. According to Jeffrey, what aspects of Wordsworth's life shaped the style and content of his poetry?
3. Summarize the advice Jeffrey might give Wordsworth.

Applying the Reading Strategy

Analyzing a Writer's Basic Assumptions

Answer the following questions to determine the scale of critical values that Jeffrey applies to Wordsworth's poetry.

1. (a) Does Jeffrey agree that Wordsworth's poetry has originality? Explain. (b) Summarize the relationship Jeffrey sees between originality and self-indulgence or "intoxication."
2. What does Jeffrey see as the foundation for good poetry: originality and genius, which are the properties of an individual, or tact and polish, which represent an agreement in taste among many people? Support your answer.

Activity

Writing a Review

Francis Jeffrey was not the first person and will not be the last to write an essay on Wordsworth's poems. Read or review William Wordsworth's "Lines Composed a Few Miles Above Tintern Abbey" (p. 666). Write your own review of this poem. As you write, determine whether the poem suffers from the faults ascribed to the Romantics by Jeffrey or whether Jeffrey's assumptions left him unable to appreciate Wordsworth's poetry.

Comparing Informational Materials

Compare Jeffrey's review from the early 1800s with a contemporary view of Wordsworth's poetry. Write an essay answering these questions: Are the scale of critical values similar in both reviews? Did tastes shift significantly from the time of one essay to the time of the other? Use the chart to help you compare the critiques presented in the two reviews.

	Jeffrey's Review	Contemporary Review
Similarities		
Differences		

Prepare to Read

The Rime of the Ancient Mariner ◆ Kubla Khan

Samuel Taylor Coleridge (1772–1834)

The poetry of Samuel Taylor Coleridge stands at the place where real life slips into dreams and facts are reborn as fantasies. More than any other Romantic poet, he dared to journey inward— deep into the world of the imagination. His explorations came at a price, though. The imagination that fed his poetry also allowed him to avoid a reckoning with his own serious problems, including poor health and self-doubt.

Early Fantasies Coleridge was born in Ottery St. Mary on the Devon coast of England, the last of ten children. At an early age, he developed the habit of retreating into a world of books and fantasy. Even as a child, his response to literature was powerful. After reading an intense tale from the *Arabian Nights*, for example, he recalled feeling "haunted by specters whenever I was in the dark." When he was nine, his father died, and Coleridge was sent to school in London. Later, he went to Cambridge University, where he became a riveting public speaker, mesmerizing audiences with his originality and intelligence.

Utopian Plans At Cambridge, Coleridge's hunger for new ideas led him into radical politics. He became a friend of the poet Robert Southey. Inspired by the early promise of the French Revolution, the two men planned to form a settlement in Pennsylvania based on their utopian political ideas. The plan collapsed, however, when Southey's aunt refused to fund their project.

A Literary Breakthrough In 1795, Coleridge and his wife, Sara Fricker, moved to Somerset, where he became a friend of poet William Wordsworth. In 1798, the two poets published *Lyrical Ballads*, a joint collection of their works. The four poems that make up Coleridge's contribution to the volume deal with spiritual matters and include his masterpiece "The Rime of the Ancient Mariner." The collection of poems slowly gained critical attention. In the end, it caused a revolution in poetic style and thought, firmly establishing the movement known as Romanticism.

Twin Poles Coleridge and Wordsworth represented two opposing sides of the movement. While Wordsworth explored the language and experience of common people in natural settings, Coleridge often celebrated the strange and the exotic. Both, however, were committed to reaching truths about the human soul deeper than those conventional poetry could express.

Success and Difficulty As Coleridge's fame grew, he suffered increasingly from asthma and rheumatism and began to rely heavily on painkillers, which dulled his creative powers. Seeking to improve his health by visiting warmer climates, he spent two years in Malta and then traveled through Italy. His journey brought him little relief from pain and contributed to the collapse of his marriage. When he returned to England in 1806, Coleridge separated from his wife and moved near the Wordsworth family. By 1810, however, even this friendship was shattered. Wordsworth felt that the poet was irresponsible, and the two men never regained their close connection.

Throughout these dark days, Coleridge kept writing on many subjects and gave lectures on Shakespeare and Milton. Visits with Coleridge had a great impact on the young crop of Romantics writing at that time. Mary Shelley, the author of *Frankenstein*, often described her admiration for Coleridge's groundbreaking poetic works.

A Romantic Legacy Perhaps Coleridge's greatest legacy is his insight into the power of imagination in literature and life, a power that shapes reality and enables freedom. A magical blend of thought and emotion lies at the heart of his works, in which the unreal (but true) becomes compellingly real.

Preview

Connecting to the Literature

Like your own dreams, these poems will sweep you off to fantasy realms where truths of life—such as courage, beauty, and redemption—stand out vividly.

Literary Analysis

Poetic Sound Devices

Romantic poetry like that of Coleridge achieves some of its emotional effect and beauty through **poetic sound devices,** including the following:

- **Alliteration** is the repetition of a consonant sound at the beginnings of words: "The fair <u>b</u>reeze <u>b</u>lew, the white <u>f</u>oam <u>f</u>lew, . . ."
- **Consonance** is the repetition of similar final consonant sounds in stressed syllables with dissimilar vowel sounds: "a frightful fie<u>nd</u> / Doth close behi<u>nd</u>. . . ."
- **Assonance** is the repetition of a vowel sound in stressed syllables with dissimilar consonant sounds: "The western w<u>a</u>ve was all afl<u>a</u>me."
- **Internal rhyme** is the use of rhymes within a poetic line: "With heavy th<u>ump</u>, a lifeless l<u>ump</u>, . . ."

Comparing Literary Works

Poetic sound devices give poetry a flavor all its own. So, too, does the **language of fantasy** in which Coleridge builds his dream world. For instance, in "The Rime of the Ancient Mariner," he uses archaic words—terms no longer in common use—such as *eftsoons* ("immediately"). In "Kubla Khan," he uses exotic-sounding place-names, such as Xanadu. As you read, compare the various ways in which Coleridge uses words to emphasize the difference between poetry and everyday speech, creating a contrast between fantasy-world and reality.

Reading Strategy

Analyzing Poetic Effects

Analyzing poetic effects, such as sound devices, will help you appreciate poetry. As you read, use a chart like the one shown. Find examples of alliteration, consonance, assonance and internal rhyme and identify their effects.

Vocabulary Development

averred (ə vʉrd′) *v.* stated to be true (p. 690)

sojourn (sō′ jʉrn) *v.* stay for a while (p. 697)

expiated (eks′ pē āt′ id) *v.* atoned; made amends for, especially by suffering (p. 704)

reverence (rev′ ər əns) *n.* deep respect (p. 708)

sinuous (sin′ yo͞o əs) *adj.* bending; winding (p. 711)

tumult (to͞o′ mult′) *n.* noisy commotion (p. 711)

Passage

The ship drove fast, loud roared the blast, / And southward aye we fled.

Sound Device

1. Internal rhyme: "fast / blast"
2. Assonance: "loud / southward"

Image

Ship fleeing the storm

Effect of Sound on Image

1. Rhyme emphasizes speed and abruptness.
2. Assonance fits the howling of the wind

THE RIME OF THE ANCIENT MARINER

Samuel Taylor Coleridge

Engraving by Gustave Doré for "The Rime of the Ancient Mariner" by Samuel Taylor Coleridge

▲ **Critical Viewing** Identify two elements in this engraving that create a gloomy, suspense-filled atmosphere. **[Analyze]**

Background

Coleridge used dreams as the basis of many of his great poems. "The Rime of the Ancient Mariner" was based on a dream reported by his friend John Cruikshank. Starting with the dream as raw material, Coleridge and Wordsworth began to elaborate upon it. Wordsworth suggested that the act that would drive the entire poem was a crime committed at sea. Using this idea and his own lively imagination, Coleridge wrote a poem that has chilled and enthralled audiences to this day. (The margin notes to the left of the poem were written by the poet.)

Argument

How a Ship having passed the Line[1] was driven by storms to the cold Country towards the South Pole: and how from thence she made her course to the tropical Latitude of the Great Pacific Ocean; and of the strange things that befell: and in what manner the Ancyent Marinere came back to his own Country.

Part I

An ancient Mariner meeteth three Gallants bidden to a wedding feast and detaineth one.

It is an ancient Mariner,
And he stoppeth one of three.
"By thy long gray beard and glittering eye,
Now wherefore stopp'st thou me?"

5 "The Bridegroom's doors are opened wide,
And I am next of kin;
The guests are met, the feast is set:
May'st hear the merry din."

He holds him with his skinny hand,
10 "There was a ship," quoth he.
"Hold off! unhand me, graybeard loon!"
Eftsoons[2] his hand dropped he.

The Wedding Guest is spellbound by the eye of the old seafaring man and constrained to hear his tale.

He holds him with his glittering eye—
The Wedding Guest stood still,
15 And listens like a three years' child:
The Mariner hath his will.

The Wedding Guest sat on a stone:
He cannot choose but hear;
And thus spake on that ancient man,
20 The bright-eyed Mariner.

"The ship was cheered, the harbor cleared,
Merrily did we drop

The Mariner tells how the ship sailed southward with a good wind and fair weather till it reached the Line.

Below the kirk,[3] below the hill,
Below the lighthouse top.

25 "The Sun came up upon the left,
Out of the sea came he!
And he shone bright, and on the right
Went down into the sea.

---

1. **Line** Equator.
2. **Eftsoons** immediately.
3. **kirk** church.

Reading Check
What effect does the ancient Mariner have on the Wedding Guest?

The Rime of the Ancient Mariner ◆ 687

"Higher and higher every day,
30 Till over the mast at noon[4] —"
The Wedding Guest here beat his breast,
For he heard the loud bassoon.

The Wedding Guest
heareth the bridal
music; but the
Mariner continueth
his tale.

The bride hath paced into the hall.
Red as a rose is she;
35 Nodding their heads before her goes
The merry minstrelsy.

The Wedding Guest he beat his breast,
Yet he cannot choose but hear;
And thus spake on that ancient man
40 The bright-eyed Mariner.

The ship driven by
a storm toward
the South Pole.

"And now the Storm blast came, and he
Was tyrannous and strong:
He struck with his o'ertaking wings,
And chased us south along.

45 "With sloping masts and dipping prow,
As who pursued with yell and blow
Still treads the shadow of his foe,
And forward bends his head,
The ship drove fast, loud roared the blast,
50 And southward aye[5] we fled.

"And now there came both mist and snow.
And it grew wondrous cold;
And ice, mast-high, came floating by,
As green as emerald.

The land of ice, and
of fearful sounds,
where no living
thing was to
be seen.

55 "And through the drifts the snowy clifts[6]
Did send a dismal sheen;
Nor shapes of men nor beasts we ken[7]—
The ice was all between.

"The ice was here, the ice was there,
60 The ice was all around;
It cracked and growled, and roared and howled,
Like noises in a swound![8]

Literary Analysis
**Poetic Sound Devices and
the Language of Fantasy**
What archaic (outdated)
word-form appears in
lines 37–40?

Reading Strategy
Analyzing Poetic Effects
Find one line in this verse
that contains the long and
the short sound of the
same vowel. What
emphasis does this
alternation create?

---

4. **over . . . noon** The ship has reached the equator.
5. **aye** ever.
6. **clifts** icebergs.
7. **ken** knew.
8. **swound** swoon.

Engraving by Gustave Doré for "The Rime of the Ancient Mariner" by Samuel Taylor Coleridge

▲ **Critical Viewing** From the expression on the Wedding Guest's face (figure on far left), what can you infer about his reaction to the ancient Mariner? **[Infer]**

*Till a great sea
bird, called the
Albatross, came
through the snow-
fog, and was
received with great
joy and hospitality.*

"At length did cross an Albatross,
Thorough[9] the fog it came;
65 As if it had been a Christian soul,
We hailed it in God's name.

"It ate the food it ne'er had eat,[10]
And round and round it flew.
The ice did split with a thunder-fit;
70 The helmsman steered us through!

Literary Analysis
Poetic Sound Devices
Identify one sound device
used in lines 67–70.

*And lo! the
Albatross proveth
a bird of good omen,
and followeth the
ship as it returned
northward through
fog and floating ice.*

"And a good south wind sprung up behind;
The Albatross did follow,
And every day, for food or play,
Came to the mariner's hollo!

75 "In mist or cloud, on mast or shroud,[11]
It perched for vespers[12] nine;
Whiles all the night, through fog-smoke
    white,
Glimmered the white Moonshine."

*The ancient Mariner
inhospitably killeth
the pious bird of
good omen.*

"God save thee, ancient Mariner!
80 From the fiends, that plague thee thus!—
Why look'st thou so?"[13] "With my crossbow
I shot the Albatross."

Part II
"The Sun now rose upon the right:[14]
Out of the sea came he,
85 Still hid in mist, and on the left
Went down into the sea.

"And the good south wind still blew behind,
But no sweet bird did follow.
Nor any day for food or play
90 Came to the mariners' hollo!

Reading Strategy
Analyzing Poetic Effects
How does the use of
alliteration and internal
rhyme in lines 91–94 give
a fatal feeling to the
Mariner's deed?

averred (ə vʉrd´) *v.*: stated
to be true

*His shipmates cry
out against the
ancient Mariner for
killing the bird of
good luck.*

"And I had done a hellish thing,
And it would work 'em woe:
For all <u>averred</u>, I had killed the bird
That made the breeze to blow.

---

  9. thorough through.
10. eat (et) old form of *eaten*.
11. shroud *n.* ropes stretching from the ship's side to
    the masthead.
12. vespers evenings.
13. God . . . so spoken by the Wedding Guest.
14. The Sun . . . right The ship is now headed north.

Engraving by Gustave Doré for "The Rime of the Ancient Mariner" by Samuel Taylor Coleridge

◀ **Critical Viewing**
What effects does the
artist, Gustave Doré, use
to capture the eerie mood
of the poem? [**Analyze**]

95   Ah wretch! said they, the bird to slay,
    That made the breeze to blow!

*But when the fog
cleared off, they
justify the same,
and thus make
themselves accom-
plices in the crime.*

    "Nor dim nor red, like God's own head,
    The glorious Sun uprist;[15]
    Then all averred, I had killed the bird
100 That brought the fog and mist.
    'Twas right, said they, such birds to slay,
    That bring the fog and mist.

*The fair breeze
continues; the ship
enters the Pacific
Ocean, and sails
northward, even till
it reaches the Line.
The Ship hath been
suddenly becalmed.*

    "The fair breeze blew, the white foam flew,
    The furrow[16] followed free;
105 We were the first that ever burst
    Into that silent sea.

    "Down dropped the breeze, the sails
        dropped down,
    'Twas sad as sad could be;

---

15. **uprist** arose.
16. **furrow** ship's wake.

☑ **Reading Check**

What has the ancient
Mariner done to the
Albatross?

And we did speak only to break
110 The silence of the sea!

"All in a hot and copper sky,
The bloody Sun, at noon,
Right up above the mast did stand,
No bigger than the Moon.

115 "Day after day, day after day,
We stuck, nor breath nor motion;
As idle as a painted ship
Upon a painted ocean.

And the Albatross
begins to be
avenged.

"Water, water, everywhere,
120 And all the boards did shrink;
Water, water, everywhere,
Nor any drop to drink.

"The very deep did rot: O Christ!
That ever this should be!
125 Yea, slimy things did crawl with legs
Upon the slimy sea.

"About, about, in reel and rout[17]
The death fires[18] danced at night;
The water, like a witch's oils,
130 Burned green, and blue and white.

A Spirit had
followed them;
one of the invisible
inhabitants of this
planet, neither
departed souls
nor angels. They
are very numerous,
and there is no
climate or element
without one or more.

"And some in dreams assurèd were
Of the Spirit that plagued us so;
Nine fathom deep he had followed us
From the land of mist and snow.

135 "And every tongue, through utter drought,
Was withered at the root;
We could not speak, no more than if
We had been choked with soot.

"Ah! well a-day! what evil looks
140 Had I from old and young!
Instead of the cross, the Albatross
About my neck was hung.

The shipmates, in
their sore distress,
would fain throw
the whole guilt on
the ancient Mariner:
in sign whereof they
hang the dead sea
bird round his neck.

---

17. rout disorderly crowd.
18. death fires St. Elmo's fire, a visible electrical discharge
from a ship's mast, believed by sailors to be an omen
of disaster.

Reading Strategy
Analyzing Poetic Effects
How does the repetition
of words in lines 115–119
contribute to the image
of the stilled ship?

Reading Strategy
Analyzing Poetic Effects
What effect does the
increased concentration
of sound devices in lines
127–130 have?

Part III

"There passed a weary time. Each throat
Was parched, and glazed each eye.
145 A weary time! a weary time!
How glazed each weary eye,
When looking westward, I beheld
A something in the sky.

The ancient Mariner beholdeth a sign in the element afar off.

"At first it seemed a little speck,
150 And then it seemed a mist;
It moved and moved, and took at last
A certain shape, I wist.[19]

"A speck, a mist, a shape, I wist!
And still it neared and neared:
155 As if it dodged a water sprite,
It plunged and tacked and veered.

At its nearer approach, it seemeth him to be a ship; and at a dear ransom he freeth his speech from the bonds of thirst.

"With throats unslaked, with black lips baked,
We could nor laugh nor wail;
Through utter drought all dumb we stood!
160 I bit my arm, I sucked the blood,
And cried, A sail! a sail!

A flash of joy:

"With throats unslaked, with black lips baked,
Agape they heard me call:
Gramercy![20] for joy did grin,
165 And all at once their breath drew in,
As they were drinking all.

And horror follows. For can it be a ship that comes onward without wind or tide?

"See! see! (I cried) she tacks no more!
Hither to work us weal;[21]
Without a breeze, without a tide,
170 She steadies with upright keel!

"The western wave was all aflame.
The day was well nigh done!
Almost upon the western wave
Rested the broad bright Sun;
175 When that strange shape drove suddenly
Betwixt us and the Sun.

It seemeth him but the skeleton of a ship.

"And straight the Sun was flecked with bars,
(Heaven's Mother send us grace!)

---

19. wist knew.
20. Gramercy (grə mur′ sē): great thanks.
21. work us weal assist us.

Reading Strategy
Analyzing Poetic Effects
What poetic effect does Coleridge use in lines 149–153 to build suspense?

Literary Analysis
Poetic Sound Devices and the Language of the Fantastic How does the line "Hither to work us weal" give the sense that these events are taking place in a strange, distant era?

Reading Check

What causes the sailors to suffer?

As if through a dungeon grate he peered
180 With broad and burning face.

And its ribs are seen
as bars on the face
of the setting Sun.

"Alas! (thought I, and my heart beat loud)
How fast she nears and nears!
Are those *her* sails that glance in the Sun,
Like restless gossameres?[22]

The Specter Woman
and her Death-
mate, and no other
on board the skele-
ton ship.

185 "Are those *her* ribs through which the Sun
Did peer, as through a grate?
And is that Woman all her crew?
Is that a Death? and are there two?
Is Death that woman's mate?

Like vessel, like
crew! Death and
Life-in-Death have
diced for the ship's
crew, and she (the
latter) winneth the
ancient Mariner.

190 "*Her* lips were red, *her* looks were free,
Her locks were yellow as gold;
Her skin was as white as leprosy,
The Nightmare Life-in-Death was she,
Who thicks man's blood with cold.

195 "The naked hulk alongside came,
And the twain were casting dice;
'The game is done! I've won! I've won!'
Quoth she, and whistles thrice.

No twilight within
the courts of
the Sun.

"The Sun's rim dips; the stars rush out:
200 At one stride comes the dark;
With far-heard whisper, o'er the sea,
Off shot the specter bark.

At the rising of
the Moon,

"We listened and looked sideways up!
Fear at my heart, as at a cup,
205 My lifeblood seemed to sip!
The stars were dim, and thick the night,
The steersman's face by his lamp
    gleamed white;
From the sails the dew did drip—
Till clomb[23] above the eastern bar
210 The hornèd[24] Moon, with one bright star
Within the nether tip.

One after another,

"One after one, by the star-dogged Moon,[25]
Too quick for groan or sigh,

---

22. **gossameres** floating cobwebs.
23. **clomb** climbed.
24. **hornèd** crescent.
25. **star-dogged Moon** omen of impending evil to sailors.

Literary Analysis
Poetic Sound Devices and the Language of the Fantastic In what way does the name of the woman—Life-in-Death—add to the eerie, mysterious atmosphere of the story?

Reading Strategy
Analyzing Poetic Effects Does the alliteration in line 208 help you imagine what is being described? Explain.

Engraving by Gustave Doré for "The Rime of the Ancient Mariner" by Samuel Taylor Coleridge

▲ **Critical Viewing** What reactions to the sighting of the other ship would you expect from the sailors? Can you find such reactions in the engraving? Explain. **[Connect]**

Each turned his face with a ghastly pang,
215 And cursed me with his eye.

His shipmates drop down dead.

"Four times fifty living men,
(And I heard nor sigh nor groan)
With heavy thump, a lifeless lump,
They dropped down one by one.

But Life-in-Death begins her work on the ancient Mariner.

220 "The souls did from their bodies fly—
They fled to bliss or woe!
And every soul, it passed me by,
Like the whizz of my crossbow!"

Part IV

The Wedding Guest feareth that a Spirit is talking to him;

"I fear thee, ancient Mariner!
225 I fear thy skinny hand!
And thou art long, and lank, and brown,
As is the ribbed sea sand.

"I fear thee and thy glittering eye,
And thy skinny hand, so brown."

But the ancient Mariner assureth him of his bodily life, and proceedeth to relate his horrible penance.

230 "Fear not, fear not, thou Wedding Guest!
This body dropped not down.

"Alone, alone, all, all alone,
Alone on a wide wide sea!
And never a saint took pity on
235 My soul in agony.

He despiseth the creatures of the calm,

"The many men, so beautiful!
And they all dead did lie:
And a thousand thousand slimy things
Lived on; and so did I.

And envieth that they should live, and so many lie dead.

240 "I looked upon the rotting sea,
And drew my eyes away;
I looked upon the rotting deck,
And there the dead men lay.

"I looked to heaven, and tried to pray;
245 But or[26] ever a prayer had gushed,
A wicked whisper came, and made
My heart as dry as dust.

"I closed my lids, and kept them close,
And the balls like pulses beat;

---

26. or before.

For the sky and the sea and the sea and the sky
Lay like a load on my weary eye,
And the dead were at my feet.

But the curse liveth
for him in the eye of
the dead men.

"The cold sweat melted from their limbs,
Nor rot nor reek did they;
255 The look with which they looked on me
Had never passed away.

"An orphan's curse would drag to hell
A spirit from on high;
But oh! more horrible than that

In his loneliness and
fixedness he year-
neth towards the
journeying Moon,
and the stars that
still sojourn, yet
still move onward;
and everywhere the
blue sky belongs to
them, and is their
appointed rest, and
their native country
and their own
natural homes,
which they enter
unannounced, as
lords that are cer-
tainly expected and
yet there is a silent
joy at their arrival.

260 Is the curse in a dead man's eye!
Seven days, seven nights, I saw that curse,
And yet I could not die.

"The moving Moon went up the sky,
And nowhere did abide:
265 Softly she was going up,
And a star or two beside—

"Her beams bemocked the sultry main,[27]
Like April hoarfrost spread;
But where the ship's huge shadow lay,
270 The charmèd water burned alway
A still and awful red.

"Beyond the shadow of the ship,
I watched the water snakes:
They moved in tracks of shining white,
275 And when they reared, the elfish light
Fell off in hoary flakes.

By the light of the
Moon he beholdeth
God's creatures of
the great calm.

"Within the shadow of the ship
I watched their rich attire:
Blue, glossy green, and velvet black,
280 They coiled and swam; and every track
Was a flash of golden fire.

Their beauty and
their happiness.

"O happy living things! no tongue
Their beauty might declare:
A spring of love gushed from my heart,

He blesseth them in
his heart.

285 And I blessed them unaware;
Sure my kind saint took pity on me,
And I blessed them unaware.

---

27. **main** open sea.

Reading Strategy
Analyzing Poetic Effects
What effect is created by
the repetition in line 250?
How does this effect
mirror the Mariner's
situation?

sojourn (sō´ jurn) v. stay
for a while

☑**Reading Check**

What has happened to
the other sailors?

The spell begins to break.

"The selfsame moment I could pray;
And from my neck so free
290 The Albatross fell off, and sank
Like lead into the sea.

Part V

"Oh sleep! it is a gentle thing,
Beloved from pole to pole!
To Mary queen the praise be given!
295 She sent the gentle sleep from Heaven,
That slid into my soul.

By grace of the holy Mother, the ancient Mariner is refreshed with rain.

"The silly[28] buckets on the deck.
That had so long remained,
I dreamed that they were filled with dew;
300 And when I awoke, it rained.

"My lips were wet, my throat was cold,
My garments all were dank;
Sure I had drunken in my dreams,
And still my body drank.

305 "I moved, and could not feel my limbs:
I was so light—almost
I thought that I had died in sleep,
And was a blessèd ghost.

He heareth sounds and seeth strange sights and commotions in the sky and the element.

"And soon I heard a roaring wind:
310 It did not come anear;
But with its sound it shook the sails,
That were so thin and sere.[29]

"The upper air burst into life!
And a hundred fire flags sheen,[30]
315 To and fro they were hurried about!
And to and fro, and in and out,
The wan stars danced between.

"And the coming wind did roar more loud,
And the sails did sigh like sedge;[31]
320 And the rain poured down from one
       black cloud;
The Moon was at its edge.

---

28. **silly** empty.
29. **sere** dried up.
30. **fire flags sheen** the aurora australis, or southern lights, shone.
31. **sedge** *n.* rushlike plant that grows in wet soil.

Literary Analysis
Poetic Sound Devices and the Language of the Fantastic What does the connection of the two events in lines 288–291 add to the fairy-tale quality of the story?

Literary Analysis
Poetic Sound Devices Which repeated consonant sound in lines 303–304 creates alliteration?

Engraving by Gustave Doré for "The Rime of the Ancient Mariner" by Samuel Taylor Coleridge

▲ **Critical Viewing** Which details support the mood of hopelessness in this illustration? **[Support]**

The Rime of the Ancient Mariner ◆ 699

"The thick black cloud was cleft, and still
The Moon was at its side:
Like waters shot from some high crag,
325 The lightning fell with never a jag,
A river steep and wide.

The bodies of the
ship's crew are
inspired[32] and the
ship moves on;

"The loud wind never reached the ship,
Yet now the ship moved on!
Beneath the lightning and the Moon
330 The dead men gave a groan.

"They groaned, they stirred, they all uprose,
Nor spake, nor moved their eyes;
It had been strange, even in a dream,
To have seen those dead men rise.

335 "The helmsman steered, the ship moved on:
Yet never a breeze up-blew;
The mariners all 'gan work the ropes,
Where they were wont[33] to do;
They raised their limbs like lifeless tools—
340 We were a ghastly crew.

"The body of my brother's son
Stood by me, knee to knee;
The body and I pulled at one rope,
But he said nought to me."

345 "I fear thee, ancient Mariner!"
"Be calm, thou Wedding Guest!
'Twas not those souls that fled in pain,
Which to their corses[34] came again,
But a troop of spirits blessed:

But not by the souls
of the men, nor by
demons of earth or
middle air, but by
a blessed troop of
angelic spirits,
sent down by the
invocation of the
guardian saint.

350 "For when it dawned—they dropped their arms,
And clustered round the mast;
Sweet sounds rose slowly through
    their mouths,
And from their bodies passed.

"Around, around, flew each sweet sound,
355 Then darted to the Sun;
Slowly the sounds came back again,
Now mixed, now one by one.

Literary Analysis
Poetic Sound Devices
Find an example of
assonance—the repetition
of vowel sounds in
unrhymed syllables—in
lines 331–334.

Literary Analysis
Poetic Sound Devices
Find an example of
alliteration—the repetition
of initial consonant
sounds—in lines 350–353.

---

32. **inspired** inspirited
33. **wont** accustomed.
34. **corses** corpses.

"Sometimes a-dropping from the sky
I heard the skylark sing;
360 Sometimes all little birds that are,
How they seemed to fill the sea and air
With their sweet jargoning![35]

"And now 'twas like all instruments,
Now like a lonely flute;
365 And now it is an angel's song,
That makes the heavens be mute.

"It ceased; yet still the sails made on
A pleasant noise till noon,
A noise like of a hidden brook
370 In the leafy month of June,
That to the sleeping woods all night
Singeth a quiet tune.

"Till noon we quietly sailed on,
Yet never a breeze did breathe;
375 Slowly and smoothly went the ship,
Moved onward from beneath.

*The lonesome Spirit
from the South Pole
carries on the ship
as far as the Line,
in obedience to the
angelic troop, but
still requireth
vengeance.*

"Under the keel nine fathom deep,
From the land of mist and snow,
The spirit slid; and it was he
380 That made the ship to go.
The sails at noon left off their tune,
And the ship stood still also.

"The Sun, right up above the mast,
Had fixed her to the ocean:
385 But in a minute she 'gan stir,
With a short uneasy motion—
Backwards and forwards half her length
With a short uneasy motion.

*The Polar Spirit's
fellow demons, the
invisible inhabitants
of the element, take
part in his wrong;
and two of them
relate, one to the
other, that penance
long and heavy for
the ancient Mariner
hath been accorded
to the Polar Spirit,
who returneth
southward.*

"Then like a pawing horse let go,
390 She made a sudden bound:
It flung the blood into my head,
And I fell down in a swound.

"How long in that same fit I lay,
I have not to declare;
395 But ere my living life returned,

---

35. **jargoning** singing.

Reading Strategy
Analyzing Poetic Effects
How does the alliteration
in lines 373–376 enhance
the description of the
boat's smooth progress?

✓**Reading Check**

What happens to the
bodies of the Mariner's
shipmates?

Engraving by Gustave Doré for "The Rime of the Ancient Mariner" by Samuel Taylor Coleridge

I heard and in my soul discerned
Two voices in the air.

"'Is it he?' quoth one, 'Is this the man?
By him who died on cross,
400   With his cruel bow he laid full low
The harmless Albatross.

"The spirit who bideth by himself
In the land of mist and snow,

He loved the bird that loved the man
405 Who shot him with his bow.'

"The other was a softer voice,
As soft as honeydew:
Quoth he, 'The man hath penance done,
And penance more will do.'

Part VI

FIRST VOICE

410 "'But tell me, tell me! speak again,
Thy soft response renewing—
What makes that ship drive on so fast?
What is the ocean doing?'

SECOND VOICE

"'Still as a slave before his lord,
415 The ocean hath no blast;
His great bright eye most silently
Up to the Moon is cast—

"'If he may know which way to go;
For she guides him smooth or grim.
420 See, brother, see! how graciously
She looketh down on him.'

FIRST VOICE

"'But why drives on that ship so fast,
Without or wave or wind?'

SECOND VOICE

"'The air is cut away before,
425 And closes from behind.

"'Fly, brother, fly! more high, more high!
Or we shall be belated:
For slow and slow that ship will go,
When the Mariner's trance is abated.'

430 "I woke, and we were sailing on
As in a gentle weather:
'Twas night, calm night, the moon was high;
The dead men stood together.

"All stood together on the deck,
435 For a charnel dungeon[36] fitter;

---

36. **charnel dungeon** vault where corpses or bones are deposited.

The Mariner hath been cast into a trance; for the angelic power causeth the vessel to drive northward faster than human life could endure.

The super-natural motion is retarded; the Mariner awakes, and his penance begins anew.

Literary Analysis
Poetic Sound Devices and the Language of Fantasy
How do the two voices contribute to Coleridge's creation of a dream world?

Literary Analysis
Poetic Sound Devices
What instance of assonance can you find in lines 414–417?

✔**Reading Check**
What do the two voices discuss?

The Rime of the Ancient Mariner ◆ 703

All fixed on me their stony eyes,
That in the Moon did glitter.

"The pang, the curse, with which they died,
Had never passed away;
440 I could not draw my eyes from theirs,
Nor turn them up to pray.

"And now this spell was snapped; once more
I viewed the ocean green,
And looked far forth, yet little saw
445 Of what had else been seen—

"Like one, that on a lonesome road
Doth walk in fear and dread,
And having once turned round walks on,
And turns no more his head;
450 Because he knows, a frightful fiend
Doth close behind him tread.

"But soon there breathed a wind on me,
Nor sound nor motion made:
Its path was not upon the sea,
455 In ripple or in shade.

"It raised my hair, it fanned my cheek
Like a meadow-gale of spring—
It mingled strangely with my fears,
Yet it felt like a welcoming.

460 "Swiftly, swiftly flew the ship,
Yet she sailed softly too:
Sweetly, sweetly blew the breeze—
On me alone it blew.

"Oh! dream of joy! is this indeed
465 The lighthouse top I see?
Is this the hill? is this the kirk?
Is this mine own countree?

"We drifted o'er the harbor bar,
And I with sobs did pray—
470 O let me be awake, my God!
Or let me sleep alway.

"The harbor bay was clear as glass,
So smoothly it was strewn![37]

The curse is finally expiated.

And the ancient Mariner beholdeth his native country.

expiated (ēk´ spē āt´ əd) *v.* atoned; made amends for, especially by suffering

Literary Analysis
Poetic Sound Devices
Find the assonance and alliteration in lines 460–463.

---

37. strewn spread.

And on the bay the moonlight lay,
475 And the shadow of the Moon.

"The rock shone bright, the kirk
    no less,
That stands above the rock;
The moonlight steeped in silentness
The steady weathercock.

480 "And the bay was white with
    silent light,
Till rising from the same,
Full many shapes, that shadows were,
In crimson colors came.

"A little distance from the prow
485 Those crimson shadows were:
I turned my eyes upon the deck—
Oh, Christ! what saw I there!

"Each corse lay flat, lifeless and flat,
And, by the holy rood!^{38}
490 A man all light, a seraph^{39} man,
On every corse there stood.

"This seraph band, each waved
    his hand:
It was a heavenly sight!
They stood as signals to the land,
495 Each one a lovely light;

"This seraph band, each waved
    his hand,
No voice did they impart—
No voice; but oh! the silence sank
Like music on my heart.

500 "But soon I heard the dash of oars,
I heard the Pilot's cheer;
My head was turned perforce away
And I saw a boat appear.

"The Pilot and the Pilot's boy,
505 I heard them coming fast:

*The angelic spirits
leave the dead
bodies,*

*And appear in their
own forms of light.*

---

38. **rood** cross.
39. **seraph** angel.

The British Tradition

The Tradition of Fantasy

Coleridge's "Rime of the Ancient Mariner"—written in a dreamlike language, set in an indeterminate past, and filled with supernatural events—is part of the British tradition of fantasy literature. Writers of works of fantasy set out to create a realm distinct from the everyday world of their readers—a never-never land ruled by strange laws.

The fantasy tradition began as long ago as Sir Thomas Malory's *Morte d'Arthur*, (p. 176), which is set in a vanished past that had become a myth by Malory's own day. The idea of a vanished past fascinated writers long after Malory, reappearing in the work of Alfred, Lord Tennyson, who resorted to Arthurian and mythological elements in many poems, as in "The Lady of Shalott" (p. 821).

Fantasy writers like Coleridge use strange settings and supernatural tales to break the spell of ordinary life. By plunging us into a wild, unfamiliar world, they remind us that human imagination can always envision worlds beyond the one into which we are born—a power that enables scientific discoveries and social reforms as well as great poetry.

 Reading Check

What place does the Mariner sail near?

Dear Lord in Heaven! it was a joy
The dead men could not blast.

"I saw a third—I heard his voice:
It is the Hermit good!
510 He singeth loud his godly hymns
That he makes in the wood.
He'll shrieve[40] my soul, he'll
        wash away
The Albatross's blood.

Part VII

*The Hermit of
the Wood,*

"This Hermit good lives in that wood
515 Which slopes down to the sea.
How loudly his sweet voice he rears!
He loves to talk with marineres
That come from a far countree.

"He kneels at morn, and noon,
        and eve—
520 He hath a cushion plump:
It is the moss that wholly hides
The rotted old oak-stump.

"The skiff boat neared; I heard them talk.
'Why, this is strange, I trow![41]
525 Where are those lights so many and fair,
That signal made but now?'

*Approacheth the
ship with wonder.*

"'Strange, by my faith!' the Hermit said—
'And they answered not our cheer!
The planks looked warped! and see those sails,
530 How thin they are and sere!
I never saw aught like to them,
Unless perchance it were

"'Brown skeletons of leaves that lag
My forest brook along;
535 When the ivy tod[42] is heavy with snow,
And the owlet whoops to the wolf below,
That eats the she-wolf's young.'

"'Dear Lord! it hath a fiendish look'
(The Pilot made reply)

---

40. shrieve (shrēv) absolve from sin.
41. trow believe.
42. tod bush.

Reading Strategy
Analyzing Poetic Effects
These lines are less
crowded with sound
devices than the lines
describing the Mariner's
nightmarish sea journey.
How does this shift in
language match the
shift in mood?

Literary Analysis
**Poetic Sound Devices and
the Language of Fantasy**
Which word in lines
523–526 might Coleridge
have borrowed from
medieval tales of knights?

540 'I am a-feared'—'Push on, push on!'
　　Said the Hermit cheerily.

　　"The boat came closer to the ship,
　　But I nor spake nor stirred;
　　The boat came close beneath the ship,
545 And straight[43] a sound was heard.

　　"Under the water it rumbled on,
　　Still louder and more dread:
　　It reached the ship, it split the bay;
　　The ship went down like lead.

550 "Stunned by that loud and dreadful sound,
　　Which sky and ocean smote,
　　Like one that hath been seven days drowned
　　My body lay afloat;
　　But swift as dreams, myself I found
555 Within the Pilot's boat.

　　"Upon the whirl, where sank the ship,
　　The boat spun round and round;
　　And all was still, save that the hill
　　Was telling of the sound.

560 "I moved my lips—the Pilot shrieked
　　And fell down in a fit;
　　The holy Hermit raised his eyes,
　　And prayed where he did sit.

　　"I took the oars; the Pilot's boy,
565 Who now doth crazy go,
　　Laughed loud and long, and all the while
　　His eyes went to and fro.
　　'Ha! ha!' quoth he, 'full plain I see,
　　The Devil knows how to row.'

570 "And now, all in my own countree,
　　I stood on the firm land!
　　The Hermit stepped forth from the boat,
　　And scarcely he could stand.

　　"'O shrieve me, shrieve me, holy man!'
575 The Hermit crossed his brow.[44]

---

43. straight immediately.
44. crossed his brow made the sign of the cross on his
　　forehead.

Reading Strategy
Analyzing Poetic Effects
Which poetic effects
contribute to the impact
of lines 556–559?

☑ **Reading Check**

Who helps the Mariner
when the ship sinks?

'Say, quick,' quoth he, 'I bid thee say—
What manner of man art thou?'

"Forthwith this frame of mine was wrenched
With a woeful agony,
580 Which forced me to begin my tale;
And then it left me free.

"Since then, at an uncertain hour,
That agony returns:
And till my ghastly tale is told,
585 This heart within me burns.

"I pass, like night, from land to land;
I have strange power of speech;
That moment that his face I see,
I know the man that must hear me:
590 To him my tale I teach.

"What loud uproar bursts from that door!
The wedding guests are there:
But in the garden bower the bride
And bridemaids singing are:
595 And hark the little vesper bell,
Which biddeth me to prayer!

"O Wedding Guest! this soul hath been
Alone on a wide wide sea:
So lonely 'twas, that God himself
600 Scarce seemèd there to be.

"O sweeter than the marriage feast,
'Tis sweeter far to me,
To walk together to the kirk
With a goodly company!—

605 "To walk together to the kirk,
And all together pray,
While each to his great Father bends,
Old men, and babes, and loving friends
And youths and maidens gay!

610 "Farewell, farewell! but this I tell
To thee, thou Wedding Guest!
He prayeth well, who loveth well
Both man and bird and beast.

**Reading Strategy
Analyzing Poetic Effects**
What effect does the
alliteration in line 590
featuring *tale*—a word
that appears in each of
the preceding two
stanzas—have?

reverence (rĕv´ ər əns) *n.*
deep respect

"He prayeth best, who loveth best
615 All things both great and small;
For the dear God who loveth us,
He made and loveth all."

The Mariner, whose eye is bright,
Whose beard with age is hoar,
620 Is gone; and now the Wedding Guest
Turned from the bridegroom's door.

He went like one that hath been stunned
And is of sense forlorn:
A sadder and a wiser man,
625 He rose the morrow morn.

Review and Assess

Thinking About the Selection

1. **Respond:** How did your reaction to the ancient Mariner change as his story went on? Explain.

2. **(a) Recall:** On what occasion does the Mariner tell his story? **(b) Interpret:** Why do you think Coleridge chose this occasion for the poem?

3. **(a) Recall:** What contradictory connections does the crew make between the Albatross and the weather? **(b) Recall:** What does the Mariner do to the Albatross? **(c) Infer:** Why does the Mariner wear the Albatross around his neck?

4. **(a) Recall:** What happens to the Mariner's shipmates after the appearance of the Specter Woman and her Death-mate? **(b) Generalize:** What might this symbolize about the effect of guilt on an individual's perceptions of and relations with others?

5. **(a) Infer:** Why does the Albatross finally fall from the Mariner's neck? **(b) Interpret:** What do you think the Albatross symbolizes? Find evidence to support your answer.

6. **(a) Recall:** What is the Mariner's lifelong penance? **(b) Analyze:** How does his story affect his listener? **(c) Draw Conclusions:** What larger lesson about human life might his story suggest?

7. **Take a Position:** In today's world, people who have been through harrowing experiences often tell their stories in books and on talk shows, just as the Mariner tells the story of his trials. Do you think this type of response is appropriate? Explain.

Kubla Khan

Samuel Taylor Coleridge

Box and Cover, Ming Dynasty, first half of 16th century, The Seattle Art Museum

◀ **Critical Viewing**
How do Coleridge's poetic images compare with the details on this sixteenth-century Chinese box cover?
[Compare and Contrast]

Background

Coleridge claimed to have dreamed his poem "Kubla Khan" line for line after falling asleep while reading a passage from a work about the founder of the great Mongol dynasty. Upon awakening, he transcribed the lines as fast as he could. When he was interrupted by a visitor, however, the lines in his head disappeared, never to be remembered. As a result, Coleridge was unable to complete the poem.

In Xanadu[1] did Kubla Khan
A stately pleasure dome decree:
Where Alph,[2] the sacred river, ran
Through caverns measureless to man
5   Down to a sunless sea.
So twice five miles of fertile ground
With walls and towers were girdled round;
And there were gardens bright with <u>sinuous</u> rills,[3]
Where blossomed many an incense-bearing tree;
10 And here were forests ancient as the hills,
Enfolding sunny spots of greenery.

But oh! that deep romantic chasm which slanted
Down the green hill athwart[4] a cedarn cover![5]
A savage place! as holy and enchanted
15 As e'er beneath a waning moon was haunted
By woman wailing for her demon lover!
And from this chasm, with ceaseless turmoil seething,
As if this earth in fast thick pants were breathing.
A mighty fountain momently was forced;
20 Amid whose swift half-intermitted burst
Huge fragments vaulted like rebounding hail,
Or chaffy grain beneath the thresher's flail;
And 'mid these dancing rocks at once and ever
It flung up momently the sacred river.
25 Five miles meandering with a mazy motion
Through wood and dale the sacred river ran,
Then reached the caverns measureless to man,
And sank in <u>tumult</u> to a lifeless ocean:
And 'mid this tumult Kubla heard from far
30 Ancestral voices prophesying war!
      The shadow of the dome of pleasure
      Floated midway on the waves;
      Where was heard the mingled measure
      From the fountain and the caves.
35 It was a miracle of rare device.[6]
A sunny pleasure dome with caves of ice!

      A damsel with a dulcimer[7]
      In a vision once I saw:

---

1. **Xanadu** (zan´ ə do͞o) indefinite area in China.
2. **Alph** probably derived from the Greek river Alpheus, the waters of which, it was believed in Greek mythology, joined with a stream to form a fountain in Sicily.
3. **rills** brooks.
4. **athwart** across.
5. **cedarn cover** covering of cedar trees.
6. **device** design.
7. **dulcimer** (dul´ sə mər) *n.* stringed musical instrument played with small hammers.

sinuous (sin´ yo͞o əs) *adj.* bending; winding

Reading Strategy
Analyzing Poetic Effects
What alliteration in lines 15–16 helps you hear the cries of the haunted woman?

tumult (to͞o´ mult´) *n.* noisy commotion

Literary Analysis
Poetic Sound Devices
Find examples of assonance and alliteration in lines 31–34.

Reading Check
What erupts continuously from the chasm?

It was an Abyssinian[8] maid,
40   And on her dulcimer she played,
Singing of Mount Abora.[9]
Could I revive within me
Her symphony and song,
To such a deep delight 'twould win me,
45 That with music loud and long,
I would build that dome in air,
That sunny dome! those caves of ice!
And all who heard should see them there,
And all should cry, Beware! Beware!
50 His flashing eyes, his floating hair!
Weave a circle round him thrice,
And close your eyes with holy dread,
For he on honeydew hath fed,
And drunk the milk of Paradise.

---

8. Abyssinian (ab ə sin´ ē ən) Ethiopian.
9. Mount Abora probably Mount Amara in Abyssinia.

Review and Assess

Thinking About the Selection

1. **(a) Recall:** Describe the pleasure dome and its setting.
   (b) Compare and Contrast: Compare the associations of the "deep romantic chasm" with those of the dome.
   (c) Analyze: What makes the pleasure dome and its setting seem beautiful? What makes them sinister?

2. **(a) Recall:** What comes from the chasm, and what are its effects? **(b) Draw Conclusions:** The pleasure dome might be thought of as a work of art. What does the existence of the chasm on the site of the dome suggest about the relation between constructive and chaotic, or "wild," forces in art?

3. **(a) Interpret:** In the last stanza, if the speaker were able to "revive" his vision, what would he do? What effect would it have on "all who heard"? **(b) Summarize:** How would "all who heard" then react to the speaker?

4. **(a) Interpret:** What does the "holy dread" experienced by "all who heard" suggest about the power of art?
   (b) Connect: What connection can you find between this "dread" and the existence of the chasm at the site of the dome?

5. **Evaluate:** Consider a work of art that has had a strong effect on you. Do you think your experience of this work supports Coleridge's views? Explain.

Review and Assess

Literary Analysis

Poetic Sound Devices

1. Find an example of the sound device **alliteration** in lines 9–12 of "The Rime of the Ancient Mariner."
2. What **sound device** does Coleridge use in the line "It cracked and growled, and roared and howled . . ." ("Rime," l. 61)?
3. What device dominates the first stanza of "Kubla Khan"? Give three examples.
4. Explain how the prevalence of sound effects in these poems creates a language suited to Coleridge's fantastic subjects.

Comparing Literary Works

5. Coleridge builds his **language of fantasy** in part from archaic words. Identify two instances of such words in the opening stanza of "The Rime of the Ancient Mariner."
6. (a) Identify four words in "Kubla Khan" that contribute to the poem's exotic atmosphere. (b) Contrast these words with the archaic words in "The Rime."
7. Using a chart like the one shown, explain how the quality of Coleridge's language suits different fantastic subjects.

Poem: _____

Subject	Setting	Events	Language	Why Suitable?

Reading Strategy

Analyzing Poetic Effects

8. (a) What mood do lines 472–483 of "The Rime of the Ancient Mariner" create? (b) What poetic devices contribute to this mood?
9. In "Kubla Khan," how do poetic devices, including repetition, contribute to the effect of lines 45–54?

Extend Understanding

10. **Cultural Connection:** Name an example of a modern "pleasure dome," and compare it with Kubla Khan's.

Quick Review

Alliteration is the repetition of a consonant sound at the beginnings of words (<u>K</u>ubla / <u>Kh</u>an).

Consonance is the repetition of similar final consonant sounds in stressed syllables with dissimilar vowel sounds (fie<u>nd</u> / behi<u>nd</u>).

Assonance is the repetition of a vowel sound in stressed syllables ending in dissimilar consonant sounds (w<u>a</u>ve / afl<u>a</u>me).

Internal rhyme is the use of rhymes within a poetic line.

In contrast to everyday language, the **language of fantasy** is used to tell of fantastic events or places.

To **analyze poetic effects,** identify the use of sound devices, images, symbols, repetition, and unusual word order, and then determine their effect on meaning or mood.

 Take It to the Net
www.phschool.com

Take the interactive self-test online to check your understanding of these selections.

Integrate Language Skills

Vocabulary Development Lesson

Word Analysis: Latin Root: -journ-

The verb *sojourn*, meaning "to visit for a while," contains the root *-journ-*, derived from French and Latin words meaning "day." Explain how the root contributes to the meaning of each of these words:

1. sojourn
2. journey
3. journalism
4. adjourn

Spelling Strategy

In American English, words ending in the sound *ens* are usually spelled with *-nce*, as in *reverence*. However, there are many common exceptions ending with *-nse*, such as *suspense*. Identify the word in each pair that is spelled correctly.

1. reverense, reverence
2. offense, offence
3. relianse, reliance
4. sense, sence

Concept Development: Antonyms

Review the words in the vocabulary list on page 685. Then, in your notebook, write the letter of the word that is the antonym of, or the word opposite in meaning to, the first word.

1. sinuous: (a) narrow, (b) straight, (c) dark

2. expiated: (a) sold, (b) atoned, (c) sinned

3. averred: (a) denied, (b) claimed, (c) wished

4. reverence: (a) respect, (b) contempt, (c) hope

5. tumult: (a) peace, (b) pleasure, (c) wealth

6. sojourn: (a) leave, (b) visit, (c) rest

Grammar and Style Lesson

Inverted Word Order

To create certain effects, poets sometimes **invert word order**, or depart from the normal English pattern of subject-verb-complement (s - v - c). In these lines, to rhyme *drowned* and *found*, Coleridge inverts the standard word order:

> Like one that hath been seven days
>
> <u>drowned</u>
>
> My body lay afloat;
>
> But swift as dreams, <u>myself</u> <u>I</u> <u>found</u> . . .
>   c s v

The inversion helps Coleridge make his rhyme and adds to the archaic sound of the poem.

Practice Rewrite these lines in standard word order.

1. That moment that his face I see, . . .
2. Red as a rose is she; . . .
3. At length did cross an Albatross, . . .
4. Nodding their heads before her goes / The merry minstrelsy.
5. Whiles all the night, . . . / Glimmered the white Moonshine.

Writing Application Write four or five poetic lines in which you invert normal word order. You may find it helpful to begin with standard word order and then invert subject, verb, and object to achieve rhyme or rhythm.

W͟G Prentice Hall Writing and Grammar Connection: Chapter 18, Section 2

Writing Lesson

Analysis of a Symbol

The Albatross in Coleridge's "The Rime of the Ancient Mariner" is a poetic symbol—a concrete image that stands for a cluster of ideas. Write an essay analyzing the meanings the Albatross takes on in the poem.

Prewriting   Using a cluster diagram, gather details from the poem about the Albatross and about the effects on the Mariner of its death. Then, group related details under headings, such as "Guilt" and "Respect for Natural Things."

Drafting   As you draft, use the headings on your prewriting lists as a guide, addressing the details you have gathered under each in turn. Link details to broader conclusions about the meaning of the Albatross.

Revising   Review your draft to highlight flat, unexciting language. Replace such passages with vivid, specific descriptions or claims.

Model: Revising for Vivid, Precise Language

The sailors praise the Albatross for bringing good weather,
a deadly calm.

then blame it for bringing ~~bad weather.~~ The Polar Spirit
wreaks its vengeance through weather, including an intense drought and a supernaturally fast wind.

~~also uses weather for its vengeance.~~

> Vivid words and added details keep the analysis interesting and precise.

Prentice Hall Writing and Grammar Connection: Chapter 14, Section 4

Extension Activities

Listening and Speaking   With a group, present a **dramatic reading** of a section of "The Rime of the Ancient Mariner." Assign parts and rehearse your reading, following these tips:

1. Each reader should take notes on the atmosphere of the section that he or she will read.
2. Readers should practice reading for sense, without pausing at line endings or overemphasizing rhymes.

Give your reading for the class. **[Group Activity]**

Research and Technology   Wordsworth and Coleridge were collaborators and friends. Research portraits, letters, and other primary sources, and write an **evaluation** of their literary friendship. As you research, consider the kind of information each source may provide. For example, a letter might suggest the warmth of a friendship.

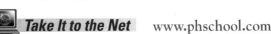 **Take It to the Net**   www.phschool.com

Go online for an additional research activity using the Internet.

Prepare to Read

She Walks in Beauty ◆ Apostrophe to the Ocean ◆ *from* Don Juan

George Gordon, Lord Byron (1788–1824)

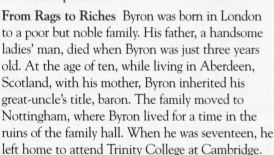

As famous for the life he led as for the poems he wrote, George Gordon, Lord Byron, came from a long line of handsome but irresponsible aristocrats. Byron lived life in the "fast lane" and was looked on with disapproval by most of his contemporaries.

From Rags to Riches Byron was born in London to a poor but noble family. His father, a handsome ladies' man, died when Byron was just three years old. At the age of ten, while living in Aberdeen, Scotland, with his mother, Byron inherited his great-uncle's title, baron. The family moved to Nottingham, where Byron lived for a time in the ruins of the family hall. When he was seventeen, he left home to attend Trinity College at Cambridge.

A Zest for Life While at Cambridge, Byron made friends, played sports, and spent money. A dashing figure, he even kept a pet bear. He also published a volume of verse, *Hours of Idleness* (1807), that received harsh criticism in Scotland's *Edinburgh Review*. In response, he wrote his first major work, the satirical poem *English Bards and Scotch Reviewers* (1809), in which he pokes fun at the prestigious magazine that gave him a terrible review.

After graduating, Byron traveled to out-of-the-way corners of Europe and the Middle East. He returned home bearing two sections of a book-length poem entitled *Childe Harold's Pilgrimage*, which depicted a young hero not unlike himself—moody, sensitive, and reckless. The work was well received, and Byron became an overnight sensation. "I awoke one morning and found myself famous," he observed.

For a time, Byron was the darling of London society. Hostesses vied to invite him to parties, and women flocked to his side. Byron became a true celebrity, a public figure of literary genius who in turn thrilled and scandalized his contemporaries. "Mad, bad, and dangerous to know" was Lady Caroline Lamb's famous description of Lord Byron.

The Byronic Hero Although Byron could be quite charming and friendly, his admirers insisted on associating him with the dark, brooding hero, impassioned by a cause, whom he so often described. Because of this persona, or adopted personality, readers throughout the nineteenth century saw Byron as the quintessential Romantic poet.

Italy and Tragedy Byron's fame and infamy grew in equal bounds. When his marriage to Annabella Milbanke broke up, the resulting scandal drove Byron from England in 1816. He would never return to the country of his birth.

Byron continued his travels through Europe, often accompanied by the poet Percy Bysshe Shelley. The two were great friends, and their poems reveal the strong influence of their mutual devotion. Eventually, Byron settled in Italy and worked on his masterful mock epic *Don Juan* (pronounced here as jo͞o´ ən). While he was there, however, tragedy struck: One of his daughters died, and Shelley drowned in a sailing accident.

A Budding Revolutionary In 1823, Byron, a champion of liberty, joined a group of revolutionaries seeking to free Greece from Turkish rule. Soon after, while training Greek rebel troops, Byron died of a rheumatic fever. Reports at the time tell of a late, poignant gesture: Dazed with fever, Byron called out in broken English and Italian, "Forward—forward—courage! Follow my example—don't be afraid!" To this day he is revered in Greece as a national hero.

Preview

Connecting to the Literature

In the popular imagination, writers and other creative people are often pictured as moody and unconventional. Two centuries ago, Lord Byron set the standard for the restless, rebellious "artistic temperament."

Literary Analysis

Figurative Language

Poetry usually contains **figurative language,** or language not meant to be taken literally. Figurative language includes these devices:

- **Similes**—direct comparisons of dissimilar things using *like* or *as*
- **Metaphors**—implied comparisons of dissimilar things, in which one thing is spoken of as if it were another kind of thing
- **Personifications**—attributions of human qualities to nonhuman subjects

These lines, addressed to the ocean, contain examples of each:

> These are thy toys, and, as the snowy flake,
> They melt into thy yeast of waves, . . .

Comparing Literary Works

In these poems, Byron uses figurative language to express the *sublime*—a sense of power in nature that escapes human understanding. To achieve the effect, poets express the infinite in sensory terms. For instance, Byron's sensory descriptions of the ocean convey the ocean's awesome, endless power—a power both divine and destructive. Compare the impressions that Byron creates of the infinite power of nature and human beauty.

Reading Strategy

Questioning

If you **question** as you read, you can focus your understanding of poetry. Begin with *who, what, where, when,* and *why* questions. Use a chart like the one shown to note and answer your questions as you read.

Vocabulary Development

arbiter (är´ bət ər) *n.* judge; umpire (p. 722)

tempests (tem´ pists) *n.* storms (p. 723)

torrid (tôr´ id) *adj.* very hot; scorching (p. 723)

fathomless (fath´ əm lis) *adj.* too deep to be measured or understood (p. 723)

retort (ri tôrt´) *v.* respond with a clever answer or wisecrack (p. 724)

insensible (in sen´ sə bəl) *adj.* unable to feel or sense anything; numb (p. 725)

credulous (krej´ oo ləs) *adj.* willing to believe; naive (p. 725)

copious (kō´ pē əs) *adj.* abundant; plentiful (p. 725)

avarice (av´ ə ris) *n.* greed (p. 725)

Passage
She walks in beauty, like the night Of cloudless climes and starry skies; . . .
Questions
1. *Who* is she? 2. *What* is her relationship with the speaker? 3. To *what* does the speaker compare her?

She Walks in Beauty

George Gordon, Lord Byron

In The Garden, (detail) Thomas Wilmer Dewing, National Museum of American Art, Washington, D.C.

Background

Lord Byron became so identified with the rebellious heroes he created—brooding figures whose ironic attitude and hidden sorrow only added to their charm—that this kind of figure became known as a Byronic hero. Such heroes are a staple of Romantic literature. They survive in modern times as a Hollywood or rock-and-roll type.

The Byronic attitude may be ironic, but Byron the poet was certainly capable of direct, sincere appreciation of beauty, as this poem demonstrates. Written to be set to music, the poem was inspired by Byron's first meeting with Lady Wilmot Horton, his cousin by marriage, who was wearing a black mourning gown with spangles.

▲ **Critical Viewing**
How does the rendering of this woman suggest some of the qualities that Byron attributes to his cousin in the poem? **[Analyze]**

She walks in beauty, like the night
　　Of cloudless climes and starry skies;
And all that's best of dark and bright
　　Meet in her aspect and her eyes:
5　Thus mellowed to that tender light
　　Which heaven to gaudy day denies.

One shade the more, one ray the less,
　　Had half impaired the nameless grace
Which waves in every raven tress,
10　　Or softly lightens o'er her face;
Where thoughts serenely sweet express
　　How pure, how dear their dwelling place.

And on that cheek, and o'er that brow,
　　So soft, so calm, yet eloquent,
15　The smiles that win, the tints that glow,
　　But tell of days in goodness spent,
A mind at peace with all below,
　　A heart whose love is innocent!

Literary Analysis
Figurative Language
With what kind of poetic comparison does Byron capture the reader's imagination in the opening lines?

Review and Assess

Thinking About the Selection

1. **Respond:** Do you think the speaker idealizes the subject of "She Walks in Beauty"? Explain.

2. **(a) Recall:** To what does the speaker compare the lady's beauty? **(b) Interpret:** What might "that tender light" in line 5 be?

3. **(a) Recall:** What would have "half impaired" the lady's grace? **(b) Interpret:** What does this claim suggest about the lady's beauty?

4. **(a) Connect:** In lines 11–18, what is the woman's appearance said to reveal about her character? **(b) Compare and Contrast:** How is the focus of the last six lines different from the focus of the opening lines? **(c) Draw Conclusions:** Does Byron's portrayal emphasize the spiritual or the physical aspect of the lady? Explain.

5. **(a) Evaluate:** Do you agree that goodness is an inherent part of beauty? Explain. **(b) Relate:** Do you think people today put too much emphasis on physical beauty? Explain.

▶**Critical Viewing** Byron speaks of the sea with "music in its roar." Does this artist succeed in visually communicating the sound of the ocean? [**Assess**]

from Childe Harold's Pilgrimage
Apostrophe to the Ocean

George Gordon, Lord Byron

There is a pleasure in the pathless woods,
There is a rapture on the lonely shore,
There is society, where none intrudes,
By the deep sea, and music in its roar;
5   I love not man the less, but nature more,
From these our interviews, in which I steal
From all I may be, or have been before,
To mingle with the universe, and feel
What I can ne'er express, yet cannot all conceal.

Reading Strategy
Questioning List three questions you might ask after reading the first stanza.

Shipwreck, J.C.C. Dahl, Munich Neue Pinakothek/Kavaler

10   Roll on, thou deep and dark blue ocean—roll!
           Ten thousand fleets sweep over thee in vain;
           Man marks the earth with ruin—his control
           Stops with the shore; upon the watery plain
           The wrecks are all thy deed, nor doth remain
15   A shadow of man's ravage, save[1] his own,
           When, for a moment, like a drop of rain,
           He sinks into thy depths with bubbling groan,
Without a grave, unknelled, uncoffined, and unknown.

---

1. **save** except.

✔Reading Check

According to the speaker, what impact does humanity's power have on the ocean?

His steps are not upon thy paths—thy fields
20 Are not a spoil for him—thou dost arise
And shake him from thee; the vile strength he wields
For earth's destruction thou dost all despise,
Spurning him from thy bosom to the skies,
And send'st him, shivering in thy playful spray
25 And howling, to his gods, where haply[2] lies
His petty hope in some near port or bay,
And dashest him again to earth—there let him lay.[3]

The armaments which thunderstrike the walls
Of rock-built cities, bidding nations quake,
30 And monarchs tremble in their capitals,
The oak leviathans,[4] whose huge ribs make
Their clay creator[5] the vain title take
Of lord of thee, and <u>arbiter</u> of war—
These are thy toys, and, as the snowy flake,
35 They melt into thy yeast of waves, which mar
Alike the Armada's[6] pride or spoils of Trafalgar.[7]

Thy shores are empires, changed in all save thee—
Assyria, Greece, Rome, Carthage, what are they?
Thy waters washed them power while they were free,
40 And many a tyrant since; their shores obey
The stranger, slave, or savage: their decay
Has dried up realms to deserts—not so thou,
Unchangeable, save to thy wild waves' play.
Time writes no wrinkle on thine azure brow;
45 Such as creation's dawn beheld, thou rollest now.

---

2. **haply** perhaps.
3. **lay** A note on Byron's proof suggests that he intentionally made this grammatical error for the sake of the rhyme.
4. **leviathans** (lə vī´ ə thənz) monstrous sea creatures, described in the Old Testament. Here the word means giant ships.
5. **clay creator** human beings.
6. **Armada's** refers to the Spanish Armada, defeated by the English in 1588.
7. **Trafalgar** battle in 1805 during which the French and Spanish fleets were defeated by the British fleet led by Lord Nelson.

Literary Analysis
Figurative Language
Explain how the images of destructive power in lines 20–36 create a sense of forces of nature beyond human comprehension.

arbiter (är´ bət ər) *n.* judge; umpire

Thou glorious mirror, where the Almighty's form
Glasses[8] itself in <u>tempests</u>: in all time,
Calm or convulsed—in breeze, or gale, or storm,
Icing the pole, or in the <u>torrid</u> clime
50   Dark-heaving—boundless, endless, and sublime;
The image of eternity, the throne
Of the Invisible; even from out thy slime
The monsters of the deep are made: each zone
Obeys thee; thou goest forth, dread, <u>fathomless</u>, alone.

55   And I have loved thee, ocean! and my joy
Of youthful sports was on thy breast to be
Borne, like thy bubbles, onward; from a boy
I wantoned with thy breakers—they to me
Were a delight: and if the freshening sea
60   Made them a terror—'twas a pleasing fear,
For I was as it were a child of thee,
And trusted to thy billows far and near,
And laid my hand upon thy mane—as I do here.

tempests (tem´ pists) *n.* storms

torrid (tôr´ id) *adj.* very hot; scorching

fathomless (fa*th*´ əm lis) *adj.* too deep to be measured or understood

---

8. Glasses mirrors.

Review and Assess

Thinking About the Selection

1. **Respond:** Which images from "Childe Harold's Pilgrimage" linger in your mind?

2. **(a) Recall:** What natural settings does the speaker describe in the first lines? **(b) Interpret:** What attitude toward nature do his descriptions reveal?

3. **(a) Recall:** In an apostrophe, a speaker addresses an absent person or personified quality or idea. Whom or what is the speaker addressing from line 10 on? **(b) Infer:** What is the speaker's attitude toward the subject he is addressing?

4. **(a) Recall:** How does the ocean treat such human things as cities and warships? **(b) Compare and Contrast:** What contrast between the ocean and human governments does the speaker make in lines 37–45? **(c) Draw Conclusions:** In what sense is the ocean a power that dwarfs all human endeavors?

5. **(a) Interpret:** In lines 46–54, what qualities make the ocean a reflection of "the Almighty's form"? **(b) Generalize:** What attitude toward nature do the lines encourage?

6. **Evaluate:** Is the sea still as mysterious and powerful today as it was in Byron's day? Explain.

from
Don Juan
George Gordon, Lord Byron

Background

Though it is unfinished, *Don Juan* (jo͞o´ ən) is regarded as Byron's finest work. A mock epic described by Shelley as "something wholly new and relative to the age," it satirizes the political and social problems of Byron's time.

Traditionally Don Juan, the poem's hero, is a wicked character driven by his obsession with beautiful women. In Byron's work, Don Juan is an innocent young man whose physical beauty, charm, and spirit prove to be alluring to ladies. As a result, he finds himself in many difficult situations.

During periodic pauses in the story, the narrator drifts away from the subject. In these digressions the narrator comments on the issues of the time and on life in general. In this excerpt the narrator sets aside the adventures of his hero to reflect on old age and death.

But now at thirty years my hair is gray
(I wonder what it will be like at forty?
I thought of a peruke[1] the other day)—
My heart is not much greener; and in short, I
5   Have squandered my whole summer while 'twas May,
And feel no more the spirit to <u>retort</u>; I
Have spent my life, both interest and principal,
And deem not, what I deemed, my soul invincible.

No more—no more—Oh! never more on me
10   The freshness of the heart can fall like dew,
Which out of all the lovely things we see
Extracts emotions beautiful and new,
Hived in our bosoms like the bag o' the bee:
Think'st thou the honey with those objects grew?
15   Alas! 'twas not in them, but in thy power
To double even the sweetness of a flower.

No more—no more—Oh! never more, my heart,
Canst thou be my sole world, my universe!

retort (ri tôrt´) *v.* respond with a clever answer or wisecrack

Reading Strategy
Questioning Ask yourself two questions about the speaker of *Don Juan*. Read on to find answers to your unanswered questions.

---

1. **peruke** (pə ro͞ok´) wig.

Once all in all, but now a thing apart,
20 Thou canst not be my blessing or my curse:
The illusion's gone forever, and thou art
<u>Insensible</u>, I trust, but none the worse,
And in thy stead I've got a deal of judgment,
Though heaven knows how it ever found a lodgment.

25 My days of love are over; me no more
The charms of maid, wife, and still less of widow
Can make the fool of which they made before—
In short, I must not lead the life I did do;
The <u>credulous</u> hope of mutual minds is o'er,
30 The <u>copious</u> use of claret is forbid too,
So for a good old-gentlemanly vice,
I think I must take up with <u>avarice</u>.

Ambition was my idol, which was broken
Before the shrines of Sorrow and of Pleasure;
35 And the two last have left me many a token
O'er which reflection may be made at leisure:
Now, like Friar Bacon's brazen head, I've spoken,
"Time is, Time was, Time's past,"[2] a chymic[3] treasure
Is glittering youth, which I have spent betimes—
40 My heart in passion, and my head on rhymes.

What is the end of fame? 'tis but to fill
A certain portion of uncertain paper:
Some liken it to climbing up a hill,
Whose summit, like all hills, is lost in vapor;
45 For this men write, speak, preach, and heroes kill,
And bards burn what they call their "midnight taper,"
To have, when the original is dust,
A name, a wretched picture, and worse bust.

What are the hopes of man? Old Egypt's King
50 Cheops erected the first pyramid
And largest, thinking it was just the thing
To keep his memory whole, and mummy hid:
But somebody or other rummaging
Burglariously broke his coffin's lid:
55 Let not a monument give you or me hopes,
Since not a pinch of dust remains of Cheops.

But I, being fond of true philosophy,
Say very often to myself, "Alas!

---

2. **Friar Bacon . . . Time's past** In Robert Greene's comedy *Friar Bacon and Friar Burgandy* (1594), these words are spoken by a bronze bust, made by Friar Bacon.
3. **chymic** (kim´ ik) alchemic: counterfeit.

insensible (in sen´ sə bəl) *adj.* unable to feel or sense anything; numb

credulous (krej´ ʊʊ ləs) *adj.* willing to believe; naive

copious (kō´ pē əs) *adj.* abundant; plentiful

avarice (av´ ə ris) *n.* greed

▼ **Critical Viewing**
What traits of the poem's narrator does this famous caricature of Byron share? **[Interpret]**

Lord Byron, Shaking the Dust of England off His Shoes, from "The Poet's Corner" pub. William Heinemann, 1904 (engraving by Max Beerbohm) Central Saint Martin's College of Art and Design

☑**Reading Check**

What type of experience will the speaker no longer undergo?

All things that have been born were born to die,
60 And flesh (which Death mows down to hay) is grass;
You've passed your youth not so unpleasantly,
And if you had it o'er again—'twould pass—
So thank your stars that matters are no worse,
And read your Bible, sir, and mind your purse."

65 But for the present, gentle reader! and
Still gentler purchaser! the bard—that's I—
Must, with permission, shake you by the hand,
And so your humble servant, and good-bye!
We meet again, if we should understand
70 Each other; and if not, I shall not try
Your patience further than by this short sample—
'Twere well if others followed my example.

"Go, little book, from this my solitude!
I cast thee on the waters—go thy ways!
75 And if, as I believe, thy vein be good,
The world will find thee after many days."[4]
When Southey's read, and Wordsworth understood,
I can't help putting in my claim to praise—
The four first rhymes are Southey's, every line:
For God's sake, reader! take them not for mine!

4. **Go . . . days** lines from the last stanza of Robert Southey's (1774–1843) Epilogue to
The Lay of the Laureate.

Literary Analysis
Figurative Language
How does Byron's
personification of death
make this abstract
concept vivid?

Review and Assess

Thinking About the Selection

1. **Respond:** Did you find the speaker of *Don Juan* amusing? Why?

2. **(a) Recall:** What subject does the speaker consider in
   the opening lines? **(b) Analyze:** How would you describe
   the mood of the speaker's reflections?

3. **(a) Recall:** What does the speaker say was the focus of his
   youth? **(b) Interpret:** In lines 33–40, why does the speaker
   call "glittering youth" "chymic," or counterfeit, treasure?

4. **Interpret:** What point about fame does the story of King
   Cheops make?

5. **(a) Draw Conclusions:** What do lines 65–80 suggest about
   Byron's attitude toward his own epic poem? **(b) Connect:** Is
   this attitude consistent with his "true philosophy"? Explain.

6. **Apply:** Identify a modern character who shares the disillusioned
   attitude of Byron's speaker.

Review and Assess

Literary Analysis

Figurative Language

1. Use a chart to list examples from the poems of **figurative language,** finding at least one example each of **simile, metaphor,** and **personification.** Show how each example suggests a number of different associations for what is being described.

Figurative Language	What Is Being Described	Associations Suggested

2. (a) Identify the simile in lines 10–18 of "Apostrophe to the Ocean." (b) What does the comparison suggest about the drowning man?

3. Identify and interpret the types of figurative language in the following lines: (a) "Thou glorious mirror, where the Almighty's form / Glasses itself. . . ." (b) "The freshness of the heart can fall like dew, . . ."

4. In "Apostrophe to the Ocean," what effect does the personification of the ocean have on the poem as a whole?

Comparing Literary Works

5. (a) In "She Walks in Beauty," how does Byron use imagery of the night to convey the mysterious, endless power of Lady Horton's beauty? (b) Identify three images suggesting the awesome, infinite power of nature in the "Apostrophe."

6. Compare the feelings associated with infinite power or mystery in these two poems.

7. Explain how Byron's use of such imagery expresses the Romantic faith in powers of nature that transcend reason and order.

Reading Strategy

Questioning

8. (a) List the questions you asked as you read Byron's poems and the answers you found. (b) Did **questioning** make your reading more active or focused? Explain.

Extend Understanding

9. **World Events Connection:** Describe a specific action that citizens who, like Byron, view nature with awe might advocate.

Integrate Language Skills

Vocabulary Development Lesson

Word Analysis: Latin Suffix -ous

The suffix of the word *credulous, -ous*, means "full of," and its root, *-cred-*, means "belief." *Credulous* means "full of belief" or "overly willing to believe." Using the meaning of the suffix *-ous*, define each of these terms.

1. glorious
2. spacious
3. porous
4. plenteous

Spelling Strategy

When adding the suffix *-ous* to a word ending in a vowel, drop or change the vowel.

beauty + *-ous* = beauteous

adventure + *-ous* = adventurous

Add the suffix *-ous* to each word.

1. fame
2. pity
3. prodigy

Concept Development: Antonyms

For each word, choose the letter of the word that is most nearly opposite to it in meaning.

1. arbiter: (a) defendant, (b) troublemaker, (c) judge
2. tempests: (a) storms, (b) lulls, (c) fixtures
3. torrid: (a) angry, (b) obedient, (c) freezing
4. fathomless: (a) deep, (b) measurable, (c) dry
5. retort: (a) ask, (b) reply, (c) deceive
6. insensible: (a) aware, (b) silly, (c) calm
7. credulous: (a) suspicious, (b) devious, (c) notorious
8. copious: (a) anxious, (b) typed, (c) scarce
9. avarice: (a) greed, (b) sin, (c) generosity

Grammar and Style Lesson

Subject and Verb Agreement

Verbs must agree with their **subjects** in number. Do not be misled when words intervene between the subject and the verb or when the subject comes after the verb.

> **Singular:** There is a pleasure in the pathless woods, . . .
>
> **Plural:** The monsters of the deep are made: . . .

Practice Identify the subject in each item. Then, choose the form of the verb that agrees with it.

1. The joys of the narrator of *Don Juan* (has, have) diminished.
2. There (is, are) much gray in his hair.
3. The charms of romance no longer (seems, seem) possible.
4. The fame of writers (escapes, escape) him.
5. Over the waters (goes, go) his book of verse.

Writing Application Rewrite this paragraph, correcting errors in agreement.

The works of Byron reflects his romantic attitudes. Each of his poems illustrate his talent for writing. His audience of enthusiastic readers also admires him for his deep sympathy for the downtrodden. Byron's commitment to political causes were, in the end, the reason for his death.

*W*G *Prentice Hall Writing and Grammar Connection: Chapter 23, Section 1*

Writing Lesson

Monologue

The speaker in *Don Juan* reveals his innermost thoughts and emotions in a monologue—a speech by the character spoken to himself or herself. Write a monologue for a modern Byronic hero (see the Background on page 718 for a definition). Organize your ideas so that your monologue will build dramatically.

Prewriting Jot down opinions that a Byronic hero might hold today. Next, consider your hero's circumstances and his or her attitude toward them. Then, list words and phrases that convey this attitude.

Drafting Structure your monologue to lead up to your hero's strongest expression of his or her attitude. As you draft, use words and phrases that feel appropriate for your character.

Revising Review the dramatic effect of your draft. Consider rearranging words and sentences to add drama.

Model: Revising to Structure Ideas for Effect

My life has made me the actor I am. If I am great, it

is because my life has been great, not perfect. The films

of my long career form a celluloid parade of my flaws,

mistakes, and crimes.

~~crimes and mistakes.~~ ∧

> Rearranging *crimes* and *mistakes* creates a stronger dramatic effect—the most powerful word comes last.

W̶G̶ Prentice Hall Writing and Grammar Connection: Chapter 5, Section 4

Extension Activities

Research and Technology Work with a team to develop a **proposal for a portrait** of the woman in "She Walks in Beauty."

- Conduct research into fashions, paintings, and lifestyles of Byron's day.
- Assemble the information in a detailed description of your proposed portrait.
- Explain how the portrait will reflect both the poem and the styles and life of the day. **[Group Activity]**

Listening and Speaking Deliver a **eulogy,** or farewell speech, to mourn the passing of Don Juan. In your eulogy, develop his character by including details from the poem. For each detail you include, draw a conclusion about Don Juan's character.

 **Take It to the Net** www.phschool.com

Go online for an additional research activity using the Internet.

Prepare to Read

Ozymandias ◆ Ode to the West Wind ◆ To a Skylark

Percy Bysshe Shelley (1792–1822)

When he died in a boating accident at 29, Percy Bysshe (bish) Shelley was eulogized by his fellow-poet Lord Byron as "without exception the best and least selfish man I ever knew." Yet the subject of this praise was a man whose disenchantment with the world was at least as great as his appreciation of its beauties. Shelley's disenchantment, though, only led him to pursue the good more passionately. At once modest and intense, Shelley was a poet of rare gifts. He was also a passionate reformer who believed that his time had betrayed the ideal of a perfect society.

A Loner and Rebel Born into the British upper classes, Shelley was raised on a country estate in Sussex. He attended the finest schools, including the prestigious boarding school Eton, but he was never able to settle into the routine of a student. Instead, he spent most of his time wandering the countryside and performing private scientific experiments. At Oxford University, he became a friend of Thomas Jefferson Hogg, a student whose political views were as strong as his own. The friendship further fueled Shelley's rebellious nature. When, with Hogg's encouragement and support, Shelley published the radical tract *The Necessity of Atheism*, both he and Hogg were expelled from the university.

Love and Art The expulsion estranged Shelley from his father. Instead of going home, Shelley headed for London. There, he met Harriet Westbrook. An unhappy schoolgirl, Westbrook played on his sympathies with descriptions of her miserable situation at home and at school. She persuaded him to elope, and they married. The two traveled to Ireland, where Shelley tried unsuccessfully to "deliver the Irish people from tyranny."

Shelley's development as a poet was already underway. In 1813, he had completed "Queen Mab," his first important poem. The work explored ideas of social justice that Shelley had encountered in the philosopher William Godwin's *Political Justice*. The views expressed by Shelley in the poem—that government and other institutions should be reshaped to conform to the will of the people—marks much of his subsequent poetry, even his nature poems.

Turmoil, Romance, and Tragedy Shelley's marriage, meanwhile, was in trouble. Harriet felt that she could not keep up with her husband, and she had come to question his political ideals. Meanwhile, continuing his travels in radical intellectual circles, Shelley fell in love with Mary Wollstonecraft Godwin, daughter of William Godwin and the feminist Mary Wollstonecraft. After Harriet's tragic death in 1816, Shelley and his beloved Mary Godwin married.

A Poet and an Outcast His radical politics, his tract about atheism, his separation from his first wife, his elopement—all helped make Shelley an outcast from his homeland. He and Mary eventually settled in Italy, where Byron, another famous exile, also lived. The friendship nourished the literary ambitions of all three. It was during a storytelling session with Shelley, Byron, and another friend that Mary Shelley was inspired to begin work on her famous novel *Frankenstein*. Shelley himself wrote many of his finest works in Italy, including "Ode to the West Wind," "To a Skylark," and his verse drama *Prometheus Unbound* (1820), a play predicting humanity's eventual freedom from tyranny.

An Early Death Shelley never lived to see whether his dreams of social progress came true. Today, he is often referred to as the perfect poet of the Romantic Era. His intense response to life and his deep convictions about freedom justify that title.

Preview

Connecting to the Literature

Nature's more extravagant effects—lightning slashing through the sky or snow blowing relentlessly for hours—may leave you gasping in awe or exclaiming in exasperation. Shelley carries this direct response a step further, addressing whole poems to an aspect of nature.

Literary Analysis

Imagery

Imagery is descriptive language that re-creates sensory experience. Writers may use imagery to create metaphors and other figures of speech. Poetic imagery has these characteristics:

- It appeals to any or all of the five senses.
- It often creates patterns supporting a poem's theme.

In "Ode to the West Wind," for example, Shelley uses wind images that appeal to sight, sound, and touch. As you read, think about how images and their patterns help you understand Shelley's message.

Comparing Literary Works

By gathering together powerful images of the West Wind or of a sky-lark, Shelley links these natural beings to the strivings of his own spirit. His images all depict concrete objects, such as leaves in the wind. Yet they also stir up longings and dreams. In the **Romantic philosophy** of the imagination, an image connects what is "outside" the mind with what is "inside," linking nature and spirit. Compare the specific ideas Shelley expresses through images. Then, judge how well his images capture both the longings of his spirit and the thing being described.

Reading Strategy

Responding to Imagery

You can **respond to imagery** in a poem even before you fully understand the meaning of the work. Immerse yourself in poetic images by noticing their sensory "texture"—dark or light, rough or smooth. Then, consider the associations each evokes. Use a chart like the one shown as you read.

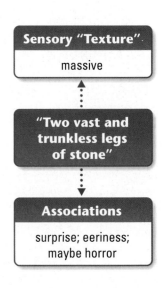

Vocabulary Development

visage (viz´ ij) *n.* face (p. 733)

verge (vʉrj) *n.* edge; rim (p. 734)

sepulcher (sep´ əl kər) *n.* tomb (p. 735)

impulse (im´ puls´) *n.* force driving forward (p. 735)

blithe (blīth) *adj.* cheerful (p. 737)

profuse (prō fyo͞os´) *adj.* abundant; pouring out (p. 737)

vernal (vʉr´ nəl) *adj.* relating to spring (p. 738)

satiety (sə tī´ ə tē) *n.* state of being filled with enough or more than enough (p. 739)

Ozymandias
Percy Bysshe Shelley

▶**Critical Viewing** How is this Egyptian statue like and unlike the one in the poem? **[Compare and Contrast]**

Background

The Ozymandias of Shelley's poem is based on an actual Egyptian pharaoh, Ramses II ("Ozymandias" was his name in Greek). Ramses II ruled during the thirteenth century B.C. and figures in the biblical story of Moses. He sponsored ambitious building projects and called for huge statues of himself to be built. According to an ancient story, one of these colossal statues was inscribed with this boast about his bold deeds: "I am Ozymandias, king of kings; if anyone wishes to know what I am and where I lie, let him surpass me in some of my exploits."

I met a traveler from an antique land
Who said: Two vast and trunkless legs of stone
Stand in the desert. Near them, on the sand,
Half sunk, a shattered visage lies, whose frown,
5   And wrinkled lip, and sneer of cold command,
Tell that its sculptor well those passions read
Which yet survive, stamped on these lifeless things,
The hand that mocked them and the heart that fed:
And on the pedestal these words appear:
10   "My name is Ozymandias, king of kings:
Look on my works, ye Mighty, and despair!"
Nothing beside remains. Round the decay
Of that colossal wreck, boundless and bare,
The lone and level sands stretch far away.

visage (viz´ ij) *n.* face

Review and Assess

Thinking About the Selection

1. **Respond:** If you could speak with the statue of Ozymandias, what question would you ask?
2. **(a) Recall:** What sight does the traveler describe?
   (b) Analyze: What overall effect does this sight have?
3. **(a) Recall:** How would you describe the expression on the face of Ozymandias? **(b) Infer:** What does his expression suggest about the kind of ruler he was?
4. **(a) Interpret:** What attitude is conveyed by the words on the pedestal? **(b) Compare and Contrast:** Compare this attitude with the opening images of the poem. **(c) Analyze:** In what sense is the inscription ironic?
5. **(a) Draw Conclusions:** What is the message of this poem? **(b) Apply:** Do you think that the message is pertinent to today's world? Why or why not?

Ode to the West Wind

Percy Bysshe Shelley

I

O wild West Wind, thou breath of Autumn's being,
Thou, from whose unseen presence the leaves dead
Are driven, like ghosts from an enchanter fleeing,

Yellow, and black, and pale, and hectic red,
5   Pestilence-stricken multitudes: O thou,
Who chariotest to their dark and wintry bed

The wingèd seeds, where they lie cold and low,
Each like a corpse within its grave, until
Thine azure sister of the Spring[1] shall blow

10 Her clarion[2] o'er the dreaming earth, and fill
(Driving sweet buds like flocks to feed in air)
With loving hues and odors plain and hill:

Wild Spirit, which art moving everywhere;
Destroyer and preserver; hear, oh, hear!

II

15 Thou on whose stream, 'mid the steep sky's commotion,
Loose clouds like earth's decaying leaves are shed,
Shook from the tangled boughs of Heaven and Ocean,

Angels[3] of rain and lightning: there are spread
On the blue surface of thine aery surge,
20 Like the bright hair uplifted from the head

Of some fierce Maenad,[4] even from the dim <u>verge</u>
Of the horizon to the zenith's height,
The locks of the approaching storm. Thou dirge

Literary Analysis
Imagery To which sense does the image in lines 18–23 mostly appeal?

verge (vʉrj) *n.* edge; rim

---

1. **sister of the Spring** the wind prevailing during spring.
2. **clarion** *n.* trumpet producing clear, sharp tones.
3. **angels** messengers.
4. **Maenad** (mē´ nad) a priestess of Bacchus, the Greek and Roman god of wine and revelry.

Of the dying year, to which this closing night
25 Will be the dome of a vast sepulcher,
Vaulted with all thy congregated might

Of vapors, from whose solid atmosphere
Black rain, and fire, and hail will burst: oh, hear!

III

Thou who didst waken from his summer dreams
30 The blue Mediterranean, where he lay,
Lulled by the coil of his crystalline streams,

Beside a pumice⁵ isle in Baiae's bay,⁶
And saw in sleep old palaces and towers
Quivering within the wave's intenser day,

35 All overgrown with azure moss and flowers
So sweet, the sense faints picturing them! Thou
For whose path the Atlantic's level powers

Cleave themselves into chasms, while far below
The sea-blooms and the oozy woods which wear
40 The sapless foliage of the ocean, know

Thy voice, and suddenly grow gray with fear,
And tremble and despoil themselves: oh, hear!

IV

If I were a dead leaf thou mightest bear;
If I were a swift cloud to fly with thee;
45 A wave to pant beneath thy power, and share

The impulse of thy strength, only less free
Than thou, O uncontrollable! If even
I were as in my boyhood, and could be

---

5. pumice (pum´ is) *n.* volcanic rock.
6. Baiae's (bā´ yēz) **bay** site of the ancient Roman resort near Naples, parts of which
lie submerged

sepulcher (sep´ əl kər) *n.*
tomb

Reading Strategy
Responding to Imagery
What associations do the
images in lines 29–36
suggest to you?

impulse (im´ puls´) *n.* force
driving forward

 **Reading Check**

In the first three sections,
what does the speaker
ask the West Wind to do?

The comrade of thy wanderings over Heaven,
50 As then, when to outstrip thy skyey speed
Scarce seemed a vision; I would ne'er have striven

As thus with thee in prayer in my sore need.
Oh, lift me as a wave, a leaf, a cloud!
I fall upon the thorns of life! I bleed!

55 A heavy weight of hours has chained and bowed
One too like thee: tameless, and swift, and proud.

V

Make me thy lyre,[7] even as the forest is:
What if my leaves are falling like its own!
The tumult of thy mighty harmonies

60 Will take from both a deep, autumnal tone,
Sweet though in sadness. Be thou, Spirit fierce,
My spirit! Be thou me, impetuous one!

Drive my dead thought over the universe
Like withered leaves to quicken a new birth!
65 And, by the incantation of this verse,

Scatter, as from an unextinguished hearth
Ashes and sparks, my words among mankind!
Be through my lips to unawakened earth

The trumpet of a prophecy! O Wind,
70 If Winter comes, can Spring be far behind?

---

7. **lyre** Aeolian (ē ō´ lē ən) lyre, or wind harp, a stringed instrument which produces musical sounds when the wind passes over it.

Literary Analysis
Imagery and Romantic Philosophy How do the images in lines 57–63 imply a connection between the speaker and nature?

Review and Assess

Thinking About the Selection

1. **(a) Recall:** What season does the poet associate with the West Wind? **(b) Interpret:** What feelings does Shelley create around the West Wind in sections II and III?

2. **(a) Recall:** What does the speaker ask of the wind in section IV? **(b) Infer:** What change in his life prompts this question?

3. **(a) Interpret:** In section V, what is the "new birth" for which the speaker asks? **(b) Interpret:** Why is the West Wind a suitable force to call on for this "new birth"?

4. **(a) Interpret:** What is the meaning of the famous final line of the poem? **(b) Analyze:** How does it tie together the poem?

To a Skylark

Percy Bysshe Shelley

Hail to thee, <u>blithe</u> spirit!
    Bird thou never wert,
That from heaven, or near it,
    Pourest thy full heart
5 In <u>profuse</u> strains of unpremeditated art.

    Higher still and higher,
    From the earth thou springest
Like a cloud of fire;
    The blue deep thou wingest,
10 And singing still dost soar, and soaring ever singest.

    In the golden lightning
    Of the sunken sun,
O'er which clouds are brightening,
    Thou dost float and run;
15 Like an unbodied joy whose race is just begun.

    The pale purple even[1]
    Melts around thy flight;
Like a star of heaven,
    In the broad daylight
20 Thou art unseen, but yet I hear thy shrill delight,

    Keen as are the arrows
    Of that silver sphere,[2]
Whose intense lamp narrows
    In the white dawn clear,
25 Until we hardly see—we feel that it is there.

    All the earth and air
    With thy voice is loud,
As, when night is bare,
    From one lonely cloud
30 The moon rains out her beams, and Heaven is overflowed.

    What thou art we know not;
    What is most like thee?
From rainbow clouds there flow not
    Drops so bright to see,
35 As from thy presence showers a rain of melody.

---

1. **even** evening.
2. **silver sphere** the morning star.

---

blithe (blīth) *adj.* cheerful

profuse (prō fyōōs´) *adj.* abundant; pouring out

Literary Analysis
Imagery To what three senses do lines 16–20 appeal?

✓**Reading Check**
Through what sense or senses does the speaker perceive the Skylark?

Like a poet hidden
    In the light of thought,
Singing hymns unbidden,
    Till the world is wrought
40 To sympathy with hopes and fears it heeded not:

Like a highborn maiden
    In a palace tower,
Soothing her love-laden
    Soul in secret hour
45 With music sweet as love, which overflows her bower:

Like a glowworm golden
    In a dell of dew,
Scattering unbeholden
    Its aerial hue
50 Among the flowers and grass, which screen it from the view!

Like a rose embowered
    In its own green leaves,
By warm winds deflowered,[3]
    Till the scent it gives
55 Makes faint with too much sweet those heavy-wingèd thieves.[4]

Sound of vernal showers
    On the twinkling grass,
Rain-awakened flowers,
    All that ever was
60 Joyous, and clear, and fresh, thy music doth surpass:

Teach us, sprite or bird,
    What sweet thoughts are thine:
I have never heard
    Praise of love or wine
65 That panted forth a flood of rapture so divine.

Chorus Hymeneal,[5]
    Or triumphal chant,
Matched with thine would be all
    But an empty vaunt,
70 A thing wherein we feel there is some hidden want.

What objects are the fountains[6]
    Of thy happy strain?
What fields, or waves, or mountains?
    What shapes of sky or plain?
75 What love of thine own kind? what ignorance of pain?

Reading Strategy
Responding to Imagery
What associations do the images in lines 51–55 suggest to you?

vernal (vʉrn´ əl) *adj.* relating to spring

---

3. **deflowered** fully open.
4. **thieves** the "warm winds."
5. **Chorus Hymeneal** (hī´ mə nē´ əl) marriage song, named after Hymen, the Greek god of marriage.
6. **fountains** sources, inspiration.

Cloud Study, 1821, John Constable, Yale Center for British Art

▲ **Critical Viewing** Which lines from Shelley's poem does this painting by the Romantic painter John Constable best illustrate? **[Connect]**

With thy clear keen joyance
　　Languor cannot be;
Shadow of annoyance
　　Never came near thee;
80 Thou lovest—but ne'er knew love's sad <u>satiety</u>.

Waking or asleep,
　　Thou of death must deem[7]
Things more true and deep
　　Than we mortals dream,
85 Or how could thy notes flow in such a crystal stream?

We look before and after,
　　And pine for what is not;

satiety (sə tī´ ə tē) *n.* state of being filled with enough or more than enough

✔Reading Check

According to the speaker, what can the skylark's song teach us?

---

7. **deem** know.

Our sincerest laughter
    With some pain is fraught;
90 Our sweetest songs are those that tell of saddest thought.

    Yet if[8] we could scorn
        Hate, and pride, and fear;
    If we were things born
        Not to shed a tear,
95 I know not how thy joy we ever should come near.

    Better than all measures
        Of delightful sound,
    Better than all treasures
        That in books are found,
100 Thy skill to poet were,[9] thou scorner of the ground!

    Teach me half the gladness
        That thy brain must know,
    Such harmonious madness
        From my lips would flow,
105 The world should listen then, as I am listening now.

---

8. if even if.
9. were would be.

Review and Assess

Thinking About the Selection

1. **(a) Recall:** In the first stanza, what does the poet claim the skylark is not? **(b) Interpret:** What point is he making? **(c) Analyze:** How do the images of light in lines 6–35 reinforce the point?

2. **(a) Recall:** To what four things does the speaker compare the bird in lines 36–55? **(b) Analyze:** What quality or power does each comparison suggest that the bird's song has?

3. **(a) Summarize:** What comparisons does the poet make between human song and the skylark's? **(b) Analyze:** Based on these comparisons, what does the speaker conclude about similarities and differences between the bird's life and human life?

4. **Interpret:** What does the speaker's use of the phrase "harmonious madness" (line 103) suggest about the difference between the skylark's song and human poetry?

5. **Evaluate:** Do you think the yearnings, speculations, and complaints that the skylark's song inspires in the speaker are as moving as the song itself? Explain.

Review and Assess

Literary Analysis

Imagery

1. Imagine filming the **imagery** of "Ozymandias." (a) Compare the camera placement you would use for lines 4–5, lines 9–11, and the final line. (b) Explain how each image helps convey Shelley's message.

2. (a) In "Ode to the West Wind," find three images indicating the power of the wind, and explain to which senses each appeals. (b) How do these images support Shelley's message of renewal?

3. (a) How do descriptions of sounds in "To a Skylark" suggest the bird's "unbodied joy"? (b) How does sound show the defect in human joy in lines 86–90?

Comparing Literary Works

4. Compare Shelley's images of the statue, the West Wind, and the skylark. (a) Which paints the strongest sensory picture of the object described? Explain. (b) Which provides the clearest sense of the ideas and feelings connected with the object? Explain.

5. In **Romantic philosophy,** the imagination connects nature and spirit. (a) What images in sections IV and V of "Ode to the West Wind" suggest such a connection? (b) Considering the light imagery and lines 36–40, how does "To a Skylark" make the connection?

6. Compare two instances in Shelley's poetry where an image connects the speaker and nature, using a chart like the one shown.

Image	How Vivid?	Associated Ideas		Link: Nature and Spirit
			····▶	

Reading Strategy

Responding to Imagery

7. Select a passage from each poem that contains images that you find striking or memorable. Explain your response to each.

Extend Understanding

8. **Media Connection:** What techniques are used in television films about nature to suggest poetic qualities?

Quick Review

Imagery is descriptive language re-creating sensory experience.

In **Romantic philosophy,** the poetic image provides a connection between nature and the human spirit.

To **respond to imagery,** take in the sensory experiences it suggests and examine the associations it has for you.

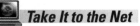 **Take It to the Net**

www.phschool.com

Take the interactive self-test online to check your understanding of these selections.

Integrate Language Skills

Vocabulary Development Lesson

Word Analysis: Latin Root -puls-

The Latin root -puls- means "push or drive." It is the base of some common words that are also used for scientific concepts. Write the letter of the definition for each numbered word, using a dictionary if needed.

1. pulse
2. compulsion
3. repulse
4. impulse
5. expulsion

a. to drive back or repel
b. a forcing out
c. brief increase in voltage or current
d. change in momentum
e. irresistible inclination

Spelling Strategy

The ending -ity is more common than -ety, which is used to avoid two i's in a row, as in satiety. In your notebook, correctly complete these words.

1. simplic ___
2. soci___
3. notori___

Concept Development: Synonyms and Antonyms

Antonyms are words that are opposite in meaning. For each vocabulary word, write the letter of its antonym in your notebook. Then, provide a synonym—a word with nearly the same meaning—for the word. Check the meanings of the word, the antonym, and the synonym in a dictionary. Explain any differences in meaning.

1. visage
2. vernal
3. blithe
4. sepulcher
5. profuse
6. verge
7. satiety
8. impulse

a. careworn
b. scarce
c. hunger
d. center
e. back
f. cradle
g. restraint
h. wintry

Grammar and Style Lesson

Subjunctive Mood

To express a wish or a condition contrary to fact, you must use a verb in the **subjunctive mood.** The past subjunctive form of be is were, used whether the subject is singular or plural.

> **Example:** If I <u>were</u> a swift cloud to fly with thee; . . . (contrary to fact)

For Romantic poets like Shelley, the subjunctive was a useful tool for expressing ideals and hopes. It allows writers to imagine and describe what is not currently true, but what they hope might one day be true.

Practice Copy the following sentences, and correct any verbs that require the subjunctive mood.

1. The speaker addressed the skylark.
2. He wishes that he was more like the bird.
3. He thinks that if he was a skylark, he would not know pain.
4. "If I was like you," he is saying, "I would know true happiness."
5. He was certain that the bird was happy.

Writing Application Using the subjunctive at least twice, describe something that you would like to change.

WG *Prentice Hall Writing and Grammar Connection: Chapter 21, Section 3*

Writing Lesson

Introductory Background on a Poem

Even in his lyric poetry, Shelley drew on the science and historical research of his time, as when he writes on the west wind. Write an introduction to one of his poems in which you explain the scientific or historical research that inspired him.

Prewriting   Select a poem, and make a list of questions to guide your research on its background. For each specific question you generate, write two questions about related, general information. Find answers to your questions, using library or Internet sources.

Model: Generating Questions to Identify Necessary Background

Did Shelley base "Ozymandias" on actual ruins?

RELATED BACKGROUND:

1. With what ancient ruins were English people of the day acquainted?

2. How much did English historians of the time know about the ancient past? About other regions of the world?

> By adding questions on background information to the first question, the writer ensures that readers will gain a good understanding of Shelley's inspiration and interests.

Drafting   Begin with an overview of Shelley's poem. Then, discuss the scientific or historical research that influenced it. Conclude with your list of sources.

Revising   Make sure the order of ideas in your draft is logical. Rearrange topics if necessary to ensure that readers will get necessary background information as they need it, not afterwards.

W̶G Prentice Hall Writing and Grammar Connection: Chapter 13, Section 3

Extension Activities

Listening and Speaking   Present a **weather report** for radio or television on the conditions in "Ode to the West Wind." Use appropriate language as follows:

1. Standard American English for clarity
2. Technical language for precision
3. Informal expressions to engage your audience

Prepare your report, including a weather map, and present it to the class.

Research and Technology   With a group, present a **cultural report** on Romantic painter John Constable's work. Conduct research to find information on his art; link his work to Romantic poetry; and find reproductions of his work. Each group member should present a section of the report to the class. **[Group Activity]**

 Take It to the Net   www.phschool.com

Go online for an additional research activity using the Internet.

Prepare to Read

Poetry of John Keats

John Keats (1795–1821)

Those who leave a lasting imprint on the world do not always live long. When the life of a groundbreaking figure is cut short, it leaves the world asking, What more might this person have achieved, if only he or she had lived longer? John Keats is such a figure. Although he died at age twenty-five, Keats left his indelible mark on literature, and this makes us wonder what more he might have accomplished had he lived longer.

A Defender of Worthy Causes Unlike his contemporaries Byron and Shelley, John Keats was not an aristocrat. Instead, he was born to working-class Londoners. As a child, he received attention for his striking good looks and his restless spirit. Keats developed a reputation for fighting, but always for a worthy cause. It was not until he and his schoolmaster's son, Charles Cowden Clarke, became friends that Keats developed an interest in poetry and became an avid reader.

From Medicine to Poetry In 1815, Keats began studying medicine at a London hospital. He had already begun writing poetry, but he earned his pharmacist's license before abandoning medicine for the literary world. In 1818, he published his first major work, *Endymion*, a long poem that the critics panned. Their negative reviews were due in part to Keats's association with the radical writer Leigh Hunt. The reviews also reflected the uneven quality of the verse itself. Despite the critical rejection, Keats did not swerve from his new career. Instead, he began writing the second of his long poems, *Hyperion*, a work he was never to complete.

A Year of Sorrow and Joy The year 1818 was significant for Keats in other ways as well. He lost his brother Tom to tuberculosis, but he also met the light of his life, Fanny Brawne, to whom he became engaged. The next year, 1819, was a period of feverish creativity. In just nine months, fired by grief, new-found love, and his own encroaching illness, Keats wrote the poems for which he is most famous, including "The Eve of St. Agnes," "La Belle Dame sans Merci," and his odes. Each is recognized as a masterpiece.

An Early Death Keats's engagement to Fanny and his burst of creativity might have been the prelude to a happy, productive life. Instead, Keats found his health deteriorating. Recognizing that like his brother, he had tuberculosis, Keats moved to Italy, hoping that the warmer climate would reverse the disease. Sadly, that hope proved false, and, in 1821, his battle with tuberculosis ended with his death. Keats wrote his own epitaph, which stresses the brevity of his life: "Here lies one whose name was writ in water."

A Legacy of Beauty Despite his early death and the fact that he composed his most important works in the space of just two years, John Keats remains one of the major influences in English poetry. Although he knew Percy Bysshe Shelley, he did not share Shelley's rebellious spirit, nor did he believe in using poetry for political statements. Keats worked as a pure artist who labored under the banner of beauty. He found in beauty the highest value our imperfect world could offer, and he put its pursuit at the center of his poetry. In masterful verse, he explored the beauty he found in the most ordinary circumstances.

At the same time, Keats was profoundly sensitive to the deep contradictions of life—of the sadness that every joy contains and the emptiness of every fulfillment. Although his best-remembered line is "'Beauty is truth, truth beauty,'" the poem in which it appears, "Ode on a Grecian Urn," implicitly contrasts the frozen world of a painted scene with the world of change and decay in which we live. For Keats, striving after what can never be attained was perhaps the true poetic task.

Preview

Connecting to the Literature

Fleeting moments, such as a beautiful sunset or a special smile, can linger in your memory. Keats explores such moments in his poems.

Literary Analysis

The Ode

An **ode** is a lyric poem, characterized by heightened emotion, that pays respect to a person or thing, usually directly addressed by the speaker.

- The **Pindaric ode** (named for the ancient Greek poet Pindar) falls in groups of three stanzas, one of which differs in form from the other two. Pindar's odes celebrated victors at the Olympic Games.
- Roman poets later developed the **Horatian ode** (also called homostrophic), which contains only one type of stanza.
- The **irregular ode** has no set pattern.

Keats created his own form of the ode, using ten-line stanzas of iambic pentameter (lines containing ten beats with a repeated pattern of weak-strong). Often those stanzas begin with a heroic quatrain (four lines rhymed *abab*) followed by a sestet (six lines rhymed in various ways). Note the various forms of Keats's odes.

Comparing Literary Works

In his odes, Keats follows the tradition of paying respect to something. Yet his odes reveal as much about him as they do about his subjects. In "Ode to a Nightingale," for instance, Keats finds himself caught by his longing for ideal beauty—a longing he cannot fulfill in real life. As you read, compare how each work dramatizes a conflict in the speaker. Analyze how the conflict is brought on by longings for what is far away.

Reading Strategy

Paraphrasing

Paraphrasing, or restating text in your own words, is a useful aid to understanding any difficult work. Using a chart like the one shown here, paraphrase difficult parts of each of Keats's poems.

Original
"When I have fears that I may cease to be . . ."
Paraphrase

Vocabulary Development

ken (ken) *n.* range of sight or knowledge (p. 747)

surmise (sər mīz′) *n.* guess; assumption (p. 747)

gleaned (glēnd) *v.* collected from bit by bit, as when gathering stray grain after a harvest (p. 748)

teeming (tēm′ iŋ) *adj.* filled to overflowing (p. 748)

vintage (vin′ tij) *n.* wine of fine quality (p. 750)

requiem (rek′ wē əm) *n.* musical composition honoring the dead (p. 752)

ON FIRST LOOKING INTO CHAPMAN'S HOMER

John Keats

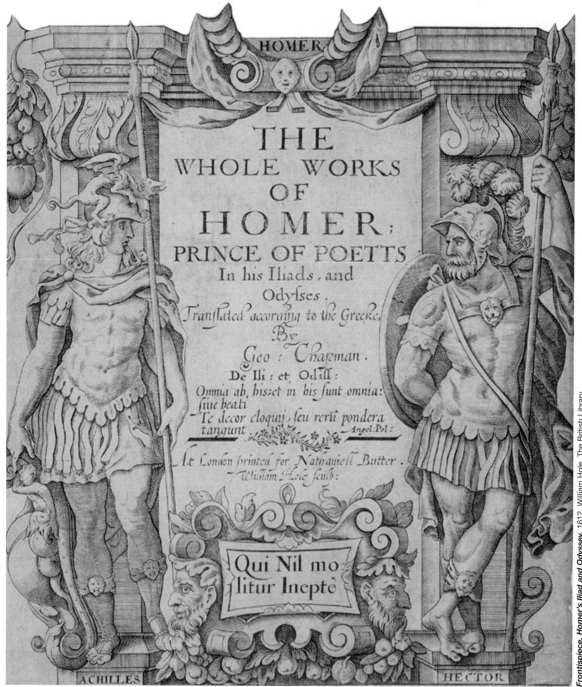

Background

Romantic poets such as Byron, Shelley, and Keats admired the culture of ancient Greece and derived inspiration from its art and literature. Keats's "Ode on a Grecian Urn" (p. 754), for instance, shows his tendency to associate ideas about beauty with antiquities, such as the beautifully adorned vases that ancient Greek society produced.

When Keats was twenty-one, his friend and former school-mate, Charles Cowden Clarke, introduced him to a translation of Homer by Elizabethan poet George Chapman. The two men spent the evening reading this book, and early the next morning Keats presented this sonnet to Clarke.

Much have I traveled in the realms of gold,
    And many goodly states and kingdoms seen;
    Round many western islands have I been
Which bards in fealty to Apollo[1] hold.
5 Oft of one wide expanse had I been told
    That deep-browed Homer ruled as his demesne;[2]
    Yet did I never breathe its pure serene[3]
Till I heard Chapman speak out loud and bold:
Then felt I like some watcher of the skies
10   When a new planet swims into his <u>ken</u>;
Or like stout Cortez[4] when with eagle eyes
    He stared at the Pacific—and all his men
Looked at each other with a wild <u>surmise</u>—
    Silent, upon a peak in Darien.[5]

Reading Strategy
Paraphrasing Paraphrase lines 5–6, paying special attention to the metaphor of a "demesne."

ken (ken) *n.* range of sight or knowledge

surmise (sər mīz´) *n.* guess; assumption

---

1. **Apollo** in Greek and Roman mythology, the god of music, poetry, and medicine.
2. **demesne** (di mān´) realm.
3. **serene** clear air.
4. **Cortez** Here, Keats was mistaken. The Pacific was discovered in 1513 by Balboa, not Cortez.
5. **Darien** (der´ ē ən) the Isthmus of Panama.

☑**Reading Check**

To what kind of things does Keats compare Chapman's translation?

◀**Critical Viewing** From the design of the engraving, what would you predict about the nature of the work to which Keats is reacting? **[Predict]**

When I Have Fears That I May Cease to Be

John Keats

When I have fears that I may cease to be
    Before my pen has <u>gleaned</u> my <u>teeming</u> brain,
Before high-piled books, in charactery,[1]
    Hold like rich garners[2] the full ripened grain;
5 When I behold, upon the night's starred face,
    Huge cloudy symbols of a high romance,
And think that I may never live to trace
    Their shadows, with the magic hand of chance;
And when I feel, fair creature of an hour,
10   That I shall never look upon thee more,
Never have relish in the fairy power
    Of unreflecting love—then on the shore
Of the wide world I stand alone, and think
Till love and fame to nothingness do sink.

gleaned (glēnd) v. collected from bit by bit, as when gathering stray grain after a harvest

teeming (tēm′ iŋ) adj. filled to overflowing

---

1. **charactery** written or printed letters of the alphabet.
2. **garners** storehouses for grain.

Review and Assess

Thinking About the Selections

1. **(a) Recall:** In the first four lines of "Chapman's Homer," what has the speaker done? **(b) Infer:** How do these lines encourage the reader to take the speaker's experience of Homer seriously?

2. **(a) Connect:** What feelings about Chapman's translation do lines 9–14 convey? **(b) Draw Conclusions:** How does the comparison of reading to a journey support these feelings?

3. **(a) Recall:** In lines 1–4 of "When I Have Fears," what does the speaker fear he will not accomplish before he dies? **(b) Interpret:** In lines 5–12, what is he concerned about missing? **(c) Evaluate:** Do the last lines offer a convincing resolution to such fears? Explain.

4. **Draw Conclusions:** What words describe Keats's character as revealed in these two poems?

5. **Apply:** Are young people today as anxious about and thrilled by the future as Keats? Explain.

John Keats, 1821, Joseph Severn, by courtesy of the National Portrait Gallery, London

▲ **Critical Viewing** From this rendering of Keats, how would you characterize him? **[Infer]**

Ode to a Nightingale

John Keats

Background

Keats composed the following ode in 1819, while living in Hampstead with his friend Charles Brown. Brown wrote the following description about how the ode was composed: "In the spring of 1819 a nightingale had built her nest near my house. Keats felt a tranquil and continued joy in her song; and one morning he took his chair from the breakfast table to the grass plot under the plum tree, where he sat for two or three hours. When he came into the house, I perceived he had some scraps of paper in his hand, and these he was quietly thrusting behind the books. On inquiry, I found those scraps, four or five in number, contained his poetic feeling on the song of our nightingale."

I

My heart aches, and drowsy numbness pains
    My sense, as though of hemlock[1] I had drunk,
Or emptied some dull opiate to the drains
    One minute past, and Lethe-wards[2] had sunk:
5 'Tis not through envy of thy happy lot,
    But being too happy in thine happiness,—
      That thou, light-winged Dryad[3] of the trees,
        In some melodious plot
    Of beechen green, and shadows numberless,
10   Singest of summer in full-throated ease.

II

O, for a draft[4] of <u>vintage</u>! that hath been
    Cooled a long age in the deep-delved earth,
Tasting of Flora[5] and the country green,

vintage (vin´ tij) *n.* wine of fine quality

Reading Strategy
Paraphrasing Restate lines 11–14 in your own words.

---

1. **hemlock** poisonous herb.
2. **Lethe-wards** toward Lethe, the river of forgetfulness in Hades, the underworld, in classical mythology.
3. **Dryad** (drī´ əd) in classical mythology, a wood nymph.
4. **draft** drink.
5. **Flora** in classical mythology, the goddess of flowers, or the flowers themselves.

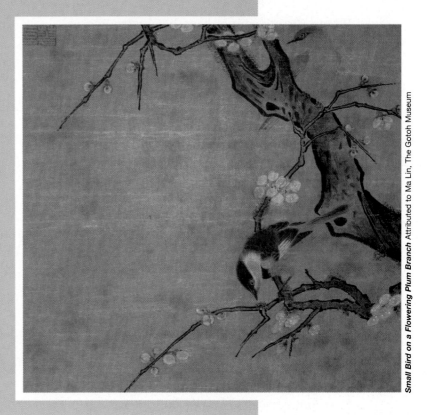

Small Bird on a Flowering Plum Branch Attributed to Ma Lin, The Gotoh Museum

Dance, and Provençal[6] song, and sunburnt mirth!
15   O for a beaker full of the warm South,
          Full of the true, the blushful Hippocrene,[7]
              With beaded bubbles winking at the brim,
                  And purple-stained mouth;
          That I might drink, and leave the world unseen,
20   And with thee fade away into the forest dim:

III

      Fade far away, dissolve, and quite forget
          What thou among the leaves hast never known,
      The weariness, the fever, and the fret
          Here, where men sit and hear each other groan;
25   Where palsy shakes a few, sad, last gray hairs,
          Where youth grows pale, and specter-thin, and dies;[8]
              Where but to think is to be full of sorrow
                  And leaden-eyed despairs,

---

6. **Provencal** (prō´ vən säl´) pertaining to Provence, a region in Southern France, renowned in the late Middle Ages for its troubadours, who composed and sang love songs.
7. **Hippocrene** (hip´ ō krēn´) in classical mythology, the fountain of the Muses on Mt. Helicon. From this fountain flowed the waters of inspiration.
8. **youth . . . dies** Keats is referring to his brother, Tom, who had died from tuberculosis the previous winter.

▲ **Critical Viewing**
Compare the mood of this painting with that of stanza III.
[Compare and Contrast]

Literary Analysis
The Ode Which sentiments in stanza III are more typical of Romantic than of traditional odes?

✔ **Reading Check**
What does the speaker wish to do along with the nightingale?

Where Beauty cannot keep her lustrous eyes,
30 Or new Love pine at them beyond tomorrow.

IV

Away! away! for I will fly to thee,
Not charioted by Bacchus[9] and his pards,
But on the viewless[10] wings of Poesy,[11]
Though the dull brain perplexes and retards:
35 Already with thee! tender is the night,
And haply[12] the Queen-Moon is on her throne,
Clustered around by all her starry Fays;[13]
But here there is no light,
Save what from heaven is with the breezes blown
40 Through verdurous[14] glooms and winding mossy ways.

V

I cannot see what flowers are at my feet,
Nor what soft incense hangs upon the boughs,
But, in embalmed[15] darkness, guess each sweet
Wherewith the seasonable month endows
45 The grass, the thicket, and the fruit-tree wild;
White hawthorn, and the pastoral eglantine;[16]
Fast fading violets covered up in leaves;
And mid-May's eldest child,
The coming musk-rose, full of dewy wine,
50 The murmurous haunt of flies on summer eves.

VI

Darkling[17] I listen; and, for many a time
I have been half in love with easeful Death,
Called him soft names in many a mused[18] rhyme,
To take into the air my quiet breath;
55 Now more than ever seems it rich to die,
To cease upon the midnight with no pain,
While thou art pouring forth thy soul abroad
In such an ecstasy!
Still wouldst thou sing, and I have ears in vain—
60 To thy high <u>requiem</u> become a sod.

> **Reading Strategy**
> **Paraphrasing** Paraphrase stanza V in one or two sentences.

> **requiem** (rek´ wē əm) *n.* musical composition honoring the dead

---

9. **Bacchus** (bak´ əs) in classical mythology, the god of wine, who was often represented in a chariot drawn by leopards ("pards").
10. **viewless** invisible.
11. **Poesy** poetic fancy.
12. **haply** perhaps.
13. **Fays** fairies.
14. **verdurous** green-foliaged.
15. **embalmed** perfumed.
16. **eglantine** (eg´ lən tīn´) sweetbrier or honeysuckle.
17. **Darkling** in the dark.
18. **mused** meditated.

VII

Thou wast not born for death, immortal Bird!
   No hungry generations tread thee down;
The voice I hear this passing night was heard
   In ancient days by emperor and clown:
65 Perhaps the selfsame song that found a path
   Through the sad heart of Ruth,[19] when, sick for home,
     She stood in tears amid the alien corn;
       The same that ofttimes hath
Charmed magic casements, opening on the foam
70   Of perilous seas, in fairylands forlorn.

VIII

Forlorn! the very word is like a bell
   To toll me back from thee to my sole self!
Adieu! the fancy cannot cheat so well
   As she is famed[20] to do, deceiving elf.
75 Adieu! adieu! thy plaintive anthem fades
   Past the near meadows, over the still stream,
     Up the hillside; and now 'tis buried deep
       In the next valley-glades:
Was it a vision, or a waking dream?
80   Fled is that music:—Do I wake or sleep?

Literary Analysis
The Ode What element of traditional odes appears in verse VII?

---

19. Ruth in the Bible (Ruth 2:1–23), a widow who left her home and went to Judah to work in the corn (wheat) fields.
20. famed reported.

Review and Assess

Thinking About the Selection

1. **(a) Recall:** How does the speaker describe his emotional state in stanza I? **(b) Infer:** What appears to have brought on this state?

2. **(a) Recall:** What wish does the speaker express in lines 19–20? **(b) Compare and Contrast:** What differences does he see between the bird's life and his own that cause him to wish this?

3. **(a) Analyze:** What is the viewpoint from which the speaker describes his surroundings in stanza V? **(b) Connect:** How does this viewpoint reflect the speaker's wish in line 21?

4. **(a) Analyze:** How does stanza VII "answer" stanza VI? **(b) Synthesize:** What similarity between death and immortality does the speaker imply?

5. **Make a Judgment:** By writing a poem full of extreme feeling, is Keats just being dramatic, or is writing such a poem a way of making peace with strong feelings? Explain.

ODE ON A GRECIAN URN

John Keats

The Orchard Vase (Column Krater),
Side A: Gathering Apples,
The Metropolitan Museum of Art

◀ **Critical Viewing**
What story can you see
in the picture decorating
this vase? **[Speculate]**

I

Thou still unravished bride of quietness
    Thou foster child of silence and slow time,
Sylvan[1] historian, who canst thus express
    A flowery tale more sweetly than our rhyme:
5 What leaf-fringed legend haunts about thy shape
    Of deities or mortals, or of both,
        In Tempe[2] or the dales of Arcady?[3]
    What men or gods are these? What maidens loath?[4]
What mad pursuit? What struggle to escape?
10   What pipes and timbrels?[5] What wild ecstasy?

II

Heard melodies are sweet, but those unheard
    Are sweeter; therefore, ye soft pipes, play on;
Not to the sensual[6] ear, but, more endeared,
    Pipe to the spirit ditties of no tone:
15 Fair youth, beneath the trees, thou canst not leave
    Thy song, nor ever can those trees be bare;
        Bold Lover, never, never canst thou kiss,
Though winning near the goal—yet, do not grieve;
    She cannot fade, though thou hast not thy bliss,
20   Forever wilt thou love, and she be fair!

III

Ah, happy, happy boughs! that cannot shed
    Your leaves, nor ever bid the Spring adieu;
And, happy melodist, unwearied,
    Forever piping songs forever new;
25 More happy love! more happy, happy love!
    Forever warm and still to be enjoyed,
        Forever panting, and forever young;
All breathing human passion far above,
    That leaves a heart high-sorrowful and cloyed,
30   A burning forehead, and a parching tongue.

IV

Who are these coming to the sacrifice?
    To what green altar, O mysterious priest,
Lead'st thou that heifer lowing at the skies,

Literary Analysis
The Ode What two figures on Keats's urn are directly addressed in stanza II?

---

1. **Sylvan** rustic, representing the woods or forest.
2. **Tempe** (tem´ pē) beautiful valley in Greece that has become a symbol of supreme rural beauty.
3. **Arcady** (är´ kə dē) region in Greece that has come to represent supreme pastoral contentment.
4. **loath** unwilling.
5. **timbrels** tambourines.
6. **sensual** involving the physical sense of hearing.

Reading Check
Describe two scenes depicted on the urn.

And all her silken flanks with garlands dressed?
35 What little town by river or seashore,
    Or mountain-built with peaceful citadel,
        Is emptied of this folk, this pious morn?
And, little town, thy streets forevermore
    Will silent be; and not a soul to tell
40   Why thou art desolate, can e'er return.

V

O Attic[7] shape! Fair attitude! with brede[8]
    Of marble men and maidens overwrought,[9]
With forest branches and the trodden weed;
    Thou, silent form, dost tease us out of thought
45 As doth eternity: Cold[10] Pastoral!
    When old age shall this generation waste,
        Thou shalt remain, in midst of other woe
Than ours, a friend to man, to whom thou say'st,
    "Beauty is truth, truth beauty,"—that is all
50   Ye know on earth, and all ye need to know.

---

7. **Attic** Attica was the region of Greece in which Athens was located; the art of the region was characterized by grace and simplicity.
8. **brede** interwoven pattern.
9. **overwrought** adorned with.
10. **Cold** unchanging.

Review and Assess

Thinking About the Selection

1. **Respond:** Do you place the same value on art that Keats does? Explain.

2. **(a) Recall:** Describe the scenes in stanzas I and II.
   (b) Infer: Why might the lover in stanza II grieve?
   (c) Interpret: Why does the speaker advise him not to grieve?

3. **(a) Recall:** Which items are called "happy" in stanza III?
   (b) Infer: What is the reason for their happiness?

4. **Draw Conclusions:** What do the speaker's comments on these painted scenes indirectly suggest about real life?

5. **(a) Interpret:** In line 49, what is the "'truth'" represented by the scenes on the urn? **(b) Connect:** How is this truth connected to the fact that the urn will remain after "old age shall this generation waste"? **(c) Make a Judgment:** Is the truth of the urn the "whole truth"? Explain.

6. **Apply:** The images on the urn do not move. What would Keats say about reruns on television? Do they also represent a kind of eternity? Explain.

Review and Assess

Literary Analysis

The Ode

1. (a) Identify the rhyme scheme of stanza I of "Ode on a Grecian Urn." (b) Is this rhyme scheme used throughout the poem? (c) Classify the **ode** as Pindaric, Horatian, or irregular.

2. What phrase does Keats use to directly address his subject in stanza I of "Ode to a Nightingale"? Identify another such phrase in the poem.

3. (a) What do Keats's two odes honor? (b) Would you say he treats his subjects with heightened emotion? Why?

Comparing Literary Works

4. (a) Compare the speaker's attitude—wonder, fear, longing—in each poem. (b) In each, an object or event represents something that the speaker desires but does not and perhaps cannot possess. Support this generalization with details from the poems.

5. Both "Ode to a Nightingale" and "Ode on a Grecian Urn" show a speaker caught between eternal beauty and the realities of life. Using a chart like the one shown, collect details to compare the relationship between the eternal and the world of time in each.

| Eternal World | Speaker's Attitude | World of Time |

6. Explain how each poem contributes to the idea that a person's self is defined by his or her deepest conflicts.

Reading Strategy

Paraphrasing

7. **Paraphrase** lines 9–10 from "Chapman's Homer."

8. Paraphrase at least one line that you find difficult in stanza VII of "Ode to a Nightingale."

Extend Understanding

9. **Cultural Connection:** What artifacts of today would speak most about our culture to the future, as the urn speaks of ancient Greece?

Integrate Language Skills

Vocabulary Development Lesson

Word Analysis: Latin Suffix *-age*

The Latin suffix *-age*, used in *vintage*, often means "condition or result of, cost or amount of, place of, collection of." A *vintage* is the "wine produced in a particular place and time." Using this information, define the following words:

1. wattage
2. storage
3. patronage
4. leverage

Spelling Strategy

In one-syllable words ending with a single vowel and consonant, double the consonant when adding *-ing*: *swim* + *-ing* = *swimming*. In words ending in *e*, drop the *e*: *bathe* + *-ing* = *bathing*. Exceptions include words like *dyeing*, in which the *e* is retained to avoid confusion with *dying*. Add *-ing* correctly to these words.

1. win
2. cringe
3. glean

Fluency: Sentence Completion

Choose words from the vocabulary list on page 745 to complete the following sentences. Write your answers in your notebook. Use each word only once, and if necessary, change the form of the word.

1. At the funeral, the organist played a mournful ___?___.
2. At harvest time, the birds ___?___ stray grain from the reaped fields.
3. Despite the evidence, he remained convinced that his initial ___?___ was correct.
4. There are many mysteries beyond our ___?___.
5. The storage room was ___?___ with supplies.
6. The wine collector carefully labeled each ___?___.

Grammar and Style Lesson

Direct Address

Terms of **direct address** are names or descriptive phrases used when speaking directly to a person or thing. Terms of direct address are set off by commas.

> **Example:** And when I feel, <u>fair creature of an hour,</u> That I shall never look upon thee more, . . .

Keats often uses terms of direct address to give poems immediacy and warmth.

Practice Identify the terms of direct address.

1. That thou, light-winged Dryad of the trees, / In some melodious plot . . .
2. Thou wast not born for death, immortal Bird!
3. Fair youth, beneath the trees, thou canst not leave / Thy song, . . .
4. Ah, happy, happy boughs! that cannot shed / Your leaves, . . .
5. To what green altar, O mysterious priest, / Lead'st thou that heifer. . . .

Writing Application Rewrite this paragraph, inserting two terms of direct address and punctuating them correctly.

I wandered through Athens thinking of you. Your memory burns in my mind. All others fade when you are near. Please stay true.

W̶G̶ Prentice Hall Writing and Grammar Connection: Chapter 27, Section 2

Writing Lesson

Response to Criticism

Scholar Douglas Bush writes of Keats: "The romantic elements in him remained . . . central, sane, normal—in everything but their intensity—and did not run into . . . excesses. . . ." Does this statement characterize Keats's poetry? Choose two of his poems, and compare them to decide.

Prewriting   List key quotations from the two poems you have selected. Identify those that express extreme feelings or ideas. Next, check for lines in which the poet qualifies or balances these feelings or ideas. Then, draw a conclusion about Keats and excess.

Drafting   Organize and draft your essay, quoting from the two poems you have selected to provide support for your points.

Revising   To analyze your draft, highlight each main point. Draw a circle around sentences that connect the point to the theme of excess. Consider adding to points not accompanied by circled text.

Model: Coding to Evaluate Unified Support

While the nightingale sings, Keats says, "Now . . . seems it rich to die," but the spell is broken when the nightingale flees. His first, excessive sentiment is balanced by his return to reality: "Do I wake or sleep?"

> The circled sentence adds unity by relating the author's point back to the theme of the essay—excess in Romantic poetry.

 Prentice Hall Writing and Grammar Connection: Chapter 14, Section 2

Extension Activities

Listening and Speaking The ancient Greek sculptures that Lord Elgin shipped to England in the 1800s had a great impact on Keats. With a group, give an **oral report** on Keats and the Elgin marbles. Divide the following tasks:

- Explaining what the Elgin marbles are
- Explaining how Keats came to know them
- Showing the influence of the experience on his poetry

Present your report to the class. **[Group Activity]**

Research and Technology Assemble a **science display** on the nightingale. Using print or Internet sources, take notes and organize them under categories such as *habitat*, *appearance*, and *behavior*. Include captioned illustrations, quotations from Keats's ode, and an annotated bibliography.

 **Take It to the Net**   www.phschool.com

Go online for an additional research activity using the Internet.

CONNECTIONS
Literature Around the World

Lyric Poetry

A lyric poem is a short poem expressing the thoughts or feelings of a single speaker. In ancient Greece, lyric poetry was verse recited or sung to the accompaniment of the stringed instrument called the lyre. Today, lyric poems provide their own verbal "music" as they express the personal thoughts and emotions of the poet.

The Romantic Lyric Poem Although lyric poems have been written for thousands of years, the Romantic Era put its special stamp on the form. The preference of Romantic poets for brief, expressive poems is not surprising, given their commitment to personal emotion. Wordsworth and Coleridge, writing in the Preface to *Lyrical Ballads* (1800), defined poetry itself as "the spontaneous overflow of powerful feelings." A second generation of poets—Shelley, Byron, and Keats—contributed their own melodies and perspectives to the Romantic lyric.

The World of the Lyric

One European contemporary of Byron's was the German poet Heinrich Heine (hīn´ riH hī nə). In his work, Heine seasoned the time-honored subject of love with a bitter-sweet flavor. His lyrics were not written for music, like those of ancient Greece, but they were later set to music by such famous composers as Robert Schumann and Franz Schubert. Writing earlier than the English Romantics, Japanese poets like Bashō (ba´ shō), Buson (bo͞o sän), and Issa (ē´ sä) anticipated the Romantics' love of nature. These writers wrote in the miniature poetic form of the haiku, which consists of three lines of five, seven, and five syllables each. Precise and simple, haiku always contain a reference to a particular season.

The Lorelei

HEINRICH HEINE
Translated by Aaron Kramer

I cannot explain the sadness
That's fallen on my breast.
An old, old fable haunts me,
And will not let me rest.

5 The air grows cool in the twilight,
And softly the Rhine[2] flows on;
The peak of a mountain sparkles
Beneath the setting sun.

More lovely than a vision,
10 A girl sits high up there;
Her golden jewelry glistens,
She combs her golden hair.

With a comb of gold she combs it,
And sings an evensong;
15 The wonderful melody reaches
A boat, as it sails along.

The boatman hears, with an anguish
More wild than was ever known;
He's blind to the rocks around him;
20 His eyes are for her alone.

—At last the waves devoured
The boat, and the boatman's cry;
And this she did with her singing,
The golden Lorelei.

---

1. **Lorelei** (lor′ ə lī) a legendary being, like the Siren, whose singing lured sailors to their doom.
2. **Rhine** (rīn) river in western Europe.

Heinrich Heine

(1797–1856)

The German poet Heinrich Heine was a brilliant love poet. He was also a gifted satirist and political writer whose fierce attacks on repression made him a controversial figure. Like the work of other late Romantics, his work reflects misgivings about the political and artistic promises of the early days of Romanticism.

HAIKU

BASHŌ

Translated by
Harold G. Henderson (first 3)
and Geoffrey Bownas (last 3)

The sun's way:
Hollyhocks turn toward it
Through all the rain of May.

———

Poverty's child—
He starts to grind the rice,
And gazes at the moon.

———

Clouds come from time to time—
And bring to men a chance to rest
From looking at the moon.

———

The cuckoo—
Its call stretching
Over the water.

———

Seven sights were veiled
In mist—then I heard
Mii Temple's bell.[1]

———

Summer grasses—
All that remains
Of soldiers' visions.

▶ **Critical Viewing**
 How does this painting reflect the changing of seasons in the first haiku? **[Interpret]**

Matsuo Bashō

(1644–1694)

Matsuo Bashō traveled widely through Japan, recording his observations and insights in poems and travel diaries.

---

1. Mii (mē′ ē′) **Temple's bell** The bell at Mii Temple is known for its extremely beautiful sound. The temple is located near Otsu, a city in southern Japan.

Crows Taking Flight Through Spring Haze, Okada Hanko (1782–1846) Hanging scroll, Edo period, dated 1841: Foundation Toyama Memorial Museum

HAIKU

YOSA BUSON

Translated by
Geoffrey Bownas

Scampering over saucers—
The sound of a rat.
Cold, cold.

———

Spring rain:
Telling a tale as they go,
Straw cape, umbrella.

———

Spring rain:
In our sedan
Your soft whispers.

———

Spring rain:
A man lives here—
Smoke through the wall.

———

Spring rain:
Soaking on the roof
A child's rag ball.

———

Fuji[1] alone
Left unburied
By young green leaves.

---

1. Fuji (foo′ jē) Mount Fuji is the highest peak in Japan (12,388 ft).

Thematic Connection
What special feelings do these haiku convey through descriptions of natural scenes?

Yosa Buson

(1716–1784)
Yosa Buson presents a Romantic view of the Japanese landscape, vividly capturing the wonder and mystery of nature.

HAIKU
KOBAYASHI ISSA

Translated by Geoffrey Bownas

Melting snow:
And on the village
Fall the children.
———

Beautiful, seen through holes
Made in a paper screen:
The Milky Way.
———

Far-off mountain peaks
Reflected in its eyes:
The dragonfly.
———

A world of dew:
Yet within the dewdrops—
Quarrels.
———

Viewing the cherry-blossom:
Even as they walk,
Grumbling.
———

With bland serenity
Gazing at the far hills:
A tiny frog.

Connecting Literature Around the World

1. Compare the speaker's troubled fascination with love in "The Lorelei" with the attitude of the speaker in another poem in this section.

2. (a) Contrast the insights into nature found in a haiku with those in another poem in this section. (b) Explain which of the poets you are comparing finds more in or expects more from nature.

Kobayashi Issa

(1763–1828)

The poetry of Kobayashi Issa captures the essence of daily life in Japan as experienced by common people, conveying his compassion for the less fortunate.

PART 3 The Reaction to Society's Ills

Forging the Anchor, 1831, William James Muller, City of Bristol Museum and Art Gallery

Prepare to Read

Speech to Parliament: In Defense of the Lower Classes ◆ A Song: "Men of England" ◆ On the Passing of the Reform Bill

George Gordon, Lord Byron (1788–1824)

Although less of a firebrand than his friend Shelley, Lord Byron was in his day a far more prominent supporter of radical reform and political liberty. In Britain, his first speech in the House of Lords defended workers who had sabotaged factory equipment that had put them out of work. (You can read a portion of that speech beginning on page 768.) Overseas, he was closely associated with the Italian freedom fighters known as the Carbonari. He lost his life in the cause of independence for Greece.

Both an aristocrat and a revolutionary, Byron was a man of extremes and contradictions. The German Romantic poet Goethe once described him as "a fiery mass of living valor hurling itself on life." Despite his contradictions, Byron consistently challenged tyranny and championed freedom. (For more on Byron, see p. 716.)

Percy Bysshe Shelley (1792–1822)

Of the major Romantic poets, Percy Bysshe Shelley was probably the most politically radical. Some of his poems are rallying cries encouraging the British working classes to rebel. Living in Italy, he wrote "A Song: 'Men of England'" in 1819 as an angry response to news of the growing economic suffering and political oppression of the working classes in England. In 1820, he decided to publish a collection of his political poems. He asked a friend if he knew of "any bookseller who would like to publish a little volume of popular songs wholly political & destined to awaken & direct the imagination of the reformers." An idealist, Shelley believed in the perfectibility of the human spirit and in the power of poetry to bring about the spiritual regeneration of humanity. (For more on Shelley, see p. 730.)

Thomas Babington Macaulay (1800–1859)

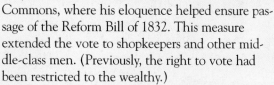

Before making his lasting mark as an insightful historian and powerful politician, Thomas Babington Macaulay won fame as a literary critic with essays published in the *Edinburgh Review*. Trained as a lawyer, he entered the House of Commons, where his eloquence helped ensure passage of the Reform Bill of 1832. This measure extended the vote to shopkeepers and other middle-class men. (Previously, the right to vote had been restricted to the wealthy.)

Macaulay continued as a force for change in the House of Commons. Pressured by the prime minister's office to vote for an amendment that would weaken an antislavery bill, Macaulay refused and offered his resignation instead. Macaulay again won a majority to his side, though, and the prime minister's office backed down.

In 1834 Macaulay accepted a government position in India, where he began a national education system and drafted a code of criminal law. He returned to England in 1838 and served again in Parliament. During periods in which his party, the Whigs, were out of power, Macaulay devoted himself to writing, producing a multivolume history of England that became a bestseller and a widely respected reference book.

Preview

Connecting to the Literature

The struggle for justice through marches, editorials, and legislation continues to make news. In nineteenth-century England, Shelley, Byron, and Macaulay added their voices to the timeless struggle.

Literary Analysis

Political Commentary

Political commentary offers opinions on political issues, building arguments on evidence and assumptions. Evaluate both the evidence and the assumptions that each writer uses. Shelley, for example, makes the argument shown, based on the assumption indicated:

> **Argument:** The common people of England should rebel because those they work for oppress them.

> **Assumption:** Duty is not a one-way street; workers and employers are bound together by mutual obligations.

Comparing Literary Works

Though each of these commentators works in a different form—speech, poem, and letter—they all seek to persuade, and each employs **persuasive devices,** including the following:

- **Rhetorical questions**—questions asked for dramatic effect, the expected answer to which is obvious
- **Balanced clauses**—two or more clauses in the same sentence that share a similar structure

Compare the types of devices each writer favors and the effectiveness of each.

Reading Strategy

Setting a Purpose for Reading

You will often get more from your reading if you first **set a purpose,** or choose a reason, for reading. Assess your own knowledge of the subject and use a graphic organizer like the one shown to set a purpose for reading these selections.

Vocabulary Development

impediments (im ped´ ə mənts) *n.* hindrances; obstructions (p. 769)

decimation (des´ ə mā´ shun) *n.* destruction or killing of one in ten, or of any large part of a group (p. 769)

efficacious (ef´ i kā´ shəs) *adj.* effective (p. 770)

emancipate (ē man´ sə pāt´) *v.* to free from slavery or oppression (p. 770)

balm (bäm) *n.* a soothing ointment; anything soothing (p. 771)

inauspicious (in´ ô spish´ əs) *adj.* not promising a good outcome; unfavorable (p. 772)

Prior Knowledge/ Interest

Byron was thought of as a "bad boy," sort of like James Dean.

Reading Purpose

How serious and well informed were his political positions?

Evidence for Answer

1.
2.

Speech to Parliament:
In Defense of the Lower Classes

George Gordon,
Lord Byron

The Workshops at the Gobelins, 1840,
Jean-Charles Develly, Musée
Carnavalet, Paris

Background

From the outbreak of the French Revolution
in 1789 until Napoleon's defeat at the Battle of
Waterloo in 1815, Britain focused on foreign affairs
at the expense of much-needed domestic reforms.
Unemployment was high, and laws such as the Corn
Law of 1815 aggravated the situation by protecting the
economic and political interests of wealthy landowners.

Even after Waterloo, reform was delayed by a dangerous cycle of protests and government crackdowns. In the
Luddite riots from 1811 to 1817, unemployed weavers in the industrial north wrecked factory equipment that they felt had endangered their
traditional livelihoods. When Parliament debated using the death penalty
for these crimes, Byron spoke out in the workers' defense.

As a person in some degree connected with the suffering county,
though a stranger not only to this House in general but to almost
every individual whose attention I presume to solicit, I must claim
some portion of your Lordships' indulgence, . . .

When we are told that these men are leagued together, not only
for the destruction of their own comfort, but of their very means of
subsistence, can we forget that it is the bitter policy, the destructive
warfare, of the last eighteen years[1] which has destroyed their comfort, your comfort, all men's comfort—that policy which, originating
with "great statesmen now no more," has survived the dead to become
a curse on the living, unto the third and fourth generation! These
men never destroyed their looms till they were become useless—

▲ **Critical Viewing**
What does the picture
suggest about working
conditions in Byron's day?
[Infer]

---

1. **bitter policy . . . last eighteen years** Byron is referring to the Napoleonic Wars,
which caused an economic depression.

worse than useless; till they were become actual <u>impediments</u> to their exertions in obtaining their daily bread.

Can you then wonder that in times like these, when bankruptcy, convicted fraud, and imputed felony are found in a station not far beneath that of your Lordships, the lowest, though once most useful, portion of the people should forget their duty in their distresses, and become only less guilty than one of their representatives? But while the exalted[2] offender can find means to baffle the law, new capital punishments must be devised, new snares of death must be spread for the wretched mechanic who is famished[3] into guilt. These men were willing to dig, but the spade was in other hands: they were not ashamed to beg, but there was none to relieve them. Their own means of subsistence were cut off; all other employments preoccupied; and their excesses, however to be deplored or condemned, can hardly be the subject of surprise.

I have traversed the seat of war in the Peninsula;[4] I have been in some of the most oppressed provinces of Turkey; but never, under the most despotic of infidel[5] governments, did I behold such squalid wretchedness as I have seen since my return, in the very heart of a Christian country. And what are your remedies? After months of inaction, and months of action worse than inactivity, at length comes forth the grand specific, the never-failing nostrum of all state physicians from the days of Draco[6] to the present time. After feeling the pulse and shaking the head over the patient, prescribing the usual course of warm water and bleeding[7]—the warm water of your mawkish police, and the lancets of your military—these convulsions must terminate in death, the sure consummation of the prescriptions of all political Sangrados.[8] Setting aside the palpable injustice and the certain inefficiency of the bill, are there not capital punishments sufficient on your statutes? Is there not blood enough upon your penal code, that more must be poured forth to ascend to heaven and testify against you? How will you carry this bill into effect? Can you commit a whole country to their own prisons? Will you erect a gibbet[9] in every field, and hang up men like scarecrows? Or will you proceed (as you must, to bring this measure into effect) by <u>decimation</u>; place the country under martial law; depopulate and lay waste all around you, and restore Sherwood Forest as an acceptable gift to the crown in its former condition of a royal chase, and an asylum for outlaws?[10] Are these the remedies for a starving and desperate

---

2. **exalted** well-born; of high rank.
3. **famished** forced by hunger.
4. **the Peninsula** Iberian Peninsula (Spain and Portugal).
5. **infidel** (in´ fə del) *n.* non-Christian.
6. **Draco** (drā´ kō) ancient Greek politician famous for his very severe code of laws.
7. **bleeding** In Byron's day, doctors often bled patients as a remedy for illness.
8. **Sangrados** doctors who bled patients.
9. **gibbet** (jib´ it) device used for hanging a person.
10. **Sherwood Forest . . . outlaws** Sherwood Forest, near Nottingham, was famous as the refuge of Robin Hood and his band of outlaws.

Literary Analysis
Political Commentary
What assumption does Byron make in the argument in this paragraph?

Literary Analysis
Political Commentary and Persuasive Devices
What reaction to these questions might Byron have expected from the legislators?

Reading Check

What punishment does the law opposed by Byron prescribe?

populace? Will the famished wretch who has braved your bayonets be appalled by your gibbets? When death is a relief, and the only relief it appears that you will afford him, will he be dragooned[11] into tranquillity? Will that which could not be effected by your grenadiers,[12] be accomplished by your executioners? If you proceed by the forms of law, where is your evidence? Those who refused to impeach their accomplices when transportation[13] only was the punishment will hardly be tempted to witness against them when death is the penalty.

With all due deference to the noble lords opposite, I think a little investigation, some previous inquiry, would induce even them to change their purpose. That most favorite state measure, so marvelously <u>efficacious</u> in many and recent instances, *temporizing*, would not be without its advantage in this. When a proposal is made to <u>emancipate</u> or relieve, you hesitate, you deliberate for years, you temporize and tamper with the minds of men; but a deathbill must be passed offhand, without a thought of the consequences.

---

11. **dragooned** (drə goōnd´) compelled by violence, especially as exerted by military troops.
12. **grenadiers** (gren´ ə dirz´) members of Britain's royal infantry.
13. **transportation** practice of sending people convicted of crimes to overseas penal colonies.

efficacious (ef´ i kā´ shəs) *adj.* effective

emancipate (ē man´ sə pāt) *v.* to free from slavery or oppression

Review and Assess

Thinking About the Selection

1. **Respond:** Did you find this speech persuasive? Why or why not?

2. **(a) Recall:** In the opening paragraph of the speech, what reason does Byron give for asking their "Lordships' indulgence"? **(b) Infer:** How would you describe Byron's tone in the opening paragraph? **(c) Analyze:** How does his tone change as the speech continues?

3. **(a) Recall:** According to Byron, why did the men wreck the looms? **(b) Compare and Contrast:** What contrast does he make between lower-class lawbreakers and upper-class lawbreakers? **(c) Infer:** What point about English society does Byron make with this contrast?

4. **(a) Analyze:** In paragraph 4, what does Byron compare to a doctor's patient? **(b) Interpret:** Explain the point Byron makes with this extended comparison.

5. **(a) Summarize:** Sum up three of Byron's arguments against the proposed bill. **(b) Evaluate:** To what extent does the address appeal to emotion? To what extent to reason?

6. **Make a Judgement:** Byron is a privileged aristocrat, not a worker or the owner of a mill. Does this fact add to or detract from the power of his speech? Explain.

A Song: "Men of England"

Percy Bysshe Shelley

Men of England, wherefore[1] plough
For the lords who lay ye low?
Wherefore weave with toil and care
The rich robes your tyrants wear?

5 Wherefore feed and clothe and save
From the cradle to the grave
Those ungrateful drones who would
Drain your sweat—nay, drink your blood?

Wherefore, Bees of England, forge
10 Many a weapon, chain, and scourge,[2]
That these stingless drones may spoil
The forced produce of your toil?

Have ye leisure, comfort, calm,
Shelter, food, love's gentle <u>balm</u>?
15 Or what is it ye buy so dear
With your pain and with your fear?

The seed ye sow, another reaps;
The wealth ye find, another keeps;
The robes ye weave, another wears;
20 The arms ye forge, another bears.

Sow seed—but let no tyrant reap:
Find wealth—let no impostor heap:
Weave robes—let not the idle wear:
Forge arms—in your defense to bear.

25 Shrink to your cellars, holes, and cells—
In halls ye deck another dwells.
Why shake the chains ye wrought? Ye see
The steel ye tempered[3] glance on ye.

With plough and spade and hoe and loom
30 Trace your grave and build your tomb
And weave your winding-sheet[4]—till fair
England be your Sepulcher.[5]

balm (bäm) *n.* a soothing ointment; anything soothing

---

1. **wherefore** for what purpose? Why?
2. **scourge** (skʉrj) whip used to inflict punishment.
3. **tempered** Made hard by alternately heating and cooling.
4. **winding-sheet** sheet for wrapping a corpse; shroud.
5. **Sepulcher** (sep´ əl kər) tomb.

✓Reading Check

According to the speaker, who benefits from the work of the "Men of England"?

ON THE PASSING OF THE REFORM BILL

Thomas Babington Macaulay

Background

By passing the Reform Bills of 1832–1835, the British Parliament sought to make Britain more democratic. The first Reform Bill dealt with Parliamentary representation. Some sparsely populated rural areas had a disproportionately large representation, whereas booming new industrial cities like Manchester had none. The bill passed the House of Commons three times, but the House of Lords voted it down each time. Finally, the prime minister forced King William IV to name fifty new members to the House of Lords. Liberal peers were appointed, and the bill finally passed. Macaulay's letter reports the first House of Commons vote on the bill.

Dear Ellis,

I have little news for you, except what you will learn from the papers as well as from me. It is clear that the Reform Bill must pass, either in this or in another Parliament.⬥ The majority of one does not appear to me, as it does to you, by any means <u>inauspicious</u>. We should perhaps have had a better plea for a dissolution⬥ if the majority had been the other way. But surely a dissolution under such circumstances would have been a most alarming thing. If there should be a dissolution now there will not be that ferocity in the public mind which there would have been if the House of Commons⬥ had refused to entertain the Bill at all.—I confess that, till we had a majority, I was half inclined to tremble at the storm which we had raised. At present I think that we are absolutely certain of victory, and of victory without commotion.

Such a scene as the division of last Tuesday I never saw, and never expect to see again. If I should live fifty years the impression of it will be as fresh and sharp in my mind as if it had just taken place. It was like seeing Caesar stabbed in the Senate House,[1] or seeing Oliver taking the mace from the table,⬥ a sight to be seen only once and

---

1. **Caesar** (sē′ zər) **stabbed in the Senate House** Emperor Julius Caesar, assassinated in the legislative council of ancient Rome.

never to be forgotten. The crowd overflowed the House in every part. When the strangers were cleared out and the doors locked we had six hundred and eight members present, more by fifty five than ever were at a division before. The Ayes and Noes* were like two vollies of cannon from opposite sides of a field of battle. When the opposition went out into the lobby,—an operation by the by which took up twenty minutes or more,—we spread ourselves over the benches on both sides of the House. For there were many of us who had not been able to find a seat during the evening. When the doors were shut we began to speculate on our numbers. Everybody was desponding. "We have lost it. We are only two hundred and eighty at most. I do not think we are two hundred and fifty. They are three hundred. Alderman Thompson has counted them. He says they are two hundred and ninety-nine." This was the talk on our benches. I wonder that men who have been long in parliament do not acquire a better coup d'œil[2] for numbers. The House when only the Ayes were in it looked to me a very fair house,—much fuller than it generally is even on debates of considerable interest. I had no hope however of three hundred. As the tellers* passed along our lowest row on the left hand side the interest was insupportable,—two hundred and ninety-one:—two hundred and ninety-two:—we were all standing up and stretching forward, telling with the tellers. At three hundred there was a short cry of joy, at three hundred and two another—suppressed however in a moment. For we did not yet know what the hostile force might be. We knew however that we could not be severely beaten. The doors were thrown open and in they came. Each of them as he entered brought some different report of their numbers. It must have been impossible, as you may conceive, in the lobby, crowded as they must have been, to form any exact estimate. First we heard that they were three hundred and three—then the number rose to three hundred and ten, then went down to three hundred and seven. Alexander Baring told me that he had counted and that they were three hundred and four. We were all breathless with anxiety, when Charles Wood who stood near the door jumped on a bench and cried out, "They are only three hundred and one." We set up a shout that you might have heard to Charing Cross[3]—waving our hats—stamping against the floor and clapping our hands. The tellers scarcely got through the crowd:—for the house was thronged up to the table, and all the floor

2. **coup d'œil** (koō dëy') glance.
3. **Charing Cross** London neighborhood some distance from the Houses of Parliament.

*L*iterature
in context Vocabulary Connection

◆ *Government Terms*

The following terms in the selection refer to British government:

Parliament the bicameral (two-house) legislative body of Britain

dissolution dismissal of Parliament in order to hold new elections; if major legislation fails, the prime minister resigns and Parliament is dissolved.

House of Commons the house of Parliament made up of elected members and led by the prime minister

House of Lords the house of Parliament whose membership is hereditary or by appointment

mace the symbol of the authority of the Speaker of the House of Commons. By demanding the removal of the mace in 1653, Puritan leader Oliver Cromwell (1599–1658) overrode Parliamentary authority and became virtual dictator of England.

Ayes and Noes respectively, votes in favor of and votes against a bill

tellers those appointed to count votes in Parliament

Westminster Palace, London, the home of the British Parliament

✓**Reading Check**

How close is the vote on the Bill?

was fluctuating with heads like the pit of a theater. But you might have heard a pin drop as Duncannon read the numbers. Then again the shouts broke out—and many of us shed tears—I could scarcely refrain. And the jaw of Peel[4] fell; and the face of Twiss[5] was as the face of a damned soul; and Herries[6] looked like Judas taking his neck-cloth off for the last operation. We shook hands and clapped each other on the back, and went out laughing, crying, and huzzaing into the lobby. And no sooner were the outer doors opened than another shout answered that within the house. All the passages and the stairs into the waiting rooms were thronged by people who had waited till four in the morning to know the issue. We passed through a narrow lane between two thick masses of them; and all the way down they were shouting and waving their hats; till we got into the open air. I called a cabriolet—and the first thing the driver asked was, "Is the Bill carried?"—"Yes, by one." "Thank God for it, Sir." And away I rode to Grey's Inn—and so ended a scene which will probably never be equalled till the reformed Parliament wants reforming; and that I hope will not be till the days of our grandchildren—till that truly orthodox and apostolical person Dr. Francis Ellis[7] is an archbishop of eighty.

---

4. **Peel** Sir Robert Peel (1788–1850), a leading member of the Tory party, which opposed the bill.
5. **Twiss** Horace Twiss, another Tory who opposed the bill.
6. **Herries** J. C. Herries, another Tory who opposed the bill.
7. **Francis Ellis** six-year-old son of Thomas Ellis.

Review and Assess

Thinking About the Selections

1. **(a) Recall:** In "A Song," what questions does the speaker ask his audience in the first stanza? **(b) Connect:** In your own words, sum up all the speaker's questions in a single ironic question to the men of England.

2. **(a) Recall:** To what does the speaker compare England's workers in stanza 3? **(b) Interpret:** In your own words, explain the point of this comparison.

3. **Draw Conclusions:** Judging from the last stanzas, what alternatives is Shelley posing in the poem? Support your answer.

4. **(a) Recall:** Summarize the events of the House of Commons vote on the Reform Bill of 1832, as reported in "On the Passing of the Reform Bill." **(b) Analyze:** In what ways does Macaulay add suspense to his account?

5. **Draw Conclusions:** How does Macaulay's final statement convey the importance of the occasion?

6. **Evaluate:** Which selection conveys the passion of politics more successfully? Explain.

Review and Assess

Literary Analysis

Political Commentary

1. Identify one implied and one stated assumption about the causes of the workers' rebellion that Byron makes in his **political commentary** "Speech to Parliament."

2. (a) What evidence does Byron present to support his argument that the "death bill" is unjust? (b) What evidence does Byron present in his argument that it will be ineffective?

3. (a) Summarize Shelley's argument in "A Song: 'Men of England.'" (b) Evaluate his arguments, using a chart like the one shown.

Evidence

Argument 1

Assumptions

Evaluation

Evaluation

Comparing Literary Works

4. (a) Find three **rhetorical questions** in Byron's speech. (b) Find three examples of **balanced clauses** in Shelley's "A Song: 'Men of England.'" (c) Compare the effect of each device on a reader.

5. (a) Contrast Macaulay's purpose and audience with Byron's or Shelley's. (b) Explain how the drama Macaulay builds in his letter adds conviction to his claim that "the Reform Bill must pass."

6. Which of these pieces do you think was probably most effective in achieving its goal? Why?

Reading Strategy

Setting a Purpose for Reading

7. List three details on which you would focus if your purpose in reading Byron's speech was to learn more about his life.

8. Choose a section from one of the selections, and show how reading it with two different purposes uncovers different details.

Extend Understanding

9. **World Events Connection:** What new technologies today threaten the jobs of workers?

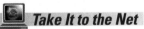

Integrate Language Skills

Vocabulary Development Lesson

Word Analysis: Latin Root -dec-

Byron asks whether Parliament desires the "decimation" of rebellious workers. The word *decimation* contains the Latin root -*dec*-, meaning "ten." *Decimation* originally referred to punishment for mutiny in the Roman army—killing every tenth person. Today, it means "any large-scale killing or destruction." The root -*dec*- appears in many words used in science and math.

Match each lettered word to its numbered definition.

1. animal with ten legs   a. decimals

2. fractions in tenths   b. deciliter

3. unit of sound intensity   c. decahedron

4. ten-sided figure   d. decapod

5. tenth of a liter   e. decibel

Concept Development: Synonyms

Replace each italicized word below with a synonym from the vocabulary list on page 767.

Byron and Shelley saw the ways of the English upper class as *hindrances* to the effort to *free* people and give them *effective* control over their own lives. These poets saw poetry not as a *salve*, but as a weapon for the *slaughter* of outmoded ideas. To them, the most *unfavorable* political sign was the stubbornness of the upper classes.

Spelling Strategy

Many adjectives, such as *inauspicious*, end in the suffix -*ious*. The *eous* spelling follows the consonants *n* and *t*: *spontaneous, courteous*. In your notebook, add *ious* or *eous* to correctly complete each word:

1. spac__   2. simultan__   3. beaut__

Grammar and Style Lesson

Correlative Conjunctions

Correlative conjunctions work in pairs to link grammatically equal words or groups of words. Correlative conjunctions include the following: *either . . . or; not only . . . but (also); both . . . and; neither . . . nor;* and *just as . . . so (too)*.

> It is clear that the Reform Bill must pass, <u>either</u> in this <u>or</u> in another Parliament.

Practice Use a pair of correlative conjunctions to combine each pair of sentences into a single sentence. Make any other changes needed.

1. (a) Byron did not write "A Song: 'Men of England.'" (b) Macaulay did not write it.

2. (a) Byron supported workers' rights. (b) Shelley supported workers' rights.

3. (a) Shelley compares English workers to bees. (b) He compares England to a tomb.

4. (a) The Tories would win the crucial vote. (b) The Whigs would win the crucial vote.

5. (a) The Whigs celebrate the passage of the bill. (b) Macaulay celebrates the passage of the bill.

Writing Application Write a short paragraph contrasting the major political parties in the United States today. Use at least three pairs of correlative conjunctions to link clauses, phrases, or words in your writing.

𝒲𝒢 Prentice Hall Writing and Grammar Connection: Chapter 17, Section 4

Writing Lesson

Editorial on a Political Issue

Byron, Shelley, and Macaulay wrote persuasively on important political issues of their time. Write an editorial about a political issue of today. Report the facts clearly and concisely. Then, present your own opinion in forceful, persuasive language.

Prewriting Browse through newspapers or newsmagazines to choose a political topic. Next, take notes on the issue, answering *who, what, where, when, why,* and *how.* Then, formulate your opinion on the issue.

Drafting As you draft, use a pyramid structure: Present the most important information first, followed by details. Conclude with a forceful statement of your opinion on the issue.

Revising Review your draft, circling vague or general words and phrases. Replace these words and phrases with forceful, persuasive language.

Model: Revising for Persuasive Language

In such a tense situation, the answer "I have no comment

at this time" represents more than indecisiveness. It is an

calculating cowardice.

act of ~~weakness.~~

> A specific description, memorably phrased, adds persuasive force.

WG Prentice Hall Writing and Grammar Connection: Chapter 7, Section 4

Extension Activities

Listening and Speaking Rehearse and deliver Byron's **speech** as he might have given it. Follow these tips:

1. Identify passages to emphasize for clarity or force. Alter the tone or volume of your voice, slow down, or add gestures for these parts.

2. Pay special attention to Byron's rhetorical questions, and deliver them forcefully for maximum impact.

Rehearse until you are confident, and then deliver your speech to the class.

Research and Technology Research an issue from this period of reform, such as the Luddite riots, the 1815 Corn Law, or the Peterloo Massacre. Then, write a **report** expressing an opinion on this issue. Use a variety of sources—such as encyclopedias, history books, and primary sources such as letters from the time— to research the issue. Then, decide what slant on the issue to take, and convey it in your report.

 **Take It to the Net** www.phschool.com

Go online for an additional research activity using the Internet.

Prepare to Read

On Making an Agreeable Marriage ◆ *from* A Vindication of the Rights of Woman

Jane Austen (1775–1817)

Modest about her own genius, Jane Austen lived a quiet life devoted to her family. Although she never married, she nonetheless explored love, beauty, and marriage in her six novels, which include *Pride and Prejudice*, *Emma*, and *Sense and Sensibility*.

A Reserved Life Austen was born in Steventon, Hampshire, the daughter of a clergyman. The seventh of eight children, she was educated largely at home by her father. In her teens, Austen began writing parodies and skits to amuse her family.

An Anonymous Novelist As an adult, Austen put her gift for keen observation to work in her novels. Capturing the absurdities of social life with satirical wit, she makes brilliant observations on human nature and shows a gift for contriving dramatic situations. The opening line of *Pride and Prejudice* illustrates her satirical sense of the realities of love and marriage: "It is a truth universally acknowledged, that a single man in possession of a good fortune, must be in want of a wife." The "must be" speaks volumes about the scheming and gossiping that went on beneath the social niceties in Austen's day.

Like most women writers of the time, Austen published anonymously. As her identity became more widely known, she was honored by the Prince Regent a few years before her death. Her novel *Emma* is dedicated to him.

Hollywood Tributes Jane Austen's sharp, satirical eye and brilliant dialogue have made her enormously popular today. All of Austen's novels have been made into feature films, and Hollywood has "rediscovered" her in recent years, making new film versions of her work.

Mary Wollstonecraft (1759–1797)

Mary Wollstonecraft, the mother of writer Mary Wollstonecraft Shelley, is recognized as one of the first major feminists. She wrote revolutionary works attacking the restrictions on women's freedom and education. The movement for women's rights has been influenced by her writings ever since.

The daughter of a textile worker and sometime farmer, Mary Wollstonecraft grew up in poverty, yet she pursued an education. She worked at various times as a lady's companion and governess. With her sisters and a friend, she established a girls' school near London. In 1787, she wrote *Thoughts on the Education of Daughters*, criticizing the poor education given to most females of her day.

A Voice for Women In 1790, when the writer Edmund Burke attacked the French Revolution, Wollstonecraft defended it in *A Vindication of the Rights of Man*. Two years later, she produced her most important work, *A Vindication of the Rights of Woman*, a landmark book on women's rights.

Wollstonecraft lived for a brief time in Paris, where she witnessed the French Revolution first-hand. Returning home to England, she joined a circle of radicals that included Thomas Paine, the defender of the American Revolution, William Blake, the poet (see p. 638), William Wordsworth, the poet (see p. 662), and the radical philosopher William Godwin. In 1797, she married Godwin. Six months later, she died from complications after giving birth to their daughter, Mary. Mary was also to become an important figure in literature: She married poet Percy Bysshe Shelley and, as Mary Wollstonecraft Shelley, wrote novels, including the famous *Frankenstein* (see p. 648).

Preview

Connecting to the Literature

"Boys will be boys. . . ." "Sugar and spice, . . . that's what little girls are made of. . . ." General assumptions like these rarely fit the facts, as these selections may suggest.

Literary Analysis

Social Commentary

Social commentary is writing or speech that offers insights into society. Social commentary can be *unconscious,* as when a writer points to a problem caused by social customs without explicitly challenging those customs. The commentary is *conscious* when a writer directly attributes a problem to social customs. As you read these selections, analyze the assumptions about women that they expose, consciously or unconsciously.

Comparing Literary Works

Austen and Wollstonecraft address widely different audiences for different purposes—Austen writes advice to her niece, and Wollstonecraft seeks to persuade the general reader. Both, however, use **persuasive techniques** that take the following forms:

- Appeals to logic based on sound reasoning
- Appeals to readers' sense of morality
- Appeals to emotion, addressing readers' feelings

As you read, compare the types of appeals that the writers use. Do they emphasize different ones? Evaluate the effectiveness of each.

Reading Strategy

Determining the Writer's Purpose

When reading, **determine the writer's purpose**—what he or she wants to accomplish—by using background knowledge and clues such as the title of the work. Use a chart like the one shown.

Vocabulary Development

scruple (skrōō´ pəl) *n.* hesitation caused by one's principles (p. 781)

amiable (ā´ mē ə bəl) *adj.* friendly; agreeable (p. 782)

vindication (vin´ də kā´ shən) *n.* act of providing justification or support for (p. 784)

solicitude (sə lis´ ə tōōd´) *n.* care; concern (p. 784)

fastidious (fas tid´ ē əs) *adj.* particular; difficult to please (p. 785)

specious (spē´ shəs) *adj.* deceptively attractive or valid; false (p. 785)

fortitude (fôrt´ ə tōōd´) *n.* courage; strength to endure (p. 785)

preponderates (prē pän´ dər āts´) *v.* dominates; causes the arm of a balance scale to tip downward (p. 786)

gravity (grav´ i tē) *n.* weight; seriousness (p. 786)

Background

Author supported equal rights.

Clues in Title

Vindication means "justification."

Direct Statements

Reports that she has done research on education

Writer's Tone

Reasonable, but she also expresses impatience, disbelief

↓

Writer's Purpose

On Making an Agreeable Marriage
Jane Austen

Marriage à la Mode: The Marriage Contract, 1743, William Hogarth, National Gallery of Art, London

▲ **Critical Viewing** In what ways does William Hogarth's (1697–1764) satirical depiction of the signing of a wedding contract echo attitudes in Austen's letter? **[Compare and Contrast]**

I feel quite as doubtful as you could be my dearest Fanny as to *when* my Letter may be finished, for I can command very little quiet time at present, but yet I must begin, for I know you will be glad to hear as soon as possible, & I really am impatient myself to be writing something on so very interesting a subject, though I have no hope of writing anything to the purpose.—I shall do very little more I dare say than say over again, what you have said before.—I was certainly a good deal surprised *at first*—as I had no suspicion of any change in your feelings, and I have no scruple in saying that you cannot be in Love. My dear Fanny, I am ready to laugh at the idea—and yet it is no laughing matter to have had you so mistaken as to your own feelings—And with all my heart I wish I had cautioned you on that point when first you spoke to me;—but tho' I did not think you then so *much* in love as you thought yourself, I did consider you as being attached in a degree—quite sufficiently for happiness, as I had no doubt it would increase with opportunity.—And from the time of our being in London together, I thought you really very much in love.—But you certainly are not at all—there is no concealing it.—What strange creatures we are!—It seems as if your being secure of him (as you say yourself) had made you Indifferent.—There was a little disgust I suspect, at the Races—& I do not wonder at it. His expressions then would not do for one who had rather more Acuteness, Penetration & Taste, than Love, which was your case. And yet, after all, I *am* surprised that the change in your feelings should be so great.—He is, just what he ever was, only more evidently & uniformly devoted to *you*. This is all the difference.—How shall we account for it?—My dearest Fanny, I am writing what will not be of the smallest use to you. I am feeling differently every moment, & shall not be able to suggest a single thing that can assist your Mind.—I could lament in one sentence & laugh in the next, but as to Opinion or Counsel I am sure none will [be] extracted worth having from this Letter.—I read yours through the very even[2] I received it—getting away by myself—I could not bear to leave off, when I had once begun.—I was full of curiosity & concern. Luckily Your Aunt C. dined at the other house, therefore I had not to maneuver away from *her*;—& as to anybody else, I do not care.—Poor dear Mr J. P![3]—Oh! dear Fanny, Your mistake has been one that thousands of women fall into. He was the *first* young Man who attached himself to you. That was the charm, & most powerful it is.—Among the multitudes however that make the same mistake with Yourself, there can be few indeed who have so little reason to regret it;—*his* Character & *his* attachment leave you nothing to be

scruple (skrōō′ pəl) *n.* hesitation caused by one's principles

Reading Strategy
Determining the Writer's Purpose What is Austen's purpose in claiming she has "no hope of writing anything to the purpose"?

✔ **Reading Check**

What news from Fanny prompts Austen's reaction?

---

1. **Fanny Knight** Fanny Austen Knight was the daughter of Austen's brother Edward.
2. **even** evening.
3. **Mr J. P.** Fanny's suitor.

ashamed of.—Upon the whole, what is to be done? You certainly *have* encouraged him to such a point as to make him feel almost secure of you—you have no inclination for any other person —His situation in life, family, friends, & above all his Character—his uncommonly amiable mind, strict principles, just notions, good habits—*all* that *you* know so well how to value, *All* that really is of the first importance—everything of this nature pleads his cause most strongly.— You have no doubt of his having superior Abilities—he has proved it at the University—he is I dare say such a Scholar as your agreeable, idle Brothers would ill bear a comparison with.—Oh! my dear Fanny, the more I write about him, the warmer my feelings become, the more strongly I feel the sterling worth of such a young Man & the desirableness of your growing in love with him again. I recommend this most thoroughly.—There *are* such beings in the World perhaps, one in a Thousand, as the Creature You & I should think perfection, where Grace & Spirit are united to Worth, where the Manners are equal to the Heart & Understanding, but such a person may not come in your way, or if he does, he may not be the eldest son of a Man of Fortune, the Brother of your particular friend, & belonging to your own County.—Think of all this Fanny. Mr J. P.– has advantages which do not often meet in one person. His only fault indeed seems Modesty. If he were less modest, he would be more agreeable, speak louder & look Impudenter;—and is not it a fine Character, of which Modesty is the only defect?—I have no doubt that he will get more lively & more like yourselves as he is more with you;—he will catch your ways if he belongs to you. And as to there being any objection from his *Goodness*, from the danger of his becoming even Evangelical,[4] I cannot admit *that.* I am by no means convinced that we ought not all to be Evangelicals, & am at least persuaded that they who are so from Reason & Feeling, must be happiest & safest.— Do not be frightened from the connection by your Brothers having most wit. Wisdom is better than Wit, & in the long run will certainly have the laugh on her side; & don't be frightened by the idea of his acting more strictly up to the precepts of the New Testament than others.—And now, my dear Fanny, having written so much on one side of the question, I shall turn round & entreat you not to commit yourself farther, & not to think of accepting him unless you really do like him. Anything is to be preferred or endured rather than marrying without Affection; and if his deficiencies of Manner &c &c[5] strike you more than all his good qualities, if you continue to think strongly of them, give him up at once.—Things are now in such a state, that you must resolve upon one or the other, either to allow him to go on as he has done, or whenever you are together behave with a coldness which may convince him that he has been deceiving himself.—I have no

amiable (ā′ mē ə bəl) *adj.* friendly; agreeable

Literary Analysis
Social Commentary What do these details reveal about the criteria for judging a suitor in Austen's day?

Literary Analysis
Social Commentary
What assumptions about responsibility in courtship does this passage reveal?

---

4. **Evangelical** of or relating to a group of earnest Church of England members active in social reform movements at the time of the letter.
5. **&c &c** et cetera (the & symbol, called an ampersand, stands for *et,* Latin for "and").

doubt of his suffering a good deal for a time, a great deal, when he feels that he must give you up;—but it is no creed of mine, as you must be well aware, that such sort of Disappointments kill any-body.—Your sending the Music was an admirable device,[6] it made everything easy, & I do not know how I could have accounted for the parcel otherwise; for tho' your dear Papa most conscientiously hunted about till he found me alone in the Din^g-parlor,[7] Your Aunt C. had seen that he had a parcel to deliver.—As it was however, I do not think anything was suspected.—We have heard nothing fresh from Anna. I trust she is very comfortable in her new home. Her Letters have been very sensible & satisfactory, with no *parade* of happiness, which I liked them the better for.—I have often known young married Women write in a way I did not like, in that respect.

You will be glad to hear that the first Edit: of M.P.[8] is all sold.— Your Uncle Henry is rather wanting me to come to Town, to settle about a 2^d Edit:—but as I could not very conveniently leave home now, I have written him my Will & pleasure, & unless he still urges it, shall not go.—I am very greedy & want to make the most of it;— but as you are much above caring about money, I shall not plague you with any particulars.—The pleasures of Vanity are more within your comprehension, & you will enter into mine, at receiving the *praise* which every now & then comes to me, through some channel or other.—

---

6. **device** trick; ruse; ploy.
7. **Ding-parlor** dining room.
8. **M.P.** Austen's novel *Mansfield Park*.

Review and Assess

Thinking About the Selection

1. **Respond:** How would you have reacted to this letter if you were Fanny? Explain.

2. **(a) Recall:** What is the "very interesting" subject Austen addresses in her letter? **(b) Interpret:** What change in her niece prompts Austen to comment "What strange creatures we are"? **(c) Summarize:** Summarize the problem that Austen is trying to help her niece resolve.

3. **(a) Recall:** What qualities does Austen find in Mr. J. P.? **(b) Interpret:** What does she mean when she writes that "Wisdom is better than Wit"?

4. **Summarize:** In one or two sentences, sum up Austen's advice to her niece about Mr. J. P.

5. **Make a Judgment:** Based on this letter, would you say Austen is a good judge of human nature? Why or why not?

from *A Vindication of the Rights of Woman*

Mary Wollstonecraft

Background

British women in the early nineteenth century had few economic or legal rights. In most cases, a woman's property was legally her father's until she married, after which the property became her husband's. Women's education focused mainly on "ladylike" accomplishments such as sewing and music. Women who showed an interest in things beyond marriage and the home were generally regarded as unfeminine. Mary Wollstonecraft focuses on the deforming effects that inadequate education had on women of her time and indicates the larger social forces holding women back.

After considering the historic page,[1] and viewing the living world with anxious <u>solicitude</u>, the most melancholy emotions of sorrowful indignation have depressed my spirits, and I have sighed when obliged to confess that either Nature has made a great difference between man and man,[2] or that the civilization which has hitherto taken place in the world has been very partial. I have turned over various books written on the subject of education, and patiently observed the conduct of parents and the management of schools; but what has been the result?—a profound conviction that the neglected education of my fellow creatures is the grand source of the misery I deplore, and that women, in particular, are rendered weak and

vindication (vin´ də kā´ shən) *n.* act of providing justification or support for

solicitude (sə lis´ ə tōōd) *n.* care; concern

---

1. **the historic page** the record of history
2. **man and man** used here in the generic sense to mean "human being and human being."

wretched by a variety of concurring causes, originating from one hasty conclusion. The conduct and manners of women, in fact, evidently prove that their minds are not in a healthy state; for, like the flowers which are planted in too rich a soil, strength and usefulness are sacrificed to beauty; and the flaunting leaves, after having pleased a <u>fastidious</u> eye, fade, disregarded on the stalk, long before the season when they ought to have arrived at maturity. One cause of this barren blooming I attribute to a false system of education, gathered from the books written on this subject by men who, considering females rather as women than human creatures, have been more anxious to make them alluring . . . than affectionate wives and rational mothers; and the understanding of the sex has been so bubbled by this <u>specious</u> homage, that the civilized women of the present century, with a few exceptions, are only anxious to inspire love, when they ought to cherish a nobler ambition, and by their abilities and virtues exact respect. . . .

The education of women has of late been more attended to than formerly; yet they are still reckoned a frivolous sex, and ridiculed or pitied by the writers who endeavor by satire or instruction to improve them. It is acknowledged that they spend many of the first years of their lives in acquiring a smattering of accomplishments; meanwhile strength of body and mind are sacrificed to libertine[3] notions of beauty, to the desire of establishing themselves—the only way women can rise in the world—by marriage. And this desire making mere animals of them, when they marry they act as such children may be expected to act—they dress, they paint, and nickname God's creatures . . . . Can they be expected to govern a family with judgment, or take care of the poor babes whom they bring into the world?

If, then, it can be fairly deduced from the present conduct of the sex, from the prevalent fondness for pleasure which takes place of ambition and those nobler passions that open and enlarge the soul, that the instruction which women have hitherto received has only tended, with the constitution of civil society, to render them insignificant objects of desire—mere propagators of fools!—if it can be proved that in aiming to accomplish them, without cultivating their understandings, they are taken out of their sphere of duties, and made ridiculous and useless when the short-lived bloom of beauty is over, I presume that *rational* men will excuse me for endeavoring to persuade them to become more masculine and respectable.

Indeed the word masculine is only a bugbear;[4] there is little reason to fear that women will acquire too much courage or <u>fortitude</u>, for their apparent inferiority with respect to bodily strength must

---

3. **libertine** immoral.
4. **bugbear** frightening imaginary creature, especially one that frightens children.

The British Tradition

The Literature of Protest
Mary Wollstonecraft writes in the tradition of protest in British literature. As early as the seventeenth century, the poet Amelia Lanier was speaking out for women's rights. By the beginning of the nineteenth century, the Romantics were urging a fair distribution of wealth and power to the working classes. Later, Charles Dickens and others would expose social problems through a newly popular form, the novel.

Twentieth-century poets, including Siegfried Sassoon, would chronicle the horrors of war. In the 1950s, the "angry young men," including Alan Sillitoe, would write grim portrayals of working-class lives. Wollstonecraft was an early voice in this tradition of protest.

fastidious (fa stid′ ē əs) *adj.* particular; difficult to please

specious (spē′ shəs) *adj.* deceptively attractive or valid; false

fortitude (fôrt′ ə to͞od) *n.* courage; strength to endure

 **Reading Check**

According to Wollstonecraft, what does the "false system of education" train women for?

render them in some degree dependent on men in the various relations of life; but why should it be increased by prejudices that give a sex to virtue, and confound simple truths with sensual reveries?

Women are, in fact, so much degraded by mistaken notions of female excellence, that I do not mean to add a paradox when I assert that this artificial weakness produces a propensity to tyrannize, and gives birth to cunning, the natural opponent of strength, which leads them to play off those contemptible infantine[5] airs that undermine esteem even whilst they excite desire. Let me become more chaste and modest, and if women do not grow wiser in the same ratio it will be clear that they have weaker understandings. It seems scarcely necessary to say that I now speak of the sex in general. Many individuals have more sense than their male relatives; and, as nothing <u>preponderates</u> where there is a constant struggle for an equilibrium without it has[6] naturally more <u>gravity</u>, some women govern their husbands without degrading themselves, because intellect will always govern.

preponderates (prē pän´ dər āts´) *v.* dominates; causes the arm of a balance scale to tip downwards

gravity (grav´ i tē) *n.* weight; seriousness

---

5. **infantine** infantile; childish.
6. **without it has** without having.

Review and Assess

Thinking About the Selection

1. **Respond:** Do you agree with Wollstonecraft that being respected is just as important as being loved? Explain.

2. **(a) Recall:** What emotional words does Wollstonecraft use in the first paragraph? **(b) Analyze:** Judging from the first paragraph, what is the author's attitude toward her subject?

3. **(a) Recall:** In the first paragraph, what comparison does the author use to describe the current state of women?
   (b) Interpret: What does she mean by the phrase "barren blooming"? **(c) Analyze:** To what cause does she attribute this "barren blooming"?

4. **(a) Recall:** According to the author, why are "notions of beauty" so important to women? **(b) Infer:** What effect does this focus on beauty have on women?

5. **(a) Interpret:** What does Wollstonecraft mean when she writes that women should become more "masculine"?
   (b) Summarize: According to the author, how do her society's notions of femininity encourage women to be childish and manipulative?

6. **Assess:** Which elements of Wollstonecraft's argument are effective? Which elements are not? Explain.

Review and Assess

Literary Analysis

Social Commentary

1. Judging from Austen's letter, and using a chart like the one shown, analyze the values of nineteenth-century courtship.

	Love	Compatibility	Money	Respectability
Examples				
Importance				

2. What unconscious **social commentary** does the letter offer on pressures that limited a woman's choices in the past?
3. Which social assumptions about men and women does Wollstonecraft challenge in *A Vindication of the Rights of Woman*?
4. Which assumptions about men's motives and desires does Wollstonecraft incorporate into her argument?

Comparing Literary Works

5. Compare the kinds of appeals used by Wollstonecraft and Austen in a chart like the one shown.

Logic	Ethics	Emotion

6. Compare the ways in which each writer handles an argument opposing her position.
7. How does each writer's audience affect her choice of **persuasive techniques**?
8. Explain which of the two works offer more effective commentary.

Reading Strategy

Determining the Writer's Purpose

9. Compare Wollstonecraft's and Austen's purposes in writing, explaining what clues you used to determine the purpose of each.
10. How does identifying a writer's purpose focus your reading?

Extend Understanding

11. **World Events Connection:** Is there still inequality in education for men and women? Support your opinion.

Quick Review

Social commentary is writing or speech that offers insights into a society and its customs.

Persuasive techniques are appeals to logic, ethics, and emotions used to convince readers.

To **determine a writer's purpose,** use clues such as direct statements and choice of title, details, and tone to determine what he or she wants to accomplish in a piece.

 Take It to the Net
www.phschool.com

Take the interactive self-test online to check your understanding of these selections.

Integrate Language Skills

Vocabulary Development Lesson

Word Analysis: Latin Root -fort-

From the Latin word *fortis*, which means "strong," comes the English root *-fort-*, which means "strength." The word *fortitude* means "strength to endure pain or misfortune." Explain how *-fort-* contributes to the meaning of the following words:

1. fortress   2. comfort   3. fortify

Spelling Strategy

Many words, such as *scruple* and *amiable*, end in *-le*. Only a few words, such as *funnel* and *novel*, end in *-el*. When choosing between *le* and *el* to spell the *uhl* sound at the end of a word, remember that the letters *d*, *p*, and *b* are usually followed by *le*. The letters *m*, *n*, *r*, and *v* are followed by *el*. Add *-le* or *-el* in each of the following items to correctly spell an English word.

1. hand__   2. doub__   3. marv__   4. quarr__

Concept Development: Synonym or Antonym?

Review the vocabulary words on page 779. Then, indicate in your notebook whether the word pairs below are synonyms—words meaning nearly the same—or antonyms—words that are opposite in meaning.

1. preponderates, dwindles
2. specious, false
3. vindication, justification
4. amiable, hostile
5. gravity, frivolity
6. solicitude, thoughtlessness
7. scruple, qualm
8. fastidious, sloppy
9. fortitude, weakness

Grammar and Style Lesson

Commas in a Series

Austen and Wollstonecraft use **commas in a series**: They separate the items in a list with commas. A **coordinating conjunction** such as *and* or *or* appears before the last item in a series. (It is common to include the comma before the conjunction, but it is also acceptable to omit it.)

> **Example:** His situation in life, family, friends, and above all his Character—

Practice Use commas to punctuate the following sentences correctly.

1. Jane Austen's novel *Pride and Prejudice* is filled with grace wit and satire.
2. Five of its characters are Jane Elizabeth Mary Kitty and Lydia Bennet.
3. Their amusements include balls visits and letter writing.
4. The Bennets meet a number of people, including Mr. Darcy Mr. Bingley and two of Mr. Bingley's sisters, at a ball.
5. Jane falls ill at the Bingleys' home is put to bed and is visited by Elizabeth.

Writing Application Write a paragraph in response to Wollstonecraft's *A Vindication of the Rights of Woman*, listing reasons you agree or disagree with her ideas. Use commas in a series to separate the reasons you list.

W͟G Prentice Hall Writing and Grammar Connection: Chapter 27, Section 2

Writing Lesson

Letter to an Author

Write a letter to either Austen or Wollstonecraft, in which you agree or disagree with her ideas. For example, you might write Austen agreeing with her views on marriage, while disagreeing with her interference in her niece's life.

Prewriting   Choose an author, and jot down your reactions to the work and the author's opinions. Find specific passages within the work with which you agree or disagree.

Drafting   As you draft, keep your audience and purpose in mind. To earn author's respect, use Standard English and a respectful tone. To catch her interest, choose words that convey enthusiasm about the topic.

Revising   Review your word choice to make sure it sets a tone that fits your purpose and audience. Circle sentences that seem uninteresting or poorly worded, and revise them to create an appropriate, consistent tone.

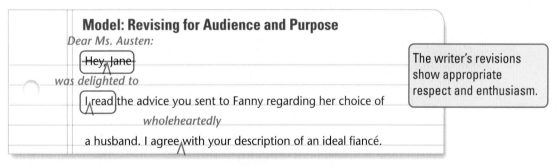

Model: Revising for Audience and Purpose

Dear Ms. Austen:

~~Hey, Jane~~

was delighted to

~~I read~~ the advice you sent to Fanny regarding her choice of

wholeheartedly

a husband. I agree with your description of an ideal fiancé.

> The writer's revisions show appropriate respect and enthusiasm.

 Prentice Hall Writing and Grammar Connection: Chapter 14, Section 2

Extension Activities

Listening and Speaking Update Austen's "conversation" about marriage in a role play of a **telephone call** between Austen and her niece.

- Update the language of the conversation to reflect the way an aunt and her niece might speak to each other today.
- Update Austen's logical, emotional, and ethical appeals to reflect today's values.

Rehearse and then present your phone call to the class.

Research and Technology Make an **annotated illustrated timeline** of the struggle for women's rights that began in the nineteenth century in England and in the United States. Highlight important dates, such as when women in each country won the right to hold property and when they won the right to vote.

 **Take It to the Net**   www.phschool.com

Go online for an additional research activity using the Internet.

CONNECTIONS
Literature and Media

The Reaction to Society's Ills

The works in this section serve as political and social commentary on the problems of early-nineteenth-century England. Shelley and Byron champion the common worker, while Macaulay joyfully describes the passage of an important reform measure. Wollstonecraft powerfully states the need for women's rights. Austen, in her private correspondence, offers a more playful commentary on social conditions.

Social Awareness Today Much of Jane Austen's insight into social circumstances and character can still be applied today. In this excerpt from the screenplay for the movie version of Jane Austen's novel *Sense and Sensibility*, Emma Thompson follows Austen and skillfully explores issues of opportunity in what appears to be an innocent conversation between two friends.

As you read, notice how Thompson uses the directions in italics to explain the emotional atmosphere in which this revealing discussion takes place. In addition, note the CAM abbreviation that indicates camera direction. EXT stands for exterior or outside shot, and the numbers indicate the scene or shot.

from Sense *and* Sensibility

Jane Austen, dramatized by Emma Thompson

After the recent death of Mr. Dashwood, his daughters Elinor, Marianne, and Margaret are trying to overcome their grief. Mr. Dashwood's eldest son and his wife, Fanny, have taken possession of the family home. Edward Ferrars, Fanny's brother, makes a great effort to comfort Margaret, the youngest, and in doing so begins to win the love of the eldest daughter, Elinor.

---

27 INT. NORLAND PARK. VELVET ROOM. ANOTHER DAY.
EDWARD *comes into the doorway and sees* ELINOR *who is listening to* MARIANNE *playing a concerto.* ELINOR *stands in a graceful, rather sad attitude, her back to us. Suddenly she senses* EDWARD *behind her and turns. He is about to turn away, embarrassed to have been caught admiring her, when he sees she has been weeping. Hastily she tries to dry her eyes. He comes forward and offers her a handkerchief, which she takes with a grateful smile. We notice his monogram in the corner: ECF.*

ELINOR. (*apologetic*)
That was my father's favorite.

EDWARD. *nods kindly.*

ELINOR.
Thank you so much for your help with Margaret, Mr. Ferrars.
She is a changed girl since your arrival.

EDWARD.
Not at all. I enjoy her company.

ELINOR.
Has she shown you her tree-house?

◀ **Critical Viewing** What can you tell from this movie still about the type of conversation Edward and Elinor are having? **[Interpret]**

Thematic Connection
What details show the social class to which these characters belong?

EDWARD.

Not yet. Would you do me the honor, Miss Dashwood? It is very fine out.

ELINOR.

With pleasure.

They start to walk out of shot, still talking.

ELINOR.

Margaret has always wanted to travel.

EDWARD.

I know. She is heading an expedition to China shortly. I am to go as her servant but only on the understanding that I will be very badly treated.

ELINOR.

What will your duties be?

EDWARD.

Sword-fighting, administering rum and swabbing.

ELINOR.

Ah.

CAM *tilts up to find* MRS. DASHWOOD *on the middle landing of the staircase, smiling down at them.* CAM *tilts up yet further to find* FANNY *on the landing above, watching* EDWARD. *and* Elinor. *with a face like a prune.*

28 EXT. NORLAND PARK. GARDENS. DAY. EDWARD *and* ELINOR *are still talking as they walk arm in arm in the late-afternoon sun.*

EDWARD.

All I want—all I have ever wanted—is the quiet of a private life but my mother is determined to see me distinguished.

ELINOR.

As?

EDWARD.

She hardly knows. Any fine figure will suit—a great orator, a leading politician, even a barrister would serve, but only on the condition that I drive my own barouche[1] and dine in the first circles.

His tone is light but there is an underlying bitterness to it.

ELINOR.

And what do you wish for?

EDWARD.

I always preferred the church, but that is not smart enough for my mother—she prefers the army, but that is a great deal too smart for me.

---

1. barouche (be rōōsh′) *n.* four-wheeled carriage with a collapsible hood and two seats on each side.

Thematic Connection
What social assumptions does Edward's joke reveal?

Thematic Connection
What social forces shape Edward's life?

ELINOR.

Would you stay in London?

EDWARD.

I hate London. No peace. A country living is my ideal—a small parish where I might do some good, keep chickens and give short sermons.

30 EXT. FIELDS NEAR NORLAND. DAY. EDWARD and ELINOR *are on horseback. The atmosphere is intimate, the quality of the conversation rooted now in their affections.*

ELINOR.

You talk of feeling idle and useless—imagine how that is compounded when one has no choice and no hope whatsoever of any occupation.

EDWARD.

Nods and smiles at the irony of it.

EDWARD.

Our circumstances are therefore precisely the same.

ELINOR.

Except that you will inherit your fortune.

He looks at her slightly shocked but enjoying her boldness.

ELINOR. *(cont.)*
We cannot even earn ours.

EDWARD.

Perhaps Margaret is right.

ELINOR.

Right?

EDWARD.

Piracy is our only option.

They ride on in silence for a moment.

EDWARD. *(cont.)*
What is swabbing exactly?

Connecting Literature and Media

1. Contrast Edward's predicament with another social problem addressed in this section.

2. Do you think Edward is as oppressed by social institutions as are any of the other men and women described in this section? Explain.

Emma Thompson

(b. 1959)

London-born Emma Thompson is one of England's most talented and successful actors, both in television and in films. She received an Academy Award for her performance in *Howard's End*, along with two nominations for performances in *The Remains of the Day* and *In the Name of the Father*. Her writing career began with her script for an adaptation of Jane Austen's novel *Sense and Sensibility*, for which she won an Academy Award.

Writing About Literature

Evaluate Literary Trends

Writing about the impact of the Romantic writers, the noted critic Isaiah Berlin stated that "The world has never been the same since, and our politics and morals have been deeply transformed by them. Certainly this has been the most radical, and indeed dramatic, not to say terrifying, change in men's outlook in modern times." For some, Romanticism represented freedom and new possibilities for self-expression. For a critic like Berlin, the movement involved a frightening rejection of reason in favor of sentiment and idealistic passion.

Following the assignment outlined in the yellow box, write an essay evaluating the impact of Romanticism.

Prewriting

Find a focus. Review the works that you have read in this unit and think about the values celebrated by Romanticism as well as their possible impact. Use these questions and an organizing chart to help you evaluate works:

- Why is this work considered Romantic? What Romantic values does the work reflect?

- How have these values affected writers and the public? Has their impact been primarily positive or negative? Why?

- What modern values or trends can I connect with these values?

Model: Assessing Values to Focus Your Response

Work	Romantic Values	My Evaluation
"... Tintern Abbey" Wordsworth	Nature as healer and teacher	This is a positive value that is often overlooked today.
"She Walks in Beauty" Byron	Admiration of beauty Physical beauty reflects spiritual depth	We value physical beauty too highly today.

Gather examples from literature. As you form your evaluation, look for specific lines that reflect the values of Romanticism. Concentrate on passages in which the poet celebrates or condemns an aspect of life or experience. These passages will help you formulate your thoughts and support your assessment.

Look for contemporary examples. To evaluate the full effects of Romanticism, you will also want to cite specific modern trends or events that show the impact of the values introduced by these writers. Review your notes on Romantic values, and freewrite on parallels in modern times. Then, list at least three ways that Romantic ideals influence today's world.

Assignment: The Legacy of Romanticism

What new values did Romantic writers celebrate? Do these values enrich our lives by emphasizing self-expression and other positive values, or do they lead to self-centered and undisciplined passion? Write an essay in which you evaluate the impact of Romantic values.

Criteria:

- Include a thesis statement that summarizes your overall evaluation of Romantic values.
- Show how two or three Romantic writers celebrate these values.
- Evaluate how these values are reflected in today's culture.
- Approximate length: 1,500 words

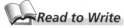
Read to Write

Review at least four Romantic works. You might begin with poems that you think are representative of the movement.

Drafting

Organize. Start with a general outline. Then, fill in details and examples. As you draft, you may reconsider the structure you have chosen.

> ### Model: Refining an Outline to Organize Ideas
>
> *Initial Outline:*
>
> **II.** Romanticism and Nature
>   **A.** "Tintern Abbey"
>   **B.** People today generally favor protecting the environment.
>   **C.** "The Rime of the Ancient Mariner"
>
> *Reorganized, Elaborated Outline:*
>
> **II.** Romanticism Celebrates Connecting With Nature
>   **A.** Examples From Romantic Writers
>   a. "Tintern Abbey": Nature as a source of wisdom
>   b. "Ancient Mariner": The mariner suffers when he violates nature
>   **B.** Contemporary Relevance: Popular Concern With the Environment
>   a. Concern over global deforestation
>   b. Antipollution laws

Use specific examples. As you draft, include specific, relevant examples from both Romantic works and contemporary life.

Revising and Editing

Review content: Begin and end powerfully. Review your opening paragraph to make sure you have introduced your evaluation clearly. Then, shape a powerful, focused conclusion.

Review style: Replace vague language. Eliminate words that are vague or imprecise. Strive for an active, vivid vocabulary.

> **Vague:** Wordsworth *likes* nature because he can *find out lots of things* and *feel really comfortable there.*
>
> **Vivid:** Wordsworth *values* nature as a *source of wisdom* and a *spiritual home.*

Publishing and Presenting

Hold a panel discussion. Find a classmate whose evaluation of Romantic values is quite different from yours. Read your essays aloud to the class, and then lead a class discussion comparing the two views.

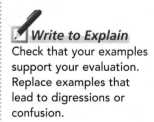 *Prentice Hall Writing and Grammar Connection: Chapter 14*

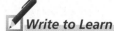 **Write to Learn**
If you cannot fill an outline section with two or three ideas, think about whether or not the heading is valid. You may need to rethink your evaluation to present an assessment you can support fully.

Write to Explain
Check that your examples support your evaluation. Replace examples that lead to digressions or confusion.

Writing WORKSHOP

Workplace Writing: Job Portfolio

A **job portfolio** includes all of the materials you submit to an employer to introduce yourself and express interest in a job. It is centered around a **résumé,** a brief, formatted summary of your educational and work experiences. In this workshop, you will write your own résumé.

Assignment Criteria Your résumé should include the following elements:

- A list, with dates and brief descriptions, of your life and work experiences, including your education
- An emphasis on skills, interests, and experiences appropriate to the type of job you are seeking
- Precise, active language, following the résumé style
- Consistent use of a clear, easy-to-understand format

To preview the criteria on which your résumé may be assessed, see the Rubric on page 799.

Prewriting

Gather facts for the résumé. Make a list of your work experiences. Also, jot down high points from your education and real-life experiences that might mark you as a good employee. List dates for all activities. In addition, note any relevant skills you may have, such as knowledge of computer applications.

Match the information to the job. Consider the job itself and what information will most interest that employer. An ad agency may want to see creativity highlighted. A bank may be more interested in your math skills.

A résumé is often taken to represent a person's entire work history. However, you may choose to omit informal or short-term work experiences, especially if their inclusion will distract from more significant experiences. You can also use the *Objective* and the *Skills* sections of your résumé to highlight the interests or accomplishments you feel will most appeal to a particular employer.

Type of Job:
something to do with computers:
-assistant Webmaster
-database maintenance

Experience to Emphasize:
-used computers at medical center
-membership in school Internet site club

Skills to Emphasize:
-HTML coding
-typing: 70 wpm

Other
-SAT math score shows my grasp of logic

Student Model

Before you begin drafting your résumé, read this student model and review the characteristics of powerful résumés.

Sarah Bailey
333 Anystreet Ave.
Independence, KY 41000
(888) 555-5555
e-mail@e-mail.com

OBJECTIVE
To obtain a position in which I can utilize my computer skills and Internet knowledge.

WORK EXPERIENCE

March 2000–present	**Nutrition Assistant,** Hermes Medical Center South, 10 Hermes Drive, Anytown, KY
	Monitored and implemented patient diets; consulted computer records, assembled individual patient trays, and communicated with nurses via hospital network.
May 1999–September 1999	**Hostess,** Fine Dining, Anytown, KY, Began as busser, promoted to hostess, July 1999; operated cash register; took responsibility for tracking receipts.

RELATED EXPERIENCE

Summer 1999	**Web Site Developer:** Assisted in setting up a Web site for school club; devised directory structure; coded HTML

EDUCATION

Fall 1996–present	Simon Kenton High School, 11132 Madison Pike, Independence, KY 41051 *Expected Graduation Date:* May 2001 *Special Courses:* Keyboarding I; Advanced Placement Calculus; Advanced Chemistry

SKILLS
- typing: 68 wpm
- HTML coding
- knowledge of Java

SPECIAL ACHIEVEMENTS
- Perfect attendance for four years
- President of National Honor Society
- Ranked first in senior class with GPA of 4.5

References available upon request

Under headings like this one, Sarah lists her work, education, and other relevant experiences.

Sarah uses precise, active language and follows the conventions of résumé style.

Throughout, Sarah emphasizes experiences and skills related to her objective.

Bullets and bold-faced headings make Sarah's format clear and easy to follow. Headings, dates, and bulleted items are consistently aligned.

Drafting

Outline your résumé. Begin by choosing and organizing your headings. Use clear, self-explanatory headings. *Education,* for example, is more direct than *Scholastic Preparation.* Organize headings effectively. No one résumé organization is best. You might use the order at right.

Play to your strengths. If you, like many high-school students, do not have an extensive employment history, list life experiences you have had that in some way relate to the job, and emphasize those.

Select and follow a format. Résumés come in a variety of formats. The model on page 797 shows one. Whatever format you choose, follow it consistently. All résumé formats share these features:

Headings	My Experiences
Education	
Work Experience	
Life Experience	
Skills	

- Your name, address, phone number, and any other contact information placed prominently at the top of the document
- A list of work experiences and other accomplishments beginning with the most recent
- Boldface or otherwise set-off names and addresses of employers
- Dates indicating your term of employment with each employer
- For each job listing, a brief indented description of your responsibilities

Follow résumé style. Do not use the pronoun *I,* but write as if it is understood. For example, write *Took responsibility for* or *Responsible for,* not *I took responsibility for.*

Revising

Revising for format. To check your formatting, follow these steps:

1. Scan your draft a few times without stopping to read. Check that items are correctly and consistently aligned. Mark items that are misaligned.

2. Scan the headings to confirm that you use boldfacing and capital letters consistently. Mark headings that need to be reformatted.

3. Scan the first line of your entries to ensure that, in each case, the information is ordered in the same pattern. Mark any inconsistencies.

When you have finished scanning your draft, go back and fix any problems.

March 2000–present **Nutrition Assistant,** Hermes Medical Center South

Hostess,
May 1999–September 1999 ˄The Frontier Inn, Anytown, KY, ~~Hostess~~

> Boldfacing this job title and moving it to the beginning of the listing makes the format of the two listings consistent.

Revise for conciseness and clarity. Use brief explanations that get at the heart of things you have done. Let strong verbs carry your message.

Wordy: Made sure that surfaces were clean; disposed of fixer used in printing and other chemicals

Concise: Maintained darkroom

Compare the model and nonmodel. Why is the model more effective?

Nonmodel	Model
Looked after patients by making sure their meals were what the doctor recommended; worked with computers, looking up records and sending e-mails.	Monitored and implemented patient diets; consulted computer records, assembled individual patient trays, and communicated with nurses via hospital network.

Publishing and Presenting

Assemble a job portfolio. To complete your job portfolio, write a cover letter to a potential employer. Include the following elements:

- Brief, pertinent introductory information about yourself
- An expression of your interest in a job
- An overview of your qualifications for the job and your reasons for interest in it
- Contact information
- A sentence thanking your reader for his or her consideration

Follow standard business letter format as you draft. Proofread your work so it is error-free.

Prentice Hall Writing and Grammar Connection: Chapter 16

Rubric for Self-Assessment

Evaluate your résumé using the following criteria and rating scale:

Criteria	Rating Scale				
	Not very				Very
How well does the résumé convey job and life experiences?	1	2	3	4	5
How appropriate is the résumé for the type of work sought?	1	2	3	4	5
How direct and dynamic is the résumé's language?	1	2	3	4	5
How clearly is the résumé organized?	1	2	3	4	5
How consistently does the writer follow the format?	1	2	3	4	5

Listening and Speaking WORKSHOP

Critiquing Persuasive Devices

The purpose of a persuasive speech is to change listeners' minds or to incite them to action. Logical arguments are not the only tools used by speakers to reach these goals. Some speakers use invalid forms of reasoning called **fallacious arguments**. Speakers may also employ powerful **rhetorical devices**, patterns of words and images that engage an audience. When critiquing a persuasive speech, identify the speaker's use of these persuasive devices.

Analyzing Fallacious Arguments

Fallacious arguments—false forms of reasoning—are attempts to win an audience's assent without earning it. As you analyze a persuasive speech, identify any fallacies, including the following:

- **Bandwagon effect:** The speaker argues that listeners should do something simply because everyone else is doing it.

- ***Ad hominem***: The speaker questions or attacks the character of those who hold the opposing point of view, without addressing their arguments.

- **False causality:** The speaker assumes that because one event followed another, the first is the cause of the second.

- **Overgeneralization:** The speaker makes a broad statement that is not supported by sufficient evidence.

> ### Feedback Form for Analyzing Persuasive Devices
>
> **Rating System**
> + = Excellent   ✔ = average   – = weak
>
> **Content**
> Arguments _____
> Word choice, imagery _____
> Drama _____
> Personal relevance _____
> Impression of speaker _____
>
> ***Answer the following question:***
> Did the speaker use any fallacious arguments?
> If so, what type? _____

Identifying Effective Rhetorical Devices

Rhetorical devices encourage an audience to share a vision of a situation, a vision also supported by the arguments a speaker offers. As you listen to a persuasive speech, identify the use of these rhetorical devices:

- **Repetition and parallelism**—To stress an idea, the speaker may make repeated use of key words or sentence structures.

- **Use of examples relevant to the audience**—To win the audience's interest, the speaker may speak directly to members' experiences.

- **Establishment of the speaker as reliable**—The presentation of credentials, a sincere manner, and accounts of the speaker's own experiences can all bring an audience to trust the speaker.

- **Creation of drama**—A speaker may frame an issue in dramatic terms: for instance, as a battle between the "little guy" and a bloated, monstrous bureaucracy.

Activity:
Listen and Analyze Analyze a persuasive speech, using the checklist shown to evaluate the speaker's use of persuasive devices.

Assessment WORKSHOP

Critical Reasoning

In the reading sections of some tests, you may be required to use critical reasoning skills. Use the following strategies to help you answer questions testing these skills:

- Identify a writer's implicit (unstated) assumptions, asking what else must be true for the writer's stated claims to be true.
- Read actively, making inferences based on the passage and testing those inferences against further details or your own knowledge.

Sample Test Item

Directions: Read the passage, and answer the question that follows.

The serious accident at the Three Mile Island nuclear facility began with a simple mechanical error. Radiation leaked into the control room. Radioactive water discharged into the Susquehanna River. A hydrogen bubble formed in the reactor, increasing the potential of a deadly explosion. People around the world were shocked by the news. Engineers prevented the core from melting down, but the facility was damaged beyond repair. The accident caused widespread fear in the nuclear industry—a change in attitude that will prevent such accidents in the future.

1. What implicit assumption does the writer make?

A The accident began as an error.

B A hydrogen bubble can cause an explosion.

C The mechanics were incompetent.

D Fear will prevent accidents.

Answer and Explanation

The correct answer is **D.** This assumption is implied in the writer's conclusion about the change of attitude in the industry. Answers *A* and *B* are stated directly as facts, so they are explicit, not implicit. *C* is incorrect because no details address the competence of the mechanics.

▶ Practice

Directions: Read the passage from "The White Umbrella" by Gish Jen, and answer the question that follows.

Sisterly embarrassment seized me. Why hadn't Mona wiped her lenses when I told her to? As she resumed abuse of the piano, I stared at the umbrella. I wanted to open it, twirl it around by its slender silver handle; I wanted to dangle it from my wrist on the way to school the way the other girls did. I wondered what Miss Crosman would say if I offered to bring it to Eugenie at school tomorrow. She would be impressed with my consideration for others; Eugenie would be pleased to have it back; and I would have possession of the umbrella for an entire night. I looked at it again, toying with the idea of asking for one for Christmas. I knew, however, how my mother would react.

"Things," she would say. "What's the matter with a raincoat? All you want is things, just like an American."

1. Which of the following describes what the umbrella means to the narrator?

A It will keep her dry when she returns from the piano lesson.

B It will irritate her mother, who does not like umbrellas.

C It will make her like the other girls.

D It will be something she has stolen from Eugenie.

The Railway Station, 1862, William Powell Frith, Royal Holloway and Bedford New College, Surrey

66 *In order that people may be happy in their work, these three things are needed: They must be fit for it. They must not do too much of it. And they must have a sense of success in it.* 99

— John Ruskin,
from *Pre-Raphaelitism*

Timeline 1833–1901

British Events

- **1833** Slavery abolished in British empire.
- **1837** Victoria becomes queen. ▼
- **1839** Michael Faraday offers general theory of electricity.
- **1843** William Wordsworth becomes poet laureate.

- **1845** Irish Potato Famine begins. ▶

- **1848** Women begin attending University of London.
- **1850 Elizabeth Barrett Browning** publishes *Sonnets from the Portuguese*.
- **1854** Britain enters Crimean War.

- **1859** Charles Darwin publishes *On the Origin of Species*.
- **1860** Florence Nightingale founds school for nurses. ▼

World Events

- **1836** United States: Ralph Waldo Emerson publishes *Nature*.
- **1841** South Pacific: New Zealand becomes a British colony.
- **1842** France: Honoré de Balzac publishes *The Human Comedy*.
- **1844** United States: Samuel F. B. Morse sends first message over a long-distance telegraph line.

- **1848** France: Revolution establishes new republic under Louis Napoleon.
- **1848** Belgium: Marx and Engels publish the *Communist Manifesto*.
- **1853** Eastern Europe: Crimean War begins.
- **1854** Japan: Trade with West reopened.
- **1854** United States: Henry David Thoreau publishes *Walden*. ▲

- **1856** France: Gustave Flaubert publishes *Madame Bovary*.
- **1857** India: Sepoy Mutiny against British.
- **1861** United States: Civil War begins.

British and World Events

- **1865** London Fire Department established.
- **1865** Lewis Carroll publishes *Alice's Adventures in Wonderland.* ▲
- **1868 Robert Browning** publishes *The Ring and the Book.*
- **1869** Debtors' prisons abolished.

- **1880** Joseph Swan installs first electric lighting. ▼
- **1884** First book (*A–ant*) of *Oxford English Dictionary* published.

- **1887** First Sherlock Holmes tale published.
- **1888** English Lawn Tennis Association founded at Wimbledon. ▶
- **1891 Thomas Hardy** publishes *Tess of the d'Urbervilles.*
- **1896 A. E. Housman** publishes *A Shropshire Lad.*
- **1901** Queen Victoria dies.

- **1865** Russia: **Leo Tolstoy** publishes *War and Peace.*
- **1865** Austria: Gregor Mendel proposes laws of heredity. ▼
- **1869** Egypt: Suez Canal completed.

- **1876** United States: Alexander Graham Bell patents telephone.
- **1879** South Africa: Zulu war against British.
- **1880** Russia: Feodor Dostoevsky publishes *The Brothers Karamazov.*
- **1884** United States: Mark Twain publishes *The Adventures of Huckleberry Finn.*

- **1894** Asia: Sino–Japanese war begins.
- **1896** Greece: First modern Olympics held.
- **1897** Russia: Anton Chekhov publishes *Uncle Vanya.*
- **1898** France: Marie and Pierre Curie discover radium.
- **1900** China: Boxer Rebellion against foreign influence.

Progress and Decline

THE VICTORIAN PERIOD
(1833–1901)

Historical Background

Living in the Victorian Age During the sixty-four years of Queen Victoria's reign, from 1837 to 1901, Britain's booming economy and rapid expansion encouraged great optimism. Factory towns grew into large cities as Britain became the world leader in manufacturing. Banks, retail shops, and other businesses expanded. These changes, in turn, spurred the growth of two important classes—an industrial working class and a modern middle class—who were able to live a better life because of the low cost and large variety of mass-produced factory goods.

Economic and military power, especially naval power, helped Britain acquire new colonies in far-flung parts of the globe. In words that could convey the confidence of the Victorian Age, Robert Browning has one of his characters exclaim, "God's in his heaven— / All's right with the world!"

A Reforming Age All was not really "right with the world" of industrial England, though. Writers exposed brutal factory conditions and stinking slums, the dark underside of a manufacturing economy. Nonetheless, Victorian reformers had great faith that their efforts could indeed make everything all right in the future. Goaded by reformers and radicals of many sorts, Victorian leaders did take steps to expand democracy and better the lot of the poor.

Two key issues—trade policy and electoral reform—dominated domestic politics during the first half of the Victorian Era. The trade controversy centered on the Corn Laws, which had long placed high tariffs on "corn" (grain). These laws discouraged food imports and helped British landlords and farmers keep food prices high, which angered the poorer classes. Popular organizations sprang up to fight the Corn Laws. Reform came in 1846 when Parliament, confronting a massive famine in Ireland (1845–1849), sought to increase the food supply by suspending the Corn Laws. Over the following decade, it established a policy of free trade that was beneficial to rising British industries.

The other burning issue of the day involved strengthening democracy. In 1838, the London radical William Lovett drew up a "People's Charter" demanding, among other things, universal suffrage for all males, not just the

Plate Presented by the Ladies of Derby to Queen Victoria on Her 1887 Golden Jubilee

▲ **Critical Viewing**
This plate honors Queen Victoria. Which details suggest the pride that the British took in their overseas empire? Explain. **[Infer]**

wealthy and middle classes. Renewed demands for electoral change led to the Second Reform Bill of 1867, which added 938,000 people to the number of voters by granting voting rights to numbers of urban workingmen. Two further acts, the Third Reform Act (1884–1885) and the Redistribution Act (1885), tripled the electorate and advanced the country toward universal male suffrage.

Reform affected many areas. Women were allowed to attend universities. Parliament passed laws to reduce the workday for women and children, to establish a system of free grammar schools, and to legalize trade unions. It voted to provide public sanitation and to regulate factories and housing. Agitation continued, however, for further reforms.

The Imperialist Urge Britons who supported a policy of imperialism could cite many arguments. Colonies would provide raw materials and markets for British industry. They would also offer a home for British settlers. Furthermore, Britain felt that it had no choice, because if it did not seize a territory, one of its European rivals would. Many Victorians tended to believe that Western civilization—commonly perceived as white, Christian, and progressive—was superior to all other cultures. This attitude led many Victorians to look condescendingly on non-Westerners as people in need of assistance. While such an attitude seems outrageous by today's standards, many people of the time sincerely believed it.

The Victorian years were generally peaceful. Britain fought only one major European war, the Crimean War (1853–1856). This war got its name from its location, the Crimea, a peninsula in southern Russia. Britain, France, and Ottoman Turkey teamed up to thwart Russian expansion, but the battles were largely inconclusive. Today, we remember the war mainly for the courageous efforts of Florence Nightingale, a military nurse regarded as the founder of modern nursing, and the daring but disastrous charge of Britain's Light Brigade. This charge was commemorated in a famous poem by Alfred, Lord Tennyson, some lines of which follow: "Theirs not to make reply, / Theirs not to reason why, / Theirs but to do and die, . . . "

Britain as a World Power Though the Liberals (formerly the Whigs) advocated limits to British rule, the Empire continued to grow. Britain acquired Hong Kong from China in 1842. Then, after a rebellion in

Close-up on Society

Victorian Political and Economic Theories

We can divide into three broad groups the political and economic theories Victorians developed to account for the changed conditions of the industrial age:

- **Laissez-faire** (les′ ā fer′) **theory** This theory holds that government should avoid meddling in the affairs of business. The French term *laissez faire* means "let it be." When allowed full freedom, the theory goes, industry will use the most efficient techniques and reach the highest possible level of prosperity.
- **Reformist liberalism** Those who held this theory believed that rapid change brings problems that *laissez-faire* policies cannot solve. They argued that government intervention and regulation were sometimes necessary to protect the rights of the weak against the strong.
- **Socialism** Some thinkers and activists favored a more far-reaching policy that would end private ownership of major industries and substitute public ownership. Supporters of this socialist position also called for sweeping government measures to promote equality and to help the poor.

1857 to 1858 by sepoys (Indian troops under British command), Britain shouldered aside the British East India Company and took direct control of India.

In the last three decades of Victoria's rule, Britain expanded its influence in Africa. It gained control of the new Suez Canal in Egypt and acquired such territories as Kenya, Uganda, Nigeria, and Rhodesia (now Zimbabwe). Britain also consolidated its control over what is now South Africa, defeating Dutch settlers there in the Boer War (1899–1902).

Victorian Thought Victorian thinkers often disagreed on the crucial issues of their times, but they shared a deep confidence in humanity's ability to better itself. The changes brought about by the Industrial Revolution stirred conflicting feelings among Victorian thinkers. On the one hand, they admired the material benefits industrialization had brought. On the other, they deplored the brutality of factory life and of industrial slums. Much debate concerned whether business should be allowed free rein or whether, for the welfare of people, the government should take a strong role in the economy.

The Victorians grappled with the religious and philosophical as well as the social implications of modern life. The theory of evolution proposed by Charles Darwin (1809–1882) in *On the Origin of Species by Means of Natural Selection* (1859), for instance, stirred bitter controversy. Darwin believed that a process he called "natural selection" explained how different forms of life evolved from previous forms. His account is quite different from the Creation story found in the Bible. Some Victorian thinkers took Darwin's theory as a direct challenge to biblical truth and traditional religious faith. Others accepted both Darwin and religion, striving to reconcile scientific and religious insights.

Literature of the Period

Romanticism and Realism Romanticism continued to influence Victorian writers, but it had by now become part of the mainstream culture. When Victorian writers confronted the rapid technological and social changes amidst which they lived, a literary movement known as Realism was born. The literature of this movement focused on ordinary people facing the day-to-day problems of life, an emphasis that reflected the trend toward democracy and the growing middle-class audience for literature.

Naturalism A related movement, known as Naturalism, sought to put the spirit of scientific observation to literary use. Naturalists crammed their novels with gritty details—the sour smells of poverty, the harsh sounds of factory life—often with the aim of promoting social reform. They directly contradicted the Romantic idea that nature mirrored human feelings and instead portrayed nature as harsh and indifferent to the human suffering it caused.

Pre-Raphaelites Rather than embracing "real" life as the advocates of Realism did, the poets and painters of the Pre-Raphaelite Brotherhood, formed in 1848, rejected the ugliness of industrial life. They turned for inspiration to the spiritual intensity of medieval Italian art, the art before the time of the painter Raphael (1483–1520).

Art in the Historical Context

Changing Sensibilities in Victorian Art

The Pre-Raphaelite Brotherhood was the most important movement in the Victorian visual arts. Founded by the painter and poet Dante Gabriel Rossetti (1828–1882), the movement rejected conventional art and sought a greater purity and "truth to nature"—in part, by painting out-of-doors.

Like the Romantic writers and artists who had found inspiration in the Gothic style of the Middle Ages, the Pre-Raphaelites turned to medieval painters as models. However, the Pre-Raphaelites also showed a Victorian spirit in regarding themselves as reformers, even if, in the case of Rossetti, the reforms related more to ways of feeling and perceiving than to detailed social programs. Rosetti is especially known for his portraits of women, which emphasize color, texture, and an earthy or sadly spiritual feminine beauty.

Although the Brotherhood lasted only a few years, the works of Rossetti, John Everett Millais, and others led to the Aesthetic Movement in literature. This later movement, fostered by Walter Pater and Oscar Wilde, rejected the materialism of Victorian life and emphasized the appreciation of sensation over truth.

▶ **Critical Viewing** Could this portrait by Rossetti, entitled *Day Dream*, be regarded as a comment on the Victorian belief in progress? Why or why not? **[Interpret]**

Day Dream, 1880, Dante Gabriel Rossetti, Victoria and Albert Museum, London, UK

Victorian Poetry The Victorian Age produced a large and diverse body of poetry. The Romantic style predominated at first, but Realism and Naturalism gained force as time went on.

Alfred, Lord Tennyson The most popular poet of the era, Alfred, Lord Tennyson (1809–1892), was influenced by earlier Romantic poets. His verse displays a keen sense of the music of language, and some of his more sentimental lyrics even reappeared in popular songs. Yet Tennyson also revealed a deeper, more thoughtful side in such powerful poems as "Ulysses" and *In Memoriam* (1850). Tennyson became poet laureate after Wordsworth died in 1850.

The Brownings Robert Browning (1812–1889) produced a body of poetry as diverse as Tennyson's, although in his lifetime he never achieved equal public acclaim. Some of Browning's poems display Romantic attitudes. Others, however, show the influence of Realism as Browning seeks to portray individuals with un-Romantic authenticity. Critics have especially admired Browning's dramatic monologues, or long speeches in which a character reveals his or her thoughts.

Elizabeth Barrett (1806–1861), Browning's wife, was the more famous poet at the time of their marriage. Today, she is remembered mostly for the beautiful love poems she wrote her husband in *Sonnets from the Portuguese* (1850).

Matthew Arnold, Thomas Hardy, and A. E. Housman One of the greatest Victorian poets to focus on "the bewildering confusion" of the Industrial Age was Matthew Arnold (1822–1888). He was haunted by

A Living Tradition

Philip Larkin Discovers Thomas Hardy

The poetry of Thomas Hardy—with its devotion to English life and landscapes, its often somber mood, and its refusal to entertain illusions—appealed greatly to the twentieth-century British poet Philip Larkin. After beginning his career under the influence of the visionary Irish poet William Butler Yeats, Larkin discovered Hardy. This account of Larkin's discovery comes from an introduction he wrote to a reprint of his first book, *The North Ship*:

> When reaction [against Yeats] came, it was undramatic, complete and permanent. In early 1946 I had some new digs [rooms] in which the bedroom faced east, so that the sun woke me inconveniently early. I used to read. One book I had at my bedside was the little blue *Chosen Poems of Thomas Hardy*: Hardy I knew as a novelist, but as regards his verse I shared Lytton Strachey's verdict that "the gloom is not even relieved by a little elegance of diction." This opinion did not last long; if I were asked to date its disappearance, I should guess it was the morning I first read "Thoughts of Phena At News of Her Death." Many years later, Vernon [the Welsh poet Vernon Watkins] surprised me by saying that Dylan Thomas had admired Hardy above all poets of this century. "He thought Yeats was the greatest by miles," he said. "But Hardy was his favorite."

Bayswater Omnibus, G. W. Joy, Museum of London

the loss of individuals' close ties to nature and with each other. Arnold was a forerunner of the more pessimistic Naturalist poets, such as Thomas Hardy (1840–1928) and A. E. Housman (1859–1936), for whom life's disappointments were a frequent subject.

Rudyard Kipling The poetry of Rudyard Kipling (1865–1936) spoke to the expansive spirit of the age, ranging across the breadth of the Empire with action-packed narrative poems like "Gunga Din" and poems written in the colorful speech of working-class soldiers in *Barrack-Room Ballads*.

Gerard Manley Hopkins While Tennyson's and Kipling's well-known lyrics turned up as popular songs, Gerard Manley Hopkins (1844–1889) remained unpublished during his own century. His innovative rhythms and deeply felt religious verse would inspire twentieth-century Modernist poets.

Victorian Drama At the beginning of the nineteenth century, playhouses were few in number. After 1843, when government restrictions were lifted, popular theater boomed. Serious dramas like Sir Arthur Wing Pinero's *The Second Mrs. Tanqueray* (1893) and satires like Oscar Wilde's *The Importance of Being Earnest* (1895) began to emerge late in the century.

Victorian Fiction If one form of literature can be seen as quintessentially Victorian, it is the novel. Members of the new middle class were avid readers, and they loved novels, especially those that reflected the major social issues of the day. Responding to the demand, weekly and monthly magazines published novels chapter by chapter in serial form. Curious readers had to continue to buy the magazine to learn what happened next. Most of the best novelists of the day wrote, at one time or another, for the magazines.

▲ **Critical Viewing**
This picture shows a scene in the interior of a horsedrawn omnibus. How do you think that the existence of public spaces such as the inside of a bus may have influenced ways of behaving in public? Explain. **[Speculate]**

The Brontë Sisters Romanticism heavily influenced early Victorian novelists, especially the three Brontë sisters: Emily Brontë (1818–1848), Charlotte Brontë (1816–1855), and the lesser-known Anne Brontë (1820–1849). The sisters were among six children raised by their father and aunt in the isolation of a northern English village. Bright and imaginative, these children relied on one another for entertainment and encouragement. They read great authors like Shakespeare and Byron, wrote verse and prose, and created fantasy worlds with names like Gondal and Angria.

Emily and Charlotte later drew on these vivid childhood experiences to create powerful works of fiction. Emily's classic *Wuthering Heights* (1847) tells the tale of the doomed passion of Catherine Earnshaw and Heathcliff, one of English fiction's outstanding Romantic heroes. Emily's sister Charlotte wrote *Jane Eyre* (1847), a novel recounting the adventures of a governess who falls in love with her mysterious employer, Mr. Rochester.

Charles Dickens The realistic elements of *Jane Eyre* probably owe much to the influence of Charles Dickens (1812–1870), who surpassed all other Victorian novelists in popularity and is regarded by many critics as the greatest novelist of the period. Dickens filled his novels with poignant, realistic details that dramatized the contrast between rich and poor in industrial England. To his eye for injustice he married a marvelous sense of humor. His novels abound in deliciously eccentric characters whose every peculiarity of speech and gesture affirms how individual people are. Among his greatest works are *David Copperfield* (1849–1850), *Bleak House* (1852–1853), and *Our Mutual Friend* (1864–1865).

Dickens also showed a sentimental side, often in the form of tear-provoking descriptions of innocents suffering in a cruel world. The most famous of these scenes is the death of Little Nell in *The Old Curiosity Shop* (1840–1841). A young girl fleeing the corrupt city in the company of her grandfather, Nell dies in her quest for a refuge. Dickens emphasized the sadness of her death, and his audience loved the experience of weeping for Little Nell. When a ship bringing the latest installment of *The Old Curiosity Shop* arrived in New York harbor, readers yelled out to the sailors before the ship docked, "Has Little Nell died?"

Realist Fiction Other, less sentimental Victorian Realists included Anthony Trollope (1815–1882) and Samuel Butler (1835–1902). George Meredith (1828–1909) produced careful psychological studies of his characters in novels such as *The Egoist* (1879).

Another important Realist, William Makepeace Thackeray (1811–1863), condemned hypocrisy in his novel *Vanity Fair* (1847–1848). Named for a fair that symbolizes worldly corruption in Puritan John Bunyan's allegory *Pilgrim's Progress* (1678, 1684), Thackeray's novel describes the rise of Becky Sharp from governess to woman of society. It uses her social climbing to reveal the immoral side of upper-class life.

Women Novelists As the novel came into its own, so did women novelists. In addition to the Brontë sisters, there were Elizabeth Gaskell

(1810–1865) and Mary Ann Evans, writing as George Eliot (1819–1880).

Charles Dickens had enormous respect for Gaskell's work in calling attention to the abuses of industrialization. Writing in his magazine *Household Words*, he commented that "there is no living English writer whose aid I would desire to enlist in preference to the authoress of *Mary Barton*." (This was the name of a novel by Gaskell that focused on life in industrial Manchester.)

Under her pen name George Eliot, Mary Ann Evans examined social issues and personal relationships in novels that fellow writer Henry James hailed as true works of art. She evoked everyday settings with careful attention to realistic specifics and focused in detail on the inner lives of her characters. *Middlemarch* (1871–1872), often considered her greatest work, describes the slow and painful maturation of its central character, Dorothea Brooke.

Edwardian London, 1901, Eugene Joseph McSwiney, Christopher Wood Gallery

Thomas Hardy and Late-Victorian Fiction As the century drew to a close, British novelists such as Thomas Hardy leaned more and more to Naturalism. (Later, Hardy would publish poetry in the same vein.) Late-Victorian readers shied away from Naturalism's dark outlook, though, preferring instead the adventure stories of writers like Robert Louis Stevenson (1850–1894) and Rudyard Kipling or the Sherlock Holmes mysteries of Sir Arthur Conan Doyle (1859–1930).

Prose Nonfiction All the great Victorian thinkers produced influential prose works. Matthew Arnold, for example, attacked the British class system in *Culture and Anarchy* (1869), his most famous work of social criticism. Other influential works included *Modern Painters* (1843) by John Ruskin (1819–1900), *On Liberty* (1859) by John Stuart Mill (1806–1873), *The Idea of a University* (1852) by John Henry Cardinal Newman (1801–1890), and *Studies in the History of the Renaissance* (1873) by Walter Pater (1839–1894). The greatest Victorian historians were Thomas Carlyle (1795–1881) and Thomas Babington Macaulay (1800–1859).

All in all, the Victorian Age produced a diverse body of literature that was entertaining, scholarly, humorous, and profound. Because the era is so close to our own times and because in it we see the beginnings of our own social problems, many of them still unresolved, Victorian literature has a special relevance to readers today. In addition, the Victorian writers were brilliant storytellers, and we read their works not only for literary appreciation and historical understanding but for pure pleasure.

▲ **Critical Viewing** Gas lighting was introduced to London during Victoria's reign. Judging by this picture, what effects do you think this advance had on street life at night? Explain. **[Infer]**

The Victorian Age

BY RICHARD LEDERER

EUPHEMISMS: THE FIG LEAVES OF LANGUAGE

Prudishness reached its golden age in the straitlaced Victorian era. Take the widely read *Lady Gough's Book of Etiquette*. Among Lady Gough's social pronouncements was that under no circumstances should books written by male authors be placed on shelves next to books written by "author-esses." Married writers, however, such as Robert and Elizabeth Barrett Browning, could be shelved together without impropriety.

So delicate were Victorian sensibilities that members of polite society would blush at the mention of anything physical. Instead of being *pregnant*, women were *in a delicate condition*, *in a family way*, or *expectant*. Women did not give birth; they experienced *a blessed event*. Their children were not born; rather, they were *brought by the stork*, or *came into the world*.

Such words and expressions are called *euphemisms* (from two Greek roots that mean "pleasant speech," "words of good omen"). A euphemism is a mild, indirect word or phrase used in place of one that is more direct or that may have an unpleasant connotation for some people. Using a euphemism is "calling a spade a heart" . . . or "telling it like it isn't."

In the Victorian Age, prudery extended even to animals and things. *Bull* was considered an indecent word, and the proper substitute was *he cow*, *male cow*, or (gasp!) *gentleman cow*. Victorian standards were so exacting that Victorians could not refer to something as vulgar as legs. They had to call them *limbs*, even when talking about the legs on a chicken or a piano. Instead of asking for a leg of chicken, they would ask for dark meat, and they went so far as to cover up piano legs with little skirts!

Children were not born but rather brought by the stork.

ACTIVITIES

1. Shakespeare's Juliet sighs, "What's in a name? A rose by any other name would smell as sweet." Would it? Write an essay in which you defend or rebut Juliet's opinion of the relationship between words and things.
2. Many occupations have taken on glorified, euphemistic titles. Nowadays, a garbage collector is called a sanitation engineer and a dogcatcher an animal control warden. Collect other examples and share them with classmates.
3. Are there any situations in which the use of euphemisms would be advisable? Explain your answer.

Relationships

Faustine, 1904 Maxwell Armfield, Museé d'Orsay, Paris, France

Prepare to Read

from In Memoriam, A.H.H. ◆ The Lady of Shalott ◆
from The Princess: Tears, Idle Tears ◆ Ulysses

Alfred, Lord Tennyson (1809–1892)

You may think of Tennyson—or any male Victorian poet—as a bearded old man whose picture belongs in a cracked, dusty book. Think again. Here is Thomas Carlyle's description of the tall, handsome but moody young Tennyson: "One of the finest looking men in the world. A great shock of rough dusty-dark hair; bright-laughing hazel eyes . . . of sallow-brown complexion, almost Indian-looking." This is the young man who was to become in middle age the most celebrated poet of Victorian England: Alfred, Lord Tennyson.

An Unhappy Childhood Tennyson was born in the rural town of Somersby in Lincolnshire, the fourth of twelve children. He was a sensitive boy who was charmed by the magical words "far, far away." His father, a clergyman, had a large library and supervised Tennyson's early education. He predicted that his son would be "the greatest Poet of the Time." At the same time, he was extremely bitter, having been disinherited by his own father. His anger poisoned the atmosphere of the Tennyson household. As a teenager, Alfred was probably eager to escape to Cambridge University.

The Power of Friendship At first, Tennyson was disappointed by Cambridge. He wrote about his studies: "None but dry-headed, calculating, angular little gentlemen can take much delight in them." Then, he met the young man who became his closest friend, Arthur Henry Hallam. They were often together, and Hallam intended to marry Tennyson's sister Emily. In 1830, with Hallam's encouragement, Tennyson published *Poems, Chiefly Lyrical*, which was followed two years later by a volume simply entitled *Poems*.

A Stunning Tragedy In 1833, however, Hallam died suddenly, leaving a void in Tennyson's life that nearly destroyed him. The poet's grief became the inspiration for some of his greatest work. Soon after Hallam's death, Tennyson began working on a series of short poems that considered questions of death, religious faith, and immortality. This series, which grew over seventeen years into an extended elegy for his friend, was published in 1850 under the title *In Memoriam, A.H.H.*

National Honor The elegy so impressed Prince Albert that in 1850, he encouraged Queen Victoria to appoint Tennyson the poet laureate of England, replacing the recently deceased Wordsworth. For the next forty years, Tennyson published regularly. One of his most celebrated works, *Idylls of the King,* a series of poems based on the legend of King Arthur, began appearing in 1859.

In 1884, Queen Victoria made Tennyson a baron, and so added the title of Lord to his name. He was the first English writer to earn this title for his literary achievements. The honor befitted one whom most Victorians regarded as the poetic voice of their age.

Land, Literature, Long Life When royalties from *In Memoriam, A.H.H.* began to flow in, Tennyson bought a farm on the Isle of Wight. There, he and his wife Emily Sellwood raised two children. Tennyson continued to publish poems into his eighties. His poetry spoke directly to the Victorians, who found reflected in it their deepest faith and deepest doubts.

An Enduring Reputation Although early twentieth-century critics faulted Tennyson for intellectual shallowness, the value of his work endures. In clear, rich, hauntingly musical language, it expresses the aspirations that sustain the human spirit.

Preview

Connecting to the Literature

When everything is going wrong, you may turn to a friend and ask: Why? When Tennyson's best friend, Arthur Hallam, died, Tennyson turned to his culture—its science, its poetry, its religion—and demanded: Tell me, why? *In Memoriam* is the result of his grief-stricken question.

Literary Analysis

The Speaker in Poetry

The **speaker** in a poem—the person who "says" its words—is not necessarily the poet. Speakers fall into the following categories:

- Fictional or real
- Generalized (not described in specific detail) or with a specific identity

Even if the speaker of a poem is fictional, he or she may resemble the poem's actual author, sharing similar situations and experiences. As you read, determine the identity of each speaker and analyze the speaker's conflict and motivation.

Comparing Literary Works

Tennyson's speakers range from well-defined individuals to nonspecific narrators. Some of his speakers have histories—they have undergone a change or suffered a loss. Using such speakers as well as other characters, he dramatizes different experiences of time, including the following:

- A perpetual present, in which nothing significant changes
- A restless movement from past accomplishment into an unknown future
- The loss of the past

As you read, compare the views of time in each poem. Consider whether each poem creates its own "time"—a moment of reflection in which the speaker sums up the past, making way for the future.

Reading Strategy

Judging a Poet's Message

One way to respond to a poem is to **judge the poet's message**—to decide how true and useful that message is. As you read, use a chart like the one shown to determine what the poet is saying and to evaluate the message.

Vocabulary Development

diffusive (di fyo͞o′ siv) *adj.* tending to spread out (p. 820)

churls (churlz) *n.* farm laborers; peasants (p. 823)

waning (wān′ iŋ) *v.* gradually becoming dimmer or weaker (p. 825)

furrows (fur′ ōz) *n.* narrow grooves, such as those made by a plow (p. 830)

The Stages of Life, Caspar David Friedrich, Museum der Bildenden Kunst, Leipzig

▲ **Critical Viewing** This painting, *The Stages of Life*, suggests that life is like a voyage. How would the speaker in the poem react to such a comparison? Explain. **[Speculate]**

from
In Memoriam, A. H. H.
Alfred, Lord Tennyson

1

I held it truth, with him who sings
    To one clear harp in divers[1] tones,
    That men may rise on stepping stones
Of their dead selves to higher things.

5   But who shall so forecast the years
    And find in loss a gain to match?

---

1. divers (dī′ vərz) *adj.* varied; having many parts.

Or reach a hand through time to catch
The far-off interest of tears?

Let Love clasp Grief lest both be drowned,
10   Let darkness keep her raven gloss.
      Ah, sweeter to be drunk with loss,
To dance with death, to beat the ground,

Than that the victor Hours should scorn
      The long result of love, and boast,
15   "Behold the man that loved and lost,
But all he was is overworn."

7

Dark house, by which once more I stand
      Here in the long unlovely street,
      Doors, where my heart was used to beat
20 So quickly, waiting for a hand,

A hand that can be clasped no more—
      Behold me, for I cannot sleep,
      And like a guilty thing I creep
At earliest morning to the door.

25 He is not here; but far away
      The noise of life begins again,
      And ghastly through the drizzling rain
On the bald street breaks the blank day.

82

I wage not any feud with Death
30   For changes wrought on form and face;
      No lower life that earth's embrace
May breed with him, can fright my faith.

Eternal process moving on,
      From state to state the spirit walks;
35   And these are but the shattered stalks,
Or ruined chrysalis of one.

Nor blame I Death, because he bare
      The use of virtue out of earth;
      I know transplanted human worth
40 Will bloom to profit, otherwhere.

For this alone on Death I wreak
      The wrath that garners in my heart;
      He put our lives so far apart
We cannot hear each other speak.

Literary Analysis
The Speaker in Poetry
What do you learn
about the speaker
in lines 21–24?

Reading Strategy
Judging a Poet's Message
In lines 29–44, what does
the poet suggest about
the consolations of faith
and philosophy?

✔ **Reading Check**

What are two of the main
feelings Tennyson conveys
in these stanzas?

45 Thy voice is on the rolling air;
        I hear thee where the waters run;
        Thou standest in the rising sun,
    And in the setting thou art fair.

    What art thou then? I cannot guess;
50   But though I seem in star and flower
        To feel thee some <u>diffusive</u> power,
    I do not therefore love thee less.

    My love involves the love before;
        My love is vaster passion now;
55   Though mixed with God and Nature thou,
    I seem to love thee more and more.

    Far off thou art, but ever nigh;
        I have thee still, and I rejoice;
        I prosper, circled with thy voice;
60 I shall not lose thee though I die.

diffusive (di fyo͞o′ siv) *adj.*
tending to spread out

Review and Assess

Thinking About the Selection

1. **Respond:** Were you moved by Tennyson's lament for his friend? Why or why not?

2. **(a) Recall:** In section 1, what idea does the speaker say he once held as truth but now doubts? **(b) Interpret:** The speaker rejects this truth in favor of a new view of grief. Paraphrase this view.

3. **(a) Recall:** By what place is the speaker standing in section 7? **(b) Interpret:** What effect does the loss of his friend have on the scene?

4. **Compare and Contrast:** Contrast the facts that, in section 82, the speaker says do not anger him with the one fact that does.

5. **(a) Interpret:** Explain the paradox in line 57: "Far off thou art, but ever nigh." **(b) Connect:** How does section 130 answer the speaker's one reason for anger in section 82?

6. **Draw Conclusions:** How have the speaker's feelings changed from the first two sections of the poem to the last two sections?

7. **Evaluate:** Would the speaker's viewpoint in section 130 reconcile you to a grief? Explain.

The Lady of Shalott

Alfred, Lord Tennyson

The Lady of Shalott, John Waterhouse, The Tate Gallery, London

▲ **Critical Viewing** What symbols of the Lady of Shalott's occupation and eventual
fate are in this painting? Explain why they are significant. **[Interpret]**

Part I

On either side the river lie
Long fields of barley and of rye,
That clothe the wold¹ and meet the sky;
And through the field the road runs by
5   To many-towered Camelot,²
And up and down the people go,
Gazing where the lilies blow³
Round an island there below,
    The island of Shalott.

10 Willows whiten, aspens quiver,
Little breezes dusk and shiver
Through the wave that runs forever
By the island in the river
    Flowing down to Camelot.
15 Four gray walls, and four gray towers,
Overlook a space of flowers,
And the silent isle imbowers
    The Lady of Shalott.

By the margin, willow-veiled,
20 Slide the heavy barges trailed
By slow horses; and unhailed
The shallop⁴ flitteth silken-sailed
    Skimming down to Camelot:
But who hath seen her wave her hand?
25 Or at the casement seen her stand?
Or is she known in all the land,
    The Lady of Shalott?

Only reapers, reaping early
In among the bearded barley,
30 Hear a song that echoes cheerly,
From the river winding clearly,
    Down to towered Camelot:
And by the moon the reaper weary,
Piling sheaves in uplands airy,
35 Listening, whispers, "'Tis the fairy
    Lady of Shalott."

Literary Analysis
The Speaker in Poetry
What does setting this poem in the days of King Arthur suggest about the poet's attitude toward the past?

---

1. **wold** rolling plains.
2. **Camelot** legendary English town where King Arthur had his court and Round Table.
3. **blow** bloom.
4. **shallop** light, open boat.

Part II

There she weaves by night and day
A magic web with colors gay.
She has heard a whisper say,
40 A curse is on her if she stay
    To look down to Camelot.
She knows not what the curse may be,
And so she weaveth steadily,
And little other care hath she,
45   The Lady of Shalott.

And moving through a mirror[5] clear
That hangs before her all the year,
Shadows of the world appear.
There she sees the highway near
50   Winding down to Camelot:
There the river eddy whirls,
And there the surly village <u>churls</u>,
And the red cloaks of market girls,
    Pass onward from Shalott.

55 Sometimes a troop of damsels glad,
An abbot on an ambling pad,[6]
Sometimes a curly shepherd lad,
Or long-haired page in crimson clad,
    Goes by to towered Camelot;
60 And sometimes through the mirror blue
The knights come riding two and two:
She hath no loyal knight and true,
    The Lady of Shalott.

But in her web she still delights
65 To weave the mirror's magic sights,
For often through the silent nights
A funeral, with plumes and lights
    And music, went to Camelot:
Or when the moon was overhead,
70 Came two young lovers lately wed;
"I am half sick of shadows," said
    The Lady of Shalott.

---

5. mirror Weavers placed mirrors in front of their looms, so that they could view the progress of their work.
6. pad easy-paced horse.

churls (churlz) *n.* farm laborers; peasants

Literary Analysis
The Speaker in Poetry
Is the speaker who tells the Lady of Shalott's story also a character in the poem? How can you tell?

✔**Reading Check**
What does the Lady of Shalott do with her time?

Part III

A bow-shot from her bower eaves,
He rode between the barley sheaves,
75 The sun came dazzling through the leaves,
And flamed upon the brazen greaves[7]
    Of bold Sir Lancelot.
A red-cross knight[8] forever kneeled
To a lady in his shield,
80 That sparkled on the yellow field,
    Beside remote Shalott.

The gemmy[9] bridle glittered free,
Like to some branch of stars we see
Hung in the golden Galaxy.[10]
85 The bridle bells rang merrily
    As he rode down to Camelot:
And from his blazoned baldric[11] slung
A mighty silver bugle hung,
And as he rode his armor rung,
90   Beside remote Shalott.

All in the blue unclouded weather
Thick-jeweled shone the saddle leather,
The helmet and the helmet feather
Burned like one burning flame together,
95   As he rode down to Camelot.
As often through the purple night,
Below the starry clusters bright,
Some bearded meteor, trailing light,
    Moves over still Shalott.

100 His broad clear brow in sunlight glowed;
On burnish'd hooves his war horse trode;
From underneath his helmet flowed
His coal-black curls as on he rode,
    As he rode down to Camelot.
105 From the bank and from the river
He flashed into the crystal mirror,
"Tirra lirra," by the river
    Sang Sir Lancelot.

She left the web, she left the loom,
110 She made three paces through the room,

---

7. **greaves** armor that protects the legs below the kneecaps.
8. **red-cross knight** refers to the Redcrosse Knight from *The Faerie Queene* by Edmund Spenser. The knight is a symbol of holiness.
9. **gemmy** jeweled.
10. **Galaxy** the Milky Way.
11. **blazoned baldric** decorated sash worn diagonally across the chest.

The British Tradition

A Crisis of Faith

When the grief-stricken Tennyson of *In Memoriam* pushes away the comforting philosophies of his day, or when he turns to the mythic past in "The Lady of Shalott," he reflects a broader crisis of faith that rocked Victorian society. The Industrial Revolution and its teeming urban masses had pushed aside the traditional bond between peasant and lord. The comfortable rhythms of a farming society had given way to surging spirals of economic boom and bust. Meanwhile, such intellectual developments as Charles Darwin's theory of evolution challenged religious beliefs.

In the midst of these social and intellectual changes, Victorian artists asked whether their cultural resources—religion, science, art—were still sufficient to guide their lives. After Tennyson, Matthew Arnold raises the question again in "Dover Beach" (1867; page 884), concluding that only personal relationships offer comfort in a confusing world. From Tennyson to Arnold to T. S. Eliot to Philip Larkin, the theme of a fractured culture, unable to answer its own questions, persists to this day.

She saw the waterlily bloom,
She saw the helmet and the plume,
    She looked down to Camelot.
Out flew the web and floated wide;
115 The mirror cracked from side to side;
"The curse is come upon me," cried
    The Lady of Shalott.

Part IV

In the stormy east wind straining,
The pale yellow woods were waning,
120 The broad stream in his banks complaining,
Heavily the low sky raining
    Over towered Camelot;
Down she came and found a boat
Beneath a willow left afloat,
125 And round about the prow she wrote
    The Lady of Shalott.

And down the river's dim expanse
Like some bold seër in a trance,
Seeing all his own mischance—
130 With a glassy countenance
    Did she look to Camelot.
And at the closing of the day
She loosed the chain, and down she lay;
The broad stream bore her far away,
135   The Lady of Shalott.

Lying, robed in snowy white
That loosely flew to left and right—
The leaves upon her falling light—
Through the noises of the night
140   She floated down to Camelot:
And as the boathead wound along
The willowy hills and fields among,
They heard her singing her last song,
    The Lady of Shalott.

145 Heard a carol, mournful, holy,
Chanted loudly, chanted lowly,
Till her blood was frozen slowly,
And her eyes were darkened wholly,
    Turned to towered Camelot.
150 For ere she reached upon the tide
The first house by the waterside,
Singing in her song she died,
    The Lady of Shalott.

Literary Analysis
The Speaker in Poetry
How does the speaker create the sense that a decisive moment has arrived?

waning (wān´ iŋ) v. gradually becoming dimmer or weaker

Reading Check

What does the Lady of Shalott do once she sees Sir Lancelot?

                Under tower and balcony,
155   By garden wall and gallery,
                A gleaming shape she floated by,
                Dead-pale between the houses high,
                    Silent into Camelot.
                Out upon the wharfs they came,
160   Knight and burgher, lord and dame,
                And round the prow they read her name,
                    The Lady of Shalott.

                Who is this? and what is here?
                And in the lighted palace near
165   Died the sound of royal cheer;
                And they crossed themselves for fear,
                    All the knights at Camelot:
                But Lancelot mused a little space;
                He said, "She has a lovely face;
170   God in his mercy lend her grace,
                    The Lady of Shalott."

Review and Assess

Thinking About the Selection

1. **Respond:** Do you think the Lady should not have decided to sail for Camelot? Explain.

2. **(a) Recall:** What does the Lady spend her time doing? Why? **(b) Interpret:** Why does the Lady glimpse only "shadows of the world"? **(c) Interpret:** Why might an artist share the complaint the Lady makes in lines 71–72?

3. **(a) Recall:** What does the Lady do after seeing Sir Lancelot in the mirror? **(b) Analyze:** How does the long description of Sir Lancelot make the knight seem like the real-life embodiment of a vision? **(c) Draw Conclusions:** Given this description of Lancelot, explain why the Lady might be said to leave her room in pursuit of her visions.

4. **(a) Draw Conclusions:** What does the fact that the Lady dies before meeting Lancelot suggest about her love for him? **(b) Make a Judgment:** Do you agree with Tennyson's implication that we can never realize our fantasies? Why or why not?

5. **Apply:** The poem suggests that the life of the imagination isolates one from reality. Do modern media, such as television and the Internet, suggest otherwise? Explain.

from The PRINCESS

Alfred, Lord Tennyson

The Princess (1847) is a long narrative poem that contains a number
of songs. Some of these songs, including the one that follows, are
considered to be among the finest of Tennyson's lyrics.

Tears, Idle Tears

Tears, idle tears, I know not what they mean,
Tears from the depth of some divine despair
Rise in the heart, and gather to the eyes,
In looking on the happy autumn fields,
5 And thinking of the days that are no more.

Fresh as the first beam glittering on a sail,
That brings our friends up from the underworld,
Sad as the last which reddens over one
That sinks with all we love below the verge;
10 So sad, so fresh, the days that are no more.

Ah, sad and strange as in dark summer dawns
The earliest pipe of half-awakened birds
To dying ears, when unto dying eyes
The casement slowly grows a glimmering square;
15 So sad, so strange, the days that are no more.

Dear as remembered kisses after death,
And sweet as those by hopeless fancy feigned
On lips that are for others; deep as love,
Deep as first love, and wild with all regret;
20 O Death in Life, the days that are no more.

✔Reading Check

What is the speaker's
reaction to the thought
of "the days that are
no more"?

Ulysses

Alfred, Lord Tennyson

Background

In this poem Tennyson extends the story of Ulysses (yoo lis´ ez´), the hero of Homer's epic the *Odyssey*. Homer's writing ends after Ulysses' triumphant return home to Ithaca. Years later, Tennyson tells us, the hero has grown restless. Although he had been away for twenty long years—ten fighting in the Trojan War and another ten making the long and adventure-filled voyage back—Ulysses finds that he is contemplating yet another journey.

It little profits that an idle king,
By this still hearth, among these barren crags,
Matched with an aged wife, I mete and dole[1]
Unequal[2] laws unto a savage race,
5   That hoard, and sleep, and feed, and know not me.
I cannot rest from travel; I will drink
Life to the lees.[3] All times I have enjoyed
Greatly, have suffered greatly, both with those
That loved me, and alone; on shore, and when
10   Through scudding drifts the rainy Hyades[4]
Vexed the dim sea. I am become a name;

Literary Analysis
The Speaker in Poetry
Who is speaking the words of this poem? How can you tell?

---

1. **mete and dole** measure and give out.
2. **unequal** unfair.
3. **lees** sediment.
4. **Hyades** (hī´ ə dēz´) group of stars whose rising was assumed to be followed by rain.

For always roaming with a hungry heart
Much have I seen and known—cities of men
And manners, climates, councils, governments,
15 Myself not least, but honored of them all—
And drunk delight of battle with my peers,
Far on the ringing plains of windy Troy.
I am a part of all that I have met;
Yet all experience is an arch wherethrough
20 Gleams that untraveled world, whose
        margin fades
Forever and forever when I move.
How dull it is to pause, to make an end,
To rust unburnished, not to shine in use!
As though to breathe were life. Life piled on life
25 Were all too little, and of one to me
Little remains; but every hour is saved
From that eternal silence, something more,
A bringer of new things; and vile it were
For some three suns to store and hoard myself,
30 And this gray spirit yearning in desire
To follow knowledge like a sinking star,
Beyond the utmost bound of human thought.
     This is my son, mine own Telemachus,
To whom I leave the scepter and the isle[5]
35 Well-loved of me, discerning to fulfill
This labor, by slow prudence to make mild
A rugged people, and through soft degrees
Subdue them to the useful and the good.
Most blameless is he, centered in the sphere
40 Of common duties, decent not to fail
In offices of tenderness, and pay
Meet[6] adoration to my household gods,
When I am gone. He works his work, I mine.
     There lies the port; the vessel puffs her sail;
45 There gloom the dark broad seas. My mariners,
Souls that have toiled and wrought, and thought with me—
That ever with a frolic welcome took
The thunder and the sunshine, and opposed
Free hearts, free foreheads—you and I are old;
50 Old age hath yet his honor and his toil;
Death closes all; but something ere the end,
Some work of noble note, may yet be done,
Not unbecoming men that strove with Gods.
The lights begin to twinkle from the rocks;
55 The long day wanes; the slow moon climbs; the deep

Ulysses, 1827, Jean-Auguste-Dominique Ingres, National Gallery of Art, Washington, D.C.

▲ **Critical Viewing**
Compare the character
of Ulysses conveyed by
this painting with the
speaker in the poem.
[Compare and Contrast]

---

5. **isle** Ithaca, an island off the coast of Greece.
6. **meet** appropriate.

Reading Check

What does Ulysses feel
the urge to do?

Moans round with many voices. Come, my friends,
'Tis not too late to seek a newer world.
Push off, and sitting well in order smite
The sounding <u>furrows</u>; for my purpose holds
60   To sail beyond the sunset, and the baths
Of all the western stars, until I die.
It may be that the gulfs will wash us down;
It may be we shall touch the Happy Isles,[7]
And see the great Achilles,[8] whom we knew.
65   Though much is taken, much abides; and though
We are not now that strength which in old days
Moved earth and heaven, that which we are, we are—
One equal temper of heroic hearts,
Made weak by time and fate, but strong in will
70   To strive, to seek, to find, and not to yield.

furrows (fur′ ōz) *n.* narrow grooves, such as those made by a plow

---

7. **Happy Isles** Elysium, or the Islands of the Blessed: in classical mythology, the place heroes went after death.
8. **Achilles** (ə kil′ ēz′) Greek hero of the Trojan War.

Review and Assess

Thinking About the Selections

1. **Respond:** Which of these two poems seems more hopeful to you? Why?

2. **(a) Recall:** What three comparisons in "Tears, Idle Tears" describe "the days that are no more"? **(b) Analyze:** What contrast does each comparison involve? **(c) Interpret:** What feelings does the line "Deep as first love, and wild with all regret" capture?

3. **(a) Recall:** In "Ulysses," how does Ulysses describe his situation? **(b) Compare and Contrast:** How does this situation contrast with his previous experiences? **(c) Draw Conclusions:** What is Ulysses' attitude toward his experiences?

4. **(a) Recall:** According to lines 58–61, what is Ulysses' purpose? **(b) Draw Conclusions:** What are Ulysses' feelings about aging? **(c) Draw Conclusions:** What is his attitude toward life in general?

5. **Speculate:** What advice might Ulysses give the speaker in "Tears, Idle Tears"?

6. **Generalize:** Why is nostalgia—the intense presence of the past accompanied by the equally intense sense that it is no more—such an attractive feeling to poets and their readers?

7. **Apply:** What type of organization might take the last line of "Ulysses" as its slogan? Explain.

Review and Assess

Literary Analysis

The Speaker in Poetry

1. (a) Who is the **speaker** of *In Memoriam*? (b) Tennyson wrote the poem in direct response to his friend's death. How does the speaker's conflict reflect one that Tennyson might have felt?

2. (a) Who is the speaker of "The Lady of Shalott"? (b) Is the speaker fictional or real, generalized or specific? Explain.

3. Why might Tennyson have identified the situation of a poet with the Lady's situation?

4. (a) Describe the conflict faced by the speaker in "Ulysses." (b) Does Tennyson see Ulysses as heroic or as selfish and self-justifying? Support your answer by quoting from the poem.

Comparing Literary Works

5. Use a chart like the one shown to compare Ulysses' view of time with the Lady of Shalott's view.

	Past	Present	Future
Ulysses	Remembers it with satisfaction: "I am a part of all that I have met"		
The Lady of Shalott	It is identical with the present: "There she weaves by night and day"		

6. Compare the speaker's relationship with the past in "Tears, Idle Tears" and in *In Memoriam*.

7. Which did Tennyson value more—the timeless world of poetry or the perishable real world? Support your view.

Reading Strategy

Judging a Poet's Message

8. (a) Summarize the poet's message in each poem. (b) Evaluate each message, explaining the basis for your evaluations.

Extend Understanding

9. **Science Connection:** Contrast the scientific approach to time with the view in one of the poems.

Quick Review

The **speaker** in a poem is the person who "says" its words. The speaker is not necessarily the poet.

To **judge a poet's message,** relate the message to experiences that you have had or know about, to judge the truth and usefulness of the message.

 Take It to the Net
www.phschool.com

Take the interactive self-test online to check your understanding of these selections.

Integrate Language Skills

Vocabulary Development Lesson

Concept Development: Medieval Words

Tennyson uses medieval English words such as *churls*, meaning "farmers" or "peasants," to add atmosphere to his poems. Many such medieval words are of Anglo-Saxon origin. Of those that are still in use, some have acquired new connotations. Today, for example, the word *churl* suggests a rude, surly person. Define the following medieval words that appear in "The Lady of Shalott," using clues to their meaning in the contexts in which they appear.

1. knight
2. reapers
3. baldric
4. plume
5. burgher

Fluency: Context

For each italicized item, write a synonym from the vocabulary list on page 817.

From the old dirt road leading to the medieval village, the *long ridges* made by the plows were clearly visible. Off in the distance, you could hear the *farm laborers* on their journey home after a hard day's work. The *spreading* scent of newly turned earth pervaded the air as the day was *growing dim*.

Spelling Strategy

In the word *churls*, the letters *ur* spell the *er* sound. In the middle of a word, this sound is also commonly spelled *er* or *ir*. In your notebook, correctly spell the words below by choosing *er*, *ir*, or *ur*.

1. et__nal   2. wh__l   3. b__den

Grammar and Style Lesson

Parallel Structure

Tennyson uses **parallel structure**—similar grammatical forms for similar ideas—to give rhythm and unity to his poems. In his poem *In Memoriam*, for example, he uses three parallel infinitive phrases—phrases containing the *to* form of a verb—to stress the compelling desire to give in to grief:

> Ah, sweeter <u>to be drunk with loss</u>, / <u>To dance with death</u>, <u>to beat the ground</u>, . . .

Poets and speakers use parallel structure to create rhythm and drama. Tennyson achieves varied effects with this device. For instance, he uses it in "The Lady of Shalott" to create chanting, fateful feeling suited to the Lady's doom.

Practice Identify the examples of parallel structure in these passages. Then, indicate whether they involve single words, phrases, or clauses.

1. My love involves the love before; / My love is vaster passion now; . . .
2. From the bank and from the river . . .
3. How dull it is to pause, to make an end, / To rust unburnished, not to shine in use!
4. One equal temper of heroic hearts, / Made weak by time and fate, but strong in will / To strive, to seek, to find, and not to yield.
5. So sad, so fresh, the days that are no more.

Writing Application Write an additional stanza for any of Tennyson's poems. Use at least one example of parallel structure.

Prentice Hall Writing and Grammar Connection: Chapter 20, Section 6

Writing Lesson

Biographical Essay

Arthur Hallam's death had a decisive influence on Tennyson's poetry. Writing *In Memoriam* gave Tennyson the money to buy his own land. Write an essay exploring the relationship between Tennyson's life and his poetry, examining cause-and-effect relations between the two.

Prewriting   Research Tennyson and his work. Outline the main events and influences in his life. Then, make a chart of his major themes and literary accomplishments. Take notes on cause-and-effect relations between the two, using a diagram like the one shown.

Model: Charting Cause-and-Effect Relationships

Life: Cause or Effect?

Work: Effect or Cause?

Drafting   In your draft, clearly discuss the cause-and-effect relations between Tennyson's life and work. Signal such relationships with transitions such as *therefore*, *because*, *as a result*, and *due to*.

Revising   Read your essay to a friend, and then ask about the connections between Tennyson's life and work. Based on your friend's response, clarify details in your essay.

W͜G *Prentice Hall Writing and Grammar Connection: Chapter 10, Section 3*

Extension Activities

Listening and Speaking   As a news anchor, present a **videotaped news report** on the discovery of the Lady of Shalott's body. Interview Lancelot, King Arthur, and an ordinary citizen for their eyewitness accounts.

- In a group, assign roles and rehearse.
- Create pacing by timing segments.
- Use lighting or staging to direct audience attention from one speaker to the next.

Videotape your broadcast, and play it for the class. **[Group Activity]**

Researching and Representing   Make **sketches of a set** for a play based on "The Lady of Shalott." Research medieval architecture and furnishings. Consult the works of pre-Raphaelite painters, who helped create the Victorians' vision of medieval England. Accompany your sketches with an annotated bibliography.

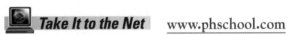 ***Take It to the Net***   www.phschool.com

Go online for an additional research activity using the Internet.

Prepare to Read

My Last Duchess ◆ Life in a Love ◆ Love Among the Ruins ◆ Sonnet 43

Robert Browning (1812–1889)

Young Robert Browning's best teacher may not have been a person, but his father's 6,000-book library. Although he had little schooling, he eagerly devoured those books, hungry for knowledge about history, art, and literature.

Inspiration and Discouragement By the time he was a teenager, Browning had decided to make poetry his life's pursuit. He published his first book, *Pauline*, at the age of twenty-one. Success was a while coming, though. A long and highly personal poem modeled after Shelley's work, *Pauline* did not sell a single copy.

Discouraged, Browning tried his hand at something less personal, a long dramatic poem called *Paracelsus*. He also wrote a play. His work still failed to attract much public notice, and his reputation was eclipsed by that of his wife, the poet Elizabeth Barrett Browning, whom he had married in 1846.

Lasting Fame In 1869, eight years after Elizabeth's death, the publication of *The Ring and the Book* turned Browning's career around. This long poem, based on an actual trial, tells the story of a murder in a series of dramatic monologues, or speeches by characters. *The Ring and the Book* achieved wide recognition for its author. It demonstrated the unique elements that Browning contributed to nineteenth-century poetry: a more down-to-earth, less "poetic" language and a renewal of the dramatic monologue, a form ideally suited to reveal character.

Today, Browning ranks with Tennyson as one of the great Victorian poets. His shorter dramatic monologues, such as "My Last Duchess," remain favorites of many.

Elizabeth Barrett Browning (1806–1861)

Like her future husband, young Elizabeth Barrett had no formal education. However, her zest for knowledge spurred her to learn eight languages on her own. By the time she was ten, she had read plays by Shakespeare, passages of *Paradise Lost*, and histories of England, Greece, and Rome. The oldest of eleven children in an upper-middle-class family, she began writing poetry as a child. By the time she reached adulthood, she had published two volumes of verse.

Frailty and Romance Elizabeth Barrett's frail health, caused by a spinal injury, made her something of a recluse. But her poetry attracted much attention, including that of Robert Browning, who wrote her a letter of appreciation. After five months of correspondence, she and Browning met and fell in love. Her father objected to their romance, but Elizabeth and Robert married in 1846 and ran away to Florence, Italy, where they had a son they nicknamed Pen and lived in happy exile. In Italy, Elizabeth Barrett took an interest in politics and wrote denunciations of slavery in the United States. She died in Florence in 1861.

Shifting Reputations It is hard for us to believe today, when Robert Browning's reputation is so great, that Elizabeth was the more famous poet during her lifetime. Her love story in verse, *Aurora Leigh* (1857), was so popular that the income from it helped support the Brownings. Also popular was her *Sonnets from the Portuguese*, a sequence of forty-four love poems written to her husband. Sonnet 43, which comes from this collection, has appeared in countless anthologies and has assured her place in the history of English poetry.

Preview

Connecting to the Literature

True love is hard to define: How does it differ from selfish possessiveness? True love may also be hard to find: Is it work, destiny, or sheer luck? The Brownings, very much in love, wrote many poems on these subjects.

Literary Analysis

Dramatic Monologue

Chaucer and Shakespeare gave us versions of the **dramatic monologue,** in which a single character delivers a speech. Robert Browning perfected the form and made it his own. His monologues contain these elements:

- A speaker who indirectly reveals his or her situation and character
- A silent listener, addressed by the speaker and implied in what the speaker says

As you read "My Last Duchess," note the skillful use of these elements.

Comparing Literary Works

The Brownings create a wide range of tones, from the dignified to the chatty. For instance, Robert Browning's monologues capture the rhythms of everyday speech through his expert use of **run-on lines**—lines ending where the flow of words forces you to read on without pause.

> But to myself they turned (since none puts by
> The curtain I have drawn for you, but I)

He and Elizabeth Barrett also use **end-stopped lines,** which end just where a speaker would pause, for a sing-song effect. Compare the poets' use of these devices.

Reading Strategy

Making Inferences About the Speaker

You make **inferences,** or educated guesses, about people every day. Similarly, you can infer the thoughts or feelings of a poem's speaker from his or her words and actions. Use a chart like the one shown to make inferences about the speakers of these poems.

Vocabulary Development

countenance (koun´ tə nəns) *n.* face (p. 837)

officious (ə fish´ əs) *adj.* meddlesome (p. 838)

munificence (myo͞o nif´ ə səns) *n.* lavish generosity (p. 838)

dowry (dou´ rē) *n.* property brought by a woman's family to her husband upon their marriage (p. 838)

eludes (ē lo͞odz´) *v.* avoids or escapes (p. 839)

vestige (ves´ tij) *n.* trace; remaining bit (p. 841)

sublime (sə blīm´) *adj.* inspiring awe through beauty or grandeur (p. 841)

minions (min´ yənz) *n.* attendants or agents (p. 841)

Words / Action of Speaker
"That's my last Duchess painted on the wall, . . ."

Overt Meaning
There on the wall is a painting of my last wife.

Inferences
The duke seems indifferent about his last wife, who is probably dead.

Antea (Portrait of a Lady), Parmigianino, Museo Nazionale di Capodimonte, Naples

▲ **Critical Viewing** Compare the character of this woman as conveyed by the painting with the character of the duchess as described by the duke. **[Compare and Contrast]**

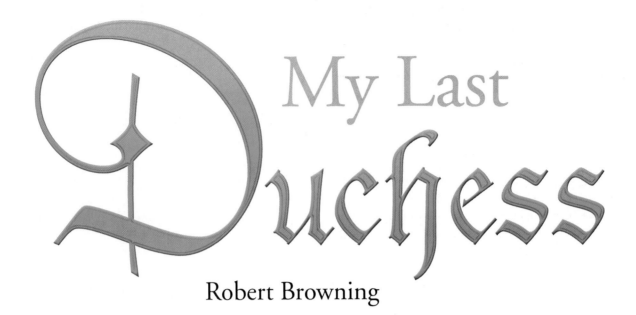

My Last Duchess

Robert Browning

Background

This poem, set in the sixteenth century in a castle in northern Italy, is based on events from the life of the duke of Ferrara, a nobleman whose first wife died after just three years of marriage. Following his wife's death, the duke began making arrangements to remarry. In Browning's poem, the duke is showing a painting of his first wife to an agent who represents the father of the woman he hopes to marry.

That's my last Duchess painted on the wall,
Looking as if she were alive. I call
That piece a wonder, now: Frà Pandolf's[1] hands
Worked busily a day, and there she stands.
5 Will't please you sit and look at her? I said
"Frà Pandolf" by design, for never read
Strangers like you that pictured <u>countenance</u>,
The depth and passion of its earnest glance,
But to myself they turned (since none puts by
10 The curtain I have drawn for you, but I)
And seemed as they would ask me, if they durst,[2]
How such a glance came there; so, not the first
Are you to turn and ask thus. Sir, 'twas not
Her husband's presence only, called that spot

countenance (koun´ tə nəns) *n.* face

✔**Reading Check**

What are the duke and his listener viewing?

---

1. **Frà Pandolf's** work of Brother Pandolf, an imaginary painter.
2. **durst** dared.

15 Of joy into the Duchess' cheek: perhaps
    Frà Pandolf chanced to say "Her mantle laps
    Over my lady's wrist too much," or "Paint
    Must never hope to reproduce the faint
    Half-flush that dies along her throat"; such stuff
20 Was courtesy, she thought, and cause enough
    For calling up that spot of joy. She had
    A heart—how shall I say?—too soon made glad,
    Too easily impressed; she liked whate'er
    She looked on, and her looks went everywhere.
25 Sir, 'twas all one! My favor at her breast,
    The dropping of the daylight in the West,
    The bough of cherries some officious fool
    Broke in the orchard for her, the white mule
    She rode with round the terrace—all and each
30 Would draw from her alike the approving speech,
    Or blush, at least. She thanked men—good! but
        thanked
    Somehow—I know not how—as if she ranked
    My gift of a nine-hundred-years-old name
    With anybody's gift. Who'd stoop to blame
35 This sort of trifling? Even had you skill
    In speech—(which I have not)—to make your will
    Quite clear to such an one, and say, "Just this
    Or that in you disgusts me; here you miss,
    Or there exceed the mark"—and if she let
40 Herself be lessoned so, nor plainly set
    Her wits to yours, forsooth,[3] and made excuse,
    —E'en then would be some stooping; and I choose
    Never to stoop. Oh sir, she smiled, no doubt,
    Whene'er I passed her; but who passed without
45 Much the same smile? This grew; I gave commands;
    Then all smiles stopped together. There she stands
    As if alive. Will 't please you rise? We'll meet
    The company below, then. I repeat,
    The Count your master's known munificence
50 Is ample warrant that no one just pretense
    Of mine for dowry will be disallowed;
    Though his fair daughter's self, as I avowed
    At starting, is my object. Nay, we'll go
    Together down, sir! Notice Neptune,[4] though,
55 Taming a sea horse, thought a rarity,
    Which Claus of Innsbruck[5] cast in bronze for me!

Literary Analysis
Dramatic Monologue
How does the duke indirectly suggest his own deeply jealous nature?

officious (ə fish´ əs) *adj.* meddlesome

Reading Strategy
Making Inferences About the Speaker How rational is the speaker being? How irrational are his underlying feelings?

munificence (myōō nif´ ə səns) *n.* lavish generosity

dowry (dou´ rē) *n.* property brought by a woman's family to her husband upon their marriage

---

3. **forsooth** in truth.
4. **Neptune** in Roman mythology, the god of the sea.
5. **Claus of Innsbruck** imaginary Austrian sculptor.

Life in a Love

Robert Browning

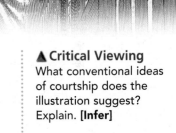

Escape me?
   Never—
   Beloved!
While I am I, and you are you,
5   So long as the world contains us both,
    Me the loving and you the loth,
While the one <u>eludes</u>, must the other pursue.
My life is a fault at last, I fear:
It seems too much like a fate, indeed!
10 Though I do my best I shall scarce succeed.
But what if I fail of my purpose here?
It is but to keep the nerves at strain,
To dry one's eyes and laugh at a fall,
And, baffled, get up and begin again,—
15 So the chase takes up one's life, that's all.
While, look but once from your farthest bound
At me so deep in the dust and dark,
No sooner the old hope goes to ground
Than a new one, straight to the self-same mark,
20 I shape me—
   Ever
   Removed!

▲ **Critical Viewing**
What conventional ideas
of courtship does the
illustration suggest?
Explain. **[Infer]**

eludes (ē lo͞odz´) v. avoids
or escapes

Review and Assess

Thinking About the Selections

1. **(a) Recall:** What complaint does the speaker make about his first wife in lines 13–24 of "My Last Duchess"? **(b) Infer:** How did he respond to her behavior? **(c) Support:** Explain what has happened to the duchess, indicating where in the poem this is revealed.

2. **(a) Recall:** To what new subject does the speaker turn in his last remark? **(b) Draw Conclusions:** What does this change of subject reveal about his character?

3. **(a) Recall:** What does the speaker of "Life in a Love" do as his beloved eludes him? **(b) Interpret:** What causes his behavior?

4. **Evaluate:** Is the speaker's "love" truly love? Explain.

5. **Apply:** Do you think irrational passions such as those in the poems still occur in modern times? Explain.

Love Among the Ruins

Robert Browning

Italian Ruins, John Claude Nattes, Victoria and Albert Museum

Where the quiet-colored end of evening smiles,
    Miles and miles
On the solitary pastures where our sheep
    Halt asleep
5 Tinkle homeward through the twilight, stray or stop
    As they crop—
Was the site once of a city great and gay
    (So they say),
Of our country's very capital, its prince
10   Ages since
Held his court in, gathered councils, wielding far
    Peace or war.

▲ **Critical Viewing**
Which phrase in the first line of Browning's poem could describe this painting? Explain.
[Support]

Now—the country does not even boast a tree,
    As you see,
15 To distinguish slopes of verdure,[1] certain rills
    From the hills
Intersect and give a name to (else they run
    Into one),
Where the domed and daring palace shot its spires
20   Up like fires
O'er the hundred-gated circuit of a wall
    Bounding all,
Made of marble, men might march on nor be pressed,
    Twelve abreast.

25 And such plenty and perfection, see, of grass
    Never was!
Such a carpet as, this summertime, o'erspreads
    And embeds
Every vestige of the city, guessed alone,
30   Stock or stone—
Where a multitude of men breathed joy and woe
    Long ago;
Lust of glory pricked their hearts up, dread of shame
    Struck them tame;
35 And that glory and that shame alike, the gold
    Bought and sold.

Now—the single little turret that remains
    On the plains,
By the caper[2] overrooted, by the gourd
40   Overscored,
While the patching houseleek's head of blossom winks
    Through the chinks—
Marks the basement whence a tower in ancient time
    Sprang sublime,
45 And a burning ring, all round, the chariots traced
    As they raced,
And the monarch and his minions and his dames
    Viewed the games.

And I know, while thus the quiet-colored eve
50   Smiles to leave
To their folding, all our many-tinkling fleece
    In such peace,
And the slopes and rills, in undistinguished gray
    Melt away—

---

1. **verdure** (vur′ jər) *n.* green plants.
2. **caper** prickly, trailing Mediterranean bush.

Love Among the Ruins ◆ 841

55 That a girl with eager eyes and yellow hair
    Waits me there
In the turret whence the charioteers caught soul
    For the goal,
When the king looked, where she looks now, breathless, dumb
60   Till I come.

But he looked upon the city, every side,
    Far and wide,
All the mountains topped with temples, all the glades'
    Colonnades,[3]

---

3. Colonnades (käl´ ə nādz´) *n.* series of columns set at regular intervals; here, groups
of trees surrounding an open area.

▼ **Critical Viewing**
What emotions might a
scene like this one evoke
in the speaker? Explain.
[Connect]

65   All the causeys,[4] bridges, aqueducts—and then,
        All the men!
    When I do come, she will speak not, she will stand,
        Either hand
    On my shoulder, give her eyes the first embrace
70   Of my face,
    Ere we rush, ere we extinguish sight and speech
        Each on each.

    In one year they sent a million fighters forth
        South and North,
75   And they built their gods a brazen pillar[5] high
        As the sky,
    Yet reserved a thousand chariots in full force—
        Gold, of course.
    Oh heart! oh blood that freezes, blood that burns!
80   Earth's returns
    For whole centuries of folly, noise and sin!
        Shut them in,
    With their triumphs and their glories and the rest!
        Love is best.

---

4. **causeys** causeways or raised roads.
5. **brazen pillar** built from the brass of captured chariots.

Reading Strategy
Making Inferences About the Speaker How does the speaker feel about the girl?

Review and Assess

Thinking About the Selection

1. **(a) Respond:** How impressed were you by the speaker's descriptions of the ancient city? Explain.

2. **(a) Recall:** What once stood where the speaker's sheep now head homeward? **(b) Compare and Contrast:** Compare the past and the present appearance of the setting.

3. **(a) Support:** In what way is the whole poem based on a contrast between past and present? **(b) Analyze:** How does Browning use the "echo" created by alternating long and short lines to emphasize both the deadness of the past and the passion of the present?

4. **(a) Analyze:** Explain how the person waiting for the speaker "replaces" the past. **(b) Interpret:** What conclusion does the speaker reach about the past and the present?

5. **Assess:** Is "Love Among the Ruins" a good title for this poem? Explain your answer.

6. **Make a Judgment:** Do you agree with the speaker's conclusion that present love is worth more than past glories? Explain.

Sonnet 43

Elizabeth Barrett Browning

How do I love thee? Let me count the ways.
I love thee to the depth and breadth and height
My soul can reach, when feeling out of sight
For the ends of Being and ideal Grace.
5   I love thee to the level of every day's
Most quiet need, by sun and candlelight.
I love thee freely, as men strive for Right;
I love thee purely, as they turn from Praise.
I love thee with the passion put to use
10 In my old griefs, and with my childhood's faith.
I love thee with a love I seemed to lose
With my lost saints—I love thee with the breath,
Smiles, tears, of all my life!—and, if God choose,
I shall but love thee better after death.

Reading Strategy
Making Inferences About the Speaker What do the references to childhood and old griefs suggest about the speaker?

Review and Assess

Thinking About the Selection

1. **Respond:** Do you find the speaker's description of the depth of her love moving? Explain.

2. **(a) Recall:** In Sonnet 43, what question does the speaker ask?
   (b) Paraphrase: Briefly summarize the speaker's answers to her own question.

3. **(a) Interpret:** In lines 9–10, what does the speaker mean by ". . . with the passion put to use / In my old griefs, . . ."?
   (b) Draw Conclusions: In what way does the kind of love expressed by the speaker in Sonnet 43 draw on all parts of her life and being?

4. **Relate:** Cite a popular song that praises love, and compare its language, attitude, and images with those of Sonnet 43.

Review and Assess

Literary Analysis

Dramatic Monologue

1. (a) Who is the speaker in "My Last Duchess," and who is the listener? (b) How can you tell when the listener interacts with the speaker? Give an example.
2. (a) Cite two lines in which the speaker reveals something negative about himself. (b) Do you think the speaker's next marriage will be successful? Explain.
3. (a) Who are the speaker and the listener in "Life in a Love"? (b) Is there interaction between them? Explain.

Comparing Literary Works

4. (a) Use a chart like the one shown to analyze the places at which a speaker would naturally pause in lines 14–22 of "My Last Duchess."

Line 14:	Her hus-	-band's pre-	-sence on-	-ly, called	that spot
Natural Pauses	no pause	no pause	no pause	**pause**	no pause

(b) How does the use of **run-on lines** and pauses within lines create a conversational rhythm?

5. Use a similar chart to analyze the rhythms of Elizabeth Barrett Browning's Sonnet 43.
6. (a) Compare the rhythms of speech in the two poems. (b) Which rhythm do you find more dramatic? Explain. (c) Which better captures general feelings in a memorable manner?

Reading Strategy

Making Inferences About the Speaker

7. Explaining the clues you use, **make inferences about the speaker's character** in (a) lines 31–43 of "My Last Duchess" and (b) lines 18–20 of "Life in a Love."
8. In "Love Among the Ruins," what can you infer about the speaker's attitude toward the ancient past? Identify the clues you use.

Extend Understanding

9. **Cultural Connection:** How important do you think it is to preserve monuments from the past, such as those Browning describes?

Quick Review

A **dramatic monologue** is a poem in which an imaginary character speaks to a silent listener.

A **run-on line** of poetry is a line that does not contain a stop or pause at the end. An **end-stopped line** ends where a speaker would pause.

To **make inferences about the speaker** of a poem, make informed guesses based on the speaker's words and actions.

 Take It to the Net
www.phschool.com
Take the interactive self-test online to check your understanding of these selections.

Integrate Language Skills

Vocabulary Development Lesson

Word Analysis: Latin Suffix -ence

The Latin suffix -ence means "quality of, or state of being." The adjective *munificent*, for example, means "very generous." Drop the suffix -ent and add -ence to form the noun *munificence*, meaning "the state of being very generous." Write the noun forms of the following words, and write the definition of each new word.

   1. innocent   **2.** prominent   **3.** permanent

Spelling Strategy

To form a noun from an adjective that ends with the suffix -ent, use the suffix -ence: *munificent* becomes *munificence*. Use the suffix -ance for adjectives ending in -ant: *elegant* becomes *elegance*. Complete each word below using -ence or -ance.

   1. intellig____   **3.** import____
   2. relev____   **4.** obedi____

Concept Development: Analogies

Complete the following analogies, using the words from the vocabulary list on page 835. Use each word only once.

1. *Chases* is to *pursuer* as ___?___ is to *escapee*.

2. *Cruelty* is to *tormentor* as ___?___ is to *benefactor*.

3. *Window* is to *curtain* as ___?___ is to *veil*.

4. *Salary* is to *employee* as ___?___ is to *husband*.

5. *Soldiers* are to *general* as ___?___ is to *king*.

6. *Plain* is to *stick figure* as ___?___ is to *masterpiece*.

7. *Totality* is to *whole* as ___?___ is to *part*.

8. *Generous* is to *philanthropist* as ___?___ is to *busybody*.

Grammar and Style Lesson

Usage: *like* and *as*

The words *like* and *as*, used to make comparisons, are not interchangeable. The word **like** is a preposition meaning "similar to." It is used to compare nouns or pronouns. The word **as**, a subordinating conjunction, is used to compare actions. It introduces a clause with a noun and verb. In some cases, the verb may be understood rather than stated.

> **Like:** Strangers <u>like you</u> . . . (prepositional phrase)
>
> **As:** Elizabeth did not live to the same age <u>as Robert</u> [did]. (subordinate clause; *did* is understood)

Practice Copy these sentences, replacing the blanks with either *like* or *as*.

1. No interpretation of Browning's *The Ring and the Book* is exactly ___?___ another.

2. The duke depicted his last duchess ___?___ he chose.

3. Before the two married, his poems were not as famous ___?___ hers.

4. Are Elizabeth Barrett Browning's sonnets ___?___ contemporary love songs?

5. "My Last Duchess" has as much conflict ___?___ a one-act play does.

Writing Application Write a paragraph comparing Sonnet 43 to "Life in a Love," using *like* and *as*.

W̖G *Prentice Hall Writing and Grammar Connection: Chapter 25, Section 2*

Writing Lesson

Written Recommendation About the Duke's Proposal

After listening to the duke in "My Last Duchess," how would you advise the father of the lady the duke hopes to marry? Give your advice in a written recommendation, clearly connecting your observations to your recommendations.

Prewriting Review the poem, noting what it reveals about the duke's character and first marriage. Gather details that will help you reach your recommendation.

Drafting Start by presenting your position. Then, explain the reasons for your recommendation. Include cause-and-effect transitions such as *as a result*, *because*, and *therefore* to link ideas.

Revising Review your draft, drawing arrows between observations and the conclusions they support. Where appropriate, add missing cause-and-effect transitions between sections connected by arrows.

Model: Revising to Indicate Cause-and-Effect Transitions

As a result of my observations,
^ I have concluded that the duke is a <u>cruel and dangerous</u>

. *Therefore,*

man, and I advise you to <u>cancel</u> your daughter's wedding

plans immediately.

> Cause-and-effect transitions clarify the link between the writer's ideas.

W͞G Prentice Hall Writing and Grammar Connection: Chapter 11, Section 4

Extension Activities

Listening and Speaking Present an **oral interpretation** of "My Last Duchess." Make decisions about your reading by marking up a copy of the poem. Consider these tips:

- Mark words that you want to emphasize.
- Note places where you should pause or change your tone.
- Indicate points at which to add gestures for dramatic effect.

Present your oral interpretation to the class.

Research and Technology With a group, prepare a **guided tour** of nineteenth-century Italy such as the Brownings might have given. Research the areas where the Brownings lived, note tourist attractions, and prepare a map showing the tour route. Incorporate your visual materials into your final word-processed document. [**Group Activity**]

 **Take It to the Net**   www.phschool.com

Go online for an additional research activity using the Internet.

CONNECTIONS
Literature Around the World
Relationships

Silence and Words The deepest poem in the world may be the words *I love you*. These words can transform and liberate, distress and bind. Yet these deep words are surrounded by silence just as deep. Lovers discover this silence when they rush to speak to the beloved, only to find that words fail them utterly.

Love and Poetry Lovers may write love poems to fill this silence. Poets may write love poems to rediscover it. Even the most boisterous poem requires a kind of quiet, a hush in which words can finally be heard for themselves. By writing on love, a poet invokes the silence and the poverty in which all speech is based—the need to be heard and to be loved. From out of this silence rushes the intoxicating whirl of images and thoughts that make up poetry—or love.

A Lover's Devotion Most of the poems in this section grew out of intense experiences of love or friendship. For example, Alfred, Lord Tennyson's *In Memoriam* expresses grief at the death of his good friend Arthur Henry Hallam. Elizabeth Barrett Browning begins to count the uncountable ways in which she loves her husband in Sonnet 43, a poem that could sum up every lover's devotion.

The poems of Sappho (saf ō) of ancient Greece and those of Charles Baudelaire (shàrl bōd ler´) of nineteenth-century France also express wholehearted devotion to a loved one. For Sappho, the loved one is Aphrodite herself, the Greek goddess of love. For Baudelaire, the beloved is a mortal woman.

Invitations to Love Both Sappho and Baudelaire wrote their poems in the form of invitations. Sappho offers a rich, alluring picture of her island to persuade Aphrodite to come from Crete and take up residence there.

Baudelaire paints for his beloved the image of a magical world of "Richness, quietness, and pleasure" where they can "live together" at peace.

You Know the Place: Then

SAPPHO   TRANSLATED BY MARY BARNARD

You know the place: then

Leave Crete and come to us
waiting where the grove is
pleasantest, by precincts

5 sacred to you; incense
smokes on the altar, cold
streams murmur through the

apple branches, a young
rose thicket shades the ground
10 and quivering leaves pour

down deep sleep; in meadows
where horses have grown sleek
among spring flowers, dill

scents the air. Queen! Cyprian![1]
15 Fill our gold cups with love
stirred into clear nectar.

---

1. **Cyprian** (sĭ′ prē ən) *n.* a reference to the goddess
Aphrodite, who was associated with the isle of Cyprus.

Sappho

(c. 610–c. 580 B.C.)

Sappho
was a lyricist
from ancient
Greece whose
works are
known for
their memorable
expressions of love
and loss. Sappho was one
of the first poets to write
in the first person rather
than from the viewpoint of
gods and Muses. Although
Sappho wrote nearly five
hundred poems, only a
small fraction of these
survive, either intact or
in fragments.

Invitation to the Voyage

Charles Baudelaire

TRANSLATED BY RICHARD WILBUR

Thematic Connection

Compare the landscapes described by Baudelaire's speaker with those described by Browning in "Love Among Ruins."

> My child, my sister, dream
> How sweet all things would seem
> Were we in that kind land to live together
> And there love slow and long,
> 5   There love and die among
> Those scenes that image you, that sumptuous[1] weather.
> Drowned suns that glimmer there
> Through cloud-disheveled[2] air
> Move me with such a mystery as appears
> 10   Within those other skies
> Of your treacherous eyes
> When I behold them shining through their tears.

---

1. **sumptuous** (sump′ chळळ əs) *adj.* magnificent or splendid.
2. **disheveled** (di shev′ əld) *adj.* disarranged and untidy.

▶**Critical Viewing**

Where, according to the speaker in this poem, might these "drowsy ships" be sailing? **[Interpret]**

There, there is nothing else but grace and measure,
Richness, quietness, and pleasure.

15   Furniture that wears
        The luster of the years
Softly would glow within our glowing chamber,
        Flowers of rarest bloom
        Proffering their perfume
20 Mixed with the vague fragrances of amber;
        Gold ceilings would there be,
        Mirrors deep as the sea,

☑ **Reading Check**

What does the speaker imagine doing?

Marine, Marcel Mouillot, Galleria d' arte Moderna, Nancy

The walls all in an Eastern splendor hung—
    Nothing but should address
25   The soul's loneliness,
Speaking her sweet and secret native tongue.

There, there is nothing else but grace and measure,
Richness, quietness, and pleasure.

    See, sheltered from the swells
30   There in the still canals
Those drowsy ships that dream of sailing forth;
    It is to satisfy
    Your least desire, they ply
Hither through all the waters of the earth.
35   The sun at close of day
    Clothes the fields of hay,
Then the canals, at last the town entire
    In hyacinth and gold:
    Slowly the land is rolled
40 Sleepward under a sea of gentle fire.

There, there is nothing else but grace and measure,
Richness, quietness, and pleasure.

Thematic Connection
What aspect of love do Baudelaire's descriptions emphasize?

Charles Baudelaire

(1821–1867)

Known as much for his unconventional lifestyle as he was for his poetry, Baudelaire was one of the most startling and innovative poets of the nineteenth century. Attempting to break away from the earlier Romantic tradition, Baudelaire created poems that are objective rather than sentimental and that celebrate the city and the artificial rather than nature. His work, however, still exhibits many of the imaginative and mystical qualities associated with Romanticism.

Connecting Literature Around the World

1. According to poets, how important is place in a friendship or love relationship? Support your answers with examples from Tennyson's *In Memoriam* and Browning's "Love Among Ruins" as well as from the poems by Sappho and Baudelaire.

2. How will the speakers in Sappho's and Baudelaire's poems feel after love has gone? Draw on a poem by Tennyson or the Brownings to support your answer.

3. Which poem in this section would you recommend for a lover to send his or her beloved? Explain your choice.

PART 2

Focus on Literary Forms: The Novel

Music and Literature, 1878, William M. Harnett, Albright-Knox Art Gallery Buffalo, New York

In an era before mass media, the new middle class looked to
the novel for entertainment, ideas, and a fictional world they
could share and discuss. Dickens, the premier British novelist,
pioneered the publication of novels in magazines, episode by

Prepare to Read

from Hard Times ◆ *from* Jane Eyre

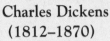

Charles Dickens
(1812–1870)

No writer since Shakespeare has occupied as important a place in popular culture as Charles Dickens. His novels have held a special appeal for critics and the public alike. They have also been dramatized time and again in plays and films.

A Childhood of Hardship Born in Portsmouth on England's southern coast, Dickens had a generally unhappy childhood. His father was sent to debtors' prison, and the boy was sent to a "prison" of his own—a factory in which he worked long hours pasting labels. Similar experiences, dramatizing the ills of the newly industrialized society, were to figure prominently in Dickens's novels.

The Birth of a Writer As a young man, Dickens held jobs as a stenographer in the courts and as a reporter for London newspapers. At twenty-one, he began to apply his keen powers of observation to producing humorous literary sketches of every-day life in London. A collection of these, *Sketches by Boz* (1836), earned him a small following, but his first novel, *The Pickwick Papers* (1837), made him the most popular writer of his day. Closely following were *Oliver Twist* (1839) and *Nicholas Nickleby* (1839).

A Serious Novelist The young Dickens reveled in the variety and peculiarity of the human character. Memorable characters like the charming Mr. Pickwick and the evil Fagin abound in his early work, but they are perhaps more like cartoons or natural forces than full-blooded characters. Dickens shows his growing mastery of characterization in *Dombey and Son* (1848) and *David Copperfield* (1850), novels of greater psychological depth. Throughout his work, Dickens offers his distinctive brand of social criticism, which is especially promi-nent in his late masterpiece *Hard Times* (1854).

Charlotte Brontë
(1816–1855)

Charlotte Brontë was part of a renowned literary family: Her sisters Anne and Emily were also writers. Their father, an Anglican clergyman, moved his family to the moors in Yorkshire in 1820, and the children were educated largely at home. Raised without their mother, who had died in 1821, the sisters, together with their brother Branwell, led a rich fantasy life that nurtured their artistic development.

Early Failure With three of her sisters, Charlotte briefly attended a boarding-school. Her experi-ences there provided material for the critical descriptions of boarding-school life at Lowood in *Jane Eyre*. Charlotte spent several years as a teacher, first of her own siblings and then at another school that she herself had briefly attended. She found this job difficult and unappealing, and in 1844 attempted to open her own school near her family home. The school's failure was quick and definite: No pupils enrolled.

Success In 1846, the three sisters published a volume of poems under the pseudonyms Currer, Ellis, and Acton Bell, but the book had little success. Charlotte had also written a novel, *The Professor*, but the book failed to find a publisher. Charlotte persevered, however, and when *Jane Eyre* was published in 1847 it met with immediate popular success.

Personal Struggle The final years of Charlotte Brontë's life were clouded by tragedy. Her brother died in 1848, and Emily and Anne died soon after. Despite her loneliness, Charlotte found the strength to complete the novels *Shirley* (1849) and *Villette* (1853). She married Arthur Bell Nicholls, her father's curate, a few months before she died.

Preview

Connecting to the Literature

You do not need to march on City Hall to make a difference. Dickens and Brontë were crusaders with their pens: Writing about the downtrodden, they won readers' sympathy for reform.

Literary Analysis

The Novel and Social Criticism

A **novel** is a long work of fiction, usually containing these elements:

- A complex plot, often including subplots and spanning a few settings
- Major and minor characters
- A significant overall theme

The novel became popular in the nineteenth century, a period of disturbing social and economic changes. Many novelists of the time included **social criticism** in their works, calling attention to society's ills. As you read, notice how each author turns particular incidents into dramatizations—and criticisms—of social trends and forces.

Comparing Literary Works

In these excerpts, both Dickens and Brontë take on a social problem—misguided educational practices. Both build their critiques using techniques of fiction. As you will see, Dickens favors comic exaggeration, and Brontë applies character analysis. Compare the techniques the writers use to make their points. Then, judge whether their effort to get a message across detracts from or adds to the literary impact of their work.

Reading Strategy

Recognizing the Writer's Purpose

Recognizing a writer's purpose can help you interpret specific incidents in a novel. A writer may write to entertain, to satirize, or to reveal a truth about life. Clues to a writer's purpose include details such as dialogue, events, and the writer's attitude toward characters. As you read, complete a chart like the one shown to help you identify each writer's purpose.

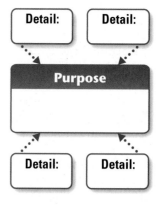

Vocabulary Development

monotonous (mə nät´ ən əs) *adj.* without variation (p. 858)

obstinate (äb´ stə nət) *adj.* stubborn; dogged (p. 859)

adversary (ad´vər ser´ ē) *n.* opponent; enemy (p. 862)

indignant (in dig´ nənt) *adj.* outraged; filled with righteous anger (p. 862)

approbation (ap´ rə bā shən) *n.* official approval or sanction (p. 862)

obscure (əb skyoor´) *adj.* not easily seen; not generally known (p. 866)

comprised (kəm prīzd´) *v.* consisted of; included (p. 866)

sundry (sun´ drē) *adj.* various; miscellaneous (p. 866)

The Curious Workshop of Charles Dickens: Making Myths

Even if you have never read a novel by Charles Dickens, you have encountered his work. Characters such as the miser Ebenezer Scrooge and the orphan Oliver Twist stepped out from Dicken's books long ago to take up a life as old friends in musicals and cartoons. The very word *Dickensian* names a special region of the imagination, a region criss-crossed by obscure city streets, each inhabited by leering villains, honest clerks, wide-eyed innocents, and a host of knotty eccentrics, a-glee with their own special knacks and nervous twitches.

Defining Dickens This generalized picture of Dickens and his works is based on his 15 novels (one incomplete) and his Christmas stories, most published in serial form in magazines. Dicken's popularity in his own lifetime was enormous. With his first major effort, *The Pickwick Papers* (1836–1837), and for decades after, he held Victorian England spellbound, raptly awaiting the publication of the next chapter of *Oliver Twist* (1837–1839) or *Great Expectations* (1860–1861). When his character Little Nell of *The Old Curiosity Shop* (1840–1841) died, England was torn by grief.

Reformer and Myth-Maker Dickens took his popularity as a responsibility, an opportunity to use influence for social improvement. In his day, the Industrial Revolution had washed over England, leaving sprawling slums overcrowded with the new working class, riddled with epidemic fatal diseases. Dickens's stories of hard times and injured innocents challenged the forces that smothered compassion and nursed vice in the new society.

A Curious Workshop Yet Dickens does more than tell moral stories about social injustice. The most distinctive characteristic of his work might be called its mythical or fairy-tale like quality. In the shadow of the harsh, gray factories choking London with smoke and slums, Dickens set up his own workshop of the imagination. There, he cobbled together ingenious new myths of crime and redemption. The trademark of his work is stamped most clearly on his characters.

"A Perpetual Summer of Being Themselves" There are no John Smiths or Jane Joneses among Dickens's characters. From Samuel Pickwick to Wilkins Micawber to Uriah Heep, each character's name is a distinctive concoction of syllables, a two-word poem. The quirkiness of character names only reflects the quirkiness of the characters themselves. From the Rumplestiltskin-like Daniel Quilp of *The Old Curiosity Shop* to the hopelessly optimistic Mr. Micawber of *David Copperfield* (1849–1850), Dickens compounded characters of peculiar turns of speech and singular mannerisms, some endearing, some frightening. As essayist G. K. Chesterton notes, these characters are so much themselves, it seems they will exist for ever, passing from one adventure to another like Paul Bunyan or Anansi in folklore. They live, Chesterton writes, "in a perpetual summer of being themselves."

Wicked Woods, Safe Havens Under Dickens's fairy-tale pen, the economic and social challenges of Victorian times reappear as a grotesque landscape, the literary equivalent of the woods in which the witch lives. Here is the description of landscape surrounding a new railroad:

> Everywhere were bridges that led nowhere; thoroughfares that were wholly impassable; Babel towers of chimneys, wanting half their height; temporary wooden houses and enclosures, in the most unlikely situations; carcasses of ragged tenements, and fragments of unfinished walls and arches, and piles of scaffolding, and wildernesses of bricks, and giant forms of cranes, and tripods straddling above nothing. There were a hundred thousand shapes and substances of incompleteness. . . .

Yet Dickens also creates islands of safety and refuge, such as the permanently beached boat in which David Copperfield finds happiness with the Peggoty family. In settings such as these, both Dickens's social criticism and his childlike attunement to the fairy-tale dimension of life have a place.

Dickens and Victorian England

Dickens ruled over the imagination of Victorian England as a kind of father-figure, by turns jolly and stern. He amuses his readers even while reprimanding their faults, and is never far from a childlike enjoyment of his own antics. Though there is much that is simply sentimental in Dickens, there are also depths of psychological realism, an unflagging faith in redemption, and the eternal exuberance in human variety. Modern readers can still warm themselves at the cheerful glow of his work.

Selected Characters of Dickens

Type	Sketch
Hero	**David Copperfield, *David Copperfield.*** A runaway, young David must make his way through the world to discover whether or not he is "the hero of my own life."
Villain	**Daniel Quilp, *The Old Curiosity Shop.*** A malevolent dwarf, charmed by his own ugliness and its power to frighten others, Quilp schemes for the sheer pleasure of mischief.
Morally Challenged	**Paul Dombey, *Dombey and Son.*** The egocentric businessman Dombey is wounded by the death of his son, through whom he thought to perpetuate his own self-image.
True-Hearted Grotesque	**Newman Noggs, *Nicholas Nickelby.*** "Goggle-eyed," by turns wooden and twitchy, Noggs rarely speaks but expresses emotion by explosively cracking his knuckles. He finds his courage when it is necessary to save Nicholas Nickelby.

from HARD TIMES

Charles Dickens

Background

Of the many beliefs in his society with which Dickens took issue, the Utilitarianism of philosopher Jeremy Bentham (1748–1832) particularly irritated him. Bentham believed that statistics and logic could be applied to all human affairs, and he viewed human beings as essentially interested only in their own happiness. He saw the purpose of society as "the greatest happiness for the greatest number," with happiness calculated in terms of individual pleasures and pains. Dickens believed Utilitarianism discounted or even sought to negate virtues like imagination and sympathy. In *Hard Times*, Dickens used his character Mr. Gradgrind to poke fun at this philosophy.

Chapter 1
The One Thing Needful

"Now, what I want is, Facts. Teach these boys and girls nothing but Facts. Facts alone are wanted in life. Plant nothing else, and root out everything else. You can only form the minds of reasoning animals upon Facts: nothing else will ever be of any service to them. This is the principle on which I bring up my own children, and this is the principle on which I bring up these children. Stick to Facts, sir!"

The scene was a plain, bare, <u>monotonous</u> vault of a schoolroom, and the speaker's square forefinger emphasized his observations by underscoring every sentence with a line on the schoolmaster's sleeve. The emphasis was helped by the speaker's square wall of a forehead, which had his eyebrows for its base, while his eyes found commodious cellarage in two dark caves, overshadowed by the wall. The emphasis was helped by the speaker's mouth, which was wide, thin, and hard set. The emphasis was helped by the speaker's voice, which was inflexible, dry, and dictatorial. The emphasis was helped by the speaker's hair, which bristled on the skirts of his bald head, a plantation of firs to keep the wind from its shining surface, all covered with knobs, like

monotonous (mə nät´ ən əs) *adj.* without variation

the crust of a plum pie, as if the head had scarcely warehouse-room for the hard facts stored inside. The speaker's <u>obstinate</u> carriage, square coat, square legs, square shoulders—nay, his very neckcloth, trained to take him by the throat with an unaccommodating grasp, like a stubborn fact, as it was—all helped the emphasis.

"In this life, we want nothing but Facts, sir; nothing but Facts!"

The speaker, and the schoolmaster, and the third grown person present, all backed a little, and swept with their eyes the inclined plane of little vessels, then and there arranged in order, ready to have imperial gallons of facts poured into them until they were full to the brim.

obstinate (äb´ stə nət) *adj.* stubborn; dogged

Chapter 2
Murdering the Innocents

Thomas Gradgrind, sir. A man of realities. A man of fact and calculations. A man who proceeds upon the principle that two and two are four, and nothing over, and who is not to be talked into allowing for anything over. Thomas Gradgrind, sir—peremptorily Thomas—Thomas Gradgrind. With a rule and a pair of scales, and the multiplication table always in his pocket, sir, ready to weigh and measure any parcel of human nature, and tell you exactly what it comes to. It is a mere question of figures, a case of simple arithmetic. You might hope to get some other nonsensical belief into the head of George Gradgrind, or Augustus Gradgrind, or John Gradgrind, or Joseph Gradgrind (all suppositious, non-existent persons), but into the head of Thomas Gradgrind—no, sir!

In such terms Mr. Gradgrind always mentally introduced himself, whether to his private circle of acquaintance, or to the public in general. In such terms, no doubt, substituting the words "boys and girls," for "sir," Thomas Gradgrind now presented Thomas Gradgrind to the little pitchers before him, who were to be filled so full of facts.

Indeed, as he eagerly sparkled at them from the cellarage before mentioned, he seemed a kind of cannon loaded to the muzzle with facts, and prepared to blow them clean out of the regions of childhood at one discharge. He seemed a galvanizing apparatus, too, charged with a grim mechanical substitute for the tender young imaginations that were to be stormed away.

"Girl number twenty," said Mr. Gradgrind, squarely pointing with his square forefinger, "I don't know that girl. Who is that girl?"

"Sissy Jupe, sir," explained number twenty, blushing, standing up, and curtseying.

"Sissy is not a name," said Mr. Gradgrind. "Don't call yourself Sissy. Call yourself Cecilia."

"It's father as calls me Sissy, sir," returned the young girl in a trembling voice, and with another curtsey.

"Then he has no business to do it," said Mr. Gradgrind. "Tell him he mustn't. Cecilia Jupe. Let me see. What is your father?"

"He belongs to the horse-riding, if you please, sir."

Mr. Gradgrind frowned, and waved off the objectionable calling with his hand.

Literary Analysis
The Novel and Social Criticism What outlook is Dickens criticizing through Gradgrind's identification of Sissy Jupe by a number?

 **Reading Check**

What does Gradgrind aim to do for students?

"We don't want to know anything about that, here. You mustn't tell us about that, here. Your father breaks horses, don't he?"

"If you please, sir, when they can get any to break, they do break horses in the ring, sir."

"You mustn't tell us about the ring, here. Very well, then. Describe your father as a horsebreaker. He doctors sick horses, I dare say?"

"Oh yes, sir."

"Very well, then. He is a veterinary surgeon, a farrier and horsebreaker. Give me your definition of a horse."

(Sissy Jupe thrown into the greatest alarm by this demand.)

"Girl number twenty unable to define a horse!" said Mr. Gradgrind, for the general behoof of all the little pitchers. "Girl number twenty possessed of no facts, in reference to one of the commonest of animals! Some boy's definition of a horse. Bitzer, yours."

The square finger, moving here and there, lighted suddenly on Bitzer, perhaps because he chanced to sit in the same ray of sunlight which, darting in at one of the bare windows of the intensely whitewashed room, irradiated Sissy. For, the boys and girls sat on the face of the inclined plane in two compact bodies, divided up the center by a narrow interval; and Sissy, being at the corner of a row on the sunny side, came in for the beginning of a sunbeam, of which Bitzer, being at the corner of a row on the other side, a few rows in advance, caught the end. But, whereas the girl was so dark-eyed and dark-haired, that she seemed to receive a deeper and more lustrous color from the sun when it shone upon her, the boy was so light-eyed and light-haired that the self-same rays appeared to draw out of him what little color he ever possessed. His cold eyes would hardly have been eyes, but for the short ends of lashes which, by bringing them into immediate contrast with something paler than themselves, expressed their form. His short-cropped hair might have been a mere continuation of the sandy freckles on his forehead and face. His skin was so unwholesomely deficient in the natural tinge, that he looked as though, if he were cut, he would bleed white.

"Bitzer," said Thomas Gradgrind. "Your definition of a horse."

"Quadruped. Graminivorous. Forty teeth, namely twenty-four grinders, four eye-teeth, and twelve incisive. Sheds coat in the spring; in marshy countries, sheds hoofs, too. Hoofs hard, but requiring to be shod with iron. Age known by marks in mouth." Thus (and much more) Bitzer.

▲ **Critical Viewing**
Judging from the details in this engraving, what was school like in London during Victorian times? **[Speculate]**

London School for Orphan Boys, Wood engraving, 1870

"Now girl number twenty," said Mr. Gradgrind. "You know what a horse is."

She curtseyed again, and would have blushed deeper, if she could have blushed deeper than she had blushed all this time. Bitzer, after rapidly blinking at Thomas Gradgrind with both eyes at once, and so catching the light upon his quivering ends of lashes that they looked like the antennae of busy insects, put his knuckles to his freckled forehead, and sat down again.

The third gentleman now stepped forth. A mighty man at cutting and drying, he was; a government officer; in his way (and in most other

Reading Check

What type of answer to his question does Gradgrind accept?

people's too), a professed pugilist; always in training, always with a system to force down the general throat like a bolus,[1] always to be heard of at the bar of his little Public-office, ready to fight all England. To continue in fistic phraseology, he had a genius for coming up to the scratch, wherever and whatever it was, and proving himself an ugly customer. He would go in and damage any subject whatever with his right, follow up with his left, stop, exchange, counter, bore his opponent (he always fought All England[2]) to the ropes, and fall upon him neatly. He was certain to knock the wind out of common sense, and render that unlucky adversary deaf to the call of time. And he had it in charge from high authority to bring about the great public-office Millennium, when Commissioners should reign upon earth.

adversary (ad′ vər ser′ ē) *n.* opponent; enemy

"Very well," said this gentleman, briskly smiling, and folding his arms. "That's a horse. Now, let me ask you girls and boys, Would you paper a room with representations of horses?"

After a pause, one half of the children cried in chorus, "Yes, sir!" Upon which the other half, seeing in the gentleman's face that Yes was wrong, cried out in chorus, "No, sir!"—as the custom is, in these examinations.

Reading Strategy
Recognizing the Writer's Purpose What does the reaction of the class hint about Dickens's purpose in this scene?

"Of course, No. Why wouldn't you?"

A pause. One corpulent slow boy, with a wheezy manner of breathing, ventured the answer, Because he wouldn't paper a room at all, but would paint it.

"You *must* paper it," said Thomas Gradgrind, "whether you like it or not. Don't tell *us* you wouldn't paper it. What do you mean, boy?"

"I'll explain to you, then," said the gentleman, after another and a dismal pause, "why you wouldn't paper a room with representations of horses. Do you ever see horses walking up and down the sides of rooms in reality—in fact? Do you?"

"Yes, sir!" from one half. "No, sir!" from the other.

"Of course no," said the gentleman, with an indignant look at the wrong half. "Why, then, you are not to see anywhere, what you don't see in fact; you are not to have anywhere, what you don't have in fact. What is called Taste, is only another name for Fact."

indignant (in dig′ nənt) *adj.* outraged; filled with righteous anger

Thomas Gradgrind nodded his approbation.

"This is a new principle, a discovery, a great discovery," said the gentleman. "Now, I'll try you again. Suppose you were going to carpet a room. Would you use a carpet having a representation of flowers upon it?"

There being a general conviction by this time that "No, sir!" was always the right answer to this gentleman, the chorus of No was very strong. Only a few feeble stragglers said Yes; among them Sissy Jupe.

approbation (ap′ rə bā′ shən) *n.* official approval or sanction

"Girl number twenty," said the gentleman, smiling in the calm strength of knowledge.

Sissy blushed, and stood up.

---

1. **bolus** small, round mass, often of chewed food.
2. **fought All England** fought according to the official rules of boxing.

"So you would carpet your room—or your husband's room, if you were a grown woman, and had a husband—with representations of flowers, would you," said the gentleman. "Why would you?"

"If you please, sir, I am very fond of flowers," returned the girl.

"And is that why you would put tables and chairs upon them, and have people walking over them with heavy boots?"

"It wouldn't hurt them, sir. They wouldn't crush and wither if you please, sir. They would be the pictures of what was very pretty and pleasant, and I would fancy—"

"Ay, ay, ay! but you mustn't fancy," cried the gentleman, quite elated by coming so happily to his point. "That's it! You are never to fancy."

"You are not, Cecilia Jupe," Thomas Gradgrind solemnly repeated, "to do anything of that kind."

"Fact, fact, fact!" said the gentleman. And "Fact, fact, fact!" repeated Thomas Gradgrind.

"You are to be in all things regulated and governed," said the gentleman, "by fact. We hope to have, before long, a board of fact, composed of commissioners of fact, who will force the people to be a people of fact, and of nothing but fact. You must discard the word Fancy altogether. You have nothing to do with it. You are not to have, in any object of use or ornament, what would be a contradiction in fact. You don't walk upon flowers in fact; you cannot be allowed to walk upon flowers in carpets. You don't find that foreign birds and butterflies come and perch upon your crockery. You never meet with quadrupeds going up and down walls; you must not have quadrupeds represented upon walls. You must use," said the gentleman, "for all these purposes, combinations and modifications (in primary colors) of mathematical figures which are susceptible of proof and demonstration. This is the new discovery. This is fact. This is taste."

The girl curtseyed, and sat down. She was very young, and she looked as if she were frightened by the matter of fact prospect the world afforded.

"Now, if Mr. M'Choakumchild," said the gentleman, "will proceed to give his first lesson here, Mr. Gradgrind, I shall be happy, at your request, to observe his mode of procedure."

Mr. Gradgrind was much obliged. "Mr. M'Choakumchild, we only wait for you."

So, Mr. M'Choakumchild began in his best manner. He and some one hundred and forty other schoolmasters, had been lately turned at the same time, in the same factory, on the same principles, like so many pianoforte legs. He had been put through an immense variety of paces, and had answered volumes of head-breaking questions. Orthography, etymology, syntax, and prosody, biography, astronomy, geography, and general cosmography, the sciences of compound proportion, algebra, land-surveying and leveling, vocal music, and drawing from models, were all at the ends of his ten chilled fingers. He had worked his stony way into Her Majesty's most Honorable

Literary Analysis
The Novel and Social Criticism How does Dickens exaggerate his characters' reaction to make a point about social trends?

**Reading Check**

Why does the third gentleman object to horses on wallpaper and flowers on rugs?

Privy Council's Schedule B, and had taken the bloom off the higher branches of mathematics and physical science, French, German, Latin, and Greek. He knew all about all the Water Sheds of all the world (whatever they are), and all the histories of all the peoples, and all the names of all the rivers and mountains, and all the productions, manners, and customs of all the countries, and all their boundaries and bearings on the two-and-thirty points of the compass. Ah, rather overdone, M'Choakumchild. If he had only learnt a little less, how infinitely better he might have taught much more!

He went to work in this preparatory lesson, not unlike Morgiana in the Forty Thieves:[3] looking into all the vessels ranged before him, one after another, to see what they contained. Say, good M'Choakumchild. When from thy boiling store, thou shalt fill each jar brim full by and by, dost thou think that thou wilt always kill outright the robber Fancy lurking within—or sometimes only maim him and distort him!

---

3. **Morgiana in the Forty Thieves** In the tale "Ali Baba and the Forty Thieves," Ali Baba's clever servant, Morgiana, saves him from the thieves who are hiding in large jars.

Review and Assess

Thinking About the Selection

1. **Respond:** How did you feel about Mr. Gradgrind's theory of education?

2. **(a) Recall:** What does Mr. Gradgrind believe is the key to all learning? **(b) Connect:** In what ways does he put this belief into practice? **(c) Interpret:** What attitude does the description of the children as "little pitchers" reflect?

3. **(a) Recall:** What is the profession of the "third gentleman" who is visiting the classroom? **(b) Summarize:** What is his view of "Fact" and imagination?

4. **(a) Compare and Contrast:** Compare and contrast Sissy's and Bitzer's performances in the classroom. **(b) Analyze:** With whom does Dickens's expect the reader to sympathize? Why?

5. **(a) Draw Conclusions:** What conclusion does Dickens want the reader to draw about the three adults in the classroom? Explain. **(b) Draw Conclusions:** What conclusion does Dickens want the reader to draw about the kind of children this type of education will produce? Explain.

6. **Make a Judgment:** How much responsibility does a system of education have for the type of adults children become? Explain.

from *Jane Eyre*

Charlotte Brontë

Chapter 6

The next day commenced as before, getting up and dressing by rushlight; but this morning we were obliged to dispense with the ceremony of washing: the water in the pitchers was frozen. A change had taken place in the weather the preceding evening, and a keen northeast wind, whistling through the crevices of our bedroom windows all night long, had made us shiver in our beds, and turned the contents of the ewers to ice.

Before the long hour and a half of prayers and Bible reading was over, I felt ready to perish with cold. Breakfast time came at last, and this morning the porridge was not burnt; the quality was eatable, the quantity small; how small my portion seemed! I wished it had been doubled.

In the course of the day I was enrolled a member of the fourth class, and regular tasks and occupations were assigned to me: hitherto, I had only been a spectator of the proceedings at Lowood, I was now to become an actor therein. At first, being little accustomed to learn by heart, the lessons appeared to me both long and difficult: the frequent change from task to task, too, bewildered me; and I was glad, when, about three o'clock in the afternoon, Miss Smith put into my hands a border of muslin two yards long, together with needle, thimble, etc., and sent me to sit in a quiet corner of the school room, with directions to hem the same. At that hour most of the others were sewing likewise; but one class still stood round Miss Scatcherd's chair reading, and as all was quiet, the subject of their lessons could be heard, together with the manner in which each girl acquitted herself, and the animadversions or commendations of Miss Scatcherd on the performance. It was English history; among the readers, I observed my

✔ **Reading Check**

How has the narrator's role at Lowood changed?

acquaintance of the verandah; at the commencement of the lesson, her place had been at the top of the class, but for some error of pronunciation or some inattention to stops, she was suddenly sent to the very bottom. Even in that <u>obscure</u> position, Miss Scatcherd continued to make her an object of constant notice: she was continually addressing to her such phrases as the following:—

"Burns" (such it seems was her name: the girls here, were all called by their surnames, as boys are elsewhere), "Burns, you are standing on the side of your shoe, turn your toes out immediately." "Burns, you poke your chin most unpleasantly, draw it in." "Burns, I insist on your holding your head up: I will not have you before me in that attitude," etc. etc.

A chapter having been read through twice, the books were closed and the girls examined. The lesson had <u>comprised</u> part of the reign of Charles I, and there were <u>sundry</u> questions about tonnage and poundage, and ship-money, which most of them appeared unable to answer; still, every little difficulty was solved instantly when it reached Burns: her memory seemed to have retained the substance of the whole lesson, and she was ready with answers on every point. I kept expecting that Miss Scatcherd would praise her attention; but, instead of that, she suddenly cried out:—

"You dirty, disagreeable girl! you have never cleaned your nails this morning!"

Burns made no answer: I wondered at her silence.

"Why," thought I, "does she not explain that she could neither clean her nails nor wash her face, as the water was frozen?"

My attention was now called off by Miss Smith, desiring me to hold a skein of thread: while she was winding it, she talked to me from time to time, asking whether I had ever been at school before, whether I could mark, stitch, knit, etc.; till she dismissed me, I could not pursue my observations on Miss Scatcherd's movements. When I returned to my seat, that lady was just delivering an order, of which I did not catch the import; but Burns immediately left the class, and going into the small inner room where the books were kept, returned in half a minute, carrying in her hand a bundle of twigs tied together at one end. This ominous tool she presented to Miss Scatcherd with a respectful courtesy; then she quietly, and without being told, unloosed her pinafore, and the teacher instantly and sharply inflicted on her neck a dozen strokes with the bunch of twigs. Not a tear rose to Burns's eye; and, while I paused from my sewing, because my fingers quivered at this spectacle with a sentiment of unavailing and impotent anger, not a feature of her pensive face altered its ordinary expression.

"Hardened girl!" exclaimed Miss Scatcherd, "nothing can correct you of your slatternly habits: carry the rod away."

Burns obeyed: I looked at her narrowly as she emerged from the book closet; she was just putting back her handkerchief into her pocket, and the trace of a tear glistened on her thin cheek.

obscure (əb skyōōr′) *adj.* not easily seen; not generally known

comprised (kəm prīz′ d) *v.* consisted of; included

sundry (sun′ drē) *adj.* various, miscellaneous

**Literary Analysis
The Novel and Social Criticism** What does the strange relationship between Miss Scatcherd and Burns suggest about how teachers "ruled" their classrooms in Victorian times?

The play-hour in the evening I thought the pleasantest fraction of the day at Lowood: the bit of bread, the draught of coffee swallowed at five o'clock had revived vitality, if it had not satisfied hunger; the long restraint of the day was slackened; the school room felt warmer than in the morning: its fires being allowed to burn a little more brightly to supply, in some measure, the place of candles, not yet introduced; the ruddy gloaming,[1] the licensed uproar, the confusion of many voices gave one a welcome sense of liberty.

On the evening of the day on which I had seen Miss Scatcherd flog her pupil, Burns, I wandered as usual among the forms and tables

---

1. **ruddy gloaming** glowing twilight; the sunset.

▲ **Critical Viewing**
How well does this still from a movie version of *Jane Eyre* match your vision of Jane and Burns? Explain. **[Evaluate]**

☑ **Reading Check**

What does the narrator think is unusual about Burns's reaction to the charge of uncleanliness?

and laughing groups without a companion, yet not feeling lonely: when I passed the windows, I now and then lifted a blind and looked out; it snowed fast, a drift was already forming against the lower panes; putting my ear close to the window, I could distinguish from the gleeful tumult within, the disconsolate moan of the wind outside.

Probably, if I had lately left a good home and kind parents, this would have been the hour when I should most keenly have regretted the separation: that wind would then have saddened my heart; this obscure chaos would have disturbed my peace: as it was I derived from both a strange excitement, and reckless and feverish, I wished the wind to howl more wildly, the gloom to deepen to darkness, and the confusion to rise to clamor.

Jumping over forms, and creeping under tables, I made my way to one of the fire-places: there, kneeling by the high wire fender, I found Burns, absorbed, silent, abstracted from all round her by the companionship of a book, which she read by the dim glare of the embers.

"Is it still 'Rasselas'?"[2] I asked, coming behind her.

"Yes," she said, "and I have just finished it."

And in five minutes more she shut it up. I was glad of this.

"Now," thought I, "I can perhaps get her to talk." I sat down by her on the floor.

"What is your name besides Burns?"

"Helen."

"Do you come a long way from here?"

"I come from a place further north; quite on the borders of Scotland."

"Will you ever go back?"

"I hope so; but nobody can be sure of the future."

"You must wish to leave Lowood?"

"No: why should I? I was sent to Lowood to get an education; and it would be of no use going away until I have attained that object."

"But that teacher, Miss Scatcherd, is so cruel to you?"

"Cruel? Not at all! She is severe: she dislikes my faults."

"And if I were in your place I should dislike her: I should resist her; if she struck me with that rod, I should get it from her hand; I should break it under her nose."

"Probably you would do nothing of the sort: but if you did, Mr. Brocklehurst would expel you from the school; that would be a great grief to your relations. It is far better to endure patiently a smart which nobody feels but yourself, than to commit a hasty action whose evil consequences will extend to all connected with you—and, besides, the Bible bids us return good for evil."

"But then it seems disgraceful to be flogged, and to be sent to stand in the middle of a room full of people; and you are such a great girl: I am far younger than you, and I could not bear it."

Literary Analysis
The Novel and Social Criticism How does Brontë address both individual ethics and social problems in this dialogue?

---

2. **Rasselas** *The History of Rasselas, Prince of Abyssinia,* a moralizing novel by Samuel Johnson.

"Yet it would be your duty to bear it, if you could not avoid it: it is weak and silly to say you *cannot bear* what it is your fate to be required to bear."

I heard her with wonder: I could not comprehend this doctrine of endurance; and still less could I understand or sympathize with the forbearance she expressed for her chastiser. Still I felt that Helen Burns considered things by a light invisible to my eyes. I suspected she might be right and I wrong; but I would not ponder the matter deeply: like Felix,[3] I put it off to a more convenient season.

"You say you have faults, Helen: what are they? To me you seem very good."

"Then learn from me, not to judge by appearances: I am, as Miss Scatcherd said, slatternly; I seldom put, and never keep, things in order; I am careless; I forget rules; I read when I should learn my lessons; I have no method; and sometimes I say, like you, I cannot *bear* to be subjected to systematic arrangements. This is all very provoking to Miss Scatcherd, who is naturally neat, punctual, and particular."

"And cross and cruel," I added; but Helen Burns would not admit my addition: she kept silence.

"Is Miss Temple as severe to you as Miss Scatcherd?"

At the utterance of Miss Temple's name, a soft smile flitted over her grave face.

"Miss Temple is full of goodness; it pains her to be severe to anyone, even the worst in the school: she sees my errors, and tells me of them gently; and, if I do anything worthy of praise, she gives me my meed liberally. One strong proof of my wretchedly defective nature is that even her expostulations, so mild, so rational, have not influence to cure me of my faults; and even her praise, though I value it most highly, cannot stimulate me to continued care and foresight."

"That is curious," said I: "it is so easy to be careful."

Reading Strategy
Recognizing the Writer's Purpose What opinion does Brontë want you to form of Helen in this paragraph?

"For *you* I have no doubt it is. I observed you in your class this morning, and saw you were closely attentive: your thoughts never seemed to wander while Miss Miller explained the lesson and questioned you. Now, mine continually rove away: when I should be listening to Miss Scatcherd, and collecting all she says with assiduity,[4] often I lose the very sound of her voice; I fall into a sort of dream. Sometimes I think I am in Northumberland, and that the noises I hear round me are the bubbling of a little brook which runs through Deepden, near our house;—then, when it comes to my turn to reply, I have to be wakened; and, having heard nothing of what was read for listening to the visionary brook, I have no answer ready."

"Yet how well you replied this afternoon."

"It was mere chance: the subject on which we had been reading had interested me. This afternoon, instead of dreaming of Deepden,

---

3. **Felix** in the Bible, governor of Judea who released Paul from prison and deferred his trial until a more "convenient season" (Acts 24:25).
4. **assiduity** (as´ ə dyo͞o´ ə tē) *n.* constant care and attention; diligence.

Reading Check
What faults does Helen Burns attribute to herself?

I was wondering how a man who wished to do right could act so unjustly and unwisely as Charles the First sometimes did; and I thought what a pity it was that, with his integrity and conscientiousness, he could see no farther than the prerogatives of the crown. If he had but been able to look to a distance, and see how what they call the spirit of the age was tending! Still, I like Charles— I respect him— I pity him, poor murdered king! Yes, his enemies were the worst: they shed blood they had no right to shed. How dared they kill him!"

Helen was talking to herself now: she had forgotten I could not very well understand her— that I was ignorant, or nearly so, of the subject she discussed. I recalled her to my level.

"And when Miss Temple teaches you, do your thoughts wander then?"

"No, certainly, not often; because Miss Temple has generally something to say which is newer to me than my own reflections: her language is singularly agreeable to me, and the information she communicates is often just what I wished to gain."

▲ **Critical Viewing**
Judging from the excerpt from the novel, what problems do you think might lie in wait for Jane and her future employer Mr. Rochester, pictured here? **[Speculate]**

"Well, then, with Miss Temple you are good?"

"Yes, in a passive way: I make no effort; I follow as inclination guides me. There is no merit in such goodness."

"A great deal: you are good to those who are good to you. It is all I ever desire to be. If people were always kind and obedient to those who are cruel and unjust, the wicked people would have it all their own way: they would never feel afraid, and so they would never alter, but would grow worse and worse. When we are struck at without a reason, we should strike back again very hard; I am sure we should—so hard as to teach the person who struck us never to do it again."

"You will change your mind, I hope, when you grow older: as yet you are but a little untaught girl."

"But I feel this, Helen: I must dislike those who, whatever I do to please them, persist in disliking me; I must resist those who punish me unjustly. It is as natural as that I should love those who show me affection, or submit to punishment when I feel it is deserved."

". . . Love your enemies; bless them that curse you; do good to them that hate you and despitefully use you."

"Then I should love Mrs. Reed, which I cannot do; I should bless her son John, which is impossible."

In her turn, Helen Burns asked me to explain; and I proceeded forthwith to pour out, in my way, the tale of my sufferings and resentments. Bitter and truculent when excited, I spoke as I felt, without reserve or softening.

Helen heard me patiently to the end: I expected she would then make a remark, but she said nothing.

"Well," I asked impatiently, "is not Mrs. Reed a hard-hearted, bad woman?"

"She has been unkind to you, no doubt; because, you see, she dislikes your cast of character, as Miss Scatcherd does mine: but how minutely you remember all she has done and said to you! What a singularly deep impression her injustice seems to have made on your heart! No ill usage so brands its record on my feelings. Would you not be happier if you tried to forget her severity, together with the passionate emotions it excited? Life appears to me too short to be spent in nursing animosity or registering wrongs. We are, and must be, one and all, burdened with faults in this world: but the time will soon come when, I trust, we shall put them off in putting off our corruptible bodies; when debasement and sin will fall from us with this cumbrous frame of flesh, and only the spark of the spirit will remain,—the impalpable principle of life and thought, pure as when it left the Creator to inspire the creature: whence[5] it came it will return; perhaps again to be communicated to some being higher than man—perhaps to pass through gradations of glory, from the pale human soul to brighten to the seraph![6] Surely it will never,

---

5. **whence** the place from which.
6. **seraph** angel of the highest order.

Literary Analysis
The Novel and Social Criticism What characteristic of the novel is reflected in this reference to events earlier in the story?

✔ **Reading Check**
What reason does Helen Burns give to encourage Jane to forgive Mrs. Reed?

on the contrary, be suffered to degenerate from man to fiend? No; I cannot believe that: I hold another creed; which no one ever taught me, and which I seldom mention; but in which I delight, and to which I cling: for it extends hope to all: it makes Eternity a rest—a mighty home, not a terror and abyss. Besides, with this creed, I can so clearly distinguish between the criminal and his crime; I can so sincerely forgive the first while I abhor the last: with this creed revenge never worries my heart, degradation never too deeply disgusts me, injustice never crushes me too low: I live in calm, looking to the end."

Helen's head, always drooping, sank a little lower as she finished this sentence. I saw by her look she wished no longer to talk to me, but rather to converse with her own thoughts. She was not allowed much time for meditation: a monitor, a great rough girl, presently came up, exclaiming in a strong Cumberland accent—

"Helen Burns, if you don't go and put your drawer in order, and fold up your work this minute, I'll tell Miss Scatcherd to come and look at it!"

Helen sighed as her reverie fled, and getting up, obeyed the monitor without reply as without delay.

Review and Assess

Thinking About the Selection

1. **Respond:** Do you relate more to Helen's or to Jane's attitude toward life? Explain.

2. **(a) Recall:** For what offense does Miss Scatcherd punish Helen Burns? **(b) Infer:** When punished, why does Helen make every effort to hold back tears?

3. **(a) Recall:** Which teacher does Helen particularly like? **(b) Analyze:** Why does Helen find that there is "no merit" in being good in this teacher's class?

4. **(a) Summarize:** Describe Jane's personality in a few sentences. **(b) Interpret:** Why might she wish "the wind to howl more wildly, the gloom to deepen to darkness"? **(c) Analyze:** What is Helen's criticism of Jane's reaction to Mrs. Reed?

5. **(a) Compare and Contrast:** Compare Jane's and Helen's reactions to mistreatment. **(b) Make a Judgment:** Do you think each has something to teach the other? Explain.

6. **(a) Draw Conclusions:** Helen and Jane might be seen as two sides of the author's personality. Explain. **(b) Evaluate:** Why might a novelist need both "sides" to write successfully?

7. **Apply:** What features of modern schools could improve life at Lowood? Explain your choices.

Review and Assess

Literary Analysis

The Novel and Social Criticism

1. (a) In the selection from the **novel** *Hard Times*, which details make the setting vivid? (b) How do they contribute to a **criticism of society**?

2. Summarize the viewpoint that Dickens criticizes.

3. (a) What does Jane and Helen's discussion in *Jane Eyre* reveal about the character of each? (b) What does it reveal about the school?

4. (a) If Helen and Jane were writers, which would write social criticism? Which one might not? Explain. (b) What does your answer suggest about Brontë's pupose in including both characters?

Comparing Literary Works

5. (a) Identify three examples in which Dickens uses comic exaggeration to criticize Gradgrind and his fellows. (b) Explain how Brontë develops interest in Helen Burns, showing her first from a distance, then in conversation.

6. Use a chart like the one shown to compare these techniques.

Passage	Intended Effect on Reader	Intended Message	Enjoyment Value

(a) Which selection held your interest better? (b) Did either seem motivated solely by the writer's desire to convey a message?

Reading Strategy

Recognizing the Writer's Purpose

7. Choose an example of each of the following elements that help clarify the writer's purpose, explaining your choice: (a) the name of a character in *Hard Times*, (b) a character's statement or dialogue in *Jane Eyre*, (c) a description of a place in either work.

Extend Understanding

8. **World Events Connection:** Dickens hints at some elements of education that Gradgrind neglects. Do modern schools address these elements? Explain.

Integrate Language Skills

Vocabulary Development Lesson

Word Analysis: Greek Prefix *mono-*

The Greek prefix *mono-* means "single" or "alone." It is used to form some words in common use as well as many scientific and technical words. Explain how the prefix *mono-* contributes to the meaning of each of the following words, using a dictionary if needed.

1. monologue
2. monorail
3. monopoly
4. monofilament
5. monotreme

Spelling Strategy

In words like *indignant*, the *g* and *n* each stand for a separate sound. Sometimes, however, *gn* stands for only the *n* sound, as in *sign*. In these cases, it usually follows the letters *ai*, *ei*, or *i*. In your notebook, correctly complete the spelling of these *gn* words.

1. des__gner
2. for__gn
3. camp__gn
4. mal__gned

Concept Development: Antonyms

Write the letter of the word that is opposite in meaning to the first word.

1. monotonous: (a) lengthy, (b) loud, (c) varied
2. obstinate: (a) still, (b) cooperative, (c) taciturn
3. adversary: (a) friend, (b) turncoat, (c) enemy
4. indignant: (a) worthy, (b) pleased, (c) angry
5. approbation: (a) freedom, (b) disapproval, (c) sin
6. obscure: (a) prominent, (b) sad, (c) realistic
7. comprised: (a) noted, (b) agreed, (c) excluded
8. sundry: (a) mixed, (b) tedious, (c) homogeneous

Grammar and Style Lesson

Punctuation of Dialogue

To **punctuate dialogue** correctly, enclose in quotation marks the exact words said by the characters. Commas and periods always fall within the final quotation mark. Question marks and exclamation marks also fall within the quotation marks when they are part of the quotation. Otherwise, question marks and exclamation marks go outside the quotation marks.

Examples: "Sissy Jupe, give me the Facts!"

Did the gentleman say, "I will try you again"?

"Hardened girl!" exclaimed Miss Scatcherd, "nothing can correct you. . . ."

Practice Copy these passages, correctly punctuating the dialogue.

1. Sissy is not a name, said Mr. Gradgrind.
2. Girl number twenty unable to define a horse! said Mr. Gradgrind, . . .
3. Bitzer, said Thomas Gradgrind. Your definition of a horse.
4. Yes, she said, I have just finished it.
5. Well, I asked impatiently, is not Mrs. Reed a hard-hearted, bad woman?

Writing Application Write a brief dialogue between Jane and Helen. Be sure to punctuate each speaker's words correctly.

W⟋*G* *Prentice Hall Writing and Grammar Connection: Chapter 27, Section 4*

Writing Lesson

Annotated Bibliography on Victorian Education

The excerpts from Dickens and Brontë present vivid pictures of education in the Victorian Age. Compile an annotated bibliography—a bibliography with descriptions and evaluations of sources—on the topic. Include both primary sources, or sources from the times, and secondary sources.

Prewriting   Use both print materials and the Internet to develop your bibliography. Find primary sources—letters and journals by students and teachers—and secondary ones, or materials written by historians. Consult style guides, and select a style for your bibliography, such as the MLA style.

Drafting   Prepare your bibliography, writing annotations that show why each source is unique and valuable. Follow your chosen style.

Model: Drafting Annotations for Primary Sources

McPhail, Ellie. Letter to her mother. 1888. Collection of Teacher's School, Anytown University, Anytown. Ellie's letter, describing an incident in which the class helped one girl get away with cheating, shows how in some cases students would go against their own basic values to protect one another.

> The writer's annotation shows the unique insight provided by this source.

Revising   Review your bibliography, using an appropriate style guide, to make sure you have correctly presented the information about each source.

Prentice Hall Writing and Grammar Connection: Chapter 31, Section 2

Extension Activities

Listening and Speaking In a **debate,** use the ideas of these selections to inspire a discussion of the basic values of today's educational system. Prepare arguments of the following kinds:

- Inductive—arguments that lead from representative examples to generalizations
- Deductive—arguments that apply principles to specific cases

Help teammates rehearse their arguments. Then, hold your debate before the class. **[Group Activity]**

Research and Technology Devise three research questions and use them to research and write a **biography of Charles Dickens's childhood.** Note parallels between events in his early life with events in his fiction. In your word-processed report, include a graphic timeline outlining important events in Dickens's early life.

 **Take It to the Net**   www.phschool.com

Go online for an additional research activity using the Internet.

CONNECTIONS
Literature Around the World
The Novel

Charles Dickens's *Hard Times* and Charlotte Brontë's *Jane Eyre* were triumphs in their own day. Their success was an example of the huge popularity of the novel during the nineteenth century. A novel is a long work of fiction with a relatively complicated plot, many major and minor characters, a significant theme, and various settings. Nineteenth-century novelists explored the full scope of human experience, from love to war, from riches to poverty. This approach, along with the growing literacy rate, guaranteed the popularity of the form. The novel was an international success, thriving in France, the United States, and Russia as well as England.

The Russian Novel

The Russian novelist Leo Tolstoy was considered the greatest of the nineteenth-century Russian writers. In 1869, he published *War and Peace*, his masterful historical novel about Napoleon's 1812 invasion of Russia. In this novel, Tolstoy weaves together numerous plots and settings with more than 500 characters. The novel was immediately recognized as a masterpiece for its graphic depiction of war, its insights into Russian life, and its exploration of the meaning of existence.

In the following excerpt from *War and Peace*, Tolstoy defends Mikhail Kutuzov, a military general, when his tactics are criticized. Tolstoy presents the general as noble and true to himself and his people—a contrast with the glory-hungry Napolean, leader of Russia's enemy, France. As you read, note the ways in which Tolstoy brings Kutuzov to life as a character.

The Return of the Troops from the Crimera, Boulevard des Italiens, in front of the Hanover Pavillon, December, 1855. *c.* 19th century / Emmanuel Masses / Musée Carnavalet, Paris, France, Roger-Viollet Paris

from WAR AND *Peace*

LEO TOLSTOY

CHAPTER V

In 1812 and 1813[1] Kutuzov[2] was openly accused of blunders. The Tsar[3] was dissatisfied with him. And in a recent history inspired by promptings from the highest quarters, Kutuzov is spoken of as a designing, intriguing schemer, who was panic-stricken at the name of Napoleon, and guilty through his blunders at Krasnoe and Berezina of robbing the Russian army of the glory of complete victory over the French. Such is the lot of men not recognized by Russian intelligence as "great men," *grands hommes;* such is the destiny of those rare and always solitary men who divining the will of Providence submit their personal will to it. The hatred and contempt of the crowd is the punishment of such men for their comprehension of higher laws.

Strange and terrible to say, Napoleon, the most insignificant tool of history, who never even in exile displayed one trait of human dignity, is the subject of the admiration and enthusiasm of the Russian historians; in their eyes he is a *grand homme.*

Kutuzov, the man who from the beginning to the end of his command in 1812, from Borodino to Vilna, was

---

1. **In 1812 and 1813** In June 1812, Napoleon and his troops invaded Russia. Their retreat from Russia began in October 1812.
2. **Kutuzov** Mikhail Illarionovich Kutuzov (1745–1813); commander in chief of all Russian forces during Napoleon's invasion.
3. **Tsar** Czar Alexander I, emperor of Russia, 1801–1825.

Reading Check

How do the majority of Russians view Kutuzov?

never in one word or deed false to himself, presents an example exceptional in history of self-sacrifice and recognition in the present of the relative value of events in the future. Kutuzov is conceived of by historians as a nondescript, pitiful sort of creature, and whenever they speak of him in the year 1812, they seem a little ashamed of him.

And yet it is difficult to conceive of an historical character whose energy could be more invariably directed to the same unchanging aim. It is difficult to imagine an aim more noble and more in harmony with the will of a whole people. Still more difficult would it be to find an example in history where the aim of any historical personage has been so completely attained as the aim towards which all Kutuzov's efforts were devoted in 1812.

Kutuzov never talked of "forty centuries looking down from the Pyramids," of the sacrifices he was making for the fatherland, of what he meant to do or had done.[4] He did not as a rule talk about himself, played no sort of part, always seemed the plainest and most ordinary man, and said the plainest and most ordinary things. He wrote letters to his daughters and to Madame de Staël,[5] read novels, liked the company of pretty women, made jokes with the generals, the officers, and the soldiers, and never contradicted the people, who tried to prove anything to him. When Count Rastoptchin galloped up to him at Yautsky bridge, and reproached him personally with being responsible for the loss of Moscow, and said: "Didn't you promise not to abandon Moscow without a battle?" Kutuzov answered: "And I am not abandoning Moscow without a battle," although Moscow was in fact already abandoned. When Araktcheev came to him from the Tsar to say that Yermolov was to be appointed to the command of the artillery, Kutuzov said: "Yes, I was just saying so myself," though he had said just the opposite a moment before. What had he, the one man who grasped at the time all the vast issues of events, to do in the midst of that dull-witted crowd? What did he care whether Count

Thematic Connection
What social criticism is Tolstoy offering here?

▼ **Critical Viewing**
Using the map, determine why Napoleon's armies might have had trouble getting supplies when they invaded Russia. **[Hypothesize]**

Napoleon's Invasion of Russia, 1812

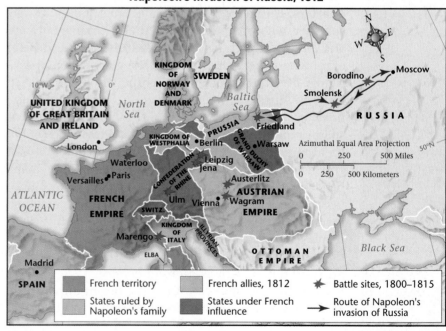

---

4. **"forty centuries . . ." . . . had done** references to Napoleon's reflections on his own place in history.
5. **Madame de Staël** Anne-Louise-Germaine de Staël (1766–1817) French-Swiss woman of letters; regarded as personal enemy of Napoleon and banished from Paris.

Rastoptchin put down the disasters of the capital to him or to himself? Still less could he be concerned by the question which man was appointed to the command of the artillery.

This old man, who through experience of life had reached the conviction that the thoughts and words that serve as its expression are never the motive force of men, frequently uttered words, which were quite meaningless—the first words that occurred to his mind.

But heedless as he was of his words, he never once throughout all his career uttered a single word which was inconsistent with the sole aim for the attainment of which he was working all through the war. With obvious unwillingness, with bitter conviction that he would not be understood, he more than once, under the most difficult circumstances, gave expression to his real thought. His first differed from all about him after the battle of Borodino,[6] which he alone persisted in calling a victory, and this view he continued to assert verbally and in reports and to his dying day. He alone said that *the loss of Moscow is not the loss of Russia.* In answer to the overtures for peace, his reply to Lauriston was: *There can be no peace, for such is the people's will.* He alone during the retreat of the French said that *all our maneuvers are unnecessary; that everything is being done of itself better than we could desire; that we must give the enemy a "golden bridge"; that the battles of Tarutino, of Vyazma, and of Krasnoe, were none of them necessary; that we must keep some men to reach the frontier with; that he wouldn't give one Russian for ten Frenchmen.* And he, this intriguing courtier, as we are told, who lied to Araktcheev to propitiate[7] the Tsar, he alone dared to face the Tsar's displeasure by telling him at Vilna that *to carry the war beyond the frontier would be mischievous and useless.*

But words alone would be no proof that he grasped the significance of events at the time. His actions—all without the slightest deviation—

Portrait of Kutuzov, Prince of Smolensk, George Dawe, Hermitage, St. Petersburg, Russia

▲ **Critical Viewing**
Compare and contrast this rendering of Kutuzov with the description of him in the story.
[Compare and Contrast]

---

6. **battle of Borodino** Kutuzov was pressured into fighting this battle against his better judgment. Although the outcome was inconclusive, Kutuzov lost half his troops.
7. **propitiate** (prō pish′ ē āt′) v. to cause to become favorably inclined.

✔ **Reading Check**
According to Tolstoy, how did Kutuzov treat words?

were directed toward the one threefold aim: first, to concentrate all his forces to strike a blow at the French; secondly, to defeat them; and thirdly, to drive them out of Russia, alleviating as far as was possible the sufferings of the people and the soldiers in doing so.

He, the lingerer Kutuzov, whose motto was always "Time and Patience," the sworn opponent of precipitate action, he fought the battle of Borodino, and made all his preparations for it with unwonted solemnity. Before the battle of Austerlitz he foretold that it would be lost, but at Borodino, in spite of the conviction of the generals that the battle was a defeat, in spite of the fact, unprecedented in history, of his army being forced to retreat after the victory, he alone declared in opposition to all that it was a victory, and persisted in that opinion to his dying day. He was alone during the whole latter part of the campaign in insisting that there was no need of fighting now, that it was a mistake to cross the Russian frontier and to begin a new war. It is easy enough now that all the events with their consequences lie before us to grasp their significance, if only we refrain from attributing to the multitude the aims that only existed in the brains of some dozen or so of men.

But how came that old man, alone in opposition to the opinion of all, to gauge so truly the importance of events from the national standard, so that he never once was false to the best interests of his country?

The source of this extraordinary intuition into the significance of contemporary events lay in the purity and fervor of patriotic feeling in his heart.

It was their recognition of this feeling in him that led the people in such a strange manner to pick him out, an old man out of favor, as the chosen leader of the national war, against the will of the Tsar. And this feeling alone it was to which he owed his exalted position, and there he exerted all his powers as commander-in-chief not to kill and maim men, but to save them and have mercy on them.

This simple, modest, and therefore truly great figure, could not be cast into the false mold of the European hero, the supposed leader of men, that history has invented.

To the flunky no man can be great, because the flunky has his own flunky conception of greatness.

Leo Tolstoy

(1828–1910)

Leo Tolstoy was a nineteenth-century Russian writer whose shattering spiritual crisis late in life led him to radical religious and political beliefs. After briefly attending law school, Tolstoy joined the army in 1851. While serving as an artillery officer, Tolstoy spent most of his free time writing, and by 1852 Tolstoy had published his first novel, *A History of My Childhood*. His novels *War and Peace* (1869) and *Anna Karenina* (1876), a portrait of the lives of the Russian upper classes, are among the most popular of his works. After his crisis of faith, he devoted himself to moral tales and pamphlets. His last novel, finished when he was 71, is entitled *Resurrection*.

Connecting Literature Around the World

1. Compare and contrast the methods by which Dickens, Brontë, and Tolstoy develop their main characters. Which author's characterization do you think is the most effective? Explain.

2. Which of the three novels represented in this section would you prefer to read? Explain.

The Empire and Its Discontents

Miniature photographic portraits commemorating the 1897
Jubilee Victoria: (adult and child) Alexandra and George V

Prepare to Read

Dover Beach ◆ Recessional ◆
The Widow at Windsor

Matthew Arnold
(1822–1888)

Much of Matthew Arnold's poetry concerns a theme as relevant today as it was in the nineteenth century: the isolation of individuals from one another and from society. In fact, in the 1960s, the American novelist Norman Mailer used a modified quotation from Arnold's poem "Dover Beach" for the title of his book about a Vietnam War protest, *Armies of the Night*.

A Social Conscience While attending Oxford University, Arnold developed the social conscience that was to guide his career as a public servant, poet, and literary critic. In 1851, he became Inspector of Schools, and in performing this job he did much to improve education throughout Great Britain. All the while, he remained a poet at heart, although his first two collections, published in 1849 and 1852, met with little success.

Literary Achievement Arnold's literary fortunes changed in 1853 when he published *Poems*, with its long preface that established him as a major critic. *New Poems*, published in 1867, contained Arnold's celebrated "Dover Beach."

A Return to Culture After completing this collection, Arnold believed that he had said everything he could in poetry. From that point on he wrote prose, such as the social criticism of the essays in *Culture and Anarchy* (1869). In this book, he attacks Victorian complacency and materialism, arguing that culture should open our minds to what is true and valuable. Arnold's idea of culture still influences critics today.

Rudyard Kipling
(1865–1936)

Rudyard Kipling's works are known for their celebration of the British Empire, yet they also warn of the costs of world dominion. While praising the benefits of imperialism, he emphasizes the responsibility of the British to bring their "civilized" ways to other parts of the world.

Early Success Kipling was born to British parents in India, one of Britain's largest colonies. At the age of six, he was placed by his parents in a foster home in England, and later, at a chaotic boarding school. One critic speculates that the theme of self-preservation in Kipling's work was inspired by experiences at the boarding school that tested his courage. Kipling would later immortalize his school days in a collection of stories called *Stalky and Co.* (1899). In 1882, Kipling returned to India to work as a journalist. During the next seven years, he published a number of witty poems and stories, and by the time he returned to England in 1889, he was a celebrity.

Kipling's Achievements Kipling is known as a Victorian author because he produced his best work before the death of Queen Victoria in 1901. In its great variety, that work includes poetry, short stories, and novels. Some of his books have become children's classics, such as *The Jungle Books* (1894, 1895), *Captains Courageous* (1897), and *Kim* (1901).

For years, Kipling was the most popular English poet, and in 1907 he became the first English writer to receive the Nobel Prize for Literature.

Preview

Connecting to the Literature

Some Victorians proclaimed that the British Empire and the Victorian Era were perfect. Matthew Arnold's "Dover Beach" and Rudyard Kipling's "Recessional" both show the truth behind this boasting assertion.

Literary Analysis

Mood as a Key to Theme

Poems contain emotional thoughts and thoughtful emotions. With thought and emotion so closely linked, the **mood,** or feeling, that a poem calls up is bound to be related to its central idea, or **theme.** Read poetry with your feelings—responding to emotionally charged words and images—and you will find your way to its ideas.

In "Dover Beach," for example, the crash of waves brings "The eternal note of sadness in." This mood of sadness leads you to the theme of the poem, which concerns a world with "neither joy, nor love, nor light."

Comparing Literary Works

The moods in these poems relate to a characteristic dilemma of the Victorian Period. The era was marked by increasing scientific progress, material prosperity, and British domination of the globe, yet each of these successes brought with it fresh anxieties:

- Scientific progress brought a greater questioning of religious faith.
- Material prosperity for some brought greater poverty for others.
- Expansion of the Empire brought heavy responsibilities.

Compare the ways in which these poems present and address such issues.

Reading Strategy

Drawing Conclusions

By **drawing conclusions** about what you read—making generalizations based on evidence—you can link elements that seem unrelated. In "The Widow at Windsor," for example, it may be unclear at first why a "widow" has a "gold crown" and "ships on the foam." However, the later reference to "Missis Victorier's sons" leads to the conclusion that the widow is Queen Victoria. Use a graphic organizer like this one to draw further conclusions about the poems.

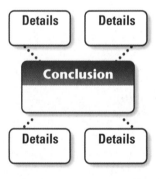

Vocabulary Development

tranquil (traŋ′ kwil) *adj.* calm; serene; peaceful (p. 884)

cadence (kād′ əns) *n.* measured movement (p. 884)

turbid (tʉr′ bid) *adj.* muddy or cloudy; stirred up and confused (p. 885)

dominion (də min′ yən) *n.* rule; control (p. 887)

contrite (kən trīt′) *adj.* willing to repent or atone (p. 887)

Dover Beach

Matthew Arnold

The sea is calm tonight.
The tide is full, the moon lies fair
Upon the straits;[1] on the French coast the light
Gleams and is gone; the cliffs of England stand,
5   Glimmering and vast, out in the tranquil bay.
Come to the window, sweet is the night air!

Only, from the long line of spray
Where the sea meets the moon-blanched land,
Listen! you hear the grating roar
10   Of pebbles which the waves draw back, and fling,
At their return, up the high strand,[2]
Begin, and cease, and then again begin,
With tremulous cadence slow, and bring
The eternal note of sadness in.

---

1. **straits** Straits of Dover, between England and France.
2. **strand** shore.

tranquil (traŋ´ kwəl) *adj.*
calm; serene; peaceful

cadence (kād´ əns) *n.*
measured movement

▼ **Critical Viewing**
Does this photograph
capture the "eternal note
of sadness" Arnold
describes? Explain.
[Support]

15 Sophocles[3] long ago
    Heard it on the Aegaean,[4] and it brought
    Into his mind the <u>turbid</u> ebb and flow
    Of human misery; we
    Find also in the sound a thought,
20 Hearing it by this distant northern sea.

    The Sea of Faith
    Was once, too, at the full, and round earth's shore
    Lay like the folds of a bright girdle furled.
    But now I only hear
25 Its melancholy, long, withdrawing roar,
    Retreating, to the breath
    Of the night wind, down the vast edges drear
    And naked shingles[5] of the world.

    Ah, love, let us be true
30 To one another! for the world, which seems
    To lie before us like a land of dreams,
    So various, so beautiful, so new,
    Hath really neither joy, nor love, nor light,
    Nor certitude, nor peace, nor help for pain;
35 And we are here as on a darkling[6] plain
    Swept with confused alarms of struggle and flight,
    Where ignorant armies clash by night.

---

3. **Sophocles** (säf´ ə klēz´) Greek tragic dramatist (496?–406 B.C.).
4. **Aegean** (ē jē´ ən) arm of the Mediterranean Sea between Greece and Turkey.
5. **shingles** *n.* beaches covered with large, coarse, waterworn gravel.
6. **darkling** *adj.* in the dark.

turbid (tʉr´ bid) *adj.* muddy or cloudy; stirred up and confused

Literary Analysis
Mood as a Key to Theme
How do the feelings that the final stanza evokes relate to its message in lines 29–30?

Review and Assess

Thinking About the Selection

1. **(a) Recall:** Where are the speaker and his "love," and what do they hear and see? **(b) Interpret:** Why do you think the scene suggests to the speaker "the eternal note of sadness"?

2. **(a) Recall:** What does the speaker say has happened to "The Sea of Faith"? **(b) Interpret:** What does he mean by this remark?

3. **(a) Recall:** In the last stanza, what does the speaker say that he and his "love" should do? **(b) Draw Conclusions:** What problem does the speaker believe that they can alleviate if they follow his urging?

4. **Take a Position:** Is Arnold's message in the final stanza a satisfactory response to "human misery" today? Why or why not?

RECESSIONAL[1]

Rudyard Kipling

Queen Victoria's Diamond Jubilee procession in London in 1897

Background

In 1897, a national celebration called the "Diamond Jubilee" was held in honor of the sixtieth anniversary of Queen Victoria's reign. The occasion prompted a great deal of boasting about the strength and greatness of the empire. Kipling responded to the celebration by writing this poem, reminding the people of England that the British empire might not last forever.

God of our fathers, known of old—
    Lord of our far-flung battle-line—
Beneath whose awful Hand we hold
    <u>Dominion</u> over palm and pine—
5 Lord God of Hosts, be with us yet
Lest we forget—lest we forget!

The tumult and the shouting dies—
    The Captains and the Kings depart—
Still stands Thine ancient Sacrifice,
10   An humble and a <u>contrite</u> heart.[2]
Lord God of Hosts, be with us yet,
Lest we forget—lest we forget!

Far-called, our navies melt away—
    On dune and headland sinks the fire[3]—
15 Lo, all our pomp of yesterday
    Is one with Nineveh[4] and Tyre![5]
Judge of the Nations, spare us yet,
Lest we forget—lest we forget!

dominion (də min´ yən) *n.* rule; control

contrite (kən trīt´) *adj.* willing to repent or atone

---

1. **Recessional** *n.* hymn sung at the end of a religious service.
2. **An . . . heart** allusion to the Bible (Psalms 51:17) "The sacrifices of God are a broken spirit: a broken and contrite heart, O God, thou wilt not despise."
3. **On . . . fire** Bonfires were lit on high ground all over Britain as part of the opening ceremonies of the Jubilee celebration.
4. **Nineveh** (nin´ ə və) ancient capital of the Assyrian Empire, the ruins of which were discovered buried in desert sands in the 1850s.
5. **Tyre** (tīr) once a great port and the center of ancient Phoenician culture, now a small town in Lebanon.

◀ **Critical Viewing** Does the Diamond Jubilee, shown here, seem to reflect the pride against which Kipling warns? Explain. **[Connect]**

If, drunk with sight of power, we loose
20   Wild tongues that have not Thee in awe—
Such boasting as the Gentiles use
        Or lesser breeds without the Law—6
Lord God of Hosts, be with us yet,
Lest we forget—lest we forget!

25   For heathen heart that puts her trust
        In reeking tube7 and iron shard8—
All valiant dust that builds on dust,
        And guarding calls not Thee to guard—
For frantic boast and foolish word,
30   Thy mercy on Thy People, Lord!

---

6. **Such boasting . . . Law** allusion to the Bible (Romans 2:14) "For when the Gentiles, which have not the law, do by nature the things contained in the law, these, having not the law, are a law unto themselves."
7. **tube** barrel of a gun.
8. **shard** fragment of a bombshell.

Reading Strategy
Drawing Conclusions
What do the final two stanzas suggest about the behavior that may have prompted Kipling to write this poem?

Review and Assess

Thinking About the Selection

1. **Respond:** Do you think "Recessional" is relevant to contemporary society? Explain.

2. **(a) Recall:** To whom is this poem addressed? **(b) Interpret:** For whom is the message of the poem really meant?

3. **(a) Recall:** What is the literal meaning of the title of the poem? **(b) Interpret:** What double meaning is contained in the title? **(c) Analyze:** How is this ambiguity appropriate to the mood of the poem?

4. **(a) Recall:** Paraphrase the first stanza of the poem. **(b) Analyze:** According to this stanza, what is the relationship between God and empire? Explain.

5. **(a) Recall:** In lines 15 and 16, what happens to "our pomp of yesterday"? **(b) Infer:** What qualities and actions does the speaker condemn? **(c) Draw Conclusions:** What is the theme of the poem?

6. **Apply:** Britain is no longer an empire. Does this fact bear out Kipling's warning? Explain.

7. **Make a Judgment:** Is Kipling condemning the very existence of the British empire, or is he advocating a more humble approach to the responsibilities of empire? Explain.

8. **Connect:** Would this poem, or one like it, be suitable to present at a presidential inauguration? Why or why not?

The Widow at Windsor

Rudyard Kipling

'Ave you 'eard o' the Widow at Windsor
    With a hairy gold crown on 'er 'ead?
She 'as ships on the foam—she 'as millions at 'ome,
    An' she pays us poor beggars in red.
5   (Ow, poor beggars in red!)
There's 'er nick on the cavalry 'orses,
    There's 'er mark on the medical stores—
An' 'er troops you'll find with a fair wind be'ind
    That takes us to various wars.
10   (Poor beggars!—barbarious wars!)
    Then 'ere's to the Widow at Windsor,
          An' 'ere's to the stores an' the guns,
    The men an' the 'orses what makes up the forces
          O' Missis Victorier's sons.
15   (Poor beggars! Victorier's sons!)

Walk wide o' the Widow at Windsor,
    For 'alf o' Creation she owns:
We'ave bought 'er the same with the sword an' the flame,
    An' we've salted it down with our bones.
20   (Poor beggars!—it's blue with our bones!)
Hands off o' the sons o' the widow,
    Hands off o' the goods in 'er shop.
For the kings must come down an' the emperors frown

▲ Critical Viewing

What elements of this portrait of Queen Victoria do you think the speaker of the poem might point out? Explain. **[Connect]**

✔Reading Check

Where does the speaker say the Widow leaves her mark?

When the Widow at Windsor says "Stop!"
25   (Poor beggars!—we're sent to say "Stop!")
      Then 'ere's to the Lodge o' the Widow,
           From the Pole to the Tropics it runs—
      To the Lodge that we tile with the rank an' the file,
           An' open in form with the guns.
30   (Poor beggars!—it's always they guns!)

We 'ave 'eard o' the Widow at Windsor,
      It's safest to leave 'er alone:
For 'er sentries we stand by the sea an' the land
      Wherever the bugles are blown.
35   (Poor beggars!—an' don't we get blown!)
      Take 'old o' the Wings o' the Mornin',
      An' flop round the earth till you're dead;
But you won't get away from the tune that they play
      To the bloomin' old rag over'ead.
40   (Poor beggars!—it's 'ot over'ead!)
      Then 'ere's to the sons o' the Widow,
           Wherever, 'owever they roam.
     'Ere's all they desire, an' if they require
           A speedy return to their 'ome.
45   (Poor beggars!—they'll never see 'ome!)

Literary Analysis
Mood as a Key to Theme
What do the remarks in parentheses suggest about the speaker's attitude toward the empire?

Review and Assess

Thinking About the Selection

1. **Respond:** What images, ideas, or lines in this poem do you find most striking? Explain.

2. **(a) Recall:** Who is the Widow at Windsor?
   (b) Infer: What is surprising about the speaker's decision to describe this woman in this way?

3. **(a) Recall:** Who is the speaker of this poem?
   (b) Analyze: Would you describe the speaker's tone as disloyal or disrespectful? Explain.

4. **(a) Recall:** What various remarks of the speaker's appear in parentheses? **(b) Make a Judgment:** How would the poem be different if the remarks in parentheses were deleted? Why?

5. **(a) Recall:** According to the last line of the poem, what fate awaits the soldiers? **(b) Draw Conclusions:** Why does Kipling describe the Empire from the perspective of a common soldier?

6. **Hypothesize:** In what circumstances, if any, would poets or songwriters of today choose to have a speaker use dialect, as Kipling does? Explain.

Review and Assess

Literary Analysis

Mood as a Key to Theme

1. Fill in a chart like the one shown here by describing the **mood** evoked by images from "Dover Beach." Then, using what you have written as a clue, state the **theme** of the poem.

Image	Where It Appears	Mood It Evokes

2. Explain how the mood of sternness and solemnity in "Recessional" relates to the theme of the poem.

3. Use the mood in "The Widow at Windsor" to explain which of these sentences best describes the theme of the poem: (a) Maintaining the Empire seems ridiculous to the soldiers who must do it. (b) Maintaining the Empire is a deadly serious game, played at the expense of the common soldier.

Comparing Literary Works

4. Compare and contrast the ways in which these poems treat the anxieties brought on by advances in science, prosperity, and empire.

5. How do both "Recessional" and "The Widow at Windsor" reflect different perspectives on the responsibilities and dangers that come with empire?

Reading Strategy

Drawing Conclusions

6. Use Arnold's descriptions of the night throughout "Dover Beach" and his use of the word "night" in line 37 to **draw conclusions** about whether he is pessimistic or optimistic.

7. Basing your answer on the concluding two lines of each stanza in "Recessional," what conclusion can you draw about Kipling's message?

8. Draw a conclusion about Kipling's reason for including the parenthetical remarks in "The Widow at Windsor."

Extend Understanding

9. **Social Studies Connection:** Could any of these poems be applied to the social conditions of today? Explain.

Quick Review

The **mood** of a work of literature is the feeling it generates.

The **theme** is the central message or insight into life it presents or an important question it explores.

To **draw conclusions** about what you read, make generalizations based on evidence in the text.

 Take It to the Net
www.phschool.com
Take the interactive self-test online to check your understanding of these selections.

Integrate Language Skills

Vocabulary Development Lesson

Word Analysis: Latin Root -domi-

Kipling uses *dominion*, or "rule," to refer to the power of the British Empire. This word contains the Latin root *-domi-*, which means "lord" or "master." Use your knowledge of this root to define these *-domi-* words.

1. domain   **2.** dominant   **3.** domineer

Spelling Strategy

Words ending in a long vowel sound followed by a single consonant sound often have a silent *e*, as in *contrite*. However, there are other ways to spell such words. Choose the correctly spelled word from each pair.

1. combein, combine   **2.** delight, delite

Concept Development: Antonyms

Review the words in the vocabulary list on page 883, and study the vocabulary words in the context of the selections. Then, in your notebook, match each word in the first column with its antonym, or the word opposite in meaning, in the second column.

1. tranquil   **a.** clear

2. cadence   **b.** unrepentant

3. dominion   **c.** agitated

4. turbid   **d.** powerlessness

5. contrite   **e.** turmoil

Grammar and Style Lesson

Present Tense

The **present tense** of a verb often expresses an action or a state of being that is occurring now. It can also express a general idea that is true at all times. Both Arnold and Kipling use the present tense effectively in expressing a generalization.

> **Occurring Now:** . . . the light / Gleams and is gone . . .
>
> **Generalization:** . . . the world . . . Hath really neither joy, nor love, . . .

Through the use of present tense, poets can make stirring or alarming statements about life in general. They can also skillfully weave together images of a present moment with general truths or symbolic images, as Arnold does in "Dover Beach."

Practice On your paper, identify the present tense verb in each of these passages from the poems. Tell whether each expresses a truth or an action or state of being occurring now.

1. The sea is calm tonight.

2. . . . you hear the grating roar / Of pebbles . . .

3. . . . we are here as on a darkling plain . . .

4. The tumult and the shouting dies— . . .

5. It's safest to leave 'er alone: . . .

Writing Application Change each statement into a generalization by using a present tense verb and, if necessary, adding or deleting words.

1. The winning of empires required great sacrifices.

2. For me, the ebb and flow of the tide represented the cycles of life.

WG Prentice Hall Writing and Grammar Connection: Chapter 21, Section 1

Writing Lesson

Response to Criticism

Critic Walter E. Houghton writes that the Victorian Age was characterized by "widespread doubt about the nature of man, society, and the universe." Using evidence from the poems by Arnold and Kipling, support or refute this assertion.

Prewriting Review the poems, using a chart like this one to gather evidence about Victorian doubt or Victorian self-confidence.

Model: Gathering Details

Poem:			
	Images	Mood(s)	Theme(s)
Doubt			
Self-confidence			

Drafting Referring to your chart, formulate a thesis statement agreeing or disagreeing with Houghton. Then, support your thesis with the evidence you have gathered from these poems. Consider organizing your response by devoting a paragraph to each selection.

Revising Be sure that, as support, you have referred to images, moods, and themes. To make your points more effectively, quote specific phrases and lines.

 Prentice Hall Writing and Grammar Connection: Chapter 14, Section 2

Extension Activities

Listening and Speaking With partners, prepare an **oral interpretation** of "Recessional" for the class.

- Pause only when the punctuation dictates.
- Use a tone of voice that evokes the proper mood.
- Consider using music, paintings, photographs, and maps to enhance the reading. However, do not overuse media.

Rehearse your presentation until you are comfortable. Pay special attention to the handling of any media. Then present your interpretation to the class. [**Group Activity**]

Research and Technology View a film based on Kipling's works, such as *Captains Courageous* (1937) or *Kim* (1950). Read the work as well to get a feeling for Kipling's prose style. Then, write a **film review,** evaluating both the effectiveness of the film and its faithfulness to the book. In discussing changes to the story in the film version, remember that visual and verbal storytelling have different demands and requirements.

 **Take It to the Net** www.phschool.com

Go online for an additional research activity using the Internet.

Prepare to Read

Condition of Ireland ◆
Progress in Personal Comfort

Newspapers and Progress

The British Empire in the nineteenth century measured itself with a yardstick called *progress*. People wondered whether things were better in the present than they had been in the past and whether present trends would lead to a more reasonable future. These two articles from Victorian newspapers give two very different answers to these questions—one a cry of outrage and the other an exclamation of pride.

The Newspaper as Evaluator of Progress

The idea of progress was perhaps born with the modern newspaper. To even ask whether progress has been made, the mind must view the world as a collection of measurable facts—the number of people fed, of miles traveled, of dieases cured. By bringing together news from near and far, Victorian newspapers assembled an image of such a world.

The most important British newspaper was *The Times* of London. From the beginning of the nineteenth century, this paper established a reputation for independent, objective reporting. Its circulation increased from 5,000 in 1815 to 40,000 in 1850.

Other newspapers also entered the market. Less expensive than *The Times*, *The Daily Telegraph* (founded in 1855) covered the news and offered thoughtful editorials. *The Illustrated London News*, in which "The Condition of Ireland" appeared, was founded as a weekly in 1842, breaking new ground in its use of graphics. It featured thirty-two woodcuts in its first edition and was also the first British periodical to use photographs.

Public Opinion These papers brought opinions as well as news to a vast public, appealing to it as witness, critic, and even judge of events. It is this era that gave meaning to a concept that is still important today: public opinion. The period also provided the overall standard by which the public could judge events, personalities, and policies: Were social conditions fairer or more efficient than they had been, and would they be even more so in the future?

THE ILLUSTRATED LONDON NEWS

No. 344.—Vol. XIII.]   FOR THE WEEK ENDING SATURDAY, NOVEMBER 18, 1848.   [SIXPENCE

Progress and Reform The author of the essay "Condition of Ireland" uses this standard of progress in criticizing English policies toward the Irish. Even though these policies were based on up-to-date economic ideas, apparent progress in economic theory spelled actual disaster in Ireland. The author judges this situation and the seemingly progressive theories that caused it by applying an ideal of progress based on common sense: the efficient and reasonable use of resources.

Progress and "Conveniences" Other Victorians used the yardstick of progress with more cheering results. Sydney Smith (1771–1845), ordained in the Church of England, was a prolific writer and preacher of his time. He was a co-founder in 1802 of *The Edinburgh Review*, a periodical to which he also contributed. In his articles, he often expressed progressive viewpoints on such serious matters as parliamentary reform, prisons, slavery, and religious freedom.

Smith was also famous for his witty essays and conversation, and his wit is evident in the essay included here. He celebrates the progress made in the area of personal comfort—innovations, large and small, that seem to have come out of nowhere but that now feel indispensable: streetlighting, railways, umbrellas.

Preview

Connecting to the Literature

In your lifetime, you have witnessed remarkable examples of technological progress. Whether you have witnessed social progress is a subject open to debate. These two essays of Victorian Britain gauge social and technological progress, respectively.

Literary Analysis

Journalistic Essay

Journalistic essays are short prose pieces that provide perspectives on current events or trends. Unlike essayists who explore the world to learn about themselves, journalistic essayists construct serious or trivial stories out of the day's jumble of news. They may take one of these approaches:

- They may use the voice of an all-knowing witness or judge, as in "Condition of Ireland,"
- They may offer individual opinions about common concerns, as in "Progress in Personal Comfort."

Look for these different approaches in the two essays.

Comparing Literary Works

Writers use deliberate approaches in keeping with their subject and audience. "Condition of Ireland," an essay on a major public issue, addresses readers as concerned citizens. It takes a serious attitude toward its subject and suggests a dramatic struggle between right and wrong. By contrast, "Progress in Personal Comfort" focuses on convenience and addresses readers as amused observers of their own individual lives and habits. It uses humor and exaggeration to make its points. Compare and contrast the effectiveness of these different approaches in achieving distinct goals.

Reading Strategy

Distinguishing Emotive and Informative Language

Emotive language uses words, phrases, and examples for emotional effect. **Informative language** conveys facts.

As an aid to understanding these authors' biases and opinions, use a chart like this one to distinguish between emotive and informative language.

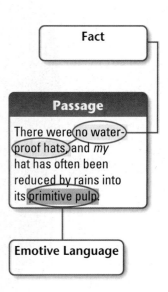

Vocabulary Development

requisites (rek´ wə zits) *n.* things necessary for a given purpose (p. 897)

sanction (saŋk´ shən) *n.* authorized approval or permission (p. 898)

exonerate (eg zän´ ər āt´) *v.* free from a charge of guilt; declare or prove blameless (p. 898)

melancholy (mel´ ən käl´ ē) *adj.* sad; depressing (p. 899)

indolence (in´ də ləns) *n.* idleness; laziness (p. 899)

depredation (dep´ rə dā´ shən) *n.* act or instance of robbing, plundering, or laying waste (p. 900)

Condition of IRELAND:

Illustrations of the New Poor-Law

The Illustrated London News,
December 15, 1849

▶ **Critical Viewing** Compare the portrayal of the Irish in this picture with the portrayal of the Irish in the article. **[Compare and Contrast]**

Woman Begging at Clonakilty, James Mahony, The Illustrated London News, 1847

Background

By the early 1840s, the potato had become a staple of the Irish diet. Nearly one half of the Irish relied almost completely on potatoes for sustenance. Then, disease ruined several potato crops, leading to the Irish potato famine of 1845–1849. Because the Irish people had become so dependent on potatoes, the impact was devastating. British economic policies only worsened the situation.

More than a million Irish people died of starvation and starvation-related diseases by 1851. More than a million and a half emigrated, many to the United States and Canada. However, despite these terrible losses and a continuing population decline, the Irish rallied to preserve their heritage.

This article was one of a series in which *The Illustrated London News* presented, in words and pictures, the plight of the Irish in the midst of the famine. The *News* took a clear stand against British policies and proposed other solutions.

The present condition of the Irish, we have no hesitation in saying, has been mainly brought on by ignorant and vicious legislation. The destruction of the potato for one season, though a great calamity, would not have doomed them, fed as they were by the taxes of the state and the charity of the world, to immediate decay; but a false theory, assuming the name of political economy,[1] with which it has no more to do than with the slaughter of the Hungarians by General Haynau,[2] led the landlords and the legislature to believe that it was a favorable opportunity for changing the occupation of the land and the cultivation of the soil from potatoes to corn.[3] When more food, more cultivation, more employment, were the requisites for maintaining the Irish in existence, the Legislature and the landlords went about introducing a species of cultivation that could only be successful by requiring fewer hands, and turning potato gardens, that nourished the maximum of human beings, into

---

1. **political economy** theory of economics and society.
2. **General Haynau** Julius Jacob; an Austrian general notorious for the brutality with which he suppressed uprisings by the Hungarians and other peoples who revolted against the Austrian empire in the 1840's. When Haynau visited London in 1850, he was attacked by outraged mobs.
3. **corn** (Brit.) grain.

Literary Analysis
Journalistic Essay What is the role of the pronoun "we" in a journalistic essay?

requisites (rek´ wə zits) *n.* things necessary for a given purpose

✔**Reading Check**

According to this article, what caused the "present condition of the Irish"?

pasture grounds for bullocks,[4] that nourished only the minimum. The Poor-Law, said to be for the relief of the people and the means of their salvation, was the instrument of their destruction. In their terrible distress, from that temporary calamity with which they were visited, they were to have no relief unless they gave up their holdings.[5] That law, too, laid down a form for evicting the people, and thus gave the <u>sanction</u> and encouragement of legislation to exterminate them. Calmly and quietly, but very ignorantly— though we cheerfully <u>exonerate</u> the parties from any malevolence; they only committed a great mistake, a terrible blunder, which in legislation is worse than a crime—but calmly and quietly from Westminster itself, which is the center of civilization, did the decree go forth which has made the temporary but terrible visitation[6] of a potato rot the means of exterminating, through the slow process of disease and houseless starvation, nearly the half of the Irish.

The land is still there, in all its natural beauty and fertility. The sparkling Shannon, teeming with fish, still flows by their doors, and might bear to them, as the Hudson and Thames bear to the people of New York and of London, fleets of ships laden with wealth. The low grounds or *Corcasses* of Clare are celebrated for their productiveness. The country abounds in limestone: coal, iron, and lead have been found. It has an area of 827,994 acres, 372,237 of which are uncultivated, or occupied by woods or water. It is estimated that there are 296,000 acres of unoccupied land; and that of these 160,000 are capable of cultivation and improvement. Why are they not cultivated and improved, as the wilds of America are cultivated and improved by the brethren of the Irish? Why are these starving people not allowed and encouraged to plant their potato-gardens on the wastes? Why are they not married to the unoccupied soil, as a humane politician proposes to provide for the starving needlewomen of the metropolis by marrying them to the *Currency Lads* of New South Wales?[7]

The Irish Famine

British economic policies, which are attacked in this essay, worsened the famine:

- The British government had promoted large farms that hired workers and exported cash crops, driving small family farms out of business. The Poor Law actually required that anyone farming a quarter acre or less give up his land before he could receive government aid. Without land, poor families could not raise crops during the famine.

- The Corn (grain) Law (1846), made wheat available at a cheaper price, but did not help Irish peasants, who had no money to buy it.

- The Poor Law provided no relief for the able-bodied unemployed except employment—and residence— in prisonlike workhouses.

---

4. **bullocks** oxen.
5. **The Poor-Law . . . gave up their holdings** The Poor-Law determined how aid was to be given to the poor. During the famine, farmers with small farms ("holdings") were required to give them up before they would be given aid.
6. **visitation** divine punishment or reward.
7. **needlewomen . . . New South Wales** Probably referring to a scheme encouraging emigration to Australia. The "New Currency Lads" are native-born Australians.

sanction (saŋk´ shən) *n.* authorized approval or permission

exonerate (eg zän´ ər āt´) *v.* free from a charge of guilt; declare or prove blameless

A more important question cannot be asked. There is about Kilrush, and in Clare, and throughout Ireland, the doubly <u>melancholy</u> spectacle of a strong man asking for work as the means of getting food; and of the fertile earth wooing his labors, in order to yield up to him its rich but latent[8] stores: yet it lies idle and unfruitful. Why is not this doubly melancholy spectacle destroyed by their union, and converted into life and happiness, as oxygen and hydrogen, each in itself destructive, become, when united as water, the pabulum[9] of existence? We shall fully consider that question before we quit the subject, but we shall now only say that the whole of this land, cultivated and uncultivated, is owned by a few proprietors—that many of them are absentees[10] — that almost all are in embarrassed circumstances—and that, from ignorance, or false theory, or <u>indolence</u>, they prefer seeing the land covered with such misery as we have described, to either bringing the land under cultivation themselves, or allowing the people to cultivate it. Their greatest ambition, apparently, is to get rid of the people.

melancholy (mel′ ən käl′ ē) *adj.* sad; depressing

Reading Strategy
Distinguishing Emotive and Informative Language What, if any, is the emotional effect of the scientific analogy regarding oxygen and hydrogen?

indolence (in′ də lens) *n.* idleness; laziness

---

8. **latent** potential; not yet actual.
9. **pabulum** nourishing substance.
10. **absentees** Many landowners who rented to small Irish farmers lived in England and were thought to lack sufficient motivation to make the best use of their lands.

Review and Assess

Thinking About the Selection

1. **Respond:** Does this article move you to outrage on behalf of the Irish, or does it leave you cold? Explain.

2. **(a) Recall:** What does the article say is the "current condition" of the Irish? **(b) Interpret:** What measures, according to the article, would have kept the famine from becoming a crisis?

3. **(a) Recall:** According to the article, what British measures were mainly responsible for the condition of the Irish? **(b) Infer:** What do you think were the ultimate objectives of these measures? Why?

4. **(a) Recall:** Summarize what the article says about Ireland's natural resources. **(b) Analyze:** Considering the overall purpose of this article, why do you think the author included the passage on Ireland's natural resources?

5. **(a) Recall:** What does the article say is the obvious solution to Ireland's difficulties? **(b) Analyze:** The article poses a solution as a series of questions. Why is this more effective and persuasive than making a simple statement?

6. **(a) Connect:** In what regions of the world today is famine still a threat? **(b) Draw Conclusions:** What are the best ways of overcoming this threat? Explain.

Progress
in Personal Comfort
SYDNEY SMITH

I t is of some importance at what period a man is born. A young man, alive at this period, hardly knows to what improvements of human life he has been introduced; and I would bring before his notice the following eighteen changes which have taken place in England since I first began to breathe in it the breath of life—a period amounting now to nearly seventy-three years.

Gas[1] was unknown: I groped about the streets of London in all but the utter darkness of a twinkling oil lamp, under the protection of watchmen in their grand climacteric,[2] and exposed to every species of <u>depredation</u> and insult.

I have been nine hours in sailing from Dover to Calais before the invention of steam. It took me nine hours to go from Taunton to

depredation (dep´ rə dā´ shən) *n.* act or instance of robbing, plundering or laying waste

---

1. **gas** coal gas, piped under the streets of London and used in street lamps after 1814.
2. **climacteric** old age; a period of great change associated in some theories with the age of 63.

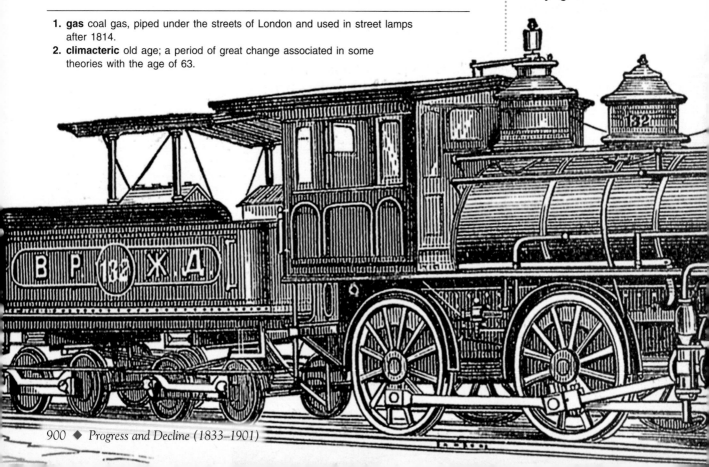

Bath, before the invention of railroads, and I now go in six hours from Taunton to London! In going from Taunton to Bath, I suffered between 10,000 and 12,000 severe contusions,[3] before stone-breaking Macadam[4] was born.

I paid £15 in a single year for repairs of carriage-springs on the pavement of London; and I now glide without noise or fracture, on wooden pavements.

I can walk, by the assistance of the police, from one end of London to the other, without molestation; or, if tired, get into a cheap and active cab, instead of those cottages on wheels, which the hackney coaches[5] were at the beginning of my life.

I had no umbrella! They were little used, and very dear. There were no waterproof hats, and *my* hat has often been reduced by rains into its primitive pulp.

---

3. **contusions** bruises.
4. **Macadam** (mə kad′ əm) road-surfacing made of small stones bound with adhesive.
5. **cheap and active cab . . . hackney coaches** Hackney coaches were used four-wheeled carriages for hire. The faster two-wheeled hansom cabs appeared in London in the 1830s.

Reading Strategy
Distinguishing Emotive and Informative Language Identify two examples each of emotive and informative language in the essay's third paragraph.

✓**Reading Check**

What are three examples of progress that Smith cites?

◀**Critical Viewing** Would Mr. Smith have described this locomotive as old-fashioned or up-to-date? Explain. **[Analyze]**

I could not keep my smallclothes in their proper place, for braces were unknown.[6] If I had the gout, there was no colchicum. If I was bilious, there was no calomel. If I was attacked by ague, there was no quinine.[7] There were filthy coffee houses instead of elegant clubs. Game could not be bought. Quarrels about uncommuted tithes[8] were endless. The corruption of Parliament, before Reform, infamous.[9] There were no banks to receive the savings of the poor. The Poor Laws were gradually sapping the vitals of the country; and whatever miseries I suffered, I had no post to whisk my complaints for a single penny[10] to the remotest corners of the empire; and yet, in spite of all these privations, I lived on quietly, and am now ashamed that I was not more discontented, and utterly surprised that all these changes and inventions did not occur two centuries ago.

I forgot to add, that as the basket of stage coaches, in which luggage was then carried, had no springs, your clothes were rubbed all to pieces. . . .

---

6. **smallclothes . . . braces** There were no suspenders to support his trousers.
7. **If I had the gout . . . there was no quinine** Gout, bilious conditions, and ague are afflictions. Colchicum, calomel, and quinine are remedies.
8. **uncommuted tithes** taxes paid to the Church in the form of produce, "commuted" (changed to) an equivalent payment in money in 1840.
9. **The corruption of Parliament . . . infamous** Before the reforms of the 1800s, the House of Commons was dominated by a few corrupt, wealthy landowners.
10. **I had no post . . . single penny** Penny postage, in the form of an adhesive stamp, was first introduced in England in 1840.

Review and Assess

Thinking About the Selection

1. **(a) Recall:** Over what period of time did the changes that Smith reports take place? **(b) Infer:** What lack of knowledge does Smith suggest is the reason for a "young man" to take these changes for granted?

2. **(a) Recall:** What are two improvements in public safety and two in public transportation that Smith reports?
   (b) Infer: Judging from Smith's account, how uncomfortable was life before these improvements? Explain.

3. **(a) Recall:** Does Smith consider the possibility that people in the future might find his world uncomfortable?
   (b) Infer: What reason can you give for his including or not including such a consideration? Explain.

4. **(a) Generalize:** In your opinion, what advances other than those in personal comfort are also a sign of progress? Explain.
   (b) Make a Judgment: Which types of advances do you consider the most essential to progress? Why?

Review and Assess

Literary Analysis

Journalistic Essay

1. In the **journalistic essay** "Condition of Ireland," the author writes as a judge, saying "we . . . exonerate the parties. . . ." Find another passage in which the author writes as a judge, and explain your choice.

2. Look at the picture on page 896. What, if anything, does it add to the attack on the government's legislation in "Condition of Ireland"?

3. Is Sidney Smith's subject, "personal comfort," better treated humorously or seriously? Why?

4. Is Smith's focus in "Progress in Comfort" compatible with his progressive viewpoints on matters like parliamentary reform? Why or why not?

Comparing Literary Works

5. Fill in a chart like this one with examples indicating the writer's approach in each essay.

Exaggeration	Humor	Moral Drama: Good vs. Evil

6. Which essay is more persuasive? Explain your choice, using examples from each essay.

Reading Strategy

Distinguishing Emotive and Informative Language

7. **Distinguish emotive and informative language** in the sentence beginning, "In their terrible distress, . . ." in the first paragraph of "Condition of Ireland."

8. In these passages, identify examples of emotive and informative language: (a) The description of natural resources in "Condition of Ireland," and (b) Smith's description of the penny post.

Extend Understanding

9. **Science Connection:** Using a specific example, demonstrate how quickly technology changes today.

Quick Review

Journalistic essays are short prose pieces that provide a perspective on current events or trends.

Emotive language uses words, phrases, and examples for emotional effect.

Informative language conveys facts.

 Take It to the Net
www.phschool.com

Take the interactive self-test online to check your understanding of these selections.

Integrate Language Skills

Vocabulary Development Lesson

Concept Development: "Humor" Words

In "Condition of Ireland," the author describes the plight of the Irish as *melancholy*, meaning "sad" or "depressing." *Melancholy* originally meant "black bile," one of the four humors, or liquids, that people once believed governed health and personality. The other three were *blood*, *yellow bile* or *choler*, and *phlegm*. Use sentence context to write a definition for each "humor" word italicized below. Then, check a dictionary to confirm your definitions.

1. Despite the setbacks, she remained *sanguine*.
2. Some people are sunny throughout the day, but he always seems to be *bilious* first thing in the morning.
3. Yelling "fire" just might get him going, but he is a pretty *phlegmatic* fellow.
4. She is so *choleric* that she will snap at you for the slightest thing.
5. It fills me with *bile* to see him get away with so much.

Grammar and Style Lesson

Coordinating Conjunctions

A **coordinating conjunction** links two sentence parts of the same grammatical kind. There are seven coordinating conjunctions: *and, but, or, nor, yet, so,* and *for.* Such conjunctions appear in both these essays, as this example demonstrates.

Example: They were little used, and very dear.

Practice In your notebook, complete each sentence by filling in the blank with a suitable coordinating conjunction.

1. He could not keep his smallclothes in their proper place, ___?___ braces were unknown.

Concept Development: Synonyms

Match each word in the first column with the word in the second column that is most similar in meaning.

1. requisites   a. destruction
2. sanction   b. absolve
3. exonerate   c. approval
4. melancholy   d. sad
5. indolence   e. necessities
6. depredation   f. idleness

Spelling Strategy

To form the plural of many nouns, add *-s* or *-es*. For example, *requisite* becomes *requisites*. In your notebook, write the plural form of each of the following nouns.

1. sanction   4. coach
2. depredation   5. potato
3. famine   6. essay

2. He now glides without noise ___?___ fracture.
3. Calmly and quietly, ___?___ very ignorantly, did the decree go forth.
4. He could walk without being bothered, ___?___ he could take a cab.
5. Their greatest ambition was to get rid of the people, ___?___ they would not allow the people to cultivate the land.

Writing Application In a letter to a modern newspaper, comment on advances in comfort. Use three coordinating conjunctions.

W͜G Prentice Hall Writing and Grammar Connection: Chapter 17, Section 4

Writing Lesson

Comparison and Contrast of Viewpoints

One of these essays reveals a crisis in the Empire, and the other suggests that things are getting better. Compare and contrast the essays, focusing on the viewpoints of the era that they express.

Prewriting Use a chart like this one to record the viewpoints expressed in the essays and the support for each. Then, draw a conclusion about the similarities and differences between the viewpoints.

Model: Comparing Viewpoints

Viewpoints on Empire	Support for Viewpoints	Conclusions on Similarities/Differences
"Condition . . ."		
"Progress . . ."		

Drafting Incorporate your conclusion into a thesis statement. Support your thesis by comparing the viewpoints expressed in the essays, using transition words such as *similarly, in contrast,* and *by comparison.*

Revising Review your paper to be sure that you have supported your thesis statement and that you have indicated in your conclusion which viewpoint is more convincing. If your thesis needs further support, scan your chart for evidence that you might not have included.

 Prentice Hall Writing and Grammar Connection: Chapter 9, Section 2

Extension Activities

Listening and Speaking Prepare a **comic monologue** about how inconvenient a "convenience" like a computer can be.

- Start with rhetorical questions: "What is it about my computer that is so *personal?*"
- Use parallel structure to help the audience follow your thoughts: "My *TV* set is not personal. My *microwave* is not personal."

As you continue to plan, provide a humorous perspective on computer problems. Then, deliver your monologue to an audience, using gestures to enhance the humor.

Research and Technology Write a **report** on a Victorian newspaper. Include a graphic, such as a newspaper illustration. One source might be books or Web sites on *The Illustrated London News.* Include a statistical table on newspaper circulation. For figures, scan articles on the history of newspapers or of British newspapers in encyclopedias.

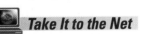 **Take It to the Net**   www.phschool.com

Go online for an additional research activity using the Internet.

READING INFORMATIONAL MATERIALS

Web Sites

About Web Sites

The **Internet,** an electronic communications network that connects computers around the world, allows users unlimited access to a great variety of information. The World Wide Web, the most commonly accessed part of the Internet, is made up of a vast collection of **Web sites** put up by individuals and organizations around the world. A Web site typically consists of a **home page** linked to several other pages on the site. Each page consists of the set of graphics, text, sound, and video that is presented in a browser window.

The Web has become a valuable tool for conducting research. As with any tool, you must be familiar with its nature in order to use it well.

Reading Strategy

Evaluating Credibility of Sources

To use the Web properly, always evaluate the credibility of a site before using the information it presents. First, ask what the authors' or sponsors' motives are. If those responsible for the site support a particular viewpoint, the site may focus on certain details at the expense of others. Are the authors experts in their field? If so, they will be careful with facts—if only to protect their reputations. If not, they may be careless in their presentation of facts.

You can find out about the authors of "The Victorian Web" by clicking on the button labeled "Who Created the Victorian Web?" This information will help you evaluate the credibility of information on the site. For instance, the author providing information on Victorian public health is a history professor, so you can probably trust his claims. You might want to double-check claims found in the work of students, especially if the claims seem extraordinary or inconsistent.

Using a graphic organizer like the one shown, list each link on the site, as shown on pages 907 and 908, and evaluate the information you find there.

Link	Credibility	My Reasoning
Victorianism	Mixed	The link probably discusses historical issues, but the site is created largely by people studying literature and the other arts—not history.
Gender Matters		
Social Context		

The Victorian Web

With the spread of Web technology, sites sponsored by scholars and institutions of learning, like this site, have proliferated. They enable users to conveniently find the latest research on a topic. Not all sites, however, are carefully fact-checked and updated. To check credentials of those who created this site, turn to page 908.

The Victorian Web

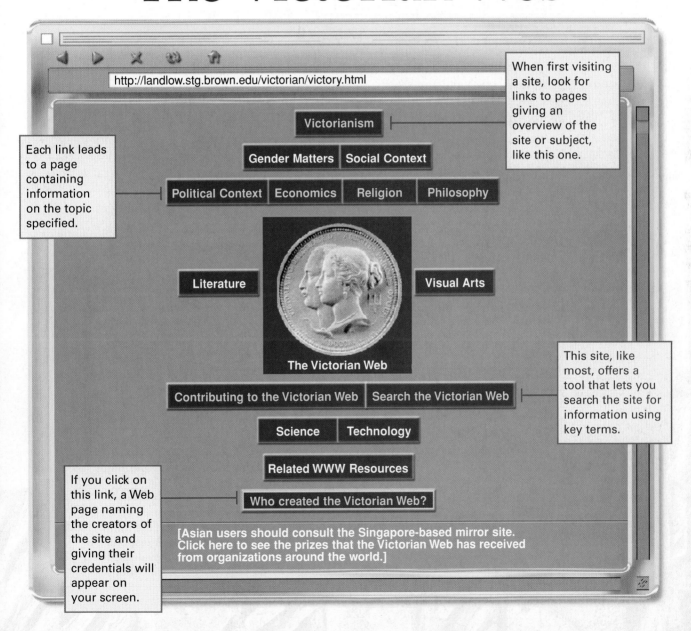

http://landlow.stg.brown.edu/victorian/victory.html

When first visiting a site, look for links to pages giving an overview of the site or subject, like this one.

Victorianism

Gender Matters Social Context

Each link leads to a page containing information on the topic specified.

Political Context Economics Religion Philosophy

Literature

Visual Arts

The Victorian Web

Contributing to the Victorian Web Search the Victorian Web

This site, like most, offers a tool that lets you search the site for information using key terms.

Science Technology

Related WWW Resources

If you click on this link, a Web page naming the creators of the site and giving their credentials will appear on your screen.

Who created the Victorian Web?

[Asian users should consult the Singapore-based mirror site. Click here to see the prizes that the Victorian Web has received from organizations around the world.]

Internal Page

Shown here is the page linked to the button labeled "Who created the Victorian Web?" on the site's home page (see page 907).

The respectable credentials of the main author of the site are presented here.

This passage explains the original purpose and motive for compiling the information on the site: to aid students taking particular courses at a university.

http://landlow.stg.brown.edu/victorian/misc/credits.html

Credits: Who Created the Victorian Web?

George P. Landow, Professor of English and Art History, Brown University

 The Victorian Web

The Victorian Web and *Context32*

 he Victorian Web is the WWW translation of Brown University's **Context 61,** which serves as a resource for courses in Victorian literature. These materials ultimately derive from **Context 32,** the Intermedia web that provided contextual information for English 32, "Survey of English Literature From 1700 to the Present." **Context 32** was begun in Spring 1985 as part of Brown University's Institute for Research in Information and Scholarship (IRIS) Intermedia project, which IBM, Apple Computers, the Annenberg/CPB Project, and other sources funded.

George P. Landow designed and edited the entire web, made many of the links, and is responsible for most of the materials on the individual authors and works as well as those on Biblical typology. He authored multiple lexias throughout the web and selected both the external criticism cited and most of the visual images. All captions for images are his. Under his direction David Cody wrote many of the general materials and chose many of the original digitized images, and Glenn Everett wrote some of the basic materials on Romantic and Victorian poets including timelines. The following year Kathryn Stockton created many of the documents on feminism and literary theory.

Anthony S. Wohl, Professor of History at Vassar College, generously contributed much of the material on Victorian public health, race and class issues, and anti-Catholic prejudice in Victorian England. This work draws upon both his published and unpublished writings.

Specific information on other contributors and the information for which each is responsible allows users to evaluate the credibility of each page.

Check Your Comprehension

1. (a) Who created this Web site? (b) What are his credentials?
   (c) Explain the responsibility he has for the information on the site.
2. Who wrote materials on Romantic and Victorian poets?

Apply the Reading Strategy

Evaluating the Credibility of Sources

To evaluate the quality, possible bias, and credibility of research material you locate online, check the source of the information. Use the following questions to help you evaluate the sources of "The Victorian Web":

1. Explain whether you would give higher credibility to materials written by Professor Landow than to materials by his students.
2. Name two links on the home page that you would be inclined to trust. Name two links you would consider more cautiously. Explain your reasoning.

Activity

Designing a Web Site

Use a chart like the one shown to sketch the design of a Web site on a topic in British literature.

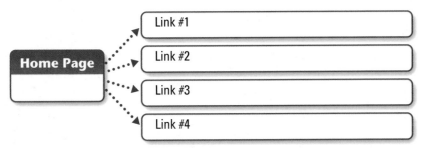

Answer to the following questions when creating your design:

1. Which page should you design first for your Web site?
2. Is there a hierarchy of topics—for example, from general to specific—that should guide your organization?

Comparing Informational Materials

Comparing Credits Pages

Find a Web site on a topic that interests you. Examine the credits for this Web site to determine whether you can trust the information presented. Compare the credits for this site with the credits for the Victorian Web. Explain which site you would rate as more credible.

CONNECTIONS
Literature Past and Present
The Empire and Its Discontents

The Two Sides of Success During the Victorian Era, Great Britain made great conquests in science and technology and exercised imperial power around the globe. The writers in this section show that British success had two sides. Sydney Smith, for example, notes the progress in personal comfort that made life easier—at least for the privileged. In sharp contrast, the article from *The Illustrated London News* reveals the harsh "aid" given the Irish by the British during the potato famine. Surveying the spirit of the times, Matthew Arnold tries to rescue meaning from a world of sadness, disillusionment, and alienation.

Discontents that Survive In "Recessional," Kipling warns that the Empire might not last forever. History has proved him right. Countries once under England's rule, such as India, are now independent. In Northern Ireland, though, still under British rule, the discontents have outlived the Empire. There, Protestants loyal to England battle with Catholics who want union with the Republic of Ireland to the south.

A New Ideal of Progress Many people of goodwill, such as Judge Catherine McGuinness, are trying to assuage the conflict. This selection is a speech by Judge McGuinness to the Forum for Peace and Reconciliation (1995), which attempted to bring together Protestants and Catholics in Northern Ireland. Her speech shows that, through the Empire is gone, ideals of progress still thrive.

Opening Statement for the

INAUGURAL SESSION OF THE FORUM FOR PEACE AND RECONCILIATION

— JUDGE CATHERINE McGUINNESS —

I am happy to welcome all who are here today in Dublin Castle, participants in the Forum, observers and distinguished guests.

The Forum for Peace and Reconciliation has been established by the Government in accordance with the intentions expressed in the Joint Declaration, to consult on, and examine, ways in which lasting peace, stability and reconciliation can be established by agreement among all the people of Ireland, and on the steps required to remove barriers of distrust, on the basis of promoting respect for the equal rights and validity of both traditions and identities. In accordance with its terms of reference it will also explore ways in which new approaches can be developed to serve economic interests common to both parts of Ireland.

It will be a fundamental principle of the Forum that all differences in relation to the exercise of the right to self-determination of the people of Ireland, and to all other matters, will be resolved exclusively by peaceful and democratic means. The purpose of the Forum will be to provide an opportunity to both major traditions, as well as to others, to assist in

Thematic Connection
What idea of progress would McGuinness embrace?

**Reading Check**
What is the ultimate aim of the Forum?

identifying and clarifying issues which could most contribute to creating a new era of trust and cooperation. Participation in the Forum will be entirely without prejudice to the position on constitutional issues held by any Party.

It is clear that major negotiations regarding Ireland's future, North and South, are now taking place and will continue to take place elsewhere. This Forum is a consultative and advisory body, which I hope will create a background of mutual understanding against which those other negotiations may more readily move forward.

The Forum is inclusive in its nature; already it contains members from all of the island of Ireland. I very much hope that in the future other Parties and other individuals will feel able to join in our deliberations. The forum does not represent a threat to any section of the people of Ireland. As I have already said, participation in it is entirely without prejudice to the position on constitutional issues held by any Party. The only entry test is a commitment to "peaceful and democratic means."

This Forum is about people rather than about territory. It is about people's right to live peacefully on this island "which we love and for whose welfare we pray," as that courageous Presbyterian minister, James Armour of Ballymoney, once said. All who live in Ireland must be made to feel that their right to be here is unquestioned and that they and their traditions are valued, whether they arrived here a few years ago or whether their ancestors came here four thousand years or four hundred years ago. People's rights and freedoms should not be affected by their religion, by their political or social outlook, by their economic standing, by their race, or by the country of origin of their ancestors. "Ireland, as distinct from her people, is nothing to me" said James Connolly, in a ringing denunciation of mindless so-called patriotism. James Connolly, who established Ireland's first republican and socialist party, and who was executed following the 1916 Rising, was born in Scotland of Ulster parents, and first arrived in Ireland as a British soldier in the Royal Scots Regiment.

The people of this country have many origins; these strands are woven together to make us what we are. My own personal background is, perhaps, an illustration. My great great grandfather, William Ellis, was twice Lord Mayor of York in England in 1799 and 1807. My great grandfather arrived in this country as a soldier in the 93rd Sutherland Highlanders regiment in 1803. He married a Clare woman whose mother's name was Morony. Their son settled in Spanish Point in County Clare, my own father's place of origin. My mother, whose family had both Irish and Scottish ancestors, came from Tullamore in County Offaly. My parents spent virtually all their adult life in Dunmurry, near Belfast. I was born into the Belfast Protestant community, a "Child of the Rectory," and spent my childhood there. I in my turn have spent my adult life in Dublin. My love for Ulster is deep-rooted and my Protestant background is strong, but I am nonetheless proud to be a citizen of Ireland.

Thematic Connection
Contrast McGuinness's ideals with the ideals of the British Empire in Victorian times.

▶ **Critical Viewing**
What elements in this photograph of McGuinness as she delivers her speech point to the solemnity of the occasion? **[Deduce]**

To say that this country faces many problems is to understate the position. In each jurisdiction the level of unemployment and under-employment is far too high; some of those in paid work or working in the home are exploited. There is poverty and deprivation in Dublin and in Belfast, in Leitrim and in Tyrone. Poverty and hardship dominate the lives of far too many people in Ireland, Protestant and Catholic, whether their government is in Dublin or in London. Of this we must not lose sight; it is part and parcel of the Irish situation and cannot be ignored. The economic aspects of the work of this Forum are vitally important.

We cannot pretend that the armed conflict of the past twenty-five years did not happen; nor can we say that it left no legacy. We mourn all those who died; we think of all who were wounded, some of whom will suffer from their injuries all their lives; we grieve for bereaved and broken families; we are conscious of homes where there are empty chairs; we know that all wars are cruel, bloody, harsh and merciless. We rejoice at the ending of violence. We salute all those who have worked for peace and who ultimately brought about the silence of the guns. Some of those are now members of this Forum; others are unsung, and wish to remain so; they each have earned the thanks and respect of us all.

This Forum is described as a Forum for Peace and Reconciliation. I would almost rather reverse the wording of the title and call it a forum for reconciliation and peace. At present we have a cessation of violence and the continuing peace process, but reconciliation is truly a prerequisite for a real and lasting peace. If we are to be reconciled we must be able to admit the errors and mistakes of the past; we must be able to express regret for past wrongs. Yet each of us must be able to retain pride and confidence in our history and in our traditions. Reconciliation can grow where there is both honesty and confidence, and where the old fears of each other are put behind us.

Unionist, socialist, republican, nationalist, liberal, conservative, feminist and all other views have legitimate rights and should be heard. There is no political test here; there is no censorship; there is openness. No party or group or tradition has a monopoly of wisdom. We hope to help banish hatred, incitement to hatred and intolerance from the politics of Ireland, and to lead through reconciliation to a true and lasting peace.

Catherine McGuinness

(b. 1934)

Judge Catherine McGuinness is the chairperson of the Forum for Peace and Reconciliation and judge of the High Court of Ireland. The conflict in Northern Ireland divides Catholics, who largely favor union with Ireland, and Protestants, who largely prefer the existing union with Britain. Combining a strong Protestant background with fierce pride in her Irish citizenship, McGuiness thus enjoys a unique perspective on the conflict in Northern Ireland. She has dedicated her career to seeking a lasting peace and an improved quality of life for all of the Irish.

Connecting Literature Past and Present

1. According to McGuinness's speech, what are the major issues dividing Northern Ireland?
2. Explain how two of the other selections in this section relate to these issues.

PART 4

Gloom and Glory

Past and Present (no. 2), Augustus Leopold Egg, Tate Gallery, London

Prepare to Read

Remembrance ◆ The Darkling Thrush ◆ "Ah, Are You Digging on My Grave?"

Emily Brontë (1818–1848)

Although some literary critics of the time attacked Emily Brontë for the violent passions expressed in her novel *Wuthering Heights* (1847), her dark Romanticism is now regarded as the essence of her genius.

A Writer's Beginnings Brontë grew up in the Yorkshire moorlands, a barren wasteland in the north of England, where her father was a clergyman. When Emily was just three, her mother died. Emily and her sisters, Charlotte and Anne, were educated at home for the most part and were often on their own.

Homesickness In 1835, Charlotte became a teacher at a school some distance from her home. Emily accompanied her as a pupil, but she quickly returned home. Three years later, she took a teaching position herself but resigned after six months.

Several years later, Charlotte and Emily devised another plan to support themselves as teachers. They would establish and run a school for girls in their own town of Haworth. To learn the skills they needed for this enterprise, they traveled to Brussels, Belgium. There, many people they met admired Emily for her Romantic temperament. However, Emily became homesick again and, after learning of her aunt's death, went home for good.

A Career Cut Short As adults, the three sisters published a book of poetry. The twenty-one poems that Emily contributed are considered the best of the collection. Emily's first and only novel, *Wuthering Heights*, was published in 1847. It tells the story of a tragic love affair played out against the mysterious landscape of the Yorkshire moors. The book is now considered a classic.

Wuthering Heights is the culminating expression of Emily's fiery imagination. A year after the book was published she died of tuberculosis.

Thomas Hardy (1840–1928)

Thomas Hardy, who was unusual in being both a great novelist and a great poet, was born in Dorset, a region of southwest England. He used this region as the basis for the imaginary county of Wessex that is the setting of many of his novels.

Early Life The son of a stonemason, Hardy grew up in a rural cottage near a tract of wasteland. He received a fine education at a local school, although he never went on to study at a university. As a teenager, he began working for a local architect, and he eventually became a draftsman for an architect who specialized in churches.

While on a business trip to Cornwall, at the southwestern tip of England, Hardy met the woman who later became his first wife. She encouraged him in his literary activities, and soon he committed himself entirely to writing.

The Novelist Hardy used his writing to elaborate his own pessimistic view of life. In tragic novels like *Tess of the D'Urbervilles* (1891) and *Jude the Obscure* (1895), he showed the difficulty people experience when trying to rise above their circumstances.

The Poet The bleakness of Hardy's fiction disturbed readers, and the response to *Jude the Obscure* was so hostile that Hardy abandoned fiction and returned to writing poetry, a form of writing he had pursued in the 1860s.

A Poetic Legacy Hardy's poetry marks a transition from Victorian verse to the Modernist movement of the twentieth century. In his use of strict meter and stanza structure, Hardy was unmistakably Victorian. However, his nonpoetic language and odd rhymes, his devotion to English characters and the English countryside, and his fatalistic outlook inspired twentieth-century poets like Philip Larkin.

Preview

Connecting to the Literature

Loss of some kind—of love, of friends, of youth—enters everyone's life. Responses to loss can vary widely, from anger to intense sorrow. Both Brontë's "Remembrance" and Hardy's "Ah, Are You Digging on My Grave?" address loss through death, but in very different ways.

Literary Analysis

Stanza Structure and Irony

Poets have a number of ways of addressing a reader's expectations. **Stanzas,** for instance, are repeated groupings of two or more verse lines with a definite pattern of line length, rhythm, and, frequently, rhyme. Stanzas are often units of meaning comparable to paragraphs in prose, and the **stanza structure** of a poem is the pattern of stanzas from which it is built. While stanza structure creates an expectation of a regular pattern, **irony** challenges expectations by creating a contradiction between reality and appearance or between what is said and what is meant.

Both stanza structure and irony relate to the expectations that a poem sets up and then fulfills or does not fulfill. In reading these poems, for example, notice these patterns:

- The arrangement of the first stanza leads you to expect a similar arrangement in the others.
- Irony surprises you by not fulfilling expectations.

Comparing Literary Works

Brontë's and Hardy's poems deal in different ways with the theme of absence—the sense of something missing, whether it is a loved one, a sign of hope, or the knowledge that people remember the speaker. Compare the ways in which the speakers in these poems feel about an absence and succeed or fail in handling it.

Reading Strategy

Reading Stanzas as Units of Meaning

Many poetic stanzas express a single main idea, as paragraphs do in prose. By **reading stanzas as units of meaning,** noticing how each stanza builds on the preceding one, you can often get a better understanding of what the writer is saying. Use a chart like this one to understand the logical progression of stanzas in each poem.

Vocabulary Development

languish (laŋ´ gwish) v. become weak; suffer from longing (p. 920)

rapturous (rap´ chər əs) adj. filled with joy and love; ecstatic (p. 920)

gaunt (gônt) adj. thin and bony, as from great hunger or age (p. 922)

terrestrial (tə res´ trē əl) adj. relating to the earth or to this world (p. 922)

"Remembrance"

Stanza 1

Speaker had a true love who died and whom she may be forgetting.

Stanza 2

Etc.

Remembrance
Emily Brontë

Background

Victorian poets wrote in many voices and many styles. Some writers, like Emily Brontë, are classified as Romantic because they explore and celebrate the human soul, the wildness of nature, and the powers of the imagination. Thomas Hardy, however, embraced Naturalism, which focused on the victimization of ordinary people by social and natural forces.

The poems that follow call to mind both Romanticism and Naturalism. Although Brontë wrote before the start of the Naturalist movement, her poem contains an attitude that is usually exhibited by Naturalist poets, and Hardy's poems contain instances of Romanticism, which is Brontë's specialty.

Cold in the earth, and the deep snow piled above thee!
Far, far removed, cold in the dreary grave!
Have I forgot, my Only Love, to love thee,
Severed at last by Time's all-wearing wave?

5 Now, when alone, do my thoughts no longer hover
Over the mountains, on that northern shore;
Resting their wings where heath and fern-leaves cover
Thy noble heart for ever, ever more?

Cold in the earth, and fifteen wild Decembers
10 From those brown hills have melted into spring—
Faithful indeed is the spirit that remembers
After such years of change and suffering!

◀ **Critical Viewing** In what ways might the woman in this painting represent the poem's speaker? **[Analyze]**

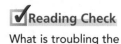

Reading Check
What is troubling the poem's speaker?

Sweet Love of youth, forgive if I forget thee
While the World's tide is bearing me along:
15 Other desires and other hopes beset me,
Hopes which obscure but cannot do thee wrong.

No later light has lightened up my heaven,
No second morn has ever shone for me:
All my life's bliss from thy dear life was given—
20 All my life's bliss is in the grave with thee.

But when the days of golden dreams had perished
And even Despair was powerless to destroy,
Then did I learn how existence could be cherished,
Strengthened and fed without the aid of joy;

25 Then did I check the tears of useless passion,
Weaned my young soul from yearning after thine;
Sternly denied its burning wish to hasten
Down to that tomb already more than mine!

And even yet, I dare not let it <u>languish</u>,
30 Dare not indulge in Memory's <u>rapturous</u> pain;
Once drinking deep of that divinest anguish,
How could I seek the empty world again?

Reading Strategy
Reading Stanzas as Units of Meaning How do lines 25–28 elaborate on the idea in lines 21–24?

languish (laŋ´ gwish) *v.* become weak; suffer from longing

rapturous (rap chər us) *adj.* filled with joy and love; ecstatic

Review and Assess

Thinking About the Selection

1. **Respond:** Were you disappointed by the speaker's final decision about his or her beloved? Why or why not?

2. **(a) Recall:** How long ago did the speaker's love die? **(b) Interpret:** What does the speaker mean by, "No later light has lightened up my heaven"?

3. **(a) Recall:** What does the speaker plan to do? **(b) Interpret:** Why is the speaker afraid to give in to his or her old feelings?

4. **(a) Draw Conclusions:** In your own words, express the basic conflict of the poem's speaker. **(b) Analyze:** How does the speaker handle this conflict?

5. **Evaluate:** Can it be desirable in some circumstances to lead an existence "without . . . joy"? Explain.

6. **Make a Judgment:** In ancient times lyric poems like this one were accompanied by music. Which of these types of music would make the best accompaniment for this poem: country, jazz, folk, rock, or hip-hop? Explain your choice.

The Darkling Thrush[1]

Thomas Hardy

I leant upon a coppice gate[2]
    When Frost was specter-gray,
And Winter's dregs made desolate
    The weakening eye of day.
5   The tangled bine-stems[3] scored the sky
    Like strings of broken lyres,
And all mankind that haunted nigh
    Had sought their household fires.

The land's sharp features seemed to be
10   The Century's corpse[4] outleant,
His crypt the cloudy canopy,
    The wind his death-lament.

---

1. **darkling** *adj.* in the dark.
2. **coppice** (kop´ is) **gate** gate leading to a thicket, or small wood.
3. **bine-stems** twining stems.
4. **Century's corpse** This poem was written on December 31, 1900, the last day of the nineteenth century.

▲ **Critical Viewing** Why might Hardy have chosen a thrush like the one pictured to symbolize hope? **[Speculate]**

✓**Reading Check**

Where is the speaker standing?

The ancient pulse of germ[5] and birth
    Was shrunken hard and dry,
15 And every spirit upon earth
    Seemed fervorless as I.

At once a voice arose among
    The bleak twigs overhead
In a full-hearted evensong
20   Of joy illimited;
An aged thrush, frail, <u>gaunt</u>, and small,
    In blast-beruffled plume,
Had chosen thus to fling his soul
    Upon the growing gloom.

25 So little cause for carolings
    Of such ecstatic sound
Was written on <u>terrestrial</u> things
    Afar or nigh around,
That I could think there trembled through
30   His happy good-night air
Some blessed Hope, whereof he knew
    And I was unaware.

gaunt (gônt) *adj.* thin and bony, as from great hunger or age

terrestrial (tə res´ trē əl) *adj.* relating to the earth or to this world

---

5. **germ** seed or bud.

Review and Assess

Thinking About the Selection

1. **Respond:** Does the ending of this poem surprise you? Why or why not?

2. **(a) Recall:** In which season and time of year is this poem set? **(b) Classify:** In the first two stanzas, what details and images does Hardy use to convey the mood of the setting?

3. **(a) Recall:** What does the speaker suddenly hear and see in the third stanza? **(b) Compare and Contrast:** How does the mood in the third stanza differ from that in the first two?

4. **(a) Recall:** Summarize what the speaker says in the final stanza. **(b) Draw Conclusions:** Do you agree with critics who assert that Hardy longs to believe there is reason for hope but does not really think so? Why or why not?

5. **Speculate:** If Hardy had seen the end of the twentieth century, do you think he would he have felt the same way that he did at the end of the nineteenth? Explain.

"Ah, Are You Digging on My Grave?"

Thomas Hardy

"Ah, are you digging on my grave
    My loved one?—planting rue?"
—"No: yesterday he went to wed
One of the brightest wealth has bred.
5 'It cannot hurt her now,' he said,
    'That I should not be true.'"

"Then who is digging on my grave?
    My nearest dearest kin?"
—"Ah, no: they sit and think, 'What use!
10 What good will planting flowers produce?
No tendance of her mound can loose
    Her spirit from Death's gin.'"[1]

---

1. gin *n.* trap.

✔ Reading Check

Who is the speaker of
this poem?

"But some one digs upon my grave?
    My enemy?—prodding sly?"
15 —"Nay: when she heard you had passed the Gate
That shuts on all flesh soon or late,
She thought you no more worth her hate,
    And cares not where you lie."

"Then, who is digging on my grave?
20   Say—since I have not guessed!"
—"O it is I, my mistress dear,
Your little dog, who still lives near,
And much I hope my movements here
    Have not disturbed your rest?"

25 "Ah, yes! *You* dig upon my grave . . .
    Why flashed it not on me
That one true heart was left behind!
What feeling do we ever find
To equal among human kind
30   A dog's fidelity!"

"Mistress, I dug upon your grave
    To bury a bone, in case
I should be hungry near this spot
When passing on my daily trot.
35 I am sorry, but I quite forgot
    It was your resting-place."

Review and Assess

Thinking About the Selection

1 **Respond:** Do you feel sorrow for the speaker in this poem? Why or why not?

2. **(a) Recall:** In each of the first three stanzas, who does the speaker think is digging? **(b) Infer:** What do the responses tell you about the people thought to be digging?

3. **(a) Recall:** Who is actually digging on the grave? **(b) Analyze:** What effect does Hardy achieve by withholding this information?

4. **(a) Recall:** What reason does the digger give for digging? **(b) Draw Conclusions:** What point about human vanity and self-esteem is Hardy making in this poem?

5. **Assess:** Do you think the message of this poem is overly pessimistic? Why or why not?

The British
Tradition

The Literature of Pessimism
The final stanza of the poem suggests a pessimistic view of life. Hardy is famous for the pessimism of his novels and poems—specifically, his belief that the world is in the hands of blind fate and that a person cannot easily escape the social and economic situation into which he or she is born. Hardy passed on this strain of pessimism to the twentieth-century poet Philip Larkin. However, Hardy was not unique among Victorian poets in his pessimism. In poems like "Dover Beach" (page 884), Matthew Arnold writes about people's isolation in a confused and frightening world. Tennyson, however, was more optimistic. He concludes his elegy *In Memoriam, A.H.H.* (page 818) with a reaffirmation of his faith in God.

Review and Assess

Literary Analysis

Stanza Structure and Irony

1. Complete a chart like the one shown to determine whether each poem uses a consistent **stanza structure.**

Stanza	Number of lines	Rhyme scheme	Meter
1			
2			
3			

2. What is ironic about the phrases "rapturous pain" and "divinest anguish" in the final stanza of "Remembrance"?

3. (a) How do lines 25–30 of "Ah, Are You Digging on My Grave?" disappoint a reader's expectations for an established stanza structure? (b) How does the last stanza use **irony** to disappoint a character's expectations in a drastic way?

Comparing Literary Works

4. Compare and contrast the types of absence that these poems address.

5. Which of the three speakers seems to experience the sorrow of loss most keenly? Why?

6. Which speaker seems best able to handle the absence of a sign of remembrance or hope? Explain.

Reading Strategy

Reading Stanzas as Units of Meaning

7. **Read stanzas as units of meaning** in "Remembrance" to show how the speaker gradually works out an answer to the question in the first stanza.

8. (a) In "The Darkling Thrush," which stanza introduces a shift in meaning? Explain. (b) In "Ah, Are You Digging on My Grave?" what important shift in meaning occurs between the last two stanzas?

Extend Understanding

9. **Science Connection:** Do you think that recent advances in science and technology show that Hardy's ironic pessimism is outdated? Explain.

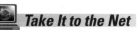

Integrate Language Skills

Vocabulary Development Lesson

Word Analysis: Latin Root *-terr(a)-*

The Latin root *-terr(a)-* comes from the Latin word for "earth." *Terrestrial,* which contains this root, means "of the earth or of this world." Explain how each of these *-terr(a)-* words relates to the meaning of the root.

1. terrain **2.** terrestrial **3.** subterranean

Spelling Strategy

Words ending in silent *e* drop the *e* before adding suffixes starting with vowels: rapture + -ous = rapturous. Words ending in *-ge* do not drop the *e*: outrage + -ous = outrageous. In your notebook, complete these spellings:

1. nerve + -ous **2.** advantage + -ous

Fluency: Word Choice

Review the vocabulary words listed on page 917 and study their use in the context of the selections. Then, in your notebook, replace the underlined word or phrase with the correct vocabulary word.

Although Emily Brontë's hero in *Wuthering Heights* is an <u>earthly</u> being, he has an almost supernatural aura and a fateful destiny. When parted from his beloved Cathy, he begins to <u>weaken</u> and becomes <u>very thin</u>. After his reunion with Cathy, Heathcliff is <u>extremely happy</u>.

Grammar and Style Lesson

Pronoun Case Following *than* or *as*

Than and *as* are conjunctions when they introduce clauses, or sentence parts containing a subject and a verb. When a pronoun follows *than* or *as*, it may function as the subject or object of the verb in the clause. The **case,** or form, of a pronoun varies depending on whether the pronoun is used as a subject or an as object. Use the nominative case for pronouns used as subjects and the objective case for pronouns used as objects. The **case of a pronoun following *than* or *as*** must be correct even if words are missing in the comparison.

> And every spirit upon earth
> Seemed fervorless as <u>I</u> [was].

I is the subject of the incomplete comparison *I was.* Mentally fill in missing words to determine the correct pronoun in such cases.

Practice On your paper, write the correct pronoun for each incomplete construction, and identify the missing words that complete the comparison.

1. Charlotte Brontë's *Jane Eyre* pleased me more than (he, him).

2. Charlotte's sister Emily was as talented as (she, her).

3. In Hardy's poem, the bird had more hope than (he, him).

4. The dog was as forgetful as (I, me).

5. Considering Brontë and Hardy as writers, I like her more than (he, him).

Writing Application Write a paragraph comparing the bird and the dog as messengers in Hardy's two poems. Use at least one incomplete construction involving a pronoun.

W̶G̶ Prentice Hall Writing and Grammar Connection: Chapter 22, Section 1

Writing Lesson

Comparative Analysis of Literary Sources

Poets like Thomas Hardy and Emily Brontë are often subjects of biography, literary analysis, or critical review. In an essay, analyze the credibility or possible bias of two sources of information about one of these writers.

Prewriting   Decide which poet or work you would like to use as the subject for your research. Then, use a chart like the one shown to identify sources and analyze their reliability. To aid your analysis, imagine you are writing a paper using these sources.

Model: Analyzing Sources

Source	Contents	Analysis
Online review	Praise; personal response	Writer is not an expert
Encyclopedia	Facts about Hardy's life	No real analysis of work
Scholarly article	Discussion of a specific theme in Hardy's poetry	Well-supported; quotes lines from poetry

Drafting   Choose two distinctly different sources. Briefly describe the contents of each. Then, compare and contrast their value to a student of literature.

Revising   Review your essay to make sure you have clearly shown the relative value of each source. Consider adding quotations from the sources to support the points you make about their tone, content, and bias or lack of bias.

 Prentice Hall Writing and Grammar Connection: Chapter 31, Section 2

Extension Activities

Research and Technology With several classmates, learn more about the remarkably creative Brontë family, and write a brief **biography** of their lives and accomplishments.

- Consult biographies, encyclopedias, and Web sites.
- Enhance your narrative with graphics, such as a Brontë family tree or a map of Yorkshire.

Make your biography available to classmates.
[Group Activity]

Listening and Speaking With a partner, give a **dramatic reading** of "Ah, Are You Digging on My Grave?" for the class. Review the poem to determine how your characters' motives and personalities should influence the tones and gestures you use.

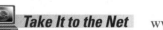 **Take It to the Net**   www.phschool.com

Go online for an additional research activity using the Internet.

Prepare to Read

God's Grandeur ◆ Spring and Fall: To a Young Child ◆ To an Athlete Dying Young ◆ When I Was One-and-Twenty

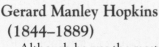

Gerard Manley Hopkins (1844–1889)

Although he was the most innovative poet of the Victorian period, Hopkins never published a collection of his work during his lifetime. It was not until 1918 that his work was published and a generation of poets could read and be influenced by his startling poetry.

Devotion to God and Nature This quietly rebellious poet was born just outside London, the oldest of nine children in a prosperous middle-class family. Although physically slight, he would perch fearlessly at the top of a tree and sway in the wind while observing the landscape. He began to write poetry in grammar school, a practice he continued at Oxford University, where he studied the classics.

During his third year at Oxford, Hopkins decided to become a Catholic priest in the Jesuit order—a decision that dismayed his parents, who were devout Anglicans. The discipline of Hopkins's religious vocation was sometimes at odds with his writing of verse. He temporarily gave up poetry but continued to keep detailed notebooks that recorded his fascination with words and his love of nature.

Inscape In the mid-1870s, while studying theology in Wales, he began to write poetry again, stimulated by the Welsh language and encouraged by his religious mentor. Somewhat earlier, Hopkins had found in the medieval theologian Duns Scotus a verification of his own ideas about the individuality of all things. Hopkins called this precious individuality *inscape*, and he tried to capture it in highly original poems like "God's Grandeur." He also experimented with new rhythms in his verse.

From early 1884 on, he taught at a Jesuit college in Dublin. There, he died of typhoid fever just before his forty-fifth birthday.

A. E. Housman (1859–1936)

A man of solitary habits and harsh self-discipline, Housman was also capable of creating delicately crafted poems, full of gentle regret.

Challenges of Youth Housman grew up in Worcestershire, a region northwest of London. His childhood came to an end on his twelfth birthday, when his mother died. Later, at Oxford University, his despair over an unrequited love darkened his life still further. Perhaps because of this double grief, his poetry has bitter undertones.

Upon leaving Oxford, where he had studied classical literature and philosophy, Housman went to work in the Patent Office. Determined to prove himself in the classics, he studied Greek and Latin at night and wrote scholarly articles. In 1892, his hard work paid off when he was appointed to a position as professor of Latin at University College in London.

Literary Success Although Housman spent most of his life engaged in teaching and in scholarly pursuits, he is most remembered for three slender volumes of poetry that are as romantic and melancholy as any ever written. His first and most famous collection of verse, *A Shropshire Lad* (1896), has as its central character a young man named Terence. In later years, Housman claimed, ironically, that he had "never spent much time" in Shropshire.

Housman's image is that of an emotionless intellectual, but his poems display deep feelings. In his view, the goal of poetry is to "transfuse emotion," not to transmit thought. A well-written poem, he maintained, should affect the reader like a shiver down the spine or a punch in the stomach.

Preview

Connecting to the Literature

As you grow, your ideas change. Several of these poems, examine how the passing of time colors emotions and changes priorities.

Literary Analysis

Rhythm and Meter

Poetry with a regular **rhythm,** or movement, is **metrical verse,** which is divided into combinations of syllables called **feet.** The following are various feet and the pattern of stressed and unstressed syllables they contain:

- **Iambic:** unstressed, stressed, as in *the time*
- **Trochaic:** stressed, unstressed, as in *grandeur*
- **Anapestic:** unstressed, unstressed, stressed, as in *to the low*

Lines with three, four, and five feet are **trimeter, tetrameter,** and **pentameter,** respectively. Iambic pentameter is a five-foot line with iambic feet, and trochaic tetrameter is a four-foot line with trochaic feet. Housman uses regular meters like iambic and trochaic tetrameter, but Hopkins invents rhythms like these:

- **counterpoint rhythm**—two opposing rhythms appear together, for example, two trochaic feet in an iambic line:
  The world is charged with the grandeur of God.

- **sprung rhythm**—all feet begin with a stressed syllable (sometimes marked with an accent) and contain a varying number of unstressed syllables. Sprung rhythm is complex, but its result is clear: densely stressed lines with many echoing consonant and vowel sounds.

Comparing Literary Works

Beauty, or the loveliness of the world, and mortality, or the certainty of death, are two connected themes that these poets explore. Look for the ways in which they express their own unique perspectives on these traditional themes.

Reading Strategy

Applying Biography

By **applying biography,** or what you know about poets' lives, to their work, you can gain a better insight into their poetry. Review the information on page 928, and use a chart like this one to apply biography to these selections.

Vocabulary Development

grandeur (gran´ jər) *n.* splendor; magnificence (p. 931)

blight (blīt) *n.* condition of withering (p. 932)

rue (rōō) *n.* sorrow; regret (p. 934)

Bird's Nest, Ros. W. Jenkins, Warrington Museum and Art Gallery

▲ **Critical Viewing** How does this painting reflect Hopkins's ideas in "God's Grandeur"? **[Apply]**

God's Grandeur

Gerard Manley Hopkins

Background

Surprisingly, when Gerard Manley Hopkins died, none of his obituaries mentioned that he was a poet and only a few friends were aware of this fact. One of these friends was Robert Bridges, an Oxford classmate and later the British poet laureate. Bridges had corresponded with Hopkins and took an interest in his experiments with rhythm. It was through Bridges's efforts that a volume of Hopkins's poetry was published for the first time in 1918. Today, Bridges is little known, but his once-obscure friend Gerard Manley Hopkins is a famous Victorian poet.

The world is charged with the grandeur of God.
   It will flame out, like shining from shook foil;[1]
   It gathers to a greatness, like the ooze of oil
Crushed.[2] Why do men then now not reck his rod?[3]
5 Generations have trod, have trod, have trod;
   And all is seared with trade; bleared, smeared with toil;
   And wears man's smudge and shares man's smell: the soil
Is bare now, nor can foot feel, being shod.

And for all this, nature is never spent;
10   There lives the dearest freshness deep down things;
And though the last lights off the black West went
   Oh, morning, at the brown brink eastward, springs—
Because the Holy Ghost over the bent
   World broods with warm breast and with ah! bright wings.

grandeur (gran´ jər) *n.* splendor, magnificence

---

1. **foil** *n.* tinsel.
2. **crushed** squeezed from olives.
3. **reck his rod** heed God's authority.

SPRING AND FALL: TO A YOUNG CHILD

GERARD MANLEY HOPKINS

Márgarét, áre you gríeving
Over Goldengrove unleaving?
Leáves, líke the things of man, you
With your fresh thoughts care for, can you?
5 Áh! ás the heart grows older
It will come to such sights colder
By and by, nor spare a sigh
Though worlds of wanwood[1] leafmeal[2] lie;
And yet you wíll weep and know why.
10 Now no matter, child, the name:
Sórrow's spríngs áre the same.
Nor mouth had, no nor mind, expressed
What heart heard of, ghost[3] guessed:
It ís the <u>blight</u> man was born for,
15 It is Margaret you mourn for.

---

1. **wanwood** (wän´ wood) pale wood.
2. **leafmeal** ground-up decomposed leaves.
3. **ghost** spirit.

Literary Analysis
Rhythm and Meter
Identify a visual clue that proves that this poem is written in sprung rhythm.

blight (blīt) *n.* condition of withering

Review and Assess

Thinking About the Selections

1. **(a) Recall:** According to Hopkins in "God's Grandeur," what has been the impact on nature of humanity's behavior? **(b) Analyze:** What opposition or conflict does he explore in lines 1–8 of "God's Grandeur"? **(c) Draw Conclusions:** How does Hopkins resolve that opposition?

2. **(a) Recall:** What makes Margaret unhappy in "Spring and Fall"? **(b) Interpret:** Explain how the poem's speaker suggests that Margaret will both outgrow and not outgrow this sadness.

3. **(a) Recall:** According to the speaker, how will Margaret change as she grows older? **(b) Draw Conclusions:** What lesson does the speaker offer to Margaret in this poem?

4. **Speculate:** Judging by "God's Grandeur," would Hopkins support the ecology movement if he were alive today? Explain.

To an Athlete Dying Young

A. E. Housman

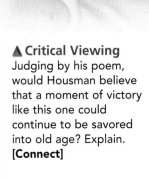

The time you won your town the race
We chaired you through the marketplace;
Man and boy stood cheering by,
And home we brought you shoulder-high.

5 Today, the road all runners come,
Shoulder-high we bring you home,
And set you at your threshold down,
Townsman of a stiller town.

Smart lad, to slip betimes away
10 From fields where glory does not stay
And early though the laurel[1] grows
It withers quicker than the rose.

Eyes the shady night has shut
Cannot see the record cut,
15 And silence sounds no worse than cheers
After earth has stopped the ears:

Now you will not swell the rout
Of lads that wore their honors out,
Runners whom renown outran
20 And the name died before the man.

So set, before its echoes fade,
The fleet foot on the sill of shade.
And hold to the low lintel up
The still-defended challenge cup.

25 And round that early-laureled head
Will flock to gaze the strengthless dead,
And find unwithered on its curls
The garland briefer than a girl's.

▲ **Critical Viewing**
Judging by his poem, would Housman believe that a moment of victory like this one could continue to be savored into old age? Explain. **[Connect]**

---

1. **laurel** symbol of victory.

When I Was One-and-Twenty

A. E. Housman

When I was one-and-twenty
    I heard a wise man say,
"Give crowns and pounds and guineas[1]
    But not your heart away;
5 Give pearls away and rubies
    But keep your fancy free."
But I was one-and-twenty,
    No use to talk to me.

When I was one-and-twenty
10   I heard him say again,
"The heart out of the bosom
    Was never given in vain;
'Tis paid with sighs a plenty
    And sold for endless <u>rue</u>."
15 And I am two-and-twenty,
    And oh, 'tis true, 'tis true.

rue (r$\overline{oo}$) *n.* sorrow; regret

---

1. **crowns . . . guineas** denominations of money.

Review and Assess

Thinking About the Selections

1. **(a) Recall:** What visual image appears in each of the first two stanzas of "To an Athlete"? **(b) Contrast:** How do the meanings of the two images differ?

2. **(a) Recall:** In "To an Athlete," what are three advantages of dying young, according to the speaker? **(b) Interpret:** Does the speaker entirely mean what he says about these advantages? Explain.

3. **(a) Recall:** In "When I Was One-and-Twenty," what advice does the speaker receive, and how does he react? **(b) Interpret:** What clues are there in the poem that Housman is mocking his speaker?

4. **Make a Judgment:** Which poem conveys the most compassionate view of human mortality— "Spring and Fall," "To an Athlete," or "When I Was One-and-Twenty"? Explain.

Review and Assess

Literary Analysis

Rhythm and Meter

1. (a) Use scansion symbols (˘ ´) to identify the **feet** in line 5 of "God's Grandeur." (b) Explain how your scan demonstrates that the line uses **counterpoint rhythm.**

> Generations have trod, have trod, have trod; . . .

2. "Spring and Fall" is written with **sprung rhythm**. Using the stresses in line 11, indicate how many feet that line has.

3. (a) How does the counterpoint rhythm in line 5 of "God's Grandeur" support the meaning of the line? (b) In "Spring and Fall," how do the three stresses in line 11 reinforce the meaning of the line?

4. (a) Show that in lines 1–8 of "To an Athlete," the **meter** includes five **iambic tetrameter** lines and three **trochaic tetrameter** lines. (b) How do the trochaic lines reinforce the idea of a "stiller town"?

Comparing Literary Works

5. (a) In "God's Grandeur," does Hopkins think the beauty of nature is enduring? Explain. (b) In "Spring and Fall," does he express the same perspective on the endurance of nature's beauty as he does in "God's Grandeur"? Why or why not?

6. Would the speakers in "Spring and Fall" and "To an Athlete" agree that deep sorrow is the right response to the realization that life and earthly beauty are fleeting? Explain.

Reading Strategy

Applying Biography

7. **Apply biography** by finding a passage in "God's Grandeur" that reflects Hopkins's love of nature. Then, explain your choice.

8. Find a passage in "To an Athlete" that reflects Housman's underlying sadness. Explain your choice.

Extend Understanding

9. **Physical Education Connection:** Do you agree with Housman in "To an Athlete" that aging can bring only sadness to an athlete? Why or why not?

Quick Review

The regular **rhythms,** or movements, of **metrical verse** are measured in units called **feet,** which combine stressed (´) and unstressed (˘) syllables.

Examples of feet are **iambic** (˘ ´), **trochaic** (´ ˘), and **anapestic** (˘ ˘ ´).

Examples of metrical lines are **trimeter** (three feet), **tetrameter** (four feet), and **pentameter** (five feet).

In a **counterpoint rhythm,** two opposing rhythms appear together.

In **sprung rhythm,** all feet begin with a stressed syllable and contain a varying number of unstressed syllables.

Applying biography, or facts about a poet's life, to a poem, can help you understand it better.

 Take It to the Net
www.phschool.com
Take the interactive self-test online to check your understanding of these selections.

Integrate Language Skills

Vocabulary Development Lesson

Concept Development: Coined Words

Hopkins's fascination with language can be seen in the way he coins, or invents, words. For example, he combines *wan*, meaning "pale," and *wood* to make *wanwood*, a new word to describe pale autumn trees. Similarly, he coins *leafmeal* to describe fallen dead leaves ground into a kind of meal. Imitate Hopkins, and replace each phrase with a lively new combination word that others will understand.

1. the very end of summer
2. chilly mornings right after dawn
3. snow-covered lawns
4. tall, bare trees

Concept Development: Analogies

On your paper, complete the following analogies with words from the vocabulary list on page 929.

1. *accomplishment : pride ::* ___?___ *: mourning*
2. *shabbiness : shack ::* ___?___ *: palace*
3. *broadness : wideness :: remorse:* ___?___

Spelling Strategy

Words that contain a long *i* sound followed by a *t* are often spelled with the letter combination *ight*, as in the word *blight*. Choose the correctly spelled word from each pair.

1. kight, kite
2. night, nite
3. fright, frite
4. brite, bright

Grammar and Style Lesson

Capitalization of Compass Points

Compass points referring to places are capitalized, like proper nouns, but those indicating direction are not. For example, in the second stanza of "God's Grandeur," *West* is capitalized because it refers to a specific region, but *eastward* is not because it merely points in a direction.

> And for all this, nature is never spent;
> There lives the dearest freshness deep
>   down things;
> And though the last lights off the black
>   <u>West</u> went [**place**]
> Oh, morning, at the brown brink
>   <u>eastward</u> springs . . . [**direction**]

Practice In your notebook, choose a capital or lowercase letter for each compass point.

1. Housman's Shropshire is located <u>n/N</u>orthwest of London.
2. The Shropshire lad would have traveled <u>s/S</u>outheast to get to London.
3. Hopkins traveled <u>n/N</u>orthwest from London to attend Oxford University.
4. Worcestershire, Housman's birthplace, is in the <u>w/W</u>est of England.
5. Ireland, where Hopkins served as a priest, is an island <u>w/W</u>est of England.

Writing Application Using compass points, write instructions for a tourist traveling from London to Oxford, the alma mater of both these poets.

WG *Prentice Hall Writing and Grammar Connection: Chapter 26*

Writing Lesson

Analytical Essay

Choose one of the four poems in this group, and write an analytical essay about it that presents and supports a thesis, or central idea, about its meaning.

Prewriting Review the poem, jotting down answers to questions like these: Who is the poem's speaker? What new perspectives does the speaker offer on a traditional theme, like beauty or mortality?

Drafting Use your notes to write a thesis statement that summarizes the poem's central insight into life. Then, develop your thesis in a series of paragraphs, citing details from the poem for support.

Revising To improve your draft, look for points at which you can support your ideas with examples.

Model: Revising to Strengthen Support

The surprises in the rhythms of "God's Grandeur" contribute to the theme that nature is not worn out. *For example, the sentence beginning in line 2 slips over the brink into line 3 and ends, surprisingly, with the first word of line 4—"Crushed."*

> A specific example from the poem provides support for a general statement.

W̶G̶ Prentice Hall Writing and Grammar Connection: Chapter 14, Section 4

Extension Activities

Research and Technology Both Hopkins and Housman attended Oxford University. Use readings, photographs, recordings, film clips, and artifacts to give a **multimedia presentation** on Oxford and its importance to British poetry.

- Devise three questions to guide your research, focusing on famous poets who attended Oxford.
- Develop strategies for recording and organizing your findings.

Then, write a script that shows how and when you will use the items you have gathered, and follow it in giving your presentation.

Listening and Speaking With several classmates, give oral interpretations of the Hopkins and Housman poems as part of a **Victorian Poetry Contest.** Each reader should review his or her poem's meter and meaning, work out difficult pronunciations, and develop appropriate gestures. Have members of the audience vote on the best presentation. **[Group Activity]**

 **Take It to the Net** www.phschool.com

Go online for an additional research activity using the Internet.

Cycles The Victorian Era marks a time of glorious progress for the British Empire. It also marks the beginning of its decline. The poems in this section reflect on the passing of glory as part of a cyclical process. For example, in Gerard Manley Hopkins's poem "Spring and Fall: To a Young Child," the poet provides a contrast between the innocence of childhood and the experiences of loss that disrupt and eventually bring that innocence to an end. Thomas Hardy and A. E. Housman juxtapose the glory of life with the gloom of death. In "Ah, Are You Digging on My Grave?" Hardy uses the cycle of life and death to question our natural belief in our own importance.

Eternity Like the other poets in this section, their contemporary Arthur Rimbaud (àr tür′ ram bō′) focuses on the cycles of life. His affirmation of these cycles in "Eternity" is at once stark and joyous, as he voices the possibility that the only thing that is eternal is the cycle of change itself. As you read "Eternity," note what is temporary and what is truly eternal.

Eternity

Arthur Rimbaud
Translated by Frances Golffing

I have recovered it.
What? Eternity.
It is the sea
Matched with the sun.

5   My sentinel soul,
Let us murmur the vow
Of the night so void
And of the fiery day.

Of human sanctions,
10   Of common transports,
You free yourself:
You soar according . . .

From your ardor[1] alone,
Embers of satin,
15   Duty exhales,
Without anyone saying: at last.

Never a hope;
No genesis.
Skill with patience . . .
20   Anguish is certain.

I have recovered it.
What? Eternity.
It is the sea
Matched with the sun.

---

1. ardor (är´ dər) *n.* emotional warmth; passion

Thematic Connections
How does the image of the sun and the sea express the idea of a cycle?

Arthur Rimbaud

(1854–1891)
Arthur Rimbaud first earned recognition for his poetry at age eight and was published when he was only fifteen. His abrupt decision at the age of nineteen to stop writing poetry and embark on a life of adventure has made him a touchstone figure of the passion and peril of the artistic life, inspiring scores of writers, musicians, and other artists down to the present.

Rimbaud spent the remainder of his life traveling throughout Africa and the Middle East. By the time of his death, the poetry of his youth had begun to influence other writers.

Writing About Literature

Analyze Literary Periods

The industrial progress of the Victorian Age transformed the world. With the development of a modern middle class and the rapid growth of industrial cities, this era brought the days of aristocrats and peasants in Europe to a close and ushered in a life closer to the one people live today. Victorian authors frequently served as insightful commentators on progress, judging the positive or negative effects—the glories and the miseries—of these dramatic changes. In the spirit of these Victorian authors, use the assignment in the yellow box to write an essay in which you analyze the impact of a specific social change on Victorian literature.

Prewriting

Find a focus. Begin by reviewing the major changes of the Victorian Age. You can find an overview of the era in the unit introduction on pages 804–813. Then, identify a specific change that had a significant impact on the literature of the period. Fill out a chart like the one shown, using these questions to guide you:

- What changes made the greatest difference to Victorian life?
- What new ideas contributed to social changes?
- How did writers respond to these changes? In what literary forms did they respond?

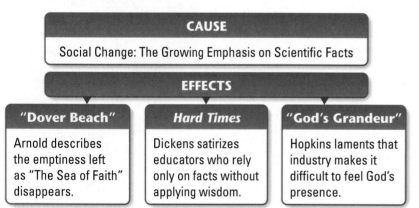

CAUSE

Social Change: The Growing Emphasis on Scientific Facts

EFFECTS

"Dover Beach"	*Hard Times*	"God's Grandeur"
Arnold describes the emptiness left as "The Sea of Faith" disappears.	Dickens satirizes educators who rely only on facts without applying wisdom.	Hopkins laments that industry makes it difficult to feel God's presence.

Gather details. Look for works that describe specific social, political, or economic circumstances. Also, review works that may indirectly express a more general reaction to the upheavals of the day. When you find a work that applies to your analysis, conduct a thorough rereading. Look for details of word choice or images that will add depth to your analysis.

Write a working thesis. Your thesis statement can guide your prewriting analysis. As your thoughts on the subject change, adjust your thesis statement to reflect your revised analysis.

Assignment: The Effect of Social Change on Literature

Identify a key change in British society or economy, and trace its impact on Victorian literature.

Criteria:

- Include a thesis statement that identifies the social change you will analyze and introduces your view of its impact on Victorian literature.
- Discuss at least three Victorian works from this unit, demonstrating how they reflect the change that you have identified.
- Approximate length: 1,500 words

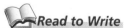
Read to Write

Consider yourself a detective as you review the texts you have read. Look for clues concerning a particular motive for writing—an author's response to social changes.

Drafting

Clarify your thesis statement. As you begin to draft, take time to make sure that your thesis statement clearly states what you want to express in your essay. This statement will guide your entire draft, so slow down and focus your thesis effectively.

Model: Focusing a Thesis

Unfocused: Science replaced faith, so Victorian authors had to warn their readers about what was happening.

Focused: As the scientific outlook replaced faith in the Victorian mind, authors of the era often warned readers about the values being lost in the race to progress.

Organize. Consider the relative strength of each of your examples when deciding the order in which you will discuss them. To leave your reader with a strong impression, you might choose to save your most effective or emphatic example for last.

Revising and Editing

Review content: Check your connections. Make sure that you introduce and explain each example you present so that your readers understand its relevance. Add transitions where necessary.

Review style: Use a variety of sentences. Include a mix of simple, compound, complex, and compound-complex sentences to create flowing prose. Identify passages lacking variety, and combine or break apart sentences in them.

Repeated sentence types: Hopkins says that humans have lost respect for the natural world. He charges that we have crushed the truest evidence of God's presence. The poem suggests that God's presence has been obscured by industrial development.

Varied sentences: Hopkins criticizes humans for losing respect for the natural world and, as a result, crushing the truest evidence of God's presence. In his view, God's presence has been obscured by industrial development.

Publishing and Presenting

Develop an oral presentation. Develop a brief talk for your class in which you present your analysis. After your presentation, ask for questions and comments from your audience.

W̶G̶ Prentice Hall Writing and Grammar Connection: Chapter 14

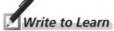
Write to Learn
If you have trouble writing a clear thesis statement, you might need to change your essay's focus. Do not feel tied to your original idea—your second or third attempts might generate better results.

Write to Explain
You can use phrases such as "more significantly" or "most importantly" to share your evaluations with readers. These transitional phrases can clarify your position and highlight the key insights within your analysis.

Writing WORKSHOP

Research: Research Paper

A **research paper** is a work in which a writer explains or narrates a particular set of facts or group of events, documenting his or her claims by citing credible sources such as reference works and experiments. In this workshop, you will perform a historical investigation and write a research report analyzing the similarities and differences in the sources you examine.

Assignment Criteria Your research paper should include the following elements:

- A clear thesis statement explaining your purpose and conclusions
- A presentation of the details of the event, drawing on several primary and secondary sources
- A comparison of the sources and an analysis of any differences in the information they present
- Conclusions about the event, taking into account your evaluation of the validity and reliability of source information
- Complete and accurate citations with a formal Works-Cited list

To preview the criteria on which your report may be assessed, see the Rubric on page 947.

Prewriting

Choose a topic. For this type of report, the best topic is a historical event about which there are differing opinions and for which a variety of primary and secondary sources are available. Because primary sources—items like letters, diaries, and interviews—are often harder to find than secondary ones, use a library catalog and the Internet to make sure that such sources are available for a topic before making your final selection.

Difficult topic:	Daily life of medieval peasants (few primary sources available)
Workable topic:	Working conditions in early industrial England

Do the research. Use a library for secondary sources such as books and encyclopedias. Use the Internet for secondary sources such as online newspapers and magazines and for many primary sources. List and briefly summarize all sources.

Choose varied documents. Make sure that your sources represent varied viewpoints. Settle on at least two primary and two secondary sources.

> **TOPIC: Battle of New Orleans**
>
> **CATALOG SCAN:**
>
> **Many Secondary Sources**
> Horsman, R. *The War of 1812.*
> London: Eyre & Spottiswoode, 1969.
>
> **Some Primary Sources On-Line**
> Jackson, A. Address to His Troops.
> 8 January 1815. 4 April 2000
> <http://www.hillsdale.edu/dept/
> History/Documents/War/America/
> 1812/South/1815-Jackson.htm>.

Student Model

Before you begin drafting your report, read this student model and review the characteristics of a powerful research paper.

Eric Southard
Lawrence, KS

A "Blessing" or a Blunder: British Defeat in the Battle of New Orleans

One of the most stirring battles of the War of 1812, the Battle of New Orleans, was actually fought weeks after the war was officially over. The battle concluded with the rousing defeat of the British by American troops under Andrew Jackson. At the time, Jackson attributed his victory to "the blessing of heaven" (Jackson, Address to His Troops). Yet it is fairly clear that misjudgments by the leaders of the British had as much to do with Jackson's victory as good fortune.

> Eric identifies his thesis in his opening paragraph.

In early 1814, what would later be called the War of 1812 had already been fought for almost two years. Having finally won the war against France, the British were stepping up their efforts on the American front. (Carter 6).

> Next, Eric provides readers with general background on his subject.

The city of New Orleans, holding a total of $15 million in stored merchandise, enticed the British military with the promise of prize money (Carter 91). Because of its situation at the mouth of the Mississippi, the capture of New Orleans would cut off resources from several states, including Kentucky, Tennessee, and Ohio, which were active in the attacks on Canada (Mahon 340).

Word of the British intentions reached William Claiborn, the Governor of Louisiana, through the pirate chieftain Jean Lafitte, who had been approached for assistance by the British. After several urgent requests from the governor, Major General Andrew Jackson arrived in New Orleans on December 1st, 1814 (Horsman 237).

Jackson established fortifications and reinforced forts in the region of New Orleans. Gunboats were placed in Lake Borgne and Lake Pontchartrain to the north, two of the most likely routes of attack (Carter 114). On December 12th, only 11 days after Jackson had arrived in New Orleans, the small boats of the British fleet, under the command of Admiral Alexander Cochrane, entered Lake Borgne. The British had completely destroyed all five American boats by December 14th. On the 23rd, after they had finished their lengthy disembarkation, the British forces captured the plantation of Jacques Villere on the Mississippi and encamped there, less than seven miles away from New Orleans (Horsman 240).

> Eric gives a detailed account of events leading up to the battle, drawing on a variety of sources.

Jackson quickly attacked the British but with equivalent casualties on either side (Hickey, *Forgotten Conflict* 209), and on December 24, he retreated two miles to take up position behind a small canal (Horsman 240). The canal was widened and deepened and a large earthwork, or rampart, was placed on the upper bank, where the American forces would make their stand. Slaves, militia, regulars, and even Jean Laffite's pirates labored side by side with shovel and pick to form these ramparts, which were to prove vital to the American side in the coming battle (Carter 188).

In the meantime, the British received reinforcements from Jamaica led by Major-General Edward Pakenham (Carter 192). After bringing up a quantity of artillery and then watching it destroyed by American fire, Pakenham decided to wait until further reinforcements arrived to try again (Lord 330–31). Until the troops of General Lambert, 1,700 in all, arrived on January 6, the British were mostly idle (Carter 239). Jackson used the time to shore up the rampart, which was by this time about five to eight feet tall and 20 feet thick (Tallant 145). A smaller, unfinished line, manned by fewer than one thousand troops, was established across the river (Carter 237).

The Battle of New Orleans was decided on January 8, 1815. Events unfolded on both sides of the river. Early in the morning, Colonel Thornton of the British took about 450 troops across the Mississippi River (Carter 245). The poorly armed American troops were surprised and took flight from the unfinished line into the swamps. In an address later that day to the troops on that side of the river, Jackson said, "no words can express the mortification I felt, at witnessing the scene on the opposite bank" (Jackson, Address).

The significance of the abandoned position may be disputed. Some historians describe it as poorly placed. Jackson saw things in a different light. Writing to Madison on the day of the battle, Jackson noted that "This unfortunate rout had totally changed the aspect of affairs." Once the British occupied the other side of the river, he said, "they occupied a position from which they might annoy us without hazard, and by means of which they might have been able to defeat, in great measure, the effects of our success on this side of the river." Jackson reported that he immediately began to prepare to dislodge the British from the new position. Fortunately, the British simply withdrew from the position during a cease-fire. "I need not tell you with how much eagerness I immediately regained possession of the position he had thus hastily quitted" (Jackson, Letter 9 January 1815). While Jackson's perspective may have been distorted by the rush of events, he clearly assigned great value to the position.

The main conflict, in any case, was on the other side of the river. There, the British strategy was to advance three columns of soldiers to the American line. Sent ahead of the other troops, the 44th Regiment was put in charge of carrying the ladders and equipment for climbing the rampart. Half of the regiment would put them in place, while the other half would provide covering fire. It was not an easy plan to execute, as events would soon show (Carter 242).

At daybreak, a single rocket was fired: the call to attack. The three columns, under Generals Gibbs, Keane, and Rennie, began to advance on the American line. The main column under Gibbs halted because the men of the 44th had not yet managed to get the heavy ladders in place. Suddenly,

> Eric cites sources on his Works-Cited list properly, following MLA style.

> Eric contrasts different views of the same event, noting why a primary source—Jackson's letter—might give an evaluation different from that of later commentators.

> Although his main concern is accuracy, Eric also adds drama to his narrative.

the fog lifted, leaving the troops in plain view of the American line. The Americans began to fire, and the British lines began to falter (Lord 336).

Rennie, in charge of the column nearest to the river, moved toward the far right end of Jackson's line. Decimated by American fire, they pressed on nonetheless, taking cover 50 feet from the main line (Carter 255). Keane, in the center column, was supposed to support whichever of the other columns needed help. He regrettably chose to move toward Gibb's column, which was in dire straits indeed. Had he moved toward Rennie's column, they probably would have broken through the line. The British pressed valiantly on, but most fell before they even came close to the American line (Carter 258 and Lord 336). The British fled the field. The Americans launched no counterattack, content to let the defeated foe withdraw unopposed.

Though Andrew Jackson steeled himself for another attack (Jackson, Letter, 9 January 1815), it never came. General Lambert, now in command of the entire British force, decided not to bring the reserves up from the rear. Thornton returned to headquarters, excited by his capture of the American position on the other side of the river, but Lambert decided not to push on the opposite bank. Supplies were running low and Lambert, despite Admiral Cochrane's suggestion of another attack, decided to retreat permanently. The British left Louisiana on February 4 and never returned.

In the heat of battle, Jackson's estimate of the importance of the position captured by Thornton may have been exaggerated. If his estimate was correct, however, then Lambert may have made a major error in withdrawing.

While General Jackson sincerely felt that the victory was a "blessing from heaven," it was as much due to the ineptitude of the British commanders, four of whom—Rennie, Gibbs, Keane, Pakenham—paid for their strategic mistakes with their lives (Mahon 366–369). If there could be any blessing from such a tragedy, perhaps it lay in the future, for this was to be the last time that Americans and English would ever fire on each other as enemies.

Works-Cited List

Carter, Samuel. *Blaze of Glory: The Fight for New Orleans.* New York: St. Martin's Press, 1971.

Hickey, Donald R. *The War of 1812: Forgotten Conflict.* Chicago: University of Illinois Press, 1989.

Horsman, Reginald. *The War of 1812.* London: Eyre & Spottiswoode, 1969.

Jackson, A. Address to His Troops. 8 January 1815. 4 April 2000 <http://www.hillsdale.edu/dept/History/Documents/War/America/1812/South/1815-Jackson.htm>.

Letter to the Secretary of War. 9 January 1815. 4 April 2000 <http://www.hillsdale.edu/dept/History/Documents/War/America/1812/South/1815.01.09-Jackson.htm>.

Lord, Walter. *The Dawn's Early Light.* New York: W.W. Norton & Co., 1972.

Mahon, John K. *The War of 1812.* Gainesville: University of Florida Press, 1972.

Tallant, Robert. *The Pirate Lafitte and the Battle of New Orleans.* New York: Random House, 1951.

Using a variety of sources, Eric reconstructs the details of the battle.

Eric clearly states his conclusions in his final paragraph.

Eric provides a complete, detailed, and properly formatted list of all the works he has cited in his report.

Eric follows MLA style, a standard citation style, in citing his primary sources.

Drafting

Establish your organizational plan. Decide whether you will present conclusions about your sources as part of your introduction or build toward them throughout the paper. Use one of the plans in this chart.

Write an effective introduction.
Use the opening paragraph to set the stage and establish the overall direction. Introduce the issue, and clarify background details such as time, place, and relevant political and social conditions.

Use sources well. As you draft, use a mix of paraphrases and direct quotations. Do not string quotes together without interpretation.

Analyze sources. When discussing different versions of an event or when introducing special evidence, describe your sources. Explain the differences among them or their unique perspective by analyzing the writers' circumstances and motives.

Document your information. As you draft, underline sentences for which you will need to cite sources. Include notes identifying the sources you will credit. After you finish drafting, format citations according to a standard format, such as MLA style.

Effective Organizations	
Introduction	**Introduction**
present historical context give thesis statement DRAW CONCLUSION	present historical context establish issue in thesis statement
Body	**Body**
PROVE CONCLUSION present/analyze/compare sources	present/analyze/compare sources LEAD TO CONCLUSION
Closing	**Closing**
summarize	DRAW CONCLUSION

Revising

Revise to give proper credit. Commonly known facts need not be credited within the body of the paper, but lesser-known facts, as well as quotations and writers' opinions, should be.

1. Have a partner read your draft and mark any statements that must be documented with the source of the information.

2. Add additional credits as needed.

3. Reread your draft. Combine and condense information as needed to avoid excessive or repetitious references.

Model: Marking for Complete Citations

Jackson quickly attacked the British but with equivalent

(Hickey, *Forgotten Conflict* 209),

casualties on either side, and on December 24, he retreated

(Horsman 240).

two miles to take up position behind a small canal.

> These specific factual claims, which are not common knowledge, require a cited source.

Revise to establish validity and reliability of sources. Make sure that you give enough information in your text about each source to establish its credibility and relevance and to show the perspective it represents.

Vague: Joseph Hebergram testified about child labor practices.

Stronger: *Sixteen-year-old* Joseph Hebergram testified *before the Sadler Committee about his own experiences as a child worker.*

Publishing and Presenting

Prepare your Works-Cited list. Your paper is ready for presentation only after you add your Works-Cited list, an alphabetical list of all of the sources cited in your paper, properly formatted. Follow MLA or another widely accepted style to assemble the list. (See pages R30—R31 for more guidance.) The list should appear at the end of your paper. Note that some teachers prefer a bibliography in which you list all the sources you consulted during your research.

Present your report orally. Use your report as the basis of an oral presentation. Follow these suggestions:

- Review your paper beforehand so that your delivery is smooth.
- Pace your speech. Speak slowly enough to give listeners a chance to understand and follow your points, without dragging.
- As you present, project your confidence in the potential interest of your topic to listeners.
- Vary your voice and tone when presenting primary sources, giving expression to the feelings the source may show.
- Share photos and other graphics by enlarging them or circulating them to the class.

 Prentice Hall Writing and Grammar Connection: Chapter 13

Rubric for Self-Assessment

Evaluate your research paper using the following criteria and rating scale:

Criteria	Rating Scale				
	Not very				Very
How clear and accurate a summary is the thesis statement?	1	2	3	4	5
How clear and well-documented is the presentation of the event?	1	2	3	4	5
How effectively are source materials analyzed and compared?	1	2	3	4	5
How strong are the conclusions about the event?	1	2	3	4	5
How complete and accurate are the citations and Works-Cited list?	1	2	3	4	5

Listening and Speaking WORKSHOP

Delivering a Persuasive Speech

A **persuasive speech** is one intended to alter listeners' views and to persuade them to take action. Use the strategies presented in this workshop and the chart below to prepare and deliver a persuasive speech.

Preparing Your Argument

To begin, identify the goals of your speech and the techniques you will use to accomplish them.

Identify your persuasive goals. To bring listeners to take a specific action, you may need to persuade them about facts, encourage them to accept a certain judgment, or bring them to feel a certain way about the issue. Use a chart like the one shown to identify the goals you need to accomplish in your speech.

Choose the appropriate persuasive techniques. In order to achieve each of your persuasive goals, you must choose an effective technique. Persuasive techniques include these:

- **Inductive reasoning**—Forming generalizations based on a selection of representative cases
- **Deductive reasoning**—Applying a general principal to a specific case to draw a conclusion
- **Parallelism**—Repeating sentence patterns or grammatical structure to build persuasive force
- **Imagery**—Using descriptive language to paint a scene, set a tone, or suggest an emotion
- **Irony**—Using words or contrasts in a situation to bring an audience to recognize surprising or amusing contradictions

Persuasive Goals and Techniques

- **What facts do you need your audience to recognize?**

  Techniques to Accomplish Goal:

- **What judgments or opinions do you want them to share?**

  Techniques to Accomplish Goal:

- **What emotional reactions do you want to encourage in them?**

  Techniques to Accomplish Goal:

- **What action do you want them to take?**

  Techniques to Accomplish Goal:

Delivering Your Speech

One of the most important persuasive tools you can use is yourself— your manner of engaging with the audience and presenting yourself. When you are giving your speech, remember to do the following:

- Establish eye contact with the audience to convey sincerity and hold audience members' attention.
- Use a confident but courteous manner. Speaking shyly or too aggressively will draw attention away from your point and place it on you.
- Speak slowly for emphasis of a serious point.

Activity:
Prepare and Deliver Choose a topic for a persuasive speech. Gather support, and draft your speech, using at least three of the techniques listed above. Deliver your speech to the class.

Assessment WORKSHOP

Paired Passages

In some tests, you are asked to read paired passages and answer questions comparing them. Use these strategies for such questions:

- Note the similarities and differences between the two passages.
- Write a one-sentence summary of each.

Test-Taking Strategy

Remember to review the information presented in *both* passages before answering a question.

Sample Test Item

Directions: Read the passages, and then answer the question that follows.

Passage 1

Some argue that hunters interfere with nature. On the contrary, hunters are not disruptive; they help keep animal populations healthy. Wild animals become too numerous when they lack natural predators. Hunting is a humane practice that quickly kills animals that would otherwise die of starvation.

Passage 2

The number of game hunters has declined. About 20 percent of the hunters who stopped hunting quit because they believe it is wrong. Some object to the killing of animals for decorative purposes. Other ex-hunters are repelled by the prevalence of guns and violence in society.

1. What is the relationship between the main ideas of the two passages?

A They offer opposing moral views.

B They address different aspects of hunting.

C They discuss people's positions on hunting.

D They contrast the motives of hunters and ex-hunters.

Answer and Explanation

The correct answer is *C.* Answer *A* is incorrect because Passage 2 does not take a moral position on hunting. *B* is too general. *D* is incorrect because Passage 1 does not discuss hunters' motives.

▶ Practice

Directions: Read the passages. (The first is from "The Way to Rainy Mountain" by N. Scott Momaday. The second is from Elie Wiesel's acceptance speech for the Nobel Peace Prize.) Then, choose the letter of the best answer to the question that follows.

Passage 1

I returned to Rainy Mountain in July. My grandmother had died in the spring, and I wanted to be at her grave. She had lived to be very old and at last infirm. Her only living daughter was with her when she died, and I was told that in death her face was that of a child.

Passage 2

I remember: it happened yesterday or eternities ago. A young Jewish boy discovered the kingdom of night. I remember his bewilderment, I remember his anguish. It all happened so fast. The ghetto. The deportation. The sealed cattle car. The fiery altar upon which the history of our people and the future of mankind were meant to be sacrificed.

1. These passages are similar because

A both involve death.

B both involve injustices done to others.

C both authors feel a need to remember.

D (*A* and *C*)

The City Rises, 1911, (tempura on card). Umberto Boccioni. Jesi Collection, Milan

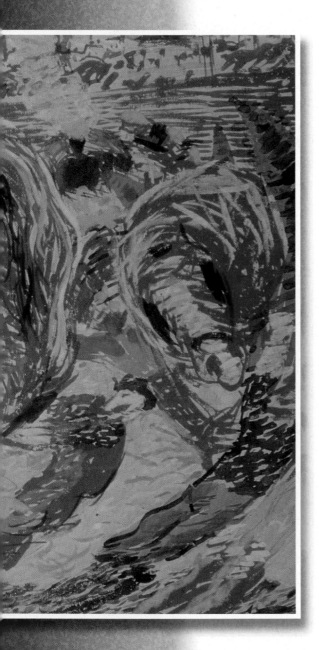

** ❝ *We are living at one of the great turning points of history. . . . Yesterday, we split the atom. We assaulted that colossal citadel of power, the tiny unit of the substance of the universe. And because of this, the great dream and the great nightmare of centuries of human thought have taken flesh and walk beside us all, day and night.* ❞**

— Doris Lessing,
from "The Small, Personal Voice"

Timeline 1901–Present

British Events

- **1901** Edward VII becomes king.
- **1902 Joseph Conrad** publishes *Heart of Darkness*.
- **1914** Britain enters World War I. ▼

British Women! — the Royal Air Force needs your help

as CLERKS, WAITRESSES, COOKS, experienced MOTOR CYCLISTS & in many other capacities. Full particulars from the nearest EMPLOYMENT EXCHANGE. ENROL AT ONCE IN THE

W·R·A·F.
WOMEN'S ROYAL AIR FORCE

- **1918** Women over thirty achieve right to vote.

- **1922** Irish Free State formed.
- **1922 T. S. Eliot** publishes *The Waste Land*.
- **1922 James Joyce** publishes *Ulysses*.
- **1939** Britain enters World War II. ▼
- **1940 Winston Churchill** becomes prime minister.

- **1945 George Orwell** publishes *Animal Farm*.
- **1947** India and Pakistan gain independence.
- **1949** Irish Free State becomes Republic of Ireland. ▲
- **1952** Elizabeth II becomes queen.
- **1954** Roger Bannister breaks four-minute mile. ▶

World Events

- **1903** Orville and Wilbur Wright build first successful airplane.
- **1905** Germany: Albert Einstein proposes theory of relativity.
- **1917** Austria: Sigmund Freud publishes *Introduction to Psychoanalysis*.
- **1917** Russia: Czar overthrown; Bolsheviks seize power.

- **1920** India: **Mohandas Gandhi** leads nonviolent protests.
- **1927** United States: Charles Lindbergh flies solo to Paris.
- **1939** Europe: Hitler invades Poland; World War II begins.
- **1941** United States: Japan bombs Pearl Harbor; United States enters World War II.

- **1945** Japan: World War II ends as Japan surrenders.
- **1948** Middle East: Israel established.
- **1949** China: Mao Zedong establishes People's Republic.
- **1955** United States: Martin Luther King, Jr., leads civil rights bus boycott.
- **1957** Russia: Sputnik I, first satellite launched.

British and World Events

- **1962 Doris Lessing** publishes *The Golden Notebook*.
- **1965** Miniskirt becomes fashionable.
- **1967** The Beatles release *Sgt. Pepper's Lonely Hearts Club Band*.
- **1972** Britain imposes direct rule on Northern Ireland.

- **1975** North Sea oil production begins. ▼

- **1979** Margaret Thatcher becomes first woman prime minister. ▶
- **1979 V. S. Naipaul** publishes *A Bend in the River*.
- **1989** Parliament privatizes national electric and water companies.

- **1991 Nadine Gordimer** wins Nobel Prize for Literature.
- **1997 Tony Blair** elected Prime Minister.
- **1997** Scotland and Wales gain right to form separate parliaments.
- **1997** Hong Kong reverts from British to Chinese rule.
- **2000** Celebration of New Year's Eve in the Millennium Dome.

- **1960** Germany: Berlin Wall built.
- **1963** United States: President John F. Kennedy assassinated.
- **1964** Vietnam: American troops join fighting.
- **1969** United States: Apollo 11 lands on moon. ▲

- **1977** Africa: Djibouti, last remaining European colony, granted independence.
- **1979** Iran: Ayatollah Khomeini overthrows Shah.
- **1980** United States: Ronald Reagan elected president.
- **1989** Germany: Berlin Wall torn down; reunification of East and West Germany follows.

- **1991** Eastern Europe: Soviet Union dissolved.
- **1994** South Africa: Nelson Mandela elected president.
- **2001** Serbia: Slobodan Milosevic arrested.
- **2001** United States: Hijacked planes crash into the World Trade Center in New York and the Pentagon in Washington, D.C., on the same day. Thousands of lives are lost.

A Time of Rapid Change

THE MODERN AND POSTMODERN PERIODS (1901–PRESENT)

Historical Background

The twentieth century dawned bright with promise. Progress in science and technology was helping to make life easier and the world more comprehensible. Yet, while steady advances in communications and transportation drew the world closer together, the scourge of modern warfare soon wrenched it apart. In World War I (1914–1918) about 8.5 million soldiers died from wounds or diseases, and estimates of the total dead, civilian and military, as a result of World War II (1939–1945) vary from 35 to 60 million.

The Edwardian Age The rigid class distinctions and moral certainties of Victorian times lingered on into the Edwardian Age (1901–1910), named for Victoria's son and successor, Edward VII. However, rapid changes were beginning to undermine the customs and assumptions of the Victorian Age, changes that ranged from the widespread use of electricity to protests aimed at gaining women the vote. By the time George V was crowned in 1910, the nineteenth-century way of life was fading into memory.

Art in the Historical Context

Pablo Picasso and Modern Art

While Edwardian England was experiencing the Indian summer of the nineteenth century, men and women unknown at the time were reinventing the arts for a new era. One of the greatest of these "unknowns" was the Spanish painter Pablo Picasso.

In 1900, Picasso arrived in Paris, a center of artistic activity. There, about six years later, he devised a type of painting that critics named Cubism. It fragmented the canvas into what the art historian H. W. Janson describes as "chunks of solidified space," which seemed to resemble cubes.

▶ **Critical Viewing** (a) In your own words, tell in detail how this painting differs from a more conventional picture of the subject it portrays. (b) Explain how Picasso's Cubism might reflect changes in the pace and texture of life that were occurring at the beginning of the twentieth century. **[Connect]**

Head of a Woman, Pablo Picasso, Prado, Madrid, Spain

World War I In 1914, long-standing tensions among the nations of Europe exploded, ignited by the assassination of Austria-Hungary's archduke Francis Ferdinand. When Germany invaded neutral Belgium, Britain joined with France to stop the aggression. The people of Great Britain went to war optimistically, expecting an easy victory. Soon, however, Britons and others recoiled in horror as the realities of poison gas, massive artillery barrages, and the terrible futility of trench warfare became evident.

In 1917, in the midst of war, revolution broke out in Russia, resulting in the overthrow of the czar and the establishment of the world's first communist state, the Soviet Union. By the time the armistice was signed on November 11, 1918, other empires and monarchies had also been swept away, including imperial Germany and the Austro-Hungarian Empire. An uneasy peace followed, its harsh terms spelled out in the Treaty of Versailles.

Between the Wars The disillusioned youth of postwar Europe were known as the "lost generation." Some young people masked their lack of purpose with the pursuit of pleasure—fast cars, wild jazz, and giddy fads. Not all was disenchantment or frivolity, of course. British women age thirty and over won the right to vote in 1918, and in 1928, the voting age for all women became twenty-one, the same as that for men.

The future, however, was being determined by political developments in Europe, exhausted and desperate after the Great War. Adolf Hitler began aggressively to expand Germany's borders. However, only when Germany invaded Poland on September 1, 1939, did Britain admit that Hitler could not be stopped without violent intervention.

World War II The second of the global wars was even more destructive than World War I. Hitler's attempt to eradicate the Jewish people brought death to about 6 million Jews. The German invasion of Russia in 1941 killed soldiers and civilians by the millions. Fighting raged from Europe to North Africa, from the mountains of Burma and China to the Hawaiian Islands. Massive bombing raids turned London, Dresden, and Tokyo into infernos.

The darkest days for Britain came in 1940, when France had fallen and Britain alone bore the brunt of German air attacks. Inspired by Prime Minister Winston Churchill, Britain fought on and was joined in 1941 by two powerful allies, the United States and the Soviet Union.

Finally, in August of 1945, American atomic bombs blasted into cinder and ash two Japanese cities, Hiroshima and Nagasaki, bringing the war to a brutal and abrupt end. The death toll by then had mounted to at least four times that of World War I.

The End of an Empire In 1922, the Irish Free State, consisting of 26 of Ireland's 32 counties, had won independence from Britain. After World War II, the British Empire suffered further dramatic losses. In Asia and Africa, nationalist leaders challenged colonial rule and gained freedom for their people. Unfortunately, ethnic, racial, and border conflicts led to bloodshed in many of the newly independent former colonies. On the

Gas Mask

▲ **Critical Viewing**
Gas masks such as this one were a standard part of a soldier's equipment during World War I. What does the look of this mask suggest about the war? **[Draw Conclusions]**

Continent, British power declined sharply, and an "iron curtain" divided Eastern and Western Europe. The United States and the Soviet Union now dominated the world.

However, by the 1960s, Britons had apparently put many of their troubles behind them. From rock music to "mod" clothing, Britain influenced fashions around the world. However, basic industries—textiles, steelmaking, shipbuilding—that had been vital to Britain were no longer competing successfully. Factories were forced to close their gates.

British society was also changing rapidly in a number of ways. In the 1950s and 1960s, London's black population increased significantly as immigrants from Britain's former colonies arrived in the city. Many black Londoners settled in Brixton, an area south of the Thames River. The discrimination that they encountered triggered the Brixton riots of April 1981. Today, London's multiracial population includes Caribbean islanders, Indians, Bangladeshis, Pakistanis, and Africans.

Flapper Dancing the Charleston

Contemporary Britain Margaret Thatcher, a member of the Conservative Party and the first female prime minister, came to power in 1979 and took a fairly hands-off approach to the economy. Prosperity resulted for some, but many Britons did not benefit from "Thatcherism." She resigned her office in 1990, to be replaced by her own handpicked Conservative party successor, John Major. In 1997, however, Major was defeated by Tony Blair, the Labor candidate.

Many problems and challenges remain as Britain adjusts to a rapidly changing world. Its participation in the European Community—a trading bloc of several hundred million people—should be a benefit, but it is still in the early stages. In Northern Ireland, the Good Friday Agreement, approved in May 1998, provides for the participation of all political parties in local government. As a result, the prospects for peace have improved, but there is still the threat of sectarian violence. Wales and Scotland voted in 1997 to set up their own parliaments, and the entire nation ponders the monarchy's role in the twenty-first century.

Tradition has always been strong in Great Britain. As in previous times of trial, Britons can turn to the past as a source of pride and comfort while moving forward into the swirl and bustle of contemporary life.

Literature of the Period

Modernism and Postmodernism Modernism, with its commitment to creating new forms, was perhaps the most important artistic movement of the twentieth century. Many Modernists used images as symbols, leading to indirect, evocative work. They often presented experiences in fragments, rather than as a coherent whole.

The Postmodernist period in English literature refers to the time from 1965 to the present. It has been characterized by what critics William Harmon and C. Hugh Holman call "continuance and completion." However, dramatists like Harold Pinter and Tom Stoppard have experimented significantly with dialogue, sequencing, and the relationships between literature and reality. Pinter's repetitious, enigmatic dialogue, for example, creates a strangely mixed aura of absurdity and menace. In his play *Betrayal*, he reverses the usual plot sequence by tracing a relationship from its end to its beginning.

Modernism and Poetry Modernism in poetry developed with the Imagist movement, founded about 1912 by Americans Ezra Pound and Hilda Doolittle (H.D.) in collaboration with Britons Richard Aldington and F. S. Flint. Imagists stressed the use of precise visual images and unadorned, concise language.

Under the influence of Ezra Pound, William Butler Yeats (1865–1939) adopted the clearer language advocated by the Imagists. Yeats, whose work spans several literary eras, was perhaps the greatest twentieth-century poet. During the heyday of Modernism, he achieved the directness and drama that inform his powerful, visionary works. However, the preeminent Modernist poet was T. S. Eliot (1888–1965), an American who went to live in Britain. Eliot's poem *The Waste Land* (1922) not only reflects the despair of the period after World War I, but also makes daring use of a collage of "voices" to link the present with the past. This experimental technique was, in a way, similar to the Cubist collages that Picasso and others assembled and painted after 1910.

Georgian Poets and War Poets The Georgian poets—who included Robert Graves (1895–1985), Edmund Blunden (1896–1974), and Walter de la Mare (1873–1956)—named themselves for George V, the reigning British monarch at the time the group was formed (1911). The Georgians rebelled against what

▼ **Critical Viewing**
During "the Blitz," which lasted from September, 1940, to May, 1941, German planes dropped bombs on London almost every night. Name two reasons why people would have taken shelter in subways during air raids.
[Infer]

Scenes from the Blitz: Londoners Sheltering in Underground Station

Point /Counterpoint

World War I Poets: "Not the Best" or a Valuable Resource?

Two critics debate whether the poets who experienced and wrote about the horrors of World War I were simply "not the best . . . of their time" or continue to be a valuable resource for literature.

"Not the Best" ". . . the poets involved in the First World War were not the best, perhaps, of their time, though it is always possible that, had they survived, Owen and even Sorley might have been. But as it is, the map read differently. What Pound and Eliot and Yeats had begun before the war they continued after it: a revolution in English poetry that leaves both unreformed and reformed Georgians in the loop of a by-pass. Owen and Jones and Graves are of sufficient stature to endure, but it could hardly be claimed that they influenced many successors. . . . In general they have had admirers rather than imitators. . . . In a not altogether rhetorical sense, all poetry written since 1918 is war poetry; and Yeats and Eliot and Auden have contributed more to it than Rosenberg or Blunden, or even than Owen and David Jones."

—Francis Hope, "Tommy's Tunes,"
The Review, No. 15 (April 1965)

A Valuable Resource "It is true that Eliot and Pound (and in a different way, Yeats) leave the war poets 'in the loop of a by-pass,' if the Eliot-Pound direction is regarded as the only desirable way forward for English poetry; but only someone totally committed to such a direction would see the poets as trapped in a disused by-pass. Francis Hope would seem to believe that not only did the war poets have few 'followers' but that, apart from the three he mentions, they are not of 'sufficient stature' (the cliché suggests the dead weight of the evaluating attitude) 'to endure.' Yet easy and obvious connections can be made between Rosenberg and Keith Douglas, between Edward Thomas and Alun Lewis. . . . Francis Hope's mild fanaticism would . . . disregard [the war poets] . . . at a time when we are in need of as much vitality . . . as we can find."

—John Silkin, *Out of Battle:
The Poetry of the Great War*

they regarded as the self-consciously knowing air of Victorian poetry. They published several anthologies in the years before Eliot's *Waste Land* appeared, but as a result of Eliot's Modernist triumph, the work of these poets fell into neglect. Some critics have argued, however, that such notable war poets as Wilfred Owen (1893–1918) and Edward Thomas (1878–1917) were Georgians.

In addition to Owen and Thomas, poets who wrote about and died in World War I include Rupert Brooke (1887–1915), Isaac Rosenberg (1890–1918), and Charles Hamilton Sorley (1895–1915). Poets who survived the conflict are Robert Graves (1895–1985), David Jones (1895–1974), and Siegfried Sassoon (1886–1967).

Auden and Others In the 1930s and 1940s, such poets as W. H. Auden (1907–1973), Louis MacNeice (1907–1963), and Stephen Spender (1909–1995) showed an increasing concern with political and social issues, though they did not abandon subtle symbolism and imagery. By contrast, Romanticism flared into wild brilliance in the poetry of Dylan Thomas (1914–1953).

During the 1950s and 1960s, British poets of "the Movement"—such as Philip Larkin (1922–1985), Donald Davie (1922–1995), and Thom Gunn (b. 1929)—rebelled against the type of Romanticism that Thomas expressed. They tried to capture everyday experiences in colloquial, yet tightly wrought, language.

The Crossword Puzzle David Hockney

Although she was born at about the same time as poets of the Auden generation and published her *Selected Poems* in 1962, Stevie Smith does not fit into any group. Called an "acrobat of simplicity" by Muriel Rukeyser, Smith gave her shrewdly childlike poems the feel of popular songs and nursery rhymes.

Noteworthy British poets of recent years, such as Ted Hughes (1930–1998), Peter Redgrove (b. 1932), and the Irish-born Seamus Heaney (b. 1939) display a visionary intensity. Penelope Shuttle (b. 1947) has written poetry that spins "fairytalelike" fantasies or looks attentively at the smallest events in nature. Two remarkable poets from former British colonies in the West Indies are James Berry (b. 1925), a Jamaican, and Nobel Prize-winner Derek Walcott (b. 1930), from the island of St. Lucia.

Twentieth-Century Drama George Bernard Shaw (1856–1950) dominated late Victorian, Edwardian, and early modern drama. His witty plays manage to evoke laughter while examining social issues. Influenced by the Irish Literary Revival, John Millington Synge (1871–1909) vividly captures Irish rural life in plays like *The Playboy of the Western World* (1907). In the depression years of the 1930s, Noel Coward (1899–1973) won attention with a series of smartly sophisticated dramas and musicals.

Angry Young Men and Absurdists In the 1950s and 1960s, a group of dramatists known as Britain's "angry young men," which included John

▲ **Critical Viewing**
British-born David Hockney's paintings and art works are groundbreaking and influential. (a) How does Hockney's use of photographs in this piece "break up" images? (b) What does this "breaking up" suggest about the relation between still images and time? (c) Why did he match this technique with a crossword puzzle as his subject? **[Speculate]**

Osborne, used realistic techniques in plays attacking the injustices of Britain's class system. A second strain of contemporary British drama, the theater of the absurd, uses disconnected dialogue and action to depict life itself as a pointless series of misfortunes. Dublin-born Samuel Beckett (1906–1989), author of *Waiting for Godot* (1952), pioneered this type of work, which has also influenced Harold Pinter (b. 1930) and Tom Stoppard (b. 1937).

Twentieth-Century Fiction The Edwardian Age produced a number of brilliant writers of realist and naturalist fiction. Joseph Conrad, one of the pioneers of psychological realism, examines internal conflicts and themes of courage and loyalty in tales like *Lord Jim* (1900), as well as issues of colonialism and injustice in *Heart of Darkness* (1902). D. H. Lawrence (1885–1930) unleashes a savage hatred of conventional British manners and morals in his novels, among them *Sons and Lovers* (1913). E. M. Forster opposes the hypocrisies of society in a gentler fashion in such novels as *A Passage to India* (1924).

Perhaps the greatest pioneer of Modernist fiction was the Irish writer James Joyce (1882–1941). Joyce revolutionized the form and structure of both the short story and the novel. His brilliant novel *Ulysses* (1922) contains a great variety of innovative techniques, including stream of consciousness—the technique of immersing readers in the associational, disjointed flow of one or more characters' thoughts—and the use of myth to structure everyday occurrences. The novelist Virginia Woolf (1882–1941) also uses stream of consciousness, in novels like *To the Lighthouse* (1927).

Political and social issues gained attention among novelists like Aldous Huxley (1894–1963) and George Orwell (1903–1950) in the 1930s and 1940s. Huxley's *Brave New World* (1932) and Orwell's *1984* (1949) paint frightening pictures of the future based on the present. Two of Britain's most popular novelists are Graham Greene (1904–1991), author of *The Power and the Glory* (1940), and P. G. Wodehouse (1881–1975), a brilliant humorist. More recent British novelists include William Golding (1911–1993), who won the Nobel Prize for Literature in 1983; Anthony Burgess (1917–1993); Kingsley Amis (1922–1995); John Fowles (b. 1926); and Alan Sillitoe (b. 1928).

In literature, as in other aspects of British life, women have been highly visible and productive in recent decades. Irish-born Iris Murdoch (1919–1999) is known for her intricate novels exploring human relationships, among them *The Message to the Planet* (1989). Doris Lessing (b. 1919) grew up in Rhodesia (now Zimbabwe) and has gained fame for a series of novels set in Africa, including *The Four-Gated City* (1969). Nobel Prize-winner Nadine Gordimer (b. 1923) writes novels and short stories that examine the moral and political dilemmas of racially divided South Africa, where she lives.

Canada Tower, London,Corbis

▲ **Critical Viewing**
This glass-and-steel office building has left its mark on contemporary London. Compare and contrast it with more traditional images of the city. **[Compare and Contrast]**

From Former Colonies In more recent years, a number of talented writers from what used to be the far-flung British Empire have enriched English literature. Among these are Frank Sargeson (1903–1982) of New Zealand; Patrick White (1912–1990), the Nobel Prize-winner from Australia; Wilson Harris (b. 1921) of Guyana; Chinua Achebe (b. 1930) and Nobel Prize-winner Wole Soyinka (b. 1934), both of Nigeria. V. S. Naipaul (b. 1932), a writer from the island of Trinidad, has achieved success with both fiction and nonfiction. The award-winning novel *In a Free State* (1971) is one of his finest works.

These ex-colonial writers are busy making classics for a new age. Borrowing a famous line from Shakespeare's *The Tempest*, we can say that they are transforming English literature "into something rich and strange."

A Living Tradition

Seamus Heaney Summons Joyce's Ghost

To serve the future, writers draw from the past, studying the works of their predecessors. However, writers can also summon the ghosts of their dead colleagues—not with a séance, but with words. That is exactly what contemporary Irish poet Seamus Heaney does when he wants advice from his great Modernist forbear James Joyce. At the end of "Station Island," a long poem that is "a sequence of dream encounters with familiar ghosts," Heaney gets some emphatic wisdom about writing from Joyce's apparition.

from "Station Island," XII

His voice eddying with the vowels of all rivers
came back to me, though he did not speak yet,
a voice like a prosecutor's or a singer's,

cunning, narcotic, mimic, definite
as a steel nib's° downstroke, quick and clean,   °pen point's
and suddenly he hit a litter basket

with his stick, saying, "Your obligation
is not discharged by any common rite.°   °ritual
What you must do must be done on your own

so get back in harness. The main thing is to write
for the joy of it. . . .

let others wear the sackcloth and the ashes.°   °symbols of
Let go, let fly, forget.   repentance
You've listened long enough. Now strike your note."

THE CHANGING ENGLISH LANGUAGE

Britspeak, A to ZED

BY RICHARD LEDERER

At the end of World War II, Winston Churchill tells us, the Allied leaders nearly came to blows over a single word during their negotiations when some diplomats suggested that it was time to "table" an important motion. For the British, table meant that the motion should be put on the table for discussion. For the Americans it meant just the opposite—that it should be put on the shelf and dismissed from discussion.

This confusion serves to illustrate the truth of George Bernard Shaw's pronouncement that "England and America are two countries divided by a common language." Or, as Oscar Wilde put it, "We have really everything in common with America nowadays, except, of course, language." Wilde made this comment when he heard that audiences in New York weren't queuing up to see his plays. Instead, they were waiting in line.

SEPARATED BY THE SAME LANGUAGE

Many of the most beguiling misunderstandings can arise where identical words have different meanings in the two cultures and lingoes. When an American exclaims, "I'm mad about my flat," he is upset about his tire. When a Brit exclaims, "I'm mad about my flat," she is not bemoaning the "puncture" of her "tyre"; she is delighted with her apartment.

British	American
gangway	aisle
hair grip	bobby pin
ironmonger	hardware store
serviette	napkin
fortnight	two weeks
zed	the letter $\underline{Z}$ [pronounced-zē]
prawn	shrimp

When a Brit points out that you have "a ladder in your hose," the situation is not as bizarre as you might at first think. Quite simply, you have a run in your stocking.

Our buses are their coaches. When a hotel in the British Isles posts a large sign proclaiming, "No football coaches allowed," the message is not directed at the Don Shulas and Joe Paternos of the world. *No football coaches allowed* means "No soccer buses permitted."

With the increasing influence of film, radio, television, and international travel, the two main streams of the English language are rapidly converging like the streets of a circus (British for "traffic circle"). Nonetheless, there are scores of words, phrases, and spellings about which Brits and Yanks still do not agree.

ACTIVITIES

1. If you choose to rent an automobile in the UK, with it will come a whole new vocabulary. Be sure to fill it with petrol, not gas. Investigate other differences between the words that Brits and Americans have for vehicles and roadways.

2. Define these words in American English first, then British English: biscuit, braces, chemist, chips, crisp, lift, plaster, pudding, spectacles, tin, torch.

Waking From the Dream

The Children Enter the Palace of Luxury Frederick Cayley Robinson, The Fine Art Society, London

Prepare to Read

Poetry of William Butler Yeats

William Butler Yeats (1865–1939)

The twentieth century was a time of change, marked by unprecedented world wars, revolutions, technological innovations, and a mass media explosion. Even as the winds of change threatened to sweep away old traditions, the Irish poet William Butler Yeats delved deep into his nation's mythological past for insight. Winner of the Nobel Prize for Literature in 1923, Yeats is generally regarded as one of the finest poets of the century. His return to the past helped earn him an abiding place in the future.

Born in Dublin, Ireland, Yeats was educated there and in London. His heart lay to the west, though, in County Sligo, where he spent childhood vacations with his grandparents. In the shadow of Sligo's barren mountains, the young Yeats was immersed in the mythology and legends of Ireland. This experience led to a lifelong enthusiasm for the roots of Irish culture.

Philosophical Influences After three years of studying painting in Dublin, Yeats moved to London to pursue a literary career. He became a friend of the poet Arthur Symons, who awakened his interest in the symbolic, visionary poetry of William Blake and the delicate, musical verse of the French Symbolists. Yeats's early poems show Symbolist influences as well as an affinity with the Pre-Raphaelites, a group of nineteenth-century British painters and writers who turned to medieval art as they strove for simplicity and beauty. Symbolism, Pre-Raphaelite elements, and Irish myths combined in Yeats's first important collection of verse, *The Wanderings of Oisin*, published in 1889.

Political and Personal Influences In the 1890s, Yeats led the Irish Literary Revival, helping to establish the Irish Literary Society based in London and the Irish National Literary Society based in Dublin. He also became involved in politics and supported the movement for Irish independence from England.

Perhaps some of Yeats's political activity was spurred by his love for a beautiful Irish actress and revolutionary named Maud Gonne. This attraction lasted his entire life, but it was never reciprocated. To his sorrow—after many refusals of his marriage proposals—Gonne chose to marry a soldier. It was only many years later that Yeats himself married.

From Poetry to Plays to Poetry As the century turned, Yeats became interested in drama. He joined with his friend Lady Augusta Gregory in founding the Irish National Theatre Society. In 1892, Yeats had written *The Countess Cathleen*, a play that was to become one of his most popular dramatic works. With the acquisition and opening of the Abbey Theatre in Dublin, Yeats turned increasingly to writing plays, producing such works as *On Baile's Strand* (1904) and *Deirdre* (1907). When Yeats returned to poetry, it was with a new voice, subtler and more powerful than the one he had used before. The poems in *The Tower* (1928) show Yeats at the height of his abilities. "Sailing to Byzantium" dates from this period of his work.

Ireland's Hero In 1922, Yeats was appointed a senator of the new Irish Free State. On his seventieth birthday, he was hailed by his nation as the greatest living Irishman. Though his quarrels with the tastes and politics of middle-class Ireland were often fierce, no one could deny his stature. He continued to write up until a day or two before his death in France. One of his last poems contains his famous epitaph: "Cast a cold eye / On life, on death. / Horseman, pass by!"

Preview

Connecting to the Literature

Life turns in cycles—holidays and seasons repeat. Yeats believed that civilizations also had cycles, each lasting two thousand years.

Literary Analysis

Symbolism

In literature, a **symbol** is an image, character, object, or action that fulfills these functions:

- It stands for something beyond itself, such as a general idea.
- It gives rise to a number of associations.
- It intensifies feelings and adds complexity to meaning by concentrating these associations together.

The swans in "The Wild Swans at Coole" combine associations of beauty (they are graceful and attractive), purity (they are white), freedom (they are wild), and the eternal (they return year after year). Like other strong symbols, the swans support multiple meanings: They symbolize both the cycle of nature and the speaker's lost youth. As you read, explore the meanings of Yeats's symbols.

Comparing Literary Works

In "The Wild Swans at Coole," Yeats builds multiple meanings by contrasting two encounters with the swans, one past and one present. He weaves his symbol from personal experiences. In other poems, though, he builds multiple meanings by turning to traditional symbols, such as the mythological Sphinx in "The Second Coming." As you read, compare the types of symbols Yeats uses and consider the different effect of each.

Reading Strategy

Applying Literary Background

No poem is written in a vacuum. A writer's experiences, beliefs, and knowledge shape his or her works. As you read, **apply literary background**—information about history, literature, and the writer's life—to aid your understanding. Use a chart like the one shown.

Background

Anarchy vs. Civilization: Yeats was interested in the rise and fall of civilizations.

Phrase or Image

"Mere anarchy is loosed upon the world, . . ."

Vocabulary Development

clamorous (klam´ ər əs) *adj.* loud and confused; noisy (p. 969)

conquest (kän´ kwest´) *n.* the winning of the submission or affection of (p. 970)

anarchy (an´ ər kē) *n.* absence of government; disorder (p. 971)

conviction (kən´ vik´ shən) *n.* belief; faith (p. 971)

paltry (pôl´ trē) *adj.* practically worthless; insignificant (p. 973)

artifice (ärt´ ə fis) *n.* skill; the product of skill, especially a skillfull deception (p. 974)

Her Signal, Norman Garstin, The Royal Cornwall Museum, Truro

▲ **Critical Viewing** The mood in "When You Are Old" is gentle and bittersweet. What elements in this painting mirror that mood? **[Classify]**

When You Are Old

William Butler Yeats

When you are old and gray and full of sleep,
And nodding by the fire, take down this book,
And slowly read, and dream of the soft look
Your eyes had once, and of their shadows deep;

5   How many loved your moments of glad grace,
And loved your beauty with love false or true,
But one man loved the pilgrim soul in you,
And loved the sorrows of your changing face;

And bending down beside the glowing bars,
10   Murmur, a little sadly, how Love fled
And paced upon the mountains overhead
And hid his face amid a crowd of stars.

Review and Assess

Thinking About the Selection

1. **(a) Recall:** What does the speaker request of the person to whom the poem is addressed? **(b) Infer:** Who is this person?

2. **(a) Recall:** In line 7, what does the speaker claim distinguishes his love from that of others? **(b) Interpret:** Does the speaker intend this claim to inspire regret? Explain.

3. **Interpret:** What do lines 10–12 suggest about what the speaker wants his beloved to acknowledge?

4. **Draw Conclusions:** What does the speaker gain by imagining the words the person addressed will "murmur"?

5. **Make a Judgment:** Do you think this poem is comforting? Why or why not?

The Lake Isle of Innisfree

William Butler Yeats

I will arise and go now, and go to Innisfree,
And a small cabin build there, of clay and wattles[1] made:
Nine bean-rows will I have there, a hive for the honeybee,
And live alone in the bee-loud glade.

5 And I shall have some peace there, for peace comes dropping slow,
Dropping from the veils of the morning to where the cricket sings;
There midnight's all a glimmer, and noon a purple glow,
And evening full of the linnet's wings.[2]

I will arise and go now, for always night and day
10 I hear lake water lapping with low sounds by the shore:
While I stand on the roadway, or on the pavements gray,
I hear it in the deep heart's core.

---

1. **wattles** stakes interwoven with twigs or branches.
2. **linnet's wings** wings of a European singing bird.

Review and Assess

Thinking About the Selection

1. **Respond:** Based on the speaker's descriptions, would you like to visit Innisfree? Why or why not?

2. **(a) Recall:** What "comes dropping slow" at Innisfree?
   (b) Infer: How does life at Innisfree contrast with the speaker's current surroundings?

3. **(a) Analyze:** What imagery in the second stanza unites the various times of day? **(b) Analyze:** What images in the last stanza unite the various places? **(c) Interpret:** What mood does this unity inspire?

4. **Draw Conclusions:** In what way does the poem itself create the feeling the speaker hopes to find in Innisfree?

5. **Compare and Contrast:** Do you think that this poem and "When You Are Old" suggest that writing poetry is a way of compensating for disappointments? Why or why not?

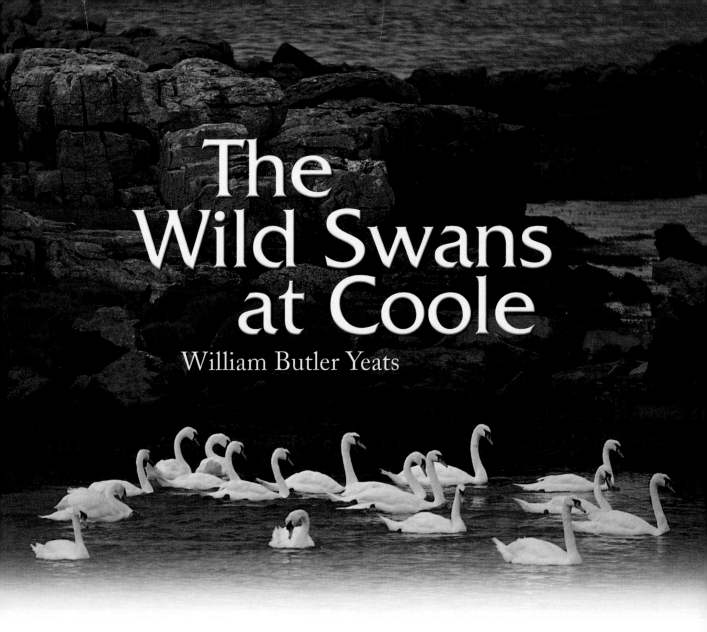

The Wild Swans at Coole

William Butler Yeats

The trees are in their autumn beauty,
The woodland paths are dry,
Under the October twilight the water
Mirrors a still sky;
5 Upon the brimming water among the stones
Are nine-and-fifty swans.

The nineteenth autumn has come upon me
Since I first made my count;
I saw, before I had well finished,
10 All suddenly mount
And scatter wheeling in great broken rings
Upon their <u>clamorous</u> wings.

▲ **Critical Viewing**
Why might Yeats describe drifting swans such as these as "mysterious" and "beautiful"? **[Infer]**

clamorous (klam´ər əs) *adj.* loud and confused; noisy

☑ **Reading Check**
How much time has passed since the speaker last saw the swans?

I have looked upon those brilliant creatures,
And now my heart is sore.
15 All's changed since I, hearing at twilight,
The first time on this shore,
The bell-beat of their wings above my head,
Trod with a lighter tread.

Unwearied still, lover by lover,
20 They paddle in the cold
Companionable streams or climb the air;
Their hearts have not grown old;
Passion or <u>conquest</u>, wander where they will,
Attend upon them still.

25 But now they drift on the still water,
Mysterious, beautiful;
Among what rushes will they build,
By what lake's edge or pool
Delight men's eyes when I awake some day
30 To find they have flown away?

conquest (kän´ kwest´) *n.*
the winning of the sub-
mission or affection of

Review and Assess

Thinking About the Selection

1. **Respond:** Have you ever been moved by the sight of an animal, as the swans move the speaker? Explain.

2. **(a) Recall:** Where is the poem set? **(b) Interpret:** How does the time of year reflect the speaker's place in life?
   (c) Analyze: Which details suggest the passing of time?

3. **(a) Recall:** While the speaker is counting the swans, what do they suddenly do? **(b) Interpret:** What reflection does their action prompt in the speakers?

4. **(a) Infer:** What has changed in the speaker since he first heard the swans? **(b) Compare and Contrast:** How does the swans' condition contrast with that of the speaker?

5. **(a) Interpret:** The speaker says he will "awake some day / To find they have flown away. . . ." What event might this flight represent for him? **(b) Draw Conclusions:** How does this imagined absence increase the poignancy of the sight of the swans?

6. **(a) Interpret:** In what way does the sight of the swans help the speaker measure the passage of time? **(b) Apply:** Compare this experience with another way in which people measure the passage of time, such as viewing family photographs or videos.

The Second Coming

William Butler Yeats

▲ **Critical Viewing**
Judging from this image, what associations might Yeats be emphasizing by using a falcon as a symbol? **[Connect]**

Background

In 1925, Yeats published *A Vision*, a work that explained the mythology, symbolism, and philosophy that he strove to express in his poetry. Yeats believed that history occurs in two-thousand-year cycles, during which a particular civilization is born, grows, and decays. Each civilization then gives way to a new one that is the direct opposite of it. Yeats believed that the society of the early twentieth century was decaying and would lead to another sort of rebirth, very different from the birth of Christ. These ideas are vividly expressed in the poem "The Second Coming."

Turning and turning in the widening gyre
The falcon cannot hear the falconer;
Things fall apart; the center cannot hold;
Mere <u>anarchy</u> is loosed upon the world,
5 The blood-dimmed tide is loosed, and everywhere
The ceremony of innocence is drowned;
The best lack all <u>conviction</u>, while the worst
Are full of passionate intensity.[1]

anarchy (an´ ər kē) *n.* absence of government; disorder

conviction (kən´ vik´ shən) *n.* belief; faith

---

1. Mere . . . intensity refers to the Russian Revolution of 1917.

Surely some revelation is at hand;
10 Surely the Second Coming is at hand.
The Second Coming! Hardly are those words out
When a vast image out of *Spiritus Mundi*[2]
Troubles my sight: somewhere in sands of the desert
A shape with lion body and the head of a man,[3]
15 A gaze blank and pitiless as the sun,
Is moving its slow thighs, while all about it
Reel shadows of the indignant desert birds.
The darkness drops again; but now I know
That twenty centuries[4] of stony sleep
20 Were vexed to nightmare by a rocking cradle,[5]
And what rough beast, its hour come round at last,
Slouches towards Bethlehem to be born?

---

2. **Spiritus Mundi** (spir´ i təs mōͻn´dē) Universal Spirit or Soul, in which the memories of the entire human race are forever preserved.
3. **A . . . man** the Sphinx, a monster in Greek mythology that posed a riddle to passing travelers and destroyed those who could not answer it. The answer to the riddle was "man."
4. **twenty centuries** historical cycle preceding the birth of Christ.
5. **rocking cradle** cradle of Jesus Christ.

Review and Assess

Thinking About the Selection

1. **Respond:** Do you agree that in the modern world "Things fall apart"? Explain.

2. **(a) Recall:** In the first two lines of the poem, why does the falcon not return to the falconer, as it ordinarily would?
   (b) Analyze: Why is the image of the falcon an effective introduction to Yeats's ideas about order and innocence?

3. **(a) Recall:** At the beginning of the second stanza, what does the speaker believe is at hand? **(b) Interpret:** What era of history might the vision in lines 11–17 represent? Explain.
   (c) Interpret: In what sense did a past birth in Bethlehem bring this era to an end?

4. **(a) Analyze:** What birth does the speaker predict will end the modern era? **(b) Draw Conclusions:** How does the traditional idea of the Second Coming differ from what the speaker is envisioning?

5. **Evaluate:** Yeats draws on his own theories of history for the theme and imagery of this poem. Why might the poem be appreciated even by readers who do not share his beliefs?

6. **Apply:** In your opinion, do any contemporary events bear out Yeats's vision of history? Explain.

Ravenna: City and Port of Classis. Mosaic, late 6th century, from Basilicia of St. Apollinare Nuovo

SAILING TO BYZANTIUM

William Butler Yeats

I

That is no country for old men. The young
In one another's arms, birds in the trees
—Those dying generations—at their song,
The salmon-falls, the mackerel-crowded seas,
5 Fish, flesh, or fowl, commend all summer long
Whatever is begotten, born, and dies.
Caught in that sensual music all neglect
Monuments of unaging intellect.

II

An aged man is but a <u>paltry</u> thing,
10 A tattered coat upon a stick, unless
Soul clap its hands and sing, and louder sing
For every tatter in its mortal dress,
Nor is there singing school but studying
Monuments of its own magnificence;
15 And therefore I have sailed the seas and come
To the holy city of Byzantium.[1]

---

1. **Byzantium** (bi zan´ shē əm) ancient capital of the Eastern Roman (or Byzantine) Empire and the seat of the Greek Orthodox Church; today, Istanbul, Turkey. For Yeats, Byzantium symbolized the world of art as opposed to the world of time and nature.

▲ **Critical Viewing** In what way do the colors and textures of this Byzantine mosaic convey the idea that the ships have arrived at a wondrous place? **[Interpret]**

paltry (pôl´ trē) *adj.* practically worthless; insignificant

✔**Reading Check**

What does his age motivate the speaker to do?

III

O sages standing in God's holy fire
As in the gold mosaic of a wall,[2]
Come from the holy fire, perne in a gyre,[3]
20 And be the singing-masters of my soul.
Consume my heart away; sick with desire
And fastened to a dying animal
It knows not what it is; and gather me
Into the <u>artifice</u> of eternity.

IV

25 Once out of nature I shall never take
My bodily form from any natural thing,
But such a form as Grecian goldsmiths make
Of hammered gold and gold enameling
To keep a drowsy Emperor awake;
30 Or set upon a golden bough to sing[4]
To lords and ladies of Byzantium
Of what is past, or passing, or to come.

artifice (ärt´ə fis) *n.* skill; the product of skill; especially a skillful deception

---

2. **sages . . . wall** wise men portrayed in mosaic on the walls of Byzantine churches.
3. **perne . . . gyre** spin in a spiraling motion.
4. **To . . . sing** Yeats wrote, "I have read somewhere that in the Emperor's palace at Byzantium was a tree made of gold and silver, and artificial birds that sang."

Review and Assess

Thinking About the Selection

1. **(a) Recall:** What do the people and things of the country referred to in the first stanza "commend"? What do they "neglect"? **(b) Interpret:** What "country" is Yeats describing in the first stanza?

2. **(a) Recall:** What is an "aged man," according to the second stanza? **(b) Interpret:** Why might the aged not belong to the "country" of the first stanza?

3. **(a) Interpret:** Why must the soul "clap its hands and sing" in line 11? **(b) Draw Conclusions:** What does the second stanza suggest about the reason people create works of art?

4. **(a) Interpret:** In the third stanza, what does the speaker ask the sages to change in him? **(b) Draw Conclusions:** What does this request reveal about the speaker's faith in artistic production?

5. **Interpret:** In the last stanza, how does the speaker hope to escape nature?

6. **Make a Judgment:** In your view, which is a "dream"— Byzantium or the world of what "is begotten, born, and dies"?

Review and Assess

Literary Analysis

Symbolism

1. (a) What associations does the speaker in "The Lake Isle of Innisfree" build around the **symbol** of Innisfree? (b) Explain two things Innisfree might symbolize.

2. Explain what the dry "woodland paths," "October twilight," and the "still sky" symbolize in "The Wild Swans at Coole."

3. (a) In "The Second Coming," what symbol does Yeats use for the era of civilization preceding Christ? (b) What multiple meanings is he able to create by not naming it directly?

4. (a) In "Sailing to Byzantium," what do the monuments in lines 8 and 14 symbolize? (b) Find two examples in this poem of Yeats's use of Byzantine art to symbolize perfection.

Comparing Literary Works

5. Using a chart like the one shown, compare the effect and meaning of the swans in "The Wild Swans at Coole" with those of the Sphinx in "The Second Coming."

Symbol:_____

Personal / Traditional	Vivid / Flat	Rich / Poor in Associations	Easy / Hard to Interpret

6. Based on Yeats's poems, do you think symbols based on personal associations, such as Innisfree, are more compelling than traditional symbols such as the Sphinx? Explain.

Reading Strategy

Applying Literary Background

7. Review the information on page 964. (a) What events in Yeats's life might have inspired "When You Are Old"? (b) What experiences might have inspired "Sailing to Byzantium"?

8. How does knowing the historical era in which Yeats wrote "The Second Coming" help you interpret the first stanza?

Extend Understanding

9. **Science Connection:** Compare Yeats's idea of historical cycles with the scientific view of time.

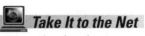

Integrate Language Skills

Vocabulary Development Lesson

Word Analysis: Latin Root -ques-

The root -ques- means "to seek or acquire." It appears in the word *conquest*, referring to "an acquisition by force." Write a definition for each word, showing how the root affects its meaning:

1. quest
2. inquest
3. request
4. question

Spelling Strategy

To form an adjective with the suffix -ous, the ending of the word base may be altered and the suffix may be spelled -eous: *instant* becomes *instantaneous* and *miscellany* becomes *miscellaneous*. Use -ous to form adjectives from the following:

1. right   2. clamor   3. beauty

Concept Development: Synonyms

In your notebook, write the letter of the word below whose meaning is closest to that of the word from the vocabulary list on page 965.

1. clamorous: (a) angry, (b) peaceful, (c) loud
2. conquest: (a) victory, (b) failure, (c) riches
3. anarchy: (a) peace, (b) systematicity, (c) disorder
4. conviction: (a) belief, (b) system, (c) violence
5. paltry: (a) magnificent, (b) trivial, (c) lying
6. artifice: (a) acquisitiveness, (b) beauty, (c) ingenuity

Grammar and Style Lesson

Noun Clauses

In his poetry, Yeats often uses **noun clauses** to connect one image or complex thought to another. A noun clause contains a subject and a verb. Noun clauses frequently begin with *how, that, who, whom, which, what, whatever, whether, whoever,* or *whomever*. A noun clause can function as subject, direct object, or object of a preposition.

Direct Object: Fish, flesh, or fowl, commend all summer long / <u>Whatever is begotten, born, and dies.</u>

Object of Preposition: . . . to sing . . . / . . . Of <u>what is past, or passing, or to come.</u>

Many noun clauses, like the ones in the examples, create a "blank" that the reader's imagination must fill in.

Practice Identify the noun clause and its function in each of the following passages.

1. Murmur, a little sadly, how Love fled. . . .
2. Dropping from the veils of the morning to where the cricket sings; . . . /
3. . . . now I know / That twenty centuries of stony sleep / Were vexed to nightmare . . .
4. It knows not what it is; . . .
5. . . . . and dream . . . / . . . / How many loved your moments of glad grace, . . .

Writing Application Write a sentence using the clause given in the function indicated.

1. What the Irish National Movement sought . . . (subject)
2. . . . that the twentieth century was a time of decay. (direct object)

Prentice Hall Writing and Grammar Connection: Chapter 19, Section 3

Writing Lesson

Response to Criticism

Scholar Reuben A. Brower wrote that Yeats succeeded "by letting his dreamlike symbols materialize to express and connect conflict he could never resolve outside his poetry." Write an essay expressing your agreement or disagreement. Supply any background information readers may need.

Prewriting Divide Brower's statement into parts—for instance, "dreamlike symbols" or "symbols expressing conflict." Under each, list examples from Yeats's poems. Then, review your notes and write your opinion of Brower's statement.

Drafting As you draft, support your evaluation with examples from the poems. Keep your audience in mind. Explain any details with which they may not be familiar.

Revising Review your essay, marking off difficult ideas or references. For each, ask yourself whether the reader needs more background. Supply any missing information.

Model: Revising to Address Knowledge Level of Readers

Yeats uses the Sphinx, a mythological figure with the body of a lion and the head of a person, to symbolize the era before Christ.

∧When Yeats describes the [Sphinx,] he creates a dreamlike image.

> The writer realizes that readers need more background on the Sphinx and so adds this sentence.

W/G Prentice Hall Writing and Grammar Connection: Chapter 14, Section 4

Extension Activities

Listening and Speaking Deliver an **oral interpretation** of one poem from each of the following Irish poets: Yeats, J. M. Synge, George Russell ("A.E."), and James Stephens.

- Focus on pacing and volume, speaking slowly and loudly enough for listeners.
- Read with the meaning of the poem in mind, finding and emphasizing words that carry the weight of each image or idea.
- Read expressively, but do not let expression overwhelm the music or sense of the verse.

Research and Technology Referring to "Sailing to Byzantium," develop three specific research questions about Byzantine society and art. Carry out your research, and develop a **visual display** presenting some of Byzantium's treasures, showing their connection to Yeats's poem and the aspects of Byzantine culture they illustrate.

 **Take It to the Net** www.phschool.com

Go online for an additional research activity using the Internet.

Prepare to Read

Preludes ◆ Journey of the Magi ◆ The Hollow Men

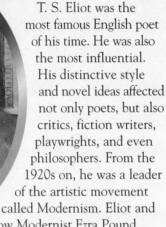

T. S. Eliot (1888–1965)

T. S. Eliot was the most famous English poet of his time. He was also the most influential. His distinctive style and novel ideas affected not only poets, but also critics, fiction writers, playwrights, and even philosophers. From the 1920s on, he was a leader of the artistic movement called Modernism. Eliot and fellow Modernist Ezra Pound transformed English-language poetry, grounding their work in the power of images rather than in individual sentiment.

Eliot's poetry is sometimes difficult to understand because it is filled with subtle, even obscure allusions to myth, history, religion, and other literature. His themes, however, are universal. In his poems, plays, and essays, he raises fundamental questions about human aspirations and the nature of civilized society.

Crossing the Atlantic Born Thomas Stearns Eliot in St. Louis, Missouri, he was educated at prestigious Harvard University. He went on to study at Oxford University in England and at the Sorbonne in Paris. The outbreak of World War I in 1914 found Eliot in England, where he lived for most of his adult life, eventually becoming a citizen of Britain.

In 1915, Eliot married the sensitive, intelligent, and witty Vivien Haigh-Wood. While writing poetry and critical reviews, Eliot taught school, worked for the banking firm of Lloyd's, and in 1925 took an editorial position with the publishing company that became Faber and Faber.

Early Work Because of its unconventional style, Eliot's earliest work was greeted with less than universal acclaim, although the American poet Ezra Pound, who was also living in England during this period, was a vocal supporter from the beginning. Pound saw that Eliot spoke in an authentic new voice and offered an original, if bleak, vision. From *Prufrock and Other Observations* (1917) through *The Waste Land* (1922) and "The Hollow Men" (1925), Eliot portrayed the modern world as one of fragmented experiences and despair. Eliot may have been responding to World War I, an event that damaged the faith of many. At the same time, the war may have prompted readers to catch up with Eliot, who had written works such as "Preludes" and "The Love Song of J. Alfred Prufrock" before the war.

A Spiritual Rebirth Eventually, Eliot found an answer to despair in religion. In 1927, he joined the Church of England and became a devout Anglican. His new faith shaped the writing of "Journey of the Magi" (1927), *Ash Wednesday* (1930), and the *Four Quartets* (1935–1943), which he completed during World War II.

As he grew older, Eliot turned his attention increasingly to poetic drama and literary criticism. Although the verse plays *Murder in the Cathedral* (1935) and *The Cocktail Party* (1950) are often performed, none of his plays have gained the critical admiration accorded his poetry. As a literary critic, though, Eliot had a profound influence on his contemporaries. His re-evaluations of past poetry shaped the tastes of a generation. In 1948, the same year in which his philosophical work *Notes Toward the Definition of Culture* appeared, Eliot received the Nobel Prize for Literature.

Poet's Corner In 1967, on the second anniversary of Eliot's death, a memorial to the poet was unveiled in the Poet's Corner of Westminster Abbey in London. In this gesture, Eliot's status as one of the most significant voices in twentieth-century English literature was confirmed in stone.

Preview

Connecting to the Literature

Long before special effects and music videos, Modernist poets were cutting rapidly from one image to another, creating dreamlike sequences rich with implied meaning. Eliot's poems are masterpieces of this technique.

Literary Analysis

Modernism

Modernism was an early twentieth-century movement in the arts, responding to the fragmented world created by mass society and industrialism. The work of Modernists is characterized by the following features:

- A new objectivity or impersonality, in which a work is built from images and allusions, not direct statements of thoughts and feelings
- A rejection of realistic depictions of life in favor of the use of images for artistic effect
- Critical attention to the spiritual troubles of modern life

In "Preludes," for example, the image "The showers beat / On broken blinds . . ." indirectly expresses the sadness of a world deprived of spiritual life. As you read, notice the Modernist characteristics of these poems.

Comparing Literary Works

Eliot applies the spirit and techniques of Modernism in various ways.

- "Preludes" juxtaposes snapshots of modern city life to convey a sense of its futility and spiritual exhaustion.
- "Journey of the Magi" takes the conventional form of a dramatic speech, yet it is also imagistic and addresses spiritual homelessness.
- "The Hollow Men" juxtaposes snapshots, not from life, but from literature. It indicts the modern lack of passion and vision.

As you read, compare what each poem shows about Modernism.

Reading Strategy

Interpreting

Modernist works may suggest themes without stating them directly. Readers must **interpret** these themes by linking different passages in a work and drawing conclusions from the patterns they find. Use a chart like the one shown to analyze patterns in the poems.

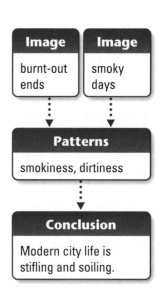

Vocabulary Development

galled (gôld) *adj.* injured or made sore by rubbing or chafing (p. 984)

refractory (ri frak´ tər ē) *adj.* hard to manage; stubborn (p. 984)

dispensation (dis´ pən sā´ shən) *n.* religious system or belief (p. 985)

supplication (sup´ lə kā´ shən) *n.* act of praying or pleading (p. 990)

tumid (tōō´ mid) *adj.* swollen (p. 991)

Modernism and Beyond

At the beginning of the twentieth century, the world woke up and discovered that it had changed. Electricity, engines, telephones, radios—the globe sizzled and crackled with new energy. Airplanes, machine guns, chemical warfare—human beings were now equipped to destroy each other with horrendous efficiency. The First World War (1914–1918) claimed ten million lives. The Russian Revolution foreshadowed deep international political changes. Disillusionment with established standards in politics and society was common.

In this climate of change and uncertainty, artists broke with the past and began to pursue new ideals and visions. They began to see themselves not just as preservers of culture but as creators of culture; they did not simply follow traditions, but participated in the creation of new ones.

The dramatic trends in the arts in the early twentieth century are collectively known as Modernism (1890–1945). For a basic grasp of Modernism, you might start with one simple modern development: the photograph.

Photographs and Images A photograph is a window into the past. When you take a photograph, you record what is happening now. Years later, the photograph will still tell you exactly what the world looked like at that moment.

Modernism could be thought of as a complex response to what photographs imply. On the one hand, Modernists such as the American poet Ezra Pound (1885–1972) and the British poet T. S. Eliot wrote poetry as if they were taking snapshots of the world and then cutting and pasting them into collages. Eliot celebrated what he called objectivity in poetry. Eliminating the outpourings of sentiment or the dramatic speeches of past poetry, he relied on images, well-chosen and artfully rendered, to encapsulate a feeling or perspective.

On the other hand, the British Modernist novelist Virginia Woolf perfected techniques for conveying an individual's moment-by-moment experience. For Woolf, the mind is like a camera filming continuously. Unlike a camera, though, her writing does not record the moment—it records what the moment looks like to an individual. In a way, her idea is the exact opposite of a photograph. A photograph shows us exactly what the world looks like; Woolf suggests that what the world looks like depends on who is looking.

Visual Arts Photography makes a good analogy for Modernist literary developments. It had a clear impact on painting. Photography now had the job of recording literal appearances, so artists were freed from the necessity of directly imitating the look of things. The revolutionary French painter Paul Cézanne (1839–1906) began to emphasize the canvas as a two-dimensional arrangement of form and color. His work led to the innovations of Modernists such as Pablo Picasso (1881–1973). In 1907, Picasso created a stir by unveiling *Les Desmoiselles d'Avignon,* the first Cubist painting—a picture in which multiple perspectives on the subject are depicted simultaneously.

Past and Present Time is a central theme of Modernism. The word *modern* comes from the Latin word *modus*, meaning "just now." The "Modern" period, then, includes any event that has recently passed. A photographer is quite "modern": He or she captures whatever has happened just now. Every moment is equal to every other, another present to be captured. Yet Eliot was deeply preoccupied with the thought that the past and present are quite unequal. In a poem like "Journey of the Magi" (p. 984), Eliot portrays the present as a time of despair, an emptiness left behind when the past has disappeared.

Modernism	Postmodernism
• Viewed the massive casualties of World War I as undercutting pretensions to rationality and civilization	• Viewed World War II, with the Holocaust and the dropping of the A-bomb, as undercutting assumptions of life's meaning
• Influenced by Freud's studies of the unconscious and a new interest in the art of primitive peoples	• Influenced by studies of media and language and by the explosive growth of information technology
• Confidence that the work of art is a unique and powerful creation with its own individual aura	• Conviction that culture endlessly duplicates and copies itself
• Belief that "high" culture and "low" culture are separated by a meaningful dividing line and that a work of fine art is inherently superior to a cartoon	• Loss of belief in the meaningful dividing line between "high" culture and "low" culture, so that in Pop Art, the subject matter of fine art can be a cartoon

Making the New At the same time that Eliot seemed to mourn the past, Modernism also turned toward the future. Modernist fiction writers broke with traditional narrative methods. Describing how characters saw their lives became more important than constructing a traditional plot, and endings were sometimes unresolved. Joseph Conrad (1857–1924), for example, a precursor to Modernist novelists, used abrupt shifts of time and space and multiple points of view, echoing Woolf's concern with the power of individual perspective to shape reality. Modernist poets, too, favored experimentation over traditional forms and rhyme schemes. Their poems draw images from a variety of sources such as history, everyday life, and other texts and cultures.

Music Around the year 1900, important changes were also taking place in music. Like Modernist literature and art, much of this music, by composers such as Arnold Schoenberg (1874–1951) and Igor Stravinsky (1882–1971), breaks with traditional ideas and prescribes its own methods for composition. In music, the power of the artist to create as well as implement rules is especially clear.

Beyond Modernism The Modernist literary movement climaxed in 1922, when both James Joyce's *Ulysses* and T. S. Eliot's *The Waste Land* were published. In ensuing decades, the arts took another turn in the developments known as Postmodernism (see chart), a movement that replaced the hopes Modernism placed on innovative artistic breakthroughs with a sometimes cynical questioning of the nature of art and perception. The Modernist legacy lives on, though, in the continuing drive for the new.

▲ **Critical Viewing**
Which themes listed on the chart are reflected in contemporary television programs? Explain your choices.
[Connect]

PRELUDES

T. S. Eliot

I

The winter evening settles down
With smell of steaks[1] in passageways.
Six o'clock.
The burnt-out ends of smoky days.
5 And now a gusty shower wraps
The grimy scraps
Of withered leaves about your feet
And newspapers from vacant lots;
The showers beat
10 On broken blinds and chimney-pots,
And at the corner of the street
A lonely cab-horse steams and stamps.
And then the lighting of the lamps.

II

The morning comes to consciousness
15 Of faint stale smells of beer
From the sawdust-trampled street
With all its muddy feet that press
To early coffee-stands.
With the other masquerades
20 That time resumes,
One thinks of all the hands
That are raising dingy shades
In a thousand furnished rooms.

III

You tossed a blanket from the bed,
25 You lay upon your back, and waited;
You dozed, and watched the night revealing
The thousand sordid images
Of which your soul was constituted;
They flickered against the ceiling.
30 And when all the world came back

Literary Analysis
Modernism What fragmented images of a city scene appear in this stanza?

---

1. **steaks** In 1910, when this poem was composed, steaks were inexpensive and were commonly eaten by members of the lower class.

And the light crept up between the shutters
And you heard the sparrows in the gutters,
You had such a vision of the street
As the street hardly understands;
35 Sitting along the bed's edge, where
You curled the papers from your hair,
Or clasped the yellow soles of feet
In the palms of both soiled hands.

IV

His soul stretched tight across the skies
40 That fade behind a city block,
Or trampled by insistent feet
At four and five and six o'clock;
And short square fingers stuffing pipes,
And evening newspapers, and eyes
45 Assured of certain certainties,
The conscience of a blackened street
Impatient to assume the world.

I am moved by fancies that are curled
Around these images, and cling:
50 The notion of some infinitely gentle
Infinitely suffering thing.

Wipe your hands across your mouth, and laugh;
The worlds revolve like ancient women
Gathering fuel in vacant lots.

Review and Assess

Thinking About the Selection

1. **Respond:** Does the poem make beauty from ugliness? Explain.

2. **(a) Recall:** In Prelude I, what is the time of year and the time of day? **(b) Interpret:** What cycle of time takes place from Prelude I to Prelude IV? **(c) Support:** What effect does the poet achieve by representing this complete cycle?

3. **(a) Draw Conclusions:** What is the character of modern life as Eliot depicts it? **(b) Compare and Contrast:** Contrast this character with "The notion of some infinitely gentle / Infinitely suffering thing" (lines 50–51)? **(c) Speculate:** Based on this contrast, what do you think the "thing" might be?

4. **Apply:** Think of a sight in a modern city that conveys joy. How might Eliot react to that image?

Journey of the Magi

T. S. Eliot

Background

In his work, Eliot often uses *allusions*—indirect references to people, places, events, or works of literature. "Journey of the Magi," for instance, is a dramatic monologue spoken by one of the three wise men ("magi") who, according to the Bible, visited the infant Jesus. In the poem, the speaker uses modern conversational language to describe events, making vividly present the spiritual agony of a man who lived long ago.

"A cold coming we had of it,
Just the worst time of the year
For a journey, and such a long journey:
The ways deep and the weather sharp,
5   The very dead of winter."[1]
And the camels <u>galled</u>, sore-footed, <u>refractory</u>,
Lying down in the melting snow.
There were times we regretted
The summer palaces on slopes, the terraces,
10   And the silken girls bringing sherbet.
Then the camel men cursing and grumbling
And running away, and wanting their liquor and women,
And the night-fires going out, and the lack of shelters,
And the cities hostile and the towns unfriendly
15   And the villages dirty and charging high prices:
A hard time we had of it.
At the end we preferred to travel all night,
Sleeping in snatches,
With the voices singing in our ears, saying
20   That this was all folly.

galled (gôld) *adj.* injured or made sore by rubbing or chafing

refractory (ri frak´ tər ē) *adj.* hard to manage; stubborn

---

1. **"A . . . winter"** Adapted from a part of a sermon delivered by 17th-century Bishop Lancelot Andrewes: "A cold coming they had of it at this time of year, just the worst time of the year to take a journey, and specially a long journey in. The ways deep, the weather sharp, the days short, the sun farthest off . . . the very dead of winter."

Then at dawn we came down to a temperate valley,
Wet, below the snow line, smelling of vegetation;
With a running stream and a water-mill beating the darkness,
And three trees on the low sky,
25 And an old white horse galloped away in the meadow.
Then we came to a tavern with vine-leaves over the lintel,
Six hands at an open door dicing for pieces of silver,
And feet kicking the empty wine-skins.
But there was no information, and so we continued
30 And arrived at evening, not a moment too soon
Finding the place; it was (you may say) satisfactory.

    All this was a long time ago, I remember,
And I would do it again, but set down
This set down
35 This: were we led all that way for
Birth or Death? There was a Birth, certainly,
We had evidence and no doubt. I had seen birth and death,
But had thought they were different; this Birth was
Hard and bitter agony for us, like Death, our death.
40 We returned to our places, these Kingdoms,
But no longer at ease here, in the old dispensation,
With an alien people clutching their gods.
I should be glad of another death.

dispensation (dis´ pən sā´ shən) *n.* religious system or belief

Review and Assess

Thinking About the Selection

1. **Respond:** Do you feel sympathy for the speaker? Explain.

2. **(a) Recall:** What event has the speaker in "Journey of the Magi" gone to witness? **(b) Compare and Contrast:** How do the descriptions of the journey compare to that of the descriptions of the event? **(c) Interpret:** Why might the speaker say so little about one and so much about the other?

3. **(a) Interpret:** How has the event changed the speaker's relation to his own people? **(b) Draw Conclusions:** Consider the speaker's own religious traditions. What does he mean when he says "this Birth was/ . . . like Death, our death." (lines 38–39)?

4. **(a) Compare and Contrast:** In what way is Eliot's choice of details similar in the first stanzas of "Preludes" and "Journey of the Magi"? **(b) Draw Conclusions:** What do you think Eliot was trying to achieve in each case?

5. **(a) Apply:** Do you think that modern society would make poets like Eliot feel as the speaker in the poem does? Explain.

Critical Commentary on "The Hollow Men"

How It Was Written

T.S. Eliot had written a long poem called *The Waste Land*. He used sections that had been edited out of *The Waste Land* as the basis for "The Hollow Men." He often worked this way, building a poem from pieces that had been written independently and using discarded fragments of one poem to create the next.

He explained this process of working in a craft interview with Donald Hall (*The Paris Review*, No. 21). Hall begins this part of the interview by pointing out that two minor poems of Eliot's, probably "Eyes that last I saw in tears" and "The wind sprang up at four o'clock," sound to him like "The Hollow Men":

Interviewer. Are any of your minor poems actually sections cut out of longer works? There are two that sound like "The Hollow Men."

Eliot. Oh, those were the preliminary sketches. Those things were earlier. Others I published in periodicals but not in my collected poems . . .

Interviewer. You seem often to have written poems in sections. Did they begin as separate poems? I am thinking of "Ash Wednesday," in particular.

Eliot. Yes, like "The Hollow Men," it originated out of separate poems. As I recall, one or two early drafts of parts of "Ash Wednesday" appeared in *Commerce* [a magazine] and elsewhere. Then gradually I came to see it as a sequence. That's one way in which my mind does seem to have worked throughout the years poetically—doing things separately and then seeing the possibility of fusing them together, altering them, and making a kind of whole of them.

The Theme of "The Hollow Men"

It makes sense to assume that "The Hollow Men," which uses fragments discarded from *The Waste Land*, is thematically related to this earlier, longer poem. *The Waste Land*, as the word "waste" in its title suggests, deals with a

sense of emotional and spiritual barrenness after the destruction wrought by World War I. (Eliot began the poem in 1921, three years after the end of the war.) Throughout the poem, however, Eliot uses allusions to past works of literature in order to compare the present with other historical moments. "The Hollow Men," published in 1925, also deals with a barren and empty (hollow) existence. Although it is quieter than *The Waste Land* and less rhythmically varied, it resembles the earlier poem in its use of literary allusions to convey this theme of barrenness and to compare the present with other historical eras.

Using Allusions to Interpret the Poem

Critics have identified four key allusions in the poem:

- Joseph Conrad's story "Heart of Darkness"
- A historical reference to the Gunpowder Plot of 1605, in which Guy Fawkes and other Catholics seeking revenge for the anti-Catholic laws under James I plotted to blow up the king and Parliament
- Shakespeare's *Julius Caesar*, with its account of the assassination of Caesar
- Dante's *Divine Comedy*, a medieval Italian poem which describes the three realms of the afterlife according to Roman Catholic belief: inferno, purgatory, and paradise

More details about these allusions appear in specific footnotes to the poem. The following information explains how to use the allusions to build meaning from this difficult work.

Joseph Conrad's "Heart of Darkness" Kurtz, referred to in a line introducing the poem, is a mysterious character in Conrad's "Heart of Darkness." He travels to the Belgian Congo on a mission to uplift and educate the Congolese people. However, he develops his own little kingdom in which he exercises absolute power over the people he intended to save. It is only when he is dying that he sees the "horror" of what he has done and how he has been, in Conrad's words, a "hollow sham," or fake. Yet Kurtz is in some ways the best of the white men that Conrad's narrator encounters. His tragic downfall, therefore, exposes the hollowness of his noble ideals and of the whole colonial enterprise. That enterprise is supported by a host of administrators and clerks who seem like ghosts wandering in a twilight world. It is these men who are most like the

speakers in Eliot's poem, a chorus of paralyzed nonentities: "We are the hollow men. . . ." Eliot may also be suggesting that this chorus includes his readers.

The Gunpowder Plot The hollow men are also like the effigies of Guy Fawkes burned to commemorate the uncovering of the Gunpowder Plot. Fawkes himself was tortured until he revealed the names of his co-conspirators. His dream of a powerful explosion that would destroy the government of England was therefore not realized. As Eliot writes at the end of the poem, "This is the way the world ends / Not with a bang but a whimper." Just as Fawkes is now only a straw figure to be burned, so the speakers of Eliot's poem are as helpless and ineffective as straw dummies: "Leaning together / Headpiece filled with straw. Alas!"

Shakespeare's *Julius Caesar* This play deals with another conspiracy to betray a leader. Brutus, a high-minded Roman, is lured by flattery into a plot to assassinate the Roman ruler Julius Caesar. Section V of "The Hollow Men" quotes lines from Shakespeare's play in which Brutus experiences the night-marelike emptiness of the time before the deed. Like Kurtz in Conrad's story, Brutus is a tragic figure, a self-deluded man who commits murder in the name of high ideals. In this sense, he too is a form of hollow man.

Dante's *Divine Comedy* Brutus is one of the betrayers that Dante punishes in the lowest circle of his inferno. The speakers in Eliot's poem are also being punished for their spiritual emptiness in a kind of inferno: a "dead land" (line 39); a "cactus land" (line 40); a "valley of dying stars" (line 54). It does not appear that these speakers will gain salvation, but Eliot uses images drawn from Dante's description of paradise to suggest the existence of higher realms: ". . . the perpetual star / Multifoliate rose . . ." (lines 63–64). "The Hollow Men" is therefore a poem about spiritual despair that contains only the slightest hints that such despair can be overcome. In terms of Dante's work, it is like an inferno (a realm of punishment) that is almost without the promise of a purgatory or a paradise.

Eliot's Theory of Tradition

Eliot's allusions create a distinctive, dreamlike world for a reader to explore. They also reflect his theory of poetry. In an essay, Eliot compares the poet to a catalyst in a chemical reaction. A catalyst adds nothing of itself, but without it, the reaction will not take place. The poet's mind is the catalyst that causes images and feelings to combine in a poem, but the poem does not necessarily reflect the poet's own life. For Eliot, a tradition of past literature was a key source of ingredients for the reaction. Eliot's allusions reflect both of these values: impersonality and tradition.

THE HOLLOW MEN

T.S. Eliot

Background

As in "Journey of the Magi," Eliot uses allusions at the beginning of "The Hollow Men" to help him contrast the past with the present. For example, "A penny for the Old Guy" is a traditional cry of children on Guy Fawkes Day. Fawkes was executed for attempting to blow up the king and Parliament on November 5, 1605. He is one of the "lost / Violent souls" of the past who contrast with the "hollow men" of today.

Mistah Kurtz[1]*—he dead.*

A penny for the Old Guy[2]

I

We are the hollow men
We are the stuffed men
Leaning together
Headpiece filled with straw. Alas!
5 Our dried voices, when
We whisper together
Are quiet and meaningless
As wind in dry grass
Or rats' feet over broken glass
10 In our dry cellar

Shape without form, shade without color,
Paralyzed force, gesture without motion;

---

1. **Mistah Kurtz** character in Joseph Conrad's "Heart of Darkness" who hopes to improve the lives of native Africans, but who finds instead that he is corrupted by his power over them.
2. **A . . . Guy** traditional cry used by children on Guy Fawkes Day (November 5), celebrating the execution of a famous English traitor of the same name. The "Old Guy" refers to stuffed dummies representing Fawkes.

✔Reading Check

How does the speaker characterize the sounds made by the hollow men?

Those who have crossed
With direct eyes, to death's other Kingdom[3]
15 Remember us—if at all—not as lost
Violent souls, but only
As the hollow men
The stuffed men.

Reading Strategy
Interpreting What pattern of images does Eliot create in lines 13–21?

II

Eyes I dare not meet in dreams
20 In death's dream kingdom
These do not appear:
There, the eyes are
Sunlight on a broken column
There, is a tree swinging
25 And voices are
In the wind's singing
More distant and more solemn
Than a fading star.
Let me be no nearer
30 In death's dream kingdom
Let me also wear
Such deliberate disguises
Rat's coat, crowskin, crossed staves
In a field[4]
35 Behaving as the wind behaves
No nearer—

Not that final meeting
In the twilight kingdom

III

This is the dead land
40 This is cactus land
Here the stone images
Are raised, here they receive
The supplication of a dead man's hand
Under the twinkle of a fading star.

45 Is it like this
In death's other kingdom
Waking alone
At the hour when we are
Trembling with tenderness
50 Lips that would kiss
Form prayers to broken stone.

supplication (sup′ lə kā′ shən) *n.* act of praying or pleading

---

3. **Those . . . kingdom** allusion to Dante's *Paradiso,* in which those "with direct eyes" are blessed by God in Heaven.
4. **crossed . . . field** scarecrows.

IV

The eyes are not here
There are no eyes here
In this valley of dying stars
55 In this hollow valley
This broken jaw of our lost kingdoms

In this last of meeting places
We grope together
And avoid speech
60 Gathered on this beach of the <u>tumid</u> river[5]

Sightless, unless
The eyes reappear
As the perpetual star[6]
Multifoliate rose[7]
65 Of death's twilight kingdom
The hope only
Of empty men.

V

Here we go round the prickly pear
Prickly pear prickly pear
70 *Here we go round the prickly pear*
At five o'clock in the morning.[8]

Between the idea
And the reality
Between the motion
75 And the act[9]
Falls the Shadow

For Thine is the Kingdom[10]

Between the conception
And the creation
80 Between the emotion
And the response
Falls the Shadow

---

5. **river** from Dante's *Inferno,* the river Acheron, which the dead cross on the
   way to Hell.
6. **star** traditional symbol for Christ.
7. **Multifoliate rose** rose with many leaves. Dante describes paradise as such
   a rose in his *Paradiso.* The rose is a traditional symbol for the Virgin Mary.
8. **Here . . . morning** adaptation of a common nursery rhyme. A prickly pear
   is a cactus.
9. **Between . . . act** reference to *Julius Caesar,* Act II, Scene i, 63–65: "Between the
   acting of a dreadful thing / And the first motion, all the interim is / Like a phantasma
   or hideous dream."
10. **For . . . Kingdom** from the ending of the Lord's Prayer.

The British Tradition

The Literary Magazine
   No institution played
a more important role
in the development of
Modernism than the literary magazine. These modest periodicals
were published on both sides of
the Atlantic. In England, Eliot
founded *The Criterion* (later
called *The New Criterion*) in 1922.
The first issue featured Eliot's celebrated poem *The Waste Land.*
In the United States, the premier
literary magazine was *The Dial.*
During the 1920s, it published
the work of Eliot, W. B. Yeats,
Ezra Pound, and D. H. Lawrence.
Another important journal, *The
Egoist,* serialized *A Portrait of
the Artist as a Young Man,* James
Joyce's first major work, in 1914
to 1915.

   These literary magazines
were grandchildren of eighteenth-
century periodicals such as
Joseph Addison's *The Spectator.*
Instead of focusing on manners
and social observations, however,
Modernist periodicals dedicated
themselves to promoting new
trends in art. The profound impact
of Eliot's work would perhaps not
have been as great if it had not
found a home in such journals.

tumid (tōō´ mid) *adj.*
swollen

✔Reading Check

To what kingdom does
the speaker refer?

Between the desire
85 And the spasm
Between the potency
And the existence
Between the essence
And the descent
90 Falls the Shadow

For Thine is the Kingdom

For Thine is
Life is
For Thine is the

95 *This is the way the world ends*
This is the way the world ends
This is the way the world ends
Not with a bang but a whimper.

---

11. Life . . . long Quotation from Joseph Conrad's *An Outcast of the Islands.*

Review and Assess

Thinking About the Selection

1. **Respond:** If you wanted to make a music video of this poem, which images from it would you use? Why?

2. **(a) Recall:** Which words are used to describe the hollow men in the first ten lines? **(b) Infer:** What do the images of wind in Parts I and II suggest about the hollow men?

3. **(a) Recall:** In Part V, what repeatedly "falls"?
   (b) Interpret: How is this action related to the poem's theme?

4. **(a) Analyze:** To what literary work and to which historical event does Eliot allude in the quotations at the beginning of the poem? **(b) Interpret:** In what way are Kurtz, a "hollow sham," and Guy Fawkes, a traitor, superior to the hollow men?

5. **Evaluate:** Do you think the nursery rhymes and other fragmented allusions that Eliot uses in Part V are effective in conveying the speakers' plight? Explain.

6. **(a) Draw Conclusions:** What overall point about the modern spiritual condition is Eliot making in the poem?
   (b) Make a Judgment: Do you think Eliot's point is fair, or do you think he is too harsh? Support your judgment.

Review and Assess

Literary Analysis

Modernism

1. Identify three images in the "Preludes" that suggest the **Modernist** view that modern life is empty. Explain your choices.

2. What Modernist qualities characterize "The Hollow Men"? Use a chart like the one shown to help you in answering.

Passage	Fragmented Images vs. Realistic Pictures	Critical of Modern Life?

3. (a) What escape from modern despair does "Journey of the Magi" suggest? (b) What despair appears in the poem?

Comparing Literary Works

4. (a) Quoting passages in support, identify two aspects of Modernism illustrated by the "Preludes." (b) Does "Journey of the Magi" also illustrate these aspects? Explain, quoting from the poem.

5. Compare the use of allusion—brief references to literature—in "The Hollow Men" with the use of images in the "Preludes." How are they similar?

6. Which poem is easiest to relate to? Explain.

7. Why might Eliot have found it necessary to turn to past literature to make a point about what is missing in the present?

Reading Strategy

Interpreting

8. (a) Find two patterns of images in the "Preludes." (b) What theme does each pattern reflect?

9. (a) In "Journey of the Magi," what pattern of images appears in the first stanza? (b) How does this pattern reinforce the idea that the journey has changed the Magi?

10. (a) Find four references to eyes in "The Hollow Men." (b) What does this pattern of images suggest about the hollow men?

Extend Understanding

11. **Cultural Connection:** To what extent does Eliot's criticism of the hollow men apply to people today? Explain.

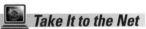

Integrate Language Skills

Vocabulary Development Lesson

Word Analysis: Latin Root -fract-

The Latin root -fract- means "to break." A refractory animal is one that "breaks away." The root -fract- appears in some scientific and mathematical terms, such as *fraction*. A fraction is a part "broken away" from a larger whole. Explain how the root -fract- contributes to the meaning of each italicized word.

1. Although her motives were good, she was guilty of an *infraction* of the law.
2. When white light is *refracted*, it produces a spectrum.
3. A *fractal* is an irregular shape made up of an infinity of irregular parts.
4. The *fractious* boys caused a good deal of trouble at school.
5. The *fracto-stratus* clouds were ragged and appeared in long, threadlike layers.

Concept Development: Analogies

Choose the word from the vocabulary list on page 979 that best completes each analogy.

1. burning : charred :: chafing : ____?____
2. category : group :: system : ____?____
3. contempt : insult :: humility : ____?____
4. knife : dull :: river : ____?____
5. prudent : thoughtless :: obedient : ____?____

Spelling Strategy

When adding a suffix to words ending in two consonants, keep both consonants. For example, adding the suffix -ed to the word *gall* forms the word *galled*. Choose from the suffixes -ed, -ment, -ship, and -ing to generate another English word from each of the following words.

1. hard	3. align	5. delight
2. content	4. swarm	6. risk

Grammar and Style Lesson

Adjectival Modifiers

Using a variety of phrases and clauses as modifiers, Eliot links diverse images. Among the structures that Eliot uses as **adjectival modifiers** are the following:

Prepositional Phrase: The burnt-out ends of smoky days. . . . (Phrase modifies *ends*.)

Participial Phrase: Headpiece filled with straw. . . . (Phrase modifies *headpiece*.)

Adjective Clause: . . . hands / That are raising dingy shades . . . (Clause modifies *hands*.)

Practice Identify the adjectival modifiers in these lines, and explain their effect:

1. "Preludes," lines 14–18
2. "Preludes," lines 26–28
3. "Journey of the Magi," lines 10–12
4. "The Hollow Men," lines 47–51
5. "The Hollow Men," lines 58–60

Writing Application Write a brief profile of the speaker in "Journey of the Magi," using a series of adjectival modifiers to describe your subject, as Eliot does. Identify the grammatical structure of each modifier.

WG *Prentice Hall Writing and Grammar Connection: Chapter 19, Sections 1–3*

Writing Lesson

Response to Criticism

In an essay, respond to the following comparison: "'Preludes' suggests humanity is trapped in a dreary, meaningless cycle of time. In 'Journey of the Magi,' Eliot's symbolic world has a new center: the Incarnation. Nevertheless, the poem's speaker is profoundly displaced. Like 'Preludes,' the poem invokes what is of highest value by showing how far from it we are."

Prewriting	Gather details from the poems concerning time and the condition of displacement or not belonging. Then, jot down a few conclusions about Eliot's attitude towards these themes.
Drafting	Begin with a general statement of your response to the quotation. As you draft, support your response with details from the poems.
Revising	Jot down a few details about each of your main points on a self-sticking note. Attach the notes to your draft, and compare each note to the paragraph it concerns. In cases where a detail appears in a note but not in the draft, consider adding it.

Model: Revising for Elaboration

"Preludes"—coarseness despair, but also an "infinitely gentle thing"

In the "Preludes," the speaker has "The notion of some infinitely gentle / Infinitely suffering thing." Similarly, ~~Just like in "Preludes,"~~ the speaker in "Journey of the Magi" has an idea of spiritual truth, but there is nothing and no one in his homeland who also recognizes this truth.

Replacing a vague assertion of similarity with a specific detail strengthens the main point.

W/*G* *Prentice Hall Writing and Grammar Connection: Chapter 14, Section 4*

Extension Activities

Listening and Speaking Is Eliot's view of modern life valid or distorted? Form teams and hold a **debate on Modernism**. Prepare arguments using

- Analogy—a comparison that explains the relationship between two things
- Induction—the derivation of a general conclusion from a sampling of specific cases

Help teammates strengthen their arguments, and then hold your debate before the class. [Group Activity]

Research and Technology Write a **cultural report** on Modernism in the visual arts. Compare Eliot's subject matter and his techniques to such Modernist developments as collage and Cubism. Incorporate reproductions of art-works in your word-processed report.

 **Take It to the Net**   www.phschool.com

Go online for an additional research activity using the Internet.

Prepare to Read

In Memory of W. B. Yeats ◆ Musée des Beaux Arts ◆ Carrick Revisited ◆ Not Palaces

W. H. Auden (1907–1973)

Much as T. S. Eliot became established as the poetic voice of the 1920s, so Wystan Hugh Auden emerged as the voice of the 1930s. As a young poet, Auden was greatly influenced by Eliot's work, particularly *The Waste Land*. He soon developed his own poetic style, however, characterized by versatility, wit, and dazzling technique.

Born in York, England, Auden had early dreams of becoming an engineer but gravitated to poetry instead. His commitment to social justice and his opposition to fascism made him a poetic spokesperson for the political left. In 1939, Auden left England for the United States, where he taught at a number of universities. He became an American citizen in 1946. From 1956 to 1960, he taught at Oxford as Professor of Poetry.

Achievements in Poetry Auden's early poems, along with works by his friends Louis MacNeice and Stephen Spender, appeared in *Oxford Poetry*, a series of annual collections of verse by the university's undergraduates. Auden's first published collection, entitled *Poems*, appeared in 1930. Full of cryptic images and references, Auden's verse struck some readers of the day as impenetrable. His more straightfoward second collection, *On This Island* (1937), generated greater enthusiasm. In 1948, Auden won a Pulitzer Prize for the collection *The Age of Anxiety*.

A Versatile Poet Auden wrote equally well in the idiom of the street or in the archaic measures of *Beowulf*. His voice is original, achieving a kind of personable intimacy even as he makes polished pronouncements on the general human condition. With Yeats and Eliot, he is among the most highly regarded British poets of the twentieth century.

Louis MacNeice (1907–1963)

Louis MacNeice was the son of a Protestant clergyman in Belfast, Northern Ireland. A gifted youth, he began to write poetry at age seven. His first collection, *Blind Fireworks*, appeared in 1929, followed six years later by *Poems*, the volume that established his reputation. During the 1930s, MacNeice taught classical literature. In 1941, he joined the British Broadcasting Corporation, writing radio plays in verse.

Today, many consider MacNeice second only to Auden among the poets of their generation. His poetry is restrained and precise, with overtones of melancholy. It is the poetry of a man who, as the poet Edwin Muir put it, "is never swept off his feet."

Stephen Spender (1909–1995)

No poet of the 1930s provided a more honest picture of the era between the wars than did Stephen Spender. Much of his early poetry deals with the world of the thirties, the "low dishonest decade" that saw the world lurch from depression to fascism to war. Yet Spender, never a pessimist, celebrates technology at the same time as he confronts the problems of industrial progress.

Born in London and educated at Oxford, Spender's first important book, *Poems* (1933), was published while he was living in Germany. A political activist, Spender promoted antifascist propaganda in Spain during its Civil War (1936–1939). He later coedited the literary magazine *Horizon* and the political, cultural, and literary review *Encounter*.

Preview

Connecting to the Literature

You just spent three hours finishing up your short story. You are tired, you are elated—but what exactly did you do? You put words on a page and moved them around until they rang true—but has all that work changed anything? These poets address similar questions about art generally.

Literary Analysis

Theme

The **theme** of a literary work is its central concern or purpose, or the central question that it raises. A poet may approach theme from these angles:

- Making direct statements expressing a theme
- Indicating a theme through word choice and imagery

In the poem "In Memory of W. B. Yeats," for example, Auden explores the link between poetry and life. Statements like "poetry makes nothing happen" (line 36) speak directly to this theme. The imagery of the "dark cold day" of Yeats's death is an indirect clue to the theme.

Comparing Literary Works

A central theme in poetry is the nature of poetry itself. Renaissance poets, for instance, wrote poems claiming that their verse immortalized their subjects. Modern poets offer a range of ideas on poetry.

- "In Memory of W. B. Yeats" suggests that poetry cannot change reality. However, by "singing" our limitations—failure, death— poetry affirms life and so causes joy.
- "Not Palaces" suggests that poems can change reality by inspiring and fueling social change.

As you read, compare the questions the poems raise about poetry.

Reading Strategy

Paraphrasing

To understand poetry, it is often helpful to **paraphrase** dense or difficult lines by restating the writer's words in your own words. This chart shows how you might paraphrase two lines from "In Memory of W. B. Yeats." Use a similar chart to paraphrase complex passages as you read.

Vocabulary Development

sequestered (si kwes´ tərd) *adj.* kept apart from others (p. 1001)

topographical (täp´ ə graf´ i kəl) *adj.* representing the surface features of a region (p. 1005)

affinities (ə fin´ i tēz) *n.* family connections; sympathies (p. 1006)

prenatal (prē nāt´ əl) *adj.* existing or taking place before birth (p. 1006)

intrigues (in trēgz´) *v.* plots or schemes (p. 1007)

Lines

"And snow disfigured the public statues; / The mercury sank in the mouth of the dying day."

Paraphrase

Snow fell all over town. The temperature fell as the day ended.

In Memory of
W. B. Yeats

W. H. Auden

▲ **Critical Viewing** Does this photograph of Yeats present him as the mortal man described in parts 1 and 2 of Auden's poem or as the great writer eulogized in part 3? **[Interpret]**

Background

The 1930s was a decade poised between a worldwide economic depression and the impending devastation of World War II. The complex concerns of the period are reflected in the poems of the Auden circle, which included Auden himself, Spender, MacNeice, and C. Day Lewis. The political urgencies of the times—the opposition to fascism and the movement for social justice for the working classes—shaped much of the poetry the Auden circle wrote then. Yet along with their social concerns, each of these poets shared a deep sense of a specifically poetic vocation—to make something happen in language.

1

He disappeared in the dead of winter:
The brooks were frozen, the airports almost deserted,
And snow disfigured the public statues;
The mercury sank in the mouth of the dying day.
5   O all the instruments agree
The day of his death was a dark cold day.

Far from his illness
The wolves ran on through the evergreen forests,
The peasant river was untempted by fashionable quays;[1]
10 By mourning tongues
The death of the poet was kept from his poems.

But for him it was his last afternoon as himself,
An afternoon of nurses and rumors;
The provinces of his body revolted,
15 The squares of his mind were empty,
Silence invaded the suburbs,
The current of his feeling failed: he became his admirers.

Now he is scattered among a hundred cities
And wholly given over to unfamiliar affections;
20 To find his happiness in another kind of wood
And be punished by another code of conscience.
The words of a dead man
Are modified in the guts of the living.

But in the importance and noise of tomorrow
25 When the brokers are roaring like beasts on the floor
      of the Bourse,[2]

---

1. **quays** (kēz) wharfs with facilities for loading or unloading ships.
2. **Bourse** (boŏrs) Paris Stock Exchange.

Literary Analysis
Theme How does the image in lines 22–23 relate to the theme of the relationship between poetry and life?

**Reading Check**

According to the speaker, where is Yeats now?

And the poor have the sufferings to which they are
        fairly accustomed,
And each in the cell of himself is almost convinced of
        his freedom;
A few thousand will think of this day
As one thinks of a day when one did something
        slightly unusual.

30 O all the instruments agree
    The day of his death was a dark cold day.

2

You were silly like us: your gift survived it all;
The parish of rich women, physical decay,
Yourself; mad Ireland hurt you into poetry.
35 Now Ireland has her madness and her weather still,
For poetry makes nothing happen: it survives
In the valley of its saying where executives
Would never want to tamper; it flows south
From ranches of isolation and the busy griefs,
40 Raw towns that we believe and die in; it survives,
A way of happening, a mouth.

3

Earth, receive an honored guest;
William Yeats is laid to rest:
Let the Irish vessel lie
45 Emptied of its poetry.

Time that is intolerant
Of the brave and innocent,
And indifferent in a week
To a beautiful physique,

50 Worships language and forgives
Everyone by whom it lives;
Pardons cowardice, conceit
Lays its honors at their feet.

Time that with this strange excuse
55 Pardoned Kipling and his views,[3]
And will pardon Paul Claudel,[4]
Pardons him for writing well.

---

3. **Kipling . . . views** English writer Rudyard Kipling (1865–1936) was a supporter of imperialism.
4. **pardon Paul Claudel** (klō del´) French poet, dramatist, and diplomat. Paul Claudel (1868–1955) had antidemocratic political views, which Yeats at times shared.

In the nightmare of the dark
All the dogs of Europe bark,
60 And the living nations wait,
Each <u>sequestered</u> in its hate;

Intellectual disgrace
Stares from every human face,
And the seas of pity lie
65 Locked and frozen in each eye.

Follow, poet, follow right
To the bottom of the night,
With your unconstraining voice
Still persuade us to rejoice;

70 With the farming of a verse
Make a vineyard of the curse,
Sing of human unsuccess
In a rapture of distress;

In the deserts of the heart
75 Let the healing fountain start,
In the prison of his days
Teach the free man how to praise.

sequestered (si kwes´ tərd)
adj. kept apart from others

Review and Assess

Thinking About the Selection

1. **(a) Recall:** What kept "The death of the poet" from his poems? **(b) Interpret:** What does the speaker mean by saying Yeats "became his admirers"?

2. **Interpret:** What does the second section suggest about the sources and effects of poetry?

3. **(a) Interpret:** Considering the kind of fame great past poets enjoy, why does the speaker say that time "Worships language and forgives / Everyone by whom it lives"? **(b) Interpret:** What kind of poetry might poets produce who "Sing of human unsuccess / In a rapture of distress; . . ."?

4. **Summarize:** Summarize the view of poetry presented in the poem.

5. **Analyze:** In phrases such as "ranches of isolation," Auden combines the abstract and the specific. Identify three other images that combine abstract ideas and concrete details.

6. **Evaluate:** Is Auden's style suited to an elegy, a poem of mourning? Explain.

▲ **Critical Viewing** In this painting by Brueghel, the drowning Icarus appears in the lower right. What is Brueghel implying about the place of suffering in life? **[Interpret]**

The Fall of Icarus, Pieter Brueghel, Musée Royaux des Beaux-Arts de Belgique, Bruxelles

Musée des Beaux Arts[1]

W. H. AUDEN

About suffering they were never wrong,
The Old Masters: how well they understood
Its human position; how it takes place
While someone else is eating or opening a window or just
     walking dully along;
5 How, when the aged are reverently, passionately waiting

---

1. **Musée des Beaux Arts** Museum of Fine Arts in Brussels, Belgium, which contains Brueghel's *Icarus*.

For the miraculous birth, there always must be
Children who did not specially want it to happen, skating
On a pond at the edge of the wood:
They never forgot
10   That even the dreadful martyrdom must run its course
Anyhow in a corner, some untidy spot
Where the dogs go on with their doggy life and the
      torturer's horse
Scratches its innocent behind on a tree.

In Brueghel's *Icarus*,[2] for instance: how everything turns away
15   Quite leisurely from the disaster; the ploughman may
Have heard the splash, the forsaken cry,
But for him it was not an important failure; the sun shone
As it had to on the white legs disappearing into the green
Water; and the expensive delicate ship that must have seen
20   Something amazing, a boy falling out of the sky,
Had somewhere to get to and sailed calmly on.

---

2. **Brueghel's** (brü´ gəlz) ***Icarus*** (ik´ ə rəs) *The Fall of Icarus,* a painting by Flemish
  painter Pieter Brueghel (1525?–1569). In Greek mythology, Icarus flies too close to
  the sun. The wax of his artificial wings melts, and he falls into the sea.

Review and Assess

Thinking About the Selection

1. **(a) Recall:** Who are the "Old Masters"? **(b) Interpret:** What general device used by the Old Masters does the speaker discuss?

2. **(a) Recall:** What disaster do the "ploughman" and the "ship" witness? **(b) Compare and Contrast:** How do their responses contrast with the gravity of the event?

3. **(a) Infer:** What is the relation of the children to the important events near them? **(b) Connect:** Is the attitude of the ploughman to Icarus' fall similar? Explain.

4. **(a) Analyze:** Look at Brueghel's *The Fall of Icarus* (p. 1002). What does the artist imply by showing only Icarus' legs in the right corner of the picture? **(b) Infer:** What does Brueghel, an Old Master, realize about the place of suffering in the world?

5. **Support:** Which of these statements best captures the sense of the poem? (a) A person's suffering belongs to him or her in a way that not even pity can change. (b) Suffering gives meaning to innocent everyday life and vice versa. Support your choice.

6. **(a) Apply:** Identify two examples of indifference to suffering today. **(b) Relate:** What might Auden say about them?

Carrick Revisited

Louis MacNeice

▼ **Critical Viewing** In "Carrick Revisited," MacNeice explores the relationship between a person's childhood home and his or her identity. What memories might a person have growing up in the setting shown in this photograph? **[Speculate]**

Back to Carrick,[1] the castle as plumb assured
As thirty years ago—Which war was which?
Here are new villas, here is a sizzling grid
But the green banks are as rich and the lough[2] as hazily lazy
5 And the child's astonishment not yet cured.

Who was—and am—dumbfounded to find myself
In a <u>topographical</u> frame—here, not there—
The channels of my dreams determined largely
By random chemistry of soil and air;
10 Memories I had shelved peer at me from the shelf.

Fog-horn, mill-horn, corncrake and church bell
Half-heard through boarded time as a child in bed
Glimpses a brangle of talk from the floor below
But cannot catch the words. Our past we know
15 But not its meaning—whether it meant well.

topographical (täp´ ə graf´ ik əl) *adj.* representing the surface features of a region

---

1. **Carrick** shortened form of Carrickfergus, a town in Northern Ireland.
2. **lough** (läkh) lake, specifically Belfast Lough. Carrickfergus is situated on the northern shore of Belfast Lough.

Time and place—our bridgeheads into reality
But also its concealment! Out of the sea
We land on the Particular and lose
All other possible bird's-eye views, the Truth
20 That is of Itself for Itself—but not for me.

Torn before birth from where my fathers dwelt,
Schooled from the age of ten to a foreign voice,
Yet neither western Ireland nor southern England
Cancels this interlude; what chance misspelt
25 May never now be righted by my choice.

Whatever then my inherited or acquired
Affinities, such remains my childhood's frame
Like a belated rock in the red Antrim³ clay
That cannot at this era change its pitch or name—
30 And the prenatal mountain is far away.

---

3. Antrim county in Northern Ireland in which Carrickfergus is located.

affinities (ə fin´ i tēz) *n.* family connections; sympathies

prenatal (prē nāt´ əl) *adj.* existing or taking place before birth

Review and Assess

Thinking About the Selection

1. **Respond:** Do you empathize with the poet's "astonishment" on returning to his birthplace? Explain.

2. **(a) Recall:** Where does the speaker find himself at the beginning of the poem?
   (b) Compare and Contrast: According to the first stanza, what has changed and what has remained the same?

3. **(a) Recall:** What discovery dumbfounds the poet?
   (b) Interpret: What relationship does the speaker discover between the imagination—which enables us to picture ourselves in any circumstances—and the facts of his personal history?

4. **(a) Interpret:** What effect do the specifics of the place have on the speaker's imagination? **(b) Interpret:** What does the speaker mean in saying "Our past we know / But not its meaning. . . ." **(c) Speculate:** What task concerning the past might MacNeice assign to poetry?

5. **(a) Interpret:** Why does the speaker call his childhood in Carrick an "interlude"? **(b) Draw Conclusions:** How is MacNeice's identity, as described in this poem, influenced by two cultures but separate from both?

6. **Extend:** Name two ways in which issues of identity are even more complex today than when MacNeice was writing.

Not Palaces

Stephen Spender

Background

In this poem's unifying metaphor, Spender says that he will not build old-fashioned poems that are like palaces—beautiful, ornate structures remote from the masses. Instead, he hopes to build active, modern poetry, more like the steel and glass skyscrapers that began with the International and Bauhaus architectural styles of the 1920s and 1930s. These buildings create dynamic spaces by combining strikingly simple forms with superior industrial craftsmanship. Walter Gropius, the founder of the Bauhaus school, sought to integrate architecture and the other arts. Gropius's school shared a social agenda related to that in Spender's poem: Seeking to bring beauty into the lives of the working classes, rather than serving the wealthy, they turned to modern techniques of mass production. Though skyscrapers may have since come to symbolize a corporate elite, in Spender's day, some saw in them the promise of true social equality.

Not palaces, an era's crown
Where the mind dwells, <u>intrigues</u>, rests:
Architectural gold-leaved flower
From people ordered like a single mind,
5 I build: this only what I tell:

intrigues (in trēgz´) v. plots or schemes

It is too late for rare accumulation,
For family pride, for beauty's filtered dusts;
I say, stamping the words with emphasis,
Drink from here energy and only energy
10 To will this time's change.
Eye, gazelle, delicate wanderer,
Drinker of horizon's fluid line;
Ear that suspends on a chord
The spirit drinking timelessness;
15 Touch, love, all senses;
Leave your gardens, your singing feasts,
Your dreams of suns circling before our sun,
Of heaven after our world.
Instead, watch images of flashing glass
20 That strike the outward sense, the polished will,
Flag of our purpose which the wind engraves.
No spirit seek here rest. But this: No one
Shall hunger: Man shall spend equally;
Our goal which we compel: Man shall be man.

Review and Assess

Thinking About the Selection

1. **Respond:** Do you prefer "palaces"—ornate, traditional artworks—to modern art? Why or why not?

2. **(a) Recall:** In lines 1–7, what does the speaker say he will not do? **(b) Interpret:** What vision of art is he rejecting?

3. **(a) Recall:** What reason does the poet give for rejecting the "accumulation" of rarities? **(b) Interpret:** What connection does the speaker make between his poem and social progress in lines 9–10?

4. **(a) Interpret:** What might the poet mean by "images of flashing glass"? **(b) Compare and Contrast:** How does this image contrast with the palaces described in the poem's opening?

5. **(a) Infer:** What does the speaker tell the senses to leave in lines 16–18? **(b) Interpret:** What should the senses attend to instead?

6. **(a) Analyze:** What does Spender think the job of poetry once was? **(b) Analyze:** What does he think it should be now?

7. **Relate:** In "In Memory of W. B. Yeats," Auden writes that although "poetry makes nothing happen," it teaches us a kind of joy in what is. Would Spender agree with Auden's ideas? Explain your answer.

Review and Assess

Literary Analysis

Theme

1. What details of the ploughman's response to the disaster in "Musée des Beaux Arts" help convey the poem's **theme**?

2. The theme of "Carrick Revisited" may be summed up in the question "What creates an artist's identity?" (a) What clue to the theme does the setting provide? (b) Identify two passages that express the theme directly. (c) Does MacNeice fully answer this question? Explain.

3. In "Not Palaces," Spender advocates rejecting old artistic attitudes. In what way does his architectural imagery express this theme?

Comparing Literary Works

4. Use a chart like the one shown to compare the ideas in these poems about the nature of art.

Poem	Central Issues	Supporting Passages	Interpretation
"In Memory of W. B. Yeats"	What difference does art make?	"Teach the free man how to praise."	

5. Both "In Memory of W. B. Yeats" and "Carrick Revisited" question the connection between the particulars of an artist's life and his or her work. Compare their answers.

6. (a) Which of these poets believe that art in some sense rises above life? (b) Which do not? Explain, using examples. (c) With which poet's view of art do you agree? Why?

Reading Strategy

Paraphrasing

7. (a) **Paraphrase** lines 32–41 of "In Memory of W. B. Yeats." (b) Paraphrase a section of a poem of your choice.

8. (a) How did paraphrasing help you understand these lines? (b) What is lost in the translation?

Extend Understanding

9. **Science Connection:** MacNeice analyzes his identity. Using ideas of heredity and environment, how might a scientist respond?

Quick Review

The **theme** of a literary work is its central concern or purpose, or the main question it raises.

To **paraphrase**, restate a writer's words in your own words.

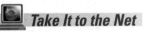 **Take It to the Net**

www.phschool.com

Take the interactive self-test online to check your understanding of these selections.

Integrate Language Skills

Vocabulary Development Lesson

Word Analysis: Greek Root -top-

The Greek root -top- means "place" or "surface." The word *topographical*, used by MacNeice, means "relating to a map of the surface features of a place." Explain how the root -top- contributes to the meanings of these words from science and mathematics:

1. topology   2. topography   3. topical

Spelling Strategy

In words that end in a vowel and *r, -er* is the most common spelling. Nouns formed from verbs that end in *-ate, -ess,* or *-ct* use *-or:* as in *generate, generator; profess, professor; act, actor.* Choose the correctly spelled word from each pair below.

1. achiever, achievor
2. communicater, communicator
3. dissenter, dissentor

Concept Development: Synonyms

Review the vocabulary list on page 997. For each numbered word below, write the letter of its synonym, the word or phrase that has the meaning closest to it.

1. sequestered: (a) convicted, (b) kept apart, (c) silent

2. intrigues: (a) schemes, (b) fails, (c) deceives

3. topographical: (a) reflecting a person's life, (b) atypical, (c) representing a place

4. affinities: (a) immensities, (b) ends, (c) attractions

5. prenatal: (a) before birth, (b) naive, (c) not natural

Grammar and Style Lesson

Parallel Structure

Poets often use **parallel structure**—repeated use of the same grammatical form or pattern—to make their writing memorable and effective. These lines from "Not Palaces" contain parallel prepositional phrases.

> **Example:** It is too late <u>for rare accumulation,</u>
> <u>For family pride,</u> <u>for beauty's filtered</u>
> <u>dusts;</u> . . .

Practice Rewrite each underscored item to make the sentence structure parallel.

1. Time worships language and <u>is pardoning</u> cowardice.

2. Suffering takes place while someone is eating or <u>opens</u> a window.
3. This is no time for collecting objects or <u>to admire</u> beautiful artifacts in museums.
4. I am not interested in building palaces or <u>the creation of</u> rare objects.
5. MacNeice tried his hand at various genres, including poetry, drama, and <u>translating in verse.</u>

Writing Application Write three sentences on art that use parallel structure to produce an effective rhythm. Your sentences might connect gerunds such as *writing* and *creating* or infinitive phrases such as *to inspire* and *to create.*

Prentice Hall Writing and Grammar Connection: Chapter 20, Section 6

Writing Lesson

Poem About an Artwork

Auden's poem "Musée des Beaux Arts" was inspired by a Brueghel painting. Choose another painting or a photograph, and respond to it in a poem of your own. To convey one main impression, establish and maintain a strong, consistent tone.

Prewriting For five minutes, write down whatever comes to mind about the artwork you have chosen. Review your notes, and circle the most interesting details. Use these notes as the basis for your draft.

Drafting Choose a logical organization. You might begin with a physical description and then describe your emotional response. As you draft, concentrate on choosing words that will result in a strong, consistent tone—whether it be wonder, amusement, or disappointment.

Revising Ask a partner to summarize the main impression of your poem. Make adjustments if your partner's response does not match your intentions.

Model: Revising to Strengthen a Main Impression

bold
A blue stripe splits the canvas in two,
  Mocking, laughing—
~~Challenging the viewer,~~ "On which side are you?"

> Flatly descriptive language is revised to suggest the self-confident energy of the painting.

WG *Prentice Hall Writing and Grammar Connection: Chapter 6, Section 4*

Extension Activities

Listening and Speaking Present a **group reading** of "In Memory of W.B. Yeats." To prepare, follow these tips:

- Analyze the various moods and tones of each section.
- Identify the most appropriate tone, volume, and pace for each.
- Assign each section as a separate part, and rehearse your reading.

When you have rehearsed sufficiently, present your reading to the class.

Research and Technology With a group, install an **art exhibition** of works in the spirit of "Not Palaces." Determine which twentieth-century artists pursue the same ideals as Spender. Then, collect copies of artworks for display. Devise strategies for highlighting the features you want to address. Produce your exhibition. **[Group Activity]**

 **Take It to the Net** www.phschool.com

Go online for an additional research activity using the Internet.

Mission Statements

About Mission Statements

Suppose that you want to volunteer your spare time working for a charitable organization. To learn the group's objectives, it may help to read its mission statement. A **mission statement** is a document provided by a company, a charitable organization, or another group to identify itself and describe its guiding purpose, specific objectives, and daily activities. Mission statements help introduce the organization to the general public. They can also help nonprofit organizations obtain government grants.

Reading Strategy

Interpreting the Organization of a Mission Statement

The organization of a mission statement is imperative to its success. To engage casual browsers, the statement must make basic information easy to find. At the same time, the statement must contain enough facts to satisfy those who desire specific information. The following organizational strategies are commonly used in mission statements and other documents that give a brief, businesslike overview of a subject:

- Short and concise boldfaced subheads to allow readers to quickly take in the main points covered
- Short, focused paragraphs and groups of bulleted items to allow readers the opportunity to follow ideas easily
- The organization of points in order of importance to focus readers' attention
- The organization of details in chronological order to allow readers to follow the order in which steps are taken to accomplish objectives.

The National Gallery, located in London, was established in 1824 with Parliament's purchase of a private collection of art. Its mission statement appears on the following pages. Use a chart like the one shown to help you determine whether it uses organizational strategies successfully.

Organizational Strategy	Purpose	Effectiveness

The National Gallery
Role and Objectives

Role

The National Gallery houses the national Collection of Western European paintings from around 1250 to 1900.

The Gallery's aim is to care for, enhance and study its Collection, so as to offer the fullest access to the pictures for the education and enjoyment of the widest possible public now and in the future. It aims for the highest international standards in all its activities.

The Collection belongs to the people of the United Kingdom. It is open, free of charge, to all.

The Gallery serves a very wide and diverse public, which includes:

- those who visit the Gallery of London—both those who visit frequently and those who visit only occasionally;
- those who see its pictures while they are on loan elsewhere, both inside and outside the UK, and those who know the Collection through publications, multimedia and TV;
- those who live nearby as well as those who live further away in the United Kingdom and overseas;
- every age group—from children to pensioners;
- the socially excluded and the privileged; the uninformed and the specialist; and those with special needs;
- the worldwide community of museums and galleries;
- and, most importantly, future generations.

Objectives

The Gallery aims to:

Care for the Collection

- keep the pictures in the nation's Collection safe for future generations by maintaining a secure and appropriate environment for them, monitoring their condition regularly, and undertaking suitable restoration or conservation;
- do everything possible to secure the pictures from fire, theft and other hazards;
- do everything possible to ensure that pictures loaned out are in sound enough condition to travel safely.

Large heads clearly divide the mission statement into sections.

An important introductory statement is set off in boldface.

Objectives are listed in order of importance, with the most important appearing first.

Enhance the Collection

- acquire great pictures across the whole range of European painting to enhance the Collection now and for future generations.

Study the Collection

- encourage all aspects of scholarship on the Collection, researching and documenting the pictures to the highest international standards, and ensuring that this work is disseminated.

Provide Access to the Collection for the Education and Enjoyment of the Widest Possible Public

- encourage the public to use the Collection as their own by maintaining free admission, during the most convenient possible hours, to as much as possible of the permanent Collection;
- display the pictures well;
- promote knowledge of the Collection and encourage the public to visit it;
- help the widest possible public both in the Gallery and beyond to understand and enjoy the paintings, taking advantage of the opportunities created by modern technology;
- offer the highest possible standards in services for our visitors.

Stand as a National and International leader in All Its Activities

- work with other regional museums and galleries in the United Kingdom.
- enhance the national and international standing of the Gallery.

Check Your Comprehension

1. Who owns the National Gallery's Collection?
2. How is the National Gallery going to enhance its Collection in the future?
3. What steps does the National Gallery take to ensure that its Collection receives proper care?
4. What is the National Gallery's general purpose?

Applying the Reading Strategy

Organizing a Mission Statement

After reading the National Gallery's mission statement, use the information within it to answer the following questions:

5. Briefly scan the subheads within the mission statement. (a) Write a summary based on your scan of the points covered. (b) Read the brochure. Does it cover everything predicted by your summary? Explain.
6. (a) Are the details within the mission statement organized in the order of their importance or in chronological order? (b) Is this organization strategy effective?
7. How does grouping related details help provide a more clearly defined mission statement?
8. Does the organization of this mission statement help you understand the National Gallery's goals and objectives? Explain.

Activity

Writing a Mission Statement

Many high schools have a number of clubs and societies. Before a student decides to join a particular organization, he or she might want to read a mission statement to ensure that he or she agrees with the group's goals and objectives. Choose an organization in your school, research it, and write a mission statement for it. Use the Web shown to help you devise the subheads for your mission statement.

Comparing Informational Materials

Evaluating Mission Statements

Most organizations and businesses have mission statements that are easily obtained by the general public. Read and compare a mission statement from a business or museum in your area with the mission statement from the National Gallery. Which mission statement is more effective in the presentation of its message? Explain your evaluation.

Prepare to Read

Shooting an Elephant

George Orwell (1903–1950)

Many television reports today are on-the-scene newscasts or in-depth documentaries, showing people in the middle of an event. These reports, like best-selling "nonfiction novels," give us not just facts but a close-up, personal perspective on events. George Orwell pioneered this first-person style of reporting. Whether writing on the Spanish Civil War or life among the downtrodden, he penetrated prejudice and dishonest politics to expose the truth in a simple act—telling what he had seen, what he knew. He still stands as a figure of political and literary honesty, challenging us to tell the truth simply and directly.

Becoming an Officer Orwell was born Eric Blair in colonial India, was educated in England, and then joined the Imperial Police in Burma. His experiences there were typical of the small group of young Englishmen recruited as police officers for the British Empire. These men had no experience of police work and no knowledge of the country they would police. Their training in Burma consisted of memorizing laws and procedures and learning the native languages. They lived apart from the Burmese, who resented British rule.

Orwell was keenly aware of the inequities of imperialism. As an officer of the Burmese police, he headed a native-born police force of 13,000. Among the 90 officers, Englishmen held almost all the top ranks—a few white men governing 13 million Asians.

Disillusioned In 1928, after five years of service as an imperial police officer, the disillusioned Orwell resigned. His first novel, *Burmese Days* (1934), describes these bitter years. "Shooting an Elephant," one of his most famous essays, is based on a defining experience from this period.

Becoming George Orwell Orwell seemed to have a talent for immersing himself in difficult situations and then writing about them with extraordinary insight. Every book that emerged from an Orwell experience was a one-of-a-kind classic. In *Down and Out in Paris and London* (1933), for example, Orwell describes what it is like to be poor in two big cities.

In a strange way, his experience of life's shabbiness gave him a stronger sense of identity. After his journeys on the seamier side of things, he published and lived under a new name: George Orwell.

Adventuring During the 1930s, Orwell gave himself to political causes. In *The Road to Wigan Pier* (1937), he wrote about the English coal miners with whom he had lived. Then, during the Spanish Civil War (1936–1939), he fought for democracy with anarchists and socialist Republicans. He witnessed the infighting among the groups defending the Spanish government, infighting that enabled the Fascists to win. In his book on that crisis, *Homage to Catalonia* (1938), Orwell blamed the interference of the Soviet Union for undermining the Republican cause—a charge that made him unpopular with his fellow leftists. The book is a gripping adventure story, one in which the narrator's cool presence of mind allows him to recall in precise detail his experience of being wounded.

A Political Prophet During World War II, Orwell wrote political and literary journalism. In 1945, he published *Animal Farm*, a satirical fable attacking both fascism and communism. In 1949, he shared a dark vision of the future in his novel *1984*, in which a dictator rules by controlling all thought and language. The year 1984 has passed, but George Orwell's lifelong commitment to political freedom and to the honest use of language is as relevant as ever.

Preview

Connecting to the Literature

It is time to give your speech. You reach the front of the room, only to realize that you have lost your notes, your topic still confuses you, and your hands are clammy with sweat. If you have had an experience like this one, you know a little about how Orwell feels in this memoir.

Literary Analysis

Irony

Orwell uses irony to underscore the no-win situation he faced in Burma. **Irony** is a device that brings out a contradiction between appearance and reality. It can take a few forms, including the following:

- **Verbal irony**—an intentional clash between the words chosen to talk about a thing and its reality; for example, calling a tall person "Shorty"

- **Irony of situation**—an opposition between the pattern of events and expectations or hopes; for example, on the day you are kicked off the team, someone you admire tells you she is eager to see you play.

As you read, notice how Orwell uses both kinds of irony.

Connecting Literary Elements

Tone is a writer's attitude toward the reader and the subject, as expressed in word choice, sentence structure, and other elements of style. Orwell's direct, matter-of-fact sentences achieve a conversational tone. In addition, his simple observations create a tone of ironic detachment—as when he sums up the complex Burmese situation with, "All this was perplexing and upsetting." As you read, notice the way Orwell develops his tone.

Reading Strategy

Recognizing the Writer's Attitudes

To understand the full meaning of a text, move beyond the words on the page to **recognize the writer's attitudes** toward his or her subject. To analyze Orwell's attitudes, use a chart like the one shown.

Vocabulary Development

prostrate (präs´ trāt) *adj.* overcome; lying face downward (p. 1020)

imperialism (im pir´ ē əl iz´ əm) *n.* policy of forming an empire and securing economic power by conquest and colonization (p. 1020)

despotic (des pät´ ik) *adj.* tyrannical (p. 1020)

squalid (skwäl´ id) *adj.* miserably poor; wretched (p. 1020)

dominion (də min´ yən) *n.* rule or power over a territory (p. 1022)

senility (si nil´ ə tē) *n.* mental deterioration due to old age (p. 1025)

> **Attitude Toward Imperialism**
>
> "... imperialism was an evil thing ..."

> **Attitude Toward Burmese**
>
> "... my rage against the evil-spirited little beasts who tried to make my life impossible."

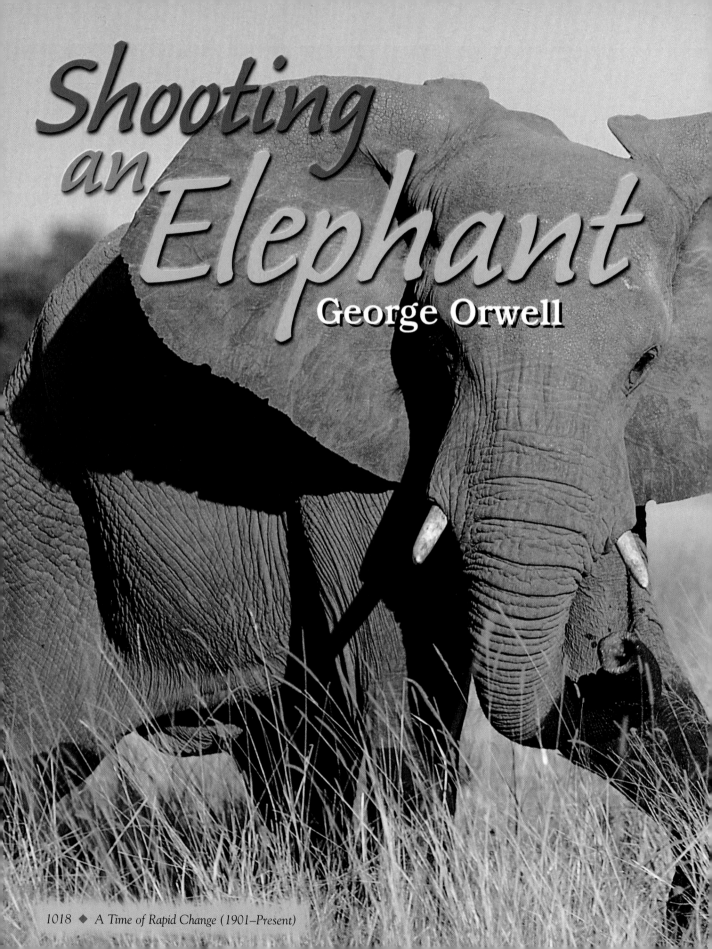

Shooting an Elephant

George Orwell

Background

Hoping to secure a better trade route with China, Great Britain fought several wars against Burma during the 1800s, finally conquering the country in 1885. Although the desired "golden path" to China did not prosper, Burma provided Britain with other economic opportunities, such as the export of Burmese rice. Many Burmese, however, were unwilling to accept British rule. Opponents of the British formed the Anti-Fascist People's Freedom League, led by Aung San. The group was instrumental in winning Burma's independence from Britain in 1948. In this essay, Orwell writes of the days of English rule in Burma.

*I*n Moulmein, in lower Burma, I was hated by large numbers of people—the only time in my life that I have been important enough for this to happen to me. I was subdivisional police officer of the town, and in an aimless, petty kind of way anti-European feeling was very bitter. No one had the guts to raise a riot, but if a European woman went through the bazaars alone somebody would probably spit betel juice over her dress. As a police officer I was an obvious target and was baited whenever it seemed safe to do so. When a nimble Burman tripped me up on the football field and the referee (another Burman) looked the other way, the crowd yelled with hideous laughter. This happened more than once. In the end the sneering yellow faces of young men that met me everywhere, the insults hooted after me when I was at a safe distance, got badly on my nerves. The young Buddhist priests were the worst of all. There were several thousands of them in the town and none of them seemed to have anything to do except stand on street corners and jeer at Europeans.

All this was perplexing and upsetting. For at that time I had already made up my mind that imperialism was an evil thing and the sooner I chucked up my job and got out of it the better. Theoretically—and secretly, of course—I was all for the Burmese and all against their oppressors, the British. As for the job I was doing, I hated it more bitterly than I can perhaps make clear. In a job like that you see the dirty work of Empire at close quarters. The wretched prisoners huddling in the stinking cages of the lockups, the gray, cowed faces of the long-term convicts, the

Reading Strategy
Recognizing the Writer's Attitudes Identify Orwell's conflicting attitudes in these opening paragraphs.

✔**Reading Check**
According to Orwell, how do the Burmese view the English?

◀ **Critical Viewing** Does this photograph depict a useful beast or a dangerous menace? Explain. **[Make a Judgment]**

scarred buttocks of the men who had been flogged with bamboos—all these oppressed me with an intolerable sense of guilt. But I could get nothing into perspective. I was young and ill educated and I had had to think out my problems in the utter silence that is imposed on every Englishman in the East. I did not even know that the British Empire is dying, still less did I know that it is a great deal better than the younger empires that are going to supplant it. All I knew was that I was stuck between my hatred of the empire I served and my rage against the evil-spirited little beasts who tried to make my job impossible. With one part of my mind I thought of the British Raj[1] as an unbreakable tyranny, as something clamped down, *in saecula saeculorum,*[2] upon the will of <u>prostrate</u> peoples; with another part I thought that the greatest joy in the world would be to drive a bayonet into a Buddhist priest's guts. Feelings like these are the normal byproducts of <u>imperialism</u>; ask any Anglo-Indian official, if you can catch him off duty.

One day something happened which in a roundabout way was enlightening. It was a tiny incident in itself, but it gave me a better glimpse than I had had before of the real nature of imperialism—the real motives for which <u>despotic</u> governments act. Early one morning the subinspector at a police station the other end of the town rang me up on the phone and said that an elephant was ravaging the bazaar. Would I please come and do something about it? I did not know what I could do, but I wanted to see what was happening and I got onto a pony and started out. I took my rifle, an old .44 Winchester and much too small to kill an elephant, but I thought the noise might be useful *in terrorem.*[3] Various Burmans stopped me on the way and told me about the elephant's doings. It was not, of course, a wild elephant, but a tame one which had gone "must."[4] It had been chained up, as tame elephants always are when their attack of "must" is due, but on the previous night it had broken its chain and escaped. Its mahout,[5] the only person who could manage it when it was in that state, had set out in pursuit, but had taken the wrong direction and was now twelve hours' journey away, and in the morning the elephant had suddenly reappeared in the town. The Burmese population had no weapons and were quite helpless against it. It had already destroyed somebody's bamboo hut, killed a cow and raided some fruit stalls and devoured the stock; also it had met the municipal rubbish van and, when the driver jumped out and took to his heels, had turned the van over and inflicted violences upon it.

The Burmese subinspector and some Indian constables were waiting for me in the quarter where the elephant had been seen. It was a very poor quarter, a labyrinth of <u>squalid</u> bamboo huts, thatched with

prostrate (präs′ trāt) *adj.* overcome; lying face downward

imperialism (im pir′ ē əl iz′əm) *n.* policy of forming an empire and securing economic power by conquest and colonization

despotic (de spät′ ik) *adj.* tyrannical

squalid (skwäl′ id) *adj.* miserably poor; wretched

---

1. **Raj** (räj) rule.
2. *in saecula saeculorum* (in sē′ kōō lə sē′ kōō lôr′ əm) Latin for "forever and ever."
3. *in terrorem* Latin for "for terror."
4. **must** into a dangerous, frenzied state.
5. **mahout** (mə hōōt′) elephant keeper and rider.

palm leaf, winding all over a steep hillside. I remember that it was a cloudy, stuffy morning at the beginning of the rains. We began questioning the people as to where the elephant had gone and, as usual, failed to get any definite information. That is invariably the case in the East; a story always sounds clear enough at a distance, but the nearer you get to the scene of events the vaguer it becomes. Some of the people said that the elephant had gone in one direction, some said that he had gone in another, some professed not even to have heard of any elephant. I had almost made up my mind that the whole story was a pack of lies, when we heard yells a little distance away. There was a loud scandalized cry of "Go away, child! Go away this instant!" and an old woman with a switch in her hand came round the corner of a hut, violently shooing away a crowd of naked children. Some more women followed, clicking their tongues and exclaiming; evidently there was something that the children ought not to have seen. I rounded the hut and saw a man's dead body sprawling in the mud. He was an Indian, a black Dravidian[6] coolie,[7] almost naked, and he could not have been dead many minutes. The people said that the elephant had come suddenly upon him round the corner of the hut, caught him with its trunk, put its foot on his back and ground him into the earth. This was the rainy season and the ground was soft, and his face had scored a trench a foot deep and a couple of yards long. He was lying on his belly with arms crucified and head sharply twisted to one side. His face was coated with mud, the eyes wide open, the teeth bared and grinning with an expression of unendurable agony. (Never tell me, by the way, that the dead look peaceful. Most of the corpses I have seen looked devilish.) The friction of the great beast's foot had stripped the skin from his back as neatly as one skins a rabbit. As soon as I saw the dead man I sent an orderly to a friend's house nearby to borrow an elephant rifle. I had already sent back the pony, not wanting it to go mad with fright and throw me if it smelled the elephant.

The orderly came back in a few minutes with a rifle and five cartridges, and meanwhile some Burmans had arrived and told us that the elephant was in the paddy fields[8] below, only a few hundred yards away. As I started forward practically the whole population of the quarter flocked out of the houses and followed me. They had seen the rifle and were all shouting excitedly that I was going to shoot the elephant. They had not shown much interest in the elephant when he

---

6. **Dravidian** (drə vid′ ē ən) belonging to the race of people inhabiting southern India.
7. **coolie** laborer.
8. **paddy fields** rice fields.

𝓛iterature
in context Vocabulary Connection

Vocabulary of Empire

The key terms in Orwell's political vocabulary often have Latin origins:

- *Imperialism* comes from a Latin word for "command" or "empire."

- *Dominion* comes from a Latin word meaning "lord" or "master."

Supporters of British imperialism may have chosen Latinate words to describe the British Empire as a way of suggesting a comparison with the glory of the Roman Empire. However, critics like Orwell seized the word *imperialism*, and it gained strongly negative connotations.

Some meanings reflect history inaccurately. In an irony that Orwell would have appreciated, the word *despot* is derived from a Greek term for "ruler." Even though our ideas of democracy come from ancient Greece, where some rulers strove for democratic goals, the term has come to describe the opposite of a democratic leader—an oppressive tyrant.

✔Reading Check

What has the elephant done that shows how dangerous it is?

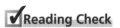

was merely ravaging their homes, but it was different now that he was going to be shot. It was a bit of fun to them, as it would be to an English crowd; besides they wanted the meat. It made me vaguely uneasy. I had no intention of shooting the elephant—I had merely sent for the rifle to defend myself if necessary—and it is always unnerving to have a crowd following you. I marched down the hill, looking and feeling a fool, with the rifle over my shoulder and an ever-growing army of people jostling at my heels. At the bottom, when you got away from the huts, there was a metaled road[9] and beyond that a miry waste of paddy fields a thousand yards across, not yet plowed but soggy from the first rains and dotted with coarse grass. The elephant was standing eight yards from the road, his left side toward us. He took not the slightest notice of the crowd's approach. He was tearing up bunches of grass, beating them against his knees to clean them, and stuffing them into his mouth.

I had halted on the road. As soon as I saw the elephant I knew with perfect certainty that I ought not to shoot him. It is a serious matter to shoot a working elephant—it is comparable to destroying a huge and costly piece of machinery—and obviously one ought not to do it if it can possibly be avoided. And at that distance, peacefully eating, the elephant looked no more dangerous than a cow. I thought then and I think now that his attack of "must" was already passing off; in which case he would merely wander harmlessly about until the mahout came back and caught him. Moreover, I did not in the least want to shoot him. I decided that I would watch him for a little while to make sure that he did not turn savage again, and then go home.

But at that moment I glanced round at the crowd that had followed me. It was an immense crowd, two thousand at the least and growing every minute. It blocked the road for a long distance on either side. I looked at the sea of yellow faces above the garish clothes—faces all happy and excited over this bit of fun, all certain that the elephant was going to be shot. They were watching me as they would watch a conjurer about to perform a trick. They did not like me, but with the magical rifle in my hands I was momentarily worth watching. And suddenly I realized that I should have to shoot the elephant after all. The people expected it of me and I had got to do it; I could feel their two thousand wills pressing me forward, irresistibly. And it was at this moment, as I stood there with the rifle in my hands, that I first grasped the hollowness, the futility of the white man's dominion in the East. Here was I, the white man with his gun, standing in front of the unarmed native crowd—seemingly the leading actor of the piece; but in reality I was only an absurd puppet pushed to and fro by the will of those yellow faces behind. I perceived in this moment that when the white man turns tyrant it is his own freedom that he destroys. He becomes a sort of hollow, posing dummy, the conventionalized figure of a sahib.[10] For

Literary Analysis
Irony How does Orwell's description of the crowd's reaction create situational irony?

dominion (də min′ yən) *n.* rule or power over a territory

Literary Analysis
Irony What ironic observation does Orwell share here?

---

9. **metaled road** road in which the pavement is reinforced with metal strips.
10. **sahib** (sä′ ib) Indian word for European gentleman.

it is the condition of his rule that he shall spend his life in trying to impress the "natives," and so in every crisis he has got to do what the "natives" expect of him. He wears a mask, and his face grows to fit it. I had got to shoot the elephant. I had committed myself to doing it when I sent for the rifle. A sahib has got to act like a sahib; he has got to appear resolute, to know his own mind and do definite things. To come all that way, rifle in hand, with two thousand people marching at my heels, and then to trail feebly away, having done nothing—no, that was impossible. The crowd would laugh at me. And my whole life, every white man's life in the East, was one long struggle not to be laughed at.

But I did not want to shoot the elephant. I watched him beating his bunch of grass against his knees with that preoccupied grandmotherly air that elephants have. It seemed to me that it would be murder to shoot him. At that age I was not squeamish about killing animals, but I had never shot an elephant and never wanted to. (Somehow it always seems worse to kill a *large* animal.) Besides, there was the beast's owner to be considered. Alive, the elephant was worth at least a hundred pounds, dead, he would only be worth the value of his tusks, five pounds, possibly. But I had got to act quickly. I turned to some experienced-looking Burmans who had been there when we arrived, and asked them how the elephant had been behaving. They all said the same thing: he took no notice of you if you left him alone, but he might charge if you went too close to him.

It was perfectly clear to me what I ought to do. I ought to walk up to within, say, twenty-five yards of the elephant and test his behavior. If he charged, I could shoot; if he took no notice of me, it would be safe to leave him until the mahout came back. But also I knew that I was going to do no such thing. I was a poor shot with a rifle and the ground was soft mud into which one would sink at every step. If the elephant charged and I missed him, I should have about as much chance as a toad under a steamroller. But even then I was not thinking particularly of my own skin, only of the watchful yellow faces behind. For at that moment, with the crowd watching me, I was not afraid in the ordinary sense, as I would have been if I had been alone. A white man mustn't be frightened in front of "natives"; and so, in general, he isn't frightened. The sole thought in my mind was that if anything went wrong those two thousand Burmans would see me pursued, caught, trampled on, and reduced to a grinning corpse like that Indian up the hill. And if that happened it was quite probable that some of them would laugh. That would never do. There was only one alternative. I shoved the cartridges into the magazine and lay down on the road to get a better aim.

The crowd grew very still, and a deep, low, happy sigh, as of people who see the theater curtain go up at last, breathed from innumerable throats. They were going to have their bit of fun, after all. The rifle was a beautiful German thing with cross-hair sights. I did not then know that in shooting an elephant one would shoot to cut an imaginary bar running from ear hole to ear hole. I ought, therefore, as the elephant was sideways on, to have aimed straight at his ear-hole;

Reading Strategy
Recognizing the Writer's Attitudes What attitude toward the elephant does Orwell communicate here?

Reading Check

What is the main reason Orwell gives for deciding to shoot the elephant?

actually I aimed several inches in front of this, thinking the brain would be further forward.

When I pulled the trigger I did not hear the bang or feel the kick— one never does when a shot goes home—but I heard the devilish roar of glee that went up from the crowd. In that instant, in too short a time, one would have thought, even for the bullet to get there, a mysterious, terrible change had come over the elephant. He neither stirred nor fell, but every line of his body had altered. He looked suddenly stricken, shrunken, immensely old, as though the frightful impact of the bullet had paralyzed him without knocking him down. At last, after what seemed a long time—it might have been five seconds,

▲ **Critical Viewing**
Judging from the details in this photograph, what made Orwell (third from left in back row) and his fellow officers conspicuous and therefore possible targets for ridicule? **[Analyze]**

I dare say—he sagged flabbily to his knees. His mouth slobbered. An enormous senility seemed to have settled upon him. One could have imagined him thousands of years old. I fired again into the same spot. At the second shot he did not collapse but climbed with desperate slowness to his feet and stood weakly upright, with legs sagging and head drooping. I fired a third time. That was the shot that did for him. You could see the agony of it jolt his whole body and knock the last remnant of strength from his legs. But in falling he seemed for a moment to rise, for as his hind legs collapsed beneath him he seemed to tower upward like a huge rock toppling, his trunk reaching skyward like a tree. He trumpeted, for the first and only time. And then down he came, his belly toward me, with a crash that seemed to shake the ground even where I lay.

I got up. The Burmans were already racing past me across the mud. It was obvious that the elephant would never rise again, but he was not dead. He was breathing very rhythmically with long rattling gasps, his great mound of a side painfully rising and falling. His mouth was wide open—I could see far down into caverns of pale pink throat. I waited a long time for him to die, but his breathing did not weaken. Finally I fired my two remaining shots into the spot where I thought his heart must be. The thick blood welled out of him like red velvet, but still he did not die. His body did not even jerk when the shots hit him, the tortured breathing continued without a pause. He was dying, very slowly and in great agony, but in some world remote from me where not even a bullet could damage him further. I felt that I had got to put an end to that dreadful noise. It seemed dreadful to see the great beast lying there, powerless to move and yet powerless to die, and not even to be able to finish him. I sent back for my small rifle and poured shot after shot into his heart and down his throat. They seemed to make no impression. The tortured gasps continued as steadily as the ticking of a clock.

senility (si nil′ ə tē) *n.* mental deterioration due to old age

Reading Strategy
Recognizing the Writer's Attitudes What does Orwell's detailed description of the elephant's collapse suggest about his attitude toward the grim side of life?

Reading Check

What happens to the elephant after Orwell's first shot?

In the end I could not stand it any longer and went away. I heard later that it took him half an hour to die. Burmans were bringing dahs[11] and baskets even before I left, and I was told they had stripped his body almost to the bones by the afternoon.

Afterward, of course, there were endless discussions about the shooting of the elephant. The owner was furious, but he was only an Indian and could do nothing. Besides, legally I had done the right thing, for a mad elephant has to be killed, like a mad dog, if its owner fails to control it. Among the Europeans opinion was divided. The older men said I was right, the younger men said it was a shame to shoot an elephant for killing a coolie, because an elephant was worth more than any Coringhee[12] coolie. And afterward I was very glad that the coolie had been killed; it put me legally in the right and it gave me a sufficient pretext for shooting the elephant. I often wondered whether any of the others grasped that I had done it solely to avoid looking a fool.

---

11. dahs (däz) knives.
12. Coringhee (cor in´ gē) Southern Indian.

Review and Assess

Thinking About the Selection

1. **Respond:** If you were in the narrator's position, would you give up your job? Why or why not?

2. **(a) Recall:** Why did the Burmese hate George Orwell?
   (b) Analyze: Why does this hatred cause conflict in him?
   (c) Interpret: What does this conflict show about Orwell?

3. **(a) Recall:** Why does Orwell think that the elephant need not be killed? **(b) Analyze Cause and Effect:** What is the primary factor influencing Orwell's decision to shoot the elephant? **(c) Interpret:** What does this decision, and his honesty about it, suggest about his character?

4. **(a) Draw Conclusions:** How does Orwell's ultimate decision show that "when the white man turns tyrant it is his own freedom that he destroys"? **(b) Modify:** If Orwell had not shot the elephant, would that have changed the meaning of the essay? Why or why not?

5. **(a) Compare and Contrast:** Compare Orwell's calm, detailed description of the dying elephant with his reactions to it at the time. **(b) Draw Conclusions:** What relationship between life and the act of writing does this contrast suggest?

6. **(a) Evaluate:** How fairly does Orwell evaluate his own actions? **(b) Make a Judgment:** Do you think that Orwell comes across as an admirable man in this selection? Explain.

Review and Assess

Literary Analysis

Irony

1. What **irony** lies in Orwell's fantasy of attacking a Buddhist priest?

2. What type of irony—verbal or situational—lies in Orwell's comment about the crowd following him: "They were going to have their bit of fun, after all." Explain your categorization.

3. Use a chart like the one shown to analyze Orwell's use of irony. Then, choose the two most effective examples.

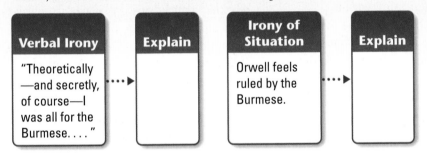

Verbal Irony

"Theoretically —and secretly, of course—I was all for the Burmese...."

Explain

Irony of Situation

Orwell feels ruled by the Burmese.

Explain

4. Do you think that Orwell's sense of irony reflects his privileged position in Burma? Explain.

Connecting Literary Elements

5. (a) Find examples of Orwell's use of dashes and of phrases such as "sort of." (b) What do such elements add to his **tone**?

6. (a) Identify and analyze three passages in which style, sentence length, or word choice create a distinctive tone. (b) Based on these passages, what would you say is the tone of the essay?

7. (a) Describe another tone that Orwell might have chosen for his essay. (b) Explain whether or not it would have been more effective.

Reading Strategy

Recognizing the Writer's Attitude

8. Describe Orwell's conflicting attitudes in the paragraph beginning "It was perfectly clear to me what I ought to do."

9. What does this conflict reveal about his views of imperialism?

Extend Understanding

10. **Career Connection:** What do you think would be the best training for a journalist like Orwell? Why?

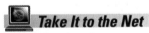

Integrate Language Skills

Vocabulary Development Lesson

Concept Development: Words About Politics

Use your knowledge of the political words in this essay to define these words:

    1. imperialism   **2.** dominion   **3.** despotic

Spelling Strategy

When adding a suffix beginning with a vowel to a multisyllable word, double the final consonant of the word only if the last syllable is stressed: *begin + -er = beginner*. Otherwise, do not double it: *imperial + -ism = imperialism*. Add the suffix indicated to these words:

    1. colonial *(-ism)*   **3.** regret *(-able)*

    2. diplomat *(-ic)*   **4.** question *(-er)*

Fluency: Context

Copy the following paragraph into your notebook. Using context clues in the paragraph, replace each italicized word or phrase with a word from the vocabulary list on page 1017.

As a veteran of summer camps from Maine to Wyoming, I can tell you about some of the *wretched* conditions under which many *tyrannical* counselors force one to live. Under their *rule*, the camp is run like a colony under *a policy of political and economic control*, which leaves some campers totally *overcome* with fear instead of overwhelmed with the joy of the outdoors. Only *mental decay* could lead me to forget my traumatic summer experiences.

Grammar and Style Lesson

Participial Phrases: Restrictive and Nonrestrictive

Participial phrases—participles with their modifiers or complements—modify nouns and pronouns. Restrictive participial phrases are essential to the meaning of the words they modify and are not set off by commas. Nonrestrictive phrases are not essential and are set off by commas.

> **Restrictive:** The wretched prisoners huddling in the stinking cages of the lockups, . . . (tells which prisoners)
>
> **Nonrestrictive:** Some more women followed, clicking their tongues and exclaiming; . . . (does not tell which women)

Participial phases allow writers to fill in details of a scene even as they narrate a main action.

Practice Write each participial phrase and the word it modifies. Identify the phrase as restrictive or nonrestrictive.

  1. It was . . . a labyrinth of squalid bamboo huts, thatched with palm leaf, . . .

  2. I . . . saw a man's dead body sprawling in the mud.

  3. I marched down the hill, looking and feeling a fool, . . .

  4. . . . peacefully eating, the elephant looked no more dangerous than a cow.

  5. . . . in reality I was only an absurd puppet pushed to and fro. . . .

Writing Application Write about Orwell's experiences, using two restrictive and two nonrestrictive participial phrases.

W͞G Prentice Hall Writing and Grammar Connection: Chapter 19, Section 2

Writing Lesson

Essay in Orwell's Style

Orwell's style is plainspoken, but it is nonetheless distinctive. Write an essay in his style on a problem you once encountered.

Prewriting   Reread Orwell's essay, jotting down notes on his style. Then, choose an experience on which to write and outline the details.

Drafting   Begin, as Orwell does, with a general account of your response to your experience. Then, present events in clear order, relating each detail to your general response. As you draft, "listen" to what you write to make sure it sounds like Orwell.

Revising   Review Orwell's essay, and then review your draft. Highlight any parts that are inconsistent with his style. For instance, look for long, elaborate sentences or vague, flowery descriptions. Rewrite or eliminate such passages to create a consistent style.

Model: Revising for Consistent Style

I had only gone along with the others for fear of being laughed at. ~~When those rotten cowards Johnny and Rafael ran away, leaving me all alone to face our parents, I thought, "This really stinks!"—I mean, can you believe what they did?~~

When Johnny and Rafael ran away, I now had a different fear to face: being the only one blamed.

> Eliminating a long, impassioned sentence makes the style more consistent with Orwell's. The new sentence adds irony like Orwell's.

WG   *Prentice Hall Writing and Grammar Connection: Chapter 4, Section 4*

Extension Activities

Listening and Speaking Burma became independent after World War II. With a group, prepare and deliver an **audiovisual presentation** about Burmese independence. Your presentation should link historical facts to Orwell's essay. Use these materials:

- Historic timeline
- Photographs for overhead projection
- Recordings of Burmese music

Discuss which audiovisual aids will be practical and effective. Have each group member direct one section of the presentation. **[Group Activity]**

Research and Technology In 1991, a Burmese freedom fighter, Aung San Suu Kyi, won the Nobel Peace Prize. Write a brief **biography** comparing her political positions and practices to Orwell's. Consult primary sources such as San's essays, speeches, and letters. Confirm facts by locating information in more than one source.

 **Take It to the Net**   www.phschool.com

Go online for an additional research activity using the Internet.

Prepare to Read

The Demon Lover

Elizabeth Bowen (1899–1973)

The fiction of Elizabeth Bowen is distinguished by her subtle observation of landscape, by her innovative and believable use of the supernatural, and by her haunting portrayal of England during one of the darkest eras of the country's history—World War II, which lasted from 1939 to 1945.

A Troubled Childhood Bowen was born into comfortable circumstances. Her parents were wealthy, and she grew up in Dublin and on their country estate in County Cork, Ireland. Early in life, though, she suffered serious losses. Her father had a breakdown when she was seven years old, and he was confined to an institution. She and her mother moved to England, where, Bowen later said, she and her mother waged a "campaign of not noticing" her father's absence. When Bowen was thirteen, her mother died of cancer. Bowen was not allowed to attend the funeral.

From Life Into Art As an adult, Bowen was to write about such experiences of the denial of emotion and about the helplessness of the heart to understand itself or others in the absence of love. In her characters' insecure lives, in the damage that is done them when their feelings are not acknowledged, one can still trace the marks left by Bowen's own early abandonment.

A Writer's Life After her mother's death, Bowen lived with her relatives and then attended boarding school until she was seventeen, when she moved to London. Her one ambition was to write, and her family's money was enough to support her as she wrote her first short stories.

Her first collection of short stories, published in 1923, received little attention. Through the 1930s, while living with her husband in Oxford, she perfected her craft, publishing regularly. In 1938, she completed *The Death of the Heart*, one of her best-known works. The novel is about the disillusionment of an innocent teenage girl, taken in by uncaring relatives after her mother's death.

The War and After During the war, Bowen observed England's hardships keenly and with compassion. She incorporated the brutal realities of the war—air raids, blackouts, betrayal—into some of her best stories. By using a wartime setting and playing on the heightened emotions and perceptions people have at such times, Bowen was able to expose the innermost workings of her characters' minds.

After the war, Bowen widened her literary activities to include literary criticism and book reviews. She wrote for such journals as the *Tatler* and contributed scripts to the British Broadcasting Company, which programmed all British radio and television broadcasts at the time. In 1948, she was honored by the prestigious award Commander, Order of the British Empire (C.B.E.). In 1949, she published *The Heat of the Day*, a much acclaimed novel. Set in wartime London, the novel movingly juxtaposes a tragic love affair with the larger crisis of the nation.

After the death of her husband in 1952, Bowen returned to Ireland. Her later novels—including, *A World of Love* (1955), *The Little Girls* (1964), and *Eva Trout* (1969)—exhibit a more symbolic, more poetic style than her earlier works. All of her work, however, testifies to her sensitivity to finer shades of emotion and her eye for telling details.

Bowen defined the novel as the "non-poetic statement of poetic truth." Guided by the hardships she had undergone, working in a deceptively simple style, she achieved this goal admirably.

Preview

Connecting to the Literature

Becoming a "ghost" is easy; it's just a trick of time and place. Walk by your old elementary school . . . linger in your old home just before moving. . . . All it takes to become a ghost—or perhaps to see one—is a sideways step out of familiar routines, as "The Demon Lover" suggests.

Literary Analysis

The Ghost Story

A **ghost story** is a tale in which part of the past—typically, a dead person—seems to make a supernatural appearance in the present. Many good ghost stories are characterized by these elements:

- An eerie or mysterious atmosphere
- The suggestion that supernatural forces are at work
- An open possibility that the eerie events they recount have a "natural" explanation

By suggesting—not directly asserting—the activity of supernatural forces and by causing the reader to hesitate between "natural" and "supernatural" interpretations of events, a ghost story eerily blurs the line between the familiar and the unfamiliar. As you read "The Demon Lover," analyze these elements of a ghost story, using a chart like the one shown.

Past ···▶ Present

Familiar ···▶ Unfamiliar

Natural ···▶ Supernatural

Connecting Literary Elements

Some of the best ghost stories contain **ambiguity**—they support two or more divergent interpretations. In literature, words may be used in intentionally ambiguous ways to add layers of meaning. As you read, notice how Bowen adds to the mysterious quality of her tale through ambiguity, making readers wonder whether the "ghost" in the story is a dead man or a hallucination brought on by unresolved feelings about the past.

Reading Strategy

Responding to the Story

The first step in understanding literature is also the most basic—**responding to the story** as you read, whether with puzzlement or terror. Your next step is to judge how the writer evoked that response. As you read, note your reactions and look for what the writer has done to elicit them.

Vocabulary Development

spectral (spek´ trəl) *adj.* ghostly (p. 1034)

dislocation (dis´ lō kā´ shən) *n.* condition of being out of place (p. 1035)

arboreal (är bôr´ ē´ əl) *adj.* of, near, or among trees (p. 1035)

circumscribed (sur´ kəm skrībd´) *adj.* limited; having a definite boundary (p. 1035)

aperture (ap´ ər chər´) *n.* opening (p. 1038)

THE DEMON Lover

Elizabeth Bowen

Background

World War II was a fact of daily life in the London of the 1940s. After decisive victories in Europe, Germany determined to break Britain with a steady bombardment focused on London. During "the Blitz," from September 1940 to May 1941, German planes dropped bombs on the city almost every night. Whole communities were evacuated periodically, leaving street after street of deserted buildings. Elizabeth Bowen lived in London during this time, and the eerie quality of "The Demon Lover" stems from her experience of a time when war's horrors had become all too "ordinary."

Toward the end of her day in London Mrs. Drover went round to her shut-up house to look for several things she wanted to take away. Some belonged to herself, some to her family, who were by now used to their country life. It was late August; it had been a steamy, showery day: at the moment the trees down the pavement glittered in an escape of humid yellow afternoon sun. Against the next batch of clouds, already piling up ink-dark, broken chimneys and parapets stood out. In her once familiar street, as in any unused channel, an unfamiliar queerness had silted up; a cat wove itself in and out of railings, but no human eye watched Mrs. Drover's return. Shifting some parcels under her arm, she slowly forced round her latchkey in an unwilling lock, then gave the door, which had warped, a push with her knee. Dead air came out to meet her as she went in.

The staircase window having been boarded up, no light came down into the hall. But one door, she could just see, stood ajar, so she went quickly through into the room and unshuttered the big window in there. Now the prosaic woman, looking about her, was more perplexed than she knew by everything that she saw, by traces of her long former habit of life—the yellow smoke stain up the white marble mantel-piece, the ring left by a vase on the top of the escritoire,[1] the bruise in the wallpaper where, on the door being thrown open widely, the china handle had always hit the wall. The piano, having gone away to be stored, had left what looked like claw marks on its part of the parquet.[2] Though not much dust had seeped in, each object wore a film of another kind; and, the only ventilation being the chimney, the whole drawing room smelled of the cold hearth. Mrs. Drover put down her parcels on the escritoire and left the room to proceed upstairs; the things she wanted were in a bedroom chest.

She had been anxious to see how the house was—the part-time caretaker she shared with some neighbors was away this week on his holiday, known to be not yet back. At the best of times he did not look in often, and she was never sure that she trusted him. There were some cracks in the structure, left by the last bombing, on which she was anxious to keep an eye. Not that one could do anything—

A shaft of refracted daylight now lay across the hall. She stopped dead and stared at the hall table—on this lay a letter addressed to her.

She thought first—then the caretaker *must* be back. All the same, who, seeing the house shuttered, would have dropped a letter in at the box? It was not a circular, it was not a bill. And the post office redirected, to the address in the country, everything for her that came through the post. The caretaker (even if he *were* back) did not know she was due in London today—her call here had been planned to be a surprise—so his negligence in the manner of this letter, leaving it to wait in the dusk and the dust, annoyed her. Annoyed, she picked up the letter, which bore no stamp. But it cannot be important, or they would know . . . She took the letter rapidly upstairs with her, without a stop to look at the writing till she reached what had been her bedroom, where she let in light. The room looked over the garden and other gardens: the sun had gone in; as the clouds sharpened and lowered, the trees and rank lawns seemed already to smoke with dark. Her reluctance to look again at the letter came from the fact that she felt intruded upon—and by someone contemptuous of her ways. However, in the tenseness preceding the fall of rain she read it: it was a few lines.

> DEAR KATHLEEN,
> You will not have forgotten that today is our anniversary, and the day we said. The years have gone by at once slowly and fast. In view of the fact that nothing has changed, I shall rely upon you to

---

1. **escritoire** (es´ krə twär´) *n.* a writing desk or table.
2. **parquet** (pär kā´) *n.* flooring of inlaid woodwork in geometric forms.

Literary Analysis
The Ghost Story How does Bowen prepare the reader for the suggestion that there is something supernatural about the letter?

**Reading Check**
What does Mrs. Drover unexpectedly discover in her vacant house?

keep your promise. I was sorry to see you leave London, but was satisfied that you would be back in time. You may expect me, therefore, at the hour arranged.
Until then . . . K.

Mrs. Drover looked for the date: it was today's. She dropped the letter onto the bedsprings, then picked it up to see the writing again—her lips, beneath the remains of lipstick, beginning to go white. She felt so much the change in her own face that she went to the mirror, polished a clear patch in it and looked at once urgently and stealthily in. She was confronted by a woman of forty-four, with eyes starting out under a hatbrim that had been rather carelessly pulled down. She had not put on any more powder since she left the shop where she ate her solitary tea. The pearls her husband had given her on their marriage hung loose round her now rather thinner throat, slipping into the V of the pink wool jumper her sister knitted last autumn as they sat round the fire. Mrs. Drover's most normal expression was one of controlled worry, but of assent. Since the birth of the third of her little boys, attended by a quite serious illness, she had had an intermittent muscular flicker to the left of her mouth, but in spite of this she could always sustain a manner that was at once energetic and calm.

Turning from her own face as precipitately as she had gone to meet it, she went to the chest where the things were, unlocked it, threw up the lid and knelt to search. But as rain began to come crashing down she could not keep from looking over her shoulder at the stripped bed on which the letter lay. Behind the blanket of rain the clock of the church that still stood struck six—with rapidly heightening apprehension she counted each of the slow strokes. "The hour arranged . . . My God," she said, "*What hour?* How should I . . . ? After twenty-five years. . . ."

The young girl talking to the soldier in the garden had not ever completely seen his face. It was dark; they were saying goodbye under a tree. Now and then—for it felt, from not seeing him at this intense moment, as though she had never seen him at all—she verified his presence for these few moments longer by putting out a hand, which he each time pressed, without very much kindness, and painfully, on to one of the breast buttons of his uniform. That cut of the button on the palm of her hand was, principally, what she was to carry away. This was so near the end of a leave from France that she could only wish him already gone. It was August 1916. Being not kissed, being drawn away from and looked at intimidated Kathleen till she imagined <u>spectral</u> glitters in the place of his eyes. Turning away and looking back up the lawn she saw, through branches of trees, the drawing-room window alight; she caught a breath for the

The British Tradition

In "The Demon Lover," Bowen hardly mentions World War II—the war appears only as the implied explanation for the Drovers' flight from their home. Bowen's story, though, captures the oppressive atmosphere of the Blitz, a time when familiar routines were routinely shattered by blackouts, air-raid sirens, and explosions. The menace Mrs. Drover confronts is not a bombing raid, but like the Blitz itself, it is a menace that lurks behind the most ordinary scenes.

Literary writers frequently engage with events of their time using the imagination to fashion a meaning from history. In *Gulliver's Travels*, Jonathan Swift criticized the political and social absurdities of his day. In poetry, Matthew Arnold lamented the spirit of the Victorian Age, while later poets such as Wilfred Owen condemned the horrors of World War I.

Such literary works may satisfy a reader's need to find sense in the jumble of historical events. At the same time, these works may challenge events, refusing to assent to the values they represent. In her portrait of Mrs. Drover, who lives a life cracked by war, Bowen may be suggesting that our world is haunted by madness, a madness that spawned two world wars less than thirty years apart.

spectral (spek´ trəl) *adj.* ghostly

moment when she could go running back there into the safe arms of her mother and sister, and cry: "What shall I do, what shall I do? He has gone."

Hearing her catch her breath, her fiancé said, without feeling: "Cold?"

"You're going away such a long way."

"Not so far as you think."

"I don't understand?"

"You don't have to," he said. "You will. You know what we said."

"But that was—suppose you—I mean, suppose."

"I shall be with you," he said, "sooner or later. You won't forget that. You need do nothing but wait."

Only a little more than a minute later she was free to run up the silent lawn. Looking in through the window at her mother and sister, who did not for the moment perceive her, she already felt that unnatural promise drive down between her and the rest of all humankind. No other way of having given herself could have made her feel so apart, lost and foresworn. She could not have plighted a more sinister troth.

Kathleen behaved well when, some months later, her fiancé was reported missing, presumed killed. Her family not only supported her but were able to praise her courage without stint because they could not regret, as a husband for her, the man they knew almost nothing about. They hoped she would, in a year or two, console herself—and had it been only a question of consolation things might have gone much straighter ahead. But her trouble, behind just a little grief, was a complete <u>dislocation</u> from everything. She did not reject other lovers, for these failed to appear: for years she failed to attract men— and with the approach of her thirties she became natural enough to share her family's anxiousness on this score. She began to put herself out, to wonder; and at thirty-two she was very greatly relieved to find herself being courted by William Drover. She married him, and the two of them settled down in this quiet, <u>arboreal</u> part of Kensington; in this house the years piled up, her children were born and they all lived till they were driven out by the bombs of the next war. Her movements as Mrs. Drover were <u>circumscribed</u>, and she dismissed any idea that they were still watched.

As things were—dead or living the letter writer sent her only a threat. Unable, for some minutes, to go on kneeling with her back exposed to the empty room, Mrs. Drover rose from the chest to sit on an upright chair whose back was firmly against the wall. The desuetude[3] of her former bedroom, her married London home's whole air of being a cracked cup from which memory, with its reassuring power, had either evaporated or leaked away, made a crisis—and at just this crisis the letter writer had, knowledgeably, struck. The hollowness of the house this evening canceled years on years of voices, habits and steps. Through the shut windows she only heard rain fall

---

3. **desuetude** (des′ wi tⱵod′) *adj.* condition of not being used any more.

Literary Analysis
The Ghost Story and Ambiguity In what two ways might Kathleen's fiancé's remarks be interpreted?

dislocation (dis′ lō kā′ shən) *n.* condition of being out of place

arboreal (är bôr′ ē′ əl) *adj.* of, near, or among trees

circumscribed (sʉr′ kəm skrībd′) *adj.* limited; having a definite boundary

**Reading Check**

What happens to Kathleen's fiancé after he returns to war?

on the roofs around. To rally herself, she said she was in a mood—and, for two or three seconds shutting her eyes, told herself that she imagined the letter. But she opened them—there it lay on the bed.

On the supernatural side of the letter's entrance she was not permitting her mind to dwell. Who, in London, knew she meant to call at the house today? Evidently, however, this had been known. The caretaker, *had* he come back, had had no cause to expect her: he would have taken the letter in his pocket, to forward it, at his own time, through the post. There was no other sign that the caretaker had been in—but, if not? Letters dropped in at doors of deserted houses do not fly or walk to tables in halls. They do not sit on the dust of empty tables with the air of certainty that they will be found. There is needed some human hand—but nobody but the caretaker had a key. Under circumstances she did not care to consider, a house can be entered without a key. It was possible that she was not alone now. She might be being waited for, downstairs. Waited for—until when? Until "the hour arranged." At least that was not six o'clock; six has struck.

She rose from the chair and went over and locked the door.

The thing was, to get out. To fly? No, not that: she had to catch her train. As a woman whose utter dependability was the keystone of her family life she was not willing to return to the country, to her husband, her little boys and her sister, without the objects she had come up to fetch. Resuming work at the chest she set about making up a number of parcels in a rapid, fumbling-decisive way. These, with her shopping parcels, would be too much to carry; these meant a taxi—at the thought of the taxi her heart went up and her normal breathing resumed. I will ring up the taxi now; the taxi cannot come too soon; I shall hear the taxi out there running its engine, till I walk calmly down to it through the hall. I'll ring up—But no: the telephone is cut off . . . She tugged at a knot she had tied wrong.

The idea of flight . . . He was never kind to me, not really. I don't remember him kind at all. Mother said he never considered me. He was set on me, that was what it was—not love. Not love, not meaning a person well. What did he do, to make me promise like that? I can't remember—But she found that she could.

She remembered with such dreadful acuteness that the twenty-five years since then dissolved like smoke and she instinctively looked for the weal[4] left by the button on the palm of her hand. She remembered not only all that he said and did but the complete suspension of *her* existence during that August week. I was not myself—they all told me so at the time. She remembered—but with one white burning blank as where acid has dropped on a photograph: *under no conditions* could she remember his face.

So wherever he may be waiting, I shall not know him. You have no time to run from a face you do not expect.

Literary Analysis
The Ghost Story In this paragraph, how do Mrs. Drover's fear of the supernatural and her attention to practical details blur the lines between the familiar world and the unknown?

---

4. **weal** *n.* raised mark, line, or ridge on the skin caused by an injury.

Ox House, Shaftsbury, 1932, John R. Biggs

◀ **Critical Viewing**
Compare the suggestion
of "life" this engraving
gives to material objects
with the role of objects
in the story. Are they a
threat, a consolation, or
indifferent? [**Compare
and Contrast**]

The thing was to get to the taxi before any clock struck what could be the hour. She would slip down the street and round the side of the square to where the square gave on the main road. She would return in the taxi, safe, to her own door, and bring the driver into the house with her to pick up the parcels from room to room. The idea of the taxi driver made her decisive, bold; she unlocked her door, went to the top of the staircase and listened down.

She heard nothing—but while she was hearing nothing the passé[5] air of the staircase was disturbed by a draft that traveled up to her face. It emanated from the basement: down there a door or window was being opened by someone who chose this moment to leave the house.

The rain had stopped; the pavements steamily shone as Mrs. Drover let herself out by inches from her own front door into the empty street. The unoccupied houses opposite continued to meet her look with their damaged stare. Making toward the thoroughfare and the taxi, she tried not to keep looking behind. Indeed, the silence was so intense—one of those creeks of London silence exaggerated this summer by the damage of war—that no tread could have gained on hers unheard. Where her street debouched on the square where people went on living, she grew conscious of, and checked, her unnatural pace. Across the open end of

---

5. passé (pa sā´) *adj.* stale.

✓ **Reading Check**

What does Mrs. Drover
struggle to avoid?

the square two buses impassively passed each other; women, a perambulator,[6] cyclists, a man wheeling a barrow signalized, once again, the ordinary flow of life. At the square's most populous corner should be—and was—the short taxi rank. This evening, only one taxi—but this, although it presented its blank rump, appeared already to be alertly waiting for her. Indeed, without looking round the driver started his engine as she panted up from behind and put her hand on the door. As she did so, the clock struck seven. The taxi faced the main road. To make the trip back to her house it would have to turn—she had settled back on the seat and the taxi *had* turned before she, surprised by its knowing movement, recollected that she had not "said where." She leaned forward to scratch at the glass panel that divided the driver's head from her own.

The driver braked to what was almost a stop, turned round and slid the glass panel back. The jolt of this flung Mrs. Drover forward till her face was almost into the glass. Through the <u>aperture</u> driver and passenger, not six inches between them, remained for an eternity eye to eye. Mrs. Drover's mouth hung open for some seconds before she could issue her first scream. After that she continued to scream freely and to beat with her gloved hands on the glass all round as the taxi, accelerating without mercy, made off with her into the hinterland of deserted streets.

aperture (ap´ ər chər´) *n.* opening

---

6. perambulator *n.* baby carriage.

![header bar]

Review and Assess

Thinking About the Selection

1. **Respond:** Do you feel sympathetic toward Mrs. Drover? Why or why not?

2. **(a) Recall:** Why is the appearance of the letter in Mrs. Drover's house unexpected? **(b) Infer:** Why is she so upset by it?

3. **(a) Recall:** Before returning to the war, what had Mrs. Drover's fiancé promised her? **(b) Analyze:** Identify three points at which she feels that she is being watched, and describe what each moment adds to the story. **(c) Draw Conclusions:** What does this feeling suggest about her guilt toward her fiancé?

4. **(a) Analyze:** Identify three references in the story to "traces," marks left behind by objects or actions.
   (b) Interpret: In what sense are ghosts and memories also traces? **(c) Draw Conclusions:** How do the references to traces suggest and support the story's theme?

5. **Draw Conclusions:** What does Mrs. Drover's fate suggest about the importance of habit and the familiar in human life?

Review and Assess

Literary Analysis

The Ghost Story

1. Find examples in the tale of each of these characteristics of a **ghost story:** (a) the intrusion of the past and, (b) the suggestion of supernatural explanations for events.

2. (a) Identify two details hinting at supernatural influences in Kathleen's last meeting with her fiancé. Explain your choice. (b) Name two details that make the parting seem psychologically realistic and not supernatural. Explain your choice.

3. (a) Find two passages that contrast the familiar with the eerie. In each, what allows the strange to "leak into" the familiar? (b) What do these passages suggest about Bowen's view of the fragility of life?

Connecting Literary Elements

4. (a) Identify two examples of **ambiguity** in phrases in the story's opening paragraph. (b) Explain how they hint at the eerie events to come.

5. (a) In what two ways might events in the story be interpreted? (b) Does the evidence favor one over the other? Explain.

6. Either Mrs. Drover or her fiancé might be the "demon lover" of the title. Explain, showing how this ambiguity sheds light on the story.

Reading Strategy

Responding to the Story

7. What was your **response** to the atmosphere at the beginning of the story? Explain.

8. Use an organizer like the one shown to analyze your responses to events in the story and the devices Bowen uses to elicit them.

Detail	My Response	Technique
Sight of letter on table	It feels a little creepy.	Appearance announced with sudden break in Mrs. Drover's thoughts.

Extend Understanding

9. **Psychology Connection:** Mrs. Drover is haunted by an unresolved problem from the past. According to psychologists, how may a person be "haunted" by the past?

Integrate Language Skills

Vocabulary Development Lesson

Word Analysis: Latin Root *-loc-*

The word *dislocation*, formed from the Latin root *-loc-*, meaning "place," means "the condition of being out of place." Using your knowledge of the root, define the following words:

1. locomotion
2. local
3. relocating

Spelling Strategy

When adding the suffix *-tion* to a verb that ends in *-te*, first drop these letters. Then, add the suffix *-tion: dislocate, dislocation.* For each of these words ending in *-tion*, give the related verb.

1. notation
2. equation
3. inflation

Fluency: Words in Context

Review the vocabulary list on page 1031. Then, in your notebook, explain whether the italicized word in each of the sentences below is used correctly. Let the context created by the sentence guide you.

1. I was relieved when I touched not a *spectral* presence, but solid flesh.
2. Given the pollution in the world's waterways, I am surprised that more *arboreal* species are not endangered.
3. Take whatever you wish; my generosity is strictly *circumscribed*.
4. The letter fit through the *aperture*.
5. The doctor has caused a permanent *dislocation* of your shoulder; you should feel fine in a day or two.

Grammar and Style Lesson

Sentence Beginnings: Participial Phrases

Bowen begins some sentences with participial phrases. A **participle** is a verb form usually ending in *-ed* or *-ing*. A **participial phrase** is a participle, together with its modifiers and complements. The whole phrase acts as an adjective.

> **Participial Phrase:** Shifting some parcels under her arm, she slowly forced round her latchkey . . . (modifies *she*)
>
> **Participle:** Shocked, she stopped to catch her breath. (modifies *she*)

When a sentence begins with a participial phrase, it seems to start "in the middle" of an action that is already underway—an effect that draws readers in. For clarity, a participial phrase should be placed next to the word it modifies.

Practice Identify the participial phrases and the words they modify.

1. The piano, having been sent away, had left claw marks on the floor.
2. The cracks, left by the last bombing, ran down the wall.
3. The soldier, entering the lighted room, pulled his hat down to cover his face.
4. The young girl, halting the conversation, ran away from the soldier.
5. Pulling away from the stand, the taxi sped down the street.

Writing Application Write a brief paragraph about the story from the perspective of the demon lover. Use three participial phrases.

W̶G̶ Prentice Hall Writing and Grammar Connection: Chapter 19 Section 2

Writing Lesson

Sequel

Write a sequel to "The Demon Lover," answering the question, What happened next? To ensure that your sequel is well-connected with the original, use clear and logical organization.

Prewriting Jot down questions that "The Demon Lover" leaves unanswered. Then, suggest answers to these questions. Select a few of these answers as a starting point.

Drafting Outline the events in your story in a logical way. As you draft, give only enough information to prepare readers for what happens next. Choose logical places to fill in background from the original story.

Revising Number the main events in your story in chronological order. Review out-of-sequence passages. For each, consider whether your order will confuse readers or whether it creates a desirable effect. Reorganize your draft as necessary.

Model: Revising to Create Clear and Logical Organization

(3) Shaking off his surprise, he stepped through the now open door. (2) Someone had prepared the way for him, almost as if he were expected. (1) The day before, the door had been rusted shut.

Placing the description of event 2 after event 3 heightens the tension. Event 1 should be narrated earlier in the story.

Prentice Hall Writing and Grammar Connection: Chapter 5, Section 3

Extension Activities

Listening and Speaking Choose a ghost story that you find especially effective for a spooky **story reading.** Prepare, using these strategies:

- Read the text through several times.
- Note passages where a hushed tone will give a chill or where a raised voice and rapid speech will build suspense.
- Incorporate and practice using visual or sound effects to enhance your retelling.

Dim the lights, and present your reading to the class.

Research and Technology With a group, present a **history report** on life in London during the Blitz, linking your research to Bowen's story. Each group member should cover an aspect of the topic, such as historical background or daily life. Consult varied sources, including photographs and other primary sources.

 **Take It to the Net** www.phschool.com

Go online for an additional research activity using the Internet.

CONNECTIONS
Literature Around the World

> ## Waking From the Dream

Awakenings The writers in this section respond to the disconcerting, often violent, changes of the twentieth century. These upheavals mark their work with imagery of dreams and disillusion. Bowen in "The Demon Lover" and Yeats in "The Second Coming" stress the nightmarish aspects of war and of historical cycles. In "Preludes," T. S. Eliot portrays an awakening of the soul to a confused and fragmented world. In "Shooting an Elephant," Orwell shows how, as a young imperial police officer, he first awakened to the detrimental effects of colonialism.

"From Starry Bullet-holes" Yehuda Amichai (yə hoo´ də ä´ mi khī), Anna Akhmatova (ak mä´ tō və) and Bei Dao (bä dou) also record awakenings to the century's grim realities. Akhmatova, writing just after a bitter civil war in Russia (1918–1920), describes both the "misery" she sees around her and the "miraculous" that she senses. Amichai, a veteran of Israel's wars, shows the devastating and far-reaching effects of an act of terrorism. Bei Dao writes the "Testament" of a prisoner about to be executed by the Chinese government. Although soon to die, this man holds out the possibility that his death will be a source of renewal: "From starry bullet-holes / the blood-red dawn will flow."

Thrust 1959, Adolph Gottlieb, The Metropolitan Museum of Art

▶**Critical Viewing** In what ways does this image illustrate Amichai's poem? [**Connect**]

The Diameter of the Bomb

Yehuda Amichai
Translated by Chana Bloch

The diameter of the bomb was thirty centimeters
and the diameter of its effective range about seven meters,
with four dead and eleven wounded.
And around these, in a larger circle
5 of pain and time, two hospitals are scattered
and one graveyard. But the young woman
who was buried in the city she came from,
at a distance of more than a hundred kilometers,
enlarges the circle considerably,
10 and the solitary man mourning her death
at the distant shores of a country far across the sea
includes the entire world in the circle.
And I won't even mention the crying of orphans
that reaches up to the throne of God and
15 beyond, making
a circle with no end and no God.

Connecting Literature Around the World

1. Auden's "In Memory of W. B. Yeats" and Orwell's "Shooting an Elephant" both deal with the impact of historical events on individual lives. Compare one of these selections with Amichai's poem.

2. Compare the effect that war has on the speaker's vision of the world in this poem with the effect of war on Bowen's Mrs. Drover.

3. How would Auden's speaker in "Musée des Beaux Arts" respond to the vision of suffering in "The Diameter of the Bomb"? Why?

Yehuda Amichai

(1924–2000)

Born in Germany, Israeli poet Yehuda Amichai emigrated to Palestine prior to the start of World War II. He then fought in nearly all of Israel's wars and wrote poetry that expresses the thoughts and feelings of a whole generation of Israelis. In his poems, written in Hebrew, he skillfully combines biblical phrases and down-to-earth, everyday language.

Everything Is Plundered

Anna Akhmatova
Translated by Stanley Kunitz

Everything is plundered, betrayed, sold,
Death's great black wing scrapes the air,
Misery gnaws to the bone.
Why then do we not despair?

5　By day, from the surrounding woods,
cherries blow summer into town;
at night the deep transparent skies
glitter with new galaxies.

And the miraculous comes so close
10　to the ruined, dirty houses—
something not known to anyone at all,
but wild in our breast for centuries.

Anna Akhmatova

(1889–1966)

Russian poet Anna Akhmatova began writing poems at age eleven. During her long life, she experienced and wrote about a host of devastating events, from the Russian Revolution to the oppression of Stalin's dictatorship. Stalin banned her work for a time, but in 1940, the ban was lifted. She continued to write and publish until her death.

Connecting Literature Around the World

1. How would the speaker in Eliot's "Preludes" respond to Akhmatova's poem? Explain.

2. How would the speaker in Yeats's "The Wild Swans at Coole" respond to the poem? Explain.

3. Akhmatova refers to the miraculous—the survival of the beautiful amid the upheavals of life—as "something not known to anyone at all, / but wild in our breast for centuries." Does this "something" only make its presence felt through poetry? Explain.

Anna Akhmatova, N. I. Altman. The Granger Collection.

▲ **Critical Viewing** Does the Anna Akhmatova depicted in the portrait seem as
if she could have written this poem? Why or why not? **[Compare and Contrast]**

TESTAMENT[1]

Bei Dao

Translated by Donald Finkel and Xueliang Chen

Perhaps the time has come.
I haven't left a will,
just one pen, for my mother.

I'm no hero, you understand.
5 This isn't the year for heroes.
I'd just like to be a man.

The horizon still divides
the living from the dead,
but the sky's all I need.

10 I won't kneel on the earth—
the firing squad might block
the last free breaths of air.

From starry bullet-holes
the blood-red dawn will flow.

---

1. **Testament** (Tes´ tə ment) *n.* will; also, a statement of one's beliefs.

Bei Dao

(b. 1949)

Bei Dao is a Chinese poet whose work is—in the words of one of his translators, Bonnie S. McDougall—a "complex reaction to the pressures of a brutalized and corrupt society." He was traveling abroad during the Tiananmen Square massacre (June 4, 1989), in which the Chinese government violently ended pro-democracy rallies. Since that time, Bei has lived in exile from China.

Connecting Literature Around the World

1. Eliot criticizes modern people for a lack of self-definition and decisiveness. How would the speaker in this poem answer his criticism?

2. (a) In this poem and in other poems in this section, do events in the modern world appear senseless? (b) Can poetry make meaning out of senseless events? Explain, using two works for support.

Conflicts Abroad and at Home

A Balloon Site, Coventry, 1940, Dame Laura Knight, Imperial War Museum

Prepare to Read

The Soldier ◆ Wirers ◆ Anthem for Doomed Youth ◆ Birds on the Western Front

Rupert Brooke (1887–1915)

Rupert Brooke had striking good looks, personal charm, and high intelligence. Before World War I began, Brooke had already established himself as a serious poet. He traveled a great deal, writing essays as well as poetry. When war broke out in 1914, he joined the Royal Navy. Tragically, he died from blood poisoning while on a mission to defeat the Turks.

Brooke's war sonnets, traditional and idealistic, were among the last from the soldier-poets of World War I to express wholehearted patriotism. The prolonged, inhuman slaughter of trench warfare extinguished the idealism of many of them.

Siegfried Sassoon (1886–1967)

Born into a wealthy family in Kent, England, Siegfried Sassoon published poetry while still in his twenties. In 1914, he joined the army and showed such reckless courage in battle that he earned the nickname "Mad Jack," along with a medal for gallantry.

By 1916 or 1917, though, Sassoon's attitude toward war had changed. He began to write starkly realistic "trench poems" about war's agonies. He was wounded early in 1917 and, while recovering, wrote a statement condemning the war. Partly to defuse his criticism and partly to protect him from its consequences, he was placed in a hospital for victims of shell shock.

Sassoon survived the war and lived almost fifty years longer, but he wrote little to match his wartime verses.

Wilfred Owen (1893–1918)

Always interested in literature, Wilfred Owen studied at London University, later worked as a tutor, and joined the army in 1915. A respected officer, he was wounded three times in 1917 and won a medal for outstanding bravery in 1918. Owen's work, at first an imitation of Keats's, became grittier and angrier under the influence of Siegfried Sassoon, whom he had met at a military hospital in 1917. It was a terrible loss to English poetry when Owen was killed in battle just one week before the end of the war.

Having published only five poems during his lifetime, Owen was unknown as a poet until Sassoon published a collection of his work, *Poems,* in 1920. Today, Owen is regarded as one of the greatest war poets in the English language. In the Preface to his poems, he is quoted as writing, "My subject is War, and the pity of War. The Poetry is in the pity. . . ."

Saki (H. H. Munro) (1870–1916)

Brought up from an early age by strict and unsympathetic aunts, Saki endured an unhappy childhood. However, he went on to become the author of many witty and humorous short stories. He also took revenge on his aunts by mocking bossy aunts in a number of the short stories he wrote. Dry, sometimes malice-tinged, his mockery is directed at those who lack imagination.

When the Great War broke out, Saki refused a commission as an officer, preferring instead to serve as an enlisted man. He was killed in the Battle of the Somme two years after volunteering.

Preview

Connecting to the Literature

World War I, the first example of mechanized warfare on an international scale, brought untold suffering and devastation. It also inspired millions of words—patriotic, indignant, or disillusioned. These authors were among the firsthand witnesses who suffered from and wrote about this cataclysmic event.

Literary Analysis

Tone

The **tone** of a literary work is the writer's attitude toward the readers and toward the subject. A writer's choice of words and details conveys the tone of a work. For example, in these lines from Rupert Brooke's "The Soldier," the underlined words and phrases communicate a tone of patriotic devotion and wistful memory:

> Her sights and sounds; dreams happy as her day;
> And laughter, learnt of friends; and gentleness,
> In hearts at peace, under an English heaven.

Be alert to the way phrases and details in these poems convey various tones.

Comparing Literary Works

In a way, these selections are like letters sent home by soldiers during World War I. These "letters" each contain a message about the war for those who are back in England, removed from the fighting. In figuring out these messages, use tone as a clue—identify words and phrases that reveal each writer's attitude toward the war and toward civilian readers. Then, compare and contrast the messages about the war that these writers convey.

Reading Strategy

Making Inferences

Because writers often suggest rather than state elements like tone, theme, and speaker, readers must **make inferences,** or educated guesses, about them based on clues in the text. Use a chart like the one shown to make inferences about tone and other elements in these works.

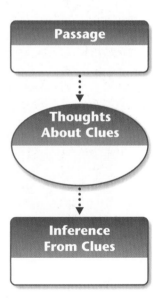

Vocabulary Development

stealthy (stel´ thē) *adj.* secretive; furtive (p. 1052)

desolate (des´ ə lit) *adj.* deserted; forlorn (p. 1052)

mockeries (mäk´ ər ēz) *n.* futile or disappointing efforts; ridicule (p. 1053)

pallor (pal´ ər) *n.* lack of color; paleness (p. 1053)

laudable (lôd´ ə bəl) *adj.* worthy of praise (p. 1054)

requisitioned (rek´ wə zish´ ənd) *v.* requested or applied for with a formal written order (p. 1055)

disconcerted (dis´ kən sʉrt´ əd) *adj.* embarrassed or confused (p. 1057)

The Soldier

Rupert Brooke

"With faith — we shall not sleep"

BUY VICTORY BONDS

▲ **Critical Viewing** How does the sentiment expressed in this poster relate to that in "The Soldier"? **[Connect]**

Background

World War I (1914–1918) pitted Great Britain, France, Russia, Japan, Italy, and later the United States (the Allies) against Germany, Austria-Hungary, and Turkey (the Central Powers). The war was fought not only in Europe but also in regions like the Middle East and Asia Minor. Typical of this conflict, especially in Western Europe, was trench warfare. Armies faced each other in defensive trenches protected by barbed wire. Periodically, one army would attack another in the face of machine-gun and artillery fire. Such warfare and the illnesses resulting from life in filthy trenches led to a total loss of about 8.5 million soldiers.

If I should die, think only this of me:
    That there's some corner of a foreign field
That is forever England. There shall be
    In that rich earth a richer dust concealed;
5 A dust whom England bore, shaped, made aware,
    Gave, once, her flowers to love, her ways to roam,
A body of England's, breathing English air,
Washed by the rivers, blest by suns of home.

And think, this heart, all evil shed away,
10   A pulse in the eternal mind, no less
      Gives somewhere back the thoughts by England given;
Her sights and sounds; dreams happy as her day;
    And laughter, learnt of friends; and gentleness,
      In hearts at peace, under an English heaven.

Literary Analysis
Tone What are three adjectives that describe the tone of this poem? Explain.

Review and Assess

Thinking About the Selection

1. **(a) Recall:** How does the speaker ask his readers to remember him, should he die? **(b) Infer:** Why would the speaker go off to war, knowing he could be killed?

2. **(a) Recall:** Name some of the things England has given the speaker. **(b) Interpret:** What is the "richer dust" to which the speaker refers?

3. **(a) Recall:** In lines 9 and 10, what does the speaker say his "heart" will become? **(b) Interpret:** What does the speaker mean by this statement?

4. **Take a Position:** Brooke's attitude has been called a "ridiculous anachronism"—something outdated—in the face of modern warfare. Do you agree or disagree? Why?

Wirers[1] Siegfried Sassoon

Drawing of Tanks, World War I

"Pass it along, the wiring party's going out"—
And yawning sentries mumble, "Wirers going out."
Unraveling; twisting; hammering stakes with muffled thud,
They toil with <u>stealthy</u> haste and anger in their blood.

5 The Boche[2] sends up a flare. Black forms stand rigid there,
Stock-still like posts; then darkness, and the clumsy ghosts
Stride hither and thither, whispering, tripped by clutching
    snare
Of snags and tangles.
            Ghastly dawn with vaporous coasts
10 Gleams <u>desolate</u> along the sky, night's misery ended.

Young Hughes was badly hit; I heard him carried away,
Moaning at every lurch; no doubt he'll die today.
But *we* can say the front-line wire's been safely mended.

▲ Critical Viewing
Which details in this painting support Sassoon's depiction of warfare? Explain. **[Connect]**

stealthy (stel´ thē) *adj.* secretive; furtive

desolate (des´ ə lit) *adj.* deserted; forlorn

---

1. **wirers** soldiers who were responsible for repairing the barbed-wire fences that protected the trenches in World War I.
2. **Boche** (bōsh) French slang for a German soldier.

Anthem *for* Doomed Youth

Wilfred Owen

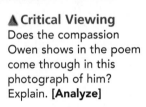

What passing-bells for these who die as cattle?
Only the monstrous anger of the guns.
Only the stuttering rifles' rapid rattle
Can patter out their hasty orisons.[1]

5 No <u>mockeries</u> for them from prayers or bells,
Nor any voice of mourning save the choirs—
The shrill, demented choirs of wailing shells;
And bugles calling for them from sad shires.[2]

What candles may be held to speed them all?
10 Not in the hands of boys, but in their eyes
Shall shine the holy glimmers of good-byes.
The <u>pallor</u> of girls' brows shall be their pall;
Their flowers the tenderness of patient minds,
And each slow dusk a drawing-down of blinds.

---

1. **orisons** (ôr´ i zəns) *n.* prayers.
2. **shires** (shīrz) *n.* any of the counties of England.

▲ Critical Viewing
Does the compassion Owen shows in the poem come through in this photograph of him? Explain. **[Analyze]**

mockeries (mäk´ ər ēz) *n.* futile or disappointing efforts; ridicule

pallor (pal´ ər) *n.* lack of color; paleness

Review and Assess

Thinking About the Selections

1. **Respond:** Which of these two poems conveys the horrors of war more effectively for you? Explain.

2. **(a) Recall:** What are the men getting ready to do at the beginning of "Wirers"? **(b) Infer:** How do the men feel about the job they have to do?

3. **(a) Recall:** In "Wirers," what happens in the course of the mission? **(b) Draw Conclusions:** What is the speaker's attitude toward the mission and toward the war? Explain.

4. **(a) Recall:** In lines 9–14 of "Anthem for Doomed Youth," what conventional signs of mourning are mentioned?
   (b) Analyze: What do Owen's suggested replacements for these signs have in common?

5. **Make a Judgment:** Which of these poems better captures the horrors of mechanized warfare? Why?

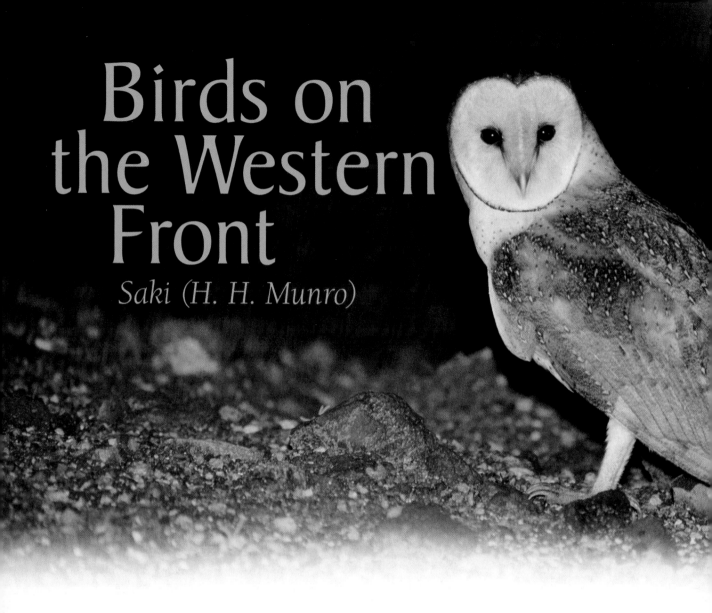

Birds on the Western Front

Saki (H. H. Munro)

Considering the enormous economic dislocation which the war operations have caused in the regions where the campaign[1] is raging, there seems to be very little corresponding disturbance in the bird life of the same districts. Rats and mice have mobilized and swarmed into the fighting line, and there has been a partial mobilization of owls, particularly barn owls, following in the wake of the mice, and making <u>laudable</u> efforts to thin out their numbers. What success attends their hunting one cannot estimate; there are always sufficient mice left over to populate one's dug-out and make a parade-ground and race-course of one's face at night. In the matter of nesting accommodation the barn owls are well provided for; most of

▲ **Critical Viewing**
According to Saki, how is the war affecting owls like this one? **[Connect]**

laudable (lôd´ ə bəl) *adj.* worthy of praise

---

1. **campaign** battles being fought against the Germans during World War I.

the still intact barns in the war zone are <u>requisitioned</u> for billeting[2] purposes, but there is a wealth of ruined houses, whole streets and clusters of them, such as can hardly have been available at any previous moment of the world's history since Nineveh and Babylon[3] became humanly desolate. Without human occupation and cultivation there can have been no corn, no refuse, and consequently very few mice, and the owls of Nineveh cannot have enjoyed very good hunting; here in Northern France the owls have desolation and mice at their disposal in unlimited quantities, and as these birds breed in winter as well as in summer, there should be a goodly output of war owlets to cope with the swarming generations of war mice.

Apart from the owls one cannot notice that the campaign is making any marked difference in the bird life of the country-side. The vast flocks of crows and ravens that one expected to find in the neighborhood of the fighting line are nonexistent, which is perhaps rather a pity. The obvious explanation is that the roar and crash and fumes of high explosives have driven the crow tribe in panic from the fighting area; like many obvious explanations, it is not a correct one. The crows of the locality are not attracted to the battlefield, but they certainly are not scared away from it. The rook is normally so gun-shy and nervous where noise is concerned that the sharp banging of a barn door or the report of a toy pistol will sometimes set an entire rookery in commotion; out here I have seen him sedately busy among the refuse heaps of a battered village, with shells bursting at no great distance, and the impatient-sounding, snapping rattle of machine-guns going on all round him; for all the notice that he took he might have been in some peaceful English meadow on a sleepy Sunday afternoon. Whatever else German frightfulness may have done it has not frightened the rook of North-Eastern France; it has made his nerves steadier than they have ever been before, and future generations of small boys, employed in scaring rooks away from the sown crops in this region, will have to invent something in the way of super-frightfulness to achieve their purpose. Crows and magpies are nesting well within the shell-swept area, and over a small beech-copse I once saw a pair of crows engaged in hot combat with a pair of sparrow-hawks, while considerably higher in the sky, but almost

---

2. **billeting** (bil´ it iŋ) *adj.* designated for sleeping by written order as soldiers' quarters.
3. **Nineveh** (nin´ ə və) **and Babylon** (bab´ ə lən) two great and prosperous ancient civilizations that fell to ruin and desolation.

requisitioned (rek´ wə zish´ ənd) v. requested or applied for with a formal written order

Literary Analysis
Tone What tone does Saki use in this description of the rook?

✔**Reading Check**

Apart from its effect on owls, is the war having a strong influence on bird life? Why or why not?

directly above them, two Allied battle-planes were engaging an equal number of enemy aircraft.

Unlike the barn owls, the magpies have had their choice of building sites considerably restricted by the ravages of war; the whole avenues of poplars, where they were accustomed to construct their nests, have been blown to bits, leaving nothing but dreary-looking rows of shattered and splintered trunks to show where once they stood. Affection for a particular tree has in one case induced a pair of magpies to build their bulky, domed nest in the battered remnants[4] of a poplar of which so little remained standing that the nest looked almost

▲ **Critical Viewing**
Does the scene in this photograph correspond to any of Saki's descriptions? Explain. **[Connect]**

---

4. remnants (rem´ nənts) *n.* remainder; what is left over.

bigger than the tree; the effect rather suggested an archiepiscopal enthronement[5] taking place in the ruined remains of Melrose Abbey. The magpie, wary and suspicious in his wild state, must be rather intrigued at the change that has come over the erst-while[6] fearsome not-to-be-avoided human, stalking everywhere over the earth as its possessor, who now creeps about in screened and sheltered ways, as chary of showing himself in the open as the shyest of wild creatures.

The buzzard, that earnest seeker after mice, does not seem to be taking any war risks, at least I have never seen one out here, but kestrels[7] hover about all day in the hottest parts of the line, not in the least <u>disconcerted</u>, apparently, when a promising mouse-area suddenly rises in the air in a cascade of black or yellow earth. Sparrow-hawks are fairly numerous, and a mile or two back from the firing line I saw a pair of hawks that I took to be red-legged falcons, circling over the top of an oak-copse. According to investigations made by Russian naturalists, the effect of the war on bird life on the Eastern front has been more marked than it has been over here. "During the first year of the war rooks disappeared, larks no longer sang in the fields, the wild pigeon disappeared also." The skylark in this region has stuck tenaciously to the meadows and crop-lands that have been seamed and bisected with trenches and honeycombed with shell-holes. In the chill, misty hour of gloom that precedes a rainy dawn, when nothing seemed alive except a few wary waterlogged sentries[8] and many scuttling rats, the lark would suddenly dash skyward and pour forth a song of ecstatic jubilation that sounded horribly forced and insincere. It seemed scarcely possible that the bird could carry its insouciance[9] to the length of attempting to rear a brood in that desolate wreckage of shattered clods and gaping shell-holes, but once, having occasion to throw myself down with some abruptness on my face, I found myself nearly on the top of a brood of young larks. Two of them had already been hit by something, and were in rather a battered condition, but the survivors seemed as tranquil and comfortable as the average nestling.

At the corner of a stricken wood (which has had a name made for it in history, but shall be nameless here), at a moment when lyddite and shrapnel[10] and machine-gun fire swept and raked and bespattered that devoted spot as though the artillery of an entire Division had suddenly concentrated on it, a wee hen-chaffinch flitted wistfully to and fro, amid splintered and falling branches that had never a green bough left on them. The wounded lying there, if any of them noticed the small bird, may well have wondered why anything having

168th Infantry French and American Raiding Party, Badonviller, France, March 1918

---

5. **archiepiscopal** (är′ kē ə pis′ kə pəl) **enthronement** ceremony during which the rank and duties of archbishop are conferred.
6. **erst-while** (ʉrst′ hwīl′) *adv.* formerly.
7. **kestrels** (kes′ trəlz) *n.* small reddish-gray European falcons.
8. **sentries** (sen′ trēz) *n.* men of military guard that are posted to warn others of danger.
9. **insouciance** (in sōō′ sē əns) *n.* the state of being calm and untroubled.
10. **lyddite** (lid′ it) **and shrapnel** (shrap′ nəl) *n.* Lyddite is a powerful explosive, and shrapnel is a collection of fragments scattered by an exploding shell or bomb.

Reading Strategy
Making Inferences
What can you infer about Saki's feelings toward nature and war from his description of humans as now resembling "the shyest of wild creatures"?

disconcerted (dis′ kən sʉrt′ əd) *adj.* embarassed or confused

Reading Check

What has been the effect of the war on bird life in the region of the Eastern front?

wings and no pressing reason for remaining should have chosen to stay in such a place. There was a battered orchard alongside the stricken wood, and the probable explanation of the bird's presence was that it had a nest of young ones whom it was too scared to feed, too loyal to desert. Later on, a small flock of chaffinches blundered into the wood, which they were doubtless in the habit of using as a highway to their feeding-grounds; unlike the solitary hen-bird, they made no secret of their desire to get away as fast as their dazed wits would let them. The only other bird I ever saw there was a magpie, flying low over the wreckage of fallen tree-limbs; "one for sorrow," says the old superstition. There was sorrow enough in that wood.

The English gamekeeper, whose knowledge of wild life usually runs on limited and perverted lines, has evolved a sort of religion as to the nervous debility[11] of even the hardiest game birds; according to his beliefs a terrier trotting across a field in which a partridge is nesting, or a mouse-hawking kestrel hovering over the hedge, is sufficient cause to drive the distracted bird off its eggs and send it whirring into the next county.

The partridge of the war zone shows no signs of such sensitive nerves. The rattle and rumble of transport, the constant coming and going of bodies of troops, the incessant rattle of musketry and deafening explosions of artillery, the night-long flare and flicker of star-shells, have not sufficed to scare the local birds away from their chosen feeding grounds, and to all appearances they have not been deterred from raising their broods. Gamekeepers who are serving with the colors might seize the opportunity to indulge in a little useful nature study.

---

11. **debility** (də bil′ ə tē) *n.* weakness or feebleness of body.

Review and Assess

Thinking About the Selection

1. **Respond:** Did you find Saki's slant on war surprising? Explain your reaction.

2. **(a) Recall:** Briefly describe the reactions to the war of barn owls, larks, and chaffinches. **(b) Evaluate:** Which bird's reaction seems most surprising? Explain.

3. **(a) Recall:** Describe the change in human behavior witnessed by the magpie (page 1057, top). **(b) Infer:** What does this change suggest about the state of humanity?

4. **Draw Conclusions:** What do you think is Saki's purpose in writing this description of wildlife in a war zone? Explain.

5. **Take a Position:** Do you think any wildlife would survive in a full-scale modern war? Why or why not?

Review and Assess

Literary Analysis

Tone

1. Using a chart like this one, briefly describe the **tone** in two or three key passages from each work.

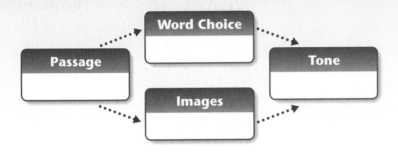

2. (a) Of the four selections, which is the least angry in tone? Explain.
   (b) Which is the most sarcastic? Explain.
3. (a) Which of the selections has the most surprising tone or mixture of tones? Why? (b) What is less surprising about the tone or tones of the other selections?

Comparing Literary Works

4. For English civilians of the time, which of these selections probably conveyed the most positive message about the conflict? Explain.
5. (a) Which selections are most concerned with war's destruction? Why? (b) Which criticize how the war is being run? Explain.
6. Compare the attitudes that these writers seem to have toward civilian readers.

Reading Strategy

Making Inferences

7. (a) **Make inferences** about the speaker's role in the action of "Wirers." For example, can you figure out whether he goes on this mission? (b) What details led you to your conclusions? Explain.
8. Make inferences about Owen's purpose in altering funeral rituals in lines 9–14 of "Anthem for Doomed Youth." Explain your reasoning.

Extend Understanding

9. **Science Connection:** What advances in military technology do these selections describe or hint at?

Quick Review

Tone is the writer's attitude toward the readers or toward the subject of a work.

Making inferences means using clues in a work to make educated guesses about the writer's intended meaning.

 Take It to the Net
www.phschool.com
Take the interactive self-test online to check your understanding of these selections.

Integrate Language Skills

Vocabulary Development Lesson

Word Analysis: The Latin Root -laud-

The word *laudable* means "worthy of praise." Knowing that the root *-laud-* means "praise," define the italicized words.

1. *laudatory* reviews
2. to *laud* a performance

Spelling Strategy

In words that end in *-y* preceded by a consonant, change the *y* to *i* before adding an ending, except when adding *-ing: stealthy + -ily = stealthily*, but *carry + -ing = carrying.*

Spell the word that results from each change:

1. *lazy* as an adverb
2. the plural of *enemy*

Concept Development: Synonyms

In your notebook, choose the letter of the word that is the closest in meaning to the first word.

1. stealthy: (a) smart, (b) furtive, (c) honest
2. desolate: (a) forlorn, (b) crowded, (c) happy
3. mockeries: (a) ridicule, (b) bravery, (c) praise
4. pallor: (a) care, (b) paleness, (c) friends
5. laudable: (a) praiseworthy, (b) low, (c) awesome
6. requisitioned: (a) wasted, (b) needed, (c) ordered
7. disconcerted: (a) untuned, (b) confused, (c) aided

Grammar and Style Lesson

Adjective Clauses With *Who* and *Whom*

When *who* and *whom* are used in **adjective clauses,** which modify nouns, the correct form is determined by the use of the word in the clause. **Who** is used for subjects and subject complements. **Whom** is used for objects of verbs or prepositions.

> **Subject in Clause:** What passing-bells for these <u>who die as cattle</u>?
>
> **Direct Object in Clause:** A dust <u>whom England bore</u>, . . .

Practice In your notebook, correctly complete each sentence with *who* or *whom*. Then, identify the pronoun's function in the clause.

1. Brooke, (whom, who) wrote "The Soldier," died before seeing battle.
2. The talented and intelligent Brooke, (who, whom) was born in 1887, was the son of a school official.
3. Owen, (who, whom) Sassoon befriended and encouraged, was wounded several times in battle.
4. Owen, (who, whom) was killed a week before the war ended, once wrote about "the pity of war."
5. Sassoon, without (who, whom) Owen would be unknown, wrote his best poems during the war.

Writing Application Write a short paragraph about young soldiers who die in wartime, incorporating details that you encountered in these selections. Include adjective clauses that use *who* and *whom.*

W͞G *Prentice Hall Writing and Grammar Connection: Chapter 22, Section 2*

Writing Lesson

Critical Response

Charles Sorley said of Brooke's patriotism, "He has clothed his attitude in fine words; but he has taken the sentimental attitude." In a critical response, agree or disagree with this observation, comparing "The Soldier" with Sassoon's "Wirers."

Prewriting Review "The Soldier" and "Wirers," jotting down details that are sentimental—that show an optimistic overemphasis of noble and positive emotions—or unsentimental.

Drafting Write a thesis statement reflecting your opinion of Sorley's observation. To structure the body of your essay, consider using an organization similar to the one shown here.

Model: Organizing a Critical Response

Paragraph 1	Paragraph 2	Paragraph 3	Paragraph 4	Paragraph 5
Thesis mentioning Sorley's observation	Definition of *sentimental*	Analysis of "The Soldier" in terms of definition	Comparison of "The Soldier" with "Wirers"	Conclusion

Revising Be sure that your definition of *sentimental* matches the arguments you make in the rest of your essay. Confirm that you have supported your response with details from both poems.

 Prentice Hall Writing and Grammar Connection: Chapter 14, Section 3

Extension Activities

Listening and Speaking With classmates, hold a **debate** on this resolution: "There are occasions when war is necessary." Consider these issues:

- The costs of war, such as suffering and loss of life and resources
- The possible benefits of war, such as self-defense and overcoming oppression

Use statistics and accounts in histories and primary sources as support. Help teammates strengthen their arguments. Then, present your debate in class. **[Group Activity]**

Research and Technology Write a **report** on trench warfare in World War I. Begin with a specific research focus, such as the daily routines of soldiers in the trenches. Look for information in various sources, including works like Paul Fussell's *The Great War in Modern Memory*, documentary videos, and Web sites with oral histories.

 **Take It to the Net** www.phschool.com

Go online for an additional research activity using the Internet.

Prepare to Read

Wartime Speech ◆ Defending Nonviolent Resistance

Sir Winston Churchill (1874–1965)

At times during World War II, it might have seemed as if the fate of freedom depended on the gruff voice of Winston Churchill, prime minister of England. Broadcast worldwide, even to Nazi-occupied Europe, this voice spoke with memorable eloquence, as in this tribute to the Royal Air Force: "Never in the field of human conflict was so much owed by so many to so few."

Truly, it might be said of Churchill himself: Never in the field of human conflict was so much owed by so many to just one!

Churchill the Warrior Directly descended from the dukes of Marlborough, Churchill was educated at Harrow and the Royal Military College at Sandhurst. After serving as a soldier and a journalist in Cuba, India, and South Africa, he was first elected to Parliament in 1900 and went on to play an important role in the government during World War I.

In the 1930s, Churchill vigorously criticized government policies, warning against the ominous ambitions of Nazi Germany. He became prime minister in May 1940, after World War II had broken out, and went on to play a key role in the victory of the Allies.

Churchill the Writer Amazingly, Churchill found time to write, despite a busy public career. During the 1930s, he produced a four-volume historical work on his ancestor, the first Duke of Marlborough. His monumental six-volume history entitled *The Second World War* (1948–1954) is now regarded as a classic. Following this work, Churchill wrote *A History of the English-Speaking Peoples*, completed in 1958. He was awarded the Nobel Prize for Literature in 1953.

Mohandas K. Gandhi (1869–1948)

Mohandas K. Gandhi held no political office in his native India, yet few leaders have had such a decisive impact on their country's destiny. He was never a military officer, yet he waged three great wars of supreme importance to world history—battling colonialism, racism, and violence.

Finding a Mission Born in the northwestern Indian state of Gujarat, Gandhi went to London to study law when he was eighteen. From 1893 to 1914, he worked for an Indian law firm in South Africa. His experiences there as a victim of racial discrimination led him to join and lead protest campaigns on behalf of the Indian community in that British-ruled colony. When he returned to India, he became the leader of the Indian National Congress and led the fight for independence from Britain.

Passive Resistance Working fearlessly for independence, Gandhi gradually developed the principles of his philosophy of *satyagraha*, "devotion to truth", or nonviolent resistance, which was to have worldwide influence, notably on the American civil rights leader Martin Luther King, Jr. Using this technique, Gandhi led thousands in acts of peaceful civil disobedience that clogged the jails and confounded the British.

Gandhi also devoted himself to improving the lot of India's lowest castes—social groups defined by ancestry and occupation—and he worked for harmony between the country's two major religions, Hinduism and Islam. India gained independence in August 1947, but to Gandhi's distress, Pakistan was established as a separate dominion. A little more than five months afterward, Gandhi was assassinated by a Hindu fanatic.

Preview

Connecting to the Literature

The speeches included here demonstrate that Winston Churchill and Mohandas K. Gandhi took great risks to assert their beliefs.

Literary Analysis

Speech

A **speech** is an oral presentation on an important issue. Three elements of a speech are its *purpose*, the reason for its presentation; its *occasion*, the event that inspires it; and its *audience*, those who hear it at the time or who hear or read it later.

In historically significant speeches, the speaker often transforms the occasion and the audience. Gandhi does this when, speaking at his own trial, he redefines his "crime" as a legitimate act of protest—a "duty."

Comparing Literary Works

Both Churchill and Gandhi use the following **rhetorical devices**—special patterns of language—to make their ideas memorable and to stir emotions:

- **Repetition,** the repeating of key words and concepts
- **Parallelism,** similar ideas expressed in similar grammatical forms
- **Allusions,** references to well-known people, places, and events
- **Dramatic alternatives,** the posing of sharply contrasting alternatives

However, the writers do not use these devices in the same ways. For example, as befits a radio address, Churchill's uses of parallelism are briefer and punchier than Gandhi's. Compare these speakers' use of other devices.

Reading Strategy

Identifying Main Points and Support

The **main points** in a speech are the key ideas that the speaker wishes to convey. The **support** consists of the facts, examples, or reasons that explain or justify these ideas. Use a chart like this one to identify main points and support as you read these speeches.

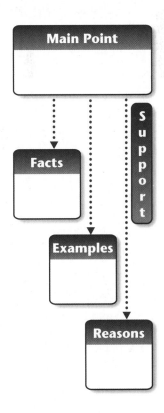

Vocabulary Development

intimidated (in tim′ ə dāt′ əd) *v.* made afraid; frightened (p. 1065)

endurance (en dŏŏr′ əns) *n.* ability to last or continue (p. 1065)

formidable (fôr′ mə də bəl) *adj.* hard to overcome (p. 1065)

invincible (in vin′ sə bəl) *adj.* unconquerable (p. 1065)

retaliate (ri tal′ ē āt′) *v.* pay back an injury or wrong (p. 1066)

disaffection (dis′ ə fek′ shən) *n.* discontent; disillusionment (p. 1068)

diabolical (dī′ ə bäl′ i kəl) *adj.* evil (p. 1068)

extenuating (ek sten′ yōō āt′ iŋ) *adj.* lessening the seriousness of; excusing (p. 1069)

excrescence (eks kres′ əns) *n.* abnormal or disfiguring outgrowth (p. 1069)

▲ **Critical Viewing** Sir Winston Churchill is shown here making a radio broadcast. In what ways does the presentation of a radio speech differ from a speech given in person? **[Compare and Contrast]**

WARTIME SPEECH

Sir Winston Churchill
BBC, London, 19 May 1940

Background

When Churchill gave this speech, his first radio address as prime minister, France was Britain's only ally in opposing German aggression. Germany had already overrun several other countries. Soon after this speech was delivered, France surrendered.

I speak to you for the first time as Prime Minister in a solemn hour for the life of our country, of our Empire, of our Allies, and, above all, of the cause of Freedom. A tremendous battle is raging in France and Flanders.[1] The Germans, by a remarkable combination of air bombing and heavily armored tanks, have broken through the French defenses north of the Maginot Line,[2] and strong columns of their armored vehicles are ravaging the open country, which for the first day or two was without defenders. They have penetrated deeply and spread alarm and confusion in their track. Behind them there are now appearing infantry in lorries,[3] and behind them, again, the large masses are moving forward. The regroupment of the French armies to make head against, and also to strike at, this intruding wedge has been proceeding for several days, largely assisted by the magnificent efforts of the Royal Air Force.

We must not allow ourselves to be <u>intimidated</u> by the presence of these armored vehicles in unexpected places behind our lines. If they are behind our Front, the French are also at many points fighting actively behind theirs. Both sides are therefore in an extremely dangerous position. And if the French Army, and our own Army, are well handled, as I believe they will be; if the French retain that genius for recovery and counter-attack for which they have so long been famous; and if the British Army shows the dogged <u>endurance</u> and solid fighting power of which there have been so many examples in the past—then a sudden transformation of the scene might spring into being.

It would be foolish, however, to disguise the gravity of the hour. It would be still more foolish to lose heart and courage or to suppose that well-trained, well-equipped armies numbering three or four millions of men can be overcome in the space of a few weeks, or even months, by a scoop, or raid of mechanized vehicles, however <u>formidable</u>. We may look with confidence to the stabilization of the Front in France, and to the general engagement of the masses, which will enable the qualities of the French and British soldiers to be matched squarely against those of their adversaries. For myself, I have <u>invincible</u> confidence in the French Army and its leaders. Only a very small part of that splendid army has yet been heavily engaged; and only a very small part of France has yet been invaded. There is good evidence to show that practically the whole of the specialized and mechanized forces of the enemy have been already thrown into the battle; and we know that very heavy losses have been inflicted upon them. No officer or man, no brigade or division, which grapples at close quarters with the enemy, wherever encountered, can fail to make a worthy contribution to the general result. The Armies must cast away the idea of resisting behind concrete lines or natural obstacles, and must realize that mastery can only be

---

1. **Flanders** (flan´ dərz) region in Northwest Europe, on the North Sea, that includes Northwest France and the provinces of East Flanders and West Flanders in Belgium.
2. **Maginot** (mazh´ ə nō´) **Line** heavy fortifications built before World War II on the Eastern frontier of France; they did not prevent invasion during World War II.
3. **lorries** (lôr´ ēz) *n.* British for "trucks."

intimidated (in tim´ ə dāt´ ed) *v.* made afraid; frightened

endurance (en door´ əns) *n.* ability to last or continue

formidable (fôr´ mə də bəl) *adj.* hard to overcome

invincible (in vin´ sə bəl) *adj.* unconquerable

✔**Reading Check**

According to Churchill, what military victories have the Germans won?

regained by furious and unrelenting assault. And this spirit must not only animate the High Command, but must inspire every fighting man.

In the air—often at serious odds—often at odds hitherto[4] thought overwhelming—we have been clawing down three or four to one of our enemies; and the relative balance of the British and German Air Forces is now considerably more favorable to us than at the beginning of the battle. In cutting down the German bombers, we are fighting our own battle as well as that of France. My confidence in our ability to fight it out to the finish with the German Air Force has been strengthened by the fierce encounters which have taken place and are taking place. At the same time, our heavy bombers are striking nightly at the taproot of German mechanized power, and have already inflicted serious damage upon the oil refineries on which the Nazi effort to dominate the world directly depends.

We must expect that as soon as stability is reached on the Western Front, the bulk of that hideous apparatus of aggression which gashed Holland into ruin and slavery in a few days, will be turned upon us. I am sure I speak for all when I say we are ready to face it; to endure it; and to retaliate against it—to any extent that the unwritten laws of war permit. There will be many men, and many women, in this island who when the ordeal comes upon them, as come it will, will feel comfort, and even a pride—that they are sharing the perils of our lads at the Front—soldiers, sailors and airmen, God bless them—and are drawing away from them a part at least of the onslaught they have to bear. Is not this the appointed time for all to make the utmost exertions in their power? If the battle is to be won, we must provide our men with ever-increasing quantities of the weapons and ammunition they need. We must have, and have quickly, more airplanes, more tanks, more shells, more guns. There is imperious need for these vital munitions. They increase our strength against the powerfully armed enemy. They replace the wastage of the obstinate struggle; and the knowledge that wastage will speedily be replaced enables us to draw more readily upon our reserves and throw them in now that everything counts so much.

Our task is not only to win the battle—but to win the War. After this battle in France abates[5] its force, there will come the battle for our island—for all that Britain is, and all that Britain means. That will be the struggle. In that supreme emergency we shall not hesitate to take every step, even the most drastic, to call forth from our people the last ounce and the last inch of effort of which they are capable. The interests of property, the hours of labor, are nothing compared with the struggle for life and honor, for right and freedom, to which we have vowed ourselves.

I have received from the Chiefs of the French Republic, and in particular from its indomitable Prime Minister, M. Reynaud, the most sacred pledges that whatever happens they will fight to the

---

4. **hitherto** (hith´ ər tōō) adv. until this time.
5. **abates** (ə bāts´) v. makes less in amount.

end, be it bitter or be it glorious. Nay, if we fight to the end, it can only be glorious.

Having received His Majesty's commission, I have found an administration of men and women of every party and of almost every point of view. We have differed and quarreled in the past; but now one bond unites us all—to wage war until victory is won, and never to surrender ourselves to servitude and shame, whatever the cost and the agony may be. This is one of the most awe-striking periods in the long history of France and Britain. It is also beyond doubt the most sublime. Side by side, unaided except by their kith and kin in the great Dominions and by the wide Empires which rest beneath their shield—side by side, the British and French peoples have advanced to rescue not only Europe but mankind from the foulest and most soul-destroying tyranny which has ever darkened and stained the pages of history. Behind them—behind us—behind the armies and fleets of Britain and France—gather a group of shattered States and bludgeoned races: the Czechs, the Poles, the Norwegians, the Danes, the Dutch, the Belgians—upon all of whom the long night of barbarism will descend, unbroken even by a star of hope, unless we conquer, as conquer we must; as conquer we shall.

Today is Trinity Sunday. Centuries ago words were written to be a call and a spur to the faithful servants of Truth and Justice; "Arm yourselves, and be ye men of valor, and be in readiness for the conflict; for it is better for us to perish in battle than to look upon the outrage of our nation and our altar. As the Will of God is in Heaven, even so let it be."

Reading Strategy
Identifying Main Points and Support What do you think is the main point of the paragraph beginning, "Having received . . ."?

Review and Assess

Thinking About the Selection

1. **Respond:** Do Churchill's words still have the power to stir a listener? Explain.

2. **(a) Recall:** What new development in the war does Churchill report at the beginning of his speech? **(b) Analyze:** What answers does Churchill provide to any concerns that this development might cause?

3. **(a) Recall:** For what future crisis does Churchill prepare his listeners? **(b) Analyze:** With what double mission does he try to inspire his listeners so that they will meet the crisis?

4. **(a) Analyze:** Describe the tone of this speech, providing examples in support. **(b) Draw Conclusions:** Judging by his tone, how confident is Churchill of his public support? Explain your reasoning.

5. **Connect:** Does any politician today speak with the same force and urgency as Churchill does in this speech? Explain.

DEFENDING NONVIOLENT RESISTANCE

Mohandas K. Gandhi

The following speech was given by Mohandas Gandhi before he was sentenced to six years in prison for stirring up rebellion. Gandhi, India's spiritual leader, worked to achieve political goals through nonviolent resistance. Through boycotts and passive refusal, he helped India gain freedom from British rule.

Before I read this statement, I would like to state that I entirely endorse the learned advocate general's remarks in connection with my humble self. I think that he was entirely fair to me in all the statements that he has made, because it is very true, and I have no desire whatsoever to conceal from this court the fact that to preach <u>disaffection</u> toward the existing system of government has become almost a passion with me; and the learned advocate general is also entirely in the right when he says that my preaching of disaffection did not commence with my connection with *Young India*, but that it commenced much earlier; and in the statement that I am about to read, it will be my painful duty to admit before this court that it commenced much earlier than the period stated by the advocate general. It is the most painful duty with me, but I have to discharge that duty knowing the responsibility that rests upon my shoulders, and I wish to endorse all the blame that the learned advocate general has thrown on my shoulders, in connection with the Bombay occurrences, Madras occurrences, and the Chauri Chaura occurrences.[1] Thinking over these deeply and sleeping over them night after night, it is impossible for me to dissociate myself from the <u>diabolical</u> crimes of Chauri Chaura or the mad outrages of Bombay. He is quite right when he says that as a man of responsibility, a man having received a fair share of education, having had a fair share of experience of this world, I should have known the consequences of every one of my acts. I know that I was playing with fire. I ran the risk, and if I was set free, I would still do the same. I have felt it this morning that I would have failed in my duty, if I did not say what I said here just now.

I wanted to avoid violence, I want to avoid violence. Nonviolence is the first article of my faith. It is also the last article of my creed. But I

Reading Strategy
Identifying Main Points and Support What is the main point in the first paragraph of the speech?

disaffection (dis´ ə fek´ shən) *n.* discontent; disillusionment

diabolical (dī´ ə bäl´ ik əl) *adj.* evil

---

1. **Bombay . . . Chauri Chaura occurrences** outbreaks of violence in Indian cities and villages.

had to make my choice. I had either to submit to a system which I considered had done an irreparable harm to my country, or incur the risk of the mad fury of my people bursting forth, when they understood the truth from my lips. I know that my people have sometimes gone mad. I am deeply sorry for it, and I am therefore here to submit not to a light penalty but to the highest penalty. I do not ask for mercy. I do not plead any <u>extenuating</u> act. I am here, therefore, to invite and cheerfully submit to the highest penalty that can be inflicted upon me for what in law is a deliberate crime and what appears to me to be the highest duty of a citizen. The only course open to you, the judge, is, as I am just going to say in my statement, either to resign your post or inflict on me the severest penalty, if you believe that the system and law you are assisting to administer are good for the people. I do not expect that kind of conversation, but by the time I have finished with my statement, you will perhaps have a glimpse of what is raging within my breast to run this maddest risk which a sane man can run.

I owe it perhaps to the Indian public and to the public in England to placate[2] which this prosecution is mainly taken up that I should explain why from a staunch loyalist and cooperator I have become an uncompromising disaffectionist and non-cooperator. To the court too I should say why I plead guilty to the charge of promoting disaffection toward the government established by law in India.

My public life began in 1893 in South Africa in troubled weather. My first contact with British authority in that country was not of a happy character. I discovered that as a man and as an Indian I had no rights. More correctly, I discovered that I had no rights as a man because I was an Indian.

But I was not baffled. I thought that this treatment of Indians was an <u>excrescence</u> upon a system that was intrinsically and mainly good. I gave the government my voluntary and hearty cooperation, criticizing it freely where I felt it was faulty but never wishing its destruction.

Consequently, when the existence of the empire was threatened in 1899 by the Boer challenge,[3] I offered my services to it, raised a volunteer ambulance corps, and served at several actions that took place for the relief of Ladysmith. Similarly in 1906, at the time of the Zulu revolt, I raised a stretcher-bearer party and served till the end of the "rebellion." On both these occasions I received medals and was even mentioned in dispatches. For my work in South Africa I was given by Lord Hardinge a Kaiser-i-Hind Gold Medal. When the war broke out in 1914 between England and Germany,[4] I raised a volunteer ambulance corps in London consisting of the then resident Indians in London, chiefly students. Its work was acknowledged by the authorities to be valuable. Lastly, in India, when a special appeal was made at the War Conference in Delhi in 1918 by

Literary Analysis
Speech With what words does Gandhi redefine the situation by shifting the guilt from himself to the British? Explain.

extenuating (ek sten´ yoo āt´ iŋ) *adj.* lessening the seriousness of; excusing

excrescence (eks kres´ əns) *n.* abnormal or disfiguring outgrowth

---

2. **placate** (plā´ kāt´) *v.* to stop from being angry.
3. **Boer challenge** rebellion in South Africa against British rule; the British suppressed the rebellion in 1902 after resorting to guerrilla warfare.
4. **the war . . . between England and Germany** World War I.

**Reading Check**

What choice does Gandhi offer the judge?

Lord Chelmsford[5] for recruits, I struggled at the cost of my health to raise a corps in Kheda, and the response was being made when the hostilities ceased and orders were received that no more recruits were wanted. In all these efforts at service I was actuated by the belief that it was possible by such services to gain a status of full equality in the empire for my countrymen.

The first shock came in the shape of the Rowlatt Act,[6] a law designed to rob the people of all real freedom. I felt called upon to lead an intensive agitation against it. Then followed the Punjab horrors beginning with the massacre at Jallianwala Bagh[7] and culminating in crawling orders, public floggings, and other indescribable humiliations. I discovered too that the plighted word of the prime minister to the Mussulmans of India regarding the integrity of Turkey and the holy places of Islam was not likely to be fulfilled. But in spite of the forebodings and the grave warnings of friends, at the Amritsar Congress in 1919, I fought for cooperation and working with the Montagu-Chelmsford reforms,[8] hoping that the prime minister would redeem his promise to the Indian Mussulmans, that the Punjab wound would be healed, and that the reforms, inadequate and unsatisfactory though they were, marked a new era of hope in the life of India.

But all that hope was shattered. The Khilafat promise was not to be redeemed. The Punjab crime was whitewashed, and most culprits went not only unpunished but remained in service and in some cases continued to draw pensions from the Indian revenue, and in some cases were even rewarded. I saw too that not only did the reforms not mark a change of heart, but they were only a method of further draining India of her wealth and of prolonging her servitude.

I came reluctantly to the conclusion that the British connection had made India more helpless than she ever was before, politically and economically. A disarmed India has no power of resistance against any aggressor if she wanted to engage in an armed conflict with him. So much is this the case that some of our best men consider that India must take generations before she can achieve the dominion status. She has become so poor that she has little power of resisting famines. Before the British advent, India spun and wove in her millions of cottages just the supplement she needed for adding to her meager agricultural resources. This cottage industry, so vital for India's existence, has been ruined by incredibly heartless and inhuman processes as described by English witnesses. Little do town dwellers know how the semistarved masses of India are slowly sinking to lifelessness. Little do they know that their miserable comfort represents the brokerage they

▼ **Critical Viewing** How does this depiction of Gandhi reflect his beliefs about violence? **[Draw Conclusions]**

---

5. **Lord Chelmsford** viceroy or governor as representative of Edwin Montagu, Secretary of State.
6. **Rowlatt Act** series of repressive acts that limited the powers of the Indian people.
7. **the massacre at Jallianwala Bagh** Under orders of General R. H. Dyer, fifty British soldiers opened fire on a crowd of peaceful Indians, firing 1,650 rounds of ammunition. The general was dismissed from his duties.
8. **Montagu-Chelmsford reforms** formally known as The Government of India Act of 1919; an attempt to slowly place power in Indian hands.

get for the work they do for the foreign exploiter, that the profits and the brokerage are sucked from the masses. Little do they realize that the government established by law in British India is carried on for this exploitation of the masses. No sophistry,[9] no jugglery in figures can explain away the evidence that the skeletons in many villages present to the naked eye. I have no doubt whatsoever that both England and the town dwellers of India will have to answer, if there is a God above, for this crime against humanity which is perhaps unequaled in history. The law itself in this country has been used to serve the foreign exploiter. My unbiased examination of the Punjab Martial Law cases has led me to believe that at least 95 percent of convictions were wholly bad. My experience of political cases in India leads me to the conclusion that in nine out of every ten the condemned men were totally innocent. Their crime consisted in the love of their country. In ninety-nine cases out of a hundred justice has been denied to Indians as against Europeans in the courts of India. This is not an exaggerated picture. It is the experience of almost every Indian who has had anything to do with such cases. In my opinion, the administration of the law is thus prostituted consciously or unconsciously for the benefit of the exploiter.

The greatest misfortune is that Englishmen and their Indian associates in the administration of the country do not know that they are engaged in the crime I have attempted to describe. I am satisfied that many Englishmen and Indian officials honestly believe that they are administering one of the best systems devised in the world and that India is making steady though slow progress. They do not know that a subtle but effective system of terrorism and an organized display of force, on the one hand, and the deprivation of all powers of retaliation or self-defense, on the other, have emasculated the people and induced in them the habit of simulation. This awful habit has added to the ignorance and the self-deception of the administrators. Section 124-A, under which I am happily charged, is perhaps the prince among the political sections of the Indian Penal Code[10] designed to suppress the liberty of the citizen. Affection cannot be manufactured or regulated by law. If one has an affection for a person or system, one should be free to give the fullest expression to his disaffection, so long as he does not contemplate, promote, or incite to violence. But the section under which Mr. Banker [a colleague in nonviolence] and I are charged is one under which mere promotion of disaffection is a crime. I have studied some of the cases tried under it, and I know that some of the most loved of India's patriots have been convicted under it. I consider it a privilege, therefore, to be charged under that section. I have endeavored to give in their briefest outline the reasons for my disaffection. I have no personal ill will against any single administrator, much less can I have any disaffection toward the king's person. But I hold it to be a virtue

Literary Analysis
Speech and Rhetorical Devices What is an example of parallelism in this paragraph?

---

9. **sophistry** (säf´ is trē) *n.* unsound or misleading arguments.
10. **Section 124-A . . . Penal Code** Gandhi was charged with sedition, inciting people to riot against British rule.

✔**Reading Check**

According to Gandhi, what harm has Britain done to India?

to be disaffected toward a government which in its totality has done more harm to India than any previous system. India is less manly under the British rule than she ever was before. Holding such a belief, I consider it to be a sin to have affection for the system. And it has been a precious privilege for me to be able to write what I have in the various articles, tendered in evidence against me.

In fact, I believe that I have rendered a service to India and England by showing in non-cooperation the way out of the unnatural state in which both are living. In my humble opinion, non-cooperation with evil is as much a duty as is cooperation with good. But in the past, non-cooperation has been deliberately expressed in violence to the evildoer. I am endeavoring to show to my countrymen that violent non-cooperation only multiplies evil and that as evil can only be sustained by violence, withdrawal of support of evil requires complete abstention from violence. Nonviolence implies voluntary submission to the penalty for non-cooperation with evil. I am here, therefore, to invite and submit cheerfully to the highest penalty that can be inflicted upon me for what in law is a deliberate crime and what appears to me to be the highest duty of a citizen. The only course open to you, the judge, is either to resign your post, and thus dissociate yourself from evil if you feel that the law you are called upon to administer is an evil and that in reality I am innocent, or to inflict on me the severest penalty if you believe that the system and the law you are assisting to administer are good for the people of this country and that my activity is therefore injurious to the public weal.[11]

---

11. **weal** (wēl) *n.* well-being; welfare.

Literary Analysis
Speech In what way is Gandhi judging the judge in the final paragraph of the speech?

Review and Assess

Thinking About the Selection

1. **(a) Recall:** How does Gandhi plead to the charges against him? **(b) Infer:** Why do you think he resists the strategy of claiming to be innocent?

2. **(a) Recall:** What are three missions Gandhi has undertaken to help the British? **(b) Infer:** Why do you think he describes these missions here?

3. **(a) Recall:** Identify three reasons for Gandhi's "disaffection" toward the British system of rule. **(b) Draw Conclusions:** Why does Gandhi consider it a privilege to be charged with "promoting disaffection"?

4. **Take a Position:** Some claim that Gandhi's policy of *satyagraha*, nonviolent resistance, was ideal for use against the British, who had a conscience, but that it would not have worked against the Nazis. Explain why you agree or disagree.

Review and Assess

Literary Analysis

Speech

1. Use a chart like the one shown to identify the elements in each **speech**.

Speaker	Purpose	Audience	Occasion

2. (a) How does Churchill's purpose motivate him to redefine a frightening occasion as an inspiring opportunity? (b) Which words transform his listeners from scattered individuals to a committed group? Explain.

3. (a) How does Gandhi attempt to redefine the role of the judge, his primary audience? (b) What larger audience might Gandhi be addressing? Explain. (c) How does Gandhi's purpose motivate him to transform a narrowly defined occasion into one with greater meaning?

Comparing Literary Works

4. Identify examples of these **rhetorical devices** in both speeches: (a) repetition, (b) parallelism, (c) allusion, (d) dramatic alternatives.

5. Choose one of these devices. Comparing and contrasting its use in the two speeches, decide which speaker employs it more effectively.

6. Although Gandhi did not deliver his speech on the radio, would it have been as effective a radio address as Churchill's? Explain.

Reading Strategy

Identifying Main Points and Support

7. (a) What is the **main point** of Gandhi's ninth paragraph ("I came reluctantly . . .")? (b) Which details provide **support** for it?

8. (a) What are two main points in Churchill's speech? (b) List several details he uses to support each point.

Extend Understanding

9. **Media Connection:** What different speechmaking skills do radio, television, and a public appearance require? Explain.

Quick Review

A **speech** is an oral presentation in which a speaker addresses an important issue. Three elements of a speech are its *purpose*, the reason for its presentation; its *occasion*, the event that gives rise to it; and its *audience*, those who hear it immediately or view, hear, or read it later.

Rhetorical devices, or uses of language designed to persuade, include repetition, parallelism, dramatic alternatives, and allusions.

To **identify main points and support,** find the most important ideas in a work and the examples, facts, and reasons that strengthen them.

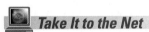 **Take It to the Net**
www.phschool.com

Take the interactive self-test online to check your understanding of these selections.

Integrate Language Skills

Vocabulary Development Lesson

Word Analysis: Latin Root *-dur-*

The Latin root *-dur-* means "hard" or "lasting," and *endurance* means "the toughness to withstand pain, exhaustion, or wear." Use this knowledge to write definitions of the following words. Then, verify your definitions in a dictionary.

1. durable
2. duress
3. endure
4. duration

Spelling Strategy

Adding a prefix to a word never changes the spelling of the base word. For example, adding the prefix *dis-* to *affection* yields the word *disaffection*. Spell the words that result from the following combinations of prefixes and base words.

1. *dis-* + appoint
2. *in-* + tolerable
3. *re-* + educate
4. *mis-* + statement

Grammar and Style Lesson

Parallel Structure

Parallel structure is the use of the same grammatical form to express similar ideas.

> **Infinitive Phrases:** Our task is <u>not only to win the battle</u>—but <u>to win the War.</u>

Writers use parallel structure to create a rhythm of ideas. This rhythm creates the sense that each idea "belongs" or is necessary, adding to its persuasive force.

Practice On your paper, rewrite each sentence below, correcting errors of faulty parallelism.

1. Either to disguise the gravity of the hour or surrendering prematurely to despair would be a great mistake.

Fluency: Words in Context

In your notebook, replace each italicized word or phrase with a word from the vocabulary list on page 1063. Your choices should be guided by the context created by the paragraph.

Churchill was not *frightened* by the Nazi offensive. He counted on the *toughness* of the British people and their ability to resist a foe, no matter how *fearsome* or apparently *unconquerable*. He knew that the British would *revenge themselves* against the Nazis and not give way to *discontent* as a result of Hitler's victories and *evil* plans. For Churchill, the Nazis were an *abnormal outgrowth* that had to be eliminated. No *excusing* circumstances could justify surrender to the Germans.

2. The British were ready to face Hitler's aggression, enduring it, and to retaliate against it.
3. Churchill's administration included every party and representing a complete spectrum of opinion.
4. Gandhi's choice was submitting to a harmful system or to run the risk of stirring up anger.
5. Gandhi said affection cannot be either manufactured or regulating it by law.

Writing Application As the judge to whom Gandhi appeals, write a response to his speech. In an effort to match Gandhi's persuasive skill, include two examples of parallel structure.

Writing Lesson

Persuasive Speech

Churchill's and Gandhi's speeches were persuasive because each communicated viewpoints in a strong, effective style. Follow their lead by writing an effective persuasive speech on an issue important to you.

Prewriting   Choose an issue and an audience. Then, list your main points and the facts, reasons, and examples you will use to support them. Also, note any questions that your audience might have, and write answers to them.

Drafting   Include support for your main points, and reinforce them with rhetorical devices such as repetition and parallel structure. Strengthen support by using allusions and presenting dramatic alternatives.

Revising   Read your draft aloud to a classmate. If he or she has questions you did not anticipate, revise your speech to deal with them. If sentences expressing your main points sound flat, add rhetorical devices to dramatize them.

Model: Adding Rhetorical Devices

neither frivolous nor fanciful.

Creating a new park is ~~important.~~ It may be the most

important action the town council takes this year.

By using parallelism of adjectives, the writer states the main point more forcefully.

 *Prentice Hall Writing and Grammar Connection: Chapter 7, Section 4*

Extension Activities

Listening and Speaking Conduct a **panel discussion** to consider how Gandhi might have responded to the Nazis if he had been in Churchill's place. Discuss Gandhi's possible actions and the types of arguments he would have made, including appeals to

- Logic, with clear arguments
- Emotions, with specific, charged examples
- Ethics, with references to his core values

To conclude, decide which appeals Gandhi might have favored. **[Group Activity]**

Research and Technology View a film on Gandhi's or Churchill's life. (A possible choice is *Gandhi*, directed by Richard Attenborough.) Devise a strategy for taking notes on the film. Then, compare the information in the film with information from a print source, such as a biography of Gandhi or of Churchill. Use your notes to write a **critique** of the film.

 **Take It to the Net**   www.phschool.com

Go online for an additional research activity using the Internet.

Prepare to Read

The Fiddle

Alan Sillitoe (b. 1928)

Growing up in poverty left a permanent impression on Alan Sillitoe. Much of his writing revolves around the struggles of the working poor, those whose hard labor results in a hand-to-mouth existence—the experience of never having enough money to get ahead of the immediate needs of self and family.

A Short Military Career The son of an often unemployed tannery worker, Sillitoe grew up in Nottingham, an industrial city northwest of London. He left school at the age of fourteen and worked in a bicycle plant and a plywood mill. At the same time, he enrolled in the Air Training Corps. In 1946, he joined the Royal Air Force and, for a time, was a radio operator in Malaya. There, he contracted the tuberculosis that eventually led to his discharge. His illness entitled him to a pension, which he collected for thirteen years, until he was pronounced cured.

A Focused Writer Sillitoe had begun to write while in Malaya, and his small pension enabled him to survive without having to get a job. In his 1995 autobiography, *Life Without Armour*, he refers to this period of his life: "Such an extended period of cosseting merely for doing my duty turned into a much appreciated case of patronage." Sillitoe spent six years in France and Spain, writing and rewriting several books. He ended up scrapping the manuscripts of nine completed novels, finally publishing *Saturday Night and Sunday Morning*. This novel, which describes the numbing effects of working-class life on a tough young man, met with instant success. It won the Author's Club Prize for the best English novel of 1958 and was later made into a movie starring Albert Finney. Of Sillitoe's work, one critic remarked, "For the first time, English working-class life is treated . . . as a normal subject matter for a writer."

"Angry Young Men" In 1959, Sillitoe published a short story collection entitled *The Loneliness of the Long Distance Runner*, perhaps his most famous work. The title story, later made into a film starring Tom Courtenay and Michael Redgrave, tells of a young juvenile delinquent in an English reform school. The boy runs in order to escape his oppressive surroundings and gain a sense of freedom.

These early works earned Sillitoe a place among a group of writers—known as the "Angry Young Men"—who believed that British social and political traditions had become outmoded.

Like the other "Angry Young Men," Sillitoe explored the theme of rebellion. His heroes, firmly rooted in the working classes, sought self-discovery by opposing much of organized society.

The scope of Sillitoe's subject matter has broadened to some extent in his later works, although he has remained primarily a chronicler of working-class people who must scratch out a living as best they can. He is one of the more prolific British writers of our time, having published more than forty books, including novels, short story collections, plays, essays, children's stories, and an autobiography.

The Story Behind the Story During his childhood, Alan Sillitoe lived for a time in a tiny cottage in Nottingham, England, near the River Leen. After a week of rain, the Sillitoes' cottage was flooded and had to be abandoned. The River Leen and the cottages on its banks are the setting of "The Fiddle." Perhaps Sillitoe's former neighbors served as inspiration for the story's characters.

Preview

Connecting to the Literature

You may feel carefree on a sunny day or gloomy when you walk down a dark street. Just as your environment affects your mood, the time and place of a story affects the outlook of each character. This is especially true in "The Fiddle," set in a mining town.

Literary Analysis

Setting and Atmosphere

A story's **setting** is the time and place in which the characters live. The general setting of "The Fiddle" is an English coal-mining town in the 1930s, but the setting also includes the characters' customs and beliefs. Various details of the setting contribute to the **atmosphere,** the overall feeling, or mood, of the work. In the following passage from "The Fiddle," the underlined words describe the physical setting and the word *ruinous* suggests an atmosphere of bleak poverty.

> On the <u>banks of the sinewy River Leen,</u> where <u>it flowed through Radford,</u> stood <u>a group of cottages called Harrison's Row.</u> There must have been <u>six to eight of them,</u> all in a <u>ruinous condition,</u> <u>but lived in</u> nevertheless.

As you read, look for key words and phrases that establish the setting and suggest the atmosphere of the selection.

Connecting Literary Elements

An author brings a setting to life through his or her **style,** or approach to writing. Style includes such elements as word choice, images, and rhythm. In "The Fiddle," Sillitoe uses simple words, clear images, and informal speech. As a result, the narrator seems like one of the neighbors. In reading, notice how the informal style invites you to feel like a part of the neighborhood circle.

Reading Strategy

Predicting the Effect of Setting

A story's setting can shape the characters' personalities and actions. As you read, make educated guesses about the outcome of the story by using a chart like this one to **predict the effects of the setting** on the characters' lives.

Vocabulary Development

persistent (pər sist′ ənt) *adj.* continuing without letup (p. 1079)

obliterate (ə blit′ ər āt′) *v.* destroy utterly (p. 1080)

sublimity (sə blim′ ə tē) *n.* quality of being majestic or noble (p. 1081)

harried (har′ ēd) *v.* harassed; worried by repeated requests (p. 1082)

The Fiddle

Alan Sillitoe

Background

   This story is set during the 1930s in a town dependent on coal mining. The coal industry has been crucial to the British economy for generations, but the conditions in which miners work have often been brutal. Until the mid-1600s, miners were often serfs or paroled convicts whose safety was of little concern to mine operators. By the twentieth century, both working conditions and wages had improved. Yet the miners and their families still led difficult lives, especially during the economic depression of the 1930s.

   On the banks of the sinewy River Leen, where it flowed through Radford, stood a group of cottages called Harrison's Row. There must have been six to eight of them, all in a ruinous condition, but lived in nevertheless.

   They had been put up for stockingers[1] during the Industrial Revolution a hundred years before, so that by now the usual small red English housebricks had become weatherstained and, in some places, almost black.

   Harrison's Row had a character all of its own, both because of its situation, and the people who lived there. Each house had a space of

---

1. **stockingers** *n.* stocking weavers.

▼ **Critical Viewing**
What effect do you think this setting would have on residents? **[Analyze Cause and Effect]**

pebbly soil rising in front, and a strip of richer garden sloping away from the kitchen door down to the diminutive River Leen at the back. The front gardens had almost merged into one piece of common ground, while those behind had in most cases retained their separate plots.

As for the name of the isolated row of cottages, nobody knew who Harrison had been, and no one was ever curious about it. Neither did they know where the Leen came from, though some had a general idea as to where it finished up.

A rent man walked down cobblestoned Leen Place every week to collect what money he could. This wasn't much, even at the best of times which, in the "thirties," were not too good—though no one in their conversation was able to hark back to times when they had been any better.

From the slight rise on which the houses stood, the back doors and windows looked across the stream into green fields, out towards the towers and pinnacles of Wollaton Hall in one direction, and the woods of Aspley Manor in the other.

After a warm summer without much rain the children were able to wade to the fields on the other side. Sometimes they could almost paddle. But after a three-day downpour when the air was still heavy with undropped water, and colored a menacing gun-metal blue, it was best not to go anywhere near the river, for one false slip and you would get sucked in, and be dragged by the powerful current along to the Trent some miles away. In that case there was no telling where you'd end up. The water seemed to flow into the River Amazon[2] itself, indicated by the fact that Frankie Buller swore blind how one day he had seen a crocodile snapping left and right downstream with a new-born baby in its mouth. You had to be careful—and that was a fact. During the <u>persistent</u> rain of one autumn water came up over the gardens and almost in at the back doors.

Harrison's Row was a cut-off place in that not many people knew about it unless they were familiar with the district. You went to it along St. Peter's Street, and down Leen Place. But it was delightful for the kids who lived there because out of the back gardens they could go straight into the stream of the Leen. In summer an old tin hip bath would come from one of the houses. Using it for a boat, and stripped to their white skins, the children were happy while sun and weather lasted.

The youths and older kids would eschew this fun and set out in a gang, going far beyond, to a bend of the canal near Wollaton Pit where the water was warm—almost hot—due to some outlet from the mine itself. This place was known as "'otties," and they'd stay all day with a bottle of lemonade and a piece of bread, coming back late in the evening looking pink and tired as if out of a prolonged dipping in the ritual bath. But a swim in 'otties was only for the older ones, because a boy of four had once been drowned there.

Harrison's Row was the last of Nottingham where it met the countryside. Its houses were at the very edge of the city, in the days

---

2. **River Amazon** largest, most powerful river in South America.

Literary Analysis

Setting What do you learn about the setting from the first four paragraphs of the story?

persistent (pər sis′ tənt) *adj.* continuing without letup

Reading Check

What do the children and older kids of Harrison's Row do for fun?

before those numerous housing estates had been built beyond. The line of dwellings called Harrison's Row made a sort of outpost bastion before the country began.

Yet the houses in the city didn't immediately start behind, due to gardens and a piece of wasteground, which gave to Harrison's Row a feeling of isolation. It stood somewhat on its own, as if the city intended one day to leapfrog over it and <u>obliterate</u> the country beyond.

On the other hand, any foreign army attacking from the west, over the green fields that glistened in front, would first have to flatten Harrison's Row before getting into the innumerable streets of houses behind.

Across the Leen, horses were sometimes to be seen in the fields and, in other fields beyond, the noise of combine harvesters could be heard at work in the summer. Children living there, and adults as well, had the advantage of both town and country. On a fine evening late in August one of the unemployed husbands might be seen looking across at the noise of some machinery working in a field, his cap on but wearing no shirt, as if wondering why he was here and not over there, and why in fact he had ever left those same fields in times gone by to be forced into this bit of a suburb where he now had neither work nor purpose in life. He was not bitter, and not much puzzled perhaps, yet he couldn't help being envious of those still out there in the sunshine.

In my visions of leaving Nottingham for good—and they were frequent in those days—I never reckoned on doing so by the high road or railway. Instead I saw myself wading or swimming the Leen from Harrison's Row, and setting off west once I was on the other side.

A tale remembered with a laugh at that time told about how young Ted Griffin, who had just started work, saw two policemen one day walking down Leen Place towards Harrison's Row. Convinced they had come to arrest him for meter-breaking, he ran through the house and garden, went over the fence, jumped into the Leen—happily not much swollen—waded across to the field, then four-legged it over the railway, and made his way to Robins Wood a mile or so beyond. A perfect escape route. He stayed two days in hiding, and then crept home at night, famished and soaked, only to find that the police had not come for him, but to question Blonk next door, who was suspected of poaching. When they did get Ted Griffin he was pulled out of bed one morning even before he'd had time to open his eyes and think about a spectacular escape across the Leen.

Jeff Bignal was a young unmarried man of twenty-four. His father had been killed in the Great War,[3] and he lived with his mother at Number Six Harrison's Row, and worked down nearby Radford Pit. He was short in height, and plump, his white skin scarred back and front with livid blue patches where he had been knocked with coal at the mine face. When he went out on Saturday night he brilliantined his hair.

obliterate (ə blit′ ə rāt) v. destroy utterly

---

3. **Great War** World War I.

After tea in summer while it was still light and warm he would sit in his back garden playing the fiddle, and when he did everybody else came out to listen. Or they opened the doors and windows so that the sound of his music drifted in, while the woman stayed at the sink or wash-copper, or the man at his odd jobs. Anyone with a wireless would turn it down or off.

Even tall dark sallow-faced elderly Mrs. Deaffy (a kid sneaked into her kitchen one day and thieved her last penny-packet of cocoa and she went crying to tell Mrs. Atkin who, when her youngest came in, hit him so hard with her elbow that one of his teeth shot out and the blood washed away most of the cocoa-stains around his mouth)—old Mrs. Deaffy stood by her back door as if she weren't stone deaf any more and could follow each note of Jeffrey Bignal's exquisite violin. She smiled at seeing everyone occupied, fixed or entranced, and therefore no torment to herself, which was music enough to her whether she could hear it or not.

And Blonk, in the secretive dimness of the kitchen, went on mending his poaching nets before setting out with Arthur Bede next door on that night's expedition to Gunthorpe by the banks of the Trent, where the green escarpment between there and Kneeton was riddled with warrens and where, so it was said, if you stood sufficiently still the rabbits ran over your feet, and it was only necessary to make a quick grab to get one.

Jeff sat on a chair, oblivious to everybody, fed up with his day's work at the pit and only wanting to lose himself in his own music. The kids stopped splashing and shouting in the water, because if they didn't they might get hauled in and clouted with just the right amount of viciousness to suit the crime and the occasion. It had happened before, though Jeff had always been too far off to notice.

His face was long, yet generally cheerful—contrary to what one would expect—a smile settling on it whenever he met and passed anybody on the street, or on his way to the group of shared lavatories at the end of the Row. But his face was almost down and lost to the world as he sat on his chair and brought forth his first sweet notes of a summer's evening.

It was said that a neighbor in the last place they had lived had taught him to play like that. Others maintained it was an uncle who had shown him how. But nobody knew for sure because when someone asked directly he said that if he had any gift at all it must have come from God above. It was known that on some Sundays of the year, if the sun was out, he went to the Methodist chapel on St. Peter's Street.

He could play anything from "Greensleeves" to "Mademoiselle from Armentières." He could do a beautiful heart-pulling version of Handel's *Largo*, and throw in bits from *The Messiah* as well. He would go from one piece to another with no rhyme or reason, from ridiculousness to sublimity, with almost shocking abruptness, but as the hour or so went by it all appeared easy and natural, part of a long piece coming from Jeff Bignal's fiddle while the ball of the sun went down behind his back.

Literary Analysis
Setting, Atmosphere, and Style Which elements of style in this paragraph help bring the setting to life?

sublimity (sə blim′ ə tē) *n.* quality of being majestic or noble

✔**Reading Check**
Who is Jeff Bignal?

To a child it seemed as if the songs lived in the hard collier's muscle at the top of his energetic arm, and that they queued one by one to get out. Once free, they rushed along his flesh from which the shirtsleeves had been rolled up, and split into his fingertips, where they were played out with ease into the warm evening air.

The grass in the fields across the stream was livid and lush, almost blue, and a piebald horse stood with bent head, eating oats out of a large old pram whose wheels had long since gone. The breeze wafted across from places farther out, from Robins Wood and the Cherry Orchard, Wollaton Roughs and Bramcote Hills and even, on a day that was not too hot, from the tops of the Pennines in Derbyshire.

Jeff played for himself, for the breeze against his arm, for the soft hiss of the flowing Leen at the end of the garden, and maybe also for the horse in the field, which took no notice of anything and which, having grown tired of its oats in the pram, bent its head over the actual grass and began to roam in search of succulent pastures.

In the middle of the winter Jeff's fiddling was forgotten. He went into the coal mine before it was light, and came up only after it had got dark. Walking down Leen Place, he complained to Blonk that it was hard on a man not to see daylight for weeks at a time.

"That's why I wain't go anywhere near the bleddy pit," Blonk said vehemently, though he had worked there from time to time, and would do so again when <u>harried</u> by his wife and children. "You'd do better to come out on a bit o' poaching with me and Arthur," he suggested.

It was virtually true that Jeff saw no daylight, because even on Sunday he stayed in bed most of the day, and if it happened to be dull there was little enough sky to be seen through his front bedroom window, which looked away from the Leen and up the hill.

The upshot of his complaint was that he would do anything to change such a situation. A man was less than an animal for putting up with it.

"I'd do anything," he repeated to his mother over his tea in the single room downstairs.

"But what, though?" she asked. "What can you do, Jeff?"

"Well, how do I know?" he almost snapped at her. "But I'll do summat,[4] you can be sure of that."

He didn't do anything till the weather got better and life turned a bit sweeter. Maybe this improvement finally got him going, because it's hard to help yourself towards better things when you're too far down in the dumps.

On a fine blowy day with both sun and cloud in the sky Jeff went out in the morning, walking up Leen Place with his fiddle under his arm. The case had been wiped and polished.

In the afternoon he came back without it.

"Where's your fiddle?" Ma Jones asked.

He put an awkward smile on to his pale face, and told her: "I sold it."

"Well I never! How much for?"

harried (har′ ēd) v. harassed; worried by repeated requests

Reading Strategy
Predicting the Effect of Setting What do you think Jeff might do to escape the mines?

---

4. **summat** something.

He was too shocked at her brazen question not to tell the truth: "Four quid."

"That ain't much."

"It'll be enough," he said roughly.

"Enough for what, Jeff?"

He didn't say, but the fact that he had sold his fiddle for four quid rattled up and down the line of cottages till everybody knew of it. Others swore he'd got ten pounds for it, because something that made such music must be worth more than a paltry four, and in any case Jeff would never say how much he'd really got for it, for fear that someone would go in and rob him.

They wondered why he'd done it, but had to wait for the answer, as one usually does. But there was nothing secretive about Jeff Bignal, and if he'd sold his music for a mess of pottage he saw no point in not letting them know why. They'd find out sooner or later, anyway.

All he'd had to do was make up his mind, and he'd done that lying on his side at the pit face while ripping coal out with his pick and shovel. Decisions made like that can't be undone, he knew. He'd brooded on it all winter, till the fact of having settled it seemed to have altered the permanent expression of his face, and given it a new look which caused people to wonder whether he would ever be able to play the fiddle again anyway—at least with his old spirit and dash.

With the four quid he paid the first week's rent on a butcher's shop on Denman Street, and bought a knife, a chopper, and a bit of sharpening stone, as well as a wooden block. Maybe he had a quid or two more knocking around, though if he had it couldn't have been much, but with four quid and a slice of bluff he got enough credit from a wholesaler at the meat market downtown to stock his shop with mutton and beef, and in a couple of days he was in trade. The people of Harrison's Row were amazed at how easy it was, though nobody had ever thought of doing it themselves.

Like a serious young man of business Mr. Bignal—as he was now known—parted his hair down the middle, so that he didn't look so young any more, but everyone agreed that it was better than being at Radford Pit. They'd seen how he had got fed up with selling the sweat of his brow.

No one could say that he prospered, but they couldn't deny that he made a living. And he didn't have to suffer the fact of not seeing daylight for almost the whole of the winter.

Six months after opening the shop he got married. The reception was held at the chapel on St. Peter's Street, which seemed to be a sort of halfway house between Harrison's Row on the banks of the Leen and the butcher's shop on Denman Street farther up.

Everybody from Harrison's Row was invited for a drink and something to eat; but he knew them too well to let any have either chops or chitter-lings (or even black puddings) on tick[5] when they came into his shop.

---

5. **tick** credit.

Literary Analysis
Setting, Atmosphere, and Style Which words and phrases in this paragraph are examples of Sillitoe's informal style?

 **Reading Check**
What does Jeff finally do with his fiddle?

The people of Harrison's Row missed the sound of his fiddle on long summer evenings, though the children could splash and shout with their tin bathtub undisturbed, floundering through shallows and scrambling up to grass on the other bank, and wondering what place they'd reach if they walked without stopping till it got dark.

Two years later the Second World War began, and not long afterwards meat as well as nearly everything else was put on the ration. Apart from which, Jeff was only twenty-six, so got called up into the army. He never had much chance to make a proper start in life, though people said that he came out all right in the end.

The houses of Harrison's Row were condemned as unfit to live in, and a bus depot stands on the site.

The packed mass of houses on the hill behind—forty years after Jeff Bignal sold his violin—is also vanishing, and high-rise hencoops (as the people call them) are put in their place. The demolition crew knock down ten houses a day—though the foreman told me there was still work for another two years.

Some of the houses would easily have lasted a few more decades, for the bricks were perfect, but as the foreman went on: "You can't let them stand in the way of progress"—whatever that means.

The people have known each other for generations but, when they are moved to their new estates and blocks of flats,[6] they will know each other for generations more, because as I listen to them talking, they speak a language which, in spite of everything and everyone, never alters.

---

6. flats apartments.

Review and Assess

Thinking About the Selection

1. **(a) Recall:** What does Jeff Bignal do in the summer when he comes home from the coal mines? **(b) Connect:** What is the connection between Jeff's fiddle and his status in the town?

2. **(a) Recall:** When Jeff complains to his friend Blonk about working in the mines, what does Blonk say in response?
   (b) Compare and Contrast: How is Jeff's attitude toward the coal mines different from his friend's?

3. **(a) Recall:** What does Jeff finally do with his fiddle?
   (b) Interpret: What does the fiddle symbolize? Explain.
   (c) Draw Conclusions: What theme does this symbol reveal?

4. **Generalize:** Do you think that the necessities of earning a living should take precedence over the pursuit of beauty? Why or why not?

Review and Assess

Literary Analysis

Setting and Atmosphere

1. Fill in a chart like this one to explain how details of the **setting** create an ominous **atmosphere** in "The Fiddle."

Description of Setting	Ominous Atmosphere
Passage From Story	Which Details? Why?

2. Using examples from the story as support, explain the effects that descriptions of the River Leen have on the atmosphere of this story.

3. Describe the effects of the fiddle, an element of setting, on the story's atmosphere.

Connecting Literary Elements

4. Using examples from the story, illustrate these aspects of the author's **style:** (a) conversational language, (b) clear images, (c) a sense that the narrator is part of the neighborhood.

5. (a) Referring to one passage, explain how the author's style brings the setting to life. (b) Describe the author's attitude towards the setting in the passage—is he amused, concerned, detached, accepting, or angry?

6. How might the style and the setting have changed if the narrator had been a social worker? Explain.

Reading Strategy

Predicting the Effect of Setting

7. What effect did the fiddle, an important detail of the setting, have on the outcome of events?

8. (a) Speculate about the effects that World War II had on Jeff's life. (b) Why do you think the author was not more specific about them?

9. Which elements of the setting pointed most strongly to a particular outcome in the story? Why?

Extend Understanding

10. **Science Connection:** How do Jeff's feelings about the mine in winter illustrate what scientists have learned about the link between sunlight and mood?

Quick Review

The **setting** of a story is the time and place in which the events occur. A story's setting contributes to its **atmosphere,** its overall feeling or mood.

A writer's **style,** or typical way of writing, can help bring a story's setting to life. Style may include such elements as word choice, images, and rhythm.

To **predict the effects of a setting,** make educated guesses about how the details of the setting will influence characters' decisions and actions.

 Take It to the Net
www.phschool.com
Take the interactive self-test online to check your understanding of the selection.

Integrate Language Skills

Vocabulary Development Lesson

Latin Word Origins: *Sublime*

The word *sublimity* contains the Latin prefix *sub-*, meaning "up to," and the root *-limen-*, meaning "lintel, the horizontal crosspiece over a door." *Sublimity* is therefore "the quality of being uplifted or noble."

Explain how the origin of *sublime* influences the meaning of these scientific words:

1. To *sublimate* is to purify or refine a substance. (chemistry)
2. To *sublime* a substance is to change it directly from a solid to a gaseous state. (chemistry)
3. To *sublimate* is to express unacceptable impulses in constructive forms. (psychology)

Concept Development: Analogies

Using the vocabulary words on page 1077, complete each analogy by forming a new word pair with the same relationship as the first pair.

1. organized : neat :: persevering : ___?___
2. believe : disprove :: create : ___?___
3. boring : routine :: awe-inspiring : ___?___
4. ideas : inspired :: responsibilities : ___?___

Spelling Strategy

Sometimes the suffix *-ity* is spelled *-ety* to avoid a double *i* when the base word part already ends in *i*, as in *society*. In your notebook, add *-ity* or *-ety* to complete these words:

1. intens___   2. agil___   3. anxi___

Grammar and Style Lesson

Vary Sentence Beginnings

If every sentence in a story began with the word *the*, the resulting monotonous rhythm would catch your attention, maybe even annoy you. By **varying sentence beginnings**—starting sentences with different parts of speech or sentence elements—a writer avoids monotomy. The right introductory word, phrase, or clause can propel you from one event to the next. To see how good writers vary sentence beginnings, note examples from the story:

Introductory Adverb: <u>Sometimes</u> they could almost paddle.

Introductory Phrase: <u>In that case</u> there was no telling where you'd end up.

Introductory Clause: <u>When they did get Ted Griffin</u>, he was pulled out of bed. . . .

Practice In your notebook, identify each of the italicized sentence beginnings as subject, adverb, phrase, or clause.

1. *Allan Sillitoe* grew up in Nottingham, England.
2. *By age fourteen*, he was earning enough to help his family.
3. *Fortunately*, he passed the necessary tests to join the Royal Air Force.
4. *When he was twenty-one*, he knew that he wanted to be a writer.
5. *Eventually*, he became famous as one of England's "Angry Young Men."

Writing Application In your notebook, rewrite sentences 1–5 above. Have each begin with one of the following sentence parts: subject, adverb, clause, or phrase.

 Prentice Hall Writing and Grammar Connection: Chapter 20, Section 3

Writing Lesson

Description of a Setting

Sillitoe describes Harrison's Row with phrases like "small red English housebricks . . . weatherstained . . . almost black" to support an overall impression of neglect. Choose a place that you know, and describe it just as vividly.

Prewriting   Gather details that express the feeling you want to convey. Consider all five senses.

Drafting   Convey an overall impression, as Sillitoe does in his opening paragraphs. Then, support that impression by including sensory descriptions arranged in a logical way, such as spatial order.

Revising   Be sure that your descriptions support the overall impression. If your organizing principle seems too mechanical, use a more interesting one. For example, you might use accounts of children's play to describe a place, as Sillitoe does.

Model: Revising to Clarify Organization

As you approach the basketball court, you
~~You~~ hear the sound of sneakers squeaking and the broken rhythm of the bouncing ball. Suddenly, voices rise out of the noise as players call excitedly to teammates.

> The additional text helps organize the spatial description.

W̶G Prentice Hall Writing and Grammar Connection: Chapter 6, Section 4

Extension Activities

Research and Technology Research and present a **multimedia report** on Britain's "Angry Young Men": Alan Sillitoe, John Osborne, and Arnold Wesker, among others. Include items like these:

- Charts illustrating the British class system, against which these writers rebelled
- Readings from the works of these writers
- Clips from films based on their works: *The Loneliness of the Long-Distance Runner* (1962) and *Look Back in Anger* (1959)

After gathering materials, write a script to guide your presentation. Rehearse presenting your materials, and give your report for the class.

Listening and Speaking With several classmates, stage a **debate** on this resolution: Old neighborhoods like Harrison's Row should be torn down and replaced by new housing. Use arguments that appeal to logic with cause-and-effect relationships, to ethics with statements of values, and to emotions with charged language. Also, consider general issues, such as when, if ever, progress justifies disruption of traditional ways. **[Group Activity]**

 **Take It to the Net**   www.phschool.com

Go online for an additional research activity using the Internet.

Prepare to Read

The Distant Past

William Trevor (b. 1928)

Like his protagonists in "The Distant Past," William Trevor was born into a Protestant family in the largely Catholic Republic of Ireland. This experience of being outside the dominant culture gave him a sympathy for the outsiders about whom he writes in his short stories and novels. Trevor himself has said, "I think the feeling of not belonging is very strong in me. In order to write about people, you have got actually to stand back quite a distance."

An Unusual Education The son of a bank manager who moved around a great deal, Trevor attended thirteen different schools. For long periods, however, he was left simply to roam the countryside, occasionally being tutored by neighboring farmers or clergymen. Still, he completed his formal education, graduating from Trinity College in Dublin in 1950. His unusual education probably helped develop his ability as a fiction writer to present clear insights about many different kinds of people and circumstances.

Finding His Art After college, Trevor taught school to support his wife and young family while devoting his creative energies to sculpture. Eventually, his sculpture became too abstract to interest him. "There weren't any people in it anymore, and I didn't like it," he says.

After abandoning sculpture, he took up fiction writing, he says, to express a humanity that he could not find in the visual arts. His art background helps him describe the craft of writing: "A short story is like an impressionist painting. You cut down everything enormously and you get the effects from one big splash or explosion. You have to cut to the very edge. What excites me is to go as far as I can."

A Pessimistic View Trevor earned a living as an advertising copywriter in London. He also achieved immediate success in his new art, publishing short stories in magazines as fast as he could write them. His stories and novels explore a wide variety of subjects and themes. He displays a deep understanding of human nature, often portraying the pointless misunderstandings that develop between individuals or groups of people. Trevor admits that his view of life is pessimistic. The "villain" in his stories is usually circumstance. People's lives are troubled—and sometimes crushed—by historical events that are beyond their control. "I'm very interested in the sadness of fate, the things that just happen to people," Trevor remarks.

Acclaim for Stories Today, William Trevor is recognized as one of the greatest living writers of short stories in the English language. In fact, critics have compared his stories to those of Anton Chekhov, Muriel Spark, and James Joyce. He has been praised for the "gritty detail" of his stories, his lack of sentimentality, and the subtle sense of humor that infuses his work.

Novelist and Playwright Having lived in both Ireland and England, Trevor is comfortable setting his fiction in either place. He has received awards from literary societies in both countries. In addition to his accomplishments as a short-story writer, Trevor is an acclaimed novelist. His works of full-length fiction include *The Old Boys* (1964) and *The Silence in the Garden* (1988). He has also written dozens of plays, many for television and many based on his own stories or those of other writers, such as Charles Dickens, Thomas Hardy, Graham Greene, and Elizabeth Bowen.

Preview

Connecting to the Literature

Joining a group means uniting with others. However, it can also mean separating from those who belong to different groups. In "The Distant Past," a brother and sister support a viewpoint and share a loyalty that is unpopular in their town. This story suggests that some differences can never really be overcome.

Literary Analysis

Social Conflict

Conflict, a struggle between opposing forces, is at the heart of most stories. Some conflicts are individual and personal; others are communal or universal. **Social conflict** refers to a struggle between those with opposing loyalties, interests, and views about the society in which they live. The underlined words in the following passage indicate a conflict about large social issues.

> They attended on Sundays St. Patrick's Protestant Church, <u>a place that matched their mood, for prayers were still said there for the King whose sovereignty their country had denied.</u>

In reading, notice how social conflict separates the two main characters from everyone else.

Connecting Literary Elements

Trevor explores the way social conflict in Ireland affects his characters' **motives,** the reasons and explanations for their actions. He seems to ask readers to consider this question: What role do social conflicts play in shaping people's motives and everyday behavior? As you read, figure out how he would answer this question—and whether you agree with him.

Reading Strategy

Questioning Causes and Effects

In reflecting on social conflicts and motives, you must determine why certain things happen. You can do this by **questioning causes and effects,** asking yourself what actions or conditions (causes) bring about other actions or conditions (effects). Use a chart like this one to question causes and effects as you read. Remember that the effect of one event can also be the cause of a later event.

Vocabulary Development

countenance (koun´ tə nəns) *n.* face; facial features (p. 1090)

adversity (ad vʉr´ sə tē) *n.* misfortune (p. 1091)

sovereignty (säv´ rən tē) *n.* supreme political authority (p. 1092)

anachronism (ə nak´ rə niz´ əm) *n.* something out of its proper time in history (p. 1093)

internment (in tʉrn´ mənt) *n.* confinement; a form of imprisonment often practiced during a war (p. 1096)

Event/
Condition #1

Middletons stay loyal to Britain.

Cause/Effect

Event/
Condition #2

Cause/Effect

Event/
Condition #3

The DISTANT PAST

William Trevor

Background

After five years of insurrection by the Irish against the British government, beginning with the Easter Rising in 1916, Ireland was divided. In the South, the Irish Free State was created. With 26 of Ireland's 32 counties and a Catholic majority, the Free State began as a self-governing dominion of the British Commonwealth. In 1948 it left the Commonwealth to become the Republic of Ireland, a separate country. In the North, the remaining six counties, all with a Protestant majority, were given home rule under British sovereignty.

The story is set in a town in the Republic of Ireland, not far from the border with Northern Ireland.

I n the town and beyond it they were regarded as harmlessly peculiar. Odd, people said, and in time this reference took on a burnish of affection.

They had always been thin, silent with one another, and similar in appearance: a brother and sister who shared a family face. It was a bony <u>countenance</u>, with pale blue eyes and a sharp, well-shaped nose and high cheekbones. Their father had had it too, but unlike them their father had been an irresponsible and careless man, with red flecks in his cheeks that they didn't have at all. The Middletons of Carraveagh the family had once been known as, but now the brother and sister were just the Middletons, for Carraveagh didn't count any more, except to them.

countenance (koun´ tə nəns) *n.* face; facial features

▶ **Critical Viewing**
How does the image of this house illustrate the Middletons' relationship with the townspeople?
[Apply]

They owned four Herefords,[1] a number of hens, and the house itself, three miles outside the town. It was a large house, built in the reign of George II,[2] a monument that reflected in its glory and later decay the fortunes of a family. As the brother and sister aged, its roof increasingly ceased to afford protection, rust ate at its gutters, grass thrived in two thick channels all along its avenue. Their father had mortgaged his inherited estate, so local rumor claimed, in order to keep a Catholic Dublin woman in brandy and jewels. When he died, in 1924, his two children discovered that they possessed only a dozen acres. It was locally said also that this <u>adversity</u> hardened their will and that because of it they came to love the remains of Carraveagh more than they could ever have loved a husband or a wife. They blamed for their ill-fortune the Catholic Dublin woman whom they'd never met and they blamed as well the new national regime, contriving in their eccentric way to relate the two. In the days of the union jack[3] such women would have known their place—wasn't it all part and parcel?

adversity (ad vʉr´ sə tē) *n.* misfortune

---

1. **Herefords** *n.* breed of cattle.
2. **reign of George II** 1727–1760.
3. **union jack** British flag; symbol of British rule.

✔**Reading Check**

How do the townspeople regard the Middletons?

Twice a week, on Fridays and Sundays, the Middletons journeyed into the town, first of all in a trap[4] and later in a Ford Anglia car. In the shops and elsewhere they made, quite gently, no secret of their continuing loyalty to the past. They attended on Sundays St. Patrick's Protestant Church, a place that matched their mood, for prayers were still said there for the King whose <u>sovereignty</u> their country had denied. The revolutionary regime would not last, they quietly informed the Reverend Packham—what sense was there in green-painted pillar boxes[5] and a language that nobody understood?

On Fridays, when they took seven or eight dozen eggs to the town, they dressed in pressed tweeds and were accompanied over the years by a series of red setters, the breed there had always been at Carraveagh. They sold the eggs in Keogh's grocery and then had a drink with Mrs. Keogh in the part of her shop that was devoted to the consumption of refreshment. They enjoyed the occasion, for they liked Mrs. Keogh and were liked by her in return. Afterwards they shopped, chatting to the shopkeepers about whatever news there was, and then they went to Healy's Hotel for a few more drinks before driving home.

. . . In spite of their loyalty to the past, they built up convivial relationships with the people of the town. Fat Driscoll, who kept the butcher's shop, used even to joke about the past when he stood with them in Healy's Hotel or stood behind his own counter cutting their slender chops or thinly slicing their liver. "Will you ever forget it, Mr. Middleton? I'd ha' run like a rabbit if you'd lifted a finger at me." Fat Driscoll would laugh then, rocking back on his heels with a glass of stout in his hand or banging their meat on to his weighing-scales. Mr. Middleton would smile. "There was alarm in your eyes, Mr. Driscoll," Miss Middleton would murmur, smiling also at the memory of the distant occasion.

Fat Driscoll, with a farmer called Maguire and another called Breen, had stood in the hall of Carraveagh, each of them in charge of a shotgun. The Middletons, children then, had been locked with their mother and father and an aunt into an upstairs room. Nothing else had happened: the expected British soldiers had not, after all, arrived and the men in the hall had eventually relaxed their vigil. "A massacre they wanted," the Middletons' father said after they'd gone. . . . "Bloody ruffians."

The Second World War took place. Two Germans, a man and his wife called Winkelmann who ran a glove factory in the town, were suspected by the Middletons of being spies for the Third Reich.[6] People laughed, for they knew the Winkelmanns well and could lend no credence to the Middletons' latest fantasy—typical of them, they explained to the Winkelmanns, who had been worried. Soon after the War the Reverend Packham died and was replaced by the Reverend Bradshaw, a younger

Literary Analysis
Social Conflict What social conflict is revealed in this paragraph?

sovereignty (säv′ rən tē) *n.* supreme political authority

▼ **Critical Viewing**
In a town this size, would it be easier to conceal a social conflict than it would be in a city? Why or why not? **[Analyze]**

man who laughed also and regarded the Middletons as an <u>anachronism</u>. They protested when prayers were no longer said for the Royal Family in St. Patrick's, but the Reverend Bradshaw considered that their protests were as absurd as the prayers themselves had been. Why pray for the monarchy of a neighboring island when their own island had its chosen President now? The Middletons didn't reply to that argument. In the Reverend Bradshaw's presence they rose to their feet when the BBC played "God Save the King," and on the day of the coronation of Queen Elizabeth II they drove into the town with a small union jack propped up in the back window of their Ford Anglia. "Bedad, you're a holy terror, Mr. Middleton!" Fat Driscoll laughingly exclaimed, noticing the flag as he lifted a tray of pork steaks from his display shelf. The Middletons smiled. It was a great day for the Commonwealth of Nations, they replied, a remark which further amused Fat Driscoll and which he later repeated in Phelan's public house. "Her Britannic Majesty," guffawed his friend Mr. Breen.

Situated in a valley that was noted for its beauty and with convenient access to rich rivers and bogs over which gamebirds flew, the town benefited from post-war tourism. Healy's Hotel changed its title and became, overnight, the New Ormonde. Shopkeepers had their shop-fronts painted and Mr. Healy organized an annual Salmon Festival. Even Canon Kelly, who had at first commented severely on the habits of

Reading Strategy
Questioning Causes and Effects What causes Fat Driscoll to react with amusement to the Middletons' loyalties, rather than with anger?

☑ **Reading Check**

What did Fat Driscoll do at Carraveagh when the Middletons were children?

the tourists, and in particular on the summertime dress of the women, was in the end obliged to confess that the morals of his flock remained unaffected. "God and good sense," he proclaimed, meaning God and his own teaching. In time he even derived pride from the fact that people with other values came briefly to the town and that the values esteemed by his parishioners were in no way diminished. . . .

From the windows of their convent the Loretto nuns observed the long, sleek cars with G.B. plates; English and American accents drifted on the breeze to them. Mothers cleaned up their children and sent them to the Golf Club to seek employment as caddies. Sweet shops sold holiday mementoes. The brown, soda and currant breads of Murphy-Flood's bakery were declared to be delicious. Mr. Healy doubled the number of local girls who served as waitresses in his dining room, and in the winter of 1961 he had the builders in again, working on an extension for which the Munster and Leinster Bank had lent him twenty-two thousand pounds.

But as the town increased its prosperity Carraveagh continued its decline. The Middletons were in their middle sixties now and were reconciled to a life that became more uncomfortable with every passing year. Together they roved the vast lofts of their house, placing old paint tins and flowerpot saucers beneath the drips from the roof. At night they sat over their thin chops in a dining room that had once been gracious and which in a way was gracious still, except for the faded appearance of furniture that was dry from lack of polish and of a wallpaper that time had rendered colorless. In the hall their father gazed down at them, framed in ebony and gilt, in the uniform of the Irish Guards. He had conversed with Queen Victoria, and even in their middle sixties they could still hear him saying that God and Empire and Queen formed a trinity unique in any worthy soldier's heart. In the hall hung the family crest, and on ancient Irish linen the Cross of St. George.[7]

The dog that accompanied the Middletons now was called Turloch, an animal whose death they dreaded for they felt they couldn't manage the antics of another pup. Turloch, being thirteen, moved slowly and was blind and a little deaf. He was a reminder to them of their own advancing years and of the effort it had become to tend the Herefords and collect the weekly eggs. More and more they looked forward to Fridays, to the warm companionship of Mrs. Keogh and Mr. Healy's chatter in the hotel. They stayed longer now with Mrs. Keogh and in the hotel, and idled longer in the shops, and drove home more slowly. Dimly, but with no less loyalty, they still recalled the distant past and were listened to without ill-feeling when they spoke of it and of Carraveagh as it had been, and of the Queen whose company their careless father had known.

The visitors who came to the town heard about the Middletons and were impressed. It was a pleasant wonder, more than one of them

---

7. **St. George** patron saint of England.

Literary Analysis
Social Conflict and Motives What motivates the Middletons to look forward to Fridays, even though they do not share the loyalties of the townspeople?

remarked, that old wounds could heal so completely, that the Middletons continued in their loyalty to the past and that, in spite of it, they were respected in the town. When Miss Middleton had been ill with a form of pneumonia in 1958 Canon Kelly had driven out to Carraveagh twice a week with pullets and young ducks that his housekeeper had dressed. "An upright couple," was the Canon's public opinion of the Middletons, and he had been known to add that eccentric views would hurt you less than malice. "We can disagree without guns in this town," Mr. Healy pronounced in his cocktail room, and his visitors usually replied that as far as they could see that was the result of living in a Christian country. That the Middletons bought their meat from a man who had once locked them into an upstairs room and had then waited to shoot soldiers in their hall was a fact that amazed the seasonal visitors. You lived and learned, they remarked to Mr. Healy.

The Middletons, privately, often considered that they led a strange life. Alone in their two beds at night they now and again wondered why they hadn't just sold Carraveagh forty-eight years ago when their father had died—why had the tie been so strong and why had they in perversity encouraged it? They didn't fully know, nor did they attempt to discuss the matter in any way. Instinctively they had remained at Carraveagh, instinctively feeling that it would have been cowardly to go. Yet often it seemed to them now to be no more than a game they played, this worship of the distant past. And at other times it seemed as real and as important as the remaining acres of land, and the house itself.

"Isn't that shocking?" Mr. Healy said one day in 1967. "Did you hear about that, Mr. Middleton, blowing up them post offices in Belfast?"

Mr. Healy, red-faced and short-haired, spoke casually in his Cocktail Room, making midday conversation. He had commented in much the same way at breakfast-time, looking up from the *Irish Independent*. Everyone in the town had said it too: that the blowing up of sub-post offices in Belfast was a shocking matter.

"A bad business," Fat Driscoll remarked, wrapping the Middletons' meat. "We don't want that old stuff all over again."

"We didn't want it in the first place," Miss Middleton reminded him. He laughed, and she laughed, and so did her brother. Yes, it was a game, she thought—how could any of it be as real or as important as the afflictions and problems of the old butcher himself, his rheumatism and his reluctance to retire? Did her brother, she wondered, privately think so too?

"Come on, old Turloch," he said, stroking the flank of the red setter with the point of his shoe, and she reflected that you could never tell what he was thinking. Certainly it wasn't the kind of thing you wanted to talk about.

"I've put him in a bit of mince," Fat Driscoll said, which was something he often did these days, pretending the mince would otherwise be thrown away. There'd been a red setter about the place that night when he waited in the hall for the soldiers; Breen and Maguire had pushed it down into a cellar, frightened of it.

"There's a heart of gold in you, Mr. Driscoll," Miss Middleton murmured, nodding and smiling at him. He was the same age as she was, sixty-six—he should have shut up shop years ago. He would have, he'd once told them, if there'd been a son to leave the business to. As it was, he'd have to sell it and when it came to the point he found it hard to make the necessary arrangements. "Like us and Carraveagh," she'd said, even though on the face of it it didn't seem the same at all.

Every evening they sat in the big old kitchen, hearing the news. It was only in Belfast and Derry, the wireless said; outside Belfast and Derry you wouldn't know anything was happening at all. On Fridays they listened to the talk in Mrs. Keogh's bar and in the hotel. "Well, thank God it has nothing to do with the South," Mr. Healy said often, usually repeating the statement.

The first British soldiers landed in the North of Ireland, and soon people didn't so often say that outside Belfast and Derry you wouldn't know anything was happening. There were incidents in Fermanagh and Armagh, in border villages and towns. One Prime Minister resigned and then another one. The troops were unpopular, the newspapers said; internment became part of the machinery of government. In the town, in St. Patrick's Protestant Church and in the Church of the Holy Assumption, prayers for peace were offered, but no peace came.

"We're hit, Mr. Middleton," Mr. Healy said one Friday morning. "If there's a dozen visitors this summer it'll be God's own stroke of luck for us."

"Luck?"

"Sure, who wants to come to a country with all that malarkey in it?"

"But it's only in the North."

"Tell that to your tourists, Mr. Middleton."

The town's prosperity ebbed. The border was more than sixty miles away, but over that distance had spread some wisps of the fog of war. As anger rose in the town at the loss of fortune so there rose also the

▲ Critical Viewing
What do these flags symbolize to the characters in the story? **[Analyze]**

internment (in tʉrn´ mənt) *n.* confinement; a form of imprisonment often practiced during war

kind of talk there had been in the distant past. There was talk of atrocities and counteratrocities, and of guns and gelignite[8] and the rights of people. There was bitterness suddenly in Mrs. Keogh's bar because of the lack of trade, and in the empty hotel there was bitterness also.

On Fridays, only sometimes at first, there was a silence when the Middletons appeared. It was as though, going back nearly twenty years, people remembered the union jack in the window of their car and saw it now in a different light. It wasn't something to laugh at any more, nor were certain words that the Middletons had gently spoken, nor were they themselves just an old, peculiar couple. Slowly the change crept about, all around them in the town, until Fat Driscoll didn't wish it to be remembered that he had ever given them mince for their dog. He had stood with a gun in the enemy's house, waiting for soldiers so that soldiers might be killed—it was better that people should remember that.

One day Canon Kelly looked the other way when he saw the Middletons' car coming and they noticed this movement of his head, although he hadn't wished them to. And on another day Mrs. O'Brien, who had always been keen to talk to them in the hotel, didn't reply when they addressed her.

The Middletons naturally didn't discuss these rebuffs but they each of them privately knew that there was no conversation they could have at this time with the people of the town. The stand they had taken and kept to for so many years no longer seemed ridiculous in the town. Had they driven with a union jack now they would, astoundingly, have been shot.

"It will never cease." He spoke disconsolately one night, standing by the dresser where the wireless was.

She washed the dishes they'd eaten from, and the cutlery. "Not in our time," she said.

"It is worse than before."

"Yes, it is worse than before."

They took from the walls of the hall the portrait of their father in the uniform of the Irish Guards because it seemed wrong to them that at this time it should hang there. They took down also the crest of their family and the Cross of St. George, and from a vase on the drawing-room mantelpiece they removed the small union jack that had been there since the coronation of Queen Elizabeth II. They did not remove these articles in fear but in mourning for the *modus vivendi*[9] that had existed for so long between them and the people of the town. They had given their custom to a butcher who had planned to shoot down soldiers in their hall and he, in turn, had given them mince for their dog. For fifty years they had experienced, after suspicion had seeped away, a tolerance that never again in the years that were left to them would they know.

---

8. **gelignite** *n.* explosive.
9. **modus vivendi** (vi ven′ dī) Latin for "manner of getting along."

Literary Analysis
Social Conflict and Motives At this point, do townspeople seem motivated more by social pressure or by their own individual judgments? Explain.

**Reading Check**

What happens to the town's prosperity during the troubles?

One November night their dog died and he said to her after he had buried it that they must not be depressed by all that was happening. They would die themselves and the house would become a ruin because there was no one to inherit it, and the distant past would be set to rest. But she disagreed: the *modus vivendi* had been easy for them, she pointed out, because they hadn't really minded the dwindling of their fortunes while the town prospered. It had given them a life, and a kind of dignity: you could take a pride out of living in peace.

He did not say anything and then, because of the emotion that both of them felt over the death of their dog, he said in a rushing way that they could no longer at their age hope to make a living out of the remains of Carraveagh. They must sell the hens and the four Herefords. As he spoke, he watched her nodding, agreeing with the sense of it. Now and again, he thought, he would drive slowly into the town, to buy groceries and meat with the money they had saved, and to face the silence that would sourly thicken as their own two deaths came closer and death increased in another part of their island. She felt him thinking that and she knew that he was right. Because of the distant past they would die friendless. It was worse than being murdered in their beds.

Review and Assess

Thinking About the Selection

1. **Respond:** Would you describe the Middletons as odd, foolish, or courageous, or would you use some other adjective? Explain.

2. **(a) Recall:** Who is responsible for the Middletons' reduced economic position? Whom do they blame? **(b) Connect:** How does the decline in the Middletons' fortunes parallel the decline of the British Empire?

3. **(a) Recall:** What kind of relationship do the Middletons have with the townspeople through most of the story? **(b) Analyze:** What, if anything, is unexpected or surprising about this relationship?

4. **(a) Recall:** How is the town altered by the violence in the North? **(b) Analyze Cause and Effect:** What is the link between these changes and the changes in the town's attitudes toward the Middletons? **(c) Draw Conclusions:** What does the change in attitude toward the Middletons suggest about human nature?

5. **Evaluate:** Do you agree with Mr. Middleton that he and his sister would have been better off "murdered"? Explain.

6. **Speculate:** Do your observations and reading suggest that the "distant past" can influence events in the present? Why or why not?

Review and Assess

Literary Analysis

Social Conflict

1. What is the **social conflict** between the Middletons and the townspeople?
2. Using a chart like this one, show how this social conflict changes or does not change in response to various outside events.

Outside Events	Anglo–Irish War (Fat Driscoll at Carraveagh)	World War II	Period of Prosperity After World War II	Beginning of "The Troubles"
Effects on Social Conflict				

3. How do the changes in Fat Driscoll's relationship with the Middletons reflect changes in Ireland's level of conflict?
4. Explain the links among these items: the social conflict in the story, the title of the story, and the theme of the story.

Connecting Literary Elements

5. What do you think is the **motive** for the Middletons' "continuing loyalty to the past"?
6. What motivates the townspeople to think of the Middletons for many years "as harmlessly peculiar"?
7. (a) Do you think the author sees the social conflict between his characters as being motivated primarily by their independent choices or by social pressures? Explain. (b) Would Trevor say his character can escape "the distant past"? Explain.

Reading Strategy

Questioning Causes and Effects

8. Show a **cause** for each of the following events and an **effect** that results from each: (a) The Middletons drive into town with a small Union Jack. (b) Tourists stop coming to the town.

Extend Understanding

9. **History Connection:** What events of today will influence future events when our times are the "distant past"? Explain.

Integrate Language Skills

Vocabulary Development Lesson

Word Analysis: Latin Suffix -ity (-ty)

In "The Distant Past," two characters experience *adversity* ("misfortune") because they insist on the *sovereignty* ("ruling power") of the British crown. Both words contain the suffix *-ity* (or *-ty*), meaning "the state or the quality of." In your notebook, add *-ity* to each word—deleting a final *e* if necessary—and use the new word in a sentence.

1. serene   2. civil   3. adverse

Spelling Strategy

Adding the suffix *-ment* changes certain verbs to nouns without affecting the spelling of the word root: *intern* + *-ment* = *internment*. In your notebook, add *-ment* to these verbs:

1. pay   2. enjoy   3. improve

Fluency: Sentence Completion

Review the vocabulary list on page 1089. Then, choose the word from the vocabulary list that best completes each sentence.

1. The townspeople regarded the Middletons as an ___?___.

2. The Middletons did not question the ___?___ of the English king.

3. Financial ___?___ bore down on them after their father's death.

4. Kindly eyes sparkled from the sister's careworn ___?___.

5. Townspeople shuddered, horrified, at news of the unjust ___?___ of innocent citizens.

Grammar and Style Lesson

Restrictive and Nonrestrictive Adjective Clauses

A subordinate clause is a group of words that contains a subject and a verb but cannot stand alone as a sentence. An **adjective clause** is a subordinate clause that modifies a noun or pronoun. A **restrictive adjective clause** contains essential information, so it is not set off by commas. In contrast, a **nonrestrictive adjective clause** contains information that is not essential, so it is set off by commas.

Restrictive: Mr. Healey doubled the number of local girls who served as waitresses in his dining room, . . . (essential: tells which *girls*)

Nonrestrictive: Fat Driscoll, who kept the butcher's shop, used even to joke about the past. . . . (nonessential: modifies *Driscoll*)

Practice In your notebook, underline each adjective clause and add commas where needed:

1. The Middletons who had once lived comfortably found themselves impoverished.

2. They rode to town where they had friendly encounters with the townspeople.

3. The dog that accompanied them was a red setter.

4. The shopkeepers with whom they did business considered them odd.

5. They made the trip back to their rundown home which they called Carraveagh.

Writing Application Write five sentences about "The Distant Past," using an adjective clause in each and inserting commas around the clause where necessary.

𝒲𝒢 *Prentice Hall Writing and Grammar Connection: Chapter 19, Section 3*

Writing Lesson

Persuasive Poster

During "The Troubles," the Middletons or some townspeople might have created a persuasive poster to advocate their side of the conflict. Design a poster that one of the factions might have displayed.

Prewriting Review the historical background in the box on page 1095. Then, choose a side, and note poster ideas on a chart like this one.

Model: Planning Key Features of a Persuasive Poster

	Headline	Visual Image	Text
Tips for Feature	Brief and catchy	Communicates instantly; goes with headline	Briefly persuades viewer to think or act in a certain way
Notes			

Drafting Referring to your chart, (1) write a one-sentence headline that tells viewers what they should know or do, (2) draw or find a visual to support your headline, and (3) write a few brief sentences to inform or direct viewers.

Revising Display your poster, and have classmates role-play a group of townspeople viewing it. Ask them to evaluate whether it takes a position that one side in the conflict would have endorsed and whether it is persuasive. Make changes based on their comments.

 Prentice Hall Writing and Grammar Connection: Chapter 8, Section 3

Extension Activities

Research and Technology With classmates, stage a **celebration of Irish culture** that includes music, food, and storytelling.

- Gather information from history books and Web sites.
- Interview Irish members of the community
- Find tapes and CDs of Irish music to play
- Find recipes from which to prepare Irish foods.

Schedule and present your celebration. [**Group Activity**]

Listening and Speaking Imagine that Miss Middleton has died. As Fat Driscoll, give the **eulogy** at her funeral service. Present a vivid and honest portrait of the deceased and your relationship with her. To play the role of Fat Driscoll convincingly, review the story to determine the speech patterns and humor that suit his character.

 **Take It to the Net** www.phschool.com

Go online for an additional research activity using the Internet.

Prepare to Read

Follower ◆ Two Lorries ◆ Outside History

Seamus Heaney (b. 1939)

Born in County Derry, Northern Ireland, Seamus Heaney has devoted much of his poetry to the life and history of his homeland. He is a gifted traditionalist whom the American poet Robert Lowell called "the most important Irish poet since Yeats." Heaney has earned that high praise with visionary books of poetry, like *Seeing Things* (1991) and *The Spirit Level* (1996), and with his brilliant lectures on poetry, collected in *The Redress of Poetry* (1995).

A Happy Childhood The eldest of nine children, Heaney spent a happy childhood on a farm that had been in his family for generations. He has said that his deep regard for tradition grew from his early experiences in the countryside.

Leaving Home Heaney first published as an undergraduate at Queen's University in Belfast, Northern Ireland. In 1972, having struggled with the role of the artist in Northern Ireland's troubled political climate, he left and settled in the independent Irish Republic. His departure was called an artistic necessity by some and by others a betrayal. Heaney nevertheless remains the leading Irish poet—Republican or Northern.

Popular Success Heaney's accessible and deeply felt poetry has achieved a popularity that is rare among modern poets. Readers around the world have generated a strong demand for his poems, including his best-selling translation of *Beowulf* (2000). His readings are well attended by enthusiastic fans.

Since 1984, he has been Boylston Professor of Rhetoric and Poetry at Harvard. From 1989 to 1994 he also held the chair of Professor of Poetry at Oxford. In 1995, Heaney received the Nobel Prize for Literature.

Eavan Boland (b. 1944)

Eavan Boland was born in Dublin, the capital of the Republic of Ireland. Her father was a diplomat who, she says, "recognized the importance of poetry to civilization." Her mother was a painter, who also "was totally in tune with what poetry tried to do."

Away From Ireland During much of Boland's early life, she was away from Ireland. When she was five, her father became ambassador to Great Britain and the family moved to London. Later, Boland was sent to school in New York City. There, she experienced anti-Irish hostility and felt "a great sense of isolation." Returning to Ireland when she was fifteen, Boland found "a great imaginative release."

A Personal Yet Public Poet Since 1967, she has published several acclaimed volumes of poetry, including *The War Horse* (1975), *In Her Own Image* (1980), *Night Feed* (1982), and *In a Time of Violence* (1994). Boland's poetry is notable for its intense focus on her personal experiences— she freely shares incidents from her life to uncover universal themes and insights. Her 1995 collection of essays, *Object Lessons: The Life of the Woman and Poet in Our Time*, combines her explorations of history, autobiography, and poetry. In addition to publishing poetry, she writes reviews and teaches at universities in both England and the United States.

Married to a novelist and the mother of two daughters, Boland often writes about domestic life, but she shuns the label "woman poet." She says poetry should create only statements that are "bound to be human." Unwilling to yoke poetry to a political program, she notes that "My poetry begins for me where certainty ends."

Preview

Connecting to the Literature

Take over your older brother's paper route. . . . Get a driver's license, and drive yourself to all the places your mom used to take you. . . . The past has a habit of reappearing every time you grow. In these poems, Heaney and Boland explore ways in which the past repeats itself.

Literary Analysis

Diction and Style

To create a literary work, a writer must make choices about diction and other elements of style.

- **Diction** refers to a writer's typical choice of words—formal or informal, homespun or intellectual.
- **Style** takes in a writer's whole manner of expression, including his or her word choice, use of forms and rhythms (traditional or otherwise), and themes and imagery.

A poem is a work in words, and style and diction—both formed from patterns of words—are as crucial to what a poem is and how it affects you as its message is. As you read, identify the characteristics of Heaney's and Boland's styles.

Comparing Literary Works

Heaney and Boland both write poems exploring their relationship to the past, but in very different styles. Heaney's style is marked by his use of traditional forms like the **sestina** ("Two Lorries"), which recycles six words to end each line. His language is precise and down to earth. Boland works in a freer form and blends the abstract and concrete in her imagery. As you read, compare the effect of each writer's style on your experience of the poem.

Reading Strategy

Summarizing

Summarizing a poem—restating its key points in brief—can help you focus on its central images and ideas. You might summarize an entire poem or an individual stanza. Use a chart like the one shown to summarize the poems or individual stanzas in them.

Vocabulary Development

furrow (fur´ ō) *n.* narrow groove made in the ground by a plow (p. 1106)

nuisance (nōō´ səns) *n.* act, thing, or condition causing trouble (p. 1106)

inklings (iŋk´ liŋz) *n.* indirect suggestions; vague ideas (p. 1109)

mortal (môr´ təl) *adj.* of that which must eventually die (p. 1110)

ordeal (ôr dēl´) *n.* difficult or painful experience that tests one (p. 1110)

Passage

I wanted to grow up and plow,
To close one eye, stiffen my arm.
All I ever did was follow
In his broad shadow round the farm.
("Follower")

Main Points

Son following his father; looking up to him; wanting to be like him.

Summary

I wanted to be a farmer, like my father.

Follower

Seamus Heaney

My father worked with a horse plow,
His shoulders globed like a full sail strung
Between the shafts and the furrow.
The horses strained at his clicking tongue.

5 An expert. He would set the wing
And fit the bright steel-pointed sock.
The sod rolled over without breaking.
At the headrig, with a single pluck

Of reins, the sweating team turned round
10 And back into the land. His eye

Narrowed and angled at the ground,
Mapping the <u>furrow</u> exactly.

I stumbled in his hobnailed wake,
Fell sometimes on the polished sod;
15 Sometimes he rode me on his back
Dipping and rising to his plod.

I wanted to grow up and plow,
To close one eye, stiffen my arm.
All I ever did was follow
20 In his broad shadow round the farm.

I was a <u>nuisance</u>, tripping, falling,
Yapping always. But today
It is my father who keeps stumbling
Behind me, and will not go away.

furrow (fur′ ō) *n.* narrow groove made in the ground by a plow

nuisance (noo′ səns) *n.* act, thing, or condition causing trouble

Review and Assess

Thinking About the Selection

1. **Respond:** Have you ever felt about an adult the way the speaker feels about his father in "Follower"? Explain.

2. **(a) Recall:** In "Follower," what is the father doing?
   (b) Interpret: Why does the boy want "To close one eye" and "stiffen" his "arm"?

3. **(a) Recall:** Give two examples of precise words Heaney uses to describe tools, actions, or other things associated with farming. **(b) Analyze:** How does the use of such words help convey the child's fascination with his father's life?

4. **(a) Compare and Contrast:** How does the relationship between father and son shift at the end of "Follower"?
   (b) Draw Conclusions: What difference between his childhood view of his father and his own experience of adulthood does the speaker see?

5. **Generalize:** Do people's relations with their parents always leave lasting marks or burdens? Explain.

6. **Hypothesize:** Do you think the speaker would still feel that his father was shadowing him if the two had talked about the son's feelings for his father? Explain.

7. **Apply:** Do you think that father-son relationships like the one Heaney describes have become less common in our times? Explain.

Two Lorries
Seamus Heaney

Background

For large parts of its history, Ireland was under English control. Since the 1920s, Ireland has been partitioned into the Irish Republic in the South and Ulster, or Northern Ireland, which remains allied with Great Britain. Northern Ireland has been a focus of conflict between Protestants and Catholics. The Ulster Protestants generally support British rule of Northern Ireland. For the most part, Northern Irish Catholics want "the British out" and Ireland united. From the late 1960s on, this conflict has produced terrorism by Catholics and Protestants. Heaney's poem refers to a bombing incident sparked by this ongoing struggle, while Boland's poem reflects on the speaker's present responsibilities to the Irish past.

It's raining on black coal and warm wet ashes.
There are tire-marks in the yard, Agnew's old lorry[1]
Has all its cribs down and Agnew the coalman
With his Belfast accent's sweet-talking my mother.
5 Would she ever go to a film in Magherafelt?
But it's raining and he still has half the load

To deliver farther on. This time the lode
Our coal came from was silk-black, so the ashes
Will be the silkiest white. The Magherafelt
10 (Via Toomebridge) bus goes by. The half-stripped lorry
With its emptied, folded coal-bags moves my mother:
The tasty ways of a leather-aproned coalman!

And films no less! The conceit of a coalman . . .
She goes back in and gets out the black lead
15 And emery paper, this nineteen-forties mother,
All business round her stove, half-wiping ashes
With a backhand from her cheek as the bolted lorry
Gets revved and turned and heads for Magherafelt

1. **lorry** truck.

Reading Strategy
Summarizing What happens during the first coalman's visit?

✔**Reading Check**

What does the coalman invite the speaker's mother to do?

And the last delivery. Oh, Magherafelt!
20   Oh, dream of red plush and a city coalman
As time fastforwards and a different lorry
Groans into shot, up Broad Street, with a payload
That will blow the bus station to dust and ashes . . .
After that happened, I'd a vision of my mother,

25   A revenant[2] on the bench where I would meet her
In that cold-floored waiting-room in Magherafelt,
Her shopping bags full up with shoveled ashes.
Death walked out past her like a dust-faced coalman
Refolding body-bags, plying his load
30   Empty upon empty, in a flurry

Of motes and engine-revs, but which lorry
Was it now? Young Agnew's or that other,
Heavier, deadlier one, set to explode
In a time beyond her time in Magherafelt . . .
35   So tally bags and sweet-talk darkness, coalman.
Listen to the rain spit in new ashes

As you heft a load of dust that was Magherafelt,
Then reappear from your lorry as my mother's
Dreamboat coalman filmed in silk-white ashes.

---

2. revenant (rev´ ə nənt) *n.* one who returns; ghost.

Review and Assess

Thinking About the Selection

1. **(a) Recall:** What are the two incidents described in "Two
   Lorries"? **(b) Analyze:** What details connect the two?

2. **(a) Infer:** How is the coalman who "sweet-talk[s]" Heaney's
   mother a threat to the young Heaney? **(b) Connect:** What
   connection can you find between this threat and the threat
   of terrorism in Northern Ireland, Heaney's "motherland"?

3. **(a) Hypothesize:** In Heaney's view, what might the coalman's
   invitation to a movie, not meant or taken seriously, have in
   common with the promises and results of terrorist politics?
   (b) Compare and Contrast: What differences distinguish
   the two?

4. **(a) Draw Conclusions:** Judging from "Two Lorries," how
   would you describe Heaney's attitude toward the Irish conflicts?
   (b) Evaluate: Do you think that writing a poem like "Two
   Lorries" is a form of political activism? Explain.

Starry Night Over the Rhone River, Vincent van Gogh, Musée d'Orsay, Paris, France

▲ **Critical Viewing** Compare the stars in the painting with those in the poem. Do both suggest the eternal, or does one suggest the explosive? **[Compare and Contrast]**

Outside History
Eavan Boland

There are outsiders, always. These stars—
these iron <u>inklings</u> of an Irish January,
whose light happened

    thousands of years before
5 our pain did: they are, they have always been
    outside history.

inklings (iŋk´ liŋz) *n.*
indirect suggestions;
vague ideas

✔**Reading Check**

According to the speaker,
what is outside history?

They keep their distance. Under them remains
a place where you found
you were human, and

10 a landscape in which you know you are <u>mortal</u>.
And a time to choose between them.
I have chosen:

Out of myth into history I move to be
part of that <u>ordeal</u>
15 whose darkness is

only now reaching me from those fields,
those rivers, those roads clotted as
firmaments[1] with the dead.

How slowly they die
20 as we kneel beside them, whisper in their ear.
And we are too late. We are always too late.

---

1. **firmaments** *n.* the heavens.

mortal (môr´ tǝl) *adj.* of
that which must eventu-
ally die

ordeal (ôr dēl´) *n.* difficult
or painful experience that
tests one

Review and Assess

Thinking About the Selection

1. **Respond:** Do you think Boland is too pessimistic when she writes, "We are always too late"? Explain.

2. **(a) Recall:** What is the speaker viewing at the opening of the poem? **(b) Interpret:** Why does the speaker claim this sight is "outside history"?

3. **(a) Interpret:** According to the speaker, what two things lie under the stars? **(b) Interpret:** Why must the speaker choose between them?

4. **(a) Analyze:** What image does the speaker use to contrast the "ordeal" of history with the stars? **(b) Infer:** Who are "the dead" in line 18? **(c) Interpret:** Is acknowledging the dead a way of becoming part of the "ordeal"? Explain.

5. **Hypothesize:** What might it mean to live in myth instead of in history?

6. **(a) Evaluate:** In writing this poem, does Boland become part of a larger "ordeal," or is that itself a myth? Explain. **(b) Defend:** How might you justify a person's right to stay uninvolved in a conflict?

Review and Assess

Literary Analysis

Diction and Style

1. Explain how Heaney's **style** and **diction** in "Follower" fit the subject of the poem.

2. Complete this chart to analyze Boland's **style** in "Outside History." Then, summarize the distinctive elements of her style.

	Diction	Imagery	Rhythm/ Rhyme	Form
Examples				
Conclusion				

3. (a) What restrictions might the **sestina** form in "Two Lorries" place on Heaney? (b) What advantage might it have?

Comparing Literary Works

4. (a) Contrast Heaney's diction, as exemplified in words such as "headrig," "hobnailed," and "leather-aproned," with Boland's, as exemplified in phrases such as "iron inklings," "out of myth," and "clotted as firmaments." (b) Which poet's diction is more conversational? Which is more abstract? Explain.

5. (a) How does Heaney's diction and style help him to re-create the past? Explain, using examples. (b) How does Boland make abstract ideas of history vivid?

6. Compare the way in which both poets use their poetry to find a way into the past.

Reading Strategy

Summarizing

7. Write a **summary** of "Two Lorries," including a comparison of the two incidents the poet recalls.

8. Write a summary of "Outside History."

Extend Understanding

9. **World Events Connection:** Should Irish literature be studied as its own tradition, separate from British literature? Explain.

Integrate Language Skills

Vocabulary Development Lesson

Word Analysis: Latin Root -mort-

The word *mortal* means "subject to death." This word contains the Latin root -mort-, which means "death." Using this information, define the italicized words.

1. He studied to be a *mortician*.
2. The *mortality* rate for smokers is high.
3. Poetry made her *immortal*.
4. The *mortuary* was respectfully silent.

Spelling Strategy

When forming regular plurals, add -es only if the noun ends in h, s, or x. Write the plurals of these nouns:

1. excess
2. republic
3. context
4. equinox

Fluency: Context

Copy this paragraph into your notebook, and fill in each blank with the most appropriate word from the vocabulary list on page 1103. Let the context created by the paragraph guide your choices. Use each word only once.

    When, as a child, Seamus Heaney followed his father around the farm, he may have made a ___?___ of himself. However, young Seamus's tripping over a ___?___ was probably more a source of amusement than an ___?___ for his father. One thing is sure, no ___?___ that his father was ___?___ had yet reached young Seamus Heaney.

Grammar and Style Lesson

Concrete and Abstract Nouns

Heaney and Boland use **concrete nouns,** which name things that can be sensed and counted, and **abstract nouns,** which name general aspects of things, such as a quality.

Concrete Nouns: shafts, furrow, horses, sod

Abstract Nouns: death, myth, place

Boland achieves a distinctive effect by using abstract nouns such as *myth* and *history* as if they were concrete ("Out of myth into history I move . . ."). She also uses concrete nouns such as *fields* in a symbolic way, as if they were abstract. In this way, she creates images that integrate intellectual concerns, the imagination, and the emotions.

Practice Identify which underlined nouns are concrete and which are abstract.

1. My father worked with a horse <u>plow</u>, . . .
2. All I ever did was follow / In his broad <u>shadow</u>. . . .
3. The <u>conceit</u> of a coalman . . .
4. . . . a <u>landscape</u> in which you know you are mortal.
5. . . . I move to be / part of that <u>ordeal</u>. . . .

Writing Application Write four sentences to describe a memory that is important to you. In two sentences, use only concrete nouns. In the other two, use only abstract nouns. Then, read the sentences aloud, and compare the impact of your sentences.

WG Prentice Hall Writing and Grammar Connection: Chapter 17, Section 1

Writing Lesson

Poem With a Strong Central Image

Heaney and Boland build their poems around strong central images, such as the lorry-driving coalman in "Two Lorries." Write a poem around such an image, carefully choosing words for meaning and sound.

Prewriting Draw on your memories or on photographs or artworks for inspiration. Choose a topic and the central image you will develop.

Drafting Decide on the form you will follow, and then begin drafting. As you draft, let ideas flow. Do not worry about formal problems, such as missing rhymes. You can fix them when you revise.

Revising Review your central image to determine whether it is effective and to confirm that it is reflected in details throughout the poem. Consider revising word choices or adding details to increase its impact.

Model: Revising to Strengthen a Central Image

wheezes

The ancient elevator ~~climbs~~ up another floor,

skin,

Thin metal ~~frame,~~ shuddering door.

spits

It groans, halts, and ~~lets~~ us out on four.

> By revising word choices to personify the elevator, the writer strengthens the central image in a description of an office building.

Prentice Hall Writing and Grammar Connection: Chapter 6, Connected Assignment

Extension Activities

Listening and Speaking Prepare and give an **interpretive reading** of a poem by Heaney or Boland. To prepare:

- Check the pronunciation of any words of which you are unsure.
- Effectively highlight the "soundscape" of the poem—for instance, you might linger over repeated vowel sounds in the opening stanza of "Follower."

Rehearse your reading, and then present it to the class.

Research and Technology With a group, write a conflict report on the "Troubles," the ongoing strife in Northern Ireland. Relate your research to "Two Lorries" and "Outside History." Consider incorporating: photographs, population maps, timelines, and public opinion graphs. **[Group Activity]**

 **Take It to the Net** www.phschool.com

Go online for an additional research activity using the Internet.

Prepare to Read

No Witchcraft for Sale

Doris Lessing
(b. 1919)

Freely admitting her deep desire to influence others through her works of fiction, Doris Lessing has said that publishing a story or novel is "an attempt to impose one's personality and beliefs on other people. If a writer accepts this responsibility, he must see himself . . . as an architect of the soul."

Exposing Injustice One of the ways that Lessing fulfills this responsibility is by writing about social injustice, challenging ideas of race and women's roles. Her own experiences give her a unique perspective on the problems caused when cultures conflict. In much of her writing, Lessing explores the intricate connections between personal experience and political reality.

She was born in Persia (now Iran), the daughter of a British bank clerk. When she was five, her family moved to the British colony of Rhodesia (now the independent country of Zimbabwe) in southcentral Africa. Her memoir *Under My Skin* (1994) describes some ways that Europeans mistreated Africans, displacing them from their lands and suppressing their traditions.

Reflecting on the era of British rule in Africa, Lessing noted that many of the British immigrants honestly thought that colonization would be good for Africa. She suggests that this kind of misguided belief is enough to make us "wonder which of the idealisms that make our hearts beat faster will seem wrong-headed to people a hundred years from now."

Experience Shapes a Writer Lessing's talent for writing developed as a response to a variety of experiences, including a childhood she described as a mixture of some pleasure and much pain. Strictly disciplined by her mother at home and by teachers at school, the young Lessing sought refuge in reading and in explorations of nature with her brother.

Acknowledging that unhappy childhoods sometimes lead people to become fiction writers, Lessing adds, "Of course, I wasn't thinking in terms of being a writer then—I was just thinking about how to escape, all the time."

Her father's bitter memories of World War I were another striking influence on the developing writer's world view. Lessing absorbed them as a kind of "poison." She would later comment that "We are all of us made by war, twisted and warped by war, but we seem to forget it."

Personal and Political Themes The turbulent influences that drove Lessing to write also taught her about the relationship between individuals and society. Early works such as her first novel, *The Grass Is Singing* (1950), and *African Stories* (1964), reflect her awareness of European injustices against Africans. Martha Quest, the heroine of a five-novel series by Lessing called *Children of Violence* (1952–1969), faces private battles that reflect global conflicts. *The Golden Notebook* (1962), Lessing's best-known novel, explores social issues through one woman's persistent search for identity. The dominant theme in her works is the free woman who struggles for individuality and equality despite social assumptions and pressures.

An Artist's Responsibility Throughout her writing career, Lessing has honored her responsibility to her audience. Her works have explored the roles of women in modern society, the evils of racism, and the limits of idealism in solving problems facing society. Her vision is broad; her voice is direct and challenging.

Preview

Connecting to the Literature

You may be a friend of the captain of the team, but when she unfairly decides to bench you during a big game, friendship suddenly seems less important than power. In this story, Lessing explores a conflict between a servant and his masters, who are also his friends.

Literary Analysis

Cultural Conflict

Many British stories of the mid-twentieth century reflect the conflicts of British colonialism, the rule of other regions by Britain. These conflicts include **cultural conflicts**—disagreements arising from differences in beliefs and values. As you read, note how Lessing shows the connections among cultural, political, and personal conflicts.

Connecting Literary Elements

Every conflict has at least two sides, so the **point of view** from which a struggle is reported is significant. Different types of point of view include

- **First person point of view:** The story is told by a character involved in the action.
- **Limited third-person point of view:** The narrator is outside the action but tells the story as it was experienced by one character.
- **Omniscient third-person point of view:** The narrator is outside the action and presents more information than any one character could have, such as details about the thoughts of a number of characters.

As you read, determine the point of view Lessing uses and how her use of it—the information she gives and does not give—affects your understanding of the conflicts in the story.

Reading Strategy

Analyzing Cultural Differences

To appreciate and understand a story involving conflicts between cultures, **analyze the cultural differences**—the contrast in customs, beliefs, and values—that contribute to the problems. Use a Venn diagram like the one shown to analyze cultural conflict in "No Witchcraft for Sale."

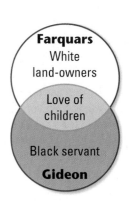

Vocabulary Development

reverently (rev´ ər ənt lē) *adv.* with deep respect or awe (p. 1116)

defiantly (di fī´ ənt lē) *adv.* disobediently; in open resistance (p. 1117)

efficacy (ef´ i kə sē) *n.* power to produce intended effects (p. 1118)

incredulously (in krej´ oo ləs lē) *adv.* in a manner expressing doubt or disbelief (p. 1120)

skeptical (skep´ ti kəl) *adj.* doubting; not easily persuaded (p. 1120)

No Witchcraft for Sale

Doris Lessing

Background

By 1924, the year Lessing's family moved to Southern Rhodesia (now Zimbabwe), the country had been under British control for just two decades. Previously, the region had been ruled by a succession of black African empires. Under British and then white Rhodesian rule, the political rights of black Rhodesians were limited, and most blacks were constrained to work as low-paid servants.

The Farquars had been childless for years when little Teddy was born; and they were touched by the pleasure of their servants, who brought presents of fowls and eggs and flowers to the homestead when they came to rejoice over the baby, exclaiming with delight over his downy golden head and his blue eyes. They congratulated Mrs. Farquar as if she had achieved a very great thing, and she felt that she had—her smile for the lingering, admiring natives was warm and grateful.

Later, when Teddy had his first haircut, Gideon the cook picked up the soft gold tufts from the ground, and held them <u>reverently</u> in his hand. Then he smiled at the little boy and said: "Little Yellow Head." That became the native name for the child. Gideon and Teddy were great friends from the first. When Gideon had finished his work, he would lift Teddy on his shoulders to the shade of a big tree, and play with him there, forming curious little toys from twigs and leaves and grass, or shaping animals from wetted soil. When Teddy learned to walk it was often Gideon who crouched before him, clucking encouragement,

▲ **Critical Viewing**
Using this picture and the title, predict what this story will be about. **[Predict]**

reverently (rev´ ər ənt lē) *adv.* with deep respect or awe

finally catching him when he fell, tossing him up in the air till they both became breathless with laughter. Mrs. Farquar was fond of the old cook because of his love for her child.

There was no second baby; and one day Gideon said: "Ah, missus, missus, the Lord above sent this one; Little Yellow Head is the most good thing we have in our house." Because of that "we" Mrs. Farquar felt a warm impulse toward her cook; and at the end of the month she raised his wages. He had been with her now for several years; he was one of the few natives who had his wife and children in the compound and never wanted to go home to his kraal,[1] which was some hundreds of miles away. Sometimes a small piccanin who had been born the same time as Teddy, could be seen peering from the edge of the bush, staring in awe at the little white boy with his miraculous fair hair and Northern blue eyes. The two little children would gaze at each other with a wide, interested gaze, and once Teddy put out his hand curiously to touch the black child's cheeks and hair.

Gideon, who was watching, shook his head wonderingly, and said: "Ah, missus, these are both children, and one will grow up to be a baas, and one will be a servant"; and Mrs. Farquar smiled and said sadly, "Yes, Gideon, I was thinking the same." She sighed. "It is God's will," said Gideon, who was a mission boy. The Farquars were very religious people; and this shared feeling about God bound servant and masters even closer together.

Teddy was about six years old when he was given a scooter, and discovered the intoxications of speed. All day he would fly around the homestead, in and out of flowerbeds, scattering squawking chickens and irritated dogs, finishing with a wide dizzying arc into the kitchen door. There he would cry: "Gideon, look at me!" And Gideon would laugh and say: "Very clever, Little Yellow Head." Gideon's youngest son, who was now a herdsboy, came especially up from the compound to see the scooter. He was afraid to come near it, but Teddy showed off in front of him. "Piccanin," shouted Teddy, "get out of my way!" And he raced in circles around the black child until he was frightened, and fled back to the bush.

"Why did you frighten him?" asked Gideon, gravely reproachful.[2]

Teddy said <u>defiantly</u>: "He's only a black boy," and laughed. Then, when Gideon turned away from him without speaking, his face fell. Very soon he slipped into the house and found an orange and brought it to Gideon, saying: "This is for you." He could not bring himself to say he was sorry; but he could not bear to lose Gideon's affection either. Gideon took the orange unwillingly and sighed. "Soon you will be going away to school, Little Yellow Head," he said wonderingly, "and then you will be grown up." He shook his head gently and said, "And that is how our lives go." He seemed to be putting a distance between himself and Teddy, not because of resentment, but in the way a person accepts

Reading Strategy
Analyzing Cultural Differences What cultural values do the Farquars and Gideon share?

defiantly (di fī´ ənt lē) *adv.* disobediently; in open resistance

---

1. **kraal** (kräl) village of South African natives, usually fenced in with a stockade.
2. **reproachful** (ri prōch´ fəl) *adj.* expressing blame.

☑ **Reading Check**

What is Gideon's role in the Farquar household?

something inevitable. The baby had lain in his arms and smiled up into his face: the tiny boy had swung from his shoulders and played with him by the hour. Now Gideon would not let his flesh touch the flesh of the white child. He was kind, but there was a grave formality in his voice that made Teddy pout and sulk away. Also, it made him into a man: with Gideon he was polite, and carried himself formally, and if he came into the kitchen to ask for something, it was in the way a white man uses toward a servant, expecting to be obeyed.

But on the day that Teddy came staggering into the kitchen with his fists to his eyes, shrieking with pain, Gideon dropped the pot full of hot soup that he was holding, rushed to the child, and forced aside his fingers. "A snake!" he exclaimed. Teddy had been on his scooter, and had come to a rest with his foot on the side of a big tub of plants. A tree-snake, hanging by its tail from the roof, had spat full into his eyes. Mrs. Farquar came running when she heard the commotion. "He'll go blind," she sobbed, holding Teddy close against her. "Gideon, he'll go blind!" Already the eyes, with perhaps half an hour's sight left in them, were swollen up to the size of fists: Teddy's small white face was distorted by great purple oozing protuberances.[3] Gideon said: "Wait a minute, missus, I'll get some medicine." He ran off into the bush.

Mrs. Farquar lifted the child into the house and bathed his eyes with permanganate.[4] She had scarcely heard Gideon's words; but when she saw that her remedies had no effect at all, and remembered how she had seen natives with no sight in their eyes, because of the spitting of a snake, she began to look for the return of her cook, remembering what she heard of the <u>efficacy</u> of native herbs. She stood by the window, holding the terrified, sobbing little boy in her arms, and peered helplessly into the bush. It was not more than a few minutes before she saw Gideon come bounding back, and in his hand he held a plant.

"Do not be afraid, missus," said Gideon, "this will cure Little Yellow Head's eyes." He stripped the leaves from the plant, leaving a small white fleshy root. Without even washing it, he put the root in his mouth, chewed it vigorously, and then held the spittle there while he took the child forcibly from Mrs. Farquar. He gripped Teddy down between his knees, and pressed the balls of his thumbs into the swollen eyes, so that the child screamed and Mrs. Farquar cried out in protest: "Gideon, Gideon!" But Gideon took no notice. He knelt over the writhing child, pushing back the puffy lids till chinks of eyeball showed, and then he spat hard, again and again, into first one eye, and then the other. He finally lifted Teddy gently into his mother's arms, and said: "His eyes will get better." But Mrs. Farquar was weeping with terror, and she could hardly thank him: it was impossible to believe that Teddy could keep his sight. In a couple of hours the swellings were gone: the eyes were inflamed and tender but Teddy could see. Mr. and Mrs. Farquar went to Gideon in the kitchen and thanked him over and over again. They felt

Literary Analysis
Cultural Conflict How do Gideon and Teddy manage the differences in their social status to protect their vulnerable emotions?

efficacy (ef´ i kə sē) *n.* power to produce intended effects

Reading Strategy
Analyzing Cultural Differences When Teddy is injured by the snake, what do the reactions of Gideon and Mrs. Farquar show about their cultural differences and similarities?

---

3. **protuberances** (prō too̅´ bər əns iz) *n.* bulges; swellings.
4. **permanganate** (pər maŋ´ gə nāt´) salt of permanganic acid.

helpless because of their gratitude: it seemed they could do nothing to express it. They gave Gideon presents for his wife and children, and a big increase in wages, but these things could not pay for Teddy's now completely cured eyes. Mrs. Farquar said: "Gideon, God chose you as an instrument for His goodness," and Gideon said: "Yes, missus, God is very good."

Now, when such a thing happens on a farm, it cannot be long before everyone hears of it. Mr. and Mrs. Farquar told their neighbors and the story was discussed from one end of the district to the other. The bush is full of secrets. No one can live in Africa, or at least on the veld,[5] without learning very soon that there is an ancient wisdom of leaf and soil and season—and, too, perhaps most important of all, of the darker tracts of the human mind—which is the black man's heritage. Up and down the district people were telling anecdotes, reminding each other of things that had happened to them.

"But I saw it myself, I tell you. It was a puff-adder bite. The kaffir's[6] arm was swollen to the elbow, like a great shiny black bladder. He was groggy after half a minute. He was dying. Then suddenly a kaffir walked out of the bush with his hands full of green stuff. He smeared something on the place, and next day my boy was back at work, and all you could see was two small punctures in the skin."

This was the kind of tale they told. And, as always, with a certain amount of exasperation, because while all of them knew that in the bush of Africa are waiting valuable drugs locked in bark, in simple-looking leaves, in roots, it was impossible to ever get the truth about them from the natives themselves.

The story eventually reached town; and perhaps it was at a sun-downer party, or some such function, that a doctor, who happened to be there, challenged it. "Nonsense," he said. "These things get exaggerated in the telling. We are always checking up on this kind of story, and we draw a blank every time."

Anyway, one morning there arrived a strange car at the homestead, and out stepped one of the workers from the laboratory in town, with cases full of test-tubes and chemicals.

Mr. and Mrs. Farquar were flustered and pleased and flattered. They asked the scientist to lunch, and they told the story all over again, for the hundredth time. Little Teddy was there too, his blue eyes sparkling with health, to prove the truth of it. The scientist explained how humanity might benefit if this new drug could be offered for sale; and the Farquars were even more pleased: they were kind, simple people, who liked to think of something good coming about because of them. But when the scientist began talking of the money that might result, their manner showed discomfort. Their feelings over the miracle (that was how they thought of it) were so strong and deep and religious, that

▲ **Critical Viewing**
In what ways does the expression and appearance of this southern African illustrate the wisdom of Gideon's generation? **[Evaluate]**

---

5. **veld** in South Africa, open grassy country, with few bushes and almost no trees.
6. **kaffir's** belonging to a black African; in South Africa, a contemptuous term.

it was distasteful to them to think of money. The scientist, seeing their faces, went back to his first point, which was the advancement of humanity. He was perhaps a trifle perfunctory:[7] it was not the first time he had come salting the tail of a fabulous bush secret.[8]

Eventually, when the meal was over, the Farquars called Gideon into their living room and explained to him that this baas, here, was a Big Doctor from the Big City, and he had come all that way to see Gideon. At this Gideon seemed afraid; he did not understand; and Mrs. Farquar explained quickly that it was because of the wonderful thing he had done with Teddy's eyes that the Big Baas had come.

Gideon looked from Mrs. Farquar to Mr. Farquar, and then at the little boy, who was showing great importance because of the occasion. At last he said grudgingly: "The Big Baas want to know what medicine I used?" He spoke <u>incredulously</u>, as if he could not believe his old friends could so betray him. Mr. Farquar began explaining how a useful medicine could be made out of the root, and how it could be put on sale, and how thousands of people, black and white, up and down the continent of Africa, could be saved by the medicine when that spitting snake filled their eyes with poison. Gideon listened, his eyes bent on the ground, the skin of his forehead puckering in discomfort. When Mr. Farquar had finished he did not reply. The scientist, who all this time had been leaning back in a big chair, sipping his coffee and smiling with <u>skeptical</u> good humor, chipped in and explained all over again, in different words, about the making of drugs and the progress of science. Also, he offered Gideon a present.

There was silence after this further explanation, and then Gideon remarked indifferently that he could not remember the root. His face was sullen and hostile, even when he looked at the Farquars, whom he usually treated like old friends. They were beginning to feel annoyed; and this feeling annulled[9] the guilt that had been sprung into life by Gideon's accusing manner. They were beginning to feel that he was unreasonable. But it was at that moment that they all realized he would never give in. The magical drug would remain where it was, unknown and useless except for the tiny scattering of Africans who had the knowledge, natives who might be digging a ditch for the municipality in a ragged shirt and a pair of patched shorts, but who were still born to healing, hereditary healers, being the nephews or sons of the old witch doctors whose ugly masks and bits of bone and all the uncouth[10] properties of magic were the outward signs of real power and wisdom.

The Farquars might tread on that plant fifty times a day as they passed from house to garden, from cow kraal to mealie field, but they would never know it.

---

7. **perfunctory** (pər fuŋk´ tə rē) *adj.* done without care or interest.
8. **salting . . . bush secret** allusion to the humorous and ironic advice given to children about how to catch a bird—by putting salt on its tail. In other words, the scientist does not really expect to capture a valuable bit of information.
9. **annulled** (ə nuld´) *v.* did away with; neutralized.
10. **uncouth** (un kōōth´) *adj.* uncultured; crude; strange.

incredulously (in krej´ oo ləs lē) *adv.* in a manner expressing doubt or disbelief

skeptical (skep´ ti kəl) *adj.* doubting; not easily persuaded

Literary Analysis
Cultural Conflict How is the Farquar's earlier reaction to the scientists offer of money similar to Gideon's reaction to their request?

But they went on persuading and arguing, with all the force of their exasperation; and Gideon continued to say that he could not remember, or that there was no such root, or that it was the wrong season of the year, or that it wasn't the root itself, but the spit from his mouth that had cured Teddy's eyes. He said all these things one after another, and seemed not to care they were contradictory. He was rude and stubborn. The Farquars could hardly recognize their gentle, lovable old servant in this ignorant, perversely obstinate African, standing there in front of them with lowered eyes, his hands twitching his cook's apron, repeating over and over whichever one of the stupid refusals that first entered his head.

And suddenly he appeared to give in. He lifted his head, gave a long blank angry look at the circle of whites, who seemed to him like a circle of yelping dogs pressing around him, and said: "I will show you the root."

They walked single file away from the homestead down a kaffir path. It was a blazing December afternoon, with the sky full of hot rain clouds. Everything was hot: the sun was like a bronze tray whirling overhead, there was a heat shimmer over the fields, the soil was scorching underfoot, the dusty wind blew gritty and thick and warm in their faces. It was a terrible day, fit only for reclining on a verandah with iced drinks, which is where they would normally have been at that hour.

From time to time, remembering that on the day of the snake it had taken ten minutes to find the root, someone asked: "Is it much further, Gideon?" And Gideon would answer over his shoulder, with angry politeness: "I'm looking for the root, baas." And indeed, he would frequently bend sideways and trail his hand among the grasses with a gesture that was insulting in its perfunctoriness. He walked them through the bush along unknown paths for two hours, in that melting destroying heat, so that the sweat trickled coldly down them and their heads ached. They were all quite silent: the Farquars because they were angry, the scientist because he was being proved right again; there was no such plant. His was a tactful silence.

At last, six miles from the house, Gideon suddenly decided they had had enough; or perhaps his anger evaporated at that moment. He picked up, without an attempt at looking anything but casual, a handful of blue flowers from the grass, flowers that had been growing plentifully all down the paths they had come.

He handed them to the scientist without looking at him, and marched off by himself on the way home, leaving them to follow him if they chose.

When they got back to the house, the scientist went to the kitchen to thank Gideon: he was being very polite, even though there was an amused look in his eyes. Gideon was not there. Throwing the flowers

Literature in context World Events

Colonial Rhodesia

Starting in the 1400s, Southern Rhodesia was ruled by a series of Shona empires. British exploitation of the area began in the late 1800s, when Cecil Rhodes brought the British South Africa Company to mine gold there, crushing outbursts of violent resistance by the local peoples. White Rhodesians voted to become a British colony in 1922.

In 1965, Rhodesia declared independence from Britain, and in 1969 a new constitution was enacted to ensure that the black majority would never rule the country. It was only in the 1970s, after years of civil war and the deaths of more than 250,000 guerrilla fighters, that blacks were granted equal rights. In 1980, Rhodesia became officially independent, changing its name to Zimbabwe ("house of stone"), the name of an ancient Shona city.

Zimbabwe (Rhodesia)

✔ **Reading Check**

What does Gideon finally do in response to requests that he identify the plant?

casually into the back of his car, the eminent visitor departed on his way back to his laboratory.

Gideon was back in his kitchen in time to prepare dinner, but he was sulking. He spoke to Mr. Farquar like an unwilling servant. It was days before they liked each other again.

The Farquars made inquiries about the root from their laborers. Sometimes they were answered with distrustful stares. Sometimes the natives said: "We do not know. We have never heard of the root." One, the cattle boy, who had been with them a long time, and had grown to trust them a little, said: "Ask your boy in the kitchen. Now, there's a doctor for you. He's the son of a famous medicine man who used to be in these parts, and there's nothing he cannot cure." Then he added politely: "Of course, he's not as good as the white man's doctor, we know that, but he's good for us."

After some time, when the soreness had gone from between the Farquars and Gideon, they began to joke: "When are you going to show us the snake-root, Gideon?" And he would laugh and shake his head, saying, a little uncomfortably: "But I did show you, missus, have you forgotten?"

Much later, Teddy, as a schoolboy, would come into the kitchen and say: "You old rascal, Gideon! Do you remember that time you tricked us all by making us walk miles all over the veld for nothing? It was so far my father had to carry me!"

And Gideon would double up with polite laughter. After much laughing, he would suddenly straighten himself up, wipe his old eyes, and look sadly at Teddy, who was grinning mischievously at him across the kitchen: "Ah, Little Yellow Head, how you have grown! Soon you will be grown up with a farm of your own . . ."

Review and Assess

Thinking About the Selection

1. **Respond:** Do you sympathize with Gideon's resistance? Explain.

2. **(a) Recall:** How does "Little Yellow Head" get his nickname?
   (b) Infer: How does this nickname emphasize the differences between the Farquars and their servants?

3. **(a) Recall:** How does Gideon save Teddy's sight?
   (b) Interpret: In what way does this incident reveal an aspect of Gideon previously unknown to the Farquars?

4. **(a) Analyze:** What effect does the scientist's visit have on the Farquars' relationship with Gideon? **(b) Draw Conclusions:** Why does Gideon refuse to share his knowledge?

5. **Interpret:** What do Gideon's last words to Teddy mean?

6. **Make a Judgment:** Do you think Gideon's decision to withhold information about the plant is justified? Explain.

Review and Assess

Literary Analysis

Cultural Conflict

1. Using a chart like the one shown, identify three incidents in the story that reflect **cultural conflict.** Explain your choices.

2. (a) Summarize the viewpoint of each side in this conflict. (b) How is the conflict political, personal, and cultural?
3. In what way does the story both resolve and leave unresolved the conflict between Gideon and the Farquars?
4. Do you think Lessing could have communicated the same message in a newspaper article? Why or why not?

Connecting Literary Elements

5. From what **point of view** is the story told? Explain.
6. (a) Does the narrator identify more closely with either cultural perspective? (b) What details help you decide?
7. How would the story be different if it had been told from Gideon's perspective?
8. (a) Does Lessing successfully use point of view to reflect the fact that, as a white Rhodesian, her knowledge of the experience of blacks is limited? Explain. (b) Does this use of point of view show respect for the experience of black Rhodesians? Explain.

Reading Strategy

Analyzing Cultural Differences

9. Identify two incidents that reflect Teddy's or his family's sense of superiority over black Africans.
10. (a) What values do the Farquars and Gideon share? Support your answer with details. (b) What values set them apart?

Extend Understanding

11. **World Events Connection:** In what other countries or times could a story with the same theme be set? Explain.

Quick Review

Cultural conflicts are disagreements arising from differences in customs, beliefs, and values.

The **point of view,** or perspective, from which a story is told determines the scope and kind of information the narrator gives readers.

Point of view is defined by the relation of the narrator to the story. In **first-person point of view,** the narrator is a character inside the story. In **third-person point of view,** the narrator is outside the story. **Limited third-person point of view** filters the story through the experience of one character.

To **analyze cultural differences,** consider the contrasts between the customs, beliefs, and values of two groups.

 Take It to the Net
www.phschool.com
Take the interactive self-test online to check your understanding of the selection.

Integrate Language Skills

Vocabulary Development Lesson

Word Analysis: Forms of *skeptical*

The word *skeptical* means "inclined to doubt or question." Consider this definition as you answer each of the following questions.

1. What did the ancient philosophers called *Skeptics* believe about knowledge?
2. What might a *skeptical* store owner do when a stranger presents a personal check?

Spelling Strategy

In many scientific or philosophical words derived from Greek, the letter *k* is used to spell the *k* sound, as in *skeptical* and *kleptomania*. Use this knowledge to correct the spelling errors below.

1. The light entering the crystal created a caleidoscopic pattern.
2. Cinesiolgists study sceletons.

Concept Development: Synonyms

Synonyms are pairs of words that share nearly the same meaning. In your notebook, write the letter of the word that is the synonym of the word from the vocabulary list on page 1115.

1. reverently: (a) politely, (b) respectfully, (c) slyly
2. defiantly: (a) disobediently, (b) wryly, (c) strongly
3. efficacy: (a) stamina, (b) reliability, (c) effectiveness
4. incredulously: (a) disbelievingly, (b) sincerely, (c) vaguely
5. skeptical: (a) trusting, (b) irate, (c) suspicious

Grammar and Style Lesson

Correct Use of *like* and *as*

Do not confuse **like** and **as.** The subordinating conjunctions *as*, *as if*, and *as though* introduce a subordinate clause, which has its own subject and verb. The preposition *like* introduces a prepositional phrase that includes an object and modifiers.

Subordinating Conjunction: They congratulated Mrs. Farquar as if she had achieved a very great thing. . . .

Preposition: He spoke to Mr. Farquar like an unwilling servant.

Remember that the verb in a clause introduced by *as*, *as if*, or *as though* may be understood, not directly stated.

Practice In your notebook, correctly complete each comparison with the conjunction *as*, *as if*, or *as though* or with the preposition *like*.

1. Teddy's hair was colored ___?___ straw.
2. At first, Gideon stared ___?___ he did not understand.
3. The scientist looked ___?___ he were skeptical.
4. The noon sun was ___?___ a furnace.
5. Teddy laughed ___?___ he had said something clever.

Writing Application Write a paragraph describing how Gideon saved Teddy from blindness, using *like* and *as* to make at least two comparisons.

W͞G *Prentice Hall Writing and Grammar Connection: Chapter 25, Section 2*

Writing Lesson

Problem-and-Solution Essay

The Farquars and Gideon have a problem: The Farquars cannot understand Gideon's uncooperativeness, and he feels betrayed by them. In an essay, offer a solution to this problem. Make your explanations precise and complete.

Prewriting Take notes on the problem between Gideon and the Farquars. Review your notes to propose a few possible solutions.

Drafting Begin your draft by describing the problem. Then, introduce your solutions. Specify any conditions that would have to be met to implement each solution, and explain each step in logical order.

Revising As you review your draft, mark off steps that are incomplete or imprecise. Add details to answer the questions *why*, *for how long*, *what kind*, and so on.

Model: Revising to Elaborate for Precision

First,
a person, such as Lessing, who has insight into both white and black worlds.

Gideon and the Farquars should talk with ~~someone else.~~

The person can help "translate" their concerns. Then,

Gideon should visit with white doctors and the

Farquars should visit with black healers.

~~they should be exposed to each other's culture.~~

> Precise descriptions help a reader understand exactly *who* and *what* is involved in the solution.

Prentice Hall Writing and Grammar Connection: Chapter 11, Section 3

Extension Activities

Listening and Speaking Form two teams and hold a **debate on colonialism.** Using details from Lessing's story, consider whether the benefits colonialism may bring outweigh the injustices it may involve. Keep the following tips in mind:

- Use details from the story to support your main points.
- Use parallelism—the expression of related ideas in similar grammatical forms—to make your arguments memorable.

Hold your debate before the class.
[Group Activity]

Research and Technology Research the discovery of medicines derived from plants in Africa, such as the one used by Gideon in the story. Prepare an **oral report on medical botany** for your class. Consult both print and electronic sources, including books, magazines, and Web sites. Consider experts you might interview, such as doctors or the staff at plant nurseries or nature preserves.

 **Take It to the Net**   www.phschool.com

Go online for an additional research activity using the Internet.

CONNECTIONS
Literature Past and Present
Conflicts at Home and Abroad

A Time of Testing As the writers in this section demonstrate, moral and social values have been tested by the twentieth-century conflicts involving Britain. The soldier poets Siegfried Sassoon and Wilfred Owen, for example, show how traditional notions of patriotism were destroyed by the horrors of trench warfare in World War I. Later, in World War II, Winston Churchill rallied the English to their traditional values in order to oppose the fascist tyranny of Adolf Hitler.

British belief in the value and permanence of the Empire was also tested during the twentieth century. Gandhi's speech illustrates the struggles of Indians to assert their own national identity in the face of British oppression. Stories by Lessing and Trevor and poems by Heaney and Boland address conflicts in South Africa and Ireland, conflicts that are a legacy of imperial rule.

A New Britain With many of Britain's major external conflicts settled, Prime Minister Tony Blair of England has expressed a new vision of British citizenship. In his speech "The Rights We Enjoy, the Duties We Owe," Blair calls for a moral approach to social issues. Rejecting the notion of doing one's "own thing" and the urge to look out only for oneself, he reaffirms the importance of rights and responsibilities. He argues for "practical policies" guided by values that stress "the good of all."

The Rights We Enjoy, The Duties We Owe

from *New Britain: My Vision of a Young Country*

TONY BLAIR

Thematic Connection
How does Blair redefine the idea of self-interest in this opening paragraph, as Gandhi redefines the idea of a law in his speech?

Individuals prosper best within a strong and cohesive society. Especially in a modern world, we are interdependent. Unless we act together to provide common services, prepare our industry and people for industrial and technological challenge, and guarantee a proper system of law and government, we will be worse off as individuals. In particular, those without the best start in life through birth are unlikely to make up for it without access to the means of achievement. Furthermore—though this may be more open to debate—a society which is fragmented and divided, where people feel no sense of shared purpose, is unlikely to produce well-adjusted and responsible citizens.

But a strong society should not be confused with a strong state, or with powerful collectivist institutions. That was the confusion of early Left[1] thinking. It was compounded by a belief that the role of the state was to grant rights, with the language of responsibility spoken far less fluently. In a further strain of thinking, connected with the libertarian Left, there was a kind of social individualism espoused,[2] where you "did your own thing." In fact this had very little to do with any forms of left-of-center philosophy recognizable to the founders of the Labor Party.[3]

The reaction of the Right,[4] after the advent of Mrs. Thatcher, was to stress the notion of the individual as against the state. Personal responsibility was extolled.[5] But then a curious thing happened. In a mirror-image of the Left's confusion, the Right started to define personal responsibility as responsibility not just for yourself but to

---

1. **Left** of those with liberal or socialist views.
2. **espoused** (e spouzd´) *v.* advocated.
3. **Labor Party** British political party.
4. **the Right** those with conservative or authoritarian political views.
5. **extolled** (eks tōld´) *v.* praised highly.

Labour

▲ **Critical Viewing**
In what ways does this photograph present Tony Blair as a leader?
[Evaluate]

yourself. Outside of a duty not to break the law, responsibility appeared to exclude the broader notion of duty to others. It became narrowly acquisitive[6] and rather destructive. The economic message of enterprise—of the early 1980s—became a philosophy of "Get what you can."

All over the Western world, people are searching for a new political settlement which starts with the individual but sets him or her within the wider society. People don't want an overbearing state, but they don't want to live in a social vacuum either. It is in the search for this different, reconstructed, relationship between individual and society that ideas about "community" are found. "Community" implies a recognition of interdependence, but not overweening[7] government power. It accepts that we are better equipped to meet the forces of change and insecurity through working together. It provides a basis for the elements of our character that are cooperative as well as competitive, as part of a more enlightened view of self-interest.

People know they face a greater insecurity than ever before: a new global economy; massive and rapid changes in technology; a labor market where half the workers are women; a family life that has been

---

6. **acquisitive** (ə kwiz′ ə tiv) *adj.* eager to acquire possessions.
7. **overweening** (ō′ vər wēn′ iŋ) *adj.* arrogant; excessively proud.

altered drastically; telecommunications and media that visit a common culture upon us and transform our expectations and behavior.

This insecurity is not just about jobs or mortgages—though of course these are serious problems. It is about a world that in less than a lifetime has compressed the historical change of epochs. It is bewildering. Even religion—once a given—is now an exception. And of course the world has the nuclear weapons to destroy itself many times over. Look at our children and the world into which they are growing. What parent would not feel insecure?

People need rules which we all stand by, fixed points of agreement which impose order on chaos. That does not mean a return to the old hierarchy of deference. That is at best nostalgia, at worst reactionary. We do not want old class structures back. We do not want women chained to the sink. We do not want birth rather than merit to become once again the basis of personal advancement. Nor does it mean bureaucracy and regulation. Bad and foolish rules are bad and foolish rules, but they do not invalidate the need to have rules.

Duty is the cornerstone of a decent society. It recognizes more than self. It defines the context in which rights are given. It is personal; but it is also owed to society. Respect for others—responsibility to them— is an essential prerequisite of a strong and active community. It is the method through which we can build a society that does not subsume our individuality but allows it to develop healthily. It accords instinct with common sense. It draws on a broader and therefore more accurate notion of human nature than one formulated on insular[8] self-interest. The rights we receive should reflect the duties we owe. With power should come responsibility.

Duty Is a Labor Value

The assertion that each of us is our brother's keeper has motivated the Labor movement since the mid nineteenth century. It is time to reassert what it really means.

The Left has always insisted that it is not enough to argue that our only duty is not to infringe on the lives and rights of others— what might be called negative duty. A minimal community creates a society of minimal citizens. It is a broader notion of duty that gives substance to the traditional belief of the Left in solidarity. This was well understood by the early pioneers of socialism. William Morris[9] put it colorfully: "Fellowship is life, and lack of fellowship is death."

But solidarity[10] and fellowship are the start of the story, and not the end, because they will be achieved only on the basis of both social equality and personal responsibility.

The historians of *English Ethical Socialism*, Norman Dennis and A.H. Halsey, argue that William Cobbett,[11] who lived before the word

> **Thematic Connection**
> What difficulties have twentieth-century people faced in doing their duty to society? Think of Sassoon's or Owen's view of British rule.

---

8. insular (in´ sə lər) *adj.* detached or isolated.
9. William Morris early English socialist (1834–1896).
10. solidarity (säl´ ə dar´ ə tē) *n.* the unity of individuals in a common cause.
11. William Cobbett (käb´ it) English journalist and reformer (1763–1835).

"socialism" achieved common currency, took it for granted that people stood a better chance of having a happy life if they were not selfish. They write that "a person matching Cobbett's ideal, therefore, was one who enjoyed the rights and performed the duties of citizenship."

Early socialists like Robert Owen understood very clearly that a society which did not encourage people voluntarily to carry out their responsibilities to others would always be in danger of slipping either into the anarchy[12] of mutual indifference—and its corollary, the domination of the powerless by the powerful—or the tyranny of collective coercion, where the freedom of all is denied in the name of the good of all.

Ethical socialists have long asserted that there was and is a distinctive socialist view of both human nature and social morality. R.H. Tawney[13] put it clearly in the 1920s: "Modern society is sick through the absence of a moral ideal," he wrote. "What we have been witnessing . . . both in international affairs and in industry, is the breakdown of society on the basis of rights divorced from obligations." And G.D.H Cole said that "A socialist society that is to be true to its egalitarian principles of human brotherhood must rest on the widest possible diffusion of power and responsibility, so as to enlist the active participation of as many of its citizens in the tasks of democratic self-government."

In his book *Liberals and Social Democrats*, the historian Peter Clarke drew a distinction between "moral reformers" and "mechanical reformers." The moral reformers were the ethical socialists like Tawney and Morris. They looked around the communities in which they lived, and called for a new moral impulse to guide them. The mechanical reformers, on the other hand, concentrated on the technicalities of social and economic reform. They were severely practical in their outlook.

Values without practical policies are useless; but policies without a set of values guiding them give no sense of meaning or direction to public life.

---

12. **anarchy** (an´ ər kē) *n.* complete absence of government.
13. **Robert Tawney** (tô´ nē) British economic historian (1880–1962).

Tony Blair

(b. 1953)

Tony Blair, Britain's youngest prime minister in modern times, is a skillful orator and noted speech writer. Educated as an attorney, he became a member of Parliament in 1983. He went on to become leader of the Labor Party in 1994, transforming it into what became known as the "New Labor Party." In May 1997, Blair became the first prime minister elected from the Labor Party in eighteen years.

Connecting Literature Past and Present

1. What common ideas of duty might Blair and Churchill share?
2. How might Blair respond to Gandhi's claim that it was his duty to break the law?
3. How might Blair respond to Owens's anthem to those who lost their lives doing their duty in World War I?
4. Choose one of the short stories in this section. Explain how, in the story's setting, duties or rights have become disconnected from an ideal of human dignity and happiness.

Focus on Literary Forms:
The Short Story

The Snack Bar, 1930, Edward Burra, Tate Gallery, London

The short story was the perfect form for a century in a hurry. It had all the elements of a novel—plot, setting, character, theme—but on a smaller scale. It could take you to the house next door, to Ireland, or to Southeast Asia, but wherever you went you got back quickly. It could also display the latest fictional techniques, sometimes taking you right into a character's mind.

Prepare to Read

The Lagoon ◆ Araby

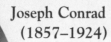

Joseph Conrad
(1857–1924)

It is accomplishment enough to become one of the most distinguished novelists of your age, but to do so in your third language is an achievement almost without parallel. Born in Poland, Joseph Conrad mastered English only after acquiring Polish, his native language, and Russian.

At Sea in the World Orphaned at the age of eleven, Conrad fled his Russian-occupied homeland when he was sixteen. He landed first in France and later in England. He spent the next six years as an apprentice seaman. The voyages Conrad made to the corners of the globe—Asia, Africa, and South America—became the vivid settings of much of his fiction. In 1886, he became a master mariner and an English citizen.

A Storytelling Life Conrad published his first novel, *Almayer's Folly*, when he was in his late thirties. In 1897, *The Nigger of the "Narcissus"* appeared. Three masterpieces followed: *Lord Jim* (1900); *Youth*, a collection of shorter pieces that includes his famous "Heart of Darkness" (1902); and *Nostromo* (1904).

Although many of Conrad's works may be read as thrilling tales of the sea, the notion of "voyage" in a work by Conrad translates to a voyage of self-discovery. The question of loyalty, so crucial for the survival of a ship's crew, appears as a question of the general frailty of human relationships and the limits of self-knowledge. The menacing jungles, vast oceans, and exotic people that confront the characters become metaphors for the hidden depths of the self. Telling tales set around the globe, Conrad charts a geography of the human soul.

James Joyce
(1882–1941)

The Dublin writer James Joyce's innovations in plot, character, and language make him one of the most challenging and distinguished writers of the twentieth century.

Experimentation Joyce's family and teachers wanted him to become a priest, but he pursued his own way as a writer. In 1904, he left Ireland for the continent. Ten years later, he published a landmark collection of short stories entitled *Dubliners*. These deceptively simple tales focus on the psychological conflicts of ordinary people. In the course of each story, the main character is forced to alter his or her perspective on life.

In 1916, Joyce published *A Portrait of the Artist as a Young Man*, a semiautobiographical work. Like Joyce, the novel's main character is in conflict with his Irish roots and chooses to become a writer.

Mature Fiction *A Portrait of the Artist* reveals a heightened awareness of language and an immersion in the minds of characters. Joyce carried these characteristics to a new level in *Ulysses* (1922). A stream-of-consciousness novel that roughly parallels Homer's *Odyssey*, the work presents a day in the life of three Dubliners. *Ulysses* represents a liberation of the novel from old ideas. Using a variety of styles and techniques, it places a new and thoroughly modern emphasis on the play of language.

In his final novel, *Finnegans Wake* (1939), Joyce took his fascination with words a step further. Written in what one scholar terms "a dream language of Joyce's own invention," it explores the author's view of human existence. With such radical innovations, Joyce guaranteed his place as one of the re-inventors of modern fiction.

Preview

Connecting to the Literature

Losing something important is a painful experience. Perhaps just as painful, though, is the discovery that something has lost its importance to you. Each of these stories explores a discovery of loss.

Literary Analysis

Plot Devices

Both Conrad and Joyce use **plot devices** to achieve innovative effects as they relate the events of a story.

- In "The Lagoon," Conrad tells a **story within a story**—a tale told by a character within a framing fictional narrative.
- In "Araby," Joyce builds toward an **epiphany**—a character's sudden insight, which forms the climax of the story.

As you read, notice how these devices structure the stories.

Comparing Literary Works

As these selections reveal, plot devices have a close connection with the **theme,** or central concern, of a story. "The Lagoon" is told by a neutral narrator outside the story—but the story within this story is told in the first person, with passion. By juxtaposing these two points of view, Conrad announces his theme: the relation of passion and the act of storytelling. Joyce's epiphany depends on a similar contrast in point of view, the contrast between the narrator's passion at the time of the story and his later detachment. As you read, compare the implications that these plot devices have for the theme of the stories in which they are used.

Reading Strategy

Picturing the Action and Situation

To better appreciate a well-crafted short story, pause occasionally to **picture the action and situation,** using your imagination to help you understand the characters' reactions to events. Use a graphic organizer like the one shown to aid you.

Vocabulary Development

portals (pôr′ təlz) *n.* doors (p. 1135)

invincible (in vin′ sə bəl) *adj.* unconquerable (p. 1136)

propitiate (prō pish′ ē āt) *v.* win the goodwill of; appease (p. 1136)

conflagration (kän′ flə grā′ shən) *n.* great fire (p. 1138)

august (ô gust′) *adj.* worthy of great respect; inspiring awe (p. 1139)

imperturbable (im′ pər tʉr′ bə bəl) *adj.* calm; not easily ruffled (p. 1147)

litanies (lit′ ən ēz) *n.* prayers in which a congregation repeats a fixed response; repetitive recitations (p. 1148)

garrulous (gar′ ə ləs) *adj.* talkative (p. 1150)

derided (di rīd′ id) *v.* made fun of; ridiculed (p. 1152)

Story Passage

A breath of warm air touched the two men's faces and passed on with a mournful sound. . . .

Action and Situation

Arsat pauses in his story. In the silence, a wind passes.

Characters' Inner Responses

Both characters may be uneasy—Arsat because of his memories and the narrator because of Arsat's distress.

The Lagoon

Joseph Conrad

Background

Between 1883 and 1888, Conrad sailed the Malay Archipelago—a group of Pacific islands that includes the Philippines and Indonesia—in British merchant ships. He used the knowledge he acquired of the region—of its language, landscape, and customs—to enrich his seafaring tales. It is likely that Captain William Lingard, revered as a spellbinding storyteller among sailors of the Malay settlements, was the model for Marlowe, who appears as the narrator of several Conrad stories.

The white man, leaning with both arms over the roof of the little house in the stern of the boat, said to the steersman—

"We will pass the night in Arsat's clearing. It is late."

The Malay[1] only grunted, and went on looking fixedly at the river. The white man rested his chin on his crossed arms and gazed at the wake of the boat. At the end of the straight avenue of forests cut by the intense glitter of the river, the sun appeared unclouded and dazzling, poised low over the water that shone smoothly like a band of metal. The forests, somber and dull, stood motionless and silent on each side of the broad stream. At the foot of big, towering trees trunkless nipa palms rose from the mud of the bank, in bunches of leaves enormous and heavy, that hung unstirring over the brown swirl of eddies. In the stillness of the air every tree, every leaf, every bough, every tendril of creeper and every petal of minute blossoms seemed to have been bewitched into an immobility perfect and final. Nothing moved on the river but the eight paddles that rose flashing regularly, dipped together with a single splash; while the steersman swept right and left with a periodic and sudden flourish of his blade describing a glinting semicircle above his head. The churned-up water frothed alongside with a confused murmur. And the white man's canoe,

---

1. **Malay** (mā´ lā) native of the Malay peninsula in Southeast Asia.

advancing up stream in the short-lived disturbance of its own making, seemed to enter the <u>portals</u> of a land from which the very memory of motion had forever departed.

The white man, turning his back upon the setting sun, looked along the empty and broad expanse of the sea-reach. For the last three miles of its course the wandering, hesitating river, as if enticed irresistibly by the freedom of an open horizon, flows straight into the sea, flows straight to the east—to the east that harbors both light and darkness. Astern of the boat the repeated call of some bird, a cry discordant and feeble, skipped along over the smooth water and lost itself, before it could reach the other shore, in the breathless silence of the world.

The steersman dug his paddle into the stream, and held hard with stiffened arms, his body thrown forward. The water gurgled aloud; and suddenly the long straight reach seemed to pivot on its center, the forests swung in a semicircle, and the slanting beams of sunset touched the broadside of the canoe with a fiery glow, throwing the slender and distorted shadows of its crew upon the streaked glitter of the river. The white man turned to look ahead. The course of the boat had been altered at right-angles to the stream, and the carved dragonhead of its prow was pointing now at a gap in the fringing

portals (pôr təlz) *n.* doors

☑**Reading Check**

What is the white man's destination?

The Lagoon ◆ 1135

bushes of the bank. It glided through, brushing the overhanging twigs, and disappeared from the river like some slim and amphibious creature leaving the water for its lair in the forests.

The narrow creek was like a ditch: tortuous, fabulously deep; filled with gloom under the thin strip of pure and shining blue of the heaven. Immense trees soared up, invisible behind the festooned draperies of creepers. Here and there, near the glistening blackness of the water, a twisted root of some tall tree showed amongst the tracery of small ferns, black and dull, writhing and motionless, like an arrested snake. The short words of the paddlers reverberated loudly between the thick and somber walls of vegetation. Darkness oozed out from between the trees, through the tangled maze of the creepers, from behind the great fantastic and unstirring leaves; the darkness, mysterious and <u>invincible</u>; the darkness scented and poisonous of impenetrable forests.

The men poled in the shoaling[2] water. The creek broadened, opening out into a wide sweep of a stagnant lagoon. The forests receded from the marshy bank, leaving a level strip of bright green, reedy grass to frame the reflected blueness of the sky. A fleecy pink cloud drifted high above, trailing the delicate coloring of its image under the floating leaves and the silvery blossoms of the lotus. A little house, perched on high piles, appeared black in the distance. Near it, two tall nibong palms, that seemed to have come out of the forests in the background, leaned slightly over the ragged roof, with a suggestion of sad tenderness and care in the droop of their leafy and soaring heads.

The steersman, pointing with his paddle, said, "Arsat is there. I see his canoe fast between the piles."

The polers ran along the sides of the boat glancing over their shoulders at the end of the day's journey. They would have preferred to spend the night somewhere else than on this lagoon of weird aspect and ghostly reputation. Moreover, they disliked Arsat, first as a stranger, and also because he who repairs a ruined house, and dwells in it, proclaims that he is not afraid to live amongst the spirits that haunt the places abandoned by mankind. Such a man can disturb the course of fate by glances or words; while his familiar ghosts are not easy to <u>propitiate</u> by casual wayfarers upon whom they long to wreak the malice of their human master. White men care not for such things, being unbelievers and in league with the Father of Evil, who leads them unharmed through the invisible dangers of this world. To the warnings of the righteous they oppose an offensive pretense of disbelief. What is there to be done?

So they thought, throwing their weight on the end of their long poles. The big canoe glided on swiftly, noiselessly, and smoothly, toward Arsat's clearing, till, in a great rattling of poles thrown down, and the loud murmurs of "Allah[3] be praised!" it came with a gentle knock against the crooked piles below the house.

Reading Strategy
Picturing the Action and Situation As you picture the boat ride, what contrasts strike you?

invincible (in vin´ sə bəl)
adj. unconquerable

propitiate (pro pish´ ē āt´)
v. win the good will of; appease

---

2. **shoaling** shallow.
3. **Allah** (al´ ə) Muslim name for God.

The boatmen with uplifted faces shouted discordantly, "Arsat! O Arsat!" Nobody came. The white man began to climb the rude ladder giving access to the bamboo platform before the house. The juragan[4] of the boat said sulkily, "We will cook in the sampan,[5] and sleep on the water."

"Pass my blankets and the basket," said the white man curtly.

He knelt on the edge of the platform to receive the bundle. Then the boat shoved off, and the white man, standing up, confronted Arsat, who had come out through the low door of his hut. He was a man young, powerful, with a broad chest and muscular arms. He had nothing on but his sarong.[6] His head was bare. His big, soft eyes stared eagerly at the white man, but his voice and demeanor were composed as he asked, without any words of greeting—

"Have you medicine, Tuan?"[7]

"No," said the visitor in a startled tone. "No. Why? Is there sickness in the house?"

"Enter and see," replied Arsat, in the same calm manner, and turning short round, passed again through the small doorway. The white man, dropping his bundles, followed.

In the dim light of the dwelling he made out on a couch of bamboos a woman stretched on her back under a broad sheet of red cotton cloth. She lay still, as if dead; but her big eyes, wide open, glittered in the gloom, staring upward at the slender rafters, motionless and unseeing. She was in a high fever, and evidently unconscious. Her cheeks were sunk slightly, her lips were partly open, and on the young face there was the ominous and fixed expression—the absorbed, contemplating expression of the unconscious who are going to die. The two men stood looking down at her in silence.

"Has she been long ill?" asked the traveler.

"I have not slept for five nights," answered the Malay, in a deliberate tone. "At first she heard voices calling her from the water and struggled against me who held her. But since the sun of today rose she hears nothing—she hears not me. She sees nothing. She sees not me—me!"

He remained silent for a minute, then asked softly—

"Tuan, will she die?"

"I fear so," said the white man sorrowfully. He had known Arsat years ago, in a far country in times of trouble and danger, when no friendship is to be despised. And since his Malay friend had come unexpectedly to dwell in the hut on the lagoon with a strange woman, he had slept many times there, in his journeys up and down the river. He liked the man who knew how to keep faith in council and how to fight without fear by the side of his white friend. He liked him—not so much perhaps as a man likes his favorite dog—but still

---

4. **juragan** (jŏŏ rä′ gän) captain or master.
5. **sampan** small flat-bottomed boat with a cabin formed by mats.
6. **sarong** long, brightly colored strip of cloth worn like a skirt.
7. **Tuan** (twan) Malayan for "sir."

✔**Reading Check**

What is wrong in Arsat's house?

he liked him well enough to help and ask no questions, to think sometimes vaguely and hazily in the midst of his own pursuits, about the lonely man and the long-haired woman with audacious face and triumphant eyes, who lived together by the forests—alone and feared.

The white man came out of the hut in time to see the enormous conflagration of sunset put out by the swift and stealthy shadows that, rising like a black and impalpable vapor above the treetops, spread over the heaven, extinguishing the crimson glow of floating clouds and the red brilliance of departing daylight. In a few moments all the stars came out above the intense blackness of the earth, and the great lagoon gleaming suddenly with reflected lights resembled an oval patch of night sky flung down into the hopeless and abysmal night of the wilderness. The white man had some supper out of the basket, then collecting a few sticks that lay about the platform, made up a small fire, not for warmth, but for the sake of the smoke, which would keep off the mosquitos. He wrapped himself in his blankets and sat with his back against the reed wall of the house, smoking thoughtfully.

Arsat came through the doorway with noiseless steps and squatted down by the fire. The white man moved his outstretched legs a little.

"She breathes," said Arsat in a low voice, anticipating the expected question. "She breathes and burns as if with a great fire. She speaks not; she hears not—and burns!" He paused for a moment, then asked in a quiet, incurious tone—

"Tuan . . . will she die?"

The white man moved his shoulders uneasily, and muttered in a hesitating manner—

"If such is her fate."

"No, Tuan," said Arsat calmly. "If such is my fate. I hear, I see, I wait. I remember . . . Tuan, do you remember the old days? Do you remember my brother?"

"Yes," said the white man. The Malay rose suddenly and went in. The other, sitting still outside, could hear the voice in the hut. Arsat said: "Hear me! Speak!" His words were succeeded by a complete silence. "O Diamelen!" he cried suddenly. After that cry there was a deep sigh. Arsat came out and sank down again in his old place.

They sat in silence before the fire. There was no sound within the house, there was no sound near them; but far away on the lagoon they could hear the voices of the boatmen ringing fitful and distinct on the calm water. The fire in the bows of the sampan shone faintly in the distance with a hazy red glow. Then it died out. The voices ceased. The land and the water slept invisible, unstirring and mute. It was as though there had been nothing left in the world but the glitter of stars streaming, ceaseless and vain, through the black stillness of the night.

The white man gazed straight before him into the darkness with wide-open eyes. The fear and fascination, the inspiration and the wonder of death—of death near, unavoidable, and unseen, soothed the unrest of his race and stirred the most indistinct, the most intimate

Literary Analysis
Plot Devices Is the narrator of the story closer in point of view to the white man or Arsat? Explain.

conflagration (kän´ flə grā´ shən) *n.* great fire

Reading Strategy
Picturing the Action and Situation What type of impression dominates as you picture the scene in this paragraph?

of his thoughts. The ever-ready suspicion of evil, the gnawing suspicion that lurks in our hearts, flowed out into the stillness round him—into the stillness profound and dumb, and made it appear untrustworthy and infamous, like the placid and impenetrable mask of an unjustifiable violence. In that fleeting and powerful disturbance of his being the earth enfolded in the starlight peace became a shadowy country of inhuman strife, a battlefield of phantoms terrible and charming, <u>august</u> or ignoble, struggling ardently for the possession of our helpless hearts. An unquiet and mysterious country of inextinguishable desires and fears.

A plaintive murmur rose in the night; a murmur saddening and startling, as if the great solitudes of surrounding woods had tried to whisper into his ear the wisdom of their immense and lofty indifference. Sounds hesitating and vague floated in the air round him, shaped themselves slowly into words; and at last flowed on gently in a murmuring stream of soft and monotonous sentences. He stirred like a man waking up and changed his position slightly. Arsat, motionless and shadowy, sitting with bowed head under the stars, was speaking in a low and dreamy tone—

". . . for where can we lay down the heaviness of our trouble but in a friend's heart? A man must speak of war and of love. You, Tuan, know what war is, and you have seen me in time of danger seek death as other men seek life! A writing may be lost; a lie may be written; but what the eye has seen is truth and remains in the mind!"

"I remember," said the white man quietly. Arsat went on with mournful composure—

"Therefore I shall speak to you of love. Speak in the night. Speak before both night and love are gone—and the eye of day looks upon my sorrow and my shame; upon my blackened face; upon my burnt-up heart."

A sigh, short and faint, marked an almost imperceptible pause, and then his words flowed on, without a stir, without a gesture.

"After the time of trouble and war was over and you went away from my country in the pursuit of your desires, which we, men of the islands, cannot understand, I and my brother became again, as we had been before, the sword bearers of the Ruler. You know we were men of family, belonging to a ruling race, and more fit than any to carry on our right shoulder the emblem of power. And in the time of prosperity Si Dendring showed us favor, as we, in time of sorrow, had showed to him the faithfulness of our courage. It was a time of peace. A time of deer hunts and cock fights; of idle talks and foolish squabbles between men whose bellies are full and weapons are rusty. But the sower watched the young rice shoots grow up without fear, and the traders came and went, departed lean and returned fat into the river of peace. They brought news too. Brought lies and truth mixed together, so that no man knew when to rejoice and when to be sorry. We heard from them about you also. They had seen you here and had seen you there. And I was glad to hear, for I remembered the stirring

august (ô gust´) *adj.* worthy of great respect; inspiring awe

Literary Analysis
Plot Devices and Point of View What shift in point of view alerts you to the fact that a story within a story begins here?

**Reading Check**
What does Arsat say his story concerns?

times, and I always remembered you, Tuan, till the time came when my eyes could see nothing in the past, because they had looked upon the one who is dying there—in the house."

He stopped to exclaim in an intense whisper, "O Mara bahia! O Calamity!" then went on speaking a little louder.

"There's no worse enemy and no better friend than a brother, Tuan, for one brother knows another, and in perfect knowledge is strength for good or evil. I loved my brother. I went to him and told him that I could see nothing but one face, hear nothing but one voice. He told

▲ **Critical Viewing**
Compare the mood of Arsat's story with the feelings you associate with a setting such as this one. [**Compare and Contrast**]

me: 'Open your heart so that she can see what is in it—and wait. Patience is wisdom. Inchi Midah may die or our Ruler may throw off his fear of a woman!'. . . I waited! . . . You remember the lady with the veiled face, Tuan, and the fear of our Ruler before her cunning and temper. And if she wanted her servant, what could I do? But I fed the hunger of my heart on short glances and stealthy words. I loitered on the path to the bath houses in the daytime, and when the sun had fallen behind the forest I crept along the jasmine hedges of the women's courtyard. Unseeing, we spoke to one another through the scent of flowers, through the veil of leaves, through the blades of long grass that stood still before our lips; so great was our prudence, so faint was the murmur of our great longing. The time passed swiftly . . . and there were whispers amongst women—and our enemies watched— my brother was gloomy, and I began to think of killing and of a fierce death. . . . We are of a people who take what they want—like you whites. There is a time when a man should forget loyalty and respect. Might and authority are given to rulers, but to all men is given love and strength and courage. My brother said, 'You shall take her from their midst. We are two who are like one.' And I answered, 'Let it be soon, for I find no warmth in sunlight that does not shine upon her.' Our time came when the Ruler and all the great people went to the mouth of the river to fish by torchlight. There were hundreds of boats, and on the white sand, between the water and the forests, dwellings of leaves were built for the households of the Rajahs.[8] The smoke of cooking fires was like a blue mist of the evening, and many voices rang in it joyfully. While they were making the boats ready to beat up the fish, my brother came to me and said, 'Tonight!'

Reading Strategy
Picturing the Action and Situation As you picture the situation among Arsat, his beloved, his ruler, and Inchi Midah, his beloved's mistress, what attitude does each convey?

---

8. **Rajahs** (rä´ jəz) Malayan chiefs.

✔**Reading Check**
What do Arsat and his brother decide to do?

I looked to my weapons, and when the time came our canoe took its place in the circle of boats carrying the torches. The lights blazed on the water, but behind the boats there was darkness. When the shouting began and the excitement made them like mad we dropped out. The water swallowed our fire, and we floated back to the shore that was dark with only here and there the glimmer of embers. We could hear the talk of slave girls amongst the sheds. Then we found a place deserted and silent. We waited there. She came. She came running along the shore, rapid and leaving no trace, like a leaf driven by the wind into the sea. My brother said gloomily, 'Go and take her; carry her into our boat.' I lifted her in my arms. She panted. Her heart was beating against my breast. I said, 'I take you from those people. You came to the cry of my heart, but my arms take you into my boat against the will of the great!' 'It is right,' said my brother. 'We are men who take what we want and can hold it against many. We should have taken her in daylight.' I said, 'Let us be off'; for since she was in my boat I began to think of our Ruler's many men. 'Yes. Let us be off,' said my brother. 'We are cast out and this boat is our country now—and the sea is our refuge.' He lingered with his foot on the shore, and I entreated him to hasten, for I remembered the strokes of her heart against my breast and thought that two men cannot withstand a hundred. We left, paddling downstream close to the bank; and as we passed by the creek where they were fishing, the great shouting had ceased, but the murmur of voices was loud like the humming of insects flying at noonday. The boats floated, clustered together, in the red light of torches, under a black roof of smoke; and men talked of their sport. Men that boasted, and praised, and jeered—men that would have been our friends in the morning, but on that night were already our enemies. We paddled swiftly past. We had no more friends in the country of our birth. She sat in the middle of the canoe with covered face; silent as she is now; unseeing as she is now—and I had no regret at what I was leaving because I could hear her breathing close to me—as I can hear her now."

He paused, listened with his ear turned to the doorway, then shook his head and went on.

"My brother wanted to shout the cry of challenge—one cry only—to let the people know we were freeborn robbers who trusted our arms and the great sea. And again I begged him in the name of our love to be silent. Could I not hear her breathing close to me? I knew the pursuit would come quick enough. My brother loved me. He dipped his paddle without a splash. He only said, 'There is half a man in you now—the other half is in that woman. I can wait. When you are a whole man again, you will come back with me here to shout defiance. We are sons of the same mother.' I made no answer. All my strength and all my spirit were in my hands that held the paddle—for I longed to be with her in a safe place beyond the reach of men's anger and of women's spite. My love was so great, that I thought it could guide me to a country where death was unknown, if I could only escape from

Reading Strategy
Picturing the Action and Situation What details in this account of the elopement stand out for you?

Literary Analysis
Plot Devices What do the pauses in Arsat's story indicate to the white man and the reader about Arsat's emotional state?

Inchi Midah's fury and from our Ruler's sword. We paddled with haste, breathing through our teeth. The blades bit deep into the smooth water. We passed out of the river; we flew in clear channels amongst the shallows. We skirted the black coast; we skirted the sand beaches where the sea speaks in whispers to the land; and the gleam of white sand flashed back past our boat, so swiftly she ran upon the water. We spoke not. Only once I said, 'Sleep, Diamelen, for soon you may want all your strength.' I heard the sweetness of her voice, but I never turned my head. The sun rose and still we went on. Water fell from my face like rain from a cloud. We flew in the light and heat. I never looked back, but I knew that my brother's eyes, behind me, were looking steadily ahead, for the boat went as straight as a bushman's dart, when it leaves the end of the sumpitan.[9] There was no better paddler, no better steersman than my brother. Many times, together, we had won races in that canoe. But we never had put out our strength as we did then—then, when for the last time we paddled together! There was no braver or stronger man in our country than my brother. I could not spare the strength to turn my head and look at him, every moment I heard the hiss of his breath getting louder behind me. Still he did not speak. The sun was high. The heat clung to my back like a flame of fire. My ribs were ready to burst, but I could no longer get enough air into my chest. And then I felt I must cry out with my last breath. 'Let us rest!' . . . 'Good!' he answered; and his voice was firm. He was strong. He was brave. He knew not fear and no fatigue . . . My brother!"

A murmur powerful and gentle, a murmur vast and faint; the murmur of trembling leaves, of stirring boughs, ran through the tangled depths of the forests, ran over the starry smoothness of the lagoon, and the water between the piles lapped the slimy timber once with a sudden splash. A breath of warm air touched the two men's faces and passed on with a mournful sound—a breath loud and short like an uneasy sigh of the dreaming earth.

Arsat went on in an even, low voice:

"We ran our canoe on the white beach of a little bay close to a long tongue of land that seemed to bar our road; a long wooded cape going far into the sea. My brother knew that place. Beyond the cape a river has its entrance, and through the jungle of that land there is a narrow path. We made a fire and cooked rice. Then we lay down to sleep on the soft sand in the shade of our canoe, while she watched. No sooner had I closed my eyes than I heard her cry of alarm. We leaped up. The sun was halfway down the sky already, and coming in sight in the opening of the bay we saw a prau[10] manned by many paddlers. We knew it at once; it was one of our Rajah's praus. They were watching the shore, and saw us. They beat the gong, and turned the head of the prau into the bay. I felt my heart become weak within my

9. **sumpitan** (sump´ ə tän) Malayan blowgun which discharges poisonous darts.
10. **prau** (prou) swift Malayan boat with a large sail.

Literary Analysis
Plot Devices How do the descriptions of the setting in which Arsat tells his tale provide a kind of commentary on his tale?

✔Reading Check

Have Arsat, his brother, and Diamelen escaped the Rajah? Explain.

The Lagoon ◆ 1143

breast. Diamelen sat on the sand and covered her face. There was no escape by sea. My brother laughed. He had the gun you had given him, Tuan, before you went away, but there was only a handful of powder. He spoke to me quickly: 'Run with her along the path. I shall keep them back, for they have no firearms, and landing in the face of a man with a gun is certain death for some. Run with her. On the other side of that wood there is a fisherman's house—and a canoe. When I have fired all the shots I will follow. I am a great runner, and before they can come up we shall be gone. I will hold out as long as I can, for she is but a woman—that can neither run nor fight, but she has your heart in her weak hands.' He dropped behind the canoe. The prau was coming. She and I ran, and as we rushed along the path I heard shots. My brother fired—once —twice—and the booming of the gong ceased. There was silence behind us. That neck of land is narrow. Before I heard my brother fire the third shot I saw the shelving shore, and I saw the water again: the mouth of a broad river. We crossed a grassy glade. We ran down to the water. I saw a low hut above the black mud, and a small canoe hauled up. I heard another shot behind me. I thought, 'That is his last charge.' We rushed down to the canoe; a man came running from the hut, but I leaped on him, and we rolled together in the mud. Then I got up, and he lay still at my feet. I don't know whether I had killed him or not. I and Diamelen pushed the canoe afloat. I heard yells behind me, and I saw my brother run across the glade. Many men were bounding after him. I took her in my arms and threw her into the boat, then leaped in myself. When I looked back I saw that my brother had fallen. He fell and was up again, but the men were closing round him. He shouted, 'I am coming!' The men were close to him. I looked. Many men. Then I looked at her. Tuan, I pushed the canoe! I pushed it into deep water. She was kneeling forward looking at me, and I said, 'Take your paddle,' while I struck the water with mine. Tuan, I heard him cry. I heard him cry my name twice; and I heard voices shouting, 'Kill! Strike!' I never turned back. I heard him calling my name again with a great shriek, as when life is going out together with the voice—and I never turned my head. My own name! . . . My brother! Three times he called—but I was not afraid of life. Was she not there in that canoe? And could I not with her find a country where death is forgotten—where death is unknown!"

The white man sat up. Arsat rose and stood, an indistinct and silent figure above the dying embers of the fire. Over the lagoon a mist drifting and low had crept, erasing slowly the glittering images of the stars. And now a great expanse of white vapor covered the land; it flowed cold and gray in the darkness, eddied in noiseless whirls round the tree-trunks and about the platform of the house, which seemed to float upon a restless and impalpable illusion of a sea. Only far away the tops of the trees stood outlined on the twinkle of heaven, like a somber and forbidding shore—a coast deceptive, pitiless and black.

▲ **Critical Viewing**
What aspects of Conrad's story does this photograph capture? What aspects does it fail to capture? **[Connect]**

Arsat's voice vibrated loudly in the profound peace.

"I had her there! I had her! To get her I would have faced all mankind. But I had her—and—"

His words went out ringing into the empty distances. He paused, and seemed to listen to them dying away very far—beyond help and beyond recall. Then he said quietly—

"Tuan, I loved my brother."

A breath of wind made him shiver. High above his head, high above the silent sea of mist the drooping leaves of the palms rattled together with a mournful and expiring sound. The white man stretched his legs. His chin rested on his chest, and he murmured sadly without lifting his head—

"We all love our brothers."

Arsat burst out with an intense whispering violence—

"What did I care who died? I wanted peace in my own heart."

He seemed to hear a stir in the house —listened—then stepped in noiselessly. The white man stood up. A breeze was coming in fitful puffs. The stars shone paler as if they had retreated into the frozen depths of immense space. After a chill gust of wind there were a few seconds of perfect calm and absolute silence. Then from behind the black and wavy line of the forests a column of golden light shot up into the heavens and spread over the semicircle of the eastern horizon. The sun had risen. The mist lifted, broke into drifting patches, vanished into thin flying wreaths; and the unveiled lagoon lay, polished and black, in the heavy shadows at the foot of the wall of trees. A white eagle rose over it with a slanting and ponderous flight, reached the clear sunshine and appeared dazzlingly brilliant for a moment, then soaring higher, became a dark and motionless speck before it vanished into the blue as if it had left the earth forever. The white man, standing gazing upward before the doorway, heard in the hut a confused and broken murmur of distracted words ending with a loud groan. Suddenly Arsat stumbled out with outstretched hands, shivered, and stood still for some time with fixed eyes. Then he said—

"She burns no more."

Before his face the sun showed its edge above the treetops, rising steadily. The breeze freshened; a great brilliance burst upon the lagoon, sparkled on the rippling water. The forests came out of the clear shadows of the morning, became distinct, as if they had rushed nearer—to stop short in a great stir of leaves, of nodding boughs, of swaying branches. In the merciless sunshine the whisper of unconscious life grew louder, speaking in an incomprehensible voice round the dumb darkness of that human sorrow. Arsat's eyes wandered slowly, then stared at the rising sun.

"I can see nothing," he said half aloud to himself.

"There is nothing," said the white man, moving to the edge of the platform and waving his hand to his boat. A shout came faintly over the lagoon and the sampan began to glide toward the abode of the friend of ghosts.

Reading Strategy
Picturing the Action and Situation What expression do you think is on each character's face when Arsat concludes his story within a story?

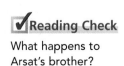
Reading Check

What happens to Arsat's brother?

"If you want to come with me, I will wait all the morning," said the white man, looking away upon the water.

"No, Tuan," said Arsat softly. "I shall not eat or sleep in this house, but I must first see my road. Now I can see nothing—see nothing! There is no light and no peace in the world; but there is death—death for many. We were sons of the same mother—and I left him in the midst of enemies; but I am going back now."

He drew a long breath and went on in a dreamy tone:

"In a little while I shall see clear enough to strike—to strike. But she has died, and . . . now . . . darkness."

He flung his arms wide open, let them fall along his body, then stood still with unmoved face and stony eyes, staring at the sun. The white man got down into his canoe. The polers ran smartly along the sides of the boat, looking over their shoulders at the beginning of a weary journey. High in the stern, his head muffled up in white rags, the juragon sat moody, letting his paddle trail in the water. The white man, leaning with both arms over the grass roof of the little cabin, looked back at the shining ripple of the boat's wake. Before the sampan passed out of the lagoon into the creek he lifted his eyes. Arsat had not moved. He stood lonely in the searching sunshine; and he looked beyond the great light of a cloudless day into the darkness of a world of illusions.

Review and Assess

Thinking About the Selection

1. **(a) Recall:** Why does Arsat ask the white man if he has medicine? **(b) Infer:** What is Arsat's state of mind?

2. **(a) Recall:** What does Arsat's brother do while Arsat and Diamelen run to the canoe? **(b) Analyze Cause and Effect:** What motivates Arsat to leave his brother behind? **(c) Speculate:** How else could he have responded, and what might have been the results?

3. **(a) Interpret:** Following Diamelen's death, Arsat says, "I can see nothing," and the white man replies, "There is nothing." What does each statement mean? **(b) Connect:** How might this dialogue relate to the story's final line?

4. **(a) Analyze:** Find three examples of Conrad's descriptions in the story of sounds, including descriptions of silence and speech. What do these images suggest about the act of storytelling? **(b) Draw Conclusions:** What is Arsat's purpose in telling his story? **(c) Evaluate:** Does he achieve it? Explain.

5. **(a) Draw Conclusions:** What do you think Conrad would recommend to people as a way to deal with past mistakes or regrets? **(b) Make a Judgment:** Would you agree? Explain.

Araby

James Joyce

North Richmond Street, being blind,[1] was a quiet street except at the hour when the Christian Brothers' School set the boys free. An uninhabited house of two stories stood at the blind end, detached from its neighbors in a square ground. The other houses of the street, conscious of decent lives within them, gazed at one another with brown <u>imperturbable</u> faces.

The former tenant of our house, a priest, had died in the back drawing room. Air, musty from having been long enclosed, hung in all the rooms, and the waste room behind the kitchen was littered with old useless papers. Among these I found a few paper-covered books, the pages of which were curled and damp: *The Abbot,* by Walter Scott, *The Devout Communicant* and *The Memoirs of Vidocq.*[2] I liked the last best because its leaves were yellow. The wild garden behind the house contained a central apple tree and a few straggling bushes under one of which I found the late tenant's rusty bicycle pump. He had been a very charitable priest: in his will he had left all his money to institutions and the furniture of his house to his sister.

When the short days of winter came dusk fell before we had well eaten our dinners. When we met in the street the houses had grown somber. The space of sky above us was the color of ever-changing violet and toward it the lamps of the street lifted their feeble lanterns. The cold air stung us and we played till our bodies glowed. Our shouts echoed in the silent street. The career of our play brought us through the dark muddy lanes behind the houses where we ran the gantlet of the rough tribes from the cottages, to the back doors of the dark dripping gardens where odors arose from the ashpits, to the dark odorous stables where a coachman smoothed and combed the horse or shook music from the buckled harness. When we returned to the street, light from the kitchen windows had filled the areas. If my uncle was seen turning the corner we hid in the shadow until we had seen him safely housed. Or if Mangan's sister came out on the doorstep to call her brother in to his tea we watched her from our

---

1. **blind** a dead end.
2. ***The Abbot . . . Vidocq*** a historical tale, a religious manual, and the remembrances of a French adventurer, respectively.

imperturbable (im′ pər tur′ bə bəl) *adj.* calm; not easily ruffled

 **Reading Check**

When and where does the story take place?

shadow peer up and down the street. We waited to see whether she would remain or go in and, if she remained, we left our shadow and walked up to Mangan's steps resignedly. She was waiting for us, her figure defined by the light from the half-opened door. Her brother always teased her before he obeyed and I stood by the railings looking at her. Her dress swung as she moved her body and the soft rope of her hair tossed from side to side. Every morning I lay on the floor in the front parlor watching her door. The blind was pulled down to within an inch of the sash so that I could not be seen. When she came out on the doorstep my heart leaped. I ran to the hall, seized my books and followed her. I kept her brown figure always in my eye and, when we came near the point at which our ways diverged, I quickened my pace and passed her. This happened morning after morning. I had never spoken to her, except for a few casual words, and yet her name was like a summons to all my foolish blood.

Literary Analysis
Plot Devices and Point of View What effect does the use of first-person point of view have on your impression of Mangan's sister?

Her image accompanied me even in places the most hostile to romance. On Saturday evenings when my aunt went marketing I had to go to carry some of the parcels. We walked through the flaring streets, jostled by drunken men and bargaining women, amid the curses of laborers, the shrill <u>litanies</u> of shop-boys who stood on guard by the barrels of pigs' cheeks, the nasal chanting of street singers, who sang a *come-all-you* about O'Donovan Rossa,[3] or a ballad about the troubles in our native land. These noises converged in a single sensation of life for me: I imagined that I bore my chalice safely through a throng of foes. Her name sprang to my lips at moments in strange prayers and praises which I myself did not understand. My eyes were often full of tears (I could not tell why) and at times a flood from my heart seemed to pour itself out into my bosom. I thought little of the future. I did not know whether I would ever speak to her or not or, if I spoke to her, how I could tell her of my confused adoration. But my body was like a harp and her words and gestures were like fingers running upon the wires.

litanies (lit´ ən ēz) *n.* prayers in which a congregation repeats a fixed response; repetitive recitations

One evening I went into the back drawing room in which the priest had died. It was a dark rainy evening and there was no sound in the house. Through one of the broken panes I heard the rain impinge upon the earth, the fine incessant needles of water playing in the sodden beds. Some distant lamp or lighted window gleamed below me. I was thankful that I could see so little. All my senses seemed to desire to veil themselves and, feeling that I was about to slip from them, I pressed the palms of my hands together until they trembled, murmuring: *"O love! O love!"* many times.

Reading Strategy
Picturing the Action and Situation Which vivid details in this passage help you form a mental picture of the scene?

At last she spoke to me. When she addressed the first words to me I was so confused that I did not know what to answer. She asked me was I going to *Araby.* I forget whether I answered yes or no. It would be a splendid bazaar, she said; she would love to go.

"And why can't you?" I asked.

---

3. *come-all-you* . . . Rossa opening of a ballad about an Irish hero.

St. Patrick's Close, Walter Osborne, Courtesy of the National Gallery of Ireland

◀ **Critical Viewing**
Why might the prospect of a fair or bazaar be appealing to someone who lived in a setting such as this? **[Infer]**

While she spoke she turned a silver bracelet round and round her wrist. She could not go, she said, because there would be a retreat[4] that week in her convent.[5] Her brother and two other boys were fighting for their caps and I was alone at the railings. She held one of the spikes, bowing her head towards me. The light from the lamp opposite our door caught the white curve of her neck, lit up her hair that rested there and, falling, lit up the hand upon the railing. It fell over one side of her dress and caught the white border of a petticoat, just visible as she stood at ease.

"It's well for you," she said.

"If I go," I said, "I will bring you something."

What innumerable follies laid waste my waking and sleeping thoughts after that evening!

---

4. retreat *n.* period of retirement or seclusion for prayer, religious study, and meditation.
5. convent *n.* school run by an order of nuns.

Literary Analysis
Plot Devices In what way might the narrator's comments on his own past thoughts and feelings prepare for an epiphany?

✔ **Reading Check**
What does the narrator promise Mangan's sister?

Araby ◆ 1149

I wished to annihilate the tedious intervening days. I chafed against the work of school. At night in my bedroom and by day in the classroom her image came between me and the page I strove to read. The syllables of the word *Araby* were called to me through the silence in which my soul luxuriated and cast an Eastern enchantment over me.

I asked for leave to go to the bazaar on Saturday night. My aunt was surprised and hoped it was not some Freemason[6] affair. I answered few questions in class. I watched my master's face pass from amiability to sternness; he hoped I was not beginning to idle. I could not call my wandering thoughts together. I had hardly any patience with the serious work of life which, now that it stood between me and my desire, seemed to me child's play, ugly monotonous child's play.

On Saturday morning I reminded my uncle that I wished to go to the bazaar in the evening. He was fussing at the hallstand, looking for the hat brush, and answered me curtly:

"Yes, boy, I know."

As he was in the hall I could not go into the front parlor and lie at the window. I left the house in bad humor and walked slowly toward the school. The air was pitilessly raw and already my heart misgave me.

When I came home to dinner my uncle had not yet been home. Still it was early. I sat staring at the clock for some time and, when its ticking began to irritate me, I left the room. I mounted the staircase and gained the upper part of the house. The high cold empty gloomy rooms liberated me and I went from room to room singing. From the front window I saw my companions playing in the street. Their cries reached me weakened and indistinct and, leaning my forehead against the cool glass, I looked over at the dark house where she lived. I may have stood there for an hour, seeing nothing but the brown-clad figure cast by my imagination, touched discreetly by the lamplight at the curved neck, at the hand upon the railings and at the border below the dress.

When I came downstairs again I found Mrs. Mercer sitting at the fire. She was an old garrulous woman, a pawnbroker's widow, who collected used stamps for some pious purpose. I had to endure the gossip of the tea table. The meal was prolonged beyond an hour and still my uncle did not come. Mrs. Mercer stood up to go: she was sorry she couldn't wait any longer, but it was after eight o'clock and she did not like to be out late, as the night air was bad for her. When she had gone I began to walk up and down the room, clenching my fists. My aunt said:

"I'm afraid you may put off your bazaar for this night of Our Lord."

At nine o'clock I heard my uncle's latchkey in the hall door. I heard him talking to himself and heard the hallstand rocking when it had received the weight of his overcoat. I could interpret these signs.

Reading Strategy
Picturing the Action and Situation As you picture the narrator daydreaming, do you also share the daydream? Explain.

garrulous (gar′ ə ləs) *adj.* talkative

---

6. **Freemason** Free and Accepted Masons, an international secret society.

When he was midway through his dinner I asked him to give me the money to go to the bazaar. He had forgotten.

"The people are in bed and after their first sleep now," he said.

I did not smile. My aunt said to him energetically:

"Can't you give him the money and let him go? You've kept him late enough as it is."

My uncle said he was very sorry he had forgotten. He said he believed in the old saying: *All work and no play makes Jack a dull boy.* He asked me where I was going and, when I had told him a second time he asked me did I know *The Arab's Farewell to His Steed.*[7] When I left the kitchen he was about to recite the opening lines of the piece to my aunt.

I held a florin[8] tightly in my hand as I strode down Buckingham Street toward the station. The sight of the streets thronged with buyers and glaring with gas recalled to me the purpose of my journey. I took my seat in a third-class carriage of a deserted train. After an intolerable delay the train moved out of the station slowly. It crept onward among ruinous houses and over the twinkling river. At Westland Row Station a crowd of people pressed to the carriage doors; but the porters moved them back, saying that it was a special train for the bazaar. I remained alone in the bare carriage. In a few minutes the train drew up beside an improvised wooden platform. I passed out onto the road and saw by the lighted dial of a clock that it was ten minutes to ten. In front of me was a large building which displayed the magical name.

I could not find any sixpenny entrance and, fearing that the bazaar would be closed, I passed in quickly through a turnstile, handing a shilling to a weary-looking man. I found myself in a big hall girdled at half its height by a gallery. Nearly all the stalls were closed and the greater part of the hall was in darkness. I recognized a silence like that which pervades a church after a service. I walked into the center of the bazaar timidly. A few people were gathered about the stalls which were still open. Before a curtain, over which the words *Café Chantant*[9] were written in colored lamps, two men were counting money on a salver.[10] I listened to the fall of the coins.

Remembering with difficulty why I had come I went over to one of the stalls and examined porcelain vases and flowered tea sets. At the door of the stall a young lady was talking and laughing with two young gentlemen. I remarked their English accents and listened vaguely to their conversation.

"O, I never said such a thing!"

"O, but you did!"

---

7. **The Arab's . . . His Steed** popular nineteenth-century poem.
8. **florin** two shilling coin of the time.
9. *Café Chantant* café with musical entertainment.
10. **salver** tray usually used for the presentation of letters or visiting cards.

The British Tradition

The Irish Tradition

Joyce's stories are a modern addition to the rich cultural legacy of Ireland. Irish literature began with an oral tradition of epics and flourished through the medieval period, when Irish monasteries guarded learned culture amid an inflowing tide of Danish and Germanic invaders. Bede's *History* is a culminating testament to the Irish preservation of learning on the islands—Irish books and Irish teaching flowing into Bede's England made the work possible.

Although the Irish cultural tradition is strong, centuries of rule by the English in Ireland and the Irish struggles against that rule have raised questions of cultural identity. When W. B. Yeats reinvigorated Irish poetry, he helped to launch the Irish Literary Revival. This literary assertion of Irish identity was also a political gesture reinforcing the movement to free Ireland. Since Yeats, writers such as Joyce, Louis MacNeice, and Seamus Heaney have made the Irish identity, as well as the splits it suffered under English rule, a theme for literary exploration.

✓ **Reading Check**

In what way does the narrator's uncle delay the narrator's arrival at Araby?

"O, but I didn't!"

"Didn't she say that?"

"Yes. I heard her."

"O, there's a . . . fib!"

Observing me the young lady came over and asked me did I wish to buy anything. The tone of her voice was not encouraging; she seemed to have spoken to me out of a sense of duty. I looked humbly at the great jars that stood like Eastern guards at either side of the dark entrance to the stall and murmured:

"No, thank you."

The young lady changed the position of one of the vases and went back to the two young men. They began to talk of the same subject. Once or twice the young lady glanced at me over her shoulder.

I lingered before her stall, though I knew my stay was useless, to make my interest in her wares seem the more real. Then I turned away slowly and walked down the middle of the bazaar. I allowed the two pennies to fall against the sixpence in my pocket. I heard a voice call from one end of the gallery that the light was out. The upper part of the hall was now completely dark.

Gazing up into the darkness I saw myself as a creature driven and <u>derided</u> by vanity; and my eyes burned with anguish and anger.

derided (di rīd′ id) v. made fun of; ridiculed

Review and Assess

Thinking About the Selection

1. **Respond:** Have you ever had doubts or ambivalent feelings about a promise like those of the narrator? Explain.

2. **(a) Recall:** What does Mangan's sister do to make a trip to the bazaar so important to the narrator? **(b) Analyze:** Describe three scenes that establish the narrator's feelings for her.

3. **(a) Recall:** Describe the narrator's experience at Araby. **(b) Analyze Causes and Effects:** What features of the Araby bazaar conflict with the narrator's expectations?

4. **(a) Evaluate:** Did you find the narrator's descriptions of his neighborhood and childhood colorful, even romantic? Explain. **(b) Connect:** Do his descriptions make the ordinary world as exciting and interesting as the world he hopes to find at the bazaar?

5. **(a) Draw Conclusions:** What has the narrator lost by the end of the story? **(b) Draw Conclusions:** What might he have gained?

6. **Apply:** Should the dreams of youth be protected, or can a disillusioning experience like the narrator's teach a valuable lesson? Explain.

Review and Assess

Literary Analysis

Plot Devices

1. Conrad uses the **plot device** of a **story within a story** in "The Lagoon." What specific information would you lack if "The Lagoon" had been narrated entirely in the first person by Arsat?
2. Why do you think Conrad chose to have Arsat narrate his own story?
3. (a) Where in "Araby" does the **epiphany** occur? (b) What does the narrator in "Araby" suddenly realize?
4. Explain in what sense the narrator's epiphany in "Araby" is as much a loss of vision as it is a gain of insight.

Comparing Literary Works

5. Contrast the mood of the parts of "The Lagoon" narrated by Arsat with the mood of the framing story, narrated in the third-person.
6. Use a chart like the one shown to compare how each story uses plot devices to establish distance between an experience of passion and the act of telling a story about passion.

7. (a) Compare the way that each story creates an "outsider's" perspective on a narrator's obsessive, passionate concerns. (b) Explain how plot devices add to the **theme** of each story.

Reading Strategy

Picturing the Action and Situation

8. Write a paragraph describing a scene in "The Lagoon."
9. Write a paragraph describing the narrator's feelings when he experiences his epiphany in "Araby."

Extend Understanding

10. **Psychology Connection:** How important do you think story-telling is in the mourning process? Why?

Quick Review

Writers use **plot devices** to achieve innovative effects.

A **story within a story** is a tale told by a character within a fictional narrative.

An **epiphany**—a profound revelation experienced by a character—gives a story a psychological climax.

The **theme** of a work is its central concern, the question about life that it raises, or the message it sends.

To better understand the characters' actions and inner lives, pause to **picture the action and situation** in scenes of a narrative.

 Take It to the Net
www.phschool.com
Take the interactive self-test online to check your understanding of these selections.

Integrate Language Skills

Vocabulary Development Lesson

Word Analysis: Latin Root -vinc-

Early in Conrad's "The Lagoon," you will find the word *invincible*, which means "unconquerable." *Invincible* is formed with the root *-vinc-*, which comes from a Latin verb meaning "to conquer." Write definitions for the following words, explaining how the meaning of the root affects the meaning of the word.

   1. convince   **2.** evince   **3.** invincibility

Spelling Strategy

If a noun ends in the letter y preceded by a consonant, form the plural by dropping the y and adding *-ies*: *litany* becomes *litanies*. Write the plural form of each of the following words:

   1. gallery

   2. cry

   3. family

Concept Development: Synonyms

Choose the synonym for the first word in each item.

   1. portals: (a) arteries, (b) doors, (c) chairs
   2. invincible: (a) unconquerable, (b) warriorlike, (c) facile
   3. propitiate: (a) appease, (b) refuse, (c) resign
   4. conflagration: (a) battle, (b) dispute, (c) fire
   5. august: (a) portly, (b) virtuous, (c) awe-inspiring
   6. imperturbable: (a) indifferent, (b) calm, (c) ruthless
   7. litanies: (a) lawsuits, (b) prayers, (c) cries
   8. garrulous: (a) talkative, (b) coy, (c) rich
   9. derided: (a) ejected, (b) ridiculed, (c) exaggerated

Grammar and Style Lesson

Adverb Clauses

Conrad and Joyce both use **adverb clauses**—subordinate clauses that modify a verb, an adjective, or an adverb.

> **Adverb Clause:** . . . the repeated call of some bird . . . skipped along over the smooth water and lost itself, <u>before it could reach the other shore</u>, . . . (modifies *lost* by telling when)

Practice In your notebook, identify the adverb clause in each sentence and the word(s) it modifies.

   1. Before the sampan passed out of the lagoon into the creek, he lifted his eyes.

   2. And since his Malay friend had come unexpectedly to dwell in the hut on the lagoon with a strange woman, he had slept many times there, ...

   3. When we met in the street, the houses had grown somber.

   4. I . . . heard the hallstand rocking when it had received the weight of his overcoat.

   5. I lingered before her stall, though I knew my stay was useless, . . .

Writing Application Write a brief account of a journey you have taken into another "world," using at least three adverb clauses.

Writing Lesson

Personal Essay

Conrad's "The Lagoon" abounds with descriptions of silence and repeated uses of the word *nothing*. Write an essay tracing these images through the story, mapping them against events in Arsat's tale and in the framing narrative. Conclude with a general insight into the relationship of silence, storytelling, passion, and "nothing" in the story.

Prewriting   Review the story, taking notes on images of silence and "nothing" and the narration surrounding each. Draft a few statements of what the references suggest. Consider the extent to which Arsat's story-telling is an interruption of silence.

Drafting   As you draft, present your ideas in logical sequence. Relate each idea to your central insight into the story.

Revising   Highlight vague passages in you draft. For each, review "The Lagoon," and jot down notes showing how the story supports your ideas. Consider incorporating your new ideas to improve vague passages.

Model: Revising to Sharpen Insight

Like the bird's cry described by Conrad, Arsat's story "loses

itself" in the void. It cannot make up for his brother's or for

Diamelen's death.

Arsat badly wants to tell his story. Silence, though, surrounds

him. ~~His words do not make any difference in his situation.~~

> A reference to Conrad's image helps focus the writer's point.

Prentice Hall Writing and Grammar Connection: Chapter 14, Section 4

Extension Activities

Listening and Speaking With a group, hold a **literary trial** of Arsat to determine whether he is responsible for his brother's death. Divide the roles of defense team, prosecution, and judge.

- Use concrete images and evidence from Arsat's account to help you state your case.
- Use figurative language—striking comparisons and images—to present your ideas.

Present your arguments before the "jury" (the class), and have them return a verdict.
[Group Activity]

Research and Technology Develop a **research presentation** on poster art at the turn of the twentieth century, such as might have been used to advertise Araby. Explore art books, galleries, and Web sites. Then, write a brief report on the history of such posters. Produce a poster for Araby, and present it with your report.

 **Take It to the Net**   www.phschool.com

Go online for an additional research activity using the Internet.

Prepare to Read

The Lady in the Looking Glass: A Reflection ◆
The First Year of My Life

Virginia Woolf (1882–1941)

Virginia Woolf revolutionized modern fiction as one of the pioneers of the stream-of-consciousness technique. This device allows readers to tune in directly to the flow of thoughts and images in a character's mind.

A Literary Life Woolf came from a prim and proper Victorian family, but it was one in which literature was prized. Her father, the renowned editor Leslie Stephen, made sure that his daughter grew up surrounded by books. At the age of twenty-three, Woolf began contributing reviews to *The Times* of London. Later, she and her husband, author Leonard Woolf, made their house in the Bloomsbury section of London into a meeting place for writers and intellectuals. This circle of thinkers became known as the Bloomsbury Group.

Revolutionizing Fiction Woolf's first two novels were not unusual, but *Jacob's Room* (1922) shattered the conventions of fiction by telling the story of a young man's life entirely through an examination of his room. (She also uses this device in "The Lady in the Looking Glass: A Reflection.") Woolf continued to refine her fluid, inward-looking style with three more stream-of-consciousness novels—*Mrs. Dalloway* (1925), *To the Lighthouse* (1927), and *The Waves* (1931). In her more revolutionary works, she virtually abolishes a traditional plot, preferring to concentrate on what she called "an ordinary mind on an ordinary day."

Depression and Tragedy Woolf suffered episodes of severe depression brought on by poor health and the turmoil of World War II. In 1941, she drowned. Today, she is recognized as one of the defining forces of modern fiction.

Muriel Spark (b. 1918)

The Scottish novelist Muriel Spark is best known for her novel *The Prime of Miss Jean Brodie* (1961), which has been successfully adapted for both the stage and the screen.

A Prolific Career Born and educated in Edinburgh, Scotland, Spark began her literary career as an editor and biographer. After winning a short-story competition sponsored by the *Observer*, a Sunday newspaper, she focused her writing efforts on fiction. A number of her early stories were set in central Africa, where she had spent several years of her youth. Her first collection, *The Go-Away Bird and Other Stories*, was published in 1958.

Novels and Faith In 1954, after Spark converted to Roman Catholicism, she searched for ways to apply the psychological and spiritual insights of her new faith to her fiction. Many of her novels, including *The Mandelbaum Gate* (1965), *Territorial Rights* (1979), and *The Only Problem* (1984), reveal a writer preoccupied with questions of good and evil.

Perverse Whimsy At the same time, an element of perverse whimsy enters much of her work. Spark's narratives make leaps and loops, and it is sometimes hard to tell how far her narrators can be trusted. It is as if she wishes to caution us against being deceived by the ideal of an all-knowing—or completely self-knowing—narrator. We are all limited creatures, she seems to be saying, and when we try to narrate the stories of our lives, we often deceive ourselves.

Carefully crafted, suspenseful, witty, and morally charged, Spark's novels and short stories are distinctive contributions to modern literature.

Preview

Connecting to the Literature

As you sit in the dentist's office, you glance at a magazine cover featuring a model who looks like your friend who just got into college—and suddenly you wonder if you forgot to mail your application. The mind flows by such associations, as Woolf shows in her stream-of-consciousness narration.

Literary Analysis

Point of View: Modern Experiments

Searching for forms suited to modern experience, writers experiment with **point of view,** the perspective from which a story is told.

- **Stream-of-consciousness** narration follows the flowing, branching currents of thought in a character's mind.

- **An omniscient narrator**—one with access to more information than any single character could have—may be used in surprising ways.

Woolf uses the stream-of-consciousness technique in "The Lady in the Looking Glass." Spark's omniscient narrator in "My First Year" is herself—as a baby who knows "everything." As you read, note the effect these experiments have on your experience of the events in the stories.

Comparing Literary Works

Both these works experiment with point of view, enabling the writers to explore the connection between appearance and reality in unique ways. Woolf sifts through the outward appearance of a character's life to reach its reality. By contrast, Spark's narrator takes in a hodgepodge of events to find ironic contrasts between reality and people's descriptions of it. Compare the ways in which these stories contrast appearance and reality.

Reading Strategy

Questioning

Experimental works offer great rewards but also place great demands on readers. Find your way in the story by continually **asking questions** as you read. Use a chart such as the one shown.

Vocabulary Development

suffused (sə fyōozd´) *v.* spread throughout; filled (p. 1158)

transient (tran´ shənt) *n.* that which passes quickly (p. 1159)

upbraidings (up brād´ iŋz) *n.* stern words of disapproval; scoldings (p. 1160)

evanescence (ev´ ə nes´ əns) *n.* vanishing or tendency to vanish (p. 1162)

reticent (ret´ ə sənt) *adj.* silent; reserved (p. 1162)

omniscient (äm nish´ ənt) *adj.* having infinite knowledge; knowing all (p. 1164)

authenticity (ô thən tis´ ə tē) *n.* reality; genuineness (p. 1165)

discerned (di surnd´) *v.* perceived clearly; recognized as separate (p. 1165)

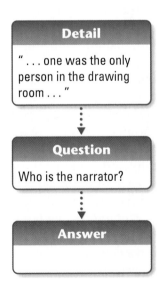

Detail

" . . . one was the only person in the drawing room . . . "

Question

Who is the narrator?

Answer

The Lady in the Looking Glass: A Reflection

Virginia Woolf

People should not leave looking glasses hanging in their rooms any more than they should leave open checkbooks or letters confessing some hideous crime. One could not help looking, that summer afternoon, in the long glass that hung outside in the hall. Chance had so arranged it. From the depths of the sofa in the drawing room one could see reflected in the Italian glass not only the marble-topped table opposite, but a stretch of the garden beyond. One could see a long grass path leading between banks of tall flowers until, slicing off an angle, the gold rim cut it off.

The house was empty, and one felt, since one was the only person in the drawing room, like one of those naturalists who, covered with grass and leaves, lie watching the shyest animals—badgers, otters, king-fishers—moving about freely, themselves unseen. The room that afternoon was full of such shy creatures, lights and shadows, curtains blowing, petals falling—things that never happen, so it seems, if someone is looking. The quiet old country room with its rugs and stone chimney pieces, its sunken bookcases and red and gold lacquer cabinets, was full of such nocturnal creatures. They came pirouetting across the floor, stepping delicately with high-lifted feet and spread tails and pecking allusive beaks as if they had been cranes or flocks of elegant flamingoes whose pink was faded, or peacocks whose trains were veiled with silver. And there were obscure flushes and darkening too, as if a cuttlefish had suddenly <u>suffused</u> the air with purple; and the room had its passions and rages and envies and sorrows coming over it and clouding it, like a human being. Nothing stayed the same for two seconds together.

Reading Strategy
Questioning What questions about the narrator does this paragraph prompt?

suffused (sə fyōozd′) v. spread throughout; filled

But, outside, the looking glass reflected the hall table, the sunflowers, the garden path so accurately and so fixedly that they seemed held there in their reality unescapably. It was a strange contrast—all changing here, all stillness there. One could not help looking from one to the other. Meanwhile, since all the doors and windows were open in the heat, there was a perpetual sighing and ceasing sound, the voice of the <u>transient</u> and the perishing, it seemed, coming and going like human breath, while in the looking glass things had ceased to breathe and lay still in the trance of immortality.

transient (tran´ shənt) *n.* that which passes quickly

✔**Reading Check**

Where is the narrator?

The Garden of Love, (detail), Walter Richard Sickert, The Fitzwilliam Museum, Cambridge

▲ **Critical Viewing** This story is a stream-of-consciousness narrative, in which thoughts, dreams, and ideas blend together to reveal a story. What aspects of this painting mirror this style of writing? **[Interpret]**

The Lady in the Looking Glass: A Reflection ◆ 1159

Half an hour ago the mistress of the house, Isabella Tyson, had gone down the grass path in her thin summer dress, carrying a basket, and had vanished, sliced off by the gilt rim of the looking glass. She had gone presumably into the lower garden to pick flowers; or as it seemed more natural to suppose, to pick something light and fantastic and leafy and trailing, traveler's-joy, or one of those elegant sprays of convolvulus that twine round ugly walls and burst here and there into white and violet blossoms. She suggested the fantastic and the tremulous convolvulus rather than the upright aster, the starched zinnia, or her own burning roses alight like lamps on the straight posts of their rose trees. The comparison showed how very little, after all these years, one knew about her; for it is impossible that any woman of flesh and blood of fifty-five or sixty should be really a wreath or a tendril. Such comparisons are worse than idle and superficial—they are cruel even, for they come like the convolvulus itself trembling between one's eyes and the truth. There must be truth; there must be a wall. Yet it was strange that after knowing her all these years one could not say what the truth about Isabella was; one still made up phrases like this about convolvulus and traveler's-joy. As for facts, it was a fact that she was a spinster; that she was rich; that she had bought this house and collected with her own hands—often in the most obscure corners of the world and at great risk from poisonous stings and Oriental diseases— the rugs, the chairs, the cabinets which now lived their nocturnal life before one's eyes. Sometimes it seemed as if they knew more about her than we, who sat on them, wrote at them, and trod on them so carefully, were allowed to know. In each of these cabinets were many little drawers, and each almost certainly held letters, tied with bows of ribbon, sprinkled with sticks of lavender or rose leaves. For it was another fact—if facts were what one wanted—that Isabella had known many people, had had many friends; and thus if one had the audacity to open a drawer and read her letters, one would find the traces of many agitations, of appointments to meet, of <u>upbraidings</u> for not having met, long letters of intimacy and affection, violent letters of jealousy and reproach, terrible final words of parting—for all those interviews and assignations had led to nothing—that is, she had never married, and yet, judging from the masklike indifference of her face, she had gone through twenty times more of passion and experience than those whose loves are trumpeted forth for all the world to hear. Under the stress of thinking about Isabella, her room became more shadowy and symbolic; the corners seemed darker, the legs of chairs and tables more spindly and hieroglyphic.

▼ **Critical Viewing** In what way does this image, like the story, suggest that mirrors show the truth? **[Connect]**

upbraidings (up brād′ iŋz) *n.* stern words of disapproval; scoldings

Suddenly these reflections were ended violently and yet without a sound. A large black form loomed into the looking glass; blotted out everything, strewed the table with a packet of marble tablets veined with pink and gray, and was gone. But the picture was entirely altered. For the moment it was unrecognizable and irrational and entirely out of focus. One could not relate these tablets to any human purpose. And then by degrees some logical process set to work on them and began ordering and arranging them and bringing them into the fold of common experience. One realized at last that they were merely letters. The man had brought the post.

There they lay on the marble-topped table, all dripping with light and color at first and crude and unabsorbed. And then it was strange to see how they were drawn in and arranged and composed and made part of the picture and granted that stillness and immortality which the looking glass conferred. They lay there invested with a new reality and significance and with a greater heaviness, too, as if it would have needed a chisel to dislodge them from the table. And, whether it was fancy or not, they seemed to have become not merely a handful of casual letters but to be tablets graven with eternal truth—if one could read them, one would know everything there was to be known about Isabella, yes, and about life, too. The pages inside those marble-looking envelopes must be cut deep and scored thick with meaning. Isabella would come in, and take them, one by one, very slowly, and open them, and read them carefully word by word, and then with a profound sigh of comprehension, as if she had seen to the bottom of everything, she would tear the envelopes to little bits and tie the letters together and lock the cabinet drawer in her determination to conceal what she did not wish to be known.

The thought served as a challenge. Isabella did not wish to be known—but she should no longer escape. It was absurd, it was monstrous. If she concealed so much and knew so much one must prize her open with the first tool that came to hand—the imagination. One must fix one's mind upon her at that very moment. One must fasten her down there. One must refuse to be put off any longer with sayings and doings such as the moment brought forth—with dinners and visits and polite conversations. One must put oneself in her shoes. If one took the phrase literally, it was easy to see the shoes in which she stood, down in the lower garden, at this moment. They were very narrow and long and fashionable —they were made of the softest and most flexible leather. Like everything she wore, they were exquisite. And she would be standing under the high hedge in the lower part of the garden, raising the scissors that were tied to her waist to cut some dead flower, some overgrown branch. The sun would beat down on her face, into her eyes; but no, at the critical moment a veil of cloud covered the sun, making the expression of her eyes doubtful—was it mocking or tender, brilliant or dull? One could only see the indeterminate outline of her rather faded, fine face looking at the sky. She was thinking, perhaps, that she must order a new

Literary Analysis
Point of View What effect does the narrator's attention to the workings of his or her own mind have on the narration?

Literary Analysis
Point of View In what way does this paragraph illustrate the use of stream-of-consciousness narration?

✔**Reading Check**

What interrupts the narrator's reflection?

net for the strawberries; that she must send flowers to Johnson's widow; that it was time she drove over to see the Hippesleys in their new house. Those were the things she talked about at dinner certainly. But one was tired of the things that she talked about at dinner. It was her profounder state of being that one wanted to catch and turn to words, the state that is to the mind what breathing is to the body, what one calls happiness or unhappiness. At the mention of those words it became obvious, surely, that she must be happy. She was rich; she was distinguished; she had many friends; she traveled—she bought rugs in Turkey and blue pots in Persia. Avenues of pleasure radiated this way and that from where she stood with her scissors raised to cut the trembling branches while the lacy clouds veiled her face.

Here with a quick movement of her scissors she snipped the spray of traveler's-joy and it fell to the ground. As it fell, surely some light came in too, surely one could penetrate a little farther into her being. Her mind then was filled with tenderness and regret. . . . To cut an overgrown branch saddened her because it had once lived, and life was dear to her. Yes, and at the same time the fall of the branch would suggest to her how she must die herself and all the futility and <u>evanescence</u> of things. And then again quickly catching this thought up, with her instant good sense, she thought life had treated her well; even if fall she must, it was to lie on the earth and molder sweetly into the roots of violets. So she stood thinking. Without making any thought precise—for she was one of those <u>reticent</u> people whose minds hold their thoughts enmeshed in clouds of silence—she was filled with thoughts. Her mind was like her room, in which lights advanced and retreated, came pirouetting and stepping delicately, spread their tails, pecked their way; and then her whole being was suffused, like the room again, with a cloud of some profound knowledge, some unspoken regret, and then she was full of locked drawers, stuffed with letters, like her cabinets. To talk of "prizing her open" as if she were an oyster, to use any but the finest and subtlest and most pliable tools upon her was impious and absurd. One must imagine—here was she in the looking glass. It made one start.

She was so far off at first that one could not see her clearly. She came lingering and pausing, here straightening a rose, there lifting a pink to smell it, but she never stopped; and all the time she became larger and larger in the looking glass, more and more completely the person into whose mind one had been trying to penetrate. One verified her by degrees—fitted the qualities one had discovered into this visible body. There were her gray-green dress, and her long shoes, her basket, and something sparkling at her throat. She came so

▲ Critical Viewing
Make an analogy comparing an unopened letter like this one with Isabella as seen by the narrator. **[Connect]**

evanescence (ev´ ə nes´ əns) *n.* vanishing or tendency to vanish

reticent (ret´ ə sənt) *adj.* silent; reserved

gradually that she did not seem to derange the pattern in the glass, but only to bring in some new element which gently moved and altered the other objects as if asking them, courteously, to make room for her. And the letters and the table and the grass walk and the sunflowers which had been waiting in the looking glass separated and opened out so that she might be received among them. At last there she was, in the hall. She stopped dead. She stood by the table. She stood perfectly still. At once the looking glass began to pour over her a light that seemed to fix her; that seemed like some acid to bite off the unessential and superficial and to leave only the truth. It was an enthralling spectacle. Everything dropped from her—clouds, dress, basket, diamond—all that one had called the creeper and convolvulus. Here was the hard wall beneath. Here was the woman herself. She stood naked in that pitiless light. And there was nothing. Isabella was perfectly empty. She had no thoughts. She had no friends. She cared for nobody. As for her letters, they were all bills. Look, as she stood there, old and angular, veined and lined, with her high nose and her wrinkled neck, she did not even trouble to open them.

People should not leave looking glasses hanging in their rooms.

Review and Assess

Thinking About the Selection

1. **Respond:** How did you feel toward Isabella Tyson by the end of the story?

2. **(a) Recall:** Where are the narrator and Isabella, respectively, at the opening of the story? **(b) Infer:** From what perspective does the narrator observe Isabella? **(c) Speculate:** Who might the narrator be? Explain.

3. **(a) Recall:** Briefly describe the layout and furnishings of the room in the story. **(b) Summarize:** How does the looking glass "guide" the narrator to an understanding of Isabella? **(c) Interpret:** What does the last sentence of the story, repeated from the beginning, mean?

4. **(a) Draw Conclusions:** In the story, what is the relation between imagination and "the hard wall" of the truth? **(b) Make a Judgment:** Is Isabella really "perfectly empty," or has the narrator's imagination run dry? Explain.

5. **Criticize:** Does Woolf succeed in creating a vivid portrait of Isabella? Why or why not?

6. **(a) Apply:** Do you think that you can ever "fasten someone down" and know his or her true nature with certainty? Explain. **(b) Take a Position:** Is the fact that a person is easy to get to know a mark his or her integrity? Explain.

The First Year of My Life

Muriel Spark

Background

The title of Spark's story refers to 1918, the final year of World War I. For over three years, Britain—allied with France, Italy, Russia, and the United States—had fought against Germany, Austria-Hungary, and Turkey. Spark's narrator "observes" a number of wartime events and leaders.

I was born on the first day of the second month of the last year of the First World War, a Friday. Testimony abounds that during the first year of my life I never smiled. I was known as the baby whom nothing and no one could make smile. Everyone who knew me then has told me so. They tried very hard, singing and bouncing me up and down, jumping around, pulling faces. Many times I was told this later by my family and their friends; but, anyway, I knew it at the time.

You will shortly be hearing of that new school of psychology, or maybe you have heard of it already, which after long and far-adventuring research and experiment has established that all of the young of the human species are born <u>omniscient</u>. Babies, in their waking hours, know everything that is going on everywhere in the world; they can tune in to any conversation they choose, switch on to any scene. We have all experienced this power. It is only after the first year that it was brainwashed out of us; for it is demanded of us by our immediate environment that we grow to be of use to it in a practical way. Gradually, our know-all brain-cells are blacked out, although traces remain in some individuals in the form of E.S.P., and in the adults of some primitive tribes.

It is not a new theory. Poets and philosophers, as usual, have been there first. But scientific proof is now ready and to hand. Perhaps the final touches are being put to the new manifesto[1] in some cell at Harvard University. Any day now it will be given to the world, and the world will be convinced.

> **omniscient** (äm nish´ ənt) *adj.* having infinite knowledge; knowing all

---

1. **manifesto** (man´ ə fes´ tō) *n.* public declaration of motives and intentions.

Let me therefore get my word in first, because I feel pretty sure, now, about the <u>authenticity</u> of my remembrance of things past. My autobiography, as I very well perceived at the time, started in the very worst year that the world had ever seen so far. Apart from being born bedridden and toothless, unable to raise myself on the pillow or utter anything but farmyard squawks or police-siren wails, my bladder and my bowels totally out of control, I was further depressed by the curious behavior of the two-legged mammals around me. There were those black-dressed people, females of the species to which I appeared to belong, saying they had lost their sons. I slept a great deal. Let them go and find their sons. It was like the special pin for my nappies[2] which my mother or some other hoverer dedicated to my care was always losing. These careless women in black lost their husbands and their brothers. Then they came to visit my mother and clucked and crowed over my cradle. I was not amused.

"Babies never really smile till they're three months old," said my mother. "They're not *supposed* to smile till they're three months old."

My brother, aged six, marched up and down with a toy rifle over his shoulder:

> The grand old Duke of York
> He had ten thousand men;
> He marched them up to the top of the hill
> And he marched them down again.
>
> And when they were up, they were up.
> And when they were down, they were down.
> And when they were neither down nor up
> They were neither up nor down.

"Just listen to him!"
"Look at him with his rifle!"

I was about ten days old when Russia stopped fighting. I tuned in to the Czar,[3] a prisoner, with the rest of his family, since evidently the country had put him off his throne and there had been a revolution not long before I was born. Everyone was talking about it. I tuned in to the Czar. "Nothing would ever induce me to sign the treaty of Brest-Litovsk,"[4] he said to his wife. Anyway, nobody had asked him to.

At this point I was sleeping twenty hours a day to get my strength up. And from what I <u>discerned</u> in the other four hours of the day I knew I was going to need it. The Western Front on my frequency was sheer blood, mud, dismembered bodies, blistered crashes, hectic flashes of light in the night skies, explosions, total terror. Since it was

---

2. **nappies** (nap´ ēz) *n.* British term for diapers.
3. **Czar** Czar Nicholas II of Russia, who was removed from power during the Russian Revolution of 1917.
4. **treaty of Brest-Litovsk** treaty in which Russia's new Communist government made peace with Germany and withdrew from the war eight months before its end.

---

authenticity (ô´ thən tis´ ə tē) *n.* reality; genuineness

Literary Analysis
Point of View Does the narrator understand everything that she "knows"? Explain.

Reading Strategy
Questioning What question might you ask about the author's purpose in including this scene with the narrator's brother? Explain.

discerned (di zʉrnd´) *v.* perceived clearly; recognized as separate

 **Reading Check**

What does the narrator claim to have known during the first year of her life?

plain I had been born into a bad moment in the history of the world, the future bothered me, unable as I was to raise my head from the pillow and as yet only twenty inches long. "I truly wish I were a fox or a bird," D. H. Lawrence[5] was writing to somebody . . . I fell asleep.

Red sheets of flame shot across the sky. It was 21 March, the fiftieth day of my life, and the German Spring Offensive[6] had started before my morning feed. Infinite slaughter. I scowled at the scene, and made an effort to kick out. But the attempt was feeble. Furious, and impatient for some strength, I wailed for my feed. After which I stopped wailing but continued to scowl.

> The grand old Duke of York
> He had ten thousand men . . .

They rocked the cradle. I never heard a sillier song. Over in Berlin and Vienna the people were starving, freezing, striking, rioting and yelling in the streets. In London everyone was bustling to work and muttering that it was time the whole . . . business was over.

The big people around me bared their teeth; that meant a smile, it meant they were pleased or amused. They spoke of ration cards[7] for meat and sugar and butter.

---

5. **D. H. Lawrence** (1885–1930) English novelist and poet.
6. **German Spring Offensive** After signing the peace treaty with Russia in March of 1918, Germany began to push to win the war along the western front.
7. **ration cards** used to limit individuals' purchases of goods that were in short supply during the war.

▲ Critical Viewing This story takes place in 1918, the last year of World War I. Judging by this photograph from the time, would you say the soldiers pictured were excited, weary, or numb? **[Infer]**

Literary Analysis
Point of View How does this paragraph demonstrate Spark's unusual form of omniscient narration?

"Where will it all end?"

I went to sleep. I woke and tuned into Bernard Shaw[8] who was telling someone to shut up. I switched over to Joseph Conrad[9] who, strangely enough, was saying precisely the same thing. I still didn't think it worth a smile, although it was expected of me any day now. I got on to Turkey. Women draped in black huddled and chattered in their harems; yak-yak-yak. This was boring, so I came back to home base.

In and out came and went the women in British black. My mother's brother, dressed in his uniform, came coughing. He had been poison-gassed in the trenches. *"Tout le monde à la bataille!"*[10] declaimed Marshal Foch[11] the old swine. He was now Commander-in-Chief of the Allied Forces. My uncle coughed from deep within his lungs, never to recover but destined to return to the Front. His brass buttons gleamed in the firelight. I weighed twelve pounds by now; I stretched and kicked for exercise, seeing that I had a lifetime before me, coping with this crowd. I took six feeds a day and kept most of them down by the time the *Vindictive* was sunk in Ostend harbor,[12] on which day I kicked with special vigor in my bath.

In France the conscripted[13] soldiers leapfrogged over the dead on the advance and littered the fields with limbs and hands, or drowned in the mud. The strongest men on all fronts were dead before I was born. Now the sentries[14] used bodies for barricades and the fighting men were unhealthy from the start. I checked my toes and fingers, knowing I was going to need them. *The Playboy of the Western World* was playing at the Court Theatre in London, but occasionally I beamed over to the House of Commons[15] which made me drop off gently to sleep. Generally, I preferred the Western Front[16] where one got the true state of affairs. It was essential to know the worst, blood and explosions and all, for one had to be prepared, as the boy scouts said. Virginia Woolf[17] yawned and reached for her diary. Really, I preferred the Western Front.

In the fifth month of my life I could raise my head from my pillow and hold it up. I could grasp the objects that were held out to me. Some of these things rattled and squawked. I gnawed on them to get my teeth started. "She hasn't smiled yet?" said the dreary old aunties.

---

8. **Bernard Shaw** George Bernard Shaw (1856–1950), British dramatist and critic.
9. **Joseph Conrad** (1857–1924) English novelist, born in Poland.
10. *Tout le monde à la bataille* (too̅ lə mônd´ ä lä bä tī´) The whole world into the battle!
11. **Marshal Foch** (fôsh) Ferdinand Foch, a French general who, after March 1918, became commander of all Allied forces on the Western Front.
12. *Vindictive* **was sunk in Ostend harbor** referring to a ship sunk in May 1918 by Allied forces to block the harbor of Ostend, Belgium, used by the Germans as a submarine base.
13. **conscripted** (kən skript´ əd) *adj.* enrolled for compulsory service in the armed service.
14. **sentries** (sen´ trēs) *n.* men of the military guard.
15. **House of Commons** lower house of British Parliament.
16. **Western Front** 450-mile-long battlefront starting in Belgium and moving across France. This line is where the allies and Germany engaged in trench warfare from 1914 to 1918.
17. **Virginia Woolf** (1882–1941) English novelist and critic.

Reading Strategy
Questioning What questions do the references to Conrad and Shaw suggest to you?

Reading Check

Identify two different kinds of scenes of which the narrator is aware.

The First Year of My Life ◆ 1167

My mother, on the defensive, said I was probably one of those late smilers. On my wavelength Pablo Picasso[18] was getting married and early in that month of July the Silver Wedding of King George V and Queen Mary was celebrated in joyous pomp at St. Paul's Cathedral. They drove through the streets of London with their children. Twenty-five years of domestic happiness. A lot of fuss and ceremonial handing over of swords went on at the Guildhall where the King and Queen received a check for $53,000 to dispose of for charity as they thought fit. *Tout le monde à la bataille!* Income tax in England had reached six shillings in the pound. Everyone was talking about the Silver Wedding; yak-yak-yak, and ten days later the Czar and his family, now in Siberia, were invited to descend to a little room in the basement. Crack, crack, went the guns; screams and blood all over the place, and that was the end of the Romanoffs.[19] I flexed my muscles. "A fine healthy baby," said the doctor; which gave me much satisfaction.

Tout le monde à la bataille! That included my gassed uncle. My health had improved to the point where I was able to crawl in my playpen. Bertrand Russell[20] was still cheerily in prison for writing something seditious about pacifism. Tuning in as usual to the Front Lines it looked as if the Germans were winning all the battles yet losing the war. And so it was. The upper-income people were upset about the income tax at six shillings to the pound. But all women over thirty got the vote. "It seems a long time to wait," said one of my drab old aunts, aged twenty-two. The speeches in the House of Commons always sent me to sleep which was why I missed, at the actual time, a certain oration by Mr. Asquith[21] following the armistice on 11 November.[22] Mr. Asquith was a greatly esteemed former prime minister later to be an Earl, and had been ousted by Mr. Lloyd George.[23] I clearly heard Asquith, in private, refer to Lloyd George as "that . . . Welsh goat."

---

18. **Pablo** (pä´ blō) **Picasso** (pi kä´ sō) (1881–1973) Spanish painter and sculptor.
19. **Romanoffs** (rō mə nôfs´) ruling family of Russia from 1613 to 1917.
20. **Bertrand Russell** (1872–1970) British philosopher, mathematician, and writer.
21. **Mr. Asquith** (as´ kwith) Herbert Henry Asquith (1852–1928), Prime Minister of Britain from 1908–1916.
22. **armistice on 11 November** the agreement that brought World War I to an end.
23. **Mr. Lloyd George** David Lloyd George (1863–1945), British Prime Minister from 1916 to 1922.

Reading Strategy
Questioning What questions might this paragraph lead you to ask about the writer's purpose?

▼ **Critical Viewing** What does the one-year-old in this photograph seem to be thinking? Contrast her probable thoughts with those of the narrator. **[Compare and Contrast]**

The armistice was signed and I was awake for that. I pulled myself on to my feet with the aid of the bars of my cot. My teeth were coming through very nicely in my opinion, and well worth all the trouble I was put to in bringing them forth. I weighed twenty pounds. On all the world's fighting fronts the men killed in action or dead of wounds numbered 8,538,315 and the warriors wounded and maimed were 21,219,452. With these figures in mind I sat up in my high chair and banged my spoon on the table. One of my mother's black-draped friends recited:

> I have a rendezvous with Death
> At some disputed barricade,
> When spring comes back with rustling shade
> And apple blossoms fill the air—
> I have a rendezvous with Death.[24]

Most of the poets, they said, had been killed. The poetry made them dab their eyes with clean white handkerchiefs.

Next February on my first birthday, there was a birthday-cake with one candle. Lots of children and their elders. The war had been over two months and twenty-one days. "Why doesn't she smile?" My brother was to blow out the candle. The elders were talking about the war and the political situation. Lloyd George and Asquith, Asquith and Lloyd George. I remembered recently having switched on to Mr. Asquith at a private party where he had been drinking a lot. He was playing cards and when he came to cut the cards he tried to cut a large box of matches by mistake. On another occasion I had seen him putting his arm around a lady's shoulder in a Daimler motor car, and generally behaving towards her in a very friendly fashion. Strangely enough she said, "If you don't stop this nonsense immediately, I'll order the chauffeur to stop and I'll get out." Mr. Asquith replied, "And pray, what reason will you give?" Well anyway it was my feeding time.

The guests arrived for my birthday. It was so sad, said one of the black widows, so sad about Wilfred Owen[25] who was killed so late in the war, and she quoted from a poem of his:

> What passing-bells for these who die as cattle?
> Only the monstrous anger of the guns.[26]

The children were squealing and toddling around. One was sick and another wet the floor and stood with his legs apart gaping at the puddle. All was mopped up. I banged my spoon on the table of my high chair.

> But I've a rendezvous with Death
> At midnight in some flaming town;

24. **I . . . Death** from the poem "I Have a Rendezvous with Death" by American poet Alan Seeger, killed in war.
25. **Wilfred Owen** (1893–1918) English poet.
26. **What . . . guns** from Wilfred Owen's "Anthem for Doomed Youth" (see p. 1053 for the complete poem).

Literary Analysis
Point of View How does the contrast between the speaker's babyish actions and her knowledge contrast with the typical role of a first-person narrator?

Literary Analysis
Point of View In what way does Spark's use of point of view suggest that she has cut and pasted her story together from different points of view?

Reading Check
What occurs in the narrator's life after the armistice?

When spring trips north again this year,
And I to my pledged word am true,
I shall not fail that rendezvous.

More parents and children arrived. One stout man who was warming his behind at the fire, said, "I always think those words of Asquith's after the armistice were so apt. . . ."

They brought the cake close to my high chair for me to see, with the candle shining and flickering above the pink icing. "A pity she never smiles."

"She'll smile in time," my mother said, obviously upset.

"What Asquith told the House of Commons just after the war," said that stout gentleman with his backside to the fire, "—so apt, what Asquith said. He said that the war has cleansed and purged the world . . . I recall his actual words: 'All things have become new. In this great cleansing and purging it has been the privilege of our country to play her part. . . .'"

That did it. I broke into a decided smile and everyone noticed it, convinced that it was provoked by the fact that my brother had blown out the candle on the cake. "She smiled!" my mother exclaimed. And everyone was clucking away about how I was smiling. For good measure I crowed like a demented raven. "My baby's smiling," said my mother.

"It was the candle on her cake," they said.

. . . . Since that time I have grown to smile quite naturally, like any other healthy and house-trained person, but when I really mean a smile, deeply felt from the core, then to all intents and purposes it comes in response to the words uttered in the House of Commons after the First World War by the distinguished, the immaculately dressed and the late Mr. Asquith.

Review and Assess

Thinking About the Selection

1. **(a) Recall:** What special power does the narrator possess?
   (b) Infer: Sum up what you learn about World War I from the narrator's "news briefs" and from the poems.

2. **Interpret:** What statement is the narrator making with her first smile?

3. **Support:** Why does Spark's attempt to combine details of her infancy with the history of the time seem absurd?

4. **(a) Compare and Contrast:** Compare Spark's idea of a "firsthand account" with the typical use of this notion.
   (b) Draw Conclusions: What does Spark's version of a "firsthand account" say about our attempts to tell of war?

5. **Apply:** Is the message of the story relevant today? Explain.

Review and Assess

Literary Analysis

Point of View: Modern Experiments

1. Give three examples of the use of the **stream-of-consciousness** technique in Woolf's narrative.

2. (a) How does the literal reflection of Isabella in the mirror serve as a climax for the narrator's mental reflections? (b) What does this climax reveal about Isabella?

3. (a) How does Spark explain her unusual omniscient narrator? (b) In what way is a person telling about her own infancy like a historian, reporter, or politician telling the story of a war?

Comparing Literary Works

4. Compare Spark's narrative technique to Woolf's, using a chart like the one shown.

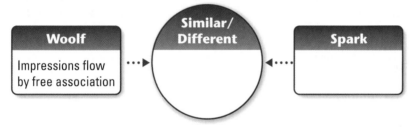

Woolf	Similar/ Different	Spark
Impressions flow by free association		

5. What does Woolf's use of the stream-of-consciousness technique show about how we construct a picture of another person?

6. What contrast between the reality and the representation of war does the narrator make in "The First Year of My Life"?

7. Which story offers more hope for our ability to penetrate appearances and discover reality? Explain.

Reading Strategy

Questioning

8. (a) In Woolf's story, what questions about the narrator might you ask? (b) What answers does the story suggest?

9. (a) What questions arise from the final paragraph of Spark's story? (b) What light do these questions shed on the theme?

Extend Understanding

10. **Science Connection:** How might a psychologist gain insight into a person through the person's free associations?

Quick Review

Point of view is the perspective from which a story is told.

Stream-of-consciousness narration presents the flow of thoughts in a character's mind.

An **omniscient narrator** knows more than any single character can.

To understand a work of fiction, ask **questions** as you read based on details in the work.

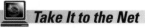 **Take It to the Net**
www.phschool.com
Take the interactive self-test online to check your understanding of these selections.

Integrate Language Skills

Vocabulary Development Lesson

Word Analysis: Latin Prefix -trans-

The Latin prefix -trans-, meaning "through" or "across," appears in the word *transient*, meaning "passing through quickly." Use the meaning of the prefix to define these phrases from the social sciences.

1. transnational corporation
2. social transaction
3. transatlantic communication

Spelling Strategy

When a *c* in a word creates a *sh* or *ch* sound, it may be followed by *ie*, as in *omniscient*, but not by *ei*. On your paper, complete the following words by adding the *ie* or *ei* that is needed.

1. anc__nt   2. perc__ve   3. suffic__nt

Fluency: Sentence Completions

On your paper, fill in each blank with the most suitable word from the vocabulary list on page 1157.

The ___?___ baby in Spark's story knew everything. She may have been ___?___ with regard to her power, not telling the adults, but there is no doubt as to the ___?___ of her abilities. She ___?___ events on remote battlefields, no matter how ___?___ they were. The ___?___ of human interactions, whether tender kisses or harsh ___?___ , did not protect these events from her knowledge. She was ___?___ with joy as she exercised her strange powers.

Grammar and Style Lesson

Subject-Verb Agreement in Inverted Sentences

A verb must agree in number with its subject even when the verb precedes the subject in the sentence. Such sentences, called **inverted sentences,** often begin with *here* or *there*. They may also begin with prepositional phrases. In these cases, do not be misled into thinking that the subject is *here*, *there*, or any nouns or pronouns that are part of a phrase preceding the verb.

> **Plural Subject:** There (were) her gray-green dress, and her long shoes, . . .

Inverted sentences may be used by writers to throw emphasis on the words that are out of order.

Practice On your paper, identify the subject in each sentence and choose the verb that agrees.

1. And there (was, were) obscure flushes and darkening too. . . .
2. . . . there (was, were) a perpetual sighing and ceasing sound . . .
3. In each of these cabinets (was, were) many little drawers. . . .
4. There (was, were) those black-dressed people, . . .
5. Next February on my first birthday, there (was, were) a birthday cake with one candle.

Writing Application Write a paragraph describing the reflection in a mirror in a room you know. Use two sentences in inverted form.

WG *Prentice Hall Writing and Grammar Connection: Chapter 20, Section 3*

Writing Lesson

Essay on a Literary Theme

Woolf's story suggests that our knowledge of others is clouded by the web of associations and assumptions we weave around them. Write an essay on our knowledge of others, considering whether Woolf's ideas are true or exaggerated.

Prewriting   Review the story. Use a chart like the one shown to compare Isabella as "seen" through the mirror with the "real" Isabella. Summarize Woolf's ideas about our knowledge of others. Then, jot down your own ideas about knowing others, and make a judgment about Woolf's position.

Model: Analyzing a Theme by Contrasting Details

Inference from "Mirror" View	Evidence	Inference About "Real" Isabella	Evidence

Drafting   Begin by presenting Woolf's idea of knowledge, supporting your claims with details from the story. Then, using generalizations from your own experience, explain your response to her idea.

Revising   Review your draft, adding support for your ideas where necessary.

 Prentice Hall Writing and Grammar Connection: Chapter 14, Section 2

Extension Activities

Research and Technology Before Woolf wrote her stream-of-consciousness narratives, Sigmund Freud used free association as a technique in therapy. Write a **report on cultural trends** comparing Freud's method with Woolf's technique. Begin with these steps:

- Formulate a description of Woolf's technique.
- Do preliminary research on Freud's method.
- Develop a set of clear research questions and answer them through additional research.

Listening and Speaking Lead a **discussion group** on literary responses to World War I. Begin by preparing readings of poems by Alan Seeger and Wilfred Owen, mentioned by Spark. Read aloud the poems you have chosen. Then, lead a discussion comparing the tone and mood of these poems with the tone and mood of Spark's story. **[Group Activity]**

 **Take It to the Net**   www.phschool.com

Go online for an additional research activity using the Internet.

Prepare to Read

The Rocking-Horse Winner ◆
A Shocking Accident

D. H. Lawrence (1885–1930)

During his lifetime, D. H. Lawrence's literary achievements were overshadowed by controversy. Like Percy Bysshe Shelley and Lord Byron in their day, Lawrence took unorthodox positions on politics and morality that shocked mainstream society.

Early Years Lawrence was born in Eastwood, Nottinghamshire, the son of an almost illiterate coal miner father and a more educated mother. Through her influence, he pursued a scholarship to the Nottingham High School, where he studied from 1898 to 1901. After leaving school for a job as a clerk, he contracted pneumonia and, on recovering, became a teacher.

Lawrence also began to write poems, stories, and novels, and his poetry attracted the attention of the well-known writer and editor Ford Madox Ford. In 1913, Lawrence published his first major novel, *Sons and Lovers*, a thinly disguised autobiography. Two years later, he published *The Rainbow*, which was banned in Britain.

Travels Abroad During World War I, Lawrence and his German wife, Frieda, lived in poverty in England and were unreasonably suspected of being German spies. At the end of the war, they left England and never returned. They traveled to Italy, Ceylon, Australia, Mexico, and the United States, and Lawrence used many of these locales in his fiction. In 1920, he published *Women in Love*, one of his greatest novels. A few years later, although suffering from tuberculosis, he completed *Lady Chatterley's Lover*. Shortly afterward, in the south of France, he died from that disease.

In the years since Lawrence's death, society's views of his writings have changed profoundly. Today, his fiction is widely admired for its vivid settings, fine craftsmanship, and psychological insight.

Graham Greene (1904–1991)

The search for salvation, a theme addressed by poets like T. S. Eliot, is a central concern in the fiction of novelist Graham Greene. Like Eliot, Greene was a religious convert who wrote works exploring pain, fear, despair, and alienation.

Journalism and Travel The son of a schoolmaster, Greene was born in Berkhamsted in Hertfordshire. He converted to Roman Catholicism after studying at Oxford University. Then, he began working as a copy editor in London and married. Eventually, he became a traveling freelance journalist.

Thrillers and More His journalism helped him develop the powers of observation, sensitivity to atmosphere, and simplicity of language that became hallmarks of his fiction. While traveling, he was able to scout out locations for his stories and novels.

Some of these novels, such as *Orient Express* (1932), he called "entertainments." These were an unusual type of thriller that went beyond the genre in its concern with moral issues.

Even more deeply involved with spiritual crisis, however, were such Greene classics as *Brighton Rock* (1938), *The Power and the Glory* (1940), and two novels set in Africa, *The Heart of the Matter* (1948) and *A Burnt-Out Case* (1961). In these works, Greene's concern with salvation burns with intensity.

Psychological Insight Greene's best fiction focuses on the psychology of human character rather than on plot. Many of his protagonists are people without roots or beliefs—people in pain. They may be odd, but they almost always excite the reader's curiosity and pity—and, almost always, Greene treats them with compassion as they strive to achieve salvation.

Preview

Connecting to the Literature

In each of these stories, characters look for someone whom they can trust with secrets or sensitive information.

Literary Analysis

Theme and Symbol

Most short stories contain a **theme,** a central idea or question, that the writer explores. Writers often reveal theme through a **symbol,** a person, object, or action that suggests deeper meanings. To identify symbols, look for descriptions that carry a special emphasis. In this passage from "The Rocking-Horse Winner," the underlined words suggest that the horse is a symbol:

> . . . he would sit on his big rocking horse, <u>charging madly into space</u>, with a <u>frenzy</u> that made the little girls peer at him uneasily.

As you read, identify symbols and use the meanings they suggest to figure out the author's central idea or concern.

Comparing Literary Works

Each of these stories is told from a **third-person point of view,** meaning that the narrator does not take part in the action. As you read, compare the ways in which both authors use this point of view to reveal their themes: for example, by disclosing the thoughts of characters and by creating symbols to suggest meanings. Also ask yourself how the third-person point of view is different in each story. Consider, for instance, whether Greene's narrative has the same intensity as Lawrence's.

Reading Strategy

Identifying With a Character

Identifying with a character—putting yourself in that character's place in order to understand his or her feelings, needs, problems, and goals—can help you understand the theme of a work. As you read, fill in a chart like this one to help you identify with the main characters.

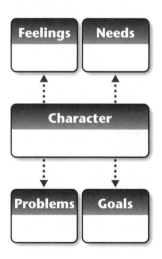

Vocabulary Development

discreet (di skrēt´) *adj.* wise; prudent (p. 1177)

brazening (brā´ zən in) *v.* daring boldly or shamelessly (p. 1179)

careered (kə rird´) *v.* rushed wildly (p. 1179)

obstinately (äb´ stə nət lē) *adv.* in a determined way; stubbornly (p. 1182)

uncanny (un kan´ ē) *adj.* mysterious; hard to explain (p. 1183)

remonstrated (ri män´ strāt´ id) *v.* objected strongly (p. 1186)

apprehension (ap´ rē hen´ shən) *n.* anxious feeling of foreboding; dread (p. 1190)

embarked (em bärkt´) *v.* engaged in something, such as a conversation (p. 1191)

intrinsically (in trin´ sik lē) *adv.* at its core; inherently; innately (p. 1193)

The Rocking-Horse Winner

D. H. Lawrence

Background

Both these stories involve wealth and class. Britain had a rigid class structure, and its upper classes tried to live at the "right" addresses, attend the "right" schools, and have the "right" friends. In "The Rocking-Horse Winner," Paul's mother is desperate to maintain upper-class appearances despite her husband's "small income." In "A Shocking Accident," Jerome attends an "expensive preparatory school"—private schools in Britain are referred to as public schools—and must deal with classmates' reactions to a tragedy that is bizarrely improper.

here was a woman who was beautiful, who started with all the advantages, yet she had no luck. She married for love, and the love turned to dust. She had bonny children, yet she felt they had been thrust upon her, and she could not love them. They looked at her coldly, as if they were finding fault with her. And hurriedly she felt she must cover up some fault in herself. Yet what it was that she must cover up she never knew. Nevertheless, when her children were present, she always felt the center of her heart go hard. This troubled her, and in her manner she was all the more gentle and anxious for her children, as if she loved them very much. Only she herself knew that at the center of her heart was a hard little place that could not feel

Literary Analysis
Theme and Symbol What ideas about the story's theme does this first paragraph suggest?

love, no, not for anybody. Everybody else said of her: "She is such a good mother. She adores her children." Only she herself, and her children themselves, knew it was not so. They read it in each other's eyes.

There were a boy and two little girls. They lived in a pleasant house, with a garden and they had <u>discreet</u> servants, and felt themselves superior to anyone in the neighborhood.

Although they lived in style, they felt always an anxiety in the house. There was never enough money. The mother had a small income and the father had a small income, but not nearly enough for the social position which they had to keep up. The father went into town to some office. But though he had good prospects, these prospects never materialized. There was always the grinding sense of the shortage of money, though the style was always kept up.

At last the mother said, "I will see if *I* can't make something." But she did not know where to begin. She racked her brains, and tried this thing and the other, but could not find anything successful. The failure made deep lines come into her face. Her children were growing up, they would have to go to school. There must be more money, there must be more money. The father, who was always very handsome and expensive in his tastes, seemed as if he never *would* be able to do anything worth doing. And the mother, who had a great belief in herself, did not succeed any better, and her tastes were just as expensive.

And so the house came to be haunted by the unspoken phrase: *There must be more money! There must be more money!* The children could hear it all the time, though nobody said it aloud. They heard it at Christmas, when the expensive and splendid toys filled the nursery. Behind the shining modern rocking horse, behind the smart doll's house, a voice would start whispering: "There *must* be more money! There *must* be more money!" And the children would stop playing, to listen for a moment. They would look into each other's eyes to see if they had all heard. And each one saw in the eyes of the other two that they too had heard. "There *must* be more money! There *must* be more money!"

It came whispering from the springs of the still-swaying rocking horse, and even the horse, bending his wooden, champing head,

▲ **Critical Viewing**
Would the casual observer have seen Paul's family in the way that this family is depicted? Explain. **[Connect]**

discreet (di skrēt´) *adj.* wise; prudent

✓**Reading Check**
What does the mother feel toward her children?

heard it. The big doll, sitting so pink and smirking in her new pram,[1] could hear it quite plainly, and seemed to be smirking all the more self-consciously because of it. The foolish puppy, too, that took the place of the teddy bear, he was looking so extraordinarily foolish for no other reason but that he heard the secret whisper all over the house: "There *must* be more money."

Yet nobody ever said it aloud. The whisper was everywhere, and therefore no one spoke it. Just as no one ever says: "We are breathing!" in spite of the fact that breath is coming and going all the time.

"Mother!" said the boy Paul one day. "Why don't we keep a car of our own? Why do we always use uncle's, or else a taxi?"

"Because we're the poor members of the family," said the mother.

"But why *are* we, mother?"

"Well—I suppose," she said slowly and bitterly, "it's because your father has no luck."

The boy was silent for some time.

"Is luck money, mother?" he asked, rather timidly.

"No, Paul! Not quite. It's what causes you to have money."

"Oh!" said Paul vaguely. "I thought when Uncle Oscar said *filthy lucker,* it meant money."

"*Filthy lucre* does mean money," said the mother. "But it's lucre, not luck."

"Oh!" said the boy. "Then what *is* luck, mother?"

"It's what causes you to have money. If you're lucky you have money. That's why it's better to be born lucky than rich. If you're rich, you may lose your money. But if you're lucky, you will always get more money."

"Oh! Will you! And is father not lucky?"

"Very unlucky, I should say," she said bitterly.

The boy watched her with unsure eyes.

"Why?" he asked.

"I don't know. Nobody ever knows why one person is lucky and another unlucky."

"Don't they? Nobody at all? Does *nobody* know?"

"Perhaps God! But He never tells."

"He ought to, then. And aren't you lucky either, mother?"

"I can't be, if I married an unlucky husband."

"But by yourself, aren't you?"

"I used to think I was, before I married. Now I think I am very unlucky indeed."

"Why?"

"Well—never mind! Perhaps I'm not really," she said.

The child looked at her, to see if she meant it. But he saw, by the lines of her mouth, that she was only trying to hide something from him.

"Well, anyhow," he said stoutly, "I'm a lucky person."

"Why?" said his mother, with a sudden laugh.

He stared at her. He didn't even know why he had said it.

1. **pram** baby carriage.

Literary Analysis
Theme and Symbol How does this secret whispering help reveal a potential theme?

Reading Strategy
Identifying With a Character If you were Paul, what impact might this exchange have on you?

"God told me," he asserted, <u>brazening</u> it out.

"I hope He did, dear!" she said, again with a laugh, but rather bitter.

"He did, mother!"

"Excellent!" said the mother, using one of her husband's exclamations.

The boy saw she did not believe him; or rather, that she paid no attention to his assertion. This angered him somewhere, and made him want to compel her attention.

He went off by himself, vaguely, in a childish way, seeking for the clue to "luck." Absorbed, taking no heed of other people, he went about with a sort of stealth, seeking inwardly for luck. He wanted luck, he wanted it, he wanted it. When the two girls were playing dolls, in the nursery, he would sit on his big rocking horse, charging madly into space, with a frenzy that made the little girls peer at him uneasily. Wildly the horse <u>careered</u>, the waving dark hair of the boy tossed, his eyes had a strange glare in them. The little girls dared not speak to him.

When he had ridden to the end of his mad little journey, he climbed down and stood in front of his rocking horse, staring fixedly into its lowered face. Its red mouth was slightly open, its big eye was wide and glassy bright.

"Now!" he would silently command the snorting steed. "Now take me to where there is luck! Now take me!"

And he would slash the horse on the neck with the little whip he had asked Uncle Oscar for. He *knew* the horse could take him to where there was luck, if only he forced it. So he would mount again, and start on his furious ride, hoping at last to get there. He knew he could get there.

"You'll break your horse, Paul!" said the nurse.

"He's always riding like that! I wish he'd leave off!" said his elder sister Joan.

But he only glared down on them in silence. Nurse gave him up. She could make nothing of him. Anyhow he was growing beyond her.

One day his mother and his Uncle Oscar came in when he was on one of his furious rides. He did not speak to them.

"Hallo! you young jockey! Riding a winner?" said his uncle.

"Aren't you growing too big for a rocking horse? You're not a very little boy any longer, you know," said his mother.

But Paul only gave a blue glare from his big, rather close-set eyes. He would speak to nobody when he was in full tilt. His mother watched him with an anxious expression on her face.

At last he suddenly stopped forcing his horse into the mechanical gallop, and slid down.

"Well, I got there!" he announced fiercely, his blue eyes still flaring, and his sturdy long legs straddling apart.

"Where did you get to?" asked his mother.

"Where I wanted to go to," he flared back at her.

brazening (brā´ zən iŋ) v. daring boldly or shamelessly

careered (kə rird´) v. rushed wildly

**Reading Check**

What does Paul do to find "the clue to 'luck'"?

"That's right, son!" said Uncle Oscar. "Don't you stop till you get there. What's the horse's name?"

"He doesn't have a name," said the boy.

"Gets on without all right?" asked the uncle.

"Well, he has different names. He was called Sansovino last week."

"Sansovino, eh? Won the Ascot.[2] How did you know his name?"

"He always talks about horse races with Bassett," said Joan.

The uncle was delighted to find that his small nephew was posted with all the racing news. Bassett, the young gardener who had been wounded in the left foot in the war, and had got his present job through Oscar Cresswell, whose batman[3] he had been, was a perfect blade of the "turf."[4] He lived in the racing events, and the small boy lived with him.

Oscar Cresswell got it all from Bassett.

"Master Paul comes and asks me, so I can't do more than tell him, sir," said Bassett, his face terribly serious, as if he were speaking of religious matters.

"And does he ever put anything on a horse he fancies?"

"Well—I don't want to give him away—he's a young sport, a fine sport, sir. Would you mind asking him yourself? He sort of takes a pleasure in it, and perhaps he'd feel I was giving him away, sir, if you don't mind."

Bassett was serious as a church.

The uncle went back to his nephew, and took him off for a ride in the car.

"Say, Paul, old man, do you ever put anything on a horse?" the uncle asked.

The boy watched the handsome man closely.

"Why, do you think I oughtn't to?" he parried.

"Not a bit of it! I thought perhaps you might give me a tip for the Lincoln."[5]

The car sped on into the country, going down to Uncle Oscar's place in Hampshire.

"Honor bright?" said the nephew.

"Honor bright, son!" said the uncle.

"Well, then, Daffodil."

"Daffodil! I doubt it, sonny. What about Mirza?"

"I only know the winner," said the boy. "That's Daffodil!"

"Daffodil, eh?"

There was a pause. Daffodil was an obscure horse comparatively.

"Uncle!"

"Yes, son?"

"You won't let it go any further, will you? I promised Bassett."

Literary Analysis
Theme and Symbol
Bassett and the small boy "live" in the racing events. What might this detail suggest about their lives?

Reading Strategy
Identifying With a Character If you were Paul, would you feel loyal to Bassett? Why or why not?

---

2. **Ascot** major English horse race.
3. **batman** British military officer's orderly.
4. **blade . . . "turf"** horse-racing fan.
5. **Lincoln** major English horse race.

"Bassett be hanged, old man! What's he got to do with it?"

"We're partners! We've been partners from the first! Uncle, he lent me my first five shillings, which I lost. I promised him, honor bright, it was only between me and him: only you gave me that ten-shilling note I started winning with, so I thought you were lucky. You won't let it go any further, will you?"

The boy gazed at his uncle from those big, hot, blue eyes, set rather close together. The uncle stirred and laughed uneasily.

"Right you are, son! I'll keep your tip private. Daffodil, eh! How much are you putting on him?"

"All except twenty pounds," said the boy. "I keep that in reserve."

The uncle thought it a good joke.

"You keep twenty pounds in reserve, do you, you young romancer? What are you betting, then?"

"I'm betting three hundred," said the boy gravely. "But it's between you and me, Uncle Oscar! Honor bright?"

The uncle burst into a roar of laughter.

"It's between you and me all right, you young Nat Gould,"[6] he said, laughing. "But where's your three hundred?"

"Bassett keeps it for me. We're partners."

"You are, are you! And what is Bassett putting on Daffodil?"

"He won't go quite as high as I do, I expect. Perhaps he'll go a hundred and fifty."

"What, pennies?" laughed the uncle.

"Pounds," said the child, with a surprised look at his uncle. "Bassett keeps a bigger reserve than I do."

Between wonder and amusement, Uncle Oscar was silent. He pursued the matter no further, but he determined to take his nephew with him to the Lincoln races.

"Now, son," he said, "I'm putting twenty on Mirza, and I'll put five for you on any horse you fancy. What's your pick?"

"Daffodil, uncle!"

"No, not the fiver on Daffodil!"

"I should if it was my own five," said the child.

"Good! Good! Right you are! A fiver for me and a fiver for you on Daffodil."

The child had never been to a race meeting before, and his eyes were blue fire. He pursed his mouth tight, and watched. A Frenchman just in front had put his money on Lancelot. Wild with excitement, he flayed his arms up and down, yelling *Lancelot! Lancelot!* in his French accent.

Daffodil came in first, Lancelot second, Mirza third. The child, flushed and with eyes blazing, was curiously serene. His uncle brought him five five-pound notes: four to one.

"What am I to do with these?" he cried, waving them before the boy's eyes.

---

6. **Nat Gould** famous English sportswriter and authority on horse racing.

Literary Analysis

Theme, Symbol, and Third-Person Point of View What does the narrator suggest about Paul's need by describing his eyes as "blue fire"?

Reading Check

What kind of a partnership does Paul have with Bassett?

"I suppose we'll talk to Bassett," said the boy. "I expect I have fifteen hundred now; and twenty in reserve; and this twenty."

His uncle studied him for some moments.

"Look here, son!" he said. "You're not serious about Bassett and that fifteen hundred, are you?"

"Yes, I am. But it's between you and me, uncle! Honor bright!"

"Honor bright all right, son! But I must talk to Bassett."

"If you'd like to be a partner, uncle, with Bassett and me, we could all be partners. Only you'd have to promise, honor bright, uncle, not to let it go beyond us three. Bassett and I are lucky, and you must be lucky, because it was your ten shillings I started winning with. . . ."

Uncle Oscar took both Bassett and Paul into Richmond Park for an afternoon, and there they talked.

"It's like this, you see, sir," Bassett said. "Master Paul would get me talking about racing events, spinning yarns, you know, sir. And he was always keen on knowing if I'd made or if I'd lost. It's about a year since, now, that I put five shillings on Blush of Dawn for him— and we lost. Then the luck turned, with that ten shillings he had from you, that we put on Singhalese. And since that time, it's been pretty steady, all things considering. What do you say, Master Paul?"

"We're all right when we're *sure*," said Paul. "It's when we're not quite sure that we go down."

"Oh, but we're careful then," said Bassett.

"But when are you *sure*?" smiled Uncle Oscar.

"It's Master Paul, sir," said Bassett, in a secret, religious voice. "It's as if he had it from heaven. Like Daffodil now, for the Lincoln. That was as sure as eggs."

"Did you put anything on Daffodil?" asked Oscar Cresswell.

"Yes, sir. I made my bit."

"And my nephew?"

Bassett was <u>obstinately</u> silent, looking at Paul.

"I made twelve hundred, didn't I, Bassett? I told uncle I was putting three hundred on Daffodil."

"That's right," said Bassett, nodding.

"But where's the money?" asked the uncle.

"I keep it safe locked up, sir. Master Paul, he can have it any minute he likes to ask for it."

"What, fifteen hundred pounds?"

"And twenty! And *forty*, that is, with the twenty he made on the course."

"It's amazing!" said the uncle.

"If Master Paul offers you to be partners, sir, I would, if I were you; if you'll excuse me," said Bassett.

Oscar Cresswell thought about it.

"I'll see the money," he said.

They drove home again, and sure enough, Bassett came round to the garden house with fifteen hundred pounds in notes. The twenty pounds reserve was left with Joe Glee, in the Turf Commission deposit.

Reading Strategy
Identifying With a Character In what way does Bassett serve as a substitute father or older brother for Paul?

obstinately (äb′ stə nət lē) *adv.* in a determined way; stubbornly

"You see, it's all right, uncle, when I'm *sure!* Then we go strong, for all we're worth. Don't we, Bassett?"

"We do that, Master Paul."

"And when are you sure?" said the uncle, laughing.

"Oh, well, sometimes I'm *absolutely* sure, like about Daffodil," said the boy, "and sometimes I have an idea; and sometimes I haven't even an idea, have I, Bassett? Then we're careful, because we mostly go down."

"You do, do you! And when you're sure, like about Daffodil, what makes you sure, sonny?"

"Oh, well, I don't know," said the boy uneasily. "I'm sure, you know, uncle; that's all."

"It's as if he had it from heaven, sir," Bassett reiterated.

"I should say so!" said the uncle.

But he became a partner. And when the Leger was coming on, Paul was "sure" about Lively Spark, which was a quite inconsiderable horse. The boy insisted on putting a thousand on the horse, Bassett went for five hundred, and Oscar Cresswell two hundred. Lively Spark came in first, and the betting had been ten to one against him. Paul had made ten thousand.

"You see," he said. "I was absolutely sure of him."

Even Oscar Cresswell had cleared two thousand.

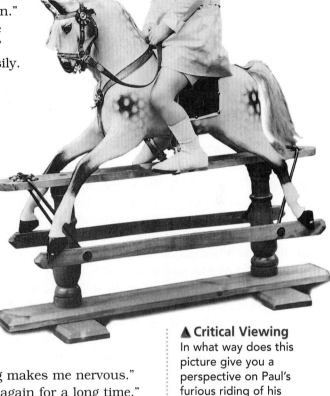

▲ **Critical Viewing**
In what way does this picture give you a perspective on Paul's furious riding of his rocking horse? Explain. **[Connect]**

"Look here, son," he said, "this sort of thing makes me nervous."

"It needn't, uncle! Perhaps I shan't be sure again for a long time."

"But what are you going to do with your money?" asked the uncle.

"Of course," said the boy, "I started it for mother. She said she had no luck, because father is unlucky, so I thought if *I* was lucky, it might stop whispering."

"What might stop whispering?"

"Our house! I *hate* our house for whispering."

"What does it whisper?"

"Why—why"—the boy fidgeted—"why, I don't know! But it's always short of money, you know, uncle."

"I know it, son, I know it."

"You know people send mother writs, don't you, uncle?"

"I'm afraid I do," said the uncle.

"And then the house whispers like people laughing at you behind your back. It's awful, that is! I thought if I was lucky . . ."

"You might stop it," added the uncle.

The boy watched him with big blue eyes, that had an <u>uncanny</u> cold fire in them, and he said never a word.

"Well then!" said the uncle. "What are we doing?"

uncanny (un kan´ ē) *adj.* mysterious; hard to explain

✓**Reading Check**
Why does Paul want to win money?

"I shouldn't like mother to know I was lucky," said the boy.

"Why not, son?"

"She'd stop me."

"I don't think she would."

"Oh!"—and the boy writhed in an odd way—"I *don't* want her to know, uncle."

"All right, son! We'll manage it without her knowing."

They managed it very easily. Paul, at the other's suggestion, handed over five thousand pounds to his uncle, who deposited it with the family lawyer, who was then to inform Paul's mother that a relative had put five thousand pounds into his hands, which sum was to be paid out a thousand pounds at a time, on the mother's birthday, for the next five years.

"So she'll have a birthday present of a thousand pounds for five successive years," said Uncle Oscar. "I hope it won't make it all the harder for her later."

Paul's mother had her birthday in November. The house had been "whispering" worse than ever lately, and even in spite of his luck, Paul could not bear up against it. He was very anxious to see the effect of the birthday letter, telling his mother about the thousand pounds.

When there were no visitors, Paul now took his meals with his parents, as he was beyond the nursery control. His mother went into town nearly every day. She had discovered that she had an odd knack of sketching furs and dress materials, so she worked secretly in the studio of a friend who was the chief "artist" for the leading drapers. She drew the figures of ladies in furs and ladies in silk and sequins for the newspaper advertisements. This young woman artist earned several thousand pounds a year, but Paul's mother only made several hundreds, and she was again dissatisfied. She so wanted to be first in something, and she did not succeed, even in making sketches for drapery advertisements.

She was down to breakfast on the morning of her birthday. Paul watched her face as she read her letters. He knew the lawyer's letter. As his mother read it, her face hardened and became more expressionless. Then a cold, determined look came on her mouth. She hid the letter under the pile of others, and said not a word about it.

"Didn't you have anything nice in the post for your birthday, mother?" said Paul.

"Quite moderately nice," she said, her voice cold and absent.

She went away to town without saying more.

But in the afternoon Uncle Oscar appeared. He said Paul's mother had had a long interview with the lawyer, asking if the whole five thousand could not be advanced at once, as she was in debt.

"What do you think, uncle?" said the boy.

"I leave it to you, son."

"Oh, let her have it, then! We can get some more with the other," said the boy.

Reading Strategy
Identifying With a Character How would you feel about your mother's reaction to the letter if you were Paul? Why?

"A bird in the hand is worth two in the bush, laddie!" said Uncle Oscar.

"But I'm sure to *know* for the Grand National; or the Lincolnshire; or else the Derby.[7] I'm sure to know for *one* of them," said Paul.

So Uncle Oscar signed the agreement, and Paul's mother touched the whole five thousand. Then something very curious happened. The voices in the house suddenly went mad, like a chorus of frogs on a spring evening. There were certain new furnishings, and Paul had a tutor. He was *really* going to Eton,[8] his father's school, in the following autumn. There were flowers in the winter, and a blossoming of the luxury Paul's mother had been used to. And yet the voices in the house, behind the sprays of mimosa and almond blossom, and from under the piles of iridescent cushions, simply trilled and screamed in a sort of ecstasy: "There *must* be more money! Oh-h-h! There *must* be more money! Oh, now, now-w! now-w-w—there *must* be more money!—more than ever! More than ever!"

It frightened Paul terribly. He studied away at his Latin and Greek with his tutors. But his intense hours were spent with Bassett. The Grand National had gone by: he had not "known," and had lost a hundred pounds. Summer was at hand. He was in agony for the Lincoln. But even for the Lincoln he didn't "know," and he lost fifty pounds. He became wild-eyed and strange, as if something were going to explode in him.

"Let it alone, son! Don't you bother about it!" urged Uncle Oscar. But it was as if the boy couldn't really hear what his uncle was saying.

"I've got to know for the Derby! I've *got* to know for the Derby!" the child reiterated, his big blue eyes blazing with a sort of madness.

His mother noticed how overwrought he was.

"You'd better go to the seaside. Wouldn't you like to go now to the seaside, instead of waiting? I think you'd better," she said, looking down at him anxiously, her heart curiously heavy because of him.

But the child lifted his uncanny blue eyes.

"I couldn't possibly go before the Derby, mother!" he said. "I couldn't possibly!"

"Why not?" she said, her voice becoming heavy when she was opposed. "Why not? You can still go from the seaside to see the Derby with your Uncle Oscar, if that's what you wish. No need for you to wait here. Besides, I think you care too much about these races. It's a bad sign. My family has been a gambling family, and you won't know till you grow up how much damage it has done. But it has done damage. I shall have to send Bassett away, and ask Uncle Oscar not to talk racing to you, unless you promise to be reasonable about it; go away to the seaside and forget it. You're all nerves!"

"I'll do what you like, mother, so long as you don't send me away till after the Derby," the boy said.

7. **Grand National . . . Derby** major English horse races.
8. **Eton** prestigious private school in England.

Literary Analysis

Theme, Symbol, and Third-Person Point of View If the story were told from Paul's point of view, would you know about the mother's "curiously heavy" feelings concerning Paul? Why or why not?

 Reading Check

What present does Paul give his mother?

"Send you away from where? Just from this house?"

"Yes," he said, gazing at her.

"Why, you curious child, what makes you care about this house so much, suddenly? I never knew you loved it!"

He gazed at her without speaking. He had a secret within a secret, something he had not divulged, even to Bassett or to his Uncle Oscar.

But his mother, after standing undecided and a little bit sullen for some moments, said:

"Very well, then! Don't go to the seaside till after the Derby, if you don't wish it. But promise me you won't let your nerves go to pieces! Promise you won't think so much about horse racing and *events*, as you call them!"

"Oh, no!" said the boy, casually. "I won't think much about them, mother. You needn't worry. I wouldn't worry, mother, if I were you."

"If you were me and I were you," said his mother, "I wonder what we should do!"

"But you know you needn't worry, mother, don't you?" the boy repeated.

"I should be awfully glad to know it," she said wearily.

"Oh, well, you *can*, you know. I mean you *ought* to know you needn't worry!" he insisted.

"Ought I? Then I'll see about it," she said.

Paul's secret of secrets was his wooden horse, that which had no name. Since he was emancipated from a nurse and a nursery governess, he had had his rocking horse removed to his own bedroom at the top of the house.

"Surely you're too big for a rocking horse!" his mother had <u>remonstrated.</u>

"Well, you see, mother, till I can have a *real* horse, I like to have *some* sort of animal about," had been his quaint answer.

Literary Analysis
Theme and Symbol In the paragraph beginning, "Paul's secret . . . ," which words or phrases suggest that the rocking horse is a symbol?

remonstrated (ri män′ strāt id) *v.* objected strongly

"Do you feel he keeps you company?" she laughed.

"Oh, yes! He's very good, he always keeps me company, when I'm there," said Paul.

So the horse, rather shabby, stood in an arrested prance in the boy's bedroom.

The Derby was drawing near, and the boy grew more and more tense. He hardly heard what was spoken to him, he was very frail, and his eyes were really uncanny. His mother had sudden strange seizures of uneasiness about him. Sometimes, for half an hour, she would feel a sudden anxiety about him that was almost anguish. She wanted to rush to him at once, and know he was safe.

Two nights before the Derby, she was at a big party in town, when one of her rushes of anxiety about her boy, her firstborn, gripped her heart till she could hardly speak. She fought with the feeling, might and main, for she believed in common sense. But it was too strong. She had to leave the dance and go downstairs to telephone to the country. The children's nursery governess was terribly surprised and startled at being rung up in the night.

"Are the children all right, Miss Wilmot?"

"Oh yes, they are quite all right."

"Master Paul? Is he all right?"

"He went to bed as right as a trivet.[9] Shall I run up and look at him?"

"No!" said Paul's mother reluctantly. "No! Don't trouble. It's all right. Don't sit up. We shall be home fairly soon." She did not want her son's privacy intruded upon.

"Very good," said the governess.

---

9. right as a trivet perfectly right.

Literary Analysis
Theme, Symbol, and Third-Person Point of View Does the third-person narrator's insight into the mother's anxiety make you feel more sympathy for her? Explain.

**Reading Check**

Why is Paul especially tense just before the Derby?

It was about one o'clock when Paul's mother and father drove up to their house. All was still. Paul's mother went to her room and slipped off her white fur cloak. She had told her maid not to wait up for her. She heard her husband downstairs, mixing a whisky-and-soda.

And then, because of the strange anxiety at her heart, she stole upstairs to her son's room. Noiselessly she went along the upper corridor. Was there a faint noise? What was it?

She stood, with arrested muscles, outside his door, listening. There was a strange, heavy, and yet not loud noise. Her heart stood still. It was a soundless noise, yet rushing and powerful. Something huge, in violent, hushed motion. What was it? What in God's name was it? She ought to know. She felt that she *knew* the noise. She knew what it was.

Yet she could not place it. She couldn't say what it was. And on and on it went, like madness.

Softly, frozen with anxiety and fear, she turned the door handle.

The room was dark. Yet in the space near the window, she heard and saw something plunging to and fro. She gazed in fear and amazement.

Then suddenly she switched on the light, and saw her son, in his green pajamas, madly surging on his rocking horse. The blaze of light suddenly lit him up, as he urged the wooden horse, and lit her up, as she stood, blond, in her dress of pale green and crystal, in the doorway.

"Paul!" she cried. "Whatever are you doing?"

"It's Malabar!" he screamed, in a powerful, strange voice. "It's Malabar!"

His eyes blazed at her for one strange and senseless second, as he ceased urging his wooden horse. Then he fell with a crash to the ground, and she, all her tormented motherhood flooding upon her, rushed to gather him up.

But he was unconscious, and unconscious he remained, with some brain fever. He talked and tossed, and his mother sat stonily by his side.

"Malabar! It's Malabar! Bassett, Bassett, I *know* it's Malabar!"

So the child cried, trying to get up and urge the rocking horse that gave him his inspiration.

"What does he mean by Malabar?" asked the heart-frozen mother.

"I don't know," said the father, stonily.

"What does he mean by Malabar?" she asked her brother Oscar.

"It's one of the horses running for the Derby," was the answer.

And, in spite of himself, Oscar Cresswell spoke to Bassett, and himself put a thousand on Malabar: at fourteen to one.

The third day of the illness was critical: they were watching for a change. The boy, with his rather long, curly hair, was tossing ceaselessly on the pillow. He neither slept nor regained consciousness, and his eyes were like blue stones. His mother sat, feeling her heart had gone, turned actually into a stone.

In the evening, Oscar Cresswell did not come, but Bassett sent a message, saying could he come up for one moment, just one moment?

Literary Analysis
Theme and Symbol In what way is the rocking horse connected with the whispering of the house?

Paul's mother was very angry at the intrusion, but on second thoughts she agreed. The boy was the same. Perhaps Bassett might bring him to consciousness.

The gardener, a shortish fellow with a little brown moustache and sharp little brown eyes, tiptoed into the room, touched his imaginary cap to Paul's mother, and stole to the bedside, staring with glittering, smallish eyes at the tossing, dying child.

"Master Paul!" he whispered. "Master Paul! Malabar came in first all right, a clean win. I did as you told me. You've made over seventy thousand pounds, you have; you've got over eighty thousand. Malabar came in all right, Master Paul."

"Malabar! Malabar! Did I say Malabar, mother? Did I say Malabar? Do you think I'm lucky, mother? I knew Malabar, didn't I? Over eighty thousand pounds! I call that lucky, don't you, mother? Over eighty thousand pounds! I knew, didn't I know I knew? Malabar came in all right. If I ride my horse till I'm sure, then I tell you, Bassett, you can go as high as you like. Did you go for all you were worth, Bassett?"

"I went a thousand on it, Master Paul."

"I never told you, mother, that if I can ride my horse, and *get there*, then I'm absolutely sure—oh, absolutely! Mother, did I ever tell you? I *am* lucky!"

"No, you never did," said the mother.

But the boy died in the night.

And even as he lay dead, his mother heard her brother's voice saying to her: "My God, Hester, you're eighty-odd thousand to the good, and a poor devil of a son to the bad. But, poor devil, poor devil, he's best gone out of a life where he rides his rocking horse to find a winner."

Literary Analysis
Theme and Symbol In explaining the meaning of Paul's brief life, what would you add to his uncle's final words about him?

Review and Assess

Thinking About the Selection

1. **Respond:** Which character in this story did you find most likable? Least likable? Explain.

2. **(a) Recall:** From the point of view of Paul's mother, what is the main problem of the family? **(b) Infer:** What does the mother's statement that the father is "unlucky" suggest about her values?

3. **(a) Recall:** Over the course of the story, how does Paul react to the house's "whispers"?
   (b) Analyze Cause and Effect: Why is he affected as he is?

4. **(a) Recall:** What does Uncle Oscar say at the end of the story? **(b) Interpret:** Do you think Uncle Oscar is speaking for the author? Why or why not?

5. **Take a Position:** What, if anything, is more important than the luck and money that Paul's mother wanted so desperately?

A Shocking Accident

Graham Greene

1

Jerome was called into his housemaster's room in the break between the second and the third class on a Thursday morning. He had no fear of trouble, for he was a warden— the name that the proprietor and headmaster of a rather expensive preparatory school had chosen to give to approved, reliable boys in the lower forms (from a warden one became a guardian and finally before leaving, it was hoped for Marlborough or Rugby, a crusader). The housemaster, Mr. Wordsworth, sat behind his desk with an appearance of perplexity and <u>apprehension</u>. Jerome had the odd impression when he entered that he was a cause of fear.

"Sit down, Jerome," Mr. Wordsworth said. "All going well with the trigonometry?"

"Yes, sir."

"I've had a telephone call, Jerome. From your aunt. I'm afraid I have bad news for you."

"Yes, sir?"

"Your father has had an accident."

"Oh."

Mr. Wordsworth looked at him with some surprise. "A serious accident."

"Yes, sir?"

Jerome worshipped his father: the verb is exact. As man re-creates God, so Jerome re-created his father—from a restless widowed author into a mysterious adventurer who traveled in far places—Nice, Beirut, Majorca, even the Canaries. The time had arrived about his eighth birthday when Jerome believed that his father either "ran guns" or was a member of the British Secret Service. Now it occurred to him that his father might have been wounded in "a hail of machine-gun bullets."

Mr. Wordsworth played with the ruler on his desk. He seemed at a loss how to continue. He said, "You knew your father was in Naples?"

"Yes, sir."

"Your aunt heard from the hospital today."

"Oh."

Mr. Wordsworth said with desperation, "It was a street accident."

"Yes, sir?" It seemed quite likely to Jerome that they would call it

apprehension (ap´ rē hen´ shən) *n.* anxious feeling of foreboding; dread

Reading Strategy
Identifying With a Character If you were Jerome, what might be your reasons for romanticizing your absent father's job?

a street accident. The police, of course, had fired first; his father would not take human life except as a last resort.

"I'm afraid your father was very seriously hurt indeed."

"Oh."

"In fact, Jerome, he died yesterday. Quite without pain."

"Did they shoot him through the heart?"

"I beg your pardon. What did you say, Jerome?"

"Did they shoot him through the heart?"

"Nobody shot him, Jerome. A pig fell on him." An inexplicable convulsion took place in the nerves of Mr. Wordsworth's face; it really looked for a moment as though he were going to laugh. He closed his eyes, composed his features, and said rapidly, as though it were necessary to expel the story as rapidly as possible, "Your father was walking along a street in Naples when a pig fell on him. A shocking accident. Apparently in the poorer quarters of Naples they keep pigs on their balconies. This one was on the fifth floor. It had grown too fat. The balcony broke. The pig fell on your father."

Mr. Wordsworth left his desk rapidly and went to the window, turning his back on Jerome. He shook a little with emotion.

Jerome said, "What happened to the pig?"

2

This was not callousness on the part of Jerome as it was interpreted by Mr. Wordsworth to his colleagues (he even discussed with them whether, perhaps, Jerome was not yet fitted to be a warden). Jerome was only attempting to visualize the strange scene and to get the details right. Nor was Jerome a boy who cried; he was a boy who brooded, and it never occurred to him at his preparatory school that the circumstances of his father's death were comic—they were still part of the mystery of life. It was later in his first term at his public school, when he told the story to his best friend, that he began to realize how it affected others. Naturally, after that disclosure he was known, rather unreasonably, as Pig.

Unfortunately his aunt had no sense of humor. There was an enlarged snap-shot of his father on the piano: a large sad man in an unsuitable dark suit posed in Capri with an umbrella (to guard him against sunstroke), the Faraglioni rocks forming the background. By the age of sixteen Jerome was well aware that the portrait looked more like the author of *Sunshine and Shade* and *Rambles in the Balearics* than an agent of the Secret Service. All the same, he loved the memory of his father: he still possessed an album filled with picture-postcards (the stamps had been soaked off long ago for his other collection), and it pained him when his aunt <u>embarked</u> with strangers on the story of his father's death.

"A shocking accident," she would begin, and the stranger would compose his or her features into the correct shape for interest and commiseration. Both reactions, of course, were false,

but it was terrible for Jerome to see how suddenly, midway in her rambling discourse, the interest would become genuine. "I can't think how such things can be allowed in a civilized country," his aunt would say. "I suppose one has to regard Italy as civilized. One is prepared for all kinds of things abroad, of course, and my brother was a great traveler. He always carried a water-filter with him. It was far less expensive, you know, than buying all those bottles of mineral water. My brother always said that his filter paid for his dinner wine. You can see from that what a careful man he was, but who could possibly have expected when he was walking along the Via Dottore Manuele Panucci on his way to the Hydrographic Museum that a pig would fall on him?" That was the moment when the interest became genuine.

Jerome's father had not been a distinguished writer, but the time always seems to come, after an author's death, when somebody thinks it worth his while to write a letter to *The Times Literary Supplement* announcing the preparation of a biography and asking to see any letters or documents or receive any anecdotes from friends of the dead man. Most of the biographies, of course, never appear—one wonders whether the whole thing may not be an obscure form of blackmail and whether many a potential writer of a biography or thesis finds the means in this way to finish his education at Kansas or Nottingham. Jerome, however, as a chartered accountant, lived far from the literary world. He did not realize how small the menace really was, nor that the danger period for someone of his father's obscurity had long passed. Sometimes he rehearsed the method of recounting his father's death so as to reduce the comic element to its smallest dimensions—it would be of no use to refuse information, for in that case the biographer would undoubtedly visit his aunt, who was living to a great old age with no sign of flagging.

It seemed to Jerome that there were two possible methods—the first led gently up to the accident, so well prepared that the death came really as an anticlimax. The chief danger of laughter in such a story was always surprise. When he rehearsed this method Jerome began boringly enough.

"You know Naples and those high tenement buildings? Somebody once told me that the Neapolitan always feels at home in New York just as the man from Turin feels at home in London because the river runs in much the same way in both cities. Where was I? Oh, yes, Naples, of course. You'd be surprised in the poorer quarters what things they keep on the balconies of those skyscraping tenements— not washing, you know, or bedding, but things like livestock, chickens or even pigs. Of course the pigs get no exercise whatever and fatten all the quicker." He could imagine how his hearer's eyes would have glazed by this time. "I've no idea, have you, how heavy a pig can be, but those old buildings are all badly in need of repair. A balcony on the fifth floor gave way under one of those pigs. It struck the third-floor balcony on its way down and sort of ricocheted into the street. My father was on the way to the Hydrographic Museum when the

Reading Strategy
Identifying With a Character Why do you think Jerome is so desperate to reduce "the comic element" in the story of the accident?

pig hit him. Coming from that height and that angle it broke his neck." This was really a masterly attempt to make an <u>intrinsically</u> interesting subject boring.

intrinsically (in trin´ sik lē) *adv.* at its core; inherently; innately

The other method Jerome rehearsed had the virtue of brevity.

"My father was killed by a pig."

"Really? In India?"

"No, in Italy."

"How interesting. I never realized there was pig-sticking in Italy. Was your father keen on polo?"

In course of time, neither too early nor too late, rather as though, in his capacity as a chartered accountant, Jerome had studied the statistics and taken the average, he became engaged to be married: to a pleasant fresh-faced girl of twenty-five whose father was a doctor in Pinner. Her name was Sally, her favorite author was still Hugh Walpole, and she had adored babies ever since she had been given a doll at the age of five which moved its eyes and made water. Their relationship was contented rather than exciting, as became the love affair of a chartered accountant; it would never have done if it had interfered with the figures.

One thought worried Jerome, however. Now that within a year he might himself become a father, his love for the dead man increased; he realized what affection had gone into the picture-postcards. He felt a longing to protect his memory, and uncertain whether this quiet love of his would survive if Sally were so insensitive as to laugh when she heard the story of his father's death. Inevitably she would hear it when Jerome brought her to dinner with his aunt. Several times he tried to tell her himself, as she was naturally anxious to know all she could that concerned him.

"You were very small when your father died?"

"Just nine."

"Poor little boy," she said.

"I was at school. They broke the news to me."

"Did you take it very hard?"

"I can't remember."

"You never told me how it happened."

"It was very sudden. A street accident."

"You'll never drive fast, will you, Jemmy?" (She had begun to call him "Jemmy.") It was too late then to try the second method—the one he thought of as the pig-sticking one.

They were going to marry quietly at a registry-office and have their honeymoon at Torquay. He avoided taking her to see his aunt until a week before the wedding, but then the night came, and he could not have told himself whether his apprehension was more for his father's memory or the security of his own love.

The moment came all too soon. "Is that Jemmy's father?" Sally asked, picking up the portrait of the man with the umbrella.

"Yes, dear. How did you guess?"

"He has Jemmy's eyes and brow, hasn't he?"

Reading Strategy
Identifying With a Character Why do you think Jerome feels that Sally's laughter could menace his "quiet love" for his father?

**Reading Check**

What two methods of narrating his father's death does Jerome rehearse?

"Has Jerome lent you his books?"

"No."

"I will give you a set for your wedding. He wrote so tenderly about his travels. My own favorite is *Nooks and Crannies.* He would have had a great future. It made that shocking accident all the worse."

"Yes?"

How Jerome longed to leave the room and not see that loved face crinkle with irresistible amusement.

"I had so many letters from his readers after the pig fell on him." She had never been so abrupt before.

And then the miracle happened. Sally did not laugh. Sally sat with open eyes of horror while his aunt told her the story, and at the end, "How horrible," Sally said. "It makes you think, doesn't it? Happening like that. Out of a clear sky."

Jerome's heart sang with joy. It was as though she had appeased his fear forever. In the taxi going home he kissed her with more passion than he had ever shown, and she returned it. There were babies in her pale blue pupils, babies that rolled their eyes and made water.

"A week today," Jerome said, and she squeezed his hand. "Penny for your thoughts, my darling."

"I was wondering," Sally said, "what happened to the poor pig?" "They almost certainly had it for dinner," Jerome said happily and kissed the dear child again.

Literary Analysis
Theme and Symbol
What does the contrast between Sally's reaction and those of other characters suggest about the theme?

Review and Assess

Thinking About the Selection

1. **Respond:** Were you surprised by the way that this story ended? Why or why not?

2. **(a) Recall:** Which two characters use the phrase "a shocking accident" to describe the death of Jerome's father?
   (b) Compare and Contrast: How do the reactions of these two characters to the death compare to Jerome's reaction?

3. **(a) Recall:** How does Jerome protect himself from the embarrassing aspects of the death? **(b) Analyze:** What are some inner conflicts Jerome experiences about his father's death?

4. **(a) Recall:** How does Sally react when she hears the story?
   (b) Infer: What does Sally's reaction reveal to Jerome about her character? **(c) Draw Conclusions:** Are Jerome's conflicts about his father's death resolved at the end of the story? Why or why not?

5. **Take a Position:** One implication of the "shocking accident" might be that what happens in life is basically beyond our control. Do you agree with this idea? Why or why not?

Review and Assess

Literary Analysis

Theme and Symbol

1. Using the terms *love and money*, state a central question, issue, or concern that expresses the **theme** in "The Rocking-Horse Winner."
2. Complete a chart like this with (a) passages illustrating the **symbolic** meanings of the rocking horse and (b) explanations linking these meanings to the theme.

Symbolic Meanings	Passages That Illustrate	Links to Overall Theme
• Frantic effort to satisfy an unsatisfiable need • Frightening power of desires and wishes		

3. For "A Shocking Accident," explain how the accident might symbolize either of these meanings: (a) that which makes no sense (b) that which is unacceptable according to upper-class notions.
4. Use the symbolic meanings of the accident to state the story's theme.

Comparing Literary Works

5. Show that "The Rocking-Horse Winner" and "A Shocking Accident" are similar in using the **third-person point of view.**
6. In which story does the point of view work most effectively to reveal the theme? Explain.
7. In which story is the third-person narrative more like a fairy tale and in which is it more like an anecdote? Explain.

Reading Strategy

Identifying With a Character

8. **Identify with the character** Paul in "A Rocking-Horse Winner," and express his most important goal.
9. In "A Shocking Accident," what makes Jerome most uneasy about telling the story of his father's death? Why?

Extend Understanding

10. **Psychology Connection:** How might a child psychologist try to help Paul in "A Rocking-Horse Winner"?

Integrate Language Skills

Vocabulary Development Lesson

Word Analysis: Latin Prefix *ob-*

The Latin prefix *ob-* can mean "against," "opposed to," "before," or "to." *Obstinately* means "as if standing against" or "stubbornly." Speculate how the meaning of the prefix influences the definitions of the words below. Then, use a dictionary containing word origins to verify your speculations.

1. object (*verb*) **2.** obligation **3.** obnoxious

Spelling Strategy

To form an adverb from words of two or more syllables ending in *-c,* you usually add the ending *-ally.* For example, *instrinsic* becomes *intrinsically.* On your paper, change the adjectives below into adverbs. Use a dictionary to check your spellings.

1. problematic   **2.** public   **3.** thematic

Fluency: Words in Context

Answer each question, and explain your answer.

1. Do *discreet* people gossip?
2. Is *brazening* out a lie easy?
3. Did Paul ride until the horse *careered?*
4. Was Paul *obstinately* determined to win?
5. Were Paul's eyes *uncanny?*
6. Had Paul's mother *remonstrated* with him about riding the rocking-horse?
7. Did Jerome feel *apprehension* about describing his father's death?
8. Did Jerome's aunt *embark* on the death with strangers?
9. Was the story of Jerome's father's death *intrinsically* dull?

Grammar and Style Lesson

Subjunctive Mood

The **subjunctive mood** of a verb states a wish or a condition contrary to fact. The subjunctive is also used in *that* clauses of recommendation, resolution, command, or demand. The subjunctive form appears in

- Certain forms of the verb *to be*—the present is *be* and the past is *were*
- The third-person singular of other verbs, usually used without the final *s*

> **Condition Contrary to Fact:** If you <u>were</u> me and I <u>were</u> you . . . I wonder what we should do! (form of *to be*)

> **That Clause of Command:** Paul's mother insisted that he <u>stop</u> rocking. (third-person singular without *-s*)

Practice Identify the correct verb for each sentence.

1. She insisted that the child (goes, go) to a first-class boarding school.
2. Bassett and Paul thought it essential that they (are, be) sure of a winner before betting.
3. Paul wished that she (wasn't, weren't) so worried.
4. It had seemed for a moment as if the housemaster (was, were) going to laugh.
5. Jerome thought that if Sally (was, were) insensitive, their engagement might end.

Writing Application As Paul's mother, write a paragraph about what you wish for your son. Use the subjunctive mood at least twice to express your hopes, wishes, or fears.

 Prentice Hall Writing and Grammar Connection: Chapter 21, Section 3

Writing Lesson

Product Description

Advertisers use the same techniques of symbolism that Lawrence does. Demonstrate this truth for yourself by writing a product description of a new toy. Sell the toy to parents and children by making it into a symbol of wonder, knowledge, or power.

Prewriting   Sketch the toy, and make notes about its function, size, sounds, color, and moving parts. Jot down the quality or qualities that it will symbolize.

Drafting   Describe the toy, in action. Using a word bank of vivid verbs and adverbs, like the one shown below, choose the ones that will suggest the symbolic meanings you want to convey.

Model: Consulting a Word Bank

	Knowledge	Magic	Power
Verbs	appreciate, recognize, grasp	charm, enchant, conjure	sway, control, arm, energize
Adverbs	keenly, perceptively, intelligently	hypnotically, magically, hauntingly	powerfully, strongly, irresistibly

Revising   Have a partner read the description to identify the quality or qualities the toy symbolizes. If your partner fails to interpret the toy correctly, insert verbs and adverbs that will suggest the correct symbolism.

 Prentice Hall Writing and Grammar Connection: Chapter 8, Section 2

Extension Activities

Listening and Speaking Imagine that you are playing the character of Jerome in a play adapted from "A Shocking Accident." Rehearse and deliver a **soliloquy**—a speech made by a character who is alone—about other people's reactions to your father's death. In your rehearsal, pay particular attention to pacing, gestures, and staging, and keep these goals in mind:

- Expressing emotion
- Adding drama and sentence variety

Then, present your speech to the class.

Research and Technology With a group, research Graham Greene's travels, and create a **multimedia travelogue** following in the footsteps of the novelist. Each person might focus on a different country, finding suitable music, readings, and slides. However, work together to script your presentation. [**Group Activity**]

 *Take It to the Net*   www.phschool.com

Go online for an additional research activity using the Internet.

Defining the short story as a form is no easy task. All short stories are brief works of fiction. They generally have simpler plots than novels. In addition, a short story tends to reveal character at a crucial moment rather than developing it through many incidents. Yet, as each story in this section shows, one writer's idea of a story may be quite different from another's.

Masters of Storytelling In "The Lagoon," Conrad uses elements that appear in much of his fiction: a tale of betrayal set in an exotic, dreamlike place and a story-within-a-story narrative. In "Araby," as in many of his other stories, Joyce builds to an epiphany —a character's flash of awareness that illuminates the story's meaning. Woolf and Spark use unusual narrative devices in their stories—a stream-of-consciousness narration that mirrors the random thoughts in a character's mind and an omniscient point of view attributed to an infant. Each of these writers helped make the short story an important literary form in the twentieth century. At the same time, each redefines the form.

Argentine writer Jorge Luis Borges uses storytelling techniques as original as those of early twentieth-century English writers. His tale "The Book of Sand," for example, is a fantastic story inspired by philosophical speculations about infinity. Told by a first-person narrator, it replaces conventional action with the "adventure" of an unfolding idea. The tale may be brief, but it will cause you to think about its narrator's discovery and dilemma for a long time.

THE BOOK OF
SAND

Jorge Luis Borges

Translated by
Andrew Hurley

...thy rope of sands...

—George Herbert (1593–1633)[1]

The line consists of an infinite number of points; the plane, of an infinite number of lines; the volume, of an infinite number of planes; the hypervolume, of an infinite number of volumes... No—this, *more geometrico*,[2] is decidedly not the best way to begin my tale. To say that the story is true is by now a convention of every fantastic tale; mine, nevertheless, *is* true.

I live alone, in a fifth-floor apartment on Calle Belgrano.[3] One evening a few months ago, I heard a knock at my door. I opened it, and a stranger stepped in. He was a tall man, with blurred, vague features, or perhaps my nearsightedness made me see him that way. Everything about him spoke of honest poverty: he was dressed in gray, and carried a gray valise. I immediately sensed that he was a foreigner. At first I thought he was old; then I noticed that I had been misled by his sparse hair, which was blond, almost white, like the Scandinavians'. In the course of our conversation, which I doubt lasted more than an hour, I learned that he hailed from the Orkneys.[4]

I pointed the man to a chair. He took some time to begin talking. He gave off an air of melancholy, as I myself do now.

"I sell Bibles," he said at last.

"In this house," I replied, not without a somewhat stiff, pedantic[5] note, "there are several English Bibles, including the first one, Wyclif's.[6] I also have Cipriano de Valera's, Luther's (which is, in literary terms, the worst of the lot), and a Latin copy of the Vulgate.[7] As you see, it isn't exactly Bibles I might be needing."

After a brief silence he replied.

"It's not only Bibles I sell. I can show you a sacred book that might interest a man such as yourself. I came by it in northern India, in Bikaner."[8]

He opened his valise and brought out the book. He laid it on the table. It was a clothbound octavo[9] volume that had clearly passed through many hands. I examined it; the unusual heft of it surprised me. On the spine was printed *Holy Writ*, and then *Bombay*.[10]

Thematic Connection

What connection can you see between a story about a book, such as this one, and a story that tells the story of a story, such as Conrad's "The Lagoon"?

---

1. **George Herbert** English metaphysical poet whose poem "The Collar" refers to religious principles of conduct as God's "rope of sands."
2. *more geometrico* (môr′ ā gā′ ō me′ tri cō) "by the method of geometry," a learned Latin phrase. The philosopher Benedict de Spinoza (1632–1677), who wrote on the infinite, described his method using this phrase.
3. **Calle Bellgrano** street in Buenos Aires, capital of Argentina.
4. **Orkneys** Orkney Islands; group of islands north of Scotland.
5. **pedantic** (pe dan′ tic) *adj.* stressing minor or trivial points of learning unnecessarily.
6. **Wyclif's** (wik′ lifs) John Wyclif (or Wycliffe; 1330–1384), English religious reformer who, in the late 1300s, made the first translation of the Bible into English from the official Latin version.
7. **Capriano de Valera's . . . Vulgate** different translations of the Bible.
8. **Bikaner** (bē kə nir′) city in northwest India.
9. **octavo** (äk tā′ vō) *n.* page size of a book, made up of printer's sheets folded into eight leaves: the usual size of each leaf is six by nine inches.
10. **Bombay** (bäm′ bā′) seaport in west India.

"Nineteenth century, I'd say," I observed.

"I don't know," was the reply. "Never did know."

I opened it at random. The characters were unfamiliar to me. The pages, which seemed worn and badly set, were printed in double columns, like a Bible. The text was cramped, and composed into versicles.[11] At the upper corner of each page were Arabic numerals. I was struck by an odd fact: the even-numbered page would carry the number 40,514, let us say, while the odd-numbered page that followed it would be 999. I turned the page; the next page bore an eight-digit number. It also bore a small illustration, like those one sees in dictionaries: an anchor drawn in pen and ink, as though by the unskilled hand of a child.

It was at that point that the stranger spoke again.

"Look at it well. You will never see it again."

There was a threat in the words, but not in the voice.

I took note of the page, and then closed the book. Immediately I opened it again. In vain I searched for the figure of the anchor, page after page. To hide my discomfiture, I tried another tack.

"This is a version of Scripture in some Hindu language, isn't that right?"

"No," he replied.

Then he lowered his voice, as though entrusting me with a secret.

"I came across this book in a village on the plain, and I traded a few rupees and a Bible for it. The man who owned it didn't know how to read. I suspect he saw the Book of Books as an amulet. He was of the lowest caste;[12] people could not so much as step on his shadow without being defiled. He told me his book was called the Book of Sand because neither sand nor this book has a beginning or an end."

He suggested I try to find the first page.

I took the cover in my left hand and opened the book, my thumb and forefinger almost touching. It was impossible: several pages always lay between the cover and my hand. It was as though they grew from the very book.

"Now try to find the end."

I failed there as well.

"This can't be," I stammered, my voice hardly recognizable as my own.

"It can't be, yet it *is*," the Bible peddler said, his voice little more than a whisper. "The number of pages in this book is literally infinite. No page is the first page; no page is the last. I don't know why they're numbered in this arbitrary way, but perhaps it's to give one to understand that the terms of an infinite series can be numbered any way whatever."

Then, as though thinking out loud, he went on.

"If space is infinite, we are anywhere, at any point in space. If time is infinite, we are at any point in time."

Thematic Connection
How does Borges's presentation of the idea of infinity compare and contrast with the presentation of a sequence of events in other stories?

---

11. versicles (vur´ si kəlz) *n.* short verses or verse parts from the Bible used in prayers with melodies.

12. lowest caste (kast) *n.* lowest social class in Indian society; the class of "untouchables."

His musings irritated me.

"You," I said, "are a religious man, are you not?"

"Yes, I'm Presbyterian. My conscience is clear. I am certain I didn't cheat that native when I gave him the Lord's Word in exchange for his diabolic[13] book."

I assured him he had nothing to reproach himself for, and asked whether he was just passing through the country. He replied that he planned to return to his own country within a few days. It was then that I learned he was a Scot, and that his home was in the Orkneys. I told him I had great personal fondness for Scotland because of my love for Stevenson[14] and Hume.[15]

"And Robbie Burns,"[16] he corrected.

As we talked I continued to explore the infinite book.

"Had you intended to offer this curious specimen to the British Museum then?" I asked with feigned indifference.

"No," he replied, "I am offering it to you," and he mentioned a great sum of money.

I told him, with perfect honesty, that such an amount of money was not within my ability to pay. But my mind was working; in a few moments I had devised my plan.

"I propose a trade," I said. "You purchased the volume with a few rupees and the Holy Scripture; I will offer you the full sum of my pension, which I have just received, and Wyclif's black-letter Bible. It was left to me by my parents."

"A black-letter Wyclif!" he murmured.

I went to my bedroom and brought back the money and the book. With a bibliophile's[17] zeal he turned the pages and studied the binding.

"Done," he said.

I was astonished that he did not haggle. Only later was I to realize that he had entered my house already determined to see the book. He did not count the money, but merely put the bills into his pocket.

We chatted about India, the Orkneys, and the Norwegian jarls[18] that had once ruled those islands. Night was falling when the man left. I have never seen him since, nor do I know his name.

▲ Critical Viewing
What qualities of the books in this picture convey the same atmosphere as the book in the story? **[Connect]**

---

13. diabolic (dī´ə bäl´ik) *adj.* of the devil; evil.
14. Stevenson Robert Louis Stevenson, (1850–1894); noted Scottish novelist, poet, and essayist.
15. Hume (hyo̅o̅m) David Hume, (1711–1776); noted Scottish philosopher and historian, prominent in the period known as the Scottish Enlightenment.
16. Robbie Burns Robert Burns, (1759–1796); famous Scottish poet.
17. bibliophile's (bib´ lē ə filz´) *n.* of a person who loves books.
18. jarls (yärlz) *n.* chieftains or noblemen in early Scandinavia.

I thought of putting the Book of Sand in the space left by the Wyclif, but I chose at last to hide it behind some imperfect volumes of the *Thousand and One Nights*.

I went to bed but could not sleep. At three or four in the morning I turned on the light. I took out the impossible book and turned its pages. On one, I saw an engraving of a mask. There was a number in the corner of a page—I don't remember now what it was—raised to the ninth power.

I showed no one my treasure. To the joy of possession was added the fear that it would be stolen from me, and to that, the suspicion that it might not be truly infinite. Those two points of anxiety aggravated my already habitual misanthropy.[19] I had but few friends left, and those, I stopped seeing. A prisoner of the Book, I hardly left my house. I examined the worn binding and the covers with a magnifying glass, and rejected the possibility of some artifice. I found that the small illustrations were spaced at two-thousand-page intervals. I began noting them down in an alphabetized notebook, which was very soon filled. They never repeated themselves. At night, during the rare intervals spared me by insomnia, I dreamed of the book.

Summer was drawing to a close, and I realized that the book was monstrous. It was cold consolation to think that I, who looked upon it with my eyes and fondled it with my ten flesh-and-bone fingers, was no less monstrous than the book. I felt it was a nightmare thing, an obscene thing, and that it defiled and corrupted reality.

I considered fire, but I feared that the burning of an infinite book might be similarly infinite, and suffocate the planet in smoke.

I remembered reading once that the best place to hide a leaf is in the forest. Before my retirement I had worked in the National Library, which contained nine hundred thousand books; I knew that to the right of the lobby a curving staircase descended into the shadows of the basement, where the maps and periodicals are kept. I took advantage of the librarians' distraction to hide the Book of Sand on one of the library's damp shelves; I tried not to notice how high up, or how far from the door.

I now feel a little better, but I refuse even to walk down the street the library's on.

---

19. **misanthropy** (mis an′ thrə pē) *n.* hatred or distrust of people.

Jorge Luis Borges

(1899–1986)

Jorge Luis Borges (hôr′ he lōō ēs′ bôr′ hes) was an Argentine writer known for his inventive, fantastic short stories and poetry. The strangeness of his tales recalls the fiction of Edgar Allan Poe.

Borges stories deal with universal themes like the meaning of time and infinity and the nature of personal identity. He received the International Publisher's Prize in 1961.

Connecting Literature Around the World

1. Compare Borges's story with another story in this section. (a) What are their general similarities? (b) What are their major differences?
2. In several stories in this section, a character or narrator discovers something fundamentally disquieting about life. Compare these discoveries in two of the selections.

PART 4

From the National to the Global

Political World, Kenneth Eward

Prepare to Read

Do Not Go Gentle into That Good Night ◆ Fern Hill ◆ The Horses ◆ The Rain Horse

Dylan Thomas (1914–1953)

Playful with language and exuberant about life, Thomas gained remarkable popularity in his lifetime. However, he also had a darker side, evident in his poems of death and the loss of childhood innocence.

A Young Poet Dylan Thomas was born in Swansea in southwestern Wales, an industrial city. However, he often visited his maternal grandfather's farm, which he describes in "Fern Hill." With the encouragement of his father, an English teacher, he became interested in poetry at an early age. Before turning twenty, he had already written—at least in early form—many of his best-known poems. As a teenager, he also produced source books of ideas that served as a basis for later works.

Journeys Abroad At the age of twenty-one, Thomas went to London, where he worked in journalism, broadcasting, and filmmaking for a number of years. In 1940, he published a collection of humorous stories about his childhood and youth, *Portrait of the Artist as a Young Dog*. In 1950, he made the first of four trips to the United States. Audiences here embraced him not only for his theatrical readings of his poems but also for the freshness and complexity of his poetic voice.

Though he continued to publish poetry, two of the later works for which he is best known are prose: Under Milkwood, a "play for voices," and A Child's Christmas in Wales, a memoir.

An Artist's Problems Although acclaimed at an early age, Thomas struggled with poverty and alcoholism through most of his adult life. He died while on tour in the United States, where he had planned to collaborate on an opera with Igor Stravinsky.

Ted Hughes (1930–1998)

Born in rural West Yorkshire, Hughes spent much of his youth hunting and fishing with his brother. These experiences contributed to his lifelong interest in the beauty and violence of nature, recurring themes in his work.

Hughes and His Father It would be a mistake, however, to ignore the violence of World War I as an influence on Hughes. He was born well after the war, but his father had had a traumatic experience in that conflict. He was among a handful of men to survive the destruction of his regiment. Hughes once said that as a child, he was strongly affected by his father's silence about this experience.

Hughes himself served in the Royal Air Force and then studied archaeology and anthropology at Pembroke College, Cambridge, where he met the American poet Sylvia Plath. He married Plath in 1956, but they later separated.

A Variety of Work Hughes is best known for his volumes of poetry *Hawk in the Rain, Crow,* and *Moortown*. In these and other works, he uses free verse and powerful, direct speech to express a yearning for a lost wholeness with the natural world. In exploring this theme, which appears in "Horses" and "The Rain Horse," he was strongly influenced by the prose and poetry of D. H. Lawrence.

Hughes was a versatile writer who, in addition to poetry and fiction, wrote books for children. He even wrote a play in a language he invented. One of his final publications was *Tales from Ovid* (1997), a translation of many verse stories from the Latin poet Ovid's *Metamorphoses*. Hughes was poet laureate of England from 1984 until his death.

Preview

Connecting to the Literature

Even if you live in a city, nature is your home. In these poems and stories, the writers consider how sweet and strange a home nature can be.

Literary Analysis

Voice

The **voice** of a poet is his or her "sound" on the page. A poet's voice is based on elements like word choice, sound devices, pace, attitude, and even patterns of vowels and consonants. These two poets have different voices, Thomas tumbling words out in a rush and Hughes "speaking" in separate little blips of images:

- *Thomas, in "Fern Hill"*: "All the sun long it was running, it was lovely, . . . "
- *Hughes, in "The Horses"*: "Not a leaf, not a bird"

Listen for the different voices of these poets as you read their poems.

Comparing Literary Works

Because they have different "voices," these two poets use different poetic forms and meters. To complement his tight, closed way of speaking, Hughes employs loose, unrhyming couplets and the open rhythms of free verse. In contrast, Thomas reigns in his headlong speech with tight poetic forms like the **villanelle**—a nineteen-line poem in which lines 1 and 3 of the opening stanza appear regularly throughout and the rhyme scheme is *aba aba aba aba aba abaa*. In reading these poets, compare the ways in which their voices relate to the forms and rhythms they use.

Reading Strategy

Judging the Writer's Message

In **judging a writer's message,** you test what a writer says against your own experience and your past reading. For example, in "Do Not Go Gentle," Thomas says that the dying should fight against death. Does your experience or reading suggest that this is good advice? Use a chart like this one to record a poet's message and your evaluation of it.

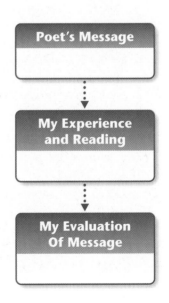

Vocabulary Development

grieved (grēvd) *v.* felt deep grief for; mourned (p. 1207)

transfiguring (trans fig′ yər iŋ) *adj.* changing or transforming, especially in a way that glorifies (p. 1213)

exasperated (eg zas′ pər āt′ id) *adj.* extremely annoyed (p. 1213)

nondescript (nän′ di skript′) *adj.* lacking identifying characteristics; bland (p. 1214)

malevolent (mə lev′ ə lənt) *adj.* wishing harm to others (p. 1218)

Do Not Go Gentle into That Good Night

Dylan Thomas

▲ **Critical Viewing** In what ways is the main boat in this painting an apt image of the soul's struggle against the "good night"? **[Analyze]**

Do not go gentle into that good night,
Old age should burn and rave at close of day;
Rage, rage against the dying of the light.

Though wise men at their end know dark is right,
5 Because their words had forked no lightning they
Do not go gentle into that good night.

Good men, the last wave by, crying how bright
Their frail deeds might have danced in a green bay,
Rage, rage against the dying of the light.

10 Wild men who caught and sang the sun in flight,
And learn, too late, they grieved it on its way,
Do not go gentle into that good night.

Grave men, near death, who see with blinding sight
Blind eyes could blaze like meteors and be gay,
15 Rage, rage against the dying of the light.

And you, my father, there on the sad height,
Curse, bless, me now with your fierce tears, I pray.
Do not go gentle into that good night.
Rage, rage against the dying of the light.

Literary Analysis
Voice and Villanelle In lines 4–15, how does the last line of each stanza stop the movement of the poem?

grieved (grēvd) v.
felt deep grief for; mourned

Review and Assess

Thinking About the Selection

1. (a) **Recall:** What is the "good night" mentioned in the title of "Do Not Go Gentle into That Good Night"? (b) **Infer:** What specific event is Thomas facing in the poem?

2. (a) **Recall:** Where in the poem does the word *grave* appear? (b) **Analyze:** What double meaning does the word have?

3. (a) **Recall:** What are four types of men Thomas describes in the poem? (b) **Infer:** Does Thomas suggest that each has regrets as he comes to the end of his life? Explain.

4. (a) **Recall:** What advice does the speaker give in lines 3, 9, 15, and 19? (b) **Interpret:** Considering the speaker's advice in these lines, why do you think he refers to the night as "good"?

5. **Evaluate:** Would this poem have been better if Thomas had chosen to work with a less restrictive form than villanelle? Why or why not?

6. **Take a Position:** Should people respond to death and life as intensely as Thomas does in this poem? Why or why not?

Fern Hill

Dylan Thomas

Now as I was young and easy under the apple boughs
About the lilting house and happy as the grass was green,
⠀⠀⠀⠀The night above the dingle starry,
⠀⠀⠀⠀⠀⠀Time let me hail and climb
5⠀⠀⠀⠀⠀⠀Golden in the heydays of his eyes,
And honored among wagons I was prince of the apple towns
And once below a time I lordly had the trees and leaves
⠀⠀⠀⠀⠀⠀Trail with daisies and barley
⠀⠀⠀⠀Down the rivers of the windfall light.

10⠀And as I was green and carefree, famous among the barns
About the happy yard and singing as the farm was home,
⠀⠀⠀⠀In the sun that is young once only,
⠀⠀⠀⠀⠀⠀Time let me play and be
⠀⠀⠀⠀Golden in the mercy of his means,
15⠀And green and golden I was huntsman and herdsman, the calves
Sang to my horn, the foxes on the hills barked clear and cold,
⠀⠀⠀⠀⠀⠀And the sabbath rang slowly
⠀⠀⠀⠀In the pebbles of the holy streams.

All the sun long it was running, it was lovely, the hay
20⠀Fields high as the house, the tunes from the chimneys, it was air
⠀⠀⠀⠀⠀⠀And playing, lovely and watery
⠀⠀⠀⠀⠀⠀⠀⠀And fire green as grass.
⠀⠀⠀⠀⠀⠀And nightly under the simple stars
As I rode to sleep the owls were bearing the farm away,
25⠀All the moon long I heard, blessed among stables, the nightjars[1]
⠀⠀⠀⠀⠀⠀Flying with the ricks,[2] and the horses
⠀⠀⠀⠀⠀⠀⠀⠀Flashing into the dark.

And then to awake, and the farm, like a wanderer white
With the dew, come back, the cock on his shoulder; it was all

Literary Analysis
Voice What is the contrast between Thomas's way of tumbling words out and the stanzas he uses?

---

1. **nightjars** *n.* common nocturnal birds, named for the whirring sound that the male makes.
2. **ricks** *n.* haystacks.

30   Shining, it was Adam and maiden,
           The sky gathered again
        And the sun grew round that very day.
So it must have been after the birth of the simple light
In the first, spinning place, the spellbound horses walking warm
35   Out of the whinnying green stable
           On to the fields of praise.

And honored among foxes and pheasants by the gay house
Under the new made clouds and happy as the heart was long,
        In the sun born over and over,
40   I ran my heedless ways,
        My wishes raced through the house-high hay
And nothing I cared, at my sky blue trades, that time allows
In all his tuneful turning so few and such morning songs
        Before the children green and golden
45   Follow him out of grace,

Nothing I cared, in the lamb white days, that time would take me
Up to the swallow thronged loft by the shadow of my hand,
        In the moon that is always rising,
          Nor that riding to sleep
50   I should hear him fly with the high fields
And wake to the farm forever fled from the childless land.
Oh as I was young and easy in the mercy of his means,
        Time held me green and dying
        Though I sang in my chains like the sea.

Reading Strategy
Judging the Writer's Message Is Thomas right in suggesting that a person can "wake" one day to realize that childhood has "forever fled"? Why or why not?

Review and Assess

Thinking About the Selection

1. **Respond:** Does your childhood seem like a distant memory, or are your early experiences still vivid in your mind? Explain.

2. **(a) Recall:** Which two colors does the speaker use to describe himself in his youth? **(b) Analyze:** How would you describe his feelings about his childhood?

3. **(a) Recall:** Paraphrase the final stanza. **(b) Interpret:** How does the mood change in this stanza? **(c) Infer:** What is the reason for this shift?

4. **Interpret:** What is the meaning of lines 53–54?

5. **Draw Conclusions:** What does this poem suggest about Thomas's attitude toward the different stages of life?

6. **Classify:** Into what important stages would you divide human life? Explain.

The Horses
Ted Hughes

Background

Although both Thomas and Hughes wrote of nature, they approached it differently. Thomas was fascinated by nature's double face, life and death, as demonstrated in the line "Time held me green and dying" from "Fern Hill." Hughes was often closely attuned to nature's violence, as in "The Rain Horse," or to its remote, primitive, nonhuman beauty, as in "The Horses."

I climbed through woods in the hour-before-dawn dark.
Evil air, a frost-making stillness,

Not a leaf, not a bird—
A world cast in frost. I came out above the wood

5 Where my breath left tortuous statues in the iron light.
But the valleys were draining the darkness

Till the moorline—blackening dregs of the brightening gray—
Halved the sky ahead. And I saw the horses:

Huge in the dense gray—ten together—
10 Megalith-still.[1] They breathed, making no move,

Literary Analysis
Voice How do the stanzas in this poem suggest Hughes's style of "speaking" in short bursts of images?

---

1. **Megalith-still** still as the huge stones left by ancient peoples, such as those at Stonehenge.

With draped manes and tilted hind-hooves,
Making no sound.

I passed: not one snorted or jerked its head.
Gray silent fragments

15 Of a gray silent world.

I listened in emptiness on the moor-ridge.
The curlew's[2] tear turned its edge on the silence.

Slowly detail leafed from the darkness. Then the sun
Orange, red, red erupted

20 Silently, and splitting to its core tore and flung cloud,
Shook the gulf open, showed blue,

▲ Critical Viewing
Compare and contrast
the horses in the poem
with those in the picture.
[Compare and Contrast]

Reading Check

What are the horses
doing when Hughes
sees them?

2. **curlew's** (kʉr´ lōō) *n.* of a large, brownish wading bird with long legs.

And the big planets hanging—
I turned

Stumbling in the fever of a dream, down towards
25   The dark woods, from the kindling tops.

And came to the horses.
                    There, still they stood,
But now steaming and glistening under the flow of light,

Their draped stone manes, their tilted hind-hooves
Stirring under a thaw while all around them

30   The frost showed its fires. But still they made no sound.
Not one snorted or stamped,

Their hung heads patient as the horizons,
High over valleys, in the red leveling rays—

In din of the crowded streets, going among the years, the faces,
35   May I still meet my memory in so lonely a place

Between the streams and the red clouds, hearing curlews,
Hearing the horizons endure.

Reading Strategy
Judging the Writer's Message Can a memory of something seen in nature stay with a person for years, as Hughes suggests in lines 34–35?

Review and Assess

Thinking About the Selection

1. **Respond:** What kind of place or scene would you like to remember later, "going among the years"? Why?

2. **(a) Recall:** What is the setting of the poem, its time and place? **(b) Evaluate:** How does this setting heighten the impact of events in the poem?

3. **(a) Recall:** How many times does the speaker sight the horses? **(b) Compare and Contrast:** Compare and contrast the horses in the different sightings.

4. **(a) Recall:** What actually occurs during the course of the poem? **(b) Draw Conclusions:** What view of nature do the descriptions and actions in the poem suggest? Explain.

5. **(a) Recall:** What wish does the speaker make at the end of the poem? **(b) Evaluate:** In what ways might the speaker—or anyone—draw solace from a scene like this in the future?

6. **Make a Judgment:** Does this poem provide a good argument for protecting nature against development? Explain.

The Rain Horse

Ted Hughes

A s the young man came over the hill the first thin blowing of rain met him. He turned his coat-collar up and stood on top of the shelving rabbit-riddled hedgebank, looking down into the valley.

He had come too far. What had set out as a walk along pleasantly-remembered tarmac[1] lanes had turned dreamily by gate and path and hedge-gap into a cross-ploughland trek, his shoes ruined, the dark mud of the lower fields inching up the trouser legs of his gray suit where they rubbed against each other. And now there was a raw, flapping wetness in the air that would be downpour again at any minute. He shivered, holding himself tense against the cold.

This was the view he had been thinking of. Vaguely, without really directing his walk, he had felt he would get the whole thing from this point. For twelve years, whenever he had recalled this scene, he had imagined it as it looked from here. Now the valley lay sunken in front of him, utterly deserted, shallow, bare fields, black and sodden as the bed of an ancient lake after the weeks of rain.

Nothing happened. Not that he had looked forward to any very transfiguring experience. But he had expected something, some pleasure, some meaningful sensation, he didn't quite know what.

So he waited, trying to nudge the right feelings alive with the details—the surprisingly familiar curve of the hedges, the stone gate-pillar and iron gatehook let into it that he had used as a target, the long bank of the rabbit-warren on which he stood and which had been the first thing he ever noticed about the hill when twenty years ago, from the distance of the village, he had said to himself "That looks like rabbits."

Twelve years had changed him. This land no longer recognized him, and he looked back at it coldly, as at a finally visited home-country, known only through the stories of a grandfather; felt nothing but the dullness of feeling nothing. Boredom. Then, suddenly, impatience, with a whole exasperated swarm of little anxieties about his shoes,

---

1. tarmac material used for paving.

transfiguring (trans fig´ yər iŋ) *adj.* changing or transforming, especially in a way that glorifies

exasperated (eg zas´ pər āt´ id) *adj.* extremely annoyed

✔Reading Check

In what way has the young man changed since the last time he was in this place?

and the spitting rain and his new suit and that sky and the two-mile trudge through the mud back to the road.

It would be quicker to go straight forward to the farm a mile away in the valley and behind which the road looped. But the thought of meeting the farmer—to be embarrassingly remembered or shouted at as a trespasser—deterred him. He saw the rain pulling up out of the distance, dragging its gray broken columns, smudging the trees and the farms.

A wave of anger went over him: anger against himself for blundering into this mud-trap and anger against the land that made him feel so outcast, so old and stiff and stupid. He wanted nothing but to get away from it as quickly as possible. But as he turned, something moved in his eye-corner. All his senses startled alert. He stopped.

Over to his right a thin, black horse was running across the ploughland towards the hill, its head down, neck stretched out. It seemed to be running on its toes like a cat, like a dog up to no good.

From the high point on which he stood the hill dipped slightly and rose to another crested point fringed with the tops of trees, three hundred yards to his right. As he watched it, the horse ran up to that crest, showed against the sky—for a moment like a nightmarish leopard—and disappeared over the other side.

For several seconds he stared at the skyline, stunned by the unpleasantly strange impression the horse had made on him. Then the plastering beat of icy rain on his bare skull brought him to himself. The distance had vanished in a wall of gray. All around him the fields were jumping and streaming.

Holding his collar close and tucking his chin down into it he ran back over the hilltop towards the town-side, the lee-side, his feet sucking and splashing, at every stride plunging to the ankle.

This hill was shaped like a wave, a gently rounded back lifting out of the valley to a sharply crested, almost concave front hanging over the river meadows towards the town. Down this front, from the crest, hung two small woods separated by a fallow field. The near wood was nothing more than a quarry, circular, full of stones and bracken,[2] with a few thorns and <u>nondescript</u> saplings, foxholes and rabbit holes. The other was rectangular, mainly a planting of scrub oak trees. Beyond the river smoldered the town like a great heap of blue cinders.

He ran along the top of the first wood and finding no shelter but the thin, leafless thorns of the hedge, dipped below the crest out of the wind and jogged along through thick grass to the wood of oaks. In blinding rain he lunged through the barricade of brambles at the wood's edge. The little crippled trees were small choice in the way of shelter, but at a sudden fierce thickening of the rain he took one at random and crouched down under the leaning trunk.

Still panting from his run, drawing his knees up tightly, he watched the bleak lines of rain, gray as hail, slanting through the

Reading Strategy
Judging the Writer's Message Do you think the idea that the horse might be "up to no good" comes from the young man, from Hughes, or from both of them? Explain.

nondescript (nän´ di skript´) *adj.* lacking identifying characteristics; bland

---

2. **bracken** Large, coarse ferns.

boughs into the clumps of bracken and bramble. He felt hidden and safe. The sound of the rain as it rushed and lulled in the wood seemed to seal him in. Soon the chilly sheet lead of his suit became a tight, warm mold, and gradually he sank into a state of comfort that was all but trance, though the rain beat steadily on his exposed shoulders and trickled down the oak trunk on to his neck.

All around him the boughs angled down, glistening, black as iron. From their tips and elbows the drops hurried steadily, and the channels of the bark pulsed and gleamed. For a time he amused himself calculating the variation in the rainfall by the variations in a dribble of water from a trembling twig-end two feet in front of his nose. He studied the twig, bringing dwarfs and continents and animals out of its scurfy bark. Beyond the boughs the blue shoal of the town was rising and falling, and darkening and fading again, in the pale, swaying backdrop of rain.

He wanted this rain to go on forever. Whenever it seemed to be drawing off he listened anxiously until it closed in again. As long as it lasted he was suspended from life and time. He didn't want to return to his sodden shoes and his possibly ruined suit and the walk back over that land of mud.

All at once he shivered. He hugged his knees to squeeze out the cold and found himself thinking of the horse. The hair on the nape of his neck prickled slightly. He remembered how it had run up to the crest and showed against the sky.

He tried to dismiss the thought. Horses wander about the countryside often enough. But the image of the horse as it had appeared against the sky stuck in his mind. It must have come over the crest just above the wood in which he was now sitting. To clear his mind, he twisted around and looked up the wood between the tree stems, to his left.

At the wood top, with the silvered gray light coming in behind it, the black horse was standing under the oaks, its head high and alert, its ears pricked, watching him.

A horse sheltering from the rain generally goes into a sort of stupor, tilts a hind hoof and hangs its head and lets its eyelids droop, and so it stays as long as the rain lasts. This horse was nothing like that. It was watching him intently, standing perfectly still, its soaked neck and flank shining in the hard light.

He turned back. His scalp went icy and he shivered. What was he to do? Ridiculous to try driving it away. And to leave the wood, with the rain still coming down full pelt, was out of the question. Meanwhile the idea of being watched became more and more unsettling until at last he had to twist around again, to see if the horse had moved. It stood exactly as before.

This was absurd. He took control of himself and turned back deliberately, determined not to give the horse one more thought. If it wanted to share the wood with him, let it. If it wanted to stare at him, let it. He was nestling firmly into these resolutions when the ground shook and he heard the crash of a heavy body coming down the

Literary Analysis
Voice What does the brief length of the paragraphs in this section of the story suggest about the young man's state of mind?

☑ **Reading Check**

In what way does the horse behave differently from other horses that shelter from the rain?

wood. Like lightning his legs bounded him upright and about face. The horse was almost on top of him, its head stretching forwards, ears flattened and lips lifted back from the long yellow teeth. He got one snapshot glimpse of the red-veined eyeball as he flung himself backwards around the tree. Then he was away up the slope, whipped by oak twigs as he leapt the brambles and brushwood, twisting between the close trees till he tripped and sprawled. As he fell the warning flashed through his head that he must at all costs keep his suit out of the leaf-mold, but a more urgent instinct was already rolling him violently sideways. He spun around, sat up and looked back, ready to scramble off in a flash to one side. He was panting from the sudden excitement and effort. The horse had disappeared. The wood was empty except for the drumming, slant gray rain, dancing the bracken and glittering from the branches.

He got up, furious. Knocking the dirt and leaves from his suit as well as he could he looked around for a weapon. The horse was evidently mad, had an abscess on its brain or something of the sort. Or maybe it was just spiteful. Rain sometimes puts creatures into queer states. Whatever it was, he was going to get away from the wood as quickly as possible, rain or no rain.

Since the horse seemed to have gone on down the wood, his way to the farm over the hill was clear. As he went, he broke a yard length of wrist-thick dead branch from one of the oaks, but immediately threw it aside and wiped the slime of rotten wet bark from his hands with his soaked handkerchief. Already he was thinking it incredible that the horse could have meant to attack him. Most likely it was just going down the wood for better shelter and had made a feint[3] at him in passing—as much out of curiosity or playfulness as anything. He recalled the way horses menace each other when they are galloping around in a paddock.

The wood rose to a steep bank topped by the hawthorn hedge that ran along the whole ridge of the hill. He was pulling himself up to a thin place in the hedge by the bare stem of one of the hawthorns when he ducked and shrank down again. The swelling gradient of fields lay in front of him, smoking in the slowly crossing rain. Out in the middle of the first field, tall as a statue, and a ghostly silver in the under-cloud light, stood the horse, watching the wood.

He lowered his head slowly, slithered back down the bank and crouched. An awful feeling of helplessness came over him. He felt certain the horse had been looking straight at him. Waiting for him? Was it clairvoyant?[4] Maybe a mad animal can be clairvoyant. At the same time he was ashamed to find himself acting so inanely, ducking and creeping about in this way just to keep out of sight of a horse. He tried to imagine how anybody in their senses would just walk off home. This cooled him a little, and he retreated farther down the

Reading Strategy
Judging the Writer's Message How do the young man's experiences with the horse relate to the earlier statement that "this land no longer recognized him"?

---

3. **feint** Pretend attack.
4. **clairvoyant** Having the supernatural ability to see what is not present or to read minds.

wood. He would go back the way he had come, along under the hill crest, without any more nonsense.

The wood hummed and the rain was a cold weight, but he observed this rather than felt it. The water ran down inside his clothes and squelched in his shoes as he eased his way carefully over the bedded twigs and leaves. At every instant he expected to see the prick-eared black head looking down at him from the hedge above.

At the woodside he paused, close against a tree. The success of this last manoeuvre was restoring his confidence, but he didn't want to venture out into the open field without making sure that the horse was just where he had left it. The perfect move would be to withdraw quietly and leave the horse standing out there in the rain. He crept up again among the trees to the crest and peeped through the hedge.

The gray field and the whole slope were empty. He searched the distance. The horse was quite likely to have forgotten him altogether and wandered off. Then he raised himself and leaned out to see if it had come in close to the hedge. Before he was aware of anything the ground shook. He twisted around wildly to see how he had been caught. The black shape was above him, right across the light. Its whinnying snort and the spattering whack of its hooves seemed to be actually inside his head as he fell backwards down the bank, and leapt again like a madman, dodging among the oaks, imagining how the buffet would come and how he would be knocked headlong. Halfway down the wood the oaks gave way to bracken and old roots and stony rabbit diggings. He was well out into the middle of this before he realized that he was running alone.

Gasping for breath now and cursing mechanically, without a thought for his suit he sat down on the ground to rest his shaking legs, letting the rain plaster the hair down over his forehead and watching the dense flashing lines disappear abruptly into the soil all around him as if he were watching through thick plate glass. He took deep breaths in the effort to steady his heart and regain control of himself. His right trouser turn-up was ripped at the seam and his suit jacket was splashed with the yellow mud of the top field.

Obviously the horse had been farther along the hedge above the steep field, waiting for him to come out at the woodside just as he had intended. He must have peeped through the hedge—peeping the wrong way—within yards of it.

However, this last attack had cleared up one thing. He need no longer act like a fool out of mere uncertainty as to whether the horse was simply being playful or not. It was definitely after him. He picked

Literary Analysis
Voice Through the use of such phrases as "whinnying snort" and "spattering whack," does Hughes create a voice that is distant or engaged, slow or rapid? Explain.

✔**Reading Check**
What happens when the horse attacks the young man?

up two stones about the size of goose eggs and set off towards the bottom of the wood, striding carelessly.

A loop of the river bordered all this farmland. If he crossed the little level meadow at the bottom of the wood, he could follow the three-mile circuit, back to the road. There were deep hollows in the river-bank, shoaled with pebbles, as he remembered, perfect places to defend himself from if the horse followed him out there.

The hawthorns that choked the bottom of the wood—some of them good-sized trees—knitted into an almost impassable barrier. He had found a place where the growth thinned slightly and had begun to lift aside the long spiny stems, pushing himself forward, when he stopped. Through the bluish veil of bare twigs he saw the familiar shape out in the field below the wood.

But it seemed not to have noticed him yet. It was looking out across the field towards the river. Quietly, he released himself from the thorns and climbed back across the clearing towards the one side of the wood he had not yet tried. If the horse would only stay down there he could follow his first and easiest plan, up the wood and over the hilltop to the farm.

Now he noticed that the sky had grown much darker. The rain was heavier every second, pressing down as if the earth had to be flooded before nightfall. The oaks ahead blurred and the ground drummed. He began to run. And as he ran he heard a deeper sound running with him. He whirled around. The horse was in the middle of the clearing. It might have been running to get out of the terrific rain except that it was coming straight for him, scattering clay and stones, with an immensely supple and powerful motion. He let out a tearing roar and threw the stone in his right hand. The result was instantaneous. Whether at the roar or the stone the horse reared as if against a wall and shied to the left. As it dropped back on its fore-feet he flung his second stone, at ten yards' range, and saw a bright mud blotch suddenly appear on the glistening black flank. The horse surged down the wood, splashing the earth like water, tossing its long tail as it plunged out of sight among the hawthorns.

He looked around for stones. The encounter had set the blood beating in his head and given him a savage energy. He could have killed the horse at that moment. That this brute should pick him and play with him in this <u>malevolent</u> fashion was more than he could bear. Whoever owned it, he thought, deserved to have its neck broken for letting the dangerous thing loose.

He came out at the woodside, in open battle now, still searching for the right stones. There were plenty here, piled and scattered where they had been ploughed out of the field. He selected two, then straightened and saw the horse twenty yards off in the middle of the steep field, watching him calmly. They looked at each other.

"Out of it!" he shouted, brandishing his arm. "Out of it! Go on!" The horse twitched its pricked ears. With all his force he threw. The stone soared and landed beyond with a soft thud. He re-armed and

Reading Strategy
Judging the Writer's Message Do you view a horse as a powerful force of nature, as Hughes seems to do in the paragraph beginning, "Now he noticed . . ."? Why or why not?

malevolent (mə lev′ ə lent) *adj.* wishing harm to others

threw again. For several minutes he kept up his bombardment without a single hit, working himself into a despair and throwing more and more wildly, till his arm began to ache with the unaccustomed exercise. Throughout the performance the horse watched him fixedly. Finally he had to stop and ease his shoulder muscle. As if the horse had been waiting for just this, it dipped its head twice and came at him.

He snatched up two stones and roaring with all his strength flung the one in his right hand. He was astonished at the crack of the impact. It was as if he had struck a tile—and the horse actually stumbled. With another roar he jumped forward and hurled his other stone. His aim seemed to be under superior guidance. The stone struck and rebounded straight up into the air, spinning fiercely, as the horse swirled away and went careering down towards the far bottom of the field, at first with great, swinging leaps, then at a canter,[5] leaving deep churned holes in the soil.

It turned up the far side of the field, climbing till it was level with him. He felt a little surprise of pity to see it shaking its head, and once it paused to lower its head and paw over its ear with its fore-hoof as a cat does.

"You stay there!" he shouted. "Keep your distance and you'll not get hurt."

And indeed the horse did stop at that moment, almost obediently. It watched him as he climbed to the crest.

The rain swept into his face and he realized that he was freezing, as if his very flesh were sodden. The farm seemed miles away over the dreary fields. Without another glance at the horse—he felt too exhausted to care now what it did—he loaded the crook of his left arm with stones and plunged out on to the waste of mud.

He was half-way to the first hedge before the horse appeared, silhouetted against the sky at the corner of the wood, head high and attentive, watching his laborious retreat over the three fields.

The ankle-deep clay dragged at him. Every stride was a separate, deliberate effort, forcing him up and out of the sucking earth, burdened as he was by his sogged clothes and load of stone and limbs that seemed themselves to be turning to mud. He fought to keep his breathing even, two strides in, two strides out, the air ripping his lungs. In the middle of the last field he stopped and looked around. The horse, tiny on the skyline, had not moved.

At the corner of the field he unlocked his clasped arms and dumped the stones by the gatepost, then leaned on the gate. The farm was in front of him. He became conscious of the rain again and suddenly longed to stretch out full-length under it, to take the cooling, healing drops all over his body and forget himself in the last wretchedness of the mud. Making an effort, he heaved his weight over the gate-top. He leaned again, looking up at the hill.

---

5. **canter** gait like a slow gallop.

Reading Strategy
Judging the Writer's Message How do the actions and attitudes of the young man in this story differ from those of the speaker in the poem "Horses"?

✔**Reading Check**

How does the young man defend himself against the horse?

Rain was dissolving land and sky together like a wet water-color as the afternoon darkened. He concentrated raising his head, searching the skyline from end to end. The horse had vanished. The hill looked lifeless and desolate, an island lifting out of the sea, awash with every tide.

Under the long shed where the tractors, plough, binders and the rest were drawn up, waiting for their seasons, he sat on a sack thrown over a petrol drum, trembling, his lungs heaving. The mingled smell of paraffin, creosote,[6] fertilizer, dust—all was exactly as he had left it twelve years ago. The ragged swallows' nests were still there tucked in the angles of the rafters. He remembered three dead foxes hanging in a row from one of the beams, their teeth bloody.

The ordeal with the horse had already sunk from reality. It hung under the surface of his mind, an obscure confusion of fright and shame, as after a narrowly-escaped street accident. There was a solid pain in his chest, like a spike of bone stabbing, that made him wonder if he had strained his heart on that last stupid burdened run. Piece by piece he began to take off his clothes, wringing the gray water out of them, but soon he stopped that and just sat staring at the ground, as if some important part had been cut out of his brain.

---

6. **petrol . . . paraffin, creosote** (krē´ ə sōt´) Petrol is gasoline; paraffin, wax; creosote, an oily liquid made from tar and used to preserve wood.

Reading Strategy
Judging the Writer's Message Do you agree that it is bad to feel cut off from nature, as Hughes seems to suggest in this story?

Review and Assess

Thinking About the Selection

1. **Respond:** Did the behavior of the horse surprise you? Explain.

2. **(a) Recall:** What effect has a twelve-year absence had on the man's relationship with this landscape? **(b) Infer:** What effect does the rain have on his mood and, specifically, on his feelings toward the landscape?

3. **(a) Recall:** Briefly summarize the man's interactions with the horse. **(b) Connect:** Is there a link between the behavior of the horse and the man's feelings about the landscape? Explain.

4. **(a) Make a Judgment:** Has the man been imagining the horse or, if the horse is real, the threat that it poses? Explain your opinion. **(b) Interpret:** What is the meaning of the last line of the story?

5. **Compare and Contrast:** Compare and contrast the attitudes toward nature of the speaker in "The Horses" and of the main character in "The Rain Horse."

6. **Speculate:** Do you think that many people today are out of touch with nature? Why or why not?

Review and Assess

Literary Analysis

Voice

1. Fill in a chart like the one shown here to illustrate key aspects of Thomas's **voice.**

Quality	Examples
Tumbles out words in a rush	
Shows an attitude of wonder about life	
Uses complex poetic forms	

2. Devise and fill in a similar chart for Hughes, listing these qualities: Speaks in blips and pulses; feels awe toward nature; uses free verse; bunches together words of one syllable.

3. Identify the voice in these lines as belonging to Hughes or Thomas, and explain your choice: "Dawn—a smoldering fume of dry frost, / Sky—edge of red-hot iron."

Comparing Literary Works

4. Given Hughes's poetic voice, do you think he would have chosen a form like the **villanelle** to address his dying father? Why or why not?

5. Why are the unrhymed couplets of "The Horses" unsuited to Thomas's aim in "Fern Hill"—to convey the rushing wonder of childhood?

6. If Thomas had written about the experience Hughes describes in "The Horses," how might the poem have been different?

Reading Strategy

Judging the Writer's Message

7. In "Fern Hill," Thomas suggests that children are carefree, with no awareness of death. Do you **judge this message** to be true? Explain.

8. In "The Horses" and "The Rain Horse," Hughes seems to be saying that people who live in cities are cut off from nature. Do you think this is necessarily true? Explain.

Extend Understanding

9. **Social Studies Connection:** Explain a possible link between the Industrial Revolution (the rise of factories and the decline of traditional farming life) and the theme of "The Rain Horse."

Quick Review

A writer's **voice,** his or her "sound" on the page, includes elements like word choice, sound devices, phrasing, pace, and attitude.

A **villanelle** is a nineteen-line poem in which lines 1 and 3 of the opening stanza alternate as endings of the next four stanzas and appear together at the end of the final stanza. The rhyme scheme of the villanelle is *aba aba aba aba aba abaa.*

To **judge a writer's message** test what a writer says against your own ideas and experiences.

 Take It to the Net
www.phschool.com

Take the interactive self-test online to check your understanding of these selections.

Integrate Language Skills

Vocabulary Development Lesson

Word Analysis: Latin Root -vol-

The Latin root -vol- means "to wish" or "to use one's will." In *malevolent*, it means "wishing harm." Knowing the meaning of this root, define each word.

   1. voluntary **2.** volunteer **3.** benevolent

Spelling Strategy

When forming the past tense of a verb that ends in a silent *e*, drop the *e* before adding -*ed*: *exasperate* + -*ed* = *exasperated*. In general, drop the final *e* whenever adding an ending that begins with a vowel. Some exceptions occur when the root ends in *ce* or *ge*. On your paper, add the ending indicated to each word.

   1. grieve + -*ed*   **2.** trace + -*able*

Grammar and Style Lesson

Sentence Beginnings: Adverb Clauses

Adverb clauses are subordinate clauses that modify verbs, adverbs, or adjectives. They answer the questions *when, why,* or *under what conditions.* Both Thomas and Hughes add variety to their writing by using adverb clauses to begin sentences.

> <u>As I rode to sleep</u> the owls were bearing the farm away, . . . (answers the question *when?*)

Practice Using a conjunction like *as, as if, after, because, when,* or *since,* combine each sentence pair into a single sentence beginning with an adverb clause. If necessary, replace nouns with pronouns.

   1. The young man came over the hill. The first thin blowing of rain met him.

Fluency: Sentence Completion

Review the vocabulary list on page 1205. Then, in your notebook, write the word from the vocabulary list that best fits in each blank. Use each word only once.

At first, the young man was merely ___?___ as he walked over the wet ground. His clothes were soaked, and the meadow looked dull and ___?___ . Then, suddenly, a ___?___ horse appeared and tried to attack him. As he thought about the experience later, he ___?___ ; nature, once friendly toward him, had become hostile. Although he expected his experience to be a(n) ___?___ one, his flight from the "rain horse" was a disturbing experience.

   2. He had recalled this scene in the past. He had imagined it as it looked from here.

   3. The horse seemed to have gone on down the wood. His way to the farm over the hill was clear.

   4. He fell. The warning flashed through his head that he must keep his suit out of the leaf-mold.

   5. The horse had been waiting for just this. It dipped its head twice and came at him.

Writing Application Write a paragraph about an encounter with an animal. To add variety to your paragraph and to describe events clearly, link ideas by using adverb clauses at the beginning of at least two sentences.

WG Prentice Hall Writing and Grammar Connection: Chapter 19, Section 3

Writing Lesson

Parody of a Poet's Voice

Dylan Thomas and Ted Hughes wrote in distinctive voices. Choose one of these voices and write a poem in which you parody or imitate the author's style for a humorous effect.

Prewriting   Review the characteristics of the voice you are parodying. Then, use a chart like this one to note the characteristics of the voice, ways in which you can exaggerate them, and a slightly ridiculous subject to which you can apply them.

Model: Analyzing Voice for Parody

Thomas's Voice	Ways of Exaggerating	Ridiculous Subject
1. tumbling, rushing words	make even faster	taking a math test
2.		

Drafting   Consider using the poet's own forms, rhythms, and words as a basis for your parody. Then, make substitutions that exaggerate the characteristics of the voice and refocus the poem on the ridiculous subject.

Revising   Read your poem aloud to several classmates. If they cannot identify the poet whose voice you are parodying, be sure you have included—in exaggerated form—all the main features of that poet's voice.

 Prentice Hall Writing and Grammar Connection: Chapter 14, Section 2

Extension Activities

Listening and Speaking   Listen to a recording of Dylan Thomas reading his poetry. Then, imitating Thomas's reading style, perform your own **oral interpretation** of one of the poems. Focus on these elements:

- Pronunciation, saying words correctly
- Enunciation, speaking words clearly
- Pacing, slowing down or speeding up
- Volume, speaking loudly or softly

After your performance, lead the class in a discussion of Thomas's reading style.

Research and Technology   With two classmates, give a **panel presentation** on the nature poetry of Dylan Thomas, Ted Hughes, and D.H. Lawrence. Each person can research a poet, using the poet's books, critical works about him, and Web sites. Present information on each poet and discuss their similarities and differences. Then, answer audience questions. **[Group Activity]**

 Take It to the Net   www.phschool.com

Go online for an additional research activity using the Internet.

Prepare to Read

An Arundel Tomb ◆ The Explosion ◆
On the Patio ◆ Not Waving but Drowning

Philip Larkin (1922–1985)

Philip Larkin turned what could have been a discouragement into a reason for developing poetic skill and emotional restraint. As a child in Coventry, England, his home life was dominated by a father who held him accountable to rigid standards. Larkin escaped from these pressures by building a private childhood world rich in creativity and imagination.

Deprivation Versus Daffodils Reflecting on his life, Larkin metaphorically explained how he drew inspiration from his difficult experiences when he told an interviewer, "Deprivation is for me what daffodils were for Wordsworth."

Although Larkin also developed a lifelong interest in jazz, which he came to love "even more than poetry," it was his clear-eyed, honest poetry, combining conversational language with well-crafted forms, that won him international fame. His poetry speaks of day-to-day realities, sometimes discouragingly, but is quietly haunted by realities beyond everyday life.

Peter Redgrove (b. 1932)

Like William Blake, a visionary poet with whom he is sometimes compared, Peter Redgrove does not fit into the usual categories. He lives at a distance from the literary hub of London—in Falmouth, Cornwall, the southwestern tip of England. Redgrove lives at an imaginative distance from London as well, rejecting the drab, everyday qualities so prevalent in many post-World War II British poems.

Transformation Through Imagination In his poetry, novels, television scripts, and nonfiction works, Redgrove celebrates our power to reimagine and transform our lives. His rich visual imagery reflects a heightened awareness that borders on the mystical as he speaks for stones or sees the world through the eyes of a wandering dog.

Redgrove's poems have been widely acclaimed in England, and he is the recipient of the 1997 Queen's Medal for Poetry.

Stevie Smith (1902–1971)

Stevie Smith's poems, cannot be easily classified. They are modeled, however, on familiar forms—hymns, popular songs, and nineteenth-century British and American poems. Using simple forms and language, she often evokes despair, perhaps relying on the poetic statement of bleak feelings to cleanse or banish them from life.

The author of this unusual body of work was born Florence Margaret Smith in Hull, Yorkshire. Due to her mother's ill health, she was raised mostly by her beloved Auntie Lion, with whom she continued to live in a Northern London suburb even as an adult. While working for a magazine, Smith wrote three novels and nine collections of poems.

Poems and Doodles Smith's poems can be humorous, macabre, surprising, and childlike, and she often illustrates them with sketches or doodles that echo her playful rhythms.

Some critics suggest that her work cunningly satirizes conventional forms of poetic expression, such as the hymn and the nursery rhyme, and adds dark new depths and keen irony to these traditional forms.

Preview

Connecting to the Literature

Body language can reveal deep emotions. In each of these poems, a gesture holds a clue to the meaning.

Literary Analysis

Free Verse and Meter

Free verse is poetry without regular end rhymes or the regular rhythms called **meter.** Widely used today, free verse has lines of varying lengths and an invented rhythm that suits the meaning. Redgrove uses free verse in "The Patio."

In contrast, Larkin uses regular meters that are classified by the stresses in each foot, or group of syllables, and the number of feet per line, as follows:

- **iamb**—foot with an unstressed and stressed syllable (˘ ´)
- **trochee**—foot with a stressed and unstressed syllable (´ ˘)
- **tetrameter**—verse with four feet per line

"An Arundel Tomb" uses **iambic tetrameter** with variations:

> The earl and countess lie in stone, . . .

"The Explosion" uses **trochaic tetrameter** (with some lines of iambic tetrameter):

> Shadows pointed towards the pithead: . . .

Stevie Smith adapts the **ballad stanza,** which usually alternates four- and three-beat lines and has a rhyme scheme of *abab* or *abcb*. Smith uses the scheme *abcb*—though "moaning" and "drowning" do not rhyme exactly—but her free rhythms include lines with one to six beats.

Comparing Literary Works

The rhythm of these poems adds to their **dramatic structure**—their use of contrasts to build toward a climax. Compare the ways in which these poems achieve such a climax.

Reading Strategy

Reading in Sentences

To understand a poem, **read in sentences:** Pause with punctuation, rather than automatically stopping at the ends of lines. As a reminder, mark the ends of lines in a copy of the poem with signs like these.

Sign	Means
→	Continue without pause
↱	Pause for comma, dash, or semicolon and continue
✋	Full stop for period

Vocabulary Development

effigy (ef´ i jē) *n.* portrait or statue of a person (p. 1227)

supine (soo¯´ pīn´) *adj.* lying on the back (p. 1227)

fidelity (fə del´ ə tē) *n.* faithfulness (p. 1227)

larking (lärk´ iŋ) *n.* free-spirited, whimsical fun (p. 1232)

AN ARUNDEL TOMB

Philip Larkin

Background

The inspiration for "An Arundel Tomb" was a stone monument in Chichester Cathedral, Sussex, near the site of the ancient Roman town of Arundel. The monument is a fourteenth-century table tomb (similar to the ancient Roman tombstones shown here). On it lie the effigies of Richard Fitzalan, thirteenth Earl of Arundel, and his second wife, Eleanor, holding hands (as the couple do on the Roman tombstones). Today, visitors to the cathedral can see the tomb itself and a copy of Larkin's poem inspired by the tomb.

Side by side, their faces blurred,
The earl and countess lie in stone,
Their proper habits vaguely shown
As jointed armor, stiffened pleat,
5 And that faint hint of the absurd—
The little dogs under their feet.

Such plainness of the pre-baroque
Hardly involves the eye, until
It meets his left-hand gauntlet,[1] still
10   Clasped empty in the other; and
One sees, with a sharp tender shock,
His hand withdrawn, holding her hand.

They would not think to lie so long.
Such faithfulness in effigy
15   Was just a detail friends would see:
A sculptor's sweet commissioned grace
Thrown off in helping to prolong
The Latin names around the base.

They would not guess how early in
20   Their supine stationary voyage
The air would change to soundless damage,
Turn the old tenantry[2] away;
How soon succeeding eyes begin
To look, not read. Rigidly they

25   Persisted, linked, through lengths and breadths
Of time. Snow fell, undated. Light
Each summer thronged the glass. A bright
Litter of birdcalls strewed the same
Bone-riddled ground. And up the paths
30   The endless altered people came,

Washing at their identity.
Now, helpless in the hollow of
An unarmorial age, a trough
Of smoke in slow suspended skeins[3]
35   Above their scrap of history,
Only an attitude remains:

Time has transfigured them into
Untruth. The stone fidelity
They hardly meant has come to be
40   Their final blazon,[4] and to prove
Our almost-instinct almost true:
What will survive of us is love.

---

1. **gauntlet** armored glove.
2. **tenantry** peasants farming the nobles' land.
3. **skeins** loosely coiled bunches of thread or yarn.
4. **blazon** coat of arms; a noble family's symbol.

◄ **Critical Viewing** Do engraved images and messages such as the ones on these tombstones always become an "untruth" in relation to life—as Larkin's poem seems to claim? Explain. **[Relate]**

Literary Analysis
Free Verse and Meter
How do the meters of lines 1 and 2 differ?

effigy (ef´ i jē) *n.* portrait or statue of a person

supine (soo´ pīn´) *adj.* lying on the back

fidelity (fə del´ ə tē) *n.* faithfulness

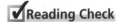
Reading Check

How did the sculptor portray the earl and countess on their tomb?

The EXPLOSION

Philip Larkin

On the day of the explosion
Shadows pointed towards the pithead:
In the sun the slagheap slept.

Down the lane came men in pitboots
5   Coughing oath-edged talk and pipe-smoke,
Shouldering off the freshened silence.

One chased after rabbits; lost them;
Came back with a nest of lark's eggs;
Showed them; lodged them in the grasses.

10   So they passed in beards and moleskins,[1]
Fathers, brothers, nicknames, laughter,
Through the tall gates standing open.

---

1. **moleskins** garments, especially trousers, of heavy cotton.

At noon, there came a tremor; cows
Stopped chewing for a second; sun,
15   Scarfed as in a heat-haze, dimmed.

The dead go on before us, they
Are sitting in God's house in comfort,
We shall see them face to face—

Plain as lettering in the chapels
20   It was said, and for a second
Wives saw men of the explosion

Larger than in life they managed—
Gold as on a coin, or walking
Somehow from the sun towards them,

25   One showing the eggs unbroken.

Literary Analysis
Free Verse, Meter, and
Dramatic Structure Why
do you think that at the
climax of the poem, the
line describing the
"unbroken" eggs breaks
the metrical pattern? ◆

Review and Assess

Thinking About the Selections

1. **Respond:** Do you find it easy to visualize what these poems describe? Why or why not?

2. **(a) Recall:** Describe the sculptured couple on whom the poet focuses in "An Arundel Tomb." **(b) Interpret:** What does the poet mean by stating that this couple has made a "supine stationary voyage"?

3. **(a) Recall:** In "An Arundel Tomb," what detail of the monument catches the speaker's eye? **(b) Interpret:** Referring to this detail, explain why "Time has transfigured" the couple "into / Untruth."

4. **(a) Recall:** What disaster occurs in "The Explosion"? **(b) Connect:** What two things in the poem last "for a second"? **(c) Interpret:** What is the meaning of the final gesture in the poem?

5. **(a) Compare and Contrast:** Compare and contrast the ways in which each poem comments on the assertion that "What will survive of us is love." **(b) Compare and Contrast:** In what way does a gesture offer a clue to the meaning of each of these poems **(c) Draw Conclusions:** Do these poems show the same optimism or pessimism about life? Explain.

6. **Speculate:** What gives the imagination the power to range over centuries or zero in on an instant, as it does in these poems?

On the Patio

Peter Redgrove

A wineglass overflowing with thunderwater
Stands out on the drumming steel table

Among the outcries of the downpour
Feathering chairs and rethundering on the awnings.

5   How the pellets of water shooting miles
Fly into the glass of swirl, and slop

Over the table's scales of rust
Shining like chained sores,

Because the rain eats everything except the glass
10   Of spinning water that is clear down here

But purple with rumbling depths above, and this cloud
Is transferring its might into a glass

In which thunder and lightning come to rest,
The cloud crushed into a glass.

15   Suddenly I dart out into the patio,
Snatch the bright glass up and drain it,

Bang it back down on the thundery steel table for a refill.

Reading Strategy
Reading in Sentences As
you read the poem, at the
end of which lines should
you come to a full stop?
Explain.

Review and Assess

Thinking About the Selection

1. **Respond:** How do you respond to the final line of the poem?
   Why?
2. **(a) Recall:** Describe the scene depicted in "On the Patio."
   (b) Connect: How do the images in the poem link what occurs
   above with what occurs below?
3. **(a) Recall:** At the end of the poem, what does the speaker do?
   (b) Interpret: What is the meaning of the speaker's final gesture?
4. **Speculate:** Why do natural phenomena like thunder and
   rain inspire heightened feelings, such as intoxication or gloom?

◄ **Critical Viewing** Does this photograph convey the power of the
"thunderwater" in the poem? Explain your answer. **[Evaluate]**

Not Waving but Drowning

Stevie Smith

Nobody heard him, the dead man,
But still he lay moaning:
I was much further out than you thought
And not waving but drowning.

5   Poor chap, he always loved larking
And now he's dead
It must have been too cold for him his heart gave way,
They said.

Oh, no no no, it was too cold always
10 (Still the dead one lay moaning)
I was much too far out all my life
And not waving but drowning.

larking (lärk´ iŋ) *n.* free-spirited, whimsical fun

Review and Assess

Thinking About the Selection

1. **Respond:** When have you seen a gesture completely misinterpreted, as in "Not Waving but Drowning"?

2. **(a) Recall:** What do "They" say about "the dead man"? **(b) Interpret:** How do "They" misinterpret the gesture and whole life of "the dead man"? **(c) Draw Conclusions:** What might "the dead man" mean when he moans, "I was much too far out all my life"?

3. **Generalize:** Using this poem as an example, explain how poetry reveals the extraordinary in the ordinary.

Review and Assess

Literary Analysis

Free Verse and Meter

1. Use a chart like this one to analyze Larkin's use of **iambic** and **trochaic tetrameter** in his two poems. Note the pattern of stresses in each line, using (´) to indicate stressed syllables and (ˇ) to indicate unstressed ones.

"An Arundel Tomb"	"The Explosion"
Their proper habits vaguely shown	It was said, and for a second
As jointed armor, stiffened pleat, . . .	Wives saw men of the explosion . . .

2. (a) How does Larkin change the meter of "The Explosion" in lines 13–14 and 25? (b) Why do you think he introduces these changes?
3. How do the **free-verse** lines in "On the Patio" reflect the setting?
4. (a) Identify a line with one beat and a line with six beats in the modified **ballad stanza** of "Not Waving." (b) How do these contrasting line lengths stress the finality of death?

Comparing Literary Works

5. Review the **dramatic structure** of "The Explosion," "On the Patio," and "Not Waving." How does the climax in each poem repeat and transform an earlier image or phrase?
6. Show how the drama in "An Arundel Tomb" and in "Not Waving but Drowning" is based on contrasts between appearance and reality.
7. Which poem ends in the most dramatic gesture? Explain.

Reading Strategy

Reading in Sentences

8. When you **read in sentences,** where do you pause at the end of the lines in "The Explosion" and where do you stop?
9. (a) Which lines in "On the Patio" require a full stop at the end? Why? (b) Which sentence in the poem describes a scene, which elaborates on the scene, and which describes an action?

Extend Understanding

10. **Performing Arts Connection:** Which poem could best be conveyed by a pantomime, a series of silent gestures? Why?

Quick Review

Free verse is poetry without regular end rhymes or the regular rhythms called **meter.**

A metric **foot** is a group of syllables with a pattern of stresses. Examples of feet are the **iamb** (unstressed, stressed) and the **trochee** (stressed, unstressed). A line in **tetrameter** has four metric feet.

A **ballad stanza** usually alternates four- and three-beat lines and has a rhyme scheme of *abab* or *abcb.*

Dramatic structure in a poem is the use of contrasts to build to an effective climax.

To **read a poem in sentences,** pause as punctuation indicates but do not automatically stop at the end of each line.

 Take It to the Net
www.phschool.com
Take the interactive self-test online to check your understanding of these selections.

Integrate Language Skills

Vocabulary Development Lesson

Word Analysis: Latin Root -fid-

The word *fidelity* means "faithfulness." It contains the root -fid-, which comes from the Latin word *fides*, meaning "faith." This root appears in the terms from economics, political science, and history that appear below. Use these terms to complete the sentences following. Then, verify your answers by using a dictionary.

fiduciary   fidelity   infidels   bona fides

1. To Renaissance Christians, the Islamic Turks were ___?___.
2. Under feudalism, vassals pledged their ___?___ to an overlord.
3. Banks require loan applicants to produce ___?___.
4. An orphan who inherited money might have a ___?___ guardian.

Concept Development: Antonyms

Select the letter of the antonym, the word opposite in meaning, of each numbered word.

1. effigy: (a) scarecrow, (b) original, (c) likeness
2. supine: (a) bright, (b) upright, (c) cowardly
3. fidelity: (a) disloyalty, (b) cowardice, (c) faithfulness
4. larking: (a) mischief, (b) bird-watching, (c) toil

Spelling Strategy

The sound *j* as the final consonant sound of an English word is almost always spelled with the letter *g*, as in *effigy*. Some exceptions to this rule are words from other languages, like *ouija board*.

On your paper, correct any misspelled words:

1. merje   2. elegy   3. collaje   4. raja

Grammar and Style Lesson

Sequence of Tenses

The poets featured in this section use different **verb tenses** to show the relationship of events in time. The **present tense** indicates events in the present or ongoing conditions. The **past tense** shows events that occurred and ended in the past. The **present perfect tense** shows events that began in the past and have continued into the present.

> **Present Tense:** The earl and countess <u>lie</u> in stone. . . .
>
> **Past Tense:** Rigidly they // <u>Persisted, linked</u> . . .
>
> **Present Perfect Tense:** Time <u>has transfigured</u> them . . .

Looking at Style Answer these questions:

1. What tense does Larkin use in lines 1–10 of "An Arundel Tomb"?
2. How does this tense draw you into the poem?
3. Where in the poem does Larkin shift to the past tense?
4. Where does he use the present perfect tense to express a key idea?
5. What is the effect of the change in tenses in "The Explosion"?

Writing Application Write a poem in free verse or meter, using the present, past, and present perfect tenses to convey a message about time.

W̶G Prentice Hall Writing and Grammar Connection: Chapter 21, Section 2

Writing Lesson

Reflective Essay

The poets in this section explore the deeper meanings of apparently ordinary sights and events, like a person waving or rain falling on a patio. Write a reflective essay that reveals an apparently ordinary event or sight to be extraordinary.

Prewriting   Recall an everyday sight or event that stirs strong emotions in you. Jot down the ideas, feelings, and comparisons it inspires. For further inspiration, review the comparisons in these poems.

Drafting   Begin by describing the event or sight. Then, referring to your notes, weave in the deeper meanings it suggests. Use transitions to introduce comparisons you make. Conclude by briefly summarizing the meanings you have discovered.

Revising   Have classmates evaluate whether you demonstrated the extraordinary within the ordinary. If not, add vivid comparisons introduced by transitions.

Model: Using Transitions to Make Comparisons

The plastic bag was ~~weird.~~ *like a misshapen leaf from a tree that never existed. . . .*

Transitions help readers understand comparisons. Other transitions that show comparisons include *as* and *similar to.*

Prentice Hall Writing and Grammar Connection: Chapter 6, Section 3

Extension Activities

Research and Technology With a team, create a **slide show** about medieval tomb statuary to help your classmates better understand "An Arundel Tomb." Use strategies like these:

- Make transparencies and photocopies of images to be shown.
- Record information about the statues on note cards.

Use your notes to prepare a script explaining how each work relates to the Arundel tomb. Then, use an overhead projector to show the transparencies in a predetermined sequence. **[Group Activity]**

Listening and Speaking Referring to "The Explosion," write and deliver a **eulogy**—a memorial speech—in honor of the miners who died. Use devices like these in your speech: *rhetorical questions,* asked to emphasize a point, not to receive an answer; and *figurative language,* like Larkin's comparison of the men to "Gold as on a coin."

Take It to the Net   www.phschool.com

Go online for an additional research activity using the Internet.

Prepare to Read

B. Wordsworth

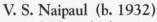

V. S. Naipaul (b. 1932)

V. S. Naipaul, who grew up in Trinidad, has earned a reputation as a brilliant writer of fiction and non-fiction books about colonialism, exile, and issues of identity in the contemporary world. He has also stirred up controversy, and some writers have accused him of taking a snobbish attitude toward Third World cultures.

A "Many-Sided Background" Naipaul, whose family came from India, was born in Trinidad, then a part of the British West Indies. There, he grew up in the Hindu culture and attended British schools. These experiences, combined with living in England and traveling all over the world, make up what Naipaul calls his "many-sided background."

In his book of autobiographical writings, *Finding the Center: Two Narratives* (1984), Naipaul recounts how his grandfather came to Trinidad as an indentured laborer. Life for such Asian Indian immigrants was certainly better than it was for the Africans enslaved in the West Indies two hundred years previously. However, the terms of indenture were not always strictly followed, and members of the Indian community faced many frustrations as a result. The next generation fared somewhat better; Naipaul's father became a popular journalist with the main Trinidadian newspaper.

Explorations in Writing Even as a student, Naipaul shared his father's talent for writing, and he won a scholarship to Oxford University. While in his final year there, he learned that his father had died. At this point, Naipaul's family wanted him to return and settle in Trinidad, but he decided to remain in Britain. He soon found work in London writing about the West Indies for radio.

Far from home, he began to write stories that drew on his memories of Trinidad. Those early stories, including "B. Wordsworth," were eventually collected in *Miguel Street* (1959). In these tales, a young narrator describes the comic and absurd elements of growing up in the West Indies. Although the narrator is about Naipaul's age, he is also quite different from Naipaul. He lives alone with his mother, unlike Naipaul, who lived with an extended family. Naipaul made some of these changes out of a need to simplify. To gain a full perspective of the community, he also created a "narrator more in tune with the life of the street than I had been."

"Fiction Never Lies" *A House for Mr. Biswas* (1961) combines the comic perspective of his early tales with poignant and universal themes to tell the story of a man similar to his father. Naipaul returned to his own youth in the novelistic memoir *A Way in the World* (1994). In justifying his choice of fictional accounts over autobiography, Naipaul explains that "an autobiography can distort, facts can be realigned. But fiction never lies. It reveals the writer totally."

Reports on Rootlessness Naipaul is drawn to writing about people living on the margins of the modern world, people who have to struggle against rootlessness and cope with sweeping change. His 1971 novel *In a Free State*, about self-exiles who meet in Africa, won Britain's prestigious Booker Prize.

Relationship With India Naipaul's preoccupation with exile and cultural identity no doubt arises from his own complex relationship with India, the country of his heritage. He has written several nonfiction books about India, including *India: An Area of Darkness* (1965), *India: A Wounded Civilization* (1977), and *India: A Million Mutinies Now* (1990). These works reflect his changing attitudes toward a civilization that shaped his family.

Preview

Connecting to the Literature

Your name is an important part of your identity. Be alert to the importance of names in this story, whose title is a famous poet's name that a character has adapted for himself.

Literary Analysis

First-Person Narrator

The point of view from which a story is told determines how you see and understand what occurs.

- A **first-person narrator** participates in the events of the story and refers to himself or herself as "I" or to his or her group or family as "we." This type of narrator shares his or her own thoughts and feelings about events.
- A **third-person narrator** is outside the action, refers to the characters as "he" or "she," and reveals the thoughts and feelings of several characters.

In "B. Wordsworth," Naipaul uses a first-person narrator to re-create Trinidad in the 1940s:

At about ten an Indian came in his dhoti and white jacket, and <u>we</u> poured a tin of rice into the sack he carried on his back.

When reading, remember that the narrator is not the same person as the author, and ask yourself how the narrator's perspective affects the story.

Connecting Literary Elements

Naipaul's use of a first-person narrator affects the **characterization** of the two main people in this story, their development as fictional characters. You learn about the narrator through what he says, does, and thinks. However, because you see B. Wordsworth through the narrator's eyes, you can only guess what he thinks. As you read, compare your reactions to B. Wordsworth with the narrator's boyish responses.

Reading Strategy

Responding to Characters

You will become more involved in a story by **responding to characters,** noting your reactions to their words, actions, and thoughts. Use a chart like this one to record these personal responses as you read.

Vocabulary Development

rogue (rōg) *n.* wandering beggar or tramp; scoundrel (p. 1238)

patronize (pā´ trən īz´) *v.* to be a customer of a particular merchant or store (p. 1242)

distill (di stil´) *v.* to obtain the essential part (p. 1242)

keenly (kēn´ lē) *adv.* sharply; intensely (p. 1243)

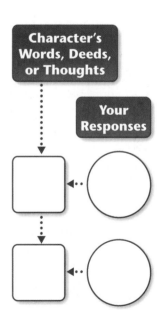

B. Wordsworth

V. S. Naipaul

Background

This story is set in Trinidad, probably in the 1940s. Trinidad, which became independent in 1962, had been a British colony since 1802. From 1845 to 1917, it had received indentured workers emigrating from India. Naipaul's grandfather had been such a worker, borrowing money for passage and laboring for years to pay off the debt. With a diverse population and with the culture of Britain, the colonial power, held up as "superior," cultural identity and names were key issues in Trinidad.

Three beggars called punctually every day at the hospitable houses in Miguel Street. At about ten an Indian came in his dhoti[1] and white jacket, and we poured a tin of rice into the sack he carried on his back. At twelve an old woman smoking a clay pipe came and she got a cent. At two a blind man led by a boy called for his penny.

Sometimes we had a <u>rogue</u>. One day a man called and said he was hungry. We gave him a meal. He asked for a cigarette and wouldn't go until we had lit it for him. That man never came again.

The strangest caller came one afternoon at about four o'clock. I had come back from school and was in my home-clothes. The man said to me, "Sonny, may I come inside your yard?"

He was a small man and he was tidily dressed. He wore a hat, a white shirt and black trousers.

I asked, "What you want?"

He said, "I want to watch your bees."

We had four small gru-gru palm trees[2] and they were full of uninvited bees.

I ran up the steps and shouted, "Ma, it have a man outside here. He say he want to watch the bees."

rogue (rōg) *n.* wandering beggar or tramp; scoundrel

Literary Analysis
First-Person Narrator
What is your impression of the narrator? Explain.

---

1. **dhoti** (dō′ tē) traditional loincloth worn by Hindu men.
2. **gru-gru** (grōō′ grōō′) **palm trees** West Indian palms that yield edible nuts.

My mother came out, looked at the man and asked in an unfriendly way, "What you want?"

The man said, "I want to watch your bees."

His English was so good, it didn't sound natural, and I could see my mother was worried.

She said to me, "Stay here and watch him while he watch the bees."

The man said, "Thank you, Madam. You have done a good deed today."

He spoke very slowly and very correctly as though every word was costing him money.

We watched the bees, this man and I, for about an hour, squatting near the palm trees.

The man said, "I like watching bees. Sonny, do you like watching bees?"

I said, "I ain't have the time."

He shook his head sadly. He said, "That's what I do, I just watch. I can watch ants for days. Have you ever watched ants? And scorpions, and centipedes, and congorees[3]—have you watched those?"

I shook my head.

I said, "What you does do, mister?"

He got up and said, "I am a poet."

I said, "A good poet?"

He said, "The greatest in the world."

"What your name, mister?"

"B. Wordsworth."

"B for Bill?"

"Black. Black Wordsworth. White Wordsworth[4] was my brother. We share one heart. I can watch a small flower like the morning glory and cry."

I said, "Why you does cry?"

"Why, boy? Why? You will know when you grow up. You're a poet, too, you know. And when you're a poet you can cry for everything."

I couldn't laugh.

He said, "You like your mother?"

"When she not beating me."

Man From the Village, Carlton Murrell

▲ **Critical Viewing**
How does the attitude of the man in the painting compare with that of B. Wordsworth? **[Compare and Contrast]**

---

3. **congorees** (kän´ gər ēz) Conger or Congo eels; large, scaleless eels found in the warm waters of the West Indies.

4. **White Wordsworth** English Romantic poet William Wordsworth (1770–1850).

☑ **Reading Check**

How does the narrator meet B. Wordsworth?

He pulled out a printed sheet from his hip-pocket and said, "On this paper is the greatest poem about mothers and I'm going to sell it to you at a bargain price. For four cents."

I went inside and I said, "Ma, you want buy a poetry for four cents?"

My mother said, "Tell that blasted man I haul his tail away from my yard, you hear."

I said to B. Wordsworth, "My mother say she ain't have four cents."

B. Wordsworth said, "It is the poet's tragedy."

And he put the paper back in his pocket. He didn't seem to mind.

I said, "Is a funny way to go round selling poetry like that. Only calypsonians[5] do that sort of thing. A lot of people does buy?"

He said, "No one has yet bought a single copy."

"But why you does keep on going round, then?"

He said, "In this way I watch many things, and I always hope to meet poets."

I said, "You really think I is a poet?"

"You're as good as me," he said.

And when B. Wordsworth left, I prayed I would see him again.

About a week later, coming back from school one afternoon, I met him at the corner of Miguel Street.

He said, "I have been waiting for you for a long time."

I said, "You sell any poetry yet?"

He shook his head.

He said, "In my yard I have the best mango tree in Port-of-Spain.[6] And now the mangoes are ripe and red and very sweet and juicy. I have waited here for you to tell you this and to invite you to come and eat some of my mangoes."

He lived in Alberto Street in a one-roomed hut placed right in the center of the lot. The yard seemed all green. There was the big mango tree. There was a coconut tree and there was a plum tree. The place looked wild, as though it wasn't in the city at all. You couldn't see all the big concrete houses in the street.

He was right. The mangoes were sweet and juicy. I ate about six, and the yellow mango juice ran down my arms to my elbows and down my mouth to my chin and my shirt was stained.

My mother said when I got home, "Where you was? You think you is a man now and could go all over the place? Go cut a whip for me."

She beat me rather badly, and I ran out of the house swearing that I would never come back. I went to B. Wordsworth's house. I was so angry, my nose was bleeding.

---

5. **calypsonians** (kə lip sō′ nē ənz) those who sing calypso songs; the characteristic satirical street singers of Trinidad.
6. **Port-of-Spain** seaport capital of Trinidad and Tobago.

B. Wordsworth said, "Stop crying, and we will go for a walk."

I stopped crying, but I was breathing short. We went for a walk. We walked down St. Clair Avenue to the Savannah and we walked to the race-course.

B. Wordsworth said, "Now, let us lie on the grass and look up at the sky, and I want you to think how far those stars are from us."

I did as he told me, and I saw what he meant. I felt like nothing, and at the same time I had never felt so big and great in all my life. I forgot all my anger and all my tears and all the blows.

When I said I was better, he began telling me the names of the stars, and I particularly remembered the constellation of Orion the Hunter,[7] though I don't really know why. I can spot Orion even today, but I have forgotten the rest.

Then a light was flashed into our faces, and we saw a policeman. We got up from the grass.

The policeman said, "What you doing here?"

B. Wordsworth said, "I have been asking myself the same question for forty years."

Reading Strategy
Responding to Characters
How does the way in which B. Wordsworth treats the angry and crying narrator affect your response to Wordsworth?

We became friends, B. Wordsworth and I. He told me, "You must never tell anybody about me and about the mango tree and the coconut tree and the plum tree. You must keep that a secret. If you tell anybody, I will know, because I am a poet."

I gave him my word and I kept it.

I liked his little room. It had no more furniture than George's front room,[8] but it looked cleaner and healthier. But it also looked lonely.

One day I asked him, "Mister Wordsworth, why you does keep all this bush in your yard? Ain't it does make the place damp?"

He said, "Listen, and I will tell you a story. Once upon a time a boy and girl met each other and they fell in love. They loved each other so much they got married. They were both poets. He loved words. She loved grass and flowers and trees. They lived happily in a single room, and then one day, the girl poet said to the boy poet, 'We are going to have another poet in the family.' But this poet was never born, because the girl died, and the young poet died with her, inside her. And the girl's husband was very sad, and he said he would never touch a thing in the girl's garden. And so the garden remained, and grew high and wild."

I looked at B. Wordsworth, and as he told me this lovely story, he seemed to grow older. I understood his story.

We went for long walks together. We went to the Botanical Gardens and the Rock Gardens. We climbed Chancellor Hill in the late afternoon and watched the darkness fall on Port-of-Spain, and watched the lights go on in the city and on the ships in the harbor.

---

7. **constellation of Orion** (ō rī´ ən) **the Hunter** group of stars named after a mythological giant who was killed accidentally by the goddess of hunting, Diana.
8. **George's front room** George is a character in one of the companion stories in Naipaul's book, *Miguel Street*.

✔**Reading Check**

What does B. Wordsworth do when the narrator, angry and crying, comes to see him?

He did everything as though he were doing it for the first time in his life. He did everything as though he were doing some church rite.

He would say to me, "Now, how about having some ice cream?"

And when I said, yes, he would grow very serious and say, "Now, which café shall we patronize?" As though it were a very important thing. He would think for some time about it, and finally say, "I think I will go and negotiate the purchase with that shop."

The world became a most exciting place.

One day, when I was in his yard, he said to me, "I have a great secret which I am now going to tell you."

I said, "It really secret?"

"At the moment, yes."

I looked at him, and he looked at me. He said, "This is just between you and me, remember. I am writing a poem."

"Oh." I was disappointed.

He said, "But this is a different sort of poem. This is the greatest poem in the world."

I whistled.

The Red House, Carlton Murrell

He said, "I have been working on it for more than five years now. I will finish it in about twenty-two years from now, that is, if I keep on writing at the present rate."

"You does write a lot, then?"

He said, "Not any more. I just write one line a month. But I make sure it is a good line."

I asked, "What was last month's good line?"

He looked up at the sky, and said, *"The past is deep."*

I said, "It is a beautiful line."

B. Wordsworth said, "I hope to distill the experiences of a whole month into that single line of poetry. So, in twenty-two years, I shall have written a poem that will sing to all humanity."

I was filled with wonder.

▲ **Critical Viewing**
Do you think this could be B. Wordsworth's house? Why or why not? **[Connect]**

patronize (pā´ trən īz´) v. to be a customer of a particular merchant or store

distill (di stil´) v. to obtain the essential part

Our walks continued. We walked along the sea-wall at Docksite one day, and I said, "Mr. Wordsworth, if I drop this pin in the water, you think it will float?"

He said, "This is a strange world. Drop your pin, and let us see what will happen."

The pin sank.

I said, "How is the poem this month?"

But he never told me any other line. He merely said, "Oh, it comes, you know. It comes."

Or we would sit on the sea-wall and watch the liners come into the harbor.

But of the greatest poem in the world I heard no more.

I felt he was growing older.

"How you does live, Mr. Wordsworth?" I asked him one day.

He said, "You mean how I get money?"

When I nodded, he laughed in a crooked way.

He said, "I sing calypsoes in the calypso season."

"And that last you the rest of the year?"

"It is enough."

"But you will be the richest man in the world when you write the greatest poem?"

He didn't reply.

One day when I went to see him in his little house, I found him lying on his little bed. He looked so old and so weak, that I found myself wanting to cry.

He said, "The poem is not going well."

He wasn't looking at me. He was looking through the window at the coconut tree, and he was speaking as though I wasn't there. He said, "When I was twenty I felt the power within myself." Then, almost in front of my eyes, I could see his face growing older and more tired. He said, "But that—that was a long time ago."

And then—I felt it so <u>keenly</u>, it was as though I had been slapped by my mother. I could see it clearly on his face. It was there for everyone to see. Death on the shrinking face.

He looked at me, and saw my tears and sat up.

He said, "Come." I went and sat on his knees.

He looked into my eyes, and he said, "Oh, you can see it, too. I always knew you had the poet's eye."

He didn't even look sad, and that made me burst out crying loudly.

He pulled me to his thin chest, and said, "Do you want me to tell you a funny story?" and he smiled encouragingly at me.

But I couldn't reply.

He said, "When I have finished this story, I want you to promise that you will go away and never come back to see me. Do you promise?"

I nodded.

Literary Analysis

First-Person Narrator and Characterization What do you know about B. Wordsworth's ambitious plan that the narrator does not seem to know?

keenly (kēn´ lē) *adv.* sharply; intensely

Reading Check

What does the narrator suddenly realize is going to happen to B. Wordsworth?

He said, "Good. Well, listen. That story I told you about the boy poet and the girl poet, do you remember that? That wasn't true. It was something I just made up. All this talk about poetry and the greatest poem in the world, that wasn't true, either. Isn't that the funniest thing you have heard?"

But his voice broke.

I left the house, and ran home crying, like a poet, for everything I saw.

I walked along Alberto Street a year later, but I could find no sign of the poet's house. It hadn't vanished, just like that. It had been pulled down, and a big, two-storied building had taken its place. The mango tree and the plum tree and the coconut tree had all been cut down, and there was brick and concrete everywhere.

It was just as though B. Wordsworth had never existed.

Literary Analysis
First-Person Narrator
How would the story be different if it were told by a third-person narrator? Explain.

Review and Assess

Thinking About the Selection

1. **Respond:** When the narrator is with B. Wordsworth, the world becomes "a most exciting place." What simple things make the world "exciting" for you? Why?

2. **(a) Recall:** What reason does B. Wordsworth give for wanting to come into the boy's yard? **(b) Compare and Contrast:** How is B. Wordsworth different from the other visitors who are described?

3. **(a) Recall:** What does the *B* in B. Wordsworth's name stand for? **(b) Interpret:** What does B. Wordsworth mean when he calls the boy "a poet"?

4. **Draw Conclusions:** B. Wordsworth "did everything as though he were doing it for the first time." In what way does this make B. Wordsworth "a poet"?

5. **(a) Infer:** What does the story of the boy poet and the girl poet suggest about B. Wordsworth? **(b) Interpret:** Why does he tell the boy that the story is untrue?

6. **(a) Infer:** What do you think B. Wordsworth's motivation is for spending time with the boy? **(b) Draw Conclusions:** What does the boy gain from knowing B. Wordsworth?

7. **Make a Judgment:** Do you think that B. Wordsworth's choice of a name shows (a) the harmful effects of colonialism on the identity and self-worth of colonized peoples, (b) the pride that colonized peoples can assert, or (c) a combination of both? Explain your answer.

Review and Assess

Literary Analysis

First-Person Narrator

1. Cite two pieces of evidence that indicate that the story is told by a **first-person narrator** rather than a **third-person narrator.**
2. Fill in a chart like this one to show how parts of the story might be different if B. Wordsworth were the first-person narrator.

Narrator	Characters' First Meeting	Knowledge of B. Words- worth's Past	B. Words- worth's Death	Mystery About B. Wordsworth
Boy				
B. Wordsworth				

3. (a) How is the narrator's voice different from the boy's dialogue? (b) Explain how this difference suggests B. Wordsworth's effect on the boy.

Connecting Literary Elements

4. Explain how a detail from each of the following categories adds to the **characterization** of B. Wordsworth: (a) what the narrator says about him, (b) what he says, (c) his name.
5. What do you learn about B. Wordsworth indirectly through his way of dealing with the narrator's anger?
6. Does the characterization of B. Wordsworth show that an author can develop a character in ways that escape a first-person narrator's awareness? Explain.

Reading Strategy

Responding to Characters

7. To which of the two main characters do you **respond** more strongly? Explain.
8. What is your response to B. Wordsworth's belief that it is possible and desirable to "cry for everything"? Explain.

Extend Understanding

9. **Psychology Connection:** What importance, if any, do role models like B. Wordsworth have in a young person's development? Explain.

Quick Review

A **first-person narrator** participates in the events of the story and refers to himself or herself as "I."

A **third-person narrator** does not take part in the story and refers to characters as "he" or "she."

Characterization, the process by which a writer develops a character, includes what a character says, does, and thinks, as well as the reaction of other characters to him or her.

To **respond to a character,** note your personal reactions to a character's words, thoughts, and actions.

 Take It to the Net
www.phschool.com
Take the interactive self-test online to check your understanding of the selection.

Integrate Language Skills

Vocabulary Development Lesson

Word Analysis: Forms of *patron*

Patronize means "to be a customer" or "to be kind but in a snobbish way." The word, with its hint of power, comes from a Latin root meaning "protector," "defender," or "father." Its various forms reflect this meaning. A *patron* of the arts is "a person of wealth and power who supports artists." *Patronage* refers to both "business given to a store," and "the power to grant favors in order to gain political advantage."

On your paper, complete each sentence using one of the following words:

patronize   patron   patronage

1. A ____?____ of the arts, she gave generously to the orchestra.
2. Some believe that ____?____ leads to corruption in politics.
3. I always ____?____ that fruit store.

Grammar and Style Lesson

Pronoun Case in Compound Constructions

For compound constructions, use the **case**—nominative or objective form—that would be correct if the pronoun were used alone.

> **Nominative Case:** We became friends, B. Wordsworth and I. (appositive of subject, *we*)
>
> **Objective Case:** This is just between you and me . . . (object of the preposition *between*)

Practice In your notebook, write each sentence using the correct pronoun or pronouns.

1. The poet and (I, me) shared a mango.

Spelling Strategy

When adding the suffix -*ly*, do not change the end of the word except in three situations. For words that end in two *l*'s, drop one *l* (*full, fully*). For words that end in a consonant + -*le*, drop the *e* (*able, ably*). For many adjectives with two or more syllables that end in -*c*, add -*ally* (*intrinsic, intrinsically*). In your notebook, add -*ly* to each of the following adjectives.

1. quiet   2. shrill   3. romantic

Fluency: Clarification

Explain answers to these questions:

1. Would a *keenly* observant poet describe or gloss over details?
2. Can a 1,000-page novel *distill* meaning?
3. Does a *rogue* promote society's rules?
4. Would you *patronize* a forest or a snack bar?

2. We watched the bees, this man and (I, me), for about an hour.
3. It was a secret between (he, him) and (I, me).
4. It was as if the stars glowed for (he, him) and (I, me).
5. A calypsonian sang my friend and (I, me) a song.

Writing Application Write a paragraph in which the narrator of the story reflects on B. Wordsworth after B. Wordsworth's death. In your paragraph, use the nominative and objective cases of pronouns once each in compound constructions.

*W*G *Prentice Hall Writing and Grammar Connection: Chapter 22, Section 1*

Writing Lesson

Account of a Remarkable Person

The narrator of Naipaul's story will never forget the remarkable B. Wordsworth. Write an account of a remarkable person you have met, using yourself as a first-person narrator.

Prewriting   Choose a subject. Then, jot down traits that make your subject remarkable. Select a scene involving you and the subject that reveals this person's memorable personality.

Drafting   As a first-person narrator, write an account of the scene. Like Naipaul, characterize your subject using your reactions and your subject's words and actions.

Revising   Show your account to several classmates to see whether your subject's remarkable qualities have come through. If not, replace vague adjectives with precise ones and add dialogue that conveys the flavor of the subject's personality.

Model: Adding Precise Details as Support

resonant   *lilting*

Mrs. Walcott's ~~pleasant~~ voice and Jamaican accent made everything she said sound ~~true.~~ *like a melody. On that occasion, she declared, "Hear the sounds behind the sounds."*

> The writer replaces vague language with precise adjectives and a simile and adds a vivid quotation.

Prentice Hall Writing and Grammar Connection: Chapter 6, Section 2

Extension Activities

Listening and Speaking   With a team, create a **multimedia tour** of Trinidadian calypso festivals. Include elements like these:

- Recordings of calypso singers
- Slides showing festivals
- T-shirts with stage names of singers, like Lord Melody
- Demonstrations of instruments, like the *shak-shak* (maraca)

Arrange the elements you choose so that they will be most effective. Then, share your tour with the class. **[Group Activity]**

Research and Technology   Research British colonialism in the West Indies. Then, design a **classroom exhibit** that reflects British influence on this region. Use the organization of your research notes to structure the exhibit. For example, if you date your note cards by decade, arrange your exhibit by decade. Caption items clearly, produce a map of the exhibit, and open your exhibit to the class.

 **Take It to the Net**   www.phschool.com

Go online for an additional research activity using the Internet.

Prepare to Read

The Train from Rhodesia

Nadine Gordimer (b. 1923)

The fiction of Nadine Gordimer has been shaped by her life in South Africa and by her firm opposition to the former government's policy of apartheid, an institutional form of racial separation and prejudice. Initially honored for her short fiction, Gordimer says that, in time, she found the short story "too delicate for what I have to say." In her longer works, as well as in her short stories, she has had a great deal to say about racial division and its harmful effects on oppressed and oppressor alike. The South African government responded by banning some of her work. Nevertheless, Gordimer has built an international reputation as a writer.

Small Town Origins Gordimer was born in Springs, South Africa, a small town near Johannesburg. Her mother took her out of the local private school when she was eleven. From then until she was sixteen, she "read tremendously" and wrote much fiction. She published her first adult short story, "Come Again Tomorrow," when she was fifteen. She continued to write short stories during her year of study at the University of Witwatersrand.

Literary Success *The Soft Voice of the Serpent* (1952) was the first collection of her stories to be published in the United States. Following the critical success of that book, Gordimer's stories appeared in such leading American magazines as *The New Yorker, The Atlantic Monthly,* and *Harper's Magazine.* These stories often describe the entrapment of whites who inherited political and economic power in the closed society of South Africa under apartheid. Frequently, as in "The Train from Rhodesia," she builds a tale around a fleeting but sharply focused moment of insight.

Although politics is a perpetual concern of Gordimer's, she does not turn fiction into sermonizing. A reviewer in *The Times Literary Supplement* noted that Gordimer "is never guilty of pushing her characters to the sideline in order to make an overt political point—a fact which, paradoxically, enables her to demonstrate South Africa's political oddities more exactly." Even though the regime of apartheid that Gordimer criticized ended in 1991, the truths that she uncovered through her characters endure.

Compassionate Observer In all her fiction—including such novels as *A Guest of Honor* (1970), *The Conservationist* (1974), and *Burger's Daughter* (1979)—Gordimer shows an ability to write from different vantage points. She portrays with insight Anglos (South Africans of English ancestry), Afrikaners (South Africans of Dutch ancestry), and black South Africans, describing her characters in a variety of economic and social settings. She writes as a compassionate observer of the human condition. In lyric tones, yet without sentimentality, she pictures the South African scene with awareness and humanity, stressing themes of understanding, honesty, and forgiveness.

"Luminous Symbol" Until she was thirty, Gordimer had never been outside South Africa. Since then, however, she has traveled widely and lectured in a number of top United States universities, including Princeton, Columbia, and the University of Michigan. She has also won a great many literary awards, including the Nobel Prize for Literature in 1991. Called by one observer "a luminous symbol of at least one white person's understanding of the black man's burden," she is without doubt one of the leading novelists writing in English.

Preview

Connecting to the Literature

You may have seen a single lie ruin a whole friendship. When an entire society is based on lies that are told to justify injustice, these lies can spoil even the happiest of times, as the couple in the story discovers.

Literary Analysis

Conflict and Theme

Writers dramatize their **themes,** or central insights, by showing characters in the midst of a **conflict,** an inner or outer struggle. In a simple story, the conflict between a good character and a bad one suggests a simple theme: Good will triumph over evil. In more complex stories, however, these generalizations may apply:

- Conflicts reflect tangled contradictions in life, not simple choices or clear lessons.
- Themes may take the form of implied questions to which various characters offer various answers.
- Conflicts need not be resolved. Instead, a story may deepen a conflict, reformulate it, or replace it with a new conflict.

As you read, determine what questions or problems are posed by the conflict in "The Train from Rhodesia."

Connecting Literary Elements

A conflict in a story may powerfully dramatize a theme, yet the story may never state that theme directly. Through conflicts, images, symbols, and other devices, a writer may establish an **implied theme.** As you form your interpretation of the theme of Gordimer's story, consider what she gains by stating it indirectly rather than directly.

Reading Strategy

Reading Between the Lines

Writers do not always describe the details of a situation. Even characters may appear to be unaware of the reasons for their own reactions. When you encounter gaps in a writer's explicit explanations, **read between the lines—** deduce the details or connections that the writer is indicating. Use a chart like the one shown to help you read between the lines of this story.

Vocabulary Development

impressionistic (im presh′ ən is′ tik) *adj.* conveying a picture through quickly sketched suggestions of details (p. 1251)

elongated (ē lôn′ gāt id) *adj.* lengthened; stretched (p. 1251)

segmented (seg′ ment id) *adj.* divided into joined parts (p. 1253)

splaying (splā′ iŋ) *v.* spreading out (p. 1253)

atrophy (a′ trə fē) *v.* waste away (p. 1254)

Passage

The mane of the lion figurine shows "that the artist had delight in the lion."

What Is Missing

A direct statement of the figurine's effect on the young woman

What Is Implied

The young woman is moved by the truth of the figurine and by the joyful vision of the artist who created it.

The Train from Rhodesia

Nadine Gordimer

Background

This story is set at a time when South Africa and Rhodesia (now Zimbabwe) enforced policies of racial separation, called apartheid in South Africa, ensuring the continued privileges of a white minority and its domination over the black majority.

The train came out of the red horizon and bore down toward them over the single straight track.

The stationmaster came out of his little brick station with its pointed chalet roof, feeling the creases in his serge uniform in his legs as well. A stir of preparedness rippled through the squatting native vendors waiting in the dust; the face of a carved wooden animal, eternally surprised, stuck out of a sack. The stationmaster's barefoot children wandered over. From the gray mud huts with the untidy heads that stood within a decorated mud wall, chickens, and dogs with their skin stretched like parchment over their bones, followed the piccanins[1] down to the track. The flushed and perspiring west cast a reflection, faint, without heat, upon the station, upon the tin shed marked "Goods," upon the walled kraal,[2] upon the gray tin house of the stationmaster and upon the sand, that lapped all around, from sky to sky, cast little rhythmical cups of shadow, so that the sand became the sea, and closed over the children's black feet softly and without imprint.

The stationmaster's wife sat behind the mesh of her veranda. Above her head the hunk of a sheep's carcass moved slightly, dangling in a current of air.

They waited.

The train called out, along the sky; but there was no answer; and the cry hung on: I'm coming . . . I'm coming . . .

The engine flared out now, big, whisking a dwindling body behind it; the track flared out to let it in.

Creaking, jerking, jostling, gasping, the train filled the station.

---

1. **piccanins** *n.* native children.
2. **kraal** (kräl) *n.* fenced-in enclosure for cattle or sheep.

Here, let me see that one—the young woman curved her body further out of the corridor window. Missus? smiled the old boy, looking at the creatures he held in his hand. From a piece of string on his gray finger hung a tiny woven basket; he lifted it, questioning. No, no, she urged, leaning down toward him, across the height of the train, toward the man in the piece of old rug; that one, that one, her hand commanded. It was a lion, carved out of soft dry wood that looked like spongecake; heraldic, black and, white, with <u>impressionistic</u> detail burnt in. The old man held it up to her still smiling, not from the heart, but at the customer. Between its Vandyke[3] teeth, in the mouth opened in an endless roar too terrible to be heard, it had a black tongue. Look, said the young husband, if you don't mind! And round the neck of the thing, a piece of fur (rat? rabbit? meerkat?); a real mane, majestic, telling you somehow that the artist had delight in the lion.

All up and down the length of the train in the dust the artists sprang, walking bent, like performing animals, the better to exhibit the fantasy held toward the faces on the train. Buck, startled and stiff, staring with round black and white eyes. More lions, standing erect, grappling with strange, thin, <u>elongated</u> warriors who clutched spears and showed no fear in their slits of eyes. How much, they asked from the train, how much?

Give me penny, said the little ones with nothing to sell. The dogs went and sat, quite still, under the dining car, where the train breathed out the smell of meat cooking with onion.

A man passed beneath the arch of reaching arms meeting gray-black and white in the exchange of money for the staring wooden eyes, the stiff wooden legs sticking up in the air; went along under the voices and the bargaining, interrogating the wheels. Past the dogs; glancing up at the dining car where he could stare at the faces, behind glass, drinking beer, two by two, on either side of a uniform railway vase with its pale dead flower. Right to the end, to the guard's van, where the stationmaster's children had just collected their mother's two loaves of bread; to the engine itself, where the stationmaster and the driver stood talking against the steaming complaint of the resting beast.

The man called out to them, something loud and joking. They turned to laugh, in a twirl of steam. The two children careered over the sand, clutching the bread, and burst through the iron gate and up the path through the garden in which nothing grew.

Passengers drew themselves in at the corridor windows and turned into compartments to fetch money, to call someone to look. Those sitting inside looked up: suddenly different, caged faces, boxed in, cut

---

3. Vandyke (van dīk´) *adj.* tapering to a point, like a Vandyke beard.

impressionistic (im presh´ ən is´ tik) *adj.* conveying a picture through quickly sketched suggestions of details

elongated (i lôŋ´ gāt´ id) *adj.* lengthened; stretched

Reading Strategy
Reading Between the Lines What does the behavior of the dogs suggest about the community around the train station?

**Reading Check**

What attracts the interest of the young woman on the train?

off, after the contact of outside. There was an orange a piccanin would like. . . . What about that chocolate? It wasn't very nice. . . .

A young girl had collected a handful of the hard kind, that no one liked, out of the chocolate box, and was throwing them to the dogs, over at the dining car. But the hens darted in, and swallowed the chocolates, incredibly quick and accurate, before they had even dropped in the dust, and the dogs, a little bewildered, looked up with their brown eyes, not expecting anything.

—No, leave it, said the girl, don't take it. . . .

Too expensive, too much, she shook her head and raised her voice to the old boy, giving up the lion. He held it up where she had handed it to him. No, she said, shaking her head. *Three-and-six?*[4] insisted her husband, loudly. Yes baas! laughed the boy. Three-and-six?—the young man was incredulous. Oh leave it—she said. The young man stopped. Don't you want it? he said, keeping his face closed to the boy. No, never mind, she said, leave it. The old native kept his head on one side, looking at them sideways, holding the lion. Three-and-six, he murmured, as old people repeat things to themselves.

The young woman drew her head in. She went into the coupé[5] and sat down. Out of the window, on the other side, there was nothing; sand and bush; a thorn tree. Back through the open doorway, past the figure of her husband in the corridor, there was the station, the voices, wooden animals waving, running feet. Her eye followed the funny little valance of scrolled wood that outlined the chalet roof of the station; she thought of the lion and smiled. That bit of fur round the neck. But the wooden buck, the hippos, the elephants, the baskets that already bulked out of their brown paper under the seat and on the luggage rack! How will they look at home? Where will you put them? What will they mean away from the places you found them? Away from the unreality of the last few weeks? The man outside. But he is not part of the unreality; he is for good now. Odd . . . somewhere there was an idea that he, that living with him, was part of the holiday, the strange places.

Outside, a bell rang. The stationmaster was leaning against the end of the train, green flag rolled in readiness. A few men who had got down to stretch their legs sprang on to the train, clinging to the observation platforms, or perhaps merely standing on the iron step, holding the rail; but on the train, safe from the one dusty platform, the one tin house, the empty sand.

There was a grunt. The train jerked. Through the glass the beer drinkers looked out, as if they could not see beyond it. Behind the flyscreen, the stationmaster's wife sat facing back at them beneath the darkening hunk of meat.

Literature in context History Connection

Apartheid

In Gordimer's story, the interactions between white passengers and black vendors reflect the social regime called apartheid ("apartness" in the language of Dutch South Africans). Under apartheid in South Africa, blacks were restricted to living in certain areas. To travel through a white area, they were required to carry passes—even if they worked every day in such areas. Public places—such as schools, restaurants, and hotels—were segregated by law. Whites lived as privileged rulers in the country. Blacks lived for the most part in poverty, stripped of political power. It was only in the closing decades of the twentieth century that blacks, after violent struggles, gained political rights in South Africa and Rhodesia.

---

4. **three-and-six** three shillings and sixpence.
5. **coupé** (kōō pāʹ) n. half-compartment at the end of a train, with seats on only one side.

There was a shout. The flag drooped out. Joints not yet coordinated, the <u>segmented</u> body of the train heaved and bumped back against itself. It began to move; slowly the scrolled chalet moved past it, the yells of the natives, running alongside, jetted up into the air, fell back at different levels. Staring wooden faces waved drunkenly, there, then gone, questioning for the last time at the windows. Here, one-and-six baas!—As one automatically opens a hand to catch a thrown ball, a man fumbled wildly down his pocket, brought up the shilling and sixpence and threw them out; the old native, gasping, his skinny toes <u>splaying</u> the sand, flung the lion.

The piccanins were waving, the dogs stood, tails uncertain, watching the train go: past the mud huts, where a woman turned to look, up from the smoke of the fire, her hand pausing on her hip.

The stationmaster went slowly in under the chalet.

The old native stood, breath blowing out the skin between his ribs, feet tense, balanced in the sand, smiling and shaking his head. In his opened palm, held in the attitude of receiving, was the retrieved shilling and sixpence.

The blind end of the train was being pulled helplessly out of the station.

The young man swung in from the corridor, breathless. He was shaking his head with laughter and triumph. Here! he said. And waggled the lion at her. One-and-six!

What? she said.

He laughed. I was arguing with him for fun, bargaining—when the train had pulled out already, he came tearing after. . . . One-and-six baas! So there's your lion.

She was holding it away from her, the head with the open jaws, the pointed teeth, the black tongue, the wonderful ruff of fur facing her. She was looking at it with an expression of not seeing, of seeing something different. Her face was drawn up, wryly, like the face of a discomforted child. Her mouth lifted nervously at the corner. Very slowly, cautious, she lifted her finger and touched the mane, where it was joined to the wood.

But how could you, she said. He was shocked by the dismay of her face.

Good heavens, he said, what's the matter?

If you wanted the thing, she said, her voice rising and breaking with the shrill impotence of anger, why didn't you buy it in the first place? If you wanted it, why didn't you pay for it? Why didn't you take it decently, when he offered it? Why did you have to wait for him to run after the train with it, and give him one-and-six? One-and-six!

She was pushing it at him, trying to force him to take it. He stood astonished, his hands hanging at his sides.

But you wanted it! You liked it so much? —It's a beautiful piece of work, she said fiercely, as if to protect it from him.

You liked it so much! You said yourself it was too expensive—

Reading Strategy
Reading Between the Lines What does the writer's choice of the words *blind, pulled,* and *helplessly* suggest about the fate of those on the train?

Literary Analysis
Conflict and Theme What does the conflict between the husband and wife suggest about the way in which racism poisons perception?

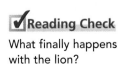**Reading Check**

What finally happens with the lion?

Oh *you*—she said, hopeless and furious. *You* . . . . She threw the lion onto the seat.

He stood looking at her.

She sat down again in the corner and, her face slumped in her hand, stared out of the window. Everything was turning around inside her. One-and-six. One-and-six. One-and-six for the wood and the carving and the sinews of the legs and the switch of the tail. The mouth open like that and the teeth, the black tongue, rolling, like a wave. The mane round the neck. To give one-and-six for that. The heat of shame mounted through her legs and body and sounded in her ears like the sound of sand pouring, pouring, pouring. She sat there, sick. A weariness, a tastelessness, the discovery of a void made her hands slacken their grip, <u>atrophy</u> emptily, as if the hour was not worth their grasp. She was feeling like this again. She had thought it was something to do with singleness, with being alone and belonging too much to oneself.

She sat there not wanting to move or speak, or to look at anything, even; so that the mood should be associated with nothing, no object, word or sight that might recur and so recall the feeling again. . . . Smuts blew in grittily, settled on her hands. Her back remained at exactly the same angle, turned against the young man sitting with his hands drooping between his sprawled legs, and the lion, fallen on its side in the corner.

The train had cast the station like a skin. It called out to the sky, I'm coming, I'm coming; and again, there was no answer.

atrophy (a′ trə fē) *v.* waste away

Review and Assess

Thinking About the Selection

1. **(a) Recall:** Who comes to meet the train from Rhodesia?
   (b) Infer: What does the interaction between these people and the passengers indicate about the story's theme?

2. **(a) Analyze:** Why does the lion impress the young woman?
   (b) Interpret: Why is the young woman angry when her husband bargains for and obtains the lion at a low price?

3. **(a) Draw Conclusions:** What have the husband and the wife discovered about each other by the end of the story?
   (b) Speculate: How might their marriage fare, given this episode? Explain.

4. **Interpret:** What do you think the train and the station symbolize in this story?

5. **Apply:** In the story, social assumptions about whites bargaining with black vendors prevent a man from seeing the true value of a statue. In your own experience, do social assumptions often cloud people's perceptions? Explain.

Review and Assess

Literary Analysis

Conflict and Theme

1. Why does a **conflict** erupt between the young woman and her husband when he buys the lion at such a low price?

2. (a) How does the shame that the young woman feels reveal an inner conflict, one in which she struggles with herself? (b) Why might she explain her inner "void" differently from the way she once did?

3. To define the **theme** of the story, explain what questions the woman's conflicts raise about her society.

Connecting Literary Elements

4. Use a chart like the one shown to explain how the images in the description of the arrival of the train establish the **implied theme**.

Detail	Implication	Link to Theme
"the sand . . . closed over the children's black feet . . . without imprint."	Blacks in the area lead anonymous, vanishing lives.	Whites deny or suppress what is of value in the lives of blacks in the area.

5. Analyze the argument between the woman and the man. (a) What different connections does each see between "liking," "wanting," and "buying"? (b) How does this argument help establish the theme?

6. The woman does not effectively articulate her viewpoint. (a) What does this inability suggest about the problem she faces? (b) Why might requiring the reader to interpret her point add to the effectiveness of the story?

Reading Strategy

Reading Between the Lines

7. What conflict is suggested by the contrast between the "bent" artists and the "elongated" statues of lion-hunting warriors?

8. What attitude toward beauty is implied in the lines "One-and-six. One-and-six for the wood and the carving and the sinews. . . ."?

Extend Understanding

9. **Visual Arts Connection:** Contrast the lion in the story with a toy animal you might find in an American souvenir shop. What does this contrast suggest about the cultures in which the figures originate?

Quick Review

Writers dramatize **themes,** or central insights or questions, by showing characters in the midst of a **conflict,** an inner or outer struggle.

Writers often establish an **implied theme** through conflicts, images, symbols, and other devices.

Read between the lines to understand details and connections that a writer only suggests.

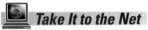 **Take It to the Net**
www.phschool.com
Take the interactive self-test online to check your understanding of the selection.

Integrate Language Skills

Vocabulary Development Lesson

Word Analysis: Greek Prefix *a-*

The word *atrophy* means "waste away." It combines the Greek prefix *a-*, meaning "without" or "not," with a word that means "to feed." *Atrophy* names what happens when something, such as a muscle or a skill, is *not* nourished.

The prefix *a-* acts like a negative sign, contradicting the root to which it is affixed. It appears in many words related to science, mathematics, and the social sciences. If the root word to which it is joined begins with a vowel (or sometimes with an *h*), the prefix *a-* becomes *an-*.

Define each of the following words, consulting your dictionary as needed:

1. atypical
2. amorphous
3. asymmetrical
4. anaerobic

Fluency: Context

In the role of the woman in the story, write a diary entry about the incident at the station. Use all the words from the vocabulary list on page 1249 in your entry.

Spelling Strategy

To add *-ist, -ing,* or *-ish* to a word that ends in *y*, retain the *y* and simply add the suffix. The word *splay*, for example, retains its final *y*, to become *splaying*. Add the suffix *-ist, -ing,* or *-ish* to form another English word from each of the words listed.

1. journey
2. boy
3. essay
4. worry
5. gray
6. simplify

Grammar and Style Lesson

Nominative Absolutes

Gordimer piles up details to add immediacy to her descriptions of the bustle at a train station when a train pulls in. She often uses **nominative absolutes,** phrases consisting of a noun or pronoun modified by a participial phrase. A nominative absolute is not grammatically linked with any single word in the sentence. Instead, it adds additional details about the topic of the sentence.

> **Example:** The old native stood, breath blowing out the skin between his ribs. . . .

Practice Identify the nominative absolute in each sentence.

1. The stationmaster was leaning against the end of the train, green flag rolled in readiness.

2. Joints not yet coordinated, the segmented body of the train . . . bumped back against itself.

3. . . . the old native, gasping, his skinny toes splaying the sand, flung the lion.

4. If you wanted the thing, she said, her voice rising and breaking with the shrill impotence of anger, why didn't you buy it in the first place?

5. She sat down again in the corner and, her face slumped in her hand, stared out of the window.

Writing Application Write a description of the new couple's home, including the artifacts they have collected while on their honeymoon, using three nominative absolutes. Underline each nominative absolute in your description.

W͛G Prentice Hall Writing and Grammar Connection: Chapter 19, Section 2

Writing Lesson

Analysis of Storytelling Technique

Gordimer suggests the central problem of her story by weaving together parts of conversation and half-glimpsed events. Write an analysis of her use of imagery and dialogue, explaining how they serve indirectly to establish her theme.

Prewriting Review the story, noting passages in which a description, an event, or an utterance adds a particular mood or suggests a parallel with social circumstances.

Drafting Discuss story elements in logical order. Relate imagery and dialogue to the theme. Conclude your essay by discussing the overall effect of Gordimer's technique.

Revising Review your draft, circling areas in which you link ideas. Add transitions, such as *in addition*, *by contrast*, *despite*, and *furthermore*, to clarify connections.

Model: Clarifying Connections With Transitions

When the girl throws candies out the window, she
Instead, as Gordimer describes it, "the
intends them for the dogs. "The hens darted in, and
In this image,
swallowed the chocolates." Gordimer anticipates her
main character's difficulty.

> Added transitions strengthen the connections between ideas.

W̶G Prentice Hall Writing and Grammar Connection: Chapter 14, Section 3

Extension Activities

Listening and Speaking With a group, hold a **debate** on this proposition: *One should always pay a fair price for a thing.* Use the following strategies:

- **Inductive arguments:** general conclusions drawn from particular instances
- **Deductive arguments:** conclusions drawn by applying general premises to a specific case

Hold your debate in class. [**Group Activity**]

Research and Technology Research and write a brief **historical report** on South Africa. In your word-processor draft, incorporate charts, spreadsheets, and other informative graphics.

 **Take It to the Net** www.phschool.com

Go online for an additional research activity using the Internet.

Prepare to Read

from Midsummer, XXIII ◆ *from* Omeros, *from* Chapter XXVIII ◆ From Lucy: Englan' Lady

Derek Walcott (b. 1930)

Nobel Prize-winner Derek Walcott, one of the most renowned contemporary poets writing in English, has roots in two worlds. Both of his grandmothers were descended from enslaved Africans, and both of his grandfathers were white colonials. Throughout his life, Walcott has reflected upon his contrasting heritages. These reflections propel his poems, which may carry the reader from tropical Trinidad to ancient Greece to Shakespeare's England, sometimes in a single line of poetry.

Early Success Walcott, born on the Caribbean Island of St. Lucia, graduated from the University of the West Indies. He published the first of his many books of poetry, *Twenty-five Poems*, when he was just a teenager. Subsequent collections include *The Gulf* (1970), *Sea Grapes* (1976), *Collected Poems 1948–1984* (1986), and *Tiepolo's Hound* (2000).

In 1959, Walcott, also an accomplished playwright, founded the Trinidad Theatre Workshop. His play *Dream on Monkey Mountain* won an Obie in 1971. More recently, Walcott collaborated with songwriter and composer Paul Simon on a Broadway musical, *The Capeman* (1997).

High Honors Walcott's 1990 book *Omeros*, which draws on the epics of the ancient Greek poet Homer, ensured him the Nobel Prize for Literature in 1992. The Swedish Academy, when granting the award, concluded that "West Indian culture has found its great poet." Such a role entails responsibilities, and Walcott's poetry often reflects on the traditions to which he belongs.

James Berry (b. 1925)

Born in a small village on the island of Jamaica and now living in Britain, James Berry draws from his many varied experiences to infuse English poetry with vivid fresh language. His work combines imagery and rhythms from his rural West Indian background with the snap and style of urban London.

Experiences of Poverty Berry's childhood experiences of poverty are all too typical in the West Indies. He had to leave school at age fourteen to help support his family. During World War II, he traveled to the United States to find work. After living in several places, including Harlem, he returned to Jamaica, discouraged by the prejudice he encountered in the States. In 1948, Berry left for England, where he began to write.

Crossing the Gaps In both prose and in poetry, Berry tells the stories of people whom history usually ignores. His books include *A Thief in the Village*, a collection of stories for children that was a Coretta Scott King Honor Book in 1989. He has also written a novel, *Ajeemah and His Son*, a story from the days of slavery. His poetry makes musical use of both English and the Creole language of his native island. Collections include *Fractured Circles* (1979) and *Lucy's Letters and Loving* (1982). In whatever form Berry writes, he works to cross the gaps between cultures and races. Lucy's simple, wise commentary on the Queen in "From Lucy: Englan' Lady" shows how powerful the results can be.

Preview

Connecting to the Literature

The language that you speak is part of you, but what makes it yours? Are some ways of speaking it more truly yours—more natural to you—than others? These poets explore some of the different "languages" that make up English. They also demonstrate how a poet makes a language his or her own.

Literary Analysis

Theme and Context

Understanding the **context** of a work—the historical moment in which it originates—can help you better appreciate its **theme**—the central issue it explores. The themes of the poems given here are general: the responsibilities of an artist and the burden of a social role. Their context, though, is the meeting of two specific cultures—British and Caribbean. Note the forms that this encounter takes, whether as a dialogue or as a collision.

Comparing Literary Works

In these poems, Walcott and Berry consider and address the literary tradition in which they write. Each in his own way both pledges allegiance to this tradition and questions it. Their techniques for engaging with the tradition include the following:

- **Allusions**—brief references to literary works, people, or events. An allusion implies that the writer and the reader "own" a common culture.
- **Political critique of art**—examination of the political implications of art. Such critique often questions the "ownership" of art, raising the question of who produces, judges, and learns to appreciate it.

Compare the ways in which these poets address and expand their traditions.

Reading Strategy

Applying Background Information

Sometimes you must **apply background information** to understand a poem. For example, to understand Walcott's response to the Brixton riots in *Midsummer*, XXIII, it is useful to know that the riots erupted in London among Caribbean immigrants. Use a chart like the one shown to help you apply background information to these poems. (You will find such information in footnotes and in the Background feature, page 1260.)

Vocabulary Development

antic (an´ tik) *adj.* odd and funny; silly (p. 1261)

rancor (raŋ´ kər) *n.* continuing, bitter hate or ill will (p. 1261)

eclipse (i klips´) *n.* dimming or extinction of power or glory (p. 1261)

inducted (in duk´ tid) *v.* brought formally into an organization (p. 1261)

Passage

. . . a Brixton riot tunneled by water hoses; . . .

↓

Background Information

Residents of the South London district of Brixton rioted in April 1981.

↓

Interpretation

"Tunneled by water hoses": The police sprayed rioters with high-pressure water from fire-hoses to disperse them.

---

from Midsummer XXIII

Derek Walcott

Background

In colonial times, British settlers brought enslaved Africans to work on their plantations in the West Indies. These slaves were freed in the 1830s, and in the 1960s and 1970s, the islands won their independence. Many present-day West Indians have emigrated to Britain in search of opportunity, only to encounter prejudice and hardships. Their frustrations erupted in the April 1981 riots in the neighborhood of Brixton, London, to which Walcott reacts in *Midsummer*, XXIII.

> With the stampeding hiss and scurry of green lemmings,
> midsummer's leaves race to extinction like the roar
> of a Brixton riot tunneled by water hoses;
> they seethe towards autumn's fire—it is in their nature,
> 5 being men as well as leaves, to die for the sun.
> The leaf stems tug at their chains, the branches bending
> like Boer cattle under Tory whips that drag every wagon
> nearer to apartheid.[1] And, for me, that closes

---

1. **Boer** (bōr) **cattle . . . apartheid** In the 1600s, the Boers, people of Dutch descent, colonized South Africa, where apartheid (racial segregation) was later practiced. The Tories held power in Britain when it won control of South Africa in the Boer War (1899–1902).

the child's fairy tale of an <u>antic</u> England—fairy rings,
10   thatched cottages fenced with dog roses,
a green gale lifting the hair of Warwickshire.
I was there to add some color to the British theater.
"But the blacks can't do Shakespeare, they have no experience."
This was true. Their thick skulls bled with <u>rancor</u>
15   when the riot police and the skinheads exchanged quips
you could trace to the Sonnets,[2] or the Moor's <u>eclipse</u>.[3]
Praise had bled my lines white of any more anger,
and snow had <u>inducted</u> me into white fellowships,
while Calibans[4] howled down the barred streets of an empire
20   that began with Caedmon's raceless dew,[5] and is ending
in the alleys of Brixton, burning like Turner's ships.[6]

---

2. **the Sonnets** William Shakespeare's sequence of 154 sonnets, noted for their passionate, often witty inquiries into love and rivalry.
3. **the Moor's eclipse** In Shakespeare's *Othello,* Othello the Moor (a black North African) is destroyed by the scheming of his white lieutenant, Iago.
4. **Calibans** Caliban is a deformed creature in Shakespeare's play *The Tempest.* Enslaved by the enchanter Prospero, Caliban has been interpreted as a native who rebels against his island's "colonizer," Prospero.
5. **Caedmon's** (kad´ mənz) **raceless dew** poetry written by the earliest known English poet, Caedmon (seventh century).
6. **Turner's ships** British artist J. M. W. Turner (1775–1851) rendered atmospheric oil paintings of, among other subjects, ships burning in battle.

antic (an´ tik) *adj.* odd and funny; silly

rancor (raŋ´ kər) *n.* continuing, bitter hate or ill will

eclipse (ē klips´) *n.* dimming or extinction of power or glory

inducted (in dukt´ id) *v.* brought formally into an organization

Review and Assess

Thinking About the Selection

1. **(a) Recall:** Toward what are midsummer's leaves racing?
   (b) Interpret: What mood does this race create for the poem?

2. **(a) Recall:** What event "closes" for the speaker "the child's fairy tale of an antic England"? **(b) Infer:** Why is this event disillusioning? **(c) Connect:** Why does Walcott's reason for being in England at the time make the event especially significant for him?

3. **(a) Draw Conclusions:** What does the speaker mean when he says that the "empire / . . . is ending / in the alleys of Brixton"? **(b) Connect:** What common idea or pattern connects the midsummer leaves, Walcott's disillusionment, and the crisis in England?

4. **Infer:** Judging by the poem, has Walcott come to terms with belonging to both black and white traditions? Explain.

5. **Make a Judgment:** Do you think black artists such as Walcott should withdraw from "white fellowships" to protest racial injustices? Explain.

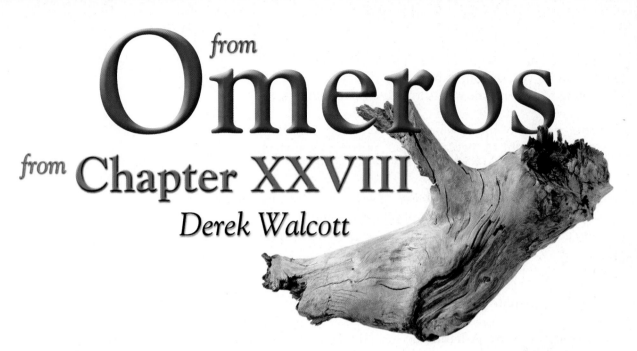

from Omeros
from Chapter XXVIII
Derek Walcott

Now he heard the griot[1] muttering his prophetic song
of sorrow that would be the past. It was a note, long-drawn
and endless in its winding like the brown river's tongue:

"We were the color of shadows when we came down
5 with tinkling leg-irons to join the chains of the sea,
for the silver coins multiplying on the sold horizon,

and these shadows are reprinted now on the white sand
of antipodal[2] coasts, your ashen ancestors
from the Bight of Benin, from the margin of Guinea.[3]

10 There were seeds in our stomachs, in the cracking pods
of our skulls on the scorching decks, the tubers[4]
withered in no time. We watched as the river-gods

changed from snakes into currents. When inspected,
our eyes showed dried fronds[5] in their brown irises,
15 and from our curved spines, the rib-cages radiated

like fronds from a palm-branch. Then, when the dead
palms were heaved overside, the ribbed corpses
floated, riding, to the white sand they remembered,

---

1. **griot** (grē′ ō) *n.* in West African cultures, a poet/historian/performer who preserves and passes on the oral tradition.
2. **antipodal** (an tip′ ə dəl) *adj.* situated on opposite sides of the earth.
3. **the Bight** (bīt) **of Benin** (be nēn′) **. . . Guinea** (gin′ ē) area of west central Africa that came to be known as the Slave Coast.
4. **tubers** (to͞ob′ ərz) *n.* thick, fleshy parts of underground stems, such as potatoes.
5. **fronds** (frändz) *n.* leaves of a palm; also the leaflike parts of seaweed.

Literary Analysis
Theme and Context
What two diverse contexts does Walcott invoke by having a griot speak in an epic?

**Reading Check**

To what does the griot compare the enslaved people?

to the Bight of Benin, to the margin of Guinea.
20 So, when you see burnt branches riding the swell,
     trying to reclaim the surf through crooked fingers,

     after a night of rough wind by some stone-white hotel,
     past the bright triangular passage of the windsurfers,
     remember us to the black waiter bringing the bill."

25 But they crossed, they survived. There is the epical splendor.
     Multiply the rain's lances, multiply their ruin,
     the grace born from subtraction as the hold's iron door

     rolled over their eyes like pots left out in the rain,
     and the bolt rammed home its echo, the way that thunder-
30 claps perpetuate their reverberation.

     So there went the Ashanti one way, the Mandingo another,
     the Ibo another, the Guinea.⁶ Now each man was a nation
     in himself, without mother, father, brother.

---

6. the Ashanti (ə shan´ tĭ) . . . **the Mandingo** (man dĭŋ´ gō) . . . **the Ibo** (ē´ bō´) . . .
the Guinea (gĭn´ ē) names of West African peoples.

Review and Assess

Thinking About the Selection

1. **Respond:** What sights connect you to a larger past, as the burnt branches connect the speaker to the past in the poem?

2. **(a) Recall:** What event does the griot describe in lines 4–24 of this excerpt from *Omeros*? **(b) Analyze:** How does the griot use plant imagery to link past and present?

3. **(a) Recall:** What happens to members of the different West African peoples once they are brought across the sea? **(b) Interpret:** What does Walcott mean when he says, "Now each man was a nation / in himself"?

4. **(a) Interpret:** What might Walcott mean by "the grace born from subtraction" (line 27)? **(b) Draw Conclusions:** According to the poem, what positive result does the slave trade have?

5. **Draw Conclusions:** Would you say that Walcott's main aim is to dramatize past experiences or to better understand the origins of the present? Explain.

6. **Make a Judgment:** In this excerpt, does Walcott pass too quickly over the suffering inflicted by the slave trade? Explain.

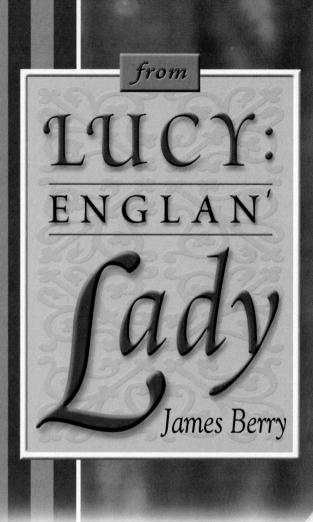

from

LUCY: ENGLAN'
Lady

James Berry

You ask me 'bout the lady. Me dear,
old center here still shine
with Queen. She affec' the place
like the sun: not comin' out oft'n
5 an' when it happ'n everybody's out
smilin' as she wave a han'
like a seagull flyin' slow slow.

An' you know she come from
dust free rooms an' velvet
10 an' diamond. She make you feel
this on-an'-on[1] town, London,
where long long time deeper than mind.[2]

Elizabeth II

---

1. **on-an'-on** extraordinary.
2. **deeper . . . mind** more than can be comprehended.

▲ **Critical Viewing** Does Queen Elizabeth show the "strain keepin' good graces" referred to in the poem? Explain. **[Analyze]**

✓Reading Check

According to the speaker, what effect does an appearance by the Queen have?

An' han's after han's[3] die away,
makin' streets, putt'n' up bricks,
15 a piece of brass, a piece of wood
an' plantin' trees: an' it give
a car a halfday job gett'n' through.

An' Leela, darlin', no, I never
meet the Queen in flesh. Yet
20 sometimes, deep deep, I sorry for her.
Everybody expec' a show
from her, like she a space touris'
on earth. An' darlin', unless
you can go home an' scratch up[4]
25 you' husban', it mus' be hard
strain keepin' good graces for
all hypocrite faces.

Anyhow, me dear, you know what
ole time people say,
30 "Bird sing sweet for its nest."[5]

---

3. **han's after han's** many generations.
4. **scratch up** lose your temper at.
5. **"Bird . . . nest"** Jamaican proverb, referring to the nightingale's habit of singing loudest near its nest. It means, "Those closest to home are the most contented."

Review and Assess

Thinking About the Selection

1. **(a) Recall:** Where does the speaker of the poem live?
(b) Infer: Has Leela, the person whom the speaker addresses, ever been there? Explain how you know. **(c) Infer:** About what does Leela appear to be curious?

2. **(a) Recall:** To what does Lucy compare the appearance of the Queen? **(b) Interpret:** Why does the Queen make Lucy "feel" the full extent of London?

3. **(a) Summarize:** What problems does Lucy think the Queen has as a result of her position? **(b) Analyze:** In what way do Lucy's perceptions bring the Queen back to human size and, at the same time, make Lucy seem as if she observes life from the center of things?

4. **Apply:** How might Lucy respond to a contemporary American celebrity? Explain.

5. **Evaluate:** Is Berry's use of Jamaican dialect effective in creating a distinctive, authentic voice for Lucy? Explain.

Review and Assess

Literary Analysis

Theme and Context

1. Explain how the **context** of *Midsummer*—a clash between cultures—ignites a conflict in the poet's mind.

2. The excerpt from *Omeros* tells in epic style how blacks, including Walcott's ancestors, arrived in the Caribbean. In what way is Walcott's **theme** a response to a context?

3. (a) What general concern about social roles does Berry explore in "From Lucy: Englan' Lady"? (b) Explain how his choice of speaker makes his presentation of this theme effective.

Comparing Literary Works

4. (a) Compare Walcott's use of **allusions** in *Midsummer* and *Omeros* with Berry's in "From Lucy." Use a chart like the one shown.

Allusion	Literary/ Scholarly?	News/ Popular Trends?	Folksy?
"'Bird sing sweet for its nest.'"			Yes: It is a country proverb.

(b) What do the poets' use of allusions suggest about their respective places in the British literary tradition?

5. (a) Compare the **political critiques** implied by Walcott's choice of speaker in *Omeros* and by Berry's choice of speaker in "From Lucy." (b) Judging by *Midsummer* and "From Lucy," how would each poet answer the question, Who owns English literature?

Reading Strategy

Applying Background Information

6. Walcott expresses the conflict of a divided heritage in *Midsummer*. How does he deal with that heritage in the excerpt from *Omeros*?

7. How does Berry's background and his residence in London help explain the word choice and subject matter of "From Lucy"?

Extend Understanding

8. **Cultural Connection:** Do you think the media exclude speakers who, like those in Berry's and Walcott's poems, offer a fresh, alternative perspective on events? Explain.

Quick Review

A **theme** is the central issue raised by a literary work.

A theme can be better understood by appreciating its **context,** the historical moment in which it originates.

Allusions are brief references without explanation to people, events, and other literary works.

A **political critique of art** is the examination of the historical and political implications of a work of art.

To **apply background information** about a literary work, consider its author or its context in order to understand it.

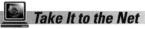 **Take It to the Net**
www.phschool.com
Take the interactive self-test online to check your understanding of these selections.

Integrate Language Skills

Vocabulary Development Lesson

Word Analysis: Latin Root -duc-

The word *inducted*, which means "led into a group," is formed from the Latin root *-duc-*, meaning "to lead." The root also appears in many scientific terms. Explain how this root contributes to the definition of each of the following words.

1. conduct   2. deduce   3. ductile

Spelling Strategy

The hard final *c* sound in an adjective is usually made by the letter *c* alone, as in the word *antic*. Add the correct ending to each italicized word.

1. Your plan to complete that *sta__* of homework in an hour is hardly *realist__*.
2. I was *frant__* when I discovered there was no place to *par__* at the mall.

Grammar and Style Lesson

Commonly Confused Words: *affect* and *effect*

Two commonly confused words are *affect* and *effect*. Though their meanings are related, they are quite different. **Affect** is most often a verb meaning "to influence." It can also be a noun meaning "mood; feeling" or a verb meaning "to put on; to make a pretense of being or having." **Effect** is most often a noun meaning "result." It can also be a verb meaning "bring about."

> **Verb:** How will this change <u>affect</u> you?
>
> **Noun:** What is the <u>effect</u> of the change?

In most cases, you can avoid confusing these words by deciding whether you want a verb meaning "to influence" (*affect*) or a noun meaning "result" (*effect*).

Concept Development: Synonyms

Synonyms are pairs of words that share nearly the same meaning. In your notebook, write the letter of the word that is a synonym of the word from the vocabulary list on page 1259.

1. rancor: (a) joyfulness, (b) musicality (c) hatred, (d) frustration, (e) sweetness

2. inducted: (a) anticipated, (b) concluded, (c) lost, (d) generalized, (e) initiated

3. antic: (a) oppositional, (b) dangerous, (c) herbivorous, (d) zany, (e) disappointing

4. eclipse: (a) outburst, (b) conflagration, (c) extinction (d) omission, (e) tumult

Practice Choose the correct word to complete each sentence.

1. Berry's stay in Harlem had a direct (affect, effect) on his ideas about prejudice.
2. Walcott's background has (effected, affected) the kind of poetry he writes.
3. Berry's poetry has (effected, affected) changes in West Indians' outlook.
4. Was Walcott more (effected, affected) by the Brixton riot than Berry was?
5. Readers respond strongly to Lucy's kindly (effect, affect).

Writing Application Write a paragraph based on one of the sentences above, using the words *affect* and *effect* twice.

W͞G *Prentice Hall Writing and Grammar Connection: Chapter 25, Section 2*

Writing Lesson

Script for the Multimedia Presentation of a Poem

In their poems, Walcott and Berry conjure up vivid scenes and lively speakers. Plan a multimedia presentation of one of their poems. Prepare a script describing the audiovisual aids that will bring out the imagery, rhythms, and spirit of the work.

Prewriting Choose one of the poems, and make a list of photographs, artwork, music, video clips, and sound effects that will highlight its theme and images.

Drafting Draft your script, clearly showing the line-by-line relationship between the text and the sounds and images you will use. Match strong audiovisual effects with the central ideas in the poem.

Model: Following Script Format

SPEAKER: She affec' the place

    [VISUAL: video slide of bright sun in sky]

like the sun: not comin' out oft'n

    [VISUAL: sky dissolves into photo of crowd]

    [AUDIO: fade in sound of happy crowd cheering]

an' when it happ'n everybody's out

> Bracketed directions clearly convey the timing of audiovisual effects with the reading of the poem.

Revising Make sure that the format of your script is clear and easy to follow. Adjust the script to achieve the clearest, strongest arrangement of multimedia elements.

𝒲𝒢 *Prentice Hall Writing and Grammar Connection: Chapter 28, Section 3*

Extension Activities

Listening and Speaking Prepare a **recitation** of Berry's poem, with special attention to the oral interpretation of the speaker's dialect.

- Prepare by listening to recorded examples of West Indian speech or by consulting with West Indians in your community.
- Follow Berry's own advice for reading a dialect poem: "Feel out the rhythms. . . . Then express it with your own easy natural voice."

Deliver your reading before the class.

Research and Technology With a group, prepare a **Caribbean culture festival.** Showcase the language, food, and music of Jamaica, St. Lucia, and other islands in the region. Provide informational note cards or audiotapes for the various exhibits, as well as a detailed map of the festival. **[Group Activity]**

Take It to the Net www.phschool.com

Go online for an additional research activity using the Internet.

Prepare to Read

A Devoted Son

Anita Desai (b. 1937)

Anita Desai's father was Indian and her mother, German. This unusual heritage may have contributed to her understanding of people from many different cultures. She displays this understanding in finely crafted novels and short stories about conflicts among characters of different generations and backgrounds. These works of fiction have gained her a reputation as one of the most gifted Indian novelists writing in English.

A Diverse Heritage Desai was born in the northern Indian town of Mussoorie, located at the foot of the Himalaya Mountains. She grew up in a large house in the old section of Delhi, India's capital city. "There were a great many books in the house and we were all bookworms," Desai recalls.

Choosing a Language Because of its unique heritage, Desai's family spoke three languages: Hindi, English, and German. Desai first learned English at school. When asked why she chose to write in it, Desai explained "it had a tremendous effect that the first thing you saw written and the first thing you ever read was English. It seemed to me the language of books. I just went on writing it because I always wanted to belong to this world of books."

Desai was part of a new development in Indian literature—the Indian writing in English. Writing literature is itself in tension with traditional Indian culture. Desai points out that "at one time all literature was recited rather than read and that remains the tradition in India. It is still rather a strange act to buy a book and read it, an unusual thing to do."

Early Work and Recognition A precocious writer, Desai finished her first English story when she was seven and published for the first time when she was nine. After graduating from Delhi University, the newly married Desai joined the Writers Workshop in Calcutta. In 1963, she published her first novel, *Cry the Peacock*, a portrayal of the despair of a young married woman. This novel was followed by *Bye-Bye, Blackbird* (1968), *Fire on the Mountain* (1977), and *Clear Light of Day* (1980). This last novel, a study of complex family relationships, was nominated for England's prestigious Booker Prize. The critic Victoria Glendinning said of this work, "Quiet writing, like Anita Desai's, can be more impressive than stylistic fireworks." In many works, she uses this quiet power to explore the struggle of women in Indian culture with the roles imposed on them by tradition.

Teaching and Writing After winning success as a writer, Desai also pursued a teaching career. She has taught, for example, at Cambridge University in England and at Smith College in Massachusetts. She continues to publish, examining the gulf between reality and delusion in recent novels.

The Clash of Cultures Another theme of her work, evident in *Baumgartner's Bombay* (1989) and in *Journey to Ithaca* (1995), is the contrast between Indian and modern European perspectives. *Journey to Ithaca*, for example, features a European couple who travel to India on a quest for spiritual meaning. Her 1999 novel *Fasting, Feasting*, a runner-up for the Booker Prize, relates how a brother and sister accommodate, each in a different way, the pressures of their strict and traditional parents. The clash between modern and traditional Indian values is also addressed in "A Devoted Son," which first appeared in her collection of short stories *Games at Twilight* (1978).

Preview

Connecting to the Literature

The modern world, with its powerful technology and instantaneous communications, seems to make wishes come true. As "A Devoted Son" shows, though, one should be careful what one wishes for.

Literary Analysis

Static and Dynamic Characters

Lifelike and believable characters in literature are often fluid—they change as the story unfolds. Some characters remain the same, however.

- **Static characters** are figures in a work who do not change. They may represent a social role or a particular attitude.
- **Dynamic characters** are figures who undergo a major change. The change may be one that they have chosen or one that is thrust upon them. Writers use such characters to develop truths about life or psychological insights.

In "A Devoted Son," only one character is dynamic. Consider whether this character is someone who embraces change or is someone who, despite preference and belief, is forced by events to change.

Connecting Literary Elements

Authors sometimes use characters as symbols to represent ideas or general attitudes. Static characters are particularly useful as symbols: Because they do not change, they can effectively represent one thing. When you read a story with many static characters, such as "A Devoted Son," consider whether the author is using these characters as symbols to represent specific cultural beliefs, traditional roles, or social trends.

Reading Strategy

Evaluating Characters' Decisions

Like people in life, characters in literary works make choices. You can **evaluate characters' decisions** just as you would assess your own. When a character makes an important choice, use organized questioning to evaluate the decision and its effect on future actions. This organizer shows one approach you might apply.

Vocabulary Development

exemplary (eg zem′ plə rē) *adj.* of that which should serve as a model (p. 1273)

filial (fil′ ē əl) *adj.* expected of a son or daughter (p. 1273)

encomiums (en kō′ mē əmz) *n.* formal expressions of great praise (p. 1273)

complaisant (kəm plā′ zənt) *adj.* agreeable; willing to please (p. 1273)

fathom (fath′ əm) *v.* understand thoroughly (p. 1276)

Character's Decision

Rakesh decides to become a doctor.

↓

Criteria

- Is decision right for character?
- Effect on other characters.
- Would I make a similar decision?

↓

Evaluation

A Devoted Son

Anita Desai

Background

Since India won its independence from Britain in 1947, modernization has resulted in dramatic contrasts between old and new. In this story, Desai dramatizes the conflict between the traditional respect shown parents, symbolized in the custom of touching one's father's feet, with the modern education that parents ask their children to acquire.

When the results appeared in the morning papers, Rakesh scanned them barefoot and in his pajamas, at the garden gate, then went up the steps to the verandah where his father sat sipping his morning tea and bowed down to touch his feet.

"A first division, son?" his father asked, beaming, reaching for the papers.

"At the top of the list, papa," Rakesh murmured, as if awed. "First in the country."

Bedlam broke loose then. The family whooped and danced. The whole day long visitors streamed into the small yellow house at the end of the road to congratulate the parents of this *Wunderkind*,[1] to slap Rakesh on the back and fill the house and garden with the sounds and colors of a festival. There were garlands and halwa,[2] party clothes and gifts (enough fountain pens to last years, even a watch or two), nerves and temper and joy, all in a multicolored whirl of pride and great shining vistas newly opened: Rakesh was the first son in the family to receive an education, so much had been sacrificed in order to send him to school and then medical college, and at last the fruits of their sacrifice had arrived, golden and glorious.

To everyone who came to him to say "*Mubarak*, Varmaji, your son has brought you glory," the father said, "Yes, and do you know what is the first thing he did when he saw the results this morning? He came

Reading Strategy
Evaluating Characters' Decision What decision did the family make regarding Rakesh?

---

1. *Wunderkind* person who achieves remarkable success at an early age.
2. **halwa** (häl vä′) (also halva) Middle Eastern sweet confection made of sesame flour and honey.

and touched my feet. He bowed down and touched my feet." This moved many of the women in the crowd so much that they were seen to raise the ends of their saris and dab at their tears while the men reached out for the betel-leaves[3] and sweetmeats that were offered around on trays and shook their heads in wonder and approval of such exemplary filial behavior. "One does not often see such behavior in sons any more," they all agreed, a little enviously perhaps. Leaving the house, some of the women said, sniffing, "At least on such an occasion they might have served pure *ghee*[4] sweets," and some of the men said, "Don't you think old Varma was giving himself airs? He needn't think we don't remember that he comes from the vegetable market himself, his father used to sell vegetables, and he has never seen the inside of a school." But there was more envy than rancor[5] in their voices and it was, of course, inevitable—not every son in that shabby little colony at the edge of the city was destined to shine as Rakesh shone, and who knew that better than the parents themselves?

And that was only the beginning, the first step in a great, sweeping ascent to the radiant heights of fame and fortune. The thesis he wrote for his M.D. brought Rakesh still greater glory, if only in select medical circles. He won a scholarship. He went to the USA (that was what his father learnt to call it and taught the whole family to say—not America, which was what the ignorant neighbors called it, but, with a grand familiarity, "the USA") where he pursued his career in the most prestigious of all hospitals and won encomiums from his American colleagues which were relayed to his admiring and glowing family. What was more, he came *back*, he actually returned to that small yellow house in the once-new but increasingly shabby colony, right at the end of the road where the rubbish vans tipped out their stinking contents for pigs to nose in and rag-pickers to build their shacks on, all steaming and smoking just outside the neat wire fences and well-tended gardens. To this Rakesh returned and the first thing he did on entering the house was to slip out of the embraces of his sisters and brothers and bow down and touch his father's feet.

As for his mother, she gloated chiefly over the strange fact that he had not married in America, had not brought home a foreign wife as all her neighbors had warned her he would, for wasn't that what all Indian boys went abroad for? Instead he agreed, almost without argument, to marry a girl she had picked out for him in her own village, the daughter of a childhood friend, a plump and uneducated girl, it was true, but so old-fashioned, so placid, so complaisant that she slipped into the household and settled in like a charm, seemingly too lazy and too good-natured to even try and make Rakesh leave home and set up independently, as any other girl might have done. What was more, she was pretty—really pretty, in a plump, pudding

---

3. **betel-leaves** leaves of a climbing evergreen shrub which are chewed in the East with betel nut parings and a little lime.
4. *ghee* clarified butter, often used in Indian cooking.
5. **rancor** bitter, lasting hate.

exemplary (eg zem′ plə rē) *adj.* of that which should serve as a model

filial (fil′ ē əl) *adj.* expected of a son or daughter

encomiums (en kō′ mē əmz) *n.* formal expressions of great praise

complaisant (kəm plā′ zənt) *adj.* agreeable; willing to please

✔**Reading Check**

What has Rakesh accomplished?

way that only gave way to fat—soft, spreading fat, like warm wax—after the birth of their first baby, a son, and then what did it matter?

For some years Rakesh worked in the city hospital, quickly rising to the top of the administrative organization, and was made a director before he left to set up his own clinic. He took his parents in his car—a new, sky-blue Ambassador with a rear window full of stickers and charms revolving on strings—to see the clinic when it was built, and the large sign-board over the door on which his name was printed in letters of red, with a row of degrees and qualifications to follow it like so many little black slaves of the regent.[6] Thereafter his fame seemed to grow just a little dimmer—or maybe it was only that everyone in town had grown accustomed to it at last—but it was also the beginning of his fortune for he now became known not only as the best but also the richest doctor in town.

However, all this was not accomplished in the wink of an eye. Naturally not. It was the achievement of a lifetime and it took up Rakesh's whole life. At the time he set up his clinic his father had grown into an old man and retired from his post at the kerosene dealer's depot at which he had worked for forty years, and his mother died

----

6. **regent** ruler; governor.

Reading Strategy
Evaluating Characters' Decisions What seems to guide the decisions that Rakesh makes about his life?

soon after, giving up the ghost with a sigh that sounded positively happy, for it was her own son who ministered to her in her last illness and who sat pressing her feet at the last moment—such a son as few women had borne.

For it had to be admitted—and the most unsuccessful and most rancorous of neighbors eventually did so—that Rakesh was not only

▼ **Critical Viewing**
How comfortable do you imagine it is for a man such as Rakesh or the businessman in the photograph to dwell among those less fortunate than himself? **[Speculate]**

a devoted son and a miraculously good-natured man who contrived somehow to obey his parents and humor his wife and show concern equally for his children and his patients, but there was actually a brain inside this beautifully polished and formed body of good manners and kind nature and, in between ministering to his family and playing host to many friends and coaxing them all into feeling happy and grateful and content, he had actually trained his hands as well and emerged an excellent doctor, a really fine surgeon. How one man—and a man born to illiterate parents, his father having worked for a kerosene dealer and his mother having spent her life in a kitchen—had achieved, combined and conducted such a medley of virtues, no one could <u>fathom</u>, but all acknowledged his talent and skill.

It was a strange fact, however, that talent and skill, if displayed for too long, cease to dazzle. It came to pass that the most admiring of all eyes eventually faded and no longer blinked at his glory. Having retired from work and having lost his wife, the old father very quickly went to pieces, as they say. He developed so many complaints and fell ill so frequently and with such mysterious diseases that even his son could no longer make out when it was something of significance and when it was merely a peevish whim. He sat huddled on his string bed most of the day and developed an exasperating habit of stretching out suddenly and lying absolutely still, allowing the whole family to fly around him in a flap, wailing and weeping, and then suddenly sitting up, stiff and gaunt, and spitting out a big gob of betel-juice as if to mock their behavior.

He did this once too often: there had been a big party in the house, a birthday party for the youngest son, and the celebrations had to be suddenly hushed, covered up and hustled out of the way when the daughter-in-law discovered, or thought she discovered, that the old man, stretched out from end to end of his string bed, had lost his pulse; the party broke up, dissolved, even turned into a band of mourners, when the old man sat up and the distraught daughter-in-law received a gob of red spittle right on the hem of her organza sari.[7] After that no one much cared if he sat up crosslegged on his bed, hawking and spitting, or lay down flat and turned gray as a corpse. Except, of course, for that pearl amongst pearls, his son Rakesh.

It was Rakesh who brought him his morning tea, not in one of the china cups from which the rest of the family drank, but in the old man's favorite brass tumbler, and sat at the edge of his bed, comfortable and relaxed with the string of his pajamas dangling out from under his fine lawn night-shirt, and discussed or, rather, read out the morning news to his father. It made no difference to him that his father made no response apart from spitting. It was Rakesh, too, who, on returning from the clinic in the evening, persuaded the old man to come out of his room, as bare and desolate as a cell, and take the

fathom (fath´ əm) v. understand thoroughly

Literary Analysis
Static and Dynamic Characters In what way is Rakesh's father changing? What events precede this change?

---

7. **organza sari** Saris are traditional garments worn by Indian women, consisting of lengths of cotton, silk, or other cloth wrapped around the waist and draped over one shoulder; organza is a sheer, stiffened fabric.

evening air out in the garden, beautifully arranging the pillows and bolsters on the divan in the corner of the open verandah. On summer nights he saw to it that the servants carried out the old man's bed onto the lawn and himself helped his father down the steps and onto the bed, soothing him and settling him down for a night under the stars.

All this was very gratifying for the old man. What was not so gratifying was that he even undertook to supervise his father's diet. One day when the father was really sick, having ordered his daughter-in-law to make him a dish of *soojie halwa* and eaten it with a saucerful of cream, Rakesh marched into the room, not with his usual respectful step but with the confident and rather contemptuous stride of the famous doctor, and declared, "No more *halwa* for you, papa. We must be sensible, at your age. If you must have something sweet, Veena will cook you a little *kheer*,[8] that's light, just a little rice and milk. But nothing fried, nothing rich. We can't have this happening again."

The old man who had been lying stretched out on his bed, weak and feeble after a day's illness, gave a start at the very sound, the tone of these words. He opened his eyes—rather, they fell open with shock—and he stared at his son with disbelief that darkened quickly to reproach. A son who actually refused his father the food he craved? No, it was unheard of, it was incredible. But Rakesh had turned his back to him and was cleaning up the litter of bottles and packets on the medicine shelf and did not notice while Veena slipped silently out of the room with a little smirk that only the old man saw, and hated.

Halwa was only the first item to be crossed off the old man's diet. One delicacy after the other went—everything fried to begin with, then everything sweet, and eventually everything, everything that the old man enjoyed.

The meals that arrived for him on the shining stainless steel tray twice a day were frugal to say the least—dry bread, boiled lentils, boiled vegetables and, if there were a bit of chicken or fish, that was boiled too. If he called for another helping—in a cracked voice that quavered theatrically—Rakesh himself would come to the door, gaze at him sadly and shake his head, saying, "Now, papa, we must be careful, we can't risk another illness, you know," and although the daughter-in-law kept tactfully out of the way, the old man could just see her smirk sliding merrily through the air. He tried to bribe his grandchildren into buying him sweets (and how he missed his wife now, that generous, indulgent and illiterate cook), whispering, "Here's fifty paise," as he stuffed the coins into a tight, hot fist. "Run down to the shop at the crossroads and buy me thirty paise worth of *jalebis*,[9] and you can spend the remaining twenty paise on yourself. Eh? Understand? Will you do that?" He got away with it once or twice but then was found out, the conspirator was scolded by his father and smacked by his mother and Rakesh came storming into the room, almost tearing his hair as he shouted through

---

8. *kheer* rice pudding traditionally served as a dessert in southern India.
9. *jalebis* Indian sweet made by frying a coil of batter and then soaking it in syrup.

Literary Analysis
Static and Dynamic Characters Does Rakesh's "rather contemptuous stride" show a change in his character? In what way is he still the ideal son in this scene?

Reading Strategy
Evaluating Characters' Decisions What does Rakesh seem to disregard in his decision about his father's diet? Is his choice wise? Explain.

**Reading Check**
What does Rakesh change in his father's life?

▲ **Critical Viewing** Identify three details in this photograph that illustrate the story's theme of ambition and the conflict between the modern and the traditional. **[Interpret]**

compressed lips, "Now papa, are you trying to turn my little son into a liar? Quite apart from spoiling your own stomach, you are spoiling him as well—you are encouraging him to lie to his own parents. You should have heard the lies he told his mother when she saw him bringing back those *jalebis* wrapped up in filthy newspaper. I don't allow anyone in my house to buy sweets in the bazaar, papa, surely you know that. There's cholera in the city, typhoid, gastroenteritis[10]—I see these cases daily in the hospital, how can I allow my own family to run such risks?" The old man sighed and lay down in the corpse position. But that worried no one any longer.

There was only one pleasure left in the old man now (his son's early morning visits and readings from the newspaper could no longer be called that) and those were visits from elderly neighbors. These were not frequent as his contemporaries were mostly as decrepit and helpless as he and few could walk the length of the road to visit him any more. Old Bhatia, next door, however, who was still spry enough to refuse, adamantly, to bathe in the tiled bathroom indoors and to insist on carrying out his brass mug and towel, in all seasons and usually at impossible hours, into the yard and bathe noisily under the garden tap, would look over the hedge to see if Varma were out on his verandah and would call to him and talk while he wrapped his *dhoti*[11] about him and dried the sparse hair on his head, shivering with enjoyable exaggeration. Of course these conversations, bawled across the hedge by two rather deaf old men conscious of having their entire households overhearing them, were not very satisfactory but Bhatia occasionally came out of his yard, walked down the bit of road and came in at Varma's gate to collapse onto the stone plinth built under the temple tree. If Rakesh was at home he would help his father down the steps into the garden and arrange him on his night bed under the tree and leave the two old men to chew betel-leaves and discuss the ills of their individual bodies with combined passion.

"At least you have a doctor in the house to look after you," sighed Bhatia, having vividly described his martyrdom to piles.

"Look after me?" cried Varma, his voice cracking like an ancient clay jar. "He—he does not even give me enough to eat."

"What?" said Bhatia, the white hairs in his ears twitching. "Doesn't give you enough to eat? Your own son?"

"My own son. If I ask him for one more piece of bread, he says no, papa, I weighed out the *ata* myself and I can't allow you to have more than two hundred grams of cereal a day. He *weighs* the food he gives me, Bhatia—he has scales to weigh it on. That is what it has come to."

"Never," murmured Bhatia in disbelief. "Is it possible, even in this evil age, for a son to refuse his father food?"

Reading Strategy
Evaluating Characters' Decisions What problems does Rakesh's decision to forbid his father sweets cause?

Reading Check

What does Varma complain about to his friend?

---

10. **cholera . . . typhoid, gastroenteritis** dangerous infectious diseases causing fever or intestinal problems.
11. *dhoti* cloth worn by male Hindus, the ends being passed through the legs and tucked in at the waist.

"Let me tell you," Varma whispered eagerly. "Today the family was having fried fish—I could smell it. I called to my daughter-in-law to bring me a piece. She came to the door and said no. . . ."

"Said no?" It was Bhatia's voice that cracked. A *drongo*[12] shot out of the tree and sped away. *"No?"*

"No, she said no, Rakesh has ordered her to give me nothing fried. No butter, he says, no oil. . . ."

"No butter? No oil? How does he expect his father to live?"

Old Varma nodded with melancholy triumph. "That is how he treats me—after I have brought him up, given him an education, made him a great doctor. Great doctor! This is the way great doctors treat their fathers, Bhatia," for the son's sterling personality and character now underwent a curious sea change. Outwardly all might be the same but the interpretation had altered: his masterly efficiency was nothing but cold heartlessness, his authority was only tyranny in disguise.

There was cold comfort in complaining to neighbors and, on such a miserable diet, Varma found himself slipping, weakening and soon becoming a genuinely sick man. Powders and pills and mixtures were not only brought in when dealing with a crisis like an upset stomach but became a regular part of his diet—became his diet, complained Varma, supplanting the natural foods he craved. There were pills to regulate his bowel movements, pills to bring down his blood pressure, pills to deal with his arthritis and, eventually, pills to keep his heart beating. In between there were panicky rushes to the hospital, some humiliating experience with the stomach pump and enema, which left him frightened and helpless. He cried easily, shriveling up on his bed, but if he complained of a pain or even a vague, gray fear in the night, Rakesh would simply open another bottle of pills and force him to take one. "I have my duty to you papa," he said when his father begged to be let off.

"Let me be," Varma begged, turning his face away from the pills on the outstretched hand. "Let me die. It would be better. I do not want to live only to eat your medicines."

"Papa, be reasonable."

"I leave that to you," the father cried with sudden spirit. "Leave me alone, let me die now, I cannot live like this."

"Lying all day on his pillows, fed every few hours by his daughter-in-law's own hand, visited by every member of his family daily—and then he says he does not want to live 'like this,'" Rakesh was heard to say, laughing, to someone outside the door.

"Deprived of food," screamed the old man on the bed, "his wishes ignored, taunted by his daughter-in-law, laughed at by his grandchildren—*that* is how I live." But he was very old and weak and all anyone heard was an incoherent croak, some expressive grunts and cries of genuine pain. Only once, when old Bhatia had come to see him and they sat together under the temple tree, they heard him cry, "God is calling me—and they won't let me go."

---

12. *drongo* black bird with a long forked tail.

Literary Analysis
Static and Dynamic Characters The narrator says Rakesh's character "now underwent a curious sea change." Which character has really changed and which one has stayed the same?

Reading Strategy
Evaluating Characters' Decisions What new view does this paragraph give of the family's decision to send Rakesh to medical school?

The quantities of vitamins and tonics he was made to take were not altogether useless. They kept him alive and even gave him a kind of strength that made him hang on long after he ceased to wish to hang on. It was as though he were straining at a rope, trying to break it, and it would not break, it was still strong. He only hurt himself, trying.

In the evening, that summer, the servants would come into his cell, grip his bed, one at each end, and carry it out to the verandah, there sitting it down with a thump that jarred every tooth in his head. In answer to his agonized complaints they said the doctor sahib had told them he must take the evening air and the evening air they would make him take—thump. Then Veena, that smiling, hypocritical pudding in a rustling sari, would appear and pile up the pillows under his head till he was propped up stiffly into a sitting position that made his head swim and his back ache.

"Let me lie down," he begged. "I can't sit up any more."

"Try, papa, Rakesh said you can if you try," she said, and drifted away to the other end of the verandah where her transistor radio vibrated to the lovesick tunes from the cinema that she listened to all day.

So there he sat, like some stiff corpse, terrified, gazing out on the lawn where his grandsons played cricket,[13] in danger of getting one of their hard-spun balls in his eye, and at the gate that opened onto the dusty and rubbish-heaped lane but still bore, proudly, a newly touched-up signboard that bore his son's name and qualifications, his own name having vanished from the gate long ago.

At last the sky-blue Ambassador arrived, the cricket game broke up in haste, the car drove in smartly and the doctor, the great doctor, all in white, stepped out. Someone ran up to take his bag from him, others to escort him up the steps. "Will you have tea?" his wife called, turning down the transistor set. "Or a Coca-Cola? Shall I fry you some *samosas*?"[14] But he did not reply or even glance in her direction. Ever a devoted son, he went first to the corner where his father sat gazing, stricken, at some undefined spot in the dusty yellow air that swam before him. He did not turn his head to look at his son. But he stopped gobbling air with his uncontrolled lips and set his jaw as hard as a sick and very old man could set it.

"Papa," his son said, tenderly, sitting down on the edge of the bed and reaching out to press his feet.

Old Varma tucked his feet under him, out of the way, and continued to gaze stubbornly into the yellow air of the summer evening.

"Papa, I'm home."

Varma's hand jerked suddenly, in a sharp, derisive movement, but he did not speak.

"How are you feeling, papa?"

---

13. **cricket** open-air game played between two teams and utilizing a ball, bats, and wicket.
14. ***samosas*** triangular pastries fried in clarified butter or oil, containing spiced vegetables or meat.

Literary Analysis
Static and Dynamic Characters Compare the father's character at the end of the story with that of the betel-juice spitter of earlier scenes.

**Reading Check**

How does Varma respond to his son's treatment?

Then Varma turned and looked at his son. His face was so out of control and all in pieces, that the multitude of expressions that crossed it could not make up a whole and convey to the famous man exactly what his father thought of him, his skill, his art.

"I'm dying," he croaked. "Let me die, I tell you."

"Papa, you're joking," his son smiled at him, lovingly. "I've brought you a new tonic to make you feel better. You must take it, it will make you feel stronger again. Here it is. Promise me you will take it regularly, papa."

Varma's mouth worked as hard as though he still had a gob of betel in it (his supply of betel had been cut off years ago). Then he spat out some words, as sharp and bitter as poison, into his son's face. "Keep your tonic—I want none—I want none—I won't take any more of—of your medicines. None. Never," and he swept the bottle out of his son's hand with a wave of his own, suddenly grand, suddenly effective.

His son jumped, for the bottle was smashed and thick brown syrup had splashed up, staining his white trousers. His wife let out a cry and came running. All around the old man was hubbub once again, noise, attention.

He gave one push to the pillows at his back and dislodged them so he could sink down on his back, quite flat again. He closed his eyes and pointed his chin at the ceiling, like some dire prophet, groaning, "God is calling me—now let me go."

Review and Assess

Thinking About the Selection

1. **Respond:** At the end of the story, with whom do you sympathize more—Rakesh or his father, Varma? Explain.

2. **(a) Recall:** What is the first thing Rakesh does when he sees his excellent exam results? **(b) Infer:** What values does Rakesh's behavior reflect?

3. **(a) Recall:** Name three things about which Rakesh and Varma come to disagree. **(b) Interpret:** How do these disagreements reflect the central conflict of the story?

4. **(a) Analyze:** Is the central conflict a struggle between two traditions or between a tradition and itself? Explain. **(b) Distinguish:** In what ways is this conflict specifically Indian and in what ways is it universal?

5. **(a) Evaluate:** Do you think Rakesh's behavior is truly devoted? Explain. **(b) Generalize:** What does this story suggest about the relationship between devotion and compassion?

6. **Make a Judgment:** Drawing on the story, explain how you think adult children should care for their parents.

Review and Assess

Literary Analysis

Static and Dynamic Characters

1. Are Rakesh's mother and wife **static** or **dynamic characters**? Explain your classifications.
2. By the end of the story, what new perspective has Varma developed on his "devoted son"?
3. Compare Rakesh and Varma at the beginning, middle, and end the story. Which of the two is dynamic? Explain.
4. How does Desai use static and dynamic characters to reflect the fate of traditional beliefs in the modern world?

Connecting Literary Elements

5. Which character in the story most clearly symbolizes traditional roles in India? Why?
6. Use a chart like the one below to interpret Rakesh's actions.

7. (a) What is the effect of Rakesh's actions? (b) Draw a conclusion about what Rakesh symbolizes.
8. Are symbolic characters the same as stereotypes, depictions representing an entire group by a few exaggerated characteristics? Explain.

Reading Strategy

Evaluating Characters' Decisions

9. **Evaluate** Rakesh's decisions concerning his father's diet. Consider Rakesh's motives, the effect of his decisions on his father, and your own ideas of what is reasonable.
10. (a) Why does the family decide to make sacrifices for Rakesh's education? (b) Was this decision unwise? Explain.

Extend Understanding

11. **Cultural Connection:** Judging from the story, what attitudes toward the elderly prevail in India? Explain.

Quick Review

A **static character** is a figure in a literary work who does not change.

A **dynamic character** is a figure who undergoes a significant change.

To **evaluate a characters' decision,** analyze why it was made, determine its effects, and assess whether or not it was effective or wise.

 Take It to the Net
www.phschool.com

Take the interactive self-test online to check your understanding of the selection.

Integrate Language Skills

Vocabulary Development Lesson

Word Analysis: Latin Root -fil-

The word *filial*, meaning "suitable to or due from a son or daughter," contains the Latin root *-fil-*, meaning "son or daughter." Explain how the root helps define each of these words.

  1. filiation   2. affiliate   3. unaffiliated

Spelling Strategy

Nouns that end in *-um* and *-us* usually have Latin roots. In addition to regular plurals formed by adding *s* or *es*, these nouns have classical plurals in which *um* becomes *a* and *us* becomes *i*. For example, *encomium* becomes *encomia*, and *focus* becomes *foci*. In formal or technical contexts, the classical plural may be preferred. Give the two plurals for each of these nouns.

  1. aquarium   2. radius   3. syllabus

Fluency: Context

Write the word from the vocabulary list on page 1271 that best fits in each sentence. Use the context suggested by the sentence to help you choose the correct word.

  1. Rakesh won ___?___ for his superior talents.

  2. The faithful son felt that he had fulfilled his ___?___ obligations.

  3. Most of the neighbors considered Rakesh a(n) ___?___ son.

  4. Varma could not ___?___ the change in his relationship with Rakesh.

  5. Despite the effects of his actions, Rakesh could be described as ___?___.

Grammar and Style Lesson

Sentence Variety

Desai uses **sentence variety**—sentences of different lengths—to heighten drama and reinforce meaning. In the example, two short simple sentences are followed by a long simple sentence.

Example: Bedlam broke loose then. The family whooped and danced. The whole day long visitors streamed into the small yellow house at the end of the road to congratulate the parents of this *Wunderkind*, to slap Rakesh on the back and fill the house and garden with the sounds and colors of a festival.

In the example, the short sentences convey the suddenness of the eruption. The long sentence suggests a long day in which one conversation flows into another.

Practice Rewrite each item below, revising its length. Add details or break single sentences into parts, as necessary.

  1. Bedlam broke loose then.
  2. The thesis he wrote for his M.D. brought Rakesh still greater glory, if only in select medical circles.
  3. It was the achievement of a lifetime. . . .
  4. A son who actually refused his father the food he craved?
  5. Outwardly all might be the same but the interpretation had altered: . . . his authority was only tyranny in disguise.

Writing Application Using varied sentences, write a paragraph evaluating Rakesh's decisions.

 Prentice Hall Writing and Grammar Connection: Chapter 19, Section 4

Writing Lesson

Proposal for a Program for the Elderly

As Anita Desai's story shows, "care" for the elderly may not always contribute to their happiness. Review the story for ways in which Rakesh fails to address his father's deepest needs. Then, write an illustrated proposal advocating a program in which students help elders while avoiding the mistakes of Rakesh's approach.

Prewriting   Brainstorm with a group to establish the details of your program. For example, you might establish structured visits to seniors that include socializing and conducting oral-history interviews. Choose effective images to illustrate your proposal.

Drafting   State the objectives of your program clearly, using active verbs with positive associations, like *broaden*, *teach*, and *serve*. Arrange images and text for the best effect.

Revising   Exchange papers with a classmate, and review each other's proposals. Find and replace words or images that sour your positive tone.

Model: Revising to Improve Persuasive Impact

puts   *miles ahead of*

The factor that ~~differentiates~~ this program ~~from~~ others

is the input of the elderly themselves.

> More active, forceful phrasing enhances the persuasive effect of this sentence.

 Prentice Hall Writing and Grammar Connection: Chapter 7, Section 4

Extension Activities

Listening and Speaking Choose a scene from the story. With a partner, perform a **role play** of the scene. As you prepare, follow these performance tips:

- Practice improvising dialogue to add spontaneity to your role play.
- Explore some ways to extend the scene beyond the story.
- Write a brief narrated introduction to set the scene.

After rehearsing, perform your role play for classmates. [**Group Activity**]

Research and Technology Write a **social services report** comparing how India and the United States provide for their elderly. Use library and Internet reference sources to collect current data and reports. Based on your comparisons, draw a conclusion about needed improvements in both systems. Present your findings to the class, using graphs to illustrate your comparative statistics.

 **Take It to the Net**   www.phschool.com

Go online for an additional research activity using the Internet.

Prepare to Read

from We'll Never Conquer Space

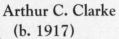

Arthur C. Clarke (b. 1917)

With more than one hundred million copies of his books in print worldwide, Arthur C. Clarke may be the most successful science-fiction writer of all time. The extensive appeal of his books is probably due to their distinctive combination of technical expertise and touches of poetry.

A Scientific Start As a child, Clarke's natural curiosity led him to explore science and space with unflagging enthusiasm. He created his own map of the moon based on observations he made with a homemade telescope. At the age of twelve, when he started to read a mass-circulation magazine called *Amazing Stories,* Clarke discovered science fiction, the genre in which he would have such success.

Imagining Satellites During World War II, Clarke's interest in scientific matters led to his service as a radar instructor in the Royal Air Force. At the end of the war, he drew on his wartime experience and his passion for space in an article for *Wireless World* magazine. The piece, entitled "Extra-Terrestrial Relays," explained how television and telephone signals could be bounced off relay stations—satellites—sent into orbit by rocket. Clarke described, in essence, the methods used today for television and other broadcasting.

Nearly twenty years later, in 1962, as if in answer to Clarke's prediction, the Communications Satellite Corporation (COMSAT) was authorized by Congress to manage commercial communication satellite systems. Clarke modestly commented that the article he had written in the 1940s had advanced telecommunications by "15 minutes."

Many others, however, disagree with his humble assessment: They consider Clarke "the godfather of global communication."

A Writer's Perspective Since the early 1950s, Clarke has worked full time as a writer, producing more than seventy works of fiction and nonfiction. Among his most famous science-fiction novels are *Childhood's End* (1953) and *The City and the Stars* (1956).

One of his earliest stories, "The Sentinel" (1951), provided the germ of an idea for the epic film *2001: A Space Odyssey* (1968). As filmed by British director Stanley Kubrick, this poetic classic combines several different narratives, including the tale of a sentient, murderous computer named HAL 9000. Clarke has summarized the film as an exploration of "man's place in the pecking order of cosmic intelligence." While working on the film, Clarke was also writing a novel based on the same material. The novel was published a few months after the film was released. Many readers find that the novel helps explain some of the film's beautiful but opaque images.

Distant Yet Connected Since 1956, Clarke has lived in Colombo, Sri Lanka. Fascinated by the region's spectacular underwater realms, he became an avid scuba diver and undersea explorer. An extensive media center helps Clarke stay in touch with the larger world, pursuing his curiosity about new technological and scientific discoveries.

Exploration of the Possible Like his distinguished contemporaries Isaac Asimov and Ray Bradbury, Clarke has established credibility with his audience through an impressive command of science. But while his speculations are grounded in hard facts, he turns them to lyrical, romantic ends in his science-fiction works.

Challenging the notion that science fiction is escapism, Clarke has asserted that the genre is "virtually the only kind of writing that's dealing with real problems and possibilities. . . ."

Preview

Connecting to the Literature

If you were to predict how technology will change your daily life in twenty-five years, you might work from a mix of guesses and facts. In this essay, Clarke uses all the science at his fingertips to make a prediction.

Literary Analysis

Prophetic Essay

All of us make guesses about the future. In a **prophetic essay,** a writer makes bold, systematic predictions. A prophetic essay has these features:

- It is a brief work of nonfiction.
- It makes predictions about the future of a large collective, such as a nation, people, or planet.
- It may give warnings against complacency or pride, as the prophets in the Bible do.
- It uses ringing, memorable phrases to impress predictions on readers' memories or to reinforce warnings.

Notice how the predictions in the prophetic essay "We'll Never Conquer Space" also serve as a warning against overconfidence.

Connecting Literary Elements

Analogies are extended comparisons that help a reader grasp an idea by showing how it parallels a more familiar idea. Clarke uses a number of analogies to explain unfamiliar concepts. For example, he compares the situation of colonists in space with that of settlers on islands. As you read, notice how such analogies help you grasp abstract or hard-to-picture ideas by comparing those ideas with clear, understandable images.

Reading Strategy

Challenging the Text

When you **challenge a text,** you critically question the statements it makes. You treat it like a friend you can argue with rather than like an authority whose words you must accept. When you read a provocative statement in this essay, ask yourself questions like those shown in the chart.

Vocabulary Development

ludicrous (lŏo͞ʹ di krəs) *adj.* absurd; ridiculous (p. 1288)

irrevocable (ir revʹ ə kə bəl) *adj.* unable to be undone or canceled (p. 1289)

instantaneous (inʹ stən tāʹ nē əs) *adj.* done or happening in an instant (p. 1290)

enigma (i nigʹ mə) *n.* riddle; perplexing statement, person, or situation (p. 1291)

inevitable (in evʹ i tə bəl) *adj.* unavoidable; certain to happen (p. 1292)

zenith (zēʹ nith) *n.* highest point of something, especially of the sky or celestial sphere (p. 1294)

> **Provocative Statement**
>
> **"We'll Never Conquer Space"**
>
> - Do Clarke's arguments fully support this sweeping claim?
> - *Never* and *always* are unconditional, and statements using them can be proved wrong with a single counterexample. Is there such a counterexample to Clarke's claim?

from

We'll Never Conquer Space

Arthur C. Clarke

Background

Clarke wrote this essay in 1960, at the brink of the era of space exploration. Three years earlier, in 1957, *Sputnik* had become the first satellite launched into space. The year after Clarke wrote the essay, in 1961, Alan Shepard became the first American to enter space. Over the next sixteen years, human beings were to land on the moon (1969) and explore Mars via remote probes (1997). Yet Clarke's caution about the limits on the human conquest of space has yet to be tested.

Man will never conquer space. Such a statement may sound <u>ludicrous</u>, now that our rockets are already 100 million miles beyond the moon and the first human travelers are preparing to leave the atmosphere. Yet it expresses a truth which our forefathers knew, one we have forgotten—and our descendants must learn again, in heartbreak and loneliness.

Our age is in many ways unique, full of events and phenomena which never occurred before and can never happen again. They distort our thinking, making us believe that what is true now will be true forever, though perhaps on a larger scale. Because we have annihilated distance on this planet, we imagine that we can do it once again. The facts are far otherwise, and we will see them more clearly if we forget the present and turn our minds towards the past.

To our ancestors, the vastness of the earth was a dominant fact controlling their thoughts and lives. In all earlier ages than ours, the world was wide indeed, and no man could ever see more than a tiny fraction of its immensity. A few hundred miles—a thousand, at the most—was

ludicrous (lo͞o′ di krəs) *adj.* absurd; ridiculous

infinity. Only a lifetime ago, parents waved farewell to their emigrating children in the virtual certainty that they would never meet again.

And now, within one incredible generation, all this has changed. Over the seas where Odysseus wandered for a decade, the Rome-Beirut Comet whispers its way within the hour. And above that, the closer satellites span the distance between Troy and Ithaca[1] in less than a minute.

Psychologically as well as physically, there are no longer any remote places on earth. When a friend leaves for what was once a far country, even if he has no intention of returning, we cannot feel that same sense of <u>irrevocable</u> separation that saddened our forefathers. We know that he is only hours away by jet liner, and that we have merely to reach for the telephone to hear his voice.

In a very few years, when the satellite communication network is established, we will be able to see friends on the far side of the earth as easily as we talk to them on the other side of the town. Then the world will shrink no more, for it will have become a dimensionless point.

Forever Too Large

But the new stage that is opening up for the human drama will never shrink as the old one has done. We have abolished space here on the little earth; we can never abolish the space that yawns between the stars. Once again we are face to face with immensity and must accept its grandeur and terror, its inspiring possibilities and its dreadful restraints. From a world that has become too small, we are moving out into one that will be forever too large, whose frontiers will recede from us always more swiftly than we can reach out towards them.

Consider first the fairly modest solar, or planetary, distances which we are now preparing to assault. The very first Lunik[2] made a substantial impression upon them, traveling more than 200 million miles from the earth—six times the distance to Mars. When we have harnessed nuclear energy for spaceflight, the solar system will contract until it is little larger than the earth today. The remotest of the planets will be perhaps no more than a week's travel from the earth, while Mars and Venus will be only a few hours away.

This achievement, which will be witnessed within a century, might appear to make even the solar system a comfortable, homely place, with such giant planets as Saturn and Jupiter playing much the same role in our thoughts as do Africa or Asia today. (Their qualitative differences of climate, atmosphere and gravity, fundamental though they are, do not concern us at the moment.) To some extent this may

---

1. **Odysseus . . . Troy and Ithaca** Odysseus was the King of Ithaca and hero of Homer's *Odyssey.* Troy and Ithaca are the ancient cities marking the beginning and end of his wanderings across the Mediterranean Sea in the *Odyssey.* The Comet was an airplane, one of the fastest at the time the essay was written.
2. **Lunik** name given by American journalists to Luna I, an unmanned Soviet space probe of 1959.

Reading Strategy
Challenging the Text
What event or trend could you use to challenge Clarke's statement that the world is "shrinking"?

irrevocable (ir rev′ ə kə bəl) *adj.* unable to be undone or canceled

Reading Check

What effect does Clarke say technology is having on distances on Earth?

be true, yet as soon as we pass beyond the orbit of the moon, a mere quarter-million miles away, we will meet the first of the barriers that will separate the earth from her scattered children.

The marvelous telephone and television network that will soon enmesh the whole world, making all men neighbors, cannot be extended into space. It will never be possible to converse with anyone on another planet.

Do not misunderstand this statement. Even with today's radio equipment, the problem of sending speech to the other planets is almost trivial. But the messages will take minutes—sometimes hours—on their journey, because radio and light waves travel at the same limited speed of 186,000 miles a second.

Twenty years from now you will be able to listen to a friend on Mars, but the words you hear will have left his mouth at least three minutes earlier, and your reply will take a corresponding time to reach him. In such circumstances, an exchange of verbal messages is possible—but not a conversation.

Even in the case of the nearby moon, the 2½ second time-lag will be annoying. At distances of more than a million miles, it will be intolerable.

"Time Barrier"

To a culture which has come to take <u>instantaneous</u> communication for granted, as part of the very structure of civilized life, this "time barrier" may have a profound psychological impact. It will be a perpetual reminder of universal laws and limitations against which not all our technology can ever prevail. For it seems as certain as anything can be that no signal—still less any material object—can ever travel faster than light.

The velocity of light is the ultimate speed limit, being part of the very structure of space and time. Within the narrow confines of the solar system, it will not handicap us too severely, once we have accepted the delays in communication which it involves. At the worst, these will amount to 20 hours—the time it takes a radio signal to span the orbit of Pluto, the outermost planet.

Between the three inner worlds the earth, Mars, and Venus, it will never be more than 20 minutes—not enough to interfere seriously with commerce or administration, but more than sufficient to shatter those personal links of sound or vision that can give us a sense of direct contact with friends on earth, wherever they may be.

It is when we move out beyond the confines of the solar system that we come face to face with an altogether new order of cosmic reality. Even today, many otherwise educated men—like those savages who can count to three but lump together all numbers beyond four—cannot grasp the profound distinction between solar and stellar space. The first is the space enclosing our neighboring worlds, the planets; the second is that which embraces those distant suns, the stars, and it is literally millions of times greater.

Reading Strategy
Challenging the Text
Consider E-mail, invented after Clarke wrote the essay. How important is direct conversation in conducting business across a distance?

instantaneous (in´ stən tā´ nē əs) *adj.* done or happening in an instant

Literary Analysis
Prophetic Essay In what way is Clarke's prediction of "a perpetual reminder of . . . limitations" like a prophet's warning against excessive pride?

There is no such abrupt change of scale in terrestrial affairs. To obtain a mental picture of the distance to the nearest star, as compared with the distance to the nearest planet, you must imagine a world in which the closest object to you is only five feet away—and then there is nothing else to see until you have traveled a thousand miles.

Many conservative scientists, appalled by these cosmic gulfs, have denied that they can ever be crossed. Some people never learn; those who 60 years ago scoffed at the possibility of flight, and ten (even five!) years ago laughed at the idea of travel to the planets, are now quite sure that the stars will always be beyond our reach. And again they are wrong, for they have failed to grasp the great lesson of our age—that if something is possible in theory, and no fundamental scientific laws oppose its realization, then sooner or later it will be achieved.

One day, it may be in this century, or it may be a thousand years from now, we shall discover a really efficient means of propelling our space vehicles. Every technical device is always developed to its limit (unless it is superseded by something better) and the ultimate speed for spaceships is the velocity of light. They will never reach that goal, but they will get very close to it. And then the nearest star will be less than five years' voyaging from the earth.

Our exploring ships will spread outwards from their home over an ever-expanding sphere of space. It is a sphere which will grow at almost—but never quite—the speed of light. Five years to the triple system of Alpha Centauri, 10 to the strangely-matched doublet Sirius A and B, 11 to the tantalizing <u>enigma</u> of 61 Cygni,[3] the first star suspected to possess a planet. These journeys are long, but they are not impossible. Man has always accepted whatever price was necessary for his explorations and discoveries, *and the price of Space is Time.*

Even voyages which may last for centuries or millennia will one day be attempted. Suspended animation has already been achieved in the laboratory, and may be the key to interstellar travel. Self-contained cosmic arks which will be tiny traveling worlds in their own right may be another solution, for they would make possible journeys of unlimited extent, lasting generation after generation.

The famous Time Dilation effect predicted by the Theory of Relativity,[4] whereby time appears to pass more slowly for a

Astronaut Buzz Aldrin on moon near Lunar Module, during Apollo 11, NASA

▼ Critical Viewing
Does the suit worn by astronauts support Clarke's argument that space cannot be "conquered"? Explain. **[Make a Judgment]**

---

3. **Alpha Centauri . . . 61 Cygni** Alpha Centauri is a system of three stars in the constellation of the Centaur; one of these, Proxima Centauri, is the star closest to Earth besides the sun. Sirius, known as the Dog Star, is the brightest star in Earth's sky; it is actually two stars orbiting each other, one of which (Sirius B), is only as big as the earth. 61 Cygni is a binary star in the constellation Cygnus, the Swan.

4. **Theory of Relativity** In physics, the theory that measurements of an object's physical properties will vary depending on the relative motion of the observer and the observed object: Only the speed of light is constant. One consequence of the theory is that time, as measured by an external observer, will slow down on an object moving close to the speed of light. In theory, a person traveling near the speed of light would age at a slower rate than a person traveling more slowly (the "Time Dilation effect" referred to by Clarke).

enigma (e nig′ mə) *n.* riddle; perplexing statement, person, or situation

✓Reading Check

What barrier will space travel force people to confront?

traveler moving at almost the speed of light, may be yet a third. And there are others.

Looking far into the future, therefore, we must picture a slow (little more than half a billion miles an hour!) expansion of human activities outwards from the solar system, among the suns scattered across the region of the galaxy in which we now find ourselves. These suns are on the average five light-years apart; in other words, we can never get from one to the next in less than five years.

To bring home what this means, let us use a down-to-earth analogy. Imagine a vast ocean, sprinkled with islands—some desert, others perhaps inhabited. On one of these islands an energetic race has just discovered the art of building ships. It is preparing to explore the ocean, but must face the fact that the very nearest island is five years' voyaging away, and that no possible improvement in the technique of ship-building will ever reduce this time.

In these circumstances (which are those in which we will soon find ourselves) what could the islanders achieve? After a few centuries, they might have established colonies on many of the nearby islands and have briefly explored many others. The daughter colonies might themselves have sent out further pioneers, and so a kind of chain reaction would spread the original culture over a steadily expanding area of the ocean.

▼ **Critical Viewing**
Does this picture convey a sense of these immense distances as clearly as Clarke's prose? Explain. **[Analyze]**

But now consider the effects of the <u>inevitable</u>, unavoidable time-lag. There could be only the most tenuous contact between the home island and its offspring. Returning messengers could report what had happened on the nearest colony—five years ago. They could never bring information more up to date than that, and dispatches from the more distant parts of the ocean would be from still further in the past—perhaps centuries behind the times. There would never be news from the other islands, but only history.

Independent "Colonies"

All the star-borne colonies of the future will be independent, whether they wish it or not. Their liberty will be inviolably protected by Time as well as Space. They must go their own way and achieve their own destiny, with no help or hindrance from Mother Earth.

At this point, we will move the discussion on to a new level and deal with an obvious objection. Can we be sure that the velocity of light is indeed a limiting factor? So many "impassible" barriers have been shattered in the past; perhaps this one may go the way of all the others.

Large spiral galaxy, Andromeda with two small companion galaxies, NASA

We will not argue the point, or give the reasons why scientists believe that light can never be outraced by any form of radiation or any material object. Instead, let us assume the contrary and see just where it gets us. We will even take the most optimistic possible case and imagine that the speed of transportation may eventually become infinite.

Picture a time when, by the development of techniques as far beyond our present engineering as a transistor is beyond a stone axe, we can reach anywhere we please instantaneously, with no more effort than by dialing a number. This would indeed cut the universe down to size and reduce its physical immensity to nothingness. What would be left?

Everything that really matters. For the universe has two aspects—its scale, and its overwhelming, mind-numbing complexity. Having abolished the first, we are now face-to-face with the second.

What we must now try to visualize is not size, but quantity. Most people today are familiar with the simple notation which scientists use to describe large numbers; it consists merely of counting zeroes, so that a hundred becomes 10^2, a million, 10^6, a billion, 10^9 and so on. This useful trick enables us to work with quantities of any magnitude, and even defense budget totals look modest when expressed as $\$5.76 \times 10^9$ instead of $\$5,760,000,000$.

The number of other suns in our own galaxy (that is, the whirlpool of stars and cosmic dust of which our sun is an out-of-town member, lying in one of the remoter spiral arms) is estimated at about 10^{11}—or written in full, 100,000,000,000. Our present telescopes can observe something like 10^9 other galaxies, and they show no sign of thinning out even at the extreme limit of vision.

There are probably at least as many galaxies in the whole of creation as there are stars in our own galaxy, but let us confine ourselves to those we can see. They must contain a total of about 10^{11} times 10^9 stars, or 10^{20} stars altogether. 1 followed by 20 other digits is, of course, a number beyond all understanding.

Before such numbers, even spirits brave enough to face the challenge of the light-years must quail. The detailed examination of all the grains of sand on all the beaches of the world is a far smaller task than the exploration of the universe.

And so we return to our opening statement. Space can be mapped and crossed and occupied without definable limit; but it can never be conquered. When our race has reached its ultimate achievements, and the stars themselves are scattered no more widely than the seed of Adam, even then we shall still be like ants crawling on the face of the earth. The ants have covered the world but have they conquered it—for what do their countless colonies know of it, or of each other?

The British Tradition

Finding a Place in the World

Clarke's essay poses the question, What is the place of humanity in the universe? With each shift in history, the literature of the British tradition has returned to this question—whether it is in the mingled yearnings for home and for the sea in the Anglo-Saxon poem "The Seafarer" (p. 16) or in Bede's definition of England as a homeland (p. 74) or in Milton's cosmic explorations in *Paradise Lost* (p. 468). Swift brought his satirical eye to the question in *Gulliver's Travels* (p. 514), finding that we are neither small enough (nor unreasonable enough) for Lilliput nor big enough (nor good enough) for Brobdingnag. Sydney Smith took on the issue in perhaps its smallest form: How physically comfortable can we be in the world? (see p. 900).

Many of these writers, like Clarke, uncover a kind of universal human homelessness—a way in which the world leaves us with persistent, unsatisfied desires or unanswered questions. By affirming this condition, these writers remind us of our limits. At the same time, they affirm a special kind of freedom—a freedom to challenge or to celebrate these limits and the life they define.

✔Reading Check

What second obstacle does Clarke see to truly conquering space?

So it will be with us as we spread outwards from Mother Earth, loosening the bonds of kinship and understanding, hearing faint and belated rumors at second—or third—or thousandth-hand of an ever-dwindling fraction of the entire human race.

Though Earth will try to keep in touch with her children, in the end all the efforts of her archivists and historians will be defeated by time and distance, and the sheer bulk of material. For the number of distinct societies or nations, when our race is twice its present age, may be far greater than the total number of all the men who have ever lived up to the present time.

We have left the realm of human comprehension in our vain effort to grasp the scale of the universe; so it must always be, sooner rather than later.

When you are next outdoors on a summer night, turn your head towards the <u>zenith</u>. Almost vertically above you will be shining the brightest star of the northern skies—Vega of the Lyre,[5] 26 years away at the speed of light, near enough the point-of-no-return for us short-lived creatures. Past this blue-white beacon, 50 times as brilliant as our sun, we may send our minds and bodies, but never our hearts.

For no man will ever turn homewards from beyond Vega, to greet again those he knew and loved on the earth.

---

5. **Vega of the Lyre** star in the northern constellation, Lyra, and the fourth brightest of the stars in Earth's night sky.

Reading Strategy
Challenging the Text
In his arguments about information lag, what is Clarke assuming about the length of human life? Do you agree?

zenith (zē´ nəth) *n.* highest point of something, especially of the sky or celestial sphere

Review and Assess

Thinking About the Selection

1. **(a) Recall:** What reason does Clarke offer for claiming that a true conversation with someone on another planet is impossible? **(b) Classify:** What distinction does Clarke make between exchanging messages and having a conversation?

2. **(a) Recall:** What technological goal will be reached within a century, according to Clarke? **(b) Draw Conclusions:** Why would this achievement not help humans "conquer space"?

3. **(a) Compare and Contrast:** According to Clarke, how is conquering space different from conquering regions of the Earth? **(b) Infer:** What implications does Clarke think that conquering space would have for human society?

4. **Evaluate:** Has Clarke made a persuasive argument about the impossibility of conquering space? Explain.

5. **Apply:** If Clarke's warning about human limitations was taken seriously throughout our society, what effect might it have on human pride and ambition?

Review and Assess

Literary Analysis

Prophetic Essay

1. (a) Summarize the prediction that Clarke makes in this **prophetic essay.** (b) Identify two specific facts that support it.
2. (a) Choose two memorable phrases or sentences in the essay. (b) Explain how they add to the essay's persuasive power.
3. (a) Identify at least four strategies that Clarke uses to support his prophecy. (b) Explain which one you think is most effective.
4. Do you think Clarke's prophecy would have a good influence if it were taken to heart by people? Explain, describing the effect you think the prophecy might have on people's outlook.

Connecting Literary Elements

5. (a) What point does Clarke make with the **analogy** of an ocean sprinkled with islands? (b) What associations make the image of islands especially effective?
6. Use a chart like the one below to interpret the analogy that compares ants on Earth with humans exploring space.

Things Compared	Similarities Emphasized	What Is Explained

7. Evaluate Clarke's use of analogies. Does he use them to oversimplify complex issues or to make it easier to grasp difficult concepts? Explain.

Reading Strategy

Challenging the Text

8. Clarke states "Man has always accepted whatever price was necessary for his explorations. . . ." Write a few sentences **challenging** this statement, and decide whether or not you agree.
9. The word *may* can signal that an author is guessing rather than giving facts. Find and challenge one of Clarke's guesses.

Extend Understanding

10. **Science Connection:** How are scientific prophecies different from the predictions of popular culture, such as fortunetelling and astrology?

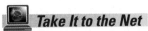

Integrate Language Skills

Vocabulary Development Lesson

Word Analysis: Latin Suffixes
-ible and *-able*

The suffixes *-ible* and *-able* both mean "able to," "having qualities of," "worthy of," or "capable of." Something *incredible* is "not able to be believed." Something *irrevocable* is "not able to be altered." Change each word following into a related word that ends in *-ible* or *-able*.

   1. define   **2.** resist   **3.** combustion

Spelling Strategy

The prefix *in-* or *im-*, meaning "not," changes to *ir-* when added to a word that begins with an *r*, as in the word *irrevocable*. Add the prefix *in-*, *im-*, or *ir-* to the following words:

   1. regular   **2.** capable   **3.** responsible

Concept Development: Synonyms

Choose the letter of the word or words closest in meaning to the first word.

1. ludicrous: (a) frisky, (b) morbid, (c) absurd

2. irrevocable: (a) rapid, (b) unalterable, (c) fickle

3. instantaneous: (a) immediate, (b) faulty, (c) risky

4. enigma: (a) quotation, (b) riddle, (c) archive

5. inevitable: (a) unavoidable, (b) sudden, (c) direct

6. zenith: (a) depth, (b) revolution, (c) peak

Grammar and Style Lesson

Linking Verbs and Subject Complements

Linking verbs, such as *seem* or *be*, connect the subject with words that complete the sentence. A **subject complement** is the noun, pronoun, or adjective that follows a linking verb and identifies or describes the subject.

>   S   LV
> **Example:** . . . the vastness of the earth <u>was</u> a
>   SC
>   dominant fact. . . .

The overuse of linking verbs can make writing dull. However, one effective stylistic use of this grammatical device is to make a vivid, surprising comparison, as when Clarke writes "A few hundred miles . . . was infinity."

Practice Identify the linking verb and the subject complement in each sentence.

1. Our age is in many ways unique, . . .
2. . . . the world was wide indeed, . . .
3. A few hundred miles . . . was infinity.
4. . . . the problem of sending speech to other planets is almost trivial.
5. The detailed examination of all the grains of sand on all the beaches of the world is a far smaller task than the exploration of the universe.

Writing Application Find five proverbs that use linking verbs, such as "Home is where the heart is." Explain why this grammatical structure is common in proverbs.

W͚G Prentice Hall Writing and Grammar Connection: Chapter 18, Section 3

Writing Lesson

Analysis of an Argument

Arthur C. Clarke argues that space cannot be conquered. His argument depends on a few basic assumptions, such as his notion of what it means to "conquer" a domain. Write an essay in which you identify, analyze, and evaluate these assumptions.

Prewriting Briefly outline the points in Clarke's essay. For each, identify the assumptions that he makes about the universe or about society.

Drafting In your draft, analyze each of Clarke's assumptions in turn. Then, evaluate each in terms of plausibility, support by scientists, and any other factor that seems appropriate.

Revising Review your draft, circling passages in which you connect two of Clarke's ideas. Draw an arrow from each circled statement to a sentence that further analyzes these ideas. If you cannot find such a sentence, consider elaborating on the circled statement.

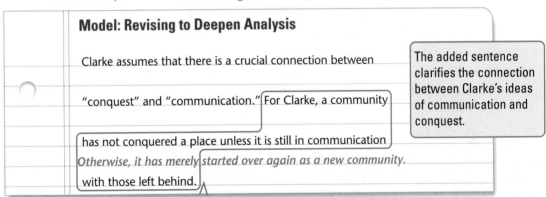

Model: Revising to Deepen Analysis

Clarke assumes that there is a crucial connection between

"conquest" and "communication." For Clarke, a community

has not conquered a place unless it is still in communication

Otherwise, it has merely started over again as a new community.

with those left behind.

The added sentence clarifies the connection between Clarke's ideas of communication and conquest.

*W*G *Prentice Hall Writing and Grammar Connection: Chapter 14, Section 4*

Extension Activities

Listening and Speaking Hold a **panel discussion** about the implications of Clarke's essay, both for the future of space travel and for our idea of humanity's place in the cosmos. Panelists should follow these guidelines:

- Use technical language when appropriate.
- Use figurative language, including analogies, to explain unfamiliar concepts.

Hold your discussion before the class.
[Group Activity]

Research and Technology Construct a **museum exhibit** that dramatizes Clarke's ideas. Use a variety of research strategies to build an effective exhibit. For instance, you might contact a local university for advice and to arrange the taping of interviews with professors.

 **Take It to the Net** www.phschool.com

Go online for an additional research activity using the Internet.

Writing About Literature

Evaluate Literary Trends

A poem like *Beowulf* was intended to reach an entire community—to thrill, instruct, and dazzle any Anglo-Saxon who heard it sung. Is it still possible for one poem to appeal to everyone? Many modern poets write poems rich in ambiguity and nuance as they explore the complexities of contemporary life. Some critics feel that, as a result, modern poetry has become too obscure and difficult to reach a large body of readers. Following the assignment outlined in the yellow box, write an essay in which you present your own views about the accessibility of poetry.

Prewriting

Find a focus. Begin by evaluating some of the poems you have read in this unit. Answer the questions below and fill in a chart like the one shown to help you organize your thoughts.

- Does the author's style include nuance (subtle shades of meaning) and ambiguity (words and ideas that may be interpreted in a variety of ways)? How?
- Do the nuances and ambiguities reflect aspects of a subject or feeling, or are they simply used for effect?
- Does the author use allusions (brief, unexplained literary references)?
- What needs of readers can this poem satisfy? What purpose of the writer's does it fulfill?

Model: Gathering Details for an Evaluation

Poem	Accessibility (1 = very accessible; 5 = very obscure)	Author's Purpose	Reader's Needs
Midsummer, XXIII Walcott	4	The complexity of the poem helps Walcott explore ambiguous feelings about his identity.	It does not fill a need for easy answers. It does enhance our perceptions of social problems and make us question the role of literature in life.

Gather support. As you form an opinion of a poem, jot it down and copy one or two lines or images from the poem that support it.

Compare evaluations. The topic of this essay is readers' reactions, so you may want to discuss your chosen poems in a group. Make generalizations based on the group's responses.

Assignment: The Audience for Modern Poetry

How accessible should poetry be? Write an essay in which you consider the reasons that many modern poets create complex and challenging works that require multiple readings. Then, provide an evaluation of the role that accessibility or community should play in shaping a poet's voice.

Criteria:

- Include a thesis statement that addresses the role of accessibility in modern poetry.
- Analyze several modern poems, including examples of easily accessible poetry as well as more challenging poems.
- Approximate length: 1,500 words

Read to Write

Do not limit your review to poems you remember enjoying. When you re-read and analyze a poem, you may discover that your opinion of it is very different from your first impression.

Drafting

Organize. Make an outline to help you find the basic organization of your essay. Use each major heading to write several paragraphs relating to that single topic. You may find it useful to create a fairly detailed outline in which you break down major headings into subheadings. When you draft from a detailed outline, you might write a complete paragraph for each subheading, with each detail beneath the subheading developed into a sentence.

Conclude effectively. In your concluding paragraph, review and tie together the ideas you have discussed in the body of your essay. Finish your essay with a strong statement about the importance of accessibility to modern poetry.

✎ **Write to Learn**

An outline can guide your first draft, but feel free to add ideas that occur to you while you write. Later, when you revise, make sure that your added ideas are coherent and relevant.

Model: Tying Together Points in an Effective Conclusion

Eliot's and Walcott's references are obscure. Their sentiments are ambiguous, a mixture of irony, guilt, and detachment. These features alone would discourage the majority of readers. In addition, both writers emphasize their inability to belong fully to a community. Yet, as I have argued, if their predicament is the predicament of the modern individual, then we need poetry like Eliot's and Walcott's to let us know we are not alone. That knowledge is itself a kind of community.

> A clear, memorable concluding sentence ties together the writer's ideas.

Revising and Editing

Review content: Assess emotional language. Your opinions should be expressed in logical, careful language. Eliminate unsupportable superlatives—for example, *completely without value*—and strengthen opinions that seem weak or vague.

Review style: Avoid ambiguity. Poetry may or may not benefit from ambiguity, but essay writing needs to be clear. Replace statements that are vague or could be interpreted more than one way.

Unclear: Modern poetry is complicated because of life.

Clear: Modern poetry's complexity reflects the confusion and chaos of modern life.

✎ **Write to Explain**

In your essay, you may wish to include classmates' thoughts from a group discussion. Be sure to identify the source of any observation.

Publishing and Presenting

Plan a poetry reading. Hold a classroom or school poetry reading in which students read modern poems. Alternate these readings with student evaluations of the poems, adapted or abridged from your essays. Student readers should lead audience discussions of the poems and evaluations.

𝒲𝒢 *Prentice Hall Writing and Grammar Connection: Chapter 14*

Writing WORKSHOP

Exposition: Multimedia Report

In a **multimedia report,** you organize words, images, and sounds into a coherent, informative, and lively presentation of a topic. In this workshop, you will assemble information into a developed multimedia script.

Assignment Criteria Your multimedia script should do the following:

- Combine words, images, and sound to present information and give the "flavor" of a topic
- Organize information in a clear, consistent manner
- Pace elements to create a coherent, even dramatic flow of sound, images, and information
- Use varied media (videos, audio recordings, spoken words, and so on) appropriate to each aspect of the topic
- Conclude with a strong, memorable ending

To preview the criteria on which your multimedia report may be assessed, see the Rubric on page 1303.

Prewriting

Choose a topic. The topic of your report must be one for which materials from several media are available. You might conduct a **media flip-through,** browsing magazines and television programs for a topic. Choose a topic that is of interest to your audience. If you do not have a specific audience in mind, choose a topic of general interest. Begin by giving your presentation a focus.

Example Focus: Zion Canyon National Park, yesterday and today

Select media materials appropriately. The media elements you choose must be varied and work well with your topic. The equipment needed to present them must also be available—old phonograph records, for instance, are useless without a turntable. Be aware that packing a script with too many elements—charts, images, sound effects, and audio clips—can lead to an unwieldy and potentially confusing presentation.

Collect relevant materials. Collect audiovisual materials for possible use. Depending on the topic, you may find what you need in libraries, on the Internet, or in a collection of your own.

Sketch an outline. First, outline your topic. Then, think of the audiovisual elements that will best explain, illustrate, or set a mood for each aspect of your topic. Do a rough storyboard indicating where you expect to incorporate the various media materials.

Selecting Material

Renaissance Portraits

I. Raphael

portraits show high individuality

VISUALS

-portrait of Baldassare Castiglione

AUDIO

-music that expresses courtliness

II. Later Renaissance Art

Titan (Venice)

VISUALS

-map showing Venice

AUDIO

-baroque music such as Vivaldi or Bach

Student Model

Before you begin drafting your script, read this student model and review the characteristics of a strong multimedia script.

Kate Vengraitis
Maplewood, NJ

Raphael's Art of the Portrait

Text	Audio and Video
[Cue AUDIO.] In the fifteenth and sixteenth centuries, art underwent a drastic change. [Cue VIDEO SLIDESHOW.] Each artist developed a unique style, sometimes blatantly trying to break the rules, other times creating innovative techniques. One common focus for Renaissance artists was the portrayal of individual personality. [Fade music.]	AUDIO: brass theme from Mussorgsky's *Pictures at an Exhibition.* VIDEO: Rapid dissolve from one slide to the next: Raphael's *Baldassare Castiglione* to Bronzio's *Portrait of a Young Man* to Titian's *Man with the Glove.*
[Cue SLIDE A.] In the Early Renaissance, portraits remained somewhat formal. By the High Renaissance, though, there is a clear focus on the personality of the subject, as in this portrait by Raphael. [Cue SLIDE B; pause.] In this portrait, *Baldassare Castiglione,* every detail helps communicate the subject's inner self. The background remains a stately neutral shade, free of decoration, appropriate for a man such as Baldassare Castiglione, the author of a handbook on genteel behavior.	SLIDE A: Timeline: Early / High Renaissance SLIDE B: Raphael's *Baldassare Castiglione.*
[Cue AUDIO.] The pose exhibits the man's elegant manner, his head and hands placed in the perfectly calm demeanor which a man of his stature would be expected to display. [Show SLIDE C; pause, then back to SLIDE B.]	AUDIO: selection from Bach's *The Well-Tempered Clavier.* SLIDE C: Detail of Castiglione's hands. SLIDE B
[Cue MUSIC.] [Cue VIDEO SLIDESHOW.] As this painting attests, Renaissance painters discovered complex ways to give insight into the individuality of their subjects.	AUDIO: Same as at opening. VIDEO SLIDESHOW: Same as at opening.

Dramatic theme music and a sampling of portraits establishes the tone and topic of the presentation.

Transitions and pauses keep the flow of the presentation smooth.

Kate chooses music to reflect the melancholy mood of this portrait.

Information is consistently organized, with each new main idea illustrated by a slide.

Both the audiovisual and textual parts of Kate's conclusion are strong and memorable.

Drafting

Write the text. Your narrated text is the glue that holds the elements of your presentation together. As you draft, follow your outline. Remember that your narration must clearly guide an audience by explaining the relevance of materials and creating transitions.

Select and position media sources. As you write the text, make final decisions on which sources to include.

- **Use script format.** Use a format such as that modeled on page 1301, to clearly coordinate narration with other elements.
- **Consider variety and flow.** As you choose audiovisual elements, focus on illustrating or setting the tone for each main point. Then, review your script to improve variety and pacing.

Prepare equipment. Assemble CD players, projectors, and any other equipment needed. Set media items such as CDs to the exact sections you will use. Enlist an assistant, or videotape your presentation.

Variety	
AVOID:	Photograph after photograph of the same scene
IMPROVEMENT:	A photograph of the scene, followed by a map showing its location

Pacing	
AVOID:	Ten minutes of the same music, interrupted by one minute of a different piece
IMPROVEMENT:	Two different pieces of music: One playing for a few minutes at the beginning, the other playing briefly in the middle, and then the opening theme repeated during the conclusion

Revising

Revise to improve media handling. Make sure your script will flow smoothly when you present it to an audience.

1. Give a partner a copy of your script. Then, give your presentation.

2. Have your partner star in red any places where you spoke too quickly, seemed to lose your place, or had trouble making the media work.

3. Work on the trouble areas. Practice reading until your pace is right and you are comfortable. Consider dropping a visual or two if necessary.

Model: Editing for Smooth Flow

(Cue AUDIO) The pose exhibits the man's elegant manner, his head and hands	AUDIO: selection from Bach's *Well-Tempered Clavier*
☆ (Show SLIDE C) placed in the perfectly calm demeanor which a man of his stature would be expected to display.	SLIDE C: Detail of Castiglione's hands.
(Show SLIDE B)	SLIDE B: Raphael's *Baldassare Castiglione.* Full length.
(Show SLIDE C; pause, then back to	

> Katie postpones showing Slide C to make her delivery smoother and to provide better pacing for the audience.

Revise to strengthen transitions. If you have included many sounds and images, your audience may grow confused about where your presentation is going. Transitions indicate when you are moving to a new point.

Vague: . . . traffic congestion. Here, the situation improved dramatically.

Clear: . . . traffic congestion. *The next photo shows how* the situation improved dramatically *after strict driving restrictions were imposed.*

Compare the model and nonmodel. Why is the model an improvement?

Nonmodel	Model
(Cue SLIDE B: High Renaissance portrait) In the Early Renaissance, portraits remained somewhat formal. By the High Renaissance, though, there is a clear focus on the personality of the subject.	(Cue SLIDE A: Timeline) In the Early Renaissance, portraits remained somewhat formal. By the High Renaissance, though, there is a clear focus on the personality of the subject, as in this portrait by Raphael. (Cue SLIDE B: High Renaissance portrait)

Publishing and Presenting

Present your report. Make your final presentation to your class or another interested audience. Follow these suggestions:

- Have everything set up in the presentation area in advance.
- Speak slowly and confidently.
- Do not get flustered if you make a mistake. Keep a sense of humor.

W̶G Prentice Hall Writing and Grammar Connection: Chapter 13

Rubric for Self-Assessment

Evaluate your multimedia script using the following criteria and rating scale.

Criteria	Rating Scale				
	Not very				**Very**
How interesting, varied, and appropriate are your media elements?	1	2	3	4	5
How well organized is your presentation of information?	1	2	3	4	5
How smoothly does the text lead into the various media elements?	1	2	3	4	5
How effective are the pacing and the transitions from one segment to the next?	1	2	3	4	5
How strong and memorable is your ending?	1	2	3	4	5

Listening and Speaking WORKSHOP

Analyzing Bias in News Media

One day, you turn on the television to discover that every channel is flooded with outraged accusations against a politician. On one channel, though, you happen to catch an expert explaining away the charges. The next day, the story seems to have vanished without a trace. You may have just been a witness to **media bias**.

The **news media** include all forms in which news and opinion are delivered to the public, from television to the Internet. **Bias** is an unacknowledged or concealed tendency to favor one side over another in a controversy. For instance, by presenting accusations against someone without giving equal time to his or her defense, the media show bias against the person. When following a news story, analyze the possible bias of reports.

Taking It Apart

While bias in the news may be subtle, there are certain techniques that critical viewers look out for:

- Emotionally charged language that suggests a point of view
- Hasty generalizations based on only a few cases
- Inflammatory images that elicit strong emotions from the audience
- Facts and images that reflect only one point of view
- The ordering of stories to emphasize or downplay the significance of a particular story

Evaluating the Whole

When analyzing a news story, ask yourself the following questions:

- What do you believe public response to the newscast will be? Who will benefit from this response?
- Was important information or an important perspective left out of the newscast? Why do you think this choice was made?
- Did the newscast use any elements indicating bias, such as inflammatory images or emotionally charged language?

Once you have detected bias in a news story, then you can critically weigh the information presented and form your own opinions.

Activity:
View and Analyze Using a chart like the one shown, compare the coverage of the same news story on two different television stations. Use your comparison to help you detect bias.

	Media Source 1	Media Source 2
Charged language		
Generalizations		
Images		
Perspectives included		
Slot for story (first, last, middle / before or after commercial)		

Assessment WORKSHOP

Strategy, Organization, and Style

On some tests, you may be asked to read a passage and answer questions about its organization and use of language. Use these strategies to help you answer such questions:

- Outline in logical order the events or ideas that the passage presents. Next to each item on your outline, write the number of the corresponding sentence or paragraph. Use the outline to help you answer questions about reordering the parts of the passage.
- Jot down a note summing up the purpose of the passage—to persuade readers to a given opinion or to inform them about a given topic. Refer to this note when answering questions about main ideas, supporting details, or sentences that do not belong.

Sample Test Item

Directions: Read the passage, and then answer the question that follows.

(1) Millions of people communicate over the Internet. (2) Some choose a custom-made home entertainment center. (3) Technology certainly has made the world seem smaller. (4) As communication technologies advance, consumers can choose among many devices designed to make their lives easier. (5) Many people carry cell phones.

1. Choose the sentence sequence that is most logical.

   A NO CHANGE

   B 4, 2, 5, 1, 3

   C 3, 1, 4, 2, 5

   D 1, 4, 2, 3, 5

Answer and Explanation

The correct answer is *B.* It is the most logical because (4) is the topic sentence of the passage. Answers *A* and *D* are incorrect because each entails starting the paragraph with an isolated detail. Answer *C* is incorrect because it involves breaking up the list of examples that support the main idea, creating the impression that they support different ideas.

▶ Practice

Directions: Read the passage, and then answer the questions that follow.

(1) It is time for everyone to realize that these laws make sense. (2) Several cities have enacted laws prohibiting the playing of boomboxes in public. (3) When will people learn to turn off those obnoxious boomboxes in public places? (4) Such laws have returned peace to city streets. (5) Too often citizens are assaulted by high-volume noise.

1. Choose the most logical sentence sequence:

   A 3, 5, 2, 4, 1

   B 1, 2, 3, 5, 4

   C 5, 3, 1, 2, 4

   D 4, 2, 1, 3, 5

2. Which of these sentences best summarizes the main idea of the passage?

   A Boomboxes are obnoxious.

   B More laws are needed to control the chaotic element in society.

   C Citizens need legal protections against noise in public places.

   D People are rude.

RESOURCES

Following are some suggestions for longer works that will give you the opportunity to experience the fun of sustained reading. Each of the suggestions further explores one of the themes in this book. Many of the titles are included in the Prentice Hall Literature Library.

Unit One

Grendel
John Gardner

Once again we meet Beowulf's foe, but this time we get the story from Grendel's point of view. This retelling of the epic poem begins with the monster attacking Hrothgar's meadhall and men, and it ends right after his fight with Beowulf, as Grendel is about to die. *Grendel* is a funny, intriguing examination of the way we look at monsters, heroes, and the worlds that we create with both.

The Once and Future King
T. H. White

This novel is a magical retelling of the legend of Arthur—from the adventure-filled days of Arthur's youth to the golden age of Camelot to the final scene in which the old, broken king lies alone on the battlefield at Salisbury. In this unforgettable tale, the characters of the legend come to life, as they experience the wonders and horrors of magic, suffer victory and defeat in battle, and grapple with matters of love, betrayal, and honor.

Unit Two

Hamlet
William Shakespeare

One of Shakespeare's greatest tragedies, *Hamlet* is the tale of a young man forced to confront and question all that he formerly believed to be true. As the play begins, Prince Hamlet is mourning the death of his father, the King of Denmark. He must also accept the new marriage of his mother to his uncle, who now rules Denmark. As Hamlet struggles with these changes, the ghost of his father appears to him and tells Hamlet that he was poisoned by his brother. He urges Hamlet to avenge his murder. The revenge of Hamlet and its aftermath are the heart of the play.

The Tempest
William Shakespeare

This drama—a tale of magic, mystery, and love—takes place on what at first appears to be a deserted island. Prospero, his daughter Miranda, the spirit Ariel, and the man-monster Caliban inhabit the island. Through his magic and the aid of Ariel, Prospero is able to lure to the island a boat that carries his brother Antonio, who had dispossessed him of his throne. Prospero works his magic to arrive at a wonderful marriage for his daughter and the Prince of Naples and to reclaim his rightful title as the Duke of Milan.

Unit Three

Robinson Crusoe
Daniel Defoe

Defoe's *Robinson Crusoe* marked the beginning of the modern English novel. It is, however, a novel populated mostly by a single character. In 1659, Crusoe is shipwrecked on an island off the coast of South America and begins a twenty-eight-year stay on the island. Although specific history is not alluded to, Crusoe is very much a product of his time—he grew up during England's Civil War and the Restoration. Crusoe's attempts to create a decent society and improve his own moral character echo England's struggles to restore itself after the political turmoil of the Civil War.

Gulliver's Travels
Jonathan Swift

Swift's *Gulliver's Travels* is a children's story, a fantasy, a parody of travel books, and a sophisticated satire of English politics all in one. This masterpiece describes four voyages of Lemuel Gulliver, a ship's physician, to exotic lands. Gulliver begins in Lilliput, where the inhabitants are one twelfth the size of human beings. By the story's end, the playful elements have yielded to a bitter indictment of humankind's corruption of reason. Swift's unique combination of allegory—using settings, objects, or characters to stand for ideas and qualities beyond themselves—has made his work appealing to all audiences.

Suggested Titles Related to Thematic Units

Unit Four

Pride and Prejudice
Jane Austen

With her usual comic flair and common sense, Jane Austen explores the pressure on women to succeed in the marriage market. Mrs. Bennet, all too aware of this market's demands, shamelessly pursues marriage for each of her daughters. Although one of them, Elizabeth, is socially inferior to the arrogant Mr. Darcy, he loses his heart to her all the same. This victory of romance shows that feelings are at least as important as shrewd calculations of matchmakers. Austen's common sense prevails over pounds and shillings.

Emma
Jane Austen

Austen has great fun with her heroine Emma Woodhouse. Emma has appointed herself matchmaker for her community, meddling in almost everyone's affairs. Although her friend Mr. Knightly cautions her against the reckless pursuit of marital bliss for others, she learns the folly of her ways only through bitter experience. Also, she realizes almost too late that her frantic activity has led her to ignore her own happiness and the person best suited to guarantee it: the same Mr. Knightly who has been her loyal friend.

Unit Five

Wuthering Heights
Emily Brontë

The setting of *Wuthering Heights* is the wild and windy moors of northern Yorkshire. Central to the story is the romantic and brooding Heathcliff, a gypsy adopted into a family and mistreated by his foster brother. The story revolves around Heathcliff's thwarted love for Catherine and his revenge on those who mistreated him. By the end of the tale, Heathcliff's passion is spent, and happiness becomes possible for two of the younger members of the family, who are able to make a new beginning.

The Importance of Being Earnest
Oscar Wilde

Mocking the social conventions of the Victorian Era, *The Importance of Being Earnest* is one of the wittiest comedies ever written. Jack Worthing invents a mischievous younger brother named Ernest to allow him to adventure in London. Algernon Moncrieff appears at Jack's home assuming the identity of Ernest Worthing to meet Jack's attractive ward, Cecily Cardew. Both men have told their romantic interests that their names are Ernest because the women want to marry men named Ernest!

Unit Six

Heart of Darkness
Joseph Conrad

Conrad explores the human mind and the effects of colonialism in this great novel that has inspired many other writers. Conrad's narrator, the river steamer captain Marlow, tells a group of friends about an ominous journey into the heart of the African jungle. Mysterious, grotesque tales about the white ivory trader Kurtz pale in comparison with the reality Marlow finds when he meets the man. In Conrad's classic tale, the "heart of darkness" is both the human heart and the oppressive colonial system.

Pygmalion
George Bernard Shaw

Like his professor of phonetics, Henry Higgins, Shaw believed in the power of language to break down class barriers. In Shaw's play, the overbearing Higgins transforms Eliza Doolittle, a cockney flower girl, into an elegant woman. Neither character foresees, however, that falling in love may complicate the process of Eliza's transformation. Nearly half a century after it was written, Shaw's comedy became the basis of the enormously successful musical *My Fair Lady*.

A Passage to India
E. M. Forster

Forster's novel is a classic portrayal of clashing cultures. Adela Quested, a young British visitor to India, falsely accuses Aziz, a likable Indian doctor, of assaulting her on a tour of the Malabar Caves. As the British and Indian characters react to this accusation, the reader sees the cultural differences between them. Forster shows that in a colonial situation, these differences inevitably lead to misunderstandings.

GLOSSARY

abasement (ə bās´ mənt) *n.*: Condition of being put down or humbled

abated (ə bāt´ id) *v.*: Lessened

abrogated (ab´rō gāt´ id) *v.*: Repealed; annulled

absolution (ab´ sə lōō´ shən) *n.*: Act of freeing someone of a sin or of a criminal charge

acceded (ak sēd´ id) *v.*: Yielded (to); agreed

adjure (ə jŏŏr´) *v.*: Appeal earnestly

admonish (ad män´ ish) *v.*: Advise; caution

adroitly (ə droit´ lē) *adv*: With physical or mental skill

adulterations (ə dul´ tər ā´ shənz) *n.*: Impurities; added ingredients that are improper or inferior

adversary (ad´ vər ser´ ē) *n.*: Opponent

adversity (ad vur´ sə tē) *n.*: Misfortune

affinities (ə fin´ i tēz) *n.*: Family connections; sympathies

affluence (af´ lōō əns) *n.*: Abundant wealth

aldermen (ôl´ dər mən) *n.*: Chief officers in a shire, or district

alters (ôl´ tərs) *v.*: Changes

amiable (ā´ mē ə bəl) *adj.*: Friendly

amorous (am´ə rəs) *adj.*: Full of love

anachronism (ə nak´ rə niz´ əm) *n.*: Something out of its proper time in history

anarchy (an´ ər kē) *n.*: Absence of government; confusion, disorder, and violence

anatomize (ə nat´ ə mīz´) *v.*: Dissect in order to examine structure

antic (an´ tik) *adj.*: Odd and funny

aperture (ap´ ər chər) *n.*: Opening

apothecary (ə päth´ ə kər´ ē) *n.*: pharmacist; druggist

appendage (ə pen´ dij) *n.*: Something added on

apprehension (ap´ rē hen´ shən) *n.*: Anxious feeling of foreboding; dread

approbation (ap´ rə bā´ shən) *n.*: Official approval, sanction, or commendation

arbiter (är´ bət ər) *n.*: Judge; umpire

arboreal (är bôr´ ē əl) *adj.*: Of, near, or among trees

artifice (ärt´ə fis) *n.*: Skill; skillful illusion

aspire (ə spīr´) *v.*: Rise high, yearn, or seek after

assault (ə sôlt´) *v.*: Violently attack

assay (a sā´) *v.*: try or attempt

assignations (as´ ig nā´ shənz) *n.*: Appointments to meet

asunder (ə sun´ dər) *adv.*: Into parts or pieces

atrophy (a´ trə fē) *v.*: Waste away

augment (ôg ment´) *v.*: Make greater; enlarge

august (ô gust´) *adj.*: Worthy of great respect

authenticity (ô´ thən tis´ ə tē) *n.*: Quality or state of being authentic; genuineness

avarice (av´ ər is) *n.*: Greed

averred (ə vurd´) *v.*: Stated to be true

avouches (ə vouch´ ez) *v.*: Asserts positively; affirms

balm (bäm) *n.*: Anything healing or soothing

barricaded (bar´ i kād´ id) *v.*: Blocked

blight (blīt) *n.*: Condition of withering

blithe (blīth) *adj.*: Cheerful

brazening (brā´ zən iŋ) *v.*: Daring boldly or shamelessly

breach (brēch) *n.*: Breaking open; the opening created by a break; failure to fullfill an agreement

cadence (kād´ əns) *n.*: Measured movement

cant (kant) *n.*: Insincere or meaningless talk

capital (kap´ ət əl) *n.*: Wealth in money or property

caprices (kə prē´ sis) *n.*: Whims

careered (kə rird´) *v.*: Rushed wildly

certify (surt´ ə fī´) *v.*: Declare a thing true or accurate; verify; attest

chronicle (krän´ i kəl) *n.*: Historical record

churls (churlz) *n.*: Farm laborers; peasants

circumscribed (sur´ kəm skrībd´) *adj.*: Limited; having a definite boundary

clamorous (klam´ ər əs) *adj.*: Noisy

combustible (kəm bus´ tə bəl) *adj.*: Capable of igniting and burning; flammable

commission (kə mish´ ən) *n.*: Authorization; act of giving authority to an individual

compassionate (kəm pash´ ən it) *adj.*: Sympathizing; pitying

complaisant (kəm plā´ zənt) *adj.*: Agreeable; willing to please

comprised (kəm prīzd´) *v.*: Consisted of; included or contained

confiscation (kän´ fis kā´ shən) *n.*: Official act of seizing private property

conflagration (kän´ flə grā´ shən) *n.*: Great fire

confounded (kən found´ id) *adj.*: Confused; bewildered; mixed together indiscriminately

conjecture (kən jek´ chər) *v.*: Guess

conquest (kän´ kwest´) *n.*: The winning of another's affection or submission

contention (kən ten´ shən) *n.*: Dispute; argument

contentious (kən ten´ shəs) *adj.*: Quarrelsome

contrite (kən trīt´) *adj.*: Willing to repent or atone

conviction (kən´ vik´ shən) *n.*: Belief; faith

copious (kō´ pē əs) *adj.*: Abundant; plentiful

countenance (koun´ tə nəns) *n.*: Face

covetousness (kuv´ ət əs ness) *n.*: Greediness

coyness (koi´ nis) *n.*: Shyness; aloofness, often as part of a flirtation

credulity (krə dōō´ lə tē) *n.*: Tendency to believe too readily

credulous (krej´ ŏŏ ləs) *adj.*: Tending to believe too readily

dauntless (dônt´ lis) *adj.*: Fearless; cannot be intimidated

decimation (des´ ə mā´ shun) *n.*: Destruction or killing of one in ten or of any large part of a group

defiantly (di fī´ ənt lē) *adv.*: Disobediently; with resistance

deign (dān) *v.*: condescend; lower oneself

depredation (dep´ rə dā´ shən) *n.*: Act or instance of robbing, plundering, or laying waste

derided (di rīd´ id) *v.*: Made fun of; ridiculed

derision (di rizh´ ən) *n.*: Contempt or ridicule

desolate (des´ ə lit) *adj.*: Deserted; forlorn

despotic (de spät´ ik) *adj.*: Tyrannical

destitute (des´ tə tōōt) *adj.*: Lacking

devise (de vīz´) *v.*: work out or create; plan

diabolical (dī´ ə bäl´ i kəl) *adj.*: Evil

diffusive (di fyōō´siv) *adj.*: Tending to spread out

disabused (dis´ ə byōōzd´) *adj.*: Freed from false ideas

disaffection (dis´ ə fek´ shən) *n.*: Discontent; disillusionment

discerned (di zurnd´) *v.*: Recognized as separate or different

disconcerted (dis´ kən surt´ əd) *adj.*: Embarrassed and confused

discoursing (dis kôrs´ iŋ) *v.*: Talking about; discussing

discreet (dis krēt´) *adj.*: Wise; prudent

discretion (di skresh´ ən) *n.*: Good judgment; prudence

dislocation (dis´ lō kā´ shən) *n.*: Condition of being out of place

dispensation (dis´ pən sā´ shən) *n.*: Religious system or belief

distemper (dis tem´ pər) *n.*: Infectious disease such as a plague

distill (di stil´) *v.*: Obtain the essential part

divert (də vurt´) *v.*: Amuse; entertain; distract

dominion (də min´ yən) *n.*: Rule or power to rule; a governed territory

dowry (dou´ rē) *n.*: Property that a woman brings to her husband at marriage

eclipse (ē klips´) *n.*: Dimming or extinction of fame or glory

efficacious (ef´ i kā´ shəs) *adj.*: Effective

efficacy (ef´ i kə sē) *n.*: Power to produce intended effects

effigy (ef´ i jē) *n.*: Portrait or statue of a person

elongated (ē lôŋ´ gāt´ id) *adj.*: Lengthened; stretched

eludes (ē lōōdz´) *v.*: Avoids or escapes

emancipate (ē man´ sə pāt) *v.*: Free from slavery or oppression

embarked (em bärkt´) *v.*: Engaged in something, such as a conversation

embellishments (em bel´ ish mənts) *n.*: Decorative touches; ornamentation

encomiums (en kō´ mē əms) *n.*: Formal expressions of great praise

endurance (en door´ əns) *n.*: Ability to last or continue

enigma (i nig´ mə) *n.*: Riddle; perplexing statement, person, or situation

enquiry (en kwīr´ ē) *n.*: Question; investigation

entreated (en trēt´ id) *v.*: Begged; pleaded

equivocate (ē kwiv´ə kāt) *v.*: Use terms that have two or more meanings to mislead purposely or deceive

evanescence (ev´ ə nes´ əns) *n.*: Vanishing or tendency to vanish

exasperated (eg zas´ pər āt´ id) *adj.*: Extremely annoyed; out of patience

excrescence (eks kres´ əns) *n.*: Abnormal or disfiguring outgrowth

exemplary (eg zem´ plə rē) *adj.*: Serving as a model or example; of that which should be imitated

exonerate (eg zän´ ər āt´) *v.*: Free from a charge of guilt; declare or prove blameless

expedient (ek spē´ dē ənt) *n.*: Device used in an emergency

expiated (ĕkʹ spē ātʹ id) *v.:* Atoned; made amends for, especially by suffering

expostulate (eks pästʹ chə lātʹ) *v.:* Reason earnestly with

extenuating (ek stenʹ yōō ātʹ iŋ) *adj.:* Lessening the seriousness of; excusing

fastidious (fas tidʹ ē əs) *adj.:* Particular; difficult to please

fathom (fath'əm) *v.:* Understand thoroughly

fathomless (fath'əm lis) *adj.:* Too deep to be measured or understood

feigned (fānd) *v.:* Made a false show of; pretended

fervent (furʹ vənt) *adj.:* Having or showing great warmth of feeling

fidelity (fə delʹ ə tē) *n.:* Faithfulness

filial (filʹ ē əl) *adj.:* Expected of a son or daughter

forage (fôrʹ ij) *n.:* Food grazed for by animals

forfeited (fôrʹ fit id) *v.:* Gave up, as a penalty

formidable (fôrʹ mə də bəl) *adj.:* Causing fear or dread

fortitude (fôrtʹ ə tōōd) *n.:* Courage; strength to endure

fraudulent (frôʹ jə lənt) *adj.:* Characterized by deceit or trickery

furrow (furʹ ō) *n.:* Narrow groove, such as that made in the ground by a plow

galled (gôld) *adj.:* Injured or made sore by rubbing or chafing

garnished (gärʹ nisht) *adj.:* Decorated; trimmed

garrulous (garʹ ə ləs) *adj.:* Talkative

gaunt (gônt) *adj.:* Very thin and angular

gleaned (glēnd) *v.:* Collected bit by bit, as when gathering stray grain after a harvest

grandeur (granʹ jər) *n.:* Splendor; magnificence

gravity (gravʹ i tē) *n.:* Seriousness

grieved (grēvd) *v.:* Caused to feel deep grief; mourned; felt deep grief for

grievous (grēvʹ əs) *adj.:* Causing sorrow; hard to bear

guile (gīl) *n.:* Artful trickery; cunning

habituate (hə bichʹ ōō ātʹ) *v.:* Make used to

harbingers (härʹ bin jərs) *n.:* Forerunners

harried (harʹ ēd) *v.:* Harassed

hoary (hôrʹ ē) *adj.:* White or gray with age

ignoble (ig nōʹ bəl) *adj.:* Not noble; common

ignominy (igʹ nə minʹ ē) *n.:* Humiliation; dishonor; disgrace

illumine (i lōōʹ mən) *v.:* Light up

impediments (im pedʹə mənts) *n.:* Obstructions

imperial (im pirʹ ē əl) *adj.:* Of an empire; having supreme authority

imperialism (im pirʹ ē əl izʹəm) *n.:* Policy of forming an empire and securing economic power by conquest and colonization

imperturbable (imʹ pər turʹ bə bəl) *adj.:* Calm; not easily ruffled

importuning (imʹ pôr tōōnʹ iŋ) *v.:* Pleading with

impressionistic (im preshʹ ən isʹ tik) *adj.:* Conveying a quick, overall picture

impudence (imʹ pyōō dəns) *n.:* Lack of shame; rudeness

impulse (imʹ puls') *n.:* Force driving forward

inauspicious (inʹ ô spishʹəs) *adj.:* Not promising a good outcome; unfavorable

incitement (in sītʹ mənt) *n.:* Act of urging; encouragement

inconstancy (in känʹ stən sē) *n.:* Fickleness; changeableness

inconstantly (in känʹ stənt lē) *adv.:* Changeably; in a fickle way

incredulously (in krejʹ ōo ləs lē) *adv.:* In a manner expressing doubt or disbelief

inculcated (in kulʹ kātʹ id) *v.:* Impressed upon the mind by frequent repetition

indignant (in digʹnənt) *adj.:* Outraged; filled with righteous anger

indissoluble (inʹ di sälʹ yōō bəl) *adj.:* Not able to be dissolved or undone

indolence (inʹ də ləns) *n.:* Idleness; laziness

inducted (in duktʹ id) *v.:* Brought formally into an organization

inevitable (in evʹ i tə bəl) *adj.:* Unavoidable; certain to happen

infirmity (in furʹ mə tē) *n.:* Physical or mental defect; illness

ingenuous (in jenʹ yōō əs) *adj.:* Naive; simple

inklings (iŋkʹ liŋz) *n.:* Indirect suggestions; vague ideas

innumerable (i nōōʹ mər ə bəl) *adj.:* Too many to count

insensible (in senʹ sə bəl) *adj.:* Unable to feel or sense anything; numb

instantaneous (inʹ stən tāʹ nē əs) *adj.:* Done or happening in an instant

intemperance (in temʹ pər əns) *n.:* Lack of restraint

intermit (inʹ tər mit') *v.:* Stop for a time

internment (in turnʹ mənt) *n.:* Confinement, especially during war

interred (in turdʹ) *v.:* Buried

intimidated (in timʹ ə dāt əd) *v.:* Made afraid; frightened

intrigues (in trēgzʹ) *n.:* Plots or schemes secretly or underhandedly

intrinsically (in trinʹ sik lē) *adv.:* At its core; inherently; innately

invincible (in vinʹ sə bəl) *adj.:* Unconquerable

irrevocable (ir revʹ ə kə bəl): *adj.:* Unable to be undone or canceled

judicious (jōō dishʹ əs) *adj.:* Showing good judgment

keenly (kēnʹ lē) *adv.:* Sharply; intensely

ken (ken) *n.:* Range of sight or knowledge

laity (lāʹ i tē) *n.:* Those not initiated into the priesthood or other profession

lamentable (lamʹ ən tə bəl) *adj.:* Distressing

languish (laŋʹ gwish) *v.:* Become weak; droop

languished (laŋʹ gwisht) *adj.:* Weakened; dulled

largesse (lär jesʹ) *n.:* Nobility of spirit

larking (lärkʹ iŋ) *n.:* Free-spirited, whimsical fun

laudable (lôdʹ ə bəl) *adj.:* Worthy of praise

liege (lēj) *n.:* Lord or king

litanies (litʹən ēz) *n.:* Prayers in which a congregation repeats a fixed response; repetitive recitations

loathsome (lōth'səm) *adj.:* Disgusting

ludicrous (lōōʹ di krəs) *adj.:* Absurd; ridiculous

malevolence (mə levʹ ə ləns) *n.:* Ill will; spitefulness

malevolent (mə levʹ ə lent) *adj.:* Wishing harm to others

malicious (mə lishʹ əs) *adj.:* Deliberately harmful; destructive

malignity (mə ligʹ nə tē) *n.:* Strong desire to harm others

massive (masʹ iv) *adj.:* Big and solid; bulky

maxim (maksʹ im) *n.:* Briefly expressed general truth or rule of conduct

melancholy (melʹ ən kälʹ ē) *adj.:* Sad; depressing

minions (minʹ yənz) *n.:* Attendants or agents

mockeries (mäkʹ ər ēz) *n.:* Ridicule; futile or disappointing efforts

monotonous (mə nätʹ ən əs) *adj.:* Having little variation

mortal (môrʹ təl) *adj.:* Of that which must eventually die

multitudinous: (mulʹ tə tōōdʹ 'n əs) *adj.:* Existing in great numbers

munificence (myōō nifʹ ə səns) *n.:* Lavish generosity

nocturnal (näk turʹ nəl) *adj.:* Occurring at night

nondescript (nänʹ di skriptʹ) *adj.:* Lacking identifying characteristics; bland

nuisance (nōōʹ səns) *n.:* act, thing, or condition causing trouble

obdurate (äbʹ dōor it) *adj.:* Stubborn; unyielding

obliquely (ə blēkʹ lē) *adv.:* At a slant; indirectly

obliterate (ə blitʹ ə rāt) *v.:* Destroy utterly

obscure (əb skyoorʹ) *adj.:* Not easily seen; not generally known

obstinate (äbʹ stə nət) *adj.:* Stubborn; dogged; mulish

odious (ōʹ dē əs) *adj.:* Hateful; disgusting

officious (ə fishʹ əs) *adj.:* Meddlesome

omniscient (äm nishʹ ənt) *adj.:* Having infinite knowledge; knowing all things

ordeal (ôr dēlʹ) *n.:* Difficult or painful experience that tests one

pallor (palʹ ər) *n.:* Lack of color; paleness

palpable (palʹ pə bəl) *adj.:* Capable of being touched or felt

paltry (pôlʹ trē) *adj.:* Practically worthless; insignificant

patronize (pāʹ trə nīz) *v.:* To be a customer of a particular merchant or store

penury (penʹ yōō rē) *n.:* Poverty

peril (perʹ əl) *n.:* Exposure to harm

pernicious (pər nishʹ əs) *adj.:* Causing serious injury; deadly

persistent (pər sisʹ tənt) *adj.:* Continuing without letup

perturbation (purʹ tər bāʹ shən) *n.:* Disturbance

phantasm (fanʹ tazʹ əm) *n.:* Supernatural form or shape; ghost; figment of the mind

piety (pīʹ ə tē) *n.:* Devotion to sacred duties

platitude (platʹ ə tōōd) *n.:* Statement lacking originality

plebeian (plē bēʹ ən) *adj.:* Common; not aristocratic

portals (pôrʹ təlz) *n.:* Doors; gateways

prating (prātʹ iŋ) *n.:* Chatter

predominance (prē dämʹ ə nəns) *n.:* Superiority

prefiguring (prē figʹ yer iŋ) *v.:* Resembling and so suggesting beforehand

prenatal (prē nātʹ əl) *adj.:* Before birth

preponderates (prē pän´ də rāts´) v.: Dominates; causes the arm of a balance scale to tip downward

presumption (prē zump´ shən) n.: Audacity; tending to assume certain things

prevarication (pri var´ i kā´ shən) n.: Evasion of truth

prime (prīm) n.: Best stage of a thing or process

pristine (pris tēn´) adj.: Original; unspoiled

procured (prō kyoord´) v.: Obtained

prodigal (präd´ i gəl) adj.: Recklessly wasteful

prodigious (prō dij´ əs) adj.: Enormous

profanation (präf´ ə nā´ shən) n.: Action showing disrespect for something sacred

profuse (prō fyoos´) adj.: Abundant; pouring out

promontories (präm´ ən tôr´ ēz) n.: Parts of high land sticking out into the sea or other body of water

propagators (präp´ ə gāt´ ərz) n.: Those who cause something to happen or to spread

propitiate (prə pish´ ē āt) v.: Win the goodwill of; appease

prostrate (präs´ trāt) adj.: Defenseless; in a prone or lying position

purge (purj) v.: Purify; cleanse

rancor (raŋ´ kər) n.: Ill will

ransacked (ran´ sakt´) v.: Searched through for plunder; pillaged; robbed

rapture (rap´ chər) n.: Joy; great pleasure

rapturous (rap´ chər us) adj.: Ecstatic

ravaged (rav´ ijd) v.: Destroyed

recompense (rek´ əm pens´) n.: Reward; payment in return for something

redress (ri dres´) n.: Compensation, as for a wrong

refractory (ri frak´ tər ē) adj.: Hard to manage; stubborn

remnant (rem´ nənt) n.: What is left over

remonstrated (ri män´ strāt id) v.: Objected strongly

reparation (rep´ ə rā´ shən) n.: Something making up for wrong or injury

requiem (rek´ wē əm) n.: Musical composition honoring the dead

requisites (rek´ wə zits) n.: Things necessary for a given purpose

requisitioned (rek´ wə zish´ ənd) v.: Requested or applied for with a formal written order

retaliate (ri tal´ ē āt´) v.: Return an injury or wrong

reticent (ret´ ə sənt) adj.: Silent; reserved

retort (ri tôrt´) v.: Respond with a clever answer or wisecrack

reverence (rev´ ər əns) n.: Deep respect

reverently (rev´ ər ənt lē) adv.: With deep respect or awe

righteous (rī´ chəs) adj.: Acting in a just, upright manner; doing what is right

rogue (rōg) n.: Scoundrel; wandering beggar

roused (rouzd) v.: Stirred up; risen from cover

rue (roo) n.: Sorrow; regret

sanction (saŋk´ shən) n.: Authorized approval or permission

sanguine (saŋ´ gwin) adj.: Confident; cheerful

satiety (sə tī´ ə tē) n.: State of being filled to excess

schism (siz´ əm) n.: Division of a group into factions

scope (skōp) n.: Range of perception or understanding

scruple (skroo´ pəl) n.: Hesitation caused by one's conscience or principles; uneasy feeling; qualm

segmented (seg´ ment id) adj.: Separated into parts

semblance (sem´ bləns) n.: Appearance; image

senility (si nil´ə tē) n.: Mental and physical decay due to old age

sentinel (sen´ ti nəl) n.: Person or animal that guards or watches over

sequestered (si kwes´ tərd) v.: Kept apart from others

sinuous (sin´ yoo əs) adj.: Bending; winding

skeptical (skep´ ti kəl) adj.: Doubting; not easily persuaded

sloth (slôth) n.: Laziness; idleness

sojourn (sō´ jurn) v.: Stay for a while

solace (säl´ is) n.: Comfort; relief

solicitous (sə lis´ ə təs) adj.: Showing care or concern

solicitude (sə lis´ ə tood´) n.: Care; concern

sordid (sôr´ did) adj.: Unclean; dirty

sovereign (säv´ rən) adj.: Supreme in power, rank, or authority

sovereignty (säv´ rən tē) n.: Supreme political authority

specious (spē´ shəs) adj.: Deceptively attractive or valid; false

spectral (spek´ trəl) adj.: Ghostly

speculation (spek´ yoo lā´ shən) n.: Train of thought on a subject, especially one using hypotheses or guesses

splaying (splā´ iŋ) v.: Spreading

squalid (skwäl´ id) adj.: Miserably poor; wretched

stagnant (stag´ nənt) adj.: Motionless; stale

stature (stach´ ər) n.: Height of a person standing; development, growth, or level of achievement

stead (sted) n.: Position of a person as filled by a replacement or substitute

stealthy (stel´ thē) adj.: Sly; furtive

stoic (stō´ ik) n.: Person indifferent to joy, grief, pleasure, or pain

stranded (stran´ did) v.: Forced into shallow water or onto a beach; left helpless

stringent (strin´ jənt) adj.: Strict

sublime (sə blīm´) adj.: Inspiring awe through greatness or beauty

sublimity (sə blim´ ə tē) n.: Quality of being majestic or noble

subsequently (sub´ si kwənt lē) adv.: At a later time

succor (suk´ ər) v.: Help; aid; relieve

suffused (sə fyoozd´) v.: Spread throughout

sullen (sul´ ən) adj.: Gloomy; dismal

sundry (sun´ drē) adj.: Various; miscellaneous

supine (soo pīn´) adj.: Lying on the back

suppliant (sup´ lē ənt) adj.: Beseeching prayerfully; imploring

supplication (sup´ lə kā´ shən) n.: Act of praying or pleading

surmise (sər mīz´) n.: Guess; assumption

symmetry (sim´ ə trē) n.: Balanced form; the beauty resulting from such balance

tarry (tar´ ē) v.: Delay or linger

teeming (tēm´ iŋ) adj.: Filled to overflowing

temperate (tem´ pər it) adj.: Mild

tempests (tem´ pists) n.: Storms

tempestuous (tem pes´ choo əs) adj.: Turbulent; violently stormy

terrestrial (tə res´ trē əl) adj.: Relating to Earth or to things of this world

timorous (tim´ ər əs) adj.: Timid

topographical (täp´ə graf´ i kəl) adj.: Relating to a map of the surface features of a region, including its elevations, rivers, mountains, and so on

torrid (tôr´ id) adj.: Very hot; scorching

tranquil (tran´ kwil) adj.: Calm; serene

transcendent (tran sen´ dənt) adj.: Surpassing; beyond all limits

transfiguring (trans fig´ yər iŋ) adj.: Changing the appearance of a thing or person, especially so as to glorify it

transgress (trans gres´) v.: Violate a law or command

transient (tran´ shənt) adj.: Temporary; passing through quickly

treachery (trech´ ər ē) n.: Betrayal of trust, faith, or allegiance

treasons (trē´ zenz) n.: Betrayals of one's country or oath of loyalty

trepidation (trep´ ə dā´ shən) n.: Trembling

trifles (trī´ fəlz) n.: Things of little value or importance; trivial matters

tumid (too´ mid) adj.: Swollen

tumult (too´ mult) n.: Noisy commotion

turbid (tur´ bid) adj.: Muddy or cloudy; stirred up; confused

uncanny (un kan´ ē) adj.: Mysterious; hard to explain

ungenial (un jēn´ yəl) adj.: Unfriendly

upbraidings (up brād´ iŋz) n.: Stern words of disapproval; scoldings

vales (vāls) n.: Valleys; hollows; depressed stretches of ground

valor (val´ ər) n.: Marked courage or bravery

venerable (ven´ ər ə bəl) adj.: Commanding respect by virtue of age, character, or rank

vernal (vurn´ əl) adj.: Relating to spring

vestige (ves´ tij) n.: Trace; remaining bit

vindication (vin´ də kā´ shən) n.: Act of providing justification or support for

vintage (vin´ tij) n.: Wine of fine quality

visage (viz´ ij) n.: Person's face or expression

wan (wän) adj.: Sickly; pale

waning (wān´ iŋ) v.: Gradually becoming dimmer

winsome (win´ səm) adj.: Having a charming, attractive appearance or manner

winsomeness (win´ səm niss) n.: Charm; winning quality

writhing (rith´ iŋ) adj.: Making twisting or turning motions

zenith (zē´ nith) n.: Highest point of something, especially of the sky or celestial sphere

LITERARY TERMS HANDBOOK

ALLEGORY An *allegory* is a literary work with two or more levels of meaning—a literal level and one or more symbolic levels. The events, settings, objects, or characters in an allegory—the literal level—stand for ideas or qualities, such as goodness, tyranny, salvation, and so on. Allegorical writing was common in the Middle Ages. Spenser revived the form in *The Faerie Queene,* and John Bunyan revived it yet again in *The Pilgrim's Progress.* Some modern novels, such as George Orwell's *Animal Farm,* can be read as allegories.

ALLITERATION *Alliteration* is the repetition of initial consonant sounds in accented syllables. Coleridge uses the alliteration of both *b* and *f* sounds in this line from *The Rime of the Ancient Mariner:*

> The fair breeze blew, the white foam flew.

Especially in poetry, alliteration is used to emphasize and to link words, as well as to create musical sounds.

See also Anglo-Saxon Poetry.

ALLUSION *Allusion* is a reference to a well-known person, place, event, literary work, or work of art.

AMBIGUITY *Ambiguity* is the effect created when words suggest and support two or more divergent interpretations. Ambiguity may be used in literature to express experiences or truths that are complex or even contradictory. For instance, the title of Elizabeth Bowen's short story "The Demon Lover," on page 1032, is ambiguous: It can refer either to the main character, who is a lover of a "demon" (a past love that she has not resolved), to the past that haunts her, or to her demonic lover, a ghost who haunts her. This ambiguous use of words reflects a larger ambiguity in the story.

See also Irony.

ANALOGY An *analogy* is an extended comparison of relationships. It is based on the idea or insight that the relationship between one pair of things is like the relationship between another pair. Unlike a metaphor, another form of comparison, an analogy involves an explicit comparison, often using the word *like* or *as.*

See also Metaphor *and* Simile.

ANAPEST *See* Meter.

ANGLO-SAXON POETRY The rhythmic poetry composed in the Old English language before A.D. 1100 is known as *Anglo-Saxon poetry.* It generally has four accented syllables and an indefinite number of unaccented syllables in each line. Each line is divided in half by a caesura, or pause, and the halves are linked by the alliteration of two or three of the accented syllables. The following translation from "Wulf and Eadwacer" shows the alliteration and caesuras used in Anglo-Saxon poetry:

> I waited for my Wulf // with far-Wandering yearnings,
> When it was rainy weather // and I sat weeping.

Anglo-Saxon poetry was sung or chanted to the accompaniment of a primitive harp; it was not written but was passed down orally.

See also Alliteration, Caesura, *and* Kenning.

ARCHETYPAL LITERARY ELEMENTS *Archetypal literary elements* are patterns in literature found around the world. For instance, the occurrence of events in threes is an archetypal element of fairy tales. Certain character types, such as mysterious guides, are also archetypal elements of such traditional stories. According to some critics, these elements express in symbolic form truths about the human mind.

ASSONANCE *Assonance* is the repetition of vowel sounds in stressed syllables containing dissimilar consonant sounds. Robert Browning uses assonance in this line in "Andrea del Sarto":

> Ah, but man's reach should exceed his grasp. . . .

The long *e* sound is repeated in the words *reach* and *exceed.* The syllables containing these sounds are stressed and contain different consonants: *r-ch* and *c-d.*

See also Consonance.

BALLAD A *ballad* is a song that tells a story, often about adventure or romance, or a poem imitating such a song. Most ballads are divided into four- or six-line stanzas, are rhymed, use simple language, and depict dramatic action. Many ballads employ a repeated refrain. Some use incremental repetition, in which the refrain is varied slightly each time it appears.

BLANK VERSE *Blank verse* is unrhymed poetry usually written in iambic pentameter (see Meter). Occasional variations in rhythm are introduced in blank verse to create emphasis, variety, and naturalness of sound. Because blank verse sounds much like ordinary spoken English, it is often used in drama, as by Shakespeare, and in poetry. The following lines come from Wordsworth's blank-verse poem "Lines Composed a Few Miles Above Tintern Abbey," on page 666:

> For thou | art with | me here | upon | the banks
> Of this | fair riv | er; thou | my dear | est Friend

See also Meter.

CAESURA A *caesura* is a natural pause in the middle of a line of poetry. In Anglo-Saxon poetry, a caesura divides each four-stress line in half and thus is essential to the rhythm.

See also Anglo-Saxon Poetry.

CARPE DIEM A Latin phrase, *carpe diem* means "seize the day" or "make the most of passing time." Many great literary works have been written with the *carpe diem* theme.

CHARACTER A person (though not necessarily a human being) who takes part in the action of a literary work is known as a character. Characters can be classified in different ways. A character who plays an important role is called a *major character*. A character who does not is called a *minor character*. A character who plays the central role in a story is called the *protagonist*. A character who opposes the protagonist is called the *antagonist*. A *round character* has many aspects to his or her personality. A *flat character* is defined by only a few qualities. A character who changes is called *dynamic*; a character who does not change is called *static*.

See also Characterization.

CHARACTERIZATION *Characterization* is the act of creating and developing a character. A writer uses *direct characterization* when he or she describes a character's traits explicitly. Writers also use *indirect characterization*. A character's traits can be revealed indirectly in what he or she says, thinks, or does; in a description of his or her appearance; or in the statements, thoughts, or actions of other characters.

See also Character.

CLIMAX The *climax* is the high point of interest or suspense in a literary work. Often, the climax is also the crisis in the plot, the point at which the protagonist changes his or her understanding or situation. Sometimes, the climax coincides with the *resolution*, the point at which the central conflict is ended.

See also Plot.

COMEDY A *comedy* is a literary work, especially a play, that has a happy ending. A comedy often shows ordinary characters in conflict with their society. Types of comedy include *romantic comedy,* which involves problems among lovers, and the *comedy of manners,* which satirically challenges the social customs of a sophisticated society. Comedy is often contrasted with tragedy, in which the protagonist meets an unfortunate end.

See also Drama *and* Tragedy.

CONCEIT A *conceit* is an unusual and surprising comparison between two very different things. This special kind of metaphor or complicated analogy is often the basis for a whole poem. During the Elizabethan Age, sonnets commonly included Petrarchan conceits. *Petrarchan conceits* make extravagant claims about the beloved's beauty or the speaker's suffering, with comparisons to divine beings, powerful natural forces, and objects that contain a given quality in the highest degree. Spenser uses a Petrarchan conceit when he claims in Sonnet 1, on page 236, that the "starry light" of his beloved's eyes will make his book happy when she reads it.

Seventeenth-century *metaphysical* poets used elaborate, unusual, and highly intellectual conceits, as in the conceit of the compass in John Donne's "A Valediction: Forbidding Mourning," on page 424.

See also Metaphor.

CONFLICT A *conflict* is a struggle between opposing forces. Sometimes, this struggle is internal, or within a character. At other times, the struggle is external, or between the character and some outside force. The outside force may be another character, nature, or some element of society such as a custom or a political institution. Often, the conflict in a work combines several of these possibilities.

See also Plot.

CONNOTATION *Connotation* refers to the associations that a word calls to mind in addition to its dictionary meaning. For example, the words *home* and *domicile* have the same dictionary meaning. However, the first has positive connotations of warmth and security, whereas the second does not.

See also Denotation.

CONSONANCE *Consonance* is the repetition of final consonant sounds in stressed syllables containing dissimilar vowel sounds. Samuel Taylor Coleridge uses consonance in these lines from *The Rime of the Ancient Mariner*, on page 686:

> a frightful fie*nd* / Doth close behi*nd* him tread.

Fiend and the stressed syllable in *behind* have the same final consonant sounds but different vowel sounds.

See also Assonance.

COUPLET A *couplet* is a pair of rhyming lines written in the same meter. A *heroic couplet* is a rhymed pair of iambic pentameter lines. In a *closed couplet*, the meaning and grammar are completed within the two lines. These lines from Alexander Pope's *An Essay on Criticism* are a closed heroic couplet:

> True ease in writing comes from art, not chance,
> As those move easiest who have learned to dance.

Shakespearean sonnets usually end with heroic couplets.

See also Sonnet.

DACTYL See Meter.

DENOTATION *Denotation* is the objective meaning of a word—that to which the word refers, independent of other associations that the word calls to mind. Dictionaries list the denotative meanings of words.

See also Connotation.

DIALECT *Dialect* is the form of a language spoken by people in a particular region or group. Dialects differ from one another in grammar, vocabulary, and pronunciation. Robert Burns used a Scots dialect in poems like "Auld Lang Syne":

> Should auld acquaintance be forgot,
> And never brought to min'?
> Should auld acquaintance be forgot,
> And days o' auld lang syne?

DIALOGUE *Dialogue* is a conversation between characters. Writers use dialogue to reveal character, to present events, to add variety to narratives, and to interest readers. Dialogue in a story is usually set off by quotation marks and paragraphing. Dialogue in a play script generally follows the name of the speaker.

DIARY A *diary* is a personal record of daily events, usually written in prose. Most diaries are not written for publication; sometimes, however, interesting diaries or diaries written by influential people are published. One example of a published diary is that of Samuel Pepys, a selection from which appears on page 496.

See also Journal.

DICTION *Diction* is a writer's word choice. It can be a major determinant of the writer's style. Diction can be described as formal or informal, abstract or concrete, plain or ornate, ordinary or technical.

See also Style.

DIMETER *See* Meter.

DRAMA A *drama* is a story written to be performed by actors. It may consist of one or more large sections, called acts, which are made up of any number of smaller sections, called scenes.

Drama originated in the religious rituals and symbolic reenactments of primitive peoples. The ancient Greeks, who developed drama into a sophisticated art form, created such dramatic forms as tragedy and comedy.

The first dramas in England were the miracle plays and morality plays of the Middle Ages. Miracle plays told biblical stories. Morality plays, such as *Everyman*, were allegories dealing with personified virtues and vices. The English Renaissance saw a flowering of drama in England, culminating in the works of William Shakespeare, who wrote many of the world's greatest comedies, tragedies, histories, and romances. During the Neoclassical Age, English drama turned to satirical comedies of manners that probed the virtues of upper-class society. In the Romantic and Victorian ages, a few good verse plays were written, including Percy Bysshe Shelley's *The Cenci* and *Prometheus Unbound*. The end of the nineteenth and beginning of the twentieth centuries saw a resurgence of the drama in England and throughout the English-speaking world. Great plays of the Modern period include plays by Bernard Shaw, Christopher Fry, T. S. Eliot, Harold Pinter, and Samuel Beckett.

DRAMATIC MONOLOGUE A *dramatic monologue* is a poem in which an imaginary character speaks to a silent listener. During the monologue, the speaker reveals his or her personality, usually at a moment of crisis. Robert Browning's "My Last Duchess," on page 836, is a dramatic monologue.

ELEGY An *elegy* is a solemn and formal lyric poem about death. It may mourn a particular person or reflect on a serious or tragic theme, such as the passing of youth or beauty. See Thomas Gray's "Elegy Written in a Country Churchyard," on page 570.

See also Lyric Poem.

END-STOPPED LINE An *end-stopped* line is a line of poetry concluding with a break in the meter and in the meaning. This pause at the end of a line is often punctuated by a period, comma, dash, or semicolon. These lines from "Away, Melancholy," by Stevie Smith, are end-stopped:

> Are not the trees green,
> The earth as green?
> Does not the wind blow,
> Fire leap and the rivers flow?

See also Run-on Line.

EPIC An *epic* is a long narrative poem about the adventures of gods or of a hero. *Beowulf*, on page 38, is a *folk epic*, one that was composed orally and passed from storyteller to storyteller. The ancient Greek epics attributed to Homer—the *Iliad* and the *Odyssey*—are also folk epics. The *Aeneid*, by the Roman poet Virgil, and *The Divine Comedy*, by the Italian poet Dante Alighieri, are examples of literary epics from the Classical and Medieval periods, respectively. John Milton's *Paradise Lost*, a selection from which appears on page 468, is also a literary epic. Milton's goal in creating *Paradise Lost* was to write a Christian epic similar in form and equal in value to the great epics of antiquity. An epic presents an encyclopedic portrait of the culture in which it was produced.

Epic conventions are traditional characteristics of epic poems, including an opening statement of the theme; an appeal for supernatural help in telling the story (an invocation); a beginning *in medias res* (Latin: "in the middle of things"); catalogs of people and things; accounts of past events; and descriptive phrases.

See also Kenning.

EPIGRAM An *epigram* is a brief statement in prose or in verse. The concluding couplet in an English sonnet may be epigrammatic. An essay may be written in an epigrammatic style.

EPIPHANY *Epiphany* is a term introduced by James Joyce to describe a moment of insight in which a character recognizes a truth. In Joyce's "Araby," on page 1147, the boy has an epiphany when he sees the falsity of his dream.

EPITAPH An *epitaph* is an inscription written on a tomb or burial place. In literature, epitaphs include serious or humorous lines written as if intended for such use, like the epitaph in Thomas Gray's "Elegy Written in a Country Churchyard," on page 570.

See Epic.

ESSAY An *essay* is a short nonfiction work about a particular subject. Essays are of many types but may be classified by tone or style as formal or informal. Addison's breezy style and tongue-in-cheek descriptions make "The Aims of *The Spectator*," on page 592, an instance of an informal essay. An essay is often classed by its main purpose as descriptive, narrative, expository, argumentative, or persuasive.

EXTENDED METAPHOR *See* Metaphor.

FICTION *Fiction* is prose writing about imaginary characters and events. Some writers of fiction base their stories on real events, whereas others rely solely on their imaginations.

See also Narration and Prose.

FIGURATIVE LANGUAGE *Figurative language* is writing or speech not meant to be interpreted literally. Poets and other writers use figurative language to paint vivid word pictures, to make their writing emotionally intense and concentrated, and to state their ideas in new and unusual ways.

Among the figures of speech making up figurative language are hyperbole, irony, metaphor, metonymy, oxymoron, paradox, personification, simile, and synecdoche.

See also the entries for individual figures of speech.

FOLKLORE The stories, legends, myths, ballads, riddles, sayings, and other traditional works produced orally by illiterate or semiliterate peoples are known as *folklore*. Folklore influences written literature in many ways. The beheading contest in *Sir Gawain and the Green Knight*, on page 162, is an example of folklore.

FOOT *See* Meter.

FREE VERSE *Free verse* is poetry not written in a regular, rhythmical pattern, or meter. Instead of having metrical feet and lines, free verse has a rhythm that suits its meaning and that uses the sounds of spoken language in lines of different lengths. Free verse has been widely used in twentieth-century poetry. An example is "The Galloping Cat," by Stevie Smith:

All the same I
Intend to go on being
A cat that likes to
Gallop about doing good
So
Now with my bald head I go,
Chopping the untidy flowers down, to and fro.

GOTHIC *Gothic* is a term used to describe literary works that make extensive use of primitive, medieval, wild, mysterious, or natural elements. Gothic novels, such as Mary Wollstonecraft Shelley's *Frankenstein*, the Introduction to which appears on page 650, often depict horrifying events set in gloomy castles.

HEPTAMETER *See* Meter.

HEXAMETER *See* Meter.

HYPERBOLE *Hyperbole* is a deliberate exaggeration or overstatement. In "Song," on page 422, John Donne uses this figure of speech:

When thou sigh'st, thou sigh'st not wind,
but sigh'st my soul away

See also Figurative Language.

IAMBIC PENTAMETER *See* Meter.

IMAGE An *image* is a word or phrase that appeals to one or more of the senses—sight, hearing, touch, taste, or smell. In a famous essay on *Hamlet*, T. S. Eliot explained how a group of images can be used as an "objective correlative." By this phrase, Eliot meant that a complex emotional state can be suggested by images that are carefully chosen to evoke this state.

See also Imagery.

IMAGERY *Imagery* is the descriptive language used in literature to re-create sensory experiences. Imagery enriches writing by making it more vivid, setting a tone, suggesting emotions, and guiding readers' reactions.

IRONY *Irony* is the general name given to literary techniques that involve surprising, interesting, or amusing contradictions. In *verbal irony*, words are used to suggest the opposite of their usual meaning. In *dramatic irony*, there is a contradiction between what a character thinks and what the reader or audience knows to be true. In *irony of situation*, an event occurs that directly contradicts expectations.

JOURNAL A *journal* is a daily autobiographical account of events and personal reactions. Daniel Defoe adapted this form to fictional use in *A Journal of the Plague Year*, an excerpt from which appears on page 503.

See also Diary.

KENNING A *kenning* is a metaphorical phrase used in Anglo-Saxon poetry to replace a concrete noun. In "The Seafarer," on page 16, the cuckoo is called "summer's sentinel" and the sea, "the whale's home."

See also Anglo-Saxon Poetry *and* Epic.

LEGEND A *legend* is a widely told story about the past that may or may not be based in fact. A legend often reflects a people's identity or cultural values, generally with more historical truth than that in a myth. English legends include the stories of King Arthur (retold in *Morte d'Arthur*, a selection from which appears on page 176) and Robin Hood.

See also Myth.

LYRIC POEM A *lyric poem* is a poem expressing the observations and feelings of a single speaker. Unlike a narrative poem, it presents an experience or a single effect, but it does not tell a full story. Types of lyric poems include the elegy, the ode, and the sonnet.

METAPHOR A *metaphor* is a figure of speech in which one thing is spoken of as though it were something else, as in "death, that long sleep." Through this identification of dissimilar things, a comparison is suggested or implied.

An *extended metaphor* is developed at length and involves several points of comparison. A mixed metaphor occurs when two metaphors are jumbled together, as in "The thorns of life rained down on him."

A *dead metaphor* is one that has been so overused that its original metaphorical impact has been lost. Examples of dead metaphors include "the foot of the bed" and "toe the line."

See also Figurative Language.

METAPHYSICAL POETRY The term *metaphysical poetry* describes the works of such seventeenth-century English poets as Richard Crashaw, John Donne, George Herbert, and Andrew Marvell. Characteristic features of metaphysical poetry include intellectual playfulness, argument, paradoxes, irony, elaborate and unusual conceits, incongruity, and the rhythms of ordinary speech. Examples of metaphysical poems in this textbook include Donne's "Song," on page 450, and Marvell's "To His Coy Mistress," on page 446.

METER *Meter* is the rhythmical pattern of a poem. This pattern is determined by the number and types of stresses, or beats, in each line. To describe the meter of a poem, you must scan its lines. Scanning involves marking the stressed and unstressed syllables, as follows:

> Ĭ ween | thăt, whén | thĕ grave's | dărk wáll
>
> Dĭd first | hĕr form | rĕtaín,
>
> Thĕy thought | thĕir heárts | coŭld ne'er | rĕcáll
> The light | ŏf jóy | ăgaín.
> —Emily Brontë, "Song"

As you can see, each stressed syllable is marked with a slanted line (´) and each unstressed syllable with a horseshoe symbol (˘) . The stresses are then divided by vertical lines into groups called feet. The following types of feet are common in English poetry:

1. *Iamb:* a foot with one unstressed syllable followed by one stressed syllable, as in the word *afraid*
2. *Trochee:* a foot with one stressed syllable followed by one unstressed syllable, as in the word *heather*
3. *Anapest:* a foot with two unstressed syllables followed by one stressed syllable, as in the word *disembark*
4. *Dactyl:* a foot with one stressed syllable followed by two unstressed syllables, as in the word *solitude*
5. *Spondee:* a foot with two stressed syllables, as in the word *workday*
6. *Pyrrhic:* a foot with two unstressed syllables, as in the last foot of the word *unspeak | ably*
7. *Amphibrach:* a foot with an unstressed syllable, one stressed syllable, and another unstressed syllable, as in the word *another*
8. *Amphimacer:* a foot with a stressed syllable, one unstressed syllable, and another stressed syllable, as in *up and down*

A line of poetry is described as *iambic*, *trochaic*, *anapestic*, or *dactylic* according to the kind of foot that appears most often in the line. Lines are also described in terms of the number of feet that occur in them, as follows:

1. *Monometer:* verse written in one-foot lines:

> Soúnd thĕ Flúte!
>
> Nów it's múte.
>
> Birds dĕlíght
>
> Dáy ănd Níght.
>
> —William Blake, "Spring"

2. *Dimeter:* verse written in two-foot lines:

> Ŏ Róse | thŏu art sick.
>
> The invís | ĭblĕ wórm.
>
> Thăt fliés | ĭn thĕ níght
>
> Ĭn thĕ hów | lĭng stórm:
>
> Hăs found | ŏut thy béd
>
> Ŏf crim | sŏn jóy: . . .
>
> —William Blake, "The Sick Rose"

3. *Trimeter:* verse written in three-foot lines:

> Ĭ wént | tŏ thĕ Gárd | ĕn ŏf Lóve
>
> Ănd sáw | whăt Ĭ név | ĕr hăd séen:
>
> Ă Cháp | ĕl wăs built | ĭn thĕ mídst,
>
> Whĕre Ĭ uśed | tŏ pláy | ŏn thĕ green.
>
> —William Blake, "The Garden of Love"

4. *Tetrameter:* verse written in four-foot lines:

> Ĭ wánd | ĕr thró' | each chárt | ĕr'd stréet
>
> Néar whĕre | thĕ chárt | ĕr'd Thámes |
> > doĕs flów

Aňd maŕk | iň év | erý faće | Ǐ meét

Márks ǒf | weákněss, | márks ǒf | wóe.

—William Blake, "The Little Black Boy"

A six-foot line is called a *hexameter*. A line with seven feet is a *heptameter*.

A complete description of the meter of a line tells both how many feet there are in the line and what kind of foot is most common. Thus, the stanza from Emily Brontë's poem, quoted at the beginning of this entry, would be described as being made up of alternating iambic tetrameter and iambic trimeter lines. Poetry that does not have a regular meter is called *free verse*.

See also Free Verse.

METONYMY *Metonymy* is a figure of speech that substitutes something closely related for the thing actually meant. In the opening line of "The Lost Leader," Robert Browning says, "Just for a handful of silver he left us," using "silver" to refer to money paid for a betrayal.

See also Figurative Language.

MIRACLE PLAY *See* Drama.

MOCK EPIC A *mock epic* is a poem about a trivial matter written in the style of a serious epic. The incongruity of style and subject matter produces comic effects. Alexander Pope's *The Rape of the Lock,* on page 532, is a mock epic.

See also Epic.

MODERNISM *Modernism* describes an international movement in the arts during the early twentieth century. Modernists rejected old forms and experimented with the new. Literary Modernists—such as James Joyce, W. B. Yeats, and T. S. Eliot—used images as symbols. They presented human experiences in fragments, rather than as a coherent whole, which led to new experiments in the forms of poetry and fiction.

MONOLOGUE A *monologue* is a speech or performance given entirely by one person or by one character.

See also Dramatic Monologue *and* Soliloquy.

MOOD *Mood*, or *atmosphere*, is the feeling created in the reader by a literary work or passage. Mood may be suggested by the writer's choice of words, by events in the work, or by the physical setting. Nadine Gordimer begins "The Train from Rhodesia," on page 1250, with a description of the hot, sandy train station that sets a mood mixing boredom and confinement with the eager expectation of the train.

See also Setting *and* Tone.

MORALITY PLAY *See* Drama.

MYTH A *myth* is a fictional tale, originally with religious significance, that explains the actions of gods or heroes, the causes of natural phenomena, or both. Allusions to characters and motifs from Greek, Roman, Norse, and Celtic myths are common in English literature. In addition, mythological stories are often retold or adapted.

See also Legend.

NARRATION *Narration* is writing that tells a story. The act of telling a story is also called narration. The *narrative*, or story, is told by a character or speaker called the *narrator*. Biographies, autobiographies, journals, reports, novels, short stories, plays, narrative poems, anecdotes, fables, parables, myths, legends, folk tales, ballads, and epic poems are all narratives, or types of narration.

See also Point of View.

NARRATIVE POEM A *narrative poem* is a poem that tells a story in verse. Three traditional types of narrative poems include ballads, epics, and metrical romances.

NATURALISM *Naturalism* was a literary movement among writers at the end of the nineteenth century and during the early decades of the twentieth century. The Naturalists depicted life in its grimmer details and viewed people as hopeless victims of natural laws.

See also Realism.

NEOCLASSICISM *Neoclassicism* was a literary movement of the late seventeenth and the eighteenth centuries in which writers turned to classical Greek and Roman literary models and standards. Like the ancients, Neoclassicists, such as Alexander Pope, stressed order, harmony, restraint, and the ideal. Much Neoclassical literature dealt with themes related to proper human conduct. The most popular literary forms of the day—essays, letters, early novels, epigrams, parodies, and satires—reflected this emphasis.

See also Romanticism.

NOVEL A *novel* is an extended work of fiction that often has a complicated plot, many major and minor characters, a unifying theme, and several settings. Novels can be grouped in many ways, based on the historical periods in which they are written (such as Victorian), on the subjects and themes that they treat (such as Gothic or regional), on the techniques used in them (such as stream of consciousness), or on their part in literary movements (such as Naturalism or Realism). Among the early novels were Samuel Richardson's *Pamela* and *Clarissa* and Henry Fielding's *Tom Jones.* Other classic English novels include Jane Austen's *Pride and Prejudice,* Sir Walter Scott's *Waverley*, Charles Dickens's *David Copperfield,* and George Eliot's *The Mill on the Floss.* Major twentieth-century novelists include James Joyce, Virginia Woolf, D. H. Lawrence, Henry James, Graham Greene, and Patrick White. A *novella*—for example, Joseph Conrad's *Heart of Darkness*— is not as long as a novel but is longer than a short story.

OBJECTIVE CORRELATIVE *See* Image.

OCTAVE *See* Stanza.

ODE An *ode* is a long, formal lyric poem with a serious theme. It may have a traditional structure with stanzas grouped in threes, called the *strophe*, the *antistrophe*, and the *epode*. Odes often honor people, commemorate events, or respond to natural scenes.

See also Lyric Poem.

ONOMATOPOEIA *Onomatopoeia* is the use of words that imitate sounds. Examples of such words are *buzz, hiss, murmur,* and *rustle*. Onomatopoeia is used to create musical effects and to reinforce meaning.

ORAL TRADITION *Oral tradition* is the body of songs, stories, and poems preserved by being passed from generation to generation by word of mouth. Among the many materials composed or preserved through oral tradition in Great Britain are *Beowulf*, on page 38, and the folk ballads on pages 194–200. In his *Morte d'Arthur*, a selection from which begins on page 176, Sir Thomas Malory drew on Arthurian legends from the oral tradition. Shakespeare drew on materials from the oral tradition to create the sprites and fairies of *A Midsummer Night's Dream* and the witches of *Macbeth*, on page 300. Folk epics, ballads, myths, legends, folk tales, folk songs, proverbs, and nursery rhymes are all products of the oral tradition.

See also Ballad, Folklore, Legend, *and* Myth.

OXYMORON An *oxymoron* is a figure of speech that fuses two contradictory ideas, such as "freezing fire" or "happy grief," thus suggesting a paradox in just a few words.

See also Figurative Language *and* Paradox.

PARABLE A *parable* is a short, simple story from which a moral or religious lesson can be drawn. The most famous parables are those in the New Testament, an example of which appears on page 279.

PARADOX A *paradox* is a statement that seems to be contradictory but that actually presents a truth. In "Love's Growth," John Donne presents the following paradox:

Methinks I lied all winter, when I swore
My love was infinite, if spring make it more.

Because a paradox is surprising or even shocking, it draws the reader's attention to what is being said.

See also Figurative Language *and* Oxymoron.

PARODY A *parody* is a humorous imitation of another work or of a type of work. For instance, Chaucer parodies the grand style of an epic poem in "The Nun's Priest's Tale" from *The Canterbury Tales* on page 119 by applying that style to trivial incidents.

PASTORAL *Pastoral* refers to literary works that deal with the pleasures of a simple rural life or with escape to a simpler place and time. The tradition of pastoral literature began in ancient Greece with the poetic idylls of Theocritus. The Roman poet Virgil also wrote a famous collection of pastoral poems, the *Eclogues*.

During the European Renaissance, pastoral writing became quite popular. Two famous examples are *The Countess of Pembroke's Arcadia,* by Sir Philip Sidney, and Christopher Marlowe's "The Passionate Shepherd to His Love," on page 245.

Today, the term *pastoral* is commonly applied to any work in which a speaker longs to escape to a simpler rural life. By this definition, both William Wordsworth's "The World Is Too Much With Us," on page 675, and William Butler Yeats's "The Lake Isle of Innisfree," on page 968, are pastoral poems.

PENTAMETER *See* Meter.

PERSONIFICATION *Personification* is a figure of speech in which a nonhuman subject is given human characteristics. Percy Bysshe Shelley uses personification in these lines:

Swiftly walk o'er the western wave,
Spirit of the Night!

Effective personification of things or ideas makes their qualities seem unified, like the characteristics of a person, and their relationship with the reader seem closer.

See also Figurative Language *and* Metaphor.

PLOT *Plot* is the sequence of events in a literary work. The two primary elements of any plot are characters and a conflict. Most plots can be analyzed into many or all of the following parts:

1. The *exposition* introduces the setting, the characters, and the basic situation.
2. The *inciting incident* introduces the central conflict.
3. During the *development,* the conflict runs its course and usually intensifies.
4. At the *climax,* the conflict reaches a high point of interest or suspense.
5. The *denouement* ties up loose ends that remain after the climax of the conflict.
6. At the *resolution,* the story is resolved and an insight is revealed.

There are many variations on the standard plot structure. Some stories begin *in medias res* ("in the middle of things"), after the inciting incident has already occurred. In some stories, the expository material appears toward the middle, in flashbacks. In many stories, there is no denouement. Occasionally, the conflict is left unresolved.

POETRY *Poetry* is one of the three major types, or genres, of literature, the others being prose and drama. Poetry defies simple definition because there is no single characteristic that is found in all poems and not found in all nonpoems.

Often, poems are divided into lines and stanzas. Poems

such as sonnets, odes, villanelles, and sestinas are governed by rules regarding the number of lines, the number and placement of stressed syllables in each line, and the rhyme scheme. In the case of villanelles and sestinas, the repetition of words at the ends of lines or of entire lines is required. (An example of a sestina, Seamus Heaney's "Two Lorries," appears on page 1107. An example of a villanelle, Dylan Thomas's "Do Not Go Gentle into That Good Night," appears on page 1206.) However, some poems are written in free verse. Most poems make use of highly concise, musical, and emotionally charged language. Many also use imagery, figurative language, and devices of sound like rhyme.

Types of poetry include *narrative poetry* (ballads, epics, and metrical romances); *dramatic poetry* (dramatic monologues and dramatic dialogues); *lyrics* (sonnets, odes, elegies, and love poems); and *concrete poetry* (a poem presented on the page in a shape that suggests its subject).

POINT OF VIEW The perspective, or vantage point, from which a story is told is its *point of view*. If a character within the story narrates, then it is told from the *first-person point of view*. If a voice from outside the story tells it, then the story is told from the *third-person point of view*. If the knowledge of the storyteller is limited to the internal states of one character, then the storyteller has a *limited point of view*. If the storyteller's knowledge extends to the internal states of all the characters, then the storyteller has an *omniscient point of view*.

PROSE *Prose* is the ordinary form of written language and one of the three major types of literature. Most writing that is not poetry, drama, or song is considered prose. Prose occurs in two major forms: fiction and nonfiction.

PYRRHIC *See* Meter.

QUATRAIN *See* Stanza.

REALISM *Realism* is the presentation in art of details from actual life. During the last part of the nineteenth century and the first part of the twentieth, Realism enjoyed considerable popularity among writers in the English-speaking world. Novels often dealt with grim social realities and presented realistic portrayals of the psychological states of characters.

REFRAIN A *refrain* is a regularly repeated line or group of lines in a poem or song.

See also Ballad.

REGIONALISM *Regionalism* is the tendency to confine one's writing to the presentation of the distinct culture of an area, including its speech, customs, and history. For example, the Brontës wrote about Yorkshire, Thomas Hardy wrote about Dorset and Wessex, and D. H. Lawrence wrote about Nottinghamshire.

RHYME *Rhyme* is the repetition of sounds at the ends of words. End rhyme occurs when rhyming words appear at the ends of lines. *Internal rhyme* occurs when rhyming words fall within a line. *Exact rhyme* is the use of identical rhyming sounds, as in *love* and *dove*. *Approximate,* or *slant, rhyme* is the use of sounds that are similar but not identical, as in *prove* and *glove*.

RHYME SCHEME *Rhyme scheme* is the regular pattern of rhyming words in a poem or stanza. To indicate a rhyme scheme, assign a different letter to each final sound in the poem or stanza. The following lines from Charlotte Brontë's "On the Death of Anne Brontë" have been marked:

There's little joy in life for me,	*a*
And little terror in the grave;	*b*
I've lived the parting hour to see	*a*
Of one I would have died to save.	*b*

RHYTHM *See* Meter.

ROMANCE A *romance* is a story that presents remote or imaginative incidents rather than ordinary, realistic experience. The term *romance* was originally used to refer to medieval tales of the deeds and loves of noble knights and ladies. These early romances, or tales of chivalry and courtly love, are exemplified by *Sir Gawain and the Green Knight*, on page 162, and by the extract from Malory's *Morte d'Arthur,* on page 176. During the Renaissance in England, many writers, such as Edmund Spenser in *The Faerie Queene,* drew heavily on the romance tradition. From the eighteenth century on, the term *romance* has been used to describe sentimental novels about love.

ROMANTICISM *Romanticism* was a literary and artistic movement of the eighteenth and nineteenth centuries. In reaction to Neoclassicism, the Romantics emphasized imagination, fancy, freedom, emotion, wildness, the beauty of the untamed natural world, the rights of the individual, the nobility of the common man, and the attractiveness of pastoral life. Important figures in the Romantic Movement included William Wordsworth, Samuel Taylor Coleridge, Percy Bysshe Shelley, John Keats, and George Gordon, Lord Byron.

RUN-ON LINE A *run-on line* is a line that does not contain a pause or a stop at the end. It ends in the middle of a statement and a grammatical unit, and the reader must read the next line to find the end of the statement and the completion of the grammatical unit. The beginning of Molly Holden's "The Double Nature of White" illustrates the run-on line:

White orchards are the earliest, stunning

the spirit resigned to winter's black, white thorn

sprays first the bare wet branches of the hedge.

See also End-Stopped Line.

SATIRE *Satire* is writing that ridicules or holds up to contempt the faults of individuals or groups. Satires include Jonathan Swift's prose work *Gulliver's Travels,* on page 514, and Alexander Pope's poem *The Rape of the Lock,* on page 532. Although a satire is often humorous, its purpose is not simply to make readers laugh but also to correct the flaws and shortcomings that it points out.

SCANSION *Scansion* is the process of analyzing the metrical pattern of a poem.

See also Meter.

SERMON A *sermon* is a speech offering religious or moral instruction. For example, the Sermon on the Mount, on page 278, given by Jesus on a mountain in Galilee, contains the basic teachings of Christianity.

SESTET *See* Stanza.

SETTING The *setting* is the time and place of the action of a literary work. A setting can provide a backdrop for the action. It can be the force that the protagonist struggles against and thus the source of the central conflict. It can also be used to create an atmosphere. In many works, the setting symbolizes a point that the author wishes to emphasize.

See also Mood *and* Symbol.

SHORT STORY A *short story* is a brief work of fiction. The short story resembles the longer novel, but it generally has a simpler plot and setting. In addition, a short story tends to reveal character at a crucial moment, rather than to develop it through many incidents.

SIMILE A *simile* is a figure of speech that compares two apparently dissimilar things using *like* or *as.* Christina Rossetti uses simile in "Goblin Market" to describe two sisters:

> Like two blossoms on one stem,
> Like two flakes of new-fallen snow,
> Like two wands of ivory
> Tipped with gold for awful kings.

By comparing apparently dissimilar things, the writer of a simile surprises the reader into an appreciation of the hidden similarities of the things being compared.

See also Figurative Language.

SOLILOQUY A *soliloquy* is a long speech in a play or in a prose work made by a character who is alone and thus reveals private thoughts and feelings to the audience or reader. William Shakespeare opens Act III of *Macbeth,* on page 337, with a soliloquy in which Banquo speculates on Macbeth's reaction to the witches' prophecy.

See also Monologue.

SONNET A sonnet is a fourteen-line lyric poem with a single theme. Sonnets are usually written in iambic pentameter. The *Petrarchan,* or *Italian sonnet,* is divided into two parts, an eight-line octave and a six-line sestet. The octave rhymes *abba abba*, while the sestet generally rhymes *cde cde* or uses some combination of *cd* rhymes. The octave raises a question, states a problem, or presents a brief narrative, and the sestet answers the question, solves the problem, or comments on the narrative.

The *Shakespearean,* or *English, sonnet* has three four-line quatrains plus a concluding two-line couplet. The rhyme scheme of such a sonnet is usually *abab cdcd efef gg*. Each of the three quatrains usually explores a different variation of the main theme. Then, the couplet presents a summarizing or concluding statement.

See also Lyric Poem *and* Sonnet Sequence.

SONNET SEQUENCE A *sonnet sequence* is a series or group of sonnets, most often written to or about a beloved. Although each sonnet can stand alone as a separate poem, the sequence lets the poet trace the development of a relationship or examine different aspects of a single subject. Examples of sonnet sequences are Sir Philip Sidney's *Astrophel and Stella*, Edmund Spenser's *Amoretti*, and Elizabeth Barrett Browning's *Sonnets from the Portuguese.*

See also Sonnet.

SPEAKER The *speaker* is the imaginary voice assumed by the writer of a poem; the character who "says" the poem. This character is often not identified by name but may be identified otherwise. For example, the title of William Blake's poem "The Chimney Sweeper," on page 643, identifies the speaker, a child who gives an account of his life.

Recognizing the speaker and thinking about his or her characteristics are often central to interpreting a lyric poem. In Blake's poem, for instance, the speaker's acceptance of his oppressive life is offered for the reader's evaluation.

See also Point of View.

SPONDEE *See* Meter.

SPRUNG RHYTHM The term *sprung rhythm* was used by Gerard Manley Hopkins to describe the idiosyncratic meters of his poems. The rhythm is quite varied and contains such violations of traditional metrical rules as several strong stresses in a row or feet containing more than two weak stresses.

STANZA A *stanza* is a group of lines in a poem, which is seen as a unit. Many poems are divided into stanzas that are separated by spaces. Stanzas often function like paragraphs in prose. Each stanza states and develops one main idea.

Stanzas are commonly named according to the number of lines found in them, as follows:

1. *Couplet:* a two-line stanza
2. *Tercet:* a three-line stanza
3. *Quatrain:* a four-line stanza
4. *Cinquain:* a five-line stanza
5. *Sestet:* a six-line stanza

6. *Heptastich:* a seven-line stanza
7. *Octave:* an eight-line stanza

See also Sonnet.

STYLE *Style* is a writer's typical way of writing. Determinants of a writer's style include formality, use of figurative language, use of rhythm, typical grammatical patterns, typical sentence lengths, and typical methods of organization. John Milton is noted for a grand, heroic style that contrasts with John Keats's rich, sensory style and with T. S. Eliot's allusive, ironic style.

See also Diction.

SUBLIME The *sublime* is an effect created in literature when a writer confronts a power or mystery in nature that exceeds human understanding. The effect is achieved by representing the infinite or endless in sensory terms, as when Byron characterizes the inexhaustible power of the ocean in the "Apostrophe to the Ocean" in *Childe Harold's Pilgrimage,* on page 720.

SYMBOL A *symbol* is a sign, word, phrase, image, or other object that stands for or represents something else. Thus, a flag can symbolize a country, a spoken word can symbolize an object, a fine car can symbolize wealth, and so on. In literary criticism, a distinction is often made between traditional or conventional symbols—those that are part of our general cultural inheritance—and personal symbols—those that are created by particular authors for use in particular works. For example, the lamb in William Blake's poem "The Lamb," on page 640, is a conventional symbol for peace, gentleness, and innocence. However, the tiger in Blake's poem "The Tyger," on page 641, is not a conventional or inherited symbol. Blake created this symbol specifically for this poem.

Conventional symbolism is often based on elements of nature. For example, youth is often symbolized by greenery or springtime, middle age by summer, and old age by autumn or winter. Conventional symbols are also borrowed from religion and politics. For example, a cross may be a symbol of Christianity, or the color red may be a symbol of Marxist ideology.

SYNECDOCHE *Synecdoche* is a figure of speech in which a part of something is used to stand for the whole. In the preface to his long poem entitled *Milton,* William Blake includes these lines: "And did those feet in ancient time / Walk upon England's mountains green?" The "feet" stand for the whole body, and "England's mountains green" stand for England.

See also Figurative Language.

TETRAMETER *See* Meter.

THEME *Theme* is the central idea, concern, or purpose in a literary work. In an essay, the theme might be directly stated in what is known as a thesis statement. In a serious literary work, the theme is usually expressed indirectly rather than directly. A light work, one written strictly for entertainment, may not have a theme.

TONE *Tone* is the writer's attitude toward the readers and toward the subject. It may be formal or informal, friendly or distant, personal or pompous. For example, John Keats's tone in his poem "On First Looking into Chapman's Homer," on page 746, is earnest and respectful, while James Boswell's tone in *The Life of Samuel Johnson,* which begins on page 554, is familiar and engaging.

See also Mood.

TRADITION In literary study and practice, a *tradition* is a past body of work, developed over the course of history. A literary tradition may be unified by form (the tradition of the sonnet), by language (literature in English), or by nationality (English literature). A tradition develops through the acknowledgment of works, forms, and styles as classic. It also develops through critical reappraisals, as when T. S. Eliot, in the early twentieth century, elevated seventeenth-century poet John Donne out of the shadows of critical obscurity and disfavor. Writers participate in a tradition if only by following conventions about the suitable forms and subjects for literature. They make conscious use of the tradition when they use references, stories, or forms from old literature to give authority to their work. For example, John Milton uses the classical form of the epic in *Paradise Lost,* page 468, to retell the biblical story of the Fall. Writers may also break from a tradition, as when Wordsworth rejects elevated poetic language in favor of conversational speech in poems such as "London, 1802," page 676. A tradition may also be used to question itself. For example, Derek Walcott in the extract from *Midsummer,* page 1260, uses references to Shakespeare's works to question the extent to which he, a black poet, can participate in a tradition largely maintained by white society for white society.

TRAGEDY *Tragedy* is a type of drama or literature that shows the downfall or destruction of a noble or outstanding person, traditionally one who possesses a character weakness called a *tragic flaw.* Macbeth, for example, is a brave and noble figure led astray by ambition. The *tragic hero* is caught up in a sequence of events that inevitably results in disaster. Because the protagonist is neither a wicked villain nor an innocent victim, the audience reacts with mixed emotions—both pity and fear, according to the Greek philosopher Aristotle, who defined tragedy in the *Poetics.* The outcome of a tragedy, in which the protagonist is isolated from society, contrasts with the happy resolution of a comedy, in which the protagonist makes peace with society.

See also Comedy *and* Drama.

TRIMETER *See* Meter.

TROCHEE *See* Meter.

THE WRITING PROCESS

A polished piece of writing can seem to have been effortlessly created, but most good writing is the result of a process of writing, rethinking, and rewriting. The process can roughly be divided into stages: prewriting, drafting, revising, editing, proofreading, and publishing.

It is important to remember that the writing process is one that moves backward as well as forward. Even while you are moving forward in the creation of your composition, you may still return to a previous stage—to rethink or rewrite.

Following are stages of the writing process, with key points to address during each stage.

Prewriting

In this stage, you plan out the work to be done. You prepare to write by exploring ideas, gathering information, and working out an organization plan. Following are the key steps to take at this stage.

Step 1: Analyze the writing situation. Start by clarifying your assignment, so that you know exactly what you are supposed to do.

- *Focus your topic.* If necessary, narrow the topic—the subject you are writing about—so that you can write about it fully in the space you have.
- *Know your purpose.* What is your goal for this paper? What do you want to accomplish? Your purpose will determine what you include in the paper.
- *Know your audience.* Who will read your paper influences what you say and how you say it.

Step 2: Gather ideas and information. You can do this in a number of ways:

- *Brainstorm.* When you brainstorm, either alone or with others, you come up with possible ideas to use in your paper. Not all of your ideas will be useful or suitable. You will need to evaluate them later.
- *Consult other people about your subject.* Speaking informally with others may suggest an idea or an approach you did not see at first.
- *Make a list of questions about your topic.* When your list is complete, find the answers to your questions.
- *Do research.* Your topic may require information that you do not have, so you will need to go to other sources to find information. There are numerous ways to find information on a topic.

The ideas and information you gather will become the content of your paper. Not all of the information you gather will be needed. As you develop and revise your paper, you will make further decisions about what to include and what to leave out.

Drafting

When you draft, you put down your ideas on paper in rough form. Working from your prewriting notes and your outline or plan, you develop and present your ideas in sentences and paragraphs.

Organize. First, make a rough plan for the way you want to present your information. Sort your ideas and notes. Decide what goes with what and which points are the most important. You can make an outline to show the order of ideas, or you can use some other organizing plan that works for you.

There are many ways in which you can organize and develop your material. Use a method that works for your topic. Following are common methods of organizing information in the development of a paper:

- *Chronological Order* In this method, events are presented in the order in which they occurred. This organization works best for presenting narrative material or explaining in a "how-to" format.
- *Spatial Order* In spatial order, details are presented as seen in space; for example, from left to right, top to bottom, or from foreground to background. This order is good for descriptive writing.
- *Order of Importance* This order helps readers see the relative importance of ideas. You present ideas from the most to least important or from the least to most important.
- *Main Idea and Details* This logical organization works well to support an idea or opinion. Present each main idea, and back it up with appropriate support.

Once you have chosen an organization, begin writing your draft. Do not worry about getting everything perfect at the drafting stage. Concentrate on getting your ideas down.

Write your draft in a way that works for you. Some writers work best by writing a quick draft—putting down all their ideas without stopping to evaluate them. Other writers prefer to develop each paragraph carefully and thoughtfully, making sure that each main idea is supported by details.

As you are developing your draft, keep in mind your purpose and your audience. These determine what you say and how you say it.

Do not be afraid to change your original plans during drafting. Some of the best ideas are those that were not planned at the beginning. Write as many drafts as you like, until you are happy with the results.

Develop an Essay Most papers, regardless of the topic, are developed with an introduction, a body, and a conclusion. Here are tips for developing these parts:

Introduction In the introduction to a paper, you want to engage your readers' attention and let them know the purpose of your paper. You may use the following strategies in your introduction:

- Startle your readers.
- Take a stand.
- Use an anecdote.
- Quote someone.

Body of the Paper In the body of your paper, you present your information and make your points. Your organization is an important factor in leading readers through your ideas. Elaborating on your main ideas is also important. Elaboration is the development of ideas to make your written work precise and complete. You can use the following kinds of details to elaborate your main ideas:

- Facts and statistics
- Anecdotes
- Sensory details
- Examples
- Explanations and definitions
- Quotations

Conclusion The ending of your paper is the final impression you leave with your readers. Your conclusion should give readers the sense that you have pulled everything together. Following are some effective ways to end your paper:

- Summarize and restate.
- Ask a question.
- State an opinion.
- Tell an anecdote.
- Call for action.
- Provide an insight.

Revising

Once you have a draft, you can look at it critically or have others review it. This is the time to make changes—on many levels. Revising is the process of reworking what you have written to make it as good as it can be.

Revising Your Overall Structure Start by examining the soundness of your structure, or overall organization. Your ideas should flow logically from beginning to end. You may strengthen the structure by reordering paragraphs or by adding information to fill in gaps.

Revising Your Paragraphs Next, examine each paragraph in your writing. Consider the way each sentence contributes to the point of the paragraph. As you evaluate your draft, rewrite or eliminate any sentences that are not effective.

Revising Your Sentences When you study the sentences in your draft, check to see that they flow smoothly from one to the next. Look to see that you have avoided the pattern of beginning most of your sentences in the same way, and vary your sentence length.

Revising Your Word Choice The final step in the process of revising your work is to analyze your choice of words. Consider the connotations, or associations each word suggests, and make sure that each word conveys the exact meaning you intended. Also, look for the repetition of words, and make revisions to polish your writing.

Peer Review After you have finished revising your draft, work with one or more classmates to get a fresh perspective on your writing. First, have your reviewer look at one element of your writing, and ask your reviewer a specific question to get the most focused feedback possible. Weigh the responses you receive, and determine which suggestions you want to incorporate in your draft.

Editing

When you edit, you look more closely at the language you have used to ensure that the way you expressed your ideas is the most effective.

- Replace dull language with vivid, precise words.
- Cut or change unnecessary repetition.
- Cut empty words and phrases—those that do not add anything to the writing.
- Check passive voice. Usually, active voice is more effective.
- Replace wordy expressions with shorter, more precise ones.

Proofreading

After you finish your final draft, proofread it, either on your own or with the help of a partner.

It is useful to have both a dictionary and a usage handbook available to help you check that your work is correct. Here are the tasks in proofreading:

- Correct errors in grammar and usage.
- Correct errors in punctuation and capitalization.
- Correct errors in spelling.

Publishing

Now your paper is ready to be shared with others. Consider sharing your writing with classmates, family, or a wider audience.

THE MODES OF WRITING

Writing is a process that begins with the exploration of ideas and ends with the presentation of a final draft. Often, the types of writing are grouped into modes according to form and purpose.

The modes addressed in this handbook are

- Narration
- Description
- Persuasion
- Exposition
- Research Writing
- Response to Literature
- Writing for Assessment
- Workplace Writing

NARRATION

Whenever writers tell any type of story, they are using **narration.** Although there are many kinds of narration, most narratives share certain elements, such as characters, a setting, a sequence of events, and, often, a theme. Following are some types of narration:

Autobiographical Writing Autobiographical writing tells a true story about an important period, experience, or relationship in the writer's life. An autobiographical narrative can be as simple as a description of a recent car trip or as complex as the entire story of a person's life. Effective autobiographical writing includes

- A series of events that involve the writer as the main character
- Details, thoughts, feelings, and insights from the writer's perspective
- A conflict or an event that affects the writer
- A logical organization that tells the story clearly
- Insights that the writer gained from the experience

A few types of autobiographical writing are autobiographical incidents, personal narratives, autobiographical narratives or sketches, reflective essays, eyewitness accounts, anecdotes, and memoirs.

Short Story A short story is a brief, creative narrative—a retelling of events arranged to hold a reader's attention. Most short stories include

- Details that establish the setting in time and place
- A main character who undergoes a change or learns something during the course of the story
- A conflict or a problem to be introduced, developed, and resolved

- A plot, the series of events that make up the action of the story
- A theme or generalization about life

A few types of short stories are realistic stories, fantasies, historical narratives, mysteries, thrillers, science-fiction stories, and adventure stories.

DESCRIPTION

Descriptive writing is writing that creates a vivid picture of a person, place, thing, or event. Descriptive writing can stand on its own or be part of a longer work, such as a short story. Most descriptive writing includes

- Sensory details—sights, sounds, smells, tastes, and physical sensations
- Vivid, precise language
- Figurative language or comparisons
- Adjectives and adverbs that paint a word picture
- An organization suited to the subject

Some examples of descriptive writing include description of ideas, observations, travel brochures, physical descriptions, functional descriptions, remembrances, and character sketches.

PERSUASION

Persuasion is writing or speaking that attempts to convince people to accept a position or take a desired action. When used effectively, persuasive writing has the power to change people's lives. As a reader and a writer, you will find yourself engaged in many forms of persuasion. Here are a few of them:

Persuasive Essay A persuasive essay presents your position on an issue, urges your readers to accept that position, and may encourage them to take an action. An effective persuasive essay

- Explores an issue of importance to the writer
- Addresses an issue that is arguable
- Uses facts, examples, statistics, or personal experiences to support a position
- Tries to influence the audience through appeals to the readers' knowledge, experiences, or emotions
- Uses clear organization to present a logical argument

Persuasion can take many forms. A few forms of persuasion include editorials, position papers, persuasive speeches, grant proposals, advertisements, and debates.

Advertisements An advertisement is a planned communication meant to be seen, heard, or read. It attempts to persuade an audience to buy a product or service, accept an idea, or support a cause. Advertisements may appear in printed form—in newspapers and magazines, on billboards, or as posters or flyers. They may appear on radio or television, as commercials or public-service announcements. An effective advertisement includes

- A memorable slogan to grab the audience's attention
- A call to action, which tries to rally the audience to do something
- Persuasive and/or informative text
- Striking visual or aural images
- Details that provide such information as price, location, date, and time

Several common types of advertisements are public-service announcements, billboards, merchandise ads, service ads, online ads, product packaging, and political campaign literature.

EXPOSITION

Exposition is writing that informs or explains. The information you include in expository writing is factual or based on fact. Effective expository writing reflects a well-thought-out organization—one that includes a clear introduction, body, and conclusion. The organization should be appropriate for the type of exposition you are writing. Here are some types of exposition:

Comparison-and-Contrast Essay A comparison-and-contrast essay analyzes the similarities and differences between two or more things. You may organize your essay either point by point or subject by subject. An effective comparison-and-contrast essay

- Identifies a purpose for comparison and contrast
- Identifies similarities and differences between two or more things, people, places, or ideas
- Gives factual details about the subjects being compared
- Uses an organizational plan suited to its topic and purpose

Types of comparison-and-contrast essays are product comparisons, essays on economic or historical developments, comparison and contrast of literary works, and plan evaluations.

Cause-and-Effect Essay A cause-and-effect essay examines the relationship between events, explaining how one event or situation causes another. A successful cause-and-effect essay includes

- A discussion of a cause, event, or condition that produces a specific result
- An explanation of an effect, outcome, or result

- Evidence and examples to support the relationship between cause and effect
- A logical organization that makes the explanation clear

Some appropriate subjects for cause-and-effect essays are science reports, current-events articles, health studies, historical accounts, and cause-and-effect investigations.

Problem-and-Solution Essay A problem-and-solution essay describes a problem and offers one or more solutions to it. It describes a clear set of steps to achieve a result. An effective problem-and-solution essay includes

- A clear statement of the problem, with its causes and effects summarized for the reader
- The most important aspects of the problem
- A proposal of at least one realistic solution
- Facts, statistics, data, or expert testimony to support the solution
- Language appropriate to the audience's knowledge and ability levels
- A clear organization that makes the relationship between problem and solution obvious

Some types of issues that might be addressed in a problem-and-solution essay include consumer issues, business issues, time-management issues, and local issues.

RESEARCH WRITING

Research writing is based on information gathered from outside sources, and it gives a writer the power to become an expert on any subject. A research paper—a focused study of a topic—helps writers explore and connect ideas, make discoveries, and share their findings with an audience. Effective research writing

- Focuses on a specific, narrow topic, which is usually summarized in a thesis statement
- Presents relevant information from a wide variety of sources
- Structures the information logically and effectively
- Identifies the sources from which the information was drawn

Besides the formal research report, there are many other specialized types of writing that depend on accurate and insightful research, including multimedia presentations, statistical reports, annotated bibliographies, and experiment journals.

Documented Essay A documented essay uses research gathered from outside sources to support an idea. What distinguishes this essay from other categories of research is the level and intensity of the research. In a documented essay, the writer consults a limited number of sources to elaborate an idea. In contrast, a formal research paper may include many more research sources. An effective documented essay includes

- A well-defined thesis that can be fully discussed in a brief essay
- Facts and details to support each main point
- Expert or informed ideas gathered from interviews and other sources
- A clear, coherent method of organization
- Full internal documentation to show sources of information

Subjects especially suited to the documented essay format include health issues, current events, and cultural trends.

Research Paper A research paper presents and interprets information gathered through an extensive study of a subject. An effective research paper has

- A clearly stated thesis statement
- Convincing factual support from a variety of outside sources, including direct quotations whose sources are credited
- A clear organization that includes an introduction, body, and conclusion
- A bibliography, or works-cited list, that provides a complete listing of research sources

Some research formats you may encounter include lab reports, annotated bibliographies, and multigenre research papers.

RESPONSE TO LITERATURE

When you write a **response-to-literature essay,** you give yourself the opportunity to discover *what, how,* and *why* a piece of writing communicated to you. An effective response

- Contains a reaction to a poem, story, essay, or other work of literature
- Analyzes the content of a literary work, its related ideas, or the work's effect on the reader
- Presents a thesis statement to identify the nature of the response
- Focuses on a single aspect of the work or gives a general overview
- Supports opinion with evidence from the work addressed

The following are just a few of the ways you might respond in writing to a literary work: reader's response journals, character analyses, literary letters, and literary analyses.

WRITING FOR ASSESSMENT

One of the most common types of school **assessment** is the written test. Most often, a written test is announced in advance, allowing you time to study and prepare. When a test includes an essay, you are expected to write a response that includes

- A clearly stated and well-supported thesis or main idea
- Specific information about the topic derived from your reading or from class discussion
- A clear organization

In your school career, you will probably encounter questions that ask you to address each of the following types of writing: explain a process; defend a position; compare, contrast, or categorize; and show cause and effect.

WORKPLACE WRITING

Workplace writing is probably the format you will use most after you finish school. It is used in offices, factories, and by workers on the road. Workplace writing includes a variety of formats that share common features. In general, workplace writing is fact-based writing that communicates specific information to readers in a structured format. Effective workplace writing

- Communicates information concisely to make the best use of both the writer's and the reader's time
- Includes a level of detail that provides necessary information and anticipates potential questions
- Reflects the writer's care if it is error-free and neatly presented

Some common types of workplace writing include business letters, memorandums, résumés, forms, and applications.

Summary of Grammar

Nouns A **noun** names a person, place, or thing. A **common noun,** such as *country,* names any one of a class of people, places, or things. A **proper noun,** such as *Great Britain,* names a specific person, place, or thing.

Pronouns Pronouns are words that stand for nouns or for words that take the place of nouns. **Personal pronouns** refer to the person speaking; the person spoken to; or the person, place, or thing spoken about.

	Singular	Plural
First Person	I, me, my, mine	we, us, our, ours
Second Person	you, your, yours	you, your, yours
Third Person	he, him, his, she, her, hers, it, its	they, them, their, theirs

A **reflexive pronoun** ends in *-self* or *-selves* and names the person or thing receiving an action when that person or thing is the same as the one performing the action.

> I pray you, school *yourself.* (Shakespeare, p. 355)

An **intensive pronoun** also ends in *-self* or *-selves.* It adds emphasis to a noun or pronoun.

> The raven *himself* is hoarse
> That croaks the fatal entrance of Duncan
> Under my battlements. (Shakespeare, p. 300)

Demonstrative pronouns—such as *this, that, these,* and *those*—single out specific people, places, or things.

A **relative pronoun** begins a subordinate clause and connects it to another idea in the sentence.

> Annoyed, she picked up the letter, which bore no stamp. (Bowen, p. 1032)

Interrogative pronouns are used to begin questions.

> Who casts not up his eye to the sun when it rises?
> (Donne, p. 428)

Indefinite pronouns refer to people, places, or things, often without specifying which ones.

> Nought's had, all's spent,
> Where our desire is got without content: . . .
> (Shakespeare, p. 337)

Verbs A **verb** is a word or group of words that expresses an action, a condition, or the fact that something exists, while indicating the time of the action, condition, or fact. An **action verb** tells what action someone or something is performing. An action verb is **transitive** if it directs action toward someone or something named in the same sentence.

> *Gather* ye rosebuds while ye may, . . .
> (Herrick, p. 449)

An action verb is **intransitive** if it does not direct action toward something or someone named in the same sentence.

> The thought *served* as a challenge.
> (Woolf, p. 1158)

A **linking verb** expresses the subject's condition by connecting the subject with another word.

> But after some time that order was more necessary, . . . (Defoe, p. 503)

Helping verbs are verbs added to another verb to make a single verb phrase. They indicate the time at which an action takes place or whether it actually happens, could happen, or should happen.

> Nothing but an extreme love of truth *could have* hindered me from concealing this part of my story. (Swift, p. 514)

Adjectives An **adjective** is a word used to describe what is named by a noun or pronoun or to give a noun or pronoun a more specific meaning. Adjectives answer these questions:

> What kind? *purple* hat, *happy* face
> Which one? *this* bowl, *those* cameras
> How many? *three* cars, *several* dishes
> How much? *less* attention, *enough* food

The **articles** *the, a,* and *an* are adjectives. *An* is used before a word beginning with a vowel sound. *This, that, these,* and *those* are used as **demonstrative adjectives** when they appear directly before a noun.

> Perchance he for whom *this* bell tolls may be so ill as *that* he knows not it tolls for him. . . . (Donne, p. 429)

A noun may sometimes be used as an adjective:
> *language* lesson   *chemistry* book

Adverbs An **adverb** is a word that modifies a verb, an adjective, or another adverb. Adverbs answer the questions *where, when, how,* or *to what extent.*

> She will answer *soon.* (modifies verb *will answer*)
> I was *extremely* sad. (modifies adjective *sad*)
> You called *more* often than I. (modifies adverb *often*)

Prepositions A preposition is a word that relates a noun or pronoun that appears with it to another word in the sentence. It can indicate relations of time, place, causality, responsibility, and motivation. Prepositions are almost always followed by nouns or pronouns.

> *around* the fire   *for* us
> *in* sight   *till* sunrise

Conjunctions A conjunction is used to connect other words or groups of words.

Coordinating conjunctions connect similar kinds or groups of words:

> bread *and* wine
> brief *but* powerful

Correlative conjunctions are used in pairs to connect similar words or groups of words:

> *both* Luis *and* Rosa
> *neither* you *nor* I

Subordinating conjunctions indicate the connection between two ideas by placing one below the other in rank or importance:

> The Count your master's known munificence
> Is ample warrant *that* no one just pretense
> Of mine for dowry will be disallowed; . . .
> (Browning, p. 836)

Interjections An **interjection** is a word or phrase that expresses feeling or emotion and functions independently of a sentence.

> *Ah,* love, let us be true
> To one another! . . . (Arnold, p. 884)

Sentences A **sentence** is a group of words with a subject and predicate, expressing a complete thought.

Phrases A **phrase** is a group of words without a subject and verb that functions as one part of speech. A **prepositional phrase** is a group of words that includes a preposition and a noun or pronoun.

> *before* dawn   *as a result of* the rain

An **adjective phrase** is a prepositional phrase that modifies a noun or pronoun.

> The space of sky above us was the color *of ever-changing violet.* . . . (Joyce, p. 1147)

An **adverb phrase** is a prepositional phrase that modifies a verb, an adjective, or an adverb.

> Arsat came through the doorway *with noiseless steps.* . . . (Conrad, p. 1134)

An **appositive phrase** is a noun or pronoun with modifiers, placed next to a noun or pronoun to add information and details.

> How soon hath Time, *the subtle thief of youth,*
> Stolen on his wing my three and twentieth year!
> (Milton, p. 464)

A **participial phrase** is a participle that is modified by an adjective or adverb phrase or that has a complement (a group of words that completes the participle's meaning). The entire phrase acts as an adjective.

> The boy gazed at his uncle from those big, hot, blue eyes, *set rather close together.*
> (Lawrence, p. 1176)

A **gerund** is a noun formed from the present participle of a verb (ending in *-ing*). A **gerund phrase** is a gerund with modifiers or a complement (words that complete its meaning), all acting together as a noun.

> Neither can we call this *a begging of misery* or *a borrowing of misery* . . . (Donne, p. 428)

An **infinitive phrase** is an infinitive with modifiers, complements (words completing its meaning), or a subject, all acting together as a single part of speech.

> . . . let baser things devise *To die in dust* . . .
> (Spenser, p. 238)

Clauses A **clause** is a group of words with its own subject and verb. An **independent clause** can stand by itself as a complete sentence. A **subordinate clause** cannot stand by itself as a complete sentence.

> Mr. Thomas Davies the actor, *who then kept a bookseller's shop in Russell Street, Covent Garden,* told me that Johnson was very much his friend. . . . (Boswell, p. 554)

An **adjective clause** is a subordinate clause that modifies a noun or pronoun by telling *what kind* or *which one.*

> . . . coffins were not to be had for the prodigious numbers *that fell in such a calamity as this.*
> (Defoe, p. 503)

Subordinate adverb clauses modify verbs, adjectives, adverbs, or verbals by telling *where, when, in what way, to what extent, under what condition,* or *why.*

> *As soon as I saw the dead man* I sent an orderly to a friend's house nearby. . . . (Orwell, p. 1018)

Subordinate noun clauses act as nouns.

> To confirm *what I have now said, . . .* I shall here insert a passage which will hardly obtain belief.
> (Swift, p. 514)

Summary of Capitalization and Punctuation

Capitalization

Capitalize the first word in sentences, interjections, and complete questions. Also, capitalize the first word in a quotation if the quotation is a complete sentence.

> I asked, "What do you want?" (Naipaul, p. 1238)

Capitalize all proper nouns and adjectives.

> Trinidadian   Thames River

Capitalize titles showing family relationships when they refer to a specific person unless they are preceded by a possessive noun or pronoun.

> Uncle Oscar   Mangan's sister

Capitalize the first word and all other key words in the titles of books, periodicals, poems, stories, plays, songs, and other works of art.

> *Frankenstein*   "Shooting an Elephant"

Punctuation

End Marks Use a **period** to end a declarative sentence, an imperative sentence, an indirect question, and most abbreviations.

> This tale is true, and mine. ("The Seafarer," p. 16)
>
> Let me not to the marriage of true minds
> Admit impediments. (Shakespeare, p. 255)
>
> At last she spoke to me. (Joyce, p. 1147)
>
> Mrs. Drover (Bowen, p. 1032)

Use a **question mark** to end an interrogative sentence.

> Sent he to Macduff? (Shakespeare, p. 300)

Use an **exclamation mark** after an exclamatory sentence, a forceful imperative sentence, or an interjection expressing strong emotion.

> "Hold off! unhand me, graybeard loon!"
> (Coleridge, p. 686)

Commas Use a **comma** before the conjunction to separate two independent clauses in a compound sentence.

> My heart aches, and a drowsy numbness pains
> My sense, . . . (Keats, p. 750)

Use commas to separate three or more words, phrases, or clauses in a series.

> Daffodil came in first, Lancelot second, Mirza third. (Lawrence, p. 1176)

Use commas to separate adjectives unless they must stay in a specific order.

> His *big, soft* eyes stared. . . . (Conrad, p. 1134)
>
> And *each slow* dusk a drawing-down of blinds.
> (Owen, p. 1053)

Use a comma after an introductory word, phrase, or clause.

> *When I nodded*, he laughed in a crooked way.
> (Naipaul, p. 1238)

Use commas to set off nonessential expressions.

> "Only you'd have to promise, *honor bright, uncle*, not to let it go beyond us three."
> (Lawrence, p. 1176)

Use commas with places, dates, and titles.

> Coventry, England
>
> September 1, 1939
>
> Reginald Farrars, M. P.

Use commas after items in addresses, after the salutation in a personal letter, after the closing in all letters, and in numbers of more than three digits.

> Hull Crescent, Dorchester
>
> Dear Randolph,
>
> Yours faithfully,
>
> 9,744

Use a comma to indicate words left out of parallel clauses, to set off a direct quotation, and to prevent a sentence from being misunderstood.

> In Tennyson's poetry, I admire the music; in Browning's, the sentiments.
>
> "Well—I suppose," she said slowly and bitterly, "it's because your father has no luck."
> (Lawrence, p. 1176)

Semicolons Use a **semicolon** to join independent clauses that are not already joined by a conjunction.

> The tone of her voice was not encouraging; she seemed to have spoken to me out of a sense of duty. (Joyce, p. 1147)

Use semicolons to avoid confusion when independent clauses or items in a series already contain commas.

> The Emperor concluded me to be drowned, and that the enemy's fleet was approaching in a hostile manner; but he was soon eased of his fears; for,

the channel growing shallower every step I made, I came in a short time within hearing, . . . (Swift, p. 514)

Colons Use a **colon** before a list of items following an independent clause.

Notable Victorian poets include the following: Tennyson, Browning, Arnold, Housman, and Hopkins.

Use a colon to introduce a formal or lengthy quotation.

And on the pedestal these words appear: "My name is Ozymandias, king of kings: . . ." (Shelley, p. 732)

Use a colon to introduce an independent clause that summarizes or explains the sentence before it.

The third day of the illness was critical: they were waiting for a change. (Lawrence, p. 1176)

Quotation Marks A **direct quotation** represents a person's exact speech or thoughts and is enclosed within quotation marks.

"If I go," I said, "I will bring you something." (Joyce, p. 1147)

An **indirect quotation** reports only the general meaning of what a person said or thought and does not require quotation marks.

Mother said he never considered me. (Bowen, p. 1032)

Always place a comma or a period inside the final quotation mark.

"We will each write a ghost story," said Lord Byron. . . . (Shelley, p. 650)

Always place a question mark or an exclamation mark inside the final quotation mark if the end mark is part of the quotation; if it is not part of the quotation, place it outside the final quotation mark.

The man said to me, "Sonny, may I come inside your yard?" (Naipaul, p. 1238)

Use single quotation marks for a quotation within a quotation.

"Lying all day on his pillows, . . . and then he says he does not want to live 'like this,'" Rakesh was heard to say. . . . (Desai, p. 1272)

Italicize the titles of long written works, movies, television and radio shows, lengthy works of music, paintings, and sculpture. Also, italicize foreign words not yet accepted into English and words you wish to stress.

If you are writing by hand or working in some other format that does not allow you to italicize text, underline such titles and words.

Howards End	60 Minutes
Guernica	déjà vu

Use quotation marks around the titles of short written works, episodes in a series, songs, and titles of works mentioned as parts of collections.

"The Lagoon"   "Boswell Meets Johnson"

Parentheses Use **parentheses** to set off asides and explanations only when the material is not essential or when it consists of one or more sentences.

My eyes were often full of tears (I could not tell why) and at times a flood from my heart seemed to pour itself out into my bosom. (Joyce, p. 1147)

Hyphens Use a **hyphen** with certain numbers, after certain prefixes, with two or more words used as one word, with a compound modifier, and within a word when a combination of letters might otherwise be confusing.

twenty-nine	re-create
pre-Romantic	brother-in-law

Apostrophe Add an **apostrophe** and an *s* to show the possessive case of most singular nouns and of plural nouns that do not end in -*s* or -*es*.

Blake's poems   the mice's whiskers

Add an apostrophe to show the possessive case of plural nouns ending in -*s* and -*es*.

the girls' songs   the Ortizes' car

Use an apostrophe in a contraction to indicate the position of the missing letter or letters.

His English was so good, it *didn't* seem natural. . . . (Naipaul, p. 1238)

Use an apostrophe and an -*s* to write the plurals of numbers, symbols, letters, and words used to name themselves.

5's and 20's   no *if's* or *but's*
five *a's*

Glossary of Common Usage

among, between

Among is generally used with three or more items. *Between* is generally used with only two items.

> *Among* Chaucer's characters, my favorite has always been the Wife of Bath.

> The ballad "Get Up and Bar the Door" consists largely of a dialogue *between* a man and his wife.

amount, number

Amount refers to quantity or a unit, whereas *number* refers to individual items that can be counted. *Amount* generally appears with a singular noun, and *number* appears with a plural noun.

> The *amount* of attention that great writers have paid to the Faust legend is remarkable.

> A considerable *number* of important English writers have been fascinated by the legend of King Arthur.

as, because, like, as to

To avoid confusion, use *because* rather than *as* when you want to indicate cause and effect.

> *Because* the narrator of Joyce's "Araby" is infatuated with Mangan's sister, he cannot see that he is driven by vanity.

Do not use the preposition *like* to introduce a clause that requires the conjunction *as*.

> *As* we might expect in a story by Joseph Conrad, there are two narrators in "The Lagoon."

The use of *as to* for *about* is awkward and should be avoided.

bad, badly

Use the predicate adjective *bad* after linking verbs such as *feel, look,* and *seem*. Use *badly* when an adverb is required.

> In "My Last Duchess," the Duke of Ferrara does not seem to feel *bad* about the death of his wife.

> The announcement of Lady Macbeth's death *badly* unnerves Macbeth.

because of, due to

Use *due to* if it can logically replace the phrase *caused by*. In introductory phrases, however, *because of* is better usage than *due to*.

> The classical allusions in *Paradise Lost* may be *due to* the poet's ambition to imitate the epics of Homer and Virgil.

> *Because of* the expansion of the reading public, eighteenth-century writers became less dependent on wealthy patrons.

compare, contrast

The verb *compare* can involve both similarities and differences. The verb *contrast* always involves differences. Use *to* or *with* after compare. Use *with* after contrast.

> Denise's report compared Shelley's style in "To a Skylark" *with* that of Keats in "Ode to a Nightingale."

> In Conrad's "The Lagoon," Arsat's point of view in the narration of his "story within a story" contrasts *with* the more detached third-person point of view that the author uses for the rest of the tale.

continual, continuous

Continual means "occurring again and again in succession," while *continuous* means "occurring without interruption."

> In "The Seafarer," the speaker describes *continual* hailstorms at sea.

> The white-hot fervor of "Ode to the West Wind" suggests that Shelley wrote the poem in a single *continuous* burst of inspiration.

different from, different than

The preferred usage is *different from*.

> In its simple, precise language, Housman's style is *different from* that of many other Victorian poets, including Tennyson and Hopkins.

farther, further

Use *farther* when you refer to distance. Use *further* when you mean "to a greater degree" or "additional."

> Although the sexton tries to persuade him to go no *farther,* Defoe is determined to enter the churchyard.

Boswell *further* illustrates Johnson's conversation by quoting his opinions of Sheridan and Derrick.

fewer, less

Use *fewer* for things that can be counted. Use *less* for amounts or quantities that cannot be counted.

> Wordsworth uses *fewer* end-stopped lines than Pope does.

> At the beginning of Luke's parable, the prodigal son shows *less* respect for the father than the older son does.

just, only

Only should appear directly before the word it modifies. *Just,* used as an adverb meaning "no more than," also belongs directly before the word it modifies.

> The form of the villanelle allows a poet to use *just* two rhymes.

> John Keats was *only* twenty-four when he wrote some of his greatest poems.

lay, lie

Lay is a transitive verb meaning "to set or put something down." Its principal parts are *lay, laying, laid, laid. Lie* is an intransitive verb meaning "to recline." Its principal parts are *lie, lying, lay, lain.*

> Coleridge implies that the mariner's reckless act of killing the albatross *lays* a curse on the crew.

> As Paul *lies* dead at the end of D. H. Lawrence's story, his Uncle Oscar sadly comments that the boy may be better off.

plurals that do not end in -s

The plurals of certain nouns from Greek and Latin are formed as they were in their original language. Words such as *data, criteria, media,* and *phenomena* are plural and should be treated as such. Each has its own distinctive singular form: *datum, criterion, medium, phenomenon.*

> Are the electronic *media* of the twentieth century contributing to the death of literature?

raise, rise

Raise is a transitive verb that usually takes a direct object. *Rise* is intransitive and never takes a direct object.

> In "Musée des Beaux Arts," W. H. Auden *raises* the question of our insensitivity to suffering.

In Tennyson's poem, when Lancelot passes, the Lady of Shallot *rises* from her loom and paces.

that, which, who

Use the relative pronoun *that* to refer to things. Use *which* only for things and *who* only for people. Use *that* when introducing a subordinate clause that singles out a particular thing or person.

> The contemporary poems *that* I most enjoy reading are James Berry's.

Which is usually used to introduce a subordinate clause that is not essential to identifying the thing or person in question:

> "Fern Hill," *which* reflects Dylan Thomas's brilliant ability to evoke emotional response, plays on the connotations of words.

Who can be used to introduce either essential or non-essential subordinate clauses:

> Two writers *who* helped redefine the essay are Addison and Steele. (essential)

> Addison and Steele, *who* were close friends for most of their lives, had very different personalities and careers. (nonessential)

when, where

Do not directly follow a linking verb with *when* or *where.* Also, be careful not to use *where* when your context requires *that.*

> Evaluation is ~~when you make~~ *the process of making* a judgment about the quality or value of something.

> Sandy read ~~where~~ *that* after the Brownings eloped to Italy, they spent most of their married life in Florence.

who, whom

Remember to use *who* only as a subject in clauses and sentences and *whom* only as an object.

> V. S. Naipaul, *who* wrote "B. Wordsworth," has also written some well-received novels.

> V. S. Naipaul, *whom* many critics have praised as one of the best contemporary writers in English, was born and raised in Trinidad.

Introduction to the Internet

The Internet is a series of networks that are interconnected all over the world. The Internet allows users to have almost unlimited access to information stored on the networks. Dr. Berners-Lee, a physicist, created the Internet in the 1980s by writing a small computer program that allowed pages to be linked together using key words. The Internet was mostly text-based until 1992, when a computer program called the NCSA Mosaic (National Center for Supercomputing Applications) was created at the University of Illinois. This program was the first Web browser. The development of Web browsers greatly eased the ability of the user to navigate through all the pages stored on the Web. Very soon, the appearance of the Web was altered as well. More appealing visuals were added, and sound, too, was implemented. This change made the Web more user-friendly and more appealing to the general public.

Using the Internet for Research

Key Word Search

Before you begin a search, you should identify your specific topic. To make searching easier, narrow your subject to a key word or a group of key words. These are your search terms, and they should be as specific as possible. For example, if you are looking for the latest concert dates for your favorite musical group, you might use the band's name as a key word. However, if you were to enter the name of the group in the query box of the search engine, you might be presented with thousands of links to information about the group that is unrelated to what you want to know. You might locate such information as band member biographies, the group's history, fan reviews of concerts, and hundreds of sites with related names containing information that is irrelevant to your search. Because you used such a broad key word, you might need to navigate through all that information before you could find a link or subheading for concert dates. In contrast, if you were to type in "Duplex Arena and [band name]," you would have a better chance of locating pages that contain this information.

How to Narrow Your Search

If you have a large group of key words and still do not know which ones to use, write out a list of all the words you are considering. Once you have completed the list, scrutinize it. Then, delete the words that are least important to your search, and highlight those that are most important.

These **key search connectors** can help you fine-tune your search:

AND: Narrows a search by retrieving documents that include both terms. For example: *baseball* AND *playoffs*

OR: Broadens a search by retrieving documents including any of the terms. For example: *playoffs* OR *championships*

NOT: Narrows a search by excluding documents containing certain words. For example: *baseball* NOT *history of*

Tips for an Effective Search

1. Remember that search engines can be case-sensitive. If your first attempt at searching fails, check your search terms for misspellings and try again.

2. If you are entering a group of key words, present them in order from the most important to the least important key word.

3. Avoid opening the link to every single page in your results list. Search engines present pages in descending order of relevancy. The most useful pages will be located at the top of the list. However, read the description of each link before you open the page.

4. Some search engines provide helpful tips for specializing your search. Take the opportunity to learn more about effective searching.

Other Ways to Search

Using Online Reference Sites How you search should be tailored to what you are hoping to find. If you are looking for data and facts, use reference sites before you jump onto a simple search engine. For example, you can find reference sites to provide definitions of words, statistics about almost any subject, biographies, maps, and concise information on many topics. Here are some useful online reference sites:

Online libraries

Online periodicals

Almanacs

Encyclopedias

You can find these sources using subject searches.

Conducting Subject Searches As you prepare to go online, consider your subject and the best way to find information to suit your needs. If you are looking for general information on a topic and you want your search results to be extensive, consider the subject search indexes on most search engines. These indexes, in the form of category and subject lists, often appear on the first page of a search engine. When you click on a specific highlighted word, you will be presented with a new screen containing subcategories of the topic you chose.

Evaluating the Reliability of Internet Resources

Just as you would evaluate the quality, bias, and validity of any other research material you locate, check the source of information you find online. Compare these two sites containing information about the poet and writer Langston Hughes:

Site A is a personal Web site constructed by a college student. It contains no bibliographic information or links to sites that he used. Included on the site are several poems by Langston Hughes and a student essay about the poet's use of symbolism. It has not been updated in more than six months.

Site B is a Web site constructed and maintained by the English Department of a major university. Information on Hughes is presented in a scholarly format, with a bibliography and credits for the writer. The site includes links to other sites and indicates new features that are added weekly.

For your own research, consider the information you find on Site B to be more reliable and accurate than that on Site A. Because it is maintained by experts in their field who are held accountable for their work, the university site will be a better research tool than the student-generated one.

Tips for Evaluating Internet Sources

1. Consider who constructed and who now maintains the Web page. Determine whether this author is a reputable source. Often, the URL endings indicate a source.
   - Sites ending in *.edu* are maintained by educational institutions.
   - Sites ending in *.gov* are maintained by government agencies (federal, state, or local).
   - Sites ending in *.org* are normally maintained by non-profit organizations and agencies.
   - Sites ending in *.com* are commercially or personally maintained.
2. Skim the official and trademarked Web pages first. It is safe to assume that the information you draw from Web pages of reputable institutions, online encyclopedias, online versions of major daily newspapers, or government-owned sites produce information as reliable as the material you would find in print. In contrast, unbranded sites or those generated by individuals tend to borrow information from other sources without providing documentation. As information travels from one source to another, it could have been muddled, misinterpreted, edited, or revised.
3. You can still find valuable information in the less "official" sites. Check for the writer's credentials, and then consider these factors:
   - Do not be misled by official-looking graphics or presentations.
   - Make sure that the information is updated enough to suit your needs. Many Web pages will indicate how recently they have been updated.
   - If the information is borrowed, notice whether you can trace it back to its original source.

Respecting Copyrighted Material

Because the Internet is a relatively new and quickly growing medium, issues of copyright and ownership arise almost daily. As laws begin to govern the use and reuse of material posted online, they may change the way that people can access or reprint material.

Text, photographs, music, and fine art printed online may not be reproduced without acknowledged permission of the copyright owner.

Writing Criticism

Literary criticism involves studying, analyzing, interpreting, and evaluating works of literature. It can be as brief as an answer to a question or as lengthy as an essay or a book. Following are examples of three types of criticism.

Three Types of Criticism

Analysis You are frequently asked to analyze, or break down into parts and examine, a passage or a work. Often you must support your analysis with specific references to the text. In this brief analysis, the writer uses words from the question to write a topic sentence and embeds quotations from the text as support.

> **Question** In "Heat" by H. D., how does the speaker create the impression that heat is almost a solid substance?
>
> **Answer** The speaker in "Heat" uses repetition and imagery to convey the impression that heat is almost a solid substance. By repeating the word *heat* in each of the three stanzas, the speaker emphasizes its physical presence. Further, the speaker uses images that appeal to the sense of touch in describing heat as if it were a substance. In the first stanza, the speaker asks the wind to "cut apart the heat," and in the third stanza, to "plow through it."

Biographical Criticism Critics who take a biographical approach use information about a writer's life to explain his or her work. In this passage of biographical criticism, Kenneth Silverman explains Edgar Allan Poe's preoccupation with death as Poe's response to the early death of his mother, Eliza.

> Much of his later writing, despite its variety of forms and styles, places and characters, is driven by the question of whether the dead remain dead. . . . The most persuasive and coherent explanation, . . . comes from the modern understanding of childhood bereavement. . . . [C]hildren who lose a parent at an early age, as Edgar lost Eliza Poe, . . . invest more feeling in and magnify the parent's image. . . . The young child . . . cannot comprehend the finality of death. . . .

Historical Criticism Using this approach, a critic explains how an author's work responds to the events, circumstances, or ideas of the author's historical era. In the following passage of historical criticism, Jean H. Hagstrum shows how William Blake's character Urizen symbolizes the Enlightenment ideas of Newton, Locke, and Bacon that Blake detested.

> Urizen is also an active force. Dividing, partitioning, dropping the plummet line, applying Newton's compasses to the world, he creates abstract mathematical forms. Like Locke, he shrinks the senses, narrows the perceptions, binds man to natural fact. Like Bacon, he creates the laws of prudence and crucifies passion.

Using Ideas From Research

Below are three common methods of incorporating the ideas of other writers into your work. Choose the most appropriate style by analyzing your needs in each case. In all cases, you must credit your source.

- **Direct Quotation:** Use quotation marks to indicate the exact words.

- **Paraphrase:** To share ideas without a direct quotation, state the ideas in your own words.

- **Summary:** To provide information about a large body of work, identify the writer's main idea.

Avoiding Plagiarism

Whether you are presenting a formal research paper or an opinion paper on a current event, be careful to give credit for any ideas or opinions that are not your own. Presenting someone else's ideas, research, or opinion as your own—even if you have rephrased it in different words—is plagiarism, the equivalent of academic stealing, or fraud.

You can avoid plagiarism by synthesizing what you learn: Read from several sources, and let the ideas of experts help you draw your own conclusions and form your own opinions. When you choose to use someone else's ideas or work to support your view, credit the source of the material.

Preparing a Manuscript

The presentation of your written work is important. Your work should be neat, clean, and easy to read. Follow your teacher's directions for placing your name and class, along with the title and date of your work, on the paper.

Research Papers

Most formal research papers have these features:

- Title Page
- Table of Contents or Outline
- Works-Cited List or Bibliography

Citing Sources

In research writing, cite your sources. In the body of your paper, provide a footnote, an endnote, or an internal citation, identifying the sources of facts, opinions, or quotations. At the end of your paper, provide a bibliography or a works-cited list, a list of all the sources you cite. Follow an established format, such as Modern Library Association (MLA) Style.

Works-Cited List (MLA Style)

A works-cited list must contain accurate information sufficient to enable a reader to locate each source you cite. The basic components of an entry are as follows:

- Name of the author, editor, translator, or group responsible for the work
- Title
- Place and date of publication
- Publisher

For print materials, the information required for a citation generally appears on the copyright and title pages of a work. For the format of works-cited list entries, consult the examples at right and in the chart on page R31.

Internal Citations (MLA Style)

An internal citation briefly identifies the source from which you have taken a specific quotation, factual claim, or opinion. It refers the reader to one of the entries on your works-cited list. An internal citation has the following features:

- It appears in parentheses.
- It identifies the source by the last name of the author, editor, or translator.
- It gives a page reference, identifying the page of the source on which the information cited can be found.

Punctuation An internal citation generally falls outside a closing quotation mark but within the final punctuation of a clause or sentence. For a long quotation set off from the rest of your text, place the citation at the end of the excerpt without any punctuation following.

Special Cases

- If the author is an organization, use the organization's name, in a shortened version if necessary.
- If you cite more than one work by the same author, add the title or a shortened version of the title.

Sample Works-Cited Lists

Carwardine, Mark, Erich Hoyt, R. Ewan Fordyce, and Peter Gill. *The Nature Company Guides: Whales, Dolphins, and Porpoises.* New York: Time-Life Books, 1998.
Whales in Danger. "Discovering Whales." 18 Oct. 1999. <http://whales.magna.com.au/DISCOVER>

Neruda, Pablo. "Ode to Spring." *Odes to Opposites.* Trans. Ken Krabbenhoft. Ed. and illus. Ferris Cook. Boston: Little, Brown and Company, 1995.
The Saga of the Volsungs. Trans. Jesse L. Byock. London: Penguin Books, 1990.

An anonymous work is listed by title.

Both the title of the work and of the collection in which it is found are listed.

Sample Internal Citations

It makes sense that baleen whales such as the blue whale, the bowhead whale, the humpback whale, and the sei whale (to name just a few) grow to immense sizes (Carwardine, Hoyt, and Fordyce 19–21). The blue whale has grooves running from under its chin to partway along the length of its underbelly. As in some other whales, these grooves expand and allow even more food and water to be taken in (Ellis 18–21).

Author's last name

Page numbers where information can be found

MLA Style for Listing Sources

Book with one author	Pyles, Thomas. *The Origins and Development of the English Language.* 2nd ed. New York: Harcourt Brace Jovanovich, Inc., 1971.
Book with two or three authors	McCrum, Robert, William Cran, and Robert MacNeil. *The Story of English.* New York: Penguin Books, 1987.
Book with an editor	Truth, Sojourner. *Narrative of Sojourner Truth.* Ed. Margaret Washington. New York: Vintage Books, 1993.
Book with more than three authors or editors	Donald, Robert B., et al. *Writing Clear Essays.* Upper Saddle River, NJ: Prentice-Hall, Inc., 1996.
Single work from an anthology	Hawthorne, Nathaniel. "Young Goodman Brown." *Literature: An Introduction to Reading and Writing.* Ed. Edgar V. Roberts and Henry E. Jacobs. Upper Saddle River, NJ: Prentice-Hall, Inc., 1998. 376–385. [Indicate pages for the entire selection.]
Introduction in a published edition	Washington, Margaret. Introduction. *Narrative of Sojourner Truth.* By Sojourner Truth. New York: Vintage Books, 1993, pp. v–xi.
Signed article in a weekly magazine	Wallace, Charles. "A Vodacious Deal." *Time,* 14 Feb. 2000: 63.
Signed article in a monthly magazine	Gustaitis, Joseph. "The Sticky History of Chewing Gum." *American History,* Oct. 1998: 30–38.
Unsigned editorial or story	"Selective Silence." Editorial. *Wall Street Journal,* 11 Feb. 2000: A14. [If the editorial or story is signed, begin with the author's name.]
Signed pamphlet	[Treat the pamphlet as though it were a book.]
Pamphlet with no author, publisher, or date	*Are You at Risk of Heart Attack?* n.p. n.d. [n.p. n.d. indicates that there is no known publisher or date]
Filmstrips, slide programs, and videotape	*The Diary of Anne Frank.* Dir. George Stevens. Perf. Millie Perkins, Shelley Winters, Joseph Schildkraut, Lou Jacobi, and Richard Beymer. Twentieth Century Fox, 1959.
Radio or television program transcript	"The First Immortal Generation." *Ockham's Razor.* Host Robyn Williams. Guest Damien Broderick. National Public Radio. 23 May 1999. Transcript.
Internet	*National Association of Chewing Gum Manufacturers.* 19 Dec. 1999 <http://www.nacgm.org/consumer/funfacts.html> [Indicate the date you accessed the information. Content and addresses at Web sites change frequently.]
Newspaper	Thurow, Roger. "South Africans Who Fought for Sanctions Now Scrap for Investors." *Wall Street Journal,* 11 Feb. 2000: A1+ [For a multipage article, write only the first page number on which it appears, followed by a plus sign.]
Personal interview	Smith, Jane. Personal interview. 10 Feb. 2000.
CD (with multiple publishers)	Simms, James, ed. *Romeo and Juliet.* By William Shakespeare. CD-ROM. Oxford: Attica Cybernetics Ltd.; London: BBC Education; London: HarperCollins Publishers, 1995.
Signed article from an encyclopedia	Askeland, Donald R. (1991). "Welding." *World Book Encyclopedia.* 1991 ed.

Index of Authors and Titles

Page numbers in *italics* refer to biographical information.

Index of Skills

Literary Analysis

Reading Strategies

Grammar and Style

Vocabulary

Critical Thinking and Viewing

Writing Applications

Index of Features

Curtis Brown Ltd., London "Be Ye Men of Valor" (retitled Wartime Speech), BBC London, May 19, 1940, from *Blood, Toil, Tears and Sweat: The Speeches of Winston Churchill* edited and with and introduction by David Cannadine. Speeches Copyright © 1989 by Winston Churchill MP. All rights reserved.

Harlan Davidson Inc./Forum Press Inc. Excerpt from "Book I" of *Utopia* by Thomas More, edited and translated by H. V. S. Ogden, pp. 21, 22 (Crofts Classics Series). Copyright © 1949 by Harlan Davidson, Inc.

Doubleday, a division of Random House, Inc. "Haiku" from *An Introduction to Haiku* by Harold G. Henderson, copyright © 1958 by Harold G. Henderson. Used by permission of Doubleday, a division of Random House, Inc.

Estate of Ann Stanford c/o Rosanna Norton "The Wife's Lament" by Ann Stanford from *The Women Poets in English: An Anthology.* Copyright © 1972 by Ann Stanford. Used by permission.

Faber and Faber Limited "The Chimney Sweeper" from *The Poetical Works of William Blake,* edited by John Sampson. Excerpt from Introduction from *The North Ship* by Philip Larkin. Copyright © 1966 by Philip Larkin. "The Rain Horse" by Ted Hughes from *Wodwo.* Copyright © 1967. From *Station Island* by Seamus Heaney. Copyright © Seamus Heaney, 1984. First published in 1984 by Faber and Faber Limited. "The Horses" from *The Hawk in the Rain* by Ted Hughes. Copyright © 1957, 1960 by Ted Hughes. Published in the UK in *The Hawk in the Rain* by Ted Hughes.

Farrar, Straus & Giroux, Inc. "Follower" from *Poems 1965–1975* by Seamus Heaney. Copyright © 1980 by Seamus Heaney. *Midsummer, XXIII,* from *Collected Poems 1948–1984* by Derek Walcott. Copyright © 1986 by Derek Walcott. From Chapter XXVIII of *Omeros* by Derek Walcott. Copyright © 1990 by Derek Walcott. "An Arundel Tomb" by Philip Larkin from *Collected Poems.* Copyright © 1988, 1989 by the Estate of Philip Larkin. "Two Lorries" from *The Spirit Level* by Seamus Heaney. Copyright © 1996 by Seamus Heaney. "The Prologue" from *Gilgamesh: A New Rendering in English Verse* by David Ferry. Copyright © 1992 by David Ferry. "The Explosion" from *Collected Poems* by Philip Larkin. Copyright © 1988, 1989 by the Estate of Philip Larkin.

Forum for Peace and Reconcilliation, c/o Mr. Walter Kirwan "Opening Address for The Forum for Peace and Reconciliation," by Judge Catherine McGuinness, from www.Irlgov.ie/iveagh/anglorish/forum/inaug.html.

Harcourt, Inc. "L'Invitation au Voyage" by Charles Baudelaire, translated by Richard Wilbur from *Things of This World,* copyright © 1956 and renewed 1984 by Richard Wilbur. Excerpt from William Wordsworth and Samuel Coleridge by George Meyer from *Major British Writers: Enlarged Edition, II,* edited by G. B. Harrison, Charles W. Dunn, et al. Copyright, 1954, © 1959, by Harcourt, Inc. All rights reserved. "Three excerpts from George Gordon, Lord Byron" by Northrop Frye from *Major British Writers: Enlarged Edition, II,* edited by G.B. Harrison, Charles W. Dunn, et al. Copyright, 1954, © 1959, by Harcourt, Inc. All rights reserved.

Harcourt, Inc., the Executors of the Virginia Woolf Estate, and The Society of Authors "The Lady in the Looking Glass: A Reflection" from *A Haunted House and Other Short Stories* by Virginia Woolf, copyright 1944 and renewed 1972 by Harcourt, Inc. Reprinted by permission of Harcourt, Inc.

Harcourt, Inc., and Faber and Faber Ltd. "The Hollow Men," "Preludes" and "Journey of the Magi" from *Collected Poems 1909–1962* by T. S. Eliot, copyright 1936 by Harcourt, Inc., copyright © 1964, 1963 by T. S. Eliot. Reprinted by permission.

Harcourt, Inc., and A. M. Heath & Co. Ltd. "Shooting an Elephant" from *Shooting an Elephant and Other Essays* by George Orwell, copyright © by George Orwell, 1936, by permission of Mark Hamilton as the Literary Executor of the Estate of the Late Sonia Brownell Orwell and Martin Secker and Warburg Ltd.

HarperCollins Publishers, Inc., and William Heinemann Ltd. "A Devoted Son" from *Games at Twilight and Other Stories* by Anita Desai. Copyright © 1978 by Anita Desai. Reprinted by permission of HarperCollins Publishers, Inc.

HarperCollins Publishers Ltd., U.K. "The Rights We Enjoy, the Duties We Owe" reprinted by permission of Fourth Estate, Ltd., from *New Britain: My Vision of a Young Country* by Tony Blair © 1996 by The Office of Tony Blair. Used by permission.

David Higham Associates Limited "On the Patio" from *Poems 1954–1987* by Peter Redgrove. Copyright © Peter Redgrove, 1959, 1961, 1963,1966, 1972, 1973, 1975, 1977, 1979, 1981, 1985, 1986, 1987. All rights reserved.

Henry Holt and Company, Inc., and The Society of Authors "When I Was One-and-Twenty" from *The Collected Poems of A. E. Housman* by A. E. Housman. Copyright 1939, 1940, © 1965 by Henry Holt and Company, Inc., © 1967 by Robert E. Symons. Used by permission of Henry Holt and Company, Inc.

International Publishers Co. Excerpt from "English Poets" from *Illusion and Reality* by Christopher Caudwell. Copyright © 1937, by Executor of the Estate of Christopher Caudwell. All rights reserved.

John Johnson Ltd. "Eve's Apology" from *The Poems of Shakespeare's Dark Lady: Salve Deus Judaeorum* by Emilia Lanier, introduced by A. L. Rowse. Reprinted by permission of John Johnson Ltd. for Dr. A. L. Rowse.

Alfred A. Knopf, Inc., a division of Random House, Inc. "The Demon Lover" from *The Collected Stories of Elizabeth Bowen* by Elizabeth Bowen, copyright © 1981 by Curtis Brown Ltd., Literary Executors of the Estate of Elizabeth Bowen. Used by permission of Alfred A. Knopf, a division of Random House, Inc.

Hal Leonard Publishing Corporation "New Beginning," words and music by Tracy Chapman. © 1996 EMI April Music Inc. and Purple Rabbit Music. All rights controlled and administered by EMI April Music Inc. All rights reserved. International copyright secured. Used by permission.

L. R. Lind From *Ovid: Tristia* translated by L. R. Lind. Published by The University of Georgia Press. All rights reserved. Copyright © 1975 by L. R. Lind.

Little, Brown and Company From "A World Lit Only By Fire'" by William Manchester from *The House of the Spirits.* © 1985 by Alfred A. Knopf, Inc.

Dr. Peter F. Morgan "Early Reviews of Wordsworth" from *Jeffreys' Criticism* by Francis Jeffrey, edited by Peter F. Morgan. Copyright © 1983 Peter F. Morgan. Used by permission.

The National Gallery, London "The Gallery's Role and Objectives" by The National Gallery Department Office. From *The Gallery's Roles and Objectives.*

New American Library, a division of Penguin Putnam, Inc. From *Beowulf* by Burton Raffel, translator. Translation copyright © 1963 by Burton Raffel. Afterword © 1963 by New American Library. Used by permission.

New Beacon Books Ltd. From "Lucy: Englan' Lady" from *Lucy's Letters and Loving* by James Berry. © 1982 by James Berry.

New Directions Publishing Co. "Not Waving but Drowning" from Stevie Smith, from *The Collected Poems of Stevie Smith.* Copyright © 1972 by Stevie Smith. "Far Corners of the Earth" by Tu Fu, translated by David Hinton, from *The Selected Poems of Tu Fu.* Copyright ©1989 by David Hinton. "Anthem for Doomed Youth" by Wilfred Owen, from *The Collected Poems of Wilfred Owen,* edited by C. Day Lewis. Copyright © Chatto & Windus Ltd. 1946, 1963.

New Directions Publishing Corporation, and David Higham Associates Ltd. "Do Not Go Gentle Into That Good Night" by Dylan Thomas, from *The Poems of Dylan Thomas.* Copyright © 1952 by The Trustees for the Copyrights of Dylan Thomas. "Fern Hill" by Dylan Thomas, from *The Poems of Dylan Thomas.* Copyright © 1945 by The Trustees for the Copyrights of Dylan Thomas. Reprinted by permission of New Directions Publishing Corporation, and David Higham Associates Ltd.

Newmarket Press From *The Sense and Sensibility Screenplay & Diaries* by Emma Thompson, published by Newmarket Press. Copyright © 1995 Columbia Pictures Industries, Inc. All rights reserved. Reprinted by permission of Newmarket Press, 18 East 48th Street, New York, NY 10017.

News International Syndication Articles "Death of a King" and "The New Queen" reprinted from Times Newspapers Limited, 7 February 1952. Copyright © Times Newspapers Limited, 1952.

North Point Press, a division of Farrar, Straus & Giroux, Inc. "Testament" by Bei Dao from *A Splintered Mirror: Chinese Poetry From the Democracy Movement* translated by Donald Finkel. Translation copyright © 1991 by Donald Finkel. Reprinted by permission of North Point Press, a division of Farrar, Straus & Giroux, Inc.

W. W. Norton & Company, Inc. From *Beowulf: A New Verse Translation* by Seamus Heaney. Copyright © 2000 by Seamus Heaney. "Outside History" from *Outside History: Selected Poems, 1980–1990* by Eavan Boland. Copyright © 1990 by Eavan Boland. From *Sir Gawain and the Green Knight: A New Verse Translation* by Marie Borroff, translator. Copyright © 1967 by W. W. Norton & Company, Inc. All rights reserved. Used by permission of W. W. Norton & Company, Inc.

Oxford University Press, London "God's Grandeur," "Pied Beauty," and "Spring and Fall" from *Poems of Gerard Manley Hopkins,* 4th edition, edited by W. H. Gardner and N. H. MacKenzie. "The Lamb," "The Chimney Sweeper," and "Infant Sorrow" from *The Poetical Works of William Blake* edited by John Sampson. Sonnet 43 from *The Poetical Works of Elizabeth Barrett Browning,* Oxford Edition. "To Althea" and "To Lucasta, on Going to the Wars" from *The Poems of Richard Lovelace,* edited by C. H. Wilkinson, copyright © 1953. "Kubla Khan" and "The Rime of the Ancient Mariner" from *The Poems of Samuel Taylor Coleridge.* Lines from "In Memoriam, A. H. H.," "The Lady of Shalott," lines from "The Princess," and "Ulysses" from *Alfred Tennyson: Poetical Works.* "To the Virgins, to Make Much of Time" from *The Poems of Robert Herrick* edited by L. C. Martin. From "The Life of Samuel Johnson" in *Boswell's Life of Johnson* by James Boswell, edited by C. B. Tinker. "Sonnet 31" and "Sonnet 39" from *The Poems of Sir Philip Sidney* edited by William A. Ringler, Jr. "The Passionate Shepherd to His Love" from *Marlowe's Poems,* edited by Roma Gill, Volume 1, © Roma Gill 1987, Clarendon Press, Oxford. Reprinted by permission of the publisher, Oxford University Press. "Sonnet 1" and "Sonnet 75" from *The Poetical Works of Edmund Spenser* edited by J. C. Smith and E. de Selincourt. "On Making an Agreeable Marriage" from *Jane Austen's Letters,* collected and edited by Deirdre Le Faye, copyright Deirdre Le Faye 1995. "The Middle Ages: 1000 Years of Darkness? No!" by H.W.C. Davis from *Medieval Europe.* "A Valuable Resource" by Jon Silkin from *Out of Battle: The Poetry of the Great War.* Copyright © Jon Silkin 1972. First published 1972. First issued as an Oxford University Press Paperback 1978.

Oxford University Press, Inc. From "The Wanderer," translated by Charles W. Kennedy, from *An Anthology of Old English Poetry.* Copyright © 1960 by Charles W. Kennedy. Used by permission of Oxford University Press, Inc.

Penguin Books Ltd. "How Siegfried Was Slain" from *The Nibelungenlied* translated by A. T. Hatto (Penguin Classics, Revised Edition, 1969), copyright © A. T. Hatto, 1965, 1969. From *A History of the English Church and People* by Bede, translated by Leo Sherley-Price, revised by R. E. Latham (Penguin Classics 1955, Revised edition 1968). Copyright © Leo Sherley-Price, 1955, 1968. "The Nun's Priest's Tale" and "The Prologue" to *The Canterbury Tales* by Geoffrey Chaucer, translated by Nevill Coghill (Penguin Classics 1951, Fourth revised edition 1977), copyright © 1951 by Nevill Coghill. Copyright © Nevill Coghill, 1958, 1960, 1975, 1977. Reprinted by permission of Penguin Books Ltd. "Melting Snow" by Kobayashi Issa (18 lines) from *The Penguin Book of Japanese Verse,* translated by Geoffrey Bownas and Anthony Thwaite (Penguin Books, 1964) Translation copyright © Geoffrey Bownas and Anthony Thwaite, 1964. Used by permission.

Phoebe Phillips Editions Excerpt from *The Anglo-Saxon Chronicle,* translated and collated by Anne Savage. Copyright © 1983 by Phoebe Phillips. All rights reserved.

Random House, Inc. "In Memory of W. B. Yeats" from *W. H. Auden: Collected Poems* by W. H. Auden, edited by Edward Mendelson. "Musée des Beaux Arts" from *W. H. Auden: Collected Poems* by W. H. Auden, edited by Edward Mendelson. Copyright © 1939 by W. H. Auden. All rights reserved. Used by permission of Random House, Inc. and Curtis Brown Ltd. Copyright 1940 and renewed 1968 by W. H. Auden. Reprinted by permission of Random House, Inc.

Random House, Inc., and Faber and Faber Ltd. "Not Palaces" from *Selected Poems* by Stephen Spender, copyright 1964 by

Stephen Spender. In the UK, from *Collected Poems, 1928–1985*. Copyright © 1986 by Stephen Spender. Copyright 1934 by The Modern Library, Inc. and renewed 1962 by Stephen Spender. Used by permission of Random House, Inc., and Faber and Faber Ltd.

Random House, Inc., and Heinemann Educational Publishers, a division of Reed Educational & Professional Publishing Limited From *A Man For All Seasons* by Robert Bolt, published by Heinemann Educational Books. Copyright © 1960, 1962 by Robert Bolt; copyright renewed 1988, 1990 by Robert Bolt. Reprinted by permission of Random House, Inc. and Heinemann Educational Publishers, a division of Reed Educational & Professional Publishing Limited.

Marian Reiner, Literary Agent "Haiku" by Yosa Buson from *More Cricket Songs: Japanese Haiku*, translated by Harry Behn. Copyright © 1971 by Harry Behn.

Tessa Sayle Agency "The Fiddle" from *The Second Chance and Other Stories* by Alan Silltoe. Copyright © 1981 by Allan Silltoe. First appeared in The Nottingham Press.

Scovil Chichak Galen Literary Agency, Inc. "We'll Never Conquer Space" by Arthur C. Clarke, from *Science Digest*, June 1960. Copyright © 1960 by Popular Mechanics Company. Reprinted by permission of the author and the author's agents, Scovil Chichak Galen Literary Agency, Inc.

Scribner, a division of Simon & Schuster, Inc., and A.P. Watt Ltd. "The Second Coming" from *The Poems of W.B. Yeats: A New Edition*, edited by Richard J. Finneran. Copyright © 1924 by Macmillan Publishing Company, copyright renewed © 1952 by Bertha Georgie Yeats. "Sailing to Byzantium," from *The Poems of W. B. Yeats: A New Edition*, edited by Richard J. Finneran. Copyright © 1928 by Macmillan Publishing Company, copyright renewed © 1956 by Georgie Yeats. Reprinted with the permission of Scribner, a division of Simon & Schuster, Inc.

Simon & Schuster, Inc. Excerpts from *The Analects of Confucius*, translated and annotated by Arthur Waley. Copyright © 1938 by George Allen and Unwin Ltd. "No Witchcraft for Sale," reprinted with the permission of Simon & Schuster and Jonathan Clowes Ltd. from *African Short Stories* by Doris Lessing. Copyright © 1951, 1953, 1954, 1957, 1958, 1962, 1963, 1964, 1965, 1972, 1981 by Doris Lessing.

Taylor & Francis Lines from "An Essay on Man" and Canto III and lines from Canto V from *The Rape of the Lock*, reprinted from *The Poems of Alexander Pope*, edited by John Butt. Published by Methuen & Co., Ltd, London. Used by permission.

University of California Press "You Know the Place: Then" from *Sappho: A New Translation* by Mary Barnard. Copyright © 1958 The Regents of the University of California; © renewed 1984 Mary Barnard. "The Diameter of the Bomb," translated by Chana Bloch, from *The Selected Poetry of Yehuda Amichai*, translated/edited by Chana Bloch and Stephen Mitchell. Translation copyright © 1996 by The Regents of the State of California. Used by permission.

University of Chicago Press From *The Iliad of Homer*, translated by Richmond Lattimore. Copyright © 1951, The University of Chicago. "Oedipus the King" by Sophocles from *The Complete Greek Tragedies*, Grene & Lattimore, eds., pp. 11–17. Used by permission.

University of Wisconsin Press Excerpts from "The Defense of Poesey" from *Sir Philip Sidney: Selected Prose and Poetry*, edited by Robert Kimbrough. Copyright © 1969, 1983 Robert Kimbrough.

Viking Penguin, Inc., a division of Penguin Putnam, Inc., and Barbara Levy Literary Agency "Wirers" from *Collected Poems of Siegfried Sassoon* by Siegfried Sassoon. Copyright 1918, 1920 by E.P. Dutton. Copyright 1936, 1946, 1947, 1948 by Siegfried Sassoon. Used by permission of Viking Penguin, a division of Penguin Putnam, Inc. and Barbara Levy Literary Agency for George Sassoon.

Viking Penguin, a division of Penguin Putnam, Inc., and David Higham Associates Ltd. "A Shocking Accident," copyright © 1957 by Graham Greene. In the USA from *Collected Stories of Graham Greene* by Graham Greene. In England from *Twenty-One Stories* by Graham Greene. Used by permission of Viking Penguin, a division of Penguin Putnam Inc. and David Higham Associates Ltd.

Viking Penguin, Inc., a division of Penguin Putnam, Inc. "Araby" from *Dubliners* by James Joyce, copyright 1916 by B. W. Heubsch. Definitive text copyright © 1967 by The Estate of James Joyce. "The Book of Sand" from *Collected Fictions* by Jorge Luis Borges, translated by Andrew Hurley, copyright © 1998 by Maria Kodama; translation copyright © 1998 by Penguin Putnam, Inc. "The Train from Rhodesia," copyright 1952 by Nadine Gordimer, from *Selected Stories* by Nadine Gordimer. Used by permission of Viking Penguin, a division of Penguin Putnam, Inc.

Viking Penguin, Inc., a division of Penguin Putnam, Inc., and The Bodley Head, c/o of Random House Group Ltd. "The Distant Past," from *Angels at the Ritz and Other Stories* by William Trevor, copyright © 1975 by William Trevor. Published in England by The Bodley Head. Used by permission of Viking Penguin, a division of Penguin Putnam, Inc. and The Random House Group Ltd.

Viking Penguin, Inc., a division of Penguin Putnam, Inc., and Laurence Pollinger Ltd. "The Rocking-Horse Winner," copyright © 1933 by the Estate of D. H. Lawrence, renewed © 1961 by Angelo Ravagli and C. M. Weekley, Executors of the Estate of Frieda Lawrence, from *Complete Short Stories of D.H. Lawrence* by D.H. Lawrence.

Wake Forest University Press "Carrick Revisited" from *Selected Poems of Louis MacNeice*, edited by Michael Longley. © Wake Forest University Press, 1990. Reprinted by permission of Wake Forest University Press.

Warner Bros. Publications Inc. "Cromwell: The Movie" by Ken Hughes from *Cromwell* (1970: movie). Copyright © 1970.

Warner/Chappell Music, Inc., A Division of Warner Brothers Music "Freeze Tag" written by Suzanne Vega. Song copyright © 1985 by Waifersongs Ltd. And AGF Music Ltd. (ASCAP).

Yale University Press "The Seafarer" from *Poems from the Old English*, translated by Burton Raffel. Copyright © 1960, 1964; renewed 1988, 1922 by The University of Nebraska Press. Copyright © 1994 by Burton Raffel. Used by permission.

Note: Every effort has been made to locate the copyright owner of material reprinted in this book. Omissions brought to our attention will be corrected in subsequent printings.

Library, London/New York; **638:** The Granger Collection, New York; **640:** From a Manuscript of "The Lamb" by William Blake, Lessing J. Rosenwald Collection, Courtesy of the Library of Congress, Washington, D.C.; **641:** *The Tyger*, A Page from "Songs of Innocence and Experience," William Blake, The Metropolitan Museum of Art, Rogers Fund, 1917 © Copyright 1984 by The Metropolitan Museum of Art; **643:** © Archive Photos; **648:** *Mary Shelley* (detail), c. 1840, Richard Rothwell, by courtesy of the National Portrait Gallery, London; **650–651:** *A View of Chamonix and Mt. Blanc*, Ludwig Ferdinand Schnorr von Carolsfeld, Austrian Gallery, Vienna; **653:** © Belinda Wright/DRK Photo; **659:** *Elizabeth Beale Bordley*, c. 1797, Gilbert Stuart, oil on canvas, 29-1/4 x 24", 1886.2, courtesy of the Museum of American Art of the Pennsylvania Academy of the Fine Arts, Philadelphia. Bequest of Elizabeth Mifflin; **660:** CORBIS-Bettmann; **661:** *The Wanderer Over the Sea of Clouds*, 1818, by Caspar-David Friedrich (1774–1840), Kunsthalle, Hamburg/Bridgeman Art Library, London/New York; **662:** The Granger Collection, New York; **664:** © Colin Raw/Stone; **666:** The Granger Collection, New York; **669:** Digital Imagery © Copyright 2001 PhotoDisc, Inc.; **670:** *Tintern Abbey*, J.M.W. Turner, © British Museum; **673:** *Storming of the Bastille, 14 July 1789*, Anonymous, Chateau de, Versailles, France/Art Resource, NY; **675:** Corel Professional Photos CD-ROM™; **684:** *Samuel Taylor Coleridge* (detail), by courtesy of the National Portrait Gallery, London; **686:** Engraving by Gustave Doré for "The Rime of the Ancient Mariner" by Samuel Taylor Coleridge ©1970 by Dover Publications, Inc.; **689:** Engraving by Gustave Doré for "The Rime of the Ancient Mariner" by Samuel Taylor Coleridge ©1970 by Dover Publications, Inc.; **691:** The Granger Collection, New York; **695:** Engraving by Gustave Doré for "The Rime of the Ancient Mariner" by Samuel Taylor Coleridge ©1970 by Dover Publications, Inc.; **699:** Engraving by Gustave Doré for "The Rime of the Ancient Mariner" by Samuel Taylor Coleridge ©1970 by Dover Publications, Inc.; **702:** The Granger Collection, New York; **705:** Digital Imagery © Copyright 2001 PhotoDisc, Inc.; **710:** *Box and Cover*, Ming Dynasty, first half of 16th century, lacquer, black; mother-of-pearl; wood; fabric. H. 4 in. The Seattle Art Museum, Gift of Mr. and Mrs. Louis Brechemin. Photo by Paul Macapia; **716:** Culver Pictures, Inc.; **716:** "Lord Byron, shaking the dust of England from his shoes," from *The Poet's Corner*, pub. by William Heinemann, 1904 (engraving) by Max Beerbohm (1872–1956), Central Saint Martins College of Art and Design/ Bridgeman Art Library, London/New York; **718:** *In the Garden* (detail), c. 1889, Thomas Wilmer Dewing, oil on canvas, 20-5/8 x 35", National Museum of American Art, Washington, D.C./Art Resource, NY; **720–721:** *Shipwreck*, J.C.C. Dahl, Munich Neue Pinakothek/ Kavaler/Art Resource, NY; **722:** Corel Professional Photos CD-ROM™; **730:** The Granger Collection, New York; **732:** © Diane Rawson/Photo Researchers, Inc.; **734–735:** © David Sutherland/ Stone; **739:** *Cloud Study*, 1821, John Constable, Yale Center for British Art, Paul Mellon Collection; **744:** The Granger Collection, New York; **746:** Courtesy of the Trustees of British Library; **749:** *John Keats*, 1821, Joseph Severn, by courtesy of the National Portrait Gallery, London; **751:** *Small Bird On a Flowering Plum Branch*, attributed to Ma Lin, The Goto Museum; **754:** Greek vase, terracotta, c. 460 B.C. Attributed to the Orchard Painter, Column Krater (called the "Orchard Vase"), Side A: *Women Gathering Apples*, The Metropolitan Museum of Art, Rogers Fund, 1907, (07.286.74); **760:** *Lady Lilith*, 1868, Dante Gabriel Rossetti, Delaware Art Museum, Wilmington, DE, USA/Bridgeman Art Library, London/New York; **761:** CORBIS-Bettmann; **762:** *Kobayashi Issa*, Heibonsha/Pacific Press Service; **763:** (l.) *Crows Taking Flight through Spring Haze* (1782–1846), hanging scroll, Edo period, dated 1841; Toyama Kinenkan, Saitama prefecture, Okada Hanko, Foundation Toyama Memorial Museum; **763:** (r.) Yosa Buson, Heibonsha/ Pacific Press Service; **765:** *Forging the Anchor*, 1831, by William James Muller (1812–45), City of Bristol Museum and Art Gallery/ Bridgeman Art Library, London/New York; **766:** (all) The Granger Collection, New York; **768:** *The Workshops at the Gobelins*, 1840, by Jean-Charles Develly (1783–1849), Musée Carnavalet, Paris, France/Giraudon/Bridgeman Art Library, London/New York; **771:**

Brown Brothers; **773:** SIPA Press; **778:** (l.) *Jane Austen* (detail), c. 1801—C. Auston, by courtesy of the National Portrait Gallery, London; **778:** (r.) The Granger Collection, New York; **780:** *Marriage à la Mode: The Marriage Contract*, 1743, William Hogarth, reproduced by courtesy of the Trustees, National Gallery of Art, London; **785:** Digital Imagery © Copyright 2001 PhotoDisc, Inc.; **790:** Photofest; **793:** Globe Photos; **796:** Walter Hodges/Tony Stone Images; **802–803:** *The Railway Station*, 1862, by William Powell Frith (1819–1909), Royal Holloway and Bedford New College, Surrey/Bridgeman Art Library, London/New York; **804:** (b.) The Granger Collection, New York; **804:** (t.r.) Library of Congress/CORBIS; **804:** (t.m.) Illustrated London News/CORBIS; **804:** (t.l.) © British Museum; **805:** (t.l.) *The Mad Tea Party* from First Edition of *Alice's Adventures*, Sir John Tenniel, The Granger Collection, New York; **805:** (t.r.) The Granger Collection, New York; **805:** (b.) Gary J. Shulfer; **805:** (m.) The Granger Collection, New York; **806:** The Royal Collection © Her Majesty Queen Elizabeth II; **807:** Hulton-Deutsch Collection/ CORBIS; **809:** *Day Dream*, 1880, Dante Gabriel Rosetti, Victoria & Albert Museum, London, UK/The Bridgeman Art Library, London/New York; **811:** *Bayswater Omnibus*, G.W. Joy, Museum of London; **813:** *Edwardian London*, 1901, by Eugene Joseph McSwiney (1866–1912), Christopher Wood Gallery, London/Bridgeman Art Library, London/New York; **815:** *Faustine*, 1904, Maxwell Armfield, Musée d'Orsay, Paris, France/Erich Lessing/Art Resource, NY; **816:** *Alfred Lord Tennyson* (detail), c. 1840, S. Laurence, by courtesy of the National Portrait Gallery, London; **818:** *The Stages of Life*, c. 1835 (oil on canvas) by Caspar-David Friedrich (1774–1840), Museum der Bildenden Kunste, Leipzig/Bridgeman Art Library, London/New York; **821:** Superstock; **824:** Digital Imagery © Copyright 2001 PhotoDisc, Inc.; **829:** Jean-Auguste-Dominique Ingres, *Ulysses*, 1827, Chester Dale Collection. Photograph © Board of Trustees, National Gallery of Art, Washington; **834:** (l., r.) The Granger Collection, New York; **836:** *Antea* (Portrait of a Lady), Parmigianino, Museo Nazionale di Capodimonte, Naples/Scala/Art Resource, NY; **839:** Culver Pictures, Inc.; **840:** *Italian Ruins*, John Claude Nattes, Victoria and Albert Museum/Art Resource, NY; **842:** Corel Professional Photos CD-ROM™; **848:** ©The Stock Market/Tibor Bognar; **849:** CORBIS-Bettmann; **851:** *Marine*, Marcel Mouillot, Galerie d'Art Moderne, Nancy/Art Resource, NY; **852:** CORBIS-Bettmann; **853:** *Music and Literature*, 1878, William M. Harnett, oil on canvas, 24 x 32-1/8" Albright-Knox Art Gallery, Buffalo, New York, Gift of Seymour H. Knox, 1941; **854:** (l., r.) The Granger Collection, New York; **856:** Illustration from *The Oxford Illustrated Dickens*; **857:** *Dickens's Dream*, Robert William Buss/ Bridgeman Art Library, London/New York; **858:** © Hulton Getty/Archive Photos; **860–861:** The Granger Collection, New York; **867:** Springer/CORBIS-Bettmann; **870:** *Rochester and Jane Eyre*, Frederick Walker, Private Collection/ Bridgeman Art Library, London/New York; **876–877:** *The Return of the Troops from the Crimea, Boulevard des Italiens, in front of the Hanover Pavilion, December 1855*, c. 19th century/Emmanuel Masses/Musée Carnavalet, Paris, France, Roger-Viollet Paris/Bridgeman Art Library, London/ New York; **879:** *Portrait of Koutouzov, Prince of Smolensk*, George Dawe, Hermitage, St. Petersburg, Russia/Giraudon/Art Resource, NY; **880:** *L. N. Tolstoi*, I. E. Repin, Sovfoto/Eastfoto; **881:** e.t. archive; **882:** (l.) *Matthew Arnold* (detail), 1888, G. J. Watts, by courtesy of the National Portrait Gallery, London; **882:** (r.) *Rudyard Kipling* (detail), 1899, P. Burne Jones, by courtesy of the National Portrait Gallery, London; **884:** Andrea Pistolesi/The Image Bank; **886:** The Granger Collection, New York; **887:** Private Collection/Bridgeman Art Library, London/New York; **889:** Culver Pictures, Inc.; **894:** Private Collection/Bridgeman Art Library, London/New York; **896:** *Woman Begging at Clonakilty*, James Mahony, The Illustrated London News, 1847. Photo by Grace Davies/Omni-Photo Communications, Inc.; **898:** Private Collection/ Bridgeman Art Library, London/New York; **900–901:** Culver Pictures, Inc.; **910–911:** © Joe Cornish/Stone; **913, 914:** Derek Speirs/Report Ltd; **915:** *Past and Present* (no. 2), Augustus Leopold Egg, Tate Gallery, London/Art Resource, NY; **916:** (l.) The Granger Collection, New York; **916:** (r.) *Thomas Hardy* (detail), R. G. Eres, by courtesy of the National Portrait